SPORTS AND THE LAW

TEXT, CASES, AND PROBLEMS

Seventh Edition

■ ■ ■

Paul C. Weiler
Late Friendly Professor of Law
Harvard Law School

Stephen F. Ross
Professor of Law
Lewis H. Vovakis Distinguished Faculty Scholar
The Pennsylvania State University

Michael C. Harper
Professor of Law and Barreca Labor Relations Scholar
Boston University

Jodi S. Balsam
Professor of Clinical Law
Brooklyn Law School

William W. Berry III
Montague Professor of Law
University of Mississippi School of Law

AMERICAN CASEBOOK SERIES®

WEST
ACADEMIC
PUBLISHING

American Casebook Series is a trademark registered in the U.S. Patent and Trademark Office.

COPYRIGHT © 1993 WEST PUBLISHING CO.
© 1998, 2004 West, a Thomson Business
© 2011 Thomson Reuters
© 2015, 2019 LEG, Inc. d/b/a West Academic
© 2023 LEG, Inc. d/b/a West Academic
    860 Blue Gentian Road, Suite 350
    Eagan, MN 55121
    1-877-888-1330

Printed in the United States of America

ISBN: 978-1-63659-405-7

Dedications

* * *

*By Steve Ross to Mary Wujek, Liz and Sara Kinports,
and Katheryn and Lisie Thayer*

* * *

By Michael Harper to Alma and Izzy

* * *

By Jodi Balsam to Michele, Mo, and Will

* * *

*By Will Berry to Stephanie, Eleanor, William,
and Caroline Berry*

PREFACE

The sports field has grown to become a multi-billion-dollar industry from its origins in social groups such as the Knickerbocker Club formed in the late 19th century, which provided sedentary white-collar workers with an opportunity for athletic exercise and gambling, followed by socializing and drinking. The business and law of sports in America has been the subject of this text since Professors Paul Weiler (deceased) and Gary Roberts published the first edition in 1993. Professors Roger Abrams and Stephen Ross joined the team for the fourth edition in 2011. The sixth and seventh editions have been prepared by Ross, an expert on antitrust who studies the operation of sports leagues throughout the world, Michael Harper, who focuses generally on labor and employment law, Jodi Balsam, a former sports league in-house counsel who handled far-ranging matters including antitrust, intellectual property, sports integrity, and sports torts and contracts, and Will Berry, whose sports scholarship focuses on intercollegiate sports.*

Those who have adopted the book for law school courses on the legal issues arising in the business of sports will find that, as in the past, we have abjured attempting to re-teach basic common law principles reviewed in the first year. Although the day-to-day life of most sports lawyers may principally involve contract negotiation and commercial and tort litigation, the book retains the view that the student of sports law is best served by understanding the business dynamics of sports. This is best communicated in substantial part through the lens of three foundational mainstays of Sports Law—labor law, antitrust law, and intellectual property law, each of which are becoming increasingly relevant to sports at the college level as well. We have expanded our discussion of the basic principles in each field in recognition that not all upper-level students will have studied these topics before venturing into Sports Law. We feel that this course offers an alternative means to introduce student to all three fields. The work also reflects an appreciation that much of sports law is decided not by courts but by private tribunals, with a greater emphasis on labor arbitration in the professional leagues, and internal decision-making within the unique institution of college sports, the NCAA. NCAA regulation offers an excellent case study in private control of collective endeavor.

---

* As scholars, the current co-authors come to this effort with well-established views on many of the topics discussed. That said, two of the current co-authors have been compensated by parties on some of the cases, and believe that some readers would want to know this. Jodi Balsam acted for the NFL in litigation from 1994–2007, which includes the *Sullivan* case (Chapter 8) and litigation surrounding intellectual property between the league and the Dallas Cowboys (Chapters 8 and 9) among other matters. Steve Ross consulted with plaintiffs' counsel in the *Laumann* case (Chapter 7).

This Seventh Edition reflects several other important innovations, in addition to the traditional updating of cases and principles. We begin with a chapter on sporting integrity, based on the view that this concept and its application is what makes sports law distinctive. We have reorganized portions of other chapters into a single one on equity in sports, which also addresses new equity issues. In addition to problems in bargaining dynamics in the antitrust chapters, in a number of chapters we provide problems for classes to consider in reading the cases and notes material.

After introducing the new integrity chapter, the second chapter again emphasizes the extraordinary power vested in league commissioners to solve governance problems in club-run leagues, and to address the best interests of sport. Raising the issue of the scope of external law to constrain internal sports league decisions, the edition moves to concentrated coverage of issues in labor law, including instruction in the basic principles that govern all major North American sports where players have selected unions as their exclusive bargaining representative. The casebook then turns to basic principles of antitrust law that govern closely integrated industries requiring cooperation among firms, and then examines the interaction between antitrust and labor law. The antitrust chapters are designed to provide (in Chapter 6) a basic introduction that can suffice for those teaching shorter courses or not emphasizing antitrust, and then detailing labor, product, and collegiate issues separately.

After the antitrust review, the book comprehensively examines the intersection of intellectual property law with the world of sports, and then treats the regulation of sports agents. The next three chapters consider college sports, emphasizing the role of the NCAA as a private regulatory body. We next present the aforementioned chapter on equity in sport, which includes consideration of Title IX's important impact on American athletic participation. Our last two chapters consider Olympic sports and international sport governance, and the legal regulation of health and safety in sports competitions. We hope you share our view that this edition continues to provide users with a solid grounding in the most salient of current issues.

STEPHEN F. ROSS
MICHAEL C. HARPER
JODI S. BALSAM
WILLIAM W. BERRY III

November 2022

ACKNOWLEDGMENTS

We first acknowledge our colleagues, Paul Weiler (deceased) and Gary Roberts, for their inspired decision to take a traditional casebook and turn it into the definitive textbook on the law and the business of sports. Our work has been substantially aided by Roger Abrams' contribution to the fourth and fifth additions. In addition to the insights provided in prior editions, the current co-authors would also like to acknowledge and thank the many colleagues, sports law professors, academics from other disciplines who study sports, practicing sports lawyers, and industry executives—too numerous to name—who over the years have generously shared their own expertise in helping us shape our own perspectives that we were able to apply in crafting revisions to this book.

Each of us benefited from the work of one or more research assistants on the Seventh Edition. At Penn State, Steve Ross would like to thank Faith Anderson. At Boston University School of Law, Michael Harper would like to thank Jeremy DaCruz. At Brooklyn Law School, Jodi Balsam would like to thank Angela Anastasi. At the University of Mississippi School of Law, Will Berry would like to thank William Morris.

SUMMARY OF CONTENTS

TABLE OF CONTENTS

TABLE OF CASES

The principal cases are in bold type.

———

SPORTS AND THE LAW

TEXT, CASES, AND PROBLEMS

Seventh Edition

CHAPTER 1

INTRODUCTION: DEFINING AND PROTECTING SPORTS INTEGRITY

■ ■ ■

A. THE ROLE OF SPORT IN SOCIETY

Sports are a celebration of much of what it means to be human. Sports began in pre-historic times as preparation for the hunt for food and the battle against tribal enemies. The ancient Greek Olympics date to 776 BCE; wars were suspended so that young men could travel to competitions where prizes included olive wreaths, trophies, and tax-free status for life. Striving to better oneself to defeat an opponent in a fair fight or demonstrate extraordinary feats of athletic endeavor is universally valued.

Modern professional and amateur sports began in the mid-nineteenth century, accelerated by the development of a middle class with leisure time. Competitive sports offered opportunities to build character and engage in physical activity beneficial to one's physical and mental health. As sports contests attracted spectators, they enabled vicarious participation in athletic achievement by developing fan bases and rivalries. They serve a basic human need for camaraderie and community, and for identifying with and taking pride in something greater than oneself. Sports are associated with a host of positive values, including equality of opportunity, teamwork, self-discipline, and fair play.

The reciprocal relationship between sports and societal values raises the question: what is a sport? Definitions vary but a good starting point is the ENCYCLOPEDIA OF WORLD SPORT (Oxford University Press 1999), which considers an activity a sport if it involves:

- Competition between two or more individuals or teams;

- Rules of play that allow a winner to be determined;

- A primary goal of victory; and

- Victory determined by the relative physical ability of the competitors, although strategy and chance may also play a role.

Whether an activity is considered a sport may also depend on history, culture, and political processes. *See* Stefan Szymanski and Andrew Zimbalist, NATIONAL PASTIME: HOW AMERICANS PLAY BASEBALL AND THE REST OF THE WORLD PLAYS SOCCER (Brookings Inst. Press 2005)

1

(describing how the English exported their values and traditions to other nations through the sport of soccer). Obtaining legitimacy as a sport can give rise to commercial opportunity (witness esports), and can determine the outcome of legal disputes (see Chapter 14's discussion of whether cheerleading is a sport for Title IX purposes).

Sports have grown into a multi-billion-dollar global industry, marked by increasing professionalization and commodification of sporting events. They nonetheless continue to have exceptional power to promote change, and inspire and unite people. The role of sports in society, however, is reliant on the integrity of the sports competition. Fans will refuse to engage with dishonest sports—sports that bill themselves as offering authentic, honest competition, but are actually conducted fraudulently. What fans abandon so will sponsors and other commercial partners. Thus, the very viability of sports as a social and commercial enterprise depends on its integrity, to which we devote the remainder of this chapter.

B. SPORTS INTEGRITY DEFINED

The sports industry's prosperity and its role in modern society has come to depend on the public's belief that the outcome of a sporting competition is the result of genuine effort and fair play. What also distinguishes competitive sports from most other forms of entertainment is its unscripted nature, with the possibility of an unexpected outcome. The legitimacy of the sport product and its appeal to consumers depends on the reality and perception of this unpredictability and authenticity. As one commentator has noted, "Integrity is, in a large measure, a perception, although there is a real intangible existence to it. Once lost it is very difficult to ever retrieve." Richard H. McLaren, *Corruption: Its Impact on Fair Play*, 19 MARQ. SPORTS L. REV. 15, 15–16 (2008).

In this vein, the Australian National Integrity of Sport Unit offers a useful definition of sports integrity:

> The manifestation of the ethics and values which promote community confidence in sports, resulting in fair and honest performances and outcomes, unaffected by illegitimate enhancements or external interests; and positive conduct by athletes, administrators, officials, supporters and other stakeholders, on and off the sporting arena, which enhances the reputation and standing of the sporting contest and of sport overall.

This chapter addresses the first half of this definition—conduct that directly implicates the on-field product: manipulation of sporting contests in connection with corrupt gambling schemes; other forms of sports cheating; and the use of performance enhancing drugs in sport. Chapter 2, Section D addresses off-field conduct, in the context of North American professional sports leagues and the commissioner's function to protect a league's reputation.

On-field sports integrity requires at least three components: (1) uniform rules and athlete eligibility requirements, applied consistently to ensure competition is meaningful, fair, and safe; (2) participant compliance with the rules and use of their best efforts in the course of the competition; and (3) outcome uncertainty in that the results of the competition are unpredictable and free of any outside influence, such as fixing, cheating, or proscribed performance enhancements. Erosion of any of these components of sports integrity can destabilize the livelihood of multitudes of people and businesses.

In the United States, public law sparsely addresses sports integrity. At the federal level, the 1964 Sports Bribery Act prohibits "any scheme in commerce to influence, in any way, by bribery any sporting contest, with knowledge that the purpose of such scheme is to influence by bribery that contest." 18 U.S.C. § 224. That law has seen fewer than 20 federal prosecutions after decades on the books, and none targeting professional athletes. Redundant sports bribery statutes reside in two-thirds of state penal codes, and are similarly rarely invoked. *See, e.g.*, Ariz. Rev. Stat. § 13–2309 (1978); Fla. Stat. Ann. § 838.12 (1997). Many states also prohibit tampering with or rigging a sports contest by, for example, interfering with an animal or equipment involved in the conduct of the contest. *See, e.g.*, Ky. Rev. Stat. Ann. § 518.060 (1998) (prohibiting tampering with a horse, among other things, to influence a sports contest).

Another federal law was expressly designed "to maintain sport's integrity"—the 1992 Professional and Amateur Sports Protection Act (PASPA), which largely prohibited betting or gambling on sports events. This law has been judicially repealed, as discussed in Section C of this chapter. The only government agencies that directly regulate sport are specialized units that oversee sports like horseracing and boxing.

Thus, securing the three components of sports integrity is largely a function of private law—sports governing bodies at all levels (amateur, scholastic, Olympic, professional) make rules, interpret and enforce those rules, and resolve disputes among organizing entities, athletes, and other participants. Private association law (discussed in Chapter 2) confers on these entities broad legal autonomy to promulgate and apply game rules and eligibility requirements, especially when it comes to delimiting their athletic contests to ensure fairness and competitive balance, and to determining the winners of those contests. Courts generally defer to these private processes and outcomes, and rarely abrogate or decline to enforce internal rules and authorized decisions of sports governing bodies.

Accordingly, in *Mercury Bay Boating Club Inc. v. San Diego Yacht Club*, 76 N.Y.2d 256 (1990), the New York Court of Appeals declined to intervene in a dispute over whether the advanced boat design used by the winner of an America's Cup race complied with the rules of the competition. The court observed:

> The question of whether particular conduct is "sporting" or "fair" in the context of a particular sporting event, however, is wholly distinct from the question of whether it is legal. Questions of sportsmanship and fairness with respect to sporting contests depend largely upon the rules of the particular sport and the expertise of those knowledgeable in that sport; they are not questions suitable for judicial resolution. As sporting activities evolve in light of changing preferences and technologies, it would be most inappropriate and counterproductive for the courts to attempt to fix the rules and standards of competition of any particular sport. To do so would likely result in many sporting contests being decided, not in the arena of the sport, but in the courts.

In this vein, the Seventh Circuit Court of Appeals declined to rule that a race was invalid after the Formula One governing body disqualified 14 of the 20 competing cars because of defective tires. *Bowers v. Federation Internationale de L'Automobile*, 489 F.3d 316 (7th Cir. 2007). Likewise, the Second Circuit reversed a district court's decision to review *de novo* a stock car race's results and reinstate a driver's victory, holding that the court should have deferred to NASCAR's interpretation of its own rules. *Crouch v. Nat'l Ass'n For Stock Car Auto Racing, Inc.*, 845 F.2d 397 (2d Cir. 1988). *But see PGA Tour, Inc. v. Martin*, 532 U.S. 661 (2001) (ruling under federal anti-discrimination law that a professional golf tour must adjust its rules to accommodate a disabled player; discussed in Chapter 14 on Equity in Sports).

In addition to regulating who may compete and how the competition runs its course, sports governing bodies further legislate to insulate their contests from improper outside influences. Integrity legislation typically encompasses offenses such as wagering on one's own games or sport, manipulating the course or result of a competition, equipment tampering, sabotaging or spying on an opponent, and using prohibited performance enhancing drugs. Specialized private sports courts and regulatory agencies have emerged to address disputes arising out of sport integrity violations, among other controversies. Examples include the Court of Arbitration for Sport (CAS) and the World Anti-Doping Agency (WADA) and its national counterparts, which are all described further in Chapter 15. The National Collegiate Athletic Association (NCAA) and its three divisions similarly function as regulators of sports integrity, enforcing member rules regarding, for example, athlete eligibility and academic standing, discussed in Chapters 11–13.

Consider the following example of private legislation to safeguard the integrity of sport—the Olympic Movement Code on the Prevention of the

Manipulation of Competitions, which applies to the International Olympic Committee, national Olympic committees, international sports federations, national sports governing bodies, and all subsidiary members at the regional level, denominated "Sports Organisations" [sic].

OLYMPIC MOVEMENT CODE ON THE PREVENTION OF THE MANIPULATION OF COMPETITIONS

Article 1 Definitions

1.1 "Benefit" means the direct or indirect receipt or provision of money or the equivalent such as, but not limited to, bribes, gains, gifts and other advantages including, without limitation, winnings and/or potential winnings as a result of a wager; the foregoing shall not include official prize money, appearance fees or payments to be made under sponsorship or other contracts;

1.2 "Competition" means any sports competition, tournament, match or event, organised in accordance with the rules of a Sports Organisation or its affiliated organisations, or, where appropriate, in accordance with the rules of any other competent sports organisation;

1.3 "Inside Information" means information relating to any competition that a person possesses by virtue of his or her position in relation to a sport or competition, excluding any information already published or common knowledge, easily accessible to interested members of the public or disclosed in accordance with the rules and regulations governing the relevant Competition;

1.4 "Participant" means any natural or legal person belonging to one of the following categories:

    a. "athlete" means any person or group of persons, participating in sports competitions;

    b. "athlete support personnel" means any coach, trainer, manager, agent, team staff, team official, medical or paramedical personnel working with or treating athletes participating in or preparing for sports competitions, and all other persons working with the athletes;

    c. "official" means any person who is the owner of, a shareholder in, an executive or a staff member of the entities which organise and/or promote sports competitions, as well as referees, jury members and any other accredited persons. The term also covers the executives and staff of the sports organisation, or where appropriate, other competent sports organisation or club that recognises the competition.

1.5 "Sports Betting, Bet or Betting" means any wager of a stake of monetary value in the expectation of a prize of monetary value, subject to a future and uncertain occurrence related to a sports competition.

Article 2 Violations

The following conduct as defined in this Article constitutes a violation of this Code:

2.1 Betting

Betting in relation either:
a.   to Competition in which the Participant is directly participating; or
b.   to the Participant's sport; or
c.   to any event of a multisport Competition in which he/she is a participant.

2.2 Manipulation of sports competitions

An intentional arrangement, act or omission aimed at an improper alteration of the result or the course of a sports competition in order to remove all or part of the unpredictable nature of the sports competition with a view to obtaining an undue Benefit for oneself or for others.

2.3 Corrupt conduct

Providing, requesting, receiving, seeking, or accepting a Benefit related to the manipulation of a competition or any other form of corruption.

2.4 Inside information

1.   Using Inside Information for the purposes of Betting, any form of manipulation of sports competitions or any other corrupt purposes whether by the Participant or via another person and/or entity.

2.   Disclosing Inside Information to any person and/or entity, with or without Benefit, where the Participant knew or should have known that such disclosure might lead to the information being used for the purposes of Betting, any form of manipulation of competitions or any other corrupt purposes.

3.   Giving and/or receiving a Benefit for the provision of Inside Information regardless of whether any Inside Information is actually provided.

2.5 Failure to report

1.   Failing to report to the Sports Organisation concerned or a relevant disclosure/reporting mechanism or authority, at the first available opportunity, full details of any approaches or invitations received by the Participant to engage in conduct or incidents that could amount to a violation of this Code.

2. Failing to report to the Sports Organisation concerned or a relevant disclosure/reporting mechanism or authority, at the first available opportunity, full details of any incident, fact or matter that comes to the attention of the Participant (or of which they ought to have been reasonably aware) including approaches or invitations that have been received by another Participant to engage in conduct that could amount to a violation of this Code.

2.6 Failure to cooperate

1. Failing to cooperate with any investigation carried out by the Sports Organisation in relation to a possible breach of this Code, including, without limitation, failing to provide accurately, completely and without undue delay any information and/or documentation and/or access or assistance requested by the competent Sports Organisation as part of such investigation.

2. Obstructing or delaying any investigation that may be carried out by the Sports Organisation in relation to a possible violation of this Code, including without limitation concealing, tampering with or destroying any documentation or other information that may be relevant to the investigation.

————

NOTES AND QUESTIONS

1. *Determining Sporting "Fairness."* Courts largely agree that determining sporting fairness is not suitable for judicial resolution or fan intercession. Yet, after a blown call at the 2019 NFC Championship Game ended the New Orleans Saints' playoff run, the team's fans brought multiple fraud and deceptive trade practices lawsuits against the National Football League. All were ultimately dismissed, with the Louisiana Supreme Court observing, "[I]t is not the role of judges and juries to be second-guessing the decision taken by a professional sports league purportedly enforcing its own rules." *Le Mon v. Nat'l Football League*, 277 So. 3d 1166, 1168 (2019). Are there acceptable ways to empower fans to participate in protecting a sport's integrity? Consider the 2021 "Fan-led Review of Football Governance," an independent review of English football (soccer), which recommended appointing a government regulator and convening "shadow boards" of fans to bolster financial sustainability and ownership integrity. While largely concerned with off-pitch matters, the review envisions significant outside, public intervention in sport. Is that a good idea?

2. *Olympic Code's Reach.* Every sports organization at the regional, national, and international level that is subject to the Olympic Code must adopt integrity standards at least as stringent as those in the Code, and may implement more stringent regulations. What additional regulations would you advise a sports organization to adopt? Would your answer depend on the sport? The country?

3. *Definition of "Benefit."* The Olympic Code defines "benefit" as the "provision of money or the equivalent," and then inculpates only that conduct for which such benefit was given or received. Is that definition adequate to encompass all corrupt conduct that might result in the manipulation of a sports competition? What if an athlete is induced to fix a match as a result of extortion, blackmail, or duress, as when Henry Hill, the mobster/informant immortalized in the film *Goodfellas*, threatened to break the fingers of college players who resisted bribes?

4. *Witness Cooperation in Exchange for Confidentiality.* One potential inadequacy of the Olympic Code and similar private association efforts to police sport is that sports governing bodies lack the necessary authority to subpoena evidence, compel testimony, charge witnesses with perjury, or assert jurisdiction over non-participants. Instead, one inducement for witness cooperation is the promise of confidentiality. But such promises must yield to superior judicial authority, as when the NCAA lost its bid to seal investigative reports in the Reggie Bush/USC infractions case, because they were part of the record in a college coach's defamation lawsuit. *See McNair v. Nat'l Collegiate Athletic Assn.*, 234 Cal. App. 4th 25 (2015) (discussed further in Chapter 13, Section A). The NCAA argued vociferously that breaching witness confidentiality in this way would undermine its investigative and enforcement efforts, but the court ruled that the public's First Amendment right of access to court proceedings overrides those concerns.

In a 2021 NFL investigation of sexual harassment claims against the Washington Commanders and team owner Dan Snyder, the league relied on oral reports from counsel and declined to commission a written report in large part because of the fragility of witness confidentiality assurances. Consider how this impacts the thoroughness and effectiveness of sports governing bodies' internal investigations.

5. *Importance of a "Culture of Compliance."* Chapter 2 excerpts the "Bountygate" decision, in which former NFL Commissioner Tagliabue serving as arbitrator vacated the suspensions of football players who earned cash bounties to injure opposing players. In doing so, he remarked on "the realities of NFL team workplaces" including "a code of silence" and resistance to the league's investigative and enforcement efforts. True culture change, the decision advises, requires a "safe haven" and whistleblower protections for those who report misconduct. How effective are such whistleblower protections in other industries? Do you think such protections would be as effective in team sports?

6. *Federalization of Horseracing Oversight.* One exception to government forbearance in regulating sports integrity is horseracing, commonly superintended by state commissions. In 2020, Congress passed the Horseracing Integrity and Safety Act, effectively federalizing horseracing regulations concerning doping, medication control, and racetrack safety, and creating a private entity to establish and enforce rules in those areas. 15 U.S.C. § 3501 *et seq.* Kentucky, Louisiana, Oklahoma, Texas, and West Virginia all challenged the law as constitutionally defective and harmful to state

sovereignty, and those suits are pending as of this casebook edition. Among the law's alleged defects is that the private regulator imposed nationwide and arbitrary standards on topics such as the types of horseshoes required for racing and training, and how many times a jockey may use a crop (whip) during races. Are there reasons why such regulation should not be centralized at the federal level? One justification offered for the law was doping scandals throughout the sport; does this integrity threat more than others warrant a government response?

C. SPORTS GAMBLING AND RELATED INTEGRITY RISKS

1. HISTORICAL AVERSION TO GAMBLING

In 1919, Major League Baseball (MLB) was convulsed by accusations that underworld gambling interests bribed eight members of the Chicago White Sox to throw the World Series against the Cincinnati Reds. In response, MLB appointed Judge Kenesaw Mountain Landis to the newly created Office of the Commissioner (discussed further in Chapter 2), and gave him absolute authority to restore the sport's integrity. Although all eight ballplayers were acquitted in a public trial in 1921, Commissioner Landis permanently banned them from baseball. The "Black Sox" episode demonstrates the overriding concern with how gambling can affect a sport's or league's reputation.

Baseball's aversion to gambling persisted for the next 100 years. In 1942, Commissioner Landis required Philadelphia Phillies' owner William Cox to sell his team after Landis discovered Cox had placed about a dozen small bets on the Phillies to win. Disciplinary action has been taken against players and managers merely for associating with gambling, even when no personal betting was involved. For example, Landis' successor, Albert "Happy" Chandler, suspended Dodgers' manager Leo Durocher for the 1947 season just for associating with gamblers, and Commissioner Bowie Kuhn suspended New York Yankees' owner George Steinbrenner from the baseball (though not the financial) affairs of the Yankees for paying a gambler, Howard Spira, to produce unsavory information about his own player, Dave Winfield. Indeed, in 1979 Bowie Kuhn went so far as to ban Willie Mays and Mickey Mantle from any official connections with professional baseball because they took public relations jobs with Atlantic City gambling casinos, a decision rescinded by his successor, Peter Ueberroth, in 1985. Baseball's particular anxiety about gambling is exemplified in the 1989 Pete Rose gambling controversy, discussed in detail in Chapter 2, Section B.

Other league commissioners have also acted forcefully over the decades. In 1963, NFL Commissioner Pete Rozelle suspended all-pros Paul Hornung of the Green Bay Packers and Alex Karras of the Detroit Lions for a year for betting on their own teams to win. On the other hand, in 1986, Tulane's star center John "Hot Rod" Williams was indicted for allegedly taking money and drugs from gamblers in exchange for "point shaving" in a 1985 game against Memphis State. National Basketball Association (NBA) Commissioner David Stern permitted the Cleveland Cavaliers to draft and pay Williams, but not to play him pending trial, in which Williams was ultimately acquitted by a New Orleans jury. Based on the acquittal, Stern took no action against Williams, who went on to a successful and lucrative NBA career with Cleveland and Phoenix.

Molinas Case. The only judicial ruling about the legality of severe league punishment of game participants who bet on their sport came in an antitrust suit filed by ex-NBA player Jack Molinas. *See Molinas v. NBA*, 190 F. Supp. 241 (S.D.N.Y. 1961). Molinas graduated from Columbia University in 1953 and was drafted by the NBA's Fort Wayne Pistons. In January 1954, he admitted that he had regularly bet on the Pistons to win certain games—depending on the relative point spread between the two teams. Halfway into his first NBA season, he had netted a betting profit of around $400. As soon as NBA Commissioner Maurice Podoloff learned of this practice, he suspended Molinas indefinitely for violating Section 79 of the league's constitution and Paragraph 15 of his player contract, both prohibiting any such gambling. Over the next few years, Podoloff rejected several Molinas requests for reinstatement, saying that he must never return because he was a "cancer to the league." In the meantime, Molinas attended Brooklyn Law School and was admitted to the New York State Bar.

Molinas then filed an antitrust suit against the league alleging that NBA member clubs had collectively enacted and enforced anti-gambling rules that barred any team from signing him even if they desired his services. He charged that his resulting lifetime expulsion for gambling thereby constituted an illegal antitrust conspiracy of all teams in the league to boycott his services. The court rejected Molinas' claim, concluding that league rules and player contract clauses providing for suspension of those who bet on games in which they participate "seems not only reasonable, but necessary for the survival of the league." *Id.* at 243. Chapters 6–8 of this book address the Sherman Antitrust Act's ban on "contracts, combinations, or conspiracies in restraint of trade," and the economic analysis used to determine whether a challenged practice is reasonable, which asks whether a practice enhances or diminishes consumer welfare. Although the *Molinas* decision predates modern antitrust analysis, the court implicitly found that consumers—the public—benefit from the NBA's anti-gambling stance in that it maintains their confidence in the game. Would that finding make sense in today's legalized gambling environment?

The *Molinas* court further rejected the ballplayer's claim that his conduct was not immoral because he bet only on his own team to win:

> The vice inherent in the plaintiff's conduct is that each time he either placed a bet or refused to place a bet, this operated inevitably to inform bookmakers of an insider's opinion as to the adequacy or inadequacy of the point-spread or his team's ability to win. Thus, for example, when he chose to place a bet, this would indicate to the bookmakers that a member of the Fort Wayne team believed that his team would exceed its expected performance. Similarly, when he chose not to bet, bookmakers thus would be informed of his opinion that the Pistons would not perform according to expectations. It is certainly reasonable for the league and Mr. Podoloff to conclude that this conduct could not be tolerated and must, therefore, be eliminated. The reasonableness of the league's action is apparent in view of the fact that, at that time, the confidence of the public in basketball had been shattered, due to a series of gambling incidents. Thus, it was absolutely necessary for the sport to exhume gambling from its midst for all times in order to survive.

Id. at 244. The court's logic implies that the harm from a player gambling on his team to win arises from his lack of anonymity in placing the bet. What if anonymity could be guaranteed—what other values are at stake? Consider whether allowing athletes or coaches to bet on their own teams to win might affect their own performance in the game, depending on the odds or the amount wagered.

The *Molinas* decision had an ironic aftermath. While the litigation was underway, Molinas was actually the ringleader of a nationwide scheme in which he bribed 47 basketball players from 27 schools to shave points in college games played between 1957 and 1961. He served a 10-to-15 year prison sentence after being convicted of conspiracy, bribery, and suborning perjury.

Since that scandal, college basketball and football point-shaving schemes have been the subject of at least seven criminal prosecutions (involving Auburn, San Diego, Toledo, Northwestern, Arizona State, Tulane, and Boston College), and are one reason why the NCAA prohibits student-athletes from making sports wagers of any kind including on college sports, professional sports, and even fantasy leagues. Risk of match-fixing is higher where game participants are not well remunerated, which has historically been the case in college athletics. College athletes are especially vulnerable to being groomed for corrupt gambling schemes if their playing eligibility is at risk because of poor academic performance, or if they do not have a future in professional sports. Consider whether these risks are mitigated by the changing landscape of college athletics, discussed further in Chapter 12, in which student-athletes receive greater benefits and are permitted to monetize their publicity rights.

PASPA. Concern in the late twentieth century about sports bribery scandals and about the growth of sports gambling, which some states sought to legalize to generate tax revenue, led Congress to enact the Professional and Amateur Sports Protection Act (PASPA) in 1992. Its lead sponsor was Senator Bill Bradley of New Jersey, a former basketball star with Princeton and the New York Knicks. All four major professional sports leagues and the NCAA lobbied hard for its passage. In support of the bill, then NFL Commissioner Paul Tagliabue testified before Congress:

> Sports gambling threatens the integrity of, and public confidence in, team sports. Sports lotteries inevitably foster a climate of suspicion about controversial plays and intensify cynicism with respect to player performances, coaching decisions, officiating calls and game results. Cynical or disappointed fans would come to assume "the fix was in" whenever the team they bet on failed to beat the point spread. . . . Its proliferation would appear to athletes to give official sanction to sports gambling and could threaten actual corruption of the games by undermining the ability of professional and amateur sports organizations to police themselves.

Hearings on S. 474 Before the Subcomm. On Patents, Copyrights and Trademarks, 102d Cong., 1st Sess., 25 (1991) (S. Hrg. 102–499).

PASPA prohibited states from authorizing sports gambling within their respective jurisdictions with certain grandfathered exceptions. PASPA did not directly prohibit sports gambling, but rather included two principal prohibitions. First, 28 U.S.C. § 3702(1) prohibited governmental entities from licensing or authorizing by law lotteries, sweepstakes, or gambling on amateur or professional sports. Second, 28 U.S.C. § 3702(2) barred both governmental entities and private individuals from sponsoring, operating, advertising, or promoting the same. PASPA authorized the U.S. Attorney General as well as professional and amateur sports leagues and organizations to institute a civil injunctive action to stop any state or entity suspected of violating the law. 28 U.S.C. § 3703. Thus, for more than 25 years, PASPA effectively confined lawful sports gambling in the U.S. to Nevada casinos and sports lotteries operated by three other States.

PASPA did not thwart illegal sportsbooks, whose annual "handle"— the total amount of bets placed—was estimated to have grown to between $67 billion and $150 billion in those 25 years. That growth was spurred in large part by the internet, which facilitated wagering through illegal offshore operators. Advancing digital and mobile technology allowed bettors to follow sports contests anywhere in the world and use personal devices to place bets and receive payouts without ever physically interacting with the dangerous elements associated with black market gambling. But, according to the United Nations Office on Drugs and Crime, *Global Report on Corruption in Sport* (2021), the internet also heralded an exponential increase in gambling-related corruption:

> [I]n the space of just a few years, technological innovation has transformed sports betting into a highly volatile, liquid and ill-controlled financial market. It has become possible to place large bets on a very wide range of sports involving primary and secondary competitions, professional and amateur sports, and with relative anonymity. This evolution has also facilitated the activities of those involved in competition manipulation. By fixing results in advance and placing a larger number of bets on different platforms, sizeable sums of money can be won, at minimal costs and with negligible risk of being caught. Although there is a long history of the manipulation of sports competitions, the advent of online sports betting has exacerbated the scale of the phenomenon to the point that networks have been created at both the international and national levels to bribe, coerce and threaten referees, players and club officials to manipulate competitions to ensure given outcomes or events take place during a competition.

NOTES AND QUESTIONS

1.   *Molinas and Illegal Sports Gambling.* Sports gambling was generally illegal at the time Molinas violated the NBA's gambling ban. Thus, Molinas was violating the law regardless of the type of sports wager he made. Would it have made a difference to the court's perspective on Molinas placing bets on his own team if sports gambling were legal at the time?

2.   *Gambling and the Best Interests of Sport.* Should it have made a difference to the MLB commissioner that Pete Rose always bet on his own Reds team to win? What should baseball have done to record-holding slugger Albert Belle, who in a 1997 deposition in a lawsuit admitted that he had lost tens of thousands of dollars betting with bookies on football or basketball (though never baseball) games, something that was a misdemeanor under Ohio state law? Or to all-star fielder Len Dykstra, who one year apparently lost $100,000 playing in a privately-organized and illegal poker game during the off-season? How should the NBA have dealt with Michael Jordan who, while playing for the Chicago Bulls, created a huge controversy when (with his father) he traveled down from Madison Square Garden after a playoff game with the New York Knicks to gamble at a (legal) casino in Atlantic City? What exactly is it about gambling that makes this behavior (or just associating with it) "detrimental to the best interests of the sport"? Jeffrey Standen, in *The Beauty of Bets: Wagers as Compensation for Professional Athletes*, 42 WILLAMETTE L.

REV. 639 (2006), argues that allowing betting by athletes would be in the best interest of sports.

3. *Sports Leagues as Private Attorneys General.* PASPA is a rare example of a federal statute empowering only a handful of specific private entities to serve as private attorneys general in enforcing the law. Did the public interest in limiting sports gambling justify supplementing law enforcement in this way? Or was PASPA's delegation only a result of the limited resources and/or interest of government in taking the enforcement lead on this issue?

2. CLEARING THE WAY FOR LEGAL SPORTS GAMBLING: *MURPHY V. NCAA*

The same technology that facilitated the growth of sports betting and corruption also offers some advantages in protecting game integrity, and this contributed to a softening of opposition to legalization. In the digital age, taking gambling out of the black market provides access to data to track customer activity and identify betting anomalies that suggest possible corruption. The rapidity with which times changed is evident in the op-ed article NBA Commissioner Adam Silver wrote in 2014, calling for sports gambling to be legalized and regulated. Adam Silver, *Legalize and Regulate Sports Betting*, NEW YORK TIMES, Nov. 13, 2014. Silver envisioned a legal betting regime with technological and practical safeguards to include:

> mandatory monitoring and reporting of unusual betting-line movements; a licensing protocol to ensure betting operators are legitimate; minimum-age verification measures; geo-blocking technology to ensure betting is available only where it is legal; mechanisms to identify and exclude people with gambling problems; and education about responsible gaming.

Ironically, Silver made this appeal in the midst of his league battling to stop New Jersey from authorizing sports gambling in Atlantic City casinos.

New Jersey's renewed interest in sports betting was designed to bolster state coffers in an economic downturn. In 2011, New Jersey amended its state constitution to allow the legislature to legalize the activity. When New Jersey passed a law in 2012 decriminalizing sports betting, the NBA, NFL, National Hockey League (NHL), MLB, and NCAA sough to enjoin the activity. Ultimately, in *Murphy v. NCAA,* 138 S. Ct. 1461 (2018), the Supreme Court struck down PASPA on constitutional grounds. The decision is principally about constitutional federalism and not sports law: the Court held that PASPA had unconstitutionally "commandeered" states to enforce federal law in violation of the Tenth Amendment. Nonetheless, the decision reveals important background and perceptions about how sports leagues, legislators, and regulators approach the issue.

The leagues had sought injunctive relief under PASPA grounded in their concern about reputational harm their sports would suffer if it were legal to wager on their games. Justice Alito's majority opinion began by observing that "Americans have never been of one mind about gambling, and attitudes have swung back and forth. By the end of the nineteenth century, gambling was largely banned throughout the country, but beginning in the 1920s and 1930s, laws prohibiting gambling were gradually loosened." Justice Alito traced widespread bans on gambling before and after the turn of the twentieth century, and the easing of state controls towards the end of the century. Legalized gambling increased significantly with passage of the federal Indian Gaming Regulatory Act in 1988, 25 U.S.C. § 2701 *et seq.*, permitting casinos on Indian land throughout the country. Justice Alito noted the strong opposition to sports gambling specifically. He cited claims from PASPA's legislative history and by the Act's proponents that it is particularly addictive and especially attractive to young people with a strong interest in sports, and in the past gamblers corrupted and seriously damaged the reputation of professional and amateur sports.

To briefly summarize the "anticommandeering principle," set forth largely in *New York* v. *United States*, 505 U.S. 144 (1992), and *Printz v. United States*, 521 U.S. 898 (1997), Article I, § 8 of the Constitution authorizes Congress to directly regulate citizens, but not sovereign states. In the Court's understanding, this provision preserves a "healthy balance of power between the States and the Federal Government," reduces "the risk of tyranny and abuse from either front," promotes political accountability by making clear that a mandate comes from Congress, and prevents Congress from shifting the costs of regulation to the States. Section 3702(1) of PASPA violated this principle by directly compelling the states to enact and enforce a federal regulatory program.

Significantly, the *Murphy* majority acknowledged that Congress has the power to bar state or private entities from actually sponsoring sports betting, and that it did so in § 3702(2) of PASPA. However, the Court declined to save this provision by "severing" the invalid one because it concluded that Congress would not have enacted the provision as a stand-alone law. The Court observed that the 1992 law was designed to bar both state-run sports lotteries and legalized casino sports bookmaking. The majority concluded that Congress would not have wanted to prevent states from running sports lotteries, while giving legislatures the freedom to authorize sports gambling in privately owned casinos:

> The present cases illustrate exactly how Congress must have intended § 3702(1) and § 3702(2) to work. If a State attempted to authorize particular private entities to engage in sports gambling, the State could be sued under § 3702(1), and the private entity could be sued at the same time under § 3702(2). The two sets of

provisions were meant to be deployed in tandem to stop what PASPA aimed to prevent: state legalization of sports gambling. But if, as we now hold, Congress lacks the authority to prohibit a State from legalizing sports gambling, the prohibition of private conduct under § 3702(2) ceases to implement any coherent federal policy.

Under § 3702(2), private conduct violates federal law only if it is permitted by state law. That strange rule is exactly the opposite of the general federal approach to gambling. Under 18 U.S.C. § 1955, operating a gambling business violates federal law only if that conduct is illegal under state or local law. Similarly, 18 U.S.C. § 1953, which criminalizes the interstate transmission of wagering paraphernalia, and 18 U.S.C. § 1084, which outlaws the interstate transmission of information that assists in the placing of a bet on a sporting event, apply only if the underlying gambling is illegal under state law. *See also* 18 U.S.C. § 1952 (making it illegal to travel in interstate commerce to further a gambling business that is illegal under applicable state law).

These provisions implement a coherent federal policy: They respect the policy choices of the people of each State on the controversial issue of gambling. By contrast, if § 3702(2) is severed from § 3702(1), it implements a perverse policy that undermines whatever policy is favored by the people of a State. If the people of a State support the legalization of sports gambling, federal law would make the activity illegal. But if a State outlaws sports gambling, that activity would be lawful under § 3702(2). We do not think that Congress ever contemplated that such a weird result would come to pass.

138 S. Ct. at 1483.

The Court concluded by observing:

The legalization of sports gambling is a controversial subject. Supporters argue that legalization will produce revenue for the States and critically weaken illegal sports betting operations, which are often run by organized crime. Opponents contend that legalizing sports gambling will hook the young on gambling, encourage people of modest means to squander their savings and earnings, and corrupt professional and college sports.

The legalization of sports gambling requires an important policy choice, but the choice is not ours to make. Congress can regulate sports gambling directly, but if it elects not to do so, each State is free to act on its own.

Id. at 1484–85.

Justice Ginsburg (joined by Justices Sotomayor and Breyer) dissented. She complained that the majority had deployed "a wrecking ball" to destroy PASPA, when Congress clearly had the constitutional authority to stop private parties from operating sports gambling schemes even if state law authorized them to do so. Citing precedents that require judges to engage "in a salvage rather than a demolition operation" when a statute is unconstitutional, she concluded that Congress would have wanted the constitutionally-valid prohibition on gambling to remain.

———

NOTES AND QUESTIONS

1. *On the Merits.* Do you agree with Justice Alito that Congress in 1992 would not have wanted to retain the ban on state or private sponsorship of sports betting, had it known it was constitutionally barred from prohibiting state authorization of gambling?

2. *State-by-State Basis.* Justice Alito suggests that Americans' diverse and changing views on sports gambling mean that the issue should be decided on a state-by-state basis. Do you agree? Can citizens opposed to gambling achieve their goals if their fellow residents can easily gamble out-of-state? Can Commissioner Silver achieve his objective of regulated gambling if black market bookmakers remain in states where gambling is illegal?

3. *Legal Gambling and Match-Fixing.* As Commissioner Silver suggested in his op-ed, protecting sports integrity may be easier when gambling is legal and regulated with full cooperation between sports leagues, law enforcement, gaming regulators, and bookmakers. Consider the following evidence that corruption is far higher in countries where betting is illegal and thus unregulated.

(a) A major scandal in 2013 threatened one of the fasting growing sports leagues, the Indian Premier League of cricket. Three Rajasthan Royals players and assorted illegal bookmakers were disciplined for "spot fixing." Under the scheme, the corrupt players signaled to bookies at the beginning of an over (loosely like a baseball inning, consisting of six balls bowled to the batsman by the same bowler) that they would concede a certain number of runs. When a Bollywood actor was also arrested, he further implicated a senior official of the Chennai Super Kings, who is also the son-in-law of N. Srinivasan, then chairman of the Board of Control of Cricket in India. Commenting on the scandal, an Indian newspaper opined:

> Legalising betting is another essential step towards cleaning up cricket. While players from other countries have been implicated in fixing, it is an uncomfortable fact that South Asia is the nexus of the entire enterprise. Not coincidentally, betting happens to be illegal in India but legal in a number of other cricket-playing nations like England and Australia. It should come as no surprise that driving betting underground in the country that is the hub of the sport's

economic activity will have a vitiating effect on the entire game. The current crop of guilty players may have been dealt with—but unless these larger factors are addressed, it won't be the last one.

Far from a clean sweep, DNA INDIA, Sept. 16, 2013.

(b) Legal gambling in Singapore is strictly limited to certain casinos and sports gambling is not lawful. Yet Europol revealed in February 2013 that criminals based in Singapore had orchestrated a global match-fixing corruption conspiracy that had rigged as many as 680 soccer matches across the world, including two UEFA Champions league matches and several top-flight matches in European national leagues.

(c) In China, where sports gambling is banned, massive corruption in football (soccer) was exposed in the summer of 2012, when two former Chinese Football Administrative Center directors were both sentenced to 10 years of imprisonment for taking bribes. Four prominent players in China's only trip to the World Cup in 2002 were also punished to varying degrees for taking payments to shave points or throw matches. Since then, as many as two dozen former football officials, players, coaches, and referees have been sentenced to prison and fined various amounts as the Chinese government demonstrated what it referred to as a bold attempt to clean up the corruption-plagued sport.

3. POST-*MURPHY* SPORTS GAMBLING REGULATION

(a) Federal Law

In the aftermath of *Murphy*, efforts at the federal level to re-enact constitutionally sound sports-integrity protections failed to gain traction. Many advocated deferring to the states (and tribes), given their traditional role in regulating gaming involving casinos, horse racing, lotteries, and the like. But observe that those gambling businesses offer an integrated entertainment experience where both the wager and the future contingent event on which the wager is placed—the roll of the dice, the equestrian performance—take place physically within a state that exercises regulatory oversight. The state regulator has the authority to control not only the terms and performance of the wagering contract, but also the rules and integrity of the future contingent event, for example, issuing technical standards for gaming devices such as slot machines. *See, e.g.*, Nev. Gaming Comm. Reg. 14.050 (2022).

Sports wagering is different because the underlying contingent event—the athletic contest—is (for the most part) beyond the physical and legal control of the betting operator and the state regulators. Sports contests that serve as the future contingent event for an in-state wager frequently occur beyond the state's borders. Mississippi now offers sports betting on every one of the four major professional leagues, none of which has a team located in that state. Consider whether federal involvement is necessary for gambling on future contingent events like athletic contests, which individual states have no authority to superintend. If Congress were to directly regulate sports gambling, what should that regulation cover?

With the demise of PASPA, the remaining federal statutes that target sports gambling-related behaviors and activities focus on illegal betting or the integrity of legal betting, with the exception of the first listed below:

- Sports Bribery Act criminalizes bribery to influence the outcome of a sporting contest. 18 U.S.C. § 224.

- Wire Act criminalizes cross-border wire communications that transmit "bets or wagers or information assisting in the placing of bets or wagers on any sporting event or contest." 18 U.S.C. § 1084.

- Travel Act prohibits use of the mail and other methods to send illegal gambling materials or make an illegal bet. 18 U.S.C. § 1952.

- Wagering Paraphernalia Act prohibits the transportation of gambling paraphernalia across state lines "for use in bookmaking, or wagering pools with respect to a sporting event." 18 U.S.C. § 1953.

- Illegal Gambling Business Act punishes operating a gambling business in violation of state law. 18 U.S.C. § 1955.

- Unlawful Internet Gambling Enforcement Act criminalizes the transfer of funds between a financial institution and an internet gambling website. 31 U.S.C. § 5361 *et seq.*

One ramification of these extant federal statutes is that any state that chooses to legalize sports gambling after *Murphy* may authorize the activity only within its own borders and, if permitting online sports wagers, must ensure through geo-location technology the legitimate in-state presence of every bettor.

(b) State Laws

After *Murphy*, states quickly mobilized to pass legislation legalizing, regulating, and, most pertinently, taxing sports gambling. As of this casebook edition, sports betting is legal in 35 states and the District of Columbia. The sports leagues correspondingly mobilized to lobby statehouses on behalf of their economic and integrity interests, with limited success. From their perspective, key issues that sports betting legislation must address include:

(1) The type of sports betting that can occur, and who (regulators, bookmakers, sports leagues) can approve or veto specific wagers;

(2) Procedures for identifying suspicious betting patterns and notifying relevant stakeholders;

(3) Confidential information that can be shared among law enforcers, gambling regulators, bookmakers, and leagues;

(4) Who shares in the profits from sports wagering: taxes for federal, state, and local governments, and fees for cooperation from sports leagues; and

(5) Whether players have a right to a share of the proceeds directly (this question is considered with regard to publicity rights in Chapter 9).

Because Nevada enjoyed a substantial head start over other states in operating its sports wagering system, many states looked to its regulatory model in establishing their own systems.

The Nevada Model. Nevada uses the same licensing and enforcement agents to regulate both casinos and sportsbooks, rather than creating oversight boards specific to one category of wagers. All bookmaking establishments must receive a license from state gaming authorities. Nev. Rev. Stat. § 463.0129(1)(d)(e) (2022). Nevada will not issue a license to any establishment until they present satisfactory evidence that they are financially capable of paying off all current obligations. Nev. Gaming Comm. Reg. 3.050 (2022). In addition to financial requirements, the Nevada Gaming Commission (NGC) requires all licensees to be of good character, display adequate business competence, and maintain a reputation that will not result in adverse publicity for the Nevada gambling industry as a whole. Reg. 3.090(1). The NGC also regulates the location of gambling establishments.

In Nevada, public policy seeks a cooperative, working relationship between gaming regulators and licensees. Regulators not only enforce gaming regulations, but also act as consultants, helping licensees find solutions and plan ahead. Licensees are able to use regulators as a resource to better avoid possible infractions. The state benefits because, in counseling licensees as to the best courses of action, regulators are less likely to expend resources on investigating and disciplining licensees.

Regarding the types of sports wagers permitted, bookmakers may take bets on any type of sports event or play, as long as they follow the general requirements for permitted wagers and the sports event can be recorded or proven to have or have not occurred. Reg. 22.120. Licensed sports pools may accept wagers on specific sporting events regarding who will win and whether the total points scored in a specified event will be higher or lower than a number specified for the event. Reg. 22.060(4). Nevada bookmakers may also accept "prop bets" (also known as "spot bets") on statistically discrete events beyond the outcome of the game. Common examples of prop bets are: which team will score first, how many balls or strikes will a pitcher throw in a game, which player will score the first touchdown in a game, who will shoot the most three-pointers, etc. Reg. 22.060(7).

Regarding integrity threats, the Nevada regulations offer some safeguards. Nevada bans accepting sports wagers from participants in the contest, including officials, owners, coaches, team staff, and players, Reg. 22.1205(2), and relatedly prohibits "messenger" betting, that is, placing a bet on behalf of another party. Reg. 22.060(5). But there is no official mechanism for cooperation with sports leagues and governing bodies to implement these bans. Nevada bookmakers are also required to file reports on suspicious wagers with the Nevada Gaming Control Board. Reg. 22.121(2). However, those reports are confidential and the Board may not share them with parties interested in the transaction, including the sports property, unless for "the necessary administration of their duties and responsibilities." Reg. 22.121(5).

The Board is the state's investigative and enforcement agency and acts in a prosecutorial capacity, with the NGC functioning as an adjudicator. Both the Board and the NGC have discretion to determine if an event should be considered a risk to the integrity of gaming and the protection of the public, and consultation with the sports property is not required. If a sports league has reservations about suspicious activity it discovers on its own, it can ask the Board to conduct an investigation, but has no guarantee of being kept informed.

Absent from the Nevada model, and from most state gambling laws, are provisions suggested by sports leagues on the key issues identified above. The NBA and MLB unsuccessfully lobbied for gaming states to adopt their Model Sports Wagering Act, which provided for sports league veto power over certain wagers. For example, they sought to keep states from offering bets on minor league or developmental league games, where players are paid less and might be more susceptible to bribes to throw games or shave points. They sought to limit in-game wagers, which they believe to be more vulnerable to manipulation. They sought to curtail prop bets on events that have little impact on the outcome of the game, and regarding which athletes may discount the ethical, criminal, and sporting implications of a fix. No state has conferred such veto power on the leagues.

The leagues also failed to convince any state so far to share sports gambling revenue by paying them "integrity fees" to compensate the leagues for the additional costs that legal gambling purportedly imposes on safeguarding game integrity. At this writing, only three states have adopted the leagues' proposal to require sportsbooks to purchase their official game data from the leagues at commercially reasonable rates. *See, e.g.*, Tenn. Code § 4–49–116 (2022). Nor were the leagues successful in persuading the states to stiffen their criminal laws that might address match-fixing. What would you include in a model state sports gambling statute?

(c) International Model

Contrast the U.S. legal landscape with the regulatory approach of countries that have longer experience with legal sports gambling. In Australia's State of Victoria, a "sports controlling body"—typically a sports league—initiates the process for authorizing gambling on its contests by applying to a state commission. *See* Gambling and Racing Legislation Amendment (Sports Betting) Act 2007. The state commission considers such factors as whether:

(1) the applicant has control of the event or administers the event;

(2) the applicant has adequate rules in place to ensure integrity;

(3) the applicant complies with international codes relating to integrity in sport;

(4) the applicant has resources and authority to monitor integrity systems;

(5) the applicant has clear policies on the provision of information relevant to the betting market;

(6) the applicant has a clear process for reporting the results of the event and hearing appeals relating to the results;

(7) the applicant has a clear policy of sharing information with sports betting providers in order to investigate suspicious betting activity;

(8) the applicant is the most appropriate body to be approved as the controlling body for the event;

(9) approval supports the public interest.

For events with approved betting, Victoria sportsbooks may accept wagers only if they meet three prerequisites. First, the sportsbook must have an agreement with the sports controlling body in charge of the sporting event, unless the event is wholly outside of Victoria. Second, the agreement must promote integrity by providing for information sharing. Third, the agreement must stipulate whether the sportsbook will pay a fee to the sports controlling body and specify the amount of the fee. If the sportsbook is unable to reach an agreement with a sports controlling body, the provider may apply to the commission for the right to service bets. The commission reserves the right to revoke approval for gambling on a sports event at any time for reasonable cause. In addition, Victoria created a series of new criminal offenses to make it illegal "to engage[ ] in conduct that corrupts a betting outcome of an event," defining conduct to encompass all means that might be used beyond bribery, including extortion, blackmail, and duress.

With the globalization and digitization of betting markets, a number of international public and non-governmental organizations have identified match-fixing as an increasing threat. *See* United Nations Office on Drugs and Crime, *Global Report on Corruption in Sport* (2021); Interpol and International Olympic Committee, *Handbook on Protecting Sport from Competition Manipulation* (2016). By 2011, the threat was sufficiently dire that Interpol, the inter-governmental law enforcement agency, created an Integrity in Sport unit and started issuing a bi-weekly bulletin that tracks competition manipulation. By 2016, it was estimated that match-fixing in European sports alone exceeded 1,000 contests annually, involving nations where sports gambling is largely legal.

In response, the Council of Europe promulgated the Convention on the Manipulation of Sports Competitions (the Macolin Convention), which entered into force in 2019 after being signed by 39 nations (the U.S. is not a signatory). The Macolin Convention defines match-fixing as:

> an intentional arrangement, act or omission aimed at improper alteration of the result or the course of a sports competition in order to remove all or part of the unpredictable nature of the aforementioned sports competition with a view to obtaining an undue advantage for oneself or for others.

The Convention then sets out a policy and framework to fight the manipulation of sport. Its signature innovation is the concept of the "national platform"—an official entity that joins public and private stakeholders to coordinate and centralize operational, informational, strategic, and enforcement activities relating to competition manipulation. Treaty ratifiers commit to establish an institutional structure under which disparate agencies, including police and prosecutorial entities, sports governing bodies, competition organizers, sports betting operators, and betting regulators, work together to combat sports corruption. Of note, the Convention requires signatory nations to consult with private sports organizations and betting operators regarding types of wagers and who may wager, to mitigate gambling's harms and to identify and manage risks of sports manipulation.

(d) Sports League Self-Regulation

As legal sports betting unfolded across the U.S., the major sports leagues revisited and strengthened their gambling policies, and expanded their monitoring and enforcement apparatus. All league collective bargaining agreements prohibit players from betting on the sport; provisions in league constitutions and bylaws extend that ban to club owners and personnel. In addition, the leagues have promulgated gambling policies that apply to all personnel—players, coaches, owners, game officials, league and team employees, and other staff and vendors.

The NFL's gambling policy, updated in 2018 in anticipation of PASPA's demise, set the standard ultimately followed by the other professional leagues. All personnel are prohibited from betting on football in any way at any time, and may not enter a sportsbook during the football season. A player who bets on football risks suspension or expulsion from the league. All personnel other than players are also prohibited from any other sports betting. The policy requires all personnel to give their "best efforts" in performing their duties and to never engage in any form of competition manipulation. "No tipping" rules are in place to protect confidential information that might provide others with a gambling-related advantage. Endorsements of and associations with gambling-related individuals and enterprises are off limits. All personnel are obligated to report gambling debts and policy violations, including improper solicitations or approaches made to themselves and others.

While the NFL policy bans ownership in gambling-related businesses, a loophole exists to allow personnel to own equity interests in an entity that generates less than a third of its revenue from gambling. At the time the policy was adopted this was deemed sufficient to permit owners like the Dallas Cowboys' Jerry Jones and the New England Patriots' Bob Kraft to retain significant investments in DraftKings, a fantasy sports provider. Since then, DraftKings has shifted its focus to sports betting, setting up a potential showdown. Do you think the NFL should require divestment of such interests?

The NFL's compliance efforts include staffing up its monitoring, investigating, and enforcement functions, and implementing a massive, periodic education and training program for 10,000 individuals associated with the league, whether as players, employees, consultants, vendors, or contractors. Having failed to achieve statutory compulsion of official data usage, the NFL, like the other leagues, has partnered with sports data and technology companies to generate and license official data feeds that will appeal to sportsbooks on the merits of their authenticity, accuracy and speed.

In this vein, the NFL and its member clubs have welcomed other commercial opportunities heralded by legal gambling. The 2020–2030 NFL-NFLPA Collective Bargaining Agreement provides insight into how this potential is viewed, as it expressly includes gambling revenue in the basis for determining the player salary floor and cap, and identifies multiple permissible sources for generating such revenue, including in-stadium sports books. As of 2022, that revenue is being driven by multi-year sponsorship deals with the major U.S. sports betting enterprises, including DraftKings, FanDuel, BetMGM, and Caesars, the aggregate value of which was reported to exceed $1 billion. For their money, these approved sportsbook operators obtain exclusive rights to purchase commercial inventory during NFL telecasts and to use league and club marks and logos in their marketing. Many individual clubs have separate deals with these companies to offer in-stadium sportsbooks and advertising, and to engage fans with special team-specific sweepstakes.

The NBA and MLB have adopted new policies on sports betting that largely track the NFL policy (and have similarly embarked on new gambling business partnerships). The NBA imposes especially strict requirements on referees, likely a continuing reaction to the 2007 scandal involving referee Tim Donaghy who bet on games he officiated (see more in the notes that follow). Baseball's policy diverges in its detailed approach to ownership interests in entities involved in sports betting. MLB owners are allowed to hold ownership interests of up to 10% in a sports gaming company, as long as they do not serve as an officer, director, or employee of the company and they adopt safeguards to protect confidential MLB information about players, transactions, and other league or club business. An MLB owner's interest in a sports gaming company may exceed 10% only if the company does not offer wagering on games involving: the owner's team, affiliated minor league teams, the performance of any player on such teams, or league-wide events like the All-Star Game. The NHL's gambling policy offers less detail, consistent with the sport's lower appeal to gamblers, as games are typically low scoring with fewer opportunities for specialty wagers and prop bets.

NOTES AND QUESTIONS

1.   *Times Change.* Consider how far the professional sports leagues have come since their 1992 advocacy for PASPA. As recently as 2018 in the *Murphy* litigation they sought to enjoin sports gambling as harmful to their reputations. Today, they embrace it as a key mover of fan engagement and driver of ancillary revenue. How does this change of heart mesh with their integrity concerns? To what extent does the ubiquity of legal sports gambling in the U.S. promote future corruption of athletic contests? Is there anything to learn from the European and Australian experience with legal sports betting?

2.   *Elite Athletes and Gambling.* Especially in the major U.S. professional leagues, where players are well paid celebrities, many assume the risk of exposure and league discipline is likely sufficient to deter players from prohibited gambling and gambling-related match-fixing. And yet, in 2021, Atlanta Falcons wide receiver Calvin Ridley bet $1,500 on NFL games while on a mental health leave from the team. NFL Commissioner Roger Goodell suspended Ridley indefinitely, with leave to seek reinstatement in one year, the first such gambling-related suspension in decades. Goodell's suspension letter stated:

> There is nothing more fundamental to the NFL's success—and to the reputation of everyone associated with our league—than upholding the integrity of the game. This is the responsibility of every player,

coach, owner, game official, and anyone else employed in the league. Your actions put the integrity of the game at risk, threatened to damage public confidence in professional football, and potentially undermined the reputations of your fellow players throughout the NFL.

Do you agree with the league's view that Ridley's infraction goes to a core function and responsibility of an NFL player? Some protested that the suspension was extreme in comparison to discipline imposed on other misconduct, such as domestic violence. Is such discipline hypocritical in view of the league's promotion of gambling?

3.   *Team Owners and Gambling.* A famous (and possibly apocryphal) episode of illicit sports gambling took place in 1958 when Baltimore Colts owner Carroll Rosenbloom allegedly bet $25,000 on his team to win the NFL championship game, in which the point spread was three-and-a-half points. The game was in overtime with a 17–17 tie, when the Colts drove deep into New York Giants territory and could have made an easy field goal to win. But that would have given the Colts only a three-point victory that would not cover the point spread. The Colts went for the touchdown and won, enabling Rosenbloom to collect on his wager and inviting speculation on what motivated the play-calling. Is such speculation likely to mushroom in an era in which team owners are business partners with gambling enterprises? If a particular game event or outcome would beat the odds sufficiently to imperil a partner sportsbook's liquidity, will fans suspect owner interference when that outcome is only barely and abruptly averted?

4.   *Lone-Wolf Match-Fixing.* How adequately does the evolving legal sports betting regime address the risk of "lone-wolf" match-fixing by a game participant who is suspected of unilaterally manipulating a sporting event? One example is NBA referee Tim Donaghy who from 2003 through 2007 bet on games at which he officiated. By the 2006–07 season, mobsters running the illegal sportsbook where Donaghy placed his wagers noticed his unusually high success rate, figured out his identity, and hijacked his scheme. They extorted him to pick winning bets for them to place, based on his access to non-public information, including the identity of officiating crews for upcoming games, team/referee relationships, and the physical condition of certain players.

An FBI investigation of other mob activities uncovered the gambling scheme and resulted in the criminal prosecution of Donaghy for conspiracy to commit wire fraud. He served eleven months in federal prison. Why do you think prosecutors declined to prosecute Donaghy under the Sports Bribery Act? The NBA pursued victim restitution covering the four years of Donaghy's scheme, but the court awarded only costs associated with the final 2006–07 year when Donaghy was working for the mob, because no penal code provision provided a predicate for charging Donaghy with his earlier lone-wolf conduct. *See* Jodi S. Balsam, *Criminalizing Match-Fixing as America Legalizes Sports Gambling*, 31 MARQ. SPORTS L. REV. 1 (2020).

5.   *"Tipping" a.k.a. Insider Trading.* Sports league gambling policies and many state gambling regulations prohibit bettors from using or disclosing confidential, non-public information regarding games, players, or other conditions material to placing a wager. Like insider trading rules in finance, no "tipping" rules protect the market-makers (the sportsbooks) and other traders (the bettors), as the Donaghy case illustrates. Furthermore, tipping is often the gateway to match-fixing: corrupt actors first just seek to learn something from the insider and then, once the athlete or coach or game official gives them information illegally, they blackmail the insider into fixing a match. How should leagues and regulators go about enforcing no tipping rules? Is it possible to do so without the level of public-private cooperation mandated by, for example, the Macolin Convention?

6.   *Tennis Match-Fixing.* Rampant fraud has taken place in international tennis, leading to the sport establishing a Tennis Integrity Unit and commissioning an Independent Review of Tennis Integrity. The review's *Final Report*, issued in 2019, describes a "tsunami" of fixed matches at the lower levels of the game, where undercompensated players would "sell" matches to corrupt gambling interests. The report attributed this phenomenon primarily to three factors. First, the nature of the game means only one player needs to act to throw a match, making fixing easy and detection difficult. Second, professional tennis does not offer sufficient opportunities for lower level players to earn enough to cover their costs, providing incentives to fix. Third, the International Tennis Federation's lucrative sale of official live scoring data for thousands of matches made them available for betting and facilitated the corruption. The report recommended abandoning that deal, as well as sponsorships from betting companies. Do you agree that such business partnerships are the culprit here?

While the Tennis Integrity report did not discover any evidence of a cover-up by international governing bodies, it criticized those bodies for lack of transparency, lack of personnel with betting expertise, and inadequate cooperation with law enforcement. And despite the report's disavowal of corruption at the top levels of the game, Russian tennis player Yana Sizikowa, at one time ranked in the top 350, was arrested for allegedly fixing a match at the French Open in 2020, and two Wimbledon 2021 matches were investigated for suspected fixes based on irregular betting patterns. Many of the report's recommendations addressed treatment of players, calling for better integrity training for players, improved tournament security, culling the number of professional players at the lowest levels of the sport to address "incentive problems," and disciplining any form of "tanking" in a match as an integrity offense, even without connection to a betting outcome. Do you agree that the focus of integrity efforts should be on the players? How might the men's and women's tennis tours be restructured to reduce incentives for match-fixing?

7.   *Reclaiming the Game.* Australia, a country where sports wagering has been legal for decades, launched an initiative in 2021 called "Reclaim the Game" which seeks to disassociate sports from gambling. The initiative reflects concern about problem gambling and children's overexposure to sports betting

and advertising. Top level clubs in the National Rugby League, Australian Football League, cricket, and basketball have voluntarily rejected money from sports betting agencies and bookmakers, and banned sports betting sponsorship and advertising from club apparel and stadium signage. Spain has gone a step further, enacting legislation to prohibit betting company logos from appearing on soccer jerseys. With the U.S. still in the early stages of embracing legal sports gambling, consider what limits either public or private regulators should place on gambling sponsorships and business partnerships.

D. CHEATING

The essence of organized sport is that it is played according to a set of rules that govern on-field action and sportsmanship more generally. Participants are expected to know the rules of their sport, and give their best efforts both to compete according to those rules and to deliver a winning performance. It seems simple then to define "cheating" as a game participant deliberately infringing the rules of the game in order to gain an advantage.

However, as Mitchell Berman and Richard Friedman note in THE JURISPRUDENCE OF SPORT: SPORTS AND GAMES AS LEGAL SYSTEMS (West 2021), "the ubiquity of tactical fouls suggests [that] sometimes its permissible to intentionally break the rules." For example, in basketball, late in a close game, the team with fewer points will often intentionally (and nonviolently) foul opponents to stop the clock, force them to the free throw line, and regain possession to try to take the lead. Or in football, a cornerback might intentionally interfere with a wide receiver's catch to avoid the greater evil of allowing a touchdown reception. Few would consider this cheating. On the other hand, sometimes strict compliance with the playing rules can offend the norms of the game, as in the "Bountygate" episode described in Chapter 2, when players on the NFL New Orleans Saints defense earned cash bounties for legal hits designed to injure opponents. While not technically cheating, this behavior violated sportsmanship norms and was deemed detrimental conduct justifying significant discipline for the perpetrators.

Accordingly, some have suggested that the definition of cheating should exempt situations where the "conventions of the sport" allow the rules violation. *See* Fred D'Agostino, *The Ethics of Games*, 8 J. PHIL. SPORT 7 (1981). Others would delimit cheating to *covert* or *surreptitious* rules violations to gain an advantage. *See* Warren P. Fraleigh, *Intentional Rule Violations—One More Time*, 30 J. PHIL. SPORT 166, 168 (2003). And still others, notably Pro Football Hall of Fame quarterback Joe Montana, consider stretching the boundaries of the rulebook to be a legitimate means of gaining a competitive advantage, observing "If you ain't cheating, you ain't trying." See Ryan Wilson, *Joe Montana on Patriots*, CBS SPORTS, Oct. 16, 2015.

Certainly, cheating in sports has been happening as long as people have been playing sports. One essential function of sports governing bodies is to draw the line between what is permissible to obtain a competitive edge and cheating egregious enough to invite punishment. Beyond sporting values, money and prestige are increasingly at stake in these contests. Cheating has real detrimental consequences to its victims—in terms of rankings, fan base, prize money, incentive payouts, ticket sales, sponsorships, endorsements, and broadcast and advertising revenue. In this sense, sports cheating is comparable to other economic crimes such as theft or fraud, and justifies a legal response. That response typically takes the form of league discipline for "conduct detrimental to the integrity of, or public confidence, in" the sport. Sometimes the league response is only the first stage of a protracted dispute that plays out in both private and public tribunals.

1. TAMPERING WITH EQUIPMENT: DEFLATEGATE

The challenges attendant to assessing the appropriate disciplinary response to an episode of sports cheating is evident from the lengthy saga known as "Deflategate." During the 2015 AFC Championship Game between the New England Patriots and the Indianapolis Colts, the NFL discovered that the Patriots used footballs that were underinflated relative to game requirements. NFL Rule 2 requires balls to be inflated to between 12.5 and 13.5 pounds per square inch (psi) to ensure uniformity in how games are played. League officials tested eleven Patriots' balls and found they ranged from 10.5 to 12.3 psi, below the requisite minimum inflation. The considerable degree of underinflation suggested that Patriots staff intentionally deflated the balls to make them easier to grip and throw during the cold and wet conditions that prevailed during the game.

NFL Rule 2 is supplemented with more detailed guidelines, incorporated into the Policy Manual for Member Clubs, concerning the "proper preparation" of footballs. Each team's equipment manager is responsible for preparing 12 footballs for use during a game, subject to prohibitions on altering the ball's "fundamental structure or surface characteristics." On game day, each team must deliver the balls to the referee for inspection and approval, after which tampering has disciplinary consequences according to the Policy Manual:

> Once the balls have left the locker room, no one, including players, equipment managers and coaches are allowed to alter the footballs in any way. If any individual alters the footballs, or if a non-approved ball is used in the game, the person responsible and, if appropriate, the head coach or other club personnel will be subject to discipline, including but not limited to, a fine of $25,000.

After discovering the underinflated balls at the 2015 championship game, the NFL retained attorney Theodore Wells of the Paul, Weiss law firm to conduct an independent investigation. Three months later, having interviewed 66 witnesses and reviewed hours of stadium security video footage and thousands of documents, phone messages and texts, Wells issued a 243-page report that found an intentional violation of Rule 2 and its guidelines. The evidence established that, in accordance with quarterback Tom Brady's preferences, a member of the Patriots equipment staff surreptitiously removed the footballs from the referee's holding location, brought them into a nearby bathroom, deflated them, and then returned them in time for game use. The report concluded:

> It is more probable than not that [equipment staff members Jim McNally and John Jastremski] participated in a deliberate effort to release air from Patriots game balls after the balls were examined by the referee. . . . [And] it is more probable than not that Tom Brady. . .was at least generally aware of the inappropriate activities of McNally and Jastremski involving the release of air from Patriots game balls.

> We do not believe that the evidence establishes that any other Patriots personnel participated in or had knowledge of the violation of the Playing Rules. . . .

> [I]t is unlikely that an equipment assistant and a locker room attendant would deflate game balls without Brady's knowledge and approval. . . . [McNally and Jastremski would not] personally and unilaterally engage in such conduct in the absence of Brady's awareness and consent.

Theodore V. Wells, Jr., *Investigative Report Concerning Footballs Used During the AFC Championship Game on January 18, 2015* (May 6, 2015).

The League fined the Patriots $1 million, stripped the club of two draft picks, and suspended Brady for four games without pay. In announcing the penalties, the League's designated hearing officer Troy Vincent explained:

> As you know, we regard violations of competitive rules as significant and deserving of a strong sanction, both to punish the actual violation and to deter misconduct in the future. In this case, the footballs were intentionally deflated in an effort to provide a competitive advantage to Tom Brady after having been certified by the game officials as being in compliance with the playing rules. While we cannot be certain when the activity began, the evidence suggests that January 18th was not the first and only occasion when this occurred, particularly in light of the evidence referring to deflation of footballs going back to before the beginning of the 2014 season.

> It is impossible to determine whether this activity had an effect on the outcome of games or what that effect was. There seems little question that the outcome of the AFC Championship Game

was not affected. But this has never been a significant factor in assessing discipline. There are many factors which affect the outcome of a game. It is an inherently speculative exercise to try to assign specific weight to any one factor. The key consideration in any case like this is that the playing rules exist for a reason, and all clubs are entitled to expect that the playing rules will be followed by participating teams. Violations that diminish the league's reputation for integrity and fair play cannot be excused simply because the precise impact on the final score cannot be determined.

Here, there are several factors that merit strong consideration in assessing discipline. The first is the club's prior record. In 2007 the club and several individuals were sanctioned for videotaping signals of opposing defensive coaches in violation of the Constitution and Bylaws. Under the Integrity of the Game Policy, this prior violation of competitive rules was properly considered in determining the discipline in this case.

Another important consideration identified in the Policy is "the extent to which the club and relevant individuals cooperated with the investigation." The Wells report identifies two significant failures in this respect. The first involves the refusal by the club's attorneys to make Mr. McNally available for an additional interview, despite numerous requests by Mr. Wells and a cautionary note in writing of the club's obligation to cooperate in the investigation. The second was the failure of Tom Brady to produce any electronic evidence (emails, texts, etc.), despite being offered extraordinary safeguards by the investigators to protect unrelated personal information. Although we do not hold the club directly responsible for Mr. Brady's refusal to cooperate, it remains significant that the quarterback of the team failed to cooperate fully with the investigation.

NFL releases statement on Patriots' violations, NFL.COM, May 11, 2015.

Pursuant to Article 46 of the NFL-NFLPA collective agreement, Brady appealed his suspension to Commissioner Roger Goodell. (The team did not appeal its penalties.) Goodell affirmed the discipline in a 20-page decision that relied heavily on even stronger evidence of Brady's complicity that had emerged on appeal. Namely, on the day the Wells investigative team interviewed him, Brady instructed his assistant to destroy the cellphone that he had been using in the six months surrounding the AFC Championship Game. He thereafter failed to inform the NFL of the cellphone's destruction until the day of his appeal hearing. Below is a decision excerpt addressing that development, and Brady's argument that the discipline was disproportionate and unprecedented.

FINAL DECISION ON ARTICLE 46 APPEAL OF TOM BRADY
July 28, 2015

[Commissioner Goodell reviewed the issues on appeal, the governing standards, and the extensive factual record. He detailed the evidence of Brady's involvement in the tampering scheme and failure to cooperate in the investigation, including new information discovered on appeal that he destroyed relevant and likely incriminating evidence.]

Mr. Brady's failure to cooperate and his destruction of potentially relevant evidence are significant because the ability to conduct an investigation—whether by NFL staff or by independent parties retained by the NFL—ultimately depends on cooperation. Neither the NFL nor any NFL member club has subpoena power or other means to compel production of relevant materials or testimony. Nonetheless, the NFL is entitled to expect and insist upon the cooperation of owners, League employees, club employees and players in a workplace investigation and to impose sanctions when such cooperation is not forthcoming, when evidence is hidden, fabricated, or destroyed, when witnesses are intimidated or not produced upon reasonable request, or when individuals do not provide truthful information. Moreover, in such cases, there is no question that the Hearing Officer may draw an adverse inference from the lack of cooperation and may reasonably interpret available evidence in a manner that supports findings of misconduct.

The evidence fully supports my findings that (1) Mr. Brady participated in a scheme to tamper with the game balls after they had been approved by the game officials for use in the AFC Championship Game and (2) Mr. Brady willfully obstructed the investigation by, among other things, affirmatively arranging for destruction of his cellphone knowing that it contained potentially relevant information that had been requested by the investigators. All of this indisputably constitutes conduct detrimental to the integrity of, and public confidence in, the game of professional football.

V. The Discipline

As noted above, I am very much aware of, and believe in, the need for consistency in discipline for similarly situated players. The NFLPA is wrong, however, to suggest that because no player may have been suspended before for tampering with game footballs or obstructing an investigation, a suspension cannot be issued here. Under the [Collective Bargaining Agreement (CBA)], the law of the shop is clear, as explained by Hearing Officer Henderson in the Tony McDaniel appeal:

> Each case is unique in its facts and circumstances. While it is important that similar cases be treated similarly for discipline purposes, differences are not always apparent, and it is often difficult to see those distinctions long after decisions are made.

Reliance on past decisions, without benefit of all the factors considered, is misplaced.

No prior conduct detrimental proceeding is directly comparable to this one. Here we have a player's uncoerced participation in a scheme to violate a competitive rule that goes to the integrity of the game. Unlike any other conduct detrimental proceeding of which I am aware, . . . this scheme involved undermining efforts by game officials to ensure compliance with League rules.

The scheme, which sought to secure a competitive advantage on the playing field, was coupled with not only (i) a failure to cooperate with the League's investigation, but also (ii) destruction of potentially relevant evidence with knowledge that the evidence had been sought in the investigation.

The conduct at issue here is therefore fundamentally different from that of the players who were found to have engaged in conduct detrimental in the Bounty proceeding. Commissioner Tagliabue there placed great emphasis on his view that the misconduct of the Saints' players was in large part the result of pressure from coaches and other management representatives, resulting in the players' "not hav[ing] much choice but to 'go along.'" The bounty program was largely developed and administered by the coaches, and the pressure on the players extended to "obstruction of the original investigation [which was] directed by Saints' officials." There is no evidence of any such pressure on Mr. Brady here.

To the contrary, the Wells Report documented that the Patriots' ownership, executives, coaching staff, and the head equipment manager, Mr. Schoenfeld, had no knowledge of or participation in the scheme. Those findings are not challenged on appeal. . . .

The conduct at issue here is also very different from the ball-warming incident in Minnesota last year, in which a Carolina Panthers ball attendant was observed warming a ball on the Vikings' sideline; there was no evidence of any intentional attempt to violate or circumvent the rules, no player involvement, and no effort to conceal the ball attendant's conduct. As Mr. Vincent testified, the ball never got into the game and the matter "was addressed immediately."

The conduct at issue here is also very different from the incident involving the Jets' equipment staff member who "attempted to use" unapproved equipment in plain view of the officials to prepare kicking balls prior to a 2009 game against the Patriots. There was no evidence of any player involvement. However, it bears mention that the Jets' employee was suspended from his regular game-day duties for a period longer than the suspension under review here.

In terms of the appropriate level of discipline, the closest parallel of which I am aware is the collectively bargained discipline imposed for a first violation of the policy governing performance enhancing drugs; steroid use reflects an improper effort to secure a competitive advantage in, and threatens the integrity of, the game. Since the advent of our testing for steroid use in the 1980s and now, pursuant to our Collective Bargaining Agreement, the first positive test for the use of performance enhancing drugs has resulted in a four-game suspension without the need for any finding of actual competitive effect. . . .

Tampering with the game balls after they have been approved by the game officials—an effort to undermine the game officials' responsibility to ensure that game balls are in compliance with League rules—is plainly within the scope of matters that may reasonably be judged by the Commissioner to affect the integrity of, and public confidence in, the game of professional football. Mr. Brady knows that players are subject to suspension for violations of the Playing Rules and had no reason to believe that a suspension could not be imposed for the conduct at issue here. . . .

––––––

Brady challenged the Goodell decision in federal court, but under the deferential judicial review accorded to labor arbitration awards (discussed further in Chapter 4), the Second Circuit enforced the discipline. *NFL Management Council v. NFLPA*, 820 F.3d 527 (2d Cir. 2016) (*Brady*). Responding to Brady's assertion that the Commissioner improperly relied on the destroyed cellphone in affirming the suspensions, the court ruled:

> This argument fails because, as set forth in the original disciplinary letter, Brady was punished for failing to cooperate, and it is clear from the Commissioner's decision that Brady's cell phone destruction was part and parcel of the broader claim that he had failed to cooperate. Further, as we stated with regard to general awareness, nothing in Article 46 limits the arbitrator's authority to reexamine the factual basis for a suspension by conducting a hearing. Additionally, the Commissioner did not increase the punishment as a consequence of the destruction of the cell phone—the four-game suspension was not increased. Rather, the cell phone destruction merely provided further support for the Commissioner's determination that Brady had failed to cooperate, and served as the basis for an adverse inference as to his participation in the scheme to deflate footballs.

Id. at 544. Brady served his four-game suspension at the outset of the 2016 season.

––––––

NOTES AND QUESTIONS

1. *Competitive Advantage.* The Patriots won the 2015 AFC Championship game by a score of 45–7, which likely informed the league disciplinary officer's opinion that the football deflation did not affect the outcome of the game. In penalizing cheating, should it matter whether the misconduct actually conferred a competitive advantage? If protecting public confidence in the game is the justification for punishing cheaters, what is the significance of an ESPN/ABC poll at the time that found a majority of the public believed Brady cheated and should be suspended, but further believed that most other teams also cheat? Given that the Patriots subsequently won Super Bowl XLIX, beating the Seattle Seahawks 28–24, does that establish that the cheating "didn't matter"?

2. *Patriots as Repeat Offenders—"Spygate."* The $1 million fine and lost draft pick penalties imposed on the Patriots for Deflategate reflected their repeat offender status from an earlier cheating episode, labeled "Spygate." In 2007, it was discovered that the Patriots violated the NFL Constitution and Bylaws prohibition on videotaping an opponent's sidelines to decipher their offensive and defensive signals. In imposing a $250,000 fine and loss of draft picks, Goodell wrote:

> This episode represents a calculated and deliberate attempt to avoid longstanding rules designed to encourage fair play and promote honest competition on the playing field.

Notwithstanding this condemnation, Goodell later informed a congressional inquiry that he did not believe the illegal taping "tainted the club's accomplishments." Does that comment still hold true after Deflategate, given the Patriot's recidivism? At the time of the Spygate congressional inquiry, the NFL was defending fan lawsuits seeking compensation for tickets to Patriots games at which the cheating took place. *See Mayer v. Belichick*, 605 F.3d 223 (3d Cir. 2010) (affirming dismissal of lawsuit). How effective have sports leagues been in walking the tightrope between policing integrity violations and marketing their games as honest competition?

3. *Standard of Proof.* Under NFL policy, the standard of proof for violations of competitive integrity rules is "preponderance of the evidence," meaning that "as a whole, the fact sought to be proved is more probable than not." Given the serious consequences of a finding of cheating, should the standard of proof be more demanding, for example, "clear and convincing evidence"? Or do integrity concerns justify a lower standard of proof to deter even "borderline" cheating? The Wells Report concluded only that Brady was "generally aware" of the illegal deflation—is that sufficient to meet the preponderance standard? The Goodell decision identified a stronger basis for culpability, using key new information that Brady destroyed evidence to make more specific and more incriminating findings. These additional findings also informed the Second Circuit's reasoning in sustaining the Goodell decision. Do these developments suggest that the Wells Report evidence was too weak to convict Brady?

4.   *Standard of Review.* The Second Circuit applied labor law's highly deferential standard of review to Brady's attack on the disciplinary process set forth in Article 46 of the NFL-NFLPA Collective Bargaining Agreement, stating, "If it is seriously believed that these procedures were deficient or prejudicial, the remedy was to address them during collective bargaining. Had the parties wished to otherwise limit the [Commissioner's] authority, they could have negotiated terms to do so." *Brady*, 820 F.3d at 548. Chapter 4 more fully covers challenges to commissioner disciplinary authority in the labor setting. Chapter 2 examines judicial review of private association decision-making in the context of clubs and non-union employee challenges to commissioner decisions. Note the differences in the standard of review, and consider whether Brady would have fared better in the Second Circuit under the law of private associations, rather than labor law.

5.   *Contrast "Bountygate."* Goodell's decision contrasted the player conduct at issue in Bountygate (excerpted in Chapter 2). There, the arbitrator vacated player suspensions because "the misconduct of the Saints' players was in large part the result of pressure from coaches and other management representatives." Does that distinction justify the different treatment of Brady?

6.   *Covert Conduct.* Goodell's decision also distinguished prior episodes of game-day misconduct that did not involve "effort[s] to conceal." He likened Brady's actions to players who use performance enhancing drugs and a masking agent to cover up the underlying violation, conduct that draws a six-game suspension. Why is concealment relevant to the disciplinary response to an integrity breach?

7.   *Public Law Response.* The football deflation took place at Gillette Stadium in Foxborough, Massachusetts, a state that does not define sports equipment tampering as a criminal offense. If the game had been played in neighboring Connecticut, which does have such a law, could or should Brady and the equipment staff members have been prosecuted?

8.   *Cooperation with League Investigations.* The Goodell decision discusses the imperative of cooperation with league investigations. As previously noted, private entities possess few inducements for witness cooperation, other than promising confidentiality and, as to employees, threatening repercussions for non-cooperation. What else might induce cooperation? While the Wells Report praised the Patriots for the team's "substantial cooperation," no leniency resulted. Contrast MLB's approach in the sign-stealing episode discussed next, and whether grants of immunity are an appropriate inducement to cooperation.

2.   SIGN-STEALING IN BASEBALL

Baseball pitchers and catchers traditionally used hand signals to communicate with each other about which pitch to throw to the batter. Accepted norms in Major League Baseball are that baserunners and coaches on the field can legitimately try to read the opposing team's signals with the naked eye in real time. These norms and MLB rules also permit clubs to utilize video before or after a game to attempt to decode an opponent's signs, in order to provide the club with an advantage in future games against that team. However, MLB Regulation 1–1 states that no club shall use electronic equipment *during* a game "for the purpose of stealing signs or conveying information designed to give a Club an advantage." Pursuant to his "best interests of baseball" authority, MLB Commissioner Rob Manfred has imposed significant sanctions on teams who violate this rule, including the Boston Red Sox and Houston Astros for sign stealing during seasons in which they won World Series, casting doubt on those outcomes and scandalizing baseball.

The saga began with MLB's 2014 expansion of instant replay review, which required installing clubhouse video replay rooms, usually located close to dugouts, where team personnel could scrutinize action on the field to decide whether to challenge certain calls made by umpires. The video feeds coincidentally offered the best looks at hand signals catchers flashed to pitchers, creating a situation ripe for electronic sign stealing. To deter such mischief, MLB adopted Replay Review Regulations that prohibit using phones connecting the replay room to the dugout for anything other than whether to challenge a play.

In the 2017 season, American League rivals New York Yankees and Boston Red Sox lodged cross-complaints that the other team was using video feeds to violate the electronic sign-stealing rule. After an investigation, the Commissioner's office determined that the Yankees had violated the Replay Review Regulations in the 2015 and 2016 seasons by using the replay room phone to relay information about opposing teams' signs to the dugout. The Red Sox, on the other hand, violated Regulation 1–1 by using smartwatches to relay decoded signs from the video replay room to the dugout to batters.

In his statement imposing significant fines against both teams, Commissioner Manfred elaborated on the Regulation 1–1 violation:

> In assessing the significance of this violation, the investigation established three relevant points. First, the violation in question occurred without the knowledge of ownership or front office personnel. Second, when the Red Sox learned of the Yankees' complaint, they immediately halted the conduct in question and then cooperated completely in my investigation. I have received absolute assurances from the Red Sox that there will be no future violations of this type. Third, our investigation revealed that Clubs have employed various strategies to decode signs that do not violate our rules. The Red Sox' strategy violated our rules because of the use of an electronic device.

Commissioner Manfred, Major League Baseball, *Statement on Boston Red Sox Sign-Stealing* (Sept. 15, 2017).

Meanwhile, undetected by any team or league personnel, Houston Astros players had devised their own sign-stealing scheme during the 2017 season. An Astros intern had developed an application and algorithm that allowed someone watching a live game feed to log an opposing catcher's and pitcher's sequence of hand signals and actual pitches into a spreadsheet, and then predict future pitches. Dubbed "Codebreaker," the application was used to decipher pitch signs observed on the video replay room's live game feed and communicate pitch predictions to Astros batters. After outhitting every other team in the major leagues that season, the Astros won the 2017 World Series, their first in franchise history, beating the Los Angeles Dodgers four games to three.

The Codebreaker scheme was exposed two years later, in November 2019, after the Astros had traded a pitcher who revealed the cheating, no longer deterred by a code of silence among his prior teammates. MLB staff conducted an investigation in which they interviewed 68 witnesses, including 23 current and former Astros players, and reviewed thousands of emails, texts, instant messages, video clips, and photographs. The club fully cooperated, as did the players in exchange for immunity from discipline. In a decision that outraged many fans, Commissioner Manfred disciplined only the club, senior baseball operations executives, and the bench coach.

STATEMENT OF THE COMMISSIONER (HOUSTON ASTROS SIGN-STEALING)

Jan. 13, 2020

* * *

Factual Findings

I.   Rules Violations in the 2017 Season

At the beginning of the 2017 season, employees in the Astros' video replay review room began using the live game feed from the center field camera to attempt to decode and transmit opposing teams' sign sequences (i.e., which sign flashed by the catcher is the actual sign) for use when an Astros runner was on second base. Once the sign sequence was decoded, a player in the video replay review room would act as a "runner" to relay the information to the dugout, and a person in the dugout would notify the players in the dugout or signal the sign sequence to the runner on second base, who in turn would decipher the catcher's sign and signal to the batter from second base. Early in the season, Alex Cora, the Astros' Bench Coach, began to call the replay review room on the replay phone to obtain the sign information. On at least some occasions, the employees in the replay review room communicated the sign sequence information by text message, which was received on the smart watch of a staff member on the bench, or in other cases on a cell phone stored nearby.

Approximately two months into the 2017 season, a group of players, including Carlos Beltrán, discussed that the team could improve on decoding opposing teams' signs and communicating the signs to the batter. Cora arranged for a video room technician to install a monitor displaying the center field camera feed immediately outside of the Astros' dugout. (The center field camera was primarily used for player development purposes and was allowed under MLB rules at the time when used for that purpose.) Witnesses have provided largely consistent accounts of how the monitor was utilized. One or more players watched the live feed of the center field camera on the monitor, and after decoding the sign, a player would bang a nearby trash can with a bat to communicate the upcoming pitch type to the batter. (Witnesses explained that they initially experimented with communicating sign information by clapping, whistling, or yelling, but that they eventually determined that banging a trash can was the preferred method of communication.) Players occasionally also used a massage gun to bang the trash can. Generally, one or two bangs corresponded to certain off-speed pitches, while no bang corresponded to a fastball.

Witnesses consistently describe this new scheme as player-driven, and with the exception of Cora, non-player staff, including individuals in the video replay review room, had no involvement in the banging scheme. However, witnesses made clear that everyone proximate to the Astros' dugout presumptively heard or saw the banging. In addition to players using the monitor installed near the dugout to decode signs, employees in the Astros' replay review room continued to decode sign sequences using the monitors in the room and communicate those sequences to the dugout for use when a runner was on second base. Both methods of sign stealing were used by the team in parallel throughout the 2017 season.

In August 2017, the Boston Red Sox were caught transmitting sign information from their replay review room to individuals in the dugout wearing smart watches. The incident received significant media attention, and I issued a press release on September 15, 2017 announcing the fine of the Red Sox (and a fine of the New York Yankees for improperly using the replay review room phone) that stated in relevant part:

> At the outset, it is important to understand that the attempt to decode signs being used by an opposing catcher is not a violation of any Major League Baseball Rule or Regulation. Major League Baseball Regulations do, however, prohibit the use of electronic equipment during games and state that no such equipment "may be used for the purpose of stealing signs or conveying information designed to give a Club an advantage." Despite this clear Regulation, the prevalence of technology, especially the technology used in the replay process, has made it increasingly difficult to monitor appropriate and inappropriate uses of electronic equipment. Based on the investigation by my office, I

have nonetheless concluded that during the 2017 season the Boston Red Sox violated the Regulation quoted above by sending electronic communications from their video replay room to an athletic trainer in the dugout.

Following the issuance of the press release announcing the results of the Red Sox investigation, I issued a memorandum that same day to all Clubs reiterating the rules regarding the use of electronic equipment to steal signs, and putting all Clubs on notice that future violations would be taken extremely seriously by my office. I specifically stated in the memorandum that the General Manager and Field Manager of Clubs would be held accountable for any violations of the rules in the future. Thus, all Clubs were put on notice as of September 15, 2017 that any use of electronic equipment to steal signs would be dealt with more severely by my office.

Notwithstanding the publicity surrounding the Red Sox incident, and the September 15th memorandum that I sent to all Clubs, the Astros continued to both utilize the replay review room and the monitor located next to the dugout to decode signs for the remainder of the regular season and throughout the Postseason.

II. Rules Violations in Subsequent Seasons

During the 2017–2018 offseason, and following a discussion at the General Managers' Meetings, the Commissioner's Office notified Clubs that the phone connecting the replay review room and the dugout would be monitored to ensure that it was not used for any purpose other than discussing a challenge of a play on the field. In addition, in March 2018, [MLB VP for Baseball Operations] Joe Torre issued a memorandum to all Clubs that expanded upon the prohibition against using electronic equipment to steal signs. The memorandum stated in relevant part:

> Major League Baseball Regulation 1–1 prohibits all uniformed personnel, clubhouse staff and equipment staff from using or possessing telephones or similar electronic devices, including any type of walkie-talkies, mobile phones, 'smart watches' (e.g., Apple watches), laptop computers, tablets or other communication devices, in or near the dugout, in the bullpens or on the playing field once batting practice has begun. MLBR 1–1 also prohibits the use of such devices in the clubhouse within 30 minutes of the start of a game. The prohibition includes the use of any electronic equipment that has the capability to receive electronic messages by any person occupying the bench or in the bullpen.

* * *

> Electronic equipment, including game feeds in the Club replay room and/or video room, may never be used during a game for the purpose of stealing the opposing team's signs. In this respect,

MLBR 1–1 expressly provides that "under no circumstance may electronic equipment or devices be used for the purpose of stealing signs or conveying other information designed to give a Club a competitive advantage." **To be clear, the use of any equipment in the clubhouse or in a Club's replay or video rooms to decode an opposing Club's signs during the game violates this Regulation.** (Emphasis in original.) Clubs (and Club employees) who are found to have utilized equipment in the replay or video rooms for such purposes during a game will be subject to discipline by the Commissioner's Office.

Prior to the 2018 season, and with MLB approval, the Astros relocated their replay review system to a video room located much closer to the dugout, as is the case in many ballparks throughout the league. The investigation uncovered no evidence that Astros players utilized the banging scheme in 2018. However, the Astros' replay review room staff continued, at least for part of the 2018 season, to decode signs using the live center field camera feed, and to transmit the signs to the dugout through in-person communication. At some point during the 2018 season, the Astros stopped using the replay review room to decode signs because the players no longer believed it was effective. The investigation did not reveal any attempt by the Astros to utilize electronic equipment to decode and transmit signs in the 2018 Postseason.

Prior to the 2019 season, the Commissioner's Office issued a revised policy governing sign stealing, which, among other things, included the placement of individuals retained by the Commissioner's Office in the Club's replay review rooms to ensure that no rules violations occurred (a practice that began in the 2018 Postseason). The investigation revealed no violations of the policy by the Astros in the 2019 season or 2019 Postseason.

Other than described above, the investigation did not reveal any other scheme or method utilized by the Astros to decode an opposing Club's signs from 2016 to the present.

III. Culpability of Astros Players and Employees for Rules Violations

The Astros' methods in 2017 and 2018 to decode and communicate to the batter an opposing Club's signs were not an initiative that was planned or directed by the Club's top baseball operations officials. Rather, the 2017 scheme in which players banged on a trash can was, with the exception of Cora, player-driven and player-executed. The attempt by the Astros' replay review room staff to decode signs using the center field camera was originated and executed by lower-level baseball operations employees working in conjunction with Astros players and Cora. The efforts involving the replay review room staff were mentioned in at least two emails sent to [General Manager Jeff] Luhnow, and there is conflicting evidence about conversations with Luhnow on the topic. Regardless of the level of

Luhnow's actual knowledge, the Astros' violation of rules in 2017 and 2018 is attributable, in my view, to a failure by the leaders of the baseball operations department and the Field Manager to adequately manage the employees under their supervision, to establish a culture in which adherence to the rules is ingrained in the fabric of the organization, and to stop bad behavior as soon as it occurred.

The Astros Players. Most of the position players on the 2017 team either received sign information from the banging scheme or participated in the scheme by helping to decode signs or bang on the trash can. Many of the players who were interviewed admitted that they knew the scheme was wrong because it crossed the line from what the player believed was fair competition and/or violated MLB rules. Players stated that if Manager A.J. Hinch told them to stop engaging in the conduct, they would have immediately stopped.

Although the Astros' players did not attempt to hide what they were doing from Hinch or other Astros employees, they were concerned about getting caught by players from other teams. Several players told my investigators that there was a sense of "panic" in the Astros' dugout after White Sox pitcher Danny Farquhar appeared to notice the trash can bangs. Before the game ended, a group of Astros players removed the monitor from the wall in the tunnel and hid it in an office. For the Postseason, a portable monitor was set up on a table to replace the monitor that had been affixed to the wall near the dugout.

Some Astros players told my investigators that they did not believe the sign-stealing scheme was effective, and it was more distracting than useful to hitters. I am neither in a position to evaluate whether the scheme helped Astros hitters (who were unquestionably a very talented group), nor whether it helped the Astros win any games. There are so many factors that impact the outcome of games that addressing that issue would require rank speculation. But for purposes of my decision, regardless of whether the scheme was effective or not, it violated the rules and, at a minimum, created the appearance of unfairness, and for that, it necessitates severe discipline.

I will not assess discipline against individual Astros players. I made the decision in September 2017 that I would hold a Club's General Manager and Field Manager accountable for misconduct of this kind, and I will not depart from that decision. Assessing discipline of players for this type of conduct is both difficult and impractical. It is difficult because virtually all of the Astros' players had some involvement or knowledge of the scheme, and I am not in a position based on the investigative record to determine with any degree of certainty every player who should be held accountable, or their relative degree of culpability. It is impractical given the large number of players involved, and the fact that many of those players now play for other Clubs.

But more importantly, the Club's General Manager and Field Manager are responsible for ensuring that the players both understand the rules and adhere to them. Our office issues a substantial number of detailed rules and procedures to Clubs—many of which, including the sign stealing rules, are not sent directly to players. It is the obligation of the Club, and, in this case, the General Manager and Field Manager, to educate and instruct their players on the rules governing play on the field. Here, because the Club's Bench Coach was an active participant in the scheme, and the Club's Manager was aware of the scheme and did nothing to stop it, I recognize that some players may have understood that their conduct was not only condoned by the Club, but encouraged by it. This was misconduct committed by the team, and with the exception of the individuals whom I will hold personally accountable, my disciplinary action will be directed at the team.

[The Commissioner summarized evidence that Luhnow and Hinch did not devise or direct the sign-stealing. However, he reproved Luhnow for failing to exercise adequate oversight, communicate MLB rules to staff and players, and ingrain adherence to those rules "in the fabric of the organization." He further condemned the "insular culture" of the Astros baseball operations department, which manifested itself in problematic treatment of employees and fraught relations with other clubs and the media. Similarly, the Commissioner criticized Hinch for failing to stop the sign-stealing scheme when he learned of it, or to clearly communicate his disapproval.

The Commissioner deferred discipline as to Alex Cora, who had become the Boston Red Sox field manager in 2018, and was the subject of a separate investigation into a new allegation of electronic sign-stealing by that club. The Commissioner completely exonerated Astros owner Jim Crane because he "was unaware of any of the violations of MLB rules by his Club" and had instructed Luhnow after the 2017 Red Sox discipline to "make sure that the Astros did not engage in similar conduct."]

Discipline

I find that the conduct of the Astros, and its senior baseball operations executives, merits significant discipline. I base this finding on the fact that the Club's senior baseball operations executives were given express notice in September 2017 that I would hold them accountable for violations of our policies covering sign stealing, and those individuals took no action to ensure that the Club's players and staff complied with those policies during the 2017 Postseason and the 2018 regular season. The conduct described herein has caused fans, players, executives at other MLB Clubs, and members of the media to raise questions about the integrity of games in which the Astros participated. And while it is impossible to determine whether the conduct actually impacted the results on the field, the perception of some that it did causes significant harm to the game.

[The Commissioner fined the club $5 million and forfeited its first and second round selections in the 2020 and 2021 drafts, and suspended without pay general manager Jeff Luhnow and field manager A.J. Hinch through the 2020 baseball season. Bench coach Alex Cora was ultimately suspended for the 2020 season as well.]

———

In April 2020, a few months after the Astros ruling, Commissioner Manfred issued his decision and findings in the separate investigation into Red Sox electronic sign-stealing during the 2018 season. He found that the club's video replay system operator J.T. Watkins violated MLB regulations by occasionally using game feeds to update sign sequence information he had permissibly given to players before the game. Manfred distinguished the Astros situation in that Watkins' conduct was far more limited in scope and impact, and was concealed from Red Sox coaching and front office staff, including then manager Alex Cora. Watkins was suspended for two seasons, but no other Red Sox personnel were disciplined. Based on the club's repeat offender status, it was stripped of its second round selection in the 2020 draft.

Again Manfred declined to discipline the players who were involved, stating:

> I feel bound by the agreement not to impose discipline on Red Sox players who testified truthfully in this matter. Even if I were not so bound, I do not believe that the Red Sox players who suspected that Watkins used game feeds to decode sign sequences should be held responsible for his conduct. Watkins knew of the rules and was responsible for not utilizing the replay system to decode sign sequences. Some players may have suspected that Watkins was using the replay system improperly, but they did not know that with certainty. Others had no idea how Watkins obtained the sign information. Moreover, those who suspected that Watkins was using the replay system largely did not understand that it was a violation of the rules because the evolving rules landscape had not been adequately explained to players.

Commissioner Manfred, Major League Baseball, *Decision and Findings of the Commissioner in the Red Sox Investigation* (April 22, 2020).

The Red Sox won the 2018 World Series, the season in which they engaged in illegal sign-stealing, beating the Los Angeles Dodgers four games to one. With their home team victimized two years in a row, the Los Angeles City Council unanimously approved a measure requesting that MLB award the 2017 and 2018 World Series titles to the Dodgers. MLB denied the request, and also declined to strip the guilty teams of wins or in any way rewrite the record books.

A raft of private lawsuits followed on the sign-stealing revelations, alleging various forms of collateral damage:

- Former Astros GM Jeff Luhnow sued the Astros alleging that owner Jim Crane and Commissioner Manfred negotiated the disciplinary outcome to scapegoat Luhnow, allowing the team to fire him for cause and avoid paying $22 million in guaranteed salary. *See Luhnow v. Houston Astros, LLC*, 2020–71920 (Dist. Ct. Harris Cty Tex. Nov. 9, 2020). The claims were settled for an undisclosed amount.

- Contestants in fantasy baseball contests brought a putative federal class action alleging that MLB and the Astros, Red Sox, and Yankees fraudulently concealed rules violations— the sign-stealing—that rendered player statistics unreliable. The suit was dismissed on the merits at the pleading stage. *Olson v. Major League Baseball*, 29 F.4th 59 (2d Cir. 2022).

- A legal gambler sued complaining that the cheating ruined his odds and lost his bets. The claim was dismissed on the ground that "sports fans generally have no legally cognizable right, interest, or injury to recover for violations of a professional sports league's 'own rules.'" *Oliver v. Houston Astros, LLC*, 2020 WL 1430382, at *3 (D. Nev. Mar. 23, 2020), *aff'd*, 2020 WL 2128656 (D. Nev. May 5, 2020).

- Astros season ticket holders brought putative state class actions seeking refunds claiming they were defrauded into attending games. The Astros settled the case after a Texas intermediate appellate court recommended dismissal because "claims based on how a sports team plays the game are not cognizable." *In re Houston Astros, LLC*, 2021 WL 2965268 (Tex. App. July 15, 2021).

- Toronto Blue Jay pitcher Mike Bolsinger sued the Astros alleging unfair business practices that shortened his big league career. He blamed the sign-stealing for his performance in a game that he pitched relief and gave up four runs before he was pulled from the mound. At the time, Bolsinger's team took the disastrous inning as proof that he could not perform at the major league level and sent him back to the minors, never to return. *Bolsinger v. Houston Astros, LLC*, 2020 WL 805795 (Cal. Super. Feb. 10, 2020). Although Bolsinger ultimately abandoned the suit, his plight is an example of the tangible injury that cheating can inflict.

NOTES AND QUESTIONS

1.   *Where to Draw the Line?* Given that sign stealing with the naked eye is widely accepted as part of the game, the prohibition on using technology to do so can seem arbitrary. Line-drawing in other areas—for example, which performance enhancing drugs to ban—often depends on criteria such as whether the substance poses a health risk to athletes. That risk is not present with sign stealing. What makes the Astros' conduct cheating? Because it was technologically aided? Because it was covert? Because the batting team is better able to protect itself from on-field sign-stealing than spying from other locations? Because it violates the spirit of sport? Or simply because it was in violation of a clearly expressed league rule?

2.   *Laissez-Faire Approach?* Would it be better to allow teams to freely engage in some conduct currently prohibited by their sport, because then such conduct would cease to provide a competitive advantage and simply become another part of the game? Consider, for example, prohibitions against doctoring the two essential pieces of baseball equipment—the ball and the bat. Are spitballs and corked bats cheating? Many consider the former to be merely a form of gamesmanship, while the latter to be outright cheating. Should one or the other be deregulated?

3.   *No Player Discipline.* In both the Astros and Red Sox cases, Manfred declined to impose player discipline, drawing heavy criticism from fans, the media, and many players who publicly condemned their fellow union members on both teams. Consider Manfred's explanations for staying his hand: (i) he had granted immunity for cooperation; (ii) he had announced that managers would be held responsible for sign stealing; (iii) disciplining players was impractical because of the difficulty in assigning blame. Are you convinced?

Considering that the MLB Collective Bargaining Agreement requires players to cooperate in cheating investigations, why was it necessary for Manfred to grant immunity? A player's failure to cooperate independently could have justified discipline. Furthermore, MLB memos warning clubs that managers would be held responsible for sign-stealing did not in any way imply that other culpable parties would be absolved. There is no shortage of language putting the players on notice that their conduct risked discipline, including the uniform player contract that compels players to "conform to high standards of personal conduct, fair play and good sportsmanship."

Difficulties in assigning blame might justify disciplining fewer players, but not exonerating all of them. Manfred later told the press that the MLB Players Association had threatened to file grievances against any player discipline, protracting the public spectacle around the cheating. The Players Association took the position that MLBR 1–1 effectuated a change in working conditions that required notification and bargaining (see Chapter 3), and therefore the Commissioner had no authority to discipline players for a violation. Would MLB have been better off if it nonetheless disciplined players, then lost the grievances, having made a good faith effort to hold players accountable? What position should the MLBPA have taken to douse the flames of controversy among its own membership?

4. *Competitive Impact.* Manfred's Astros decision states, "while it is impossible to determine whether the conduct actually impacted the results on the field, the perception of some that it did causes significant harm to the game." Do you agree it is impossible to determine the competitive impact of this type of cheating? Would it help to assess that impact if you learned that upon rewatching every pitch of every Astros home game during the 2017 season, a fan detected more than 1,100 "bangs" on 8,200 pitches? How would you weigh the fact that the Astros aggregate team batting average went from .247 in 2016, to .282 in 2017 (the cheating year), then back down to .255 in 2018?

5. *Counteractive Technology.* As of the 2022 season, MLB permits clubs to use "PitchCom" signaling devices, which eliminate the need for hand signals. Using a pad with buttons on the wrist of the gloved hand, a catcher can signal pitches directly to the pitcher through a listening device. This technology resembles the coach-to-quarterback headsets and helmet receivers that the NFL has been using to call plays since the 1990s. Some MLB clubs have expressed concern about hacking into the system or opponents illegally blocking signals. Many NFL teams have accused the Patriots of such mischief over the years. It seems each solution brings its own new problems and raises the question of how the regulators—the sports leagues—can keep up.

3. TANKING

The chief goal for participants in competitive sports is to win. To reach that goal, players have a duty to try, that is, to put forth "best efforts." Even so, incentive structures in some sports settings reward underperformance or "tanking"—losing games on purpose to secure some future competitive advantage. This phenomenon is also referred to as "non-gambling match-fixing."

For example, in a league with a rookie draft, a team that is unlikely to advance to post-season play might intentionally lose to earn higher draft picks that will strengthen the team going forward. The NBA has been plagued with accusations of tanking, and introduced (and continually reforms) a draft lottery system to address it. The head coach of the NFL Miami Dolphins accused the team's owner of offering him $100,000 for every loss in order to gain a draft advantage. (See Brian Flores race discrimination complaint noted in Chapter 14.) Although the ensuing investigation concluded that the comment was made in jest and no evidence suggested that the team intentionally lost games, Commissioner Goodell stated:

> Even if made in jest and not intended to be taken seriously, comments suggesting that draft position is more important than winning can be misunderstood and carry with them an unnecessary potential risk to the integrity of the game.

In 2022, the revived United States Football League announced a draft rule to avoid tanking: in the final week of the season, in a game between the two worst teams in the league, the winner instead of the loser would get the top pick in the draft.

In global soccer, promotion and relegation deter tanking to some degree as teams that end the season at the bottom of the league risk relegation to a lower (and far less lucrative) level of competition. Strategic tanking nonetheless occurs when teams are trying to maximize their chances in future matches. English Premier League rule L.19 states: "In every league match each participating club shall field a full strength team." Pursuant to this rule, the league fined teams in 2010 and 2011 for fielding weakened teams to rest players for more crucial later fixtures. And precisely because of the dire consequences of relegation, the Premier League insists on full strength to maintain the integrity of end-of-season rankings. That was a concern in the 2019–20 season, when Liverpool locked up the title early. Had Liverpool intentionally underperformed against bottom-ranked teams in tight races to avoid relegation, it would lead to significant competitive and commercial consequences for those teams.

In some forms of tournament play, tanking occurs to affect seeding or advancement. At the 2012 London Olympics, badminton introduced a round-robin format, and teams soon realized that purposely losing certain matches would improve their draw in the next round. Four women's badminton teams—two from South Korea and one each from China and Indonesia—were observed to play so poorly that they elicited boos from the spectators. All four teams were expelled from the Games for "not using one's best efforts to win." Similarly, in certain team sports that involve individual performances, like cycling or gymnastics, a coach might tell an athlete to underperform so that another athlete can progress in a competition. Tanking may also occur where tournament prize money is guaranteed, as when Bernard Tomic lost his first round match at the 2019 Wimbledon in under an hour. Officials issued a finding that he "did not perform to the required professional standard" and fined him the entirety of his first round prize money.

The challenge is in defining the nature and contours of the supposed duty to use best efforts. Does an athlete have to try to win at every moment and stage of a competition? Is it acceptable for a batter to take the first pitch to size up the pitcher? Is it okay for a tennis player to withhold her best efforts during several points or even games in order to conserve energy for a final decisive set? Does a basketball team have to play its hardest with every starter when they are up by 30 points in the fourth quarter? If a playoff slot is locked up, is it permissible for a team to rest some of its players for the post-season, as frequently happens in the NFL? Do the answers to these questions depend on the level of sport, whether the underperformance affects only part of the contest versus the outcome, or fans' expectations (and investment) in attending the contest?

Sports tanking implicates more than honest competition, but also relationships with broadcast partners, the media, and the public. An early season November 29, 2012 NBA game between the San Antonio Spurs against the Heat in Miami offers an illustration. The two teams were top contenders at the time and in fact met in the NBA finals later that season and the next. The game was highly anticipated as it was the Spurs only trip to Miami during the regular season, and it was to be aired on TNT's exclusive Thursday night national broadcast. But the Spurs were winding up a grueling five-game road trip, so Coach Gregg Popovich decided to rest four starters—Tim Duncan, Tony Parker, Manu Ginobili, and Danny Green. Without announcing his plans, Popovich sent the four players home without stopping in Miami. The game that was played that night was nonetheless close and competitive, with the Heat wining by five points.

Under league policy that prohibits resting players in a manner "contrary to the best interests of the NBA," Commissioner David Stern fined the Spurs $250,000, stating:

> The result here is dictated by the totality of the facts in this case. The Spurs decided to make four of their top players unavailable for an early season game that was the team's only regular-season visit to Miami. The team also did this without informing the Heat, the media, or the league office in a timely way. Under these circumstances, I have concluded that the Spurs did a disservice to the league and our fans.

Popovich was unrepentant, responding that he did what was best for his basketball team and the players in question, two of whom were in their late 30s and needed the respite. Other coaches spoke up for him, defending their discretion to set rosters based on what's best for the players and for the team's season-long competitive advantage.

Popovich's secrecy was a significant factor in Stern classifying the incident as a "disservice." What exactly is the disservice here? Is it that, with advance knowledge of the depleted game roster, fans might have made different ticket purchases? Or is the disservice more broadly to the values of honest competition? Most commentators attributed Stern's indignation to potential damage to the league's relationship with TNT. With advance notice, the league might have offered TNT a different game. Is there any reason why a league should not require coaching decisions to weigh the entire league's commercial advantage?

———

NOTES AND QUESTIONS

1.   *Who Is the Victim?* If an athlete or team purposely underperforms or loses a contest, where is the harm? Should we be concerned for fans who paid for tickets? Should we be concerned for business partners who invested in association with the event? Should we be concerned for television networks who lose ratings? What about the non-tanking teams—should they be able to pursue remedies for breach of fiduciary duties to a co-venturer? Or is the issue one of larger concern for societal values of fairness and honest play?

2.   *Fans as Victims.* Note that in the Spurs case, Commissioner Stern's concern for the fans' disappointment goes only so far. The NBA does not offer a policy similar to that of many Broadway shows, which allow customers to get their money back if an understudy stands in for a star. Moreover, as iterated at the end of the discussion of Astros sign-stealing, courts have consistently held that fan claims for compensation based on how a sports team plays the game or a league applies its rules are not "cognizable." Does sports' unscripted nature justify the different treatment of these two forms of entertainment?

3.   *Broadcast Partners as Victims.* The Spurs incident sabotaged a potential ratings bonanza for TNT, which had paid for exclusive Thursday night NBA programming. In condemning the Spurs, Dallas Mavericks owner Mark Cuban described the NBA's national TV contracts as its "money train"— the difference in the league being profitable or not. He criticized Popovich for not resting his stars one game earlier or one game later, rather than "when you've got our biggest customer at stake." By the same token, Cuban blasted the NBA for its scheduling decision: "It's just as stupid to put a team in their fourth game in five nights on national television. . . .You're not going to get as good of a performance, and that's what you want to show." Do Cuban's remarks suggest that the issue is not ensuring best efforts, but rather the timing of those efforts to serve commercial interests?

4.   *Covert Conduct, Redux.* Would strategic tanking offend less if it were transparent, that is, if a team or athlete was simply allowed to forfeit, rather than going through the charade of trying to lose? Or should competition organizers do a better job at structuring rules, seasons, and tournaments to reduce incentives to tank, as the NBA has tried with its draft lottery? In the Spurs case, if Popovich had announced with sufficient advance notice that player well-being compelled him to sit the team's star attractions, should the Spurs have escaped discipline?

5.   *Tanking in an Era of Legal Sports Betting.* With the legalization of sports betting, and league exploitation of the commercial opportunities it brings, how should the law treat sportsbooks that set odds based on honest competition and bettors who place wagers on a team that decides to throw a game? Should they be entitled to sue for compensation? Does your answer differ if the tanking occurs in a late-season game, when sophisticated bettors have already factored in the expectation that rosters may not feature star players (just as the stock market factors in future contingencies based on past experience)?

One result of the Spurs incident is that the NBA formalized advance reporting procedures for player injuries and game rosters. Fans, opposing teams, broadcast partners, and, incidentally, bettors are thereby able to reset expectations as to the nature of the contest. Do you think this measure is adequate to avoid the perception of tanking? Alternatively, after a suspicious game, leagues could launch an investigation or require teams to submit written explanations of roster and coaching decisions. What other steps might leagues take to deter tanking?

6.   *Blurring the Line Between Sports and Other Entertainment.* Ryan Rodenberg has commented on the increasingly "blurred line between sports and noncompetitive scripted entertainment," citing situations where organizers have manipulated sporting events for commercial gain, including car racing events that stop action to heighten suspense, tennis tournaments that eschew random draws and unevenly enforce time violations, and NFL referees who request coaches to call a timeout in order to accommodate more television commercials. *(Non)gambling Corruption in Sports*, 2 WAKE FOREST L. REV. ONLINE 32, 35, 37 (2012). How do these manipulations impact sports integrity? Does that depend on the extent to which outcome uncertainty is subverted? Consider at what point such manipulations convert a competitive sport into scripted entertainment of the sort offered by, for example: (a) World Wrestling Entertainment, where athletes participate in live action fights with pre-determined outcomes, or (b) the Harlem Globetrotters, where basketball players put on theatrical exhibitions including staged games that they always win.

E. PERFORMANCE ENHANCING DRUGS

In sports, excellence historically has been achievable only by a combination of natural physical advantages and disciplined effort. But fast-moving developments in biotechnology, medicine, and pharmaceuticals have revived basic questions about what we value in athletic achievement and whether those values can accommodate unnatural performance enhancements. Sports leagues and governing bodies now continually wrestle with what types of performance enhancements to permit or forbid. Is the touchstone to preserve fair competition by ensuring no enhancement provides a particular athlete with a net advantage over what nature and training have provided?

Governing bodies regulate permissible improvements in equipment, as with the International Tennis Federation and oversized tennis rackets, and the Fédération Internationale de Natation and high-buoyancy swimsuits. Biomechanical enhancements in response to physical disability, such as the prosthetic legs worn by runners Oscar Pistorius and Blake Leeper, are assessed for whether they result in unnatural proportions that convey an unfair advantage (discussed further in Chapter 14, Section C.3).

Performance enhancing drugs (PEDs) are a particularly fraught subject of regulation, as they have grown increasingly sophisticated, amplifying their users' competitive edge, while getting better at evading detection. In U.S. sports leagues with unionized athletes, the law surrounding the use of PEDs by players cannot be divorced from relevant labor law and provisions of collective bargaining agreements, discussed in Chapter 4. The role of international bodies, such as the World Anti-Doping Agency (WADA), in regulating PEDs is discussed in Chapter 15. This chapter addresses the topic through the lens of sports integrity: (1) why to prohibit PEDs in sport and which ones, and (2) who should regulate sports PED use and how to enforce those regulations.

1. WHY PROHIBIT PEDs AND WHICH ONES

Any number of substances might enhance one's athletic performance. For example, caffeine is a central nervous system stimulant that can make one feel more alert and active. Non-steroidal anti-inflammatory drugs like ibuprofen (Advil) and naproxen sodium (Aleve) relieve pain and swelling, accelerating recovery time from athletic injuries. WADA and other PED regulators do not consider these to be unfair performance enhancers. Rather, to fall into that category, the substance is typically one that both poses a health risk to the user and debases the integrity of the athletic contest because it provides an unfair competitive advantage. WADA will place a substance on its prohibited list if it meets two out of three criteria: (1) it has the potential to enhance or enhances sport performance; (2) it represents an actual or potential health risk to the athlete; and (3) it violates "the spirit of sport." The WADA Code defines "the spirit of sport" as "the ethical pursuit of human excellence through the dedicated perfection of each Athlete's natural talents."

At the top of prohibited substance lists is the archetypal performance enhancer—anabolic steroids, which increase muscle mass and decrease fat. While they have legitimate medical uses, steroids pose serious health risks including heart attack or stroke, liver or kidney failure, high blood pressure, and reproductive system abnormalities. Prohibited drug lists have grown to add: human growth hormone (HGH), cannabinoids, narcotics, stimulants, beta-2 agonists, beta Blockers, blood doping, and diuretics and masking agents. Combinations of these drugs and treatments can increase stamina and endurance, decrease sensation of fatigue and pain, improve mental function and behavior, reduce performance anxiety, and fuel energy production and recovery. Each of these can also have dire health consequences, both short-term and long-term.

In assessing whether a particular substance should be banned as unduly performance enhancing, some would draw the line to permit use that is medically justified as a treatment or therapy. If a pitcher blows out his elbow ligament, he should be permitted to undergo Tommy John surgery to repair it. Accordingly, should a runner with asthma be permitted to take beta-2 agonists that treat hyperventilation, even though they also improve performance? To address this thorny issue, governing bodies have promulgated "therapeutic use exemptions." WADAs version of this exemption allows the use if the athlete can demonstrate four criteria:

(1) The drug is necessary to treat an acute or chronic medical condition and the athlete would experience a significant impairment to health if it were to be withheld.

(2) The therapeutic use of the prohibited drug is highly unlikely to produce any additional enhancement of performance beyond what might be anticipated by a return to the athlete's normal state of health following the treatment.

(3) There is no reasonable permitted therapeutic alternative to the use of the prohibited drug.

(4) The necessity to use of the prohibited drug is not a consequence of prior use of a prohibited drug or method.

For many fans, the crux of the integrity concern is that athletic achievement attained through PEDs looks like a form of cheating. For some, the use of PEDs diminishes the sport's intended challenges and devalues excellence in meeting those challenges. For example, a key challenge for a hitter in baseball is to hit a homerun. During MLB's steroids era of the 1990s, players who used the drugs shattered long-standing home run records, with St. Louis Cardinal Mark McGwire hitting 70 and Chicago Cub Sammy Sosa hitting 66 in the 1998 season. Barry Bonds later broke that record, hitting 73 home runs in 2001. When evidence indicated that all these players were using steroids, many questioned the legitimacy of the new records, and whether their steroid use should disqualify them from induction into the sport's hall of fame. In golf, mental composure is essential for high-pressure putting and so, before it was banned, some professional golfers used beta blockers to steady their nerves and their hands. In 2014, golfer Christiaan Bezuidenhout was banned for two years after a positive test for the drug, despite the fact that it was medically prescribed for a debilitating stutter.

The health-related arguments for banning PEDs often distinguish between "willing" and "unwilling" users. Some argue that willing users should be allowed to make the informed choice to use a substance for its performance benefits, free of paternalistic regulation, even if it damages their health. However, viewed from the perspective of clean athletes, a laissez faire approach amounts to coercion as they will face competitive pressure to use. Steroid use victimizes nonusers by giving them three undesirable choices: lose out to the biologically enhanced, quit the game, or imperil their bodies by becoming users themselves. As physician Leon Kass reflects, "In an age of biotechnical enhancements, many athletes feel that it is impossible to compete on an even playing field without them, and that the choice to forgo performance enhancing drugs amounts to unilateral disarmament." Leon R. Kass, LEADING A WORTHY LIFE, FINDING MEANING IN MODERN TIMES (2017).

———

NOTES AND QUESTIONS

1.   *Biomechanically Enhanced Athletes.* What principles should determine whether a medical procedure provides an unfair advantage to an athlete? Does it depend on whether the procedure is urgent or elective? What about a moderately nearsighted tennis player who improves her vision through Lasik surgery? What about a golfer on the senior tour whose arthritis requires an artificial knee? What about young baseball pitchers who undergo preemptive "Tommy John" surgery to strengthen the elbow ligament? What degree of biomechanical enhancement degrades sport integrity and requires barring an athlete from competing?

2.   *Extracorporeal Training Methods.* Sports governing bodies generally do not regulate extracorporeal training methods and tools, such as the use of sensory deprivation tanks by athletes seeking faster recovery time, and travel to higher-altitude locations to improve endurance. Not every athlete can afford or has access to such training opportunities. Should that affect our perception of them as permissible ways to obtain a competitive advantage?

3.   *Coercion.* An oft-cited argument for prohibiting doping is that it coerces the unwilling to use PEDs and thereby avoid "unilateral disarmament." Why is doping any more coercive than the full-time training regimens and special diets necessary to perform at elite levels? Those efforts can also pose health risks—what differentiates them from steroid use?

4.   *Doping as Sports Fraud.* When an athlete who wins a major sporting event, MVP honors, and/or prize money is later found to have used prohibited drugs, she may be stripped of the title and winnings. Although the second place athlete who competed cleanly may move up to first place, she has been denied the moment of glory and the often transitory opportunity to capitalize on that glory through, for example, endorsements. Who is the victim in this case—the second place competitor, every athlete who competed, the event organizers? If doping is effectively a scheme to obtain money, benefits, rewards, or advantages dishonestly, should there exist remedies in civil or criminal law for sporting fraud?

5.   *Who Decides?* For many sports around the globe and the Olympics, as noted above, WADA committees determine which substances are banned. Is a global anti-doping organization the appropriate body to determine if a substance violates "the spirit" of a particular sport? Is there any reason to ban a substance if it is not both health harming and performance enhancing? If doping is prohibited to avoid athlete coercion, shouldn't athletes who are represented have their player associations negotiate which substances are banned? Or does that fail to account for effects from the use of harmful drugs on other third party interests, including those of minors tempted by the drugs?

2. REGULATORY CHALLENGES

As with match-fixing, anti-doping regulatory efforts co-exist in the private and public sectors, with the former traditionally taking the lead. Individual sports leagues and governing bodies have developed specific and comprehensive anti-doping policies, and extensive investigative and prosecutorial functions to effectuate those policies. Nonetheless, they confront the same impediments as discussed with match-fixing: a lack of necessary authority to subpoena evidence, compel testimony, or assert jurisdiction over non-participants. Self-policing is further complicated by leagues' and governing bodies' self-interest in denying the problem, and athletes' reluctance to breach the locker room code of silence.

Thus, governments have felt compelled to intervene, especially following doping scandals in the sporting world. In the U.S., public concern about anabolic steroids spiked after the 1988 Olympics when Canadian sprinter Ben Johnson was stripped of a gold medal for testing positive after a race in which he broke a world record. Soon after, Congress passed the Anabolic Steroid Act of 1990 to categorize this drug class as a controlled substance and criminalize their sale and use without a prescription. Although the Act was intended to penalize steroid use in sport, it has rarely been used to prosecute professional, Olympic, or elite-level athletes.

Congressional interest in regulating doping lay dormant for more than a decade until the MLB steroids scandal led to U.S. Senate hearings in the 2000s. At the conclusion of those hearings, Senator John McCain sponsored the Clean Sports Act of 2005, which would impose uniform drug testing and disciplinary standards for the four major U.S. professional sports. Congress ultimately did not act because the threat of legislation induced MLB and its Players Association to agree to self-police through a series of collective agreements to institute random drug testing and penalize PED users.

Congress eventually passed the Rodchenkov Anti-Doping Act of 2020 in response to the Russian state-sponsored doping scandal that tainted the Olympic Games throughout the 2010s (discussed further in Chapter 15). The Act was named after Grigory Rodchenkov, former director of WADA's Moscow laboratory, who was granted asylum in the U.S. after whistleblowing on the Russian scheme. The Rodchenkov Act makes it a crime for "any person, other than an athlete, to knowingly carry into effect, attempt to carry into effect, or conspire with any other person to carry into effect a scheme in commerce to influence by use of a prohibited substance or prohibited method any major international sports competition." 21 U.S.C. § 2402. The Act thus restructures accountability to target the perpetrators of doping fraud and treat the athletes as victims. Offenders can be sentenced to up to 10 years in prison and fined up to $1 million. Although substantial protections are available to whistleblowers, the Act also provides for sharing all information relevant to doping violations with the United States Anti-Doping Agency (USADA).

Because the Rodchenkov Act gives the U.S. extraterritorial jurisdiction, WADA, the IOC, and other anti-doping stakeholders have criticized it over concerns that it could lead to inconsistent standards and discrimination against athletes from some countries. However, as of this casebook edition, only one prosecution has been brought under the Act. The Department of Justice charged Eric Lira, a Texas doctor, with obtaining PEDs and distributing them to two foreign athletes for the purpose of cheating at the 2021 Tokyo Olympics. Significantly, unlike sports governing bodies, the FBI was able to subpoena records that showed intentional PED use by the athletes in contradiction of their denials and claims that the doping was accidental. When the FBI shared that information with USADA, both athletes were banned from competition. How does this information sharing jibe with the Act's whistleblower protections and intent to treat the athletes as victims?

In protecting honest athletes and their fans and sponsors from doping corruption, regulators often encounter conflicting investigative priorities and obstacles. Two episodes highlight these challenges—one in professional cycling and one in Major League Baseball.

Lance Armstrong and Professional Cycling. Evidence amassed during investigations by federal law enforcement and USADA established that Lance Armstrong and five other members of the U.S. professional cycling team conspired to dope from 1998 until Armstrong retired in 2009. Along the way Armstrong amassed a record-breaking seven Tour de France titles. Armstrong consistently denied using PEDs, but over time an increasing number of former teammates came forward and admitted drug use. Federal prosecutors contemplated, although ultimately dropped, criminal charges against Armstrong and others for conspiracy, fraud, and racketeering based on the cycling team's use of government money to fund the doping scheme, as the team was sponsored at the time by the United States Postal Service.

Meanwhile, USADA initiated an arbitration process that sought to invalidate all of Armstrong's competition results and ban him from racing for life. Armstrong challenged the USADA arbitration as violating his federal constitutional due process rights, but a Texas federal court disagreed and declined to intervene. *Armstrong v. Tygart*, 2012 WL 3569682 (W.D. Tex.). Armstrong nonetheless refused to participate in the USADA arbitration or contest the testimony of 11 former cycling teammates that he was the central figure in a decade-long doping scheme. In its final report, USADA concluded "that the US Postal Service Pro Cycling Team ran the most sophisticated, professionalized and successful doping program that sport has ever seen." *Reasoned Decision of the United States Anti-Doping Agency on Disqualification and Ineligibility, USADA v.*

Armstrong (Oct. 10, 2012). Armstrong was stripped of his titles, and finally in 2013 admitted to doping throughout much of his career.

A key whistleblower in advancing the cycling investigations was Armstrong's teammate Floyd Landis, who himself was suspended for doping. He later brought a False Claims Act civil suit, joined by the U.S. Postal Service, to recover from Armstrong and his teammates over $32 million in government sponsorship money on the theory it was obtained by fraud. Armstrong defended the suit by arguing the government didn't suffer any harm from the fraud because it made at least $163.7 million in benefits from the sponsorship. Ultimately, he settled the suit by paying $5 million. *See United States ex rel. Landis v. Tailwind Sports Corp.*, 51 F. Supp. 3d 9, 58 (D.D.C. 2014).

Major League Baseball's Steroid Era. For most of the 1990s and early 2000s, steroid use in MLB was widespread and largely unchecked. The MLB Players Association was adamantly opposed to any form of mandatory random drug testing, and the league looked the other way as steroid-fueled on-field performances lined the owners' pockets, epitomized by the Mark McGwire-Sammy Sosa home run race in 1998. This changed in 2002 after retired third baseman Ken Caminiti admitted in a *Sports Illustrated* exposé to doping during the season that he was named 1996 National League MVP. He estimated that half of major league players were using steroids. Law enforcement got involved after a 2003 raid on the Bay Area Laboratory Cooperative (BALCO) uncovered evidence of PED use by numerous baseball players, including all-stars Barry Bonds, Roger Clemens, and Jason Giambi. Congressional hearings ensued, featuring testimony of baseball executives and 10 ballplayers, including McGwire, Sosa, and Bonds, all of whom denied or were evasive about steroid use.

By 2004, the MLBPA was prepared to agree to the league's first anti-doping policy that allowed random drug testing. Later CBAs expanded the policy's list of prohibited substances to include HGH, and incorporated increased testing and harsher suspensions. In 2006 MLB Commissioner Bud Selig appointed former U.S. Senate majority leader George Mitchell to conduct an independent investigation of the doping allegations. Mitchell's 407-page report was a bombshell, substantiating that every MLB club had players who had been using PEDs at some point, and that everyone knew about it including the union, owners, team physicians, trainers, and even the Commissioner's office.

REPORT TO THE COMMISSIONER OF BASEBALL OF AN INDEPENDENT INVESTIGATION INTO THE ILLEGAL USE OF STEROIDS AND OTHER PERFORMANCE ENHANCING SUBSTANCES BY PLAYERS IN MAJOR LEAGUE BASEBALL (MITCHELL REPORT)

Dec. 13, 2007

* * *

B.   The Problem Is Serious

The illegal use of performance enhancing substances poses a serious threat to the integrity of the game. Widespread use by players of such substances unfairly disadvantages the honest athletes who refuse to use them and raises questions about the validity of baseball records. In addition, because they are breaking the law, users of these substances are vulnerable to drug dealers who might seek to exploit their knowledge through threats intended to affect the outcome of baseball games or otherwise.

The illegal use of these substances to improve athletic performance also carries with it potentially serious negative side effects on the human body. Steroid users place themselves at risk for psychiatric problems, cardiovascular and liver damage, drastic changes to their reproductive systems, musculoskeletal injury, and other problems. Users of human growth hormone risk cancer, harm to their reproductive health, cardiac and thyroid problems, and overgrowth of bone and connective tissue.

Apart from the dangers posed to the major league player himself, however, his use of performance enhancing substances encourages young athletes to use those substances. Young Americans are placing themselves at risk of serious harm. Because adolescents are already subject to significant hormonal changes, the abuse of steroids and other performance enhancing substances can have more serious effects on them than they have on adults.

* * *

Recommendations

1.   The Commissioner Should Establish a Department of Investigations

. . . [The MLB labor relations department's] primary responsibility [of overseeing the collective bargaining relationship] complicates the ability of the labor relations department to meet another of its responsibilities, to investigate allegations of player wrongdoing. The department must maintain good relations with the Players Association; but aggressive, thorough investigations of the alleged possession or use by players of performance enhancing substances may be inconsistent with that objective. Many of the investigations involving performance enhancing substances have not been aggressive or thorough. Before this investigation, with few exceptions, the Commissioner's Office had not conducted investigative interviews of current major league players regarding alleged possession or use of performance enhancing substances, by that player or by others.

The Commissioner's Office security department has been responsible for parts of some investigations into the use or distribution of performance enhancing substances. That department's primary function, however, is to provide security for the players and the playing environment. That also places security officials in a difficult situation when they are asked to investigate the very persons they are responsible for protecting.

The Commissioner should create a Department of Investigations, led by a senior executive who reports directly to the president of Major League Baseball. Ideally, this senior executive should have experience as a senior leader in law enforcement, with the highest credibility among state and federal law enforcement officials; the success of this department will depend in part upon how well it interacts with law enforcement authorities. The senior executive should have sole authority over all investigations of alleged performance enhancing substance violations and other threats to the integrity of the game, and should receive the resources and other support needed to make the office effective. . . .

2.   The Commissioner's Office Should More Effectively Cooperate with Law Enforcement Agencies

No matter how skilled, the Commissioner's Office's investigators face significant disadvantages in investigating illegal performance enhancing substance use compared to law enforcement officials. Law enforcement officials, of course, have a broad array of investigatory powers, including search warrants and subpoena power. Recently, law enforcement agencies have become increasingly flexible and creative in sharing with professional sports organizations information gathered during investigations. This practice makes sense because law enforcement agencies typically focus their efforts in illegal drug investigations on prosecution of the manufacturers, importers, and distributors, not on the athletes who are the end users. During these investigations, however, law enforcement agencies often accumulate evidence of use by individuals. . . .

3.   The Commissioner's Office Should Actively Use the Clubs' Powers as Employer, to Investigate Violations of the Joint Program

One of the critical tools available to all employers is the investigatory interview. Generally, an employer may compel union-represented employees to attend and truthfully respond during any interview conducted by or on behalf of the employer.

The Ferguson Jenkins arbitration decision has played a role in the interpretation of a player's rights during an investigatory interview. In Jenkins, an arbitrator ruled that the Commissioner could not impose discipline upon Jenkins for refusing to answer questions about alleged possession of drugs of abuse while Jenkins was facing criminal charges for the same conduct.

According to the Commissioner's Office and the Players Association, however, no major league player ever has been convicted of a criminal offense for the use or possession of performance enhancing substances. And, as noted elsewhere in this report, the policy of the Department of Justice, and of other prosecutors, is to prosecute the manufacturers, importers, and distributors of performance enhancing substances, not the athletes who use them. Thus, the basis on which the Jenkins arbitrator relied—pending criminal charges against the athlete based on the same conduct—will rarely be an issue. . . .

4.   All Clubs Should Have Clear, Written, and Well-Publicized Policies for Reporting Information Relating to Possible Performance Enhancing Substance Violations

Since 1991, Major League Baseball's Drug Policy has covered performance enhancing substances expressly. That policy states in part:

> If any club covers up or fails to disclose to [the Commissioner's] office any information concerning drug use by a player, the Club will be fined in an amount up to $2 million, the highest allowable amount under the Major League Constitution.

Many club personnel told us that they were not aware of the policy. The Commissioner's Office should actively publicize its policy regarding performance enhancing substances to club personnel and require each club to adopt a uniform, written policy for reporting information about possible substance violations. . . .

* * *

Conclusions

1.   The use of steroids in Major League Baseball was widespread. The response by baseball was slow to develop and was initially ineffective. For many years, citing concerns for the privacy rights of the players, the Players Association opposed mandatory random drug testing of its members for steroids and other substances. But in 2002, the effort gained momentum after the clubs and the Players Association agreed to and adopted a mandatory random drug testing program. The current program has been effective in that detectable steroid use appears to have declined. However, that does not mean that players have stopped using performance enhancing substances. Many players have shifted to human growth hormone, which is not detectable in any currently available urine test.

2.   The minority of players who used such substances were wrong. They violated federal law and baseball policy, and they distorted the fairness of competition by trying to gain an unfair advantage over the majority of players who followed the law and the rules. They—the players who follow the law and the rules—are faced with the painful choice of either being placed at a competitive disadvantage or becoming illegal users themselves. No one should have to make that choice.

3.   Obviously, the players who illegally used performance enhancing substances are responsible for their actions. But they did not act in a vacuum. Everyone involved in baseball over the past two decades— Commissioners, club officials, the Players Association, and players— shares to some extent in the responsibility for the steroids era. There was a collective failure to recognize the problem as it emerged and to deal with it early on. As a result, an environment developed in which illegal use became widespread.

4.   Knowledge and understanding of the past are essential if the problem is to be dealt with effectively in the future. But being chained to the past is not helpful. Baseball does not need and cannot afford to engage in a never-ending search for the name of every player who ever used performance enhancing substances. The Commissioner was right to ask for this investigation and report. It would have been impossible to get closure on this issue without it, or something like it. . . .

———

The Mitchell Report did not close the book on government pursuit of MLB players implicated in PED use. Three later episodes are worth mentioning. First, legendary hitter Barry Bonds had testified at a 2003 grand jury hearing on the indictment of the BALCO trainer who allegedly supplied him with steroid creams, stating that he believed they were arthritis balms. That testimony prompted a seven-year investigation into whether Bonds lied to the grand jury, resulting in an indictment for perjury and obstruction of justice. At a 2011 criminal trial, Bonds was convicted only of the obstruction charge, but that verdict was overturned on appeal. *United States v. Bonds*, 784 F.3d 582 (9th Cir. 2015) (*en banc*).

Second, at 2008 congressional hearings convened in response to the Mitchell Report, Roger Clemens, one of the game's most dominant pitchers, testified that he had never used PEDs. He too was later indicted for perjury. He was tried twice on the charge, the first a mistrial and the second an acquittal in 2012. *United States v. Clemens*, No. 1:10CR00223, 2010 WL 3260179 (D.D.C. Aug. 19, 2010) (Indictment). Clemens later admitted steroid use and expressed remorse.

Third, in 2013, another PED scandal erupted in baseball, reviving concern that doping was again rampant in MLB. Several players were accused of obtaining HGH from Biogenesis of America, a rejuvenation clinic in Miami, after a disgruntled former employee disclosed clinic records. A criminal prosecution ensued, with law enforcement sharing with MLB the names of its players who used the clinic. Thirteen MLB players were punished with lengthy suspensions of fifty or more games, including Alex Rodriguez, who was suspended for a staggering 211 games. His challenge to that suspension is discussed in Chapter 4.

NOTES AND QUESTIONS

1. *Whistleblowers.* Few athletes are willing to serve as whistleblowers of doping schemes, with the notable exception of American cyclist Floyd Landis. How should sports governing bodies deal with individuals whose own doping is uncovered in this manner? When Canadian sprinter Ben Johnson was suspended for doping at the 1988 Olympics, he asserted it was rampant in track and field, yet no other athlete came forward and he alone was sanctioned. What response would incentivize cooperation with doping investigations while meting out appropriate sanctions?

2. *Government Intervention.* It took the threat of government regulation for MLB to clean up its act. Would U.S. professional sports have been better off if Congress had enacted a uniform drug testing policy? Even if such legislation passed, would prosecutors have interest in enforcing it? Consider past experience of non-enforcement of the Sports Bribery Act, discussed earlier in this chapter, and of the Sports Agent Responsibility and Trust Act (SPARTA), discussed in Chapter 10. Consider also the failures of the criminal prosecutions of Barry Bonds and Roger Clemens. What else might explain law enforcement's deference to sports self-policing? What prospects are there for robust enforcement of the Rodchenkov Act?

3. *Sport Self-Regulation.* Are you satisfied that sport can successfully self-regulate PEDs in view of leagues' and governing bodies' vested interest in athlete performance and protecting the sport's brand from scandal? On the other hand, why might it be preferrable—for the sport and fans alike—for each sport to develop individual anti-doping policies?

4. *Players Unions and Doping.* As with allegations of on-field cheating, doping has precipitated major rifts inside players unions. The MLBPA opposed stricter doping policies for years, despite the countervailing interests of a significant segment of its membership who preferred to stay clean. The Mitchell Report states that throughout the investigation, "the Players Association was largely uncooperative," refusing to provide any relevant documents and advising players not to agree to interviews. What do you think explains the MLBPA's attitude and choices in dealing with doping at the time?

5. *Validity of Baseball Records.* The Mitchell Report observes that PED usage has raised questions about the validity of baseball records, notably home runs. However, pitchers were also using PEDs—did that sufficiently even the playing field to validate the new home run records? The record-breakers of the

steroids era—notably Mark McGwire and Sammy Sosa—are unlikely to ever be voted into the baseball hall of fame. And yet admitted steroid user Mike Piazza, one of baseball's best hitting catchers, was voted in on his third appearance on the ballot. What explains this different treatment? Is it the perception that his steroid usage was not material because he didn't break any significant records (other than most homeruns by a catcher)? What does this say about public reaction to PED usage?

6.   *Investigating Violations.* The Mitchell Report makes detailed recommendations about how a sports league should structure its investigative function with respect to PED use. As with gambling-related corruption and match-fixing, cooperation with law enforcement is deemed critical. And yet that cooperation remains largely reactive to actual incidents of illegal PED use, as in the aftermath of the Biogenesis scandal. Are there ways in which sports leagues and law enforcement might proactively collaborate that respects league autonomy and athlete privacy and dignity interests?

7.   *Athletes as Role Models.* The Mitchell Report argues for prohibiting doping by professional baseball players in part because they are role models for impressionable youth who might then also use PEDs. But adults are allowed to engage in many behaviors that we view as inappropriate for children, for example, drinking alcohol and smoking cigarettes. Yet we don't ban athletes from partaking, although some leagues ban athletes from endorsing those products and many athletes avoid them as part of their training regimens. Some athletes use their fame as a platform to advance worthy causes. It seems logical and fair to expect those athletes to live up to higher standards, but what about the rest?

CHAPTER 2

COMMISSIONER-LED PROFESSIONAL SPORTS LEAGUES IN NORTH AMERICA

■ ■ ■

The business of every sport is based on contract, specifically the voluntary undertakings by those willing to risk their time, human capital, and financial resources. Those contracts—for example, between entrepreneurs to form a league, between owners and players, and, in the form of collective bargaining agreements, between unions and leagues—give rise to numerous disputes resolved either in court or by arbitrators. It is not surprising that the law would have a role to play when so much money is involved. Not all disputes involve enforcement of private agreements. Public law often constrains how private parties might prefer to organize sporting competitions. However, public law often responds only after the private parties have failed to meet public expectations about important sporting practices.

An early illustration of a sports league's response to public expectations is the Chicago "Black Sox" scandal of 1919, raising serious issues of sporting integrity discussed in Chapter 1. The immediate diagnosis was that a major contributing cause was baseball club owners' inability to police themselves. This led to the view that owners should agree to delegate to an "independent commissioner" the responsibility to decide whether and how to protect the "best interests of the sport" from behavior that threatened the business. Every organization needs a chief executive officer. In the case of sports, someone must establish schedules and league championships, supervise officials, negotiate television and merchandising contracts, and the like.

Historically, many claimed that the office of the commissioner was the supreme voice about what truly is in the *best* interests (not just the *business* interests) of the game. League constitutions vest the commissioner with power to resolve disputes on that score among players, clubs, and other participants. Commissioners or presidents also govern individual professional sports like golf and tennis with their tours, and college sports with the NCAA, and Olympic sports with their respective governing bodies. One conspicuous exception is boxing, where a large number of "governing" organizations exist, subject to manipulation by promoters on behalf of particularly popular fighters. This example reinforces the conventional wisdom that any sport that wants to preserve its integrity needs a commissioner.

Although commissioners have always primarily served ownership, their public image has evolved over time. Baseball, the sport that gave birth in the early 1920s to an independent commissioner whose principal focus was integrity, became the first-ever league to make an owner of one of its teams the commissioner: Allen "Bud" Selig of the Milwaukee Brewers. Selig's appointment signaled a greater emphasis on the role of the commissioner as a CEO charged with expanding profitability by securing approval of his former fellow owners of initiatives that would grow revenues.

The unique office of sports commissioner raises important questions. Why would owners, who control sports as a private, for-profit business, vest power in a powerful single individual? A commissioner's actions require either legal authority—in the form of delegation in league constitutions or other agreements—or success in obtaining authority from current owners. Given this dynamic, does the public interest warrant external regulation over the power residing in a single person selected by one constituency, the team owners? Understanding the power of the commissioner informs consideration of whether sports warrant special dispensation from external rules applied to other industries, or whether there are special regulations that are warranted because of the unique nature of sport that would not apply to CEOs of other big businesses.

A. THE LEGAL STATUS OF PROFESSIONAL SPORTS LEAGUES

1. A BRIEF HISTORY

The first U.S. professional sports league was created in 1876 as the National League of Professional Base Ball Clubs. Organized by William A. Hulbert of the Chicago White Stockings, the NL was created in response to a host of problems with the loose organization known as the National Association that had been organized five years earlier. Clubs were responsible for arranging their own schedule of competition through agreements that were often breached; players were unpaid, contracts breached, and gambling and match-fixing were rampant. The solution was what we know call a "closed league" controlled by the member clubs. As an economic historian noted:

> Hulbert appealed to the owners, businessmen all, by using some simple economic logic. If the businessmen ran the teams and the players concentrated on playing ball, each party could concentrate on doing what they did best and everyone would be better off. The geographic exclusivity he promised to each club appealed to the owners as well. Exclusivity meant monopoly, and monopoly meant profit. Establishing the NL as the premier professional league, with entry strictly controlled by the monopolists themselves, also

appealed to their sense of profits. If the new league was recognized as the premier assemblage of baseball talent then it would be able to attract a greater percentage of the better players, and with no equals to bid them away, it would lower the payroll burden, leaving a larger percentage of the revenues for the owners. Another reason to concentrate the quality of talent at the top was to reduce the number of poor drawing games played against low quality competition in small towns.

Michael Haupert, *William Hulbert and the Birth of the National League*, Baseball Research Journal (spring 2015), *available at* https://sabr.org/journal/article/william-hulbert-and-the-birth-of-the-national-league/. A constitution was approved by the eight charter members: the Boston Red Stockings, Hartford Dark Blues, New York Mutuals, Philadelphia Athletics, Cincinnati Red Stockings, Louisville Grays, Chicago White Stockings, and St. Louis Brown Stockings. The constitution provided that the league was to be governed by a board of five owners chosen by lot.

As recounted by Stefan Szymanski and Andrew Zimbalist in *National Pastime: How Americans Play Baseball and the Rest of the World Plays Soccer* (Brookings Inst. Press 2005), this model was emulated by the first sports league in England, the Football League. However, because England had a national sports governing board, the powerful Football Association, who organized the lucrative knock-out FA Cup competition, Football League clubs quickly developed the very different "promotion and relegation" model, leading to what is now known as the European Model of Sport. *See* James A.R. Nafziger, "European and North American models of sports organization," in HANDBOOK ON INTERNATIONAL SPORTS LAW (James A.R. Nafziger & Stephen F. Ross, eds. Edward Elgar 2011). Back in North America, the NL model has been largely followed by the other major professional sports and retains much of the form devised by Hulbert and his compatriots nearly a century and a half ago.

2. LEAGUE CONSTITUTIONS[*]

The fundamental structure of the four major North American sports leagues is similar. The Major League Baseball (MLB) Constitution is an agreement among participating clubs (Art. I). It creates the office of a commissioner, and defines the powers delegated to this officer and means for electing and terminating a commissioner (Art. II). Although the text confers broad powers on the Commissioner (including punitive action against owners, employees, or players "that is deemed by the Commissioner not to be in the best interests of baseball" (Art. II, § 3), the text also limits authority in specific cases. *See, e.g.,* Art. II, § 4 (limiting application to matters subject to a vote of the owners). The Constitution

---

[*]   For the most recent texts of league constitutions available to us, see https://pennstatelaw.psu.edu/online-documentary-supplement.

specifies majority or super-majority votes required for various actions (Art.
V, § 2). It states (Art. VI) that *all*

> disputes and controversies related in any way to professional
> baseball between Clubs or between a Club(s) and any Major
> League Baseball entity(ies) (including in each case, without
> limitation, their owners, officers, directors, employees and
> players), other than those whose resolution is expressly provided
> for by another means in this Constitution, the Major League
> Rules, the Basic Agreement with the Major League Baseball
> Players Association, or the collective bargaining agreement with
> any representative of the Major League umpires, shall be
> submitted to the Commissioner, as arbitrator, who, after hearing,
> shall have the sole and exclusive right to decide such disputes and
> controversies and whose decision shall be final and unappealable.

The Constitution identifies the teams in the league and the
extraordinary circumstances where a team's membership can be
terminated (Art. VIII). It also specifies, by state and county, the territories
where each club shall operate, while delegating to the Commissioner the
designation of broadcast territories (Art. VIII, § 8), and specifying
broadcast rights (Art. X § 3).

3.   SPORTS LEAGUES AS JOINT VENTURES
OF CLUB OWNERS

This brief summary reflects the fundamental nature of North
American sports leagues as a contractual relationship among the clubs
participating in the competition. The nature of a sports league is a critical
issue in determining the appropriate application of the antitrust laws to
sport: Chapter 6, Section D discusses the Supreme Court's decision in
American Needle, Inc. v. National Football League, 560 U.S. 183 (2010).
There, the Court observed that each club "is a substantial, independently
owned, and independently managed business." *Id.* at 196. Because "the
financial performance of each team, while related to that of the others, does
not . . . necessarily rise and fall with that of the others," *id.*, citing *North
American Soccer League v. NFL,* 670 F.2d 1249, 1252 (2d Cir. 1982), their
corporate actions are guided by " 'separate corporate consciousnesses,' and
[their] 'objectives are' not 'common.' " 560 U.S. at 196 (citing *Copperweld
Corp. v. Indep. Tube Corp.,* 467 U.S. 752, 771 (1984). The Court's analysis
makes clear that North American sports leagues are joint ventures, which
are functionally distinct from a single enterprise. Although clubs "have
common interests in promoting the NFL brand, they are still separate,
profit-maximizing entities, and their interests . . . are not necessarily
aligned." *Id.* at 196.

The Court's characterization of sports leagues as joint ventures has
important implications for how those aggrieved by league policies might

seek judicial review. As discussed extensively in Chapters 6–8, parties can use the antitrust laws to allege that these decisions constitute unreasonable restraints of trade in violation of the Sherman Act. As detailed below in Chapter 1, Section B.4, parties can also challenge decisions under the law of private associations.

4. AN ECONOMIC ANALYSIS OF LEAGUE STRUCTURE

Unusual in business but typical in government, the structure of North American sports leagues requires the approval of multiple stakeholders to respond to changes in a dynamic social and business environment. As with public policy, changes in sports policy are rarely "Pareto efficient" (where everyone is better off, and no one is worse off). Thus, proponents of any changes in labor rules, revenue sharing, structure of the playoffs, location of teams, etc., must overcome or assuage stakeholders who are adversely affected by the change, even if the change is good for the sport as a whole.

The insights of two Nobel-prize winning economists are relevant here. Adopting a standard economic model that assumes all parties have perfect information and there are no bargaining costs, Ronald Coase's famous theorem holds that private parties will bargain toward the efficient result regardless of how legal rules allocate rights. A critical corollary to this insight, however, is Coase's view that where imperfect information and significant transaction costs are likely to inhibit efficient bargaining, then the legal system has to consider how best to allocate rights initially. Ronald Coase, *The Problem of Social Costs,* 3 J. LAW & ECON. 1 (1960). The extent to which sports leagues feature information asymmetries and bargaining costs that are not overcome by the parties is a critical issue in sports law and business.

If these dynamics significantly inhibit parties from working out efficient results, then the question arises as to why sports leagues would create governance structures that allow stakeholders to veto innovations that are actually good for the sport or league as a whole. These include control by club owners with their own individual interests, and super-majority votes by these owners. Why not vest management of the league in a corporate board of directors and a CEO?

The work of Oliver Williamson provides some answers. He explains business structures as techniques to minimize transactions costs. Thus, in a variety of contexts, granting parochial stakeholders a right to veto significant change is a means of securing agreement among the parties and avoiding costly contracting about unforeseen future events: parties can be assured their own interests will be protected as long as they have these veto rights. For example, the legal admission of a new partner to a partnership requires the entire partnership agreement to be redone. The

MLB Constitution permits the admission of new clubs with a super-majority vote, without having to deal with this hoary subject in advance.

These insights are useful as we consider a number of issues in sports law:

- When should league owners reserve authority to themselves, and when should they delegate authority to a Commissioner? To what extent can the Commissioner's authority be used to overcome information and bargaining cost problems?

- What vote should be required for important league policies? How can proponents of innovations use economic or legal strategies to overcome a bloc that can veto the proposals?

- In reviewing legal challenges to sports league decisions, to what extent can judges confidently defer to league choices?

5. FIDUCIARY DUTIES AND LEAGUE GOVERNANCE

As discussed in detail in Chapter 6, Section D, a difference between a North American sports league and an integrated company like McDonald's or General Motors is that publicly traded corporations are governed by boards of directors with fiduciary duties to the shareholders as a whole. Unlike corporations or partnerships, it does not appear that sports owners, when acting under the league constitution as the governors of the sport, are required to act like directors or partners. The word "fiduciary" does not appear in any of the four major league constitutions. Language in the NFL Constitution suggests that owners may appropriately adopt or reject policies that serve the interests of their club, rather than the league as a whole: Art. II, § 2.1(a) provides that the NFL is organized to "promote and foster the primary business of League members, each member being an owner of a professional football club located in the United States." *See also* NHL Const., Art. II, § 2.1 (same). The MLB Constitution also seems to assume that owners may act in their own interest, rather than the best interests of baseball, creating limited opportunities for the Commissioner to overrule owners' votes on rules or policies. *See* MLB Const., Art. II, § 4 (allowing Commissioner to override owners' actions on matters requiring a vote of the clubs pursuant to Art. II, § 9 [election of commissioner] or Art. V, § 2 [collective bargaining, schedules, post-season play, playing rules, broadcast rights, expansion or relocation, sale of ownership, divisional play, revenue sharing, exclusion of club from league], but only where the matter "involves the integrity of, or public confidence in, the national game of Baseball."

Claims of breach of fiduciary duty by a fellow owner have been rarely litigated. Indeed, it would appear that under Art. V of the MLB Constitution, such a claim could not be brought in court but would have to be submitted to the Commissioner as arbitrator. In one case involving ongoing disputes between maverick NFL owner Al Davis and the league, *Oakland Raiders v. NFL*, 131 Cal. App. 4th 631 (2005), a California appellate court held the other club owners held no fiduciary duty toward the Raiders regarding league policies. *But see Professional Hockey Corp. v. World Hockey Ass'n (WHA)*, 143 Cal. App. 3d 410 (1983) (representatives of each franchise on Board of Trustees of defunct league, established as a corporate entity, had a fiduciary duty to act for the benefit of the league as a whole when making decisions about common league goals).

Under general partnership law, which treats joint ventures as a type of partnership, each partner has a fiduciary duty to place the interests of the venture above his own interests unless the partnership agreement or the other partners allow otherwise. On the other hand, business associations such as limited liability companies (LLCs) typically do not include a requirement that those governing the entity must act in the best interests of the entity. *See* 1 Larry Ribstein & Robert Keatinge, *Ribstein and Keatinge on Ltd. Liab. Cos.* § 9:12 (2017). In *American Needle*, the Supreme Court cited with approval an insightful analysis, Zenichi Shishido, *Conflicts of Interest and Fiduciary Duties in the Operation of a Joint Venture*, 39 HASTINGS L. J. 63 (1987). Professor Shishido notes that, unlike for corporate directors, there exists a "duplicity of joint ventures' directors' interests. Almost all the directors of a joint venture are interlocking directors or employees of one of the parent companies; thus, they have interests not only in the joint venture but also in one of the parent companies." *Id.* at 71. Likewise, the well-recognized duty of a controlling shareholder to shareholders of subsidiary companies does not apply in a joint venture setting. He observes that when a conflict arises in the interests of a joint venture and those of "parent companies," officers of both will typically give the interests of the parent (*i.e.*, the club, in the sports league context) the higher priority. *Id.* at 73.

Consider the application of this principle to sport leagues. The next section discusses an MLB dispute arising because league executives and most owners preferred a realignment by placing the Chicago Cubs in the NL West and the Atlanta Braves in the NL East. The Cubs' ownership objected, reportedly because it feared that adding late-starting west coast games to the Cubs' schedule would detract from the television ratings of the Cubs' games broadcast on the team's corporate sibling, the Chicago superstation WGN. Putting aside the specific powers of the Commissioner in resolving this dispute, should each owner have a judicially enforceable duty to vote in favor of the interests of the league at the expense of its own team's financial rewards? Do owners of clubs in large media markets have a fiduciary duty to vote in favor of sharing their teams' television revenues with teams in smaller markets? Did Baltimore Orioles' owner Peter Angelos breach a duty to fellow owners by blocking the relocation of the failing Montreal Expos to Washington until, after over five years, a complex side deal about broadcast rights was signed? If they are not under such a duty, is that because no such legal duty exists, or because the parties to the Major League Constitution have implicitly waived each owner's duty in certain contexts when they vote on league affairs?

As a comparative note on this issue, the English Premier League's governing documents vest minimal power in their Board of Directors and assign most decisions to the twenty clubs who are "shareholders" in the governing entity. This is done because under English law (as with American law), in most circumstances shareholders do not have a fiduciary duty to adopt policies that maximize the interests of all.

B. THE HISTORY AND LEGAL AUTHORITY OF THE SPORTS LEAGUE COMMISSIONER

The origin and evolution of the unique role of Commissioner of Baseball is detailed by Andrew Zimbalist, IN THE BEST INTERESTS OF BASEBALL? THE REVOLUTIONARY REIGN OF BUD SELIG (Hoboken, N.J.: John Wiley & Sons 2006). In its 1876 Constitution, the National League vested authority in a board of directors of five randomly selected owners, who chose a President from among its ranks. The National Agreement that ended a brief inter-league war between the National and American Leagues in 1903 created a National Commission consisting of the presidents of the two leagues and a third member chosen by the other two, subject to renewal annually.

According to Zimbalist, several factors—the preservation of regulatory authority in each league president for "conduct detrimental to the general welfare of the game" (see the *Johnson* case in Section B, *infra*), the lack of owner support for the Commission, and the resistance to the leadership of American League President Ban Johnson—caused owners to seek structural reform "well before" the Black Sox Scandal broke in 1919. At the same time, when word of the "Black Sox" scandal emerged a full year later, both fans and club owners felt that the source of the problem was the lax disciplinary approach of the National Commission. The owners decided to dismantle the tripartite commission and replace it with a single, powerful commissioner. Their first pick for that position was former President William Howard Taft (an avid baseball fan who was the first chief executive to throw out the first pitch of the baseball season and may also have originated the 7th inning stretch), but he declined. (Taft was rewarded with appointment by President Harding as Chief Justice of the United States six months later.)

The man actually tagged for the Commissioner position was Kenesaw Mountain Landis, a 38-year-old federal judge in Chicago who had initially caught the owners' eye with his favorable handling of the Federal League antitrust suit a few years earlier (see Chapter 5). Landis agreed to take this new position only if the Major League Agreement was rewritten to give the commissioner the sweeping powers described in *Rose v. Giamatti*, which is discussed in the following pages. (Landis originally wanted the title "high commissioner.") *See generally*, David Pietrusza, JUDGE AND JURY: THE LIFE AND TIMES OF JUDGE KENESAW MOUNTAIN LANDIS (South Bend, IN: Diamond Communications, Inc. 1998).

On January 12, 1921, a new National Agreement created the Office of Commissioner. Prior to its enactment, Landis spoke to the owners as follows:

> It is my duty to be very frank with you. . . . I got the impression [that you] had a structure outlined which provided for authority to discharge a responsibility and that part of that authority would be control over whatever and whoever had to do with baseball.

> Another impression was that there had grown up in baseball certain evils not limited to bad baseball players; that men who controlled ball clubs in the past had been guilty of various offenses and the time had come where somebody would be given the authority, if I may put it brutally, to save you from yourselves. . . .

Quoted in Daniel Ginsburg, THE FIX IS IN: A HISTORY OF BASEBALL GAMBLING AND GAME FIXING SCANDALS 35 (Jefferson, N.C.: McFarland 1995). Threatening to refuse the position if, as the latest draft constitution suggested, his powers were limited to crooked ballplayers, the owners granted Landis plenary powers over the entire game.

A case that dramatically illustrated the unique role of a sports league commissioner with regard to game integrity is summarized below and detailed in James Reston, Jr., COLLISION AT HOME PLATE: THE LIVES OF PETE ROSE AND BART GIAMATTI (Univ. of Nebraska Press 1997). In the early winter of 1989, rumors began to filter into the Commissioner's Office that Rose, then manager of the Cincinnati Reds, had been betting on baseball games, even on games involving his own team. If true, that action would have violated a sixty-year-old Major League Rule that required a one-year suspension for anyone betting on baseball and a lifetime ban for betting on a game involving one's own team. Accordingly, on February 23, newly elected Commissioner Bart Giamatti, a classics scholar who was the former President of Yale University, hired Washington lawyer John Dowd to investigate this allegation. Giamatti acted under the authority granted him by a document known then as the "Major League Agreement" (now renamed the "Constitution"). As it was written then (see footnote * for cite to the current version), Article I, § 2, provided that "the functions of the Commissioner" include:

> (a) To investigate, either upon complaint or upon his own initiative, any act, transaction or practice charged, alleged or suspected to be not in the best interests of the national game of Baseball, with authority to summon persons and to order the

production of documents and, in cases of refusal to appear or produce, to impose such penalties as are hereinafter provided;

(b) To determine, after investigation, what preventive, remedial or punitive action is appropriate in the premises, and to take such action either against Major Leagues, Major League Clubs, or individuals, as the case may be.

In early May, after three months of investigating and interviewing some 40 witnesses, including taking sworn statements from Rose and the two key informants against him, Ron Peters and Paul Janszen, Dowd delivered to Giamatti a 225-page report (with seven volumes of evidence and exhibits) that ended with Dowd's judgment that Rose had regularly bet on Reds games (although apparently Rose always bet on his Reds to win). Giamatti immediately sent this report to Rose and his lawyers and scheduled Rose's hearing before him for late June. See Ronald J. Rychlak, *Pete Rose, Bart Giamatti, and the Dowd Report*, 68 MISS. L.J. 889 (1999) (a publication of Dowd's report and the relevant MLB governing documents).

Then, on April 18, Giamatti sent a letter to U.S. District Judge Carl Rubin, who was preparing to sentence Ron Peters for federal drug and income tax offenses. Giamatti stated in his letter that Peters had been "candid, forthright and truthful" in providing investigators "critical sworn testimony" about Rose. The Cincinnati-based Judge Rubin, an avowed Reds fan who was highly exercised by what he termed the Commissioner's "vendetta against Pete Rose," sent a copy of the letter to Reuven Katz, Rose's principal lawyer. Armed with this letter, Katz filed suit in state court to enjoin Giamatti from going any further with the disciplinary proceeding. The contention was that Giamatti had prejudged the facts of the case, and thus had denied Rose his right to a proceeding conducted with "due regard for all the principles of natural justice and fair play," as the Commissioner's own disciplinary rules required. Rose won a controversial 10-day restraining order from state court Judge Norbert Nadel, the first time the action of any sports commissioner had been enjoined. (Nadel faced re-election later that year for his judicial office, and the Rose case offered him a unique opportunity to demonstrate to his constituents his adoration of the Reds manager.) Giamatti sought to remove the case to federal district court on diversity of citizenship grounds.

In arguing for removal, the Commissioner's counsel asserted that this case should be heard only by a "national tribunal":

In the state court in Cincinnati, I need not describe Mr. Rose's standing. He is a local hero, perhaps the first citizen of Cincinnati. And Commissioner Giamatti is viewed suspiciously as a foreigner from New York, trapped in an ivory tower, and accused of bias by Mr. Rose. Your Honor, this is a textbook example of why diversity jurisdiction was created in the Federal Courts and why it exists to this very day.

But that removal could be obtained only if this case were deemed to be a dispute just between Rose, a citizen of Ohio, and Giamatti, a citizen of New York. If the Cincinnati Reds, also a citizen of Ohio in the eyes of the law, were considered a real party to this conflict, then the complete diversity of citizenship required for federal jurisdiction would be lacking. In applying the arcane rules of federal versus state court jurisdiction, the judicial opinion in *Rose v. Giamatti*, 721 F. Supp. 906, 917 (S.D. Ohio, 1989), laid bare "the reality . . . that Major League Baseball is a unique organization . . . [with] extraordinary power invested in the Commissioner."

Rose's argument was quite simple: as manager of the Reds, he was in imminent danger of losing the benefits of a contract paying him $500,000 a year because of Giamatti's violation of procedural fairness towards him. Clearly, then, the Reds were an appropriate party in Rose's lawsuit to prevent that from happening. The Commissioner's answer, which the federal court accepted, was that the contract between Rose and the Reds provided that "the Major League and Professional Baseball Agreements and Rules and all amendments thereto hereafter adopted, are hereby made a part of this contract." This feature of Rose's personal employment contract stemmed from the following provision of the Major League Agreement:

> The form of players' contract to be used by the Major Leagues, and all contracts between Major Leagues or Clubs and their officers and employees, shall contain a clause by which the parties agree to submit themselves to the discipline of the Commissioner, and to accept his decisions rendered in accordance with this Agreement.

The commissioner's disciplinary authority was reinforced by the constituent members' further agreement to "be finally and unappealably bound" by all the disciplinary decisions of the commissioner, and to "waive such right of recourse to the courts as would otherwise have existed in their favor." The judge read this web of contractual relationships as establishing a commissioner's office wielding judicial power totally independently of control by either the Reds individually or the 26 clubs collectively. (As the judge observed, the constitution ordained that "neither the Commissioner's powers nor his compensation may be diminished during his term of office.") That meant that only Rose and Giamatti were real parties to this case, which therefore was properly removable to the federal judicial arena.

The district court issued its decision removing the case to federal court on July 31, 1990. Perhaps because he was then facing even more pressing legal problems with the Internal Revenue Service, Rose agreed on August 23 to settle the baseball case on the terms that Rose would withdraw his suit, accept the Commissioner's jurisdiction and penalty, but neither admit nor deny having bet on baseball. As penalty, Giamatti declared Rose permanently ineligible to associate with any major or minor league baseball club. (After a year, however, Rose would be entitled to apply to the commissioner for termination of this lifetime ban.) Eight days later, Giamatti was dead of a heart attack, succeeded in office by his counsel and close friend, Francis "Fay" Vincent. A few months later, Rose went to jail for income tax fraud—in particular, for concealing large cash payments from baseball autograph shows (money that Rose had used to cover his large gambling losses). Rose finally admitted in his best-selling autobiography, *My Prison Without Bars*, what he told Commissioner Selig in late 2002: he had regularly placed bets with bookmakers on his Cincinnati Reds when he was managing as well as playing for them, but always on his team to win. Rose's efforts for baseball reinstatement continue, unsuccessfully, to this day.

———

The function of the league commissioner in preserving sporting integrity is not the only one served by such an office. Averting litigation is another important function, conferred via the power to arbitrate inter-club and intra-club disputes. The NHL Constitution, to illustrate, provides in Article 6.3(b)(1) that the Commissioner "shall have full and exclusive jurisdiction and authority to arbitrate and resolve . . . any dispute that involves . . . two or more holders of an ownership interest in a Member Club of the League." Individuals or entities must agree to be bound by these provisions as a condition of assuming any ownership interest in the NHL. This provision's impact was demonstrated in 2021, when minority owners of the Pittsburgh Penguins challenged the sale of majority control from Ron Burkle and Mario Lemieux to the Fenway Sports Group. Alleging that the sale violated a 2007 partnership agreement between themselves and Burkle and Lemieux, they filed a lawsuit in Delaware seeking a judgment that the sale to Fenway was void.

Without taking a position on the merits of the claim, the NHL filed a motion to compel arbitration. In *Wildfire Productions, LP v. Team Lemieux LLC*, C.A. No. 2021-1072-PAF (Del. Chanc. June 29, 2022), the court agreed. Applying the Federal Arbitration Act, the court reasoned that agreements containing arbitration clauses should be liberally construed to favor arbitration. In addition, the court upheld the Commissioner's power to compel the arbitration based on his determination that the matter in dispute could be "detrimental to the best interests of the NHL," specifically the uncertainty that could result to lengthy litigation over ownership and control of the Penguins. The court rejected an argument that the 2007 partnership agreement's grant of exclusive jurisdiction to Delaware courts, to which the NHL was not a party, superseded the minority owners' agreement with the NHL to submit all disputes to the Commissioner.

———

NOTES AND QUESTIONS

1.   *Why Should a Commissioner Decide What Is in the Best Interests of a Sport?* Why would MLB owners want a Commissioner to decide a case like that of Rose, rather than assign the decision to the ownership of the most concerned club, the Reds? Why would the owners prefer to delegate to a Commissioner rather than to an ad hoc ownership committee?

2.   *Why Should a Commissioner Arbitrate Internal Disputes?* Should owners and key executives be required, in order to be part of a league, to submit all legal dispute to a Commissioner? Should the Commissioner be required to rule impartially, as an arbitrator would, or may the Commissioner render a decision based on commercial, strategic, or other factors?

3.   *Legal Basis for Judicial Review?* On what law could Rose base any claim that he was treated unfairly by the Commissioner? Was the Commissioner, or MLB, constrained by the Due Process clause or any other constitutional provision? Was Rose limited to making common law arguments that would apply to any private association?

4.   *The Proper Role of Judges in "Civil Society."* Perhaps the most fundamental issue posed by *Rose v. Giamatti*—the theme that runs through the entire field of sports and the law—is the extent to which public law, speaking through judges, should overturn decisions made by private leagues, usually speaking through their commissioners. The challenge to the law is captured by this passage from George Will's review of Reston's book:

> Reston does not do justice to how close the *Rose* case came to becoming another case of a familiar political pathology. Yet another functioning American institution—the commissioner's office—almost became a victim of judicial overreaching. Today's courts have an unhealthy itch to supervise and fine-tune virtually every equity judgment in American life. Rose's legal strategy was to find a judge willing to insinuate himself into baseball's disciplinary procedures. If Rose had succeeded, the commissioner's office would have been irreparably damaged. Its core function, which is disciplinary, would permanently have been put in question. Another of civil society's intermediary associations—those that stand between the individual and the state—would have been broken to the saddle of government. A nanny-like judiciary would henceforth have made the commissioner's office negligible—another hitherto private institution permeated by state power.

George Will, *Foul Ball*, N.Y. Rev. of Books, June 27, 1991, at 31, 34. Do you agree with Will? Would you feel the same way had courts sought to intervene regarding the pernicious example of Judge Landis, who strictly maintained apartheid in our National Game?

C. THE LEGAL SCOPE OF THE COMMISSIONER'S AUTHORITY OVER CONDUCT DETRIMENTAL TO THE GENERAL WELFARE OF THE GAME[1]

The source and scope of any judicial scrutiny that could be given to Commissioner Giamatti's treatment of Rose can be traced in the following cases. As you read each of the decisions reproduced in this chapter, look for and reflect upon the answers to the following questions:

1. What is the source of the commissioner's authority to act in the given case? Why is this authority given to the commissioner rather than to an individual club, to an outside arbitrator, or to a public official or judge?

2. What is the scope of the commissioner's power—that is, under the asserted source of authority—in what situations is the commissioner empowered to act in cases of this type?

3. What procedures should the commissioner follow in deciding on the course of action? What is the source of these procedural requirements?

4. If there are factual doubts or disputes, what standard of proof should the commissioner employ in the given case—reasonable suspicion, preponderance of the evidence, clear and convincing evidence, or proof beyond a reasonable doubt? Or can he do whatever attracts his fancy?

5. What remedy or penalty may the commissioner employ in the specific case?

6. Finally, and most importantly, what is (and what should be) the jurisdiction of a court (or an arbitrator) to review the commissioner's action, *i.e.*, the commissioner's answers to questions two through five. What legal theories can legitimately be employed to challenge the action? What standard of review will a court use in these legal challenges?

The legal starting point is *American League Baseball Club of New York (Yankees) v. Johnson*, 179 N.Y.S. 498 (N.Y. Sup. Ct. 1919). This litigation occurred near the end of the "National Commission" era in major league governance, during which American League President Byron "Ban" Johnson was acknowledged to be the strongest figure in the game. *See* Eugene X. Murdock, BAN JOHNSON: CZAR OF BASEBALL (Westport, CN: Greenwood Press 1982). Carl Mays, a pitcher for the Boston Red Sox, walked off the field in the middle of a game, and went fishing the next day. While Johnson waited for the Red Sox to take disciplinary action, Sox

---

[1] **[Ed. note]:** This section focuses on the Commissioner's jurisdiction and judicial review. Chapter 1 considers the substantive issues involved with integrity issues such as cheating, match-fixing, and doping that often trigger the Commissioner's power.

owner Harry Frazee instead sold Mays to the Yankees (this was a rehearsal for the next such transaction between the two clubs, which involved Babe Ruth). When he learned of the sale, Johnson himself suspended Mays for "deserting his club and breaking contract," relying on § 20 of the league constitution:

> The president, in the performance of his duties, shall have the power to impose fines or penalties, in the way of suspension or otherwise, upon any manager or player who, in his opinion, has been guilty of conduct detrimental to the general welfare of the game.

Furious at losing Mays' services in the midst of the pennant race, the Yankees sued Johnson, calling him an "unmolested despot." The Yankees argued that § 24 of the AL Constitution assigned responsibility for these questions to the individual team:

> Each club belonging to this league shall have the right to regulate its own affairs, to establish its own rules, and to discipline, punish, suspend or expel its manager, players or other employees, and these powers shall not be limited to cases of dishonest play or open insubordination, but shall include all questions of carelessness, indifference, or other conduct of the player that may be regarded by the club as prejudicial to its interest, but not in conflict with any provision of the National Agreement or this constitution.

The case was heard by then Judge, later Senator, Robert Wagner of New York, who began his decision by stating:

> It is undisputed, and, indeed, a matter of common knowledge, that the commercialization of baseball is a highly profitable undertaking, rendering lucrative returns to the member clubs, to their stockholders, and to their employees. Large capital is invested in the enterprise, and the property representative of this capital consists principally of contracts with individual players, together with the reputation of the club for skill and ability in playing the game. Suspension of a player, therefore, not only interferes with his individual contract, but may also interfere with the reputation and collective ability of the club. Inasmuch as the leading clubs of the league and their players are entitled at the end of the season to certain rights and privileges which are unquestionably to be deemed property rights, this interference with an individual player would confuse and possibly destroy the rights of the respective clubs and their players, for the validity of the games in which Mays participated might be questioned.

Judge Wagner agreed with the Yankee's interpretation of the league constitution, observing that the league President had the authority to exercise disciplinary authority only "in the performance of his duties." The judge characterized this authority as follows:

> Under these rules it is the right and duty of the president to regulate the actual playing of the game on the field and to enforce the rules instituted for the governing of the game. Doubtless his powers would extend to the discipline of players for any infringement of these rules upon the field, or for an overt act committed by a player on the field in violation of the rules. Beyond that power, however, it does not seem that the president may proceed, for under the constitution he is given power to discipline only in the performance of his duties, and his duties are only such as are set forth in the constitution and playing rules.

The offense of which Mays was accused was obviously not one of those embraced within the prohibition of these rules. It was not an overt act committed on the field.

Although that literal reading of the constitution did not square with historical practice, the judge stated:

> On behalf of the defendant, contention is made that many times in the past the defendant Johnson had exercised power similar to that which he claims the right to exercise under the present circumstances, that his jurisdiction to make orders similar to the one now in dispute has never been questioned, and that the parties to a contract will be bound by the construction which their conduct and acquiescence have placed upon it. Although courts have placed great weight on the construction which parties have put upon contracts existing between them, such considerations must never violate the fundamental concepts of justice. If the original act was unauthorized, repetition does not invest the act with authority. If the construction did not convey power to the president, he cannot prescriptively acquire power by continual usurpation. If the opposite were true he would, in effect, effectuate an amendment of the constitution by usurpation. In his immortal and always useful Farewell Address, Washington said:
>
>> "If in the opinion of the people the distribution or modification of the constitutional powers be in any particular wrong, let it be corrected by an amendment in the way which the Constitution designates, but let there be no change by usurpation."
>
> So in this case there can be no change by usurpation. The structure of precedents must fall, unless laid on the foundation of authority.

Accordingly, Judge Wagner granted a permanent injunction against Mays' suspension. The Yankees' celebratory press release stated that "our fight has not been for Mays alone, but to safeguard the vested property rights of the individual club-owners against the continual encroachments on club rights by the president, who has never been clothed with the powers that he has taken unto himself."

The one reported legal challenge to Commissioner Landis' authority was a skirmish in what was ultimately an unsuccessful effort by the Commissioner to prevent MLB clubs from creating farm systems.*

MILWAUKEE AMER. ASS'N V. LANDIS
49 F.2d 298 (N.D. Ill. 1931)

LINDLEY, DISTRICT JUDGE.

* * *

Under the Major League Agreement the office of commissioner was created, and his functions were defined. . . . He was given jurisdiction to hear and determine finally any disputes between leagues and clubs or to which a player might be a party, certified to him, and authorized, in case of "conduct detrimental to baseball," to impose punishment and pursue appropriate legal remedies; to determine finally a disagreement over any proposed amendment to the rules; and "to take such other steps as he might deem necessary and proper in the interest and morale of the players and the honor of the game." Optional agreements with players were defined and assignments thereof required to be filed with, and approved by, the commissioner. The parties agreed to abide by the decisions of the latter and the discipline imposed by him under the agreement and severally waived right of recourse to the courts. Similar covenants appear in the Major-Minor agreement, the National Association agreement and the uniform contracts with players.

The Major-Minor League agreement recognizes the office of commissioner and the jurisdiction aforesaid and provides that, in case of any dispute between any Major club and any Minor club, the disputants may certify the dispute to the commissioner for decision, and that his determination shall be final.

The various agreements and rules constituting a complete code for, or charter and by-laws of, organized baseball in America, disclose a clear intent upon the part of the parties to endow the commissioner with all the attributes of a benevolent but absolute despot and all the disciplinary powers of the proverbial *pater familias*.

---

* *See* Zimbalist, IN THE BEST INTERESTS OF BASEBALL? at 44–47. The development of farm systems is detailed in a Supplemental Webnote, "Note on Waiver and Option Rules," available on the Casebook's website (http://pennstatelaw.psu.edu/SportsTextWebsite). The note also provides additional background on the disagreement between Commissioner Landis and owners over the development of farm systems.

* * *

The parties endowed the commissioner with wide powers and discretion to hear controversies that might be submitted to him and of his own initiative to observe, investigate and take such action as necessary to secure observance of the provisions of the agreements and rules, promotion of the expressed ideals of, and prevention of conduct detrimental to, baseball. The code is expressly designed and intended to foster keen, clean competition in the sport of baseball, to preserve discipline and a high standard of morale, to produce an equality of conditions necessary to the promotion of keen competition and to protect players against clubs, clubs against players, and clubs against clubs.

* * *

Certain acts are specified as detrimental to baseball, but it is expressly provided that nothing contained in the code shall be construed as exclusively defining or otherwise limiting acts, practices or conduct detrimental to baseball. It is contended that this phrase should be so construed as to include only such conduct as is similar to that expressly mentioned. However, the provisions are so unlimited in character that we can conclude only that the parties did not intend so to limit the meaning of conduct detrimental to baseball, but intended to vest in the commissioner jurisdiction to prevent any conduct destructive of the aims of the code. Apparently it was the intent of the parties to make the commissioner an arbiter, whose decisions made in good faith, upon evidence, upon all questions relating to the purpose of the organization and all conduct detrimental thereto, should be absolutely binding. So great was the parties' confidence in the man selected for the position and so great the trust placed in him that certain of the agreements were to continue only so long as he should remain commissioner.

[Infielder Fred Bennett had been "assigned" several times between the St. Louis Browns and several minor league teams, under terms that did not require the Browns to make Bennett available to other teams through waivers, but presumably gave other teams the ability to purchase Bennett's contract from the minor league club to which he had been "assigned." When Landis learned that all these clubs were secretly controlled by Browns' owner Phil Ball, he refused to approve the assignment to Milwaukee and declared Bennett a free agent.]

Plaintiffs contend that the commissioner has no power to declare a player a free agent. In his answer, the commissioner states that it is his view that, by reason of the alleged breach of the code by plaintiffs and their denial of Bennett's rights, plaintiffs have made it his duty to declare Bennett absolved from any contractual obligations which he may have had with either plaintiff and to declare him a free agent. Obviously declaring Bennett a free agent is a mere declaration of legal effect, that is, the result of finding that the St. Louis Club has forfeited its rights by violating the spirit and intent of the code. Whether there is given to the commissioner the power in so many words to declare Bennett a free agent is immaterial, since the agreements and rules grant to the commissioner jurisdiction to refuse to approve Bennett's assignment by St. Louis to Milwaukee, and to declare him absolved from the burdens of the same and of his contract with St. Louis.

* * *

It is asserted that this wide grant of jurisdiction of the commissioner is an attempt to deprive the court of its jurisdiction and that such a provision as is contained in these agreements, rules, and uniform contract is contrary to public policy. No doubt the decision of any arbiter, umpire, engineer, or similar person endowed with the power to decide may not be exercised in an illegal manner, that is fraudulently, arbitrarily, without legal basis for the same or without any evidence to justify action. The many cases cited upon the power and jurisdiction of such officials are not in serious conflict. An agreement to arbitrate a controverted question and to deprive all courts of jurisdiction, so long as in executory form, is quite commonly held void, but an actual submission to an arbiter or umpire in good faith is proper, and decision under same is binding, unless it is unsupported by evidence, or unless the decision is upon some basis without legal foundation or beyond legal recognition.

Plaintiffs submitted to the defendant as commissioner an optional contract, which under the code could not be effective unless approved by him. After ascertaining the facts, he refused to approve the same. This, if we look at it from the point of arbitration, was an executed agreement for arbitration, and called for more than ministerial action. As we have seen, the commissioner is given almost unlimited discretion in the determination of whether or not a certain state of facts creates a situation detrimental to the national game of baseball. The commissioner rightfully found that the common control of St. Louis and the named Minor Clubs by one person made it possible to create a situation whereby the clear intent of the adopted code that the players under the control of a Major club should not be kept with a Minor club more than two successive seasons without giving other Major clubs the right to claim him was clearly violated, and a result achieved highly detrimental to the national game of baseball. The facts negative any assertion that this decision was made arbitrarily or fraudulently. It was made in pursuance of jurisdiction granted to the commissioner with the expressed desire to achieve certain ends, that is, to keep the game of baseball clean, to promote clean competition, to prevent collusive or fraudulent contracts, to protect players' rights, to furnish them full opportunity to advance in accord with their abilities and to prevent their deprival of such opportunities by subterfuge, covering or other unfair conduct.

Suit dismissed.

Recent decades have witnessed a much more active use of commissioner authority in a fast-changing sports environment. Modern-day commissioners have become more involved in the business of sports, as well as in concepts of fair play, than in the other integrity issues discussed in Chapter 1. In his autobiography, *Hardball: The Education of a Baseball Commissioner*, at 173–87 and 259–64, former baseball commissioner Bowie Kuhn recounts many such cases: two of the most controversial involved maverick club owners Charlie Finley of the Oakland Athletics and Ted Turner of the Atlanta Braves.[2] Both of these cases grew out of an arbitration ruling reproduced in Chapter 5: the 1975 arbitration decision in the *Andy Messersmith/Dave McNally* grievance that eviscerated the "reserve clause" that had tied baseball players for life to their original team, and gave players the freedom to move to a new team upon expiration of their current contracts.

Among the most concerned was Athletics' owner Charles Finley. Despite an ill-advised move from Kansas City to Oakland, where the Athletics had to compete with the San Francisco Giants for support in the Bay Area, Finley had successfully used the draft system (instituted by baseball in 1965) to build the most powerful team in the game in the early 1970s: five straight divisional titles and three straight World Series championships. Unfortunately, Finley tended to treat his players like "plantation hands" (as Kuhn observed), including such stars as Reggie Jackson, Vida Blue, and Jim "Catfish" Hunter. With free agency pending, the A's appeared to risk the loss of its players. Still, Finley had a few aces up his sleeve. Because of MLB rules barring "tampering" with players currently under contract with other teams until they became free agents, Finley not only enjoyed the exclusive right to the baseball services of stars like Jackson and Blue but also the exclusive right to negotiate a new contract with them. Thus, Finley articulated the following strategy: he would sell off his current player assets, the veteran stars of his three-time World Series Champion A's, and invest the proceeds in development via the farm system of future assets—young stars who could not command high salaries through free agency. There was only one roadblock to his plan—Commissioner Kuhn.

---

[2] A revealing counterpoint to Kuhn's account of these times and these cases can be found in the memoirs of the leader of the Major League Baseball Players Association when it won free agency for its members. Marvin Miller, A WHOLE DIFFERENT BALL GAME: THE SPORT AND BUSINESS OF BASEBALL (New York: Birch Lane Press 1991).

CHARLES O. FINLEY & CO., INC. v. BOWIE KUHN

569 F.2d 527 (7th Cir. 1978)

SPRECHER, CIRCUIT JUDGE.

[Just before baseball's trading deadline of June 15, 1976, Finley and the Athletics sold the contract rights to the services of Joe Rudi and Rollie Fingers to the Boston Red Sox for $2 million and of Vida Blue to the New York Yankees for $1.5 million. (To put this in perspective, the average salary in 1976 was $51,000 and the new owners of the expansion Toronto Blue Jays paid $7 million for the franchise.) Rudi and Fingers were to become free agents upon the expiration of their contracts at the end of the 1976 season. Just before the Athletics' transaction with the Yankees, Blue signed a three-year contract extension, the benefit of which was transferred to the Yankees in this sale. The day after a quickly scheduled hearing on June 17, Commissioner Kuhn disapproved the assignments of the contracts of Rudi, Fingers, and Blue to the Red Sox and Yankees "as inconsistent with the best interests of baseball, the integrity of the game and the maintenance of public confidence in it." The Commissioner expressed his concern for (1) the debilitation of the Oakland club, (2) the loss of competitive balance in professional baseball through the buying of success by the wealthier clubs, and (3) "the present unsettled circumstances of baseball's reserve system." A week later, Finley brought this suit challenging Kuhn's authority to take such action.]

II

Basic to the underlying suit brought by Oakland and to this appeal is whether the Commissioner of baseball is vested by contract with the authority to disapprove player assignments which he finds to be "not in the best interests of baseball." In assessing the measure and extent of the Commissioner's power and authority, consideration must be given to the circumstances attending the creation of the office of Commissioner, the language employed by the parties in drafting their contractual understanding, changes and amendments adopted from time to time, and the interpretation given by the parties to their contractual language throughout the period of its existence.

* * *

[After recounting the story we read earlier about how the "Black Sox Scandal" had "proved the catalyst" for creating a commissioner position with full authority over baseball, the judge continued.]

* * *

The Major Leagues and their constituent clubs severally agreed to be bound by the decisions of the Commissioner and by the discipline imposed by him. They further agreed to "waive such right of recourse to the courts as would otherwise have existed in their favor." Major League Agreement, Art. VII, Sec. 2.

Upon Judge Landis' death in 1944, the Major League Agreement was amended in two respects to limit the Commissioner's authority. First, the parties deleted the provision by which they had agreed to waive their right of recourse to the courts to challenge actions of the Commissioner. Second the parties added the following language to Article I, 3:

> No Major League Rule or other joint action of the two Major Leagues, and no action or procedure taken in compliance with any such Major League Rule or joint action of the two Major Leagues shall be considered or construed to be detrimental to Baseball.

The district court found that this addition had the effect of precluding the Commissioner from finding an act that complied with the Major League Rules to be detrimental to the best interests of baseball.

The two 1944 amendments to the Major League Agreement remained in effect during the terms of the next two Commissioners, A.B. "Happy" Chandler and Ford Frick. Upon Frick's retirement in 1964 and in accordance with his recommendation, the parties adopted three amendments to the Major League Agreement: (1) the language added in 1944 preventing the Commissioner from finding any act or practice "taken in compliance" with a Major League Rule to be "detrimental to baseball" was removed; (2) the provision deleted in 1944 waiving any rights of recourse to the courts to challenge a Commissioner's decision was restored; and (3) in places where the language "detrimental to the best interests of the national game of baseball" or "detrimental to baseball" appeared those words were changed to "not in the best interests of the national game of Baseball" or "not in the best interests of Baseball."

* * *

III

Despite the Commissioner's broad authority to prevent any act, transaction or practice not in the best interests of baseball, Oakland has attacked the Commissioner's disapproval of the Rudi-Fingers-Blue transactions on a variety of theories which seem to express a similar thrust in differing language.

The complaint alleged that the "action of Kuhn was arbitrary, capricious, unreasonable, discriminatory, directly contrary to historical precedent, baseball tradition, and prior rulings and actions of the Commissioner." In pre-trial answers to interrogatories, Oakland acknowledged that the Commissioner could set aside a proposed assignment of a player's contract "in an appropriate case of violation of (Major League) Rules or immoral or unethical conduct."

* * *

The plaintiff has argued that it is a fundamental rule of law that the decisions of the head of a private association must be procedurally fair. Plaintiff then argued that it was "procedurally unfair" for the Commissioner to fail to warn the plaintiff that he would "disapprove large cash assignments of star players even if they complied with the Major League Rules."

In the first place it must be recalled that prior to the assignments involved here drastic changes had commenced to occur in the reserve system and in the creation of free agents. In his opinion disapproving the Rudi, Fingers and Blue assignments, the Commissioner said that "while I am of course aware that there have been cash sales of player contracts in the past, there has been no instance in my judgment which had the potential for harm to our game as do these assignments, particularly in the present unsettled circumstances of baseball's reserve system and in the highly competitive circumstances we find in today's sports and entertainment world."

Absent the radical changes in the reserve system, the Commissioner's action would have postponed Oakland's realization of value for these players. Given those changes, the relative fortunes of all major league clubs became subject to a host of intangible speculations. No one could predict then or now with certainty that Oakland would fare better or worse relative to other clubs through the vagaries of the revised reserve system occurring entirely apart from any action by the Commissioner.

In the second place, baseball cannot be analogized to any other business or even to any other sport or entertainment. Baseball's relation to the federal antitrust laws has been characterized by the Supreme Court as an "exception," an "anomaly" and an "aberration." Baseball's management through a commissioner is equally an exception, anomaly and aberration. . . . In no other sport or business is there quite the same system, created for quite the same reasons and with quite the same underlying policies. Standards such as the best interests of baseball, the interests of the morale of the players and the honor of the game, or "sportsmanship which accepts the umpire's decision without complaint," are not necessarily familiar to courts and obviously require some expertise in their application. While it is true that professional baseball selected as its first Commissioner a federal judge, it intended only him and not the judiciary as a whole to be its umpire and governor.

As we have seen in Part II, the Commissioner was vested with broad authority and that authority was not to be limited in its exercise to situations where Major League Rules or moral turpitude was involved. When professional baseball intended to place limitations upon the Commissioner's powers, it knew how to do so. In fact, it did so during the 20-year period from 1944 to 1964.

The district court found and concluded that the Rudi-Fingers-Blue transactions were not, as Oakland had alleged in its complaint, "directly contrary to historical precedent, baseball tradition, and prior rulings." During his almost 25 years as Commissioner, Judge Landis found many acts, transactions and practices to be detrimental to the best interests of baseball in situations where neither moral turpitude nor a Major League Rule violation was involved, and he disapproved several player assignments.

On numerous occasions since he became Commissioner of baseball in February 1969, Kuhn has exercised broad authority under the best interests clause of the Major League Agreement. Many of the actions taken by him have been in response to acts, transactions or practices that involved neither the violation of a Major League Rule nor any gambling, game-throwing or other conduct associated with moral turpitude. Moreover, on several occasions Commissioner Kuhn has taken broad preventive or remedial action with respect to assignments of player contracts.

On several occasions Charles O. Finley, the principal owner of the plaintiff corporation and the general manager of the Oakland baseball club, has himself espoused that the Commissioner has the authority to exercise broad powers pursuant to the best interests clause, even where there is no violation of the Major League Rules and no moral turpitude is involved.

Twenty-one of the 25 parties to the current Major League Agreement who appeared as witnesses in the district court testified that they intended and they presently understand that the Commissioner of baseball can review and disapprove an assignment of a player contract which he finds to be not in the best interests of baseball, even if the assignment does not violate the Major League Rules and does not involve moral turpitude.

* * *

We conclude that the evidence fully supports, and we agree with, the district court's finding that "[t]he history of the adoption of the Major League Agreement in 1921 and the operation of baseball for more than 50 years under it [strongly indicate] that the Commissioner has the authority to determine whether any act, transaction or practice is 'not in the best interests of baseball,' and upon such determination, to take whatever preventive or remedial action he deems appropriate, whether or not the act, transaction or practice complies with the Major League Rules or involves moral turpitude." Any other conclusion would involve the courts in not only interpreting often complex rules of baseball to determine if they were violated but also, as noted in the Landis case, the "intent of the [baseball] code," an even more complicated and subjective task.

The Rudi-Fingers-Blue transactions had been negotiated on June 14 and 15, 1976. On June 16, the Commissioner sent a teletype to the

Oakland, Boston and New York clubs and to the Players' Association expressing his "concern for possible consequences to the integrity of baseball and public confidence in the game" and setting a hearing for June 17. Present at the hearing were 17 persons representing those notified. At the outset of the hearing the Commissioner stated that he was concerned that the assignments would be harmful to the competitive capacity of Oakland; that they reflected an effort by Boston and New York to purchase star players and "bypass the usual methods of player development and acquisition which have been traditionally used in professional baseball"; and that the question to be resolved was whether the transactions "are consistent with the best interests of baseball's integrity and maintenance of public confidence in the game." He warned that it was possible that he might determine that the assignments not be approved. . . .

[In his decision] the Commissioner recognized "that there have been cash sales of player contracts in the past," but concluded that "these transactions were unparalleled in the history of the game" because there was "never anything on this scale or falling at this time of the year, or which threatened so seriously to unbalance the competitive balance of baseball." The district court concluded that the attempted assignments of Rudi, Fingers and Blue "were at a time and under circumstances making them unique in the history of baseball."

We conclude that the evidence fully supports, and we agree with, the district court's finding and conclusion that the Commissioner "acted in good faith, after investigation, consultation and deliberation, in a manner which he determined to be in the best interests of baseball" and that "[w]hether he was right or wrong is beyond the competence and the jurisdiction of this court to decide."[44]

* * *

V

Following the bench trial, the district court reached its decision in favor of the Commissioner without considering the impact of Article VII, 2 of the Major League Agreement, wherein the major league baseball clubs agreed to be bound by the Commissioner's decisions and discipline and to waive recourse to the courts.

* * *

Oakland has urged us to apply the substantive law dealing with the "policies and rules of a private association" to the Major League Agreement

---

[44]   It is beyond the province of this court to consider the wisdom of the Commissioner's reasons for disapproving the assignments of Rudi, Blue and Fingers. There is insufficient evidence, however, to support plaintiff's allegation that the Commissioner's action was arbitrary or capricious, or motivated by malice, ill will or anything other than the Commissioner's good faith judgment that these attempted assignments were not in the best interests of baseball. The great majority of persons involved in baseball who testified on this point shared Commissioner Kuhn's view.

and actions taken thereunder. Illinois has developed a considerable body of law dealing with the activities of private voluntary organizations and we agree that the validity and effect of the waiver of recourse clause should initially be tested under these decisions.

Even in the absence of a waiver of recourse provision in an association charter, "[i]t is generally held that courts . . . will not intervene in questions involving the enforcement of bylaws and matters of discipline in voluntary associations."

* * *

Viewed in light of these decisions, the waiver of recourse clause contested here seems to add little if anything to the common law nonreviewability of private association actions. This clause can be upheld as coinciding with the common law standard disallowing court interference. We view its inclusion in the Major League Agreement merely as a manifestation of the intent of the contracting parties to insulate from review decisions made by the Commissioner concerning the subject matter of actions taken in accordance with his grant of powers.

* * *

Even if the waiver of recourse clause is divorced from its setting in the charter of a private, voluntary association and even if its relationship with the arbitration clause in the agreement is ignored, we think that it is valid under the circumstances here involved. Oakland claims that such clauses are invalid as against public policy. This is true, however, only under circumstances where the waiver of rights is not voluntary, knowing or intelligent, or was not freely negotiated by parties occupying equal bargaining positions. The trend of cases in many states and in the federal courts supports the conclusion of the district court under the circumstances presented here that "informed parties, freely contracting, may waive their recourse to the court."

Although the waiver of recourse clause is generally valid for the reasons discussed above, we do not believe that it forecloses access to the courts under all circumstances. Thus, the general rule of nonreviewability which governs the actions of private associations is subject to exceptions 1) where the rules, regulations or judgments of the association are in contravention to the laws of the land or in disregard of the charter or bylaws of the association, or 2) where the association has failed to follow the basic rudiments of due process of law. Similar exceptions exist for avoiding the requirements of arbitration under the United States Arbitration Act. We therefore hold that, absent the applicability of one of these narrow exceptions, the waiver of recourse clause contained in the Major League Agreement is valid and binding on the parties and the courts.

* * *

Suit dismissed.

———

The court in *Finley v. Kuhn* endorsed a broad authority of the commissioner to nullify club transactions. Another decision, *Atlanta National League Baseball Club & Ted Turner v. Bowie Kuhn*, 432 F. Supp. 1213 (N.D. Ga. 1977), was issued between the dates of the district and appellate court rulings in *Finley v. Kuhn*. *Turner* dealt with the commissioner's authority to discipline owners and employees of the member teams, and thus raised many issues similar to those posed later in Pete Rose's case.

In July 1976, following the events described in the *Finley* case above, Major League Baseball and its Players Association negotiated a new collective agreement with an elaborate free agency system. Players with six years of service in the Major Leagues could declare their intention to become free agents before the end of October. In early November, a draft would be conducted for those "declared" free agents, under which up to twelve teams could elect to bid for any one player. Before the draft, though, only his prior club had the right to negotiate with that player.

In August 1976, Commissioner Kuhn issued a series of directives to owners that warned them against any dealings with potential free agents prior to the "reentry draft." In September 1976, the Commissioner found that the Atlanta Braves' General Manager had made improper contact with Gary Matthews of the San Francisco Giants. For this "tampering" offense the Commissioner fined the Braves $5,000 and took away the club's first pick in the winter amateur draft. Subsequently, at a cocktail party in October 1976, Braves' owner Ted Turner told Giants' owner Bob Lurie that the Braves would go as high as necessary to get Matthews. Members of the media present at this exchange published the story.

The free agent draft was conducted on November 4, and the Braves succeeded in signing Matthews on November 17. On December 30, Commissioner Kuhn upheld Lurie's complaint against Turner. Kuhn decided, however, not to disapprove Matthews' contract with the Braves. Instead, the Commissioner suspended Turner from baseball for one year, and deprived Atlanta of its first-round pick in the next summer's amateur draft. Turner and the Braves went to court to try to overturn Kuhn's ruling.

District Judge B. Avant Edenfield acknowledged the traditional broad authority of the Commissioner to "punish" baseball people "for acts considered not in the best interests" of the game. Complicating this situation, though, was the fact that the Major League Agreement among the owners had to be read in tandem with the new labor agreement between the owners and the Players Association—the document that had created both free agency and a reentry draft for players like Matthews. "The two agreements must now be read together as forming the framework for the government of Major League baseball," which meant that the powers of the Commissioner had to be interpreted "so as to avoid infringing upon the rights secured by the parties to the collective bargaining agreement." *Atlanta National League Baseball Club, Inc. v. Kuhn,* 432 F. Supp. 1213, 1221 (N.D. Ga.1977).

Even with this caveat, the judge concluded ("with some misgivings") that the Commissioner had the authority to issue and enforce directives that barred any owner from "dealing" with another team's players before the draft. With respect to the penalties for the Braves breaching that directive, the judge also found it strange that Kuhn had allowed the Braves to sign and keep Matthews, but forbade Turner, the owner, to operate his Braves team. Ultimately, though, the court did not judge this to be an "abuse of commissioner discretion."

> In Article VII, § 2, of the Major League Agreement the clubs explicitly agreed to be bound by the discipline imposed by the Commissioner and obviously intended to give him a certain amount of leeway to choose the appropriate sanction. Judicial review of every sanction imposed by the Commissioner would produce an unworkable system that the Major League Agreement endeavors to prevent. Here, Turner was warned of the suspension, he asked for the suspension, the contract specifically authorized it, and he got it.

432 F. Supp. at 1223.

The judge, however, concluded that he had the authority to rule that Commissioner Kuhn went beyond the scope of his authority by taking away from the Braves their first pick in the next June rookie draft. The court's rationale was that such a draft penalty was not one of the specific commissioner sanctions then mentioned in Article II, § 3, of the Major League Agreement [the clause has since been broadened, as noted in the new text found in the Documentary Supplement section of the text website]. Although Kuhn's counsel had emphasized the phrasing in § 3 to the effect that "punitive actions by the Commissioner . . . *may involve* any one or more of the following. . ." (emphasis added), Judge Edenfield concluded that the textual language

> seems to imply that the list of sanctions in § 3 is exclusive, and basic rules of contract construction support this conclusion. Prior to the original Major League Agreement, there were no presumed powers vested in a Commissioner. The 1921 agreement created the office of the Commissioner and defined his powers out of whole cloth. In such a situation, the maxim "Expressio unius est exclusio alterius" is particularly applicable. Moreover, in light of the fact that this contract purports to authorize the imposition of a penalty or forfeiture, it must be strictly construed.

Id. at 1225. Nor was the court persuaded by the fact that Kuhn's predecessors had regularly imposed disciplinary sanctions that were not listed in § 3, without anyone having gone off to court to seek relief.

> That the Commissioner's authority in those cases went unchallenged does not persuade this court of the Commissioner's unlimited punitive powers in light of contractual language and established rules of construction to the contrary. If the Commissioner is to have the unlimited punitive authority as he says is needed to deal with new and changing situations, the agreement should be changed to expressly grant the Commissioner that power. The deprivation of a draft choice was first and foremost a punitive sanction, and a sanction that is not specifically enumerated under § 3. Accordingly, the court concludes that the Commissioner was without the authority to impose that sanction, and its imposition is therefore void.

Id. at 1226.

Kuhn argued that even if the judge believed he had exceeded his authority, judicial review was foreclosed because he was acting as an arbitrator of a dispute between the Braves and the Giants. The court rejected the claim, reasoning that Kuhn had solicited clubs to alert his office to tampering violations, rather than passively adjudicating an inter-team dispute:

> In this respect, and bearing in mind that it was the Commissioner's own directive that he was claiming to enforce, the instant case is similar to *Professional Sports, Ltd. v. Virginia Squires Basketball*, 373 F. Supp. 946, 950 (W.D. Tex. 1974), wherein the court found an agreement to be bound by the Commissioner of Basketball's arbitration decision inapplicable where the dispute was one generated by the Commissioner himself. *See Hurd v. Illinois Bell Telephone Co.*, 136 F. Supp. 125, 155 (N.D. Ill. 1955):
>
> > The judicial mind is so strongly against the propriety of allowing one of the parties, or its especial representative, to be judge or arbitrator in its own case, that even a strained interpretation will be resorted to if necessary to avoid that result.
>
> That the Commissioner did not act as an arbitrator herein is supported by the sanctions imposed. Typically, in an arbitration dispute the arbitrator adjudicates the rights as between two parties and accords relief to one of them. Here, the Commissioner was not deciding Lurie's rights vis a vis Turner, and granting relief to Lurie; rather, a punishment was imposed which would primarily affect only Turner and the Atlanta Club.

The court is inclined to view the Commissioner's authority as deriving not from the arbitration clause of the Major League Agreement, but from Article I, § 2, where he is given the power to "INVESTIGATE, either upon complaint or upon his own initiative, any act . . . alleged or suspected to be not in the best interests of the national game of Baseball," and "TO DETERMINE, after investigation, what . . . punitive action is appropriate . . . ." (Emphasis in original.)

Id. at 1219.

———

A more important restriction on the scope of the Commissioner's powers surfaced in 1992, in a dispute arising out of the National League's expansion to include the Colorado Rockies and the Florida Marlins. This sparked an effort by several owners to review the overall two-division alignment, with the vast majority of clubs favoring a shift of the Chicago Cubs and St. Louis Cardinals to the West and Cincinnati Reds and Atlanta Braves to the East. This move would ease travel times, enhance geographic rivalries, and keep more away-game telecasts in prime time viewing in the home markets. The Cubs, however, were strongly opposed. The stated reason for their opposition was the loss of long-standing rivalries with teams such as the New York Mets. The unstated, but widely assumed, reason was that under the National League's unbalanced divisional schedule, the Cubs would play many more games in western time zones, which would impair their television ratings. The Cubs (supported by the New York Mets) exercised their right under the National League constitution to veto their transfer to another division, and thereby blocked the overall proposal.

A number of National League clubs decided to pursue the matter further and asked Commissioner Fay Vincent to order realignment through his "best interests of baseball" authority under Article I, § 2 of the Major League Agreement (MLA). The Cubs (now supported by National League President Bill White) argued to the Commissioner that his authority in this case was limited to and by Article VII of the MLA, which empowers the Commissioner to decide:

all disputes and controversies related in any way to professional baseball between clubs . . . *other than those whose resolution is expressly provided for by another means in this Agreement* . . . in the constitution of either Major League or the Basic Agreement between the Major Leagues and the Major League Baseball Players Association. (emphasis added).

When Vincent invoked his "best interests" powers and ordered that the Cubs (and the Cardinals) be shifted to the National League's Western Division, the Cubs went to federal district court in Chicago to secure an injunction blocking this move. In an unreported decision, *Chicago National League Ball Club v. Francis Vincent, Jr.*, 1992 WL 179208 (N.D. Ill. 1992), Judge Suzanne B. Conlon concluded that the Commissioner's general authority under Article I was limited by the specific language in Article VII that "no member club may be transferred to a different division without its consent." The judge was not prepared to allow the Commissioner to "unilaterally amend the National League Constitution simply because he finds that a constitutional provision or procedure is 'not in the best interests of baseball.'"

> Under Illinois rules for construing contracts, it is clear that the broad authority granted the Commissioner by Article I of the Major League Agreement is not as boundless as he suggests. Giving the language of Article I its common sense and ordinary meaning, the Commissioner's authority to investigate "acts," "transactions" and "practices" and to determine and take "preventive, remedial or punitive action" does not encompass restructuring the divisions of the National League. There has been no conduct for the Commissioner to investigate, punish or remedy under Article I. The veto exercised by the Chicago Cubs as a matter of contractual right merely resulted in the maintenance of long-standing divisional assignments reflected in the National League Constitution.

Echoing the views of the district court in *Turner*, Judge Conlon was not impressed by the long history of untrammeled commissioner authority in baseball.

> The Commissioner also cites two prior actions to support his position: Commissioner Kuhn's 1976 reversal of the National League's rejection of an expansion plan and Commissioner Ueberroth's 1985 approval of a new minority owner of the Texas Rangers. In both of these actions, the Commissioner overrode voting requirements of a league constitution. The Commissioner contends that these actions constitute "strong precedent" for his realignment decision. These incidents did not arise under comparable factual circumstances and implicated different constitutional provisions. More importantly, the fact that these actions did not result in a court challenge is neither probative nor persuasive evidence that the Commissioner in fact acted within his authority on those occasions.

Thus, the Court granted an injunction to keep the Cubs in the East, though when both leagues divided themselves into three rather than just two divisions, Chicago's baseball teams played in the central divisions of their respective circuits.

Commissioner Vincent's Cubs realignment ruling was just one controversial decision among many he made in 1992 that gradually alienated a growing number of owners, leading to a vote of no confidence and Vincent's eventual resignation (despite his protests that the Commissioner should not be subject to dismissal by the owners). The owners appointed Milwaukee Brewers' owner Allen "Bud" Selig as Chairman of the Major League Baseball Executive Committee, and placed him in charge of the game's day-to-day affairs. The owners stated publicly that no successor to Vincent would be installed as Commissioner until they had secured a new and more favorable labor agreement from the players' union.

In 1994, as an offshoot of their labor negotiations with the players, the baseball owners created an *ad hoc* Restructuring Committee to study how to alter and improve the office of commissioner. The Committee's recommendations, approved by the owners, included a number of significant revisions to the Major League Agreement.

First, the owners added a clause to Article I, § 2(a), which specified that the future commissioner would be the chair of the Player Relations Committee. This would officially make the commissioner a direct participant and partisan for the owners in the collective bargaining process, a sharp departure from the "neutral" role that previous commissioners had always claimed for themselves in player-club relations. To make sure the commissioner would not intervene unilaterally in labor matters—as Bowie Kuhn did in 1976 by ending the owners' spring training lockout of the players, and as Peter Ueberroth did in the summer of 1985 by ordering the clubs to make their financial records available to the Players Association—a new § 5 was added to Article 1:

> Sec. 5. [T]he powers of the Commissioner to act in the best interests of Baseball shall be inapplicable to any matter relating to a subject of collective bargaining between the Clubs and the Major League Baseball Players Association.

Undoubtedly with an eye on the *Chicago Cubs* case, a new § 4 was also added to Article 1 to clarify another limitation on the commissioner's power to act "in the best interests of Baseball."

> Sec. 4. Notwithstanding the provisions of Section 2, above, the Commissioner shall take no action in the best interests of Baseball that (i) requires the Clubs to take, or to refrain from taking, joint League action (by vote, agreement, or otherwise) on any of the matters requiring a vote of the Clubs at a Joint Major League Meeting that are set forth in Article I, Section 9 or in Article V, Section 2(b) or (c), or (ii) requires the member Clubs of either League to take, or to refrain from taking, League action (by vote, agreement, or otherwise) on any matter to be voted upon by Member Clubs of the League pursuant to their League Constitution; *provided, however*, that nothing in this Section 4 shall limit the Commissioner's authority to act on any matter that

involves the integrity of, or public confidence in, the national game of Baseball.

Article VII, § 1, which empowers the commissioner to arbitrate all disputes between clubs or club personnel, had this concluding sentence added to it:

> The procedure set forth in this Section is separate from and shall not alter or affect either the procedure set forth in Article V governing the role of the Commissioner at Joint Meetings of the two Major Leagues *or the Commissioner's powers to act in the best interests of Baseball under Article I.* [Emphasis added.]

The Restructuring Committee did not amend the Major League Agreement to clarify the ambiguity over the owners' power to remove a Commissioner during his term. Later reform did, however, eliminate the 80-year-old division of authority between the Commissioner and the American and National League Presidents by terminating the latter two positions and assigning to the Commissioner's office functions such as disciplining players for on-field misconduct, and hiring, assigning, and supervising umpires. The Commissioner's power to impose fines was increased from up to $250,000 to $2 million for team offenses, and to $50,000 for player (or other individual) offenses.

Significantly, the owners expanded the powers of the Commissioner to act "in the best interests of Baseball" to include financial as well as moral issues. As the new version of Section 4 states:

> ... nothing in this Section 4 shall limit the Commissioner's authority to act on any matter that involves the integrity of, or public confidence in, the national game of baseball. Integrity shall include without limitation, as determined by the Commissioner, the ability of, and the public perception that, players and clubs perform and compete at all times to the best of their abilities. Public confidence shall include without limitation the public perception, as determined by the Commissioner, that there is an appropriate level of long-term competitive balance among Clubs.

The basic structure of league governance in the other major team sports has long been similar, though not identical, to baseball's structure. For example, the National Football League's constitution gives the commissioner disciplinary authority to protect the "integrity of the sport." The National Basketball Association (under § 35 of its constitution), like the National Hockey League (under § 17 of its by-laws), gives its commissioner the authority to expel, suspend, or fine any club official, employee, or player for conduct "detrimental or prejudicial to the Association" (in the NHL, conduct "dishonorable, prejudicial to, or against the welfare of the League"). In both leagues, though, such chief executive decisions can be appealed to the Board of Governors, which consists of all the owners or their designated representatives.

Process and substance often converge when courts review disciplinary decisions in sports. Illustrative, albeit outside a Commissioner-led context, was a challenge to discipline imposed on a drag car race driver rejected in *Dixon v. Nat'l Hot Rod Ass'n*, 450 F. Supp. 3d 831 (S.D. Ind. 2020). Formally, the court enforced a covenant not to sue, specifically distinguishing *Finley v. Kuhn* by claiming that Indiana law, in contrast to Illinois law, was more reluctant to interfere in internal league decisions. It suggested, moreover, that under Indiana law:

> A voluntary association may, without direction or interference by the courts, for its government, adopt a constitution, by-laws, rules and regulations which will control as to all questions of discipline, or internal policy and management, and its right to interpret and administer the same is as sacred as the right to make them. [Citations omitted.] As a general rule courts will not interfere to control the administration of the constitution and bylaws of such association, or to enforce rights springing therefrom. [S]ee also *Freeman v. Sports Car Club of Am., Inc.*, 51 F.3d 1358, 1363–64 (7th Cir. 1995) (declining to intervene in club's expulsion of member and noting "that it is not uncommon for auto racing sanctioning bodies to require that rule decisions be non-litigable").

450 F. Supp. 3d at 846.

Yet the court did, in fact, review de novo the driver's challenge to discipline and concluded that the NHRA had abided by its own rules and had afforded the driver due process. *Id.* at 844.

———

NOTES AND QUESTIONS

1. *Compare* Finley *and* Turner. Review the *Finley* and *Turner* decisions to identify the precise basis of judicial review under the common law of private associations. Did the courts apply the same level of judicial scrutiny to Commissioner Vincent's determination that the Cubs' veto of divisional realignment was contrary to the best interests of baseball and Commissioner Kuhn's similar determination regarding cash sales of star players? Why did the district court in *Finley* express its agreement with Kuhn's conclusion that these cash sales were distinguishable from others that prior commissioners had approved? Why did the Seventh Circuit expressly reject Charlie Finley's claim that Kuhn's decision was malicious? Is *Dixon v. NHRA* correct in implying that the Seventh Circuit was too interventionist in its conclusion?

2. *Waiver of Recourse?* Would the standard of review articulated in *Finley v. Kuhn* have been any different if the "waiver of legal recourse" clause had not been included in the Major League Agreement?

3. *Private Association Law.* From what legal foothold can judges scrutinize and overturn any aspect of the decisions made by a private association such as a sports league? Should courts be more or less ready to review the decisions of a baseball commissioner than those of a union official, for example? (A classic article on the general common law in this area is Zechariah Chafee, Jr., *The Internal Affairs of Associations Not for Profit*, 43 HARV. L. REV. 993 (1930).) Does your answer depend upon whether the person challenging the commissioner is an owner, a manager, or a player? On whether the commissioner's decision infringes on specially favored public policies? For example, suppose a team executive is disciplined for speaking out against the commissioner's drug policy or the league's poor record in hiring minorities as managers, coaches, or in front office positions?

4. *Revisiting* Chicago Cubs. Return now to the *Chicago Cubs* case and consider how that case might have been resolved on an appeal to the Seventh Circuit, particularly in light of the circuit precedent in *Finley v. Kuhn*. Which of the two arguably relevant provisions of the Major League Agreement (MLA) should take precedence—Article I, regarding the "best interests" of baseball, or Article VII, regarding "disputes and controversies" in baseball? Suppose the case were to have arisen under the 1995 revisions, with both the new § 4 in Article 1 and the new sentence at the end of Article VII, § 1: would these make any difference in the legal outcome?

5. *Effect of Possible MLA Amendments.* At the 1994 Senate hearings concerning a bill to remove baseball's antitrust exemption (addressed in Chapter 5), Ohio Senator Howard Metzenbaum claimed that the cumulative effect of the pending amendments to the Major League Agreement would be to weaken the authority and power of the commissioner to protect the interests of fans and communities in baseball. Bud Selig, testifying as acting Commissioner, responded that these amendments were redefining the office in a manner that not only retained the historic authority of the commissioner's office, but, in key respects, strengthened it. Which of these views is correct— or is the answer somewhere in-between?

6. *Revisiting* Finley *on the Merits.* Ignoring for the moment the appropriate scope of judicial scrutiny of commissioner decisions, consider the merits of Commissioner Kuhn's ruling in the *Finley* case. Is there anything wrong with one owner selling a player's services to another? The world of baseball is very different in the 21st-century than it was in the mid-1970s. It is now quite common each summer to see teams out of the pennant race transfer star players to top contenders, sometimes for young talent (often to be selected and named later), and occasionally just to move a high salary player off a payroll when game attendance is dropping. While baseball still has a version of the *Kuhn* doctrine that bars explicit *sales* of players for excessive (though now much larger) sums, and the NFL expressly bars the *sale* of players for cash, this is not true of all sports. A 1989 blockbuster hockey deal sent

Wayne Gretzky from the Edmonton Oilers to the Los Angeles Kings for $15 million plus players, a deal replicated in 1992 by the Quebec Nordiques who sent Eric Lindros to the Philadelphia Flyers for $15 million and players. Would it have been in the best interests of hockey for then-NHL President John Ziegler to have disallowed either of these transactions just because of the huge sums of money involved?

D. THE COMMISSIONER'S FUNCTION IN PROTECTING THE LEAGUE'S REPUTATION

As noted above, the MLB Constitution vests the Commissioner of Baseball with authority to prevent acts "deemed by the Commissioner not to be in the best interests of Baseball." Art. II, § 3. The relevant provision of the NFL Constitution, Art. VIII, § 8.13, authorizes the Commissioner to take action against those involved with the NFL who are "guilty of conduct detrimental to the welfare of the League or professional football." (Likewise, § 8.6 gives the Commissioner the power to take action against outsiders "in the best interests of either the League or professional football."). We have previously noted how owners have recognized that someone other than themselves must exercise authority over challenges to the "best interests" of sport with regard to gambling and game-fixing, player misconduct, evasion of the spirit of labor market rules, tampering with players under contract to other clubs, and selfish exercise of business prerogatives.

One might define the "best interests of the sport" as the long-term interests of those who make the rules. In this case, legal recognition simply follows contract law. Thus, the power of a sports league (through a commissioner or collectively through the owners) to take actions against those acting in a manner detrimental to "best interests" would be construed to effectuate the parties' intent.

An alternative way to consider the "best interests of the sport" is to recognize the legal and political contexts in which sports operate. Those who do not get to make the rules—including fans, players (subject to contractual limits on owners in collective bargaining agreements), taxpayers, and groups marginalized or excluded from the sport—may turn to legislatures to impose their own conception of "the best interests of the sport" externally, through law. Even those who do make the rules (professional club owners, major colleges and universities) may find it very costly to reach agreement on rules in the best interest of the sport, when dynamic responses to changed circumstances result in winners and losers. These stakeholders may also turn to the law to impose external restraints.

In organizing these materials, we have divided this topic in two. Chapter 1 considers the substantive—and for some, objective—issues involved in sports integrity. It includes issues relevant to a sports league's reputation, including gambling, match-fixing, cheating, and doping. This section has a narrower focus: on how the Commissioner acts to protect both for commercial objectives and to limit external interference. Consider whether the specific examples are legitimate objects of concern for a commissioner, what other topics warrant Commissioner protection, and whether the reputation-protecting function of a Commissioner's power should be the sole basis for use of "best interests" powers. Consider also whether these powers are adequate to protect the interests of the sport and the public, or whether further external regulation is needed. Finally, note that external restraints—including labor, antitrust, and anti-discrimination law-are discussed in following chapters.

1. TARGETING PLAYERS FOR ON-FIELD INJURY

The authority to discipline misconduct by players or other employees who have organized unions is significantly limited by the terms and conditions of employment negotiated in collective bargaining agreements. However, in limited cases league commissioners retain authority regarding certain kinds of player misconduct, and commissioner discipline remains subject only to league constitutions with regard to owners and non-union employees (such as front office executives and coaches). The scope of the commissioner's authority is illustrated in the following decision, where NFL Commissioner Roger Goodell delegated the final authority to his predecessor, Paul Tagliabue.

IN THE MATTER OF NEW ORLEANS SAINTS PAY-FOR-PERFORMANCE ("BOUNTYGATE")

Final Decision on Appeal (December 11, 2012)

PAUL TAGLIABUE, HEARING OFFICER.

INTRODUCTION AND SUMMARY

The matter before me involves appeals by four present or former New Orleans Saints' players who are challenging findings of misconduct and disciplinary actions taken by Commissioner Roger Goodell on October 9, 2012. The players are Anthony Hargrove, Scott Fujita, Will Smith and Jonathan Vilma. The imposed discipline was the result of the National Football League's (the "NFL") investigation of allegations concerning a pay-for-performance program (the "Program") conducted by the Saints during the 2009 through 2011 seasons to reward particular plays by Saints' defensive players that ultimately incentivized rendering opposing players unable to play, and allegations concerning a specific bounty being placed on Brett Favre to injure him during the NFC Championship game against the Minnesota Vikings in January 2010.

The present appeals are a small piece of a much larger picture. Senior Saints' coaches conceived, encouraged and directed the Program. While it included performance rewards for recovering fumbles, interceptions and the like, it also came to include higher cash incentives to "cart-off" or "knockout" an opposing player. The Program eventually led to allegations of a bounty being placed on Favre. Making matters far more serious—as well as challenging for Commissioner Goodell and League investigators— Saints' coaches and managers led a deliberate, unprecedented and effective effort to obstruct the NFL's investigation into the Program and the alleged bounty. Commissioner Goodell found and properly characterized the Program, any bounty and the obstruction to be organizational misconduct by the New Orleans Saints. The Commissioner determined the misconduct to be "particularly unusual and egregious," "totally unacceptable" and to constitute "conduct detrimental" to the game of professional football and the NFL and to be a violation of the NFL Constitution and Bylaws. Commissioner Goodell fined the Saints $500,000; forfeited the team's second-round draft selections in 2012 and 2013; suspended the Saints' head coach Sean Payton for the entire 2012 NFL season; suspended Saints' general manager Mickey Loomis for eight games and fined him $500,000; suspended Saints' assistant head coach Joe Vitt for six games and fined him $100,000; and suspended the now former Saints' defensive coordinator Gregg Williams indefinitely. These suspensions thus deprived the Saints of vitally important coaching and leadership talent, and they represented a severe competitive penalty for the Saints' team, its fans and indirectly for the New Orleans / Gulf Coast region. Commissioner Goodell's findings and the resulting suspensions of these Saints' personnel are final and no longer subject to appeal.

Unlike the Saints' broad organizational misconduct, the player appeals involve sharply focused issues of alleged individual player misconduct in several different aspects of the Saints' Program. The challenges involving the four players to Commissioner Goodell's October 9, 2012 decisions can fairly be summarized as follows:

Anthony Hargrove: Commissioner Goodell found that Hargrove falsely answered questions put to him by an NFL investigator during the initial investigation of Saints' misconduct in March 2010. That investigation was obstructed in multiple ways by the Saints' head coach, senior coaches and other team officials, including their instructing Hargrove to answer questions falsely, though it remains unclear what exactly Hargrove was asked by investigators regarding the Program. Hargrove was suspended seven games, for which he was credited with having served five games, leaving a suspension of two games.

Scott Fujita: Commissioner Goodell found that Fujita offered his own incentive program to reward big plays, not including rewards for cart-offs and knockouts, and that he failed to report the existence of the Program. Two dozen other Saints' defensive players were aware of the Program, many participated in it and all were present at defensive team meetings that are central to the events under review here. Fujita was suspended for one game.

Will Smith: Commissioner Goodell found that Smith endorsed, agreed to and financially contributed to the Program. Many other Saints' defensive players participated in the Program similar to Smith without suspension. He was suspended for four games.

Jonathan Vilma: Commissioner Goodell found that Vilma endorsed, agreed to and financially contributed to the Program and offered a $10,000 bounty reward to any Saints' player who could knock Vikings' quarterback Brett Favre out of the Saints-Vikings NFC Championship game in January 2010. The evidence as to whether Vilma made such an offer is sharply disputed, but other key points are undisputed: the Saints' coaches conducted, directed and choreographed all defensive team meetings; in the same defensive team meeting where Vilma allegedly offered a bounty, the Saints' defensive coordinator, Gregg Williams, admits that he offered a $5,000 bounty reward of his own to knock Favre out of the game; and Williams admitted that he was the responsible team official who unfortunately let the team meeting get out of control. The NFL assessed fines totaling $30,000 against certain Saints' players after the Vikings game, none of which included any player here, and no Saints' player was suspended for conduct on the field. Vilma was suspended for the entire 2012 NFL season.

I affirm Commissioner Goodell's factual findings as to the four players. I conclude that Hargrove, Smith and Vilma—but not Fujita—engaged in "conduct detrimental to the integrity of, and public confidence in, the game of professional football." However, for the reasons set forth in this decision, I now vacate all discipline to be imposed upon these players.

Although I vacate all suspensions, I fully considered but ultimately rejected reducing the suspensions to fines of varying degrees for Hargrove, Smith and Vilma. My affirmation of Commissioner Goodell's findings could certainly justify the issuance of fines. However, as explained in my discussion below, this entire case has been contaminated by the coaches and others in the Saints' organization. Moreover, the League has not previously suspended or fined players for some of the activities in which these players participated and has in the recent past imposed only minimal fines on NFL Clubs—not players—of a mere $25,000 or less.

* * *

[Discussion of Tagliabue's appointment under the collective bargaining agreement omitted. This issue is discussed in Chapter 3, Section B. However, he announced he was giving "appropriate deference to Commissioner Goodell's reasonable findings" and was "reviewing the discipline for consistency of treatment, uniformity of standards for parties similarly situated and patent unfairness or selectivity." In reaching his decision, Tagliabue applied the standard set in Art. 46 of the NFL-NFLPA collective bargaining agreement: whether the misconduct was "detrimental to the integrity of, or public confidence in, the game of professional football." It slightly contrasts with the authority the Commissioner possesses under the NFL Constitution to discipline conduct "detrimental to the welfare of the League or of professional football."]

There are vital reasons why all NFL-NFLPA Collective Bargaining Agreements since the 1970s have consistently given the Commissioner the exclusive and broad authority to decide what constitutes conduct detrimental. The integrity of and public confidence in the game of professional football are essential to the playing of the game itself and are critical to public interest in NFL football and to public respect for all those participating in NFL football—owners, coaches, players, officials and executives. Equally important, the matters that can affect such integrity and public confidence evolve and change over time depending on both developments within and external to the League, and the parties to the CBAs have agreed not to operate with a static or frozen definition of conduct detrimental. . . .

FRAMEWORK FOR CONSIDERING PLAYER DISCIPLINE

Before turning to the specific issues before me, it is important to establish an understanding of how the NFL has approached important turning points related to the culture and safety of the game. In this context, it is critical to recognize that player safety in the NFL is the responsibility of everyone involved in the League. Strict enforcement of safety rules and policies serves the interests of all players and teams and is essential to the integrity of and public confidence in the game. But safety concerns have evolved—and will continue to evolve—significantly over the years.

. . . The NFL, its teams and its players have long recognized that overly aggressive playing tactics often create unacceptable retaliation cycles that encourage impermissible violence on the playing field. . . . Neither a competitive advantage nor any other justification warrants the encouragement of overly aggressive tactics or the cycle of retaliation that often ensues. Any such tactics are detrimental to the integrity of the game of professional football. . . .

* * *

The evidence before me reflects the realities of NFL team workplaces: sometimes prohibitions and policies that seem clear in the team front office or the League office become blurred in team meeting rooms and on practice fields. Techniques or programs intended to prepare teams to win sometimes ignore or contradict League rules and policies. Teams mimic each other. Coaches, staff and players move from team to team, carrying their techniques and programs with them. Sometimes techniques and programs are misdescribed or become modified or mismanaged. Shortcuts turn out to be dead ends.

As Commissioner Goodell has suggested, part of the player safety and injury challenge in the NFL may be an issue of culture. Presumably, this could mean, at least in part, that there is a pervasive, entrenched and undesirable acceptance of overly aggressive play—including financial rewards, intimidation tactics and "trash talk" to encourage aggressive play. Such a culture could include dismissive attitudes about player injury risks and player safety. Commissioner Goodell clearly recognizes that the responsibility for player safety in the NFL starts at the top, with the Commissioner and the entire League office. . . .

In this context, confronted with the events here, Commissioner Goodell correctly set out aggressively to address them. But when an effort to change a culture rests heavily on prohibitions, and discipline and sanctions that are seen as selective, ad hoc or inconsistent, then people in all industries are prone to react negatively—whether they be construction workers, police officers or football players. They will push back and challenge the discipline as unwarranted. As reflected in the record in the present appeals, they will deny, hide behind a code of silence, destroy evidence and obstruct. In other words, rightly or wrongly, a sharp change in sanctions or discipline can often be seen as arbitrary and as an impediment rather than an instrument of change. This is what we see on the record here.

For whatever reasons—entrenched pay-for-performance practices thought to be common in the NFL, bad judgment by coaches or lack of clarity in the rules or their enforcement—the Saints' coaches here resented the League's investigative/enforcement efforts and improperly resisted and blocked them. As Coach Williams put it, the strategy was to "deny, deny, deny" (New Orleans Saints Article 46 Appeal Proceedings Hr'g Tr. 1105:5–11), possibly in part to avoid tarnishing what everyone saw as an incredibly important and well-earned Saints Super Bowl victory.

As NFL counsel stated at the opening of the hearings here, the "code of locker-room silence is, indeed, strong" in the League. (Hr'g Tr. 167:4–6.) NFL counsel thus noted Jonathan Vilma's statement to the Commissioner in a September meeting, "What we say in-house is kept in-house." (Hr'g Tr. 142:2–3.) And NFL counsel continued, comparing this culture to the "blue wall of silence in another context [that] also makes investigating and proving police corruption quite difficult." (Hr'g Tr. 168:7–10.)

Regardless of what caused the Saints' coaches so strongly to resent and obstruct the League's investigation, it is critical to focus on and get to the root of these questions because clearly a League policy of "strict compliance and strict enforcement" based on well-grounded concern for player safety has not yielded a constructive outcome here. Often one way of avoiding or minimizing the severe reaction of parties subject to discipline—such as

Saints' coaches and players in this matter—and the unconscionable obstruction led by non-player personnel is to eliminate the motivation to deny. This can be done by creating a tailored type of safe haven for individuals to respond to inquiries or provide information about the destructive culture and help change it—without risk of sanction for a specified period of time. Common examples include whistleblower programs with defined and limited immunities; specified immunities for informants or witnesses in various contexts; and the use of company-managed investigative or fact-gathering panels to identify clearly the character and causes of negative cultures. Such systems are antidotes to the code of silence or culture that condones or encourages illegal or improper conduct despite organization rules and policies against such conduct.

* * *

FINDINGS AND FINAL DETERMINATION REGARDING THE FOUR PLAYERS

In challenging the discipline, all four players rely upon Commissioner Goodell's findings of wrongdoing by the Saints in each of the three respects noted above. But the players urge that there is an insufficient basis—both evidentiary and legally—for the imposition of discipline on them, asserting multiple grounds for finding the discipline to be unwarranted. Among other arguments, they contend that these players are victims of inconsistent treatment compared to how the League has disciplined—or declined to discipline—other players; that it was the Saints' coaches and other officials who created and directed the challenged activities in which the players are alleged to have participated; and that there is no evidence of any intent by any of the players to injure any opposing players—and that such intent is an essential element of any finding of culpability.

* * *

[*Anthony Hargrove*] Commissioner Goodell charged Hargrove with providing false information regarding a bounty on Brett Favre or a "pay for performance bounty program," which is presumably the Program. Although I affirm Commissioner Goodell's general finding that Hargrove contributed to the obstruction of the investigation by providing denials as instructed by his coaches, a number of factors complicate and mitigate the propriety of his remaining two-game suspension. The context of previous NFL punishment for obstruction suggests that a seven-game suspension is unprecedented and unwarranted here. In December 2010, the NFL fined Brett Favre $50,000—but did not suspend him—for obstruction of a League sexual harassment investigation. Although not entirely comparable to the present matter, this illustrates the NFL's practice of fining, not suspending players, for serious violations of this type. There is no evidence of a record of past suspensions based purely on obstructing a League investigation. In my forty years of association with the NFL, I am aware of many instances of denials in disciplinary proceedings that proved to be false, but I cannot recall any suspension for such fabrication. This is not to mitigate in any way the severity of obstruction of an investigation with substantial issues as unique as those involved here.

As a further complication, it is unclear exactly what NFL investigators asked Hargrove regarding the Program or any other alleged program and, thus, unclear whether he lied about the Program or the fact that it included cart-offs and knockouts. There is evidence in the appeals record that NFL investigators may not have asked Hargrove whether the Saints employed any particular program. The investigators focused on the alleged bounty placed on Brett Favre prior to the NFC Championship game in January 2010, which was the impetus for questioning Hargrove, who allegedly told a Vikings player of the Favre bounty. If Hargrove denied only the existence of the alleged bounty on Favre, he is no more guilty of conduct detrimental than the numerous Saints' defensive team members from the 2009–2010 season who have provided sworn statements or testimony to the same effect and who have not been suspended or otherwise disciplined.

Finally, given the comprehensive, overt and ongoing nature of the obstruction by coaches and their direct instructions to Hargrove to lie, combined with their control over his football career, it is clear that Hargrove was under tremendous pressure to follow the chain of command in order to keep his job.

I have concluded that there is not sufficient evidence to demonstrate in these unique circumstances that Anthony Hargrove's alleged misconduct is deserving of a suspension. I therefore vacate the suspension imposed on Hargrove.

[*Scott Fujita and Will Smith*] The basis of the discipline issued to Fujita and Smith centers on their participation in the Program or, in Fujita's case, creating his own performance pool.

[Tagliabue recounted the NFL's decades-long prohibitions of pay-for-performance programs and non-contract bonuses, also incorporated into collective bargaining agreements beginning in 1994.]

. . . Neither the League nor the NFLPA appears to have developed a fully articulated, concrete set of guidelines or prohibitions related to performance pools that take into account the current realities of signing bonuses, reporting bonuses, performance bonuses and other incentive arrangements often included in NFL player contracts. In addition, the NFL in its policies sends a mixed message by allowing 'kangaroo courts' where players are fined for mental lapses and other onfield mistakes but prohibiting any distributions to players via those courts. Most important, no matter what the League rules and policies are or have been, if many teams in the League allow pay-for-performance programs to operate in the locker room, as seems to be the case, and, in the main, the League has tolerated this behavior without punishment of players, then many players may not have a clear understanding that such behavior is prohibited or where the lines are between permissible and impermissible conduct.

. . . In the testimony before me, current NFL executive Troy Vincent, a former outstanding player with the Philadelphia Eagles, confirmed that during his time with the Eagles the defensive backs had created a performance pool that simply covered three types of plays—interceptions, fumble recoveries and touchdowns—none of which rewarded the purposeful injury of an opponent. Indeed, Vincent testified that the pool conducted within the Eagles in his career covered both regular season games as well as team practices. Obviously, such a program cannot reasonably be viewed as having been created or managed to injure players.

Other programs on other teams involving greater sums of money were discussed at the appeals hearings.

* * *

The record includes PowerPoint slide presentations made by the Saints' coaching staff to Saints' players following the Saints' victories in 2009 season playoff games against the Arizona Cardinals (with quarterback Kurt Warner) and the Minnesota Vikings (with quarterback Brett Favre). Several of these presentations are very graphic and suggest that the aim of the Saints' defense was to injure these quarterbacks. For example, one slide set following the game against the Cardinals includes a photo of Kurt Warner lying on the ground with a caption: "SO WE WILL JUST DESTROY EACH QUARTERBACK LEAVING EACH TEAM WITHOUT A FIELD GENERAL! ONE DOWN TWO QB's TO GO!" (Record on Appeal, Ex. 80 at 3.)

* * *

NFL players on average have short careers; their careers can end suddenly through injury or declining skills; players want to be good, cohesive members of the team, or unit, not complainers or dissenters; and players accept that they work for coaches, in "programs" conceived by coaches. These are programs for which coordinators and assistant coaches are often specially selected and hired to execute. Here we have a classic example: Head Coach Payton hired Defensive Coordinator Williams with directions to make the Saints' defense "nasty."

In such circumstances, players may not have much choice but to "go along," to comply with coaching demands or directions that they may question or resent. They may know—or believe—that from the coaches' perspective, "it's my way or the highway." Coaching legends such as George Halas and Vince Lombardi are not glorified or remembered because they offered players "freedom of choice."

* * *

[Tagliabue rejected the NFL counsel's argument that it was not important that Fujita did not offer money for hits on opponents such as cart-offs or knockouts. In the past, the NFL had disciplined clubs, but not players, for pay-for-performance bonuses.] Accordingly, the NFL's decision to suspend a player here for participating in a program for which the League typically fines a club certainly raises significant issues regarding inconsistent treatment between players and teams.

* * *

The Commissioner found that Smith's assertion that rewards for cart-offs or knockouts in the Program were offered only when an opposing player was disabled for a play or two because he had the wind knocked out of him, and not if he sustained some other type of injury, was not credible. I affirm Commissioner Goodell's judgment that rewarding players for these categories incentivizes injury of opposing players to a degree that is detrimental to the integrity of and public confidence in the game.

Within the Saints' defensive unit, Smith was one of approximately two dozen Saints' defensive players who participated in the Program. Although Commissioner Goodell found Smith's role as a defensive leader to be a basis, at least in part, for singling Smith out for discipline, this is inappropriate when most or all of the Saints' defensive unit committed the same or similar acts as those underpinning the discipline of Smith.

In addition, I am not aware of previous League discipline that similarly rested on whether or not a player was a team leader. . . . On the present record, selective prosecution of allegations of misconduct and enforcement of discipline relative to Smith cannot be sustained. Whatever the reason for such selective enforcement, it does not satisfy basic requirements for consistent treatment of player employees similarly situated. Therefore, I vacate the suspension of Will Smith.

* * *

[*Jonathan Vilma*] It is essential to recognize that Vilma is being most severely disciplined for "talk" or speech at a team meeting on the evening before the Saints-Vikings game. He is not being punished for his performance on the field and, indeed, none of the discipline of any player here relates to on-field conduct. No Saints' player was suspended for on-field play by the League after the game in question. If the League wishes to suspend a player for pre-game talk including "offers" to incentivize misconduct, it must start by imposing enhanced discipline for illegal hits that involve the kind of player misconduct that it desires to interdict. The relationship of the discipline for the off-field "talk" and actual on-field conduct must be carefully calibrated and reasonably apportioned. This is a standard grounded in common sense and fairness. It rests also on the competence of NFL officiating and the obligation and ability of the League to closely observe playing field misconduct, record it and review for illegal hits or other related misconduct.

* * *

If one were to punish certain off-field talk in locker rooms, meeting rooms, hotel rooms or elsewhere without applying a rigorous standard that separated real threats or "bounties" from rhetoric and exaggeration, it would open a field of inquiry that would lead nowhere. More specifically, there is no question that Coach Williams and other coaches orchestrated the Program to incentivize cart-offs and knockouts; carefully choreographed defensive team meetings, including presenting graphic slide presentations showing injuries to opposing players; ensured that any player who would speak at team meetings was adequately prepared or supported; and generally created an atmosphere in the 2009 season and playoffs that suggested to Saints' players that offering a $10,000 bounty to injure an opposing player was permissible behavior. . . .

Adding to the complexity, there is little evidence of the tone of any talk about a bounty before the Vikings game. Was any bounty pledged serious? Was it inspirational only? Was it typical "trash talk" that occurs regularly before and during games? The parties presented no clear answers. No witness could confirm whether Vilma had any money in his hands as he spoke; no evidence was presented that $10,000 was available to him for purposes of paying a bounty or otherwise. There was no evidence that Vilma or anyone else paid any money to any player for any bounty-related hit on an opposing player in the Vikings game.

I neither excuse nor condone the alleged offer of a bounty on Favre, whether offered by any player, coach, other Saints' employee or third party. Such conduct has no place in the game of professional football. I cannot, however, uphold a multi-game suspension where there is no evidence that a player's speech prior to a game was actually a factor causing misconduct on the playing field and that such misconduct was severe enough in itself to warrant a player suspension or a very substantial fine. Nor can I find justified a suspension where Williams and other Saints' personnel so carefully crafted an environment that would encourage and allow a player to make such an ill-advised and imprudent offer. I therefore vacate the suspension of Jonathan Vilma.

CONCLUSIONS AND ORDER

For the reasons set forth in this Final Decision on Appeal, I affirm the factual findings of Commissioner Goodell; I conclude that Hargrove, Smith, and Vilma engaged in "conduct detrimental to the integrity of, and public confidence in, the game of professional football"; and I vacate all player discipline.

/s/ Paul Tagliabue

The proceedings against the Saints were extraordinary because of the focus on off-field planning for excessive, unduly risky contact on the field. League commissioners traditionally retain the power to discipline players for on-field misconduct.

As a comparative matter, the North American reliance on the originally independent Office of the Commissioner to impose discipline contrasts with the approach in the rest of the world. Perhaps because competitions in soccer, rugby, cricket, and other sports are often international in character, a single individual (necessarily identified with one country) would not be trusted to independently resolve disputes. Thus, challenges to discipline have almost always been before respected current or former judges, represented by leading trial advocates.

For example, during the World Rugby Cup, disciplinary issues that are not resolved during a match are dealt with in a process similar to arbitration. Each game is watched by a citing commissioner, who looks for any misconduct that should be brought in front of the disciplinary panel. The disciplinary panel consists of ten appointed judicial officers who are typically experts in rugby and law. The accused player (often with their team lawyer) appears before a judicial officer with any relevant witnesses and the tournament's "designated disciplinary officer" to determine whether to uphold the citing complaint made by the citing commissioner. This decision may be appealed to a panel, which is comprised of three appeal officers (chosen from a pool of four). Daniel Saoul, *Avoiding the legal scrum: Arbitration in the Rugby World Cup*, LexisNexis Dispute Resolution, Oct. 22, 2015. Similarly, the Cherwell Cricket League of the United Kingdom performs its disciplinary hearings before a disciplinary panel appointed by the League Chairman, which consists of no less than three panelists. Cricket players are also entitled to an appeal, which takes place in front of three different appointed panelists who did not sit at the initial hearing. Cherwell Cricket League Disciplinary Regulations § 5 (2018).

2. OFFENSIVE PERSONAL BEHAVIOR AND CHANGING SOCIAL ATTITUDES

Despite the broad wording of the Commissioner's authority, poor stewardship of a franchise has not resulted in intervention to discipline or remove an owner. Consider former Los Angeles Clippers owner Donald Sterling. He exemplified the worst ownership in sports, notorious for putting profits over success, making inappropriate comments about players, and operating a franchise characterized by obscurity and irrelevance, Joshua S.E. Lee and Jaimie K. McFarlin, *Sports Scandals from the Top-Down: Comparative Analysis of Management, Owner, and Athletic Discipline in the NFL & NBA*, 23 JEFFREY S. MOORAD SPORTS L.J.

69, 86 (2016). But he did not face official rebuke until a public scandal emerged from a tabloid website's exposé of a heated argument with his mistress that she had secretly recorded. During the argument, Sterling made derogatory and racist comments about Blacks and other minorities, generally demanding she not socialize in public with Black men and singling out the legendary Magic Johnson. Sponsors withdrew support and Clippers players joined others in publicly protesting his continued ownership.

Four days after these recordings were made public, Commissioner Adam Silver banned Sterling for life and fined him $2.5 million. Silver also announced he would recommend that the Board of Governors (the other owners) invoke the powers reserved to them in the NBA Constitution to strip Sterling of his ownership. After threats and preliminary litigation, Sterling agreed to sell the Clippers to Microsoft magnate Steve Ballmer for over $2 billion.

Silver, who had recently succeeded David Stern as NBA Commissioner, announced his decision in a widely viewed press conference. He stated:

> Shortly after the release of an audio recording this past Saturday morning of a conversation that allegedly included Clippers owner Donald Sterling, the NBA commenced an investigation, which among other things, included an interview of Mr. Sterling. That investigation is now complete. The central findings of the investigation are that the man whose voice is heard on the recording and on a second recording from the same conversation that was released on Sunday is Mr. Sterling and that the hateful opinions voiced by that man are those of Mr. Sterling.

> The views expressed by Mr. Sterling are deeply offensive and harmful; that they came from an NBA owner only heightens the damage and my personal outrage. Sentiments of this kind are contrary to the principles of inclusion and respect that form the foundation of our diverse, multicultural and multiethnic league.

> I am personally distraught that the views expressed by Mr. Sterling came from within an institution that has historically taken such a leadership role in matters of race relations and caused current and former players, coaches, fans and partners of the NBA to question their very association with the league.

> To them, and pioneers of the game like Earl Lloyd, Chuck Cooper, Sweetwater Clifton, the great Bill Russell, and particularly Magic Johnson, I apologize. Accordingly, effective immediately, I am banning Mr. Sterling for life from any association with the Clippers organization or the NBA. Mr. Sterling may not attend any NBA games or practices. He may not

be present at any Clippers facility, and he may not participate in any business or player personnel decisions involving the team. He will also be barred from attending NBA Board of Governors meetings or participating in any other league activity. I am also fining Mr. Sterling $2.5 million, the maximum amount allowed under the NBA constitution. These funds will be donated to organizations dedicated to anti-discrimination and tolerance efforts that will be jointly selected by the NBA and its Players Association.

As for Mr. Sterling's ownership interest in the Clippers, I will urge the Board of Governors to exercise its authority to force a sale of the team and will do everything in my power to ensure that that happens. This has been a painful moment for all members of the NBA family. I appreciate the support and understanding of our players during this process, and I am particularly grateful for the leadership shown by Coach Doc Rivers, Union President Chris Paul and Mayor Kevin Johnson of Sacramento, who has been acting as the players' representative in this matter.

We stand together in condemning Mr. Sterling's views. They simply have no place in the NBA.

Transcript available at https://www.usatoday.com/story/sports/nba/2014/04/29/adam-silver-commissioner-opening-statement-donald-sterling/8467947/.

Silver intriguingly disclosed that in meting out punishment, he did not take into account Sterling's past behavior, which also included multiple claims that as a property owner he had engaged in racial discrimination. However, he explicitly stated that the Board of Governors would "take into account a lifetime of behavior" in determining "his overall fitness to be an owner in the NBA."

The Clippers sale mooted a number of interesting issues regarding Sterling's expulsion from the league. The relevant constitutional provision, Art. 13, sets forth ten specific grounds for expulsion. Do you agree with Commissioner Silver that one or more of these grounds were met?

(a) Willfully violate any of the provisions of the Constitution and By-Laws, resolutions, or agreements of the Association.

(b) Transfer or attempt to transfer a Membership or an interest in a Member without complying with the provisions of Article 5.

(c) Fail to pay any dues or other indebtedness owing to the Association within thirty (30) days after Written Notice from the Commissioner of default in such payment.

(d) Fail or refuse to fulfill its contractual obligations to the Association, its Members, Players, or any other third party in such a way as to affect the Association or its Members adversely.

[subsections (e), (f), and (g) all involve gambling]

(h) Disband its Team during the Season, dissolve its business, or cease its operation.

(i) Willfully fail to present its Team at the time and place it is scheduled to play in an Exhibition, Regular Season, or Playoff Game.

(j) Willfully misrepresent any material fact contained in its application for Membership in the Association.

———

In 2010, a 20-year-old college student in Milledgeville, Georgia, accused Pittsburgh Steelers' QB Ben Roethlisberger of sexual assault. The local prosecutor elected not to file criminal charges, citing insufficient evidence to secure a criminal conviction. However, Commissioner Roger Goodell suspended Roethlisberger for the first six games of the season, and refused to allow him to participate in any offseason activities until he underwent a "comprehensive behavioral evaluation by professionals." Goodell cited his reason for the suspension as "[players] are held to a higher standard as an NFL player" than those imposed by criminal law, concluding that "there is nothing about [Roethlisberger's] conduct in Milledgeville that can remotely be described as admirable, responsible, or consistent with either the values of the league or the expectations of our fans." Roethlisberger admitted taking a 20-year-old woman into the men's bathroom at a bar, and engaging in sex. Roethlisberger did not contest the ruling.

On January 14, 2010, authorities formally charged Gilbert Arenas, a guard for the Washington Wizards, with felony gun possession after bringing an unlicensed firearm outside his home into the Wizard's locker room. Arenas claims it was a joke aimed at his teammate, Javaris Crittenton. The two had an argument over a gambling debt when Arenas brought an unloaded firearm to the locker room. Crittenton then brought his own firearm into the same facility. National Basketball Association Commissioner David Stern decided to suspend Arenas without pay because his behavior showed "[he is] not currently fit to take the court." In response to his suspension, Arenas made shooting gestures with his hands. Stern thought his actions showed a blatant disregard for the situation. He therefore suspended Arenas indefinitely. Arenas entered into a plea agreement with the prosecution, agreeing to plead guilty. On March 26, 2010, Arenas was sentenced to two years' probation and 30 days in a halfway house, avoiding any jail time. Arenas continued to play for the

Washington Wizards. Team president Ernie Grunfeld decided not to void his contract, believing Arenas had changed.

When can a commissioner appropriately impose discipline for criminal misconduct? Should suspension occur, for example, as soon as a sports figure is charged with a crime? Only after a formal indictment? Only after conviction? Once a player is convicted of a serious crime, should the Commissioner impose a lifetime ban? Should re-entry be based on rehabilitation? Many of these questions are raised in the case of a star college player who pled guilty as a teenager in a juvenile court proceeding sexually abusing his young niece. S.L. Price, *Prospect and Pariah*, Sports Illustrated, May 21, 2018, at 30. Despite a stellar college career at Oregon State, the player was undrafted and left baseball after a short time playing in Mexico.

3.   BEYOND PROTECTION OF LEAGUE REPUTATION?

The sports league constitutions studied in this chapter grant Commissioners broad power to act in the league's "best interests." Courts have broadly construed this power, with great deference to the Commissioner's judgment. The specific topics covered in this Section related to matters that patently affect the league's reputation among avid fans, casual viewers, sponsors, and others who provide revenue to America's commercialized sports leagues.

As a descriptive matter, the modern sports league commissioner has become the Chief Executive Officer of a major commercial operation, who ultimately reports to club owners who have invested millions (and more frequently billions) in their franchises. Many would view skeptically the claim that these commissioners would act to protect some broader concept of a league's "best interests" beyond those necessary to preserve reputation. The question for public policy, and ultimately law, is how we can best achieve what *society* believes to be in sports' "best interests" if they diverge from the interests of owners as a collective.

In a landmark decision, MLB Commissioner Bud Selig suggested that the best interests of an individual owner may be contrary to the best interests of baseball. A settlement of litigation claims, briefly noted in a preliminary opinion in *In re Los Angeles Dodgers LLC*, 457 B.R. 308 (Bank. D. Del. 2011), precluded an important judicial decision concerning the scope of the Commissioner's best interest powers. The issue was whether the Commissioner could intervene to protect a club's long-term economic prospects from what the Commissioner believes to be improvident business decisions by the current owner. Consider whether this decision expands the "best interests" power, or fits more comfortably within the framework of reputation-protection that the other examples in this chapter have discussed.

The dispute arose when Los Angeles Dodgers' owner Frank McCourt, who had acquired the storied team from News Corporation in a leveraged transaction, found himself facing personal financial difficulties (largely due to a messy and very expensive divorce proceeding). McCourt sought to alleviate this problem by entering a new long-term media rights deal with Fox, totaling $1.7 billion over 17 years, which including an up-front cash payment of $385 million to McCourt. Under Art. VIII, § 4(f) of the MLB Constitution, this contract required the approval of the Commissioner. Selig rejected the contract as contrary to the best interests of baseball. He concluded that McCourt was harming the Dodgers' future for a quick fix of his personal financial issues, that the agreement precluded long-term maximization of media rights, and took great exception to the diversion of most of the $385 million for McCourt's personal use. Selig also expressed concern that future ownership would be locked into a below-market deal. The letter concluded:

> As the Dodgers' control owner, you have the duty to manage the Club "for its own sake, in a sound fiscal manner, and not for the benefit of another business," and a contractual commitment to operate the Dodgers "with the intention of being profitable and with respect to all operations and control in the best interests of the Los Angeles Dodgers and Major League Baseball." Instead, you have run the Club consistently for your own benefit and that of your family members, and your lifestyle, with little or no regard for the distinction between the Club's finances and your own.

Letter from Bud Selig, Comm'r, Major League Baseball, to Frank McCourt, Owner, L.A. Dodgers Baseball Club 7–8 (June 20, 2011), *quoted in* Frank J. Mallaro, Jr., Note, *Permeating the Good Old Boys Club: Why Holding the Commissioner of Baseball to a Fiduciary Duty of Loyalty is in the "Best Interests of the Game,"* 7 BROOK J. CORP. FIN. & COM. L. 475, 485 (2013).

Without an influx of cash from a new television deal, the Dodgers could not meet payroll obligations. Rather than cede control of the team to Major League Baseball, McCourt filed for Chapter 11 bankruptcy, even though such a step directly violates the Major League Agreement and can result in an owner being stripped of his ownership rights. (Article VIII § 4(ii)(*l*) of the Major League Agreement states, "the rights, privileges and other property rights of a Major League Club hereunder and under any other Baseball-related agreement may be terminated . . . if the Club in question shall . . . file a voluntary petition in bankruptcy." Article II § 3(c) of the Major League Agreement grants the Commissioner the right to suspend or remove any owner of a Major League Club.) After legal skirmishing, the bankruptcy litigation was settled. McCourt finally succumbed to financial and legal pressures and agreed with Major League Baseball that the Dodgers would be sold at auction. The team was subsequently sold to a group led by Guggenheim Partners, and including long-time baseball executive Stan Kasten and local basketball star Earvin "Magic" Johnson, for $2.2 billion. The new owners were able to obtain a 25-year media deal with Fox' rival, Time Warner Cable, valued at over $7 billion.

Are there social reasons to recognize a special trust in sports that goes beyond the "branding" inherent in other commercial products and services whose providers seek to preserve reputation? Consider the following:

> The relationship between a sports fan and a team owner or a league is not the same as between . . . the buyer of computer software and its supplier . . . in sports, no one *wants* market retribution to be swift. We hope that Los Angelenos and others who grew up as Dodger fans with Vin Scully's Hall of Fame broadcast will remain loyal despite management travails that have impeded recent performance. We honor members of Red Sox Nation who lived and died with years of ineptitude, which some believe was supernaturally imposed. With sports, the customer is not buying something that depends largely on the current behavior of the owner, but is rather buying into a tradition. . . . The 'trust' that fans place in their favorite teams is what makes sports the special entertainment and civil institution that it is.

Stephen F. Ross & Stefan Szymanski, FANS OF THE WORLD, UNITE! A (CAPITALIST) MANIFESTO FOR SPORTS CONSUMERS 6–7 (Stanford Univ. Press 2008). Do you agree? If so, when owners act commercially to breach this trust, is that contrary to the best interests of sport?

E. COMPARATIVE PERSPECTIVES

This chapter documents the evolution of professional sports leagues in North America, from the founding of baseball's National League in 1876, through the recognition that owners needed an independent commissioner to deal with integrity issues, to today's delegation of significant power and discretion to an official resembling a chief executive officer. A brief comparative glance at other nations reveals that MLB's approach to organizing professional sport, while largely emulated here, is quite different from the practices elsewhere. It provides an opportunity to consider whether North American practices are desirable and suited for our context or simply the result of custom and practice in need of rigorous reconsideration.[3]

Consider the following major ways in which North American sports differs from most of the world.

---

[3]   This comparison is detailed in Stephen F. Ross, AN ADVANCED INTRODUCTION TO GLOBAL SPORTS LAW (Edward Elgar 2021). For a comprehensive reference to English and European law, *see* Adam Lewis QC and Jonathan Taylor QC, SPORT: LAW AND PRACTICE (Bloomsbury 4th ed. 2021).

1.   *Integrated or dis-integrated from other sports institutions.* One key aspect of North American sports leagues is that their structure is wholly separate from other institutions. Other than a few specific community-oriented programs, Major League Baseball has little to do with the wholly separate entities that control Little League, interscholastic and intercollegiate baseball, traveling "pay-for-play" youth teams, and adult recreational competitions often organized by local park and recreation departments. This contrasts with the structure typical in other countries, where a national governing board sits on top of a "pyramid" of governance, with a varying degree of control over commercially successful major leagues, but also controlling the national team and regulating all aspects of youth and recreational sport. European Commission, *The European Model of Sport*, Consultation Document of DG X (September 1998) 2–3.

This approach is nominally justified by a principle of "solidarity" that calls on wealthy professional leagues to use some of their proceeds to support grass roots recreational sports. A useful example is New Zealand rugby, featuring the profitable and legendary All-Blacks. The national team has won over 75% of their matches, and since the first Rugby World Cup in 1987, they have won the trophy three times. Youth rugby is organized, with proceeds from the All-Blacks, by the NZ Rugby Union, a non-profit board. Young boys and girls (called "Small Blacks") participate at local clubs, with subsidized funding for those unable to pay fees, and with coaches trained by the NZRU. Participation rates among poor kids, and in particular Maori and Pacific Islander youth, is fairly high. European countries feature varied success, in part because European and local authorities do not rigorously enforce the principal of solidarity.

2.   *Open versus closed leagues.* All leagues seek to achieve some degree of "competitive balance" among teams. A major reason is that without the opportunity to succeed during the season to move on to the playoffs, inferior teams have nothing to play for. In the rest of the world, leagues are largely "open", with a system of "promotion and relegation" so that the worst teams drop down to a lower-tier competition and the best teams in the lower-tier move up to the top tier.

3.   *Distinguishing regulatory and commercial functions.* Clubs in the English Premier League make purely commercial decisions such as broadcast licensing or rules governing sponsorships and marketing, just as clubs in the NFL do. However, rules of the game, on-field regulations, player discipline, and similar matters are determined by the English Football Association (the FA), or federations to which the FA belongs, such as UEFA or FIFA.

4.   *The multiple functions of national governing boards (NGBs).* Governments typically grant significant discretion (either by omission or substantive legal delegation) to these NGBs. They have many functions, including (a) overseeing the commercial operation of elite professional club

competitions, (b) developing talent for and managing international representative teams and (c) regulating and funding grass-roots amateur clubs or organizations, either directly with grants or indirectly in providing services, equipment, and the like. The latter function serves in turn multiple purposes, including youth recreation, adult recreation, and the development of elite young talent.

5. *The role of government in sports governance.* Modern sport has evolved from two different models related to the role of government. The English common law permitted individuals to form associations for any purpose not specifically barred by the law, which facilitated the formation of private sporting clubs. The clubs offered competitions in sports such as football and cricket with the incidental benefit of physical exercise and the primary purpose of encouraging drinking, gambling, and socializing. Sporting clubs similarly developed in 19th-century America. Thus, sport was seen as a private function, with activities subject only to laws of general application, akin to private dining clubs, and of little concern to the public interest other than allowing individuals the freedom to choose their leisure activities.

In assessing the reasonableness of sporting rules challenged in courts of these countries, judges long exhibited significant deference to the judgment of these private sporting organizations. Consider the following observations by a British judge:

> I think that the courts must be slow to allow any implied obligation to be fair to be used as a means of bringing before the Courts for review honest decisions of bodies exercising jurisdiction over sporting and other activities which those bodies are far better fitted to judge than the Courts. This is so even where those bodies are concerned with the means of livelihood of those who take part in those activities. Concepts of natural justice and the duty to be fair must not be allowed to discredit themselves by making unreasonable requirements and imposing undue burdens, bodies such as the board which promote a public interest by seeking to maintain a high stance in a field of activity which otherwise might easily become degraded or corrupt ought not to be hampered in their work without good cause. Such bodies should not be tempted or coerced into granting licences that otherwise they would refuse by reason of the Courts having imposed on them procedure for refusal which facilitates litigation against them.... The individual must indeed be protected against impropriety; but any claim of this or anything more must be balanced against what the public interest requires.

McInnes v. Onslow-Fane, [1978] 1 W.L.R. 1520, 1535 (Ch.).

In contrast, continental European countries historically banned private associations unless expressly authorized by government, which directed sports into activities like French cycling or German gymnasiums with more demonstrable use for military purposes. European states thus adopted an "interventionist" model of sport, based on the more authoritarian society that then existed. Today the French *Loi du sport* declares "the development of physical activities, sports, and high level sports is incumbent upon the state." The Ministry of Sport promotes sports for all age group and manages government sports grants, and grants authority to NGBs in each sport.

Over time, even the English model acknowledged the vital public interest in sport. A 1966 landmark English legal decision relied on this interest in a case contesting the private Jockey Club's refusal to license women as jockeys and trainers, effectively excluding them from participating in English horseracing. The Court of Appeal held that this was an unreasonable agreement in restraint of trade and void. The decision explicitly distinguished private dining clubs from sporting organizations that assumed a monopoly regulatory position: "But we are not considering a social club, we are considering an association which exercises a virtual monopoly in an important field of human activity." *Nagle v. Feilden,* [1966] 2 QB 633 (C.A.).

Thus, the modern view of sports governance recognizes the public importance of decisions by sporting entities. Sports are now understood to "hold a singular position among leisure time activities and have an unparalleled impact on the everyday lives of billions of people." Andrei S. Markovits and Lars Rensmann, GAMING THE WORLD: HOW SPORTS ARE RESHAPING GLOBAL POLITICS AND CULTURE (Princeton Univ. Press 2010), at 1. The differences between an English private dining club and an NGB go beyond the importance of sport as a social institution. Another key difference is alternatives to those affected. If someone were excluded, even wrongfully, from the Charlton Club, he could seek membership in the Groucho Club. A female trainer could not work, and sports fans would be denied her talents, if she were excluded from the Jockey Club.

The modern view continues to evolve. Increased financial support for elite national team development and grass-roots sport come at the price of public conditions. Social problems raised by sport that are beyond the capacity of private sporting entities necessitate legal intervention, such as regulation of public safety (thus, in the UK, Parliament has enacted laws such as the Safety of Sports Grounds Act and the Football Spectators Act to deal with unsafe stadia and hooliganism, discussed further in Chapter 16, Section B.4).

In contrast, North America's commercial focus means that professional sports are largely viewed as the providers of entertainment services. As a result, the government's role is to provide external public policy concerns to sport by statute: primarily competition and employment/ labor law.

6. *Judicial review.* Although it is not clear how many cases would come out differently across the Atlantic, formally the British system of judicial review differs from the American approach outlined above in cases like *Finley v. Kuhn* and *Turner.* In the landmark decision in *Bradley v. Jockey Club,* [2005] EWCA Civ 1056, *aff'd,* [2004] EWHC 2164, Judge Richards concluded that sports governing boards were subject to supervisory review equivalent to the standard used by courts reviewing administrative agency decisions. The court concluded that, "even in the absence of any contractual relationship, the decision of the Appeal Board is subject to the supervisory jurisdiction of the court." Elaborating on this point, Judge Richards declined to follow other courts who sought to keep the law grounded in the doctrine of restraint of trade, expressly rejecting reliance on that doctrine. This is important, for it makes clear that *Bradley* applies supervisory review to anyone aggrieved by NGB decisions, not just those decisions that operate to deprive someone of their ability to practice their trade or business. On point, New Zealand courts held that courts would entertain a challenge to a controversial decision to allow the All-Blacks to tour apartheid-era South Africa as ultra vires the authority granted to the NZ Rugby Football Union under its rules. *Finnegan v. NZ Rugby FU,* [1985] 2 NZLR 159. *Bradley* emphasized the supervisory, rather than merits, review of challenges to NGB decisions. The key holding is worth quoting:

> The function of the court is not to take the primary decision but to ensure that the primary decision-maker has operated within lawful limits. It is a review function, very similar to that of the court on judicial review. Indeed, given the difficulties that sometimes arise in drawing the precise boundary between the two, I would consider it surprising and unsatisfactory if a private law claim in relation to the decision of a domestic body required the court to adopt a materially different approach from a judicial review claim in relation to the decision of a public body.

Id. ¶ 37.

Where the issue calls for discretion—as in *Bradley* where the question is the proportionality of discipline—the question for the reviewing court is "whether the Board's decision on penalty fell within the limits of its discretionary area of judgment." Here, the claim failed because Bradley had "failed to persuade me that any of the findings made by the Board went beyond those reasonably open to it on the evidence."

Three other points are worthy of emphasis. First, as with its American cousin, *Finley v. Kuhn, supra,* the court seemed to take a careful, if still modestly deferential, approach to the NGB's handling of internal precedents. On the merits, the court upheld a disciplinary punishment for revealing confidential information to gamblers, finding that the sport's Appeal Board gave "valid reasons" for distinguishing cases of lighter punishment. Second, the court accepted the application of the doctrine requiring public actors to act in a proportional manner, without exactly explaining why. Third, it remains less clear whether a reviewing court would be as deferential to pure questions of law, such as the interpretation of text, as it is toward the NGB's findings of fact and exercise of discretion.

In sum, two leading scholars conclude that an NGB "will be afforded a margin of appreciation, or latitude, in its decision-making but will still be held to account if it goes too far." Their analysis makes clear that a court's power to insist that NGBs act (1) lawfully (both in accordance with general law and faithful to their own rules), (2) with procedural fairness and (3) in a non-arbitrary way, is grounded not in established doctrines of contract law but, in the modern world, the public interest in allowing private monopoly control over sports regulation. *See* Nick De Marco et al., *Grounds for Review Arising Out of Control of the Sport,* in SPORT: LAW AND PRACTICE (Bloomsbury: 4th. Ed. 2021) (Adam Lewis & Jonathan Taylor, eds.)

CHAPTER 3

LABOR LAW AND COLLECTIVE BARGAINING IN PROFESSIONAL SPORTS

■ ■ ■

A. INTRODUCTION TO NATIONAL LABOR LAW

A basic understanding of national labor law is necessary to comprehend the operation of professional sports leagues in America. Although labor relations in professional sports in America are regulated by antitrust law as well as labor law, the Supreme Court has bestowed preeminence on the principles of national labor policy. As explained in Chapter 7, what would otherwise be treated as antitrust violations—such as unreasonable restraints on the market for players' services—can be insulated from regulation by a collective bargaining relationship between a league and a union that represents the league's athletes.

In the nineteenth century—long before the advent of sports unions—state courts considered unions to be illegal conspiracies subject to criminal prosecution whenever they withdrew the services of their members in support of demands for increased wages and improved labor conditions. As the organization of craft and some industrial workers continued into the twentieth century, courts continued to serve management's interests by granting employers injunctive relief against union-related concerted activity.

Unions eventually received support from the federal legislative branch. Congress granted unions relief from judicial injunctive interference in labor disputes—first in the Clayton Act of 1914 and then more broadly in the Norris-LaGuardia Act of 1932. In 1935, moreover, as the nation suffered from the continuing Depression, Congress provided affirmative governmental protection to the efforts of employees to bargain collectively with their employers. The Wagner Act of 1935—entitled the National Labor Relations Act (NLRA or Labor Act)—protected from employer interference the rights of employees to self-organize, to demand to bargain collectively, and to engage in concerted activities. The Labor Act established a federal agency—the National Labor Relations Board (NLRB or Labor Board)—charged with securing employee rights and with conducting secret ballot elections in which employees could vote to form or not to form a union. Congress expected the Labor Act both to foster industrial peace and to improve employee wages. Congress hoped that the processes of collective bargaining would result in stable terms of employment that reflected the relative economic power of the parties involved in the negotiations, rather than solutions imposed by government.

The Taft-Hartley Act substantially amended the Labor Act in 1947. Taft-Hartley added protections from union as well as employer restraint and the rights of employees to refrain from as well as to engage in concerted activities, including collective bargaining. In the Landrum-Griffin Act of 1959, Congress both amended the Labor Act further to close some loopholes and also addressed issues of internal union democracy in a separate statute. Since 1959, however, the statutory framework of federal labor policy has not been significantly altered.

Employees, unions, or employers that believe that an employer or a union has committed a violation of the Labor Act can file an unfair labor practice charge with a regional office of the Labor Board. Board attorneys investigate the charge. If found to have merit, the General Counsel of the Labor Board may issue a complaint that is tried before an administrative law judge (ALJ). ALJ decisions are reviewed by the Labor Board, which is empowered by the Labor Act to issue orders with equitable remedies, including the reinstatement of wrongfully discharged employees with back pay. The Labor Board also can direct an employer to bargain in good faith with a union. These orders must be enforced in a federal Circuit Court of Appeals. A party aggrieved by a Labor Board order also can appeal to a Circuit Court of Appeals for review. Courts of Appeals, however, give some deference to the Labor Board's judgment.

Unions of professional sports teams' athletes generally have been the beneficiaries of the Labor Act and the interpretive case law elaborated by the Labor Board and the courts. The Labor Board and the courts have been able to adapt labor law principles to sports unions and the distinctive work situations their members face. The seeds of modern collective action by professional athletes were sown after the enactment of the NLRA in the 1950s with the formation of player organizations in all four team sports. In each sport, organizers deliberately named these bodies associations rather than unions, because the latter term was considered appropriate only for the teams' concession vendors or maintenance crews, not for elite athletes. Not until the mid-1960s did players begin to realize that, for all their status in the outside world, if they were to induce owners to change the structure of the players' market and thereby significantly enlarge their share of league revenues, they would have to engage in full-fledged collective bargaining and concerted activity under professional union leadership.

Collective bargaining in the sports industry has proved contentious. Sports unions first had to convince club owners that they were actually real unions and not simply fraternities of sporting athletes who were satisfied simply to have the opportunity to play their chosen sport. The genuine sports unions that evolved in the 1960s in the four major team sports had to overcome the fact that on average their membership would turn over every four years because of the short careers of their members. Sports unions had to employ economic weapons and withhold the services of their members to firmly establish their legitimacy with the owners. The owners, in turn, have resorted to locking out the athletes in an effort to prove that highly paid and short-career sports workers could not maintain the solidarity needed to withstand the owners' demands. Many of these battles have focused on the system used to determine the compensation of athletes and the systems that bind an athlete to a particular club.

By the current day, for each major professional team sports league, through work stoppages, peaceful collective bargaining, and labor arbitration, unionism has transformed the rules for dealings between individual teams and players. In particular, veteran free agency has become the rule, but with different forms of salary constraints imposed on the amount that a team can offer its players. Ultimately, as professional league teams flourished more and more economically, the players began to earn a more equitable share of league revenues.

Major League Baseball experienced decades of particularly contentious labor relations. Led by Marvin Miller, the MLB Players Association (MLBPA) approached collective bargaining with the same zeal as the United Steelworkers union, where Miller had earlier served as chief economist. Baseball club owners, who generally had experienced labor relations only in non-unionized industries, found the collective bargaining process to be inhospitable. Miller and his successor Donald Fehr had to prove repeatedly to the owners each time a collective bargaining agreement (CBA) expired that the players were genuine unionists. The result was eight successive work stoppages—either union strikes or management-directed lockouts.

In 2002, however, negotiations in baseball achieved a stable relationship between owners and players. In large measure this was the result of the work of two experienced labor law experts—the late Michael Weiner, the successor to Donald Fehr as the Executive Director of the MLBPA, and Rob Manfred, now Commissioner of Major League Baseball. The two forged a productive relationship that until an off-season lockout in the winter of 2022 kept baseball free from the work stoppages that continued to afflict professional football, basketball, and hockey in the twenty-first century.

In the late 1960s, when real unionism first came to the sports world, the average salaries in baseball, hockey, basketball, and football ranged from $19,000 to $25,000. By 2020, average player salaries ranged from $2.7 million in hockey to almost $8 and a half million in basketball. Compared with the average American worker, baseball players earned 3.5 times more in salaries in 1967, while by 2018 they were making 92 times more. This huge player salary spiral has been accompanied by comparable leaps in fan attendance, television and merchandising deals, league expansion, and team franchise values. Sports unions and sports management have both flourished financially over recent decades.

The focus of this chapter and the two chapters to follow is on how federal labor law, private labor negotiations, and the use of labor arbitration have addressed employment conflicts in professional sports. Over the last eight decades, the NLRB and the courts have developed an elaborate labor law jurisprudence. The more than five decades of active union representation in professional sports has produced decisions that illustrate the important doctrinal spheres in contemporary labor law.

B. APPLICATION OF THE LABOR ACT TO SPORTS

Congress enacted the Labor Act pursuant to its power to regulate interstate commerce. The Labor Act was a key feature of President Franklin Delano Roosevelt's New Deal, based in part on the premise that unionization and collective bargaining would enhance worker's buying power and help drive the nation out of the Depression, as well as secure industrial peace. It was not at all clear, however, that the Supreme Court would find this legislative strategy constitutional. The Court had a narrow perspective on the reach of interstate commerce. In fact, the Supreme Court in 1922 had ruled in *Federal Baseball Club of Baltimore v. National League of Professional Baseball Clubs*, 259 U.S. 200 (1922), that baseball was too localized a form of business enterprise to be subject to federal antitrust law. Nevertheless, a closely divided Supreme Court, in *NLRB v. Jones & Laughlin Steel Corp.*, 301 U.S. 1 (1937), broadened that perspective and upheld the constitutional validity of the Labor Act.

Although the *Jones & Laughlin* decision did not apply the Labor Act to professional sports, it did seem to provide the Labor Board with the authority to address the issue. The Labor Board decision that ultimately did so and thereby gave professional athletes rights under the Labor Act was rendered in response to a union representation petition filed by American League umpires.

AMERICAN LEAGUE OF PROFESSIONAL BASEBALL CLUBS & ASS'N OF NATIONAL BASEBALL LEAGUE UMPIRES
180 N.L.R.B. 190 (1969)

* * *

[The Labor Board first considered whether baseball sufficiently involved interstate commerce so that the NLRA could apply.] The Board's jurisdiction under the Act is based upon the commerce clause of the Constitution, and is coextensive with the reach of that clause. . . [Notwithstanding *Federal Baseball*], since professional football and boxing have been held to be in interstate commerce and thus subject to the antitrust laws, it can no longer be seriously contended that the Court still considers baseball alone to be outside of interstate commerce. Congressional deliberations regarding the relationship of baseball and other professional team sports to the antitrust laws likewise reflect a Congressional assumption that such sports are subject to regulation under the commerce clause. It is, incidentally, noteworthy that these deliberations reveal Congressional concern for the rights of employees such as players to bargain collectively and engage in concerted activities. Additionally, legal scholars have agreed, and neither the parties nor those participating as *amici* dispute, that professional sports are in or affect interstate commerce, and as such are subject to the Board's jurisdiction. Therefore, on the basis of the above, we find that professional baseball is an industry in or affecting commerce, and as such is subject to Board jurisdiction under the Act.

* * *

Section 14(c)(1) of the National Labor Relations Act, as amended, permits the Board to decline jurisdiction over labor disputes involving any "class or category of employers, where, in the opinion of the Board, the effect of such labor dispute on commerce is not sufficiently substantial to warrant the exercise of its jurisdiction. . . ." The Employer and other employers contend that because of baseball's internal self-regulation, a labor dispute involving the American League of Professional Baseball Clubs is not likely to have any substantial effect on interstate commerce; and that application of the National Labor Relations Act to this Employer is contrary to national labor policy because Congress has sanctioned baseball's internal self-regulation. The Employer also contends that effective and uniform regulation of baseball's labor relations problems is not possible through Board processes because of the sport's international aspects.

* * *

We have carefully considered the positions of the parties, and the *amicus* briefs, and we find that it will best effectuate the mandates of the Act, as well as national labor policy, to assert jurisdiction over this Employer. We reach this decision for the following reasons.

Baseball's system for internal self-regulation of disputes involving umpires is made up of the Uniform Umpires Contract, the Major League Agreement, and the Major League Rules, which provide, among other things, for final resolution of disputes through arbitration by the Commissioner. The system appears to have been designed almost entirely by employers and owners, and the final arbiter of internal disputes does not appear to be a neutral third party freely chosen by both sides, but rather an individual appointed solely by the member club owners themselves. We do not believe that such a system is likely either to prevent labor disputes from arising in the future, or, having once arisen, to resolve them in a manner susceptible or conducive to voluntary compliance by all parties involved. Moreover, it is patently contrary to the letter and spirit of the Act for the Board to defer its undoubted jurisdiction to decide unfair labor practices to a disputes settlement system established unilaterally by an employer or group of employers. Finally, although the instant case involves only umpires employed by the League, professional baseball clubs employ, in addition to players, clubhouse attendants, bat boys, watchmen, scouts, ticket sellers, ushers, gatemen, trainers, janitors, office clericals, batting practice pitchers, stilemen, publicity, and advertising men, grounds keepers and maintenance men. As to these other categories, there is no "self-regulation" at all. This consideration is of all the more consequence for those employees in professional baseball whose interests are likely to call the Board's processes into play, the great majority are in the latter-named classifications.

We can find, neither in the statute nor in its legislative history, any expression of a Congressional intent that disputes between employers and employees in this industry should be removed from the scheme of the National Labor Relations Act.

* * *

[W]e are not here confronted with the sort of small, primarily intrastate employer over which the Board declines jurisdiction because of failure to meet its prevailing monetary standards. Moreover, it is apparent that the Employer, whose operations are so clearly national in scope, ought not have its labor relations problems subject to diverse state laws.

The Employer's final contention, that Board processes are unsuited to regulate effectively baseball's international aspects, clearly lacks merit, as many if not most of the industries subject to the Act have similar international features.

* * *

MEMBER JENKINS, dissenting:

[Member Jenkins would have declined to assert jurisdiction over baseball, reasoning that Congress' silence on whether the Labor Act covered baseball meant that the agency should not assert jurisdiction. In 1935 when it enacted the Wagner Act, Congress knew that the Supreme Court had held that baseball did not affect interstate commerce. Even if the Board had discretion to assert or decline jurisdiction, it should not do so because "[t]here is no showing that this industry is wracked with the kinds of labor disputes which are likely to constitute a burden on commerce." Any disputes that might arise could be addressed by the internal commissioner system.]

———

NOTES AND QUESTIONS

1.   *Effect on Interstate Commerce.* This decision is the first judicial or agency ruling that baseball affects interstate commerce. Impact on interstate commerce is the constitutional nexus for both the Labor Act and the antitrust laws examined in subsequent chapters. Recall your study of the developments in constitutional law in response to the New Deal. How would you determine whether a sport affects interstate commerce? What kind of evidence would you consider?

2.   *Self-Regulation of Labor Disputes?* What is your reaction to the contrasting observations by the NLRB members about the relevance of baseball's system of internal self-regulation? Does Member Jenkins realistically assume a Commissioner who is neutral between owners and employees?

3.   *Reliance Interest.* Should the Board in 1969 have weighed more heavily the reliance of the American League and its member clubs on the Supreme Court's 1922 decision in *Federal Baseball* before asserting jurisdiction under the Labor Act? The Supreme Court had reaffirmed the Sherman Act's non-coverage of baseball in *Toolson v. New York Yankees*, 346 U.S. 356 (1953), and again did so in *Flood v. Kuhn*, 407 U.S. 258 (1972). The latter decision is presented in Chapter 5 below. Consider whether the clubs' reliance interest might be stronger for non-coverage by antitrust law than for non-coverage by labor law.

————

The Board's assertion of jurisdiction over other more recently developed professional leagues in other sports is less controversial, because the Supreme Court had never held that these leagues did not operate in interstate commerce for purposes of antitrust law or any other laws. Indeed, in *Radovich v. National Football League,* 352 U.S. 445 (1957), the Court refused to extend *Federal Baseball* and applied the Clayton Act to professional football. *See also Haywood v. National Basketball Assn.,* 401 U.S. 1204 (1971) (Douglas, J., acting as Circuit Justice).

On the other hand, the determination that Congress has Commerce Clause authority to regulate professional sports leagues did not mean that the Labor Act protects all the employees of these leagues or all professional athletes. The Labor Act, as amended in 1947, expressly excludes from the definition of protected employees, "any individual having the status of an independent contractor, or any individual employed as a supervisor." 29 U.S.C. § 152(3).

The latter term "supervisor" in turn is defined broadly to include "any individual having authority, in the interest of the employer, to hire, transfer, suspend, lay off, recall, promote, discharge, assign, reward, or discipline other employees, or responsibly direct them, or to adjust their grievances, or effectively to recommend such action, if . . . such authority

. . . requires the use of independent judgment." 29 U.S.C. § 152(11). The Supreme Court has required the Board to interpret this exclusion expansively, *see, e.g., NLRB v. Kentucky River Community Care, Inc.,* 532 U.S. 706 (2001), and to continue to maintain an implied exclusion of "managerial employees" who "formulate and effectuate management policies by expressing and making operative the decision of their employers." *See NLRB v. Bell Aerospace Co.,* 416 U.S. 267 (1974). These exclusions would seem to preclude the protection not only of club presidents and general managers, but also of managers and coaches. Why do they not also preclude the coverage of umpires and referees?

Even athletes in many professional sports, such as tennis and golf, are denied the Labor Act's protection by the Act's exclusion of independent contractors. The Taft-Hartley Congress added this exclusion to require the Board to observe the common law distinction of independent contractors from employees. *See NLRB v. United Insurance Co.,* 390 U.S. 254 (1968). The Supreme Court subsequently has clarified that for purposes of federal statutes this common law distinction should follow the multifactor "right-to-control" test adopted by the Restatements of Agency. *See, e.g., Nationwide Mutual Insurance Co. v. Darden,* 503 U.S. 318 (1992). As reformulated in § 1.01 of the Restatement of Employment Law, this multifactor test determines whether the workers can perform their work in their own independent business interest.

Tennis and golf professionals operate independent businesses employing their own coaches and "teams." These athletes, rather than their tours, determine in which tournaments they will compete and when, where and how they will practice and compete. Similarly, boxers, race car drivers, horse jockeys, and mixed martial arts fighters generally are treated as independent contractors. A sports owner's use of an independent contractor designation is not determinative of workers' actual status, however. The designation of NFL cheerleaders as independent contractors by the clubs that closely control their work, for instance, seems open to challenge. *See, e.g., Ferrari v. National Football League,* 61 N.Y.S.3d 421 (2017) (certifying class to determine whether cheerleaders designated as contractors are really employees). On the other hand, officials who work only part time for a sports league may be classifiable as independent contractors rather than employees. See *Pennsylvania Interscholastic Athletic Assn., Inc. v. NLRB,* 926 F.3d 837 (D.C. Cir. 2019) (high school lacrosse referees who worked few hours a week in short season were independent contractors).

The managerial exclusion is not the only implied departure from the common law definition of employee that the Board has recognized to restrict its jurisdiction. Most importantly for college athletes, the Board has held that Congress did not intend to treat graduate students discharging compensated teaching or research responsibilities as employees when their relationship with their universities is "primarily educational." *Brown University*, 342 N.L.R.B. 483 (2004). Whether or not the President Obama-appointed Board's reversal of the *Brown* decision in *Trustees of Columbia University*, 364 N.L.R.B. No. 90 (2016) is confirmed by subsequent Boards, the Labor Board would have to determine that college athletes in at least revenue producing sports were employees under the Labor Act before it could protect their efforts to form a union. Furthermore, athletes at public universities could not be protected because the Labor Act's definition of employer excludes states and their subdivisions. For further discussion of college athlete unionization, as well as the treatment of compensation of college athletes, see Chapter 12 *infra*.

C. UNION ACTIVITY AND EMPLOYER RETALIATION

Employees covered by the NLRA gain federal administrative protection against employer retaliation for supporting a union. For most workers, this legal protection can be most important in the early days of union organization confronting employers determined to stay union-free. In professional sports, however, players had organized their associations and secured collective bargaining agreements even before they could be sure that the Labor Board would assert jurisdictional coverage. In addition, as explained below in Chapter 7, sports clubs and leagues are unusual employers because they need and want a union for their players in order to secure and retain the benefit of the implied labor exemption to the antitrust laws

The rights of employees secured by the Labor Act, however, extend beyond initial union organization to encompass any concerted activity for employee mutual aid or protection, whether or not union related. These employee rights also encompass actions in support of the union in its bargaining efforts—for example, engaging in strikes and rallying fellow employees in favor of the union and against the employer during a strike. Section 8(a)(1) of the Labor Act makes it an unfair labor practice for the employer to "interfere with, restrain, or coerce" employees engaged in any such "concerted activities," and § 8(a)(3) forbids "discrimination in regard to hire or tenure of employment to encourage or discourage membership in any labor organization."

While these employee rights and employer obligations are firmly embedded in labor jurisprudence, they are inevitably murky in application. Even a determined anti-union employer, recognizing the presence of the Labor Act in the background, is likely to be careful to direct such retaliation only against employees whose work history provides some colorable basis for discharge or other punitive action. As a result, unfair labor practice charges based on § 8 involve difficult and time-consuming examinations of both the employer's true motivation for its actions and the employee's record of performance.

This difficulty may be exacerbated in professional sports. Unlike most other workers, athletes can have no expectation of keeping their positions just because they are doing a reasonably competent job. Veteran players continuously face the threat of release and replacement by rookie challengers. The standard NFL player contract, for example, has provided:

> *Skill, Performance and Conduct.* Player understands that he is competing with other players for a position on Club's roster within the applicable player limits. If at any time, in the sole judgment of Club, Player's skill or performance has been unsatisfactory as compared with that of other players competing for positions on Club's roster, or if Player has engaged in personal conduct reasonably judged by Club to adversely affect or reflect on Club, then Club may terminate this contract. In addition, during the period any salary cap is legally in effect, this contract may be terminated if, in Club's opinion, Player is anticipated to make less of a contribution to Club's ability to compete on the playing field than another player or players whom Club intends to sign or attempts to sign, or another player or players who is or are already on Club's roster, and for whom Club needs room.

Deciding whether a club's exercise of managerial judgment about a player's relative skill was contaminated by animus against his union activities may pose a severe test for the Labor Board. This problem becomes magnified when union representatives are respected veterans who may have passed their peak performance years but still have relatively large salaries.

SEATTLE SEAHAWKS V. NFLPA & SAM MCCULLUM
292 N.L.R.B. 899 (1989)

[From 1976 through 1981, Sam McCullum was a starting wide receiver for the Seattle Seahawks. In 1981, McCullum was selected by his teammates to be their union player representative. McCullum's prominent role in union activities in the following bargaining year (leading up to the lengthy players' strike during the 1982 season) produced severe tensions with Seahawks' coach Jack Patera. In particular, Patera was upset by McCullum's orchestration of the "solidarity handshake" by his teammates with members of the opposing team at the beginning of their first pre-season game. Nevertheless, McCullum started all of the August 1982 pre-season games for the Seahawks. In a trade made at the end of training camp, however, the Seahawks obtained from the Baltimore Colts another wide receiver, Roger Carr, and McCullum was cut from the team's final roster. An unfair labor practice charge was then filed by McCullum and the NFLPA.

The evidence at trial before an administrative law judge (ALJ) showed that the Seahawks' Director of Football Operations, Mike McCormick, and its General Manager, John Thompson, had been trying for months to trade for Carr on favorable terms. Also, Jerry Rhome, the offensive coordinator, had been closely involved in deciding which of the team's four wide receivers should be let go to make room for Carr. However, the ALJ found that both of these team decisions were influenced by the Seahawks'—and especially Patera's—anti-union sentiments directed at McCullum. In this decision, a divided NLRB grapples with the Seahawks' appeal from the ALJ's ruling.

In *Wright Line*, 251 N.L.R.B. 1083 (1980), *enf'd*, 662 F.2d 899 (1st Cir. 1981), the NLRB clarified its test for determining when an employer has committed an unfair labor practice by firing an employee. Rather than simply determining whether antiunion motivation was a "cause" of the firing, the Board required the NLRB General Counsel to show only that union activities were a "motivating factor" in the employer's decision to terminate, but then allowed the employer to defend by showing that the employee would have been fired even if he had not engaged in union activities. The Supreme Court accepted this process and its ultimate "but for" test in *NLRB v. Transportation Management Corp.*, 462 U.S. 393, 400–03 (1983). The Seahawks first challenged the ALJ's ruling on the ground that it misapplied the *Wright Line* test by finding no more than that McCullum's union activities were "in part" a factor in his release.]

It is incontestable that the judge, notwithstanding his occasional use of the term "in part" to describe the extent of the Respondent's unlawful motivation, found that antiunion considerations were a motivating factor in the decision that produced McCullum's release, and that he fully considered the Respondent's *Wright Line* defense. We therefore find that his analysis fully comports with the *Wright Line* standard.

The Respondent has also excepted to the judge's implicit finding that certain remarks that Sam McCullum made in his role as the team's player representative at a February 19, 1982 press conference and that produced negative reactions from both the team's general manager, John Thompson, and its head coach, Jack Patera, are in fact protected under § 7 of the Act. In particular, the Respondent argues that McCullum's expression of his view that team doctors, whom he saw as identified with management, released injured players for games too soon, when the players were not fully recovered, constituted "disloyal" disparagement of the employer, which, pursuant to the theory of *NLRB v. Electrical Workers Local 1229 IBEW (Jefferson Standard)*, 346 U.S. 464 (1953), is not protected activity under § 7. The Respondent also argues, as to the "solidarity handshake" episode, that any hostility would naturally be against the Union—as the author of this activity throughout the league—rather than against McCullum. We disagree with both contentions.

In *Jefferson Standard*, the Supreme Court held that a union's public attacks on the quality of the employer's product were not protected under § 7 when they had no connection with the employee's working conditions or any current labor controversy. It seems indisputable, however, that the relative haste with which injured players are returned to the football field is a matter that directly affects the players' working conditions. Although McCullum's views may have been exaggerated or not soundly based, that does not withdraw the protection of the Act from them. Indeed, employees and employers frequently differ greatly in their views whether the employees are properly treated.

We do not mean to suggest, of course, that it was unlawful for either Thompson or Patera to take issue with McCullum's statements. The fact remains, however, that McCullum established himself at this press conference as a fairly aggressive union spokesman. McCullum's role as player representative was highlighted again when he and two other players approached Patera in August to apprise him of the players' intention to support the Union's "solidarity handshake" plan by engaging in such a handshake with the opposing team in the upcoming August 13 game with St. Louis. Although it was another player who mentioned the "union solidarity" symbolism of the handshake, it was McCullum who—after Patera had expressed his opposition—said that the players might go ahead and do it anyway. We agree with the judge that Patera's prediction of the subsequent fines ('I'll fine you as much as I can') and the heavy fines that the Respondent sought to impose reveal animus toward union activity for which, at this point, McCullum was the obvious focus on the team.

* * *

Finally, we address two of the Respondent's arguments concerning alleged inconsistencies between the judge's factual findings and the record evidence. . . .

First, the Respondent argues that a finding that it was seeking to obtain Carr in order to rid itself of McCullum is inconsistent with the evidence that the Respondent had declined to accept Baltimore's offer of Carr in late spring for a first round draft choice, that it had declined another Baltimore offer in August for a "high" draft choice, and that the Respondent had even toughened its position by insisting on September 2 that it would give up only a fourth round draft choice for Carr. We do not see that conduct as inconsistent with the judge's motivation finding for the reasons essentially given by the judge.

An employer may harbor an unlawful intent to rid itself of a troublesome employee but still wish to do so on the most advantageous terms possible. Furthermore, the testimony of the Respondent's own witnesses shows that they reasonably believed that Baltimore wanted to be rid at all costs of the injury-prone Carr.

* * *

It is undeniable that Rhome was responsible for rating the wide receivers throughout training camp and the pre-season games and that

Patera would reasonably take seriously his judgment, after the Carr trade, that McCullum should be released rather than Steve Largent, Byron Walker, or Paul Johns. But it is clear from Rhome's testimony that he was not consulted about the desirability of having Carr, as opposed to McCullum, at the point in the season that Carr was finally acquired. Thus, Rhome testified that he could not rate Carr because he had not seen him play very recently. Rhome obviously approached the evaluation process with the realization that Carr was not for cutting. As he testified, "You can't just eliminate Roger Carr because you just got through trading for him." Hence, having Carr as one of the wide receivers going into the new season was essentially imposed on Rhome by the trade. He made no considered judgment that an injury-prone player who had not participated in any training camp that summer and did not know Seattle's system of offensive plays would be more valuable than McCullum.

Although Carr's name was first mentioned by McCormick when he joined the Respondent's organization in March and the initial decision to make inquiries about Carr occurred after a conversation among McCormick, Patera, and Thompson about the matter, Patera made the initial call, while subsequent negotiations with Baltimore were carried out first by McCormick and later by Thompson. But Patera's role was crucial. As Thompson testified, Patera was the one to decide who would make the team. Given the time at which Carr was finally acquired—just before the opening of the season—it was clear that, as Rhome recognized, acquiring him meant bringing him onto the team. Nothing in the record suggests that efforts to acquire players would have been made without continuing consultation with the head coach. Thus, it had to be up to Patera whether negotiations to acquire Carr would continue just before the start of the season, when cuts were to be made. . . .

Given the reports that Rhome says he made to Patera about the progress of players Walker and Johns in the training camp and pre-season games, the continued pursuit of Carr is suspect. McCullum was rated a very good wide receiver in many respects—allegedly all except for the ability to go deep and catch "the bomb." But this was an area in which Johns and Walker were now rated highly, so the need to obtain Carr for that particular skill was diminishing rapidly according to the Respondent's own witnesses.

The Respondent simply has not shown that the acquisition of Roger Carr on September 3 would have occurred even in the absence of the animus of the Respondent's management—more notably, but not solely, the animus of Patera—against McCullum as an outspoken representative of union sentiment on the team. The animus against the Union's solidarity had been powerfully expressed, but thwarted in August, when the Respondent imposed fines for the 'solidarity handshake' that greatly exceeded those imposed by any other NFL team and then was forced to rescind the fines. The opportunity for the Respondent to rid itself of the most visible team symbol of that solidarity was finally seized upon in September through the acquisition of Carr.

Charges upheld.

———

NOTES AND QUESTIONS

1.   *Seahawks' Motivation?* Why do you think the Seahawks released Sam McCullum? After his release, McCullum played for the Minnesota Vikings for two seasons after which he retired from professional football, but continued to stay active in the NFL Players Association.

2.   *Difficulty of Proving Discriminatory Motive.* Could the Seahawks have avoided easily the NLRB's finding of anti-union discrimination against McCullum by a more careful sequencing of their decision making? How hard do you think it is generally for the NLRB's General Counsel to prove that personnel decisions have an anti-union motivation? Is it likely to be harder or easier for professional athletes? Does this depend somewhat on whether the player is a star or rather a marginal performer? On whether the athlete's contract is guaranteed and whether the club is operating under a salary cap?

3.   *Best Union Representatives?* Does this case have implications for an average player deciding on whom to elect as his club's union representative? Should he vote for a younger star player who is unlikely to be released but also less likely to be sympathetic to the union's goals on behalf of journeymen players, or for an older journeymen player who is more susceptible to being cut by the team but more committed to union activities? Consider also which type of player is more likely to be critical to the success of any union organized work stoppage.

4.   *Adequate Remedies?* The remedies available under the NLRA are only equitable; they do not include legal damages. Is the prospect of being ordered to provide reinstatement and back pay to discharged union activists likely to deter the normal employer who fears the impact of unionization on its labor costs? Is it more likely to deter owners of professional sports teams who have similar concerns? What if reinstatement would result in a club violating a league salary cap? Is reinstatement in any event an adequate remedy without an immediate preliminary injunction? (The Board has the discretion, but not the resources or the political will, to seek injunctions in the usual discriminatory discharge case).

5.   *Effect of Delay?* Consider also the not atypical delay in securing a final remedy in the *McCullum* case. The NLRB rendered its decision in 1989, and the D.C. Circuit eventually upheld the Board's unfair labor practice finding and $250,000 back pay award in *Nordstrom v. NLRB*, 984 F.2d 479 (D.C. Cir. 1993). That final legal ruling in this case took place *eleven years* after the Seahawks released McCullum for the reasons detailed above. What is the likely effect of such administrative-judicial delay on the protection of worker

rights of self-organization against employer retaliation? Is delay more or less significant in securing the policies of the Labor Act in the sports context?

6.   *Alternative Remedy Through Arbitration. McCullum* does not reflect the typical manner by which athletes represented by sports unions challenge allegedly unfair personnel decisions. As explained in the next chapter, arbitration systems framed in collective bargaining agreements generally can offer a better form of protection than that provided by the regulatory processes of the NLRB.

7.   *NLRA Protection for Non-Union Activities?* The "concerted activities" protected by § 7 of the NLRA from employer interference, restraint, or coercion, include not only those related to unions or collective bargaining, but also others "for mutual aid or protection," at least if the activities are not disavowed by a union with exclusive bargaining authority. This scope of protection, however, does not include activities that have no connection to enhancing or protecting employment status. Thus, § 7 presumably could protect football players' protesting the discipline of some of their fellow players for kneeling during the national anthem. Would it also protect the kneeling itself if it is directed toward protesting police mistreatment of arrestees rather than toward club or league mistreatment of employees?

8.   *Union Security Agreements.* Section 8(a)(3) of the NLRA prohibits terms of employment that "discourage" as well as those that "encourage" membership in a labor organization. This section, however, also includes a proviso that allows an employer, under certain conditions, to make an agreement with a representative union to require employees to pay the initiation fees and periodic dues required for membership in the union. One of the amendments to the NLRA contained in the Taft-Hartley Act of 1947 nonetheless empowers individual ("right-to-work") states to prohibit such union security clauses. A majority of states, many of them containing professional sports franchises, are now "right-to-work" jurisdictions where union security clauses cannot be enforced to require dues payments. *See, e.g., NFLPA v. Pro-Football, Inc.,* 857 F. Supp. 71 (D.C. 1994) (Washington Redskins players could not be compelled to pay union dues because they were primarily employed at the club's Virginia practice facilities and thus were subject to Virginia's "right-to-work" law). Regardless, strong sports unions generally have not been weakened by an inability to collect dues in multiple jurisdictions.

D. APPROPRIATE BARGAINING UNIT IN SPORTS LEAGUES

The various major professional sports leagues in the late 1960s voluntarily recognized their comparatively weak players associations on the basis of the associations' demonstration of majority support. Absent an employer's voluntary recognition, a union may petition the NLRB to conduct a secret ballot election if it can demonstrate substantial allegiance (a 30-percent "showing of interest") among the employees "in a unit appropriate" for collective bargaining. If the union receives a majority of the votes cast, the Board then certifies the union as the exclusive bargaining agent for all the employees in the unit (§ 9(c)(1)). But before any such election can be conducted, the Board must define the scope of the relevant employee constituency—that is, whether the union seeks to represent a "unit appropriate for the purposes of collective bargaining" under § 9(b) of the Labor Act.

The NLRB and the courts have developed an elaborate jurisprudence for determining whether the employees within a proposed grouping share a sufficient "community of interest" to become a recognized "bargaining unit." The Labor Board determines whether a unit proposed by a union is an appropriate bargaining unit, not whether it is the best unit or the only appropriate unit. Unions sculpt units based on whether they believe they can prevail in an election. In some instances, for example, a union may petition for a representation election in a single plant where it has support among the employees and not in all the company's plants at one time. As long as the single plant unit is an appropriate grouping of employees, the Labor Board will proceed to conduct the election.

Section 9(b) of the Labor Act authorizes the Board to choose an "employer unit, craft unit, plant unit, or subdivision thereof." It does not authorize multiemployer units. Thus, labor law has permitted bargaining in multiemployer units only where each employer and the union all consent. Nonetheless, multiemployer bargaining became a common feature of the industrial relations landscape, particularly in industries, such as trucking or construction, in which there are hosts of small firms dealing with a few large unions, such as the Teamsters or the Carpenters. Both employers and unions in these industries found they have a complementary long-term interest in bargaining that avoids labor cost competition between employers. Both the Board and the Supreme Court have fashioned doctrine to support consensual multiemployer bargaining by prohibiting any party from unilaterally withdrawing from a multiemployer unit during a particular round of bargaining just because negotiations have not gone as that party hoped. Thus, in *Charles D. Bonanno Linen Service v. NLRB*, 454 U.S. 404 (1982), the Supreme Court held that even a negotiating impasse did not warrant an employer leaving the larger multiemployer unit.

The Board, with approval from the Supreme Court, also has determined that some employees are jointly employed by more than one employer where the employees' working conditions and benefits are controlled in part by both. The Board designates some joint employer units as appropriate even without the consent of the employers. See, e.g., *Boire v. Greyhound Corp.*, 376 U.S. 473 (1964).

When a sports league recognizes a sports union as the representative of the players employed by all clubs in a single bargaining unit, it accordingly accepts a combination of multiemployer and joint employer bargaining. It should not be difficult to understand why the leagues and unions have preferred league-wide rather than individual-club bargaining. Consider, for instance, the many sports labor issues that need to be resolved consistently for all clubs in a league. But what if a league for some reason does not consent to this multiemployer, joint employer bargaining framework? Can this framework be required by the Board? Consider the following case.

NORTH AMERICAN SOCCER LEAGUE V. NLRB

613 F.2d 1379 (5th Cir. 1980)

RONEY, CIRCUIT JUDGE.

[In 1977, the National Football League Players Association (NFLPA) financed and staffed a new North American Soccer League Players Association (NASLPA), which then organized players from the 19 NASL clubs (two of which were Canadian teams) and petitioned the NLRB for certification of a single, league-wide bargaining unit. The division of authority between soccer clubs and their league (under its commissioner) was essentially the same as in other team sports. In the case of player relations, individual teams selected, compensated, traded, and released their players. However, league rules regarding rookie drafts, waivers, free agency, and the like governed such individual team player dealings, and all players were required to sign a standard NASL contract that accepted the ultimate disciplinary authority of the commissioner.

Given these facts, the Labor Board accepted the position of the Player Association that a single league-wide unit was an (though not the only) appropriate bargaining unit in an employment relationship in which the League and individual clubs were "joint employers" of the players, because both exercised a significant degree of control over their respective personnel policies. The Board majority decided, though, not to exercise jurisdiction over the two Canadian owned and based clubs, the Toronto Metros and the Vancouver Whitecaps, notwithstanding the dissent's observation that these two teams played nearly half their games in the United States and shared in both gate receipts and television revenues from this country. The League and its member clubs appealed the Board's certification of a single unit encompassing all of the players on American teams.]

* * *

Joint Employers.

Whether there is a joint employer relationship is "essentially a factual issue," and the Board's finding must be affirmed if supported by substantial evidence on the record as a whole.

The existence of a joint employer relationship depends on the control which one employer exercises, or potentially exercises, over the labor relations policy of the other. In this case, the record supports the Board's finding that the League exercises a significant degree of control over essential aspects of the clubs' labor relations, including but not limited to the selection, retention, and termination of the players, the terms of individual player contracts, dispute resolution and player discipline. Furthermore, each club granted the NASL authority over not only its own labor relations but also, on its behalf, authority over the labor relations of the other member clubs. The evidence is set forth in detail in the Board's decision and need be only briefly recounted here.

The League's purpose is to promote the game of soccer through its supervision of competition among member clubs. Club activities are governed by the League constitution, and the regulations promulgated thereunder by a majority vote of the clubs. The commissioner, selected and compensated by the clubs, is the League's chief executive officer. A board of directors composed of one representative of each club assists him in managing the League.

The League's control over the clubs' labor relations begins with restrictions on the means by which players are acquired. An annual college draft is conducted by the commissioner pursuant to the regulations, and each club obtains exclusive negotiating rights to the players it selects. On the other hand, as the Board recognized, the League exercises less control over the acquisition of "free agent" players and players "on loan" from soccer clubs abroad.

The regulations govern interclub player trades and empower the commissioner to void trades not deemed to be in the best interest of the League. Termination of player contracts is conducted through a waiver system in accordance with procedures specified in the regulations.

The League also exercises considerable control over the contractual relationships between the clubs and their players. Before being permitted to participate in a North American Soccer League game, each player must sign a standard player contract adopted by the League. The contract governs the player's relationship with his club, requiring his compliance with club rules and the League constitution and regulations. Compensation is negotiated between the player and his club, and special provisions may be added to the contract. Significantly, however, the club must seek the permission of the commissioner before signing a contract which alters any terms of the standard contract.

Every player contract must be submitted to the commissioner, who is empowered to disapprove a contract deemed not in the best interest of the League. The commissioner's disapproval invalidates the contract. Disputes between a club and a player must be submitted to the commissioner for final and binding arbitration.

Control over player discipline is divided between the League and the clubs. The clubs enforce compliance with club rules relating to practices and also determine when a player will participate in a game. The League, through the commissioner, has broad power to discipline players for misconduct either on or off the playing field. Sanctions range from fines to suspension to termination of the player's contract.

Although we recognize that minor differences in the underlying facts might justify different findings on the joint employer issue, the record in this case supports the Board's factual finding of a joint employer relationship among the League and its constituent clubs.

Having argued against inclusion of the Canadian clubs in the NLRB proceeding, petitioners contend on appeal that their exclusion renders the Board's joint employer finding, encompassing 21 clubs, inconsistent with the existence of a 24-club League. The jurisdictional determination is not before us on appeal, however, and the Board's decision not to exercise jurisdiction over the Canadian clubs does not undermine the evidentiary base of its joint employer finding.

Even assuming the League and the clubs are joint employers, they contend that *Greenhoot, Inc.*, 205 N.L.R.B. 250 (1973), requires a finding of a separate joint employer relationship between the League and each of its clubs, and does not permit all the clubs to be lumped together with the League as joint employers. In *Greenhoot*, a building management company was found to be a joint employer separately with each building owner as to maintenance employees in the buildings covered by its contracts. The present case is clearly distinguishable, because here each soccer club exercises through its proportionate role in League management some control over the labor relations of other clubs. In *Greenhoot*, building owners did not exercise any control through the management company over the activities of other owners.

Appropriate Unit.

The joint employer relationship among the League and its member clubs having been established, the next issue is whether the leaguewide unit of players designated by the Board is appropriate. Here the Board's responsibility and the standard of review in this Court are important.

The Board is not required to choose the most appropriate bargaining unit, only to select a unit appropriate under the circumstances. The determination will not be set aside "unless the Board's discretion has been exercised 'in an arbitrary or capricious manner.'"

Notwithstanding the substantial financial autonomy of the clubs, the Board found they form, through the League, an integrated group with common labor problems and a high degree of centralized control over labor relations. In these circumstances the Board's designation of a leaguewide bargaining unit as appropriate is reasonable, not arbitrary or capricious.

In making its decision, the Board expressly incorporated the reasons underlying its finding of a joint employer relationship. The Board emphasized in particular both the individual clubs' decision to form a League for the purpose of jointly controlling many of their activities, and the commissioner's power to disapprove contracts and exercise control over disciplinary matters. Under our "exceedingly narrow" standard of review, no arguments presented by petitioners require denial of enforcement of the bargaining order.

Thus the facts successfully refute any notion that because the teams compete on the field and in hiring, only team units are appropriate for collective bargaining purposes. Once a player is hired, his working conditions are significantly controlled by the League. Collective bargaining at that source of control would be the only way to effectively change by agreement many critical conditions of employment.

Order enforced.

NOTES AND QUESTIONS

1. *Why Not Require Clubs' Consent?* Note the *NASL* court's discussion of the Board's *Greenhoot* decision. The holding of this case, that competitive joint employers cannot be placed in the same multiemployer bargaining unit without each employer's consent, remains good law. Did the *NASL* court convincingly distinguish *Greenhoot*?

2. *Only Appropriate Unit?* Is a league-wide unit not only *an* appropriate unit for a professional sports league; is it also the *only* appropriate unit? Could the Board accept the request of a sports union for a single club and league, joint employer unit? Could it accept a request for a single club, single employer unit? Would a sports union have any reason for requesting less than a league-wide bargaining unit?

In seeking to end the 2012 NHL lockout, the players sought to invoke the jurisdiction of Canadian regulators over individual hockey teams located there. One effort was rejected when the Alberta Board exercised its discretion to decline to intervene because it found jurisdictional questions to be "ambiguous." Prominent labor expert Professor William Gould opined in similar proceedings in Quebec (unresolved due to the dispute's settlement) that collective bargaining has to be conducted on a league-wide basis to meet the interests of the parties, as well as of the public. Do you agree? Just as the United Steelworks are free to choose whether to engage in multi-employer bargaining with steel companies or to bargain individually, should the MLBPA be able to announce that the next round of bargaining will only be with individual clubs? Reconsider this question after studying the labor exemption to antitrust regulation treated in Chapter 7 below.

3. *Should All Athletes in Team Sports Be in the Same Bargaining Unit, Regardless of Tenure or Position?* The bargaining units in each professional league are defined to include all the positions on each club's rosters. Such units are undoubtedly included in those that are appropriate based on the Labor Board's traditional focus on whether proposed jobs in bargaining units share a "community of interests"—considering a number of factors including contact and interchange, common supervision, overlap in jobs, similar training and skills, and common working conditions. But given these factors, are these "all-position" units the only ones that could be appropriate, or might there be arguments for the appropriateness of smaller league-wide units, perhaps defined by tenure or position?

In 2019, a Board regional director summarily rejected on procedural grounds a petition to carve out running backs from the unit of all position players represented by the NFLPA. The petition claimed that running backs "have unique career structures, the current one-size fits all unit is inappropriate, and the new mini-max rookie wage contract is economically harmful to running backs but advantageous to quarterbacks." Did the petition present a compelling substantive argument for a separate running back unit?

4. *College Athlete Bargaining Units?* The General Counsel of the President Biden-appointed Labor Board has asserted that college athletes can be treated as employees subject to the Board's jurisdiction. If these athletes are so treated, would a single university unit be appropriate, notwithstanding significant regulation of collegiate athletics by the National Collegiate Athletics Association (NCAA) and various athletic conferences? Is it relevant that most universities with revenue producing sports programs, at least in football, are public universities beyond the Board's jurisdiction? *See Northwestern University,* 362 N.L.R.B. No. 167 (2015) (without deciding question of employee status, unanimous, full-Board opinion declines to assert jurisdiction over Northwestern football players seeking a unit for a single team that is regulated by NCAA and by a Big Ten conference otherwise consisting of public universities.) For further discussion, see Chapter 12 below.

E. UNION'S EXCLUSIVE BARGAINING AUTHORITY

If a majority of the employees choose to be represented for purposes of collective bargaining by a union, the union becomes the "exclusive representative of all the employees in the unit for purposes of collective bargaining" (§ 9(a) of the Labor Act). The Supreme Court, in its crucial decision in *J.I. Case Co. v. NLRB,* 321 U.S. 332 (1944), found a congressional intent underlying this provision to make the collective agreement prevail over any individually negotiated employment conditions:

> It is equally clear since the collective trade agreement is to serve the purpose contemplated by the Act, the individual contract cannot be effective as a waiver of any benefit to which the

employee otherwise would be entitled under the trade agreement. The very purpose of providing by statute for the collective agreement is to supersede the terms of separate agreements of employees with terms which reflect the strength and bargaining power and serve the welfare of the group. Its benefits and advantages are open to every employee of the represented unit, whatever the type or terms of his pre-existing contract of employment.

321 U.S. at 338.

MORIO v. NORTH AMERICAN SOCCER LEAGUE
501 F. Supp. 633 (S.D.N.Y. 1980)

MOTLEY, DISTRICT JUDGE.

[Following the NLRB's certification of the NASL Players Association as bargaining agent for NASL soccer players, the League sought (unsuccessfully) to challenge the Board's league-wide unit determination in court. While its appeal was pending, the League refused to bargain collectively with the union, and its clubs continued to negotiate new contracts with individual players. League authorities unilaterally instituted a number of changes in the general working conditions that were embodied in these contracts: the summer season was extended by two weeks; a new winter season was created; roster sizes were reduced from 30 to 26 players; and players were required to use the footwear selected by their club (absent consent by the latter). The Players Association filed unfair labor practice charges with the NLRB, alleging that this NASL conduct violated the union's exclusive bargaining authority under the NLRA; the Labor Board issued a complaint against the League and the Labor Board's General Counsel went to federal district court to secure a § 10(j) interim injunction against such negotiation of new individual contracts (by then covering 97% of league players).]

* * *

The unilateral changes which Respondents [the League and its clubs] admit have occurred since September 1, 1978, in the terms and conditions of employment, may violate the employer's obligations to bargain with the exclusive bargaining representative of the players. The duty to bargain carries with it the obligation on the part of the employer not to undercut the Union by entering into individual contracts with the employees. In *NLRB v. Katz*, 369 U.S. 736 (1962), the Supreme Court noted: "A refusal to negotiate in fact as to any subject which is within § 8(d) and about which the Union seeks to negotiate violates § 8(a)(5)."

[The judge first rejected the NASL owners' claim that they could legally refuse to negotiate at all with the players' union for the three years they had spent challenging its certification election. She then turned to the]

Respondents' most vigorous opposition, [which] comes in response to Petitioner's application for an order requiring Respondents to render voidable, at the option of the Union, all individual player contracts, whether entered into before or after the Union's certification on September 1, 1978. Respondents' claim that such power in the hands of the Union, a non-party to this action, would result in chaos in the industry and subject Respondents to severe economic loss and hardship since these individual contracts are the only real property of Respondents.

It should be noted, at the outset, that the relief requested by Petitioner is not a request to have all individual contracts declared null and void. It should be emphasized that Petitioner is not requesting that the "exclusive rights" provision of the individual contracts, which bind the players to their respective teams for a certain time, be rendered voidable. Moreover, the Board seeks an order requiring Respondents to maintain the present terms and conditions in effect until Respondents negotiate with the Union—except, of course, for the unilateral changes—unless and until an agreement or a good faith impasse is reached through bargaining with the Union. Petitioner does not, however, seek to rescind that unilateral provision which provided for the present summer schedule. The Board has consciously limited its request for relief to prevent any unnecessary disruption of Respondents' business. The Board is seeking to render voidable only those unilateral acts taken by the Respondents, enumerated above, which Respondents admit have in fact occurred.

These unilateral changes appear to modify all existing individual contracts entered into before September 1, 1978, in derogation of the Union's right to act as the exclusive bargaining agent of all employees in the unit.

The court finds that Petitioner is entitled to the temporary injunctive relief which it seeks with respect to all of the individual contracts. The individual contracts entered into since September 1, 1978, are apparently in violation of the duty of the Respondents to bargain with the exclusive bargaining representative of the players. The Act requires Respondents to bargain collectively with the Union. The obligation is exclusive. This duty to bargain with the exclusive representative carries with it the negative duty not to bargain with individual employees. *Medo Photo Supply Corp. v. NLRB,* 321 U.S. 678 (1944).

* * *

In *National Licorice Co. v. NLRB,* 309 U.S. 350 (1940), the Supreme Court held that the Board has the authority, even in the absence of the employees as parties to the proceeding, to order an employer not to enforce individual contracts with its employees which were found to have been in violation of the NLRA. Petitioner is seeking temporary relief to this effect as to those individual contracts entered into before September 1, 1978, as well as relief with respect to those contracts entered into prior to

September 1, 1978. The evidence discloses that Petitioner has reasonable cause to believe that Respondents have used, and will continue to use, the individual contracts entered into prior to September 1, 1978, to forestall collective bargaining.

[The court concluded that the Labor Board and the NASL Players Association were entitled to require NASL to "render voidable" the particular contract provisions that the union objected to—relief that "has been carefully tailored to avoid chaos in (the League's) industry and to avoid any economic hardship to (League members)."]

Injunction granted.

————

A union vested with exclusive bargaining authority under § 9(a) is entitled to eliminate all individual bargaining, even bargaining to secure better terms than the collectively negotiated minimum. As the Supreme Court explained in *J.I. Case, supra*:

> [I]t is urged that some employees may lose by the collective agreement, that an individual workman may sometimes have, or be capable of getting, better terms than those obtainable by the group and that his freedom of contract must be respected on that account. We are not called upon to say that under no circumstances can an individual enforce an agreement more advantageous than a collective agreement, but we find the mere possibility that such agreements might be made no ground for holding generally that individual contracts may survive or surmount collective ones. The practice and philosophy of collective bargaining looks with suspicion on such individual advantages. Of course, where there is great variation in circumstances of employment or capacity of employees, it is possible for the collective bargain to prescribe only minimum rates or maximum hours or expressly to leave certain areas open to individual bargaining. But except as so provided, advantages to individuals may prove as disruptive of industrial peace as disadvantages. They are a fruitful way of interfering with organization and choice of representatives; increased compensation, if individually deserved, is often earned at the cost of breaking down some other standard thought to be for the welfare of the group, and always creates the suspicion of being paid at the long range expense of the group as a whole. Such discriminations not infrequently amount to unfair labor practices. The workman is free, if he values his own bargaining position more than that of the group, to vote against representation; but the majority rules, and if it collectivizes the employment bargain, individual advantages or favors will generally in practice go in as a contribution to the

collective result. We cannot except individual contracts generally from the operation of collective ones because some may be more individually advantageous.

321 U.S. at 338–39.

Indeed, individual bargaining is unthinkable in most unionized industries. But collective bargaining in sports, as in the entertainment industry generally, has followed a different path, under which the labor agreement sets out guaranteed benefits and a minimum salary scale and then usually permits each player (or each movie star) to negotiate whatever extra remuneration the market will bear. Such individual freedom of contract operates at the sufferance of, and within parameters set by, the collective bargaining agreement—with the performer's agent serving, in a sense, as delegate for the union.

This free-market orientation first became pronounced in baseball after the free agency system was established in 1976. Not only have baseball salaries climbed dramatically higher, but also the salary range has become much wider; for example, in 2022 salaries ranged from the $700,000 minimum set forth in the parties' newly negotiated Basic Agreement, to Los Angeles Angels all-star Mike Trout's $37,166,667 salary. Nor are these figures just isolated extremes. In 1967, when Marvin Miller was appointed Executive Director of the MLBPA and set out to turn the organization into a true union, the average baseball salary was $19,000 a year and the median salary was $17,000; in 1976, just before free agency became operative, the average salary was $52,000, the median $40,000; but by the 2021 season, the median salary was less than 30% of the average salary. Thus, the outcome of sports collective bargaining is sharply different from what one finds in most unionized sectors, where the salary scale tends to tilt towards the average career veteran rather than the exceptional star.

————

NOTES AND QUESTIONS

1.   *Why Do Sports Unions Encourage Bargaining of Individual Player Contracts?* What explains the departure of sports unions from the typical union's negotiation of collective salary structures? Could such structures provide the players with salaries that are equal in the aggregate to the individually bargained salaries? How might the facilitation of individual bargaining rather than the use of collective salary structures affect the solidarity of the union members during collective bargaining negotiations or a work stoppage? How might this affect the political dynamics within the union and its leadership?

2.   *Collective Salary Structures in Bargaining in Sports.* On one occasion, a sports union sought to act like a mainstream labor union. During the 1982 negotiations in football, the NFL Players Association (NFLPA) under Ed Garvey unsuccessfully tried to establish a fixed-salary scale weighted

toward seniority and specific accomplishments. Garvey would have restructured the existing salary pattern that turns more on playing position (for example, quarterback as opposed to offensive lineman) or original draft position (for example, early in the first round rather than in a later round). Do you think Garvey's proposal would have secured the support of represented players in the long run? Why might the NFL have opposed the proposal?

After rejecting the effort of the NFLPA to institute a salary scale in the 1982 negotiations, the NFL five years later proposed a salary scale of its own, this time targeting rookies. The NFLPA (in return for somewhat relaxed veteran free agency) ultimately agreed to establish a separate salary pool for each team's annual crop of rookies. Each team was to divide up this amount in individual negotiations with its various draft picks. In 1995, though, the sports unions in both hockey and basketball used their exclusive bargaining authority rights to define a specific salary range that would be permitted for each pick in each round of the draft. Then, in 1998, the National Basketball Players Association (NBPA) became the first major sports union to agree to a cap, not just a floor, on individual player salaries—one that immediately limited such hoop greats as Tim Duncan and Kobe Bryant to $9 million in the year when they became free agents, rather than the $21 million a year deal that their counterpart Kevin Garnett had secured by signing his free agency contract just before the prior CBA had expired. Why might the NBPA have agreed to such a cap?

3. *Union Interest in Individual Contracts.* On one occasion, a sports union exercised its exclusive representative status to prevent a player from giving up any of his contract salary. In 2003, the Texas Rangers and Boston Red Sox negotiated a deal to trade Alex Rodriguez for Manny Ramirez. In order to limit its exposure under MLB's payroll tax, the Red Sox insisted that Rodriguez reduce his salary by a total of $29 million over the remaining seven years of his contract. Rodriguez (and his agent, Scott Boras) agreed. Undoubtedly, Rodriguez also felt that he could more than make up that reduction in salary by the increased value of his endorsement rights playing in Boston for a pennant contender.

The MLBPA, however, rejected the new player contract. Its contention was that the collective bargaining agreement did not permit individual players and clubs to agree to salary reductions; rather, it barred any salary reduction in a guaranteed contract unless the union was satisfied that the terms "actually or potentially provide additional benefits to the player." The MLBPA officials said they would let Rodriguez take a total seven year pay cut of $12 million (rather than the proposed $29 million) if the team would add to his contract a provision that allowed him to use the Red Sox name and logo in selling his personal publicity rights. While the team owners were fully prepared to agree to that latter term, they would not accept the additional $17 million financial cost (and potential salary tax). MLB Commissioner Bud Selig ultimately rejected the contract to avoid a union grievance and a subsequent arbitration.

Did the MLBPA best represent its membership by not allowing Alex Rodriguez to accept a reduction in his salary in order to facilitate his trade from the Rangers to the Red Sox? Suppose that rather than this Rodriguez-Red Sox deal, another player who had been paid $1.5 million annually under a multi-year contract largely to sit on his team's bench, told the union that he wanted to be traded to another lower-paying team where he could be the starting shortstop if he would agree to reduce his salary to $1.2 million a year? What should the MLBPA do, if anything?

F. DUTY TO BARGAIN IN GOOD FAITH

The Board's certification or an employer's recognition of a union as an exclusive bargaining agent imposes duties on both the employer and the union to bargain "collectively" with each other. Section 8(d) of the NLRA defines that obligation as follows:

> [T]o bargain collectively is . . . to meet at reasonable times and confer in good faith with respect to wages, hours, and other terms of employment, . . . but such obligation does not compel either party to agree to a proposal or require the making of a concession.

The principal focus of this duty is procedural, rather than substantive. As long as a party does not engage in *surface* bargaining, that is, go through the motions with no real intent to try to arrive at a settlement, the party is perfectly free to engage in *hard* bargaining and to not make concessions from its negotiating position. The statutory policy of free collective bargaining presumes that the ultimate way to break a deadlock at the bargaining table is through the economic pressure of a strike or a lockout or perhaps mere insistence, not through unfair labor practices or a petition of some sort in which one party tries to persuade the Labor Board that its position is more reasonable than the other side's. As the Supreme Court observed in *NLRB v. Insurance Agents' Int'l Union*, 361 U.S. 477 (1960):

> It must be realized that collective bargaining under a system where the Government does not attempt to control the results of negotiations, cannot be equated with an academic collective search for truth—or even with what might be thought to be the ideal of one. The parties . . . still proceed from contrary and to an extent antagonistic viewpoints and concepts of self-interest. The system has not reached the ideal of the philosophic notion that perfect understanding among people would lead to perfect agreement among them on values. The presence of economic weapons in reserve, and their actual exercise on occasion by the parties, is part and parcel of the system that the Wagner and Taft-Hartley Acts have recognized.

361 U.S. at 488–89. There is no better illustration of the Court's appraisal of collective bargaining than the sports world's experience with bargaining over free agency and salary caps during the last forty-five years.

While the law has adopted a hands-off attitude about the *content* of the collective bargain, it has been more interventionist in prescribing standards of *behavior* in the bargaining process. Perhaps the two most important doctrines are (i) an obligation of the employer (and, on occasion, the union) to supply all relevant information that is "needed by the bargaining representative for the proper performance of its duties," *see NLRB v. Acme Industrial Co.*, 385 U.S. 432, 435–36 (1967), and (ii) the obligation to refrain from unilateral changes in employment conditions, whether to the employees' benefit or detriment, at least until "impasse" has been reached in bargaining, *see NLRB v. Katz*, 369 U.S. 736, 743, 745 (1962). The assumption of the Supreme Court is that "freezing the status quo ante after a collective agreement has expired promotes industrial peace by fostering a non-coercive atmosphere that is conducive to serious negotiations on a new contract." *See Laborers Health & Welfare Trust v. Advanced Lightweight Concrete Co.*, 484 U.S. 539, 544 n. 6 (1988). Both doctrines require determining whether the issue in dispute falls within the phrase "terms and conditions of employment" under § 8(d); if the issue does not concern a term or condition, there is no obligation to provide information or to refrain from unilateral action.

The Board and the courts for several decades thus have made difficult substantive judgments about the meaning of the "terms and conditions" phrase, what is defined as the scope of "mandatory" bargaining. The important Supreme Court decision in *First National Maintenance Corp. v. NLRB*, 452 U.S. 666, 673 (1981), held that key management decisions "about the scope and direction of the enterprise," such as closings of facilities, are not mandatory subjects of bargaining, regardless of their direct impact on employee lives. The Court majority echoed the sentiment in Justice Stewart's concurring opinion in *Fibreboard Paper Products v. NLRB*, 379 U.S. 203, 223, 226 (1964), that § 8(d) does not detract from the prerogative of private business management under "the traditional principles of free enterprise" to make decisions that "lie at the core of entrepreneurial control." On the other hand, management's prerogative not to bargain about its entrepreneurial *decision*, for example, to close down a facility, does not relieve the employer of its duty to bargain with the union about the *effects* of that action on its employees. *See generally* Michael C. Harper, *Leveling the Road from* Borg-Warner to First National Maintenance: *the Scope of Mandatory Bargaining*, 68 VA. L. REV. 1447 (1982).

Bargaining about topics that are not *mandatory* is not *illegal*. Indeed, purely voluntary negotiation about *permissive* topics takes place regularly in different bargaining relationships, and each party can induce bargaining on a permissive topic by being more or less reasonable on a mandatory topic. But the line drawn between mandatory and permissive subjects is significant not only because the employer has no duty to discuss the latter topics (nor to supply information and to remain inactive about them), but also because the union is not entitled to insist—in particular, to the point of a strike—on bargaining about them. *See NLRB v. Wooster Division of Borg-Warner Corp.,* 356 U.S. 342 (1958).

Consider whether the following range of sports issues should be judged to be mandatory subjects for bargaining by owners with players.

(i)   Enlarging the regular schedule or playoffs, adopting interleague or international play, or realigning teams among the leagues and their divisions.

(ii)   Adding in the NL, or eliminating in the AL, the designated hitter in baseball.

(iii)   Instituting (or eliminating) overtime to break ties in hockey or football.

(iv)   Deciding to install artificial turf in football or baseball parks.

(v)   Using instant replay (here, consider whether mandatory bargaining required with either the players or the umpires association).

(vi)   Imposing time limits between pitches or between innings.

(vii)   Setting new rules regarding hand checking by defensive players in basketball.

(viii)   Altering the league's no gambling policies.

(ix)   Requiring players to stand at attention before fans during the playing of the national anthem.

(x)   Shifting some of a team's home games to a new location (*e.g.*, the Tampa Bar Rays playing several "home" games in Puerto Rico), as compared to full relocation of the team, or expansion into new cities or countries.

(xi)   Eliminating one or more teams in a league.

(xii)   Appointing or discharging the commissioner.

———————

The distinction between mandatory and permissive subjects proved determinative in the litigation that brought an end to the 1994–95 baseball strike. As noted above, the Labor Act requires management, even after the expiration of the collective bargaining agreement, to maintain the status quo on mandatory topics of bargaining until negotiations reach a genuine impasse. At that point management can implement the final offer it made to the union. On the other hand, if a bargaining topic is deemed a permissive subject of bargaining, management can unilaterally institute a change without violating the statute, and upon the expiration of the collective bargaining agreement, without violating the collective agreement.

In the early 1990s, baseball owners seemingly decided to reassert greater control over player salaries by enfeebling the MLBPA sufficiently to allow management to eliminate free agency and salary arbitration and install the kind of salary cap that was imposed by the other professional sports leagues. At this time, for purposes of determining salaries under the existing collective bargaining agreement, baseball players not under contract fell into three basic categories. Those in their first three seasons were limited to offers from their own team with a floor set by the CBA's guaranteed minimum amount; those players with three to six years of Major League service could have a neutral arbitrator assess and choose between their final salary proposal and the team's proposal; those with six or more years of Major League service were entitled to free agency bidding by any major league team.

The owners' first step toward overturning this system was to ensure that the commissioner would not attempt to intervene in collective bargaining as a neutral mediator. (Previously, commissioners had invoked their "best interest of baseball" powers to override owner tactics and preclude lockouts.) The owners fired Commissioner Fay Vincent and installed one of their number, Alan "Bud" Selig, the owner of the Milwaukee Brewers, as the acting commissioner. The owners then orchestrated a plan to negotiate with the MLBPA to the point of "impasse" when they would unilaterally install their new labor relations system and return the game to management predominance. In response to management's proposed changes, the MLBPA called a strike in August 1994, but management would not budge from its plan and Selig cancelled the World Series.

An essential part of the owners' plan was to hire "replacement" players who would maintain baseball until the union buckled. They contacted minor leaguers and recently retired players in preparation for spring training the following March. In mid-December 1994, the MLBPA made a new proposal to impose a significant "tax" on owners based on their total team salaries. The tax would deter (although not prohibit) individual clubs from spending freely on free agents because of the increased price of doing so.

This proposal did not satisfy the owners—it was not part of their strategy—and they declared that an "impasse" had been reached in bargaining. Baseball management then implemented its prior position on a salary cap and restricted free agency. The MLBPA responded by filing an unfair labor practice charge with the Labor Board claiming bad faith bargaining because of the unilateral change in terms and conditions of employment in the absence of a genuine impasse. Management restored the previous status quo after the Labor Board General Counsel made a tentative decision that the owners had violated the Labor Act and that a formal complaint should be issued. The General Counsel then held the Board's unfair labor practice proceedings in abeyance.

Just three days later, though, the owners informed the MLBPA that there would be no more negotiations between individual teams and players for new contracts. Instead, all player contracts for the upcoming season would have to be worked out between the owners' Player Relations Committee (PRC) and the MLBPA. In those negotiations, salary arbitration would not be available to any player, and the prior contractual ban against concerted action by owners or players would be revoked. The Association immediately filed new unfair labor practice charges against these three owner moves. President Clinton called both sides to the White House in an unsuccessful effort to secure a settlement.

In mid-March 1995, while the teams were conducting spring training with replacement squads (without a single crossover from major league strike rosters), the General Counsel of the NLRB issued a formal complaint against the owners' latest unilateral actions. The Labor Board voted 3–2 to authorize the General Counsel to seek a preliminary injunction in district court barring the owners' action. The owners did not try to defend this unilateral action on the basis that an impasse had been reached on these matters. Instead, the PRC's claim was that their three unilateral changes involved *permissive*, not *mandatory*, topics and thus their changes were not constrained by the duty to bargain in good faith. Following is the opinion by future Supreme Court Justice, and avid baseball fan, Sonia Sotomayor, hearing her first labor case on the federal district court.

SILVERMAN V. MAJOR LEAGUE BASEBALL PLAYER RELATIONS COMMITTEE

880 F. Supp. 246 (S.D.N.Y.), *aff'd*, 67 F.3d 1054 (2d Cir. 1995)

SOTOMAYOR, DISTRICT JUDGE.

* * *

Collective bargaining in the context of professional sports presents issues different from most other contexts. On the one hand, the talent of an individual athlete can provide him with extraordinary bargaining power, but on the other hand, a player may sell his talent only to a circumscribed group of owners, who have something akin to monopoly power in the sport at issue. These circumstances in professional sports have given rise to the development of the reserve/free agency system, which, perhaps not surprisingly, is quite different from other models of collective bargaining in less specialized and unique industries.

To look for guidance, then, in deciding whether the Board had reasonable cause for making its determination that the provisions changed by the Owners were mandatory, I find most helpful precedent that involves professional sports. *Accord, Wood v. Nat'l Basketball Ass'n*, 809 F.2d 954, 961 (2d Cir. 1987) (collective bargaining between athletes and their leagues "raises numerous problems with little or no precedent in standard industrial relations"). And in the sports context, courts have overwhelmingly held that the constituent parts of reserve/free agency systems are mandatory, not permissive, subjects of bargaining.

For example, this Circuit held in *Wood* that the agreement between professional basketball players and team owners "is a unique bundle of compromises," and matters such as salary caps, minimum individual salaries, fringe benefits, minimum aggregate team salaries, guaranteed revenue-sharing, and first refusal provisions are all mandatory subjects of bargaining, as "each of them is intimately related to 'wages, hours, and other terms and conditions of employment.'" *Id.* at 961–62. Likewise, in *Mackey v. Nat'l Football League*, 543 F.2d 606, 615 (8th Cir. 1976), cert. dismissed, 434 U.S. 801 (1977), the Eighth Circuit held that the Rozelle Rule, even though it does not on its face deal with wages, hours, and other terms and conditions of employment, is a mandatory subject of bargaining because it "operates to restrict a player's ability to move from one team to another and depresses player salaries." *See also, Powell v. Nat'l Football League*, 930 F.2d 1293, 1298–99 (8th Cir. 1989) (agreements establishing first refusal and compensation system are mandatory subjects).

* * *

Maintaining the reserve/free agency systems in the interim between collective bargaining agreements does not alter the rights of Owners to have the PRC represent them for purposes of negotiating a successor agreement or to continue to oppose the inclusion of the systems in any successor agreement. The Owners can, if they successfully bargain, end the free agency and salary arbitration systems, exclude the anti-collusion provision, and create an entirely new system. What they cannot do is alter particular individual's wages until the system is changed by agreement or until the parties negotiate to impasse. That is the nub of all wage negotiations which are inherently mandatory subjects of bargaining. It must be remembered that many employers are forced to continue sometimes onerous and debilitating wage obligations until the collective bargaining process runs its course, just as many employees may earn less than they would in a system that more closely duplicates the free market. Having freely entered into the free agency and reserve systems in their Basic Agreement, the Owners are bound to that system until they bargain in good faith to an impasse.

In view of the abundant case law in the professional sports context that has found that constituent parts of the reserve/free agency system are mandatory subjects of collective bargaining, I find that the Board had substantial reasonable cause to conclude, and a substantial likelihood of success ultimately in establishing, that the unilateral changes made by the Owners to the free agency system before impasse violated the rule against changes to mandatory subjects of bargaining. In summary, the Board has clearly met its injunctive remedy standard in demonstrating that the Owners committed an unfair labor practice by their unilateral abrogation of Article XX(F) and the free agency system.

For substantially similar reasons, I find that salary arbitration for reserve players is also a mandatory part of the collective bargaining process between the Players and the Owners. The Owners argue that their salary arbitration system is indistinguishable from interest arbitration clauses, which are generally classified as permissive subjects of bargaining. Thus, the Owners contend, they have no statutory obligation to preserve salary arbitration until the formation of a new collective bargaining agreement.

The Second Circuit has recognized two basic types of arbitration in the labor context: interest arbitration and rights arbitration. *New York Typographical Union No. 6 v. Printers League Section of the Assoc. of the Graphic Arts*, 919 F.2d 3, 3 n. 2 (2d Cir. 1990). Interest arbitration "concerns disputes over terms of new or renewal contracts." *Id.*; *see also Local 58, Int'l Brotherhood of Electrical Workers v. Southeastern Michigan Chapter, Nat'l Electrical Contractors Ass'n, Inc.*, 43 F.3d 1026, 1030 (6th Cir. 1995) (interest arbitrator acts as legislator in fashioning new contractual obligations, rather than as judicial officer who concentrates on construing terms of existing agreement). Rights arbitration, in contrast, is for disputes "over the interpretation or application of a contract." *Printers League*, 919 F.2d at 3 n.2. Because interest arbitration clauses involve "a mechanism for resolving disputes which may arise as to the terms of future contracts," as opposed to existing terms and conditions of employment, they are a non-mandatory topic of bargaining. *Sheet Metal Workers Local Union No. 20 and George Koch Sons, Inc.*, 306 NLRB 834 (1992).

I agree with the Board's conclusion that the salary arbitration clause at issue here is not a traditional interest arbitration clause. The distinction blurred by the Owners' argument is that new future contractual obligations are not being created by the salary arbitrator. By the time a player and owner go to salary arbitration, a UPC [Uniform Player Contract], created by the terms of the Basic Agreement, has already been entered into by the parties. The only item missing from the executed contract is a dollar amount. The Owners cannot escape the plain and unambiguous language of Article VI(F)(6), which provides:

> Form of submission: The Player and the Club shall each submit to the arbitrator and exchange with each other in advance of the hearing single salary figures for the coming season (which need not be figures offered during the prior negotiations). At the hearing, the Player and the Club shall deliver to the arbitrator a Uniform Player's Contract executed in duplicate, complete except

for the salary figure to be inserted in paragraph 2. Upon
submission of the salary issue to arbitration by either Player or
Club, the Player shall be regarded as a signed Player. . . .

Basic Agreement, Article VI(F)(g) (emphasis added); *see also id.* at Article
VI(F)(5) (within 24 hours of hearing arbitrator shall insert salary figure
awarded in the duplicate UPC's delivered to him or her). Before the
arbitrator rules, there is no question that the player will provide his
services to the club for a specified period of time and that the club will pay
for those services. The arbitrator's only task is, literally, to fill in the blank
where the salary figure goes.

Even if the salary arbitration clause contained in the Basic Agreement
is an interest arbitration clause, however, I also agree with the Board's
reasoning in *Sea Bay Manor Home for Adults*, 253 NLRB 739 (1980) and
Columbia Univ. in the City of New York, 298 NLRB 941 (1990) that interest
arbitration clauses can survive the expiration of collective bargaining
agreements where the clauses

> [are] so intertwined with and inseparable from the mandatory
> terms and conditions for the contract currently being negotiated
> as to take on the characteristics of the mandatory subjects
> themselves.

The essence of the reasoning in *Sea Bay* and *Columbia Univ.* is that in
some industries the result of collective bargaining is not to stop talking in
the future about a dispute but a recognition that the best continuing
process for the parties to establish wages is in arbitration. In these
situations, a salary arbitration is a current term of employment. That is
the situation in baseball. Salary arbitration is the collectively bargained
wage in the parties' Agreement, and the Board's view of it as such is not
clearly or otherwise erroneous. For the foregoing reasons, the Board has
sustained its burden of proving that the Owners committed unfair labor
practices both by eliminating Article XX(F) of the free agency system and
the salary arbitration provisions of the Basic Agreement.

* * *

[The court then turned to the question of whether an interim
injunction was warranted for this violation of the Labor Act. One key value
that seemed to require such immediate legal action was the public's
interest in more productive and peaceful collective bargaining in baseball.]

. . . This strike has captivated the public's attention, given the
popularity of the sport as well as the protracted nature and
well-documented bitterness of the strike. Thus, this strike is about more
than just whether the Players and Owners will resolve their differences. It
is also about how the principles embodied by federal labor law operate. In
a very real and immediate way, this strike has placed the entire concept of
collective bargaining on trial. It is critical, therefore, that the Board ensure

that the spirit and letter of federal labor law be scrupulously followed. If the Board is unable to enforce the NLRA, public confidence in the collective bargaining process will be permanently and severely undermined. . . . Issuing the injunction before Opening Day is important to ensure that the symbolic value of that day is not tainted by an unfair labor practice and the NLRB's inability to take effective steps against its perpetuation.

* * *

[The private interests of players was also a sufficient ground for injunctive relief. In particular, the judge was not persuaded by the owners' argument that monetary damages for lost pay would be sufficient to rectify any losses suffered by affected players. For example, with respect to the obstacles erected to free agent movement,]

. . . [s]alary is just one factor a free agent considers when seeking and accepting offers. A free agent may wish to join a team because of personal reasons such as family considerations, or because of promises of more playing time. Likewise, a free agent may select a team that pays less money but whose coaching staff and team roster make it a World Series contender. . . . The protections of the NLRA extend to non-monetary bargaining topics that are "terms and conditions of employment." . . . In professional baseball, whether to leave a team, where to go and why are of "deep concern" to the affected players and the loss of those choices in the terms and conditions of employment cannot be adequately recompensed by money.

* * *

[While salary arbitration seemed to be concerned purely with money (as the decision had asserted earlier), the judge believed it would be impossible to reconstruct later what would have been the appropriate arbitration verdicts. One key reason was that the systems of free agency and salary arbitration were "inextricably intertwined," such that illegal alteration of one such feature in the baseball players' market would inevitably change the product of the other.]

Similarly, to the extent the salary arbitration system is intimately intertwined with the choice for both owners and players between free agency or arbitration, it is nearly impossible to reconstruct retrospectively the factors that would have influenced each side's decision at the time of election. Hence, even though it is easier later to reconstruct the actual process of salary arbitration and more precisely determine a lost wage from that process, monetary damages are insufficient to recompense for the harm caused in eliminating the salary arbitration process as a choice in the integrated reserve/free agency systems.

* * *

Thus, a poisoning of the free agency bargaining process will also affect the wage negotiations of reserve and salary arbitration players. Conversely, the loss of salary arbitration in the reserve system skews the choice of free agency rights. The unusual wage structure in this monopoly industry makes it extraordinarily difficult if not nearly impossible to reconstruct past market conditions for purposes of retroactive damage calculations.

[Since monetary damages would be too difficult to ascertain after the fact, injunctive relief was needed before the harm was done.]

Injunction granted.

———

Judge Sotomayor rendered her decision on Friday, March 31, just before opening day of the 1995 season. The injunction transformed the situation on the field: this time the two sides agreed to "Play Ball!" The players voted on Saturday to end their strike and return to work, and the owners voted on Sunday to cancel the opening game scheduled for that night with replacements (generally referred to by unionists as "scabs"). Instead, the beginning of the regular season was postponed until April 26, and the next three weeks were devoted to signing and training the regular players.

Later that fall, the Second Circuit affirmed Judge Sotomayor's decision. *See Silverman v. MLBPRC*, 67 F.3d 1054 (2d Cir. 1995). In his opinion for the panel, Judge Winter dismissed the clubs' argument that an injunction compelling the PRC and the Clubs to observe the anti-collusion and free agency provisions of the Basic Agreement infringed on their right as a multiemployer group to bargain through an exclusive representative:

Free agency and the ban on collusion are one part of a complex method—agreed upon in collective bargaining—by which each major league player's salary is determined under the Basic Agreement. They are analogous to the use of seniority, hours of work, merit increases, or piece work to determine salaries in an industrial context. The PRC and the Clubs describe free agency and the ban on collusion as provisions undermining their right to select a joint bargaining representative because those provisions entail individual contracts with clubs. However, the argument ignores the fact that free agency is simply a collectively bargained method of determining individual salaries for one group of players. The anti-collusion provision is not designed to prevent the PRC from representing the Clubs. Rather, that provision guarantees that free agency will be a reality when permitted by the Basic Agreement. The injunction thus does not in any way prevent the PRC from bargaining as the Clubs' exclusive representative with the Players Association over the elimination of free agency in its entirety or for a modified version of the same, and thereafter from implementing any proposals incorporated into a collective bargaining agreement.

Id. at 1060.

There were no further work stoppages during the 1995 and 1996 seasons, and in December 1996, the two sides finally reached a settlement of their three-year labor dispute.

_____

NOTES AND QUESTIONS

1.   *Mandatory Subjects?* Do you agree with Judge Sotomayor's judgment that the freedom of individual clubs to sign players not under contract was a mandatory topic of bargaining? With her similar judgment regarding salary arbitration for individual players, as contrasted with interest arbitration for future collective agreements? With her similar judgment about the clubs' and players' earlier undertaking not to act "in concert" in individual salary negotiations?

2.   *Proper Doctrinal Compromise?* As a matter of general labor law policy, why should there be a bar on unilateral changes in working conditions, even when proposed at the bargaining table, until after an impasse has been reached in negotiations? Alternatively, why should the law allow unilateral changes even after impasse, rather than require the parties to reach a compromise? Should lockouts (and strikes) also be prohibited before impasse?

G. ECONOMIC CONFLICT IN SPORTS LABOR RELATIONS

Under federal labor law, the principal means for breaking deadlocks at the bargaining table are the economic pressures of strikes or lockouts, not the legal pressures of an unfair labor practice charge. Section 7 of the original Labor Act protects employees' right "to engage in concerted activities for the purpose of collective bargaining"—which of course includes engaging in strikes. After thirty years of doctrinal evolution, the Supreme Court read the Act to afford employers a reciprocal economic weapon—a lockout of their employees to force the union to compromise at the bargaining table. *See American Ship Building Co. v. NLRB*, 380 U.S. 300 (1965). As MLB's lockout of players during the 2021–22 off-season demonstrates, the employer's lockout weapon, like the union's strike weapon, can be used before impasse.

For most labor negotiations, the balance of power is also affected by another important labor law principle. Since a pronouncement in dicta in the Supreme Court's decision in *NLRB v. Mackay Radio and Telegraph*, 304 U.S. 333 (1938), employers free of associated unfair labor practices have been free to attempt to continue operating during an economic strike by hiring replacement workers who are promised that strikers will not bump them out of their jobs when the strike ends. For a period in the late twentieth century, the issue of "permanent" status for strike replacements was a prominent political issue. The use of permanent replacements, however, has never been an issue for professional athletes in the major sports leagues. Do you understand why?

The collapse of the NFLPA strike in 1987 after the NFL's three-week use of replacement players shows that a professional sports league's ability to recruit and use *temporary* replacements who have no guarantees of job security nonetheless may be a sufficient counter weapon. An employer can hire such temporary replacements even when it is the *employer* that initiates the work stoppage through a lockout. *See Local 825 International Union of Operating Engineers v. NLRB (Harter Equipment)*, 829 F.2d 458 (3d Cir. 1987).

National labor law, as explained above, does not find inconsistent with good faith bargaining employers' and unions' use of disruptive economic weapons to secure a contract settlement on their preferred terms. Nevertheless, the Board does find certain employer responses to protected strike activity to constitute impermissible retaliation against the exercise of statutory rights. An interesting exploration of where a line between such retaliation and legitimate self-defense should be located is this decision by the Labor Board involving the troubled bargaining relationship in football in the 1980s.

NFL MANAGEMENT COUNCIL AND NFLPA
309 N.L.R.B. 78 (1992)

[After its experience with the lengthy players strike in 1982, the NFL Management Council (NFLMC) decided that if the NFLPA went on strike during the 1987 contract negotiations, the league would continue its regular schedule using replacement players. The Council Executive Committee (CEC) and its Executive Director, Jack Donlan, asked CEC official (and former NFL quarterback) Eddie LeBaron, to coordinate this effort under which the clubs would rely mainly on players who were at their training camps in August that year but who had failed to make the regular roster. The NFL players did go on strike after the third game of the 1987 season. After canceling the following week's games, the NFL clubs were able to present replacement games in each of the next two weeks. The fact that these games were played induced a considerable number of striking players to cross their union teammates' picket line and return to work. The pressures felt by the general union membership forced the Association to call off the strike and send all the players back to work on Thursday, October 15th. Pursuant to the league's labor policy, however, all the clubs refused to use any of their striking veterans for that weekend's games, because these players had not reported by 1:00 p.m. on Wednesday. At the same time, the clubs used replacement players who signed as late as 4:00 p.m. on Saturday, October 17th for that Sunday's games (or by 4:00 p.m. Monday for the Monday night game). The NFLPA then filed unfair labor charges with the Labor Board on the ground that this NFL policy discriminated against those players who had exercised their statutory right to strike, and thus deprived strikers of one-sixteenth of their annual salaries for the sixteen-game season.]

* * *

The Supreme Court has recognized that "there are some practices which are inherently so prejudicial to union interests and so devoid of significant economic justification . . . that the employer's conduct carries with it an inference of unlawful intent so compelling that it is justifiable to disbelieve the employer's protestations of innocent purpose." *American Ship Building Co. v. NLRB*, 380 U.S. 300 (1965). If an employer's conduct falls within this category, "the Board can find an unfair labor practice even if the employer introduces evidence that the conduct was motivated by business considerations." *NLRB v. Great Dane Trailers*, 388 U.S. 26, 34 (1967).

On the other hand, if the impact on employee rights of the discriminatory conduct is:

> comparatively slight, an antiunion motivation must be proved to sustain the charge if the employer has come forward with evidence of legitimate and substantial business justifications for the conduct. Thus, in either situation, once it has been proved that the employer engaged in discriminatory conduct which could have adversely affected employee rights to some extent, the burden is upon the employer to establish that it was motivated by legitimate objectives since proof of motivation is most accessible to him.

Id. at 34.

Applying these principles to this case, we find as an initial matter that the Wednesday deadline rule clearly constitutes discriminatory conduct which adversely affects employee rights. On its face, the rule discriminates against strikers by applying different, and more stringent, standards for eligibility to participate in NFL games (and to be paid for such participation). Moreover, the rule also adversely affects one of the most significant rights protected by the Act—the right to strike. The Board and the courts, applying the principles of *Great Dane*, have long recognized that the right to strike includes the right to full and complete reinstatement upon unconditional application to return. *NLRB v. Fleetwood Trailer Co.*, 389 U.S. 375, 380–381 (1967); *see also Laidlaw Corp.*, 171 NLRB 1366, 1368–1369 (1968), *enf'd.*, 414 F.2d 99 (7th Cir. 1969), cert. denied 397 U.S. 920 (1970).

As in *Laidlaw*, the Respondents—in reliance on their Wednesday reporting deadline—offered the striking employees who reported for work on October 15 "less than the rights accorded by full reinstatement" (*i.e.*, the right to participate in the games scheduled for October 18–19 and to be paid for those games). Thus, the Wednesday deadline adversely affected the striking employees in the exercise of their right to strike or to cease participating in the strike, by prohibiting the full and complete reinstatement, for the October 18–19 games, of those employees who chose to return to work after the Respondents' deadline had passed.

* * *

The Respondents assert that the Wednesday deadline was justified by the Clubs' need for sufficient time to prepare returning players for game conditions. In this regard, the Respondents presented evidence that the strikers' physical condition would be expected to deteriorate as the strike progressed. In addition, NFL Management Council official Eddie LeBaron testified that players could not maintain their "football condition" without participating in practices involving physical contact. The Respondents also assert that they particularly did not wish to risk injuries to so-called franchise players.

The Respondents also assert that the rule is justified by their goal of ensuring that each Club operates from the same competitive position. Thus, the Wednesday deadline would give each Club the same amount of preparation time with returning players, prevent situations in which a replacement squad was "mismatched" against a squad composed of veterans who had reported late in the week, and ensure that Clubs could prepare for specific players during the Wednesday and Thursday practices when game plans were typically practiced.

Finally, the Respondents assert that the Wednesday deadline was justified in light of substantial administrative difficulties allegedly posed if strikers returned at a late date in the week . . .

In evaluating the Respondents' justifications, we initially note the unprecedented nature of the Wednesday deadline and the absence of any evidence that the Respondents have imposed a deadline of this type on employees outside of a strike setting. In particular, the record shows that players who withheld their services in pursuit of individual goals (*i.e.*, players holding out for a more lucrative contract) are not subject to comparable restraints on their status on their return. Rather, such players are eligible to play immediately so long as they are included in the Club's active roster. If the Club determines that the player is not in shape to play, he may be placed on an Exempt list, as noted above. However, there is no automatic disqualification from participation in NFL games, or from being paid for a game while on the Exempt list, as was the case with the striking employees in 1987. This is so whether or not the individual is considered a "franchise player." Likewise, after the 1982 strike, players were immediately restored to their prestrike status—including players who did not report or practice until the Thursday prior to the next weekend's games. . . .

It is undisputed that the Wednesday deadline was only applicable to striking players. The Respondents could and did sign nonstrikers to contracts subsequent to the date the strikers were declared ineligible; the nonstrikers were eligible to play in and were paid for the October 18–19 games. . . .

Under these circumstances, we find that the Respondents have not established legitimate and substantial justifications for the deadline rule. While it may be true that some striking employees' physical conditioning declined during the strike, the same considerations were present in the case of holdouts and of replacement players. Likewise, safety concerns did not preclude the immediate reinstatement of the striking players in 1982, even though they had been out for 57 days, while the 1987 strike lasted only 25 days. . . .

We also find that the Respondents' asserted competitiveness concerns are unpersuasive. Although the Respondents were entitled to ensure that all clubs operated under the same rules, adopting a deadline which discriminated against strikers was unnecessary to the achievement of this goal. The Respondents' argument that Clubs needed the practice time provided by the Wednesday deadline to prepare the strikers to play (and, for the purpose of those practices, needed to know who would be playing for its opponent) is contradicted by their willingness to allow nonstrikers with substantially less preparation time to play in those games. Moreover, the Respondents' claim that late-returning strikers would have a disproportionate impact on the game unless Clubs had an opportunity to prepare their players to face them would seem to contradict their prior claim that these same players were so out of shape that it would be unsafe to play them. Again, in the case of returning holdouts, replacement players, and the players returning from the 1982 strike, competitiveness concerns did not dictate the imposition of an eligibility deadline like the Wednesday deadline at issue here. We find that such concerns did not justify that deadline in 1987 either.

In addition, we find that the logistical and administrative burden of reinstating the strikers does not justify the rule either. In this regard, the Respondents' arguments are premised entirely on the burden of reinstating the entire 1100 player complement, even though the rule on its face would apply to a single striker who elected to return to work. The Respondents provide no justification for the application of the rule in these circumstances.[24] We also note that the Respondents maintained a

---

[24]   Indeed, we note that the deadline rule was anomalous in other respects as well. Thus, as the judge noted, it was applied to preclude even specialty players such as kickers from participation in the games, notwithstanding the lack of any evidence that the Respondents'

substantial complement of replacement players well after the strikers had been fully reinstated. Accordingly, we find that any administrative burden associated with maintaining two separate squads for the games on October 18–19 is not a legitimate and substantial justification for the Wednesday deadline.

* * *

Complaint upheld.

———

The NLRB directed NFL teams to compensate each striking player for the salary lost (plus interest) as a result of this unfair labor practice—estimated to total $30 million for 1,100 players. In that same first week in October 1992, a jury in an antitrust suit found the NFL liable for $30 million in trebled damages for having imposed a $1,000-a-week cap on salaries payable to 235 development squad players. Just a few months earlier, the NFL had lost its final appeal of another $30 million judgment for disputed contributions (and interest) payable to the players' pension fund. *See Bidwill v. Garvey*, 943 F.2d 498 (4th Cir. 1991). As part of a class action settlement of broader free agency-salary cap issues in January 1993, the NFL agreed to pay the players the bulk of the sums awarded by the Board and the jury in the *NFLMC* and *Bidwill* cases, respectively. The development squad antitrust case eventually made its way to the Supreme Court, with consequences considered in Chapter 7.

———

NOTES AND QUESTIONS

1.   *Treatment of "Injured Reserve" Players?* In the portion of the *NFL Management Council* decision excerpted above, the Board ruled that players who were on the active roster when the strike began were entitled to be paid for the "deadline games" played after the strike ended, despite the League's contention that they would not be ready to play that weekend. Therefore, players who were on "injured reserve" when the strike began and ended—and who were paid their normal salaries before the strike—were even more clearly entitled to payment for the "deadline games," since there was no issue about their readiness to play. But should these players also have been entitled to be paid for games cancelled or played during the strike? Does the answer to this question depend on whether injured reserve players also were on strike? If so, how would you determine whether an injured player was on strike? If you were

_____

asserted justifications applied in their case. Likewise, the rule was applied to players on injured reserve throughout the strike even though those players would not have been eligible in any event and the only effect of the Wednesday deadline was to prevent them from receiving compensation to which they would otherwise have been entitled as injured players. The Wednesday deadline was also applied to players whose next scheduled game was on Monday, October 19 even though they had as much time to prepare for a Sunday game. The Respondents admit that safety or logistical reasons could not justify the application of the rule to these individuals.

a Players Association official, would you encourage injured players to "report" for work during a strike or to maintain "solidarity" with the striking players?

2.   *What if a Common Reporting Deadline?* How could the NFL Management Council have avoided the unfair labor practice charge? Could it have simply required all players—strikers and replacements as well—to report by the same deadline, whether Wednesday or some other day of the week? What would the Labor Board have decided if those were the facts?

3.   *Work Stoppage Strategy in Sports.* Consider the broader industrial relations factors that influence the protagonists in deciding how to exercise their statutory rights in a sports labor dispute.

a.   Why did the baseball players choose to strike in August 1994 (in late-season), and the hockey owners choose to lock out in October 1995 (at the start of their season)? Why have all work stoppages in professional sports leagues since 1994 been lockouts during the off-season or at the start of the season? Does your answer suggest that there may never be another player strike?

b.   Why did MLB Commissioner Rob Manfred announce the lockout of baseball players several weeks into the off-season on December 2, 2021, and then wait six weeks to present a new proposal for a new agreement? Note that during the off-season the players negotiate new individual agreements but are not paid.

c.   Why were replacement players used during the 1987 football strike but not used in either the 1994 hockey lockout or the 1998 hockey and basketball work stoppages? Further, why were replacement players planned for baseball in the spring of 1995 before litigation aborted those plans?

d.   Why is it that football stars like Tony Dorsett, Joe Montana, and Lawrence Taylor chose to cross the players' picket line to play in replacement games in October 1987, but baseball stars like Ken Griffey, Jr., Frank Thomas, and Greg Maddux made it clear they would not do that in April 1995? (Indeed, Cal Ripken announced that he would give up his chance to break Lou Gehrig's historic consecutive games streak, rather than break his commitment to his Association teammates.) Are the explanations to be found in the structures or the cultures of the respective sports?

4.   *Service Time Versus Pay During Strike.* Why did the MLBPA make it an absolute condition to settling their three-year dispute with baseball owners in December 1996 that the latter agree to count as player "service time" the period lost because of the strike late in the 1994 season and early in 1995? Is there any difference between earning pay during a strike (which the players union did not insist upon) and earning service credit for eligibility for salary arbitration and free agency?

————

Unlike the NFL (but like the NHL and the NBA), Major League Baseball is a North American league with franchises in Toronto and previously in Montreal. The fact that a league does most of its business in the United States does not insulate it from Canadian law governing that part of its operations (just as U.S. law governs Japanese auto manufacturers for their American operations). Canadian labor law is largely within the legislative authority of provinces, such as Ontario and Quebec. Unlike the constitutional situation in the United States, the fact that a manufacturer may have plants in different provinces does not put its labor relations within the Canadian national government's authority.

The major practical significance of this constitutional situation is that the labor laws of several provinces (though not yet the Canada Labor Code) have barred use of *temporary*, as well as *permanent*, replacements in legal strikes and lockouts. That is why the Toronto Blue Jays (whose home is in Ontario) could not have used replacements for their striking players in 1995 in games played in the SkyDome (although the Montreal Expos could have because the MLBPA was not certified in Quebec). As events transpired following the *Silverman* ruling in the spring of 1995, Ontario's replacement ban never did figure directly in the League's bargaining dispute and eventual settlement with the MLBPA.

The Ontario law, however, did come into play at the end of April 1995, because the owners had begun their season with replacements for the umpires they had locked out that winter. Thus, the Umpires Association filed an unfair labor practice complaint with the Ontario Labor Board. This complaint posed the intriguing legal questions whether the umpires were employed just by the American League (based in New York) and not jointly by the Blue Jays, and even if so, whether Ontario law barred use of replacements for U.S. employees performing their regular duties in Ontario. (The flip side of that issue was whether the Blue Jays could legally use replacements for the regular players they employed in Ontario to play games outside Ontario, as the Jays did during spring training in Florida in 1995.) A panel of the Ontario Board delivered an expedited ruling in favor of the Umpires Association and barred future use of replacements in the SkyDome. The issue was rendered moot by settlement of the bargaining dispute just a few days later, but many attributed the difficulties caused by this Ontario law as being a major factor in forcing MLB to make critical concessions. This issue of Canadian labor law is potentially important for the future of North American labor relations in professional baseball, hockey, and basketball.

NOTES AND QUESTIONS

1. *How Should Labor Law Treat Replacements?* American labor law continues to permit permanent replacements based on the principal argument that employers need the permanent replacement option to be able to recruit competent workers to keep operating during a strike, and, as a result, maintain a fair balance of bargaining power in their labor disputes. In Canada, the

argument in favor of banning even temporary replacements is that blocking the employer from continuing to operate while legally striking (or locked-out) employees are out of work is necessary to maintain a fair balance of bargaining power in the same disputes. How would you appraise those competing positions about the role of law in labor disputes, based on the planned effort to use replacements in baseball in 1995 and their actual use in football during the 1987 NFL strike?

2.   *Union Treatment of Replacements During Strike.* Employees not only have a legal right to strike; they also have a right *not* to strike, free of retaliation from their union. The latter legal rule, however, does not preclude nonthreatening verbal expressions of displeasure by members of sports (and other labor) unions against "scabs" or replacements, during and after the strike.

3.   *Disparate Treatment of League Reprisals Against Dissident Owners?* A similar issue can confront owners involved in multi-employer bargaining disputes. In baseball, for example, Peter Angelos, who had represented unions in his law practice, decided not to allow his Baltimore Orioles to play games with replacements, partly because of his concern for Cal Ripken's historic pursuit of Lou Gehrig's record for consecutive games played. Some owners suggested that Angelos and the Orioles might be penalized—indeed, might have the franchise put into trusteeship—for violating the decision made by the rest of the owners. The Labor Act, which grants affirmative rights just to employees, not employers (or unions), does not prohibit such league reprisals against owner-employers, as it prohibits certain union reprisals, including fines, against player-employees who cross their teammates' picket lines, at least after resigning from the union. Is it players or owners who benefit the most from such disparate protection of dissidents in labor-management conflicts?

4.   *Preemption of Regulatory but Not Proprietary State Action.* In the spring of 1995, both the City of Baltimore and the State of Maryland enacted legislation that barred use of replacement players in Camden Yards (in order to head off any overruling of Angelos' decision by his fellow baseball owners). A number of Supreme Court decisions have made it clear that the employer's right to use replacements under federal labor law preempts any state laws to the contrary. *See, e.g., Golden State Transit Corp. v. City of Los Angeles,* 475 U.S. 608 (1986). The Maryland legislators said, though, that they were acting not in a regulatory, but in a proprietary, capacity to protect the state's and city's investment in its Camden Yards stadium. This distinction was based on the Supreme Court's allowance of state efforts to achieve labor peace on its own construction projects, *see Building & Construction Trades Council v. Associated Builders & Contractors,* 507 U.S. 218 (1993). Do you think the distinction should make a difference in the legal result in this case? Suppose, alternatively, that a city like San Francisco had taken the position in 1995 that the use of replacements by the Giants violated the terms of its lease for its public stadium, requiring the club "to field a team of major league baseball players in accordance with major league rules." Is that state action preempted?

5. *Third Party Contracts.* What are the obligations of teams using replacements to their season ticket-holders, broadcast stations, and concessionaires with whom the teams contract to deliver "major league baseball?" Are the owners permitted to deem any games played in their facilities to be "major league," whatever the quality of replacement players (or umpires)?

H. DUTY OF FAIR REPRESENTATION

During the same term that the Supreme Court delineated the scope of a union's statutorily conferred authority as exclusive bargaining representative in its *J.I. Case* decision, *supra*, the Court in *Steele v. Louisville & Nashville R.R. Co.*, 323 U.S. 192 (1944), held that any such statutory authority must implicitly create a duty of fair representation (DFR) owed by the union to individual employees. *Steele* was a Railway Labor Act case involving egregious union race discrimination. But the Court soon held that the Labor Act imposed the same duty by virtue of the exclusive bargaining authority it conferred. In *Vaca v. Sipes*, 386 U.S. 171 (1967), the Court first articulated its most authoritative description of this duty, stressing its limited scope: "[A] breach of the statutory duty of fair representation occurs only when a union's conduct toward a member of the collective bargaining unit is arbitrary, discriminatory, or in bad faith." This same standard applies for union negotiation of collective bargaining agreements as well as for union implementation of agreements. *See, e.g., Air Line Pilots Ass'n v. O'Neill*, 499 U.S. 65 (1991) (when applying the "arbitrary, discriminatory, or bad faith" standard to collective bargaining, courts must offer unions latitude "within a wide range of reasonableness.")

The *Vaca* decision involved an employee's effort to sue his employer for violation of a collective bargaining agreement between the employer and the employee's union. The Court held that the employee could not do so where the employee's claim was subject to an arbitration process that the union, without violating its DFR, had chosen not to invoke. An employee like the plaintiff in *Vaca* thus must first demonstrate that his union has violated its DFR before recovering from the employer for violating the collective bargaining agreement. *Vaca* expresses the national labor policy that the resolution of disputes that arise in the unionized workplace should be resolved by procedures set forth in a collective bargaining agreement, including arbitration. Access to these procedures is negotiated by and is typically under the control of a union. The DFR requires union decision makers to be fair and principled in using this control, but it does not require them to invoke arbitration regardless of the merits of grievances or the extent of union resources.

Suppose, for instance, that a player files a grievance alleging that his release violated a "no cut" guarantee in his contract, and the MLBPA agrees with the club and the league that the contract language will not bear that interpretation and drops the grievance rather than take it to arbitration. The player would have to sue in court both the association and the club, establish first that the union's judgment in dropping the grievance was "arbitrary, discriminatory, or in bad faith," and then try to sustain the merits of his contract claim against the team (in court, not in arbitration). If the player succeeded on both counts, the club would be responsible for the damage done by the contract violation and the union for the additional costs attributable to use of this more complex procedure, such as legal fees incurred in the lawsuit and additional salary losses incurred because it took longer to obtain a ruling in litigation than in arbitration. *See Bowen v. United States Postal Service,* 459 U.S. 212 (1983). For sports cases illustrating this process, *see, e.g., Chuy v. NFLPA,* 495 F. Supp. 137 (E.D. Pa. 1980), and *Sharpe v. NFLPA,* 941 F. Supp. 8 (D.D.C. 1996).

PETERSON V. KENNEDY AND NFLPA
771 F.2d 1244 (9th Cir. 1985)

REINHARDT, CIRCUIT JUDGE.

[James Peterson of the Tampa Bay Buccaneers signed one-year contracts for each of the 1976, 1977, and 1978 football seasons. Besides the standard injury protection clause that provided for payment of that year's salary in case of an injury occurring during any one season, Peterson's contract contained a special clause that entitled him to his salary for the 1977 and 1978 seasons if he were unable to play because of a football-related injury in a previous year. Peterson injured his knee early in the 1976 season and missed the entire year because of surgery. When Peterson reported to training camp in the summer of 1977, he was cut from the team after one week of drills. This was done pursuant to the standard player contract provision that allows the club to terminate the contract if a player's performance appears "unsatisfactory" compared to other players competing for positions on the squad.

In August 1977, after allegedly talking with Harold Kennedy, a NFLPA staff member, Peterson's agent filed a grievance under the "injury grievance procedure" in the NFL-NFLPA collective agreement in order to recover the salary due for the 1977 and 1978 seasons. The parties disputed whether the NFLPA had been informed at the outset of the special "injury protection" clause in Peterson's contract. However, when Richard Berthelson, the NFLPA General Counsel, learned of that clause in 1978, he sought to channel the grievance into the "non-injury" grievance procedure. Unfortunately, because the switch took place after the sixty days permitted for filing non-injury grievances, the contract arbitrator found the non-injury grievance to be time-barred. Meanwhile, the arbitrator ruled against Peterson's claim under the injury grievance procedure, on the ground that this particular procedure was used only to collect salary payments owed for the year during which the injury occurred.

Having lost both sides of his contract claim against the Buccaneers, Peterson sued the NFLPA for breach of the labor law duty of fair representation—in particular, by erroneously advising him to file an injury grievance and then failing to rectify this error while there still was time to do so. Although the jury found in favor of Peterson's legal claim, the trial judge granted the NFLPA's motion for judgment notwithstanding the verdict (JNOV). The principal ground was that the union's conduct amounted to no more than negligence, and negligence could not constitute unfair representation under the NLRA. Peterson appealed that ruling.]

* * *

The district court concluded that the evidence presented was legally insufficient to sustain the jury's verdict that the union breached its duty of fair representation. We agree. After reviewing all of the evidence in the light most favorable to Peterson, we conclude that the union did not breach its duty of fair representation; the record is devoid of evidence that the union acted in an arbitrary, discriminatory, or bad faith manner.

The duty of fair representation is a judicially established rule imposed on labor organizations because of their status as the exclusive bargaining representative for all of the employees in a given bargaining unit. The Supreme Court [in *DelCostello v. International Bthd. of Teamsters*, 462 U.S. 151 (1983)] recently explained the basis and scope of the duty:

> The duty of fair representation exists because it is the policy of the National Labor Relations Act to allow a single labor organization to represent collectively the interests of all employees within a unit, thereby depriving individuals in the unit of the ability to bargain individually or to select a minority union as their representative. In such a system, if individual employees are not to be deprived of all effective means of protecting their own interests, it must be the duty of the representative organization to "serve the interests of all members without hostility or discrimination toward any, to exercise its discretion with complete good faith and honesty, and to avoid arbitrary conduct."

462 U.S. at 164, n. 14.

A union breaches its duty of fair representation only when its conduct toward a member of the collective bargaining unit is "arbitrary, discriminatory, or in bad faith." The duty is designed to ensure that unions represent fairly the interests of all of their members without exercising hostility or bad faith toward any. It stands "as a bulwark to prevent arbitrary union conduct against individuals stripped of traditional forms of redress by the provisions of federal labor law."

The Supreme Court has long recognized that unions must retain wide discretion to act in what they perceive to be their members' best interests. To that end, we have "stressed the importance of preserving union discretion by narrowly construing the unfair representation doctrine." We have emphasized that, because a union balances many collective and individual interests in deciding whether and to what extent it will pursue a particular grievance, courts should "accord substantial deference" to a union's decisions regarding such matters.

A union's representation of its members "need not be error free." We have concluded repeatedly that mere negligent conduct on the part of a union does not constitute a breach of the union's duty of fair representation.

* * *

Whether in a particular case a union's conduct is "negligent", and therefore non-actionable, or so egregious as to be "arbitrary", and hence sufficient to give rise to a breach of duty claim, is a question that is not always easily answered. A union acts "arbitrarily" when it simply ignores a meritorious grievance or handles it in a perfunctory manner, for example, by failing to conduct a "minimal investigation" of a grievance that is brought to its attention. We have said that a union's conduct is "arbitrary" if it is "without rational basis," or is "egregious, unfair and unrelated to legitimate union interests." In *Robesky v. Qantas Empire Airways Ltd.*, 573 F.2d 1082, 1089–90 (9th Cir. 1978), we held that a union's unintentional mistake is "arbitrary" if it reflects a "reckless disregard" for the rights of the individual employee, but not if it represents only "simply negligence violating the tort standard of due care."

There are some significant general principles that emerge from our previous decisions. In all cases in which we found a breach of the duty of fair representation based on a union's arbitrary conduct, it is clear that the union failed to perform a procedural or ministerial act, that the act in question did not require the exercise of judgment and that there was no rational and proper basis for the union's conduct.

* * *

We have never held that a union has acted in an arbitrary manner where the challenged conduct involved the union's judgment as to how best to handle a grievance. To the contrary, we have held consistently that unions are not liable for good faith, non-discriminatory errors of judgment made in the processing of grievances. We have said that a union's conduct may not be deemed arbitrary simply because of an error in evaluating the merits of a grievance, in interpreting particular provisions of a collective bargaining agreement, or in presenting the grievance at an arbitration hearing. In short, we do not attempt to second-guess a union's judgment when a good faith, non-discriminatory judgment has in fact been made. It is for the union, not the courts, to decide whether and in what manner a particular grievance should be pursued. We reaffirm that principle here.

Sound policy reasons militate against imposing liability on unions for errors of judgment made while representing their members in the collective bargaining process. [We have] recognized that holding unions liable for such errors would serve ultimately to "defeat the employees' collective bargaining interest in having a strong and effective union." If unions were subject to liability for "judgment calls," it would necessarily undermine their discretion to act on behalf of their members and ultimately weaken their effectiveness. In the long run, the cost of recognizing such liability would be borne not by the unions but by their memberships. Not only would the direct costs of adverse judgments be passed on to the members in the form of increased dues, but, more importantly, unions would become increasingly reluctant to provide guidance to their members in collective bargaining disputes. Such a result would be inconsistent with our oft-repeated commitment to construe narrowly the scope of the duty of fair representation in order to preserve the unions' discretion to decide how best to balance the collective and individual interests that they represent.

* * *

Whether liability for a loss occasioned by ordinary negligence of the union might be spread more equitably among the membership as a whole, rather than be borne by the individual member who is harmed, is no longer an open question.

In applying the foregoing principles to the case at hand, we conclude, as a matter of law that Peterson failed to establish that the NFLPA breached its duty of fair representation. . . . The alleged error was one of judgment. Viewing the evidence in the light most favorable to Peterson, the most that can be said is that the union provided him with incorrect advice and did not alter its judgment until it was too late to rectify the error. In this case, deciding whether to file an injury or a non-injury grievance was not a purely mechanical function; the union attorneys were required to construe the scope and meaning of the injury and non-injury grievance provisions of the collective bargaining agreement and to determine which of the two grievance procedures was more appropriate. As we have indicated earlier, the answer was not as simple as a literal reading of the two contract sections might indicate.

* * *

Although the union's representatives may have erred in initially advising Peterson to file an injury grievance and in failing to recognize its mistake in time to file a non-injury grievance in its stead, we are unwilling to subject unions to liability for such errors in judgment. Accordingly, we affirm the district court's conclusion that the evidence presented was insufficient, as a matter of law, to support the jury's verdict against the union.

Appeal denied.

———

NOTES AND QUESTIONS

1. *Ministerial Versus Discretionary.* Do you understand the distinction between "ministerial" and "discretionary" actions made by the court in *Peterson v. Kennedy?* Of what relevance is it to the standard for a union's duty of fair representation? How did it apply to the facts of that case?

2. *Union's Dual Constituency.* A union serving as exclusive representative of a bargaining unit has a duty to represent each employee serving in a job within the unit, regardless of the degree of support the employee gives the union. A union thus has dual overlapping constituencies: its active members and the employees it represents. What then should be a sports union's duty toward players who have crossed over picket lines to replace striking players? Can the union negotiate lower employer contributions to a pension fund for such replacement players? Can it negotiate to provide no credit for free agency for the time the replacements played during a strike? Why is it also not a violation of the union's duty to exclude replacements from membership in the union and hence eligibility to collect a share of licensing fees?

3. *Non-Allowance of Rodriguez Trade.* Consider again the MLBPA's refusal to allow the trade of Alex Rodriguez to the Red Sox in 2004, as described above in Section E. Was that refusal a violation of the union's duty of fair representation? Why or why not?

4. *Sports Unions' Discretion in Negotiating Collective Agreements.* The "wide range of reasonableness" afforded unions by the deferential "arbitrary, discriminatory, or in bad faith" duty of fair representation standard does not restrict sports unions' good faith balancing of the interests of higher paid or more veteran players against the interests of lower paid or less experienced workers. Thus, to note two recent examples: (1) the NFLPA in 2020 was free to decide to accept or resist the NFL's proposal to add a seventeenth regular season game, though the proposal was opposed by many higher paid veterans who viewed it as a safety risk, while supported by younger lower paid players who were more interested in their share of the revenue produced by an extra game; and (2) the MLBPA in 2022 was free to choose to give greater priority in collective bargaining either to reducing the competitive balance tax that inhibits the free agency primarily benefiting star players or rather to raising the minimum salary and bonus pools for younger players who are not yet eligible for salary arbitration or free agency. In making such balances during negotiations, sports union leadership is much more constrained by the politics of their democratic unions, and the need to maintain solidarity for any work action, than by any legal standards.

5. *Unions' Duty When Employer Disciplines to Protect Other Employees.* The conflicting interests of bargaining unit members may be most salient in cases where some members are subject to discipline for taking actions that may harm other members. This may be true, for instance, in cases where an employer disciplines some unit members for sexual or racial harassment of other unit members. Sports unions confront such conflicts in cases where the

league proposes discipline against some union members for taking performance-enhancing drugs. In such cases, the union's duty in grievance administration is to ensure that the accused unit member obtains fair process under the standards set in the collective agreement. When negotiating an agreement, however, the union may balance conflicting interests, so that the standards for judging drug use or harassment may be made more strict.

CHAPTER 4

LABOR ARBITRATION IN PROFESSIONAL SPORTS

■ ■ ■

The use of negotiated private arbitration to resolve disputes over the interpretation and application of collective bargaining agreements spread with the proliferation of unionized workplaces after the passage of the Labor Act in 1935. Union leaders favored arbitration before bilaterally selected neutrals in part because of the leaders' lingering suspicion of a judiciary that had been hostile to collective worker action for over a century. These leaders also recognized that private arbitration can provide a cheaper and certainly quicker forum for resolving disputes than can courts, advantages especially important to unions with limited relative resources. Furthermore, management has been attracted to arbitration as an alternative to work stoppages over unresolved grievances during the term of collective agreements; indeed, labor relations professionals soon came to view management agreements to submit grievances to final and binding arbitration as a "quid pro quo" for a union agreement not to strike over such grievances.

Before the rise of unions in professional sports, moreover, the Supreme Court used a grant of jurisdiction provided by the Labor Management Relations Act (LMRA) in 1947 to assert law favorable to the adoption and enforcement of arbitration provisions in collective bargaining agreements. Section 301 of the LMRA grants federal courts jurisdiction over "[s]uits for violation of contracts between an employer and a labor organization . . . without respect to the amount in controversy or without regard to the citizenship of the parties." In *Textile Workers Union v. Lincoln Mills of Alabama*, 353 U.S. 448 (1957), the Court provided a constitutional basis for this grant of jurisdiction—"arising under" Article III jurisdiction—by holding that the provision must intend federal courts to fashion substantive law to govern collective agreements "from the policy of our national labor laws." The *Lincoln Mills* Court then fashioned the first principle of this new law: notwithstanding any contrary state contract law, or the anti-injunction commands of the Norris-LaGuardia Act, CBA agreements to arbitrate can be specifically enforced through injunctions, not only through damages. Doing so, the Court suggested, encourages the peaceful resolution of labor disputes in accord with national labor policy.

Three years later in a trilogy of cases involving the United Steelworkers, the Court provided further support for arbitration under labor agreements. One of the cases, *United Steelworkers of America v. Enterprise Wheel & Car Corp.*, 363 U.S. 593 (1960), held that courts should not review the merits of an arbitration award and is treated more fully in the last section of this chapter. The other two cases involved standards for the enforcement of agreements to arbitrate. In *United Steelworkers of America v. American Manufacturing Co.*, 363 U.S. 564 (1960), the Court held that a court should enforce a CBA provision to arbitrate a grievance even if the court considered the grievance "frivolous" or "patently baseless." "Whether the moving party is right or wrong is a question of contract interpretation for the arbitrator" not the court. In *United Steelworkers of America v. Warrior & Gulf Navigation Co.*, 363 U.S. 574 (1960), the Court recognized that courts must decide whether the parties to a collective agreement intended a particular dispute to be subject to the jurisdiction of the arbitrator, but it held that they should do so with a strong presumption in favor of arbitration: "[a]n order to arbitrate the particular grievance should not be denied unless it may be said with positive assurance that the arbitration clause is not susceptible of an interpretation that covers the asserted dispute. Doubts should be resolved in favor of coverage." Ten years after the *Steelworkers Trilogy*, in *Boys Market, Inc. v. Retail Clerks Union, Local 770*, 398 U.S. 235 (1970), the Court gave management further encouragement to agree to final and binding arbitration by holding that the Norris-LaGuardia Act does not preclude the specific enforcement of union commitments not to strike over grievances that are subject to resolution by neutral arbitrators.

Today labor arbitration continues to be a central part of successful collective bargaining in the unionized workplace. Although collective bargaining agreements covered less than 12% of the workforce in 2021, these CBAs almost always contain arbitration clauses to resolve disputes over interpretation and application.

The professional sports industry illustrates the importance of arbitration to successful collective bargaining. From their first collective agreements the players associations and league managements have utilized negotiated labor arbitration systems. In baseball, the owners and union have traditionally selected a single independent neutral to chair a panel of three persons charged with deciding unsettled disputes. The union selects one member of the panel, as does management. The neutral runs the hearing and, in fact, makes the determination, which is joined by one member of the panel or the other. In the NFL, NBA, and NHL, the two sides have selected a single person who becomes the sole arbitrator. In all the leagues, the parties normally choose experienced and respected arbitrators to serve as their permanent umpires. They are typically elected members of the honorary association of labor neutrals, the National Academy of Arbitrators. The arbitrators hear all disputes that the CBA assigns to independent arbitration until they are dismissed in accordance with the agreement's procedures.

A. CONTRACT INTERPRETATION THROUGH ARBITRATION

Collective bargaining agreements in some ways are similar to legislative enactments. Like legislators with different political priorities seeking acceptable compromises, parties negotiating collective agreements often agree only on general principles that require interpretation before being applied in particular cases. Sometimes the parties have a different understanding of the principles, but do not want to upset an agreement by pressing their point of view. Sometimes the parties do not anticipate the particular cases that require further interpretation. In any case, the parties anticipate that clarification can be offered in arbitration during the course of the agreement, and that renegotiation is available before signing the next agreement. The arbitration process, like the judicial process for legislation, thus can be an integral part of the development of a collective bargaining relationship.

The most important example from the sports industry of how arbitral interpretation of a collective agreement can prompt refinement of the agreement and affect future labor relations is treated in Chapter 5 on player mobility restraints. That example, the *Messersmith-McNally* decision, excerpted in Chapter 5, Section B, changed assumptions about the meaning of a clause in baseball players' individual contracts, and effectively forced Major League Baseball to bargain with the MLBPA about rules to govern free agency in baseball. The result of this bargaining was a collective agreement that not only specified when a player could become a free agent and what compensation (in the form of draft picks) was owed to the former team, but also created a draft procedure whereby a specified number of teams could secure the right to bid for the free agents the teams wanted to pursue. That last feature of the free agency system was dispensed with in the 1981 baseball agreement, but not before an arbitrator interpreted its meaning and scope in a decision that illustrates how arbitral interpretations can be a central part of the collective bargaining process.

ALVIN MOORE & ATLANTA BRAVES
MLB-MLBPA Arb. 77–18 (1977)

PORTER, ARBITRATOR.

[In April 1977, Alvin Moore signed a one-year contract with the Atlanta Braves. That contract contained a clause that said that if Moore told the Braves he was "not satisfied with his playing time by June 15, 1977," the Braves had to trade him to another team (approved by Moore). If such a trade had not been consummated before the end of the season, Moore would "become a free agent if he so desires." National League President Feeney disapproved of this "special covenant" as "inconsistent with the Reserve System Article of the new Basic Agreement." The Players Association filed a grievance on Moore's behalf, based on the Article II Recognition clause in the MLB Agreement, which permitted players to negotiate not just individual salaries above the prescribed league minimum, but also "Special Covenants ... which actually or potentially provide additional benefits to the Player." The issue for the arbitrator was whether this provision in the Moore/Braves contract met the test.]

According to the Association, there are only three valid reasons for a League President to disapprove a special covenant. He may do so: (1) if the covenant does not meet the test of Article II in that it does not "actually or potentially provide additional benefits to the Player;" (2) if the covenant violates an applicable law or is specifically prohibited by a Major League rule which is not inconsistent with the Basic Agreement (*e.g.*, if the covenant provides for the giving of a bonus for playing, pitching or batting skill or a bonus contingent on the Club's standing, types of bonuses specifically prohibited by Major League Rule 3[a]); or (3) if the covenant purports to bind some third party whom the Club and the Player have no authority to bind (*e.g.*, a covenant stating that, regardless of what a Player does on the field, an Umpire cannot eject him from a game or the League President or the Commissioner cannot discipline him). . . .

The Clubs reply that the Moore covenant strikes at the very heart of the reserve system which the parties negotiated following the Arbitration Panel's Decision No. 29, the so-called "*Messersmith-McNally*" case. In the wake of the *Messersmith-McNally* case, all players were theoretically free to play out their contracts and become free agents after an additional renewal year. Confronted by the impending collapse of the reserve system, the Clubs observe, the parties, for the first time, jointly negotiated a new reserve system and incorporated the new system in Article XVII of the 1976–1979 Basic Agreement. In the Clubs' view, Article II of the Basic Agreement does not provide authority for an individual Club and Player to negotiate what, in their opinion, is an entirely new reserve system, merely because such a system would provide a benefit to the Player. . . .

The Clubs concede that, in practice, the League Presidents have approved particular covenants which differ from and hence are arguably "inconsistent" with the provisions of the Basic Agreement. In their view, however, the inconsistencies in these approved covenants involved interests of the individual Clubs and Player alone—e.g., covenants guaranteeing a player's salary for one or more years, covenants waiving a Club's rights regarding commercial endorsements, medical examinations, etc. They did not involve covenants, such as the Moore covenant, wherein the Club and the Player sought to waive the interests of others—in this case the 25 other Clubs' interest in maintaining the kind of competitive balance among the various Clubs which the Reserve System of Article XVII was and is designed to provide.

The Moore covenant is said by the Clubs to contravene the scheme of Article XVII in three main respects. First, it grants to Moore, who presently has less than one year of Major League service, a conditional right to demand a trade, should he "not be satisfied with his playing time by June 15, 1977. . . ."

Second, if a trade is not consummated by the end of the 1977 season, the Moore covenant renders Moore eligible to become a free agent, if he so desires, despite the fact that he will then have only a little more than a year's Major League service. . . .

Third, the Moore covenant does not expressly make him subject to the [free agent] re-entry procedure, with its quota and compensation provisions. . . .

The objective of this re-entry procedure, the Clubs contend, is to provide for an even and equitable distribution of players among all the Clubs and prevent a few of the richer Clubs from buying up a disproportionate share of the available free agent talent. To permit the Atlanta Club and Player Moore to by-pass the re-entry procedure would defeat this objective and allow the Atlanta Club to waive the rights which the other 25 Clubs have in maintaining the competitive balance which the re-entry procedure is designed to foster, the Clubs conclude. They ask, accordingly, that league President Feeney's disapproval of the Moore covenant be sustained by the Panel.

* * *

In the Chairman's judgment, both parties have advanced sound positions in support of their respective claims, but each has pushed his position to an unsound extreme. For reasons to be given more fully below, the Chairman is convinced the Moore covenant can be interpreted in a way which does not impinge upon the legitimate interests of the other Clubs and could and should have been approved on that basis. No reason appears why the Atlanta Club may not accord to Moore conditional rights to demand a trade and to become a free agent under Article XVII, B(2), despite the fact that he does not have the requisite years of Major League service to claim these rights unilaterally. The 5- and 6-year service requirements for Players seeking to exercise such rights unilaterally under Article XVII, D and B(2), respectively, are for the individual Club's benefit; and no persuasive evidence or argument has been presented to show why the benefit of long-term title and reservation rights to Moore's contract may not be waived by his club. But if Atlanta may waive the length of service requirements designed for its benefit, it may not waive the reentry procedure designed for the benefit of all 26 Clubs. . . .

Negotiations between individual Clubs and Players are not . . . conducted in a vacuum. To the contrary, and at the risk of belaboring the obvious, individual Player-Club negotiations are conducted not only within the framework of applicable law but within the framework of organized professional baseball and the attendant rules, agreements and regulations by which the sport or industry is governed and by which the Association on behalf of the Players and the Clubs comprising the two Major Leagues have agreed to be bound. Within the latter framework are innumerable matters affecting the interests and rights of all the Clubs and Players, such as the number of Player contracts to which each Club may have title and reservation rights, the number of Players each Club may retain on its active roster, the length of the intra or interleague trading periods, etc. Variations in any one of these provisions might give a Player "additional benefits" but are beyond the Club's power to make. . . .

To the extent the Association seeks to push its "additional benefit" argument to the point where the Moore covenant is to be interpreted as exempting Moore from the free agent quota system and other aspects of the reentry procedure designed to protect the interests of all 26 Clubs, the Chairman believes it presses its argument too far.

* * *

Grievance upheld in part.

———

NOTES AND QUESTIONS

1.   *Arbitrator's Role?* Which clauses in the 1976 collective agreement did arbitrator Porter interpret in this decision? Did these clauses directly answer the questions posed to and answered by the arbitrator? If not, how exactly were the clauses relevant to his decision? Why did the arbitrator decide one of the questions favorably to MLB and the other favorably to the MLBPA? Was the arbitrator simply offering the parties a compromise that would make his continuing employment palatable to each, or did his opinion offer a coherent and consistent interpretation of the collective agreement?

2.   *Further Application.* In 1978, an arbitrator invalidated an individual contract signed under the 1976 agreement because it specified that, at its termination, the player would become a free agent without compensation, that is, the contracting team waived its right to whatever draft pick it would receive from a new team signing the player. What do you suppose was the arbitrator's reasoning?

3.   *Collective Bargaining Reaction to Kris Bryant Arbitration.* A more recent example of how an arbitrator's interpretation of a collective agreement affected subsequent collective bargaining over free agency concerned the MLBPA's efforts to discourage the clubs' control of players' service time to delay free agency. In the spring of 2015, Kris Bryant was considered by most experts to be the number one baseball prospect in the minor league systems. In spring training that year Bryant hit nine home runs in forty at-bats. The Chicago Cubs, who controlled his rights, nonetheless did not call Bryant up to

play on their active roster until a few weeks into the season on the day after the date that would have given him credit for a full year of service time for 2015. This ensured Bryant would be under team control through the 2021 season as Cubs President Theo Epstein promised Cubs ownership in March, 2015 in a slide presentation.

In 2019 the MLBPA filed a grievance challenging the denial of full 2015 service time to Bryant and seeking to make him eligible for free agency after the 2020 season. In a decision denying the grievance, arbitrator Mark Irvings interpreted the collective bargaining agreement to warrant the grant of service time contrary to a club's assignment to the active roster only if the club's assignment was in "bad faith." Irvings then concluded that the MLBPA did "not satisfy its burden of proving that the Cubs' assignments of Bryant were done in bad faith to mask service time manipulation" or for "a nefarious motive." Irvings in part relied on Epstein's history of never promoting promising prospects to opening day rosters, though this history might in part have reflected a desire to restrict service time.

Absent any controlling language in the collective agreement, do you think that the arbitrator should have required the MLBPA to prove bad faith rather than requiring the Cubs to carry a burden of proving their good faith? Consider that plaintiffs generally have the burden of proving breaches of the implied covenant of good faith in contracts. Consider also, however, that the Cubs had possession of the evidence of their decision-making process.

In light of the difficulty of proving bad faith motivation, the MLBPA responded to the arbitration decision by proposing and successfully securing some objective standards and incentives in the 2022 collective bargaining agreement in order to avoid cases like those of Bryant. These include granting a full year of service time to any player who finishes first or second in a league's Rookie of the Year voting. (Bryant was a unanimous pick for National League Rookie of the Year in 2015.) In addition, clubs promoting a player to an opening day roster will be eligible to receive a draft pick if the player finishes in the top three in Rookie of the Year voting or top five in MVP or Cy Young voting in either league. Does the Bryant arbitration and subsequent 2022 bargaining agreement provide an example of the flexibility in solving disputes afforded by federal labor law's reliance on private ordering?

B. ARBITRATION OF DISCIPLINARY DISPUTES

The grievances presented to neutral arbitration authorized under collective agreements most often involve challenges to the discharge or discipline of employees covered by the agreement. Even such cases may facilitate further collective bargaining and a refinement of the collective agreement. Consider the following decision.

IN RE LATRELL SPREWELL

NBA-NBPA Arb. (1998)

JOHN FEERICK, ARBITRATOR.

Facts

The Grievant entered the NBA as a player for the Warriors in 1992 as a result of the draft. From that time until his suspension on December 1, 1997, he played for the Warriors under four different head coaches, each with their own style of coaching. Although he was fined from time to time and participated, according to the record, in two physical altercations with other players,* he never was suspended from a practice or a game until the 1995/96 season. He worked hard, played hard, and achieved All-Star status. He also was the Warriors' best player and its captain by appointment of the Team.

Head Coach Peter Carlesimo joined the Warriors in June 1997, after several successful seasons with the Portland Blazers and a successful college coaching career at Seton Hall. It appears from the record that the Grievant and Head Coach had a reasonably good pre-season in terms of their relationship, though some cracks began to develop as the season opened in late October and early November 1997. During the month of November the relationship between the two deteriorated with the player wanting to be traded and the Team wanting to trade him so it might build its future in a different direction.

The record reveals that the Grievant engaged in some acts of defiance in November and felt singled out, not listened to, and blamed to some extent for the Team's lack of success. Coaches and players testified in the hearings before me that the Head Coach was not abusive toward the Grievant. There also was testimony that the Head Coach was in the Grievant's "ear" on a fairly regular basis in order to motivate him to achieve an even higher level of excellence. [Warriors Assistant Coach Mark] Grabow testified that he "felt that P.J.'s prodding of players was equally distributed among all the players but because Spree was his star and he needed Spree's offense and defensive energy, he needed Spree to be his guy and for us to be successful." In response to my question as to whether or not more was asked of the Grievant, he added, "[t]hen perhaps he did, but I never looked at it as he was picking on him or anything like that." In reply to a follow-up question by counsel, he said, "[h]e needed him more than any other player for us to be successful."

Testimony was also given that screaming and profanity in general were not an infrequent occurrence, and there was testimony that the Grievant and Donyell Marshall seemed to be singled out more than the other players. By the end of November a great deal of frustration had set

---

*   In neither altercation was he disciplined, in one the other player was disciplined.

in as a result, it appears, of the Team's failure to win more than one of its first 14 games. [Warriors Assistant Coach Bob] Staak testified: "Everybody on the team was unhappy. It was no fun at that point in time." . . .

On December 1, 1997, the Warriors engaged in a regular, closed door practice, preparing for its next game scheduled for December 3 against Cleveland. The coaches participated in different ways with the players as the Head Coach moved from one practice court to another. One of the drills that day was a three-man, two-ball exercise in which one player rebounds, another receives a pass from the rebounder and throws the ball to the third person, who takes a shot at the basket. The object of the drill is to have the shooter take as many shots as possible within a 55-second period. When the Head Coach reached the court on which the Grievant was playing with Grabow and [point guard Muggsy] Bogues, he told the Grievant to put more speed on the ball when making a pass. The practice was proceeding in a normal manner and the Head Coach spoke in a low tone and then raised his voice a bit louder, saying the words a second time. The Grievant proceeded to slam the ball down and express a number of expletives reasonably approximating "get out of my face, get the f— out of here and leave me the f— alone." The Head Coach responded: "you're the f— out of here." Thereupon, Grievant immediately either walked to or lunged at the Head Coach, placing his two hands around his neck. With his arms fully extended, the Grievant moved the Coach backwards saying, "I will kill you." Apparently no one else heard him use these words except the Head Coach, who did not believe he intended to kill him although he thought he was trying to inflict serious bodily harm. The Grievant, upset and angry, said that he used the words figuratively, as he (and others) testified, in the same manner that they are used from time to time in the sport in fight situations.

Almost as soon as the Grievant had placed his two hands around the Head Coach's neck, Grabow intervened in an effort separate the two, as others came to the area to help. Between seven and ten seconds elapsed during which the Grievant had his hands around the Coach's neck. The Head Coach remained calm and offered no resistance except toward the end when he raised his arms, palms down, toward his shoulders at about which point the Grievant's hands came free of his neck. The Head Coach testified that his breathing became more difficult toward the end of the seven to ten second period. Grievant testified that he was applying some pressure but did not intend any serious harm.

The testimony is not entirely clear as to how the Grievant came to remove his hands from the Head Coach's' neck. In response to questions concerning getting the Grievant off the Coach, Grabow said: "I was trying to get Spree off him, like the three of us were waltzing around the floor a little bit, but then I felt Tom Abdenour, our trainer, come over my shoulder and we finally got Spree's hands off of Coach and Tommy just kind of escorted Spree toward the locker room." The testimony suggests that Grievant may have removed his own hands.

After the Grievant and Head Coach were separated, Tom Abdenour took the Grievant to the door leading from the playing facility to the locker room and shower. At that point, they were joined by [Warriors assistant coach Rod] Higgins and [player Bimbo] Coles. As Grievant and Abdenour moved toward the door Grievant angrily said a number of expletives, including "trade me, get me out of here, I will kill you." The Head Coach responded with words to the effect of "I am here." In leaving the facility, Grievant slammed the door hard and knocked over the water cooler immediately inside the door. As Coles was walking through the door with Grievant to talk to him, someone told him to come back in to continue the practice. No one, it appears, joined the Grievant in the locker-room area.

With respect to the period during which he was in the locker room, between ten and 20 minutes, the Grievant testified that he reflected on all the negative things that had gone on between him and the Head Coach up to that point, including what had just happened in practice. He said: "For through that whole incident, from the time I went into the shower and put on sweats and flip-flops, I am moving fast. I never sat down and reflected on what happened or anything. I walked back out there at a fast pace."

Grievant returned to the practice facility after showering and changing. In his testimony he said that he had not calmed down at all and remained angry. Coach Grabow, apparently the first to see him upon his return, heard the Grievant say "you better get my ass out of here, get me the f— out of here." Grabow said, "he didn't say anything at that point that was threatening to anyone." He said that the Grievant was walking with "a purpose" and he (Grabow) uttered "someone grab him." [Assistant Coach Bob] Staak and then Coach Higgins tried unsuccessfully to arrest the Grievant's fast movement around the baseline toward the basket under which the Head Coach was standing as a full-court drill was in progress. Grabow, as well as [Assistant Coach Paul] Westhead, testified that the Grievant became more enraged as people grabbed him. Staak said that, in entering, there was no question that Grievant's "intent was to get closer to P.J.," adding that he was extremely mad. When Staak said, "Spree, it is bad enough. You don't want to do this," he said that Grievant's response was "get the f— out of my way, don't touch me." Others testified that upon seeing him after his return, Grievant appeared mad, enraged, angry and upset, though it was not clear at all when they saw him in relation to when Grabow first observed him.

At some point Grievant and Head Coach came within a foot or two or each other. Coach Grabow testified that as people grabbed the Grievant it "became a chaotic scene," with coaches and players being drawn closer to each other as if a melee were taking place. The testimony is quite confused at the point when Grievant and the Head Coach were within reach of each other. What is clear is that efforts were being made by those present to prevent them from having any contact. The Grievant testified that he sought to free himself from those grabbing him by kicking his feet and flailing his arms. He said it was possible that in doing so, he may have hit the Head Coach in a flailing motion. Other testimony was given that there was a moment in time when the Grievant either freed himself from the clutch of others, or at least his arms, and directed a punch at the Coach which grazed the side of his right cheek. I find that, as a melee was occurring, Grievant did direct an overhand punch which landed on the Coach in the area near his right shoulder but the testimony does not establish whether it was directed or the result of a flailing motion. Almost immediately Grievant was moved away from the Head Coach and the Head Coach was moved away as well. From that point until he left the playing facility, the Grievant was firmly in the clutch of Coach Higgins and players Ferrell and Coles. As he was leaving, Grievant uttered words similar to those he used after the first incident, including "I will kill you."

Upon leaving the playing facility, Grievant went to [Warrior General Manager Garry] St. Jean's office and said he wanted to be traded using various expletives. The General Manger, who at that point was speaking to the Grievant's agent, handed the Grievant the telephone. The Grievant shouted into it "get me out of here today, get me the f— out of here." He then strongly placed the phone on St. Jean's desk and walked out. St. Jean testified as to his concern for Grievant because of "his emotional state." . . .

[The opinion next describes the twin investigations by the Warriors and the league. Although the Warriors initially pursued the idea of trading Sprewell, by December 3 they decided that the best course was to terminate his contract. Commissioner Stern then decided to suspend Sprewell for one year.]

Legal Framework . . .

First, I begin by emphasizing that violence in the work place is not tolerated in the field of labor and employment law. The subject has been dealt with strongly by arbitrators, leading to severe discipline including termination where an assault is made on a supervisor or manager. I note as well that the idea of fairness runs throughout the field of labor and employment law, finding expression in contracts, arbitration decisions, court decisions, statutes and constitutions. Some of the elements of fairness are expressed by a number of arbitral principles. Arbitrators apply progressive discipline, take account of mitigating factors, and look to see whether discipline is consistent with prior penalties for comparable acts. Variations in penalties are appropriate depending on the circumstances and context surrounding the act in question. . . . Moreover, previous lax discipline on the part of an employer will not require similar treatment of subsequent misconduct where clear notice is given that such behavior would warrant greater discipline.

Another aspect of fairness is the notion of industrial due process. It is, however, a less exacting standard than its constitutional counterpart. As the arbitrator noted in *Cameron Iron Works*, 73 LA 878 (Marlett, 1979): "[E]mployers and unions meet in bargaining on approximately equal terms, and their contracts speak of 'just cause' rather than 'due process.' The distinction is significant. The essential question for an arbitrator is not whether disciplinary action was totally free from procedural error, but rather whether the process was fundamentally fair." An employee subject to discipline is entitled to notice of the charges, an opportunity to be heard and an adequate and fair investigation. Indeed, the California Supreme Court recently emphasized that, while employers had wide discretion in the area of employment termination, an employer's factual determination must be a "reasoned conclusion supported by substantial evidence gathered through an adequate investigation that includes notice of the claimed misconduct and a chance for the employee to respond." *Cotran v. Rollins Hudig Hall Int'l Inc.*, 17 Cal. 4th 93, 948 P.2d 412 (1998).

Sometimes notice to an employee is obviated where it is clear that the conduct would not be tolerated. Adolph M. Koven & Susan L. Smith, *Just Cause: The Seven Tests* 31, 59–161 (rev. by Donald F. Farwell, 2nd ed. 1992). Interviewing a grievant also may not be required, unless provided for by contract, although the presence or absence of such an opportunity may be relevant to a just cause termination. As for an adequate and fair investigation, the authors of a leading treatise on arbitration declare: "[E]xcept in the most obvious and heinous of situations, management must conduct a fair and impartial investigation of the incident." Elkouri & Elkouri, *How Arbitration Works* 919 (Marlin M. Volz & Edward P. Goggins eds. 5th ed. 1997) (quoting *Great Midwest Mining Corp.* 82 LA 52, 55 (Milrut, 1984)).

* * *

Against this background, I turn to the arguments made by the parties, most particularly as follows: (1) whether the standard of review of the Commissioner's one-year suspension is just cause or arbitrary and capricious; (2) whether a just cause standard of review is applicable to the termination of Grievant's Player Contract by the Warriors; (3) whether the CBA allows discipline to be imposed jointly by the Commissioner and Warriors with respect to the same conduct; (4) whether the actions taken by the Commissioner and Warriors violate double jeopardy principles of labor law; and (5) whether the actions taken by the Commissioner and Warriors are appropriate.

(1) Whether the Standard of Review of the Commissioner's One-year Suspension Is Just Cause or Arbitrary and Capricious.

The parties disagree on whether just cause or an arbitrary and capricious standard is applicable in reviewing the Commissioner's one-year suspension of the Grievant. To determine which is applicable, one must interpret the CBA. Two of the relevant provisions of the CBA are as follows:

> The parties recognize that a player may be subjected to disciplinary action for just cause by his Team or the Commissioner (or his designee). Therefore, in Grievances regarding discipline, the issue to be resolved shall be whether there has been just cause for the penalty imposed. CBA Art. XXXI, Section 14(c)

> In any Grievance that involves an action taken by the Commissioner (or his designee) concerning (I) the preservation of the integrity of, or the maintenance of public confidence in, the game of basketball, and (ii) a fine and/or suspension that results in a financial impact to the player of more than $25,000, the Grievance Arbitrator shall apply an arbitrary and capricious standard of review. CBA, AR. XXXI, Section 5(c).

Also relevant is Article 35 of the NBA Constitution entitled "Misconduct," which governs all players and is referenced in Paragraph 5 of the Uniform Player Contract. * * *

It is difficult to fashion a bright-line rule for determining conduct that implicates the integrity of our public confidence in the game of basketball. I find that such conduct would include, as in this proceeding, a well-publicized violent subversion of the most fundamental authority relationship in the game, that between player and coach. An attack on a head coach puts in jeopardy the entire structure and organization of a team, affecting its morale and the sport at large. The witnesses who testified said that they have never seen an incident before of a player attacking a head coach. Westhead put it tellingly: "I was kind of emotionally very, very concerned, concerned because this is not something that is good for a team. There was such stillness going on that it kind of cut right to the [heart] of the team, you know, player/coach, coach/player."

With respect to a review based on an arbitrary and capricious standard, the New York Court of Appeals has stated, in an administrative agency context, that it chiefly relates to whether a particular action should have been taken or is justified and whether the action is without foundation in fact. *In the Matter of Pell*, 34 N.Y. 2d 222, 231, 313 N.E. 2d 321 (1974). Under this standard, courts consider whether a determination is based on a consideration of the relevant factors and whether a clear error of judgment has been committed.

Arbitrators have followed a similar application of arbitrary and capricious. In *United Paper Workers and Rayonier, Inc.*, 1996 WL 865274, the arbitrator said that, "so long as the discharge bears a reasonable relation to the facts and surrounding circumstances, it must stand." Arbitrator Whitley P. McCoy stated that, "where an employee has violated a rule or engaged in conduct meriting disciplinary action, it is primarily the function of management to decide upon the proper penalty. If management acts in good faith upon a fair investigation and fixes a penalty not inconsistent with that imposed in other like cases, an arbitrator should not disturb it. The only circumstances under which a penalty imposed by management can be rightfully set aside are those where discrimination, unfairness, or capricious and arbitrary action are proved—in other words, where there has been abuse of discretion." *Stockham Pipe Fittings Co.*, 1 L.A. 160, 162 (1945). *See also* Elkouri and Elkouri, *supra* at 910, and Owen Fairweather, *Practice and Procedure in Labor Arbitration*, 245 (2d 1981) (great deference is owed to the employer).

Interestingly, counsel for NBPA and Grievant, in their closing oral arguments, almost said as much by expressing the view that deference should be given to the Commissioner's action under even a just cause standard. Although the arbitrary and capricious standard is applicable to this proceeding, I find that it should be read together with the just cause standard of Article XXXI, Section 14(c), which provides that "in grievances regarding discipline, the issue to be resolved shall be whether there has been just cause for the penalty imposed." (emphasis mine). As counsel for the NBA have noted in their post-hearing brief, some arbitrators have linked arbitrary and capricious with just cause. *See Lockheed Engineering Sciences Co.*, 101 L.A. 1161, 1163 (Neas, 1993); *Pepsi-Cola Bottlers Inc.*, 87 L.A. 83 (Morgan, 1986).

(2) Whether a Just Cause Standard of Review Is Applicable to the Termination of Grievant's Player Contract by the Warriors

The record establishes beyond dispute that the termination of Grievant's contract was issued as additional punishment for the incidents of December 1. The letter sent to Grievant on December 1, entitled "Notice of Suspension," expressed a specific form of discipline (a suspension of a minimum of ten games) and held out the possibility of further discipline, including an increased suspension and possible termination. Subsequently, the Warriors made a decision to terminate Grievant's contract, so as not to reward him, as Baggett testified would have been the case if he were traded. The record is beyond dispute that the termination was done to punish Grievant for what he had done on December 1. Since the disciplinary nature of this action is plain, a just cause standard of review under Section 14(c) of Article XXXI of the CBA is applicable.

As for the standard of just cause, one distinguished arbitrator has stated:

> It is ordinarily the function of an Arbitrator in interpreting a contract provision which requires "sufficient cause" as a condition precedent to discharge not only to determine whether the employee involved is guilty of wrong-doing and, if so, to confirm the employer's right to discipline where its exercise is essential to the objective of efficiency, but also to safeguard the interest of the

discharged employee by making reasonably sure that the causes for discharge were just and equitable and such as would appeal to reasonable and fair-minded persons as warranting discharge. To be sure, no standards exist to aid an Arbitrator in finding a conclusive answer to such a question and, therefore, perhaps the best he can do is to decide what reasonable man, mindful of the habits and customs of industrial life and of the standards of justice and fair dealing prevalent in the community, ought to have done under similar circumstances and in that light to decide whether the conduct of the discharged employee was defensible and the disciplinary penalty just. *Riley Stoker Corp.*, 7 L.A. 764, 767 (Platt and Lavery, 1947).

In a proceeding involving just cause, the burden of proof is with the employer and I have determined to apply a clear and convincing standard regarding material issues of dispute given the nature of the conduct and the discipline involved in this proceeding.

* * *

(5) Whether Actions Taken by the Commissioner and Warriors Are Appropriate

I finally turn to the issue of whether the applicable standards have been satisfied with respect to the discipline imposed by the Commissioner and the Team. [The arbitrator found that the NBA's investigation "was done in good faith and was fair and adequate under the exigencies of the well-publicized situation with which it was then confronted" and that Stern was not required to meet with Sprewell personally, because the relevant sections of the NBA constitution did not require a hearing. Thus, he found "that the NBA complied with the standard of industrial due process." The Warriors' investigation, however, was complicated by the simultaneous league investigation. Reliance on a telephone conversation between league investigators and Sprewell was insufficient prior to contract termination, but became irrelevant because the league effectively pre-empted the club.]

When I consider the two disciplinary actions alongside each other with respect to the same conduct and against the background of just cause, I note the following:

There has never been a case of contract termination in the history of the NBA for a physical assault or a one-year suspension for such conduct or, it appears from the record, in the sports of baseball and football. In the case of the NFL, joint action by a team and the League is prohibited as a matter of contract. Although there is no specific contract provision in the NBA, as I have found, the evidence indicates that there is no history of both the League and a team imposing discipline for the same violent conduct, on or off the court. . . . This speaks to the issue of fairness, as I see it. The major cases of violence in the NBA that were brought to my attention all involved discipline by the NBA itself and not a team. . . . In the instant matter, the two disciplines together are unprecedented, as well as the severity of each, with respect to an act of violence. Given the magnitude of the Warriors' earlier discipline of the Grievant on December 1 and the NBA having become the dominant in the investigatory process after that, I am unable to sustain the termination of the Grievant's contract as meeting a standard of just cause. . . . I also find that the conduct in question was born of anger and passion and did not constitute an act of moral turpitude which is at the core of the Team's action.

* * *

My review of the Commissioner's discipline, however, proved to be exceedingly difficult, since he is entitled to great deference as the spokesperson for the sport of basketball in the National Basketball Association and is accountable for the integrity of the League. That is his duty and it would be wrong for me to substitute my judgment for his in terms of discipline. Such is not the role of a grievance arbitrator. In approaching my responsibility in the instant matter, I considered whether I should apply to the Commissioner's decision a level of review that asked and answered whether the NBA conducted a fair and adequate investigation and rendered a fair and reasonable judgment based on what was before it as a result of that investigation. Applying such a standard, I would sustain the decision of a one-year suspension of the Grievant. . . .

I have already indicated my findings with respect to the established facts. I now add my finding that the conduct of the Grievant on December 1, 1997, which was grievous in nature, was not the result of premeditation and deliberation. I do not find that the Grievant cooled down or cooled off during the 10 to 20 minute time period between the first incident and the second incident on December 1, 1997. I do not consider the time spent by him in the locker room to have been a sufficient and adequate cooling off period under all the circumstances. The record establishes that the anger, if not rage, that erupted in the first incident fed on itself during the period he spent alone in the locker room between the incidents, continuing the fury of the first and connecting the two incidents and making them actually one. . . . The record in this long and protracted proceeding establishes, and I so find, that the Grievant never cooled off or reflected in the broad sense of that term. This finding, of course, does not justify his misconduct but is a factor to be considered in rendering a fair and just determination.

* * *

I note the Commissioner's testimony before me that if he had information indicating that the second incident on December 1 was not premeditated, he would have imposed a lesser penalty. Indeed, with respect to the incidents in question he had before him from his deputy the question of a suspension limited to the 1997/98 season. While the violence inflicted by the Grievant on his Head Coach is to be condemned, the form of the condemnation in terms of discipline must be tempered by principles of fairness, as the Commissioner recognized at the hearings. Confidence in the game of basketball is dependent not only on appropriated punishment for misconduct but also on the fairness of proceedings where that punishment is reviewed. After a great deal of reflection and consideration, I have determined to uphold the discipline imposed by the NBA, but to limit it to the 1997/98 season. In justice and fairness the Grievant should be allowed to start the 1998/99 season with this tragic event behind him instead of having it extend into the next season. In reaching this judgment, I note that a suspension for the 1997/98 season involves the loss of 68 games and $6.4 million. It is many times the aggregate suspensions imposed on other players for acts of physical violence, exceeding the total of all suspensions imposed on all players for physical altercations during the 1995/96 and 1996/97 seasons combined, and all suspensions imposed for acts of altercations during the 1992/93, 1993/94, and 1994/95 seasons combined.

I find that a penalty of 68 games is commensurate with the severity of the misconduct, addresses the wrong done to the Head Coach, the Grievant's Team, and the NBA and conveys a message that violence in the NBA will be dealt with severely, but always with due regard to principles of fairness. I also find that based on other NBA disciplinary actions with respect to violence in the sport, both on and off the court, a greater penalty would be unreasonable and disproportionate to the circumstances involved in this proceeding. As for a penalty of $6.4 million against a history of lesser penalties for misconduct not involving a Coach, I find it justified by virtue of the singularity of the misconduct and the emphasis placed on combating violence by both the NBA and NBPA. A suspension of practically an entire season is one of great severity, to be sure, but appropriate given the fact that physical altercations with a head coach strike at the very core of a structure that provides stability for a team and an organized sport.

Having concluded, I should note that the Grievant . . . has had an honorable career in the NBA. He has worked hard and played hard, has won All-Star status on a number of occasions; carried the captaincy of his Team by its appointment through December 1, 1997; and won the Team's Most Inspirational Player Award during one of his playing seasons. At the hearings before me, he conducted himself in a calm and restrained manner, even at moments that would have challenged the most even-tempered of individuals. The severity of the discipline, the commentary that has accompanied this matter, and the experience undergone by the Grievant may well equip him in the future years of his life to be an example of a person who can overcome adversity and be a role model. As Commissioner Stern noted at the conclusion of the testimonial portion of the hearings: "[Grievant] is a gifted athlete who has done well in the NBA. . . . We want Mr. Sprewell in the NBA. We expect him to be in the NBA during the '98/'99 season."

NOTES AND QUESTIONS

1. *Usual Just Cause Standard.* Most collective bargaining agreements state that discipline can be imposed on members of the bargaining unit only for "just cause." Pursuant to this standard, arbitrators determine both whether the employer had cause to impose any discipline and also whether the particular level of discipline imposed was justified, although some agreements expressly negate the latter arbitral authority. Does Arbitrator Feerick in the *Sprewell* case purport to evaluate both the league's as well as the team's discipline under a "just cause" standard, or does he claim, for his review of the league's discipline, to adopt a much more deferential "arbitrary or capricious" standard, borrowed from the review of administrative law decisions? If the latter, does Feerick actually apply a more deferential standard, or does he revert to determining whether Commissioner Stern had just cause to suspend Sprewell for the 1998–1999 season as well as for the remainder of the 1997–1998 season?

2. *Just Cause Factors.* In determining whether an employer had just cause for imposing particular discipline for particular conduct, arbitrators consider a range of factors, including whether the grievant had adequate notice of possible punishment, the grievant's past contributions to the enterprise and past disciplinary record, comparisons with the employer's treatment of other employees who engaged in similar conduct, other arbitral decisions under the same and additional similar collective agreements, whether the grievant had been subjected to multiple punishments for the same conduct, and a range of possible mitigating factors. Which of these considerations did Feerick find relevant in the *Sprewell* case?

3. *Comparative Punishments.* Were you persuaded by Feerick's comparisons with the lesser punishments imposed on other players for "physical altercations" during previous seasons in the 90s? Might the league have had good reason to distinguish those altercations?

4. *Arbitrator's Authority to Weigh Evidence.* Of what relevance was arbitrator Feerick's finding of fact, based on testimony at the hearing, that Sprewell's second attack on the coach was an expression of his original anger, rather than coolly premeditated? Note that the arbitrator cites the testimony of Commissioner Stern that he would have imposed a lesser penalty had he information that the second attack was not premeditated. Was it appropriate for the arbitrator to weigh that testimony heavily?

5. *Judicial Review?* Consider whether the league should be able to have this decision vacated on appeal, and then reconsider this question after reading the last section of this chapter on judicial review.

Recognition that the parties can modify in the next collective bargaining session any precedent established by an arbitration decision may be relevant to how closely courts should review arbitration decisions like that in *Sprewell*. Indeed, in the wake of the *Sprewell* decision, the NBA collective bargaining agreement now contains a clause, Article 6, § 10, that states that the NBA and a team shall not discipline a player for the same conduct, and that a league penalty will preclude or supersede disciplinary action by any team for the same conduct. However, this same section excepts conduct of an "egregious" nature so "lacking in justification" as to warrant a double penalty of both termination of the team's contract and suspension by the league.

Another NBA arbitration decision provides a further example of how arbitration is an extension of the collective bargaining process. In November 2004, near the end of an NBA basketball game at the palace in Auburn Hills, Michigan between the Detroit Pistons and the Indiana Pacers, a typical on-court altercation between players escalated into a brawl between visiting players and Detroit fans in the stands. The melee resulted in suspensions for numerous players. The NBPA grieved the suspensions, but the NBA claimed that the grievance arbitrator had no jurisdiction because the NBA's collective bargaining agreement then provided that the Commissioner's discipline for "on court" conduct was exclusive and could not be appealed. The arbitrator nonetheless ruled that he did have jurisdiction because the incident was in the stands and thus "obviously not on the playing court." Following the proceeding, the NBA and the players union revised the CBA to provide a fuller definition of "on the playing court" and exclusive jurisdiction for the Commissioner to impose fines of up to $50,000 and/or suspensions of up to 12 games for conduct "on the playing court." In exchange, the union obtained for its members the right to appeal to the grievance arbitrator if the discipline exceeds the Commissioner limits, even for conduct on the playing court. The new agreement also provided, however, that in such cases, as well as in cases involving the integrity of the game of basketball, the arbitrator can overturn the Commissioner's discipline only upon finding that the decision was "arbitrary and capricious," not just lacking in "just cause."

The other professional leagues also have detailed and somewhat complicated provisions dealing with the players' rights to obtain arbitral review of discipline. Each league's provisions are special to the league and each differs from those typical in collective bargaining agreements outside sports. All the agreements, like that of the NBA, distinguish discipline for conduct more directly associated with the playing of the game. For instance, MLB's agreement does not provide for arbitration before a neutral for discipline imposed for "conduct on the playing field or in the ballpark." While players cannot appeal such discipline beyond the Commissioner's office, the discipline does not result in any sacrifice of salary because suspensions for on the field conduct are not without pay.

Suspensions or other discipline for off the field conduct, including the violation of external law, may result in the loss of salary and may be appealed to an impartial arbitrator under a "just cause" standard. The agreement also states that if the Commissioner determines the league's actions involved "the preservation of the integrity of, or the maintenance of public confidence in, the game of baseball," the Commissioner's final decision "shall have the same effect as a Grievance decision of the Arbitration Panel." This authority was originally intended to cover disciplinary action for gambling and has not been used more broadly. The agreement further provides that the union has the right to reopen the agreement if the authority is used in ways the union deems "unsatisfactory."

Prior to modification in its current 2020–2030 collective agreement, the NFL's collective agreement empowered the Commissioner or his designee, and not a neutral arbitrator, to decide appeals of disciplinary fines or suspensions for conduct on the playing field other than for unnecessary roughness or unsportsmanlike conduct, or for any "conduct detrimental to the integrity of, or public confidence in, the game of professional football." NFL Commissioner Roger Goodell, however, used his unilateral authority on occasion to appoint a hearing officer with authority to act as an arbitrator. For instance, in 2012 Goodell appointed his predecessor as commissioner, Paul Tagliabue, to review the league's discipline of four New Orleans Saints players for participating in a conspiracy organized by Saints' coaches to reward players with "bounty" payments for disabling targeted players, like star quarterback Brett Favre, on other teams. Tagliabue, invoking the authority of an independent arbitrator, vacated all discipline against the players, basically because they were not the initial instigators of the conspiracy and their involvement was not sufficiently distinct from other players not disciplined. (For additional discussion of this "bounty-gate" case, see Chapter 2, Section D.1)

In 2014, Commissioner Goodell took the further step of obtaining the agreement of the NFLPA before appointing an independent retired federal judge, Barbara Jones, to review his suspension of Baltimore Ravens' running back Ray Rice based on Rice's admitted physical assault of his fiancée. Initially, the league treated the assault as a minor infraction, suspending him only for two games. However, a national furor developed after a celebrity news website released a video showing Rice punching his fiancée in an elevator, knocking her out. Commissioner Goodell subsequently suspended Rice indefinitely and the Ravens terminated his contract.

The NFLPA appealed the Rice suspension, claiming that since the Commissioner had initially imposed a two-game suspension, the subsequent indefinite suspension constituted unfair "double jeopardy." The Commissioner continued to claim publicly that he had not known about the severity of Rice's assault of his fiancée until the tape was made public. Goodell agreed with the NFLPA that in this instance, because he would have to testify as to his knowledge at the time of his initial suspension of Rice, an independent outside person should serve as the reviewing hearing officer. In her opinion after the hearing, Judge Jones, claiming the authority of an arbitrator, detailed the evidence concerning the investigatory meeting between Goodell and Rice, and concluded that Rice had adequately informed Commissioner before the first suspension of the severity of his assault. Judge Jones also found that, at the time the initial suspension was imposed, the NFL had known about the existence of the tape made in the elevator. Jones therefore vacated the Commissioner's indefinite suspension of Rice. Notably, she stated that she did so under a more deferential "arbitrary or capricious" standard, rather than under a "just cause" standard, because Article 46 does not include a "just cause" provision, unlike another article in the NFL collective agreement covering club discipline.

Other uses of Commissioner Goodell's authority in disciplinary cases under prior Article 46 are considered in the last section of this chapter on judicial review of arbitration awards. The significant publicity given some of the disciplinary cases highlighted the level of the Commissioner's Article 46 authority for the players as well as for many NFL fans. The NFL and NFLPA responded by negotiating for the 2020–2030 CBA changes in Article 46 that eliminated the Commissioner's discretion to initially determine fines or suspensions "for violating the League's Personal Conduct Policy." Instead, these penalties are to be determined by a "Disciplinary Officer" jointly selected by the NFL and NFLPA. This officer is also responsible for conducting evidentiary hearings that determine "binding findings of fact." The officer's disciplinary determination, however, is still subject to an "appeal to the Commissioner . . . limited to arguments why, based on the evidentiary record . . ., the amount of discipline, if any, should be modified."

The new Article 46 process was applied in 2022 to consider multiple allegations that star quarterback Deshaun Watson had committed sexual assaults during private massages. The NFL and NFLPA jointly chose retired federal district judge Sue L. Robinson to conduct the evidentiary hearing. Robinson determined that Watson was guilty of certain assaults and set a six game suspension penalty based on her consideration of the league's past discipline for sexual misconduct. (As noted above, consistency with prior discipline is a key feature of the "just cause" standard typically used in labor arbitration.) The NFL then invoked its right to appeal the level of punishment to the Commissioner. Goodell, however, delegated consideration of the appeal to Peter C. Harvey, a former New Jersey Attorney General who has served on NFL Committees and as the Commissioner's representative in other disciplinary cases. Before Harvey could render a decision, the parties agreed on a suspension of 11 games, a fine of five million dollars, and mandatory counseling.

C. ARBITRATION OF DRUG USAGE DISCIPLINE

The professional sports leagues, like most American employers, treat drug abuse as a significant problem. Discipline for drug abuse, and associated grievance arbitrations, since the emergence of sports unions, have addressed the use of illegal recreational drugs, like cocaine and opioids such as heroin and now fentanyl. (These prohibited drugs initially included marijuana as well, though as society and a majority of states have legalized cannabis, at least for medicinal purposes, the leagues to varying degrees have become more accepting of at least occasional offseason usage.) In the past quarter century, moreover, the focus of drug usage discipline has expanded to eliminating, or at least controlling, the use of drugs, like anabolic steroids or human growth hormones, taken to enhance athletic performance or accelerate the recovery from injury.

As discussed in detail in Chapter 1, Section D, public hostility toward performance enhancing drugs resulted in Congressional pressure, and the leagues began negotiating drug polices with the sports. Today each league prohibits the use of a range of performance enhancing drugs, imposes a schedule of penalties—including long suspensions—when a prohibited drug's presence is discovered in scheduled or non-scheduled drug tests, and provides procedures, including arbitration, through which players can challenge any penalties. MLB, the NFL, and the NBA all have especially detailed agreements with their unions. Major League Baseball, for instance, has negotiated a 120-page supplementary Joint Drug Agreement (JDA) with the MLBPA that specifies prohibited drugs (now including opioids and fentanyl), considers exemptions for the treatment of certain mental health issues, sets clear severe penalties, provides treatment plans for drug abuse, and sets special arbitration provisions. The JDA also includes forty-six pages covering the protocols for urine and blood tests. The NFL now covers these topics in two lengthy supplementary agreements with the NFLPA, one on "Substances of Abuse" and the other on "Performance-Enhancing Substances," while the NBA's collective agreement covers most of the topics in 38 pages of its collective bargaining agreement.

MLB's JDA, like the NFL and NBA agreements, requires MLB to prove only a player's use of a prohibited drug; it does not require the league to prove the player's intent or even negligence. The JDA, like the NFL agreements and the NBA collective agreement, at least formally affords players an affirmative defense of unintentional and non-negligent use. All the agreements, however, state that the player cannot demonstrate a defense by merely denying intentional use, but must have "objective" or "clear and convincing" evidence." The NFL agreements further state that a player "cannot satisfy his burden" merely by demonstrating that he "was given the substance by a Player, doctor, trainer, family member or other representative" or "that he took a mislabeled or contaminated product."

Most league penalties for violation of drug prohibitions have been based on positive drug test results, so the only possible issues in challenges would be whether adequate testing protocols were observed and whether the player could carry the very difficult burden of proving a defense of unintentional and non-negligent use. Consider the following decision, however.

MAJOR LEAGUE BASEBALL PLAYERS ASSOCIATION AND OFFICE OF THE COMMISSIONER OF BASEBALL

132 Lab. Arb. Rep. (BNA) 1397 (2014)

FREDRIC HOROWITZ, ARBITRATOR.

[Alex Rodriguez, a 38-year-old infielder with the New York Yankees, had not previously been suspended by MLB for a violation of its drug agreement with the Players Association. Anthony Bosch, who operated a clinic named Biogenesis in Miami, testified by the Arbitrator that he provided Rodriquez with performance-enhancing substances (PES) over a multi-year period, including lozenges containing testosterone, testosterone creams, injections of human growth hormone and other substances all banned under the drug agreement. Bosch designed a detailed protocol for Rodriguez indicating the days and times when he should use the banned substances.

Throughout the baseball season, Rodriguez and Bosch communicated with each other directly by telephone, text messages, and BlackBerry messages related to the doses and timing of administration of the protocol, as well as the payments for Bosch's services. After stories about Rodriguez's use of banned substances appeared in the Miami New Times, MLB investigated Rodriguez using a variety of methods to obtain information. On August 5, 2013, Commissioner Bud Selig issued Rodriguez a notice imposing a substantial suspension, and the MLBPA grieved on his behalf.]

MLB contends that Rodriguez was disciplined for just cause. MLB maintains Rodriguez committed multiple violations of the JDA [Joint Drug Agreement] over the course of three seasons by the continuous use and possession of a variety of PES [performance-enhancing substances]. MLB asserts the multiple efforts by Rodriguez to obstruct MLB's investigation of his violations of the JDA violated the Basic Agreement. MLB argues adverse inferences be drawn from Rodriguez's failure to testify under oath in this proceeding or present other witnesses to refute the evidence of his misconduct. MLB contends the penalty in this case is appropriate and

justified in light of the scope and gravity of the misconduct by Rodriguez
. . .

Rodriguez contends MLB has failed to meet its burden of proving the alleged misconduct by clear and convincing evidence. Rodriguez argues MLB did not show he possessed and used PES and that the testimony by Bosch, his notebooks, and the BBMs [BlackBerry messages] are inherently unreliable, must be stricken, and can be afforded no weight. Rodriguez contends that science establishes he did not use PES. Rodriguez also asserts MLB failed to establish he obstructed MLB's investigation of Biogenesis and Bosch. Rodriguez further maintains that all of the evidence presented by MLB is irrevocably tainted by investigatory misconduct and coercion of witnesses, including Bosch.

OPINION OF THE PANEL CHAIRMAN

This is an appeal by Alexander Rodriguez of a 211-game suspension which covered the remainder of the 2013 season and the 2014 season and was issued by MLB for alleged violations of the Basic Agreement [BA] and Joint Drug Agreement [JDA]. The Basic Agreement and JDA contain a grievance procedure which allows a Player who chooses to contest the validity of a suspension to have the matter decided by a neutral arbitrator. These collectively bargained agreements require MLB to have just cause to impose a suspension on any Player. This means that MLB carries the burden of establishing just cause in arbitration by demonstrating that some or all of the alleged offenses occurred, and, if so, that its imposed penalty is appropriate. The sole question presented by the parties for decision by this Panel is whether MLB had just cause to suspend Rodriguez for the remainder of the 2013 season and the 2014 season (211 games) . . . .

MLB contends Rodriguez repeatedly violated the JDA over a three-year period by use and possession of multiple banned substances. MLB asserts Rodriguez then aggravated his offenses by obstructing MLB's investigation in violation of the BA. MLB defends the 211-game suspension as appropriate given the nature, extent, and severity of his offenses. In defense of these allegations, Rodriguez through counsel flatly denies any use or possession of PES during the period in question. Rodriguez and the MLBPA assert no credible evidence has been presented by MLB which establishes any violation of the BA or JDA. Alternately, Rodriguez and the MLBPA argue MLB is prevented from imposing any penalty because of egregious misconduct during the course of its investigation. The MLBPA and Rodriguez further contend the 211-game penalty cannot be justified when compared to suspensions received by other Players for drug or PES violations.

A review of all the evidence and argument presented by all parties in this proceeding clearly and convincingly establishes Rodriguez committed multiple violations of the JDA and BA warranting a substantial disciplinary penalty. It follows that the suspension imposed by MLB, as reduced by this Panel, will be sustained.

JDA Violations

The evidence confirms that Rodriguez used and/or possessed three discrete PES banned by Section 2.B. of the JDA during the three-year period in question: testosterone, IGF-1, and hGH. Direct evidence of those violations was supplied by the testimony of Anthony Bosch and corroborated with excerpts from Bosch's personal composition notebooks, BBMs exchanged between Bosch and Rodriguez, and reasonable inferences drawn from the entire record of evidence.

In this case, the testimony under oath from Bosch about JDA violations by Rodriguez was direct, credible, and squarely corroborated by excerpts from several of the hundreds of pages of his personal composition notebooks that were stolen in late December 2012 or early January 2013. The original notebooks have not been located or produced. Rodriguez asserts the copies in evidence are unreliable because the originals were stolen, the copies introduced were not in order, there is no way to know if the copies are complete, the time and date of many entries are unclear, and the notebooks were never kept in a secure location while in Bosch's possession. Despite these concerns, Bosch verified the entries relied upon herein were in fact his notes made contemporaneously with the events he described. No direct evidence was presented to demonstrate the excerpts he identified from the copies of his notebooks that implicated Rodriguez had been forged or fabricated. Bosch had many clients to whom he prescribed many substances, banned or otherwise. As a practical matter, he needed to keep track of clients, protocols, and payments. Bosch elected to use those composition notebooks to record this information by hand for his own use and reference. The protocols, visits, and cash payments pertaining to Rodriguez he wrote in the excerpts he identified in this proceeding confirm and corroborate the JDA violations he has described.

Similar support for his testimony is found in the evidence of BBMs [BlackBerry messages exchanged] between Rodriguez and Bosch. Those messages corroborate the JDA violations described by Bosch as well as illustrate the course and nature of their dealings. The BBMs by and to Rodriguez address doses, timing, and administration of PES to Rodriguez, as well as payment for drugs and services. The BBMs also reflect the deliberate efforts taken by Bosch and Rodriguez to conceal their activities and to avoid a positive MLB drug test. . . . Rodriguez complains the case as presented by MLB lacks specificity concerning the precise dates and times, dosages, and frequency of the alleged violations. Rodriguez decries the absence of documentation concerning the sources of PES obtained by Bosch or introduction of samples which confirm the substances Bosch claimed he used were indeed ones banned by the JDA. Yet these and other deficiencies in MLB's case cited by Rodriguez do not eviscerate credible testimony from

Bosch about his activities in supplying and administering PES to Rodriguez over a three-year period or the BBMs and composition notebook pages that confirm the violations occurred. The only reasonable inference to be drawn from the weight of the evidence is that Rodriguez violated the JDA as alleged.

The claim by Rodriguez that science exonerates him in this case is not supported by any evidence in this record. It is recognized Rodriguez passed eleven drug tests administered by MLB from 2010 through 2012. The assertion that Rodriguez would have failed those tests had he consumed those PES as alleged is not persuasive. As advanced as MLB's program has become, no drug testing program will catch every Player. In this case, the blood testing required to detect hGH or IGF-1 had not yet been implemented in the JDA and therefore was not administered during the 2010, 2011, and 2012 seasons. With respect to testosterone, the record establishes that during the period in question it was possible for an individual to pass a drug test despite having recently used the substance, depending on variables such as the route of administration (*i.e.*, transdermal, sublingual, or intramuscular), dosage, concentration, the baseline value of the individual's natural testosterone to epitestosterone ratio ("T/E"), and how soon after use the individual's urine sample is collected. Bosch testified that he considered several of these variables when developing Rodriguez's protocols, and the BBM communications between Bosch and Rodriguez show multiple exchanges where Bosch instructed Rodriguez to use testosterone at such times, and in such forms and doses, as would prevent Rodriguez from testing positive. For these reasons, the absence of a positive test during the three years in question, in and of itself, does not and cannot overcome the unrebutted direct evidence in this record of possession and use. In any event, a positive drug test is not required to establish a violation of the JDA for use or possession of a PES.

Obstruction

MLB charges Rodriguez with violating Article XII(B) of the BA by attempting to cover-up his JDA violations through a course of conduct since January 2013 intended to obstruct and frustrate MLB's investigation of Biogenesis and Bosch. MLB accuses Rodriguez and his representatives of purchasing and then destroying the original Bosch composition notebooks, as well as deactivating and destroying his own BlackBerry to prevent MLB from learning their contents. . . . MLB alleges that Rodriguez's press release on January 29, 2013, falsely denying any relationship with Bosch, and Rodriguez's role in facilitating Bosch's own false public denial later that day, which included a commitment by Rodriguez to pay Bosch $25,000 for attorneys fees, also violated the BA. MLB further asserts that Rodriguez's attempt on May 31, 2013, to get Bosch to sign a false affidavit and the offer to pay Bosch to leave the country rather than testify in this proceeding constitute additional examples of improper conduct in violation of the BA meriting a severe disciplinary response. For his part, Rodriguez denies through counsel having possessed or destroyed Bosch's original composition notebooks, any improper attempts to influence the testimony of Medina or Bosch, or that the evidence supports any of these charges.

Deliberate efforts to obstruct an MLB investigation under the JDA, or to cover-up misconduct by a Player who is subject to such an investigation, if established, may subject a Player to additional disciplinary sanctions under Article XII(B) of the Basic Agreement. In this case, the evidence considered in its entirety supports a minimum of two such violations. Rodriguez, having himself publicly denied being treated or advised by Bosch—a denial which he knew to be false—played an active role in inducing Bosch to issue his own public denial on January 29, 2013, which Rodriguez also knew to be false. Rodriguez also attempted to induce Bosch to sign a sworn statement on May 31, 2013, attesting that Bosch never supplied Rodriguez with PES and had no personal knowledge that Rodriguez had ever used them, statements that Rodriguez also knew to be false. These actions, viewed in the context of the record as a whole, were clearly designed to cover up Rodriguez's relationship with Bosch and the fact that Rodriguez had received PES from Bosch, to inhibit MLB's efforts to investigate Rodriguez's use and possession of PES, and to avoid punishment under the JDA. The remaining allegations of obstruction, while troubling, need not be addressed because they would not affect the ultimate determination regarding the appropriate penalty in this matter.

* * *

Penalty

[The Arbitrator reduces the suspension to the entire 2014 season and postseason based on prior baseball arbitration awards.]

Conclusion

Based on the entire record from the arbitration, MLB has demonstrated with clear and convincing evidence there is just cause to suspend Rodriguez for the 2014 season and 2014 postseason for having violated the JDA by the use and/or possession of testosterone, IGF-1, and hGH over the course of three years, and for the two attempts to obstruct MLB's investigation described above, which violated Article XII(B) of the Basic Agreement. While this length of suspension may be unprecedented for a MLB Player, so is the misconduct he committed. The suspension imposed by MLB as modified herein is hereby sustained.

NOTES AND QUESTIONS

1.   *A Rare Public Arbitration.* The Alex Rodriguez case may have been the most public labor arbitration proceeding ever conducted. Even though the

proceeding itself was private and participants for the most part maintained the pledge of confidentiality that is required by the Joint Drug Agreement, attorneys for the grievant made statements to the media before the proceeding and Rodriquez appeared on sports talk radio after he walked out of the hearing, proclaimed his total innocence of the charges against him, and vowed to appeal.

2. *Burden of Proof.* Arbitrators normally require employers to carry the burden of proving that an employee engaged in conduct warranting an imposed discipline. On whom did the arbitrator place the burden of proof in this case? Under what standard of proof? Given Rodriguez's passage of all drug tests, did the evidence against him depend totally on the credibility of Bosch?

3. *Player's Lawyer's Tactics.* Note that Rodriguez, unlike almost all employees in disciplinary arbitrations, declined to testify. The absence of his testimony made it easier for the arbitrator to credit the testimony of Bosch, despite Bosch's involvement in criminal activity and his public misrepresentation of himself as a medical doctor. Why did Rodriguez's lawyer not have him testify? Rodriguez subsequently admitted use, apologized to Yankee fans, returned to play in 2015, reached several significant milestones, including 3000 hits and 2000 RBIs, and then continued to work for the Yankees after his retirement. Do you think Rodriguez was well served by his aggressive lawyers and other advisors before and during the arbitration?

4. *MLB Business Strategy.* Major League Baseball expended significant resources investigating the Biogenesis operation and then pressuring Bosch to cooperate in developing cases against not only Rodriguez, but many other ballplayers, thirteen of whom also received suspensions for their involvement with Biogenesis. Was it a wise business decision for the MLB to work to taint its own product? If players evade detection by a strong drug testing program like that of MLB and do not openly use drugs, how is MLB harmed by non-public, covert use?

5. For further consideration of how sports leagues should regulate performance enhancing drugs, see Chapter 1, Section D.

D. ARBITRATION AS AN EXCLUSIVE REMEDY; § 301 PREEMPTION

The Court's decision in *Lincoln Mills, see* page 175 *supra*, to read § 301 of the LMRA to confer federal substantive law control over collective bargaining agreements ensured that the interpretation of such agreements would not vary between states. Although state courts have concurrent jurisdiction over suits to enforce collective agreements, they must apply the federal law fashioned by the Supreme Court. Not surprisingly, the Court also has held that the states cannot circumvent the authority of federal § 301 law by using an interpretation of a collective agreement as a basis for the imposition of some state law. *See, e.g., Allis-Chalmers Corp. v. Lueck,* 471 U.S. 202, 211–12 (1985) (action on Wisconsin tort claim that company failed to implement collectively bargained disability insurance in good faith must be brought under collective agreement through grievance arbitration system). The Court in *Lueck* stressed that a further reason "to pre-empt this kind of derivative tort claim is that only that result preserves the central role of arbitration." This § 301 "preemption" of state law has been asserted in many challenges to state statutes as well as to state common law torts, including some laws relevant to drug testing and discipline. Consider the following important challenge to the NFL drug testing and discipline system.

WILLIAMS V. NATIONAL FOOTBALL LEAGUE
582 F.3d 863 (8th Cir. 2009)

SHEPHERD, J.

[The NFL and the NFLPA's 2006 collective bargaining agreement (CBA) incorporated the Policy on Anabolic Steroids and Related Substances (Policy). The Policy banned NFL players from using a number of prohibited substances, including " 'blocking' or 'masking' agents" such as "diuretics or water pills, which have been used in the past by some players to reach an assigned weight." It adopted a rule of strict liability under which "[p]layers are responsible for what is in their bodies," and explained that "a positive test result will not be excused because a player was unaware he was taking a Prohibited Substance." In 2006, several NFL players tested positive for bumetanide, a prescription diuretic and masking agent that is banned under the Policy. The NFL determined that StarCaps, a dietary supplement, contained bumetanide, although the product's label did not disclose it as an ingredient. It prohibited players from endorsing any products manufactured by Balanced Health Products, the maker of StarCaps, but did not ban StarCaps as a Prohibited Substance under the Policy or inform the players of its findings, although it knew the product contained bumetanide.

In July and August 2008, players in the NFL submitted to random testing for steroids and other substances in accordance with the Policy. Five players—Kevin Williams and Pat Williams of the Minnesota Vikings, and Charles Grant, Deuce McAllister, and Will Smith of the New Orleans Saints—tested positive for bumetanide after using StarCaps. In late September and early October 2008, all of the players were advised by letter that their positive results were a violation of the Policy, and they were suspended without pay for four games. All five players appealed their suspensions, and their appeals were heard by Jeffrey Pash, Vice President and General Counsel of the NFL, who was designated by the commissioner as the hearing officer under the Policy. Pash upheld the suspensions under the Policy's rule of strict liability.

The players filed suit in Minnesota state court. The NFL removed the action to federal court. The players sought to have Pash's decisions vacated. In addition, they raised a violation of Minnesota's Drug and Alcohol

Testing in the Workplace Act (DATWA), Minnesota's Consumable Products Act (CPA) and a variety of common law tort claims. The district court granted a preliminary injunction, which allowed the players to continue playing football while their suit proceeded. The trial court denied the players' motion for summary judgment, concluding that their common law claims were preempted by section 301 of the federal Labor Management Relations Act (LMRA), the Pash arbitration awards did not fail to draw their essence from the CBA, Mr. Pash was not a biased arbitrator, and he acted within the scope of his discretion under the Policy. The court also ruled that the NFL did not have a duty to warn the players about StarCaps, even though it knew it contained a banned substance. However, the district court concluded that the players' claims under the Minnesota statutes were not preempted by section 301 of the Labor Management Relations Act. Both parties appealed portions of the district court's order.] We affirm in all respects. . .

II.

We review the preemption issues de novo.

A.

We first consider the [state law] DATWA claim. The NFL asserts that the DATWA claim is preempted because: (1) the claim turns on analysis of the Policy in order to determine whether it "meets or exceeds" DATWA's requirements, (2) the claim requires interpretation of the Policy in order to determine whether the NFL qualifies as an employer under DATWA such that the statute's protections extend to the Players, and (3) uniform interpretation of the CBA/Policy is necessary to preserve the integrity of the NFL's business as a national organization.

We begin our analysis by reviewing the section 301 preemption doctrine. Section 301 applies to "[s]uits for violation of contracts between an employer and a labor organization," or, in other words, suits for breaches of CBAs. The Supreme Court has held that federal law exclusively governs suits for breach of a CBA, and that "the pre-emptive force of [section] 301 extends beyond state-law contract actions." Section 301 preempts state-law claims that are "substantially dependent upon analysis" of a CBA, because "the application of state law. . . might lead to inconsistent results since there could be as many state-law principles as there are States." Rather, "federal labor-law principles-necessarily uniform throughout the nation-must be employed to resolve the dispute." However, the Court has established that section 301 does not preempt state law claims merely because the parties involved are subject to a CBA and the events underlying the claim occurred on the job.

In applying the section 301 preemption doctrine, we begin with "the claim itself,", and apply a two-step approach in order to determine if the claim is sufficiently "independent" to survive section 301 preemption. First, a "state-law claim is preempted if it is 'based on' [a]. . . provision of the CBA[,]" meaning that "[t]he CBA provision at issue" actually sets forth the right upon which the claim is based. Second, section 301 preemption applies where a state-law claim "is 'dependent upon an analysis' of the relevant CBA," meaning that the plaintiff's state-law claim requires interpretation of a provision of the CBA.

DATWA governs drug and alcohol testing in the Minnesota workplace by imposing "minimum standards and requirements for employee protection" with regard to an employer's drug and alcohol testing policy. DATWA lists minimum informational requirements for the contents of drug policies. DATWA sets forth the criteria that a testing laboratory must meet in order for an employer to use its services.

DATWA also requires that an employer provide an employee, who tests positive for drug use, with "written notice of the right to explain the positive test [,]" an opportunity "to explain that result," and the ability to "request a confirmatory retest of the original sample at the employee's or job applicant's own expense . . ." DATWA precludes an employer from "discharg[ing][or] disciplin[ing] . . . an employee on the basis of a positive result . . . that has not been verified by a confirmatory test." Specifically, with respect to first-time offenders, an employer cannot discharge such an employee unless the employee is first given the opportunity to participate in treatment and refuses to participate or fails to successfully complete the program.

DATWA expressly addresses CBAs. Subdivision two of section 181.955 mandates that DATWA applies to all CBAs in effect after passage of the law in 1987. However, subdivision one of section 181.955 provides that DATWA "shall not be construed to limit the parties to a collective bargaining agreement from bargaining and agreeing with respect to a drug and alcohol testing policy that meets or exceeds, and does not otherwise conflict with, the minimum standards and requirements for employee protection. . . ."

We note that it is unclear which specific violations of DATWA that the Players are alleging, other than the failure to use certified laboratories. The amended complaint does not flesh out the claim but generally states that the "[d]efendants have violated the Players' substantive and procedural rights under the Minnesota Drug and Alcohol Testing in the Workplace Act." The district court, in discussing the DATWA claim, noted that "[a]mong other things, DATWA provides that an employee may not be disciplined on the basis of an initial positive test and requires the employer to allow the employee the right to explain a positive test[,]" and that "[t]he NFL concedes that its steroid testing procedures do not comply with the letter of Minnesota law, but argues that the differences are negligible and do not require the Court to invalidate the Williamses' positive tests for bumetanide."

First, the NFL contends that, because the Players were tested pursuant to a collectively bargained-for drug policy, DATWA liability hinges on whether the Policy affords protections that are equivalent to or greater than DATWA's mandatory protections. The NFL asserts that DATWA creates two paths to compliance such that an employer may conduct its drug testing either: (1) in compliance with DATWA or (2) pursuant to a CBA providing employees with equivalent or greater protections than DATWA. The NFL argues that this will necessarily require a court to construe the terms of the Policy in order to determine whether its protections for players "meets or exceeds" DATWA's protections such that any DATWA claim alleged by the Players is preempted by section 301. Thus, the NFL is essentially arguing that an employee has no DATWA claim if he or she is a party to a CBA that is at least as protective of the employee as DATWA. We disagree.

DATWA does not state that an employee who is a party to such a CBA cannot bring a claim under DATWA. Rather, where there is a CBA that is at least as protective of employees as DATWA, the number of possible claims an employee has against his or her employer will be affected. Where the employer complies with DATWA but not with its CBA that provides greater protection, the employee could only have a claim for breach of contract. Where the employer does not comply either with DATWA or its CBA that provides equivalent or greater protection than DATWA, the employee could potentially have two claims, a claim for breach of contract and a DATWA claim.

Here, a court would have no need to consult the Policy in order to resolve the Players' DATWA claim. Rather, it would compare the facts and the procedure that the NFL actually followed with respect to its drug testing of the Players with DATWA's requirements for determining if the Players are entitled to prevail. Such a claim is not preempted.

* * *

Second, the NFL contends that, because DATWA provides employees with a cause of action against their employers, interpretation of the CBA/Policy is required in order to determine if the NFL qualifies as an employer under DATWA. Section 301 preempts a state law claim if its "resolution . . . *depends upon the meaning* of a collective-bargaining agreement." "[T]he Supreme Court has distinguished those which require interpretation or construction of the CBA from those which only require reference to it." "An otherwise independent claim will not be preempted if the CBA need only be consulted during its adjudication." In sum, section 301 does not preempt every employment dispute, and it does not preempt all other disputes concerning CBA provisions. "Rather, the crucial inquiry is whether 'resolution of a state-law claim depends upon the meaning of a [CBA].'"

The NFL does not point to a specific provision of either the CBA or the Policy which must be interpreted. . . . Finally, the NFL argues that denying preemption and subjecting the Policy to divergent state regulations would render the uniform enforcement of its drug testing policy, on which it relies as a national organization for the integrity of its business, nearly impossible. The Ninth Circuit, sitting en banc, has rejected a similar argument. *See Cramer v. Consolidated Freightways, Inc.,* 255 F.3d 683, 695 n.9 (9th Cir. 2001) (en banc). In *Cramer,* the employer, a large trucking company, "argue[d] that the terms of CBAs affecting employees in multiple states should supersede inconsistent state laws." The Ninth Circuit observed, "This contention overreaches, however, because the LMRA certainly did not give employers and unions the power to displace any state regulatory law they found inconvenient." We think this is the proper result. . . in light of the Supreme Court's observation that:

> [T]here [is not] any suggestion that Congress, in adopting § 301, wished to give the substantive provisions of private agreements the force of federal law, ousting any inconsistent state regulation. Such a rule of law would delegate to unions and unionized employers the power to exempt themselves from whatever state labor standards they disfavored. *Clearly, § 301 does not grant the parties to a [CBA] the ability to contract for what is illegal under state law.* In extending the pre-emptive effect of § 301 beyond suits for breach of contract, it would be inconsistent with congressional intent under that section to preempt state rules that proscribe conduct, or establish rights and obligations, independent of a labor contract.

[*Allis-Chalmers Corp. v. Lueck,*] 471 U.S. 202, 211–12 (1985) (footnote omitted) (emphasis added). Therefore, the NFL's national uniformity argument fails.

In sum, the Players' DATWA claim is predicated on Minnesota law, not the CBA or the Policy, and the claim is not dependent upon an interpretation of the CBA or the Policy. Thus, the Players' DATWA claim is not preempted by section 301.

[The court similarly concludes that the Players' claim under the Minnesota Consumable Products Act is not preempted, but that the Players' common law claims for breach of fiduciary duty, aiding and abetting a breach of fiduciary duty, violations of public policy, fraud, constructive fraud, negligent misrepresentation, negligence, gross negligence, intentional infliction of emotional distress, and vicarious liability are preempted by section 301.]

[Finally, the Court dismisses objection to Pash's awards.] Thus, it is clear that the arbitrator did not "ignore" the provisions of either the 2006 or 2008 Policies when he issued the awards . . . [The NFL was under no clear public policy obligation to inform the Players that StarCaps contained bumetanide. The Union waived any objection to Mr. Pash serving as the arbitrator and his action did not demonstrate "evident partiality."] Therefore, we decline to vacate the awards on this basis. In sum, we reject each of the Union's arguments for vacating the awards. Accordingly, we affirm the district court's order confirming the awards . . . For the foregoing reasons, we affirm the judgment of the district court in all respects.

———

The state law challenge to the National Football League ultimately was unsuccessful in the Minnesota courts because bumetanide was not included in DATWA's list of covered drugs. *See Williams v. National Football League*, 794 N.W.2d 391 (Minn. App. 2011).

———

NOTES AND QUESTIONS

1.   *Why No § 301 Preemption?* Do you understand why the court in *Williams* held that the plaintiffs' claims under Minnesota's DATWA statute were not preempted by § 301 federal law? Were the players' DATWA claims in any way dependent upon the players' coverage by a collective bargaining agreement? Did adjudication of the DATWA claims in any way require consideration of the NFL's collective bargaining agreement, even as a possible affirmative defense? If not, what would preemption preserve for federal law or for an arbitrator assigned responsibility for interpretation of the agreement? *See generally* Michael C. Harper, *Limiting Section 301 Preemption: Three Cheers for the Trilogy, Only One for Lingle and Lueck*, 66 CHICAGO-KENT L. REV. 685 (1990).

2.   *Complicating Collective Bargaining?* Even if the decision correctly applies § 301 preemption law, does allowing individual states to impose regulations like those in DATWA on employers subject to multistate collective bargaining agreements, like those in professional sports, not at least complicate collective bargaining? Does the NFL now have to be careful to fashion a drug testing and disciplinary policy that complies with the law of all other states in which it offers football? Does this mean that a uniform national drug testing regime is impossible, or does state law like DATWA impose only minimum procedures that can be exceeded in private contracts?

3.   *A Special Rule for Sports Leagues?* The Court has held that federal labor law does not preclude states from requiring employers within their jurisdiction to offer the same minimum benefits to employees covered by collective agreements as those the employers are required to offer to non-unionized employees. *See, e.g., Metropolitan Life Insurance Co. v. Massachusetts*, 471 U.S. 724 (1985) (allowing Massachusetts to mandate mental health coverage in general health insurance policies, including those negotiated in collective agreements). Indeed, the Court has held that federal labor law prevents a state from discriminating against employees covered by collective agreements by exempting these employees from protections

mandated for non-union employees. *See, e.g., Lividas v. Bradshaw,* 512 U.S. 107 (1994) (California's penalties for non-payment of wages must be available to employees covered by collective agreements). Could lobbyists for the NFL and the other professional leagues nonetheless make a strong argument to Congress for preemptive federal regulation of drug testing and discipline in professional sports?

4.   *Preemption of State Law Torts.* Note that the court in *Williams* held that a range of Minnesota common law torts are preempted by § 301. It did so because resolution of all of those torts required some interpretation of the collective bargaining agreement created under federal law, either to define the duties of the NFL or to determine what player reliance was reasonable or what league actions could be treated as outrageous. This holding was in line with the Court's decision in *Lueck,* which preempted a claim based on a Wisconsin tort of bad faith insurance administration because the claim required interpretation of the collective agreement that created the insurance obligation. The § 301 preemption of tort claims most often turns on whether the common law duties allegedly breached are in part defined by a collective bargaining agreement. For a well-reasoned example involving a sports league's collective agreement, see *Carcillo v. National Hockey League,* 529 F.Supp.3d 768 (N.D. Ill. 2021) (considering preemption of concussion-related claims of retired hockey players against NFL for injuries sustained because of the league's encouragement of fighting).

E. SALARY ARBITRATION

When most sports fans think of arbitration, they imagine not *grievance,* but *salary,* arbitration. Salary arbitration, as practiced in MLB and the NHL, is distinct because it does not purport to interpret or enforce contract rights already established by the collective bargaining agreement. It instead establishes a key term in the individual player's contract, how much the player will be paid the coming season (or in hockey possibly the next two seasons), based on criteria set forth in the collective bargaining agreement. Salary arbitration, similar to grievance arbitration, involves private presentations of the contending positions of the club and the player before a neutral arbitrator, or in baseball a panel of three arbitrators. Under baseball's procedure the player's case in salary arbitration may be presented by his personal agent, although the players association also has someone present to assist the player's agent and to make sure the interests of the entire bargaining unit are protected.

Salary arbitration first emerged in hockey in the early 1970s. By contrast with football or basketball, hockey resembled baseball (at least prior to the advent of free agency) in its assumption that the player contract was perpetually renewable. That posed the question of how to fix the salary figure in each year's unilaterally renewed contract. Traditionally, that prerogative had been reserved to the owners. With the emergence of independent players associations in the late 1960s, the perceived unfairness and anti-competitiveness of this practice led to the utilization of salary arbitration—in hockey in 1970 and in baseball in 1973. The hockey and baseball systems of salary arbitration also eliminated holdouts by eligible employees. The adoption of negotiated systems of free agency in both sports did not result in the elimination of salary arbitration in either, as both systems continued to include salary arbitration for some players.

The procedures operate quite differently in the two sports. Hockey utilizes a more conventional arbitration model in which hearings are conducted after briefing before a single arbitrator during the summer in Toronto. The arbitrator issues a written decision that includes a statement of the reasons for the decision within forty-eight hours of the close of the proceedings. The arbitrator is allowed to write a contract for whatever salary and other clauses the arbitrator deems appropriate. After the arbitrator issues the award, however, a club can "walk away" from an award. Article 12 of the 2012–2022 collective bargaining agreement provides:

> If a Club has elected to arbitrate a one-year SPC, and the award issued is for $3,500,000 or more per annum, then the Club may, within forty-eight (48) hours after the award of the Salary Arbitrator is issued . . . notify the Player or his Certified Agent, if any, the NHLPA and the NHL in writing . . . that it does not intend to tender to the Player [a contract] based on the award as determined by the Salary Arbitrator. Upon receipt of that notice, the Player shall automatically be deemed to be an Unrestricted Free Agent. . . [A] Club may exercise the walk-away rights . . . not more than one (1) time in a League Year in which the Club has only one (1) salary arbitration award, one (1) time in a League Year in which the Club has two (2) salary arbitration awards, two (2) times in any League Year in which the Club has three (3) salary arbitration awards, two (2) times in any League Year in which the Club has four (4) salary arbitration awards, three (3) times in any League Year in which the Club has five (5) salary arbitration awards and so on.

A hockey player's eligibility for salary arbitration depends upon two variables: his age when he first signed a standard player contract and his years of experience in the League. For example, a player who signed at age 21 becomes eligible after three years of experience, but a player who signed at a younger age is eligible only after four years of experience.

In baseball, each salary arbitration is conducted before a three-person panel of arbitrators, normally during a three-week period in February, and each panel simply gives the final verdict without any supporting decision within 24 hours of the end of the hearing. In contrast to hockey arbitrators, baseball arbitrators cannot strike a compromise or draft any contract that they deem appropriate; the arbitrators can only select one of the two figures proposed—the club's offer or the player's demand.

Baseball's "last best offer" system of arbitration is designed to encourage settlement agreements without a hearing by increasing the risk to both sides of non-settlement. The design generally has been successful. Typically 80–90 percent of all cases submitted to arbitration have been resolved privately without the intervention of the panel of three neutrals. In fact, in 2013, although dozens of players were eligible for salary arbitration, all cases were settled and no hearings were held. In 2018, however, perhaps because of rancor generated by slower signings of free agents, twenty-two cases were submitted to a hearing, with the players prevailing in twelve. This was the most since 1990, when players prevailed in fourteen out of twenty-four cases. In 2021, there were nine hearings, with the players prevailing in four.

There are many advantages to settling a dispute short of arbitration. First, the arbitration hearing itself imposes a cost on the parties. It tends to strain the relationship between the player and his club. The result in salary arbitration is a simple one-year contract. If the parties settle instead of litigating, they can agree to a multi-year deal and be creative in designing a compensation package, including bonuses, for example, or a no-trade clause. Finally, a settlement can build the parties' relationship rather than rupture it. Both parties win to some degree. In salary arbitration, there is always one winner and one loser.

The final-offer baseball salary arbitration process—which is available only to players with a minimum level of service time—has evolved since the mid-1970s, and salaries awarded have increased considerably. Even players who lose in arbitration usually leave as multi-millionaires. Many players eligible to file for salary arbitration threaten to use the process to leverage higher pay levels. To avoid salary arbitration, some clubs have offered their junior star performers multi-year contracts at premium rates. If the clubs and their players cannot settle their salary differences through negotiations, baseball's salary arbitration provides a quick, informal, and, most importantly, final resolution of the salary dispute. There are no appeals from arbitrators' decisions, and the ballplayers report to spring training under signed one-year contracts.

In the 2022 negotiations, the MLBPA unsuccessfully attempted to expand the number of players eligible for arbitration set in the prior 2016 agreement. As that agreement provided, all players with at least three years, but fewer than six years, of major league service remain eligible for salary arbitration. A player with at least two years, but less than three years, of major league service is eligible for salary arbitration if "he has accumulated at least 86 days of service during the immediately prior season" and "he ranks in the top twenty-two percent" of the players in the two-year service group in terms of major league service. The eligibility of these "super-two's," as the parties call them, is obviously the result of a compromise reached during collective bargaining negotiations between owners and the players association.

Because baseball salary arbitration never results in supporting opinions, it is not possible to examine the arbitrators' reasoning. The opinion of hockey arbitrators, by contrast, can be lengthy. Reading these opinions offers a revealing look at what player agents and team executives have to do by way of salary comparisons and appraisals, not just for purposes of arbitration, but also for negotiation. The following decision was issued by Richard Bloch, an experienced sports neutral.

NEW JERSEY DEVILS AND SCOTT GOMEZ
NHL-NHLPA Arb. (2006)

Before RICHARD I. BLOCH, ESQ.

Facts

Scott Gomez is a 26 year old centerman for the New Jersey Devils. He has played six seasons in the NHL, all with the New Jersey club. At the end of his rookie season, 1999–00, the Player won the Calder Memorial Trophy for the outstanding rookie, was selected to the NHL all rookie team and played in the NHL All-Star game. The Player was also a member of the 2006 US Olympic Hockey Team. Gomez became a restricted Group II Free Agent with his prior contract ended on July 1, 2006. At that time, he requested arbitration for the purpose of determining his 2006–07 compensation. In accordance with the CBA, this arbitration award is to be for one year. The Club has offered Gomez $3.5 million for the 2006–07 season. The Player seeks $6.5 million.

In August of 2004, Mr. Gomez and the Club arbitrated the Player's compensation for the 2004–05 season. In his decision, Arbitrator Michel Picher echoed the Club's assessment of Mr. Gomez as a "gifted playmaker," but one whose goal production was, at the time, "relatively modest":

> . . . He has never again achieved the high of 19 goals scored in his rookie year and he has averaged 14 goals per season while playing on a highly successful Club and seeing fairly extensive powerplay action.

The arbitrator concluded Scott Gomez is "extremely good at what he does well, which is to make offensive plays and, consequently, to register a high number of assists.

In certain respects, the essence of Mr. Gomez's skill set has not changed. He remains primarily an offensive forward who cannot reasonably be described as a two-way player. The statistics, which amply bear out that assessment, need not be repeated here; the premise is not in dispute. In one significant respect, however, his performance during the

2005–06 season, with a career high 33 goals, 51 assists and 84 points suggest a certain balancing of his offensive capabilities. Even accounting for rule changes that, in the immediate past season, led to a dramatic league-wide scoring increase—goals were up by almost 18%—Gomez's offensive performance was nothing less than stellar. The Club seeks to temper the impact of his achievements by noting he has been part of a very successful team, playing on lines with the likes of Patrick Elias and Brian Gionta, for example. This contention, particularly in this case, hardly advances the resolution of this case: Good players generally play better together, and whatever the alchemy responsible for the product, the fact is Mr. Gomez and his team have been to three Stanley Cup finals during his tenure and won two of them. The Devils Club is appropriately characterized as a disciplined defensive bunch, complete with specialists who are utilized as role players: Scott Gomez has shown in the most recent season that he is increasingly stepping up to his role has a very talented offensive specialist. The evidence also supports the claim that he is among the very best 5-on-5 players in the League.

* * *

Most of the proposed comparable players have signed multi-year contacts. Such agreements often, but not always, represent a premium situation, the Club paying more for longer term personnel stability. A team wishing to ensure continued availability of a young rising star, for example, may well pay more, particularly if the player forfeits free agency rights in the process. But it is also true that a player may, for a variety of reasons, conclude that long-term security, even at a reduced annual salary, is prudent on his part. As one of the seasoned advocates has noted, "The only thing one can know is that one cannot know." And that, in the final analysis, is the point. Whether one infers a premium paid by the Club or, contrarily, an "under-market" concession by the Player, the multi-year agreement is problematical for comparison purposes. The task is made no easier when one attempts to parse the meaning of "level" agreements (repeated iterations of a single salary) as contrasted with those that are "stepped." There are simply too many dynamics, financial, psychological, tactical, and otherwise, that enter the bargaining process to reduce this aspect of comparative analysis to anything approaching science. This does not require rejection of all such agreements as *per se* inapplicable. They may, in a given case, serve to inform. It means that one must exercise extreme caution before relying on them to draw pat conclusions on comparability.

One begins with several players who cannot reasonably be viewed as comparable. Martin St. Louis is a winger with the Tampa Bay Lightening. Originally joining the NHL with Calgary, he was claimed by Tampa Bay on waivers and has played with that Club since the 2000–01 season. He won the Hart Trophy in 2003–04, at the same time winning the Art Ross

Trophy as the League's leading scorer and the Pearson Trophy, awarded by the NHLPA as the MVP. Prior to the 05–06 season, he signed a 6 year contract with the Tampa Bay Club that paid him $6.5 million in '05/'06 and will pay him $6.0, $6.0, $5.0, $4.0, and $4.0 in the outlying years of the contract term. The Player notes that St. Louis was 30 years old at signing and that St. Louis' career path is distinct from that of Gomez, leading the Player to conclude his contract is not instructive. The Arbitrator agrees.

Brad Richards, a 26-year old center with the Tampa Bay Club, entered the League prior to the 2000–01 season and, therefore, played fewer games than Gomez. However he has more goals (107 to 103) and a higher point per game average (.90 to .82). He has scored more than 20 goals in each of his NHL seasons except one and is properly regarded as an all-situational player who garners substantially more time on ice than does Gomez and has been used extensively both on the power play and in short-handed situations. Moreover, four of the five years involved in this multi-year contract ($7.8 million per year) are Unrestricted Free Agent years. Richards won the Conn Smythe Trophy as the MVP in the 2004 playoffs and was the recipient of the Lady Byng Trophy. In the overall, the Richards comparison is unenlightening.

Steve Sullivan is a veteran forward with the Nashville Predators. Originally drafted in 1994 by the Devils, he was traded to the Toronto Maple Leafs in 1996 and subsequently claimed on waivers by the Chicago Blackhawks in 1999. He was traded to Nashville during the 2003–04 season. Following that season, a very good one for Sullivan, he signed a four-year contract for the 2005 through 2009 seasons that paid $3.2M each year. Offensive production statistics favor Gomez, as do career accomplishments. On a career through platform year comparison, while Sullivan has more total goals and points (but not assists) than Gomez—he began his NHL 4 seasons before Gomez—Gomez has more points per game (.82 to .75). On a platform year comparison, Gomez has 33 goals to Sullivan's 24 and a point/game average of 1.02 to Sullivan's .91. Gomez has been to 3 Stanley Cup Finals, as indicated earlier.

In this case, circumstances surrounding the negotiation of the long-term agreement are revealing, if not the four-year agreement itself; one cannot ignore the fact that Sullivan's contract was consummated when he was 31. The promise and the performance of the 26-year old Gomez are clearly distinguishable.

Milan Hejduk is a 30-year old right winger who plays for the Colorado Avalanche. Hejduk is an accomplished player, outpacing Gomez substantially as a goal-scorer—on a career through platform year comparison (both players have participated in essentially the same number games) he had 197 goals to Gomez's 103 and .89 points per game, compared to Gomez's .82.

Name	Career	PY	GP	G	A	Pts	Pts/G	+/–	PIMs/G	ESPts	ESPts/G
Gomez, Scott	1999–00	2005–06	**476**	103	**287**	390	0.82	52	**0.67**	**271**	**0.57**
Hejduk, Milan	1998–99	2003–04	470	**197**	219	**416**	**0.89**	125	0.33	264	0.56

On a platform year comparison, Gomez fairs better, scoring 1.02 points per game to Hejduk's .91. Other statistics are closely aligned: Hejduk scored 35 goals to Gomez's 33, both players were utilized essentially the same amount of time during the games and their performance in terms of even strength production was similar, although Gomez was used more on the power play. Like Gomez, Hejduk also has substantial playoff experience. He also has a Stanley Cup ring, Olympic team membership and two All-Star games under his belt. He is, as the Club argues, one of the premier players in the League. His offensive output has been substantial and consistent, including a 50 goal season, in 02–03, a 41 goal season in 00–01 and two 30+ goal seasons. He has received numerous votes for All-Star, as well as for the Hart, Lady Byng and Selke trophies, the latter recognition being a reflection of his defensive capabilities, as well.

At age 28, following the '03–'04 season, Hejduk signed a five-year contract providing for payment of $3.7, $3.8 and $4.0 million dollars for the final three years. The Player says the contact is undervalued—Hejduk having taken a lower long-term contract in exchange for security, it is suggested. While this may be so, particularly considering the forfeiture of four UFA years, this is the type of speculation that tends to outstrip the capabilities of this very expedited fact finding process. In all, the age, length and terms of this contract make it difficult to rely upon as a benchmark.

Alex Tanguay and Scott Gomez are in many respects very comparable players. Tanguay is a 26-year old winger with the Calgary Flames. Following the 05–06 season, when he was traded by the Avalanche to the Flames, Tanguay signed a three-year contract that paid $5.0, $5.375 and $5.375 million. The two players have similar career statistics. Both entered the League in the 1999–00 season and Tanguay finished just behind Gomez in rookie scoring; both were finalists for the Calder Trophy that Gomez won. On a career through platform year comparison, the games played are reasonably close, with Tanguay holding a slight edge on a points per game basis of .89 as contrasted with Gomez's .82. Tanguay has scored more goals (137 to 103; Gomez leads in assists 287–263.) The platform year comparison is also close, with Gomez scoring a few more goals and Tanguay leading on a point per game basis.

Name	PY	GP	G	A	Pts	Pts/G	+/–	PIMs/G	ESPts	Min/G	ESPts/G	PPMin/G
Gomez, Scott	2005–06	82	33	51	84	1.02	8	42	51	18.77	13.54	5.07
Tanguay, Alex	2005–06	71	29	49	78	1.10	8	46	49	18.35	13.14	4.99

Their records in the playoffs are virtually identical.

Name	GP	G	A	Pts	Pts/G	+/–	PIMs	PIMs/G	Min/G
Gomez, Scott	86	17	34	51	0.59	8	36	0.42	15.15
Tanguay, Alex	83	18	32	50	0.60	3	28	0.34	16.58

Name	PY	GP	G	A	Pts	Pts/G	+/–	PIMs	Min/G
Gomez, Scott	2005–06	9	5	4	9	1.00	–1	6	18.11
Tanguay, Alex	2005–06	9	2	4	6	0.67	1	12	18.11

The Player argues that Tanguay benefits from having played on a line with a Hall of Fame center for his entire career (Joe Sakic and Peter Forsberg). "This," says the Player, "has no doubt freed up Tanguay from a significant amount of offensive attention, and enabled him to rack up points at a more frequent pace. He also has played on a team that has always scored a lot of goals. The argument has a family ring. Commenting on Gomez's playmaking abilities, the Club argues that "equipped with this skill, he has been lined-up with a variety of talented, all-round players who have both exploited his talent and, at the same time, compensated for his deficiencies. In 2002–03 and 2003–04 Gomez was paired primarily with Patrik Elias, the Club's leading scorer for five straight seasons . . . and an NHL All-Star. In 2005–06, Gomez was paired with the Club's leading scorer, Brian Gionta, for the entire season, and Patrik Elias in the second half of the season as well." These claims, one concludes, ultimately canceled themselves out. Once more, it is not surprise that good players play well when paired with good players. The Player again claims that Tanguay's multi-year contract is "low," that "for whatever reason, [Tanguay] agreed to a deal that was below market . . ." As proof, the Player directs the Arbitrator's attention to the contracts of Messrs. Gaborik, Hossa, Lecavalier, and Richards.

Marian Gaborik is a 24-year old winder with the Minnesota Wild. He joined the Wild as their first choice in the 2000 entry draft and has led that club in scoring 4 out of 5 NHL seasons. He has three 30+ goal seasons and the evidence supports the Club's claim that he played a major role in helping the team advance to the semi-finals in 2002–03. And, he was the high scorer for the team in those playoffs, with 17 points in 18 games, ranking third in the League that year in playoff scoring. After a slow season in 03–04, he had a strong year in 05–06, scoring 38 goals and 28 assists for a total of 66 points, averaging in 65 games, 1.01 points per game. After that season, he and the Club agreed on a three-year contract paying $5.0, $6.5 and $7.5 million dollars. In the course of this contract, Gaborik forfeited 2 years of unrestricted free agency. That, according to the Club, makes Gaborik's situation "completely different, and his contract not useful for comparison purposes, unless substantially discounted." There are, as indicated above, reasons to recognize a certain premium being paid for long-term contracts. At the same time, the performance statistics for Gaborik and Gomez are revealing. On a career through platform year basis, Gaborik has scored more goals (134 to 103) and has done so in substantially fewer games (360 as contrasted with Gomez's 476). But Gomez has more than twice the assists—287 to 140 and leads in the points per game comparison .82 to .76. Gaborik is used substantially more on short-handed situations, showing his defensive prowess. But overall time on ice (Gomez is used somewhat more in even strengths situations) is close on both a platform year and a career to platform year basis.

Name	PY	GP	G	A	Pts	Pts/Gm	PIM	PIM/G	+/–	Time on Ice Per Game			
										Total	Even	PP	SH
Gomez	2006	82	33	51	84	1.02	42	0.51	8	18.78	13.54	5.07	0.17
Gaborik	2006	65	38	28	66	1.02	64	0.99	6	18.43	12.75	5.06	0.63

Name	PY	GP	G	A	Pts	Pts/Gm	PIM	PIM/G	+/–	Time on Ice Per Game			
										Total	Even	PP	SH
Gomez	2006	476	103	287	390	0.82	320	0.67	52	16.63	13.39	3.13	0.10
Gaborik	2006	360	134	140	274	0.76	196	0.54	22	17.22	12.89	3.90	0.44

Gomez, unlike Gaborik, has substantially more playoff experience and has received some voting recognition for Byng and Selke trophies.

Marion Hossa is a 27-year old right wing with the Atlanta Thrashers. Hossa entered the NHL with the Ottawa Senators in 1997 and played with them through the 2003–04 season. Prior to the 05–06 season, Hossa was traded to Atlanta and the Thrashers signed him to a three-year contract prior to the 05–06 season that paid $5.0, $6.0 and $7.0. The platform year statistics are almost identical although the Club notes, with some justification, one concludes, that Hossa's platform year scoring was achieved in 2003–04, when scoring was considerably lower than in the most recent season.[5]

---

[5]   A note here is in order with respect to the new rules and "goal inflation". To be sure, there should be some recognition that goal production during the 05–06 season, with revised rules designed to enhance just that, was up. But the arbitrator rejects an arithmetic approach that

Name	PY	GP	G	A	Pts	Pts/Gm	PIM	PIM/G	+/–	Time on Ice Per Game			
										Total	Even	PP	SH
Gomez	2006	82	33	51	84	1.02	42	0.51	8	18.78	13.54	5.07	0.17
Hossa	2004	81	36	46	82	1.01	46	0.57	4	18.62	13.17	4.05	1.41

Name	PY	GP	G	A	Pts	Pts/Gm	PIM	PIM/G	+/–	Time on Ice Per Game			
										Total	Even	PP	SH
Gomez	2006	476	103	287	390	0.82	320	0.67	52	16.63	13.39	3.13	0.10
Hossa	2004	467	188	202	390	0.84	243	0.52	64	17.59	13.49	3.32	0.78

On a career basis, however, Hossa substantially outpaces Gomez as a consistent offensive force. In five of his six full seasons, for example, he has scored between 29 and 45 goals, for a total of 188 to Gomez's 103. Hossa is more of a two-way player and has received substantial League recognition that well surpasses Gomez, including a total of 134 All-Star Votes to Gomez's 12 on a career to platform basis. He is properly compensated higher than Gomez.

In summary, both parties in this case have presented a range of reasonably comparable players whose compensation varies, for the reasons noted above. The conclusion here, based on a careful review of each of these players and their situations results in the conclusion that Scott Gomez should receive $5 million for the 2006–07 season and shall be entitled to participate in team bonus plan.

———

NOTES AND QUESTIONS

1. *Standard for Salary Arbitration?* What exactly is arbitrator Bloch trying to determine through his comparative analysis? A "fair" salary? What Gomez would receive if he were an unrestricted free agent? Is there a difference? Should the age of Gomez compared to other players be relevant? Should his participation in the playoffs?

2. *Are Compromises Appropriate in Hockey System?* How does arbitrator Bloch's award compare to the salary levels proposed by the team and the player? Does it seem that the award was in part influenced by the arbitrator's desire to avoid fully displeasing either side? If so, is this necessarily inconsistent with the intent of the system? On the other hand, would compromising in every case render the hockey system ineffective?

3. *Why Not Adopt Last Best Offer?* Baseball's last-best-offer arbitration has historically resulted in a higher level of settlement than has hockey's more

---

would somehow apply a fixed numerical adjustment factor to any such statistics. There are simply too many variables to allow for that kind of mechanical application. It suffices to note that scoring was easier after the rule changes.

traditional system. Why might the NHL nonetheless have declined to adopt baseball's system?

4. *Baseball Criteria.* Although baseball's collective bargaining agreement expressly provides that there shall be no arbitration opinion, it does specify the criteria the arbitrators are to use.

Article VI, Section E (10) of the Basic Agreement provides:

(A)   The criteria will be the quality of the Player's contribution to his Club during the past season (including but not limited to his overall performance, special qualities of leadership and public appeal), the length and consistency of his career contribution, the record of the Player's past compensation, comparative baseball salaries . . . , the existence of any physical or mental defects on the part of the Player, and the recent performance record of the Club including but not limited to its League standing and attendance as an indication of public acceptance . . .

(B)   Evidence of the following shall not be admissible:

(i)   The financial position of the Player and the Club;

(ii)   Press comments, testimonials or similar material bearing on the performance of either the Player or the Club, except that recognized annual Player awards for playing excellence shall not be excluded;

(iii) Offers made by either Player or Club prior to arbitration;

(iv)   The cost to the parties of their representatives, attorneys, etc.;

(v)   Salaries in other sports or occupations.

The provision does not weigh these factors, however. The parties direct their arbitrators to assign "such weight to the evidence as shall appear appropriate under the circumstances."

Does the provision direct a different weighing than that taken by arbitrator Bloch in the *Gomez* case? Aside from his compromise between the parties' proposals, could Bloch's analysis in that case have been rendered under this provision?

F. JUDICIAL REVIEW OF ARBITRATION AWARDS

As stated in the introduction to this chapter, the third case in the Supreme Court's *Steelworkers* trilogy, *United Steelworkers of America v. Enterprise Wheel & Car Corp.*, 363 U.S. 593 (1960), concerned judicial enforcement of arbitral awards after they are issued. The Court held in this case that, just as a court should enforce an agreement to arbitrate regardless of its view of the strength of the merits of a grievance, so should it enforce an arbitration award regardless of its view of the merits of the arbitrator's ultimate decision. The Court stated, "[i]t is the arbitrator's construction which was bargained for, and so far as the arbitrator's decision concerns construction of the contract, the courts have no business overruling him because their interpretation of the contract is different from his." *Id.* at 599. Courts may refuse to enforce or to vacate only awards that an arbitrator manifestly based not on an attempt to implement the party's agreement, but instead based in "essence" on some other consideration, such as external law or the arbitrator's view of what the agreement should have said, *i.e.*, "his own brand of industrial justice." The Court thus directed lower courts to review arbitral decisions only to determine whether the arbitrator was attempting to construe or apply the contract, not whether the arbitrator did so correctly, or even what the court deferentially might view as reasonably or minimally competently.

Not surprisingly, some lower court judges, perhaps themselves anxious to express their "own brand of industrial justice," have resisted this restraint on their authority to review arbitral decisions. Some judges have charged arbitrators with expressing their "own brand of industrial justice" whenever the arbitrators' interpretation of an agreement varies from that of the judges. This has been particularly true when the judges find the contract language to be "clear and unambiguous," despite the arbitrator's claim of ambiguity. For a recent example from the sports world, see *United States Soccer Fed'n, Inc. v. Unites State Nat'l Soccer Team Players Ass'n*, 838 F.3d 826 (7th Cir. 2016) (arbitrator cannot resort to consideration of past practice to interpret "clear and unambiguous" specified obligations of employer under agreement).

Other judges have misinterpreted language in the *Enterprise Wheel & Car* decision that an arbitral "award is legitimate only so long as it draws its essence from the collective bargaining agreement" to mean that the award must be consistent with the "essence" of the agreement, rather than the award must be primarily based on the agreement. In response, in a series of decisions in the half century after the Trilogy, the Court has had to confirm the teaching of *Enterprise Wheel & Car*. One of the clearest of these confirmations involved an important incident in the history of labor relations in Major League Baseball.

MAJOR LEAGUE BASEBALL PLAYERS ASSOCIATION V. GARVEY
532 U.S. 504 (2001)

PER CURIAM.

The Court of Appeals for the Ninth Circuit here rejected an arbitrator's factual findings and then resolved the merits of the parties' dispute instead of remanding the case for further arbitration proceedings. Because the court's determination conflicts with our cases limiting review of an arbitrator's award entered pursuant to an agreement between an employer and a labor organization and prescribing the appropriate remedy where vacation of the award is warranted, we grant the petition for a writ of certiorari and reverse. The motions for leave to file briefs *amicus curiae* of the National Academy of Arbitrators and the Office of the Commissioner of Baseball are granted.

In the late 1980's, petitioner Major League Baseball Players Association (Association) filed grievances against the Major League Baseball Clubs (Clubs), claiming the Clubs had colluded in the market for free-agent services after the 1985, 1986 and 1987 baseball seasons, in violation of the industry's collective-bargaining agreement. A free agent is a player who may contract with any Club, rather than one whose right to contract is restricted to a particular Club. In a series of decisions, arbitrators found collusion by the Clubs and damage to the players. The Association and Clubs subsequently entered into a Global Settlement Agreement (Agreement), pursuant to which the Clubs established a $280 million fund to be distributed to injured players. The Association also designed a "Framework" to evaluate the individual player's claims, and, applying that Framework, recommended distribution plans for claims relating to a particular season or seasons.

The Framework provided that players could seek an arbitrator's review of the distribution plan. The arbitrator would determine "only whether the approved Framework and the criteria set forth therein have been properly applied in the proposed Distribution Plan." *Garvey v. Roberts,* 203 F.3d 580, 583 (CA9 2000) (Garvey I). The Framework set forth factors to be considered in evaluating players' claims, as well as specific requirements for lost contract-extension claims. Such claims were cognizable " 'only in those cases where evidence exists that a specific offer of an extension was made by a club prior to collusion only to thereafter be withdrawn when the collusion scheme was initiated.' " *Id.* at 584.

Respondent Steve Garvey, a retired, highly regarded first baseman, submitted a claim for damages of approximately $3 million. He alleged that his contract with the San Diego Padres was not extended to the 1988 and 1989 seasons due to collusion. The Association rejected Garvey's claim in February 1996, because he presented no evidence that the Padres actually offered to extend his contract. Garvey objected, and an arbitration hearing was held. He testified that the Padres offered to extend his contract for the 1988 and 1989 seasons and then withdrew the offer after they began colluding with other teams. He presented a June 1996 letter from Ballard Smith, Padres' President and CEO from 1979 to 1987, stating that, before the end of the 1985 season, Smith offered to extend Garvey's contract through the 1989 season, but that the Padres refused to negotiate with Garvey thereafter due to collusion.

The arbitrator denied Garvey's claim, after seeking additional documentation from the parties. In his award, he explained that " 'there exists . . . substantial doubt as to the credibility of the statements in the Smith letter.' " *Id.* at 586. He noted the "stark contradictions" between the 1996 letter and Smith's testimony in the earlier arbitration proceedings regarding collusion, where Smith, like other owners, denied collusion and stated that the Padres simply were not interested in extending Garvey's contract. *Ibid.* The arbitrator determined that, due to these contradictions, he " 'must reject [Smith's] more recent assertion that Garvey did not receive [a contract] extension' " due to collusion, and found that Garvey had not shown a specific offer of extension. *Ibid.* He concluded that:

> " 'the shadow cast over the credibility of the Smith testimony coupled with the absence of any other corroboration of the claim submitted by Garvey compels a finding that the Padres declined to extend his contract not because of the constraints of the collusion effort of the clubs but rather as a baseball judgment founded upon [Garvey's] age and recent injury history.' " *Ibid.*

Garvey moved in Federal District Court to vacate the arbitrator's award, alleging that the arbitrator violated the Framework by denying his claim. The District Court denied the motion. The Court of Appeals for the Ninth Circuit reversed by a divided vote. The court acknowledged that judicial review of an arbitrator's decision in a labor dispute is extremely limited. But it held that review of the merits of the arbitrator's award was warranted in this case, because the arbitrator " 'dispensed his own brand of industrial justice.' " *Id.* at 589. The court recognized that Smith's prior testimony with respect to collusion conflicted with the statements in his 1996 letter. But in the court's view, the arbitrator's refusal to credit Smith's letter was "inexplicable" and "bordered on the irrational," because a panel of arbitrators, chaired by the arbitrator involved here, had previously concluded that the owners' prior testimony was false. *Id.* at 590. The court rejected the arbitrator's reliance on the absence of other corroborating evidence, attributing that fact to Smith and Garvey's direct negotiations. The court also found that the record provided "strong support" for the truthfulness of Smith's 1996 letter. *Id.* at 591–592. The Court of Appeals reversed and remanded with directions to vacate the award.

The District Court then remanded the case to the arbitration panel for further hearings, and Garvey appealed. The Court of Appeals, again by a divided vote, explained that *Garvey I* established that "the conclusion that Smith made Garvey an offer and subsequently withdrew it because of the collusion scheme was the only conclusion that the arbitrator could draw from the record in the proceedings." [. . . T]he Court clarified that *Garvey I* "left only one possible result—the result our holding contemplated—an award in Garvey's favor." The Court of Appeals reversed the District Court and directed that it remand the case to the arbitration panel with instructions to enter an award for Garvey in the amount he claimed.

The parties do not dispute that this case arises under § 301 of the Labor Management Relations Act, 1947, 61 Stat. 156, 29 U.S.C. § 185(a), as the controversy involves an assertion of rights under an agreement between an employer and a labor organization. Although Garvey's specific allegation is that the arbitrator violated the Framework for resolving players' claims for damages, that Framework was designed to facilitate payments to remedy the Clubs' breach of the collective-bargaining agreement. Garvey's right to be made whole is founded on that agreement.

Judicial review of a labor-arbitration decision pursuant to such an agreement is very limited. Courts are not authorized to review the arbitrator's decision on the merits despite allegations that the decision rests on factual errors or misinterprets the parties' agreement. *Paperworkers v. Misco, Inc.*, 484 U.S. 29, 36 (1987). We recently reiterated that if an " 'arbitrator is even arguably construing or applying the contract and acting within the scope of his authority,' the fact that 'a court is convinced he committed serious error does not suffice to overturn his decision.' " *Eastern Associated Coal Corp. v. Mine Workers*, 531 U.S. 57, 62 (2000) (quoting *Misco, supra*, at 38). It is only when the arbitrator strays from interpretation and application of the agreement and effectively "dispenses his own brand of industrial justice" that his decision may be unenforceable. *Steelworkers v. Enterprise Wheel & Car Corp.*, 363 U.S. 593, 597 (1960). When an arbitrator resolves disputes regarding the application of a contract, and no dishonesty is alleged, the arbitrator's "improvident, even silly, factfinding" does not provide a basis for a reviewing court to refuse to enforce the award. *Misco*, 484 U.S. at 39.

In discussing the courts' limited role in reviewing the merits of arbitration awards, we have stated that " 'courts . . . have no business weighing the merits of the grievance [or] considering whether there is equity in a particular claim.' " *Id.* at 37 (quoting *Steelworkers v. American Mfg. Co.*, 363 U.S. 564 (1960)). When the judiciary does so, "it usurps a function which . . . is entrusted to the arbitration tribunal." *Id.* at 569; *see also Enterprise Wheel & Car Corp., supra*, at 599 ("It is the arbitrator's construction [of the agreement] which was bargained for . . . ").

Consistent with this limited role, we said in *Misco* that "even in the very rare instances when an arbitrator's procedural aberrations rise to the level of affirmative misconduct, as a rule the court must not foreclose further proceedings by settling the merits according to its own judgment of the appropriate result." 484 U.S. at 40–41, n. 10. That step, we explained, "would improperly substitute a judicial determination for the arbitrator's decision that the parties bargained for" in their agreement. *Ibid.* Instead, the court should "simply vacate the award, thus leaving open the possibility of further proceedings if they are permitted under the terms of the agreement." *Ibid.*

To be sure, the Court of Appeals here recited these principles, but its application of them is nothing short of baffling. The substance of the Court's discussion reveals that it overturned the arbitrator's decision because it disagreed with the arbitrator's factual findings, particularly those with respect to credibility. The Court of Appeals, it appears, would have credited Smith's 1996 letter, and found the arbitrator's refusal to do so at worst "irrational" and at best "bizarre." *Garvey I*, 203 F.3d at 590–591. But even "serious error" on the arbitrator's part does not justify overturning his decision, where, as here, he is construing a contract and acting within the scope of his authority. *Misco, supra,* at 38.

In *Garvey II*, the court clarified that *Garvey I* both rejected the arbitrator's findings and went further, resolving the merits of the parties' dispute based on the court's assessment of the record before the arbitrator. For that reason, the court found further arbitration proceedings inappropriate. But again, established law ordinarily precludes a court from resolving the merits of the parties' dispute on the basis of its own factual determinations, no matter how erroneous the arbitrator's decision. *Misco, supra,* at 40, n. 10; see also *American Mfg. Co.,* 363 U.S. at 568. Even when the arbitrator's award may properly be vacated, the appropriate remedy is to remand the case for further arbitration proceedings. *Misco, supra,* at 40, n. 10. The dissent suggests that the remedy described in *Misco* is limited to cases where the arbitrator's errors are procedural. *Post,* at 1 (opinion of STEVENS, J.) *Misco* did involve procedural issues, but our discussion regarding the appropriate remedy was not so limited. If a remand is appropriate *even* when the arbitrator's award has been set aside for "procedural aberrations" that constitute "affirmative misconduct," it follows that a remand ordinarily will be appropriate when the arbitrator simply made factual findings that the reviewing court perceives as "irrational." The Court of Appeals usurped the arbitrator's role by resolving the dispute and barring further proceedings, a result at odds with this governing law.

The fact that an earlier panel of arbitrators rejected the owners' testimony as a whole does not compel the conclusion that the panel found Smith's specific statements with respect to Garvey to be false. The arbitrator's explanation for his decision indicates that he simply found Smith an unreliable witness and that, in the absence of corroborating evidence, he could only conclude that Garvey failed to show that the Padres had offered to extend his contract. The arbitrator's analysis may have been unpersuasive to the Court of Appeals, but his decision hardly qualifies as serious error, let alone irrational or inexplicable error. And, as we have said, any such error would not justify the actions taken by the court.

For the foregoing reasons, the Court of Appeals erred in reversing the order of the District Court denying the motion to vacate the arbitrator's award, and it erred further in directing that judgment be entered in

Garvey's favor. The judgment of the Court of Appeals is reversed, and the case is remanded for further proceedings consistent with this opinion.

JUSTICE GINSBURG, concurring in part and concurring in the judgment (omitted).

JUSTICE STEVENS, dissenting (omitted).

NOTES AND QUESTIONS

1. *Meaning of "Own Brand of Industrial Justice"?* On what did the Ninth Circuit Court of Appeals base its conclusion that the arbitrator dispensed "his own brand of industrial justice?" Did the Court of Appeals do anything other than substitute its credibility judgment for that of the arbitrator? What evidence might "manifest" an arbitrator's "infidelity" to his or her "obligation" to enforce the parties' agreement rather than some independent view of what is just?

2. *Effect of Vacatur of Arbitration Award?* Note the Court's iteration of its earlier directive in the *Misco* case that where a court appropriately determines that it cannot enforce an arbitration award, even because of an arbitrator's "affirmative misconduct," the appropriate response is not to decide the case itself, but rather simply to vacate the award and remand the case, perhaps for further arbitration. An arbitrator's lack of contractual authority to issue an award against a party to a collective agreement thus does not empower a court to issue a different award. Does this mean that any action challenged by the grievance before the arbitrator, such as some disciplinary penalty, must stand, at least until challenged in a subsequent arbitration? Consider the following case.

Early in the 2014 football season a Texas grand jury indicted Adrian Peterson, the then star running back of the Minnesota Vikings, for felony injury to a child, his four-year old son. Peterson had hit his son with a tree branch as punishment. The punishment reportedly inflicted "cuts and bruises to the child's back, buttocks, ankles, legs, and scrotum, along with defensive wounds to the child's hands." Peterson subsequently stated that he would "never eliminate whooping my kids . . . because I know how being spanked has helped me in my life." After the grand jury's charge was entered, Peterson took a paid leave from the team pending adjudication of his criminal case. As explained below, however, the NFL took further action.

NATIONAL FOOTBALL LEAGUE PLAYERS ASS'N V. NATIONAL FOOTBALL LEAGUE (PETERSON)

831 F.3d 985 (8th Cir. 2016)

COLLOTON, CIRCUIT JUDGE.

During the 2014 football season, National Football League Commissioner Roger Goodell suspended Minnesota Vikings running back Adrian Peterson indefinitely for "conduct detrimental to . . . the game of professional football," and fined Peterson a sum equivalent to six games' pay. Peterson's suspension stemmed from his plea of *nolo contendere* in November 2014 to a charge of misdemeanor reckless assault on one of his children. Peterson appealed his discipline to an arbitrator, who affirmed the suspension and fine.

Peterson petitioned the district court to vacate the arbitration decision. The court granted the petition, and the League appeals. After the district court ruled, the Commissioner reinstated Peterson. He has resumed playing professional football, and this appeal does not involve his eligibility to play. The remaining dispute concerns whether the League may collect the fine imposed by the Commissioner and upheld by the arbitrator. We conclude that the parties bargained to be bound by the decision of the arbitrator, and the arbitrator acted within his authority, so we reverse the district court's judgment vacating the arbitration decision.

I.

The NFL Players Association is the exclusive collective bargaining representative for present and future players in the National Football League. Collective Bargaining Agreement (2011) [hereinafter "CBA"]. . . . Article 46 of the Agreement authorizes the Commissioner to impose discipline for "conduct detrimental to the integrity of, or public confidence in, the game of professional football." *Id.* art. 46, § 1(a). The standard NFL player contract further acknowledges that the Commissioner has the power "to fine Player in a reasonable amount; *to suspend Player for a period certain or indefinitely*; and/or to terminate this contract." . . . The Agreement does not define "conduct detrimental" or prescribe maximum or presumptive punishments for such conduct.

The Agreement establishes an exclusive arbitration process for resolving disputes over player discipline. Any player sanctioned under Article 46 for conduct detrimental to the game has the right to appeal to the Commissioner. *Id.* art. 46, §§ 1(a), 2(a). The Commissioner may hear the appeal himself, or he may designate one or more persons to serve as hearing officers. *Id.* § 2(a).

Pursuant to Article 46, the Commissioner has promulgated a Personal Conduct Policy that applies to all players. The Policy specifies behavior that may be considered "conduct detrimental," explains the types of penalties violators may receive, and describes the procedures for imposing and appealing Commissioner discipline. Players are advised that "[d]iscipline may take the form of fines, suspension, or banishment from the League," and that violators might also be required to undergo clinical evaluation or mental health treatment.

The Personal Conduct Policy effective June 1, 2013, listed various forms of off-the-field conduct, including domestic violence, that could subject a player to discipline for conduct detrimental. The Policy does not establish maximum or presumptive punishments; rather, it provides that discipline will depend on "the nature of the incident, the actual or threatened risk to the participant and others, any prior or additional misconduct . . . , and other relevant factors." An identical policy was reissued on June 1, 2014.

On August 28, 2014, Commissioner Goodell sent a letter to all NFL owners to "communicate our position and strengthen our policies on domestic violence and sexual assault." An attached memorandum to all NFL personnel explained that violations of the Personal Conduct Policy involving domestic violence would be subject to "enhanced discipline." These communications followed criticism of the League's handling of a highly publicized incident of domestic violence involving Baltimore Ravens running back Ray Rice. In July 2014, the Commissioner suspended Rice without pay for the first two games of the 2014 season and fined Rice an additional week's salary after Rice was charged with assaulting his then-fiancée. The NFL and Goodell were sharply criticized in many quarters for treating Rice too leniently.

The August 2014 communications outlined measures to "reinforce and enhance" the League's approach to domestic violence. Specifically, the memorandum announced that a first domestic violence offense would be subject to a suspension of six weeks without pay, and that more severe discipline would be imposed if aggravating circumstances were present. Goodell's letter to the owners said that the enhanced discipline was "consistent with [the League's] Personal Conduct Policy."

Adrian Peterson entered the NFL in 2007 and has spent his entire career with the Minnesota Vikings. On September 11, 2014—two weeks after Goodell issued the August 2014 communications—a Texas grand jury indicted Peterson for felony injury to a child. The indictment alleged that in May 2014, Peterson hit his four-year-old son with a tree branch as a form of corporal punishment. . . .

On November 4, 2014, Peterson pleaded *nolo contendere* to a reduced charge of reckless assault, a class A misdemeanor. Two weeks later, Goodell suspended Peterson indefinitely (for a minimum of the six games remaining in the 2014 season), fined him six-weeks' salary, and required him to meet with a League-appointed psychiatrist. Goodell relied on the "baseline discipline" of a six-game suspension that was announced in the August 2014 memorandum. Goodell also identified several aggravating circumstances that merited the lengthy suspension: the age and vulnerability of the child, the emotional and psychological trauma inflicted on a young child, and Peterson's lack of remorse and suggestion that he would not refrain from engaging in similar conduct in the future. Goodell told Peterson that he would periodically review Peterson's progress towards reinstatement, with the first review to occur in April 2015.

The Players Association appealed on Peterson's behalf under the procedures of the Collective Bargaining Agreement. The Commissioner designated Harold Henderson to hear Peterson's appeal. Henderson is the president of the Player Care Foundation, a League-affiliated charity. He previously served for sixteen years as the League's vice president for labor relations and chairman of the NFL Management Council Executive Committee. The Association asked Henderson to recuse himself from the hearing due to his close ties to League officials and his role in shaping the League's disciplinary policies. Henderson denied the request, noting that the Association had not objected to his designation as arbitrator in dozens of past disciplinary appeals.

The Players Association's primary argument before Arbitrator Henderson was that custom and practice under the Personal Conduct Policy in effect at the time of Peterson's misconduct limited the Commissioner's disciplinary authority to a maximum two-game suspension for a first-time domestic violence offense. The Association argued that Goodell was required to apply the policies in force on the date of the misconduct, and asked the arbitrator to reduce Peterson's punishment to a two-game suspension and a fine equivalent to two-weeks' salary. The Association also challenged the process by which Peterson's discipline was determined and the conditions placed on his reinstatement, accusing the League of "making up the process and punishment as it goes." . . .

The arbitrator affirmed Peterson's discipline, finding that it was "fair and consistent." He concluded that the August 2014 communications did not constitute a change of the Personal Conduct Policy, but rather "reinforce[d] that policy with initiatives to explain and enhance it." He observed that the Personal Conduct Policy, which had not been rescinded, authorized suspensions and provided that "[t]he specifics of the disciplinary response will be based on the nature of the incident" and other relevant factors. The arbitrator explained that the Commissioner has "broad discretion" under Article 46 of the Agreement and the Personal Conduct Policy, and concluded that the August 2014 pronouncements "simply reflect his current thinking on domestic violence and other incidents involving physical force."

The arbitrator quoted from a prior arbitration decision in 2010 concerning the suspension of a Miami Dolphins player:

The Commissioner has considerable discretion in assessing discipline. If he should determine that the current level of discipline imposed for certain types of conduct has not been effective in deterring such conduct, it is within his authority to increase discipline in such cases. He is not forever bound to historical precedent.

In the *Dolphins Player* case, the player argued that a one-game suspension for domestic violence was inconsistent with prior cases in which the League had imposed only fines for first-time domestic violence offenses. The arbitrator there observed, however, that "domestic violence is an area where discipline has been increased, and a suspension for a first offense is now the norm rather than the exception. [The Commissioner] should not be handcuffed by prior cases." In Peterson's case, the arbitrator reasoned that just as the Commissioner was permitted to begin suspending, rather than fining, players for first-time offenses in 2010, he had "broad discretion" to increase the magnitude of suspensions and fines in 2014 if he concluded that past sanctions had been an insufficient deterrent.

The arbitrator also rejected the Players Association's contention that the Commissioner's discipline of Peterson was inconsistent with an arbitrator's decision in the Ray Rice case. Although the Commissioner initially suspended Rice for two games, he later changed the punishment to an indefinite suspension after a website published video footage of Rice's assault. An arbitrator vacated the indefinite suspension, finding that the second suspension was an arbitrary repunishment for misconduct that already had been punished. The *Rice* arbitrator opined, however, that "[i]f this were a matter where the *first discipline imposed* was an indefinite suspension, an arbitrator would be hard pressed to find that the Commissioner had abused his discretion." Arbitrator Henderson thus concluded that the Commissioner's indefinite suspension of Peterson was not inconsistent with the reasoning in *Rice*.

The arbitrator then stated that it was unnecessary to find whether the June 2014 policy and the August 2014 communications were "a single policy or two, or which one was applied, because the result is the same in either instance." He explained that the Commissioner's discipline of Peterson fit both the Personal Conduct Policy and the August 2014 communications. The arbitrator acknowledged that Peterson's discipline was more severe than in most prior domestic violence cases, but found that the "severe beating of a four year old child" was "arguably one of the most egregious cases of domestic violence in this Commissioner's tenure." He said that "[t]here is no comparing this brutal incident to the typical violence against another adult."

The arbitrator rejected the Players Association's argument that Peterson lacked fair notice of the potential punishment. He found no evidence that Peterson knew what level of discipline had been imposed in prior domestic violence cases or that he relied in any way on an understanding about potential disciplinary measures. The arbitrator distinguished a case involving a "fine for missing the last few minutes of a Thursday practice" and other cases cited by the Association, finding no reason to believe that "Peterson might not have inflicted those injuries on his young son if he had known he could be suspended six weeks rather than two." The arbitrator saw no lack of basic fairness in the Commissioner's approach. Accordingly, the arbitrator denied the grievance and affirmed the Commissioner's discipline of Peterson.

The Players Association petitioned the district court to vacate the arbitration award. The Association argued that the case involved "the rare Arbitration Award that must be set aside" and sought to vacate the award on four grounds, alleging: (1) the Commissioner retroactively punished Peterson, in violation of the Collective Bargaining Agreement; (2) the arbitrator exceeded his authority by hypothesizing whether the Commissioner could have disciplined Peterson in the same manner prior to the August 2014 memorandum; (3) the arbitrator was evidently partial; and (4) the award violated the principle of fundamental fairness.

The district court accepted the Association's first two arguments and granted the petition. . . .

The League appeals the district court's order. After the district court ruled, the Commissioner reinstated Peterson to play football, and this appeal concerns only the monetary sanction imposed by the Commissioner and upheld by the arbitrator. . . .

II.

In an arbitration case like this one, the role of the courts is very limited. *Major League Baseball Players Ass'n v. Garvey*, 532 U.S. 504, 509 (2001) (per curiam). . . .Vacatur of an arbitration award is appropriate only when the decision does not "draw [ ] its essence from the collective bargaining agreement," and the arbitrator instead has "dispense[d] his own brand of industrial justice." *Enter. Wheel*, 363 U.S. at 597.

The gravamen of the Players Association's petition is that the arbitrator ignored "law of the shop" that forbids the retroactive application of a new disciplinary policy to Peterson. The Association maintains that industrial common law developed under the Personal Conduct Policy before Peterson's misconduct constrained the League to impose no more than a two-game suspension for a first-time domestic violence infraction. The Association argues that the Commissioner relied on a "new policy" set forth in the August 2014 communications to impose a more severe penalty on Peterson, and that the arbitrator ignored the law of the shop when he upheld the discipline. The district court, relying primarily on the *Rice* arbitration, ruled that the arbitrator "simply disregarded the law of the shop."

To be sure, "the industrial common law—the practices of the industry and the shop—is equally a part of the collective bargaining agreement although not expressed in it." *United Steel Workers v. Warrior & Gulf Nav. Co.*, 363 U.S. 574, 581–82 (1960). . . . At the same time, however, "an arbitrator's error in failing to give precedential or preclusive effect to a previous arbitration award is not alone sufficient to vacate an arbitration award." *SBC Advanced Sols., Inc. v. Commc'ns Workers, Dist. 6*, 794 F.3d 1020, 1030 (8th Cir. 2015); *see Am. Nat'l Can Co. v. United Steelworkers*, 120 F.3d 886, 892–93 (8th Cir. 1997). An arbitrator acts within his authority as long as he is arguably construing or applying the contract, even if a court disagrees with the arbitrator's construction or application. *Misco*, 484 U.S. at 38. The same holds true for the law of the shop: as long as the arbitrator is arguably construing or applying arbitral precedents, a court's disagreement with the arbitrator's application of precedent is not sufficient grounds to vacate an arbitration decision. *See Am. Nat'l Can*, 120 F.3d at 892–93.

The district court concluded that the arbitrator ignored the law of the shop set forth in the *Rice* decision—namely, that the "new policy" arising from the August 2014 communications cannot be applied retroactively. But the arbitrator addressed *Rice* head-on. . . .

The district court disagreed with the arbitrator's decision and found "no valid basis to distinguish this case from the *Rice* matter." In resolving a motion to vacate an arbitration award, however, the question for the courts is not whether the arbitrator's distinction is persuasive enough to withstand ordinary judicial review. An erroneous interpretation of a contract, including the law of the shop, is not a sufficient basis for disregarding the conclusion of the decisionmaker chosen by the parties. *Misco*, 484 U.S. at 38; *Alcan Packaging*, 729 F.3d at 843. The dispositive question is whether the arbitrator was at least arguably construing or applying the contract, including the law of the shop. The arbitrator here undoubtedly construed the *Rice* decision in reaching his decision. Disagreement with his conclusion is not a valid ground on which to vacate the decision

Aside from the *Rice* decision, the Players Association contends that the arbitrator ignored other arbitral precedents that establish a prohibition on retroactive punishment. The arbitrator, however, disagreed with the Association's premise that the Commissioner applied a "new" policy that called for discipline that was unavailable under the "old" policy. He concluded instead that the August 2014 communications "do not constitute a change" of the preexisting Personal Conduct Policy, because the communications did not effect a change in the Commissioner's disciplinary power.

The arbitrator relied on the Collective Bargaining Agreement and the law of the shop to reach this conclusion. The Agreement gives the Commissioner discretion to impose fines and suspensions for conduct detrimental to the game. The Personal Conduct Policy allows for fines and suspensions based on the nature of the incident and other relevant factors; it does not establish maximum punishments. Citing the 2010 *Dolphins Player* decision, the arbitrator reasoned that the Commissioner "is not forever bound to historical precedent," and that "[i]f he should determine that the current level of discipline imposed for certain types of conduct has not been effective in deterring such conduct, it is within his authority to increase discipline in such cases." As applied to Peterson's case, therefore, the arbitrator thought the terms of the Agreement, the law of the shop, and the Personal Conduct Policy gave the Commissioner discretion to impose a six-game suspension and fine if he concluded that shorter suspensions in prior cases had been inadequate. The arbitrator's decision on this point was grounded in a construction and application of the terms of the Agreement and a specific arbitral precedent. It is therefore not subject to second-guessing by the courts.

* * *

Article 46 and the Personal Conduct Policy by their terms place no limit on the Commissioner's authority to suspend players. In his August 2014 letter to NFL owners, Goodell described the attached memorandum and the six-game suspension for first-time domestic violence offenses as "*consistent with* our Personal Conduct Policy." App. 29 (emphasis added). And, as we have explained, the law of the shop included arbitral precedent stating that the Commissioner is not forever bound to historical precedent if prior discipline under the Personal Conduct Policy provided insufficient deterrence. In other words, the League might change its discipline without changing its policy.

The parties have delegated to the arbitrator the job of reconciling conflicting evidence. The arbitrator, having been presented with the Commissioner's statements, concluded that the August 2014 communications did not constitute a change of the Personal Conduct Policy. He necessarily found, therefore, that Goodell's statements were not admissions to the contrary. Courts are not permitted to review the merits of an arbitration decision even when a party claims that the decision rests on factual errors. *See Garvey*, 532 U.S. at 509; *Misco*, 484 U.S. at 39.

The Players Association further argues that the arbitrator ignored four arbitral decisions requiring advance notice to a player of the consequences of a violation. The arbitrator mentioned these decisions and found them distinguishable. A close reading of the prior decisions shows why. . . .

In any event, the question for a reviewing court is not whether the arbitrator's distinctions were correct, but whether the arbitrator was arguably construing and applying the contract and the law of the shop. The arbitrator applied the law of the shop . . . . We see no basis for setting aside the decision under a federal court's limited scope of review.

The Players Association also argues that the arbitrator ignored an "admission" by Commissioner Goodell, when testifying in the *Rice* case, that he could not apply retroactively the "new" policy of imposing a six-game suspension for first-time domestic violence offenses. . . .

The arbitrator obviously did not agree with the Association that Goodell's testimony in *Rice* was an admission that he could not apply a six-game suspension to Peterson. The meaning of Goodell's statement is a question of fact. Given the context of the *Rice* testimony, the arbitrator reasonably concluded that Goodell did not testify to one belief on November 5, 2014, and then act to the contrary two weeks later when he disciplined Peterson. In any case, a federal court may not set aside an arbitrator's decision based on "improvident, even silly, factfinding," so the Association's reliance on Goodell's testimony does not carry the day. *Garvey*, 532 U.S. at 509, 532 U.S. at 509 (quoting *Misco*, 484 U.S. at 39).

III.

* * *

IV.

* * *

The Association [also] asserts that Arbitrator Henderson was "evidently partial," because he demonstrated "such a degree of partiality that a reasonable person could assume that the arbitrator had improper motives." *Dow Corning Corp. v. Safety Nat'l Cas. Corp*, 335 F.3d 742, 750 (8th Cir. 2003) (quotation omitted). In *Williams v. National Football League*, 582 F.3d 863 (8th Cir. 2009), an NFL player raised a virtually identical challenge to the League's general counsel serving as an arbitrator in a dispute arising under the previous collective bargaining agreement. We held that the Association had "waived its objection to [the general counsel] serving as arbitrator by agreeing in the CBA that the Commissioner's designee . . . could serve as arbitrator." *Id.* at 885–86. Allowing the Commissioner or the Commissioner's designee to hear challenges to the Commissioner's decisions may present an actual or apparent conflict of interest for the arbitrator. But the parties bargained for this procedure, and the Association consented to it. *See* CBA art. 46 § 2(a). It was foreseeable that arbitration under the Agreement sometimes would involve challenges to the credibility of testimony from Goodell or other League employees. When parties to a contract elect to resolve disputes through arbitration, a grievant "can ask no more impartiality than inheres in the method they have chosen." *Winfrey v. Simmons Foods, Inc.*, 495 F.3d 549, 551 (8th Cir. 2007) (quotation omitted). The Association's challenge to Henderson's service as arbitrator is thus foreclosed by *Williams*, and a remand is unnecessary. *Accord Nat'l Football League Mgmt. Council v. Nat'l Football Players Ass'n*, 820 F.3d 527, 548 (2d Cir. 2016).

The Association's remaining contention is that the arbitration was "fundamentally unfair." Fundamental fairness is a not a basis for vacatur identified in the Labor Management Relations Act or the Federal Arbitration Act. The latter statute informs our analysis in labor arbitration cases. *See Granite Rock Co. v. Int'l Bhd. of Teamsters*, 561 U.S. 287, 298 n.6 (2010); *Am. Postal Workers Union v. U.S. Postal Serv.*, 754 F.3d 109, 112 n.4 (2d Cir. 2014). Even assuming for the sake of analysis that there could be grounds for vacatur that are not specified in the statutes, *cf. Hall St. Assocs., LLC v. Mattel, Inc.*, 552 U.S. 576, 589 (2008), "our narrow construction of extra-statutory review militates against" adopting a "fundamental fairness" standard. *Hoffman v. Cargill, Inc.*, 236 F.3d 458, 462 (8th Cir. 2001). *Hoffman* did not "categorically reject the possibility of such a standard," but said that it could apply only "to arbitration schemes so deeply flawed as to preclude the possibility of a fair outcome." *Id.* at 462–63.

The Players Association does not identify any structural unfairness in the Article 46 arbitration process for which it bargained. The Association's fundamental fairness argument is little more than a recapitulation of its retroactivity argument against the merits of the arbitrator's decision. We have never suggested that when an award draws its essence from the collective bargaining agreement, a dissatisfied party nonetheless may achieve vacatur of the arbitrator's decision by showing that the result is "fundamentally unfair." The Association's fairness argument does not fit within the narrow window left open for consideration in *Hoffman*, and we therefore conclude that the contention is without merit.

For the foregoing reasons, the judgment of the district court is reversed, and the case is remanded with directions to dismiss the petition.

NOTES AND QUESTIONS

1. *Basis for Reviewing Arbitrator Under § 301 Precedent?* Did the union have any basis to argue that arbitrator Henderson based his decision on his own view of "industrial justice" or fairness rather than on the discretion that he determined the agreement afforded Commissioner Goodell? If not, could the district court's decision to vacate Henderson's affirmation of Goodell's punishment have been consistent with the Court's clear directive in *Enterprise Wheel & Car Corp.*, *Misco*, and *Garvey*? Was it the arbitrator or the district judge that attempted to impose personal views on what is fair or just, regardless of the extent to which the agreement limited managerial discretion?

2. *Effect of District Court's Vacatur?* What should have been the effect of the district court's vacatur of Henderson's decision on the appeal of the punishment imposed by Commissioner Goodell? Based on the Supreme Court's decisions in *Misco* and *Garvey*, the judge had authority only to vacate the arbitral decision, not to vacate any punishment. Article 46 affords players a

right to appeal, but does not stay any punishment during the appeal. Did the district judge have any authority to enjoin punishment pending another arbitration hearing and decision? He in fact only remanded "for further proceedings before the arbitrator as permitted by the CBA."

3. *Federal Arbitration Act.* Note the Eighth Circuit's citation of the Federal Arbitration Act (FAA) when addressing the union's argument that the arbitration was "fundamentally unfair." The 1925-enacted FAA renders "enforceable" an agreement to arbitrate in any contract involving interstate commerce. When the Supreme Court rendered its decisions in *Lincoln Mills* and the Trilogy, the parties and the Justices apparently assumed that § 301 of the LMRA would have to be the basis for enforcement of agreements to arbitrate because § 1 of the FAA exempted "contracts of employment" like collective bargaining agreements. However, the Supreme Court subsequently invigorated the FAA, and in *Circuit City Stores, Inc. v. Adams*, 532 U.S. 105 (2001), held that this exemption covered employment contracts only of workers directly engaged in foreign or interstate commerce, such as railroad workers or truckers. This means that the FAA provides another basis for the enforcement of agreements to arbitrate in professional sports. Section 10 of the FAA also seems to provide further procedural grounds for vacating awards, including "evident partiality or corruption" or "refusing to hear evidence pertinent and material," but it does not provide for any judicial substantive review.

4. *The Tom Brady/Deflate-Gate Case.* For another appellate court's reversal of a district court review of an Article 46 hearing, see *NFL Management Council v. NFLPA (Brady)*, 820 F.3d 527 (2d Cir. 2016), cited in the Peterson case. There, the district court refused the NFL's request to confirm Commissioner Goodell's decision as the collectively bargained reviewer of the four-game suspension of New England Patriots quarterback Tom Brady for his involvement in the team's partial deflation of footballs he used in a playoff game (addressed in Chapter 1). The district court instead vacated Arbitrator Goodell's decision and also Brady's four-game suspension. The district court did not explain how its vacation of the suspension was consistent with *Misco* and *Garvey*, or with Article 46 of the collective agreement. The Second Circuit reversed the district court and, like the Eighth Circuit in *Peterson*, adhered to the *Enterprise Wheel & Car* standard for limited judicial review and refused to allow the district judge to impose his own standards of "fundamental fairness" or "adequate notice."

The Second Circuit in Brady also considered the union's arguments under the review standards in the FAA. The court held that Goodell's Article 46—authorized review of Brady's punishment did not suffer from "evident partiality" because the parties to a collective agreement "can ask for no more partiality than inheres in the method they have chosen." 820 F.3d at 548. The court also held that the FAA does not restrict broad arbitral control over the admission of evidence unless that control is exercised to deny "fundamental fairness."

5.   *Fundamental Fairness as a Review Standard?* The Second Circuit's interpretation of the FAA in *Brady* to allow vacatur of an arbitral award for the denial of "fundamental fairness" raises the question of whether courts can apply this standard to the review of any labor arbitration award. In another review of an Article 46 arbitration award, a district court in the Second Circuit refused to read the Brady case to expand this standard for judicial review of labor arbitration awards because doing so would be inconsistent with the jurisprudence developed by the Supreme Court under § 301 of the LMRA. *National Football Management Council v. National Football League Players Association (Elliott)*, 296 F. Supp. 3d 614 (S.D.N.Y. 2017). This decision denied a motion to vacate arbitrator Harold Henderson's acceptance of Commissioner Goodell's six-game suspension of star Dallas Cowboy running back Ezekiel Elliott for the violent physical abuse of his ex-girlfriend. The district court alternatively held that Henderson did not deny "fundamental fairness" by refusing to compel the Commissioner or the ex-girlfriend accuser to testify. The Second Circuit then declined to stay on appeal the district court's ruling, effectively defeating the NFLPA's efforts to enjoin the suspension. Do you agree that adoption of a "fundamental fairness" standard would undermine the finality and functionality of the arbitration process promised by the Court's § 301 decisions, including the Trilogy? Is the standard even implicit in the FAA grounds for vacatur quoted in note 3 above?

6.   *Do Unilaterally Appointed Arbitrators Deserve the Same Deference?* Might the departure of the district judges in the *Peterson* and *Brady* from the review standard established in *Enterprise Wheel & Car* be in part explained by the judges' discomfort with arbitrators who are not chosen by both sides? Should the Trilogy apply only when arbitrators are chosen through a bilateral arbitration process? Or would the involvement of courts in judicial review of arbitrations conducted under management-empowering provisions like Article 46 lead only to an alternative loosening of substantive constraints on management discretion?

Alternatively, should decisions by the Commissioner under Article 46 not be reviewed as arbitration decisions at all, but rather as decisions governing a private association subject to the common law arbitrariness review applied in the *Finley v. Kuhn* decision in Chapter 2, Section C. For advocacy of this position, see Stephen Ross and Roy Eisenhardt, *Clear Statement Rules and the Integrity of Labor Arbitration*, 10 ARB. L. REV. 1 (2018). Consider also the relevance to judicial review of the modifications to Article 46 noted at the end of Section B above. These modifications provide that a bilaterally chosen disciplinary officer will initially determine discipline for violation of the NFL's Personal Conduct Policy after conducting an evidentiary hearing, but also provide for a right of appeal to the Commissioner for possible modification of the discipline.

CHAPTER 5

CONTRACTUAL RESTRAINTS ON LABOR MOBILITY IN PROFESSIONAL SPORTS

■ ■ ■

Disputes about player movement from one team to another have been the central preoccupation of sports litigation since the 1870s. From the 1880s to the 1960s, the principal focus of court adjudication in professional sports was on contract law that defined the relationship between individual player and club. Teams regularly sought to enforce, and players to elude, restrictions that limited players to negotiating contracts with a single team. As suggested in the two prior chapters, these restrictions have been loosened through collective bargaining and the arbitration system it supports. By the early 1970s, moreover, unions representing players in professional sports leagues other than MLB helped launch successful federal antitrust litigation against player restraints. By the beginning of the 1980s, the players associations in each of the four major team sports—baseball, football, basketball, and hockey—had negotiated in their collective agreements new rules that specified whether and when a player could become a "free agent" and be entitled to move to any other team within that league that made him a better contract offer.

Contract law nonetheless remains relevant to current labor markets in professional sports for several reasons. First, it provides the background law that is modified by collective bargaining. Second, it continues to govern player movement between sports leagues. And third, it applies to working relationships not governed by collective agreements, including those of independent contractors, like tennis or golfing professionals, or coaches or other managerial employees of professional teams.

A. STANDARDS FOR ENFORCEMENT OF CONTRACTUAL MOBILITY RESTRAINTS

From the earliest days of American team sports, employers imposed contract terms on talented young athletes who wanted to play. Owners colluded to set limits on what they would pay their players. The contracts also contained provisions granting management the right to terminate the contract upon fairly short notice and a promise by the player only to play for that particular club and no other club.

The earliest challenges to these restraints on player mobility came not from sports unions, but from player attempts to move to clubs that did not honor the restraints because of their membership in rival leagues. For instance, in their fourth year of operation in 1879, the baseball club owners of the National League created a "reserve system" because of the owners' concern with players moving from one club to another, sometimes in the middle of a season, for modest increases in salary. This management device worked well for the owners within the National League, but the device was challenged when Ban Johnson and eight entrepreneurs created the rival American League in 1901. The American League business strategy was to induce the marquee players of the National League to jump to the Americans. Fans followed their favorites to the new league. Among the finest stars of the American League was Napoleon Lajoie, a future Hall of Fame second baseman. Lajoie had anchored the Philadelphia Phillies' infield for five seasons. His $2,400 annual salary payable under his Phillies' contract was the ceiling imposed on players' salaries by agreement of the owners of the National League. To avoid this ceiling, Lajoie moved crosstown to play in the fledgling American League for the Athletics club. The Phillies brought suit against Napoleon Lajoie, and his case was the first important sports law case decided by American courts.

PHILADELPHIA BALL CLUB V. LAJOIE
202 Pa. 210, 51 A. 973 (1902)

POTTER, JUSTICE.

The defendant in this case contracted to serve the plaintiff as a baseball player for a stipulated time. During that period he was not to play for any other club. He violated his agreement, however, during the term of his engagement, and, in disregard of his contract, arranged to play for another and a rival organization. The plaintiff, by means of this bill, sought to restrain him during the period covered by the contract. The court below refused an injunction.

* * *

The learned judge who filed the opinion in the court below, with great industry and painstaking care, collected and reviewed the English and American decisions bearing upon the question involved, and makes apparent the wide divergence of opinion which has prevailed. We think, however, that in refusing relief unless the defendant's services were shown to be of such a character as to render it impossible to replace him he has taken extreme ground. It seems to us that a more just and equitable rule is laid down in *Pom. Spec. Perf.* p. 31, where the principle is thus declared: "Where one person agrees to render personal services to another, which require and presuppose a special knowledge, skill, and ability in the employee, so that in case of a default the same service could not easily be obtained from others, although the affirmative specific performance of the contract is beyond the power of the court, its performance will be negatively enforced by enjoining its breach.... The damages for breach of such contract cannot be estimated with any certainty, and the employer cannot, by means of any damages, purchase the same service in the labor market." ... [W]hen, owing to special features, the contract involves peculiar convenience or advantage, or where the loss would be a matter of uncertainty, then the breach may be deemed to cause irreparable injury.

* * *

The court below finds from the testimony that "the defendant is an expert baseball player in any position; that he has a great reputation as a second baseman; that his place would be hard to fill with as good a player; that his withdrawal from the team would weaken it, as would the withdrawal of any good player, and would probably make a difference in the size of the audiences attending the game." We think that, in thus stating it, he puts it very mildly, and that the evidence would warrant a stronger finding as to the ability of the defendant as an expert ball player. He has been for several years in the service of the plaintiff club, and has been re-engaged from season to season at a constantly increasing salary. He has become thoroughly familiar with the action and methods of the other players in the club, and his own work is peculiarly meritorious as an integral part of the teamwork which is so essential. In addition to these features which render his services of peculiar and special value to the plaintiff, and not easily replaced, Lajoie is well known, and has great reputation among the patrons of the sport, for his ability in the position which he filled, and was thus a most attractive drawing card for the public. He may not be the sun in the baseball firmament, but he is certainly a bright particular star. We feel, therefore, that the evidence in this case justifies the conclusion that the services of the defendant are of such a unique character, and display such a special knowledge, skill, and ability, as renders them of peculiar value to the plaintiff, and so difficult of substitution that their loss will produce "irreparable injury," in the legal significance of that term, to the plaintiff. The action of the defendant in violating his contract is a breach of good faith, for which there would be no adequate redress at law, and the case, therefore, properly calls for the aid of equity in negatively enforcing the performance of the contract by enjoining against its breach.

[The court then turned to the lower court's argument that the contract lacked "mutuality of remedy," because while Lajoie was bound to "perpetually renewable" obligations, the team could release him (without pay) with just ten days' notice. The appeals court first quoted paragraphs in the contract whereby the "consideration" for Lajoie's salary was deemed to be not just performance of services, but also his "concession of the options of release and renewal," and acceptance of equitable relief against performing services for anybody else. The court then continued.]

* * *

We have, then, at the outset, the fact that the paragraphs now criticized and relied upon in defense were deliberately accepted by the defendant, and that such acceptance was made part of the inducement for the plaintiff to enter into the contract. We have the further fact that the contract has been partially executed by services rendered, and payment made therefore, so that the situation is not now the same as when the contract was wholly executory. The relation between the parties has been so far changed as to give to the plaintiff an equity, arising out of the part performance, to insist upon the completion of the agreement according to its terms by the defendant. This equity may be distinguished from the original right under the contract itself, and it might well be questioned whether the court would not be justified in giving effect to it by injunction, without regard to the mutuality or nonmutuality in the original contract. The plaintiff has so far performed its part of the contract in entire good faith, in every detail, and it would therefore be inequitable to permit the defendant to withdraw from the agreement at this late day.

The term "mutuality" or "lack of mutuality" does not always convey a clear and definite meaning. As was said in *Grove v. Hodges*, 55 Pa. 516:

> The legal principle that contracts must be mutual does not mean
> that in every case each party must have the same remedy for a
> breach by the other.

In the contract now before us the defendant agreed to furnish his skilled professional services to the plaintiff for a period which might be extended over three years by proper notice given before the close of each current year. Upon the other hand, the plaintiff retained the right to terminate the contract upon 10 days' notice and the payment of salary for that time and the expenses of defendant in getting to his home. But the fact of this concession to the plaintiff is distinctly pointed out as part of the consideration for the large salary paid to the defendant, and is emphasized as such; and owing to the peculiar nature of the services demanded by the business, and the high degree of efficiency which must be maintained, the stipulation is not unreasonable. Particularly is this true when it is remembered that the plaintiff has played for years under substantially the same regulations.

We are not persuaded that the terms of this contract manifest any lack of mutuality in remedy. Each party has the possibility of enforcing all the rights stipulated for in the agreement. It is true that the terms make it possible for the plaintiff to put an end to the contract in a space of time much less than the period during which the defendant has agreed to supply his personal services; but mere difference in the rights stipulated for does not destroy mutuality of remedy. Freedom of contract covers a wide range of obligation and duty as between the parties, and it may not be impaired, so long as the bounds of reasonableness and fairness are not transgressed. . . . We cannot agree that mutuality of remedy requires that each party should have precisely the same remedy, either in form, effect, or extent. In a fair and reasonable contract, it ought to be sufficient that each party has the possibility of compelling the performance of the promises which were mutually agreed upon.

* * *

The court cannot compel the defendant to play for the plaintiff, but it can restrain him from playing for another club in violation of his agreement. No reason is given why this should not be done, except that presented by the argument, that the right given to the plaintiff to terminate the contract upon 10 days' notice destroys the mutuality of the remedy. But to this it may be answered that, as already stated, the defendant has the possibility of enforcing all the rights for which he stipulated in the agreement, which is all that he can reasonably ask. Furthermore, owing to the peculiar nature and circumstances of the business, the reservation upon the part of the plaintiff to terminate upon short notice does not make the whole contract inequitable.

* * *

Upon a careful consideration of the whole case, we are of the opinion that the provisions of the contract are reasonable, and that the consideration is fully adequate. The evidence shows no indications of any attempt at overreaching or unfairness. Substantial justice between the parties requires that the court should restrain the defendant from playing for any other club during the term of his contract with the plaintiff.

Injunction granted.

The Lajoie litigation offered the National League its greatest victory against the rival American circuit, but it would prove short-lived. Most other courts refused to grant negative injunctions and clubs of the American League flourished at the box office. Ultimately, the economic battle was settled by negotiation and not litigation or economic warfare.

Napoleon Lajoie was, as the court stated, a "bright particular star." Over his 21-year career Lajoie had 3,251 hits and a .339 batting average. He was the first second baseman voted into the Hall of Fame, part of the eleven Immortals, with Babe Ruth and Ty Cobb.

Despite their judicial victory, the Phillies failed to retrieve their star second baseman. The Philadelphia Athletics simply traded Lajoie to their Cleveland counterparts, and the Ohio courts refused the Phillies demand to give the Pennsylvania injunction "full faith and credit." Shortly thereafter, the National and American Leagues settled their war with the 1903 Major League Agreement that established the foundation for organized baseball. Lajoie stayed with the Cleveland franchise, which was renamed the "Naps" in his honor.

NOTES AND QUESTIONS

1.   *Negative Not Affirmative Injunction.* Note that the court does not approve an affirmative injunction that would have forced Lajoie to play for the National League Phillies, but only a negative injunction against him playing for the American League Athletics.

2.   *Any Bargaining Leverage?* How could Lajoie have obtained better contract terms from the Phillies?

3.   *Adequate Mutuality?* Do you agree with the conclusion in *Lajoie* that there was mutuality in the terms of this player contract? Does mutuality mean that two parties have reached an agreement, or should it mean more than that? Should courts have broad discretion to decide whether there is sufficient mutuality or fairness to make it equitable to enforce a contract? For all contracts, or only for personal service contracts?

4.   *Unique Player?* Was Lajoie sufficiently "unique?" Weren't there other athletes who could play second base for the Phillies? (There were seven other second basemen in the National League and eight in the new American League—and many minor leagues operating all over the country in 1901.) What does the court mean when it says: "He may not be the sun in the baseball firmament, but he is certainly a bright particular star?" After he jumped to the Athletics in 1901, Lajoie led the American League in runs (145), hits (232), doubles (48), home runs (12), total bases (350), runs batted in (125), batting average (.426), on base percentage (.483), and slugging percentage (.643). Not a bad year! *Total Baseball's* sabermetric ratings show Lajoie leading the AL in the all-important statistical category of Runs Created (179). Lajoie's Total Player Rating of 8.9 more than doubled the AL runner-up.

5.   *Time to Change American Law? Lajoie* still seems to command strong support among modern American judges. *See, e.g., Marchio v. Letterlough,* 237 F. Supp. 2d 580 (E.D. Pa. 2002) (citing decisions supporting negative injunctions upon finding services are unique or extraordinary). By contrast, based on a concern that workers generally have inferior bargaining power compared to employers, many European jurisdictions explicitly permit workers to terminate definite term as well as at-will contracts with minimal penalties. *See* Frank Hendrickx, "Employment Relationships at National Level: Belgium," in REGULATING EMPLOYMENT RELATIONSHIPS IN PROFESSIONAL FOOTBALL 39, 47–48 (Michele Colucci and Frank Hendrickx eds. 2014). Furthermore, there is a school of academics and worker-rights advocates who argue against the "commodification" of labor and therefore suggest workers should not be able to contract away their right to choose for whom to work. For a summary of the literature and application of the argument to Australian sports, see Matt Nichol, *The Commodification of Labour in the Australian Football League: What is the Impact of Free Agency?,* 31 AUSTRALIAN J. OF LABOUR LAW 73 (2018). Do you agree that players should not be subject to negative injunctions that effectively force them to 'play out their contract' with

an employer for whom they no longer wish to work? How might this affect initial salaries paid players for multi-year contracts?

_____

The *Lajoie* case was actually one of the few cases in which a baseball team ever secured an injunction against its own player, but it was an important victory nonetheless. The possibility that courts might stop players from jumping to the new league raised by the Lajoie case made it critical that the two circuits reach a rapprochement, which they did in 1903. Even more important than judicial involvement were the economic realities of the time. The new American League was prospering in those cities where one of their clubs went head-to-head with a National League rival. The Nationals gave in and Ban Johnson, president of the American League, became baseball's strongman for almost two decades, until the Black Sox scandal compelled baseball's sixteen owners to find an even more dictatorial commander-in-chief, Kenesaw Mountain Landis, baseball's first commissioner (*see* Chapter 2, Section B).

_____

A series of cases in the twentieth century arose in other professional team sports when rival leagues battled over the rights to contract with important players. By the 1950s, courts had largely overcome their reluctance (notwithstanding *Lajoie*) to issue injunctions against athletes. The courts' attention shifted from the supposed inequity of the contract toward the player (its lack of mutuality) to the team's need to retain especially talented athletes. In *Central NY Basketball, Inc. v. Barnett*, 181 N.E.2d 506 (Ohio Ct. Comm. Pleas 1961), the same type of Ohio court that had refused to enforce the negative injunction against Lajoie in 1902, granted a negative injunction to the Syracuse Nationals of the NBA barring Dick Barnett from playing for another basketball team so as to pressure their stellar guard to fulfill his contract promise: "Professional players in the major baseball, football, and basketball leagues have unusual talents and skills or they would not be so employed. Such players, the defendant Barnett included, are not easily replaced." 181 N.E.2d 517.

Courts applied the equitable doctrine of "unclean hands" in two notable injunction cases involving the rivalry between the National Football League and the American Football League. In *New York Football Giants, Inc. v. Los Angeles Chargers Football Club, Inc. (Flowers)*, 291 F.2d 471 (5th Cir. 1961), the NFL's New York Giants signed Charlie Flowers, a star player for the University of Mississippi football team, to a pro football contract in December 1959 while he was still in college. If they had publicized the contract signing at that time, Flowers would have lost his NCAA eligibility to play in the New Year's Day Sugar Bowl against Mississippi's traditional rival, Louisiana State. Accordingly, Giants owner Wellington Mara acceded to Flower's request to keep the contract (and signing bonus) secret until January 2, 1960; thus, the team did not submit the contract to NFL Commissioner Pete Rozelle for his approval.

Later in December, the Los Angeles Chargers of the new American Football League offered Flowers more money to play for them. Flowers notified the Giants that he was withdrawing from their contract and returning their uncashed bonus checks. Flowers signed with the Chargers on January 1, immediately after the Sugar Bowl, and the Giants went to court seeking an injunction to nullify Flowers' contract with the Chargers and bar him from playing for the AFL team. In court, the Giants were met with "the age old but sometimes overlooked doctrine that 'he who comes into equity must come with clean hands.'"

> Here the plaintiff's [Giants'] whole difficulty arises because it admittedly took from Flowers what it claims to be a binding contract, but which it agreed with Flowers it would, in effect, represent was not in existence in order to deceive others who had a very material and important interest in the subject matter. If there had been a straightforward execution of the document, followed by its filing with the Commissioner, none of the legal problems now presented to this court to untangle would exist. We think no party had the right thus to create problems by its devious and deceitful conduct and then approach a court of equity with a plea that the pretended status which it has foisted on the public be ignored and its rights be declared as if it had acted in good faith throughout.

> When it became apparent from uncontradicted testimony of Mara that this deceit was practiced in order to bring into being the "contract" sued upon, the trial court should have dismissed the suit without more on the basis of the "clean hands" doctrine.

Id. at 474.

The commercial war between the NFL and the AFL in the early 1960s produced numerous cases of players trying to renege on secret pre-college-bowl game contracts (and bonus payments) with a team in one league in order to sign with a team in the other league. While *Flowers* reflected the standard approach to this kind of case, the Tenth Circuit in *Houston Oilers v. Neely*, 361 F.2d 36 (1966), granted an injunction despite similar misconduct by the AFL Oilers in violation of NCAA rules. In addition to the *Neely* and *Flowers* cases, see *Detroit Football Co. v. Robinson*, 186 F. Supp. 933 (E.D. La.1960), and *Los Angeles Rams Football Club v. Cannon*, 185 F. Supp. 717 (S.D. Cal. 1960), where the district courts found agreements not approved by the football league commissioner to be merely revocable offers. Interestingly, in every one of these cases the court ended up siding with the AFL team and against the NFL team. Is that just a coincidence, or did it reflect a judicial desire to assist the upstart football league against the established league that had far greater market power?

The *Neely* court made a great deal out of the fact that Ralph Neely was intelligent and sophisticated. He knew what he was doing when he helped hide the contract from his college and the NCAA. Should this be a factor on which a case should turn? What if the deception were proposed by the club, and not by the player? What if the player was relatively naive and uninformed and thus more likely to be led astray by the professional team?

The next case brings the story up to the 1970s and the competition launched against the NFL by the World Football League (WFL). In the course of his opinion, the judge describes comparable litigation involving basketball stars Rick Barry and Billy Cunningham, who were courted by both the NBA and the American Basketball Association (ABA), a competitor that emerged in the late 1960s. The interesting legal question is whether it is consistent with a player's contractual obligations to his present team to sign a contract to play for another team in the future.

CINCINNATI BENGALS V. BERGEY
453 F. Supp. 129 (S.D. Ohio 1974)

PORTER, DISTRICT JUDGE.

[Bill Bergey, a star linebacker for the Cincinnati Bengals of the NFL, earned slightly less than $40,000 per year under a non-guaranteed contract for 1974 that gave the Bengals an option on his services for 1975. In April 1974, Bergey signed a no-cut, three-year contract with the Virginia Ambassadors of the newly formed WFL, which agreed to pay Bergey $125,000 per year plus a $150,000 signing bonus. This WFL contract was designed to begin with the 1976 football season, but would be accelerated forward if the Bengals released Bergey for any reason. Bergey was one of several Bengal stars pursued by the WFL (including starting linemen such as Bob Trumpy, Bob Johnson, and Rufus Mayes), as part of a WFL effort to stockpile a large number of NFL players for the new league. The threat of competition from the WFL moved NFL teams to sharply elevate their salary levels—the Bengals offered Bergey a new five-year contract for a total of $400,000. Unsuccessful in that bidding war, the Bengals sued Bergey, the Ambassadors, and the WFL, on the grounds that Bergey's future service agreement with the WFL team undermined and interfered with the Bengals' rights under its existing contract with Bergey.

Extensive testimony was offered about the special character of football as a sport and as a business enterprise, particularly from Bengals' founder and head coach, Paul Brown, and its assistant coach, Bill Walsh. The judge concluded that, notwithstanding the special emotional demands of football, Bergey's signing of a "futures" contract with another team would not reduce his effectiveness with the Bengals during his existing contract. However, the judge felt there likely would be an adverse impact if several other Bengals' stars were to follow Bergey's lead, because "a football team is a sort of delicate mechanism, the success of whose operation is dependent upon the coordination of various cohesive units."

On the other side of the ledger, though, was the harmful effect on the WFL if its teams were barred from signing NFL contract players for promotion of this new venture. The court noted that "starting a new franchise and a new league is a risky business." It then continued . . .]

* * *

Increased television coverage of professional football games has produced a sophisticated audience. The costs of fielding a competitive team are much higher today than in 1960 [when the American Football League first played]. The cost of acquiring players of exceptional ability has contributed significantly to the substantial increase in ticket prices (though these price increases have not been proportionately as great as the increase in costs). The higher ticket prices mean that sports fans expect major league entertainment for their sports dollar. Faced with the stiff competition for the sports dollar by the NFL, as well as other professional sports organizations, the WFL seeks to ensure its future by signing established NFL players to give the new league "credibility" in the eyes of the public. The signing of professional players is also necessary to overcome the doubts of college players as to the future of the league. . . . Mr. Putnam stated that the signing of name players to future contracts is "essential" to the WFL's success, since the league's financial future is dependent in great part on the earliest possible public acceptance of the WFL as a marketer of "major league" professional football.

[Turning to the legal issues, the court considered two earlier precedents involving Rick Barry and Billy Cunningham, who had been the subject of a similar tug of war between the National Basketball Association and the American Basketball Association in the late 1960s.

Barry's case was extremely entangled. While under contract with the NBA's San Francisco Warriors for 1967–1968, Barry signed a three-year deal with the ABA's Oakland Oaks. Barry was enjoined from jumping to the Oaks for the 1967–1968 season (*see Lemat Corp. v. Barry*, 80 Cal. Rptr. 240 (Cal. App. 1969)), but he did play for Oakland in 1968–69. However, when the Oaks were bought by the Washington Capitols, Barry, who wanted to remain in the Bay area, signed a five-year contract with the Warriors. When the Capitols sought injunctive relief against the NBA team, Barry's argument was that the Oakland contract had been tainted from the outset because of the conflict with his earlier agreement with the Warriors. The Ninth Circuit rejected this argument in *Washington Capitols Basketball Club v. Barry*, 419 F.2d 472 (9th Cir.1969). There was no actionable wrong in an athlete (like any other employee) signing a new contract during the period of his existing contract, as long as "performance and consideration" under the new contract were to begin after the expiration of the existing agreement, and there was no "encouragement" to terminate the latter contract early.

A similar ruling was rendered in *Munchak Corp. v. Cunningham*, 457 F.2d 721 (4th Cir.1972), in which the court refused to nullify Cunningham's contract to play for the Carolina Cougars in the 1971–1972 season, even though the three-year agreement had been signed in August 1969 when Cunningham was under contract to the Philadelphia 76ers. The judge in the *Bergey* case then addressed and rejected the Bengals' argument that judicial precedents from basketball should not govern the assertedly different world of professional football.]

* * *

When *Barry* and *Cunningham* are applied to the case at bar, the Court can only conclude that neither the WFL nor Bergey committed a tortious or otherwise unlawful act in entering into negotiations for and reaching agreement upon a contract for Bergey's personal services to commence after the expiration of his contract with the Bengals. In the language of *Cunningham*, there are no more obligations to be protected by either party to the Bengals contract after May 1, 1976.

Plaintiff argues that the acceleration clause of Bergey's WFL contract induces Bergey to seek his release prior to his NFL contract's expiration. We reject this argument, however, because we accept as true Bergey's testimony that he has no intention of seeking an early release. And, notwithstanding plaintiff's interpretation of *Barry*, we do not read the Ninth Circuit's opinion in that case as granting to Barry the right to breach his contract. Bergey will be liable should he breach his contract while its terms are still in effect.

* * *

In short, we conclude that *Barry* and *Cunningham* support the proposition that it is not illegal for either the player or the sports organization, at the time when the player is under a valid contract to one team, to negotiate and enter into a contract with a different, competing, team and league, under the terms of which the player agrees to render his services at the expiration of his current contract.

* * *

Harm To Public Interest

* * *

Next, we flesh out the bare bones conclusion that plaintiff has failed to show an absence of harm to the public interest if an injunction is granted herein. As we view it, the "public interest" within the meaning of that phrase as it is used here is the policy such as that behind the antitrust laws to encourage to the fullest extent practicable free and open competition in the marketplace. Restraints on competition are not favored.

* * *

The Court would be blind if it did not recognize that there is a public interest of another sort. This is the concern among fans over the actual and prospective loss of key members of a team of which they are devoted followers and the effect this may have on that team's "chances." It is clear that the Court cannot take such "public interest" into consideration. The only public interest that can properly be taken into account is the policy of the law to encourage free competition in the marketplace. Hence, the denial of an injunction is not a case of the Court's turning its back on the fans and the owners of the plaintiff's franchise, as the plaintiff improperly suggested in final argument that it might be.

Harm to WFL and Plaintiff

* * *

The conclusion that plaintiff has not made a clear showing of irreparable injury to itself is a difficult one to make. One reason it is, is that there is nothing to go on because this case is unique. As pointed out by Coach Brown, in all his forty years: "I've never had one like this, where I had a football player playing for me who is also under contract to somebody else." For another, while it may be too late to close the barn door as far as Bergey and Chomyszak are concerned, the threatened damage from the loss of Bob Johnson, et al., may not occur, and will not occur, if the Bengals match any offer they get from a WFL team. The Bengals argue that the fact that in order to match WFL offers they may have to tear up existing contracts and pay more for present services is evidence of irreparable injury.

We recognize that it will cost the Bengals something to bid for the future services of its players to preserve the continuity of the team's performance when present contracts expire. We do not, however, follow the argument that that is evidence of irreparable injury. Prior to the emergence of the World Football League, the teams in the National Football League could rest in relative assurance that the services of their players presently under short term contracts would remain available beyond the termination dates should the clubs desire to offer players further contracts. The absence of a competitor league justified that self-assurance, for the NFL, until now, has been "the only game in town." With the rise of the WFL, the NFL can no longer rely upon the absence of a competitor for protection of its claims to the future services of players, for which the established teams have neither bargained nor paid consideration.

It is not the players' present services for which the clubs will have to pay more, for those are protected by contracts which can presumably be enforced in the usual manner. It is only when the NFL chooses (and such decision is likely) to join the competition for the later services of its players that it will incur these higher costs. In our best judgment, such higher costs will be attributable to competition and not unfair competition.

* * *

Injunction denied.

_____

NOTES AND QUESTIONS

1.   *Injunction Against Futures Contract?* Might there be circumstances where a team could get a negative injunction or court order nullifying a futures contract?

2.   *Effect of Multiple Contracts?* What if several starters on the team signed with another team? Might that changed circumstance warrant judicial intervention?

3.   *Alternative Remedy?* What if a player under a futures contract with another team started to play very poorly or faked an injury or started publicly trashing the current team or league? What would be the appropriate remedy?

4.   *Intraleague Anti-Tampering Policies.* North American professional sports leagues currently have anti-tampering rules—incorporated by reference in collective bargaining agreements—that prohibit teams from negotiating with or even soliciting the services of any player while he is under contract with another team. These rules effectively give clubs *two* intraleague exclusive rights for the duration of a player's contract: the right to the player's services in the sport, and the right to negotiate any potential extension of the contract. The policies also cover coaches and high-level front office employees, like general managers and team presidents. (In order to encourage teams to develop minority and women coaches and high level officials, however, the NFL has relaxed its anti-tampering policy, and has even resolved to award third round draft picks to teams whose employee is hired by another team to fill a head coaching or general manager position. For further discussion of the NFL's "Rooney Rule" initiatives, see Chapter 14.)

_____

Litigation about player contracts vividly displays the conflict between two visions of contract and its enforcement. One view pictures contracts as personal promises that create moral obligations and entitlements and are worthy of as much legal teeth as the law can sensibly provide. From this perspective, while judges might reasonably be cautious about issuing a specific order forcing a player to play for the team to which he is under contract, they should not hesitate to enjoin him from playing for another team, which because of financial pressures would then usually soon yield the first result.

An alternative conception of contract sees it as an economic instrument the law should enforce only to the extent such judicial intervention produces an efficient allocation of society's resources. Under this theory, a player should be entitled to break an initial commitment to one team as long as he is willing to pay that team for its financial losses suffered through loss of his services. The assumption is that such contract breaches will be committed only when it is socially efficient to do so—in other words, when someone else finds the player's services more valuable and thus worth enough extra money to leave the player better off after compensation damages are paid to the original team.

The cases we have read leave no doubt that in terms of bottom line results, if not underlying rationale, the courts and arbitrators (including commissioners) have embraced the first view about player contracts, enforcing the value of promise keeping. But is this judicial verdict socially desirable? Consider these specific questions about sports cases:

1. Is society (at least the sports community) better off with the athlete playing for the original team or the new team? How do you decide?

2. Is it possible to calculate the actual damages inflicted on a team if a player defects? By analogy, how would you go about calculating the tort damages payable to a team that lost a star player because of physical injuries due to someone else's fault?

3. Suppose that a court issues an injunction that forbids a player to move to another team. Is the player likely to stay and perform effectively for his original team? If not, has litigation been futile for that team? Or has the club nonetheless gained something of tangible value from the judicial order? The Coase theorem posits that the law's initial allocation of the right to an asset does not dictate its ultimate destination, so long as some voluntary transactions are permitted, are feasible regarding disposition of the asset, both parties have reasonably complete access to relevant information, and bargaining costs are not significant. What does this theorem imply for the way these legal doctrines play themselves out in sports over the longer run? Specifically, if bargaining is permitted, is the issuance of an injunction likely to impede efficient movement of players, or to ensure that the original employer is fully compensated for their own expected losses?

4. An alternative way of characterizing the issue is the following: whereas limiting the team's remedy to damages treats the contract as simply a liability rule, giving the club injunctive relief means that the contract has, in effect, conferred on the team a property right in the player's services. In the sports world, the latter term is not merely a rhetorical label. A standard feature of the player contract in every sport has been a right of the team to sell or trade the player's services to another team by assigning his contract for cash or other players' contracts. Owners have used that right to sell even the greatest players in the game—the Boston Red Sox sold Babe Ruth to the New York Yankees in 1919, and the Edmonton Oilers sold Wayne Gretzky to the Los Angeles Kings in 1988. As long ago as

Lajoie, however, courts have observed that players are paid more than generously for giving the teams that prerogative. Is this judicial sentiment apt? Is it even accurate?

———

Most interleague competition for player services disappeared from the four major U.S. professional sports leagues by the 1990s because existing leagues had either merged with their rivals or crushed them in the economic contest. Players could find teams willing to employ them in the face of a contractual restraint only by departing for a foreign league or for another sport. The next case presents an international player contract dispute in the contemporary context of a collective agreement negotiated by a players' union and interpreted by a labor arbitrator. Brian Shaw was drafted by the Boston Celtics in 1988 and signed a one-year contract. The next year after the Celtics offered Shaw a modest increase in salary, Shaw signed a two-year contract with an Italian basketball team, Il Messaggero Roma, paying him $800,000 in the first year and $900,000 in the second. That contract also gave Shaw the option to opt out of the second year if he wanted to return to the NBA.

In January of 1990, Celtics executives flew to Rome and signed Shaw to a five-year deal—with a $450,000 bonus and an average salary of slightly over $1 million a year. Shaw undertook to terminate his Il Messaggero contract during the designated window period. At that time, Shaw was without an agent, although he signed the contract in front of the United States consul in Rome. Later that spring, Shaw retained an agent, who told his client that the Celtics' contract did not reflect Shaw's potential market value and that he should not leave Il Messaggero that year. (If Shaw had played another year in Rome, he would have been a free agent and able to negotiate with any NBA club and not just the Celtics.) The Celtics took the dispute to the permanent arbitrator under the NBA Players Association collective bargaining agreement, whose terms were incorporated by reference in Shaw's (and all other players') individual contracts. The arbitrator ruled that Shaw had to deliver the registered termination letter to Il Messaggero, and a federal district judge issued an order of enforcement. Shaw appealed.

BOSTON CELTICS V. BRIAN SHAW
908 F.2d 1041 (1st Cir. 1990)

BREYER, CIRCUIT JUDGE.

* * *

II.   The Legal Merits

Shaw makes two basic categories of argument in his effort to show that the district court lacked the legal power to enter its order. First, he says that the arbitration award was itself unlawful. Second, he says that regardless of the lawfulness of the award, the district court followed improper procedures. We shall address these arguments in turn and explain why we find each not persuasive.

A.   The Arbitrator's Decision

Shaw says that the district court should not have enforced the arbitrator's award because that award was itself unlawful, for any of five separate reasons.

1.   The termination promise. Shaw argues that the arbitrator could not reasonably find that he broke a contractual promise to the Celtics because, he says, the Celtics had previously agreed with the Players Association that contracts with individual players such as Shaw would not contain promises of the sort here at issue, namely, a promise to cancel a contract to play with a different team. Shaw says that this previous agreement between the Celtics and the Players Association renders his promise to terminate Il Messaggero "null and void." To support this argument, he points to Article I, § 2 of the Collective Bargaining Agreement, which Shaw and the Celtics, through cross-reference, made part of their individual agreement. Section 2 says, "Any amendment to a Uniform Player Contract [of the type Shaw and the Celtics used], other than those permitted by this [Collective Bargaining] Agreement, shall be null and void." The Agreement permits amendments (a) "in . . . respect to the compensation . . . to be paid the player," (b) "in respect to specialized compensation arrangements," (c) in respect to a "compensation payment schedule," and (d) in respect to "protect[ion]" of compensation in the event of contract termination. Shaw says that his promise to cancel the Il Messaggero agreement was an amendment to the Uniform Players Contract that does not concern compensation, specialized compensation, compensation schedules, or compensation protection; therefore, it is "null and void."

Shaw's argument, while logical, fails to show that the arbitrator's contrary finding is unlawful. The reasons it fails are fairly straightforward. First, the argument concerns the proper interpretation of a contract negotiated pursuant to a collective bargaining agreement. Second, federal labor law gives arbitrators, not judges, the power to interpret such contracts. The Supreme Court, noting the strong federal policy favoring the voluntary settlement of labor disputes, has written that a labor arbitration award is valid so long as it "draws its essence" from the labor contract. *See United Steelworkers v. Enterprise Wheel & Car Corp.*, 363 U.S. 593, 597 (1960). An award "draws its essence" from the contract so long as the "arbitrator is even arguably construing or applying the contract and acting within the scope of his authority." *United Paperworkers Int'l v. Misco*, 484 U.S. 29, 38 (1987).

* * *

Third, one can find "plausible arguments" favoring the arbitrator's construction. Shaw's "rescission" promise defines the beginning of the compensation relationship. It also plausibly determines, at the very least, whether Shaw's compensation will begin at $1.1 million (and continue for three years) or whether it will begin at $1.2 million (and continue for only two years). More importantly, and also quite plausibly, Shaw's overall compensation might have been much different had he declined to promise to play for the Celtics in 1990–91, thereby forcing the Celtics, perhaps, to obtain the services of a replacement for that year. The NBA Commissioner, who reviews all player contracts, found that the term was related to "compensation," as did the arbitrator. We cannot say that their findings lack any "plausible" basis.

* * *

In sum, we find the arbitration award lawful; and, in doing so, it has not been necessary for us to consider the Celtics' additional argument that Shaw bears an especially heavy legal burden in this case because the Players Association does not support him.

B.   The District Court Proceedings

[The court then turned to the question whether the district court's injunction ordering Shaw to rescind "forthwith" his contract with Il Messaggero and barring him from playing basketball for anyone but the Celtics satisfied the standards for preliminary injunctive relief.]

* * *

To begin with, the Celtics have shown a clear likelihood of success on the merits. . . . The Celtics also have demonstrated irreparable harm. Without speedy relief, they will likely lose the services of a star athlete next year, *see Wright & Miller* § 2948, at 439 & n. 34 (1972) (collecting cases that have found irreparable harm "in the loss by an athletic team of the services of a star athlete"), and, unless they know fairly soon whether Shaw will, or will not play for them, they will find it difficult to plan intelligently for next season. Indeed, in his contract Shaw expressly:

> represents and agrees that he has extraordinary and unique skill and ability as a basketball player . . . and that any breach by the Player of this contract will cause irreparable injury to the Club.

Further, the court could reasonably find that the "balance of harms" favors the Celtics. Of course, a preliminary injunction, if ultimately shown wrong on the merits, could cause Shaw harm. He might lose the chance to play in the country, and for the team, that he prefers. On the other hand, this harm is somewhat offset by the fact that ultimate success on the merits—*i.e.*, a finding that Shaw was not obligated to terminate Il Messaggero after all—would likely result in the following scenario: Shaw might still be able to sign with Il Messaggero and, if not, he would always have the Celtics contract of over $5 million to fall back upon. At the same time, the court's failure to issue the injunction, if the merits ultimately favored the Celtics, could cause them serious harm of the sort just mentioned (*i.e.*, significantly increased difficulty in planning their team for next season). Given the very small likelihood that Shaw would ultimately prevail on the merits, and the "comparative" harms at stake, the district court could properly decide that the overall "balance" favored the Celtics, not Shaw.

Finally, the court could properly find that issuing a preliminary injunction would not harm the public interest. Indeed, as we have pointed out, the public interest favors court action that "effectuate[s]" the parties' intent to resolve their disputes informally through arbitration. Where the dispute involves a professional basketball player's obligation to play for a particular team, one could reasonably consider expeditious, informal and effective dispute-resolution methods to be essential, and, if so, the public interest favoring court action to "effectuate" those methods of dispute-resolution would seem at least as strong as it is in respect to work-related disputes typically arising under collective bargaining agreements. *See New England Patriots Football Club, Inc. v. University of Colorado*, 592 F.2d 1196, 1200 (1st Cir.1979) (collecting cases in which professional sports players were enjoined from playing for rival teams). Shaw, while conceding that the public also has an interest in seeing that contracts between consenting adults are honored, points to a general policy disfavoring enforcement of personal service contracts. That latter policy, however, typically prevents a court from ordering an individual to perform a personal service; it does not prevent a court from ordering an individual to rescind a contract for services and to refrain from performing a service for others.

Shaw makes an additional argument. He notes that courts will not provide equitable relief such as an injunction to a party with "unclean hands," and he argues that the Celtics' hands are not clean. To support this argument, he has submitted an affidavit saying, in effect, that he signed the contract in a weak moment. His trip to Italy had made him "homesick;" he was "depressed" by what he viewed as undeserved and "negative criticism" in the Italian press; he was not represented by an agent; the Celtics had been urging him to sign up; he read the contract only for about 20 minutes while he was driving around Rome with a Celtics official; and no one ever explained to him that if he did not sign and played with Il Messaggero for another year, he would become a "free agent," able to bargain thereafter with any American team, perhaps for an even greater salary than the Celtics were willing to pay him.

Other evidence in the record, however, which Shaw does not deny, shows that he is a college graduate; that he has played under contract with the Celtics before; that the contract is a standard form contract except for a few, fairly simple, rather clear, additions; that he had bargained with the Celtics for an offer that increased from $3.4 million (in December) to $5.4 million (less than one month later); that he looked over the contract before signing it; that he told the American consul in Rome (as he signed it) that he had read and understood it; and that he did not complain about the contract until he told the Celtics in June that he would not honor it.

Given this state of the record, the district court could easily, and properly, conclude that the Celtics' hands were not "unclean." The one case Shaw cites in support of his position, *Minnesota Muskies, Inc. v. Hudson*, 294 F. Supp. 979, 981 (M.D.N.C.1969), is not on point. The player in Muskies had a contract with Team A that permitted Team A, not the player, to renew the contract for additional years. Team B lured the player away from Team A even though it knew that Team A intended to exercise its contractual right to keep the player. The court held that this contractual interference amounted to "unclean hands" and refused Team B's request for an injunction preventing the player from returning to Team A. Here, in contrast, Il Messaggero has no contractual right to retain Shaw; whether or not the contract is renewed or rescinded is entirely up to Shaw, not Il Messaggero. Under those circumstances, we cannot find anything improper, "unclean," or unfair about the Celtics' convincing Shaw (indeed, paying Shaw) to exercise his contractual right in their favor. *Cf.* Restatement (Second) of Torts § 768 (1979).

* * *

Injunction upheld.

NOTES AND QUESTIONS

1.   *Effect of Arbitration Decision?* Unlike in *Lajoie* and *Bergey*, in *Shaw* there was an earlier adjudication of the issues by a labor arbitrator jointly appointed by the NBA and its Players Association under their collective agreement. Should this fact make a court more willing to order equitable relief against a player seeking to stay in another league?

2.   *Assignment Clause.* In the middle of the 1991–92 season, the Celtics traded an injured Shaw to the Miami Heat for the latter's equally disenchanted point guard, Sherman Douglas. Such trades are made possible by the assignment clause in the standard player contract that gives the team, the player's employer, the right to assign the personal services contract to another team in the same league. Though unthinkable in most other employment contexts, this provision is standard in athlete's contracts unless the player can negotiate a "no-trade" clause, or the collective bargaining agreement gives a veteran player some control over being traded. Should this feature of the contract influence a court's decision about whether to force the player to play

for the team with which he originally signed? For the team to which he was traded?

More generally, is this assignment clause fair and reasonable, or should it be void as against public policy? Would your answer hinge on whether the players union had agreed to the inclusion of such a clause in the standard contract? (It did.) For what reasons do club owners want such a clause? What would be the long-term effect on player-club relations if such clauses were not enforced by the courts? Does this provision, along with that requiring commissioner approval before the contract can become valid, essentially mean that the player is as much under contract to the league as to the club? Should the league, then, also be liable for any breach of contract (*i.e.*, failure to pay) by the club? *See USFL Players Ass'n v. USFL*, 650 F. Supp. 12 (D. Or. 1986) (league and clubs were not single employer, so that league could not be held liable for wages owed by member club).

3.   *Meaning of No-Trade Clause.* In *Munchak Corp. v. Cunningham*, 457 F.2d 721 (4th Cir. 1972), Billy Cunningham negotiated a "no-trade" clause in his basketball contract with the ABA's Carolina Cougars. Subsequently, the Cougars were sold and all the team's player contracts were assigned to the new owner. Cunningham sought to avoid being held to his contract by arguing that this assignment made it void. The Fourth Circuit rejected his argument and held that a standard "no assignment" clause merely meant that the player could not be traded to a different club, not that he could not be traded to a different owner of the same club. Is this a fair interpretation of general "no-trade" language? Would your answer be different if the team was sold to a new owner who immediately relocated the franchise to a different city and changed the name of the team?

4.   *Continuing Relevance.* Requests by teams in the dominant major American sports leagues to obtain injunctions like that issued against Bryan Shaw are not frequent because other leagues do not offer comparable compensation and benefits. Nonetheless, the issue may still arise, especially for soccer players who may have more attractive international playing options. For instance, in 2021, Major League Soccer (MLS) and the New York Red Bulls obtained judicial enforcement of an arbitration award that ordered midfielder Alejandro "Kaku" Romero Gamarra not to play for a Saudi Arabian soccer club in breach of his contract with the Red Bulls. Kaku unsuccessfully argued to the arbitrator that the Red Bulls had not given adequate notice of their unilateral renewal of his contract, but then continued to play in Saudi Arabia despite the American court's enforcement order.

B. THE RESERVE SYSTEM AND ITS DEMISE

As noted above, in 1879, the eight club owners of baseball's National League formulated the first reserve system in professional sports. The reserve system created a restricted market in which the players could sell their services. Each player could only negotiate with one club, creating a monopsony in economic terms. Previous to the establishment of the reserve system, players "revolved" from one club to another, sometimes in the middle of a season, seeking better pay. Under the reserve system, pay levels dropped dramatically as cartel rules controlled the movement of players.

To ease reading of the following *Chase* opinion, consider this capsule summary of the reserve system:

1. Each team in a league was entitled to list a certain number of players with whom it had a contract relationship and to which the team claimed exclusive rights.

2. All other teams in the league agreed to respect the reserve lists of their fellow league members and not to "tamper" with another team's players by inducing them to move.

3. All teams in the league agreed to sign players only to a single standard form contract. A key provision in that contract was that when its term expired, the team retained an option to renew the contract for another season with the same provisions as before—including this perpetually renewable option clause—except for salary. In case of disagreement over salary, the team had the prerogative to set the salary for the upcoming year.

4. A further feature of the reserve system was the draft, whereby major league teams agreed to select (in reverse order of finish in the previous season) from among minor league players talented enough to play in the major leagues. The modern rookie draft was actually first developed in football in 1936, emulated in basketball in the late 1940s, and adopted by baseball and hockey only in the mid-1960s. The players selected were reserved to the drafting club even before they signed the first standard form contract.

AMERICAN LEAGUE BASEBALL CLUB OF CHICAGO V. CHASE
86 Misc. 441, 149 N.Y.S. 6 (1914)

BISSELL, JUDGE.

[Hal Chase played first base for the Chicago White Sox in the American League. In March 1914 he signed a one-year contract with the Sox for the upcoming season. However, on June 15, 1914, Chase gave the White Sox notice that he was terminating the contract, and on June 20, he jumped to the Buffalo team in the new Federal Baseball League. The White Sox filed suit for breach of contract and sought an immediate injunction barring Chase from playing for Buffalo.

The court quoted from a number of provisions in Major League Baseball's National Agreement, the Rules of the National Commission, and the terms of the standard player agreement. This combination of baseball rules gave each team an "absolute right and title" to players it had "selected" (or drafted), required all players to enter into the standard contract prescribed by the National Commission and incorporated in this contract a term that gave the team the option to renew each player's contract (if the team so chose) on the same terms as in the previous year, but also gave the team the right to terminate a player's contract on ten days' notice (the provision that had generated the "mutuality" issue in the earlier *Lajoie* case).]

* * *

It appears that originally the defendant was a "selected" player; but whether he was a selected player at the time he entered the service of the plaintiff is immaterial. Had he come from the vacant lots of the cities, or the fields of the country, or from the college campus, and therefore been "a free agent" at the time he made his entry into "organized baseball," the result would have been the same. If a sale or trade is to be made by one major league club to another, section 3 of article VI governs, and "The right and title of a major league club to its players shall be absolute."

If a sale or trade is to be made by a major league club to a minor league club, section 9 of article VI governs, and the sale or trade is not absolute until waivers have been obtained from the other major league clubs. Thus a player in the highest league, without the exercise of any individual choice, may be required to take service with a club of a lower league where smaller salaries are paid, and where both the aggregate of the salary list and the salary of each individual player is subject to strict limitation under the terms of the National Agreement. No opportunity is afforded the player to solicit employment upon his own account. No right is afforded to enable him to resist an unjust limitation upon his power to earn. No consideration is afforded either himself or his family with respect to choosing a home. In short, he is placed where he must, at all times while playing in "organized baseball," consider that his home is only the place in which his services are for the time being controlled.

The baseball player, even though about to be discharged, is still a thing of value to the club owner. The termination of the obligations by the club owner pursuant to the 10-day provision is not accomplished by him without securing some return. If the player goes to another major league club, it is either in exchange for some other more desired player or players, or for the waiver price; and the same is true if the discharged player is sent to a league of lower grade.

It seems that the promotion of the ball player is also hedged about with such limitations as to make the property in him absolute whether he will accept terms or not, and to make those terms when arrived at only liberal enough to prevent the player from seeking other means of earning his livelihood.

* * *

"Organized baseball" as conducted under the terms of the National Agreement further seeks to enforce and perpetuate its title to and control of its players as follows:

Section 1, Article VI, of the National Agreement provides:

All parties to this agreement pledge themselves to recognize the right of reservation and respect contracts between players and clubs under its protection. No club operating under this agreement shall at any time negotiate for the purchase or lease of the property of another club without first securing the consent of such club.

Section 2 of Article VI is as follows:

Any club or league which harbors a player who refuses to observe his contract with a club member of any party to this agreement, or to abide by its reservation, shall be considered an outlaw organization, and its claim to contractual and territorial rights ignored.

Thus the baseball player is made a chattel; the title of the club to the player . . . is made absolute.

Section 2 of Article VI recognizes the property of the club in the player as existing under two conditions: First, under a contract; and, second, under reserve without a contract.

* * *

If the player has ideas of his own, which fail to accord with those of the club, the National Agreement enables the club to enforce its own terms, leaving the player the option to enter some other trade, calling, or profession, if he is not satisfied.

The scheme of the National Agreement to perpetuate control over a player by means of contracts apparently legal is interesting and pertinent. Each term contract, as appears by Section 1 of Article VIII, must contain a reserve clause or option to renew, and this article of the National Agreement is further enforced by Section A, Rule 17, of the National Commission, which is as follows:

A nonreserve clause in the contract of a major league player without the approval of the commission or of a minor league player without the approval of the National Board shall not be valid.

So that each new contract of the player must contain a reserve clause, and so by a series of contracts, "organized baseball" is able to perpetuate its control over the services of the player. But if, upon the other hand, a contract is at any time unobtainable, or even in fact not in good faith sought to be obtained, as the club owner might offer an immoderately low salary, then the provisions for reservation and the respecting thereof, apply and safeguard the "absolute title" of the club.

But why should a player enter into a contract when his liberty of conduct and of contract is thus curtailed? The answer is that he has no recourse. He must either take the contract under the provisions of the National Agreement, whose organization controls practically all of the good ball players of the country, or resort to some other occupation.

[The court then quoted several provisions of the National Agreement and Rules promulgated by the National Commission, which prohibited teams from using players who had not signed formal playing contracts that contained the renewable option clause.]

* * *

This somewhat extended analysis shows to what extent the contract between the plaintiff and the defendant presents reciprocal and mutual, enforceable obligations. The plaintiff can terminate the contract at any time on 10 days' notice. The defendant is bound to many obligations under the remarkable provisions of the National Agreement. The Player's Contract executed in accordance with its terms, binds him, not only for the playing season of six months from April 14th to October 14th, but also for another season, if the plaintiff chooses to exercise its option, and if it insists upon the requirement of an option clause in each succeeding contract, the defendant can be held for a term of years. His only alternative is to abandon his vocation. Can it fairly be claimed that there is mutuality in such a contract? The absolute lack of mutuality, both of obligation and of remedy, in this contract, would prevent a court of equity from making it the basis of equitable relief by injunction or otherwise. The negative covenant, under such circumstances, is without a consideration to support it, and is unenforceable by injunction.

[The court then addressed the question of whether this contractual regime in baseball violated federal antitrust law.]

The novel argument is presented with much earnestness by the learned counsel for the defendant that the combination formed by the operation of the National Agreement and the rules and regulations of the National Commission thereunder, with which the defendant is connected through his contract with the plaintiff, is in direct violation of an act to protect trade and commerce against unlawful restraints and monopolies, in force July 2, 1890, and popularly known as the Sherman Antitrust Law. It is apparent from the analysis already set forth of the agreement and rules forming the combination of the baseball business, referred to as "organized baseball," that a monopoly of baseball as a business has been ingeniously devised and created in so far as a monopoly can be created among free men; but I cannot agree to the proposition that the business of baseball for profit is interstate trade or commerce, and therefore subject to the provisions of the Sherman Act. An examination of the cases cited by the defendant confirms rather than changes my conclusion.

* * *

Baseball is an amusement, a sport, a game that comes clearly within the civil and criminal law of the state, and it is not a commodity or an article of merchandise subject to the regulation of Congress on the theory that it is interstate commerce.

[The court then turned to the question of what was the appropriate treatment under the common law of player contracts entered into within this baseball structure.]

Another question to be determined upon this motion is whether so-called "organized baseball," operating under the provisions of the National Agreement and the Rules and Contracts subsidiary thereto, is an illegal combination or monopoly in contravention of the common law. The affidavits read on the hearing of this motion show that a combination of 40 leagues, major and minor, has been formed under the terms of the National Agreement, controlling for profit the services of 10,000 players of professional baseball, practically all of the good or skillful players in the country. The analysis of the National Agreement and the Rules of the Commission, controlling the services of these skilled laborers, and providing for their purchase, sale, exchange, draft, reduction, discharge, and blacklisting, would seem to establish a species of quasi peonage unlawfully controlling and interfering with the personal freedom of the men employed. It appears that there is only one league of any importance operating independently of the National Commission, and that is the newly organized Federal League which comprises eight clubs in eight cities. "Organized baseball" is now as complete a monopoly of the baseball business for profit as any monopoly can be made. It is in contravention of the common law, in that it invades the right to labor as a property right, in that it invades the right to contract as a property right, and in that it is a combination to restrain and control the exercise of a profession or calling.

* * *

If a baseball player like the defendant, who has made baseball playing his profession and means of earning a livelihood, desires to be employed at the work for which he is qualified and is entitled to earn his best compensation, he must submit to dominion over his personal freedom and the control of his services by sale, transfer, or exchange, without his consent, or abandon his vocation and seek employment at some other kind of labor. While the services of these baseball players are ostensibly secured by voluntary contracts, a study of the system as hereinabove set forth, and as practiced under the plan of the National Agreement, reveals the involuntary character of the servitude which is imposed upon players by the strength of the combination controlling the labor of practically all of the players in the country. This is so great as to make it necessary for the player either to take the contract prescribed by the commission or abandon baseball as a profession and seek some other mode of earning a livelihood. There is no difference in principle between the system of servitude built up by the operation of this National Agreement, which as has been shown, provides for the purchase, sale, barter, and exchange of the services of baseball players—skilled laborers—without their consent, and the system of peonage brought into the United States from Mexico and thereafter existing for a time within the territory of New Mexico. The quasi peonage of baseball players under the operations of this plan and agreement is contrary to the spirit of American institutions, and is contrary to the spirit of the Constitution of the United States. . . .

The system created by "organized baseball" in recent years presents the question of the establishment of a scheme by which the personal freedom, the right to contract for their labor wherever they will, of 10,000 skilled laborers, is placed under the dominion of a benevolent despotism through the operation of the monopoly established by the National Agreement. This case does not present the simple question of a laborer who has entered into a fair contract for his personal services.

While the question of the dissolution of this combination on the ground of its illegality is not before this court for decision, it has nevertheless been thought necessary for the purpose of ascertaining whether or not this plaintiff comes into a court of equity with clean hands to inquire into the organization and operations of the combination to which the plaintiff is a party. A court of equity, insisting that "he who comes into equity must come with clean hands," will not lend its aid to promote an unconscionable transaction of the character which the plaintiff is endeavoring to maintain and strengthen by its application for this injunction. The court will not assist in enforcing an agreement which is a part of a general plan having for its object the maintenance of a monopoly, interference with the personal liberty of a citizen, and the control of his free right to labor wherever and for whom he pleases, and will not extend its aid to further the purposes and practices of an unlawful combination, by restraining the defendant from working for any one but the plaintiff.

Injunction vacated.

———

Chase casts in a different light the contracts signed by Nap Lajoie a decade earlier, or even by other athletes fifty years later. One question is whether the league arrangements justify the court's refusal to enforce individual contracts through injunctions. While over the years most courts have answered "no," a more important question is whether even a hands-off approach by courts to player contracts would be a sufficient response to the problems players have with these league arrangements.

In *Chase*, the player tried to use antitrust policy as a *shield* against a contract injunction sought by the American League Club that had reserved his services. That tactic was sufficient for Chase's purposes because another club in the rival Federal League had been prepared to bid handsomely for his services. Nonetheless, since the demise of the Federal League just a year later, Major League Baseball has faced no such competition in its players market, and other professional leagues have encountered rivals only intermittently. Whether or not a judge enforces the restrictive terms in a contract between a player and his team, if the other teams in the league have agreed not to "tamper" with the services of their respective players except under strictly defined rules and conditions (an agreement enforced by the commissioner), there will be no effective market for the players' services and the players will have to accept any salary offered by the clubs to which they are "reserved." That is why players have tried to use antitrust law as a *sword* against such an intraleague arrangement, as examined in Chapter 7.

Baseball players were never successful in using antitrust as such a sword, however, for a reason that is highlighted in a decision presented at the end of this chapter. Nonetheless, within a few years after that decision, players were able to use collective bargaining to slay the reserve system. Under the second baseball collective bargaining agreement, a neutral arbitrator, Peter Seitz, replaced Commissioner Bowie Kuhn as interpreter of both the baseball labor agreement and the player contract. Seitz was a universally respected neutral under collective bargaining agreements throughout the American economy. His work as the baseball neutral had a profound effect on the sport. Arbitrator Seitz was presented with a case that required him to construe the meaning and scope of the key components of the reserve system based on the provisions of the uniform player's contract that was negotiated by MLB and the MLBPA as part of their collective bargaining agreement.

In 1974, Jim "Catfish" Hunter had a 25–13 record with the Oakland A's, his fourth year as a 20-game winner. He had signed a two-year contract with club owner Charlie Finley for a $100,000 annual salary. Half of the salary each year would be paid to him directly; $50,000 would be paid to a deferment plan of Hunter's choice, which allowed him to avoid immediate tax liability. Apparently, Finley belatedly discovered that under Hunter's deferred compensation scheme the club could not deduct the annual $50,000 annuity payment as a business expense in the current year, and that Finley would lose control over the funds. Finley then simply refused to make the payments as he had promised. Hunter made repeated requests, but the deferred payments were not made. Hunter filed a grievance claiming he could terminate the contract for non-payment.

Section 7(a) of Hunter's Uniform Player Contract explained the implication of Finley's action. It read: "The Player may terminate this contract . . . if the Club shall default in the payments to the Player." Arbitrator Peter Seitz ruled this provision was "pellucidly clear." The contract was not ambiguous. Since Hunter no longer had a valid contract with the A's, he was a free agent and could entertain offers from any other club.

On December 31, 1974, Hunter accepted a Yankees' offer for the then unprecedented salary package of a $1 million signing bonus, and $150,000 a year for five years, life insurance benefits worth $1 million and a substantial amount of deferred compensation. Hunter's case demonstrated both the extent to which the reserve system suppressed player salaries and, for the first time, the formidable power of labor arbitration in the sports business. The decision heralded an enormous shift in power within the baseball enterprise brought about by collective bargaining. The *Hunter* case also foreshadowed the role arbitrator Peter Seitz would play the following year when the MLBPA launched a full-frontal attack on baseball's venerable reserve system. Catfish Hunter's case was, after all, a unique situation—an obstinate owner materially breached a contract freeing his star player and no other owner was upset with the decision because it involved the prodigal owner of baseball, Charlie Finley.

The following year, the Players Association submitted to the labor agreement umpire Seitz the most critical issue in the business of sports, whether a player is bound to his club in perpetuity or whether he is allowed to sell his services to any club he wishes upon the expiration of his contract term plus one option year with his current team. The status quo was the perpetual reserve system, but the MLBPA's grievance claimed that the system was not embodied in the parties' collective bargaining agreement.

NATIONAL & AMERICAN LEAGUE PROFESSIONAL BASEBALL CLUBS V. MAJOR LEAGUE BASEBALL PLAYERS ASSOCIATION (MESSERSMITH AND MCNALLY GRIEVANCES)

66 Lab. Arb. Rep. (BNA) 101 (1976)

SEITZ, ARBITRATOR.

[Andy Messersmith of the Los Angeles Dodgers and Dave McNally of the Montreal Expos had both refused to sign new player contracts at the end of the 1974 season; instead, they played the 1975 season under the terms of § 10(c) of the Uniform Player's Contract, which gave their clubs the right to renew for one year the old contract "on the same terms" (except for salary, the amount of which had recently been subjected to binding arbitration in cases of dispute). The question posed to the arbitrator was whether the contract as renewed by the club contained this option clause as well. If it did, the club could include the player indefinitely on its reserve list through use of this perpetually renewable option. If, on the other hand, the reserve option clause was spent after its first use, the two players had now become free agents. In addition to that merits issue of contract interpretation, the arbitrator faced a preliminary question whether he even had jurisdiction to entertain this issue, because of the presence of the following curious provision in the collective agreement:

> Except as adjusted or modified hereby, *this agreement does not deal with the reserve system*. The Parties have different views as to the legality and as to the merits of such system as presently constituted. This agreement shall in no way prejudice the position or legal rights of the parties or of any player regarding the reserve system. During the term of this agreement neither of the parties will resort to any form of concerted action with respect to the issue of the reserve system, and there shall be no obligation to negotiate with respect to the reserve system. (Emphasis supplied.)

In the first half of his decision, Seitz wrestled with the meaning of this apparent exclusion of the reserve clause from the collective bargaining agreement upon which his authority rested. Eventually, he concluded that he did have jurisdiction to resolve grievances about the meaning of different provisions in the collective bargaining agreement and the standard player contract. Although the parties agreed to a clause that stated that their agreement did not deal with the reserve system, a number of the provisions of the agreement served as critical features of the reserve system. Seitz's decision on "arbitrability" will be examined below in the Eighth Circuit Court of Appeals decision that affirmed Seitz's conclusion. Here, we present the arbitrator's analysis of the scope of the reserve clause in baseball.

The arbitrator first reviewed the origins and development of the reserve clause.]

* * *

The Reserve System of the leagues is nowhere defined in a sentence or a paragraph. Reference is commonly and frequently made in the press and by the news media to a "Reserve Clause;" but there is no such single clause encompassing the subject matter. It seems fair to say, on the basis of what has been presented, that the "Reserve System" refers to a complex and a congeries of rules of the leagues (and provisions in the collective Basic Agreement and the Uniform Players Contract) related to the objective of retaining exclusive control over the service of their players in the interest of preserving discipline, preventing the enticement of players, maintaining financial stability and promoting a balance or a relative parity of competitive skills as among clubs. Such "exclusive control," it is said, is exercised by a Club placing the name of a player on its "reserve list" which is distributed to the other clubs in both leagues. A player on such a list, assert the leagues, cannot "play for or negotiate with any other club until his contract has been assigned or he has been released" (Rule 4–A(a) and may not be the subject of "tampering" as described in Rule 3(g).

This system of reservation of exclusive control is historic in baseball and is traceable to the early days of the organized sport in the 19th century. Over the years, the scheme and structure of provisions designed to establish and maintain that control has been changed in expression. The leagues assert that the system was designed, initially, to combat the institutional chaos that resulted when players under contract with one club defected to another. In an effort to deal with the problem, it is represented, various versions of reserve clauses had been adopted.

The problems facing the National League in the closing years of the 19th century, however, in respect of defecting players, were not limited to the circumstances of a player defecting to another club in the league. Other leagues came into being from time to time and disappeared. The League, in 1899, in an effort to prevent defection of players to other leagues, placed in the individual player's contract a "renewal clause," so called. This clause, according to the leagues, was the legal basis for clubs applying to the courts of equity to enjoin players from "jumping" to a rival league. As Club Exhibit 16 evidences, contract renewal clauses, over time, differed in their provisions; but all gave an option to a Club to renew its contracts with players for stated periods.

[The current version of the renewal clause in MLB's Uniform Player's Contract was developed in 1947. If the Club had tendered a contract to the player by February 1 and the parties had not agreed to new contract terms by March 1, the Club had the prerogative under § 10(a) (via written notice to the player within the next ten days) "to renew the contract for the period of one year on the same terms." The only exception was salary, which the club could fix at an amount not less than 75% of the prior year's salary.]

* * *

No one challenges the right of a Club to renew a Player's contract with or without his consent, under § 10(a), "for the period of one [renewal] year." I read the record, however, as containing a contention by the leagues that when a Club renews a Player's contract for the renewal year, the contract in force during that year contains the "right of renewal" clause as one of its terms, entitling the Club to renew the contract in successive years, to perpetuity, perhaps, so long as the Player is alive and the Club has duly discharged all conditions required of it. This is challenged by the Players Association whose position it is that the contractual relationship between the Club and the Player terminates at the end of the first renewal year. Thus, it claims that there was no longer any contractual bond between Messersmith and the Los Angeles Club on September 29, 1975.

The leagues' argument is based on the language in § 10(a) of the Player's Contract that the Club "may renew this contract for the period of one year *on the same terms;*" and that among those "terms" is the right to further contract renewal.

In the law of contract construction, as I know it, there is nothing to prevent parties from agreeing to successive renewals of the terms of their bargain (even to what had been described as "perpetuity"), provided the contract expresses that intention with explicit clarity and the right of subsequent renewals does not have to be implied. . . .

There is nothing in § 10(a) which, explicitly, expresses agreement that the Players Contract can be renewed for any period beyond the first renewal year. The point the leagues present must be based upon the implication or assumption, that if the renewed contract is "on the same terms" as the contract for the preceding year (with the exception of the amount of compensation) the right to additional renewals must have been an integral part of the renewed contract. I find great difficulties, in so implying or assuming, in respect of a contract providing for the rendition of personal services in which one would expect a more explicit expression of intention. There are numerous provisions and terms in the Uniform Players Contract that are renewed in the renewal year when a Club exercises its renewal rights under § 10(a). Provision of the right to make subsequent and successive renewals is in an entirely different category, however, than the numerous terms in the Players Contract which deal with working conditions and duties which the Club and the Player owe to each other. That right, critically, concerns and involves the continued existence of the contract itself as expressing the mutual undertakings of the parties and the bargain which they struck. All of the other "terms" of the Player-Club relationship stand or fall according to whether the contract, as such, is renewed.

[The arbitrator then discussed two basketball cases—*Lemat Corp. v. Barry*, 275 Cal. App. 2d 671, 80 Cal. Rptr. 240 (1969) and *Central New York Basketball v. Barnett*, 181 N.E.2d 506 (Ohio C.P. Ct.1961), both involving similar renewal clauses. In *Barnett*, the club had argued and the court agreed, that the option clause in basketball's standard player contract was for one renewal year only, not in perpetuity, and *Barry* followed *Barnett*.]

* * *

In these circumstances I find that § 10(a) falls short of reserving to a Club the right to renew a contract at the end of the renewal year. Accordingly, I find that Messersmith [and by extension, McNally] was not under contract when his renewal year came to an end.

[The clubs advanced a second argument for their position on the merits. Under Major League Rule 4–A(a), each club was to transmit to the commissioner, by November 20th, "a list not exceeding forty (40) active and eligible players whom the clubs desire to reserve for the ensuing season . . . and thereafter no player on any list shall be eligible to play for and negotiate with any other club until his contract has been assigned or he has been released." Rule 4–A(a) was supplemented and reinforced by Rule 3(g), which provided that "to preserve discipline and competition and to prevent the enticement of players . . . there shall be no negotiations or dealings respecting employment, either present or prospective, between any player . . . and any club other than the club with which he is under contract . . . or by which he is reserved . . ."]

We now turn to the Major League Rules, as to which it has already been stated that, by virtue of § 9(a) of the Uniform Players Contract and Article XIII of the Basic Agreement, they are a part of the agreements of the parties if not inconsistent with the provisions of the Basic Agreement and the Players Contract.

The parties are in sharp conflict on this. The leagues claim that there is exclusive reservation of a player's services under Rule 4–A(a) regardless of the continued existence of any contractual relationship between the Club and the Player. Thus, Counsel for the National League asserted that:

> The club may continue the pattern of career long control over the player and that this pattern of career long control is not essentially dependent upon the renewal clause (Section 10–A) at all.

The Players Association, on the other hand, asserts that in the absence of a nexus or linkage of contract between the Player and the Club, there can be no exclusive reservation of the right to his future services.

* * *

These provisions and others in the very Rules which, allegedly, establish the kind of reservation of services for which the leagues contend, all subsume the existence of a contractual relation. The leagues would have it that it is only when there is a release or assignment that a contract must have been in existence; but even if there were no contract in existence (the players' contract having expired) a Club, by placing the name of a player on a list, can reserve exclusive rights to his services from year to year for an unstated and indefinite period in the future. I find this unpersuasive. It is like the claims of some nations that persons once its citizens, wherever they live and regardless of the passage of time, the swearing of other allegiances and other circumstances, are still its own nationals and subject to the obligations that citizenship in the nation imposes. This "status" theory is incompatible with the doctrine or policy of freedom of contract in the economic and political society in which we live and of which the professional sport of baseball ("the national game") is a part.

* * *

[Finally, Arbitrator Seitz addressed the League's concern that the absence of a lifetime reserve system would devastate baseball.]

I am not unmindful of the testimony of the Commissioner of Baseball and the Presidents of the National and American League given at the hearings as to the importance of maintaining the integrity of the Reserve System. It was represented to me that any decision of the Arbitration Panel sustaining the Messersmith and McNally grievances would have dire results, wreak great harm to the Reserve System and do serious damage to the sport of baseball.

Thus, for example, it was stated that a decision favoring these grievants would encourage many other players to elect to become free agents at the end of the renewal years; that this would encourage clubs with the largest monetary resources to engage free agents, thus unsettling the competitive balance between clubs, so essential to the sport; that it would increase enormously the already high costs of training and seasoning young players to achieve the level of skills required in professional baseball and such investments would be sacrificed if they became free agents at the end of a renewal year; that driven by the compulsion to win, owners of franchises would over extend themselves financially and improvident bidding for players in an economic climate in which, today, some clubs are strained, financially; that investors will be discouraged from putting money in franchises in which several of the star players on the club team will become free agents at the end of a renewal year and no continuing control over the players' services can be exercised; and that even the integrity of the sport may be placed in hazard under certain circumstances.

I do not purport to appraise these apprehensions. They are all based on speculations as to what may ensue. Some of the fears may be imaginary or exaggerated; but some may be reasonable, realistic and sound. After all, they were voiced by distinguished baseball officials with long experience in the sport and a background for judgment in such matters much superior to my own. However, as stated above, at length, it is not for the Panel (and especially the writer) to determine what, if anything, is good or bad about the reserve system. The Panel's sole duty is to interpret and apply the agreements and undertakings of the parties. If any of the expressed apprehensions and fears are soundly based, I am confident that the dislocations and damage to the reserve system can be avoided or minimized through good faith collective bargaining between the parties. There are numerous expedients available and arrangements that can be made that will soften the blow—if this decision, indeed, should be regarded as a blow. This decision is not the end of the line by any means. The parties, jointly, are free to agree to disregard it and compose their differences as to the reserve system in any way they see fit.

* * *

Grievance upheld.

———

NOTES AND QUESTIONS

1. *Evaluation of Policy or Interpretation?* Early in his opinion, Arbitrator Seitz emphatically stated that his role was not to evaluate the merits of baseball's reserve system, but merely to interpret the meaning of its constituent provisions. Look closely at the passages in which the arbitrator considers and selects from the alternative interpretations advanced by the Players Association and the League about the proper interpretation of the option clause in the player's contract and the reserve clause in the major league rules. Is there a distinction between evaluation and interpretation of these legal documents?

2. *A Convincing Interpretation?* Was Arbitrator Seitz correct in his reading of the collective bargaining agreement? Remember that the owners had originally designed the Reserve System in the nineteenth century to keep players from "revolving" from club to club in the nascent National League. Why would they construct a player control system that would last only for two years and would not accomplish this goal of institutional stability?

3. *Effect of Past Practice?* The parties had negotiated over the extent and reach of the Reserve System, but they could not reach an agreement. Instead, they agreed to disagree. Do you think anyone who had been at those negotiations would have been surprised by the arbitrator's conclusion that the parties had mutually agreed on a "one-year-only" option? Shouldn't their "non-agreement" on any significant change have perpetuated their hundred-year-old understanding that the Reserve System was, in fact, perpetual?

4. *Arbitrator as Bargaining Catalyst?* Could Seitz have ruled for the Players Association because he knew that this was the only way to get the parties to the bargaining table where they would be forced to address the Reserve System issue? Had the owners prevailed, would the Reserve System have remained in its historic form for a substantially longer period? If this was Seitz's strategy, is this a proper role for an arbitrator?

———

The Kansas City Royals, representing Major League Baseball, appealed the federal district court decision upholding Arbitrator Seitz's ruling, primarily arguing that he overstepped his jurisdiction. A young, local lawyer from Kansas City named Donald Fehr represented the union, the beginning of his career with the baseball labor organization.

KANSAS CITY ROYALS V. MAJOR LEAGUE
BASEBALL PLAYERS ASS'N
532 F.2d 615 (8th Cir. 1976)

HEANEY, CIRCUIT JUDGE.

* * *

We cannot say, on the basis of the evidence discussed above, that the record evinces the most forceful evidence of a purpose to exclude the grievances here involved from arbitration.

(a) The 1968 agreement clearly permitted the arbitration of grievances relating to the reserve system. It, therefore, cannot be said that the Club Owners never consented to the arbitration of such grievances. The Club Owners might have argued that they agreed to arbitrate such grievances because the Commissioner of Baseball was designated as the arbitrator, and that he, recognizing the importance of the reserve system to baseball, would interpret the disputed provisions to allow perpetual control by a Club Owner over its players. That argument, however, was not advanced before either the arbitration panel, the District Court or this Court. Moreover, the argument would not be particularly flattering to any Commissioner of Baseball.[19]

(b) Article XIV, the predecessor to Article XV, was suggested by the Players Association for rather specific purposes and the Club Owners clearly did what they could to preserve their right to argue that the reserve system remained a part of the collective bargaining agreement. Indeed, if the Club Owners' counterproposals with respect to Article XIV had been accepted, the reserve system would clearly have remained subject to arbitration.

Article XV was clearly designed to accomplish the same purposes as Article XIV. If in accomplishing these purposes the players had clearly agreed to exclude disputes arising out of the operation of the reserve system from arbitration, the Messersmith-McNally grievances would not be arbitrable. For the reasons discussed in this opinion, however, no such agreement can be found.

(c) From 1970 to 1973, a number of grievances concerning the reserve system were submitted to arbitration. The Club Owners raised no jurisdictional objections. While this fact alone is not of controlling significance, because the grievances submitted did not go to what the Club Owners regard as the "core" or "heart" of the reserve system, the

---

[19]   Mr. Bowie Kuhn, the present Commissioner of Baseball, testified, in substance, that he felt that Article X of the 1973 agreement gave him the power to withdraw a grievance from arbitration if he felt that the grievance involved the "preservation of the integrity of, or the maintenance of public confidence in, the game of baseball." He testified further that he did not withdraw these grievances from arbitration because he didn't want to do anything to adversely affect the collective bargaining process: he respected the reputation of Mr. Seitz, the impartial arbitrator, and he respected the arbitration process.

submission of grievances relating to the reserve system is certainly a fact that detracts from the Club Owners' contention that the parties clearly understood Article XIV to mean that grievances relating to the reserve system would not be subject to arbitration.

(d) The fact that Marvin Miller may have given assurances, during the 1970 negotiations, that the players would not grieve over house rules cannot be viewed as the most forceful evidence of a purpose to exclude the Messersmith-McNally grievances from arbitration. First, there is some dispute in the record as to whether Miller made such a statement. Second, assuming he did, the term "house rules" is ambiguous. Third, and we think most important, the weight of the evidence, when viewed as a whole, does not support the conclusion that Article XV was intended to preclude arbitration of any grievances otherwise arbitrable.

(e) The essence of the Club Owners' arguments on the question of arbitrability was perhaps best articulated in the testimony of Larry McPhail, President of the American League, in which he stated: "Isn't it fair to say that our strong feelings on the importance of the core of the reserve system would indicate that we wouldn't permit the reserve system to be within the jurisdiction of the arbitration procedure?" The weaknesses in this argument have been previously discussed in paragraphs (a), (b) and (c) above. We add only that what a reasonable party might be expected to do cannot take precedence over what the parties actually provided for in their collective bargaining agreement.

The Club Owners contend that even if the arbitration panel had jurisdiction, the award must be vacated. They argue that the award exceeded the scope of the panel's authority by "fundamentally altering and destroying the Reserve System as it historically existed and had been acquiesced in by the Association."

As we have previously noted, our review of the merits of an arbitration panel's award is limited. The award must be sustained so long as it "draws its essence from the collective bargaining agreement." *United Steelworkers of America v. Enterprise Wheel & Car Corp.*, 363 U.S. 593, 597 (1960).

The nub of the Club Owners' argument is that both they and the Players Association understood the reserve system to enable a club to perpetually control a player, that this understanding was reflected in the 1973 agreement, and that the arbitration panel was without authority to alter the agreed upon operation of the reserve system.

We cannot agree that the 1973 collective bargaining agreement embodied an understanding by the parties that the reserve system enabled a club to perpetually control a player. First, the agreement contained no express provision to that effect. Second, while there is evidence that the reserve system operated in such a manner in recent years, the record discloses that various Players Association representatives viewed the system as allowing a player to become a free agent by playing under a renewed contract for one year.

Moreover, it can be argued that the arbitration panel's award did not "alter" the reserve system. To the extent that the reserve system did enable a club to perpetually control a player, it was not necessarily by virtue of successive invocations of the renewal clause, or application of the reserve list and no tampering rules in the absence of a contractual obligation. Other provisions operate to deter a player from "playing out his option," as is evidenced by the fact that few players have done so. On this basis, it may be said that the arbitration panel's decision did not change the reserve system, but merely interpreted various elements thereof under circumstances which had not previously arisen.

The 1973 agreement empowered the arbitration panel to "interpret, apply or determine compliance with the provisions of agreements" between the players and the clubs. We find that the arbitration panel did nothing more than to interpret certain provisions of the Uniform Player's Contract and the Major League Rules. We cannot say that those provisions are not susceptible of the construction given them by the panel. Accordingly, the award must be sustained.

Conclusion

We hold that the arbitration panel had jurisdiction to hear and decide the Messersmith-McNally grievances, that the panel's award drew its essence from the collective bargaining agreement, and that the relief fashioned by the District Court was appropriate. Accordingly, the award of the arbitration panel must be sustained, and the District Court's judgment affirmed. In so holding, we intimate no views on the merits of the reserve system. We note, however, that Club Owners and the Players Association's representatives agree that some form of a reserve system is needed if the integrity of the game is to be preserved and if public confidence in baseball is to be maintained. The disagreement lies over the degree of control necessary if these goals are to be achieved. Certainly, the parties are in a better position to negotiate their differences than to have them decided in a series of arbitrations and court decisions. We commend them to that process and suggest that the time for obfuscation has passed and that the time for plain talk and clear language has arrived. Baseball fans everywhere expect nothing less.

* * *

Appeal dismissed.

NOTES AND QUESTIONS

1. *Final Verdict?* Having read both the arbitral and judicial opinions, what do you think was the proper construction of baseball's collective agreement as it relates to the reserve system? To what extent are your views influenced by your sentiments about the equities of the issue? If you feel that Arbitrator Seitz's reading may have been somewhat dubious, does this affect your evaluation of the *Enterprise Wheel & Car* standard for judicial review of arbitral construction of labor agreements, discussed in *Boston Celtics v. Brian Shaw, supra?* Or does this case support the national labor police that parties to labor agreements should accept the decision maker and the process for which they have contracted?

2. *Arbitrator Selection Strategy.* Recall that the parties mutually select their arbitrator and that either party can terminate the appointment if displeased with any one ruling. Such dismissal befell Tom Roberts, the baseball arbitrator in 1986, following his decision striking down the drug testing covenants in individual player contracts. The same fate overtook Peter Seitz following his *Messersmith* decision. The baseball owners actually almost dismissed Seitz before the *Messersmith* hearing because of Seitz' decision in the Jim "Catfish" Hunter case a year earlier. Indeed, Commissioner Bowie Kuhn, in his autobiography, HARDBALL, relates that the club owners rejected Kuhn's recommendation to replace Seitz. The Player Relations Committee felt that Seitz, having ruled for the Players Association in *Hunter*, would likely lean toward the owners in *Messersmith,* with that case's quite different contract footing and more momentous implications.

3. *Lasting Impact or Easy Renegotiation?* Even though a party may guess wrongly how its current arbitrator will rule, a second key difference between contract arbitration and statutory administration is that the parties can renegotiate the contractual language that an outside arbitrator may have misconstrued, a step the parties certainly cannot take with respect to an administrative interpretation of a statute without a significant Congressional detour. In fact, the baseball agreement expired around the time the *Messersmith* decision was rendered, and the agreement was renegotiated long before any more players reached free agent status. According to the Coase theorem, Seitz's interpretation of the reserve clause, right or wrong, was largely irrelevant to the real world outcome of those negotiations. Do you agree?

4. *Avoiding Mandatory Bargaining?* In order to re-establish its reserve system after *Messersmith*, did Major League Baseball need to have the consent of the Players Association? There were two contractual features of the traditional system, the perennially renewable option clause in the player contract and the anti-tampering clause in the league rules. Could baseball have simply amended its own rules to address this problem? With what risks under labor law? In industrial relations? In public relations?

The legal implication of the final-and-binding *Messersmith* ruling was that any baseball player could become a free agent simply by playing out his option year without signing a new contract. As the *Messersmith* decision was being rendered and judicially reviewed in the winter of 1975–76, the baseball collective bargaining agreement (referred to in baseball as the "Basic Agreement") was itself expiring and being renegotiated. Naturally enough, free agency became the central issue in these negotiations. After a 17-day owner lockout of the players during spring training—a work stoppage that was unilaterally ended by Commissioner Bowie Kuhn in the "best interests of the sport"—the Players Association and the owners' Player Relations Committee reached a new collective bargaining agreement in the summer of 1976.

The new contract modified free agency considerably. During his first two years in the league, a player had to accept his club's unilateral contract offers or not play, and for years three through six, the player was still contractually bound to his initial club but had the right to final-offer arbitration to establish the appropriate amount of salary. Free agency began only after six years of Major League service. The owners saw this as a significant victory. Seitz had set the players free and then the players negotiated away their rights. In fact, the Players Association understood economics better than baseball management. Had all Major League players flooded the free agent market each year, the surplus of talent would have driven down salaries. Instead, limiting free agency to players with six or more years of Major League service drove prices up, in turn affecting the salaries of all players and the salary arbitration awards that three through six-year players received.

Messersmith and its baseball progeny stand in stark contrast to what happened in football. As explained in Chapter 7, shortly after the arbitral ruling in the *Messersmith* grievance, federal appeals courts held that the NFL's restraints on competition for players violated federal antitrust laws. *See, e.g., Mackey v. NFL*, 543 F.2d 606 (8th Cir. 1976). Like their counterparts in basketball and hockey, though, the NFL Players Association subsequently agreed in collective bargaining to alternative restraints on free agency.

The post-*Mackey* regime in football allowed a player to become a free agent after five years of service. This right was largely illusory, however, in the absence of a competing football league because the collective agreement gave the incumbent team a right of first refusal over any offer made by another club to one of the team's free agent players. If the incumbent team chose not to match the offer, it was awarded specified draft picks of the new team determined by the transferring player's new salary, which was intended to compensate for the value of the player being lost. Unlike baseball, then, football did not establish any time at which a veteran player would enjoy unrestricted free agency. Experience soon made it clear that there would be little or no competitive bidding for players under this system, and as a result the NFLPA sought to emulate their baseball counterpart's success through labor arbitration.

The case of *NFL Players Association and NFL Management Council (Dutton)*, (Arbitration 1980), involved John Dutton, an All-Pro defensive lineman with the Baltimore Colts. Dutton completed his contract in 1978, received no offers from other teams as a free agent, and thus played the next "option" season with the Colts for 110% of his prior year's salary, as provided for in § 17 of Article XV (Right of First Refusal/Compensation) of the NFL labor agreement. At the expiration of the 1979 season, Dutton again sought free agent offers, but received none, even though he was one of the leading defensive ends in the league. The reason was that the NFL Management Council interpreted the prior club's right to elect first refusal or draft pick compensation as applying perpetually to any free agent, even one coming off an option year contract, not just one whose previous negotiated contract had just expired. Thus Dutton and the NFLPA sought a ruling from the football arbitrator similar to *Messersmith*—that these obstacles to free agency applied only after the expiration of the contract signed by the player, not after the year of automatic contract renewal via the collective agreement (*i.e.*, that these restraints do not exist in perpetuity).

Arbitrator Burt Luskin observed that the evidence before him indicated that, during the several months of labor negotiations in the winter and spring of 1977, neither side had ever explicitly raised or addressed the *Messersmith* question, though that decision and its impact on baseball had occurred the prior year. The football players' argument was that, absent express contract language or clear negotiating history, the general wording of § 17 must not be interpreted as creating a perpetually renewable option for the teams (though with option year salaries going up, not down, as had been the case in baseball). Arbitrator Luskin rejected this argument after he had situated § 17 within the broader array of provisions in Article XV. Section 1 seemed to subject all "veteran free agents" to this regime, not just those who "play out the options in their contracts," and § 18 created an Extreme Personal Hardship exception that denied the prior club a right of first refusal to keep the player on that team, but still granted the club a right of compensation. Given these and several other clues in related contract provisions, the arbitrator concluded that he could not "infer from the absence of affirmative or negative language that the parties reached an agreement or understanding that would serve to confer total free agent status to a veteran player who had completed a year of service pursuant to a § 17(b) contract. . . ."

Thus, Andy Messersmith was able to win free agency for his baseball counterparts, but John Dutton failed in his effort in football. While there were some textual variations in the language of the collective agreements in the two sports, differences in the negotiating scenarios that produced the language (and perhaps also in the arbitrators' philosophical inclinations) might also account for the opposite outcomes. The stark contrast between baseball's and football's labor markets after *Messersmith* and *Dutton* drove home to both players and owners (in basketball and hockey as well) what a difference a labor agreement could make. Not until the early 2000s (and following fierce legal and labor relations conflicts) did the governing rules begin to converge across the professional sports leagues.

C. CURRENT RESTRAINTS—SALARY CAPS AND TAXES

From the early 1970s to the early 1990s, collective bargaining and antitrust litigation in professional team sports were primarily targeted at securing a freer labor market for the players. By the mid-1990s, however, the focus of player-owner conflict had shifted. Owners were now prepared to accept (perhaps even embrace) free movement of players from one team to another. They insisted, though, on creation of league-wide constraints on the amount of money that individual teams could spend to induce such player movement—via salary caps or salary taxes.

This concept of free player movement with salary constraints was first proposed in the 1982 negotiations by NFLPA Executive Director Ed Garvey. Garvey's idea was that 55% of league revenues should be allocated to player compensation. The bulk of this money would be paid in fixed salary rates determined by position and seniority. The rest would be paid in bonuses for personal and team performance, as measured by statistical factors developed and administered by the NFLPA. The NFL owners, under Commissioner Pete Rozelle, rejected this salary sharing idea as "socialism in disguise," and an unacceptable inroad upon each team's property rights in a capitalist market.

Just a year later, basketball instituted a revised version of salary capping and sharing came into existence in basketball. By contrast with football, the NBA was in a sorry state in the early 1980s. Two-thirds of its teams were losing money every year, and a few (especially the Cleveland Cavaliers) were both spending and losing so much that the league office considered taking control of them. Thus, NBPA founder and leader Larry Fleisher, Commissioner Larry O'Brien, and O'Brien's chief counsel and soon to be successor, David Stern, developed a league salary formula designed to accommodate the interests of both sides. Ten years later, new football leadership (NFLPA Executive Director Gene Upshaw and Commissioner Paul Tagliabue) agreed to their own version of the salary cap after two decades of football suits and strikes over free agency. Then, in 1997 the baseball negotiators fashioned a "soft" salary tax system to settle their three-year labor battle, one they revised and strengthened in their 2002, 2006, 2011, 2016, and 2022 labor negotiations. In the aftermath of the NHL lockout of its players in 2004, the parties agreed on a salary cap system, individual salary restrictions and new free agency rules.

Salary cap and tax provisions take up dozens of densely written pages in the NBA, NFL, NHL and MLB collective agreements. In the capped leagues—the NBA, NFL and NHL—each year the league office and the players association add up the gross revenue received by all clubs from defined sources—not just gate receipts and television revenues, but also merchandising sales, luxury box and club seat rentals, and the like. An agreed-to percentage of that revenue is assigned for player compensation. Part of that compensation fund is reserved for payment of the player retirement, disability, and other benefit funds. The remainder is then divided by the number of clubs in the league to establish the cap on each team's total player compensation.

In all three leagues, this system imposes not just a ceiling on the amount that teams may pay their players, but also a floor on the amount that each team must pay in salaries. This combination of a cap and a floor means that the NBA, NHL and NFL labor agreements actually function to give players a guaranteed share in aggregate league revenues. The leagues also have developed a variety of revenue-sharing devices to ensure that each team can and does meet the specified salary floor.

There is, however, a crucial difference between the NFL, NHL and NBA versions of the salary cap. The NBA's cap is a "soft" cap because it is qualified by several complicated exceptions. Most importantly, the scheme largely exempts the amount that clubs can spend to sign their current players to new contracts. This feature has always been known as the "Larry Bird" exception, because it was inserted in the 1983 NBA collective agreement to enable the Celtics to re-sign Larry Bird for the salary they knew he was seeking without having to release or trade Bird's star teammates. The sole aim of the NBA cap, then, was to prevent the Celtics (or the Knicks and Lakers) from using large salary offers to lure players away from the Cavaliers and other smaller market teams. But because the Larry Bird exception and other exceptions allow teams to spend a much larger percentage of their revenue on player salaries than is consistent with the intent of the cap system, the collective agreement also creates a tax on the amount a team's payroll exceeds a threshold that is set significantly above the cap amount. The tax is graduated at higher levels for each 5 million dollars that the team exceeds the threshold; currently $1.50 for each of the first five million dollars in excess, rising to $3.75 for each dollar from 20 million to 25 million in excess and then $.50 more in tax for each higher 5 million dollar tier. This tax makes the NBA system a hybrid between the NFL's/NHL's hard payroll caps and MLB's payroll "luxury tax" regime. The NBA was also the first league to negotiate individual salary caps that limited the amount individual players may earn, not just a salary cap for an entire club that can be allocated among a team's players.

The NFL owners and players, and later the NHL owners and players, eventually agreed to a "hard" cap, one that forced teams to release some of their higher paid players when their overall salary budget exceeded the collectively bargained limit. The NFLPA also negotiated a graduated minimum salary for the players as well as a rookie player payroll cap that assigned to each team a maximum amount that it could pay to all of its first-year players, with the amount varying depending on how many rookies the team drafted and how high they were taken in the draft. The agreement also set forth a series of basic minima for NFL players that increase for each year of service in the league.

Baseball's negotiations in 2002 threatened to be a reprise of the strife of the mid-1990s, but the productive work of Michael Weiner for the MLBPA and Rob Manfred for MLB resulted in a last-minute settlement imposing a tax on the amount of a team's payroll that exceeded a certain pre-established threshold, with the percentage of the excess that is taxed increasing as a team goes over the threshold in successive years. The luxury tax has not operated as an effective salary cap because it has been set at a level substantially above the payroll of most teams. The tax seems intended to dampen the spending of only large market franchises. Over the years, most MLB teams have never exceeded the limit and thus have never paid what is now called the "competitive balance" tax. For the first years of the cap, only the Yankees consistently exceeded the threshold, though other clubs, including the Dodgers, Red Sox, Mets, Nationals, Cubs, Giants, and Tigers also have exceeded the tax threshold.

Baseball's most recent agreements have set multiple thresholds that impose higher taxes for higher payrolls. Under the 2022 CBA, the threshold is 230 million for the first year and 244 million for the final 2026 year. The rate for the first year of overage is 20%, but this climbs to 30% for a second consecutive year and 50% for a third consecutive year. The surcharge on these rates for overages between 20 and 40 million is 12%, for overages between 40 and 60 million is 42.5% or 45%, and for overages above 60 million is 60%. For 2022, the Dodgers projected payroll was above 288 million, the Mets was above 259 million, the Yankees was above 246 million, and the Phillies above 232 million. The Athletics and Orioles both had projected 2022 payrolls below 50 million.

————

NOTES AND QUESTIONS

1.   *Hard Cap, Soft Cap, or Tax?* What are the pros and cons of the NBA's softer cap (with its Larry Bird exception and excessive payroll tax) versus the NFL's and NHL's harder versions? Of any cap versus MLB's past or current

tax system? From the broader perspective of instruments for social control of private behavior, what are the virtues and limitations of regulatory standards as compared to tax incentives?

2. *Specific Caps or Revenue Sharing Formula?* Is it better to have the parties negotiate specific amounts for their salary ceilings (as they did in baseball), or to develop a salary-sharing formula based on a numerical percentage of overall league revenues? An obvious virtue of the formula approach is that it automatically adjusts to changes in league revenues over the longer run. Calculating revenues for purposes of applying the formula may remain contentious, however.

3. *How to Define Revenue?* An even bigger labor issue is which revenue sources should be shared with the players. For instance, should the NBA owners continue to agree to include their upward spiraling merchandising earnings in the revenue base? The simple answer (and the one the players obviously favor) is to count all owner earnings having anything to do with the sport except for franchise value appreciation. In football, though, this poses a potentially significant problem because of the lucrative stadium deals enjoyed by some but not all teams that can generate substantial revenues from luxury box suites, club seating, seat licenses, parking, and concessions. If these unshared team revenues lift the amount that teams can (and must) pay in salaries, a significant problem is posed for other teams that have not been able to extract such deals from their community's taxpayers or are situated in a market without a critical mass of moneyed local fans and businesses.

4. *What Percentage to Assign to Players?* Even when the two sides do reach an understanding about which revenues and how much revenues are to be counted, they must answer the most difficult question: the percentage to be assigned to the players. Relevant considerations may differ from sport to sport. For example, football and basketball do not face the substantial expenditures made by baseball and hockey to run farm systems that develop talent for their games. Furthermore, football teams have as many as 50 players under contract and substantial medical expenses compared to only about 15 players under contract on NBA teams that also have far fewer medical expenses per player.

5. *Adjusting to the 2020 Pandemic Season.* The three leagues with salary caps and revenue sharing systems were able to adapt flexibly to the reduced revenues that resulted from pandemic constraints. As revenues declined, the players' payrolls could decline proportionately.

MLB's tax-qualified free agency system was not as flexible. In the midst of uncertainty as the pandemic started in the U.S., on March 26, 2020, MLB and MLBPA agreed that salaries and service time would be prorated proportionate to the number of games played out of the usual 162 game schedule. MLB agreed to make its "best effort to play as many games as possible." When it became clear that fans would not be attending games, however, the incentives for the league to play games diverged from those of the players. MLB settled on a 60-game schedule which paid the players only 37% of the salaries they would have earned in a regular season. In early 2021, the

MLBPA filed a grievance asking for damages of $500 million based on the league's refusal to play 20 to 25 more games and increase the players' prorated salaries accordingly. The union cited a clause in the March 2020 agreement that the two sides would "discuss in good faith the economic feasibility of playing games in the absence of spectators," and claimed that the league did not show such good faith. The union ultimately dropped the grievance in the negotiations for its new 2022 collective bargaining agreement with the league.

D. BASEBALL'S ANTITRUST EXEMPTION

History explains why baseball players, unlike their counterparts in the other professional team sports, could not use antitrust law as well as labor law to replace the old system of almost total owner control of their labor market with the current negotiated and balanced system. The National and American Leagues emerged before the broadening of the interpretation of interstate commerce as the basis for both Congressional power and the congruent limit on the reach of antitrust law, which requires "trade or commerce among the several States." As a result, only the baseball owners could claim a reliance on the earlier narrower interpretation of interstate commerce. The following famous (or infamous) application of the principle of *stare decisis* reflects the strength of that claim.

FLOOD V. KUHN
407 U.S. 258 (1972)

JUSTICE BLACKMUN delivered the opinion of the Court.

[Curt Flood was an All-Star center fielder for the St. Louis Cardinals throughout the 1960s, helping lead his team to the World Series in 1964, 1967, and 1968. Flood's salary rose from $4,000 in his initial 1956 contract to $90,000 in 1969. In October 1969, Flood was stunned to learn that, at the age of 31, he had been traded to the Philadelphia Phillies. Although the Phillies offered him a pay raise to $100,000, Flood rejected the trade, declared himself a free agent, and filed suit to establish these rights under federal and state antitrust law (as well as under the Thirteenth Amendment's bar on "involuntary servitude"). After the lower courts had rejected his core antitrust claim based on the judicially-fashioned exemption for baseball, the Supreme Court accepted the case to take yet another look at this issue.]

* * *

For the third time in 50 years the Court is asked specifically to rule that professional baseball's reserve system is within the reach of the federal antitrust laws.[1] Collateral issues of state law and of federal labor policy are also advanced.

---

[1]   The reserve system, publicly introduced into baseball contracts in 1887, centers in the uniformity of player contracts; the confinement of the player to the club that has him under the

I

THE GAME

It is a century and a quarter since the New York Nine defeated the Knickerbockers 23 to 1 on Hoboken's Elysian Fields June 19, 1846, with Alexander Jay Cartwright as the instigator and the umpire. The teams were amateur, but the contest marked a significant date in baseball's beginnings. That early game led ultimately to the development of professional baseball and its tightly organized structure.

The Cincinnati Red Stockings came into existence in 1869 upon an outpouring of local pride. With only one Cincinnatian on the payroll, this professional team traveled over 11,000 miles that summer, winning 56 games and tying one. Shortly thereafter, on St. Patrick's Day in 1871, the National Association of Professional Baseball Players was founded and the professional league was born.

The ensuing colorful days are well known. The ardent follower and the student of baseball know of General Abner Doubleday; the formation of the National League in 1876; Chicago's supremacy in the first year's competition under the leadership of Al Spalding and with Cap Anson at third base; the formation of the American Association and then of the Union Association in the 1880s; the introduction of Sunday baseball; interleague warfare with cut-rate admission prices and player raiding; the development of the reserve "clause"; the emergence in 1885 of the Brotherhood of Professional Ball Players, and in 1890 of the Players League; the appearance of the American League, or "junior circuit," in 1901, rising from the minor Western Association; the first World Series in 1903, disruption in 1904, and the Series' resumption in 1905; the short-lived Federal League on the majors' scene during World War I years; the troublesome and discouraging episode of the 1919 Series; the home run ball; the shifting of franchises; the expansion of the leagues; the installation in 1965 of the major league draft of potential new players; and the formation of the Major League Baseball Players Association in 1966.

Then there are the many names, celebrated for one reason or another, that have sparked the diamond and its environs and that have provided tinder for recaptured thrills, for reminiscence and comparisons, and for conversation and anticipation in-season and off-season: Ty Cobb, Babe Ruth, Tris Speaker, Walter Johnson, Henry Chadwick, Eddie Collins, Lou Gehrig, Grover Cleveland Alexander, Rogers Hornsby, Harry Hooper, Goose Goslin, Jackie Robinson, Honus Wagner, Joe McCarthy, John McGraw, Deacon Phillippe, Rube Marquard, Christy Mathewson, Tommy Leach, Big Ed Delahanty, Davy Jones, Germany Schaefer, King Kelly, Big Dan Brouthers, Wahoo Sam Crawford, Wee Willie Keeler, Big Ed Walsh,

---

contract; the assignability of the player's contract; and the ability of the club annually to renew the contract unilaterally, subject to a stated salary minimum. . . .

Jimmy Austin, Fred Snodgrass, Satchel Paige, Hugh Jennings, Fred Merkle, Iron Man McGinnity, Three-Finger Brown, Harry and Stan Coveleski, Connie Mack, Al Bridwell, Red Ruffing, Amos Rusie, Cy Young, Smokey Joe Wood, Chief Meyers, Chief Bender, Bill Klem, Hans Lobert, Johnny Evers, Joe Tinker, Roy Campanella, Miller Huggins, Rube Bressler, Dazzy Vance, Edd Roush, Bill Wambsganss, Clark Griffith, Branch Rickey, Frank Chance, Cap Anson, Nap Lajoie, Sad Sam Jones, Bob O'Farrell, Lefty O'Doul, Bobby Veach, Willie Kamm, Heinie Groh, Lloyd and Paul Waner, Stuffy McInnis, Charles Comiskey, Roger Bresnahan, Bill Dickey, Zack Wheat, George Sisler, Charlie Gehringer, Eppa Rixey, Harry Heilmann, Fred Clarke, Dizzy Dean, Hank Greenberg, Pie Traynor, Rube Waddell, Bill Terry, Carl Hubbell, Old Hoss Radbourne, Moe Berg, Rabbit Maranville, Jimmie Foxx, Lefty Grove. The list seems endless.

And one recalls the appropriate reference to the "World Serious," attributed to Ring Lardner, Sr.; Ernest L. Thayer's "Casey at the Bat"; the ring of "Tinker to Evers to Chance"; and all the other happenings, habits, and superstitions about and around baseball that made it the "national pastime" or, depending upon the point of view, "the great American tragedy."

* * *

IV

THE LEGAL BACKGROUND

A. *Federal Baseball Club v. National League*, 259 U.S. 200 (1922), was a suit for treble damages instituted by a member of the Federal League (Baltimore) against the National and American Leagues and others. The plaintiff obtained a verdict in the trial court, but the Court of Appeals reversed. The main brief filed by the plaintiff with this Court discloses that it was strenuously argued, among other things, that the business in which the defendants were engaged was interstate commerce; that the interstate relationship among the several clubs, located as they were in different States, was predominant; that organized baseball represented an investment of colossal wealth; that it was an engagement in moneymaking; that gate receipts were divided by agreement between the home club and the visiting club; and that the business of baseball was to be distinguished from the mere playing of the game as a sport for physical exercise and diversion.

Mr. Justice Holmes, in speaking succinctly for a unanimous Court, said:

> The business is giving exhibitions of baseball, which are purely state affairs. . . . But the fact that in order to give the exhibitions the Leagues must induce free persons to cross state lines and must arrange and pay for their doing so is not enough to change the

character of the business. . . . [T]he transport is a mere incident, not the essential thing. That to which it is incident, the exhibition, although made for money would not be called trade or commerce in the commonly accepted use of those words. As it is put by the defendant, personal effort, not related to production, is not a subject of commerce. That which in its consummation is not commerce does not become commerce among the States because the transportation that we have mentioned takes place. To repeat the illustrations given by the Court below, a firm of lawyers sending out a member to argue a case, or the Chautauqua lecture bureau sending out lecturers, does not engage in such commerce because the lawyer or lecturer goes to another State.

If we are right the plaintiff's business is to be described in the same way and the restrictions by contract that prevented the plaintiff from getting players to break their bargains and the other conduct charged against the defendants were not an interference with commerce among the States.

* * *

B.   In the years that followed, baseball continued to be subject to intermittent antitrust attack. The courts, however, rejected these challenges on the authority of *Federal Baseball*. In some cases stress was laid, although unsuccessfully, on new factors such as the development of radio and television with their substantial additional revenues to baseball. For the most part, however, the Holmes opinion was generally and necessarily accepted as controlling authority. And in the 1952 Report of the Subcommittee on *Study of Monopoly Power*, of the House Committee on the Judiciary, H.R. Rep. No. 2002, 82d Cong., 2d Sess., 229, it was said, in conclusion:

On the other hand the overwhelming preponderance of the evidence established baseball's need for some sort of reserve clause. Baseball's history shows that chaotic conditions prevailed when there was no reserve clause. Experience points to no feasible substitute to protect the integrity of the game or to guarantee a comparatively even competitive struggle. The evidence adduced at the hearings would clearly not justify the enactment of legislation flatly condemning the reserve clause.

C.   The Court granted certiorari, in the *Toolson*, *Kowalski*, and *Corbett* cases, and, by a short per curiam (Warren, C.J., and Black, Frankfurter, Douglas, Jackson, Clark, and Minton, JJ.), affirmed the judgments of the respective courts of appeals in those three cases. *Toolson v. New York Yankees, Inc.*, 346 U.S. 356 (1953). *Federal Baseball* was cited as holding "that the business of providing public baseball games for profit between clubs of professional baseball players was not within the scope of the federal antitrust laws," and:

Congress has had the ruling under consideration but has not seen fit to bring such business under these laws by legislation having prospective effect. The business has thus been left for thirty years to develop, on the understanding that it was not subject to existing antitrust legislation. The present cases ask us to overrule the prior decision and, with retrospective effect, hold the legislation applicable. We think that if there are evils in this field which now warrant application to it of the antitrust laws it should be by legislation. Without re-examination of the underlying issues, the judgments below are affirmed on the authority of *Federal Baseball Club of Baltimore v. National League of Professional Baseball Clubs*, supra, so far as that decision determines that Congress had no intention of including the business of baseball within the scope of the federal antitrust laws.

This quotation reveals four reasons for the Court's affirmance of *Toolson* and its companion cases: (a) Congressional awareness for three decades of the Court's ruling in *Federal Baseball*, coupled with congressional inaction. (b) The fact that baseball was left alone to develop for that period upon the understanding that the reserve system was not subject to existing federal antitrust laws. (c) A reluctance to overrule *Federal Baseball* with consequent retroactive effect. (d) A professed desire that any needed remedy be provided by legislation rather than by court decree. The emphasis in *Toolson* was on the determination, attributed even to *Federal Baseball*, that Congress had no intention to include baseball within the reach of the federal antitrust laws.

[Justice Blackmun then described and quoted from *United States v. Shubert*, 348 U.S. 222 (1955), in which the Court refused to extend professional baseball's antitrust immunity to a nationwide theatre company. Chief Justice Warren's opinion stresses that the result in *Toolson* was based on *Federal Baseball* and stare decisis and concluded that "[i]f the *Toolson* holding is to be expanded—or contracted—the appropriate remedy lies with Congress."]

* * *

E.   *United States v. International Boxing Club*, 348 U.S. 236 (1955), was a companion to *Shubert* and was decided the same day. This was a civil antitrust action against defendants engaged in the business of promoting professional championship boxing contests. Here again the District Court had dismissed the complaint in reliance upon *Federal Baseball* and *Toolson*. The Chief Justice observed that "if it were not for *Federal Baseball* and *Toolson*, we think that it would be too clear for dispute that the Government's allegations bring the defendants within the scope of the Act." He pointed out that the defendants relied on the two baseball cases but also would have been content with a more restrictive interpretation of them than the *Shubert* defendants, for the boxing defendants argued that the cases immunized only businesses that involve exhibitions of an athletic nature. The Court accepted neither argument. It again noted that "*Toolson* neither overruled *Federal Baseball* nor necessarily reaffirmed all that was said in *Federal Baseball*." It stated:

> The controlling consideration in *Federal Baseball* and *Hart* was, instead, a very practical one—the degree of interstate activity involved in the particular business under review. It follows that *stare decisis* cannot help the defendants here; for, contrary to their argument, *Federal Baseball* did not hold that all businesses based on professional sports were outside the scope of the antitrust laws. The issue confronting us is, therefore, not whether a previously granted exemption should continue, but whether an exemption should be granted in the first instance. And that issue is for Congress to resolve, not this Court.

The Court noted the presence then in Congress of various bills forbidding the application of the antitrust laws to "organized professional sports enterprises"; the holding of extensive hearings on some of these; subcommittee opposition; a postponement recommendation as to baseball; and the fact that "Congress thus left intact the then-existing coverage of the antitrust laws."

Mr. Justice Frankfurter, joined by Mr. Justice Minton, dissented. "It would baffle the subtlest ingenuity," he said, "to find a single differentiating factor between other sporting exhibitions . . . and baseball insofar as the conduct of the sport is relevant to the criteria or considerations by which the Sherman Law becomes applicable to a trade or commerce." He went on:

> The Court decided as it did in the *Toolson* case as an application of the doctrine of *stare decisis*. That doctrine is not, to be sure, an imprisonment of reason. But neither is it a whimsy. It can hardly be that this Court gave a preferred position to baseball because it is the great American sport. . . . If *stare decisis* be one aspect of law, as it is, to disregard it in identical situations is mere caprice.
>
> Congress, on the other hand, may yield to sentiment and be capricious, subject only to due process. . . .
>
> Between them, this case and *Shubert* illustrate that nice but rational distinctions are inevitable in adjudication. I agree with the Court's opinion in *Shubert* for precisely the reason that constrains me to dissent in this case.

Mr. Justice Minton also separately dissented on the ground that boxing is not trade or commerce. He added the comment that "Congress has not attempted" to control baseball and boxing. The two dissenting Justices, thus, did not call for the overruling of *Federal Baseball* and *Toolson*; they merely felt that boxing should be under the same umbrella of freedom as was baseball and, as Mr. Justice Frankfurter said, they could not exempt baseball "to the exclusion of every other sport different not one legal jot or tittle from it."

F.   The parade marched on. *Radovich v. National Football League*, 352 U.S. 445 (1957), was a civil Clayton Act case testing the application of the antitrust laws to professional football. The District Court dismissed. The Ninth Circuit affirmed in part on the basis of *Federal Baseball* and *Toolson*. The court did not hesitate to "confess that the strength of the pull" of the baseball cases and of *International Boxing* "is about equal," but then observed that "[f]ootball is a team sport" and boxing an individual one.

This Court reversed with an opinion by Mr. Justice Clark. He said that the Court made its ruling in *Toolson* "because it was concluded that more harm would be done in overruling *Federal Baseball* than in upholding a ruling which at best was of dubious validity." He noted that Congress had not acted. He then said:

> All this, combined with the flood of litigation that would follow its repudiation, the harassment that would ensue, and the retroactive effect of such a decision, led the Court to the practical result that it should sustain the unequivocal line of authority reaching over many years.

> [S]ince *Toolson* and *Federal Baseball* are still cited as controlling authority in antitrust actions involving other fields of business, we now specifically limit the rule there established to the facts there involved, *i.e.*, the business of organized professional baseball. As long as the Congress continues to acquiesce we should adhere to—but not extend—the interpretation of the Act made in those cases. . . .

> If this ruling is unrealistic, inconsistent, or illogical, it is sufficient to answer, aside from the distinctions between the businesses, that were we considering the question of baseball for the first time upon a clean slate we would have no doubts. But *Federal Baseball* held the business of baseball outside the scope of the Act. No other business claiming the coverage of those cases has such an adjudication. We therefore, conclude that the orderly way to eliminate error or discrimination, if any there be, is by legislation and not by court decision. Congressional processes are more accommodative, affording the whole industry hearings and an opportunity to assist in the formulation of new legislation. The resulting product is therefore more likely to protect the industry and the public alike. The whole scope of congressional action would be known long in advance and effective dates for the legislation could be set in the future without the injustices of retroactivity and surprise which might follow court action.

* * *

G.   Finally, in *Haywood v. National Basketball Assn.*, 401 U.S. 1204 (1971), Mr. Justice Douglas, in his capacity as Circuit Justice, reinstated a District Court's injunction pendente lite in favor of a professional basketball player and said, "Basketball . . . does not enjoy exemption from the antitrust laws."

H.   This series of decisions understandably spawned extensive commentary, some of it mildly critical and much of it not; nearly all of it looked to Congress for any remedy that might be deemed essential.

I.   Legislative proposals have been numerous and persistent. Since *Toolson* more than 50 bills have been introduced in Congress relative to the applicability or nonapplicability of the antitrust laws to baseball. A few of these passed one house or the other. Those that did would have expanded, not restricted, the reserve system's exemption to other professional league sports. And the Act of Sept. 30, 1961, Pub. L. 87–331, 75 Stat. 732, and the merger addition thereto effected by the Act of Nov. 8, 1966, Pub. L. 89–800, § 6(b), 80 Stat. 1515, 15 U.S.C. §§ 1291–1295, were also expansive rather than restrictive as to antitrust exemption.

V

In view of all this, it seems appropriate now to say that:

1.   Professional baseball is a business and it is engaged in interstate commerce.

2.   With its reserve system enjoying exemption from the federal antitrust laws, baseball is, in a very distinct sense, an exception and an anomaly. *Federal Baseball* and *Toolson* have become an aberration confined to baseball.

3.   Even though others might regard this as "unrealistic, inconsistent, or illogical," the aberration is an established one, and one that has been recognized not only in *Federal Baseball* and *Toolson*, but in *Shubert, International Boxing*, and *Radovich*, as well, a total of five consecutive cases in this Court. It is an aberration that has been with us now for half a century, one heretofore deemed fully entitled to the benefit of *stare decisis*, and one that has survived the Court's expanding concept of interstate commerce. It rests on a recognition and an acceptance of baseball's unique characteristics and needs.

4.   Other professional sports operating interstate—football, boxing, basketball, and, presumably, hockey and golf—are not so exempt.

5.   The advent of radio and television, with their consequent increased coverage and additional revenues, has not occasioned an overruling of *Federal Baseball* and *Toolson*.

6.   The Court has emphasized that since 1922, baseball, with full and continuing congressional awareness, has been allowed to develop and to expand unhindered by federal legislative action. Remedial legislation has been introduced repeatedly in Congress but none has ever been enacted. The Court, accordingly, has concluded that Congress as yet has had no intention to subject baseball's reserve system to the reach of the antitrust statutes. This, obviously, has been deemed to be something other than mere congressional silence and passivity.

7.   The Court has expressed concern about the confusion and the retroactivity problems that inevitably would result with a judicial overturning of *Federal Baseball*. It has voiced a preference that if any change is to be made, it come by legislative action that, by its nature, is only prospective in operation.

8.   The Court noted in *Radovich* that the slate with respect to baseball is not clean. Indeed, it has not been clean for half a century.

This emphasis and this concern are still with us. We continue to be loath, 50 years after *Federal Baseball* and almost two decades after *Toolson*, to overturn those cases judicially when Congress, by its positive inaction, has allowed those decisions to stand for so long and, far beyond mere inference and implication, has clearly evinced a desire not to disapprove them legislatively.

Accordingly, we adhere once again to *Federal Baseball* and *Toolson* and to their application to professional baseball. We adhere also to *International Boxing* and *Radovich* and to their respective applications to professional boxing and professional football. If there is any inconsistency or illogic in all this, it is an inconsistency and illogic of long standing that is to be remedied by the Congress and not by this Court. If we were to act otherwise, we would be withdrawing from the conclusion as to congressional intent made in *Toolson* and from the concerns as to retrospectivity therein expressed. Under these circumstances, there is merit in consistency even though some might claim that beneath that consistency is a layer of inconsistency.

The petitioner's argument as to the application of state antitrust laws deserves a word. Judge Cooper rejected the state law claims because state antitrust regulation would conflict with federal policy and because national "uniformity [is required] in any regulation of baseball and its reserved system." The Court of Appeals, in affirming, stated, "[A]s the burden on interstate commerce outweighs the states' interests in regulating baseball's reserve system, the Commerce Clause precludes the application here of state antitrust law." As applied to organized baseball, and in the light of this Court's observations and holding in *Federal Baseball*, in *Toolson*, in *Shubert*, in *International Boxing*, and in *Radovich*, and despite baseball's allegedly inconsistent position taken in the past with respect to the application of state law, these statements adequately dispose of the state law claims.

* * *

[W]hat the Court said in *Federal Baseball* in 1922 and what it said in *Toolson* in 1953, we say again here in 1972: the remedy, if any is indicated, is for congressional, and not judicial, action.

The judgment of the Court of Appeals is affirmed.

JUSTICE MARSHALL, with whom JUSTICE BRENNAN concurs, dissenting.

* * *

To non-athletes it might appear that petitioner was virtually enslaved by the owners of major league baseball clubs who bartered among themselves for his services. But, athletes know that it was not servitude that bound petitioner to the club owners; it was the reserve system. The essence of that system is that a player is bound to the club with which he first signs a contract for the rest of his playing days. He cannot escape from the club except by retiring, and he cannot prevent the club from assigning his contract to any other club.

* * *

We have only recently had occasion to comment that:

> Antitrust laws in general, and the Sherman Act in particular, are the Magna Charta of free enterprise. They are as important to the preservation of economic freedom and our free-enterprise system as the Bill of Rights is to the protection of our fundamental personal freedoms. . . . Implicit in such freedom is the notion that it cannot be foreclosed with respect to one sector of the economy because certain private citizens or groups believe that such foreclosure might promote greater competition in a more important sector of the economy. (*United States v. Topco Associates, Inc.*, 405 U.S. 596, 610 (1972).)

The importance of the antitrust laws to every citizen must not be minimized. They are as important to baseball players as they are to football players, lawyers, doctors, or members of any other class of workers. Baseball players cannot be denied the benefits of competition merely because club owners view other economic interests as being more important, unless Congress says so.

Has Congress acquiesced in our decisions in *Federal Baseball Club* and *Toolson*? I think not. Had the Court been consistent and treated all sports in the same way baseball was treated, Congress might have become concerned enough to take action. But, the Court was inconsistent, and baseball was isolated and distinguished from all other sports. In *Toolson* the Court refused to act because Congress had been silent. But the Court may have read too much into this legislative inaction.

Americans love baseball as they love all sports. Perhaps we become so enamored of athletics that we assume that they are foremost in the minds of legislators as well as fans. We must not forget, however, that there are only some 600 major league baseball players. Whatever muscle they might have been able to muster by combining forces with other athletes has been greatly impaired by the manner in which this Court has isolated them. It is this Court that has made them impotent, and this Court should correct its error.

We do not lightly overrule our prior constructions of federal statutes, but when our errors deny substantial federal rights, like the right to compete freely and effectively to the best of one's ability as guaranteed by the antitrust laws, we must admit our error and correct it. We have done so before and we should do so again here.

* * *

To the extent that there is concern over any reliance interests that club owners may assert, they can be satisfied by making our decision prospective only. Baseball should be covered by the antitrust laws beginning with this case and henceforth, unless Congress decides otherwise.

Accordingly, I would overrule *Federal Baseball Club* and *Toolson* and reverse the decision of the Court of Appeals.

* * *

[Justice Marshall went on to explain that if the Court were to hold baseball subject to antitrust as a general matter, this did not mean that Flood's claim was necessarily actionable. In particular, baseball would still be entitled to offer as a defense the fact that the terms of Flood's player contract were mandatory subjects of collective bargaining between Major League Baseball and its Players Association, and thus arguably protected by the labor exemption from antitrust liability.]

NOTES AND QUESTIONS

1. *Holmes and Stare Decisis.* Justice Oliver Wendell Holmes, Jr., who wrote the Supreme Court's opinion in *Federal Baseball*, had earlier made the following observations about *stare decisis* in his famous lecture on "The Path of the Law":

> It is revolting to have no better reason for a rule of law than that it was laid down in the time of Henry IV. It is still more revolting if the

grounds upon which it was laid down have vanished long since, and that rule simply persists from blind imitation of the past.

How would (should) Justice Holmes have reacted to Justice Blackmun's adherence in *Flood* to Holmes' decision in *Federal Baseball* given that *Flood* rejected every one of the premises upon which *Federal Baseball* was founded?

2.   *Reliance for What?* Is there any reason other than the baseball owners' reliance on their antitrust exemption for the Court to continue to honor the out dated *Federal Baseball* decision? What exactly had the owners done in reliance on that decision? Was it simply the earlier purchase of their teams? Is concern about reevaluation of assets usually a sufficient argument against otherwise sensible legal change, even for change that is judicial in origin? Or might one argue that professional baseball's structure, including its minor league system, depended upon the antitrust exemption?

3.   *Union Strategy?* Can you explain why Flood would pursue his suit knowing that the Supreme Court had twice ruled that baseball did not affect interstate commerce and thus was not covered by the federal antitrust laws? The most significant business development in the sport following the *Toolson* case was the establishment of the Major League Baseball Players Association which fully funded Flood's effort. Might that explain Flood's willingness to pursue this matter?

4.   *Same Result if a Discrimination Case?* How would the *Toolson* Court in 1953 (or the *Flood* Court in 1972) have reacted if, instead of allowing Jackie Robinson to play, baseball had tried to protect its Jim Crow segregation policies from federal antitrust scrutiny? Keep in mind that the Court had greatly expanded the scope of Congress' "trade and commerce" power in the later stages of the New Deal, but Congress did not enact the Civil Rights Act barring employment discrimination until 1964.

5.   *Time for Another Reconsideration?* Does the Supreme Court's willingness to overrule a half-century old decision, *Roe v. Wade*, 410 U.S. 113 (1973), in *Dobbs v. Jackson Women's Health Organization*, 142 S. Ct. 2228 (2022), signal a new willingness to overrule other old precedents like *Federal Baseball*? Does it matter that *Federal Baseball* has always been subject to legislative modification, while—as Justice Alito stressed in his majority opinion in *Dobbs*—*Roe* was a constitutional decision that could not be overturned by Congress? Consider also whether the Curt Flood Act, treated below, has relevance to the likelihood of any further judicial consideration of baseball's antitrust immunity.

––––––––––––

The *Flood* decision was a significant loss both for baseball players and their union and for Curt Flood. Even so, Peter Seitz's arbitration decision interpreting the reserve clause was issued only four years later in 1976, and the players union has thwarted the return of the reserve system challenged by Flood. Furthermore, in 1996 the Supreme Court broadly applied another immunity from the antitrust laws, based on the existence of a collective bargaining relationship, to professional sports, in a decision considered in Chapter 7, *Brown v. Pro Football, Inc.*, 518 U.S. 231 (1996). Perhaps finding reassurance in the *Brown* decision and under renewed pressure from members of Congress threatening to eliminate the antitrust exemption because of the loss of the 1994 World Series, baseball owners finally agreed to passage of legislation to limit their exemption, at least for the major league players market where they accepted the continuation of entrenched collective bargaining. Indeed, the 1996 collective agreement included a final provision that both sides "jointly request and cooperate in lobbying Congress to pass a law clarifying that Major League Baseball players are covered under the antitrust laws . . . along with a provision that makes it clear that the passage of that bill does not change the application of the antitrust laws in any other context or with respect to any other person or entity . . . ." The legislation, aptly named the Curt Flood Act of 1998, passed two years later, less than two years after Curt Flood's untimely death at the age of 59.

CURT FLOOD ACT OF 1998
15 U.S.C. § 26b

(a) Major league baseball subject to antitrust laws

Subject to subsections (b) through (d), the conduct, acts, practices, or agreements of persons in the business of organized professional major league baseball directly relating to or affecting employment of major league baseball players to play baseball at the major league level are subject to the antitrust laws to the same extent such conduct, acts, practices, or agreements would be subject to the antitrust laws if engaged in by persons in any other professional sports business affecting interstate commerce.

(b) Limitation of section

No court shall rely on the enactment of this section as a basis for changing the application of the antitrust laws to any conduct, acts, practices, or agreements other than those set forth in subsection (a). This section does not create, permit or imply a cause of action by which to challenge under the antitrust laws, or otherwise apply the antitrust laws to, any conduct, acts, practices, or agreements that do not directly relate to or affect employment of major league baseball players to play baseball at the major league level, including but not limited to

(1) any conduct, acts, practices, or agreements of persons engaging in, conducting or participating in the business of organized professional baseball relating to or affecting employment to play baseball at the minor league level, any organized professional baseball amateur or first-year player draft, or any reserve clause as applied to minor league players;

(2) the agreement between organized professional major league baseball teams and the teams of the National Association of Professional

Baseball Leagues, commonly known as the "Professional Baseball Agreement", the relationship between organized professional major league baseball and organized professional minor league baseball, or any other matter relating to organized professional baseball's minor leagues;

(3) any conduct, acts, practices, or agreements of persons engaging in, conducting or participating in the business of organized professional baseball relating to or affecting franchise expansion, location or relocation, franchise ownership issues, including ownership transfers, the relationship between the Office of the Commissioner and franchise owners, the marketing or sales of the entertainment product of organized professional baseball and the licensing of intellectual property rights owned or held by organized professional baseball teams individually or collectively;

(4) any conduct, acts, practices, or agreements protected by Public Law 87–331 (15 U.S.C. § 1291 et seq.) (commonly known as the "Sports Broadcasting Act of 1961");

(5) the relationship between persons in the business of organized professional baseball and umpires or other individuals who are employed in the business of organized professional baseball by such persons; or

(6) any conduct, acts, practices, or agreements of persons not in the business of organized professional major league baseball.

(c) Standing to sue

Only a major league baseball player has standing to sue under this section. . . .

NOTES AND QUESTIONS

1. *Effect of Curt Flood Act?* Does this statute provide baseball more secure antitrust immunity in markets other than the major league players' labor market than that which existed before its passage? Does it at least support an argument that Congress assumed that baseball's preexisting antitrust immunity extends to markets other than the major league players' labor market, including those expressly mentioned, such as the minor league players' labor market, and the franchise expansion, location, and ownership markets? If the latter, does it weaken any argument that the *stare decisis* basis for the *Flood* decision should not extend beyond the players' market at issue in *Federal Baseball, Toolson,* and *Flood?*

2. *How Broad an Exemption?* Given the *Flood* decision and the Curt Flood Act, how broadly should courts now apply baseball's antitrust exemption? Is it at least clear that it applies to other labor markets of baseball employees? *See, e.g., Miranda v. Selig,* 860 F.3d 1237 (9th Cir. 2017) (exemption extends to minor league players market); *Wyckoff v. Office of the*

Commissioner of Baseball, 795 Fed. Appx. 26 (2d Cir. 2017) (exemption extends to baseball scouts market); *Salerno v. American League*, 429 F.2d 1003 (2d Cir.1970)) (exemption extends to umpires labor market). How about the relocation of franchises? *See City of San Jose v. Office of the Commissioner of Baseball*, 776 F.3d 686 (9th Cir. 2015) (exemption extends). The contraction of franchises? *See Major League Baseball v. Crist*, 331 F.3d 1177 (11th Cir. 2003) (exemption extends). The sale of franchises? *Compare Minnesota Twins Partnership v. State of Minnesota*, 592 N.W.2d 847 (Minn. 1999), *with Piazza v. Major League Baseball*, 8311 F. Supp. 420 (E.D. Pa. 1993). For a case applying the exemption to protect the Cubs' efforts to control the views into Wrigley Field, see *Right Field Rooftops v. Chicago Cubs Baseball Club, LLC*, 870 F.3d 682 (7th Cir. 2017).

Finally, should the exemption extend to baseball's dealings with other industries? Some pre-Flood Act cases refused to extend the exemption to baseball's dealings with concessionaires, *see Twin City Sportservice Inc. v. Charles O. Finley & Co. (Oakland Athletics)*, 365 F. Supp. 235 (N.D. Cal.1972), *rev'd on other grounds*, 512 F.2d 1264 (9th Cir.1975)); with broadcast outlets, *see Henderson Broadcasting Corp. v. Houston Sports Ass'n (Houston Astros)*, 541 F. Supp. 263 (S.D.Tex.1982); and with merchandisers, *see Fleer v. Topps Chewing Gum & Major League Baseball Players Ass'n*, 658 F.2d 139 (3d Cir. 1981). Are at least these cases still good law after the Flood Act?

3.   *MLB Control over Minor Leagues.* As suggested by § (b)(1) of the Curt Flood Act, MLB and its controlling owners seem particularly concerned about any regulation of their control of minor league baseball. Notwithstanding § (b)(1)'s apparent protection of any continuing exemption, however, antitrust lawsuits continue to be filed challenging MLB's control of the minors. In December 2021, for instance, a suit was filed by several minor league teams challenging MLB's substantial contraction of the minor league system during the pandemic. Then, in January 2022, minor league players filed in Puerto Rico district court a putative class action challenging the major league draft and the exclusive control of minor league players by individual teams.

A challenge to the minor league system also was lodged by a suit brought in 2014 to collect overtime pay for minor leaguers working more than forty hours per week in prior years. The minor leaguers would have been owed that pay under the federal Fair Labor Standards Act (FLSA) if baseball owners had not properly applied an FLSA exemption for amusement or recreational employees or could not claim any other exemption. After the Ninth Circuit Court of Appeals upheld the certification of a class action against MLB and several franchises, *see Senne v. Kansas City Royals Baseball Corp.*, 934 F.3d 918 (9th Cir. 2019), *cert. denied*, 141 S. Ct. 248 (2020), the players, represented by a former minor league pitcher, were able to obtain a substantial 185 million dollar settlement in May 2022, on the eve of trial.

The baseball owners do not have to worry about future FLSA suits, however, because their lobbyists were able to insert a specific exemption of baseball players from overtime pay regulation in the one paragraph "Save America's Pastime Act," included in the 2,232-page 2018 Omnibus Budget Act, with one Congressional sponsor and without any committee hearing or other legislative history. This exemption covers FLSA claims for future work, but does not control state wage and hour statutes, which are not preempted by the FLSA.

––––––

The *Flood* decision did more than maintain baseball's exemption from federal antitrust law. It also established an immunity for baseball from *state* antitrust law. Moreover, this immunity from state antitrust law is based on the "dormant Commerce Clause" principle of federal constitutional law that applies just as much to other sports leagues and organizations.

For instance, Dennis Partee, the San Diego Chargers' kicker faced this obstacle when he sought to strike down the NFL's version of the reserve system under California antitrust law. In *Partee v. San Diego Chargers Football Co.*, 34 Cal.3d 378, 194 Cal. Rptr. 367, 668 P.2d 674 (1983), a divided Supreme Court of California highlighted a key feature of dormant Commerce Clause jurisprudence. State business regulation is judged to impose an unreasonable burden on interstate commerce where it governs "those phases of the national commerce which, because of the need for national uniformity, demand their regulation, if any, be prescribed by a single authority." *Id.* at 677. In the majority's view, professional football clearly met that standard:

> Professional football is a nationwide business structured essentially the same as baseball. Professional football's teams are dependent upon the league playing schedule for competitive play, just as in baseball. The necessity of a nationwide league structure for the benefit of both teams and players for effective competition is evident as is the need for a nationally uniform set of rules governing the league structure. Fragmentation of the league structure on the basis of state lines would adversely affect the success of the competitive business enterprise, and differing state antitrust decisions if applied to the enterprise would likely compel all member teams to comply with the laws of the strictest state.

> We are satisfied that national uniformity required in regulation of baseball and its reserve system is likewise required in the player-team-league relationships challenged by Partee and that the burden on interstate commerce outweighs the state interests in applying state antitrust laws to those relationships.

668 P.2d at 678–79.

Another California court concluded that the same Commerce Clause principle precluded quarterback Bobby Hebert from using California's Labor Code (which makes it illegal for any business to deprive a person of the opportunity to earn his livelihood) to move freely from the New Orleans

Saints to the Los Angeles Raiders. *See Hebert v. Los Angeles Raiders*, 234 Cal. App. 3d 36, 285 Cal. Rptr. 449 (Ct. App.), *review granted and opinion superseded*, 2 Cal. Rptr. 2d 489, 820 P.2d 999 (1991). Earlier decisions to the same effect are *Matuszak v. Houston Oilers*, 515 S.W.2d 725 (Tex. Ct. Civ. App. 1974) (refusing to apply Texas antitrust law to NFL restraints on player movement), and *State of Wisconsin v. Milwaukee Braves*, 31 Wis.2d 699, 144 N.W.2d 1 (1966) (refusing to apply Wisconsin antitrust law to block the move of the Braves from Milwaukee to Atlanta).

CHAPTER 6

BASIC PRINCIPLES OF ANTITRUST LAW APPLIED TO THE SPECIAL NATURE OF THE SPORTS INDUSTRY

■ ■ ■

A. INTRODUCTION

For some sports lawyers, the constraints and strategic opportunities created by the antitrust laws form a critical part of their practice. Many, however, take the "rules of the game" as they are; perhaps daunted by the complexity of antitrust doctrine, they may engage in "willful blindness" about the interplay between antitrust and sports, leaving it to special counsel to assist on antitrust issues where necessary. Antitrust analysis is worthy of introductory consideration for all sports lawyers, and serious consideration for any sophisticated ones. Although antitrust liability may play a small role in many sports law practices, the disputes considered here provide some of the best case studies to understand the business of sports, and how this accords with economic understandings. Moreover, the potential to use antitrust litigation as a shield or a sword is a vital strategic tool for any good sports lawyer.

This chapter provides a basic summary of important antitrust principles. It considers a leading Supreme Court case that illustrates the basic structure of sports leagues and how this impacts antitrust analysis, then provides an overview of the leading Supreme Court doctrinal articulation of the "Rule of Reason" that applies to most sports antitrust litigation. For those interested in more extended treatment, the chapter concludes with consideration of how best to reconcile the tendency of sports leagues to be monopolies (or monopsonies) with situations where antitrust doctrine may not deal adequately with the resulting problems. Chapters 7 and 8 apply antitrust law to labor markets and to intra-league rules, respectively. These chapters have a two-fold focus: both to convey antitrust *doctrine*, and to review important *topics* in sports business to allow an analysis of how business strategy is and can be affected by antitrust doctrine.

The two landmark cases featured in this chapter—*NCAA v. Board of Regents* and *American Needle v. NFL*—are perhaps less important to the typical sports lawyer for their doctrinal significance to antitrust law, than to provide an important framework to understand how the sports business works. As we will see, *Board of Regents* requires consideration of (1) how league rules will affect the price, output, and quality of sports entertainment services and whether those rules are responsive to consumer preferences; (2) what are the real reasons that leagues adopt rules, and which of these reasons are legitimate; and (3) whether leagues have alternative means of achieving their goals. These concerns link together with *American Needle*'s observations about the ways in which league rules might be motivated by the individual self-interest of league members, rather than the overall interests of the league. When sports executives and lawyers consider league rules, antitrust inquiry is both relevant to legality under the Sherman Act and useful to provide strategic business insight to all stakeholders—and their effective counsel.

B. GENERAL BACKGROUND TO ANTITRUST LAW

Congress enacted the Sherman Act in 1890 as the first federal competition law. For sports lawyers, the two most relevant provisions are § 1, which prohibits "[e]very contract, combination in the form of trust or otherwise, or conspiracy, in restraint of trade or commerce among the several States, or with foreign nations," and § 2, which prohibits "monopolization." Congress supplemented this legislation with the 1914 Clayton Act; the provisions most relevant to sports lawyers are § 4, which permits anyone damaged "in their business or property" to sue antitrust violators for treble damages and attorneys' fees, and § 6 (considered in Chapter 7) relating to labor.

What do these broadly worded statutes mean? Sections 1 and 2 were meant to make criminal and tortious those acts that were simply void under the common law restraint of trade doctrine. *United States v. Addyston Pipe & Steel Co.*, 85 Fed. 271, 278–79 (6th Cir. 1898), *aff'd*, 175 U.S. 211 (1899). The common law is evolutionary, but a landmark British case still provides a useful benchmark. *Nordenfelt v. Maxim Nordenfelt Gun & Ammunication Co.*, [1894] A.C. 535, 565 (H.L.), sets forth the broad notion of reasonableness with regard to restraints of trade, which must be considered "in reference to the interests of the parties concerned and reasonable in reference to the interests of the public, so framed and so guarded as to afford adequate protection to the party in whose favour it is imposed, while at the same time it is in no way injurious to the public."

1. THE PURPOSES OF THE ANTITRUST LAWS

Although controversial within antitrust circles, for our purposes it is probably sufficient to observe that the immediate target of antitrust law, at least since the mid-1970s, is excessive market power, abused either by a single firm (like the Standard Oil or American Tobacco monopolies a century ago) or a group of firms who jointly acquire such market power through anticompetitive agreements.

Normally when one thinks of market power and its adverse effects, one does so in the context of a firm operating in a product market—selling its goods or services to consumers. Market power exists when consumers have few if any alternatives to the seller's product, thus enabling the seller to dictate terms based on profit maximization rather than competitive pressure. Economists have identified two general consequences of such market power. Consider the cartel fixing prices on beverage sweeteners. *See In re High Fructose Corn Syrup Antitrust Litig.*, 295 F.3d 651 (7th Cir. 2002); *United States v. Andreas*, 216 F.3d 645 (7th Cir. 2000). First, customers who purchase sweetened beverages have to pay higher prices (or obtain lower quality products); many of us who fancy or are even addicted to soft drinks pay the higher amount and keep on drinking, which results in a "wealth transfer" from customers to producers. Second, some folks cannot afford the higher prices, or choose not to pay, so that the overall amount of the good or service produced will drop. This inflicts a "dead-weight loss" upon the economy as a whole as total consumer utility declines, because some factors of production (labor, materials, capital, land, or equipment) that would be most efficient at making the sweetened beverages are either left unemployed or are diverted into producing other goods and services for which they are less well-suited. (Antitrust professors argue about whether wealth transfers are an appropriate basis of concern, but the cases we discuss in these three chapters do not turn on these disputes.)

Just as the power of a single seller or a cartel of conspiring rival sellers can cause *monopoly* power, a single buyer or cartel of conspiring rival buyers can cause *monopsony* power with similar anticompetitive effects. Antitrust commentators are more divided on whether the "wealth transfer" effect of lower prices for goods and services ought to be considered symmetrically with monopoly power. For example, in *Kartell v. Blue Shield of Massachusetts, Inc.*, 749 F.2d 922 (1st Cir. 1984), the First Circuit dismissed an antitrust claim filed by doctors against Blue Shield, the dominant provider of health insurance in Massachusetts, which required all doctors who performed services for Blue Shield insureds to accept its fee schedule as full payment for the service, and not charge the patient any more. As then-Judge Stephen Breyer observed,

> . . . the prices at issue here are low prices, not high prices. Of course, a buyer, as well as a seller, can possess significant market power; and courts have held that agreements to fix prices—whether maximum or minimum—are unlawful. Nonetheless, the Congress that enacted the Sherman Act saw it as a way of protecting consumers against prices that were too high, not too low. And the relevant economic conditions may be very different when low prices, rather than high prices, are at issue. These facts suggest that courts at least should be cautious—reluctant to

condemn too speedily—an arrangement that, on its face, appears
to bring low price benefits to the consumer.

749 F.2d at 930–31. *Kartell*, then, implies that at least some monopsony
power—because it may improve the situation of at least some consumers
in the marketplace—may not warrant the same kind of close antitrust
scrutiny as does monopoly power, which always threatens the interests of
all its consumers. At the same time, the court does not suggest that these
agreements are necessarily lawful.

2.   THE APPLICABLE § 1 ANTITRUST STANDARD: *PER SE* OR RULE OF REASON?

The Supreme Court has made it clear that not all restraints of trade
are illegal; rather, only those judged to be unreasonable violate § 1. *See
Standard Oil v. United States*, 221 U.S. 1 (1911). Some early sports law
decisions were influenced by an earlier antitrust doctrinal trend where
courts tended to find various business arrangements unreasonable *per se*:
that is, it was sufficient to show that the defendants had engaged in
practices such as price fixing (*United States v. Socony-Vacuum Oil Co.*, 310
U.S. 150 (1940)); market allocation (*United States v. Topco Assocs.*, 405
U.S. 596 (1972)); or group boycotts (*Klor's, Inc. v. Broadway-Hale Stores*,
359 U.S. 207 (1959)), to condemn the agreement without any further
analysis. In *Northern Pac. Ry. Co. v. United States*, 356 U.S. 1, 5 (1958),
the Court observed that "there are certain agreements or practices which
because of their pernicious effect on competition and lack of any redeeming
virtue arc conclusively presumed to be unreasonable and therefore illegal
without elaborate inquiry as to the precise harm they have caused or the
business excuse for their use."

Because these categories were vaguely defined, earlier § 1
jurisprudence allowed courts to condemn forms of conduct that the judges
disapproved of for social, political, or economic reasons. Beginning in the
mid-1970s, the Supreme Court sharply altered its antitrust stance by
either expressly overruling or drastically limiting application of the various
per se categories. The following summarizes a few such decisions—the ones
most relevant for analyzing sports law cases.

In *Broadcast Music Inc. v. Columbia Broadcasting System, Inc.*, 441
U.S. 1 (1979), the Supreme Court narrowed the *per se* approach to price
fixing by rejecting a claim that an organization that held nonexclusive
copyright licenses for the musical compositions of hundreds of composers
automatically violated the antitrust laws when it charged commercial
broadcasters a set price for the right to play all of its licensed music to
commercial broadcasters. The Court reasoned that, even though the
composers literally fixed the price for their "blanket license," it achieved
major cost savings for purchasers, who otherwise would have had to

traverse the globe to obtain individual licenses from the composer of every musical piece they wished to broadcast. They explained further:

> This substantial lowering of costs, which is of course potentially beneficial to both sellers and buyers, differentiates the blanket license from individual use licenses. The blanket license is composed of the individual compositions plus the aggregating service. Here, the whole is truly greater than the sum of its parts; it is, to some extent, a different product. The blanket license has certain unique characteristics: it allows the licensee immediate use of covered compositions, without the delay of prior individual negotiations, and great flexibility in the choice of musical material. . . . Thus, to the extent the blanket license is a different product, ASCAP is not really a joint sales agency offering the individual goods of many sellers, but is a separate seller offering its blanket license, of which the individual compositions are raw material. ASCAP, in short, made a market in which individual composers are inherently unable to compete fully effectively.

441 U.S. at 21–22. As a result, the Court directed a Rule of Reason analysis of the agreement among competing copyright holders. On remand, the lower court concluded that this blanket, but non-exclusive, license satisfied the Rule of Reason standard. *Buffalo Broadcasting Co. v. ASCAP*, 744 F.2d 917 (2d Cir. 1984) (finding terms reasonable because potential purchasers could obtain desired copyright licenses from individual holders as well as from joint licensing organizations.)

Next, the Supreme Court limited the *per se* condemnation of "group boycotts" in *Northwest Wholesale Stationers, Inc. v. Pacific Stationery & Printing Co.*, 472 U.S. 284 (1985). It held that a wholesale purchasing cooperative formed by a group of small stationery retailers was not guilty of a *per se* violation when it expelled one of its members for operating a wholesale stationery supply business in competition with the cooperative. The Court observed that the cooperative created purchasing efficiencies for its members, which in turn produced lower prices for consumers, and that enforcement of the rule against members who competed against the cooperative was arguably important for the cooperative to be able to provide these economic advantages. Refining prior precedents, the Court suggested that *per se* condemnation of group boycotts applied only to agreements where firms sought to disadvantage *competitors* by persuading or coercing suppliers or customers "to deny relationships the competitors need in the competitive struggle" and where the challenged practice was "not justified by plausible argument that they were intended to enhance overall efficiency and make markets more competitive." The Court concluded that "[u]nless the cooperative possesses market power or exclusive access to an element essential to effective competition, the conclusion that expulsion [for violating the rule] is virtually always likely to have an anticompetitive effect is unwarranted." Under this reasoning, restrictive labor practices harming players, rather than rival clubs or leagues, would not be labeled as *per se* illegal group boycotts.

In *Continental T.V., Inc. v. GTE Sylvania Inc.*, 433 U.S. 36 (1977), the Supreme Court expressly overturned the *per se* rule against a television manufacturer placing vertical territorial restrictions on its distributors. The Court reasoned that such restrictions on distributors might improve the firm's overall marketing strategy and make the company more efficient and competitive vis-a-vis its rivals, and such competition among producers would ultimately produce lower prices and higher quality for consumers. The Court noted that while vertical restraints may reduce competition among sellers of one manufacturer's brand (intrabrand competition), they might also stimulate greater competition among sellers of different manufacturers' brands (interbrand competition):

> Vertical restrictions reduce intrabrand competition by limiting the number of sellers of a particular product competing for the business of a given group of buyers. Location restrictions have this effect because of practical constraints on the effective marketing area of retail outlets. Although intrabrand competition may be reduced, the ability of retailers to exploit the resulting market may be limited both by the ability of consumers to travel to other franchised locations and, perhaps more importantly, to purchase the competing products of other manufacturers. . . .

> Vertical restrictions promote interbrand competition by allowing the manufacturer to achieve certain efficiencies in the distribution of his products. . . . Economists have identified a number of ways in which manufacturers can use such restrictions to compete more effectively against other manufacturers. For example, [manufacturers] can use the restrictions in order to induce competent and aggressive retailers to make the kind of investment on capital and labor that is often required in the distribution of products unknown to the consumer, [or] to induce retailers to engage in promotional activities or to provide service and repair facilities necessary to the efficient marketing of their products. . . . The availability and quality of such services affect a manufacturer's goodwill and the competitiveness of his product. Because of market imperfections such as the so-called "free rider" effect, these services might not be provided by retailers in a purely competitive situation, despite the fact that each retailer's benefit would be greater if all provided the services than if none did.

433 U.S. at 54–55. In an important footnote, the majority emphasized that where interbrand competition existed, it provides a "significant check" on exploitation "because of the ability of consumers to substitute a different brand of the same product." *Id.* at 52 n.19.

In conducting Rule of Reason review, courts remain more skeptical of "horizontal" restraints agreed to by rivals, while the *Sylvania* case demonstrates increasing judicial benevolence toward "vertical" restraints imposed on "downstream" firms (such as retailers or franchisees) by "upstream" companies (like manufacturers or franchisors). The Supreme Court's benign view of limits on Sylvania retailers contrasts with cases decided ten years earlier during the closing years of the Court's populist antitrust era. In *United States v. Sealy*, 388 U.S. 350 (1967), the Court held that a scheme to limit retail sales of mattresses was *per se* illegal because the "manufacturer" (Sealy) was really controlled by the retailers themselves. In *United States v. General Motors*, 384 U.S. 127 (1966), the Court condemned as *per se* illegal an agreement among GM dealers not to sell Chevrolets to unauthorized discount retailers, but Justice Fortas' opinion explicitly distinguished the challenged scheme from a plan where GM had "by unilateral action" determined that its cars should not be sold to discounters. (The insights from these cases are relied upon by Justice Stevens in the *American Needle* excerpt discussed in Section D, *infra*.)

National Society of Professional Engineers v. United States, 435 U.S. 679 (1978), clarified permissible factors to be considered during a Rule of Reason review. The Justice Department had charged the Society governing civil engineers with a *per se* violation of § 1 for adopting a rule that prohibited engineers from quoting a price in their project bids. The Society defended its price ban as necessary to protect the public from unsafe structures that engineers might design if they became too cost conscious in order to win bids and jobs. The Court rejected this argument as "nothing less than a frontal assault on the basic policy of the Sherman Act."

> The Sherman Act reflects a legislative judgment that ultimately competition will produce not only lower prices, but also better goods and services. . . . The assumption that competition is the best method of allocating resources in a free market recognizes that all elements of a bargain—quality, service, safety, and durability—and not just the immediate cost, are favorably affected by the free opportunity to select among alternative offers. Even assuming occasional exceptions to the presumed consequences of competition, the statutory policy precludes inquiry into the question whether competition is good or bad.

Id. at 695–96.

The antitrust Rule of Reason therefore requires judges and juries to balance only an agreement's effects on economic competition. Courts must weigh the injury to the consumer stemming from any increase in defendants' market power due to the arrangement (allocative inefficiency) against any benefits to the consumer that occur because defendants can make and sell their product(s) at a lower price, or make more and higher quality products at the same price (productive efficiency). This suggests that sports leagues or sports governing bodies cannot justify restrictive commercial practices on non-economic grounds, although occasionally courts will suggest that some non-economic grounds may be relevant if the objectives are salutary and not motivated by the defendants' economic self-interest. *See United States v. Brown Univ.*, 3 F.3d 658 (3d Cir. 1993) (relevant to consider whether an agreement among Ivy League colleges to standardize the size of scholarship offers to needy students "promoted the social ideal of equality of educational access and opportunity").

A challenge in applying these precedents to sports leagues arises because, akin to comparing apples and oranges, restrictive practices that leagues adopt as the purchasers of services (such as from players) are justified by sports leagues as improving the quality of the overall product for the benefit of consumers. Economists differ sharply over both the market power and the efficiency effects of any particular business arrangement, so this balancing exercise can be problematic for judges, let alone lay juries. Judge Robert Bork noted this problem in *Rothery Storage & Van Co. v. Atlas Van Lines, Inc.*, 792 F.2d 210 (D.C. Cir. 1986), an important non-sports antitrust opinion which sought to solve the problem by resurrecting the "ancillary restraints" doctrine that had first been formulated by in an early landmark decision, *United States v. Addyston Pipe & Steel Co.*, 85 Fed. 271 (6th Cir. 1898), *aff'd*, 175 U.S. 211 (1899). This venerable doctrine held that restraints are reasonable if "ancillary" to a lawful agreement among the parties, and reasonably necessary to protect the parties' "legitimate" interests. Though the Supreme Court has not yet explicitly endorsed this concept, we will see it figure in several sports law opinions reproduced in this and the following chapters.

C. APPLYING THE "RULE OF REASON" TO SPORTS LEAGUE RESTRAINTS

Two important judicial decisions teach us when and how the Rule of Reason applies to sports league restraints. The first, explored in more detail in Chapter 7, is *Mackey v. NFL*, 543 F.2d 606 (8th Cir. 1976). This was an antitrust challenge by veteran NFL players to the "Rozelle Rule" that limited the ability of NFL clubs to compete for their services, by requiring a club signing a player previously employed by another NFL club to provide substantial "compensation" that would be determined by the NFL commissioner. The Eighth Circuit employed a three-step test in finding that the NFL rule was an unreasonable restraint of trade in violation of § 1.

First, the court found that the agreement had a **significant anticompetitive effect**. The court found that the rule:

> acts as a substantial deterrent to players playing out their options and becoming free agents; that it significantly decreases players' bargaining power in contract negotiations; that players are thus

denied the right to sell their services in a free and open market; that as a result, the salaries paid by each club are lower than if competitive bidding were allowed to prevail; and that absent the Rozelle Rule, there would be increased movement in interstate commerce of players from one club to another.

Id. at 620.

Second, the court considered "whether the restraint imposed is **justified by legitimate business purposes.**" *Id.* (We consider the specific justifications offered by the NFL—harm to competitive balance, protecting the clubs' investment in scouting expenses and player development costs, and the need for player continuity on the same team, in Chapter 7.)

Third, the court examined whether the restraint "is **no more restrictive than necessary.**" In this regard, the court looked both at other alternatives, and whether the scope of the restraint was broader than necessary to achieve the NFL's stated goals.

The three-part framework utilized by *Mackey* was applied and more fully expanded by the Supreme Court in its landmark exposition of how the rule of reason applies to sports, as well as multiple other industries. The Court's observations about specific issues surrounding intercollegiate sports are considered in detail in Chapter 12.

NCAA v. BOARD OF REGENTS OF THE UNIV. OF OKLAHOMA & UNIV. OF GEORGIA ATHLETIC ASS'N
468 U.S. 85 (1984)

JUSTICE STEVENS for the Court.

* * *

History of the NCAA Television Plan

In 1938, the University of Pennsylvania televised one of its home games.[3] From 1940 through the 1950 season all of Pennsylvania's home games were televised. That was the beginning of the relationship between television and college football.

On January 11, 1951, a three-person "Television Committee," appointed during the preceding year, delivered a report to the NCAA's annual convention in Dallas. Based on preliminary surveys, the committee had concluded that "television does have an adverse effect on college football attendance and unless brought under some control threatens to seriously harm the nation's overall athletic and physical system." The

---

[3]   According to the NCAA football television committee's 1981 briefing book: "As far as is known, there were [then] six television sets in Philadelphia: and all were tuned to the game."

report emphasized that "the television problem is truly a national one and requires collective action by the colleges."

[In 1951 the NCAA adopted a television plan that permitted only one game per week to be broadcast in each area, and limited each school to two television appearances per season. The University of Pennsylvania at first insisted on televising all its home games, but after the NCAA declared it a member in bad standing and the four schools scheduled to play at Pennsylvania that year threatened to cancel the games, the school agreed to follow the NCAA plan.

Studies in each of the next five years indicated that television had an adverse effect on attendance. The NCAA continued to formulate a television policy for all its members. From the mid-1960s to the late 1970s, ABC held the exclusive network right to broadcast college football games. In 1981, the NCAA negotiated four-year agreements with both ABC and CBS, under which each network could broadcast 14 games per season in return for an annual $33 million apiece. In addition, the NCAA granted Turner Broadcasting System (TBS) exclusive cable rights for a limited number of games, for $9 million a year.

The "appearance requirements and limitations" followed the same pattern as before. Under the new contracts, over a two-year cycle each network had to carry games showing at least 82 NCAA members, with six being the maximum number for any one college team (and only four on national coverage). The NCAA's rules, as reflected in the network contracts, also barred any individual member from selling its own team's broadcast rights.

However, the [College Football Association (CFA)] members were unhappy with these restraints, and they negotiated a different contract with NBC that gave these "big-time" college football powers both more appearances and more money. The NCAA threatened any team that allowed its game to be broadcast on NBC with sanctions, not only against their football program, but against all of their sports. Thus, the Universities of Oklahoma and Georgia filed suit in an Oklahoma federal district court, and secured an injunction against any effort by the NCAA to interfere with CFA's dealings with NBC. The Supreme Court agreed to hear the NCAA's appeal.]

* * *

II

There can be no doubt that the challenged practices of the NCAA constitute a "restraint of trade" in the sense that they limit members' freedom to negotiate and enter into their own television contracts. In that sense, however, every contract is a restraint of trade, and as we have repeatedly recognized, the Sherman Act was intended to prohibit only unreasonable restraints of trade.

It is also undeniable that these practices share characteristics of restraints we have previously held unreasonable. The NCAA is an association of schools which compete against each other to attract television revenues, not to mention fans and athletes. As the District Court found, the policies of the NCAA with respect to television rights are ultimately controlled by the vote of member institutions. By participating in an association which prevents member institutions from competing against each other on the basis of price or kind of television rights that can be offered to broadcasters, the NCAA member institutions have created a horizontal restraint—an agreement among competitors on the way in which they will compete with one another. A restraint of this type has often been held to be unreasonable as a matter of law. Because it places a ceiling on the number of games member institutions may televise, the horizontal agreement places an artificial limit on the quantity of televised football that is available to broadcasters and consumers. By restraining the quantity of television rights available for sale, the challenged practices create a limitation on output; our cases have held that such limitations are unreasonable restraints of trade. Moreover, the District Court found that the minimum aggregate price in fact operates to preclude any price negotiation between broadcasters and institutions, thereby constituting horizontal price fixing, perhaps the paradigm of an unreasonable restraint of trade.

Horizontal price fixing and output limitation are ordinarily condemned as a matter of law under an "illegal per se" approach because the probability that these practices are anticompetitive is so high; a per se rule is applied when "the practice facially appears to be one that would always or almost always tend to restrict competition and decrease output." In such circumstances a restraint is presumed unreasonable without inquiry into the particular market context in which it is found. Nevertheless, we have decided that it would be inappropriate to apply a per se rule to this case. This decision is not based on a lack of judicial experience with this type of arrangement, on the fact that the NCAA is organized as a nonprofit entity, or on our respect for the NCAA's historic role in the preservation and encouragement of intercollegiate amateur athletics. Rather, what is critical is that this case involves an industry in which horizontal restraints on competition are essential if the product is to be available at all.

As Judge Bork has noted: "[S]ome activities can only be carried out jointly. Perhaps the leading example is league sports. When a league of professional lacrosse teams is formed, it would be pointless to declare their cooperation illegal on the ground that there are no other professional lacrosse teams." R. Bork, *The Antitrust Paradox* 278 (1978). What the NCAA and its member institutions market in this case is competition itself—contests between competing institutions. Of course, this would be completely ineffective if there were no rules on which the competitors agreed to create and define the competition to be marketed. A myriad of rules affecting such matters as the size of the field, the number of players on a team, and the extent to which physical violence is to be encouraged or proscribed, all must be agreed upon, and all restrain the manner in which institutions compete. Moreover, the NCAA seeks to market a particular brand of football—college football. The identification of this "product" with an academic tradition differentiates college football from and makes it more popular than professional sports to which it might otherwise be comparable, such as, for example, minor league baseball. In order to preserve the character and quality of the "product," athletes must not be paid, must be required to attend class, and the like. And the integrity of the "product" cannot be preserved except by mutual agreement; if an institution adopted such restrictions unilaterally, its effectiveness as a competitor on the playing field might soon be destroyed. Thus, the NCAA plays a vital role in enabling college football to preserve its character, and as a result enables a product to be marketed which might otherwise be unavailable. In performing this role, its actions widen consumer choice— not only the choices available to sports fans but also those available to athletes—and hence can be viewed as procompetitive. . . .

Respondents concede that the great majority of the NCAA's regulations enhance competition among member institutions. Thus, despite the fact that this case involves restraints on the ability of member institutions to compete in terms of price and output, a fair evaluation of their competitive character requires consideration of the NCAA's justifications for the restraints.

Our analysis of this case under the Rule of Reason, of course, does not change the ultimate focus of our inquiry. . . . Under the Sherman Act the criterion to be used in judging the validity of a restraint on trade is its impact on competition.

III

Because it restrains price and output, the NCAA's television plan has a significant potential for anticompetitive effects.[28] The findings of the District Court indicate that this potential has been realized. The District Court found that if member institutions were free to sell television rights, many more games would be shown on television, and that the NCAA's output restriction has the effect of raising the price the networks pay for television rights. Moreover, the court found that by fixing a price for

---

[28]   In this connection, it is not without significance that Congress felt the need to grant professional sports an exemption from the antitrust laws for joint marketing of television rights. *See* 15 U.S.C. § 1291–1295. The legislative history of this exemption demonstrates Congress' recognition that agreements among league members to sell television rights in a cooperative fashion could run afoul of the Sherman Act, and in particular reflects its awareness of the decision in *United States v. National Football League,* 116 F. Supp. 319 (E.D.Pa.1953), which held that an agreement between the teams of the National Football League that each team would not permit stations within 75 miles of the home city of another team to telecast its games on a day when that team was playing at home violated § 1 of the Sherman Act.

television rights to all games, the NCAA creates a price structure that is unresponsive to viewer demand and unrelated to the prices that would prevail in a competitive market. And, of course, since as a practical matter all member institutions need NCAA approval, members have no real choice but to adhere to the NCAA's television controls.

The anticompetitive consequences of this arrangement are apparent. Individual competitors lose their freedom to compete. Price is higher and output lower than they would otherwise be, and both are unresponsive to consumer preference.[33] This latter point is perhaps the most significant, since "Congress designed the Sherman Act as a 'consumer welfare prescription.'" A restraint that has the effect of reducing the importance of consumer preference in setting price and output is not consistent with this fundamental goal of antitrust law.[34] Restrictions on price and output are the paradigmatic examples of restraints of trade that the Sherman Act was intended to prohibit. At the same time, the television plan eliminates competitors from the market, since only those broadcasters able to bid on television rights covering the entire NCAA can compete. Thus, as the District Court found, many telecasts that would occur in a competitive market are foreclosed by the NCAA's plan.

Petitioner argues, however, that its television plan can have no significant anticompetitive effect since the record indicates that it has no market power—no ability to alter the interaction of supply and demand in the market. We must reject this argument for two reasons, one legal, one factual.

As a matter of law, the absence of proof of market power does not justify a naked restriction on price or output. To the contrary, when there is an agreement not to compete in terms of price or output, "no elaborate industry analysis is required to demonstrate the anticompetitive character of such an agreement." Petitioner does not quarrel with the District Court's finding that price and output are not responsive to demand. Thus the plan

---

[33]   The District Court provided a vivid example of this system in practice:

A clear example of the failure of the rights fees paid to respond to market forces occurred in the fall of 1981. On one weekend of that year, Oklahoma was scheduled to play a football game with the University of Southern California. Both Oklahoma and USC have long had outstanding football programs, and indeed, both teams were ranked among the top five teams in the country by the wire service polls. ABC chose to televise the game along with several others on a regional basis. A game between two schools which are not well-known for their football programs, Citadel and Appalachian State, was carried on four of ABC's local affiliated stations. The USC-Oklahoma contest was carried on over 200 stations. Yet, incredibly, all four of these teams received exactly the same amount of money for the right to televise their games.

[34]   As the District Court observed:

Perhaps the most pernicious aspect is that under the controls, the market is not responsive to viewer preference. Every witness who testified on the matter confirmed that the consumers, the viewers of college football television, receive absolutely no benefit from the controls. Many games for which there is a large viewer demand are kept from the viewers, and many games for which there is little if any demand are nonetheless televised.

is inconsistent with the Sherman Act's command that price and supply be responsive to consumer preference. We have never required proof of market power in such a case. This naked restraint on price and output requires some competitive justification even in the absence of a detailed market analysis. As a factual matter, it is evident that petitioner does possess market power. The District Court employed the correct test for determining whether college football broadcasts constitute a separate market—whether there are other products that are reasonably substitutable for televised NCAA football games. Petitioner's argument that it cannot obtain supracompetitive prices from broadcasters since advertisers, and hence broadcasters, can switch from college football to other types of programming simply ignores the findings of the District Court. It found that intercollegiate football telecasts generate an audience uniquely attractive to advertisers and that competitors are unable to offer programming that can attract a similar audience. These findings amply support its conclusion that the NCAA possesses market power. Indeed, the District Court's subsidiary finding that advertisers will pay a premium price per viewer to reach audiences watching college football because of their demographic characteristics is vivid evidence of the uniqueness of this product. Moreover, the District Court's market analysis is firmly supported by our decision in *International Boxing Club v. United States*, 358 U.S. 242 (1959), that championship boxing events are uniquely attractive to fans and hence constitute a market separate from that for non-championship events. Thus, respondents have demonstrated that there is a separate market for telecasts of college football which "rest[s] on generic qualities differentiating" viewers. It inexorably follows that if college football broadcasts be defined as a separate market—and we are convinced they are—then the NCAA's complete control over those broadcasts provides a solid basis for the District Court's conclusion that the NCAA possesses market power with respect to those broadcasts. "When a product is controlled by one interest, without substitutes available in the market, there is monopoly power." *United States v. E.I. du Pont de Nemours & Co.*, 351 U.S. 377, 394 (1956).

Thus, the NCAA television plan on its face constitutes a restraint upon the operation of a free market, and the findings of the District Court establish that it has operated to raise price and reduce output. Under the Rule of Reason, these hallmarks of anticompetitive behavior place upon petitioner a heavy burden of establishing an affirmative defense which competitively justifies this apparent deviation from the operations of a free market.

IV

[P]etitioner argues that its television plan constitutes a cooperative "joint venture" which assists in the marketing of broadcast rights and hence is procompetitive. . . .

The District Court did not find that the NCAA's television plan produced any procompetitive efficiencies which enhanced the competitiveness of college football television rights; to the contrary it concluded that NCAA football could be marketed just as effectively without the television plan. There is therefore no predicate in the findings for petitioner's efficiency justification. Indeed, petitioner's argument is refuted by the District Court's finding concerning price and output. If the NCAA's television plan produced procompetitive efficiencies, the plan would increase output and reduce the price of televised games. The District Court's contrary findings accordingly undermine petitioner's position. In light of these findings, it cannot be said that "the agreement on price is necessary to market the product at all." . . . Here production has been limited, not enhanced. No individual school is free to televise its own games without restraint. The NCAA's efficiency justification is not supported by the record.

Neither is the NCAA's television plan necessary to enable the NCAA to penetrate the market through an attractive package sale. Since broadcasting rights to college football constitute a unique product for which there is no ready substitute, there is no need for collective action in order to enable the product to compete against its nonexistent competitors. This is borne out by the District Court's finding that the NCAA's television reduces the volume of television rights sold.

V

Throughout the history of its regulation of intercollegiate football telecasts, the NCAA has indicated its concern with protecting live attendance. This concern, it should be noted, is not with protecting live attendance at games which are shown on television; that type of interest is not at issue in this case. Rather, the concern is that fan interest in a televised game may adversely affect ticket sales for games that will not appear on television.[56]

Although studies in the 1950s provided some support for the thesis that live attendance would suffer if unlimited television were permitted, the District Court found that there was no evidence to support that theory in today's market. . . .

There is, however, a more fundamental reason for rejecting this defense. The NCAA's argument that its television plan is necessary to protect live attendance is not based on a desire to maintain the integrity of college football as a distinct and attractive product, but rather on a fear

---

[56] The NCAA's plan is not even arguably related to a desire to protect live attendance by ensuring that a game is not televised in the area where it is to be played. No cooperative action is necessary for that kind of "blackout." The home team can always refuse to sell the right to telecast its game to stations in the immediate area. The NCAA does not now and never has justified its television plan by an interest in assisting schools in "blacking out" their home games in the areas in which they are played.

that the product will not prove sufficiently attractive to draw live attendance when faced with competition from televised games. At bottom the NCAA's position is that ticket sales for most college games are unable to compete in a free market. The television plan protects ticket sales by limiting output—just as any monopolist increases revenues by reducing output. By seeking to insulate live ticket sales from the full spectrum of competition because of its assumption that the product itself is insufficiently attractive to consumers, petitioner forwards a justification that is inconsistent with the basic policy of the Sherman Act. "[T]he Rule of Reason does not support a defense based on the assumption that competition itself is unreasonable." *National Society of Professional Engineers v. United States*, 435 U.S. 679, 696 (1978).

VI

Petitioner argues that the interest in maintaining a competitive balance among amateur athletic teams is legitimate and important and that it justifies the regulations challenged in this case. We agree with the first part of the argument but not the second.

Our decision not to apply a per se rule to this case rests in large part on our recognition that a certain degree of cooperation is necessary if the type of competition that petitioner and its member institutions seek to market is to be preserved. It is reasonable to assume that most of the regulatory controls of the NCAA are justifiable means of fostering competition among amateur athletic teams and therefore procompetitive because they enhance public interest in intercollegiate athletics. The specific restraints on football telecasts that are challenged in this case do not, however, fit into the same mold as do rules defining the conditions of the contest, the eligibility of participants, or the manner in which members of a joint enterprise shall share the responsibilities and the benefits of the total venture.

The NCAA does not claim that its television plan has equalized or is intended to equalize competition within any one league.[62] The plan is nationwide in scope and there is no single league or tournament in which all college football teams complete. There is no evidence of any intent to equalize the strength of teams in Division I-A with those in Division II or Division III, and not even a colorable basis for giving colleges that have no football program at all a voice in the management of the revenues

---

[62]   It seems unlikely, for example, that there would have been a greater disparity between the football prowess of Ohio State University and that of Northwestern University in recent years without the NCAA's television plan. The District Court found that in fact the NCAA has been strikingly unsuccessful if it has indeed attempted to prevent the emergence of a "power elite" in intercollegiate football. Moreover, the District Court's finding that there would be more local and regional telecasts without the NCAA controls means that Northwestern could well have generated more television income in a free market than was obtained under the NCAA regime.

generated by the football programs at other schools.[63] The interest in maintaining a competitive balance that is asserted by the NCAA as a justification for regulating all television of intercollegiate football is not related to any neutral standard or to any readily identifiable group of competitors.

The television plan is not even arguably tailored to serve such an interest. It does not regulate the amount of money that any college may spend on its football program, nor the way in which the colleges may use the revenues that are generated by their football programs, whether derived from the sale of television rights, the sale of tickets, or the sale of concessions or program advertising. The plan simply imposes a restriction on one source of revenue that is more important to some colleges than to others. There is no evidence that this restriction produces any greater measure of equality throughout the NCAA than would a restriction on alumni donations, tuition rates, or any other revenue producing activity. At the same time, as the District Court found, the NCAA imposes a variety of other restrictions designed to preserve amateurism which are much better tailored to the goal of competitive balance than is the television plan, and which are "clearly sufficient" to preserve competitive balance to the extent it is within the NCAA's power to do so. And much more than speculation supported the District Court's findings on this score. No other NCAA sport employs a similar plan, and in particular the court found that in the most closely analogous sport, college basketball, competitive balance has been maintained without resort to a restrictive television plan.

Perhaps the most important reason for rejecting the argument that the interest in competitive balance is served by the television plan is the District Court's unambiguous and well supported finding that many more games would be televised in a free market than under the NCAA plan. The hypothesis that legitimates the maintenance of competitive balance as a procompetitive justification under the Rule of Reason is that equal competition will maximize consumer demand for the product. The finding that consumption will materially increase if the controls are removed is a

---

[63] Indeed, the District Court found that the basic reason the television plan has endured is that the NCAA is in effect controlled by schools that are not restrained by the plan:

> The plaintiffs and other CFA members attempted to persuade the majority of NCAA members that NCAA had gone far beyond its legitimate role in football television. Not surprisingly, none of the CFA proposals were adopted. Instead the membership uniformly adopted the proposals of the NCAA administration which "legitimized" NCAA's exercises of power. The result was not surprising in light of the makeup of the voting membership. Of approximately 800 voting members of the NCAA, 500 or so are in Divisions II and III and are not subjected to NCAA television controls. Of the 275 Division I members, only 187 play football, and only 135 were members of Division I-A at the time of the January Convention. Division I-A was made up of the most prominent football-playing schools, and those schools account for most of the football games shown on network television. Therefore, of some 850 voting members, less than 150 suffer any direct restriction on their right to sell football games to television.

compelling demonstration that they do not in fact serve any such legitimate purpose.[68]

VII

The NCAA plays a critical role in the maintenance of a revered tradition of amateurism in college sports. There can be no question but that it needs ample latitude to play that role, or that the preservation of the student-athlete in higher education adds richness and diversity to intercollegiate athletics and is entirely consistent with the goals of the Sherman Act. But consistent with the Sherman Act, the role of the NCAA must be to preserve a tradition that might otherwise die; rules that restrict output are hardly consistent with this role. Today we hold only that the record supports the District Court's conclusion that by curtailing output and blunting the ability of member institutions to respond to consumer preference, the NCAA has restricted rather than enhanced the place of intercollegiate athletics in the Nation's life. Accordingly, the judgment of the Court of Appeals is

Affirmed.

JUSTICE WHITE with whom JUSTICE REHNQUIST joins, dissenting.

* * *

I

"While it would be fanciful to suggest that colleges are not concerned about the profitability of their ventures, it is clear that other, non-commercial goals play a central role in their sports programs." J. Weistart & C. Lowell, *The Law of Sports* § 5.12 (1979). The NCAA's member institutions have designed their competitive athletic programs "to be a vital part of the educational system." Deviations from this goal, produced by a persistent and perhaps inevitable desire to "win at all costs," have in the past led, and continue to lead, to a wide range of competitive excesses that prove harmful to students and institutions alike. . . .

The NCAA, in short, "exist[s] primarily to enhance the contribution made by amateur athletic competition to the process of higher education as distinguished from realizing maximum return on it as an entertainment commodity." In pursuing this goal, the organization and its members seek to provide a public good—a viable system of amateur athletics—that most likely could not be provided in a perfectly competitive market. "Without regulation, the desire of member institutions to remain athletically competitive would lead them to engage in activities that deny amateurism to the public. No single institution could confidently enforce its own

---

[68]   This is true not only for television viewers, but also for athletes. The District Court's finding that the television exposure of all schools would increase in the absence of the NCAA's television plan means that smaller institutions appealing to essentially local or regional markets would get more exposure if the plan is enjoined, enhancing their ability to compete for student athletes.

standards since it could not trust its competitors to do the same." Note, *Antitrust and Nonprofit Entities*, 94 Harv. L. Rev. 802, 817–18 (1981). The history of intercollegiate athletics prior to the advent of the NCAA provides ample support for this conclusion. By mitigating what appears to be a clear failure of the free market to serve the ends and goals of higher education, the NCAA ensures the continued availability of a unique and valuable product, the very existence of which might well be threatened by unbridled competition in the economic sphere.

In pursuit of its fundamental goal and others related to it, the NCAA imposes numerous controls on intercollegiate athletic competition among its members, many of which "are similar to those which are summarily condemned when undertaken in a more traditional business setting." J. Weistart & C. Lowell, *supra*, at § 5.12.b. Thus, the NCAA has promulgated and enforced rules limiting both the compensation of student-athletes, and the number of coaches a school may hire for its football and basketball programs; it also has prohibited athletes who formerly have been compensated for playing from participating in intercollegiate competition, restricted the number of athletic scholarships its members may award, and established minimum academic standards for recipients of those scholarships; and it has pervasively regulated the recruitment process, student eligibility, practice schedules, squad size, the number of games played, and many other aspects of intercollegiate athletics. One clear effect of most, if not all, of these regulations is to prevent institutions with competitively and economically successful programs from taking advantage of their success by expanding their programs, improving the quality of the product they offer, and increasing their sports revenues. Yet each of these regulations represents a desirable and legitimate attempt "to keep university athletics from becoming professionalized to the extent that profit making objectives would overshadow educational objectives." Significantly, neither the Court of Appeals nor this Court questions the validity of these regulations under the Rule of Reason.

Notwithstanding the contrary conclusion of the District Court, and the majority, I do not believe that the restraint under consideration in this case—the NCAA's television plan—differs fundamentally for antitrust purposes from the other seemingly anticompetitive aspects of the organization's broader program of self-regulation. The television plan, like many of the NCAA's actions, furthers several complementary ends. Specifically, the plan is designed "to reduce, insofar as possible, the adverse effects of live television . . . upon football game attendance and, in turn, upon the athletic and related educational programs dependent upon the proceeds therefrom; to spread football television participation among as many colleges as practicable; to reflect properly the image of universities as educational institutions; to promote college football through the use of television, to advance the overall interests of intercollegiate athletics, and to provide college football television to the public to the extent compatible with these other objectives." More generally, in my view, the television plan reflects the NCAA's fundamental policy of preserving amateurism and integrating athletics and education. Nor does the District Court's finding that the plan is intended to maximize television revenues, warrant any implication that the NCAA and its member institutions pursue this goal without regard to the organization's stated policies.

* * *

[I]t is essential at this point to emphasize that neither the Court of Appeals nor this Court purports to hold that the NCAA may not (1) require its members who televise their games to pool and share the compensation received among themselves, with other schools, and with the NCAA; (2) limit the number of times any member may arrange to have its games shown on television; or (3) enforce reasonable blackout rules to avoid head-to-head competition for television audiences. As I shall demonstrate, the Court wisely and correctly does not condemn such regulations. What the Court does affirm is the Court of Appeals' judgment that the NCAA may not limit the number of games that are broadcast on television and that it may not contract for an overall price that has the effect of setting the price for individual game broadcast rights. I disagree with the Court in these respects.

* * *

III

Even if I were convinced that the District Court did not err in failing to look to total viewership, as opposed to the number of televised games, when measuring output and anticompetitive effect and in failing fully to consider whether the NCAA possesses power to fix the package price, as opposed to the distribution of that package price among participating teams, I would nevertheless hold that the television plan passes muster under the Rule of Reason. The NCAA argues strenuously that the plan and the network contracts "are part of a joint venture among many of the nation's universities to create a product—high-quality college football—and offer that product in a way attractive to both fans in the stadiums and viewers on [television]. The cooperation in producing the product makes it more competitive against other [television] (and live) attractions." The Court recognizes that, "[i]f the NCAA faced 'interbrand' competition from available substitutes, then certain forms of collective action might be appropriate in order to enhance its ability to compete." It rejects the NCAA's proffered procompetitive justification, however, on the ground that college football is a unique product for which there are no available substitutes and "there is no need for collective action in order to enable the product to compete against its nonexistent competitors." This proposition is singularly unpersuasive.

It is one thing to say that "NCAA football is a unique product," that "intercollegiate football telecasts generate an audience uniquely attractive to advertisers and that competitors are unable to offer programming that can attract a similar audience." It is quite another, in my view, to say that maintenance or enhancement of the quality of NCAA football telecasts is unnecessary to enable those telecasts to compete effectively against other forms of entertainment. The NCAA has no monopoly power when competing against other types of entertainment. Should the quality of the NCAA's product "deteriorate to any perceptible degree or should the cost of 'using' its product rise, some fans undoubtedly would turn to another form of entertainment. . . . Because of the broad possibilities for alternative forms of entertainment," the NCAA "properly belongs in the broader 'entertainment' market rather than in . . . [a] narrower marke[t]" like sports or football.

The NCAA has suggested a number of plausible ways in which its television plan might enhance the ability of college football telecasts to compete against other forms of entertainment. Although the District Court did conclude that the plan is "not necessary for effective marketing of the product," its finding was directed only at the question whether college football telecasts would continue in the absence of the plan. It made no explicit findings concerning the effect of the plan on viewership and thus did not reject the factual premise of the NCAA's argument that the plan might enhance competition by increasing the market penetration of NCAA football. The District Court's finding that network coverage of NCAA football would likely decrease if the plan were struck down, in fact, strongly suggests the validity of the NCAA's position. On the record now before the Court, therefore, I am not prepared to conclude that the restraints imposed by the NCAA's television plan are "such as may suppress or even destroy competition" rather than "such as merely regulat[e] and perhaps thereby promot[e] competition."

IV

Finally, I return to the point with which I began—the essentially noneconomic nature of the NCAA's program of self-regulation. Like Judge Barrett, who dissented in the Court of Appeals, I believe that the lower courts "erred by subjugating the NCAA's educational goals (and, coincidentally, those which Oklahoma and Georgia insist must be maintained in any event) to the purely competitive commercialism of [an] 'every school for itself' approach to television contract bargaining." Although the NCAA does not enjoy blanket immunity from the antitrust laws, it is important to remember that the Sherman Act "is aimed primarily at combinations having commercial objectives and is applied only to a very limited extent to organizations . . . which normally have other objectives." *Klor's Inc. v. Broadway-Hale Stores, Inc.*, 359 U.S. 207, 213, n.7 (1959).

The fact that a restraint operates on nonprofit educational institutions as distinguished from business entities is as "relevant in determining whether that particular restraint violates the Sherman Act" as is the fact that a restraint affects a profession rather than a business. The legitimate noneconomic goals of colleges and universities should not be ignored in analyzing restraints imposed by associations of such institutions on their members, and these noneconomic goals "may require that a particular practice, which could properly be viewed as a violation of the Sherman Act in another context, be treated differently." The Court of Appeals, like the District Court, flatly refused to consider what it termed "noneconomic" justifications advanced by the NCAA in support of the television plan. It was of the view that our decision in *National Society of Professional Engineers v. United States*, 435 U.S. 679 (1978), precludes reliance on noneconomic factors in assessing the reasonableness of the television plan. This view was mistaken, and I note that the Court does not in so many words repeat this error.

Professional Engineers did make clear that antitrust analysis usually turns on "competitive conditions" and "economic conceptions." Ordinarily, "the inquiry mandated by the Rule of Reason is whether the challenged agreement is one that promotes competition or one that suppresses competition." The purpose of antitrust analysis, the Court emphasized, "is to form a judgment about the competitive significance of the restraint; it is not to decide whether a policy favoring competition is in the public interest, or in the interest of the members of an industry." Broadly read, these statements suggest that noneconomic values like the promotion of amateurism and fundamental educational objectives could not save the television plan from condemnation under the Sherman Act. But these statements were made in response to "public interest" justifications proffered in defense of a ban on competitive bidding imposed by practitioners engaged in standard, profit-motivated commercial activities. The primarily noneconomic values pursued by educational institutions differ fundamentally from the "overriding commercial purpose of [the] day-to-day activities" of engineers, lawyers, doctors, and businessmen, and neither *Professional Engineers* nor any other decision of this Court suggests that associations of nonprofit educational institutions must defend their self-regulatory restraints solely in terms of their competitive impact, without regard for the legitimate noneconomic values they promote.

When these values are factored into the balance, the NCAA's television plan seems eminently reasonable. Most fundamentally, the plan fosters the goal of amateurism by spreading revenues among various schools and reducing the financial incentives toward professionalism. As the Court observes, the NCAA imposes a variety of restrictions perhaps better suited than the television plan for the preservation of amateurism. Although the NCAA does attempt vigorously to enforce these restrictions, the vast potential for abuse suggests that measures, like the television plan, designed to limit the rewards of professionalism are fully consistent with, and essential to the attainment of, the NCAA's objectives. . . . The collateral consequences of the spreading of regional and national appearances among a number of schools are many: the television plan, like the ban on compensating student-athletes, may well encourage students to choose their schools, at least in part, on the basis of educational quality by reducing the perceived economic element of the choice; it helps ensure the economic viability of athletic programs at a wide variety of schools with weaker football teams; and it "promot[es] competitive football among many and varied amateur teams nationwide." These important contributions, I believe, are sufficient to offset any minimal anticompetitive effects of the television plan.

Los Angeles Memorial Coliseum Comm'n v. NFL, 726 F.2d 1381 (9th Cir. 1984), articulated another formulation of the Rule of Reason. There, the court considered the traditional doctrine of ancillary restraints that Judge Taft, in his landmark *Addyston Pipe* decision, had borrowed from the common law of restraints of trade. Under this doctrine, some agreements that restrain competition may be valid if they are "subordinate and collateral to another legitimate transaction and necessary to make that transaction effective." *Id.* at 1395 (quoting Robert Bork, *The Rule of Reason and the Per Se Concept: Price Fixing and Market Division*, 74 YALE L.J. 775, 797–798 (1965) and citing *Addyston Pipe*, 85 F. at 281–82. This formulation may simply be a restatement of the second and third inquiries under the Rule of Reason set forth in *Mackey, supra.*

The *NCAA* decision is an example of what has been called a "quick look" review under the Rule of Reason. Because of the obvious restriction in the number of games shown on television, the court considered and then rejected the defendants' business justification. In contrast, a "full rule of reason review" would require the plaintiff to establish that the challenged restraint actually resulted in higher prices, lower output, or output unresponsive to consumer preference in a properly defined relevant market. The Court cited settled antitrust doctrine in suggesting, in this regard, that the principal focus should be on whether other products which consumers view as substitutes are available in the marketplace.

Justice White noted in his *NCAA* dissent that the antitrust victory won by these CFA members might come back to haunt the CFA in its own dealings with the television networks. In the immediate aftermath of the *Board of Regents* ruling, the price of network television packages dropped sharply, after having risen from $1.1 million in 1952, to $5 million per year in the early 1960s, to $75 million per year in the early 1980s. Although there were nearly three times as many college football games on television in 1984 as in 1983 (under a CFA contract with ABC, a Big Ten/Pac Ten contract with CBS, and a host of deals between individual schools and cable networks or television sports distributors), the price per game was cut from just under $1 million to $250,000 (and total game attendance rose marginally). Not until 1990 was the CFA able to negotiate a $70 million per year deal with ABC and ESPN, in addition to a Big Ten/Pac Ten package (which by then had been awarded to ABC). Toward the end of those negotiations, Notre Dame broke away and signed a separate 5-year, $35 million deal with NBC for the rights to telecast its home games, to the great displeasure of its fellow CFA members. As we compare the pre-1984 landscape (approximately five games per week on television, with strict limits on the number of appearances for each club) to today, we see that virtually all major college football games are televised. The major conferences typically have agreements with national networks for premier games, and have created special conference networks for the remainder; these networks also provide conference-oriented features as well as broadcasts of other sports.

Chapter 12, Section D below details the torrent of antitrust litigation in recent years concerning compensation for college athletes, with principal focus on the Supreme Court's unanimous decision in *NCAA v. Alston*, 141 S. Ct. 2141 (2021). *Alston* affirmed an order requiring the NCAA to permit member schools to offer college athletes any benefits that are educationally related and up to $6,000 above scholarship funding. The Court's decision is important for purposes of this chapter's introduction to antitrust reasoning in the following respects:

(a) The decision reaffirms the application to sports of the general antitrust principle that "market forces yield the best allocation of the Nation's resources." *Id.* at 2147. But given how fast things change in the dynamic market for sports, the key goal of judicial review is not to mechanically enforce precedents, but to focus on "a careful analysis of market realities." *Id.* at 2158 (noting changes since the 1984 *Board of Regents* decision excerpted above).

(b) Reaffirming precedents, it held that *per se* condemnation of restraints, or the sort of "quick look" deferential review favoring a defendant, was appropriate "only for restraints at the opposite ends of the competitive spectrum." *Id.* Principally, a "full" rule of reason analysis can be truncated in favor of the defendant where it lacks market power. *Id.* at 2156. Thus, even though some restraints are essential to organize sporting competitions, the Rule of Reason is still the appropriate means for courts to evaluate if the specific restraint challenged in an antitrust case is not necessary for "the very competitions that consumers value." *Id.* at 2156–57, *citing with approval Chicago Professional Sports Ltd. Partnership v.*

National Basketball Assn., 95 F.3d 593, 600 (7th Cir. 1996) ("Just as the ability of McDonald's franchises to coordinate the release of a new hamburger does not imply their ability to agree on wages for counter workers, so the ability of sports teams to agree on a TV contract need not imply an ability to set wages for players").

(c) The three-step test discussed above is not a "rote checklist" but is designed to furnish "an enquiry meet for the case, looking to the circumstances, details, and logic of a restraint" to ensure that it unduly harms competition before a court declares it unlawful. *Id.*

(d) Although "antitrust law does not require businesses to use anything like the least restrictive means of achieving legitimate business purposes," and courts should not "second-guess 'degrees of reasonable necessity'", a plaintiff can prevail by demonstrating that the claimed objectives could be achieved by "substantially less restrictive alternative rules." *Id.* at 2161–62.

NOTES AND QUESTIONS

1. *Are NCAA Rules Procompetitive?* Dicta in *Board of Regents* suggests that many NCAA rules are actually procompetitive because they contribute to the creation of a unique product that would not otherwise be available—amateur athletics. From the perspective of consumer demand, is college football different from NFL football? What are the attributes of college football that differentiate it? Have those attributes changed over time? Are you persuaded by the Court's arguments that the NCAA's television rules did not significantly contribute to the preservation of amateur athletics?

2. *Market Definition.* The *Board of Regents* ruling involved the use of antitrust law to eliminate restrictive agreements that affected the supply and price of a product offered to consumers, the principal constituency of antitrust policy. A key step in Rule of Reason analysis is defining the market in which the defendant's product competes. Study the majority opinion closely. Does the Court indicate or suggest whether any one league's games should be considered as just one of the many sports and entertainment products that compete for consumer patronage, either at the live gate or on the television screen? As will be clear in later cases applying *Board of Regents,* absent a facial showing of anticompetitive effect sufficient to warrant a "quick look," courts often require either a large market share in properly defined market, or clear evidence of an actual effect on prices or output.

3. *Restraints in the Absence of Economic Dominance.* The Court upheld the trial court's findings that there were no reasonable substitutes for Division I college football subject to the NCAA's regulation. In the absence of economic dominance, collective agreements by football conferences that restricted individual member schools, where conferences were in competition with each other, received more favorable judicial treatment. *See Regents of the Univ. of*

Calif. v. American Broadcasting Cos., 747 F.2d 511 (9th Cir. 1984) (generally approving contracts but enjoining provision barring CFA members from allowing games with non-members to be televised elsewhere); and *Association of Independent Television Stations, Inc. v. College Football Ass'n*, 637 F. Supp. 1289 (W.D. Okla. 1986) (summary judgment for plaintiff rejected, *inter alia*, because of factual disputes of market power of CFA).

D. THE NATURE OF A SPORTS LEAGUE: ARE LEAGUE RULES THE PRODUCT OF A "SINGLE ENTITY" OR AN AGREEMENT AMONG COMPETING CLUB OWNERS?

Chapter 2 provided a glimpse of the distinctive structure of the sports league. In each of the four historically "major" North American team sports, the dominant league rests upon an elaborate contractual agreement among the member teams—its "constitution." Each owner holds both a franchise that the team runs in its (usually) exclusive territory and a vote in the governance of the league. Through its governing bodies, the club owners in turn develop by-laws and rules that define the rights and obligations of all participants in the enterprise—in particular, the division of revenues from gate receipts, television contracts, and marketing of the league and team names. At the apex of this structure is a commissioner who wields broad authority, subject always to the ultimate collective power of club owners, to determine and enforce "the best interests of the sport," including adjudication of disputes between league participants.

As we saw in Chapter 2, when objections are launched against the commissioner's formulation of the league's "best interests," courts have generally displayed a deferential attitude toward decisions reached through internal league councils. Courts show much less deference, however, when attacks are launched against the underlying validity of the league contract—particularly challenges under antitrust law. Three different types of non-government challengers may surface against league practices. One group consists of third parties attempting to deal with the existing league, such as players, fans, stadiums, aspiring club owners, and television networks. The second group includes team owners who may oppose a rule or policy of their league. The third type of challenger is a new league trying to develop and maintain itself as a viable competitor to the established league. Whenever these parties are adversely affected by league policies or practices, they can strategically utilize the antitrust laws to advance their goals, principally by challenges brought under § 1 of the Sherman Act, which bars any "contract, combination, or conspiracy . . . in restraint of trade," and § 2, which condemns anyone who "monopolize[s] or attempt[s] to monopolize" a market.

1. SINGLE ENTITY DEFENSE

In this setting, a crucial legal issue that underlies all § 1 sports litigation within both the product and the labor markets is: Does a sports league consist of a collection of distinct and economically competitive clubs who have come together to cooperate in some aspects of otherwise autonomous businesses—akin to the joint venture created by MGM Hotels and GVC Holdings, an online gambling operator, to take advantage of legalized sports gambling? Or is a sports league more aptly treated as a single integrated entity, analogous to a national law firm with partners based in several cities, which is thus incapable of *conspiracy* in restraint of trade when it establishes its internal operating rules and structure?

The basic premises of the "single entity defense" are that (i) the league members jointly create the athletic product offered in the broader sports and entertainment market, and those members are inherently incapable of producing anything of value independently of their league; and (ii) while each team *competes athletically* on the field in order to produce an attractive league product, they *cooperate economically* as partners within a joint venture through which they jointly create and own the business assets of the league.

The doctrinal framework for that question was set forth by the Supreme Court in *Copperweld Corp. v. Independence Tube Corp.*, 467 U.S. 752 (1984). That case held a parent corporation incapable of conspiring for purposes of § 1 with its wholly-owned subsidiary, because "a parent and a wholly owned subsidiary *always* have a 'unity of purpose or a common design'" and because "the parent may assert full control at any moment if the subsidiary fails to act in the parent's best interests." The court suggested that single entity status turns on whether the defendants "represent a sudden joining of two independent sources of economic power" or instead derive their strength from a single source of economic power. *Id.* at 771, 774.

The Supreme Court largely resolved this issue in *American Needle, Inc. v. NFL*, 560 U.S. 183 (2010), with a determination that policies established by the NFL and the other club-run major leagues constitute horizontal agreements by the club owners and not the unilateral decision of a single entity, the league itself. How the law characterizes sports leagues remains both important and controversial, however, for a number of reasons.

First, sports leagues and those who defend their practices continue to express skepticism that legal treatment of sports league policies should turn on challenges by private parties before generalist judges and juries. *See, e.g.*, Gary Roberts, *The Single Entity Status of Sports Leagues Under Section 1 of the Sherman Act: An Alternative View*, 60 TULANE L. REV. 562 (1986). Leagues continue to seek creative ways to avoid Rule of Reason inquiry of their practices. Your own analysis of this question may depend in part how well you believe courts have analyzed the issues presented in Chapters 6–8. Second, cases requiring a judicial determination as to the structure of sports leagues are relevant to whether the club-run structure of sports leagues, which are evaluated in this section, may itself be anticompetitive and contrary to the public interest. Stephen F. Ross and Stefan Szymanski, FANS OF THE WORLD, UNITE! A (CAPITALIST) MANIFESTO FOR SPORTS CONSUMERS (Stanford Univ. Press 2008). Third, understanding the economic significance of the potential differences between club-run leagues and sporting competitions organized by unitary entities is important for any student of North American sports leagues. Fourth, focusing on the specific ways in which rules adopted by club owners in their own interests can diverge from the best interests of the league provides sports executives and their counsel with strategic opportunities to block, or evade, owner self-interest. Fifth, questions remain about how league decisions concerning assets controlled by the league itself, rather than member clubs (most notably intellectual property) should be evaluated after *American Needle.* Sixth, recent efforts—effective overseas—by private equity investors to provide significant cash in return for a long-term share of a league's profits may cause leagues to reconsider the traditional club-run model that *American Needle* holds is not a single-entity.

AMERICAN NEEDLE, INC. V. NFL
560 U.S. 183 (2010)

STEVENS, J., delivered the opinion for a unanimous Court.

"Every contract, combination in the form of a trust or otherwise, or, conspiracy, in restraint of trade" is made illegal by *§ 1* of the Sherman Act, ch. 647, 26 Stat. 209, as amended, *15 U.S.C. § 1.* The question whether an arrangement is a contract, combination, or conspiracy is different from and antecedent to the question whether it unreasonably restrains trade. This case raises that antecedent question about the business of the 32 teams in the National Football League (NFL) and a corporate entity that they formed to manage their intellectual property. We conclude that the NFL's licensing activities constitute concerted action that is not categorically beyond the coverage of *§ 1.* The legality of that concerted action must be judged under the Rule of Reason.

I

Originally organized in 1920, the NFL is an unincorporated association that now includes 32 separately owned professional football teams.[1] Each team has its own name, colors, and logo, and owns related

---

[1]   The NFL was founded in Canton, Ohio as the "American Professional Football Association." *United States Football League v. National Football League,* 842 F.2d 1335, 1343 (CA2

intellectual property. Like each of the other teams in the league, the New Orleans Saints and the Indianapolis Colts, for example, have their own distinctive names, colors, and marks that are well known to millions of sports fans.

Prior to 1963, the teams made their own arrangements for licensing their intellectual property and marketing trademarked items such as caps and jerseys. In 1963, the teams formed National Football League Properties (NFLP) to develop, license, and market their intellectual property. Most, but not all, of the substantial revenues generated by NFLP have either been given to charity or shared equally among the teams. However, the teams are able to and have at times sought to withdraw from this arrangement.

Between 1963 and 2000, NFLP granted nonexclusive licenses to a number of vendors, permitting them to manufacture and sell apparel bearing team insignias. Petitioner, American Needle, Inc., was one of those licensees. In December 2000, the teams voted to authorize NFLP to grant exclusive licenses, and NFLP granted Reebok International Ltd. an exclusive 10-year license to manufacture and sell trademarked headwear for all 32 teams. It thereafter declined to renew American Needle's nonexclusive license.

American Needle filed this action in the Northern District of Illinois, alleging that the agreements between the NFL, its teams, NFLP, and Reebok violated §§ 1 and 2 of the Sherman Act. In their answer to the complaint, the defendants averred that the teams, NFL, and NFLP were incapable of conspiring within the meaning of § 1 "because they are a single economic enterprise, at least with respect to the conduct challenged." After limited discovery, the District Court granted summary judgment on the question "whether, with regard to the facet of their operations respecting exploitation of intellectual property rights, the NFL and its 32 teams are, in the jargon of antitrust law, acting as a single entity." *American Needle, Inc. v. New Orleans La. Saints*, 496 F. Supp. 2d 941, 943 (2007). The court concluded "that in that facet of their operations they have so integrated their operations that they should be deemed a single entity rather than joint ventures cooperating for a common purpose." *Ibid.*

The Court of Appeals for the Seventh Circuit affirmed. The panel observed that "in some contexts, a league seems more aptly described as a single entity immune from antitrust scrutiny, while in others a league appears to be a joint venture between independently owned teams that is subject to review under § 1." 538 F.3d 736, 741 (2008). Relying on Circuit precedent, the court limited its inquiry to the particular conduct at issue, licensing of teams' intellectual property. The panel agreed with petitioner that "when making a single-entity determination, courts must examine

---

1988). It took its current name in 1922. *Ibid.* Forty-one franchises failed in the first forty-one years of the League's existence. *Ibid.*

whether the conduct in question deprives the marketplace of the independent sources of economic control that competition assumes." *Id.*, at 742. The court, however, discounted the significance of potential competition among the teams regarding the use of their intellectual property because the teams "can function only as one source of economic power when collectively producing NFL football." *Id.*, at 743. The court noted that football itself can only be carried out jointly. *See ibid.* ("Asserting that a single football team could produce a football game . . . is a Zen riddle: Who wins when a football team plays itself"). Moreover, "NFL teams share a vital economic interest in collectively promoting NFL football . . . [to] compet[e] with other forms of entertainment." *Ibid.* "It thus follows," the court found, "that only one source of economic power controls the promotion of NFL football," and "it makes little sense to assert that each individual team has the authority, if not the responsibility, to promote the jointly produced NFL football." *Ibid.* Recognizing that NFL teams have "license[d] their intellectual property collectively" since 1963, the court held that § 1 did not apply. *Id.*, at 744.

We granted certiorari.

II

As the case comes to us, we have only a narrow issue to decide: whether the NFL respondents are capable of engaging in a "contract, combination . . . , or conspiracy" as defined by § 1 of the Sherman Act, *15 U.S.C. § 1*, or, as we have sometimes phrased it, whether the alleged activity by the NFL respondents "must be viewed as that of a single enterprise for purposes of § 1." *Copperweld Corp. v. Independence Tube Corp.*, 467 U.S. 752, 771 (1984).

* * *

The meaning of the term "contract, combination . . . or conspiracy" is informed by the " 'basic distinction' " in the Sherman Act " 'between concerted and independent action' " that distinguishes § 1 of the Sherman Act from § 2. *Copperweld*, 467 U.S., at 767 (quoting *Monsanto Co. v. Spray-Rite Service Corp.*, 465 U.S. 752, 761 (1984)). Section 1 applies only to concerted action that restrains trade. *Section 2*, by contrast, covers both concerted and independent action, but only if that action "monopolize[s]," *15 U.S.C. § 2*, or "threatens actual monopolization," *Copperweld*, 467 U.S., at 767, a category that is narrower than restraint of trade. Monopoly power may be equally harmful whether it is the product of joint action or individual action.

Congress used this distinction between concerted and independent action to deter anticompetitive conduct and compensate its victims, without chilling vigorous competition through ordinary business operations. The distinction also avoids judicial scrutiny of routine, internal business decisions.

* * *

III

We have long held that concerted action under *§ 1* does not turn simply on whether the parties involved are legally distinct entities. Instead, we have eschewed such formalistic distinctions in favor of a functional consideration of how the parties involved in the alleged anticompetitive conduct actually operate.

As a result, we have repeatedly found instances in which members of a legally single entity violated § 1 when the entity was controlled by a group of competitors and served, in essence, as a vehicle for ongoing concerted activity. In *United States v. Sealy, Inc.*, 388 U.S. 350 (1967), for example, a group of mattress manufacturers operated and controlled Sealy, Inc., a company that licensed the Sealy trademark to the manufacturers, and dictated that each operate within a specific geographic area. *Id.*, at 352–353. The Government alleged that the licensees and Sealy were conspiring in violation of § 1, and we agreed. *Id.*, at 352–354. We explained that "[w]e seek the central substance of the situation" and therefore "we are moved by the identity of the persons who act, rather than the label of their hats." *Id.*, at 353. We thus held that Sealy was not a "separate entity, but . . . an instrumentality of the individual manufacturers." *Id.*, at 356. * * *

Conversely, there is not necessarily concerted action simply because more than one legally distinct entity is involved. Although, under a now-defunct doctrine known as the "intraenterprise conspiracy doctrine," we once treated cooperation between legally separate entities as necessarily covered by § 1, we now embark on a more functional analysis.

[The court retraced the defunct doctrine, culminating in *Copperweld*'s rejection of earlier precedents and holding that an agreement between a corporation and a wholly-owned subsidiary was not subject to § 1. Here, the court read *Copperweld* as focused on the fact that both parties were controlled by a single center of decisionmaking and they control a single aggregation of economic power.]

IV

As *Copperweld* exemplifies, "substance, not form, should determine whether a[n] . . . entity is capable of conspiring under *§ 1*." 467 U.S., at 773, n. 21. This inquiry is sometimes described as asking whether the alleged conspirators are a single entity. That is perhaps a misdescription, however, because the question is not whether the defendant is a legally single entity or has a single name; nor is the question whether the parties involved "seem" like one firm or multiple firms in any metaphysical sense. The key is whether the alleged "contract, combination . . . , or conspiracy" is concerted action—that is, whether it joins together separate decisionmakers. The relevant inquiry, therefore, is whether there is a "contract, combination ... or conspiracy" amongst "separate economic actors pursuing separate economic interests," *id.*, at 769, such that the agreement "deprives the marketplace of independent centers of decisionmaking," *ibid.*, and therefore of "diversity of entrepreneurial interests," *Fraser v. Major League Soccer, L.L.C.*, 284 F.3d 47, 57 (CA1 2002) (Boudin, C. J.), and thus of actual or potential competition, *see Freeman v. San Diego Assn. of Realtors*, 322 F.3d 1133, 1148–1149 (CA9 2003) (Kozinski, J.); *Rothery Storage & Van Co. v. Atlas Van Lines, Inc.*, 792 F.2d 210, 214–215 (CADC 1986) (Bork, J.); *see also* Areeda & Hovenkamp ¶ 1462b, at 193–194 (noting that the "central evil addressed by Sherman Act *§ 1*" is the "elimin[ation of] competition that would otherwise exist").

Thus, while the president and a vice president of a firm could (and regularly do) act in combination, their joint action generally is not the sort of "combination" that § 1 is intended to cover. Such agreements might be described as "really unilateral behavior flowing from decisions of a single enterprise." Copperweld, 467 U.S., at 767. Nor, for this reason, does § 1 cover "internally coordinated conduct of a corporation and one of its unincorporated divisions," *id.*, at 770, because "[a] division within a corporate structure pursues the common interests of the whole," *ibid.*, and therefore "coordination between a corporation and its division does not represent a sudden joining of two independent sources of economic power previously pursuing separate interests," *id.*, at 770–771. Nor, for the same reasons, is "the coordinated activity of a parent and its wholly owned subsidiary" covered. *See id.*, at 771. They "have a complete unity of interest" and thus "[w]ith or without a formal 'agreement,' the subsidiary acts for the benefit of the parent, its sole shareholder." *Ibid.*

Because the inquiry is one of competitive reality, it is not determinative that two parties to an alleged *§ 1* violation are legally distinct entities. Nor, however, is it determinative that two legally distinct entities have organized themselves under a single umbrella or into a structured joint venture. The question is whether the agreement joins together "independent centers of decisionmaking." *Id.*, at 769. If it does, the entities are capable of conspiring under *§ 1*, and the court must decide whether the restraint of trade is an unreasonable and therefore illegal one.

V

The NFL teams do not possess either the unitary decisionmaking quality or the single aggregation of economic power characteristic of independent action. Each of the teams is a substantial, independently owned, and independently managed business. "[T]heir general corporate actions are guided or determined" by "separate corporate consciousnesses," and "[t]heir objectives are" not "common." Copperweld, 467 U.S., at 771; *see also North American Soccer League v. NFL*, 670 F.2d 1249, 1252 (CA2 1982) (discussing ways that "the financial performance of each team, while related to that of the others, does not . . . necessarily rise and fall with that of the others"). The teams compete with one another, not only on the playing field, but to attract fans, for gate receipts and for contracts with managerial and playing personnel. *See Brown v. Pro Football, Inc.*, 518 U.S. 231, 249 (1996); *Sullivan v. NFL*, 34 F.3d 1091, 1098 (CA1 1994); *Mid-South Grizzlies v. NFL*, 720 F.2d 772, 787 (CA3 1983); cf. *NCAA*, 468 U.S., at 99.

Directly relevant to this case, the teams compete in the market for intellectual property. To a firm making hats, the Saints and the Colts are two potentially competing suppliers of valuable trademarks. When each NFL team licenses its intellectual property, it is not pursuing the "common interests of the whole" league but is instead pursuing interests of each "corporation itself," *Copperweld*, 467 U.S., at 770; teams are acting as "separate economic actors pursuing separate economic interests," and each team therefore is a potential "independent cente[r] of decisionmaking," *id.*, at 769. Decisions by NFL teams to license their separately owned trademarks collectively and to only one vendor are decisions that "depriv[e] the marketplace of independent centers of decisionmaking," *ibid.*, and therefore of actual or potential competition. *See NCAA*, 468 U.S. at 109, n. 39 (observing a possible § 1 violation if two separately owned companies sold their separate products through a "single selling agent"); *cf.* Areeda & Hovenkamp ¶ 1478a, at 318 ("Obviously, the most significant competitive threats arise when joint venture participants are actual or potential competitors").

In defense, respondents argue that by forming NFLP, they have formed a single entity, akin to a merger, and market their NFL brands through a single outlet. But it is not dispositive that the teams have organized and own a legally separate entity that centralizes the management of their intellectual property. An ongoing § 1 violation cannot evade § 1 scrutiny simply by giving the ongoing violation a name and label. "Perhaps every agreement and combination in restraint of trade could be so labeled." *Timken Roller Bearing Co. v. United States*, 341 U.S. 593, 598 (1951).

The NFL respondents may be similar in some sense to a single enterprise that owns several pieces of intellectual property and licenses them jointly, but they are not similar in the relevant functional sense. Although NFL teams have common interests such as promoting the NFL brand, they are still separate, profit-maximizing entities, and their interests in licensing team trademarks are not necessarily aligned. *See generally* Hovenkamp, *Exclusive Joint Ventures and Antitrust Policy*, 1995 Colum. Bus. L. Rev. 1, 52–61 (1995); Shishido, *Conflicts of Interest and Fiduciary Duties in the Operation of a Joint Venture*, 39 Hastings L.J. 63, 69–81 (1987). Common interests in the NFL brand "*partially* unit[e] the economic interests of the parent firms," Broadley, *Joint Ventures and*

Antitrust Policy, 95 Harv. L. Rev. 1521, 1526 (1982) (emphasis added), but the teams still have distinct, potentially competing interests.

It may be, as respondents argue, that NFLP "has served as the 'single driver' of the teams" "promotional vehicle," " 'pursu[ing] the common interests of the whole.'" Brief for NFL Respondents 28 (quoting Copperweld, 467 U.S., at 770–771; brackets in original). But illegal restraints often are in the common interests of the parties to the restraint, at the expense of those who are not parties. It is true, as respondents describe, that they have for some time marketed their trademarks jointly. But a history of concerted activity does not immunize conduct from § 1 scrutiny. "Absence of actual competition may simply be a manifestation of the anticompetitive agreement itself." *Freeman*, 322 F.3d at 1149.

Respondents argue that nonetheless, as the Court of Appeals held, they constitute a single entity because without their cooperation, there would be no NFL football. It is true that "the clubs that make up a professional sports league are not completely independent economic competitors, as they depend upon a degree of cooperation for economic survival." *Brown*, 518 U.S., at 248. But the Court of Appeals' reasoning is unpersuasive.

The justification for cooperation is not relevant to whether that cooperation is concerted or independent action. A "contract, combination . . . or conspiracy," § 1, that is necessary or useful to a joint venture is still a "contract, combination . . . or conspiracy" if it "deprives the marketplace of independent centers of decisionmaking," *Copperweld*, 467 U.S., at 769. *See NCAA*, 468 U.S., at 113 ("[J]oint ventures have no immunity from antitrust laws"). Any joint venture involves multiple sources of economic power cooperating to produce a product. And for many such ventures, the participation of others is necessary. But that does not mean that necessity of cooperation transforms concerted action into independent action; a nut and a bolt can only operate together, but an agreement between nut and bolt manufacturers is still subject to § 1 analysis. Nor does it mean that once a group of firms agree to produce a joint product, cooperation amongst those firms must be treated as independent conduct. The mere fact that the teams operate jointly in some sense does not mean that they are immune.[7]

---

[7]   In any event, it simply is not apparent that the alleged conduct was necessary at all. Although two teams are needed to play a football game, not all aspects of elaborate interleague cooperation are necessary to produce a game. Moreover, even if leaguewide agreements are necessary to produce football, it does not follow that concerted activity in marketing intellectual property is necessary to produce football.

The Court of Appeals carved out a zone of antitrust immunity for conduct arguably related to league operations by reasoning that coordinated team trademark sales are necessary to produce "NFL football," a single NFL brand that competes against other forms of entertainment. But defining the product as "NFL football" puts the cart before the horse: Of course the NFL produces NFL football; but that does not mean that cooperation amongst NFL teams is immune from § 1 scrutiny. Members of any cartel could insist that their cooperation is necessary to produce the "cartel product" and compete with other products.

The question whether NFLP decisions can constitute concerted activity covered by § 1 is closer than whether decisions made directly by the 32 teams are covered by § 1. This is so both because NFLP is a separate corporation with its own management and because the record indicates that most of the revenues generated by NFLP are shared by the teams on an equal basis. Nevertheless we think it clear that for the same reasons the 32 teams' conduct is covered by § 1, NFLP's actions also are subject to § 1, at least with regards to its marketing of property owned by the separate teams. NFLP's licensing decisions are made by the 32 potential competitors, and each of them actually owns its share of the jointly managed assets. *Cf. Sealy*, 388 U.S., at 352–354. Apart from their agreement to cooperate in exploiting those assets, including their decisions as the NFLP, there would be nothing to prevent each of the teams from making its own market decisions relating to purchases of apparel and headwear, to the sale of such items, and to the granting of licenses to use its trademarks.

We generally treat agreements within a single firm as independent action on the presumption that the components of the firm will act to maximize the firm's profits. But in rare cases, that presumption does not hold. Agreements made within a firm can constitute concerted action covered by *§ 1* when the parties to the agreement act on interests separate from those of the firm itself, and the intrafirm agreements may simply be a formalistic shell for ongoing concerted action. *See, e.g., Topco Associates, Inc.*, 405 U.S., at 609; *Sealy*, 388 U.S., at 352–354.

For that reason, decisions by the NFLP regarding the teams' separately owned intellectual property constitute concerted action. Thirty-two teams operating independently through the vehicle of the NFLP are not like the components of a single firm that act to maximize the firm's profits. The teams remain separately controlled, potential competitors with economic interests that are distinct from NFLP's financial well-being. *See generally* Hovenkamp, 1995 Colum. Bus. L. Rev., at 52–61. Unlike typical decisions by corporate shareholders, NFLP licensing decisions effectively require the assent of more than a mere majority of shareholders. And each team's decision reflects not only an interest in NFLP's profits but also an interest in the team's individual profits. *See generally* Shusido, 39 Hastings L.J., at 69–71. The 32 teams capture individual economic benefits separate and apart from NFLP profits as a result of the decisions they make for the NFLP. NFLP's decisions thus affect each team's profits from licensing its own intellectual property. "Although the business interests of" the teams "will *often* coincide with those of the" NFLP "as an entity in itself, that commonality of interest exists in every cartel." *Los Angeles Memorial Coliseum Comm'n v. NFL*, 726 F.2d 1381, 1389 (CA9 1984) (emphasis added). In making the relevant licensing decisions, NFLP is therefore "an instrumentality" of the teams. *Sealy*, 388 U.S., at 352–354; *see also Topco Associates, Inc.*, 405 U.S., at 609.

If the fact that potential competitors shared in profits or losses from a venture meant that the venture was immune from § 1, then any cartel "could evade the antitrust law simply by creating a 'joint venture' to serve as the exclusive seller of their competing products." *Major League Baseball Properties, Inc. v. Salvino, Inc.*, 542 F.3d 290, 335 (CA2 2008) (Sotomayor, J., concurring in judgment). "So long as no agreement," other than one made by the cartelists sitting on the board of the joint venture, "explicitly listed the prices to be charged, the companies could act as monopolies through the 'joint venture.'" *Ibid.* (Indeed, a joint venture with a single management structure is generally a better way to operate a cartel because it decreases the risks of a party to an illegal agreement defecting from that agreement). However, competitors "cannot simply get around" antitrust liability by acting "through a third-party intermediary or 'joint venture'." *Id.* at 336.[9]

VI

Football teams that need to cooperate are not trapped by antitrust law. "[T]he special characteristics of this industry may provide a justification" for many kinds of agreements. *Brown*, 518 U.S., at 252 (STEVENS, J., dissenting). The fact that NFL teams share an interest in making the entire league successful and profitable, and that they must cooperate in the production and scheduling of games, provides a perfectly sensible justification for making a host of collective decisions. But the conduct at issue in this case is still concerted activity under the Sherman Act that is subject to § 1 analysis.

When "restraints on competition are essential if the product is to be available at all," *per se* rules of illegality are inapplicable, and instead the restraint must be judged according to the flexible Rule of Reason. *NCAA*, 468 U.S., at 101; *see id.*, at 117 ("Our decision not to apply a *per se* rule to this case rests in large part on our recognition that a certain degree of cooperation is necessary if the type of competition that petitioner and its member institutions seek to market is to be preserved"); *see also Dagher*, 547 U.S., at 6. In such instances, the agreement is likely to survive the Rule of Reason. *See Broadcast Music, Inc. v. Columbia Broadcasting System*,

---

[9]   For the purposes of resolving this case, there is no need to pass upon the Government's position that entities are incapable of conspiring under § 1 if they "have effectively merged the relevant aspect of their operations, thereby eliminating actual and potential competition . . . in that operational sphere" and "the challenged restraint [does] not significantly affect actual or potential competition . . . outside their merged operations." Brief for United States as *Amicus Curiae* 17. The Government urges that the choices "to offer only a blanket license" and "to have only a single headwear licensee" might not constitute concerted action under its test. *Id.* at 32. However, because the teams still own their own trademarks and are free to market those trademarks as they see fit, even those two choices were agreements amongst potential competitors and would constitute concerted action under the Government's own standard. At any point, the teams could decide to license their own trademarks. It is significant, moreover, that the teams here control NFLP. The two choices that the Government might treat as independent action, although nominally made by NFLP, are for all functional purposes choices made by the 32 entities with potentially competing interests.

Inc., 441 U.S. 1, 23 (1979) ("Joint ventures and other cooperative arrangements are also not usually unlawful . . . where the agreement . . . is necessary to market the product at all"). And depending upon the concerted activity in question, the Rule of Reason may not require a detailed analysis; it "can sometimes be applied in the twinkling of an eye." *NCAA*, 468 U.S., at 109, n. 39.

Other features of the NFL may also save agreements amongst the teams. We have recognized, for example, "that the interest in maintaining a competitive balance" among "athletic teams is legitimate and important," *NCAA*, 468 U.S., at 117. While that same interest applies to the teams in the NFL, it does not justify treating them as a single entity for *§ 1* purposes when it comes to the marketing of the teams' individually owned intellectual property. It is, however, unquestionably an interest that may well justify a variety of collective decisions made by the teams. What role it properly plays in applying the Rule of Reason to the allegations in this case is a matter to be considered on remand.

* * *

Accordingly, the judgment of the Court of Appeals is reversed, and the case is remanded for further proceedings consistent with this opinion.

It is so ordered.

<hr>

NOTES AND QUESTIONS

1. *Distinguishing* Copperweld. The Court rejected the NFL's argument that decisions by a sports league like the NFL are akin to decisions by a parent corporation vis-a-vis a subsidiary (the holding of *Copperweld*). Precisely what is it about the NFL's structure that resulted in this distinction? If the NFL were so inclined, what could it do to restructure the league in order to meet the requirements for single entity status set forth in *American Needle*?

2. *League Intellectual Property. American Needle* involved collective decisions concerning intellectual property that the member clubs each independently initially owned and developed. What about intellectual property that has always been owned and developed by the league as a whole (for example, licensing decisions concerning the NFL's famous shield)? Should it be relevant whether there is any potential conflict between the owners' interests in maximizing return on league properties and their own club interests? If the NFL owners grant a license for the shield exclusively to Anheuser-Busch for beer marketing purposes, should it matter whether some owners would prefer to allow clubs to use the shield for club beer sponsors?

In *Washington v. NFL*, 880 F. Supp. 2d 1004 (D. Minn. 2012), the district court dismissed an antitrust challenge to the NFL's refusal to either compensate players for their name, image, and likeness rights in game films used to promote the league, or to allow players to use the film for games in which they played. Invoking the single entity theory, the *Washington* court viewed *American Needle* as limited to its facts: "that teams in the NFL could not be treated as a single entity under the Sherman Act 'when it comes to the marketing of the teams' individually owned intellectual property.' " *Id.* at 1006, *citing* 560 U.S. at 204. The district court reasoned that, unlike team logos and colors, "historical football game footage, something that the individual teams do not separately own, and never have separately owned," is something that clubs "must cooperate to produce and sell . . . ; no one entity can do it alone." *Id.*

3. *Precise Antitrust Concerns That Warrant § 1 Scrutiny of Sports League Decisions.* In allowing the North American Soccer League to proceed with an antitrust challenge to a threatened NFL rule barring football owners from also owning soccer clubs, the Second Circuit reversed the trial court's embrace of the single entity defense, reasoning that the single entity defense was a "loophole" that would

> permit league members to escape antitrust responsibility for any restraint entered into by them that would benefit their league or enhance their ability to compete even though the benefit would be outweighed by its anticompetitive effects. Moreover, the restraint might be one adopted more for the protection of individual league members from competition than to help the league. . . . The sound and more just procedure is to judge the legality of such restraints according to well-recognized standards of our antitrust laws rather than permit their exemption on the ground that since they in some measure strengthen the league competitively as a "single economic entity," the combination's anticompetitive effects must be disregarded.

NASL v. NFL, 670 F.2d 1249, 1257 (2d Cir. 1982).

Is it a legitimate concern under Sherman Act § 1 that the NFL might adopt policies that "would benefit their league or enhance their ability to compete even though the benefit would be outweighed by its anticompetitive effects?" The court also suggested that the policy "might be one adopted more for the protection of individual league members from competition than to help the league," noting that the policy was the result of pressure from Minnesota Vikings and Philadelphia Eagles owners, whose clubs were facing substantial competition from NASL teams in their home cities. Do you agree that the last concern should have influenced the court?

4. *Are Rival Clubs Economic as Well as Sporting Competitors?* Justice Rehnquist dissented from the denial of certiorari in *NASL v. NFL.* He argued:

> The NFL owners are joint venturers who produce a product, professional football, which competes with other sports and other forms of entertainment in the entertainment market. Although individual NFL teams compete with one another on the playing field, they rarely compete in the marketplace. The NFL negotiates its television contracts, for example, in a single block. The revenues from

broadcast rights are pooled. Indeed, the only interteam competition occurs when two teams are located in one major city, such as New York or Los Angeles. These teams compete with one another for home game attendance and local broadcast revenues. In all other respects, the league competes as a unit against other forms of entertainment.

This arrangement, like the arrangement in *Broadcast Music, Inc. v. Columbia Broadcasting System, Inc.*, 441 U.S. 1 (1979), is largely a matter of necessity. If the teams were entirely independent, there could be no consistency of staffing, rules, equipment, or training. All of these are at least arguably necessary to permit the league to create an appealing product in the entertainment market. Thus, NFL football is a different product from what the NFL teams could offer independently, and the NFL, like ASCAP, is "not really a joint sales agency offering the individual goods of many sellers, but is a separate seller offering its [product], of which the individual [teams] are raw material. [The NFL], in short, made a market in which individual [teams] are inherently unable to compete fully effectively."

The cross-ownership rule, then, is a covenant by joint venturers who produce a single product not to compete with one another. The rule governing such agreements was set out over 80 years ago by Judge (later Chief Justice) Taft: A covenant not to compete is valid if "it is merely ancillary to the main purpose of a lawful contract, and necessary to protect the covenantee in the enjoyment of the legitimate fruits of the contract, or to protect him from the dangers of an unjust use of those fruits by the other party." *United States v. Addyston Pipe and Steel Co.*, 85 F. 271, 281 (6th Cir. 1898), *aff'd as modified*, 175 U.S. 211 (1899).

The cross-ownership rule seems to me to meet this test. Its purposes are to minimize disputes among the owners and to prevent some owners from using the benefits of their association with the joint venture to compete against it. Participation in the league gives the owner the benefit of detailed knowledge about market conditions for professional sports, the strength and weaknesses of the other teams in the league, and the methods his co-venturers use to compete in the marketplace. It is only reasonable that the owners would seek to prevent their fellows from giving these significant assets, which are in some respects analogous to trade secrets, to their competitors.

. . .

. . . it seems to me that the cross-ownership rule was narrowly drawn to vindicate the legitimate interests described above. The owners are limited only in areas where the special knowledge and skills provided by their co-owners can be expected to be of significant value. They are not prohibited from competing with the NFL in areas of the entertainment market other than professional sports. An owner may invest in television movies, rock concerts, plays, or anything else that suits his fancy.

NFL v. NASL, 459 U.S. 1074, 1077–80 (1982). Do you agree with Justice Rehnquist's analysis? Is the extensive cooperation he catalogued in the first paragraph, like the blanket license in *Broadcast Music*, necessary to produce the product? Is the cross-ownership rule narrowly tailored?

Dissenting in *Los Angeles Memorial Coliseum Comm'n v. NFL (Raiders I)*, 726 F.2d 1381 (9th Cir. 1984) (affirming antitrust liability, discussed further in Chapter 8), Judge Spencer Williams would have declined to review under Sherman Act § 1 an agreement among owners to bar the Oakland Raiders from relocating to Los Angeles. The majority emphasized that according to the NFL Constitution, the league's purpose was to "promote and foster the primary business of" the individual clubs. *Id.* at 1389. Judge Williams argued that:

> The NFL cannot truly be separated from its member clubs, which are simultaneously franchisees and franchisors. The Raiders did not, and do not now, seek to compete with the other clubs in any sense other than in their win/loss standings; they do not challenge the plethora of other ancillary regulations attendant to the league structure, including the draft, regulation and scheduling of meetings between teams, and the system of pooled and shared revenues among the clubs because they wish to remain within its beneficial ambit.
>
> . . .
>
> In the case of the member clubs, this "downstream output" is professional football, and the organ of regulation is the unincorporated, not-for-profit, association commonly known as the NFL. There is virtually no practical distinction between the League, administered by the appointed Commissioner, per se and the member clubs; the NFL represents to all clubs, including the Raiders, the least costly and most efficient manner of reaching day-to-day decisions regarding the production of their main, and collectively produced, product.
>
> [The NFL decisions challenged here were decided by a committee of club representatives, who necessarily are] acting in other than the collective interests of the member clubs, since by definition, that body's decisions are the consensus of NFL members. There is no distinct interest of the NFL, since it exists solely to coordinate the members' participation in the joint production of professional football.

Id. at 1405–06. Do you agree with Justice Rehnquist and Judge Williams that clubs do not compete in the marketplace? With Judge Williams' claim that there is no difference between the interests of the league and the interests of the clubs?

5.   *What's the Harm in Subjecting Sports Leagues to the Rule of Reason?* In his *Raiders I* dissent, Judge Williams also argued that "extreme caution is

warranted in defining precisely what competitive units exist in the marketplace. It is equally as important to permit collaboration and concerted action among branches of a single economic entity in the marketplace with impunity from the Sherman Act § 1, as it is to police conspiracies between economic competitive entities." 726 F. 2d at 1403–04. Do you agree with Judge Williams's concern that subjecting internal NFL rules to § 1's Rule of Reason effectively prevents enforcement of collective decisions over the dissent of one club member? That without the ability to engage in unfettered collaboration, the NFL will be unable (or unwilling out of fear of an unpredictable adverse antitrust ruling) to control free-riding or take advantage of economies of scale?

6. *Legislative Support for Sports Leagues Avoidance of Rule of Reason Scrutiny.* Chapter 5 traced the origins of the antitrust exemption that the Supreme Court created for baseball. After the Supreme Court had declared it would not extend the exemption to other sports in *Radovich v. NFL*, 352 U.S. 445 (1957), Congress turned its attention in earnest to the question. The House Judiciary Committee reported legislation that would explicitly apply the antitrust laws to all sports, but it created an exemption for agreements that were "reasonably necessary" to (1) the equalization of competitive playing teams, (2) the right to operate in exclusive geographic territories, (3) the preservation of public confidence in the integrity of sports contests, and (4) the regulation of broadcasting rights. H. Rep. 1720, 85th Cong. 2d Sess. (1958). On the House floor, dissenting members of the Judiciary Committee proposed a substitute amendment that would grant an absolute exemption for any rules "relating to" the player draft, the reserve clause, exclusive territories, and actions taken to preserve confidence in the honesty of sports. The amendment's supporters argued that "the present bill would force organized professional team sports to run a gauntlet of legal proceedings to save themselves from complete ruin." *Id.* at 10. They claimed that the bill was "an open invitation to every disgruntled player to litigate the fine points of the game in courts throughout the land." *Id.* at 11. The committee chair, Rep. Emanuel Celler of New York, complained that in his many years in Congress, "I have never seen more pressure exerted upon Members than during the last week, pressure directed from the headquarters of the high commissioner of baseball and his counsel." 104 Cong. Rec. 12075 (1958). However, one of the amendment's proponents responded: "Can anyone say with conviction that there is reason for foisting upon the already overburdened courts of this land an ill-suited role as arbiters of disputes within the sports family?" *Id.* at 12085 (remarks of Rep. Keating). The amendment passed the House by a voice vote, although the bill later died in the Senate. Do you think the majority that prevailed in the House of Representatives in 1958 was correct?

7. *Is Revenue Sharing Relevant to the Single Entity Question?* To what extent are the actual interests of clubs within a league unified or disparate? Inherently ordained or voluntarily negotiated? Does the degree of unity depend on the league's tradition, culture, and leadership? Compare, for example, baseball under Judge Landis in the 1920s and 1930s with baseball under Bud Selig in the 1990s. Does it depend on the degree of revenue sharing among the clubs in the league? Should the NFL clubs, which share about 60% of total

football revenue according to league-determined formulas, be deemed a different "entity" than the NHL, where less than 10% of revenues are shared? *See* Scott E. Atkinson, Linda R. Stanley & John Tschirhart, *Revenue Sharing as an Incentive in an Agency. Problem: An Example from the National Football League*, 19 RAND J. ECON. 27 (1988).

8. *Are Decisions by NFL Owners Analogous to Decisions by the Board of Directors of General Motors?* Do member clubs of a sports league compete with each other like independent oil companies or auto manufacturers, or like divisions of a single corporation (like General Motors with its various largely autonomous divisions) in which each division's economic rewards are based on its varying performance? In an opinion concerning restrictions on club broadcast rights discussed below in Chapter 8, *Chicago Professional Sports Ltd. Partnership & WGN v. NBA,* 95 F.3d 593 (7th Cir. 1996) (Bulls II), Judge Frank Easterbrook opined that decisions by the owners comprising the NBA Board of Governors were analogous to those of a corporate board of directors. He noted that "antitrust law permits, indeed encourages, cooperation inside a business organization the better to facilitate competition between that organization and other producers." *Id.* at 597–98.

Judge Easterbrook scolded the district court for rejecting the corporate analogy, based on the lower court's "quite narrow" reading of *Copperweld* as applying only because the parent and subsidiary have a 'complete unity of interest' " (quoting from 467 U.S. at 771).

> As a proposition of law, it would be silly. Even a single firm contains many competing interests. One division may make inputs for another's finished goods. The first division might want to sell its products directly to the market, to maximize income (and thus the salary and bonus of the division's managers); the second division might want to get its inputs from the first at a low transfer price, which would maximize the second division's paper profits. . . .

95 F.3d at 598.

Judge Richard Cudahy dissented from this analysis. He focused on whether "individual teams have some chance of economic gain at the expense of the league." *Id.* at 602. He noted that joint ventures, as opposed to single firms, warrant antitrust scrutiny

> for at least two reasons—(1) the venture could possess market power with respect to the jointly produced product (essentially act like a single firm with monopoly power) or (2) the fact that the venturers remain competitors in other arenas might either distort the way the joint product is managed or allow the venturers to use the joint product as a smokescreen behind which to cut deals to reduce competition in the other arenas.
>
> . . .
>
> There is potential for inefficient decisionmaking regarding the joint product of "league basketball" even when the individual teams

> engage in no economic activity outside of the league. This potential
> arises because the structure of the league is such that all "owners" of
> the league must be "owners" of individual teams and decisions are
> made by a vote of the teams. This means that the league will not
> necessarily make efficient decisions about the number of teams
> fielded or, more generally, the competitive balance among teams.
> Thus, the fact that several teams are required to make a league does
> not necessarily imply that the current makeup of the league is the
> most desirable or "efficient" one.

Id. at 602–03. Specifically, Judge Cudahy noted that because broadcast revenues are distributed unequally to clubs (each club receives more for their own locally-licensed games), a conflicting economic interest between league and clubs existed.

Is it relevant whether the internal disputes are resolved by those with a fiduciary duty to the league as a whole?

9.   *Relevance of the League's Structure of Governance. American Needle* focused on the decision-making structure of NFL Properties, a separately incorporated for-profit corporation; all major decisions are made by the 32 club owners who were equal shareholders in the corporation. Justice Stevens emphasized that "each team's decision reflects not only an interest in NFLP's profits but also an interest in the team's individual profits." Judge Cudahy, in his *Bulls II* opinion, articulated this point in more detail:

> The analogy, within the context of an ordinary firm, is to allow the
> salespeople to vote on the bonuses each is to get. Each salesperson
> has some incentive, of course, to promote the overall efficiency of the
> firm on which his or her salary, or perhaps the value of his or her firm
> stock, depends and therefore to award the larger bonuses to the most
> productive salespersons. However, in this scenario each salesperson
> has two ways of maximizing personal wealth—increasing the overall
> efficiency of the firm and redistributing income within the firm. The
> result of the vote might not be to distribute bonuses in the most
> efficient fashion. The potential for this type of inefficiency is
> particularly great when, as with the NBA, the league is "the only
> game in town" so that a team does not have the option of going
> elsewhere if it is not receiving revenues commensurate with its
> contribution to the overall league product. In any event, a group of
> team owners who do not share all revenues from all games might well
> make decisions that do not maximize the profit of the league as a
> whole.

Id. at 604–05.

a.   Compare NFL Rule 4.3, barring the Raiders from relocating to Los Angeles, with a policy of McDonald's Corporation regulating a franchisee's ability to move to another location. Consider the economic incentives of those individuals who decide where the Raiders might be located, and whether they are the same as the incentives of those individuals who decide where a branch of a multi-outlet company might be located.

b.   How would this affect antitrust scrutiny of Major League Baseball Advanced Media, a formally separate business entity that is controlled by a Board of Directors including a representative of the Commissioner's office and a number of owners? Is it relevant that these owners are charged, in adopting MLBAM rules, with a fiduciary duty to all "shareholders" (the rest of the owners)?

10.   *Judicial Recognition of Single-Entity Sports Defendants.* Some sports industry actors have successfully asserted that their decisions reflect those of a single economic entity and not an agreement among stakeholders. *See, e.g., Top Rank, Inc. v. Haymon,* 2015–2 Trade Reg. Rep. (CCH) ¶ 79,332 (C.D. Cal. Sept 17, 2015) (investors and boxing promoters were a "single enterprise" with "a complete unity of economic interest in the venture's success"); *Elite Rodeo Ass'n v. Prof'l Rodeo Cowboys Ass'n,* 159 F. Supp. 3d 738 (N.D. Tex. 2016) (defendant's board of directors had a single interest where only a small number of board members had any conflicting interests).

2.   ALTERNATIVE LEAGUE STRUCTURES

Sports fans might think that leagues can be run only collectively by member teams, because that is how the first league in the world (baseball's National League) was organized in 1876. But oldest doesn't necessarily mean best and certainly doesn't mean only. As noted in Ross and Szymanski, *supra,* at 70–71:

> The concept that an independent competition organizer [may be] more efficient has not been dreamed up by us in the pristine confines of ivory-tower academia. In developing ... NASCAR, impresario Bill France Sr. recognized, according to one observer, that to achieve success, "it would require a central racing organization whose authority outranked all drivers, car owners, and track owners." Indeed, from the early chaotic conditions of independently-owned race tracks setting different rules with no league competition, NASCAR developed into a national sport in large part because an independent entrepreneur was able to identify the best locations for racing, establish complex rules designed to produce close races with cars perceived to be similar to those driven by fans, and determine the appropriate economic rewards that would attract the best drivers, engineers and crews.

Over the years, a variety of other leagues have used different structures, in some cases to achieve efficiencies, while others seemed primarily designed with the goal of insulating the league against antitrust liability. The American Basketball League, a women's professional league that eventually lost out to the WNBA, organized itself as a pure single limited liability company that owned all of the teams and employed everyone involved from franchise executives to coaches to players. The WNBA itself was structured differently, operated by a Board of Directors of four owners with WNBA teams, four owners with no WNBA clubs, and the Commissioner's designee.

Consider the following international example from the sport of cricket. For decades, the only significant form of professional cricket featured contests between representative teams from different countries. (Imagine baseball without MLB and only the World Baseball Classic and other similar tournaments!) A proposal for a new international club competition, where privately owned franchises featuring the best players from around the world would compete, was blocked by the International Cricket Council (ICC), ostensibly because it was contrary to the self-interest of the national governing boards that controlled the ICC. Likewise, the English Cricket Board for decades blocked a new English club competition, ostensibly because it harmed the interest of county cricket clubs that were heavily subsidized to sponsor "minor league" cricket competitions between English players that attract few fans. However, when a rival organization threatened to start such a club competition in India, the Board of Control for Cricket in India (BCCI) acted quickly to overcome the sort of objections prevailing at the highest levels of international and English cricket, setting up the new Indian Premier League (IPL). This illustrates an aspect of monopoly power that is often overlooked: the effect of transactions costs when business initiatives that do not face vigorous competition require collaboration.

Faced with a credible threat from a rival league, the BCCI proceeded quickly to authorize a new cricket league structured more like NASCAR than the NFL. The BCCI appointed a five-member Board of Directors that controls the new IPL, rather than being controlled by the franchises. The league initially awarded eight franchises based on a competitive bidding process, subject to terms devised by BCCI. Contracts for franchises in a league with a relatively short season (14 games plus a playoff, over a two-month period) attracted lucrative bids, the largest one for US$117m for the Mumbai franchise. Most significantly, these highly attractive franchises were offered on terms that most North American club owners claim to be intolerable: (i) open bidding for prized locations; (ii) participation subject to rules set by someone else; (iii) clubs guaranteed a fixed and decreasing percentage of league-wide revenues based on a revenue sharing formula devised by independent board; (iv) an initial salary cap for the first year subject to change by the BCCI-controlled Board, not the club owners.

FRASER V. MAJOR LEAGUE SOCCER
284 F.3d 47 (1st Cir. 2002)

[The substantive issues relating to the league's labor policies are discussed in Chapter 7. MLS was originally designed to establish a single-entity defense against any challenge under § 1 of the Sherman Act. Rather than have each team owned by separate persons, MLS was established as a Delaware limited-liability company that would itself own and operate all the teams around the country. However, organizers came to realize that there were few, if any, wealthy sports fans prepared to put up the initial $5 million investment, plus take on the additional risk of significant start-up costs, just to be faceless investors in a league venture whose visible figures would all be in the MLS head office. Thus, MLS sold a separate special class of stock to each of its "investor-operators" who received almost full operating control over the teams in their areas. Club revenue was split 50–50 with the league, with the "investor" choosing front office and player personnel, where the games would be played, and what prices would be charged for tickets, local broadcasts, merchandise, and the like. Broadcast and national merchandising revenues were retained by the league, which used the money to pay each team's player salaries as well as league expenses, and then distributed any profits or dividends to the MLS shareholders. The special stock owned by investor-operators could be resold, allowing club owners to reap all the capital gain (or loss) that flowed out of their team's performance on the field as well as off it. MLS, like other sports leagues, is now run by those who have a substantial economic investment in "their" club, more than their investment in the league. The decision was written by the former Deputy Assistant Attorney General of the Antitrust Division.]

BOUDIN, CHIEF JUDGE:

* * *

At issue in this case is MLS's control over player employment. MLS has the "sole responsibility for negotiating and entering into agreements with, and for compensating, Players." In a nutshell, MLS recruits the players, negotiates their salaries, pays them from league funds, and, to a large extent, determines where each of them will play. For example, to balance talent among teams, it decides, with the non-binding input of team operators, where certain of the league's "marquee" players will play.

* * *

The league began official play in 1996. The following February of 1997, eight named players sued MLS, the USSF [the national governing board], and the operator/investors under various antitrust theories. . . . In count I, the players claimed MLS and its operator/investors violated Sherman Act section 1 by agreeing not to compete for player services. . . .

* * *

If ordinary investors decided to set up a company that would own and manage all of the teams in a league, it is hard to see why this arrangement would fall outside *Copperweld*'s safe harbor. Certainly the potential for competition within the firm is not enough: after all, a railroad could in theory provide alternative routes between the same cities and a grocery could locate competing branches of its chain quite near one another; yet no law requires competition within a company. It is common practice, but hardly essential, that the teams in a sports league have independent owner/managers.

* * *

Nevertheless, it is hard to treat the corporate integration as conclusive. The challenge here is primarily to the operator/investors' role as team managers, not as ordinary stockholders, and to restrictions imposed on them in that role preventing competition for player services. That a stockholder may be insulated by *Copperweld* when making ordinary governance decisions does not mean automatic protection when the stockholder is also an entrepreneur separately contracting with the company. Above all, there are functional differences between this case and *Copperweld* that are significant for antitrust policy.

First, there is a diversity of entrepreneurial interests that goes well beyond the ordinary company. MLS and its operator/investors have separate contractual relationships giving the operator/investors rights that take them part way along the path to ordinary sports team owners: they do some independent hiring and make out-of-pocket investments in their own teams; they retain a large portion of the revenues from the activities of their teams; and each has limited sale rights in its own team that relate to specific assets and not just shares in the common enterprise. One might well ask why the formal difference in corporate structure should warrant treating MLS differently than the National Football League or other traditionally structured sports leagues.

This contrasts with *Copperweld's* observation that the parent and its wholly owned subsidiary in that case shared a "complete unity of interests." 467 U.S. at 771. . . . the existence of distinct entrepreneurial interests possessed by separate legal entities distinguishes Copperweld; it further indicates that certain functions have already been disaggregated and assigned to different entities; and it makes the potential for actual competition closer to feasible realization.

Second, in this case the analogy to a single entity is weakened, and the resemblance to a collaborative venture strengthened, by the fact that the operator/investors are not mere servants of MLS; effectively, they control it, having the majority of votes on the managing board. The problem is especially serious where, as here, the stockholders are themselves potential competitors with MLS and with each other. Here, it is MLS that has two roles: one as an entrepreneur with its own assets and revenues; the other (arguably) as a nominally vertical device for producing horizontal coordination, i.e., limiting competition among operator/investors.

From the standpoint of antitrust policy, this prospect of horizontal coordination among the operator/investors through a common entity is a distinct concern. Whatever efficiencies may be thought likely where a single entrepreneur makes decisions for a corporate entity (or set of connected entities), the presumption is relaxed—and may in some contexts be reversed—where separate entrepreneurial interests can collaborate; the fixing of above market prices by sellers is the paradigm. This does not make MLS a mere front for price fixing, but it does distinguish *Copperweld* by introducing a further danger and a further argument for testing it under section 1's rule of reason.

[Here, Judge Boudin observed that antitrust law could expand *Copperweld* to "to develop functional tests or criteria for shielding (or refusing to shield)" what he called "hybrid" structures from section 1 scrutiny, or to apply the rule of reason flexibly.]

* * *

Once one goes beyond the classic single enterprise, including Copperweld situations, it is difficult to find an easy stopping point or even decide on the proper functional criteria for hybrid cases. To the extent the criteria reflect judgments that a particular practice in context is defensible, assessment under section 1 is more straightforward and draws on developed law. Indeed, the best arguments for upholding MLS's restrictions—that it is a new and risky venture, constrained in some (perhaps great) measure by foreign and domestic competition for players, that unquestionably creates a new enterprise without combining existing competitors—have little to do with its structure.

* * *

_____

Citing *Fraser, O.M. v. Nat'l Women's Soccer League, LLC*, 541 F. Supp. 3d 117 (D. Ore. 2021), rejected the NWSL's argument that it was a single-entity league. Holding that a rule barring clubs from signing players under the age of 18 was subject to the rule of reason, the court focused on each club's separate ownership and separate (a) funding for team operations, (b) revenue sources, (c) hiring of staff, (d) permission from league to spend ownership funds on individual players in excess of the league salary cap, (d) payments to non-league clubs to acquire contract rights to players.

3. NON-ANTITRUST CONTEXTS FOR CONSIDERING THE ISSUE

Whether a sports league is best viewed as a joint venture of independent clubs, a single entity comprised of separately managed divisions, or something in between, has arisen in other contexts. For example, recall from Chapter 4 that the National Labor Relations Board treated the North American Soccer League as a "joint employer" that was required to negotiate with a single bargaining unit of all players represented by its Players' Association (a decision upheld by the Fifth

Circuit). A few years later, the USFL Players' Association sued that league to collect the unpaid salaries of players for the defunct Portland Breakers' franchise. In ruling against the Players Association, the judge emphasized the difference between *joint* and *single* employer status, and held that a sports league did not exhibit the integrated operation under common ownership and management that warranted "single employer" treatment. *See USFLPA v. USFL,* 650 F. Supp. 12 (D. Or. 1986).

Bankruptcies in prior years by the NHL's Pittsburgh Penguins, Buffalo Sabres, Ottawa Senators, and Phoenix Coyotes also raise the question of whether creditors of a team should have recourse against the entire league for some or all the team's debts. Having seen in earlier chapters the league policies that establish uniform player contracts, entry-level drafts, waiver and trade rules, and restrictions on veteran free agency and salary caps, do you agree that players left unpaid by one franchise should have no recourse against the league as a whole? Is this relevant to whether a league is a single entity for antitrust purposes?

E. THE PROBLEM OF MONOPOLY IN PROFESSIONAL SPORTS

In appraising the legal policies that legislatures and courts fashion for professional sports, of paramount importance is the fact that each established sport is dominated by only one major professional league. This "monopoly" state, in turn, is the principal source of many of the conflicts that arise between the league and its constituents, and of the difficult problems that these disputes pose for traditional legal doctrines.

Previous chapters have described how player salaries and franchise values have soared during the last several decades. Underlying both trends has been a remarkable rise in the total revenues flowing into professional sports, from fans attending the games, broadcasters (and now digital distributors of content) paying huge rights fees, and product manufacturers paying for the rights to use team names and emblems. In 1950, for example, Major League Baseball's revenues from all sources barely totaled $30 million. By 2009, baseball's revenues surpassed $6.6 billion annually. Forbes magazine's annual review reported that MLB's 2017 revenue exceeded $10 billion for the first time, and predicts 2022 revenue to approach $11 billion. Other major professional sports have experienced the same kind of financial bonanza. This section considers whether the total size of the pie is due in part to the fact that there is almost always only one major league in each sport selling this product to an enthusiastic fandom—and if so, what is the law's responsibility for that state of affairs.

Chapters 7 and 8 consider several cases challenging rules that allegedly restrain trade in various markets relating to professional sports. Consider what the effect would be on many of the economic issues facing

BASIC PRINCIPLES OF ANTITRUST LAW APPLIED TO
348   THE SPECIAL NATURE OF THE SPORTS INDUSTRY   CH. 6

professional sports if two, three, or even four leagues presented viable alternatives for those who claimed to be injured by league rules.

Players—What if other baseball leagues were bidding for Curt Flood when he had to decide whether to sign a contract that permitted the Cardinals to trade him to the Phillies without his consent? What would be the economic and legal effect of challenges to the NFL, NHL, or NBA salary caps if there were rival leagues in each sport?

Television—Suppose several professional basketball leagues were seeking exposure and revenue from television networks and superstations. Would the NBA want to limit superstation coverage of one of its most popular teams? If it had done so, would the availability of other leagues and games have ameliorated the impact of the NBA's policy on television viewers who wanted to watch professional basketball?

Franchises—Suppose that the American Football League had continued as a rival to the National Football League, perhaps accompanied by one or more of the other leagues that have sought to challenge the NFL's dominance. Would there still have been only one professional football team in the Los Angeles area in the late 1970s, so that the city of Anaheim was forced to offer Rams' owner Carroll Rosenbloom 95 acres of prime real estate to induce him to move his team from the Coliseum? Or more starkly, would the NFL have left Los Angeles, the nation's second largest metropolitan area, without any team as it did for over 20 years beginning in 1995 when the Rams and Raiders left for St. Louis and Oakland? In these situations, would not the AFL have moved aggressively to occupy such a lucrative market, and would not that have encouraged the NFL to try to fill that void first? Similarly, following the demise of the WFL in the mid-1970s, would not another hypothetical league have eagerly sought to adopt the Memphis Grizzlies to establish a presence in the "football-mad" South?

Products—Although league resistance to innovations that may improve the quality of the sport only rarely generates antitrust litigation by product suppliers, such innovation has an important value for consumer welfare. The competitive pressures generated by a challenger league create an incentive for innovations that enhance enjoyment of the sport. Perhaps the best example is the American Basketball Association, whose heritage for professional basketball includes not only veteran free agency, but also the three-point shot and the slam dunk.

Fans—What is the reason why, in 2021, the average cost of going to a Major League Baseball game, according to Team Marketing Report, was $34.91, and the average premium ticket cost $253.64? These averages, of course, mask wide variation. Using 2020 data, the most expensive tickets to enter Fenway Park for a Boston Red Sox game were $167 per ticket, and the least expensive tickets to enter Camden Yards for a Baltimore Orioles game were $52 per ticket.

The assumption of some is that the best guarantee that such arrangements will enhance rather than harm social welfare is the force of market competition faced by such businesses. Courts have, however, been unwilling to embrace that position fully in sports cases. The undeniable lesson from history is that interleague competition in a single sport is very much the exception, not the rule, and even when it occurs it is usually short-lived.

For example, while organized baseball regularly faced rival leagues during its first fifty years of existence, no new league has played games since the demise of the Federal League in 1915 (that league's principal legacy being the 1922 Supreme Court decision that produced baseball's antitrust immunity). Similarly, once the National Hockey League (formed in 1917) established its dominance in that sport in the 1920s, only one competitor has come on the scene. The World Hockey Association disappeared after only six seasons, with a 1979 agreement under which the NHL absorbed four WHA teams—the Edmonton Oilers, Winnipeg Jets, Hartford Whalers, and Quebec Nordiques—while the other WHA teams folded. Likewise, the National Basketball Association (formed in 1949) faced a short-lived American Basketball League for only one season, and then struggled against the American Basketball Association for nine seasons (1967–1976) before a peace treaty brought four ABA teams—the New Jersey Nets, Denver Nuggets, Indiana Pacers, and San Antonio Spurs—into the NBA, with the other ABA teams folding.

The National Football League (formed in 1920) has faced by far the most vigorous interleague competition. The most serious challenges came from the All-American Football Conference, which lasted from 1946 to 1949, when the NFL absorbed three AAFC teams—the Cleveland Browns, San Francisco 49ers, and Baltimore Colts—and then from the American Football League, whose growing impact from 1960 through 1966 led the NFL to merge with the AFL and take in all nine AFL teams (with the blessing of an express antitrust exemption granted by Congress). This larger, more powerful NFL, with its annual Super Bowl championship, had little trouble in fending off subsequent challenges from the World Football League in the mid-1970s and the United States Football League in the mid-1980s. At the present time in football, as in all the other men's professional team sports, the established league faces no visible prospect of serious competition, despite the periodic appearance of a spring football contender.

While the above factual record is clear, the explanation for it is not. Does the historic tendency toward monopoly indicate that this is the "natural" state for professional sports, or does it reveal a failure to implement the legal policy against monopolization? This is the underlying question posed in the cases and materials in this section.

1. ANTITRUST LAW AND MONOPOLY POWER

The principal source of law in this area is § 2 of the Sherman Act, which prohibits firms from "monopolizing [or attempting to monopolize] trade and commerce," supplemented by § 7 of the Clayton Act which forbids mergers that may tend substantially to "lessen competition or tend to create a monopoly." A monopolization charge consists of two elements: the possession of monopoly market power, and the use of unacceptable means to acquire, entrench or maintain that market power. An "attempt to monopolize" claim requires a showing that the defendant has a dangerous probability of acquiring monopoly market power and has acted with the specific intent to achieve monopoly status. In both types of § 2 claims, there are essentially two elements: the first requires substantial market power of some degree; and the second, improper conduct that creates, entrenches, or enlarges that market power. To facilitate discussion, we focus upon the monopolization offense.

The first legal issue, which also has key significance for business strategy, is to apply the concept of monopoly power to the sports marketplace. From an economic point of view, monopoly is not to be equated with "bigness" as such. Companies as huge as General Motors have learned, to their chagrin, that mere size is no guarantee against the forces of market competition. *A firm has a measure of monopoly power only if it has the ability to lower the quantity or quality of its product and in turn to raise prices significantly above marginal production costs without experiencing a decrease in profits* (perhaps not even in sales). The immediate source of such market power is "inelasticity of demand": when so few consumers will substantially reduce their purchases of the firm's products in response to higher prices or lower product quality that the firm can get away with these anti-consumer practices. A long-run source is "inelasticity of supply": despite the presence of monopoly profits, barriers to entry obstruct the emergence of new competitors that would give consumers an alternative source of supply.

In practice, however, it is difficult to detect and measure monopoly power in the precise economic sense of the term, and even more difficult to demonstrate such market reality in the artificial setting of a courtroom. Consequently, courts have adopted a surrogate test for monopoly power: does the firm have a large majority of the total production (or sales) in the *relevant market*, which is defined by both a product type and a geographical area within which the products in question are viable alternatives for most buyers (or sellers)—*e.g.*, television rights to football games in the northeastern United States, tickets to sporting events in southern California, or professional football players in the United States? (Many have suggested that this is an exercise that seems as much theological as scientific.) Once the plaintiff demonstrates a sufficiently large market share (usually somewhere over 70%), the burden shifts to the defendant to show that it does not actually have the power to raise prices above or reduce output below their competitive levels without a sharp decline in sales and thus profits. Few defendants can meet the burden of proving this negative—the absence of market power—when they are found to have a huge share of some relevant market.

In thinking about § 2's ban on monopolization, it is important to remember that the two elements of a violation—monopoly market power and improper conduct—are wholly separate. A firm with monopoly power might not use that power in an improper way to maintain its monopoly. For instance, using monopoly profits to invest in newer more efficient plants probably would not constitute monopolization. *In re E.I. du Pont de Nemours & Co. (TiO₂)*, 96 F.T.C. 653 (1980). On the other hand, evidence that an industry leader had to hold elaborate dinners to persuade rivals to fix prices, while likely a criminal violation of § 1, demonstrated that the misbehaving executive's firm did not have monopoly power. *United States v. United States Steel Corp.*, 251 U.S. 417, 442 (1920). Furthermore, the conduct constituting the monopolizing act does not have to involve directly the market being monopolized.

The key task in the legal determination of monopoly power, is establishing the precise scope of the market that the defendant is alleged to dominate. Defining the relevant product market is not as easy a task as it might appear. What initially looks like an insulated enclave for a particular firm if the market is viewed narrowly often can be a strongly competitive environment when one takes account of the entire array of choices available to participants in the broader marketplace.

The National Football League, for example, has regularly argued (though without much success) that professional football faces market competition from college football, as well as from professional baseball, basketball, and other sports, and that all sports face competition from movies, concerts, theater, and other forms of entertainment. The major judicial precedent in this regard is *United States v. E.I. du Pont de Nemours & Co.*, 351 U.S. 377 (1956) (the "Cellophane" case). This case involved a § 2 complaint against du Pont, which produced 75% of the country's cellophane; cellophane, however, constituted just 20% of all "flexible packaging materials." The following passages indicate how the Supreme Court analyzes such market definition issues:

> Market delimitation is necessary under du Pont's theory to determine whether an alleged monopolist violates § 2. The ultimate consideration in such a determination is whether the defendants control the price and competition in the market for such part of trade or commerce as they are charged with monopolizing. Every manufacturer is the sole producer of the particular commodity it makes but its control in the above sense of the relevant market depends upon the availability of

alternative commodities for buyers: *i.e.*, whether there is a cross-elasticity of demand between cellophane and the other wrappings. This interchangeability is largely gauged by the purchase of competing products for similar uses, considering the price, characteristics and adaptability of the competing commodities.

. . .

If a large number of buyers and sellers deal freely in a standardized product, such as salt or wheat, we have complete or pure competition. Patents, on the other hand, furnish the most familiar type of classic monopoly. As the producers of a standardized product bring about significant differentiations of quality, design, or packaging in the product that permit differences of use, competition becomes to a greater or less degree incomplete and the producer's power over price and competition greater over his article and its use, according to the differentiation he is able to create and maintain. A retail seller may have in one sense a monopoly on certain trade because of location, as an isolated country store or filling station, or because no one else makes a product of just the quality or attractiveness of his product, as for example in cigarettes. Thus one can theorize that we have monopolistic competition in every nonstandardized commodity with each manufacturer having power over the price and production of his own product. However, this power that, let us say, automobile or soft-drink manufacturers have over their trademarked products is not the power that makes an illegal monopoly. Illegal power must be appraised in terms of the competitive market for the product.

. . .

What is called for is an appraisal of the "cross-elasticity" of demand in the trade. The varying circumstances of each case determine the result. In considering what is the relevant market for determining the control of price and competition, no more definite rule can be declared than that commodities reasonably interchangeable by consumers for the same purposes make up that "part of the trade or commerce," monopolization of which may be illegal.

351 U.S. at 380–81.

Shortly after *du Pont (Cellophane)*, the Supreme Court rendered its second decision in the litigation involving *International Boxing Club v. United States* (at 358 U.S. 242 (1959)). In its initial decision in these proceedings, at 348 U.S. 236 (1955), the Supreme Court ruled for the first time that a sport was subject to antitrust law (thereby beginning the progression of cases whereby the immunity won earlier by baseball would

be confined to that sport by *Flood v. Kuhn).* This second decision dealt with
the merits of an antitrust complaint concerning boxing. James Norris,
owner of Detroit's Olympia Arena and hockey Red Wings, and Willard
Wirtz, owner of Chicago's Stadium and Black Hawks, allegedly had formed
the International Boxing Club (IBC) to try to dominate professional boxing.
IBC used Joe Louis and Sugar Ray Robinson as the levers to win exclusive
control of the champions and contenders in boxing's heavyweight,
middleweight and welterweight divisions, and bought Madison Square
Garden to secure control of all the major sites for big time fights. The
Justice Department charged IBC with monopolizing and restraining trade
in *championship* boxing, and the district court found violations of both §§ 1
and 2 of the Sherman Act. The following is the key passage from the
Supreme Court's analysis of the merits of IBC's appeal:

> Appellants launch a vigorous attack on the finding that the
> relevant market was the promotion of *championship* boxing
> contests in contrast to *all* professional boxing events. They rely
> primarily on *United States v. du Pont & Co.,* 351 U.S. 377
> (1956). . . . The appellants argue that the "physical identity of the
> products here would seem necessarily to put them in one and the
> same market." They say that any boxing contest, whether
> championship or not, always includes one ring, two boxers and one
> referee, fighting under the same rules before a greater or lesser
> number of spectators either present at ringside or through the
> facilities of television, radio, or moving pictures.

> We do not feel that this conclusion follows. As was also said
> in *du Pont, supra,* at 404:

>> The 'market' . . . will vary with the part of commerce
>> under consideration. The tests are constant. That market is
>> composed   of   products   that   have   reasonable
>> interchangeability for the purposes for which they are
>> produced—price, use and qualities considered.

With this in mind, the lower court in the instant case found that
there exists a "separate, identifiable market" for championship
boxing contests. This general finding is supported by detailed
findings to the effect that the average revenue from all sources for
appellants' championship bouts was $154,000 compared to
$40,000 for their nonchampionship programs; that television
rights to one championship fight brought $100,000, in contrast to
$45,000 for a nontitle fight seven months later between the same
two fighters; that the average "Nielsen" ratings over a two-and-
one-half-year period were 74.9% for appellants' championship
contests, and 57.7% for their nonchampionship programs
(reflecting a difference of several million viewers between the two
types of fights); that although the revenues from movie rights for

six of appellants' championship bouts totaled over $600,000, no full-length motion picture rights were sold for a non-championship contest; and that spectators pay "substantially more" for tickets to championship fights than for nontitle fights. In addition, numerous representatives of the broadcasting, motion picture and advertising industries testified to the general effect that a "particular and special demand exists among radio broadcasting and telecasting [and motion picture] companies for the rights to broadcast and telecast [and make and distribute films of] championship contests in contradistinction to similar rights to non-championship contests."

In view of these findings, we cannot say that the lower court was "clearly erroneous" in concluding that nonchampionship fights are not "reasonably interchangeable for the same purpose" as championship contests. . . . [C]hampionship boxing is the "cream" of the boxing business, and, as has been shown above, is a sufficiently separate part of the trade or commerce to constitute the relevant market for Sherman Act purposes.

358 U.S. at 249–52.

2. MONOPOLY POWER AND EXPANSION

Another early sports monopolization case raising monopoly power and monopoly conduct issues was *American Football League v. National Football League*, 323 F.2d 124 (4th Cir. 1963). The AFL charged that the NFL had offered expansion franchises to the cities of Dallas and Minneapolis in order to frustrate the AFL's plan to move into these two prime football sites. A trial judge dismissed the antitrust suit, and the AFL appealed.

In 1959, the NFL operated with twelve teams located in eleven cities. There were two teams in Chicago and one each in Cleveland, New York, Philadelphia, Pittsburgh, Washington, Baltimore, Detroit, Los Angeles, San Francisco, and Green Bay, Wisconsin. The NFL had begun discussing expansion as early as 1956, and in 1960, it awarded two additional franchises, one in Dallas and one in Minneapolis-St. Paul. The Dallas team was to begin play in 1960 and the Minneapolis-St. Paul team in 1961. In 1961, one of the Chicago teams, the Cardinals, moved to St. Louis.

One of the applicants for the NFL's Dallas franchise was Lamar Hunt, who decided to form a new league instead. By the end of 1959, he had organized the AFL, which began with a full schedule of games in 1960. Affiliated with it were eight teams located in eight cities: Boston, Buffalo, Houston, New York, Dallas, Denver, Los Angeles, and Oakland. Significantly, the NFL had eliminated Houston as a viable candidate for a franchise because of the unavailability of an adequate stadium. Instead, the NFL had lured away the prospective owners of the AFL Minneapolis-

St. Paul franchise, who forfeited the $25,000 franchise fee already paid to AFL founder Lamar Hunt and joined the NFL as the Minnesota Vikings. Hunt and new AFL commissioner Joe Foss then searched for a new eighth team and found a willing ownership group in Oakland whose team became the Raiders. After the 1960 season, the Los Angeles AFL team moved to San Diego and the Dallas Texans, which won the first AFL championship, moved to Kansas City, as the Chiefs.

The appeals court rejected the monopolization claim. It noted that, in addition to those cities in which the AFL had franchises, AFL founder and Kansas City Chiefs' owner Lamar Hunt testified that there was substantial interest in a franchise in Vancouver, Seattle, Kansas City, Louisville, Cincinnati, Philadelphia, Jacksonville, Miami, Atlanta, St. Louis, and Milwaukee. The court rejected the AFL's claim that the market was those 17 cities where the NFL had or was seriously considering franchises.

> . . . location of the franchise is only a selection of a desirable site in a much broader, geographically unlimited market. It is not unlike the choice a chain store company makes when it selects a particular corner lot as the location of a new store. It preempts that lot when it acquires it for that purpose, but, as long as there are other desirable locations for similar stores in a much broader area, it cannot be said to have monopolized the area, or, in a legal sense, the lot or its immediate vicinity.
>
> . . .

Id. at 130. For this reason, the Fourth Circuit found that the trial court's conclusion that the NFL did not have the power to monopolize the relevant market "appears plainly correct."

> In 1959, it occupied eleven of the thirty-one apparently desirable sites for team locations, but its occupancy of some of them as New York and San Francisco-Oakland was not exclusive, for those metropolitan areas were capable of supporting more than one team. Twenty of the thirty-one potentially desirable sites were entirely open to American. Indeed, the fact that the American League was successfully launched, could stage a full schedule of games in 1960, has competed very successfully for outstanding players, and has obtained advantageous contracts for national television coverage strongly supports the District Court's finding that National did not have the power to prevent, or impede, the formation of the new league. Indeed, at the close of the 1960 season, representatives of the American League declared that the League's success was unprecedented.

Id. at 130–31.

Finally, the court rejected the AFL's complaint that the NFL, the first upon the scene, had occupied the more desirable of the thirty-one potential sites for team locations. Some locations were not exclusive, and being the first to enter a market with room for only one firm does not violate the Sherman Act, the court reasoned: "When one has acquired a natural monopoly by means which are neither exclusionary, unfair, nor predatory, he is not disempowered to defend his position fairly." *Id.* at 131.

The AFL's argument that the NFL had unlawfully expanded was, of course, impaired by the new league's very success. Perhaps a better example was Major League Baseball's response to an upstart Continental League, designed by legendary baseball executive Branch Rickey in the late 1950s. With an anchor team in New York City to fill the void created by the Dodgers and Giants relocation to the west coast, Rickey's new league included franchises in Dallas-Ft. Worth, Houston, Atlanta, Buffalo, Toronto, Minneapolis, and Denver. A critical blow to the league's viability was the decision of the National and American Leagues to add the Los Angeles Angels, Minnesota Twins, New York Mets, and Houston Astros to their leagues. For a detailed description of the league and its antitrust and legislative fights, see Michael Shapiro, *Bottom of the Ninth* (New York: Times Books 2009).

3. MONOPOLIZING CONDUCT AND MONOPOLIZING THE SUPPLY OF PLAYERS

The mere existence of monopoly power in the relevant market, however defined, is not sufficient to establish a violation of § 2 of the Sherman Act. As the Supreme Court put it in *United States v. Grinnell Corp.*, 384 U.S. 563, 570–71 (1966), a § 2 violation also requires "the willful acquisition or maintenance of that power as distinguished from growth or development as a consequence of a superior product, business acumen, or historic accident." Over the last century, courts have developed a sizable jurisprudence regarding how to distinguish legitimate from illegitimate sources of monopoly power.

From the point of view of antitrust policy, the question is not whether a monopolistic firm has exploited its power by raising prices or lowering output to maximize its profits. While this practice harms consumers in the short run (and may be subject to government regulation on that account), the presence of monopoly profits in a particular market often serves as an inducement to other firms to enter the market if they can, which in the long run creates a competitive environment for the benefit of consumers. Indeed, the prospect of new entry may discourage the established firm from fully exploiting its monopoly power in the first place. The true evil aimed at by American antitrust law, then, is action by the monopolist that excludes others from entering or remaining in the market and providing competitive balance. (This is quite different than in Europe, where Art. 102 of the European Union's Treaty makes it a violation for a firm to "abuse a dominant position," not merely to acquire or maintain it.)

Nonetheless, not all exclusionary practices warrant legal prohibition. Superior efficiency itself can effectively deter would-be competitors. But if the size or competence of an established firm allows it to develop high quality products sold at low prices that cannot be matched by its rivals, it hardly enhances consumer welfare for a judge to penalize the firm for being so efficient in its effort to satisfy its customers. The challenge in this area of antitrust law is to distinguish between those exclusionary practices by the dominant firm that benefit consumers, and hence are legally tolerable, and exclusionary practices that are improper or unfair, and thus warrant legal prohibition.

In this regard, the fairly standard monopolization claim of "predatory pricing" (as in the government's successful prosecution of Standard Oil for slicing prices below sustainable levels and then charging monopoly profits after its rivals were driven out of business) can be applied to sports leagues if they engage in "predatory spending." This occurs where an established league facing a new rival league increases spending on players to unsustainable levels, in hopes that its deeper pockets can outlast the new league and allow it to return to levels where it can pay players lower than competitive salaries because it is the only league in town. *See, e.g., USFL v. NFL*, 842 F.2d 1335, 1349 (2d Cir. 1987) (jury found that NFL adopted strategy of "spending the USFL dollar" as well as adding additional roster spaces that NFL owners, pre-merger, considered unnecessary, in order to deprive USFL of player talent).

Controlling entry into the labor market tends to be less effective in football and basketball, because every year the intercollegiate "farm clubs" in these sports "graduate" a new class of athletes of demonstrated quality and considerable renown. Perhaps this is one of the reasons why the NFL and NBA never included provisions in their player contracts that perpetually bound players to the team and prevented them from signing with teams *in a different league* (if one existed) when the contract expired. By contrast, in baseball and hockey, the intercollegiate game is much less prominent; thus the major leagues have created or supported their own farm systems to develop player talent for parent clubs. Since a network of contract restrictions bound every young player from the time he entered the minor leagues to the time he retired from the big leagues, it was crucial to the success of new leagues aspiring to big-time status to break that stranglehold. The appropriate legal vehicle was § 2 of the Sherman Act; the following decision is the principal example of its use in this context.

PHILADELPHIA WORLD HOCKEY CLUB V.
PHILADELPHIA HOCKEY CLUB
351 F. Supp. 462 (E.D. Pa. 1972)

HIGGINBOTHAM, DISTRICT JUDGE.

[This decision concerned an antitrust suit filed by the fledgling World Hockey Association (WHA) against its established rival, the National Hockey League (NHL). The WHA's primary objective was to secure a federal court injunction barring the NHL and its clubs from seeking state court injunctions to prevent more than 60 NHL players who had signed WHA contracts from moving to the WHA in apparent violation of their NHL standard player contracts. *See Boston Professional Hockey Ass'n v. Cheevers*, 348 F. Supp. 261 (D. Mass. 1972), *rev'd on other grounds*, 472 F.2d 127 (1st Cir. 1972), and *Nassau Sports v. Hampson*, 355 F. Supp. 733 (D. Minn. 1972) (both denying the negative injunction); *contra Nassau Sports v. Peters*, 352 F. Supp. 870 (E.D.N.Y. 1972) (granting the injunction). The trial judge provided an elaborate description of the structure of professional hockey, relations between the NHL and amateur and minor professional hockey leagues, the reserve system and the standard player contract, expansion of the NHL in the late 1960s, and the emergence of the WHA in the early 1970s. Specifically, Judge Higginbotham (a former Federal Trade Commissioner) described how, at the time, almost all major league hockey players came from amateur teams governed by the Canadian Amateur Hockey Association (CAHA). Since 1967, an umbrella NHL-CAHA agreement expected NHL clubs to contribute over $1 million per year for amateur player development. At the same time, the NHL began to conduct an annual draft of 150 or so of the approximately 7,000 amateur players turning 20 years of age. Specified payments were made to CAHA club members for each player drafted, and again for each of the 45 or so players who signed an NHL contract. Almost all newly drafted players began professional hockey in one of three minor hockey leagues—the American, Western, and Central Hockey Leagues—all of whose teams were either directly sponsored by, or had an affiliation or player loan arrangement with, an NHL club.]

[While the WHA planned to recruit a significant number of players from the minor professional leagues, the judge concluded that in order to succeed the WHA also needed access to players who had developed the ability to excel in the NHL. The major obstacle to the WHA's recruiting of NHL players was the NHL standard player contract. Under Clause 17 of that contract, the club was entitled to renew the contract for one year upon its expiration on the same terms as before, with the exception of the salary amount, which was set anew each year. (This was essentially the same approach that the MLB player contract followed until the *Messersmith-McNally* arbitration decision in 1976 excerpted in Chapter 5.) Since one of the terms in the existing contract was Clause 17 itself, the player contract was perpetually renewable. Similar terms were included in the standard contracts in the AHL, the WHL, and the CHL constitutions.]

The similarities of phraseology and basic incorporation of Clause 17 in the Standard Player's Contract of the AHL, CHL, WHL, and NHL is the result of a common agreement, mutual understanding, and conspiracy by the NHL and its affiliated minor leagues to maintain a monopolistic position so strong that the NHL precludes effective competition by the entry of another major professional hockey league. Through the totality of many interlocking arrangements, including the Joint Affiliation Agreement, the Pro-Amateur Agreement, and Clause 17 in the Standard Player's Contract, the NHL perpetuates a conspiracy and combination with the intent to monopolize and which monopolizes major league professional hockey. These concerted efforts were done not solely to maintain a high level of professional competition among the NHL teams, but rather the major reason was the desire to preclude others from ever having immediate access to the reservoir of players who could become part of another major professional hockey league which could be a material and viable competitor to the NHL. In the words of Mr. Clarence Campbell, President of the NHL, part of the NHL's purpose was to make certain that the NHL would always be ". . . the only major professional hockey league operating from coast-to-coast in the United States or Canada."

* * *

In August 1971, the NHL learned of the imminent formation of the WHA. In reaction, the NHL took two major steps. One was to authorize further expansion into Atlanta and Long Island, at $6 million per franchise. Long Island was crucial because the WHA had been actively negotiating for a franchise lease in the newly-constructed Nassau Coliseum, the only site available for a hockey team in the New York metropolitan area (other than Madison Square Garden, which had an exclusive hockey lease with the NHL Rangers). When the NHL awarded a franchise to Roy Boe (who also paid $4 million in territorial indemnity to the Rangers), the Nassau Coliseum signed a lease with the NHL's New York Islanders.

The NHL's other step was to form a Legal Committee that, through the Washington law firm of Covington and Burling, coordinated vigorous enforcement of the reserve clause through injunction proceedings against NHL players seeking to move to the WHA for much higher salaries.

The WHA's response was to launch this antitrust suit against the NHL. . . .

[At the heart of the WHA's case was § 2 of the Sherman Act, which prohibited monopolization. Although NHL teams had always had a perpetually renewable option clause in their Standard Player's Contract, Judge Higginbotham viewed this arrangement, which had been fashioned by NHL owners with monopoly power, to be a clearcut violation of § 2. He held] that in the circumstances of this case, the three-year restraint following the expiration of a current contract (considering this factor along with the other numerous interlocking agreements the NHL has fashioned and shaped over the years to monopolize a hockey player's professional career) is unreasonable, and in violation of § 2 of the Sherman Act.

Finally, apart from the collective bargaining negotiations relative to the arbitration of salary, there have been no modifications of Clause 17 of the Standard Player's Contract which have altered or eliminated the basic perpetual option which the NHL has over any hockey player once he has first signed a Standard Player's Contract.

B.   Monopoly Power.

* * *

Here, through the use, inter alia, of (1) Standard Players' Contracts, including the "reserve clause" in paragraph 17 of that contract, (2) the agreements between the NHL and three of the major semi-professional leagues, and (3) the agreements between the professional and semi-professional leagues and the amateur leagues, it is clear that the NHL overwhelmingly controls the supply of players who are capable and available for play in a new league where the level of internal competitions fairly approaches the levels currently existing in the NHL. In an attempt to minimize the NHL's extraordinary degree of control over the players, the NHL asserts that there are many other available players who will shortly be able to play major league professional hockey. However, the relevant market place is the market place of today, not the market place of 1980 or even the market place of 1975. A monopolist may not today excuse his present predatory practices because someday in the future his total domination of the market place may be lessened.

The NHL's monopoly power is their power to control overwhelmingly the supply of hockey players who are today available for play in any major professional league. It is that total control by the NHL which I hold is proscribed by § 2 of the Sherman Act. One who builds the most modern steel mill cannot operate without an adequate supply of iron ore. The 50,000 amateur hockey players allegedly available to the WHA are the "iron ore" from which viable competition can be built. If the WHA is to compete effectively for attendance and television rights with commensurate payments, the WHA must have a "show" which is equal or nearly equal to that of the NHL today. Since the WHA is a newcomer, the quality of play need not instantly equal that of the NHL, but there must be a prospect that the product will be nearly equal in a relatively short period of time.

Of course, I recognize that the NHL has neither prevented the birth of the infant WHA nor has the NHL caused the WHA to sustain a premature demise, but monopoly power may be restrained before its full wrath is felt.

C. *Willfulness & Intent.*

The mere possession of monopoly power in the relevant market does not alone constitute a violation of § 2 of the Sherman Act, 15 U.S.C. § 2. There must also be "(2) the willful acquisition or maintenance of that power as distinguished from growth or development as a consequence of a superior product, business acumen, or historic accident." *United States v. Grinnell*, 384 U.S. 563, 570–71 (1966).

The activities of the NHL go beyond mere possession of monopoly power in the relevant market to breach these aforementioned prohibitions articulated in *United States v. Grinnell.*

The NHL has willfully acquired and maintained its monopoly power through the use of the many agreements. . . . Its continuing and overriding goal is to maintain a monopoly over the supply of major league professional hockey players.

The NHL employs devices such as reserve clauses, Standard Player Contracts, an NHL semi-professional league Joint-Affiliation Agreement, and control over the amateurs through the Pro-Am Agreement in which the amateurs agreed to recognize the NHL as the "sole and exclusive governing body of professional hockey." If the NHL reserve clause were valid for those players whose contracts terminated in September, 1972, then the NHL would have the power, directly or indirectly, to prevent any player under "contract" to the NHL or one of its affiliated minor professional leagues from playing with any other team or league outside the NHL System.

Upon reading the self-serving tributes for its expenditure of millions of dollars to develop amateur and minor league hockey, one might infer that the millions were spent solely for the honor and glory of amateur and minor league hockey. The NHL's motives were not quite so noble; these expenditures to develop the amateur and minor professional leagues were essential to maintain the NHL's monopolistic position.

In *American Football League v. National Football League,* the Court noted:

> In 1959 the NFL had most of the ablest players under contract. However, colleges graduate annually large numbers of talented players, and, because after the season starts professional football rosters are usually limited to around 35 players, many good players are released each year after the training season and are available to be signed by clubs in any league. Moreover, NFL players become free agents after a period of years.

In contrast to the above picture of relative openness and availability of players in professional football, the NHL has a system which controls access to all professional and semi-professional players for at least three years. As my discussion, *supra*, concerning the reserve clause conclusively demonstrates, if the operation of the NHL's current reserve clause is not restrained, the NHL's control over the players is absolute for at least three years after the expiration of any current contract. Further, the value of the minor league professional hockey players as a source of supply to the major leagues is not the equivalent of college-level players in football. Moreover, the minor league professional hockey players are likewise bound by standard player contracts which contain reserve clauses materially identical to the NHL standard player contract. Finally, the general practice is that if a minor professional league player does not make the NHL team, nevertheless he is still bound by his former minor professional league contract and is thus not free to sign with another club or any other league. These differences between the football and hockey reserve systems are crucial.

Secondary evidence of the NHL's intent to maintain its control over professional hockey is its continuing policy of expansion tied to the increasing demand for hockey in the United States and also in Canada. Of course, if even this burgeoning interest in hockey in North America could nonetheless support only one supplier, then this court would be bound to conclude that the NHL enjoys a "natural monopoly." In *Ovitron Corp. v. General Motors Corp.*, 295 F. Supp. 373, 378 (S.D.N.Y. 1969), the Court noted "the natural monopolist is entitled to compete vigorously and fairly in a struggle for a market which cannot support more than one supplier."

* * *

Keeping in mind both the many agreements employed by the National Hockey League and its continuing expansion, it is apparent that the National Hockey League's intent is and was the willful acquisition and maintenance of a position as the only major professional hockey league in the United States and Canada.

* * *

The expansion of the NHL during the WHA's formative period and the creation of the WHA itself are both responses to an increased market for the sport and thus increased economic attractiveness for those entering as well as those already in the field.

Here, I do not rely solely on the expansion of the NHL to show that it had the intent to monopolize; for the President of the NHL, Clarence Campbell, has explained his league's intent as a determined drive to assure that the NHL is 'the only major professional hockey league operating from coast to coast in the United States or Canada.'

Expansion of the NHL was one factor indicative of the wrongful intent of the older league to totally monopolize hockey and remain the only major professional hockey league operating with the United States, but expansion was only one of the several threads spun in the monopolistic fabric of the NHL to blanket players from entry to another league.

Injunction granted.

4. OTHER MONOPOLISTIC PRACTICES

Courts have analyzed a host of sports business conduct to determine if it constitutes legitimate "superior skill" or "exclusionary" measures to reject a competitor. Consider:

(a) Stadium Control

Other factors limit the power of monopolists to block rivals in this manner, but in *Hecht v. Pro-Football, Inc.*, 570 F.2d 982 (D.C. Cir. 1977), the court remanded for trial a claim that the owner of the NFL's Washington franchise acted unlawfully in securing and invoking a provision of a lease precluding any other football tenant at RFK Stadium in the nation's capital. The appellate court rejected the trial judge's argument that, to prevail without proof of specific unfair practices, Hecht had to demonstrate that the Washington metropolitan area could support two professional football teams. The appellate court agreed that, if the defendants had a "natural monopoly"—that is, it was the only firm in the market because the market was not large enough to support two firms— "such a monopoly does not violate the antitrust laws unless it was acquired or maintained by exclusionary, unfair, or predatory means." *Id.* at 991. However, it reversed the instruction that Hecht bore the burden of proving that the Redskins did not have a natural monopoly; rather, it was the defendant's obligation to prove the claim. Otherwise, Circuit Judge Malcolm Wilkey reasoned,

> a defendant is entitled to remain free of competition unless the plaintiff can prove, not only that he would be a viable competitor, but also that he and defendant both would survive. This result would be ironic indeed: we cannot say that it is in the public interest to have the incumbent as its sole theatre, or its sole newspaper, or its sole football team, merely because the incumbent got there first. Assuming that there is no identity of performance, the public has an obvious interest in competition, "even though that competition be an elimination bout." "It has been the law for centuries," Justice Holmes once wrote, "that a man may set up a business in a small country town, too small to support more than one, although thereby he expects and intends to ruin some one already there, and succeeds in his intent." The

newcomer and the incumbent may both succeed, or either or both may fail; this is what competition is all about.

Id. at 991–92.

Still, the holding is narrow. To prevail, the plaintiff had to demonstrate that (1) use of RFK stadium was essential to the operation of a professional football team in Washington; (2) such stadium facilities could not practicably be duplicated by potential competitors; (3) another team could use RFK stadium in the Redskins' absence without interfering with the Redskins' use; and (4) the restrictive covenant in the lease prevented equitable sharing of the stadium by potential competitors. Thus, defendants claimed that University of Maryland's Byrd Stadium (just outside Washington in College Park) was a suitable alternative that Hecht could have used, and that Hecht might not have received an AFL franchise anyway. Because of this, Hecht finally agreed to settle the case in 1979, about nine years after it had been filed, for $200,000.

In *USFL v. NFL,* 634 F. Supp. 1155, 1176–80 (S.D.N.Y.1986), the district judge granted summary judgment to the defendant NFL against a feature of the USFL's wide-ranging antitrust claim—the allegation that NFL teams had hampered efforts by potential USFL franchises to play in stadiums where NFL teams had leases. Most of the alleged offenders were NFL teams that leased municipally-owned stadiums. The judge held that any NFL team's effort to persuade the public stadium authority not to grant a lease to a USFL rival, or at least a lease on unfavorable terms, was insulated from antitrust scrutiny by the *Noerr-Pennington* doctrine. That doctrine, based on a pair of Supreme Court decisions bearing these names, holds that a private actor's effort to persuade a public body to exercise its prerogative favorably to the petitioner's position cannot violate the Sherman Act even if done for an anticompetitive purpose. The USFL did not appeal this feature of the trial judge's ruling, which held that such First Amendment immunity to antitrust regulation applied to municipal decisions made in a commercial or a proprietary (as well as in a regulatory) capacity.

(b) Television Contracts

Even less likely, in today's world of almost unlimited television and streaming options and channels, was the claim in *USFL v. NFL,* 842 F.2d 1335 (2d Cir. 1988) that the NFL had unlawfully monopolized a key source of guaranteed revenue essential to compete. Regarding monopolizing television contracts, Judge Winter observed that the NFL's 1982–86 contracts were nonexclusive and did not forbid a network from televising another football league's games at any time when it was not broadcasting NFL games, and when the NFL's network contracts expired in 1986, the networks were free to contract with a competing league's games for all time slots. Indeed, because the NFL was forbidden by its network contracts to televise games on cable, cable television contracts were open to a competing league, although such contracts were less lucrative than network contracts.

Rather than exclusionary television contracts, the court found that the real cause of the USFL's demise was a strategy, adopted at the urging of New Jersey Generals' owner Donald Trump, to move to a fall schedule in 1986, supposedly the more natural time for fans to watch football. Rather than trying to establish itself as a long-term competitor with the NFL, Judge Winter observed that the USFL followed Trump's merger strategy, which ultimately caused the USFL's downfall. The merger strategy, the NFL argued, involved escalating financial competition for players as a means of putting pressure on NFL expenses, playing in the fall to impair NFL television revenues, shifting USFL franchises out of cities where NFL teams played into cities thought to be logical expansion (through merger) cities for the NFL, and, finally, bringing this antitrust suit. *Id.* at 1351–52.

The court affirmed a jury finding that the NFL had not monopolized access to television in the fall, a key predicate to the USFL's damages claim. Judge Winter reasoned that the jury could have found that the USFL was free to sell its rights to all three networks at the expiration of the NFL's contracts, that ABC (which at the time only showed Monday Night Football) was free to show USFL games on the weekend, that the NFL did not seek exclusionary terms, and that even if the NFL had monopolized the television market, this was not the cause of the plaintiffs' demise.

(c) Antitrust Remedies

The *USFL v. NFL* jury did find the NFL guilty of monopolization in violation of § 2 in a number of ways, including an effort to co-opt potential USFL owners such as Donald Trump or franchise locations such as Oakland (a strategy sketched in a presentation to NFL executives by Harvard Business School Professor Michael Porter, called "Conquering the USFL"). Having upheld the one-dollar damage award (that was automatically trebled to three dollars), the court also rejected the USFL's request to use these antitrust findings as a basis for sweeping injunctive relief—restructuring the NFL into two leagues, each limited to a single network contract.

> What the USFL seeks is essentially a judicial restructuring of major-league professional football to allow it to enter. Because of the explicit congressional authorization in 1966 for the NFL-AFL merger and single-league operation, the USFL does not attack the league structure directly. Instead, the USFL asks us to prevent networks from broadcasting, and fans from watching, NFL games in the hope that they will turn to the USFL. Absent a showing of an unlawful barrier to entry, however, new sports leagues must be prepared to make the investment of time, effort and money that

develops interest and fan loyalty and results in an attractive product for the media. The jury in the present case obviously found that patient development of a loyal following among fans and an adherence to an original plan that offered long-run gains were lacking in the USFL. Instead, the USFL quickly changed to a strategy of competition with the NFL in the fall, hoping thereby to force a merger of a few USFL teams into the NFL. That led to a movement of USFL teams out of large television markets and a resultant reduction in value of USFL games to television. As USFL owner and negotiator Einhorn predicted, abandoning major television markets precluded the possibility of obtaining a network contract. The USFL hoped, however, that if a merger did not occur, a jury verdict in the instant litigation followed by a decree effectively forcing a network to televise its product would save the day. Instead, the jury found that the failure of the USFL was not the result of the NFL's television contracts but of its own decision to seek entry into the NFL on the cheap.

Id. at 1380.

5. MONOPOLY LEVERAGING

Section 2 of the Sherman Act forbids those who may have lawfully obtained monopoly power in one market to leverage that power in anticompetitive ways in order to obtain monopoly power in a second market. A modern example is *United States v. Microsoft Corp.,* 253 F.3d 34 (D.C. Cir. 2001), where the courts found that Microsoft had illegally used its monopoly in the market for computer operating systems (Windows) to eliminate a rival internet browser (Netscape).

This theory may also play out in § 1 cases, where a firm with market power is accused of leveraging its power to force consumers seeking to acquire a product or service with no reasonable substitutes to acquire another product or service from them. Both §§ 1 and 2 are informed by more narrowly drafted provisions § 3 of the Clayton Act, that prohibit sellers or lessors of goods and commodities to condition their sale or lease on the understanding that the purchaser or lessee not use goods sold by a competitor, where the effect may be to substantially lessen competition. An early example of this sort of arrangement was *International Business Machines Corp. v. United States,* 298 U.S. 13 (1936), where the Court found illegal IBM's practice of tying leased machines to the purchase of unpatented punchcards (originally required for computers to read data).

On the other hand, the theory is not available where the practice, although potentially exploitive of consumers, does not affect commerce in other markets. Thus, courts have rejected challenges to the widespread NFL practice that conditions the sale of regular season tickets on the purchase of exhibition pre-season tickets. *See, e.g., Coniglio v. Highwood*

Services, Inc., 495 F.2d 1286, 1291–92 (2d Cir. 1974); *Driskill v. Dallas Cowboys Football Club*, 498 F.2d 321, 323 (5th Cir. 1974).

Another judicial ruling addressing the problem of a team using its control over a facility to secure control in a sports market, though this time in the merchandising side of the business, is *Weinberg v. Chicago Blackhawk Hockey Team*, 274 Ill. App. 3d 637, 653 N.E.2d 1322 (1995). (Although the case arose under the Illinois Antitrust Act, Illinois state courts have interpreted this statute as being substantively identical to the Sherman Act.) The Blackhawks refused to grant the plaintiff media credentials and stadium access to generate content for his unofficial game program, *The Blue Line*, which he sold outside Chicago Stadium in competition with the Blackhawks' own program, *Face Off*.

First, the court described the particular offense of "monopoly leveraging", as requiring proof:

> (1) that defendant has monopoly power in one market, (2) that defendant used this power to exact a competitive advantage for itself in a second market, (3) that the competitive advantage was not won on competitive merits, but rather stemmed from a coercive use of the monopoly power in the first market, (4) that the defendant acted with the intent to gain the unwarranted advantage in the second market and (5) the anti-competitive conduct resulted in a lessening of competition.

274 Ill. App. 3d, at 640.

The court found that the plaintiffs' complaint adequately contained allegations of fact supporting a finding of all the necessary elements.

> As to the first element, the Blackhawks unquestionably have monopoly power in National Hockey League hockey in Chicago. We note that a professional sports team, like the Blackhawks, is an absolutely unique entity providing the public with an absolutely unique product. The second element, concerning the use of monopoly power to gain an advantage in a second market, is established by the allegations relating to the Blackhawks' refusal to grant plaintiffs media credentials and press access to prevent *The Blue Line* from competing with *Face Off*. The same allegations satisfy the third element. The advantage *Face Off* has acquired was achieved not through pro-competitive efficiencies, but rather through denying plaintiffs access to the Blackhawks' games. The fourth element, intent, is supplied by the quote from the assistant director of public relations wherein he stated: "I don't think we want to set aside credentials for a publication that is conceivably competing . . . ."

The only remaining element under the monopoly leveraging theory is whether plaintiffs have sufficiently alleged that the

Blackhawks' course of conduct has had an anti-competitive effect. . . . The complaint clearly states that the Blackhawks have effectively excluded *The Blue Line* from the immediate and intimate access to the games and players to which the Blackhawks' own publication enjoys and to which one would reasonably expect any game day program to have. From the very existence of media credentials, press boxes, press rooms and press conferences, we can reasonably infer that a publication without access to these credentials, locations and events is less competitive than it would otherwise be. Through the course of conduct alleged in the complaint, plaintiffs are unable to obtain the quality of photographs, reports and interviews, including answers to plaintiffs' own questions which they would otherwise have. Denying such access necessarily makes *The Blue Line* less competitive.

Id. at 640–41.

On remand, the trial court granted summary judgment for the Blackhawks, and this time both the court of appeals and the state supreme court affirmed, on the ground that selling programs outside of one hockey arena did not constitute "a substantial part of trade or commerce" of the State of Illinois and thus the relevant market was too small to warrant application of the state's antitrust law. *Blue Line Publishing, Inc. v. Chicago Blackhawk Hockey Team*, 201 Ill. 2d 561, 786 N.E.2d 180, *aff'g* 329 Ill. App. 3d 859, 263 Ill. Dec. 895, 769 N.E.2d 97 (2002).

———

NOTES AND QUESTIONS

1.   *Starting a New League.* If you were an upstart league alleging that an established league was trying to prevent you from becoming a viable competitor, in what market would you allege that the established league held monopoly (or monopsony) market power that it most wanted to maintain? In what market are the competitive effects of a second league most immediately apparent and dramatic? What do established leagues fear most from new leagues?

2.   *Revisiting Market Definition.* In light of the *du Pont* and *International Boxing* line of analysis, how much weight should be given to the NFL's argument that its teams compete in a broad entertainment market for the patronage of fans attending games, watching television, or purchasing merchandise? Would you answer be different if the league were the WNBA or the National Lacrosse League? In any case, would such a market be a national, regional, or local market?

3.   *Is Expansion Good or Bad? Philadelphia Hockey* referred to the NHL's expansion initiative, taken at the same time that the WHA was trying

to establish itself, as further evidence of its intent to monopolize. Thinking back to the *AFL* case, can expansion that fills the public's growing demand for more franchises be an illegal erection of barriers to a new league's entry, by depriving any new entrant of the most attractive areas in which to locate profitable teams? Since all the major leagues today have approximately 30 teams, are there enough attractive markets available for a new league to have any hope of surviving in these sports? Does this make the existing major leagues illegal monopolists for having expanded into so many cities, or natural monopolists in a market where no new league could possibly survive? Remember that the 1966 NFL-AFL merger into a single league of 26 teams was given an express congressional exemption. Was that good antitrust and/or sports policy?

4.   *Can Rival Leagues Really Compete?* Does the failure of the American Basketball League, which started operations a half-year before the WNBA, support the view that there is a naturally dominant league in each sport or, given the WNBA's access to the NBA's resources and connections, new leagues fail when they have to face the power of established leagues? Or merely that start up leagues will always need deep-pocketed investors willing and able to cover inevitable large losses for several years before it can hope to become an established product in the minds of sports fans?

5.   *Predatory Spending.* Facilitated by the *Philadelphia Hockey* decision, the WHA's entry on the hockey scene resulted in a fierce bidding war for players that sent average salaries soaring and team balance sheets into the red. The same scenario took place in football and basketball, whose established leagues faced the challenge of new competitors without a perpetually renewable option in their standard player contracts. Why were teams willing to spend huge sums of money on players, irrespective of the effect on their balance sheets? Does this practice make good business sense for teams in the new league? For teams in the established league? Is there—or should there be—a legal barrier to such spending, especially by the established league?

Consider the analogy of illegal "predatory pricing" by a dominant firm faced by a new rival—*i.e.*, deliberately pricing a product below cost to force weaker firms out of the market. Should there be a similar bar to "predatory salary-paying"? If so, how would a court determine when a salary had escalated above the player's legitimate competitive market value (*i.e.*, his marginal revenue product) and become an illegitimate predatory wage level? (Recall the "natural monopoly" market hypothesis described earlier.) Why does an established league such as the NFL, the NBA, and the NHL always choose to compete by paying higher salaries to its players, rather than by charging lower prices to its fans? The explanation is crucial to understanding the peculiar features of monopoly in sports.

6.   *Challenging League Mergers.* The culmination of the legal and financial struggle between the NHL and the WHA was a 1979 agreement under which four WHA clubs moved into the NHL and the other WHA owners received monetary compensation to fold their teams. The NHL Players Association agreed not to challenge the legality of this arrangement under the

Sherman Act in return for a collective agreement containing significant modifications of labor market restrictions. An almost identical scenario occurred in basketball at about that same time. Is resolution in a collective bargaining process sufficient to allay public policy concerns about interleague mergers? If not, who should challenge such arrangements? In what circumstances, if any, should sports mergers be allowed to occur?

Should the law allow an established league to merge with all or some of the clubs in an upstart league? Under what circumstances would you permit such a merger? What is the likely alternative if such a merger is not permitted? Why did the NFL not try to merge with or buy-off the USFL? For a non-sports look at the so-called "failing company" exception to otherwise unlawful mergers, see *Citizen Publishing Co. v. United States*, 394 U.S. 131 (1969). *See also* 4A P. Areeda, H. Hovenkamp, & J. Solow, *Antitrust Law* ¶¶ 951–54 (rev. ed. 1998).

7.   *Exclusive Lease Arrangements.* If you were counsel for an NFL team negotiating a lease with a local stadium authority, would you seek an exclusivity clause of the type the Redskins had, in light of *Hecht*? Even if it turned out that § 2 prevented the team from enforcing that provision, might it still have some value to the NFL team in the event a team in a new league sought to obtain a lease?

8.   *What Is an "Essential" Facility?* In *Fishman v. Estate of Wirtz*, 807 F.2d 520 (7th Cir. 1986) (with Judge Easterbrook dissenting at length), the court found that Chicago Stadium was an "essential facility" for the NBA Chicago Bulls, which could not lawfully be withheld from Fishman, a prospective buyer of the Bulls, by the Wirtz family (owners of the Stadium and the NHL Chicago Black Hawks) in their competition to purchase the Bulls. As the *Hecht* test requires, this is a fact-based determination based on the availability of alternative sites. Does it matter that Bulls' revenues warranted bids in the $3–4 million range, compared to current franchise values in the billions?

9.   *Relevance of Stadium Access Today.* In today's marketplace, effective competition may require each club to own (or at least have total control over) its own stadium to take advantage of the many revenue streams clubs have created since *Hecht* was litigated. For example, suppose the Washington Commanders were required under the *Hecht* precedent to permit a team in the New American Football League to play at FedEx field. While this would give the rival league a venue, the stadium owner (the Commanders) would still collect all the revenue from parking, concessions, suite ownership (which often gives the owner access to all stadium events), etc.

10. *Break up the NFL?* The jury found only $1 (trebled to $3) in USFL damages because it believed that irrespective of the NFL's illegal monopolizing behavior, the USFL's business strategy and conduct was such that it would have failed anyway. However, if the purpose of private antitrust actions is to encourage private enforcement, and the NFL was found to be an illegal monopoly, why was the court unwilling to grant the USFL's requested

injunction that would have forced the NFL to divide into two independent leagues? Is the court's reasoning persuasive? Would consumer welfare and competition have been benefited by granting the requested relief?

Whatever your diagnosis of the causes of the current sports monopoly, would it be desirable or feasible for Congress or an antitrust court to break up the established leagues, all whose current divisions enjoy "big league" status in the popular mind? Each such division would be made an independent entity headed by its own commissioner: no agreements would be permitted with the other new leagues for allocation of players or franchises, or for the sale of television rights and marketing licenses. If that policy course were to be followed, should the several new leagues be entitled to (or required to) cooperate in staging a single championship playoff? In effect, should the Super Bowl or the World Series be deemed an "essential facility" that must be made accessible to each league in order to preserve a competitive sports marketplace (by analogy to the appeals court ruling in *Aspen Highlands Skiing Corp. v. Aspen Skiing Co.*, 738 F.2d 1509 (10th Cir. 1984), *aff'd on other grounds,* 472 U.S. 585 (1985))?

Among the different constituencies observed in earlier chapters—owners, players, players associations, agents, municipalities, television networks, and fans—who would win and who would lose from such a dramatically different structure to the sports world? Why? What do you think would be the likely long run result of breaking up a league into two equal parts? Would the two leagues continue to stay equal, or would one of the leagues be likely to continue to build on its perceived superiority? Would it be necessary for the Antitrust Division or the FTC to vigorously monitor league spending, to assure that neither league used any temporary advantage or perceived superiority to spend in a predatory manner to exclude its rival? If the inevitable result of multiple leagues is dominance, does this suggest a different kind of natural monopoly in sports leagues?

11. *Consequence of a Single League in Each Sport.* If each major league is judged to be a natural monopoly that it is neither desirable nor feasible to break up, should Congress deal with the economic problems created in the sports world in the manner that natural monopolies have historically been treated? A federal regulatory commission could be established to determine (or at least approve) how many franchises there would be, where they would be located, who would be allowed to own them, what television rights could be sold to whom and for how much, for how much and to whom trademarks and logos could be licensed, the length of the season, and many other important decisions that a monopolist would otherwise make against the best interests of the public. What are the pros and cons of having sports governed by such an agency?

6. ABUSE OF POWER BY SPORTS GOVERNING BOARDS

As detailed in Chapter 2, the four major North American professional leagues are controlled by club owners and operate distinctly from any national sports governing board or international federation. In other sports, the global structure has greater relevance; in addition, the availability of treble damage remedies attracts international litigation under the Sherman Act.

European case law has developed around the antitrust problems (somewhat analogous, but distinct from, monopoly leveraging discussed above) that arise when a governing board or federation exercises both regulatory power over a sport and also engages in commercial activity as the organizer of major and even dominant competitions. An early example was when the Fédération Internationale d'Automobile (FIA) sought EU approval of its regulatory and commercial agreements; the EU's Competition Directorate (roughly equivalent to the United States Department of Justice Antitrust Division) closed its inquiry only after FIA agreed to sell the commercial rights to organize Formula One to a private owner and to confine itself to regulation. A litigated decision came in a dispute between the Greek governing board for motorcycle racing and a party seeking to organize a rival competition. In *Motosykletistiki Omospondia Ellados NPID (MOTOE) v. Dimosio*, 46(4) CMLR 1327 (2009), the European court observed that:

> a system of undistorted competition, such as that provided for by the treaty, can be guaranteed only if equality of opportunity is secured between the various economic operators. To entrust a legal person such as ELPA, the National Association for Motorcycling in Greece, which itself organizes and commercially exploits motorcycling events, the task of giving the competent administration its consent to applications for authorization to organize such events, is tantamount de facto to conferring upon it the power to designate the persons authorized to organize those events and to set the conditions in which those events are organized, thereby placing that entity at an obvious advantage over its competitors. Such a right may therefore lead the undertaking which possesses it to deny other operators access to the relevant market. . .

The Advocat General, whose preliminary opinions are relied upon by European courts, noted that

> 95. Consequently, the fact that an organisation such as ELPA makes the grant of consent to the authorisation of a motorcycling event subject to the requirement that the event must not clash with other events that have already been planned and authorised cannot automatically be regarded as an abuse. However, it goes without saying in this regard that, when establishing a national Greek annual programme for motorcycling events, ELPA must not give preference to the events co-organised or marketed by it over those of other, independent organisers.

96. The pyramid structure that has developed in most sports helps to ensure that the special requirements of sport, such as uniform rules and a uniform timetable for competitions, are taken into account. An organisation such as ELPA, which is the official representative of the FIM in Greece, is part of that pyramid structure. Under its right of co-decision in the authorisation by a public body of motorcycling events, it may legitimately assert the interests of sport and, if necessary, refuse to give its consent. However, a refusal to grant consent becomes an abuse where it has no objective justification in the interests of sport, but is used arbitrarily to promote the organisation's own economic interests, to the detriment of other service providers that would like to organise, and above all market, motorcycling events on their own responsibility.

The clearest statement of European law on this point to date is the European Commission's decision in *International Skating Union v. Commission,* Case No T-93/18 (16 December 2020), barring the ISU from using its regulatory power to impose a lifetime ban on skaters' participation in its own competitions, and in Olympic qualifying competitions, if they participate in "unsanctioned" competitions organized by the ISU's commercial rivals.

These issues can arise under the Sherman Act, providing jurisdiction can be established in the United States. *Compare World Skating Fed'n v. Int'l Skating Union,* 357 F. Supp. 2d 661 (S.D.N.Y. 2005) (no jurisdiction over the federation and its president) *with Shields v. Fed'n Internationale de Natation,* Case No. 18-cv-07393-JSC, 2022 U.S. Dist. LEXIS 25140 (N.D. Cal.) (denying motion to dismiss for lack of jurisdiction). The latter pending case involves a similar effort by swimming's regulatory federation, FINA, to preclude commercial competition by threatening participating swimmers with a ban on participation in FINA tournaments critical to the Olympics.

NOTES AND QUESTIONS

1.   *Revisiting* Radovich v. NFL. A related complaint arose in *Radovich v. NFL,* 352 U.S. 445 (1957), challenging a league boycott of a player who had participated in a rival league. It alleged that the boycott harmed the plaintiff and was designed to destroy the rival All American Football Conference, and sought damages. The NFL argued factually that the plaintiff was too old to play in the NFL, and legally that football should enjoy the same immunity from antitrust litigation as baseball did. 231 F.2d 620, 621 (9th Cir. 1956). The Court, as noted in Chapter 3, reversed lower courts' dismissal of the complaint and remanded for trial. The case was settled.

2.   *The Amateur Sports Act.* Among the problems Congress sought to solve in the Amateur Sports Act, discussed below in Chapter 15, Section B, was the practice of some national federations to deny athletes the opportunity to represent the United States in the Olympics of participation in unsanctioned events, often by a rival amateur sports association. The statute requires selections to be based on sporting merit and provides for an independent arbitrator to resolve disputes. Is this a preferred way to resolve disputes about athlete eligibility?

3.   *What Is the Rationale for Excluding Athletes Based on Participation in Unsanctioned Competitions?* Recall a basic principle of the law of monopolization: it is unlawful to deliberately sacrifice short-term benefits in order to maintain monopoly power: this is called "predatory conduct." When a national team or federation bars elite athletes from participating in a major event, because they previously participated in a "rival" event, is there any reason other than the dominant federation's desire to maintain its monopoly position?

4.   *Blending Economic and Non-Economic Rationales.* As this book goes to press, the PGA Tour announced that golfers participating in a rival competition sponsored by a Saudi Arabian sovereign wealth fund would be banned from the PGA Tour. Affected golfers and the rival tour brought an antitrust suit, and the DOJ Antitrust Division launched an investigation. Is this conduct the same as banning an ice skater from the Olympics, or boycotting a player who now seeks to return to the established league? Is it significant that "rebel" golfers can still participation in the U.S. and British Opens and the Masters, which are not organized by the PGA Tour? Is it relevant that the rival tour is sponsored by the Saudi Arabian government and is viewed as an effort to sanitize their image despite significant human rights abuses?

CHAPTER 7

ANTITRUST REGULATION AND BUSINESS STRATEGY IN SPORTS LABOR MARKETS

■ ■ ■

This chapter recounts the key legal and industry consequences of antitrust litigation and its impact on the player labor market. It builds upon the legal foundation of collective bargaining discussed in Chapter 3 to analyze the business dynamics between employers with multiple and different interests and players whose union owes them a duty of fair representation.

A. ECONOMIC ANALYSIS OF RESTRAINTS IN THE PLAYERS MARKET

The landmark *Board of Regents* decision excerpted in Chapter 6 focused the attention of judges and litigants on the actual anticompetitive effect of challenged restraints. With regard to challenges in the players market, the questions include whether the restraint had the effect of misallocating resources in the player labor market, and whether some actual marketplace benefits for consumers could justify the restraint. Answering these questions requires understanding the fundamental economics of player restraints.

1. TYPES OF PLAYER RESTRAINTS

In most professional sports leagues around the world, participating clubs compete among themselves to sign players, subject to rules imposed by the league or agreed to among themselves. These rules often significantly restrain this intraleague competition for players. The labor restraints sometimes include a *reserve list*, whereby clubs will not bid for reserved players at the expiration of a contract; the player must either re-sign with his prior employer or seek employment outside the league. Some leagues use a *restricted list*, so that any club desiring a player's services agrees to provide compensation to the former employer, or to allow the former employer to match the best offer. Common among North American and Australian leagues is a *player draft*, whereby amateurs or veterans not under contract can only negotiate with the team that selects them; teams usually select in reverse order of finish from the prior season unless they trade a selection to or acquire one from another team.

In recent years, many leagues have adopted *club salary (or payroll) caps*, which prevent a club from competing for players when total player payroll exceeds a specified amount, or a more modest version of this restraint, a *luxury tax* on payrolls that exceed a certain amount, thereby making it more expensive for high-payroll teams to compete for the services of players. Some leagues also employ *individual player salary caps* that limit the amount a player can receive based on years of service within the league or his previous salary. (They often also ensure that a negotiated percentage of total league revenue is shared with players in salary, guaranteeing that players share in the league's prosperity.)

Other common practices also can significantly affect a club's ability to compete for player services. *Debt limits,* by which clubs agree not to spend more than a certain percentage of their own revenue on players, can take profligate or poorly managed clubs out of the bidding for players. North American leagues also employ *roster limits* and *waiver rules*. In combination, these provisions limit the total number of major league-quality players that any team can employ; and the existing contracts for players in excess of that number must be offered for assignment, for a modest fixed fee, to other teams (that may select in reverse order of their current position in the standings).

European football leagues have adopted regulations that limit club spending on operations to the actual revenues derived from the sport. The rules are designed to prevent both improvident spending by clubs that lack adequate resources, as well as to bar cash infusions from wealthy owners. Some North American leagues also ban another practice that may not seem at first blush to affect player restraints—significant cash sales for players still under contract, the primary means by which players are exchanged in European football. If significant cash sales are banned, clubs seeking a star player must either sign one of the few "free agents" (a player whose contract has expired, and who is not subject to any of the aforementioned restrictive rules) or arrange a trade with another club.

2. ECONOMIC EFFECTS OF PLAYER RESTRAINTS

The more restrictive of the aforementioned rules are prevalent where clubs adhering to restraints do not face significant competition from others for the services of players. For example, the NFL allows clubs to reserve players with less than four years of service (most players), has an annual draft for all rookie players, places a cap on the payroll for player personnel, and puts a specific limit on the salaries payable to the pool of rookie players.

Restraints are less prevalent where players have credible options to play elsewhere. For example, Serie A (the top Italian soccer league) seriously considered imposing a salary cap but decided against such a rule, because it was clear that the top players would simply leave Serie A and play for clubs in other European soccer leagues. Soccer, however, is the only major league sport played in the United States where serious inter-league competition exists for the world's best players. The revenue disparities between American baseball, basketball, and hockey leagues and those in other countries where these sports are played are so great that the option to play elsewhere is not a viable substitute for most players, especially the stars, and "gridiron" football is only played professionally in North America.

The most obvious and immediate effect of the imposition of player restraints by clubs with monopsony power is lower salaries for players. This restraint thus represents a significant transfer of wealth from players to clubs. If the salary restraint is too severe, it may discourage some athletes from working hard to become professionals, affect players' decisions on when to end their careers, and potentially hurt the quality of the sport. (This point was made by Judge Patricia Wald in her dissenting opinion in *Brown v. Pro-Football*, 50 F.3d 1041, 1060–61 (D.C. Cir. 1995), *aff'd*, 518 U.S. 231 (1996).) Professional athletes' next-best occupation usually pays so much below the salary they can command in their best sport, however, that restraints probably do not significantly affect the supply of players.

Another important concern is that restraints often result in the inefficient allocation of players among teams. In general, the optimal allocation of players among teams in a league will be to allow the market to place the players with the teams that value them the most. Contrary to conventional wisdom, some scholarship suggests that player restraints often *harm* competitive balance, by making it more difficult for underperforming teams to improve quickly.

3. JUSTIFICATIONS FOR PLAYER RESTRAINTS

Defenders of sports league practices limiting competition for players have offered myriad justifications, many of which would not be accepted as procompetitive in other industries. This section focuses on the economic underpinnings of oft-proffered justifications.

Economists generally reject the claim that *high salaries drive up ticket prices,* especially in the short- or medium-run. Suppose a club plays in a 50,000-seat stadium. Perhaps the club could sell out each game by charging $5/ticket. Assuming an average of $5/person profit from parking, concessions, etc., this would bring in revenue of $500,000/game. The club could also charge $995/ticket. If it could attract 500 purchasers, it could bring in about $500,000/game in revenue. But perhaps with a $20 ticket, the club could attract 35,000 fans, or revenue of $875,000/game. This illustrates that there is some profit-maximizing price for the tickets: once that level is reached, the club cannot raise prices further to pay for a higher payroll. Economists recognize one exception to the rule that higher payrolls do not affect ticket prices, but this rule counts against, rather than in favor of, player restraints. If, because of an unrestrained market for player services, a club spends more to bring in better players, then demand for seats should increase, as should price. *See* Andrew Zimbalist, "Economics 100: Higher Ticket Prices Not Caused by Payroll," *Sports Bus. J.*, July 10, 2000, at p. 46.

In the real world, things may well be more complex. The economic analysis assumes that the team owner is trying to maximize revenue; owners with non-profit or other strategic motivations might charge below-market ticket prices but then alter pricing if compelled to increase payroll costs significantly. Moreover, because ticket pricing for discretionary consumer goods like sporting events is often partially a function of public perception, an owner might be able to get away with a larger ticket price increase by blaming player salaries.

Another justification that has occasionally been asserted is the need for player restraints to *allow clubs in smaller towns to remain viable* (or, outside of North America, to allow clubs owned by supporters to compete effectively with clubs owned by investors). Owners, politicians, commentators, or ordinary fans might favor player restraints for this purpose for at least three conceptually distinct reasons. One is a business decision that the league's overall output (live attendance, television audience, merchandise sales, sponsorships, etc.) will be increased if there are many teams in many towns, even if those towns are not economically capable of supporting a profitable team that pays competitive salaries to players. Another reason to ensure that clubs remain viable in smaller towns is to preclude any possibility of entry from a rival league: even if the dominant league is established in larger towns, competition with a new league could drive up salaries significantly. Finally, there are cultural reasons to favor having clubs in major national sports located in small towns across the continent.

Smaller towns might maintain a major league club in a variety of ways, even when free market forces preclude viability. Clubs in highly profitable markets could share revenue, or national or sub-national governments could provide operating subsidies. Scholars of law and economics have observed that player restraints effectively amount to a "subsidy" to small towns and their clubs from the players, whose salaries are being reduced to achieve this goal. *See* Michael J. Trebilcock, THE COMMON LAW OF RESTRAINT OF TRADE 227–28 (Toronto: Carswell 1986). If a community determines that having a major sports team is important to the local culture, the community as a whole should provide the subsidy; if the society at large wants to preserve and enhance cultural life in mid-sized cities, then it can provide a national subsidy. To the extent that progressive citizens believe that the burden of this subsidy should fall upon those who can more easily shoulder it, then perhaps special taxes should be imposed on affluent professional athletes, as well as affluent investment brokers, movie moguls, and any others in the top income bracket.

Yet another justification for player restraints is the club's interest in recouping its *investment in training and developing players*. Of course, this problem is not unique to sports. In many industries, employers train younger workers who potentially could leave for a better offer after receiving training. Nor can the NFL and NBA invoke this claim, as they are the beneficiaries of millions of dollars of free training for their athletes by NCAA schools. Some economists have suggested that restraints of trade are unnecessary to training recoupment, because clubs that provide training to young athletes can sign them to individually negotiated, multi-year contracts that allow adequate recoupment. Trebilcock, *supra,* at 228. Indeed, this practice is common in international soccer, where elite players rarely become "free agents" playing out their contracts: if a club perceives it will be unable to re-sign a player, the player's contract is sold prior to expiration to a wealthier club for a substantial transfer fee. At the same time, FIFA regulations permit smaller clubs to obtain compensation for training services for young players who do play out their contract.

The principal economic argument in favor of player restraints is that they *help promote competitive balance*. Logically, the argument relies on three distinct propositions:

(1) fans prefer a more balanced competition;

(2) absent player restraints, the competition will be less balanced than fans prefer;

(3) player restraints actually result in improved competitive balance.

As a matter of theory and anecdotal evidence, it seems apparent that neither total imbalance nor perfect parity in any given season maximizes a sport's fan appeal. Interest seems to decline if one or a few teams dominate every year, with no one else having a remote possibility of winning a championship in the foreseeable future. For example, the All-American Football Conference in the 1940s–50s folded in large part because of complete dominance by the Cleveland Browns. On the other hand, fans seem to like the notion of dynasties being challenged. Hence, the English Premier League has shown unprecedented popularity at the same time Manchester United and now Manchester City have shown unprecedented dominance, and the NBA flourished during the era of the Chicago Bulls' dynasty and the more recent dominance of the Golden State Warriors.

At the same time, theory suggests that (except for football, where so few games are played and largely viewed on television) a league where Pittsburgh and New York won the exact same number of games and championships would not maximize appeal, in light of the much greater number of fans of New York teams than Pittsburgh teams. Many economic studies have considered this question empirically (summarized in Stefan Szymanski, *The Economic Design of Sporting Contests* 41 J. ECON. LIT. 1137 (2003)). The results are decidedly mixed, with many studies showing that more balanced competitions are not any more attractive to fans than imbalanced ones. Even a panel of consultants MLB hired to study the issue concluded that parity was not desired, advocating instead the need to adopt rules with a goal that "every well-run club has a regularly recurring hope of reaching postseason play."

Assuming that fans do indeed prefer a particular range of competitive balance, the next question is why free markets will not produce that range. Economic theory suggests that markets should promote the competitive balance fans prefer, assuming, however, that all the teams have roughly similar revenue-generating potential. All else equal (which, of course, it never is), a star player is going to be more valuable to an *inferior* team, because the marginal contribution of that player will be greater for the weaker team. When the economic value of a win is much greater for Club A than for Club B, Club A presumably will spend more for the player, even if the player is more valuable on the field to Club B. To illustrate, some data from years past suggested that each additional win (within the range of their actual success) produced about $2.4 million in revenue for the Yankees, and about $400,000 for the Pirates. Thus, if a player is predicted to add 2 wins ($4.8 million additional revenue) to the Yankees and 6 wins ($2.4 million additional revenue) for the Pirates, the Yankees are likely to win the bidding for his services. In the short run, this advances consumer preferences, as, all else equal, more fans prefer to see the Yankees than the Pirates win. But suppose the result is that fans in many smaller cities lose any hope of reaching post-season play, and stop attending games? This is a real harm, but it is not considered by the Yankees in making its bid. The Yankees are only concerned with how much they earn, not the effect on others. This is what provides the economic justification for some form of player restraints.

The foregoing, however, is economic theory, not real life. In real life, for free markets persistently to create imbalance, the clubs bidding the most actually have to succeed at buying the best players. If clubs' ability to predict the success of veteran free agents is poor—in statistical terms, if there is a weak correlation between player pay and team performance— then the beneficial influence of player restraints on competitive balance is diminished. Empirical studies summarized by Professor Szymanski, *supra*, have shown that clubs in North America do a much poorer job of matching pay with performance than do European soccer clubs. Indeed, although the labor market for hockey resulted in most teams losing money prior to 2004, over the prior three seasons 12 different teams participated in the Stanley Cup semi-finals.

4.   ALTERNATIVES TO PLAYER RESTRAINTS

One frequently mentioned alternative to player restraints is *revenue sharing*. Designing a reasonable revenue sharing scheme, however, is not easy. If all clubs shared all revenue, the result would be to remove any incentive for each club to succeed. If clubs share a portion of local revenue, the result could actually harm balance. Suppose that teams shared 1/3 of their revenue from live gate and concessions with the visiting team, and that higher attendance yields $3 million/win in large markets (like Los Angeles and New York) and $900,000/win in small markets (like Milwaukee or Kansas City). If a player is expected to produce three additional wins for each club, then the Brewers, Royals and other small market clubs will be able to claim a one-third share of the $9 million additional gate received by the large market club, but would only keep a 2/3 share of the additional $1.8 million if the player signs with their own club. *See* Stefan Szymanski, *Professional team sports are only a game: The Walrasian fixed supply conjecture model, Contest-Nash equilibrium and the invariance principle*, 5 J. SPORTS. ECON. 111 (2004). Thus, Professor Andrew Zimbalist has suggested a formula that provides revenues to teams based on weak market *potential*, which they would continue to receive regardless of their actual performance. Using this formula would provide weak market teams with additional revenues regardless of whether the wealthier teams perform better or worse, and it would provide better incentives for clubs to participate in the labor market in a manner that will facilitate the level of competitive balance that fans prefer. *See* Andrew Zimbalist, MAY THE BEST TEAM WIN: BASEBALL ECONOMICS AND PUBLIC POLICY 103–07 (Washington: Brookings Inst. Press, 2003).

5.   ANALYZING PLAYER RESTRAINTS

(a) Do Player Restraints Achieve Their Desired Pro-Competitive Objective?

Even if (1) fans prefer some level of competitive balance, and (2) free markets will not necessarily produce the level of competitive balance fans prefer, the next economic question is whether the particular restraint chosen by a league has the desired effect of promoting competitive balance.

An oft-cited economic argument against player restraints is that they are unlikely to affect the allocation of players among teams, since the large-market teams will simply find another way of getting highly valued players (economists call this claim the "invariance principle"). This is clearly true in European soccer, where an active market in the cash sale of players exists. Suppose a player is worth £4.8 million to Manchester United and £2 million to West Bromwich Albion. If the player is a free agent, he will receive up to £4.8 million and sign with Man U. If the player is reserved for life to West Bromwich and must play for a salary of £100,000, Man U would be willing to pay West Brom up to £4.7m to acquire his services. The only effect of the reserve rule is who gets the money.

This argument has less salience in North America because in practice all the major leagues prohibit or strictly limit the assignment of player contracts in return for large amounts of cash. Thus, for a player to be transferred, a trade must be arranged. The resulting bargaining difficulties can result in players remaining on one club even if more valuable to another. And, if players are more valuable to inferior teams, the result of player restraints and a ban on cash sales is a more rigid labor market, and good teams staying good, bad teams staying bad, and competitive balance getting worse.

(b) Are Player Restraints Needed Because of Irrational Club Behavior?

In an intriguing article, two leading American sports practitioners assert that sports club owners are uniquely unable to act as economically rational profit-maximizers. As a result, absent some meaningful labor market restraints, "in their relentless desire to win games," owners will "commit economic suicide." The authors' argument is succinctly put:

> The need and desire to win, the pressure from coaches, fans, and the media to be successful on the court, field, or ice, will often cloud and distort even the most astute business judgment. In order to win games, a team must sign talented players, and to sign talented players, a team may conclude it has no choice other than to meet financial demands that are *not realistic in relation to the revenues that team is able to generate.*

> One seemingly simple answer to this is just to say no to a player's financial demands. But experience teaches that those who just say no usually are not able to field the most competitive teams. In the era of free agency, if a team is not prepared to pay whatever happens to be the going rate, the better players will go elsewhere, where some other owner is willing to meet their demands, *heedless of the financial consequences* to that team or the league.

Jeffrey A. Mishkin & Shepard Goldfein, *Professional Sports Leagues Need Fiscal Responsibility*, N.Y.L.J., Aug. 7, 2000, at 12. Player restraints that are designed to ensure that payroll designs are economically rational, then, may also make economic sense.

———

NOTES AND QUESTIONS

1. *Antitrust and Player Restraints.* Do player restraints significantly restrain trade?

2. *Are Player Restraints Pretext for Lowering Payroll?* Are there any reasons to justify player restraints? In NASCAR rules are set by an independent third party. NASCAR has adopted thousands of engineering rules designed to promote competitive balance, but absolutely no restraints on competition in the labor market for talented drivers, crew chiefs, crews, or engineers. Is that relevant to your answer?

3. *Competitive Balance.* Player restraints are often justified to promote competitive balance; what does competitive balance mean and why is it desirable? Once you have defined a measure of competitive balance in a particular league, compare the current level of balance with the expected amount of balance if:

a. there are no restraints on the ability of a player to receive competing salary offers whenever the player's current contract expires;

b. players are bound for life to their initial employer, but cash sales between clubs are permitted;

c. players are bound for life to their initial employer, but cash sales between clubs are forbidden;

d. clubs adopt one or more different schemes to share revenue:

   i.   high-revenue teams are "taxed" and money redistributed to low-revenue teams

   ii. teams from large media markets are taxed and money redistributed to teams in small media markets

   iii. home teams share 1/3 of live gate with visiting team

   iv. all live gate revenue shared

   v.   all broadcast rights revenue shared

   vi. broadcast rights shared in part in equal shares, in part based on number of games the club appears on national broadcast, and in part based on actual order of finish in the competition

e. teams are subject to a fairly rigid salary cap.

4. *Are Clubs Rational?* Why would clubs accept player payrolls that they did not expect to recoup in increased revenues? What sort of player restraints can prevent or deter economic irrationality?

B. ANTITRUST ANALYSIS OF SPECIFIC PLAYER MARKET RESTRAINTS

We now turn to the key substantive issues raised in antitrust litigation by players against restraints imposed on the labor market by leagues. The major cases have taken place in football, and they concern three specific player restraints involving the rookie draft, developmental squads, and restraints on veteran free agency.

1. ROOKIE DRAFT

The draft of college players originated in football in the late 1930s and later spread to other professional sports. While there are variations across the sports, the basic structure of the draft is simple—proceeding in reverse order of finish from the prior season, each team selects a player from the pool of new players available that year, unless it trades away or acquires a draft pick in a deal with another team. (The NBA and the NHL conduct a lottery for drafting positions among the teams that miss the playoffs, but this is still heavily weighted towards the clubs with the worst records that season.) The consequence is that a player can either negotiate a contract to play with the team that selected him, or not play in the league at all (unless he can force a trade to another team, as star rookie quarterbacks John Elway and Eli Manning famously did). Reciprocally, each team is only allowed to negotiate with those players it has drafted, so if a star draft pick is not signed, the team will not be able to approach another rookie player at the same position. Thus, both sides have significant incentive to reach a deal. Nonetheless, the impact of not reaching a deal is usually going to be more severe for the player, especially when the player can turn to no other league to play his sport. In a case involving football, one player lodged an antitrust suit when he was unhappy with the contract offer from the team that drafted him.

SMITH V. PRO FOOTBALL, INC.
593 F.2d 1173 (D.C. Cir. 1978)

WILKEY, CIRCUIT JUDGE.

[James "Yazoo" Smith, an All-American defensive back at the University of Oregon, was selected by the Washington Redskins as the twelfth pick in the first round of the 1968 draft. He signed a one-year contract for a total of $50,000—$22,000 in salary and $28,000 in bonuses. Smith suffered a career-ending neck injury in the last game of the 1968 regular season, and the Redskins paid him an additional $19,800 (the amount he would have received had he played out the option year of his contract).

Two years later, Smith filed a lawsuit that, among other things, attacked the legality of the rookie draft under antitrust law. Smith contended that, but for the draft, he would have secured a more lucrative contract that would have better protected him from the financial consequences of his injury. The district court ruled that the NFL's draft violated federal antitrust law and had cost Smith $92,000—the amount the judge calculated as the difference between what Smith would have received in a "free market" without a draft, and what he actually received. These financial losses were automatically trebled to a $276,000 damage award.]

I. Background

[As noted above, the NFL uses a reverse-order-of-finish draft. In 1968 there were 16 succeeding rounds, the same order of selection being followed in each round. Each of the 26 teams had one choice per round unless they had traded their choice in that round to another team (a fairly common practice).]

The NFL draft, like similar procedures in other professional sports, is designed to promote "competitive balance." By dispersing newly arriving player talent equally among all NFL teams, with preferences to the weaker clubs, the draft aims to produce teams that are as evenly-matched on the playing field as possible. Evenly-matched teams make for closer games, tighter pennant races, and better player morale, thus maximizing fan interest, broadcast revenues, and overall health of the sport.

The draft is effectuated through the NFL's "no-tampering" rule. Under this rule as it existed in 1968, no team was permitted to negotiate prior to the draft with any player eligible to be drafted, and no team could negotiate with (or sign) any player selected by another team in the draft. The net result of these restrictions was that the right to negotiate with any given player was exclusively held by one team at any given time. If a college player could not reach a satisfactory agreement with the team holding the rights to his services, he could not play in the NFL.

* * *

The NFL player draft differs from the classic group boycott in two significant respects. First, the NFL clubs which have "combined" to implement the draft are not *competitors* in any economic sense. The clubs operate basically as a joint venture in producing an entertainment product—football games and telecasts. No NFL club can produce this product without agreements and joint action with every other team. To this end, the League not only determines franchise locations, playing schedules, and broadcast terms, but also ensures that the clubs receive equal shares of telecast and ticket revenues. These economic joint venturers "compete" on the playing field, to be sure, but here as well cooperation is essential if the entertainment product is to attain a high quality: only if the teams are "competitively balanced" will spectator interest be maintained at a high pitch. No NFL team, in short, is interested in driving another team out of business, whether in the counting-house or on the football field, for if the League fails, no one team can survive.

The draft differs from the classic group boycott, secondly, in that the NFL clubs have not combined *to exclude competitors or potential competitors* from their level of the market. Smith was never seeking to "compete" with the NFL clubs, and their refusal to deal with him has resulted in no decrease in the competition for providing football entertainment to the public. The draft, indeed, is designed not to insulate the NFL from competition, but to improve the entertainment product by enhancing its teams' competitive equality.

In view of these differences, we conclude that the NFL player draft cannot properly be described as a group boycott, at least not the type of group boycott that traditionally has elicited invocation of a *per se* rule. The "group boycott" designation, we believe, is properly restricted to concerted attempts by competitors to exclude horizontal competitors; it should not be applied, and has never been applied by the Supreme Court, to concerted refusals that are not designed to drive out competitors but to achieve some other goal.

[The court further explained why, even if not in the precise category of a *per se* illegal group boycott, the draft did not meet the general standards for *per se* condemnation from *Northern Pacific Railway*: a pernicious effect of competition and lack of any redeeming virtue.] Some form of player selection system may serve to regulate and thereby promote competition in what would otherwise be a chaotic bidding market for the services of college players. The Redskins, moreover, presented considerable evidence at trial that the draft was designed to preserve, and that it made some contribution to preserving, playing-field equality among the NFL-teams with various attendant benefits. The draft, finally, like the vertical restraints challenged in *Continental T.V.*, is "widely used" in our economy and has both judicial and scholarly support for its economic usefulness. [The Court therefore found that the Rule of Reason should apply.]

* * *

B. Rule of Reason

Under the rule of reason, a restraint must be evaluated to determine whether it is significantly anticompetitive in purpose or effect. . . . If, on analysis, the restraint is found to have legitimate business purposes whose realization serves to promote competition, the "anticompetitive evils" of the challenged practice must be carefully balanced against its "procompetitive virtues" to ascertain whether the former outweigh the latter. A restraint is unreasonable if it has the "net effect" of substantially impeding competition.

* * *

The draft that has been challenged here is undeniably anticompetitive both in its purpose and in its effect. The defendants have conceded that the draft "restricts competition among the NFL clubs for the services of graduating college players" and, indeed, that the draft "is designed to limit competition" and "to be a 'purposive' restraint" on the player-service market. The fact that the draft assertedly was designed to promote the teams' playing-field equality rather than to inflate their profit margins may prevent the draft's purpose from being described, in subjective terms, as nefarious. But this fact does not prevent its purpose from being described, in objective terms, as anticompetitive, for suppressing competition is the Telos, the very essence of the restraint.

The trial judge was likewise correct in finding that the draft was significantly anticompetitive in its *effect*. The draft inescapably forces each seller of football services to deal with one, and only one buyer, robbing the seller, as in any monopolistic market, of any real bargaining power. The draft, as the District Court found, "leaves no room whatever for competition among the teams for the services of college players, and utterly strips them of any measure of control over the marketing of their talents." The predictable effect of the draft, as the evidence established and as the District Court found, was to lower the salary levels of the best college players. There can be no doubt that the effect of the draft as it existed in 1968 was to "suppress or even destroy competition" in the market for players' services.

The justification asserted for the draft is that it has the legitimate business purpose of promoting "competitive balance" and playing-field equality among the teams, producing better entertainment for the public, higher salaries for the players, and increased financial security for the clubs. The NFL has endeavored to summarize this justification by saying that the draft ultimately has a "procompetitive" effect, yet this shorthand entails no small risk of confusion. The draft is "procompetitive," if at all, in a very different sense from that in which it is anticompetitive. The draft is anticompetitive in its effect on the market for players' services, because it virtually eliminates economic competition among buyers for the services of sellers. The draft is allegedly "procompetitive" in its effect on the playing field; but the NFL teams are not economic competitors on the playing field, and the draft, while it may heighten athletic competition and thus improve the entertainment product offered to the public, does not increase competition in the economic sense of encouraging others to enter the market and to offer the product at lower cost. Because the draft's "anticompetitive" and "procompetitive" effects are not comparable, it is impossible to "net them out" in the usual rule-of-reason balancing. The draft's "anticompetitive evils," in other words, cannot be balanced against its "procompetitive virtues," and the draft be upheld if the latter outweigh the former. In strict economic terms, the draft's demonstrated procompetitive effects are nil.

The defendants' justification for the draft reduces in fine to an assertion that competition in the market for entering players' services would not serve the best interests of the public, the clubs, or the players themselves. This is precisely the type of argument that the Supreme Court only recently has declared to be unavailing. In *National Society of Professional Engineers v. United States,* the Court held that a professional society's ban on competitive bidding violated § 1 of the Sherman Act. In so holding the Court rejected a defense that unbridled competitive bidding would lead to deceptively low bids and inferior work "with consequent risk to public safety and health," terming this justification "nothing less than a frontal assault on the basic policy of the Sherman Act." . . . The purpose of antitrust analysis, the Court concluded, "is to form a judgment about the competitive significance of the restraint; it is not to decide whether a policy favoring competition is in the public interest, or in the interest of the members of an industry. Subject to exceptions defined by statute, that policy decision has been made by Congress."

Confining our inquiry, as we must, to the draft's impact on competitive conditions, we conclude that the draft as it existed in 1968 was an unreasonable restraint of trade. The draft was concededly anticompetitive in purpose. It was severely anticompetitive in effect. It was not shown to have any significant offsetting procompetitive impact in the economic sense. Balancing the draft's anticompetitive evils against its procompetitive virtues, the outcome is plain. The NFL's defenses, premised on the assertion that competition for players' services would harm both the football industry and society, are unavailing; there is nothing of procompetitive virtue to balance, because "the Rule of Reason does not support a defense based on the assumption that competition itself is unreasonable."

We recognize . . . that professional football "may differ significantly from other business services, and, accordingly [that] the nature of the competition" for player talent may vary from an absolute "free market" norm. Given the joint-venture status of the NFL clubs, we do not foreclose the possibility that some type of player selection system might be defended as serving "to regulate and promote . . . competition" in the market for players' services. But we are faced here, as the Supreme Court was faced in *Professional Engineers*, with what amounts to a "total ban" on competition, and we agree with the District Court that this level of restraint cannot be justified. The trial judge concluded, with pardonable exaggeration, that the draft system at issue was "absolutely the most restrictive one imaginable." Even though the draft was justified primarily by the need to disperse the best players, it applied to all graduating seniors, including average players who were, in a sense, fungible commodities. It permitted college players to negotiate with only one team. If a player could not contract with that team, he *could not play at all*.

Without intimating any view as to the legality of the following procedures, we note that there exist significantly less anticompetitive alternatives to the draft system which has been challenged here. The trial judge found that the evidence supported the viability of a player selection system that would permit "more than one team to draft each player, while restricting the number of players any one team might sign." A less anticompetitive draft might permit a college player to negotiate with the team of his choice if the team that drafted him failed to make him an acceptable offer. The NFL could also conduct a second draft each year for players who were unable to reach agreement with the team that selected them the first time. Most obviously, perhaps, the District Court found that the evidence supported the feasibility of a draft that would run for fewer rounds, applying only to the most talented players and enabling their "average" brethren to negotiate in a "free market." The least restrictive alternative of all, of course, would be for the NFL to eliminate the draft entirely and employ revenue-sharing to equalize the teams' financial resources, a method of preserving "competitive balance" nicely in harmony with the league's self-proclaimed "joint-venture" status.

We are not required in this case to design a draft that would pass muster under the antitrust laws. We would suggest, however, that under the Supreme Court's decision in *Professional Engineers*, no draft can be justified merely by showing that it is a relatively less anticompetitive means of attaining sundry benefits for the football industry and society. Rather, a player draft can survive scrutiny under the rule of reason only if it is demonstrated to have positive, economically procompetitive benefits that offset its anticompetitive effects, or, at the least, if it is demonstrated to accomplish legitimate business purposes and to have a net anticompetitive effect that is insubstantial. Because the NFL draft as it existed in 1968 had severe anticompetitive effects and no demonstrated procompetitive virtues, we hold that it unreasonably restrained trade in violation of § 1 of The Sherman Act.

* * *

MacKINNON, CIRCUIT JUDGE, dissenting.

* * *

The Nature of the Business.

* * *

Professional sports teams are in some respects traditional economic units seeking to sell a product to the public. But economic competition between teams is not and cannot be the sole determinant of their behavior. Professional sports leagues are uniquely organized economic entities; the ultimate success of the league depends on the economic cooperation rather than the economic competition of its members. The product being offered to the public is more than an isolated exhibition, it is a series of connected exhibitions that culminate in the annual grand finale contest between the two teams with the best records in the League, which have demonstrated their prowess in organized, rigidly scheduled League competition. The product being offered the public is the "league sport," and the value of this product at the stadium gate and to the television networks depends on the competitive balance of the teams in the league. Spectators and television viewers are not interested in lopsided games or contests between weak teams.

In many respects, the business of professional football as carried on by the NFL resembles a "natural monopoly." The structure of the League as a single entity outside the antitrust laws was also specifically authorized in 1966 by Act of Congress. As defined by two authorities, a natural monopoly is a monopoly resulting from economies of scale, a relationship between the size of the market and the size of the most efficient firm such that one firm of efficient size can produce all or more than the market can take at a remunerative price, and can continually expand its capacity at less cost than that of a new firm entering the business. In this situation, competition may exist for a time but only until bankruptcy or merger leaves the field to one firm; in a meaningful sense, competition here is self-destructive. At the present time, the NFL, as an organized association of various teams (or firms), has a statutorily recognized monopoly over production of the "league sport" of major professional football. Anyone who wishes to watch a major professional football game must watch an NFL game, played under NFL rules with NFL teams and players. History suggests that it is easier for the NFL to expand the number of teams than it is for another league to form and operate successfully. Competition may exist for a time, as the experiences of the American Football League and the World Football League demonstrate, but in the long run such competition is destructive and many teams fail, even as they did within the NFL in its free market formative years.

The History and Effect of the Draft.

[Here Judge MacKinnon detailed a number of features of life in the NFL in the mid-1930s at the time the draft was adopted. (Note that George MacKinnon was an All-American center for the University of Minnesota Golden Gophers in the 1920s.) There were just nine teams with squads of 22 to 26 players. Though a free market existed for players coming out of college, a career in professional football was not that attractive to many players as they graduated from college. Many opted to go on to graduate or professional school, to go into business, or to begin college or high school football coaching. These alternatives were attractive as compared to the NFL, where salaries were modest, careers were short, and there was always a possibility of a permanently disabling injury. In 1936, the NFL instituted the draft after the last-place Cincinnati team had dropped out of the league. Initially covering 30 rounds, the draft had been cut to 17 rounds by the time that Smith challenged its legality under antitrust law four decades later.]

* * *

In my view, there are compelling reasons why the draft has continued so long without serious challenge. In effect a player draft is *natural for league sports.* Competitive equality among the component teams is an inherent requirement for meaningful sports competition and the survival of a conference or league high school, college, or professional and all of its members. Close rivalries are the backbone of any successful sport. When the NFL established the draft, its objective was to give each team the same fair *opportunity to* be competitive; it sought to achieve a competitive balance among all the League's teams, that is, to "try to equalize the teams." The intended result was to create a situation where each League game would become a closer contest, where spectator interest in the game and the players themselves would be increased, where the interesting individual contests would create an interesting League championship race, and where ultimately the teams and their players would benefit from the greater income resulting from the increased fan interest.

* * *

All major sports, in recognition of the need for competitive balance, have drafts. Hockey and basketball have drafts, and baseball instituted a draft when it became clear from the long domination of the New York Yankees that the farm system was not producing competitive balance.

Since the first college football player draft was held in 1936, the results sought to be accomplished have clearly been achieved. Some argue that this has been caused by other factors, but the preponderance of the factual testimony and record evidence supports a conclusion that the college player draft was the key factor which produced the competitive balance of the teams, which in turn brought about the exciting games and interesting championship races and increased public interest in the sport, which ultimately led to the huge gate receipts and large television contracts that are presently producing enormous benefits for the players themselves. There was no showing to the contrary in the 2,000 page record. The majority argue that it is television that produces the interest and the revenues but the balanced teams produced by the draft came first and caused the close contests which attracted the public and eventually television.

Since 1935, the number of teams has increased from nine to today's League of 28 teams, and the number of players per team has also been increased substantially. Instead of the small squads of around 26 players in the early days of the sport, the modern team's roster once swelled to 47 and was later reduced to 43 players. This has increased the total number of active players in the League as a whole to slightly over 1,200. Gate receipts have increased tremendously due to the increased popular interest in the game. Also important are the television revenues, which constitute a large part of each team's annual income. The NFL television contracts between the League and the television networks have distributed hundreds of millions of dollars to all teams in the League; and current news reports indicate that the payments are to be substantially increased. The lucrative television contract, made possible by an *exemption* from the antitrust laws enacted by Congress, is negotiated for all teams by the League Commissioner. These moneys are distributed *equally* to each team in the League without regard to the size of the team's local television market. In 1968 the revenues from television accounted for approximately 30% of the total revenue of the Redskins and this was approximately the same percentage as the average for all NFL teams in that year. Team revenue from gate receipts, television contracts, and other sources has increased tremendously since 1935, and the NFL teams and their players are the direct recipients of the benefits of the increased national interest in NFL games. College players, 22 years old, coming out of college in 1976 and playing in the NFL were making $20,000 to $150,000 their first year.

* * *

Due to the increased benefits afforded professional football players, the competition for graduating college football players that previously existed from lucrative coaching positions and numerous other business and professional opportunities has been successfully met, if not altogether eliminated as a practical matter. The increasing popularity of pro football and its attractiveness to graduating college players assures those interested in the success of the game, such as television and radio broadcasters and networks, stadium owners, team owners, and players already playing in the NFL, that the best college football players year after year will continue to join the professional ranks and assure the quality and attractiveness of their games. In fact, a great many players now go to college for the sole purpose of establishing a playing record which will result in their being drafted by one of the professional teams; a first-round draft choice in the professional league is viewed by many as the substantial equivalent of *summa cum laude* and first-round draft choices are generally paid much higher starting salaries.

* * *

From my analysis, the testimony of record overwhelmingly supports the conclusion that the growth of football between 1935 and 1968 was largely due to the competitive balance that the League achieved during those years and to the creation of a quality product, the "league sport." This competitive balance, and the consequential tremendous growth in public interest, which has inured greatly to the benefit of the players themselves, is in large part a result of the college player draft. . . . The draft created the competitive balance, that created the public interest, that led other cities to organize teams, that led to national expansion of the league, that enlarged the total gate receipts, that led to the large revenue-producing television contracts.

[The dissent then addressed the majority's argument that a less restrictive draft system should have been devised by the NFL.]

A pure draft takes all of the college players that are coming into the market with the teams with the poorest records having preference in the order of their won and lost records. The draft as it existed in 1968 was a pure draft, and it is submitted that the draft should be that extensive if the opportunity for maximum competitive balance is to be assured. If the draft only lasts two rounds, as the trial court here suggested, the rest of the players are left for the free market and the preponderance of those players, or at least the preponderance of the better players in that group, would go to teams with special attractions and the teams owned by super-wealthy millionaires who desire very greatly to own a winning team. Not even a complete sharing of team revenues could overcome the unfair advantage posed by wealthy owners and collateral attractions of a few cities. Large cities such as New York, Chicago, Los Angeles, and Washington offer special advantages for publicity, endorsements, and lucrative off-field jobs in business. Cities with better weather are more attractive to some players, and teams with better prospects of winning in a particular season furnish a certain attraction for some players. Larger cities with larger stadiums realize more income and hence are somewhat able to offer larger salaries than teams with smaller cities and stadiums. So are teams owned by wealthy sportsmen who place a premium on winning and are willing to support their desires with almost unlimited financial resources. The draft has substantially reduced the ability of these owners to dominate the league.

Given these factors that would permit a few teams to corner the "developing players" that in a great many instances eventually surpass developed players, drafted in the earlier rounds, it is necessary to have a draft that reaches the *maximum number of potential players who are absolutely necessary to preserve competitive balance.* When the draft does not reach that many players, the few stronger teams with the natural advantages will be able to corner the best remaining prospects who become free agents. The testimony indicated that a few "super wealthy" owners with a very deep pocketbook could obtain a very substantial advantage if there were a substantial pool of free market players.

* * *

The Rule of Reason and the College Player Draft.

* * *

[T]he important consideration is the effect of the draft. The majority concludes that the draft strips the players of "any real bargaining power," lowers their salaries, and suppresses if not destroys competition for their services. I disagree. The majority opinion and the trial court only looked at the draft from the players' side and only at a portion of that. As for bargaining power, the operation of the draft also restrains the team from dealing with other players (even though there are exceptions, discussed below). This is particularly true when a team drafts for a position, as the

Redskins did in drafting Smith as their first-round choice in 1968. The Redskins drafted Smith in the first round to fill a need at the "free safety position." In using their first-round draft choice to select a player for that particular position, they practically put all of their eggs in one basket for that year. In selecting Smith, they passed over or did not reach, all other players of nearly equal ability for that position. After the Redskins had exercised their first draft selection, these other players would be chosen by other teams with later picks, and would thus not be available in later rounds. Even if another player was later available, it would be a waste of a valuable draft choice for the Redskins to use any subsequent choice to draft for that same position, since the position needed only one player and the team had other needs to fill as well. That is the way the 1968 player draft went for the Redskins. After they had drafted Smith first to fill that position, the team practically had to sign him if they wanted to fill what they considered was a vital team vacancy. These circumstances gave Smith very substantial bargaining leverage, as his professional negotiating agent frequently reminded the Redskins. Also, a first-round draft choice commands considerable publicity in the locality, and the team is under very considerable pressure from its fans to sign the player and thereby put the first-round pick in a uniform. Smith was the beneficiary, as a first-round choice, of such public pressure.

While in a free market a player could negotiate with several teams, a team could also negotiate with several players of nearly equal ability and play one off against the others. If Smith had negotiated with the Redskins in a free market, the Redskins could also have simultaneously negotiated with the next-best prospect for free safety as well and the availability of the other player might have served to reduce the salary offers to Smith. Then if Smith and the Redskins could not come to terms, the Redskins could always opt for one of the other prospects they considered to be close to Smith in ability, well realizing, as experience has many times proven, that the ultimate development and performance of the second or third choice might eventually eclipse that of their first favored choice. Drafting college players is not an exact science.

* * *

Simply because the draft is essential to the vitality of the business does not mean that players entering the League, as opposed to veterans already playing in the League, have no interest in the existence of a draft. It would be error to suggest otherwise because without a draft a less stable League with fewer franchises and lower salaries would result. Incoming players receive salaries and bonuses far in excess of what they could command in a free market of teams in a league that did not have the competitive balance which a player draft produces. The vitality of the League, which is admittedly dependent in large measure on the balanced team competition produced by the draft, has attracted so great a public interest that the public in most localities, as referred to above, has subsidized the teams by the erection of huge stadiums without full contribution to their cost by the teams that use them. This fact has enabled salaries paid to draftees to be higher than what they would be in a free market with the attendant destructive competition, unequal competitive balance, and resulting shaky franchises. It cannot be said that rookie players have no interest in the existence of the college player draft.

In short, in my opinion, the evidentiary record here supports the conclusion that the draft also has a favorable effect on the bargaining position of players, which to a considerable extent nets out the adverse effect it has in limiting the players' right to negotiate with other teams. And this bargaining equivalency vitiates the assertion that players' salaries are depressed on account of the draft.

NOTES AND QUESTIONS

1. *Consistent Reasoning?* Is the *Smith* majority's analysis in the first part of the opinion, which defends the competitive virtues of the draft against a charge of *per se* illegality, fully compatible with its analysis in the second part of the opinion, which condemns the anticompetitive effect of the draft under the Rule of Reason?

2. *Causes of NFL Success.* In several very long footnotes, the *Smith* majority and dissent debated a number of the factual underpinnings to their respective arguments:

a. Was it the player draft, instituted in 1935, or network television, which emerged in the late 1950s, or some linkage between the two, that was the true source of pro football's economic success?

b. How much competitive balance can really be contributed by the rookie draft (or restraints on veteran free agency), given the team dynasties associated with legendary head coaches? To improve competitive balance, should sports leagues place similar limits on the ability of winning teams to hire top coaches and front office executives from other clubs?

c. Is revenue sharing among owners, not just from network and cable television and trademark licensing, but also from gate receipts and other revenue sources, the most effective means to achieve evenly balanced athletic competition? What effect might such league "socialism" have on teams' ability and incentive to pay their players higher salaries? What effect might this have on the owners' incentives to promote their team in their local market? How would your answer be different if the league had, as the NFL does today, a "hard" team salary cap (and floor)? Indeed, is there any competitive balance need for a draft at all if the league has a team salary cap as in the NFL or NBA today, or a rookie pool salary cap as in the NFL and NHL today?

3. *Legitimacy of Competitive Balance as a Justification.* The *Smith* majority seems to state that it is irrelevant for Rule of Reason analysis that a league practice such as the draft enhances competitive balance within the league. *NCAA v. Alston*, 141 S. Ct. 2141 (2021), discussed in detail in Chapter 13, explicitly refused to address the argument, although it is inconsistent with the approach of most sports law cases, such as *NCAA v. Bd. of Regents,* that look at whether restraints improve the quality of the product and enhance fan appeal (and thus output) and make the produce more responsive to consumer preference. Indeed, if a league cannot defend the legality of restrictive internal practices on the grounds that they improve the quality of the product offered to its fans, how could a less restrictive draft (or any conduct-standardizing rule) pass muster, as the *Smith* majority intimates it could in the latter part of its decision?

4. *Do Restraints Help Small-Market Clubs?* The principal argument for the draft is that it is necessary to preserve balanced athletic competition against the threat posed by big market teams. But is there any guarantee that the draft will have that effect, at least as long as teams can sell their top picks to other clubs? Consider, for example, the significance of the Quebec Nordiques dealing Eric Lindros to the Philadelphia Flyers in 1992, for $15 million and five players. (The Nordiques franchise had been purchased in 1989 for $15 million, though it became far more valuable in the late-1990s as the Stanley Cup champion Colorado Avalanche.) In addition, is it possible that the draft also obstructs achievement of competitive balance? Does not the football draft guarantee the Super Bowl winner the exclusive right to valued players, which may obstruct the ability of weaker teams to make rapid improvements in their relative strength? Can you think of ways to restructure the draft to enhance its contribution to equality on the playing field (as well as its ability to pass the Rule of Reason test)?

5. *Are Draftees Exploited?* Opponents of the draft assert that it permits exploitation of new players, who are left with no choice but to accept a "take it or leave it" offer by the drafting team, the only team with which they are permitted to deal. Yet in sports like football or basketball, top rookie draft picks sign multiyear contracts worth tens of millions of dollars, suggesting that they must have significant bargaining leverage as well. There is no doubt that collective bargaining agreements imposing limits on rookie salaries under-compensates some players, however.

In more recent collective bargaining agreements, this issue has been mooted because unions have agreed to sharp limits on salaries given to rookies in the context of overall schemes that ensure a fixed percentage of revenues will go to club payroll, thus increasing pay to veterans.

6. *Less Restrictive Alternatives.* The previous questions suggest the possibility of "more reasonable" or "less restrictive" alternatives to the current "restraint of trade" flowing from the draft. In *NCAA v. Alston*, the Supreme

Court affirmed the trial court's approach to this issue, asking plaintiffs "to show that 'substantially less restrictive alternative rules' existed that 'would achieve the same procompetitive effect as the challenged set of rules.'" It noted that courts should not accept any less restrictive alternative imagined by skilled litigators, so that "courts should not second-guess 'degrees of reasonable necessity.'" 141 S. Ct. at 2161.

Does the LRA have to achieve the exact same level of benefit, or can it achieve almost the same benefit to the league with far less adverse effects on players? For example, if a court believes that professional football with the existing draft is more procompetitive (more attractive to fans) than football without a draft, does the possibility of a less restrictive draft (one that has less anticompetitive impact on the players market) make the existing system illegal? How can a judge determine which version of the draft is more or less restrictive for players? For example, compare a three-round draft with players tied to the drafting team for two years to a six-round draft with players tied to the team for just one year. How does one compare the incremental gains to players from relaxing the draft's prohibition against teams bidding for rookies to the incremental losses to fans from a reduction in competitive athletic balance within the league (on the assumption that the draft does contribute at least some measure of competitive equality)? Alternatively, could a plaintiff advocate that greater revenue sharing within the league would accomplish the same competitive balance benefits as effectively as the draft? Should a jury then be able to find a violation if it decides that increased sharing of some unspecified revenues would also promote competitive balance? Does the process of antitrust litigation about these issues give the league sufficient guidance in designing its system for allocating new players to the teams? Does the threat of litigation give the league the incentive to explore more optimal solutions along both dimensions of this issue? And whatever restraint the league decides to adopt, isn't there always going to be some alternative that someone can imagine that is less restrictive?

2. VETERAN FREE AGENCY

Recall from Chapter 5 that none of the opinions in *Flood v. Kuhn* reached the merits of Curt Flood's claim that baseball's reserve clause was an unreasonable restraint of trade. Unlike baseball, the NFL never had a reserve clause; rather the practice evolved by the 1960s was that, at the expiration of a player's contract, he was free to sign with another team after playing out one "option year" at a 10% increase in salary. However, there was one major condition: the new team was required to provide what the commissioner judged to be "fair and equitable" compensation (by way of players, draft choices, or both) to the team that had lost the player off its roster. If the two teams could not agree on what the free agent compensation would be, the commissioner (then Pete Rozelle) would determine it, and his decision was final and unappealable. The players objected to the "Rozelle Rule" because, unless there was an upstart league competing for players at the time, this requirement effectively meant that football players had no greater opportunity than did baseball players to obtain competing offers for their services.

MACKEY V. NFL

543 F.2d 606 (8th Cir. 1976)

LAY, CIRCUIT JUDGE.

* * *

HISTORY.

* * *

[The Rozelle Rule], unchanged in form, is currently embodied in § 12.1(H) of the NFL Constitution. The ostensible purposes of the rule are to maintain competitive balance among the NFL teams and protect the clubs' investment in scouting, selecting and developing players.

During the period from 1963 through 1974, 176 players played out their options. Of that number, 34 signed with other teams. In three of those cases, the former club waived compensation. In 27 cases, the clubs involved mutually agreed upon compensation. Commissioner Rozelle awarded compensation in the four remaining cases.*

---

*   [The district court detailed these four cases:

- In 1967, Pat Fischer played out the option year with the St. Louis Cardinals and was signed by the Washington Redskins. Commissioner Rozelle awarded the Cardinals a second round draft choice in the 1969 draft and a third round draft choice in the 1970 draft.

- In 1967, Pro Bowl tight end David Parks played out the option with the San Francisco 49ers and became a free agent, subsequently signing with the New Orleans Saints. There had been no agreement on compensation between the two clubs. Commissioner Rozelle awarded as compensation from the New Orleans Saints to the San Francisco 49ers the Saints' first round draft choice in the earlier 1968 draft, and the Saints' first round draft choice in the upcoming 1969 draft. The then-superior 49ers club used the two picks awarded by Rozelle to select two future Pro Bowl starters, center Forrest Blue and tight end Ted Kwalik.

- In 1971 the New England Patriots neglected to timely exercise their option over Phil Olsen's services for the upcoming 1972 season. Commissioner Rozelle declared Olsen a free agent and no longer a member of the New England Patriots team. Olsen then signed with the Los Angeles Rams. Commissioner Rozelle awarded to the New England Patriots the Los Angeles Rams' first round draft choice in the 1972 draft and stated that additional compensation would be awarded to the Patriots from the Rams at the conclusion of the 1971 season. He also directed the Rams to pay to the Patriots the sum of $35,000 constituting Olsen's initial signing bonus and other expenses. In January 1972 Commissioner Rozelle awarded additional compensation to the New England Patriots: the Rams' third round draft choice which they had previously acquired from the Washington Redskins.

- Dick Gordon played out the option with the Chicago Bears during the 1971 season and became a free agent. Although a number of clubs thereafter expressed interest in obtaining Gordon's services, no club was able to work out a compensation agreement with the Chicago Bears. Because of this fact, no club would sign Gordon due to the unknown compensation that would be awarded should it do so. The situation was at an impasse well into the 1972 regular season. Finally, Commissioner Rozelle announced in advance of any signing what the compensation to the Chicago

[The Court first determined that the Rozelle Rule was not protected by the labor exemption. This is summarized in Section C of this chapter.]

We turn, then, to the question of whether the Rozelle Rule, as implemented, violates § 1 of the Sherman Act, which declares illegal "every contract, combination . . . or conspiracy, in restraint of trade or commerce among the several States." The district court found the Rozelle Rule to be a *per se* violation of the Act. Alternatively, the court held the Rule to be violative of the Rule of Reason standard.

* * *

PER SE VIOLATION.

* * *

There is substantial evidence in the record to support the district court's findings as to the effects of the Rozelle Rule. We think, however, that this case presents unusual circumstances rendering it inappropriate to declare the Rozelle Rule illegal per se without undertaking an inquiry into the purported justifications for the Rule.

[T]he line of cases which has given rise to *per se* illegality for the type of agreements involved here generally concerned agreements between business competitors in the traditional sense. Here, however, as the owners and Commissioner urge, the NFL assumes some of the characteristics of a joint venture in that each member club has a stake in the success of the other teams. No one club is interested in driving another team out of business, since if the League fails, no one team can survive. Although businessmen cannot wholly evade the antitrust laws by characterizing their operation as a joint venture, we conclude that the unique nature of the business of professional football renders it inappropriate to mechanically apply *per se* illegality rules here, fashioned in a different context. This is particularly true where, as here, the alleged restraint does not completely eliminate competition for players' services.

* * *

RULE OF REASON.

The focus of an inquiry under the Rule of Reason is whether the restraint imposed is justified by legitimate business purposes, and is no more restrictive than necessary.

In defining the restraint on competition for players' services, the district court found that the Rozelle Rule significantly deters clubs from negotiating with and signing free agents; that it acts as a substantial deterrent to players playing out their options and becoming free agents; that it significantly decreases players' bargaining power in contract

---

Bears would be: a first round draft choice for the draft following the 1973 football season. Immediately thereafter the Los Angeles Rams signed Gordon to a contract.]

negotiations; that players are thus denied the right to sell their services in a free and open market; that as a result, the salaries paid by each club are lower than if competitive bidding were allowed to prevail; and that absent the Rozelle Rule, there would be increased movement in interstate commerce of players from one club to another.

We find substantial evidence in the record to support these findings. Witnesses for both sides testified that there would be increased player movement absent the Rozelle Rule. Two economists testified that elimination of the Rozelle Rule would lead to a substantial increase in player salaries. Carroll Rosenbloom, owner of the Los Angeles Rams, indicated that the Rams would have signed quite a few of the star players from other teams who had played out their options, absent the Rozelle Rule. [The court then cited evidence identifying two free agent players who probably would have signed with and moved to new teams but for the Rozelle Rule's deterrent effect on the potential new teams.]

In support of their contention that the restraints effected by the Rozelle Rule are not unreasonable, the defendants asserted a number of justifications. First, they argued that without the Rozelle Rule, star players would flock to cities having natural advantages such as larger economic bases, winning teams, warmer climates, and greater media opportunities; that competitive balance throughout the League would thus be destroyed; and that the destruction of competitive balance would ultimately lead to diminished spectator interest, franchise failures, and perhaps the demise of the NFL, at least as it operates today. Second, the defendants contended that the Rozelle Rule is necessary to protect the clubs' investment in scouting expenses and player developments costs. Third, they asserted that players must work together for a substantial period of time in order to function effectively as a team; that elimination of the Rozelle Rule would lead to increased player movement and a concomitant reduction in player continuity; and that the quality of play in the NFL would thus suffer, leading to reduced spectator interest, and financial detriment both to the clubs and the players. Conflicting evidence was adduced at trial by both sides with respect to the validity of these asserted justifications.

The district court held the defendants' asserted justifications unavailing. As to the clubs' investment in player development costs, Judge Larson found that these expenses are similar to those incurred by other businesses, and that there is no right to compensation for this type of investment. With respect to player continuity, the court found that elimination of the Rozelle Rule would affect all teams equally in that regard; that it would not lead to a reduction in the quality of play; and that even assuming that it would, that fact would not justify the Rozelle Rule's anticompetitive effects. As to competitive balance and the consequences which would flow from abolition of the Rozelle Rule, Judge Larson found that the existence of the Rozelle Rule has had no material effect on competitive balance in the NFL. Even assuming that the Rule did foster competitive balance, the court found that there were other legal means available to achieve that end: *e.g.*, the competition committee, multiple year contracts, and special incentives. The court further concluded that elimination of the Rozelle Rule would have no significant disruptive effects, either immediate or long term, on professional football. In conclusion the court held that the Rozelle Rule was unreasonable in that it was overly broad, unlimited in duration, unaccompanied by procedural safeguards, and employed in conjunction with other anticompetitive practices such as the draft, Standard Player Contract, option clause, and the no-tampering rules.

We agree that the asserted need to recoup player development costs cannot justify the restraints of the Rozelle Rule. That expense is an ordinary cost of doing business and is not peculiar to professional football. Moreover, because of its unlimited duration, the Rozelle Rule is far more restrictive than necessary to fulfill that need.

We agree, in view of the evidence adduced at trial with respect to existing players turnover by way of trades, retirements and new players entering the League, that the club owners' arguments respecting player continuity cannot justify the Rozelle Rule. We concur in the district court's conclusion that the possibility of resulting decline in the quality of play would not justify the Rozelle Rule. We do recognize, as did the district court, that the NFL has a strong and unique interest in maintaining competitive balance among its teams. The key issue is thus whether the Rozelle Rule is essential to the maintenance of competitive balance, and is no more restrictive than necessary. The district court answered both of these questions in the negative.

We need not decide whether a system of inter-team compensation for free agents moving to other teams is essential to the maintenance of competitive balance in the NFL. Even if it is, we agree with the district court's conclusion that the Rozelle Rule is significantly more restrictive than necessary to serve any legitimate purposes it might have in this regard. First, little concern was manifested at trial over the free movement of average or below average players. Only the movement of the better players was urged as being detrimental to football. Yet the Rozelle Rule applies to every NFL player regardless of his status or ability. Second, the Rozelle Rule is unlimited in duration. It operates as a perpetual restriction on a player's ability to sell his services in an open market throughout his career. Third, the enforcement of the Rozelle Rule is unaccompanied by procedural safeguards. A player has no input into the process by which fair compensation is determined. Moreover, the player may be unaware of the precise compensation demanded by his former team, and that other teams might be interested in him but for the degree of compensation sought.

* * *

In sum, we hold that the Rozelle Rule, as enforced, unreasonably restrains trade in violation of § 1 of the Sherman Act.

———

From the 1978 *Smith* decision until the 1993 antitrust settlement discussed below, the NFL's rookie draft remained virtually the same other than a reduction to 12 rounds. Nonetheless, this period witnessed constant innovation and experimentation with different modes of free agency in all leagues. Collective bargaining with the players' associations produced almost all those variations. But after a bargaining impasse in 1988, NFL owners unilaterally introduced one new practice—Plan B, a less restrictive alternative to the Rozelle Rule found illegal in *Mackey*. Plan B entitled each team each year to protect 37 players on its reserve list. Protected players, whether or not their contract had expired, could move to other NFL teams only if their current team chose not to match new offers received, and then the new team had to pay compensation to the player's current team (in the form of draft picks whose number and round varied with the size of the new salary offer). By contrast, all unprotected players (even those still under contract) could try to negotiate a better deal with another club that paid no compensation to the team that lost the player (though just during the months of February and March). If a player did not receive a better offer from another club, he could return to his existing team under whatever contract he enjoyed or was able to negotiate with the latter. In the four years of Plan B, many veteran players (although no stars) moved to other clubs for sizable signing bonuses and salary increases.

In 1989, eight players, backed by the NFLPA, challenged the NFL's Plan B restrictions on each team's 37 protected players. (As we will see in the next section, the players were able to avoid application of the labor exemption defense after the district judge held that the NFLPA had successfully renounced its status as a union bargaining agent.) The merits of the antitrust issues were tried during the summer of 1992, and the jury found that Plan B violated the Rule of Reason. *McNeil v. NFL,* Civ. No. 4-90-476, 1992 WL 315292, at 1 (D. Minn. Sept. 10, 1992). In responding to a series of special interrogatories, the jury found (1) that Plan B harmed players by diminishing competition among NFL clubs for their services, (2) that nonetheless the system contributed significantly to competitive balance among NFL teams, but (3) that the system was unreasonable because it was more restrictive than necessary for that purpose.

On point (2), the players claimed that sports leagues did not need competitive balance to survive, asserting that too much parity would harm fan interest and that college football was enormously popular despite metrics suggesting it is severely imbalanced. The plaintiffs also argued that player movement restrictions harm, rather than create, competitive balance, noting that 13 different teams had won a World Series since free agency was introduced in baseball while at the same time only 7 of 28 NFL teams had won the Super Bowl, and that weaker teams are unable to improve by signing better players. The jury apparently was persuaded by the NFL's arguments that competitive balance was important to a league's attractiveness to fans, that the NFL was well-balanced, and that the NFL's best players would avoid moving to losing teams or cold-weather cities or small market teams where endorsement opportunities were far more limited. On point (3), the plaintiffs argued that a variety of other factors could address the NFL's concerns with free agency if the challenged restrictions were removed, including revenue sharing, imbalanced scheduling, investment in superior management and coaching, and qualitative ways in which players are treated.

A contentious issue in *McNeil* concerned less restrictive alternatives. Although it is well settled that a challenged agreement is unreasonable under the Rule of Reason if it is more restrictive than necessary to achieve the defendants' legitimate business purposes, Judge David Doty did not require the plaintiffs to identify the alternatives, but instead instructed the jury to place the burden on the NFL to show that no less restrictive alternatives were available. The jury found that the NFL had failed to meet this burden.

The jury found that only four of the eight plaintiffs actually suffered damages—totaling $1.6 million. Once Judge Doty rendered a final judgment with an injunctive order, the NFL appealed the verdict on several grounds, including the important issue of who had the burden of proof regarding alternatives. The case was settled by the players and owners before the Eighth Circuit issued an opinion.*

The settlement, which was part of an overall resolution of the long-standing legal and labor-relations conflict between the NFL and NFLPA, emerged from the burst of litigation that followed the *McNeil* verdict. The NFL paid $195 million to the players it had restricted under Plan B and several other NFL policies that had generated lawsuits. In *White v. NFL*, 836 F. Supp. 1458 (D. Minn. 1993), Judge Doty reviewed the settlement of the class action under Fed. R. Civ. P. 23(b) and found it to be "fair, reasonable and adequate" for the affected class. In so doing, the judge overruled objections by veteran players who disapproved of the salary cap, recent college graduates who disapproved of the special rookie salary cap provisions, and a team owner who disapproved of the settlement provision that allowed the NFLPA to control group licenses (licenses for more than five players) of player publicity rights. After the settlement, the union recertified and both sides compromised their legal and public relations positions to generate the framework for a new collective agreement, which

---

* The substantive arguments summarized above come from insightful papers delivered after the jury verdict by two of the leading litigators at the 1993 Sports Lawyers Association annual conference. *See* Jeffrey L. Kessler, "A Look at the *McNeil* Litigation and its Results," and Jeffrey Pash, "Free Agency Litigation in the National Football League." These papers are available on the Casebook Website (http://pennstatelaw.psu.edu/SportsTextWebsite).

they have extended repeatedly, through the 2020 season, with largely the same structural characteristics.

The basic architecture of the post-1993 regime as it applies to free agency remains in place today. Veteran players are unrestricted free agents when their contracts expire, but each club can protect one free agent by designating him as its "franchise" player, who is then guaranteed a salary of either the average of the highest five players in the league at his position for the most plays for the previous year or 120% of his prior year's salary (whichever is higher). In addition, each club can designate two "transition" players among its free agents. For these, the club has a right to match any offer the player receives from another team. If no such offer is received, the club must pay the player the average of the ten highest paid players in the league at his position for the most plays for the previous year or 120% of his prior year's salary. Players with three accrued seasons, but fewer than four accrued seasons at the expiration of their contracts are restricted free agents when their contracts expire, subject to the club's right of first refusal and right to receive draft choice compensation from any new club with which the player signs (as under the old agreement).

In exchange for this system of veteran free agency, the NFLPA agreed to continue the rookie draft, though with the number of rounds reduced from twelve to seven. Most important, the NFLPA accepted a team salary cap, and the owners agreed that clubs must spend a designated percentage of DGR on player costs each season (the percentage has varied over time). In the first year of free agency in 1993, average salaries shot up to $650,000 from $488,000 in 1992. In 2021, the average NFL salary was approximately $2 million. The end of this chapter reviews the bargaining dynamics that led the parties to negotiate this result.

———

NOTES AND QUESTIONS

1. *Allocation of Players.* Essentially the same questions posed earlier about the rookie draft can also be asked about the system that requires clubs who sign veteran free agents to compensate the players' former teams. Does this arrangement really contribute to stronger competition on the field, or does it inhibit the ability of weaker teams to catch up to their stronger rivals, or does it do some of both? What lessons can be drawn from baseball's experience before and after 1976, when free agency rights were given to six-year veterans? Or from comparing the level of competitiveness in baseball with that in football over the next fifteen years, with football experiencing a more restrictive scheme between 1977–94 and a less restrictive scheme (constrained by a salary cap) since then?

2. *Effect on Player Salaries.* Do limits on competition really produce unacceptable exploitation of players by the teams? Keep in mind that salaries paid by NFL clubs still soared over the same fifteen-year period. What is more

important from either an economic or equity standpoint—the *average* or the *median* salary in a sport? The average player *salary* or the average club *payroll*? The proportion of either salary figure to average club *revenues*?

3. *Proving Less Restrictive Alternatives.* As noted above, *Alston* seems to make clear that the plaintiff bears the burden of proof as to whether a challenged player restraint is overbroad. Jury instructions provide the basis of appeal, but in most cases that survive summary judgment and directed verdict motions, do you think that the allocation of burden matters? Would a jury likely find that a league has not proven the absence of a less restrictive alternative if the plaintiffs failed to suggest any? On the merits, do you believe that the NFL could achieve a desired degree of competitive balance without the Plan B restraints challenged in *McNeil*? Would any plan you can conceive of to promote competitive balance predictably survive a less restrictive alternative analysis?

———

As detailed in Chapter 6, MLS varies from the structure of most major North American sports leagues. In practice, the principal impact of this MLS variation from the NFL structure is felt in the players market. The league, not the individual clubs, employs and pays all players (but only the players) on each team. Players negotiate contracts and their salaries only with a department in the MLS office. Once MLS signs player contracts, it distributes the players among the clubs. The league does this first through a "rookie" draft, after which the team has the freedom to retain, release, or trade the player to another team, depending on how the investor-operator and his staff views the player's performance and the club's needs.

The asserted objective of this MLS structure for its players market is to avoid the fate of the North American Soccer League (NASL), in which "competition among teams . . . drove up acquisition costs of the players," thus generating "destructive, economically irrational spending" that eventually led to the dissolution of that league in the early 1980s. Complaint at 14, *Fraser v. Major League Soccer*, No. 97-10342 (D. Mass Feb. 13, 1997). Under MLS rules, each player must sign a Standard Player Agreement which gives the league the unilateral right to renew it for varying terms based on the player's age and length of contract after the negotiated contract term expires. Teams are limited to players whose total salary levels do not exceed the league's salary cap. The Standard Player Agreement assigns to the league the exclusive right to license on a group basis the player's name and image for merchandising purposes. In other leagues, player unions are largely financed by group licensing revenues.

FRASER V. MAJOR LEAGUE SOCCER
284 F.3d 47 (1st Cir. 2002)

BOUDIN, CHIEF JUDGE.

* * *

I.   BACKGROUND FACTS

Despite professional soccer's popularity abroad, the sport has achieved only limited success in this country. Several minor leagues have operated here (four such leagues exist today), but before the formation of MLS, only one other U.S. professional league—the North American Soccer League ("NASL")—had ever obtained Division I, or top-tier, status. Launched in 1968, the NASL achieved some success before folding in 1985; MLS attributes the NASL's demise in part to wide disparities in the financial resources of the league's independently owned teams and a lack of centralized control.

* * *

At issue in this case is MLS's control over player employment. MLS has the "sole responsibility for negotiating and entering into agreements with, and for compensating, Players." In a nutshell, MLS recruits the players, negotiates their salaries, pays them from league funds, and, to a large extent, determines where each of them will play. For example, to balance talent among teams, it decides, with the non-binding input of team operators, where certain of the league's "marquee" players will play.

II.   SHERMAN ACT SECTION 1

[As excerpted in Chapter 6, the appellate court reviewed the district court's summary dismissal of the plaintiffs' § 1 claim on the grounds that MLS was a single entity. It declined to definitively rule on the issue, affirming the dismissal on other grounds.]

. . . [E]ven if we assume that section 1 applies, it is clear to us that the venture cannot be condemned by *per se* rules and presents at best a debatable case under the rule of reason. More significantly, as structured by plaintiffs themselves, this case would have been lost at trial based on the jury's rejection of plaintiffs' own market definition.

* * *

The possibility that a less integrated and restrictive salary regime might make some individual salaries even higher is hardly conclusive. Without the restrictions, MLS might not exist or, if it did, might have larger initial losses and a shorter life. This would hardly enhance competition. . . . As in any other non-per se case, players would have to show that MLS exercised significant market power in a properly defined market, that the practices in question adversely affected competition in that market and that on balance the adverse effects on competition outweighed the competitive benefits.

Here, the jury said that neither the United States nor Division I delimited the relevant market—findings that imply that MLS faced significant competition for player services both from outside the United States and from non-Division I teams. That inference at a minimum creates uncertainty as to whether the jury could have found market power under section 1. However, the peculiar assemblage of evidence, including MLS-authored materials suggesting that it expected to exercise some control over player salaries, makes it impossible to rule out abstractly the possibility of a jury finding of MLS market power in a broader market.

[The court acknowledged that there theoretically "may be a broader market which plaintiffs might show (without contradicting the jury findings) in which unrestricted salary competition between the MLS operator/investors might result in somewhat higher player salaries." However, the court noted that the plaintiffs had alleged that the relevant market was "competition for Division I soccer players in the United States."]

Proof of such a market was the consistent theme of plaintiffs' *section 2* trial evidence. To be sure, had the *section 1* claim been put to trial, the plaintiffs could have sought to amend their complaint to allege a different market, but there is no obvious reason to think that they would have done so. The United States/Division I theory alleged in the complaint was the most favorable for each of their claims and the easiest to define; and the focus on a single market theory would have allowed the plaintiffs to focus their proof on a single market definition. Plaintiffs did have some incentive to allege a broader market under sections 1 and 7,[9] but that incentive existed when they filed their complaint as well.

* * *

We [ ] have every reason to think that if the *section 1* claim had not been dismissed on summary judgment it would have been presented at trial with the same market analysis alleged in the complaint. It follows that had the district court allowed the *section 1* claim, it too would have been defeated by the jury's finding that the market alleged in the complaint had not been proved. Accordingly, any error in dismissing the claim based on a single entity theory was harmless so long as the jury verdict stands. . . .

---

[9]   Whereas section 2 requires monopoly power or a prospect of it, significant market power is enough to trigger section 1's rule of reason approach; similarly, something less than monopoly power is required to condemn mergers under section 7's "substantially lessen competition" test. *Columbia Metal Culvert Co. v. Kaiser Aluminum & Chem. Corp.*, 579 F.2d 20, 27 n.11 (3d Cir. 1978).

III. SHERMAN ACT SECTION 2

At trial, players alleged three possible violations of *section 2*: that MLS monopolized the market for Division I professional soccer in the U.S.; that it attempted to monopolize that market; and that it conspired with the [United States Soccer Federation] to monopolize the same market. The jury found that players had failed to establish the relevant market as alleged; it reached no other issue in the case. The court thereafter entered judgment for the defendants on all three section 2 claims.

[The court then proceeded to uphold the jury verdict on the section 2 claims by rejecting a plethora of arguments by the players claiming that the jury instructions were faulty, and that evidence was either improperly allowed or excluded. It then concluded that the jury's finding was supported by substantial evidence.]

IV. CLAYTON ACT SECTION 7

In their final argument, players say that the district court erred in dismissing their claim that the formation of MLS violated section 7 of the Clayton Act. Count IV of the complaint alleged that, "[i]f not for this combination of assets and purchase of stock, MLS Member Teams would compete with each other for players, like teams in all other major professional sports leagues in the United States." Section 7 prohibits, with certain commerce-related conditions, stock or asset acquisitions whose effect "may be substantially to lessen competition, or to tend to create a monopoly." 15 U.S.C. § 18.

The district court granted summary judgment to the defendants on the ground that "[t]here can be no § 7 liability because the formation of MLS did not involve the acquisition or merger of existing business enterprises, but rather the formation of an entirely new entity which itself represented the creation of an entirely new market." *Fraser*, 97 F. Supp. 2d at 140. . . .

* * *

It might be argued that [this ruling] present[s] issues that a jury ought to consider; but there is one final objection that the jury did effectively consider. Even advocates of a broader reading of section 7 concede that striking down a combination that does not threaten present competition could be justified, in the hope of obtaining more competition in the future, only in already concentrated markets. . . .

Thus, even on the broader reading of section 7 and allowing room for conjectures about future effects, it would have been necessary for players to prove that MLS operates within a relevant economic market that is presently concentrated. In their section 7 count, the players alleged the same relevant United States/Division I market as in their section 1 and section 2 counts. For reasons already discussed in connection with the section 1 claim, the jury's rejection of this relevant market would also have doomed the section 7 claim based on enhancing future competition if it too had been presented.

Affirmed.

———

NOTES AND QUESTIONS

1. *Market Power Under Different Antitrust Provisions.* The amount of market power that must be shown in order to establish a § 2 violation is more than that required to establish a § 1 or Clayton Act § 7 merger violation. Judge Boudin acknowledged as much in footnote 9 of *Fraser.* Given the jury's finding that the relevant market was worldwide, and its finding, implicit in its verdict for MLS on the § 2 claims, that MLS lacked monopoly market power and a likelihood of ever acquiring it, did this result necessarily dispose of the § 1 and Clayton Act § 7 claims as well?

2. *Broader Implications.* What lesson does the *Fraser* decision hold for players in other start-up leagues who might want to challenge league player restraints under antitrust law? Would cases brought against those leagues by their players be likely to come out the same way, or are there material distinctions?

C. LABOR EXEMPTION FROM ANTITRUST

1. HISTORY AND BACKGROUND

When players in Major League Soccer and the Arena Football League began to consider how to improve their bargaining power, they initially decided not to form themselves into a labor union to engage in collective bargaining with their respective leagues. Instead, the players' initial strategy was to initiate collective antitrust litigation against the league. Arena League owners were so hostile to this tactic that they sought to force players to join a union, going so far as to threaten a lockout if the players did *not* organize! Arena league Commissioner David Baker and the team owners had publicly urged the players to form a labor union and to engage in collective bargaining, a management position that is now almost unheard-of in any other American industry. Simultaneously, a rival group of AFL players that many suspected were being supported by the league formed for the purpose of collecting enough players' signatures to force a union certification election. Thus, when the AFLPA filed its antitrust suit instead, the owners voted to cancel the upcoming 2000 season, as they had threatened to do. The initial players group then filed an unfair labor practices charge with the National Labor Relations Board (NLRB) claiming that the owners had violated § 8(a)(1) of the NLRA by coercing players in the exercise of their right not to have a union. Before the NLRB could resolve the complaint, the parties settled on terms that disposed of the antitrust litigation and established a collective agreement between players and the league.

The likely explanation for this superficially bizarre management tactic is the subject of this section. The application of the antitrust laws to labor markets raises a number of important questions, concerning the extent to which antitrust policy should be subordinate to a separate federal labor laws designed to foster and protect labor organizations and collective bargaining. This question took on real urgency in the sports world in the 1970s, because almost all the important antitrust litigation about free agency restraints was either launched or backed by the player unions that had emerged by the late 1960s in all four major professional sports.

A fundamental tension exists between antitrust law, which bars any "contract, combination, or conspiracy in restraint of trade," and labor law, which facilitates collective action among employees in dealing with their employers. Indeed, for the first two decades of its existence, judges used the Sherman Act more often against trade unions than against business corporations. *See, e.g., Loewe v. Lawlor,* 208 U.S. 274 (1908) (applying the Sherman Act to unions and their national consumer boycott against a non-union hat manufacturer).

(a) The Statutory Exemption

Concerned about this threat to their very existence, let alone their effectiveness, unions belonging to the American Federation of Labor persuaded new Democratic President Woodrow Wilson (and his chief advisor on antitrust and labor issues, Louis Brandeis) to include in the 1914 Clayton Act amendments to the Sherman Act a new § 6 which declared:

> That the labor of a human being is not a commodity or article of commerce. Nothing contained in the anti-trust law shall be construed to forbid the existence and operation of labor ... organizations, instituted for the purposes of mutual help ... or to forbid or restrain individual members of such organizations from lawfully carrying out the legitimate objects thereof; nor shall such organizations, or the members thereof, be held or construed to be illegal combinations or conspiracies in restraint of trade, under the anti-trust laws.

Samuel Gompers, founder and president of the AFL, celebrated this new section as the "Magna Carta of labor!" To buttress its legal force, Clayton Act § 20 went on to state that in disputes between employers and employees about terms and conditions of employment, collective action undertaken by employees through strikes, picketing, and boycotts, should not "be considered or held to be violations of any law of the United States."

Despite the apparent breadth of this legislative directive, the Supreme Court held in *Duplex Printing Press Co. v. Deering*, 254 U.S. 443 (1921), that the Clayton Act protected unions and their members from antitrust liability and federal court injunctions only when the union members were pursuing the "normal and legitimate objects" of a union, not when they "engage in an actual combination or conspiracy in restraint of trade." In *Duplex*, the Court held that a secondary boycott of the only major non-union printing press manufacturer in the country was outside the scope of Clayton Act protection and therefore could be enjoined under § 1 of the Sherman Act. Dissenting, Justice Brandeis argued that the injunction granted by the majority deprived unions of forms of collective action that Congress had expressly sought to legalize. *Id.* at 486.

During the Great Depression and the New Deal of the 1930s, labor was in a political position to secure the protection it thought it had won two decades earlier. Labor's first victory was the Norris-LaGuardia Act of 1932 (drafted by *Professor* Felix Frankfurter). This Act clarified that regardless of whether a labor dispute went beyond the normal bounds of conflict between an employer and its immediate employees, federal courts could not enjoin strikes, pickets, and other forms of employee self-help. Although the language of the Norris-LaGuardia Act expressly barred only federal *injunctive* remedies in "labor disputes," nine years later *Justice* Felix Frankfurter authored the Supreme Court's decision in *United States v. Hutcheson*, 312 U.S. 219 (1941), involving a criminal antitrust prosecution, which read the Act as having tacitly overruled *Duplex* and restored the Clayton Act's intended protection of labor disputes from substantive antitrust liability:

> So long as a union acts in its self-interest and does not combine with non-labor groups, the licit and the illicit under Section 20 [of the Clayton Act] are not to be distinguished by any [judicial] judgment regarding the wisdom or unwisdom, the rightness or wrongness, the selfishness or unselfishness of the end of which the particular union activities are the means.

312 U.S. at 232.

Hutcheson's interpretation of the statutory exemption limited its scope by conditioning it on the union not combining with a "non-labor group," presumably because such a combination might be used to restrain a product market to benefit that group. Subsequent decisions applying the statutory exemption thus have asked whether a union had combined with a group that might be interested in such restraint, or whether the union only had acted with those who could affect the labor market it attempted to control. *See, e.g., H. A. Artists & Assoc. v. Actors' Equity Ass'n*, 451 US. 804 (1981) (theatrical agents, though independent contractors, are part of a labor group as they perform functions that outside of special context would be performed by the union).

(b) The "Non-Statutory" Labor Exemption

Hutcheson seemed to create an anomaly by protecting unions' collective pressure on management to secure a collective bargaining agreement, but not protecting union success at obtaining an agreement with employers. This result also contradicts the 1935 National Labor Relations Act (NLRA), discussed in Chapter 3, which (1) created an affirmative right of employees to organize themselves into unions, (2) recognized the employees' chosen union as the *exclusive* bargaining agent for the employees, and then (3) imposed on the employer a duty to bargain in good faith with the union in an effort to reach a collective bargaining agreement. In the 1947 Taft-Hartley amendments to the NLRA, the duty to bargain in good faith was also imposed on unions. Furthermore, both in practice and under the law, such bargaining is often conducted on a wide-ranging multi-employer basis. As a result, collective bargaining agreements often bind, either legally or practically, some individual workers and employers who do not necessarily favor its terms.

In a series of decisions, the Supreme Court recognized the need for a "nonstatutory" (*i.e.*, implicit or implied) labor exemption for collectively bargained agreements in some cases. It has not, however, granted collective bargaining agreements the same blanket antitrust exemption that it has extended to union concerted action short of agreements with non-labor groups. The Court recognized that unions and employers may find it in their mutual interest to agree upon restrictive practices that control markets other than the labor market. *See Allen Bradley Co. v. IBEW*, 325 U.S. 797 (1945); *United Mine Workers v. Pennington*, 381 U.S. 657 (1965); *Connell Construction Co. v. Plumbers and Steamfitters*, 421 U.S. 616 (1975). In all three cases, the Court held the nonstatutory exemption inapplicable, and allowed the antitrust claim to proceed. In each, the Court found that the alleged restraint had a significant effect in the employers' product market, and that the plaintiffs were business competitors of the employers who were not members of the multiemployer unit that had signed the collective bargaining agreement. For example, in *Pennington*, the United Mine Workers had not only agreed with large mining companies to specified wages, hours, and working condition for the large companies' workers, but had promised that they would not agree to lower wages with smaller mining rivals.

A divided Court reached a different result in a case decided the same day as *Pennington, Local Union No. 189, Amalgamated Meat Cutters v. Jewel Tea Co.*, 381 U.S. 676 (1965), shielding from antitrust scrutiny provisions in a collective agreement that restricted a product market. Jewel Tea challenged a collective bargaining agreement arising out of multi-employment bargaining in which it had participated, along with myriad other employers of butchers, with the Meat Cutters Union. The union had insisted on inserting in its collective agreement with the Chicago grocery stores a provision that barred the sale of fresh meat at nighttime, in order to protect the unionized butchers from employer pressures to work in the evenings, and to protect the jobs of butchers working for small stores that did not stay open in the evening (in contrast with the Jewel supermarkets). A divided Supreme Court held that this contract term was protected from antitrust challenge by the labor exemption.

Three justices, in an opinion by Justice Douglas, would have found the bargain to be illegal under the antitrust laws, holding that antitrust concerns always trumped labor concerns. Three justices, in an opinion by Justice Goldberg, would have found any agreement between union and management on terms about which the parties were required to bargain under the NLRA always to be exempt from antitrust scrutiny. (Justice Goldberg, formerly counsel to the Steelworkers' Union and President Kennedy's Secretary of Labor, detailed the historical use of antitrust laws to harm unions and workers.) Justice White's decisive opinion (for himself and two other Justices) took a middle ground. This oft-cited passage explains the plurality's view on the scope of the exemption:

> Thus the issue in this case is whether the marketing-hours restriction, like wages, and unlike prices, is so intimately related to wages, hours and working conditions [mandatory subjects of collective bargaining under the NLRA] that the union's successful attempt to obtain that provision through bona fide, arms' length bargaining in pursuit of their own labor union policies, and not at the behest of or in combination with non-labor groups, falls within the protection of the National Labor Policy and is therefore exempt from the Sherman Act.

381 U.S. at 689–90.

This same scenario arises in the sports context, when the operation of a collectively bargained lifetime reserve clause denies a new league access to the available supply of top-flight athletes whom the new league needs to survive as a serious competitor to the established league. In *Philadelphia World Hockey Club v. Philadelphia Hockey Club*, 351 F. Supp. 462 (E.D. Pa. 1972)), the merits of which were excerpted in Chapter 6, the court found that the agreement unlawfully monopolized major league professional hockey in violation of § 2 of the Sherman Act. Before reaching the merits, however, Judge Leon Higgenbotham first held that the labor exemption was not applicable. His review of the cases discussed above led him to conclude that "those cases all involved situations where the union had been sued for its active, conspiratorial role in restraining competition of a product market, and the union, not the employer, sought to invoke the labor exemptions." *Id.* at 498. Moreover, "the cases cited above pertained to issues which furthered the interests of the union members and on which there had been extensive collective bargaining. *Id.* at 498–99. Finally:

even if, arguendo, there had been substantial arm's-length collective bargaining by the National Hockey League and the Players' Association to revise the perpetual option provision of the reserve clause, those negotiations would not shield the National Hockey League from liability in a suit by outside competitors who sought access to players under the control of the National Hockey League.

* * *

I reject the argument that an employer (National Hockey League) can conspire with or take advantage of a union to restrain competition and seriously impair the business dealings and transactions of competitors. To grant the National Hockey League an exemption in this proceeding would undermine and thwart the policies which have evolved over the years in disposing of labor-management and anti-trust disputes. I cannot compatibly reconcile the National Hockey League's monopolistic actions here with the labor exemptions from the Sherman Act. The NHL can do no more than could the employers and union in *Allen Bradley, supra*. Even if the National Hockey League was primarily concerned about the welfare of its players, its purported good intentions would be insufficient to insulate its actions. . . .

351 F. Supp. at 500.

2. JUDICIAL OPTIONS FOR THE NONSTATUTORY LABOR EXEMPTION

With respect to situations involving collective employer restraints whose direct impact is felt only inside, not also outside, the employment relationship, the following alternative formulations of the nonstatutory labor exemption have each been advanced by at least one judge or scholar.

Option 1: There should be no non-statutory exemption from antitrust at all—unions and employers should have no right to do through their agreement what would otherwise be illegal by statute.

Option 2: There should be exemption only for provisions that have been inserted in the agreement at the behest of the union for the benefit of the employees—the historic purpose of the labor exemption is to help workers, not employers.

Option 3: The exemption should protect all, but only, the terms within an existing collective agreement—the essential condition for relief from antitrust must be actual consent to the practice by the employees through their union.

Option 4: The exemption should protect all employment practices that exist in an employee unit represented by a union—since the employees now have the right under labor law to force the employer to negotiate about the practice, they should not also enjoy the right to litigate about the practice under antitrust law.

Option 5: There should be no antitrust liability at all for restraints in employment—as § 6 of the Clayton Act stated, "the labor of a human being is not a commodity or article of commerce" for purposes of antitrust law.

Consider the pros and cons of these options as we trace the history of the labor exemption in sports until its final resolution by the Supreme Court.

3. INITIAL DEVELOPMENT OF THE DOCTRINE IN THE LOWER COURTS

(a) The Outer Limits of the Exemption: It Exists but Does Not Protect All Labor-Market Restraints

In *Mackey v. NFL*, 543 F.2d 606 (8th Cir. 1976), whose factual underpinnings and substantive antitrust treatment were presented earlier in this chapter in Section C, Part 2, the Eighth Circuit **rejected Options 1 and 5**. The NFL relied on the text of Clayton Act § 6—"[t]he labor of a human being is not a commodity or article of commerce"—to argue that labor restraints are beyond the scope of the antitrust laws.

The Eighth Circuit rejected the NFL's argument:

On the surface, the language relied on by defendants lends merit to the defense. However, we cannot overlook the context in which the language arose. Section 6 of the Clayton Act was enacted for the benefit of unions to exempt certain of their activities from the antitrust laws after courts had applied the Sherman Act to legitimate labor activities. . . .

In other cases concerning professional sports, courts have not hesitated to apply the Sherman Act to club owner imposed restraints on competition for players' services. . . . In other contexts, courts have subjected similar employer imposed restraints to the scrutiny of the antitrust laws. We hold that restraints on competition within the market for players' services fall within the ambit of the Sherman Act.

543 F.2d at 617–18.

At the other extreme, the Eighth Circuit also rejected the players' attempt to narrow *Jewel Tea* to lawsuits where the union was a defendant:

We must disagree. Since the basis of the nonstatutory exemption is the national policy favoring collective bargaining, and since the exemption extends to agreements, the benefits of the exemption logically extend to both parties to the agreement. Accordingly, under appropriate circumstances, we find that a non-labor group may avail itself of the labor exemption.

Id. at 612.

The court ultimately rejected the application of the labor exemption to the challenged Rozelle Rule based on its own reading of *Jewel Tea* that required the challenged position to be "the product of bona fide arm's-length bargaining." *Id.* at 614. This test was rejected by the Supreme Court in *Brown v. Pro Football, Inc.,* 518 U.S. 231 (1996), discussed below.

(b) Application to Restraints Agreed to by the Union but Sought by Management

During the late 1970s, nascent player unions agreed to collective bargains that marginally improved wages, hours, and working conditions for players but incorporated highly restrictive rules regarding competition for player services. Individuals challenging these rules argued that the labor exemption should only, as in *Jewel Tea,* protect anti-competitive agreements inserted in a collective bargaining agreement at the behest of workers. In *McCourt v. California Sports, Inc.,* 600 F.2d 1193 (6th Cir. 1979), the Sixth Circuit rejected **Option 2** described above. The court found the non-statutory labor exemption protected the system embedded in NHL By-law 9A, incorporated in the 1976 collective agreement with the NHLPA, that required that an "equalization payment" similar to the Rozelle Rule at issue in *Mackey,* although the determination was to be made by a neutral arbitrator, rather than the commissioner. The district court had held that the challenged provision had not been negotiated in *bona fide,* arms-length bargaining. On appeal, the Sixth Circuit reversed.

> Contrary to the trial judge's conclusion, the very facts relied upon by him in his opinion illustrate a classic case of collective bargaining in which the reserve system was a central issue. It is apparent from those very findings that the NHLPA used every form of negotiating pressure it could muster. It developed an alternate reserve system and secured tentative agreement from the owner and player representatives, only to have the proposal rejected by the players. It refused to attend a proposed meeting with the owners to discuss the reserve system further. It threatened to strike. It threatened to commence an antitrust suit and to recommend that the players not attend training camp.

> For its part, the NHL, while not budging in its insistence upon By-Law Section 9A, at least in the absence of any satisfactory counter proposal by the players, yielded significantly on other issues. . . .

From the express findings of the trial court, fully supported by the record, it is apparent that the inclusion of the reserve system in the collective bargaining agreement was the product of good faith, arm's-length bargaining, and that what the trial court saw as a failure to negotiate was in fact simply a failure to succeed, after the most intensive negotiations, in keeping an unwanted provision out of the contract. This failure was a part of and not apart from the collective bargaining process, a process which achieved its ultimate objective of an agreement accepted by the parties.

600 F.2d at 1202–03.

The Second Circuit in *Wood v. NBA*, 809 F.2d 954 (2d Cir. 1987), further articulated the rationale for why anticompetitive labor market terms should be exempt if included in a collective bargaining agreement, even if the term was not sought by workers. Dismissing an antitrust challenge to a salary cap included in the CBA, Judge Ralph Winter emphasized the fundamental principle of federal labor policy (in § 9(a) of the NLRA) that "employees may eliminate competition among themselves through a governmentally supervised majority vote selecting an exclusive bargaining representative."

Federal labor policy thus allows employees to seek the best deal for the greatest number by the exercise of collective rather than individual bargaining power. Once an exclusive representative has been selected, the individual employee is forbidden by federal law from negotiating directly with the employer absent the representative's consent, *NLRB v. Allis-Chalmers Mfg. Co.*, 388 U.S. 175, 180 (1967), even though that employee may actually receive less compensation under the collective bargain than he or she would through individual negotiations. *J.I. Case Co. v. NLRB*, 321 U.S. 332, 338–39 (1944).

The gravamen of Wood's complaint, namely that the NBA-NBPA collective agreement is illegal because it prevents him from achieving his full free market value, is therefore at odds with, and destructive of, federal labor policy. It is true that the diversity of talent and specialization among professional athletes and the widespread exposure and discussions of their "work" in the media make the differences in value among them as "workers" more visible than the differences in efficiency and in value among industrial workers. High public visibility, however, is no reason to ignore federal legislation that explicitly prevents employees, whether in or out of a bargaining unit, from seeking a better deal where that deal is inconsistent with the terms of a collective agreement.

809 F.2d at 959.

Judge Winter emphasized the incompatibility of Wood's antitrust position with that feature of national labor policy that "attaches prime importance to freedom of contract between the parties to a collective agreement."

Freedom of contract is an important cornerstone of national labor policy for two reasons. First, it allows an employer and a union to agree upon those arrangements that best suit their particular interests. Courts cannot hope to fashion contract terms more efficient than those arrived at by the parties who are to be governed by them. Second, freedom of contract furthers the goal of labor peace. To the extent that courts prohibit particular solutions for particular problems, they reduce the number and quality of compromises available to unions and employers for resolving their differences.

Freedom of contract is particularly important in the context of collective bargaining between professional athletes and their leagues. Such bargaining relationships raise numerous problems with little or no precedent in standard industrial relations. As a result, leagues and player unions may reach seemingly unfamiliar or strange agreements. If courts were to intrude and to outlaw such solutions, leagues and their player unions would have to arrange their affairs in a less efficient way. It would also increase the chances of strikes by reducing the number and quality of possible compromises.

The issues of free agency and entry draft are at the center of collective bargaining in much of the professional sports industry. It is to be expected that the parties will arrive at unique solutions to these problems in the different sports both because sports generally differ from the industrial model and because each sport has its own peculiar economic imperatives. The NBA/NBPA agreement is just such a unique bundle of compromises. The draft and the salary cap reflect the interests of the employers in stabilizing salary costs and spreading talent among the various teams. Minimum individual salaries, fringe benefits, minimum aggregate team salaries, and guaranteed revenue sharing reflect the interests of the union in enhancing standard benefits applicable to all players. The free agency/first refusal provisions in turn allow individual players to exercise a degree of individual bargaining power. Were a court to intervene and strike down the draft and salary cap, the entire agreement would unravel. This would force the NBA and NBPA to search for other avenues of compromise that would be less satisfactory to them than the agreement struck down. It would also measurably increase the chances of a strike. We decline to take that step.

809 F.2d at 961–62.

4. THE SUPREME COURT SPEAKS

In 1989, NFL owners agreed to establish six-player developmental squads for each team at a league-mandated salary level of $1,000 a week. These squads were to be made up of first- or second-year players who had not made the regular 47-man roster, but whose teams wanted to keep them for practices and possible replacement of injured or poorly-performing regulars. The system was designed to eliminate the practice of teams "stashing" players who had not made the regular roster on their injured reserve list. This league initiative was not the subject of collective bargaining (let alone agreement) prior to 1989. The NFLPA applauded the creation of these squads, but insisted that developmental players' salaries be individually negotiated in the same manner as regular players' salaries. The Association filed an antitrust suit when the NFL proceeded to implement its fixed salary scale of $1,000 per week, which was not just a cap, but a huge cut in the average salary paid to this category of player (*i.e.*, to new players previously "stashed" on injured reserve), a figure that dropped from as much as $60,000 per year in 1988 to $16,000 in 1989.

In *Brown v. Pro-Football, Inc.*, 782 F. Supp. 125 (D.D.C. 1991), the district court rejected the NFL's labor exemption defense to this action, concluding that the labor exemption expired immediately upon expiration of a collective bargaining agreement (in effect Option 3 above). At trial, the jury found this salary arrangement violated the Sherman Act and awarded $10 million in damages, which was trebled to a $30 million award plus legal costs. On appeal, a divided panel of the D.C. Circuit reversed. 50 F.3d 1041 (D.C. Cir. 1995). The majority opinion held that the non-statutory labor exemption protected a league from all antitrust suits brought by or on behalf of their players' union with respect to conduct engaged in during the collective bargaining process, as long as the bargaining relationship with the union exists. NFL sought certiorari, which the Supreme Court granted.

BROWN V. PRO FOOTBALL, INC.
500 U.S. 231 (1996)

JUSTICE BREYER delivered the opinion of the Court.

[The court began by framing the specific question posed by this case as whether "club owners who had bargained to an impasse with the players union about a wage issue, and had then agreed among themselves (but not with the union) to implement the terms of their own last best bargaining offer" should have their agreement shielded by federal labor laws from antitrust attack. After sketching the history of the "implicit ('nonstatutory')" labor exemption, Justice Breyer stated that its point was to limit] . . . an antitrust court's authority to determine, in the area of industrial conflict, what is or is not a "reasonable" practice. It thereby substitutes legislative and administrative labor-related determinations for judicial antitrust-related determinations as to the appropriate legal limits of industrial conflict.

As a matter of logic, it would be difficult, if not impossible, to require groups of employers and employees to bargain together, but at the same time to forbid them to make among themselves or with each other any of the competition-restricting agreements potentially necessary to make the process work or its results mutually acceptable. Thus, the implicit exemption recognizes that, to give effect to federal labor laws and policies and to allow meaningful collective bargaining to take place, some restraints on competition imposed through the bargaining process must be shielded from antitrust sanctions. . . .

The petitioners and their supporters concede, as they must, the legal existence of the exemption we have described. They also concede that, where its application is necessary to make the statutorily authorized collective-bargaining process work as Congress intended, the exemption must apply both to employers and to employees. Nor does the dissent take issue with these basic principles. Consequently, the question before us is one of determining the exemption's scope: Does it apply to an agreement among several employers bargaining together to implement after impasse the terms of their last best good-faith wage offer? We assume that such conduct, as practiced in this case, is unobjectionable as a matter of labor law and policy. On that assumption, we conclude that the exemption applies.

Labor law itself regulates directly, and considerably, the kind of behavior here at issue—the post-impasse imposition of a proposed employment term concerning a mandatory subject of bargaining. Both the [National Labor Relations] Board and the courts have held that, after impasse, labor law permits employers unilaterally to implement changes in preexisting conditions, but only insofar as the new terms meet carefully circumscribed conditions. For example, the new terms must be "reasonably comprehended" within the employer's pre-impasse proposals (typically the last rejected proposals), lest by imposing more or less favorable terms, the employer unfairly undermined the union's status. The collective-bargaining proceeding itself must be free of any unfair labor practice, such as an employer's failure to have bargained in good faith. These regulations reflect the fact that impasse and an accompanying implementation of proposals constitute an integral part of the bargaining process.

Although the caselaw we have cited focuses upon bargaining by a single employer, no one here has argued that labor law does, or should, treat multiemployer bargaining differently in this respect. Indeed, Board and court decisions suggest that the joint implementation of proposed terms after impasse is a familiar practice in the context of multiemployer bargaining. We proceed on that assumption.

Multiemployer bargaining itself is a well-established, important, pervasive method of collective bargaining, offering advantages to both management and labor. *See* Appendix (multiemployer bargaining accounts for more than 40% of major collective-bargaining agreements, and is used in such industries as construction, transportation, retail trade, clothing manufacture, and real estate, as well as professional sports); *NLRB v. Truck Drivers*, 353 U.S. 87, 95 (1957) (*Buffalo Linen*) (Congress saw multiemployer bargaining as "a vital factor in the effectuation of the national policy of promoting labor peace through strengthened collective bargaining"); *Charles D. Bonanno Linen Service, Inc. v. NLRB*, 454 U.S. 404, 409 n.3 (1982) (*Bonanno Linen*) (multiemployer bargaining benefits both management and labor, by saving bargaining resources, by encouraging development of industry-wide worker benefits programs that smaller employers could not otherwise afford, and by inhibiting employer competition at the workers' expense). The upshot is that the practice at issue here plays a significant role in a collective-bargaining process that itself comprises an important part of the Nation's industrial relations system.

In these circumstances, to subject the practice to antitrust law is to require antitrust courts to answer a host of important practical questions about how collective bargaining over wages, hours and working conditions is to proceed—the very result that the implicit labor exemption seeks to avoid. And it is to place in jeopardy some of the potentially beneficial labor-related effects that multiemployer bargaining can achieve. That is because unlike labor law, which sometimes welcomes anticompetitive agreements conducive to industrial harmony, antitrust law forbids all agreements among competitors (such as competing employers) that unreasonably lessen competition among or between them in virtually any respect whatsoever. *See, e.g., Paramount Famous Lasky Corp. v. United States*, 282 U.S. 30 (1930) (agreement to insert arbitration provisions in motion picture licensing contracts). Antitrust law also sometimes permits judges or juries to premise antitrust liability upon little more than uniform behavior among competitors, preceded by conversations implying that later uniformity might prove desirable, *see, e.g., United States v. General Motors Corp.*, 384 U.S. 127, 142–143 (1966), or accompanied by other conduct that in context suggests that each competitor failed to make an independent decision, *see, e.g., American Tobacco Co. v. United States*, 328 U.S. 781, 809–810 (1946).

If the antitrust laws apply, what are employers to do once impasse is reached? If all impose terms similar to their last joint offer, they invite an antitrust action premised upon identical behavior (along with prior or accompanying conversations) as tending to show a common understanding or agreement. If any, or all, of them individually impose terms that differ significantly from that offer, they invite an unfair labor practice charge. Indeed, how can employers safely discuss their offers together even before a bargaining impasse occurs? A pre-impasse discussion about, say, the practical advantages or disadvantages of a particular proposal, invites a later antitrust claim that they agreed to limit the kinds of action each would later take should an impasse occur. The same is true of post-impasse discussions aimed at renewed negotiations with the union. Nor would adherence to the terms of an expired collective-bargaining agreement eliminate a potentially plausible antitrust claim charging that they had "conspired" or tacitly "agreed" to do so, particularly if maintaining the status quo were not in the immediate economic self-interest of some. All this is to say that to permit antitrust liability here threatens to introduce instability and uncertainty into the collective-bargaining process, for antitrust law often forbids or discourages the kinds of joint discussions and behavior that the collective-bargaining process invites or requires.

We do not see any obvious answer to this problem. We recognize, as the Government suggests, that, in principle, antitrust courts might themselves try to evaluate particular kinds of employer understandings, finding them "reasonable" (hence lawful) where justified by collective-bargaining necessity. But any such evaluation means a web of detailed rules spun by many different nonexpert antitrust judges and juries, not a set of labor rules enforced by a single expert administrative body, namely the Labor Board. The labor laws give the Board, not antitrust courts, primary responsibility for policing the collective-bargaining process. And one of their objectives was to take from antitrust courts the authority to determine, through application of the antitrust laws, what is socially or economically desirable collective-bargaining policy. . . . ; *see also Jewel Tea*, 381 U.S. at 716–719 (opinion of Goldberg, J.).

III

Both petitioners and their supporters advance several suggestions for drawing the exemption boundary line short of this case. We shall explain why we find them unsatisfactory.

A

Petitioners claim that the implicit exemption applies only to labor-management agreements—a limitation that they deduce from caselaw language, *see, e.g., Connell*, 421 U.S. at 622 (exemption for "some union-employer agreements"), and from a proposed principle—that the exemption must rest upon labor-management consent. The language, however, reflects only the fact that the cases previously before the Court involved collective-bargaining agreements; the language does not reflect the exemption's rationale.

Nor do we see how an exemption limited by petitioners' principle of labor-management consent could work. One cannot mean the principle literally—that the exemption applies only to understandings embodied in a collective-bargaining agreement—for the collective-bargaining process may take place before the making of any agreement or after an agreement has expired. Yet a multiemployer bargaining process itself necessarily involves many procedural and substantive understandings among participating employers as well as with the union. Petitioners cannot rescue their principle by claiming that the exemption applies only insofar as both labor and management consent to those understandings. Often labor will not (and should not) consent to certain common bargaining positions that employers intend to maintain. Similarly, labor need not consent to certain tactics that this Court has approved as part of the multiemployer bargaining process, such as unit-wide lockouts and the use of temporary replacements. *See NLRB v. Brown*, 380 U.S. 278, 284 (1965); *Buffalo Linen*, 353 U.S. at 97.

Petitioners cannot save their consent principle by weakening it, as by requiring union consent only to the multiemployer bargaining process itself. This general consent is automatically present whenever multiemployer bargaining takes place. *See Hi-Way Billboards, Inc.*, 206 N.L.R.B. 22 (1973) (multiemployer unit "based on consent" and "established by an unequivocal agreement by the parties"), *enf. denied on other grounds*, 500 F.2d 181 (5th Cir. 1974); *Weyerhaeuser Co.*, 166 N.L.R.B. 299, 299–300 (1967). As so weakened, the principle cannot help decide which related practices are, or are not, subject to antitrust immunity.

B

The Solicitor General argues that the exemption should terminate at the point of impasse. After impasse, he says, "employers no longer have a duty under the labor laws to maintain the status quo," and "are free as a matter of labor law to negotiate individual arrangements on an interim basis with the union."

Employers, however, are not completely free at impasse to act independently. The multiemployer bargaining unit ordinarily remains intact; individual employers cannot withdraw. The duty to bargain survives; employers must stand ready to resume collective bargaining. And individual employers can negotiate individual interim agreements with the union only insofar as those agreements are consistent with "the duty to abide by the results of group bargaining." Regardless, the absence of a legal "duty" to act jointly is not determinative. This Court has implied antitrust immunities that extend beyond statutorily required joint action to joint action that a statute "expressly or impliedly allows or assumes must also be immune."

More importantly, the simple "impasse" line would not solve the basic problem we have described above. Labor law permits employers, after impasse, to engage in considerable joint behavior, including joint lockouts and replacement hiring. *See, e.g., Brown*, supra, at 289 (hiring of temporary replacement workers after lockout was "reasonably adapted to the achievement of a legitimate end—preserving the integrity of the multiemployer bargaining unit"). Indeed, as a general matter, labor law often limits employers to four options at impasse: (1) maintain the status quo, (2) implement their last offer, (3) lock out their workers (and either shut down or hire temporary replacements), or (4) negotiate separate interim agreements with the union. What is to happen if the parties cannot reach an interim agreement? The other alternatives are limited. Uniform employer conduct is likely. Uniformity—at least when accompanied by discussion of the matter—invites antitrust attack. And such attack would ask antitrust courts to decide the lawfulness of activities intimately related to the bargaining process.

The problem is aggravated by the fact that "impasse" is often temporary; it may differ from bargaining only in degree; it may be manipulated by the parties for bargaining purposes; and it may occur several times during the course of a single labor dispute, since the bargaining process is not over when the first impasse is reached. How are employers to discuss future bargaining positions during a temporary impasse? Consider, too, the adverse consequences that flow from failing to guess how an antitrust court would later draw the impasse line. Employers who erroneously concluded that impasse had not been reached would risk antitrust liability were they collectively to maintain the status quo, while employers who erroneously concluded that impasse had occurred would risk unfair labor practice charges for prematurely suspending multiemployer negotiations.

The Solicitor General responds with suggestions for softening an "impasse" rule by extending the exemption after impasse "for such time as would be reasonable in the circumstances" for employers to consult with counsel, confirm that impasse has occurred, and adjust their business operations; by reestablishing the exemption once there is a "resumption of good-faith bargaining"; and by looking to antitrust law's "rule of reason" to shield—"in some circumstances"—such joint actions as the unit-wide lockout or the concerted maintenance of previously-established joint benefit or retirement plans. But even as so modified, the impasse-related rule creates an exemption that can evaporate in the middle of the bargaining process, leaving later antitrust courts free to second-guess the parties' bargaining decisions and consequently forcing them to choose their collective-bargaining responses in light of what they predict or fear that antitrust courts, not labor law administrators, will eventually decide.

C

Petitioners and their supporters argue in the alternative for a rule that would exempt post-impasse agreement about bargaining "tactics," but not post-impasse agreement about substantive "terms," from the reach of antitrust. They recognize, however, that both the Board and the courts have said that employers can, and often do, employ the imposition of "terms" as a bargaining "tactic." *See, e.g., American Ship Building Co. v.*

NLRB, 380 U.S. 300, 316 (1965). This concession as to joint "tactical" implementation would turn the presence of an antitrust exemption upon a determination of the employers' primary purpose or motive. But to ask antitrust courts, insulated from the bargaining process, to investigate an employer group's subjective motive is to ask them to conduct an inquiry often more amorphous than those we have previously discussed. And, in our view, a labor/antitrust line drawn on such a basis would too often raise the same related (previously discussed) problems. *See Jewel Tea*, 381 U.S. at 716 (opinion of Goldberg, J.) (expressing concern about antitrust judges "roaming at large" through the bargaining process).

D

The petitioners make several other arguments. They point, for example, to cases holding applicable, in collective-bargaining contexts, general "backdrop" statutes, such as a state statute requiring a plant-closing employer to make employee severance payments, *Fort Halifax Packing Co. v. Coyne*, 482 U.S. 1 (1987), and a state statute mandating certain minimum health benefits, *Metropolitan Life Ins. Co. v. Massachusetts*, 471 U.S. 724 (1985). Those statutes, however, " 'neither encouraged nor discouraged the collective-bargaining processes that are the subject of the [federal labor laws].' " *Fort Halifax*, supra, at 21 (quoting *Metropolitan Life*, supra, at 755). Neither did those statutes come accompanied with antitrust's labor-related history.

Petitioners also say that irrespective of how the labor exemption applies elsewhere to multiemployer collective bargaining, professional sports is "special." We can understand how professional sports may be special in terms of, say, interest, excitement, or concern. But we do not understand how they are special in respect to labor law's antitrust exemption. We concede that the clubs that make up a professional sports league are not completely independent economic competitors, as they depend upon a degree of cooperation for economic survival. *National Collegiate Athletic Assn. v. Board of Regents of Univ. of Okla.*, 468 U.S. 85, 101–102 (1984). In the present context, however, that circumstance makes the league more like a single bargaining employer, which analogy seems irrelevant to the legal issue before us.

We also concede that football players often have special individual talents, and, unlike many unionized workers, they often negotiate their pay individually with their employers. But this characteristic seems simply a feature, like so many others, that might give employees (or employers) more (or less) bargaining power, that might lead some (or all) of them to favor a particular kind of bargaining, or that might lead to certain demands at the bargaining table. We do not see how it could make a critical legal difference in determining the underlying framework in which bargaining is to take place. *See generally* Jacobs & Winter, *Antitrust Principles and Collective Bargaining by Athletes: Of Superstars in Peonage*, 81 Yale L.J. 1

(1971). Indeed, it would be odd to fashion an antitrust exemption that gave additional advantages to professional football players (by virtue of their superior bargaining power) that transport workers, coal miners, or meat packers would not enjoy.

. . . Ultimately, we cannot find a satisfactory basis for distinguishing football players from other organized workers. We therefore conclude that all must abide by the same legal rules.

* * *

For these reasons, we hold that the implicit ("nonstatutory") antitrust exemption applies to the employer conduct at issue here. That conduct took place during and immediately after a collective-bargaining negotiation. It grew out of, and was directly related to, the lawful operation of the bargaining process. It involved a matter that the parties were required to negotiate collectively. And it concerned only the parties to the collective-bargaining relationship.

Our holding is not intended to insulate from antitrust review every joint imposition of terms by employers, for an agreement among employers could be sufficiently distant in time and in circumstances from the collective-bargaining process that a rule permitting antitrust intervention would not significantly interfere with that process. *See, e.g.*, 50 F.3d at 1057 (suggesting that exemption lasts until collapse of the collective-bargaining relationship, as evidenced by decertification of the union); *El Cerrito Mill & Lumber Co.*, 316 N.L.R.B. at 1006–1007 (suggesting that "extremely long" impasse, accompanied by "instability" or "defunctness" of multiemployer unit, might justify union withdrawal from group bargaining). We need not decide in this case whether, or where, within these extreme outer boundaries to draw that line. Nor would it be appropriate for us to do so without the detailed views of the Board, to whose "specialized judgment" Congress "intended to leave" many of the "inevitable questions concerning multiemployer bargaining bound to arise in the future."

The judgment of the Court of Appeals is affirmed.

JUSTICE STEVENS, dissenting.

In his classic dissent in *Lochner v. New York*, 198 U.S. 45, 75 (1905), Justice Holmes reminded us that our disagreement with the economic theory embodied in legislation should not affect our judgment about its constitutionality. It is equally important, of course, to be faithful to the economic theory underlying broad statutory mandates when we are construing their impact on areas of the economy not specifically addressed by their texts. The unique features of this case lead me to conclude that the Court has reached a decision that conflicts with the basic purpose of both the antitrust laws and the national labor policy expressed in a series of congressional enactments.

I

The basic premise underlying the Sherman Act is the assumption that free competition among business entities will produce the best price levels. *National Soc. of Professional Engineers v. United States*, 435 U.S. 679, 695 (1978). Collusion among competitors, it is believed, may produce prices that harm consumers. *United States v. Socony-Vacuum Oil Co.*, 310 U.S. 150, 226, n. 59 (1940). Similarly, the Court has held, a market-wide agreement among employers setting wages at levels that would not prevail in a free market may violate the Sherman Act. *Anderson v. Shipowners' Assn. of Pacific Coast*, 272 U.S. 359 (1926).

The jury's verdict in this case has determined that the market-wide agreement among these employers fixed the salaries of the replacement players at a dramatically lower level than would obtain in a free market. While the special characteristics of this industry may provide a justification for the agreement under the rule of reason, *see National Collegiate Athletic Assn. v. Board of Regents of Univ. of Okla.*, 468 U.S. 85, 100–104 (1984), at this stage of the proceeding our analysis of the exemption issue must accept the premise that the agreement is unlawful unless it is exempt.

The basic premise underlying our national labor policy is that unregulated competition among employees and applicants for employment produces wage levels that are lower than they should be. Whether or not the premise is true in fact, it is surely the basis for the statutes that encourage and protect the collective-bargaining process, including the express statutory exemptions from the antitrust laws that Congress enacted in order to protect union activities. Those statutes were enacted to enable collective action by union members to achieve wage levels that are higher than would be available in a free market.

The statutory labor exemption protects the right of workers to act collectively to seek better wages, but does not "exempt concerted action or agreements between unions and nonlabor parties." *Connell Constr. Co. v. Plumbers*, 421 U.S. 616, 621–622 (1975). It is the judicially crafted, nonstatutory labor exemption that serves to accommodate the conflicting policies of the antitrust and labor statutes in the context of action between employers and unions.

The limited judicial exemption complements its statutory counterpart by ensuring that unions which engage in collective bargaining to enhance employees' wages may enjoy the benefits of the resulting agreements. The purpose of the labor laws would be frustrated if it were illegal for employers to enter into industry-wide agreements providing supracompetitive wages for employees. For that reason, we have explained that "a proper accommodation between the congressional policy favoring collective bargaining under the NLRA and the congressional policy favoring free competition in business markets requires that some union-employer agreements be accorded a limited nonstatutory exemption from antitrust sanctions."

Consistent with basic labor law policies, I agree with the Court that the judicially crafted labor exemption must also cover some collective action that employers take in response to a collective bargaining agent's demands for higher wages. Immunizing such action from antitrust scrutiny may facilitate collective bargaining over labor demands. So, too, may immunizing concerted employer action designed to maintain the integrity of the multi-employer bargaining unit, such as lockouts that are imposed in response to "a union strike tactic which threatens the destruction of the employers' interest in bargaining on a group basis." *NLRB v. Truck Drivers*, 353 U.S. 87 (1957).

In my view, however, neither the policies underlying the two separate statutory schemes, nor the narrower focus on the purpose of the nonstatutory exemption, provides a justification for exempting from antitrust scrutiny collective action initiated by employers to depress wages below the level that would be produced in a free market. Nor do those policies support a rule that would allow employers to suppress wages by implementing noncompetitive agreements among themselves on matters that have not previously been the subject of either an agreement with labor or even a demand by labor for inclusion in the bargaining process. That, however, is what is at stake in this litigation.

II

In light of the accommodation that has been struck between antitrust and labor law policy, it would be most ironic to extend an exemption crafted to protect collective action by employees to protect employers acting jointly to deny employees the opportunity to negotiate their salaries individually in a competitive market. Perhaps aware of the irony, the Court chooses to analyze this case as though it represented a typical impasse in an unexceptional multiemployer bargaining process. In so doing, it glosses over [several] unique features of the case that are critical to the inquiry into whether the policies of the labor laws require extension of the nonstatutory labor exemption to this atypical case.

First, in this market, unlike any other area of labor law implicated in the cases cited by the Court, player salaries are individually negotiated. The practice of individually negotiating player salaries prevailed even prior to collective bargaining. The players did not challenge the prevailing practice because, unlike employees in most industries, they want their compensation to be determined by the forces of the free market rather than by the process of collective bargaining. Thus, although the majority professes an inability to understand anything special about professional sports that should affect the framework of labor negotiations, in this business it is the employers, not the employees, who seek to impose a noncompetitive uniform wage on a segment of the market and to put an end to competitive wage negotiations.

Second, respondents concede that the employers imposed the wage restraint to force owners to comply with league-wide rules that limit the number of players that may serve on a team, not to facilitate a stalled bargaining process, or to revisit any issue previously subjected to bargaining. The employers could have confronted the culprits directly by stepping up enforcement of roster limits. They instead chose to address the problem by unilaterally forbidding players from individually competing in the labor market.

* * *

Given these features of the case, I do not see why the employers should be entitled to a judicially crafted exemption from antitrust liability. We have explained that the "the nonstatutory exemption has its source in the strong labor policy favoring the association of employees to eliminate competition over wages and working conditions." *Connell Constr. Co.*, 421 U.S. at 622. I know of no similarly strong labor policy that favors the association of employers to eliminate a competitive method of negotiating wages that predates collective bargaining, and that labor would prefer to preserve.

Even if some collective action by employers may justify an exemption because it is necessary to maintain the "integrity of the multiemployer bargaining unit," *NLRB v. Brown*, 380 U.S. 278, 289 (1965), no such justification exists here. The employers imposed a fixed wage even though there was no dispute over the pre-existing principle that player salaries should be individually negotiated. They sought only to prevent certain owners from evading roster limits and thereby gaining an unfair advantage. Because "the employer's interest is a competitive interest rather than an interest in regulating its own labor relations," *Mine Workers v. Pennington*, 381 U.S. 657, 667 (1965), there would seem to be no more reason to exempt this concerted, anticompetitive employer action from the antitrust laws than the action held unlawful in *Radovich v. National Football League*, 352 U.S. 445 (1957).

The point of identifying the unique features of this case is not, as the Court suggests, to make the case that professional football players, alone among workers, should be entitled to enforce the antitrust laws against anti-competitive collective employer action. Other employees, no less than well-paid athletes, are entitled to the protections of the antitrust laws when their employers unite to undertake anticompetitive action that causes them direct harm and alters the state of employer-employee relations that existed prior to unionization. Here that alteration occurred because the wage terms that the employers unilaterally imposed directly conflict with a pre-existing principle of agreement between the bargaining parties. In other contexts, the alteration may take other similarly anticompetitive and unjustifiable forms.

* * *

Accordingly, I respectfully dissent.

————

The Court thus adopted **Option 4**. Justice Stevens used the latter part of his dissent to document that the principal precedent cited by the majority was the earlier opinion written by Justice Goldberg in *Jewel Tea*. As Justice Stevens pointed out, in *Jewel Tea* and *Pennington*, discussed in Part 1(b) of this Section, Justice Goldberg secured only three votes for his position that any negotiations over mandatory subjects of bargaining were protected by the labor exemption. Rather, it was the three-member opinion by Justice White whose votes and opinion were decisive in both cases. Indeed, Justice Stevens went on to document Justice Goldberg's subsequent change of heart in the brief he filed with the Court in the early 1970s, on behalf of his client Curt Flood. What Justice Stevens was too polite to note in his dissent is that during the term when Justice Goldberg was unsuccessful in persuading a majority of his views in *Jewel Tea*, among his law clerks was Stephen Breyer.

————

NOTES AND QUESTIONS

1.   *Antitrust-Labor Balance?* In *Pennington*, the Supreme Court refused application of the labor exemption after finding that the union-management bargain harmed the management's rival coal producers and contractors. It concluded that the antitrust values of competition in the product market outweighed the labor law values of collective bargaining. In *Jewel Tea*, where labor relations concerns were judged stronger, the Court held that the labor exemption precluded use of antitrust law to strike down even a restraint whose immediate impact (though not its purpose) was on the product market: banning sales of meat after 6:00 p.m. is a classic example of distorting output in a manner unresponsive to consumer preference. In the *Brown* case, the petitioners argued that there was a strong antitrust interest in precluding employer collusion to eliminate a competitive labor market for development squad players, and a minimal (actually a negative) labor law interest in forcing all the NFL players either to go on strike or to decertify their union in order to allow the development squad players to use antitrust law to remove the large salary cut that the owners had collectively imposed on them. How did the Court's opinion respond to that argument?

2.   *Drawing a Line at Impasse?* All parties involved in the case recognized significant industrial relations problems in exposing to antitrust scrutiny multi-employer bargaining associations whose *raison d'etre* was to coordinate and constrain individual employer dealings with their employees.

Since unionized employees often benefit from the multiemployer bargaining process as much as do employers, everyone agreed that there had to be some measure of labor exemption for such collective employer action. The position of the Solicitor General was that employer associations such as the NFL were fully insulated from antitrust suits *before* bargaining reached an impasse, but that they lost the exemption once it was clear that impasse had been reached. (Even after that point the NFL owners would be entitled to defend their actions under all relevant antitrust doctrines.) The Court's opinion focused on this doctrinal proposal and rejected it. What are your views on this score? Which approach would foster collective bargaining?

3.   *Scope of* Brown*'s Holding?* Consider the last two paragraphs in the majority opinion in *Brown*. What limits do they suggest might be placed on the Court's holding? Does it apply only to employer, and union, bargaining tactics that are not unfair labor practices? Only to tactics that concern mandatory topics of bargaining? What temporal limits are suggested? Might union decertification necessarily negate the exemption?

4.   *Is Multiemployer Bargaining in Sports Distinguishable?* Why does Justice Stevens argue in dissent that a union's bargaining to encourage individual negotiation of player salary makes a league's unilateral imposition of a set salary different than the imposition of a wage level by a typical multiemployer consortium? Is it relevant to the scope of the exemption that in sports bargaining, it is the employers, rather than the union, that tries to avoid "the forces of the free market?" Does the majority adequately respond to Justice Stevens on this point? For an argument in support of Justice Stevens, see Michael C. Harper, *Multiemployer Bargaining, Antitrust Law, and Team Sports: The Contingent Choice of a Broad Exemption,* 38 WM & MARY L. REV. 1663 (1997).

Consider a hypothetical raised by Judge Winter in *NBA v. Williams,* 45 F.3d 684 (2d Cir. 1995), another pre-*Brown* decision applying the labor exemption: an association employing union printers, whose collective bargaining agreement with the printers union had expired, unilaterally implements its offer of a five percent wage increase rather than the ten percent increase sought by the union. In *Brown,* the players agreed with Judge Winter that such post-impasse collective action by the employers' association was immune from antitrust challenge, because the union in that industry had consented to the principle of standardized wages in place of competition among employers and individual employees; the only thing it had not agreed to was the specific standardized wage level. The players argued, however, that a key difference in the sports world is that players' unions seek to preserve or expand, not to eliminate, a competitive labor market for the setting of salaries. The players noted that sports actually resemble the entertainment, not the printers', labor market. Just as in sports, entertainment performers negotiate (through their agents) individual contract terms above the collectively-established minimum floors. If the Court had recognized this distinction, how would the exemption apply to unilateral action by NFL owners to lengthen the playing season, reduce existing pension or disability benefits, expand the commissioner's disciplinary authority, or revise the rookie draft, current restraints on free agency, and the specifics of the existing salary cap?

5. ELIGIBILITY TO PLAY IN UNIONIZED PROFESSIONAL SPORTS POST-*BROWN**

CLARETT V. NFL
369 F.3d 124 (2d Cir. 2004)

SOTOMAYOR, CIRCUIT JUDGE.

Defendant-appellant National Football League ("NFL" or "the League") appeals from a judgment of the United States District Court for the Southern District of New York (Scheindlin, J.) ordering plaintiff-appellee Maurice Clarett ("Clarett") eligible to enter this year's NFL draft on the ground that the NFL's eligibility rules requiring Clarett to wait at least three full football seasons after his high school graduation before entering the draft violate antitrust laws. In reaching its conclusion, the district court held, *inter alia,* that the eligibility rules are not immune from antitrust scrutiny under the non-statutory labor exemption.[1]

We disagree and reverse.

BACKGROUND

* * *

[The court noted that the litigation arises in the context of an ongoing collective bargaining agreement between the NFL and its players, negotiated between the NFL Management Council ("NFLMC"), which is the NFL member clubs' multi-employer bargaining unit, and the NFL Players Association ("NFLPA"), the NFL players' exclusive bargaining representative.] Despite the collective bargaining agreement's comprehensiveness with respect to, *inter alia,* the manner in which the NFL clubs select rookies through the draft and the scheme by which rookie compensation is determined, the eligibility rules for the draft do not appear in the agreement.

* * *

[The court observed that three provisions of the collective bargaining agreement refer to the NFL Constitution and Bylaws, where the draft

---

*   This Part focuses on eligibility rules for professional sports, all of which are now subject to collective bargaining agreements with players unions. Earlier cases discuss how antitrust laws would apply to eligibility rules if the labor exemption were not applicable. These can be found on the Casebook Website (http://pennstatelaw.psu.edu/SportsTextWebsite).

[1]   Because we find that the eligibility rules are immune from antitrust scrutiny under the non-statutory labor exemption, we do not express an opinion on the district court's legal conclusions that Clarett alleged a sufficient antitrust injury to state a claim or that the eligibility rules constitute an unreasonable restraint of trade in violation of the antitrust laws.

eligibility rules appear.] First, in Article III, Section 1 (Scope of Agreement), the collective bargaining agreement states:

> This Agreement represents the complete understanding of the parties as to all subjects covered herein, and there will be no change in the terms and conditions of this Agreement without mutual consent. . . . [T]he NFLPA and the Management Council waive any rights to bargain with one another concerning any subject covered or not covered in this Agreement for the duration of this Agreement, *including the provisions of the NFL Constitution and Bylaws;* provided, however, that if any proposed change in the NFL Constitution and Bylaws during the term of this Agreement could significantly affect the terms and conditions of employment of NFL players, then the [NFLMC] will give the NFLPA notice of and negotiate the proposed change in good faith.

(emphasis added). Second, Article IV, Section 2 (No Suit) provides generally that "neither [the NFLPA] nor any of its members" will sue or support a suit "relating to the presently existing provisions of the Constitution and Bylaws of the NFL as they are currently operative and administered." Third, Article IX, Section 1 (Non-Injury Grievance) makes "[a]ny dispute . . . involving the interpretation of, application of, or compliance with, . . . any applicable provision of the NFL Constitution and Bylaws pertaining to terms and conditions of employment of NFL players" subject to the grievance procedures afforded under the collective bargaining agreement.

Before the collective bargaining agreement became effective, a copy of the Constitution and Bylaws, as amended in 1992, was provided by the NFL to the NFLPA along with a letter, dated May 6, 1993, that "confirm[ed] that the attached documents are the presently existing provisions of the Constitution and Bylaws of the NFL referenced in Article IV, Section 2, of the Collective Bargaining Agreement." The May 6 letter was signed by representatives of the NFL and the NFLPA. The only other evidence presented to the district court by the NFL concerning the negotiation of the collective bargaining agreement were the two declarations of Peter Ruocco, Senior Vice President of Labor Relations at the NFLMC. In the second declaration, Ruocco attests that "[d]uring the course of collective bargaining that led to the [collective bargaining agreement], the [challenged] eligibility rule itself was the subject of collective bargaining."

* * *

DISCUSSION

Clarett argues that the NFL clubs are horizontal competitors for the labor of professional football players and thus may not agree that a player will be hired only after three full football seasons have elapsed following that player's high school graduation. That characterization, however, neglects that the labor market for NFL players is organized around a collective bargaining relationship that is provided for and promoted by federal labor law, and that the NFL clubs, as a multi-employer bargaining unit, can act jointly in setting the terms and conditions of players' employment and the rules of the sport without risking antitrust liability. For those reasons, the NFL argues that federal labor law favoring and governing the collective bargaining process precludes the application of the antitrust laws to its eligibility rules. We agree. . . .

I.

[The court first traced the history of the nonstatutory labor exemption in several Supreme Court decisions, particularly *Allen Bradley* (1945), *Pennington* (1965*), Jewel Tea* (1965), and *Connell Construction* (1975). Judge Sotomayor, as she then was, rejected Clarett's arguments that the challenged eligibility rule was not exempt. She explained her view of why the Eighth Circuit's decision in *Mackey* requiring a bona fide arms' length agreement did not properly define the limits of the non-statutory exemption.]

. . . Moreover, we disagree with the Eighth Circuit's assumption in *Mackey* that the Supreme Court's decisions in *Connell, Jewel Tea, Pennington*, and *Allen Bradley* dictate the appropriate boundaries of the non-statutory exemption for cases in which the only alleged anticompetitive effect of the challenged restraint is on a labor market organized around a collective bargaining relationship. Indeed, we have previously recognized that these decisions are of limited assistance in determining whether an athlete can challenge restraints on the market for professional sports players imposed through a collective bargaining process, because all "involved injuries to *employers* who asserted that they were being excluded from competition in the product market." *Wood v. Nat'l Basketball Ass'n,* 809 F.2d 954, 963 (2d Cir. 1987) (emphasis in original).

Clarett does not contend that the NFL's draft eligibility rules work to the disadvantage of the NFL's competitors in the market for professional football or in some manner protect the NFL's dominance in that market. *Compare N. Am. Soccer League v. Nat'l Football League*, 670 F.2d 1249 (2d Cir. 1982). He challenges the eligibility rules only on the ground that they are an unreasonable restraint upon the market for players' services. *See Clarett*, 306 F. Supp. 2d at 399. Thus, we need not decide here whether the *Mackey* factors aptly characterize the limits of the exemption in cases in which employers use agreements with their unions to disadvantage their competitors in the product or business market, because our cases have counseled a decidedly different approach where, as here, the plaintiff complains of a restraint upon a unionized labor market characterized by a collective bargaining relationship with a multi-employer bargaining unit.

Moreover, as the discussion below makes clear, the suggestion that the *Mackey* factors provide the proper guideposts in this case simply does not comport with the Supreme Court's most recent treatment of the non-statutory labor exemption in *Brown v. Pro Football, Inc.*, 518 U.S. 231 (1996).

II.

* * *

B.

* * *

. . . Our prior cases highlight a number of consequences resulting from the advent of this collective bargaining relationship that are relevant to Clarett's litigation. For one, prospective players no longer have the right to negotiate directly with the NFL teams over the terms and conditions of their employment. That responsibility is instead committed to the NFL and the players union to accomplish through the collective bargaining process, and throughout that process the NFL and the players union are to have the freedom to craft creative solutions to their differences in light of the economic imperatives of their industry. Furthermore, the NFL teams are permitted to engage in joint conduct with respect to the terms and conditions of players' employment as a multi-employer bargaining unit without risking antitrust liability. The arguments Clarett advances in support of his antitrust claim, however, run counter to each of these basic principles of federal labor law.

Because the NFL players have unionized and have selected the NFLPA as its exclusive bargaining representative, labor law prohibits Clarett from negotiating directly the terms and conditions of his employment with any NFL club [citation omitted], and an NFL club would commit an unfair labor practice were it to bargain with Clarett individually without the union's consent [citation omitted]. The terms and conditions of Clarett's employment are instead committed to the collective bargaining table and are reserved to the NFL and the players union's selected representative to negotiate. [Citation omitted.]

The players union's representative possesses "powers comparable to those possessed by a legislative body both to create and restrict the rights of those whom it represents." [Citations omitted.] In seeking the best deal for NFL players overall, the representative has the ability to advantage certain categories of players over others, subject of course to the representative's duty of fair representation. [Citation omitted.] The union representative may, for example, favor veteran players over rookies [citation omitted], and can seek to preserve jobs for current players to the detriment of new employees and the exclusion of outsiders [citations omitted]. This authority and exclusive responsibility is vested in the players' representative "once a mandatory collective bargaining

relationship is established and continues throughout the relationship."
Caldwell [*v. Am. Basketball Ass'n*, 66 F.3d 523, 528 (2d Cir. 1995)] For the
duration of that relationship, federal labor law then establishes a " 'soup-
to-nuts array' of rules, tribunals and remedies to govern [the collective
bargaining] process." *Id.* at 529 (quoting *Williams*, 45 F.3d at 693).

Clarett's argument that antitrust law should permit him to
circumvent this scheme established by federal labor law starts with the
contention that the eligibility rules do not constitute a mandatory subject
of collective bargaining and thus cannot fall within the protection of the
non-statutory exemption. Contrary to the district court, however, we find
that the eligibility rules are mandatory bargaining subjects. Though
tailored to the unique circumstance of a professional sports league, the
eligibility rules for the draft represent a quite literal condition for initial
employment and for that reason alone might constitute a mandatory
bargaining subject. *See* Caldwell, 66 F.3d at 529 (describing the mandatory
bargaining subject "pertinent" to that case as "the circumstances under
which an employer may . . . refuse to hire an employee"); R. Gorman, *Labor
Law* at 504 ("In accordance with the literal language of the Labor Act, the
parties must bargain about the requirements or 'conditions' of initial
employment."). But moreover, the eligibility rules constitute a mandatory
bargaining subject because they have tangible effects on the wages and
working conditions of current NFL players. Because the unusual economic
imperatives of professional sports raise "numerous problems with little or
no precedent in standard industrial relations," *Wood*, 809 F.2d at 961, we
have recognized that many of the arrangements in professional sports that,
at first glance, might not appear to deal with wages or working conditions
are indeed mandatory bargaining subjects, *see Silverman v. Major League
Baseball Player Relations Comm., Inc.*, 67 F.3d 1054, 1061 (2d Cir.
1995). . . . The eligibility rules in other words cannot be viewed in isolation,
because their elimination might well alter certain assumptions underlying
the collective bargaining agreement between the NFL and its players
union.

Furthermore, by reducing competition in the market for entering
players, the eligibility rules also affect the job security of veteran players.
See Fibreboard, 379 U.S. at 210–15 (recognizing union members' "vital
concern" in preserving jobs for union members); *see also Intercontinental
Container Transp. Corp. v. N.Y. Shipping Ass'n*, 426 F.2d 884, 887–88 (2d
Cir. 1970) ("[T]he preservation of jobs is within the area of proper union
concern[, and u]nion activity having as its object the preservation of jobs
for union members is not violative of the anti-trust laws." (internal
citations omitted)). Because the size of NFL teams is capped, the eligibility
rules diminish a veteran player's risk of being replaced by either a drafted
rookie or a player who enters the draft and, though not drafted, is then
hired as a rookie free agent. *See* Michael S. Jacobs & Ralph K. Winter, Jr.,
Antitrust Principles and Collective Bargaining by Athletes: Of Superstars

in Peonage, 81 Yale L.J. 1, 16 (1971) (recognizing that entry of new players through draft "has an enormous effect on those already in the unit and the collective agreement which governs them"). Consequently, as was true in *Silverman*, we find that to regard the NFL's eligibility rules as merely permissive bargaining subjects "would ignore the reality of collective bargaining in sports." *Silverman*, 67 F.3d at 1061–62.

Clarett, however, argues that the eligibility rules are an impermissible bargaining subject because they affect players outside of the union. But simply because the eligibility rules work a hardship on prospective rather than current employees does not render them impermissible. *See Wood*, 809 F.2d at 960. The eligibility rules in this respect are not dissimilar to union demands for hiring hall arrangements that have long been recognized as mandatory subjects of bargaining. [Citation omitted.] In such hiring hall arrangements, the criteria for employment are set by the rules of the hiring hall rather than the employer alone. Nevertheless, such an arrangement constitutes a permissible, mandatory subject of bargaining despite the fact that it concerns prospective rather than current employees. *Wood*, 809 F.2d at 960.

As a permissible, mandatory subject of bargaining, the conditions under which a prospective player, like Clarett, will be considered for employment as an NFL player are for the union representative and the NFL to determine. Clarett, however, stresses that the eligibility rules are arbitrary and that requiring him to wait another football season has nothing to do with whether he is in fact qualified for professional play. But Clarett is in this respect no different from the typical worker who is confident that he or she has the skills to fill a job vacancy but does not possess the qualifications or meet the requisite criteria that have been set. In the context of this collective bargaining relationship, the NFL and its players union can agree that an employee will not be hired or considered for employment for nearly any reason whatsoever so long as they do not violate federal laws such as those prohibiting unfair labor practices, or discrimination. [Citation omitted.] Any challenge to those criteria must "be founded on labor rather than antitrust law." *Caldwell*, 66 F.3d at 530.

Even accepting that an individual club could refuse to consider him for employment because he is less than three full seasons out of high school, Clarett contends that the NFL clubs invited antitrust liability when they agreed amongst themselves to impose that same criteria on every prospective player. As a consequence of the NFL's unique position in the professional football market, of course, such joint action deprives Clarett of the opportunity to pursue, at least for the time being, the kind of high-paying, high-profile career he desires. In the context of collective bargaining, however, federal labor policy permits the NFL teams to act collectively as a multi-employer bargaining unit in structuring the rules of play and setting the criteria for player employment. Such concerted action is encouraged as a matter of labor policy and tolerated as a matter of antitrust law, *see Williams*, 45 F.3d at 593, despite the fact that it "plainly involve [s] horizontal competitors for labor acting in concert to set and to implement terms of employment," *Caldwell*, 66 F.3d at 529. Multi-employer bargaining in professional sports, moreover, offers the added advantage of allowing the teams to agree with one another and, as required, bargain with the union over the host of uniform rules needed for the successful operation of the league, such as the "[n]umber of games, length of season, playoff structures, and roster size and composition." *Williams*, 45 F.3d at 689. The fact that the challenged rules govern eligibility for the NFL draft, thereby excluding some potential employees from consideration, does not render the NFL's adherence to its eligibility rules as a multi-employer bargaining unit suspect.

The threat to the operation of federal labor law posed by Clarett's antitrust claims is in no way diminished by Clarett's contention that the rules were not bargained over during the negotiations that preceded the current collective bargaining agreement. The eligibility rules, along with the host of other NFL rules and policies affecting the terms and conditions of NFL players included in the NFL's Constitution and Bylaws, were well known to the union, and a copy of the Constitution and Bylaws was presented to the union during negotiations. Given that the eligibility rules are a mandatory bargaining subject for the reasons set out above, the union or the NFL could have forced the other to the bargaining table if either felt that a change was warranted. *See* NLRB v. Katz, 369 U.S. 736, 743 (1962). Indeed, according to the declaration from the NFLMC's Vice President for Labor Relations, Peter Ruocco, this is exactly what the NFL did.

. . . In the collective bargaining agreement, the union agreed to waive any challenge to the Constitution and Bylaws and thereby acquiesced in the continuing operation of the eligibility rules contained therein—at least for the duration of the agreement. The terms of that waiver not only keep the eligibility rules in effect for the length of the agreement but also leave the NFL in control of any changes to the eligibility rules on the condition that any significant change potentially affecting the terms and conditions of players' employment would be preceded by notice to the union and an opportunity to bargain. The value of such a clause to the NFL is obvious, as control over any changes to the eligibility rules is left in the hands of management at least until the expiration of the collective bargaining agreement. Although it is entirely possible that the players union might not have agreed entirely with the eligibility rules, the union representative might not have regarded any difference of opinion with respect to the eligibility rules as sufficient to warrant the expenditure of precious time at the bargaining table in light of other important issues.

Clarett would have us hold that by reaching this arrangement rather than fixing the eligibility rules in the text of the collective bargaining agreement or in failing to wrangle over the eligibility rules at the bargaining table, the NFL left itself open to antitrust liability. Such a holding, however, would completely contradict prior decisions recognizing that the labor law policies that warrant withholding antitrust scrutiny are not limited to protecting only terms contained in collective bargaining agreements. *See Brown*, 518 U.S. at 243–44; *Caldwell*, 66 F.3d at 528–29 & n. 1. The reach of those policies, rather, extends as far as is necessary to ensure the successful operation of the collective bargaining *process* and to safeguard the "unique bundle of compromises" reached by the NFL and the players union as a means of settling their differences.[19] *Wood*, 809 F.2d at 961. It would disregard those policies completely to hold that some "particular *quid pro quo* must be proven to avoid antitrust liability," *id.* at 962 n. 5, or to allow Clarett to undo what we assume the NFL and its players union regarded as the most appropriate or expedient means of settling their differences, *id.* at 961. We have cautioned before that "[t]o the extent that courts prohibit particular solutions for particular problems, they reduce the number and quality of compromises available to unions and employers for resolving their differences." *Id.* Clarett would have us disregard our own good advice.

The disruptions to federal labor policy that would be occasioned by Clarett's antitrust suit, moreover, would not vindicate any of the antitrust policies that the Supreme Court has said may warrant the withholding of the non-statutory exemption. This is simply not a case in which the NFL is alleged to have conspired with its players union to drive its competitors out of the market for professional football. *See Pennington*, 381 U.S. at 665. Nor does Clarett contend that the NFL uses the eligibility rules as an unlawful means of maintaining its dominant position in that market. *See Allen Bradley Co.*, 325 U.S. at 809 ("The primary objective of all the Antitrust legislation has been to preserve business competition and to proscribe business monopoly."). This lawsuit reflects simply a prospective employee's disagreement with the criteria, established by the employer and the labor union, that he must meet in order to be considered for employment. Any remedies for such a claim are the province of labor law. Allowing Clarett to proceed with his antitrust suit would subvert "principles that have been familiar to, and accepted by, the nation's workers for all of the NLRA's [sixty years] in every industry except professional sports." *Caldwell*, 66 F.3d at 530. We, however, follow the Supreme Court's lead in declining to "fashion an antitrust exemption [so as to give] additional advantages to professional football players . . . that transport workers, coal miners, or meat packers would not enjoy." *Brown*, 518 U.S. at 249.

---

[19]   We therefore need not determine whether as a matter of law the Constitution and Bylaws that contained the eligibility rules were incorporated by reference into the current collective bargaining agreement.

NOTES AND QUESTIONS

1.   *Further Rejection of* Mackey. In *Mackey*, the Eighth Circuit concluded that the Rozelle Rule was not the product of genuine collective bargaining and thus would not enjoy antitrust immunity. By comparison, Judge Sotomayor explains that immunity does not require that the union achieve a good deal or even that it formally bargained over a management proposal. Which approach do you think is preferable? Which approach is consistent with the Court's opinion in *Brown*?

2.   *Scope of* Clarett *Holding*. Does Judge Sotomayor's analysis depend on finding that the union affirmatively agreed to the eligibility rule? In *O.M. by & through Moultrie v. Nat'l Women's Soccer League, LLC*, 544 F. Supp. 3d 1063 (D. Or. 2021), *appeal dismissed*, No. 21-35469 (9th Cir. Aug. 20, 2021), the district court distinguished *Clarett* because the union had not agreed to a rule barring contracts with players under the age of 18 (the rule was originated by the US Soccer Federation and continued in existence by the NWSL). Do you agree with this distinction? (The case was settled before the appeal could be resolved and the player debuted at age 15 for the Portland Thorns.)

3.   *A Viable Antitrust Claim?* Did Clarett, in any event, have any viable antitrust claim against the NFL, even in the absence of the labor exemption? Does the eligibility requirement operate like a monopsonist's restraint on the labor market, suppressing wages by limiting demand, or does it instead suppress supply and thereby inflate the wages of players?

Instead, assume, perhaps wrongly, that Clarett had standing to assert that the league's eligibility rule helps monopolize the product market. Does the rule do so, or did it provide an opportunity for a new league of competitors in that market?

4.   *Procompetitive Purpose of the Eligibility Rule?* If the rule does not have an anticompetitive purpose, why did the NFL adopt it? To please the NFLPA by limiting labor supply, as unions historically have wanted? Or might the rule have a procompetitive purpose of ensuring a higher quality product by avoiding teams feeling compelled to draft players before they are ready to play? Would it serve the competitive balance objective of the draft if a 19-year old quarterback were drafted by a dominant team and apprenticed behind an elite veteran nearing retirement? Might teams feel compelled to draft "prospects" before rival teams do so unless the "collective action" problem is solved by a rule like the NFL's?

6.   UNION RESPONSES POST-*BROWN*

During an 18-month period from the summer of 2011 until January 2013, the sports unions and the sports leagues in all four major team sports were engaged in collective bargaining and—in three out of the four sports—the use of economic weapons. The NFLPA, having unsuccessfully challenged anticompetitive labor restraints through industrial action during their failed 1987 strike, and through litigating *Brown*, developed another strategy: it arranged for its members to disclaim the union's authority to collectively negotiate on their behalf, and then proceeded with antitrust litigation. Without a collective bargaining arrangement, the players anticipated that cooperation among football clubs would not be exempt from the antitrust laws, and many of the agreements among clubs ratified previously in collective bargaining would be unlawful.

The history of this strategy is explained in *Brady* below. The NFL responded to this tactic in turn by, following due notice to union officials, locking out all players immediately following the CBA's expiration. The players tried to preempt the league's strategy by terminating the union's status as their collective bargaining agent hours before the expiration of the agreement, and then filing an antitrust challenge to the lockout. As discussed in the excerpt below, the trial judge granted an injunction against the lockout that was reversed by the court of appeals.

BRADY V. NFL

644 F.3d 661 (8th Cir. 2011)

COLLOTON, CIRCUIT JUDGE.

* * *

The League proceeded with its planned lockout on March 12, 2011. The Players moved for a preliminary injunction in the district court, urging the court to enjoin the lockout as an unlawful group boycott that was causing irreparable harm to the Players. The district court granted a preliminary injunction, and the League appealed. We conclude that the injunction did not conform to the provisions of the Norris-LaGuardia Act, 29 U.S.C. § 101 *et seq.*, and we therefore vacate the district court's order.

A.

Some historical background will place this case in context. [The court recounted the judicial application of the antitrust laws to the NFL, the NLRB's application of labor laws and recognition of the NFLPA as the exclusive bargaining representative of all NFL players, and the history of collective bargaining in the NFL. It noted the contentious history included strikes and litigation, as well as a response to continued application of the labor exemption that resulted in the NFLPA executive committee's decision to abandon the organization's collective bargaining rights in an effort to end the NFL's nonstatutory labor exemption from the antitrust laws. This decision resulted in a verdict in the *McNeil* case discussed in Section C, Part 2 above, awarding substantial damages. The appeal of that case and other issues was resolved when the parties settled ongoing litigation in *White v. NFL*, 822 F. Supp. 1389 (D. Minn. 1993).]

. . . Many disputes between the League and the players were resolved when the parties entered into a class action settlement agreement in

White. . . . The NFLPA subsequently collected authorization cards from NFL players re-designating the organization as the players' exclusive collective bargaining representative, and the NFL voluntarily recognized the NFLPA as the players' union on March 29, 1993. The district court approved the parties' Stipulation and Settlement Agreement ("SSA") in April 1993, and the NFL and the NFLPA entered into a new CBA shortly thereafter. The NFL and the NFLPA agreed to amend various portions of the SSA to conform to the provisions of the new CBA, and the district court approved the requested amendments. The court entered a consent decree incorporating the terms of the amended SSA on August 20, 1993.

[The court then described *Brown*'s holding and quoted its discussion of when the labor exemption might end.]

* * *

B.

. . . Although the NFL and the NFLPA engaged in more than two years of negotiations toward a new CBA, the League and the players were unable to reach an agreement. The League filed an unfair labor practice charge with the NLRB in February 2011, asserting that the union failed to confer in good faith. The Players say that the charge is meritless. [The NFL claimed that the union was engaged in what it termed "surface bargaining," a tactic designed to avoid reaching an agreement before the collective bargaining agreement expired so that it could disclaim its representative status and allow its members to pursue antitrust litigation and injunctive relief against the League to try to block the NFL's expected lockout. The union responded that the players sought "a fair, new and long-term deal" and it had "offered proposals and solutions on every issue" the owners had raised. The Labor Board would never rule on whether the NFLPA's strategy constituted bad faith bargaining.]

As the deadline approached, a substantial majority of NFL players voted to end the NFLPA's status as their collective bargaining representative. . . .

The League filed an amended unfair labor practice charge on March 11, alleging that the NFLPA's disclaimer was a "sham" and that the combination of a disclaimer by the union and subsequent antitrust litigation was "a ploy and an unlawful subversion of the collective bargaining process." The Players dispute the charge, citing an advice memorandum of an associate general counsel of the NLRB in *Pittsburgh Steelers, Inc.*, No. 6-CA-23143, 1991 WL 144468 (NLRB G.C. June 26, 1991). The memorandum concluded that the NLFPA's 1989 disclaimer was valid, and that it was "irrelevant" whether the disclaimer was motivated by "litigation strategy," so long as the disclaimer was "otherwise unequivocal and adhered to." *Id.* at *2 & n.8.

The Players, funded by the NFLPA, commenced this action on the same day as the disclaimer, March 11, 2011. . . .

* * *

On April 25, 2011, the district court granted the Players' motion to enjoin the lockout, rejecting the League's assertions that the court lacked jurisdiction to enter the injunction, that the court should defer to the primary jurisdiction of the NLRB, and that the League is in any event immune from antitrust liability under the nonstatutory labor exemption. The court concluded that the Norris-LaGuardia Act ("NLGA" or "Act"), 29 U.S.C. § 101 *et seq.*, which restricts the power of federal courts to issue injunctions in cases "involving or growing out of a labor dispute," *id.* § 1, was inapplicable, because the term "labor dispute" connotes a dispute between an employer and a union, and the Act therefore does not apply "absent the present existence of a union." . . .

The district court also declined to stay the action pending the NLRB's resolution of the League's pending unfair labor practice charges. The court determined that a stay would not be appropriate because the delay could cause significant hardship for the plaintiffs, and because "[t]he Board has articulated the standard under which disclaimers must be evaluated in a clear and consistent fashion, and application of that established standard requires no particular specialized expertise." Finally, the district court concluded that the nonstatutory labor exemption does not protect the League from antitrust liability related to the lockout. In the court's view, the exemption applies only to agreements concerning "mandatory subjects of collective bargaining," such as wages, hours, and other terms and conditions of employment, and an employer's imposition of a lockout is not exempted because "[a] lockout is not a substantive term or condition of employment." The court distinguished the Supreme Court's decision in *Brown* on the basis that the parties here "have left the collective bargaining framework entirely."

* * *

II.

We consider first the League's contention that the Norris-LaGuardia Act deprived the district court of jurisdiction to enter the injunction. [The recounted the history of the Act, summarized above.]

The language of the Act, however, extends well beyond the specific issues decided in [the anti-union cases that led to the Act's enactment.] The impetus for the NLGA was dissatisfaction with injunctions entered against workers in labor disputes, but the statute also requires that an injunction against an employer participating in a labor dispute must conform to the Act. [Citations omitted.] This case requires us to decide whether, and if so how, the Act applies to the district court's injunction against the League.

To determine whether the NLGA forbids or places conditions on the issuance of an injunction here, we begin with the text of the statute. *Section 1* provides that "[n]o court of the United States . . . shall have jurisdiction to issue any . . . temporary or permanent injunction in a case involving or growing out of a labor dispute, except in strict conformity with the provisions of this chapter." 29 U.S.C. § 101. As noted, the district court concluded that the Act is inapplicable to this action, because the case is not one "involving or growing out of a labor dispute."

Section 13(c) of the Act states that "[t]he term 'labor dispute' includes *any controversy concerning terms or conditions of employment*, or concerning the association or representation of persons in negotiating, fixing, maintaining, changing, or seeking to arrange terms or conditions of employment, regardless of whether or not the disputants stand in the proximate relation of employer and employee." 29 U.S.C. § 113(c) (emphasis added). This lawsuit is a controversy concerning terms or conditions of employment. The Players seek broad relief that would affect the terms or conditions of employment for the entire industry of professional football. In particular, they urge the court to declare unlawful and to enjoin several features of the relationship between the League and the players, including the limit on compensation that can be paid to rookies, the salary cap, the "franchise player" designation, and the "transition player" designation, all of which the Players assert are anticompetitive restrictions that violate § 1 of the Sherman Act. . . .

We are not convinced by the Players' contention that because § 13(c) uses the term "includes," rather than "means," to introduce the substance of a "labor dispute," Congress did not fully define the term. They urge that § 13(c) merely expanded in one respect (to disputes outside the employer-employee relationship) a preexisting definition of "labor dispute"—a definition that was not codified and that, according to the Players, extended only to disputes involving organized labor. Whatever might be the significance of the verb "include" when used in other contexts, *cf. Massachusetts v. EPA*, 549 U.S. 497 (2007) (Scalia, J., dissenting), Congress stated in § 13 of the NLGA that "labor dispute" is "defined in this section," 29 U.S.C. § 113(a), and the Supreme Court consistently has described § 13(c) as a "definition" of "labor dispute." [citations omitted]. Not only has the Supreme Court repeatedly characterized § 13(c) as a definition, but contrary to the suggestion that an established meaning should be used to narrow the text, the Court has observed that "the statutory definition itself is extremely broad," *Jacksonville Bulk Terminals, Inc.*, 457 U.S. at 712, and explained that "Congress made the definition broad because it wanted it to be broad." Order of R.R. Telegraphers, 362 U.S. at 335–36.

The Act also states expressly that "[a] case shall be held to involve or grow out of a labor dispute when the case involves persons who are engaged in the same industry, trade, craft, or occupation." 29 U.S.C. § 113(a). This case, of course, involves persons engaged in the "same industry," namely, professional football. The statute continues that such a case "shall be held to involve or grow out of a labor dispute" when "such dispute is . . . between one or more employers or associations of employers and one or more employees or associations of employees." *Id.* This dispute is between one or more employers or associations of employers (the League and the NFL teams) and one or more employees (the Players under contract). By the plain terms of the Act, this case "shall be held to involve or grow out of a labor dispute."

The district court reached a contrary conclusion by departing from the text of § 13(a). The court thought the phrase "one or more employees or associations of employees" did not encompass the Players in this dispute, because "one or more employees" means "individual *unionized* employee or employees." We see no warrant for adding a requirement of unionization to the text.

A similar argument did not persuade the Supreme Court in *New Negro Alliance v. Sanitary Grocery Co.*, 303 U.S. 552 (1938). There, a company sought an injunction against the New Negro Alliance, which the Supreme Court described as "a corporation composed of colored persons, organized for the mutual improvement of its members and the promotion of civic, educational, benevolent, and charitable enterprises." *Id.* at 555. The Alliance allegedly had conspired to picket and boycott one of the company's grocery stores to pressure the store to employ Black clerks. *Id.* at 555–56. The company claimed, among other things, that the Alliance's acts were "unlawful, [and] constitute[d] a conspiracy in restraint of trade." *Id.* at 558–59. . . .

The Supreme Court reversed. Although no labor organization was involved in the dispute, and the company argued that "a recognized labor union or unions or individual members thereof were involved" in all but one of the "labor dispute" precedents cited by the Alliance, Brief for Respondent at 24, the Court ruled that the definitions in the Act "plainly embrace the controversy which gave rise to the instant suit and classify it as one arising out of a dispute defined as a labor dispute." *New Negro Alliance*, 303 U.S. at 560. The Court observed that § 13(a) provides that a case shall be held to involve or grow out of a labor dispute "when the case involves any conflicting or competing interests in a 'labor dispute' . . . of 'persons participating or interested' therein," and ruled that the Alliance and its individual members were "persons interested in the dispute." *Id.* (internal quotation omitted). If § 13(a) were limited to controversies involving unions or unionized employees, then the Court could not have reached this conclusion.

Further confirmation that the present existence of a union is not required for a "labor dispute" comes from *NLRB v. Washington Aluminum*

Co., 370 U.S. 9 (1962). There, a group of seven employees who were "wholly unorganized" and had "no bargaining representative" or "representative of any kind to present their grievances to their employer" staged a walkout to protest cold working conditions in a machine shop. *Id.* at 14–15. Although the employees were not part of a union, the Supreme Court held that the walkout "did grow out of a 'labor dispute' within the plain meaning of the definition of that term in § 2(9) of the [National Labor Relations] Act." *Id.* at 15. The definition of "labor dispute" in the National Labor Relations Act is "virtually identical" to the definition of "labor dispute" in the NLGA, and the two provisions "have been construed consistently with one another" by the Supreme Court. *Jacksonville Bulk Terminals, Inc.*, 457 U.S. at 711 n.11; *accord* United States v. Hutcheson, 312 U.S. 219, 234 n.4 (1941).

* * *

The text of the Norris-LaGuardia Act and the cases interpreting the term "labor dispute" do not require the present existence of a union to establish a labor dispute. Whatever the precise limits of the phrase "involving or growing out of a labor dispute," this case does not press the outer boundary. The League and the players' union were parties to a collective bargaining agreement for almost eighteen years prior to March 2011. They were engaged in collective bargaining over terms and conditions of employment for approximately two years through March 11, 2011. At that point, the parties were involved in a classic "labor dispute" by the Players' own definition. Then, on a single day, just hours before the CBA's expiration, the union discontinued collective bargaining and disclaimed its status, and the Players filed this action seeking relief concerning industry-wide terms and conditions of employment. Whatever the effect of the union's disclaimer on the League's immunity from antitrust liability, the labor dispute did not suddenly disappear just because the Players elected to pursue the dispute through antitrust litigation rather than collective bargaining.

III.

[This part, an important question of labor law but unnecessary for resolution of sports law issues given Part II, discusses and rejects the Players' claim that § 4 of the Act does not apply at all to employer lockouts. One general interpretive rationale, which would seemingly apply to Part II as well, deserves inclusion in this excerpt:]

Aside from the text and structure of § 4, the Players argue that the policy of the NLGA and the legislative history support their position that § 4(a) offers no protection to employers. To be sure, the policy stated in § 2 is that the individual unorganized worker should be free from the interference, restraint, or coercion of employers in the designation of representatives, self-organization, or other concerted activities. But it does not follow that a prohibition on injunctions against employer lockouts is contrary to the policy of the Act. The Supreme Court has observed that while the Act was designed to protect workingmen, the broader purpose was "to prevent the injunctions of the federal courts from *upsetting the natural interplay of the competing economic forces of labor and capital.*" *Bhd. of R.R. Trainmen v. Chi. River & Ind. R.R. Co.*, 353 U.S. 30, 40 (1957) (emphasis added). An employer's lockout is part of this interplay; it is not the equivalent of a judicial injunction that interferes with the ability of workers to exercise organized economic power.

The Court elsewhere explained that "powerful judicial dissents," such as that of Justice Brandeis in *Duplex Printing*, urged that labor disputes were an "area of economic conflict that had best be left to economic forces and the pressure of public opinion and not subjected to the judgment of courts." *Hutcheson*, 312 U.S. at 231. In support of that view, the Brandeis dissent cited this excerpt from the 1915 Report of the Committee on Industrial Relations:

> [T]here are apparently, only two lines of action possible: First to restrict the rights and powers of employers to correspond in substance to the powers and rights now allowed to trade unions, and second, to remove all restriction which now prevent the freedom of action of both parties to industrial disputes, retaining only the ordinary civil and criminal restraints for the preservation of life, property and the public peace. The first method has been tried and failed absolutely. * * * *The only method therefore seems to be the removal of all restrictions upon both parties, thus legalizing the strike, the lockout, the boycott, the blacklist, the bringing in of strike-breakers, and peaceful picketing.*

Duplex Printing, 254 U.S. at 486 n.7 (Brandeis, J., dissenting) (emphasis added); *see also* 75 Cong. Rec. 5478 (1932) (remarks of Rep. LaGuardia) ("If the courts had administered even justice to both employers and employees, there would be no need of considering a bill of this kind now."); *id.* at 4915 (remarks of Sen. Wagner) ("The policy and purpose which give meaning to the present legislation is its implicit declaration that the Government shall occupy a neutral position, lending its extraordinary power neither to those who would have labor unorganized nor to those who would organize it and limiting its action to the preservation of order and the restraint of fraud."). A one-way interpretation of § 4(a)—prohibiting injunctions against strikes but not against lockouts—would be in tension with the purposes of the Norris-LaGuardia Act to allow free play of economic forces and "to withdraw federal courts from a type of controversy for which many believed they were ill-suited and from participation in which, it was feared, judicial prestige might suffer." *Marine Cooks & Stewards*, 362 U.S. at 369 n.7. We are not convinced that the policy of the Act counsels against our textual analysis of § 4(a). *Cf. Am. Med. Ass'n v. United States*, 317 U.S. 519, 535 (1943) ("It is not our province to define the purpose of Congress apart from what it has said in its enactments, and if [a party's] activities fall within the classes defined by the [Clayton and Norris-LaGuardia] acts, we are bound to accord [the party] . . . the benefit of the legislative provisions.").

* * *

B.

[Discussion of another technical point regarding the Norris-LaGuardia Act concerning the refusal to deal with free agents and rookies omitted.]

IV.

Given our conclusion that the preliminary injunction did not conform to the provisions of the Norris-LaGuardia Act, we need not reach the other points raised by the League on appeal. In particular, we express no view on whether the League's nonstatutory labor exemption from the antitrust laws continues after the union's disclaimer. The parties agree that the Act's restrictions on equitable relief are not necessarily coextensive with the substantive rules of antitrust law, and we reach our decision on that understanding.

The district court's order of April 25, 2011, granting a preliminary injunction is vacated, and the case is remanded for further proceedings.

BYE, CIRCUIT JUDGE, dissenting.

In 1914, after twenty years of judicial interference in labor conflicts on the side of the employers, Congress stepped in to protect organized labor by passing sections 6 and 20 of the Clayton Act. Section 20 of the Act generally prohibited the issuance of injunctions in cases involving or growing out of labor disputes. *See* 29 U.S.C. § 52. It soon became apparent, however, that what was supposed to be the "charter of liberty of labor," Felix Frankfurter & Nathan Greene, *The Labor Injunction* 164 (1930) (remarks of William Howard Taft), fell short of the promise. The *Lochner*-era judges adopted a narrow interpretation of the Act, restricting it to "trade union activities directed against an employer by his own employees." *United States v. Hutcheson*, 312 U.S. 219, 230 (1941). "[T]o protect the rights of labor in the same manner the Congress intended when it enacted the Clayton Act," *id.* at 236, Congress passed the Norris-LaGuardia Act, under which "the allowable area of union activity was not to be restricted . . . to an immediate employer-employee relation." *Id.* at 231. Through its holding in this case today, the majority reaffirms the wisdom of the old French saying used by Felix Frankfurter and Nathan Greene when describing judicial reluctance to enforce § 20 of the Clayton Act: "the more things are legislatively changed, the more they remain the same judicially." Felix Frankfurter & Nathan Greene, *The Labor Injunction* 176 (1930). Despite the repeated efforts of the legislative branch to come to the rescue of organized labor, today's opinion puts the power of the Act in the service of employers, to be used against non-unionized employees who can no longer avail themselves of protections of labor laws. Because I cannot countenance such interpretation of the Act, I must and hereby dissent.

I.

A. "Labor Dispute"

First, I have to disagree with the majority's reading of the term "labor dispute." As the majority recounts, "[t]he underlying aim of the Norris-LaGuardia Act was to restore the broad purpose which Congress thought it had formulated in the Clayton Act but which was frustrated, so Congress believed, by unduly restrictive judicial construction." *United States v. Hutcheson*, 312 U.S. at 235–36. The unequivocal goal of the new legislation was to overturn the Supreme Court's decisions in *Duplex Printing* and *Bedford Cut Stone*, which had restricted § 20 of the Clayton Act to labor union activities directed against employees' immediate employers. . . .

However, in passing the NLGA, Congress never intended to change the well-accepted calculus of the Clayton Act as the legislation for the benefit of organized labor. The Clayton Act was always understood as an attempt to assist the organized labor movement at the time its progress was impeded by judicial misuse of injunctions. *See, e.g., Hutcheson*, 312 U.S. at 229–30 (explaining § 20 of the Clayton Act "withdrew from the general interdict of the Sherman Law specifically enumerated practices of labor unions by prohibiting injunctions against them"); *Bedford Cut Stone Co. v. Journeymen Stone Cutters' Ass'n of N. Am.*, 274 U.S. 37, 56 (1927) (separate opinion by Stone, J.) (describing the Clayton Act as being concerned with "organized labor"); *Am. Steel Foundries v. Tri-City Cent. Trades Council*, 257 U.S. 184, 208–09 (1921) ("Labor unions are recognized by the Clayton Act as legal when instituted for mutual help and lawfully carrying out their legitimate objects."); *see also* Frankfurter & Green, *The Labor Injunction*, at 130–31, 139 (describing the Clayton Act's preoccupation with organized labor). It is this well-entrenched understanding of the term "labor dispute" as centered on the struggle between employers and organized labor that informs interpretation of the same definition under the NLGA. *See Bruesewitz v. Wyeth LLC*, 131 S. Ct. 1068, 1082 (2011) ("When 'all (or nearly all) of the' relevant judicial decisions have given a term or concept a consistent judicial gloss, we presume Congress intended the term or concept to have that meaning when it incorporated it into a later-enacted statute.") (citation omitted).

Like the Clayton Act, the NLGA has been consistently cited in connection with protection of unions' rights. [Citations omitted]. This interpretation is in part dictated by § 2 of the Act, which "explicitly formulated the 'public policy of the United States' in regard to the industrial conflict." *Hutcheson*, 312 U.S. at 231. Such public policy expressed concern with the plight of the "individual unorganized worker," whom Congress deemed "helpless to exercise actual liberty of contract and to protect his freedom of labor, and thereby to obtain acceptable terms and conditions of employment" when confronted with "corporate and other forms of ownership association" assumed by employers. 29 U.S.C. § 102. Commenting on the judicial respect § 2 deserves, the Supreme Court explained that "[t]here are few pieces of legislation where the congressional hearings, committee reports, and the language in the legislation itself more clearly point to the necessity for giving an Act a construction that will protect the congressional policy the Act adopted." *See Order of R.R. Telegraphers v. Chicago & N. W. R.R. Co.*, 362 U.S. 330, 335 (1960). In the NLGA's case, the congressional policy was about helping the unions.

* * *

B. "Involving or Growing Out"

Second, I must take issue with the majority's conclusion as to this case not representing the outer boundary of the phrase "involving or growing out of a labor dispute." Like the nonstatutory labor exemption, statutory exemption from antitrust liability, which rests in part on the Norris-LaGuardia Act, *Connell Construction Co.*, 421 U.S. at 621–22, lies at the intersection between labor and antitrust laws. . . . *Mackey v. NFL*, 543 F.2d 606, 613 (8th Cir. 1976) (availability of the labor exemption "turns upon whether the relevant federal labor policy is deserving of preeminence over federal antitrust policy under the circumstances of the particular case"). "While the Norris-LaGuardia Act's bar of federal-court labor injunctions is not explicitly phrased as an exemption from the antitrust laws, it has been interpreted broadly as a statement of congressional policy that the courts must not use the antitrust laws as a vehicle to interfere in labor disputes." *H.A. Artists & Associates, Inc.*, 451 U.S. at 714. The scope of the two exemptions differs somewhat—"the statutory exemption allows unions to accomplish some restraints by acting unilaterally, [whereas] the nonstatutory exemption offers no similar protection when a union and a nonlabor party agree to restrain competition in a business market," *see Connell Construction Co.*, 421 U.S. at 622,—but there is no place for the application of either at the time labor laws no longer govern and labor policy is no longer implicated.

The Supreme Court recognized as much when it explained that nonstatutory immunity from antitrust review is no longer necessary when "an agreement among employers [is] sufficiently distant in time and in circumstances from the collective-bargaining process that a rule permitting antitrust intervention would not significantly interfere with that process." *Brown*, 518 U.S. at 250. As an example of such endpoint, the Court cited "collapse of the collective-bargaining relationship, as evidenced by decertification of the union." *Id.* (quoting Brown v. Pro Football, Inc., 50 F.3d 1041, 1057 (D.C. Cir. 1995)). With the players having voted to end the NFLPA's status as their collective bargaining representative and the NFLPA likewise having disclaimed its status as the players' representative, this case has reached that endpoint.

Indeed, the League itself anticipated dissolution of antitrust remedy fetters upon disclaimer of union representation, as is evident from its concessions in previous cases. *See Powell v. NFL*, 930 F.2d 1293, 1303 n.12 (8th Cir. 1989) (describing the League's concession that "the Sherman Act could be found applicable, depending on the circumstances, . . . if the affected employees ceased to be represented by a certified union"); *see also* Appellees Special Add. at 370 (transcript of the League's Supreme Court argument in *Brown v. Pro Football, Inc.*, where the League conceded antitrust immunities would not apply when "employees ultimately elect, in good faith, . . . to give up their rights under the labor laws"). The League's view was consistent with those of the courts, who saw disassociation from the union as the point beyond which labor laws yield to the antitrust regime. *Brown*, 50 F.3d at 1057 ("If employees wish to seek the protections of the Sherman Act, they may forego unionization or even decertify their unions. We note that the NFL players took exactly this latter step after the Eighth Circuit's *Powell* decision."); *Powell*, 930 F.2d at 1305 (Heaney, J., dissenting) (criticizing the majority opinion for continuing the labor exemption for too long—in effect, "until the bargaining relationship is terminated either by a NLRB decertification proceeding or by abandonment of bargaining rights by the union"). This realization as to the players' membership in a union acting as a shield against the possibility of antitrust charges is the reason why, in the 1993 *White* settlement, the League insisted the NFLPA be reconstituted as the players' representative and the collective bargaining relationship between the parties be reestablished.

At some point in the "arising out of" spectrum, the antitrust immunities stemming from statutory and nonstatutory labor exemptions must come to an end and give way to antitrust remedies. Such point does not come a year from the union disclaimer, nor one business cycle from it, as suggested by the League's counsel. Rather, such point comes at the moment of the union disclaimer.

II.

[The dissent's disagreement with the majority's conclusion that § 4(a) protects employers is omitted. The dissent emphasized portions of the legislative history that Congress intended the Act to stop anti-union injunctions. He noted that the Norris-LaGuardia Act was explicitly intended to overrule judicial decisions that Congress felt had improperly weakened § 20 of the Clayton Act, intended to exempt collective action by workers organizing unions from antitrust liability. That section has not been construed to symmetrically exempt employer groups from antitrust liability. The dissent concluded]:

Viewing the legislative history of § 4(a) in its entirety, Congress did not intend to protect employers under the provision. *See De Arroyo*, 425 F.2d at 291 ("Our understanding of the legislative history behind section

4(a) leads us to conclude that that section was not intended as a protection for employers."). Moreover, the purpose delineated in § 2 further bolsters this conclusion. *See Baseball Players and the Antitrust Laws*, 53 Colum. L. Rev. 242, 249 n.71 (1953) ("Given the purpose of the Norris-LaGuardia Act it is improbable that an association of employers which deprives an 'individual unorganized worker' of his 'freedom of labor' comes within its protection."). Interpreting the text of § 4(a) in light of the legislative history and express policy of the NLGA, I would conclude § 4(a) does not protect employers.

In the end, I find illustrative the wise words of Judge Learned Hand:

> Of course it is true that the words used, even in their literal sense, are the primary, and ordinarily the most reliable, source of interpreting the meaning of any writing: be it a statute, a contract, or anything else. But it is one of the surest indexes of a mature and developed jurisprudence not to make a fortress out of the dictionary; but to remember that statutes always have some purpose or object to accomplish, whose sympathetic and imaginative discovery is the surest guide to their meaning.

Cabell v. Markham, 148 F.2d 737, 739 (2d Cir. 1945). In this case, "the fact remains that Congress passed the Norris-LaGuardia Act to forestall judicial attempts to narrow labor's statutory protection." *Bhd. of Maint. of Way Emps.*, 481 U.S. at 443. This is exactly what the majority has done. As a consequence, I am compelled to and must dissent.[9]

NOTES AND QUESTIONS

1.   *A Distortion of the Norris-LaGuardia Act?* Do you find it strange that the court uses a statute enacted by Congress in the mid-1930s with the immediate objective of freeing unions from judicial interference to bolster management in its labor battle with a labor organization? Remember that the federal courts took the same side in the first decade of the Sherman Act by holding repeatedly that a statute designed to attack combinations of capital was easily contorted to apply to organizations in the nascent labor movement. After *Brady*, should unions and workers conclude that self-help and private alternative dispute resolution are better tools for achieving institutional goals than is antitrust litigation? Consider that a broad interpretation of the statutory labor exemption works in favor of professional athletes in individual, non-unionized sports. In *Confederacion Hipica de Puerto Rico, Inc. v.*

---

[9]   Although the majority confines its analysis to the NLGA, I remain strongly convinced the other traditional injunction factors favor the Players. *See Minn. Citizens Concerned for Life, Inc. v. Swanson*, 640 F.3d 304, 310 (8th Cir. 2011) (setting forth the factors a court must consider). For the reasons set forth in my prior dissent, *see Brady v. NFL*, 640 F.3d 785, 794–96 (8th Cir. 2011) (Bye, J., dissenting), which have only intensified given the current juncture, I would affirm the district court.

Confederacion de Jinetes Puertorriquenos, Inc., 30 F.4th 306 (1st Cir. 2022), the First Circuit reversed a permanent injunction in favor of racetrack owners who claimed that a jockey association work stoppage over employment conditions amounted to an illegal group boycott under § 1. The court found the activity protected by the statutory labor exemption, despite the jockeys' status as independent contractors, explaining that they "sought higher wages and safer working conditions, making this a core labor dispute."

2. *An Even Broader Interpretation of the Labor Exemption.* For an argument that the literal language of § 6 takes all labor market restraints outside the scope of federal antitrust law, *see* Gary Roberts, *Reconciling Federal Labor and Antitrust Policy: The Special Case of Sports League Labor Market Restraints,* 75 GEO. L.J. 19, 26–58 (1986), and *Brown v. Pro Football, Inc.: The Supreme Court Gets It Right For The Wrong Reasons,* 42 THE ANTITRUST BULLETIN 595, 618–24 (Fall 1997). If Roberts' arguments were accepted, even non-union players, and other workers, would never be able to seek antitrust protection from their employers' restrictive labor market practices. Do you agree that this could have been Congress' intent when passing the Clayton Act in response to labor's lobbying?

3. *Were Damages Available?* What if the players had not sought an injunction of the lockout, but had sought only the treble damages available under antitrust law? Had settlement not ensued, how should a court have ruled on the application of *Brown?*

4. *Disclaimer or Decertification as an Option.* Aside from the reach of the labor exemption, another problem with the strategy of disclaiming collective bargaining and suing the owners is that even if the owners were found to have violated the antitrust laws by locking out the players, there would be no union available to resolve the underlying labor dispute. The individual players could not claim to represent the bargaining unit. In fact, although the NFL Players Association announced it was defunct, it stood ready to resume collective bargaining once the owners' lockout was enjoined. Neither the courts nor the Labor Board ruled on the legality of this strategy. After management ultimately prevailed in court, the NFL recognized the NFLPA's status as the players' collective bargaining representative on July 30, 2011, and the parties proceeded to negotiate terms for a new collective bargaining agreement. The agreement became effective after ratification by the players on August 4, 2011.

5. *Disclaimer Versus Decertification?* Under labor law, a union can disclaim when 50% of members show they do not want to be represented by a union; a union is decertified following an election among workers in the bargaining unit, following a petition signed by 30% of the members. However, once a union has been decertified, there cannot be a new election to certify a union for 12 months. *See* 29 U.S.C. § 159. Some observers have suggested that a complete decertification, which would bar the union from representing players for over a year and involves more procedural requirements, is the appropriate point for terminating protection of the labor exemption. Another option would be to bar unions from withdrawing from multi-employer

bargaining and cutting deals with individual employers during a particular "bargaining cycle." Are either of these workable and desirable standards?

D. THE BUSINESS DYNAMICS OF REGULATING SPORTS LABOR MARKETS

The doctrinal questions about when and how the Sherman Act applies to professional sports leagues' labor restraints also generate important and more broadly applicable insights into the underlying business dynamics involved. Such insights may affect a public policy evaluation of the correctness of judicial interpretations, allow lawyers who counsel "in the shadow" of these rules and collective agreements to better understand them, and create potential opportunities for third-party stakeholders to interact strategically with owners and players' unions to achieve their own goals.

Foundational Concepts in Studying Bargaining Dynamics

Launching an antitrust lawsuit against a sports league's labor rules presumes that success will actually change things: that the landscape will be different if the plaintiff wins than if the plaintiff loses. Nobel laureate Ronald Coase observed that the established rules do not matter in a world of perfect information and zero transaction costs. The proper inference from the existence of all the material in Sections B and C of this chapter is that the process of adopting and negotiating over labor market rules is an endeavor featuring significant differences in information as well as costly bargaining.

Less abstractly, keep in mind that labor restraints in North American professional sports leagues are initially the product of agreements among the member clubs, and then the result of collective bargaining between the clubs and players unions during which both sides have a duty to bargain in good faith. Recall from Chapter 3 that union executives representing players owe a Duty of Fair Representation to all members of the union, and that ultimately any agreement must be approved by the membership or their elected representatives. Recall from Chapter 6's discussion of the *American Needle* case that professional sports leagues are governed by their member clubs, whose interests relate to the overall profitability of the league as well as to specific profits for their own club. Consider these dynamics in the following exercises, which can either be thought experiments, group projects, or topics for class discussion.

A third key concept to consider is that these considerations don't take place in a vacuum. Sports leagues have histories and contexts, and any change from the status quo will make some stakeholders better off and others worse off. Consider how parties strategically interact to make it easier or more difficult to implement changes in the status quo.

First Exercise: Constructing Labor Market Rules

Consider the Rozelle Rule that was successfully challenged in the *Mackey* litigation. Prior to 1947, the NFL had a reserve clause similar to the baseball rule that was unsuccessfully challenged in *Flood v. Kuhn*. In that year, however, owners adopted an "option system" that allowed a club to renew a player's contract for an additional year, but only one year, at 90% of his prior year's salary. However, it appeared that no player had taken advantage of this option to secure a large raise from a rival club. As described in Lionel S. Sobel, PROFESSIONAL SPORTS AND THE LAW 109 (New York: Law Arts Publishers 1977), playing out an option "is a risky thing for a professional athlete to do." Such a strategy would mean that

> a player must accept at least a 10% cut in pay, which in reality could amount to a much greater cut from what the player could have earned had he been willing to sign a new contract. . . . The player must face the risk he might be injured while playing out the option. And he must do all this without knowing in advance what salary any other team might be willing to pay him . . .

Prior to the 1963 season, however, star receiver R. C. Owens (purportedly the originator of the "alley oop catch") played out his option with the San Francisco 49ers and signed with the Baltimore Colts. Thereafter, Commissioner Pete Rozelle announced a new rule that he would award players or draft picks of the acquiring club to the former club "as the Commissioner in his sole discretion deems fair and equitable."

1. Why did the owners substitute an option system for a reserve clause in 1947? (Hint: review the defenses to an injunction if a player wanted to switch to a rival league raised in Chapter 5 and note that the NFL was in a "war" with the All-American Football Conference at that time.)

2. Why was the 1963 change imposed by Commissioner Rozelle rather than adopted by league owners?

3. Would Baltimore Colts' owner Carroll Rosenbloom have supported the Rozelle Rule?

4. After the 1963 season, the Los Angeles Rams had a 3-year record of 10–31. Would they have been in favor of the Rozelle Rule's continuance? If not, do you think it likely they could have prevailed on fellow owners to overturn the rule?

5. Why wasn't anyone worried that the NFL would be hurt as players who could not receive rival bids from other NFL clubs would seek employment elsewhere? (Consider the *Fraser v. MLS* case earlier in the chapter.)

Second Exercise: Negotiating Rules with the Union

Consider the situation facing the NBA in the early 1980s. After a costly "war" with the rival American Basketball Association in the 1970s, a planned merger was preliminarily enjoined in a suit brought by NBA players. (The litigation history is recounted in *Robertson v. NBA*, 72 F.R.D. 64 (S.D.N.Y. 1976).) Following extensive pre-trial proceedings and voluminous discovery, the players and the NBA reached a settlement in 1976 that included extensive free agency subject to a "right of first refusal" by the player's current employer.

Despite the end to inter-league rivalry, the league was struggling in part due to continued imprudent spending by some clubs, poor consumer perception because of well-publicized instances of drug abuse, and other factors. Famously, weeknight NBA finals games were broadcast after the late-night news on tape delay.

The strategy successfully implemented by David Stern as Executive Vice President and later Commissioner of the NBA, and upheld against antitrust challenge in *Wood, supra*, resulted in continued free agency for veteran players but subject to a salary cap on overall team payroll, pegged at a fixed percentage of basketball revenue earned by the clubs. The cap contained several exceptions, the most important of which (the "Larry Bird exception") allowed teams to re-sign their own players regardless of the cap.

1. Prior to the attempted merger with the ABA, the NBA owners were able to resist their players' demands for free agency; once they sought to merge, they conceded partial free agency to get a settlement of the players' litigation; by 1982, the owners were proposing a salary cap. Why couldn't the NBA owners just adhere to strict limits on competition for players that prevailed in the NFL until 1994?

2. Why would the owners of the Boston Celtics, New York Knicks, and Los Angeles Lakers agree to a salary cap (albeit a "soft" one with the Larry Bird exception)?

3. In the two prior seasons before the 1982 agreement, the Cleveland Cavaliers' record was 43–121. Why would the Cavaliers have wanted a salary cap to limit their ability to spend on new players?

4. Why would a majority of owners agree to give the Celtics such an advantage in re-signing Larry Bird?

5. Why were the owners able to get player agreement for a salary cap in 1982, when the players insisted on uncapped free agency subject only to a right of first refusal in 1976?

6. Why would the NBPA agree to a scheme where top rookies were paid minimal terms if drafted by teams with no cap room?

7. Should MLB players adopt this approach to improve overall spending by baseball clubs?

Third Exercise: Individual "Rights" Versus General Welfare

The NBA's "one and done" rule—barring clubs from signing players until they are both 19 years of age and one year removed from high school—remains controversial in many quarters (and, by the time you study this, may soon be amended by agreement of the owners and the players' association). Legally, the Second Circuit's decision in *Clarett* would seem to shield the rule from antitrust challenge. Consider a proposed change to raise the minimum age for participating in the NBA to 20, and assume that the effect will be that some players will remain in college for two years, while other players will opt to move from high school to the NBA's wholly-owned developmental league, denominated the G League after its name sponsor Gatorade.

1. Given that all rookies have to go into the draft, and are subject to the salary cap, why would NBA clubs want to limit their ability to sign the next Kevin Garnett/Lebron James?

2. Some NBA clubs currently have G League affiliate teams, while others do not; should this affect an owner's position on changing the rule?

3. Would the National Basketball Players Association support raising the age limit? If not, would they demand huge or modest concessions from the owners in order to amend the collective bargaining agreement in this manner?

4. How would the small number of teenagers who might be immediately drafted into the NBA absent the rule voice their objections to a higher age limit?

5. Which other stakeholders might oppose increasing the minimum age?

6. What would the following stakeholders think about the proposal:

   a. college basketball coaches and athletic directors?

   b. entrepreneurs who own GLeague franchises with affiliate relationships with a "parent" NBA club?

   c. CBS Sports (which currently holds the broadcast rights to G League games)?

7. What actions can third-party stakeholders take in order to influence the NBA-NBPA negotiations?

Fourth Exercise: Maneuvering to Advantage in the Future

Following the 2010–11 NBA season, the league's collective bargaining agreement with its players expired. When negotiations did not result in an agreement, the league locked out the players through December; at that time the parties agreed to a new bargain. The key features include maintenance of the salary cap regime from prior agreements, albeit with a lower percentage of revenues going to players. Meanwhile, the union's executive director from the 2011 negotiations, Billy Hunter, was replaced by Michele Roberts, the first female sports union leader.

1. Why did the NBA owners lock out the players, instead of negotiating to impasse and then imposing their own rules?

2. Assuming that the owners are not inclined either to increase revenues or to loosen the salary cap restrictions on player compensation, should the NBPA decertify as a union upon expiration of the agreement (in contrast to a disclaimer used by the NFLPA, a decertification prevents workers from forming a new union for 12 months)?

   a. Would such a decertification clearly constitute an end to the owners' immunity from antitrust suit under the labor exemption?

   b. Would such a decertification lead a court to conclude that an ensuing lockout was not a "labor dispute" for purposes of the Norris-LaGuardia Act?

   c. Would a lockout constitute a violation of § 1 of the Sherman Act?

   d. Would the current salary cap restrictions constitute a violation of § 1?

3. If the NBPA decertified, should the NBA:

   a. Continue operations and litigate any antitrust challenges?

   b. File a claim with the National Labor Relations Board alleging that the decertification is a form of bad faith bargaining?

   c. Implement a lock out until the players either agree to a new collective bargaining agreement or settle any class action litigation?

   d. Seek to implement a new set of rules that strengthen their likelihood of success in antitrust litigation?

CHAPTER 8

BUSINESS STRATEGY AND ANTITRUST SCRUTINY OF INTERNAL LEAGUE REGULATION OF INTER-CLUB COMPETITION

■ ■ ■

This chapter concludes our study of antitrust and business strategy with a detailed examination of how the law treats the relationship between clubs and their league. The significance of this inquiry can be seen in the economic trends in sports over the last few decades. Despite spiraling player costs, baseball and football franchises that sold for approximately $7 million in 1967 are now selling for billions of dollars. The same has been true for hockey and basketball. The NHL charged $2 million for an expansion franchise in 1967 and $650 million to establish the Seattle Kraken in 2021. Joe Tsai paid $3.3 billion for the NBA's Brooklyn Nets in 2019.

Franchise values continue to increase because league revenues from all sources (*i.e.*, ticket sales, luxury boxes and club seats, ancillary stadium revenues, television, merchandise licensing, and internet rights) continue to rise. This upward trend was displayed even more dramatically in the use of taxpayer dollars to build new stadiums and arenas. The concept of a "new" stadium is short-lived, as many stadiums built in the 1960s and 1970s were replaced in the 1990s, when taxpayers contributed more than $10 billion of the $15 billion total spent to replace many of those "ancient" facilities with far more luxurious sites in which to watch the games.

The cycle repeated in this century, with Atlanta as the "poster child" for this phenomenon: the NFL Falcons moved to Mercedes-Benz Stadium in 2017 after 25 years in the Georgia Dome and the MLB Braves moved to Truist Park after only 20 years in Turner Field. In 2022, New York state officials agreed to provide $600 million for a new stadium for the Buffalo Bills. State and local governments have also been generous with taxpayer money to fund soccer-only stadiums for MLS teams: since 2003, 19 soccer-specific facilities have been constructed. The smaller size of soccer stadiums, however, provides a business model for some owners to incorporate real estate development opportunities in their facilities plans and thereby reduce public subsidy.

Recognizing these financial trends is important for two reasons. First, although a more favorable legal environment has enabled players to secure a larger share of the game's revenues—player salaries have gone up somewhat more than franchise prices—the lion's share of salary increases is attributable to increases in the game's revenues that also enlarge ownership profits (or for some teams reduce ownership losses). Sports over the past few decades serve as an apt illustration of what the eminent British economist Alfred Marshall called the first "law" of labor economics: the employer's demand for labor is derived from the consumer's demand for the goods and services produced by that labor.

The second reason to be conscious of the explosion in team values is the law's importance to this economic trend. This chapter explores the legal structure of sports ownership within a league, and how this structure influences franchise values and the amount of revenue teams and leagues extract from fans who attend the games, broadcasters and advertisers that televise the games, merchandisers that draw upon the team's names and logos that are seen in the games, and communities that subsidize the facilities in which the games are played. The focus of this chapter is both on antitrust doctrine (for lawyers primarily concerned about doctrine) and on the key topics that consume the attention of sports executives, topics on which legal restraints largely come from antitrust.

A. FRANCHISE OWNERSHIP RULES

It takes more than financial wherewithal to purchase an interest in a major league sports team. All leagues have rules about who may own their clubs, and these rules may differ depending on whether the transaction is for a minority or controlling interest. The rules invite litigation when the result is the rejection of a prospective owner. The parties inevitably frame the issue differently. To the league, the question is whether the rejected applicant should be their partner in their joint effort to compete with other forms of entertainment. Others may perceive the rejection as an agreement by owners to exclude a new rival who may be more effective in competing with them.

An early illustration was litigation arising out of the NBA's rejection of the application by Irving Levin and Harold Lipton to purchase the Boston Celtics from Ballantine Brewery in 1972. Levin alleged that they were rejected because of their personal and business associations with Sam Schulman, the maverick owner of the Seattle SuperSonics, who was allegedly a "troublemaker." The NBA denied this, claiming that its conflict-of-interest rules precluded approval: Levin and Schulman were both employees of the same corporation and Levin owned a minority interest in the Sonics. Federal district judge Richard Owen did not venture into the merits of the contrary views asserted by the parties about the nature and legitimacy of the grounds for rejection. Instead, he summarily dismissed the claim on the ground that this case presented no antitrust concerns:

> While it is true that the antitrust laws apply to a professional athletic league, and that joint action by members of a league can have antitrust implications, this is not such a case. Here the plaintiffs wanted to join with those unwilling to accept them, not to compete with them, but to be partners in the operation of a sports league for plaintiffs' profit. Further, no matter which reason one credits for the rejection, it was not an anti-competitive reason. Finally, regardless of the financial impact of this rejection upon the plaintiffs, if any, the exclusion of the plaintiffs from membership in the league did not have an anticompetitive effect nor an effect upon the public interest. The Celtics continue as an operating club, and indeed are this year's champion.

> The law is well established that it is competition, and not individual competitors, that is protected by the antitrust laws. . . .

> It is also clear that where the action the plaintiffs attack, the rejection from co-partnership, has neither anticompetitive intent nor effect, that conduct is not violative of the antitrust laws. . . .

Levin v. NBA, 385 F. Supp. 149, 152 (S.D.N.Y. 1974).

League advocates can read *Levin* broadly to support the claim that league membership is akin to joining a law or accounting firm partnership, an issue about which competition law has little to say. Challengers can read *Levin* more narrowly, emphasizing that the court found no claim that the NBA's rejection of Levin as an owner was "an anti-competitive reason."

In some cases, the parties agree on the "reason" but disagree as to whether it is anticompetitive. All of the major U.S. sports leagues have rules against the same owner controlling multiple teams. European soccer varies this approach because of its somewhat unusual structure, where clubs primarily compete in domestic leagues, but some also compete in competitions sponsored by UEFA, the European governing body. UEFA adopted a rule in 1998 that bars a single person or entity from owning a majority interest in two different teams that participate in the same European-wide competition, on the theory that such common ownership would compromise the appearance of honest competition. The English National Investment Company (ENIC) owned teams in both Greece and The Czech Republic who qualified for the UEFA Cup competition in 1998. Because of the newly adopted rule, the Greek team was disqualified from participating. An interim order (*i.e.*, a preliminary injunction) of the Court of Arbitration for Sport (CAS) allowed both teams to participate in the UEFA Cup. Meanwhile, the case proceeded to a trial in March 1999. In July 1999, the CAS rendered an opinion upholding the UEFA ban on multiple ownership, deciding that the rule did not violate European or

Swiss competition law. Subsequently, in 2003, the European Commission (the executive body of the European Union) issued an opinion that the UEFA rule was consistent with Art. 81 of the Treaty of Rome (the analogue to Sherman Act § 1). Compare MLS, which for a time operated with several investors controlling multiple teams, a process that ended in 2015 when AEG divested the Houston Dynamo, retaining LA Galaxy.

North American sports leagues have a variety of ownership rules, largely dealing with a proposed owner's finances and character. The major source of antitrust litigation about specific sports ownership rules in the United States concerns a now-abandoned NFL policy restricting owners' ability to control clubs in *other* leagues, and a separate policy against any NFL franchise being owned by publicly-traded corporations. Cross-ownership rules were not enforced in other major leagues: for many years Atlanta's MLB, NBA, and NHL teams had the same ownership, and today the same entities control the Chicago White Sox and Bulls and the New York Knicks and Rangers. A grandfathered exception to the NFL's still-continuing policy against public ownership is the Green Bay Packers, which has always been a not-for-profit corporation owned by citizens of Green Bay, Wisconsin, under a special statute passed by the Wisconsin legislature. Recently, the owners sustained this requirement but voted to require new owners to personally acquire only 30 percent of the team when the team is purchased. Thereafter, pieces of the team can be distributed to family members with, eventually, the controlling owner personally owning as little as one percent of the team. The NFL enforces these rules by requiring three-quarters of the clubs to approve any change in ownership of a team.

The legal groundwork for antitrust analysis of ownership rules was set forth in *North American Soccer League v. NFL,* 670 F.2d 1249 (2d Cir. 1982). Although the challenged policy is no longer in effect, the court's analysis retains its precedential vitality.

The court acknowledged the NFL's legitimate interest in maintaining the loyalty of club owners to their common business venture, but found that the facts demonstrated that there was "no market necessity or threat of disloyalty by cross-owners which would justify the ban." The court found that there were less restrictive ways to achieve the NFL's interests.

SULLIVAN V. NFL
34 F.3d 1091 (1st Cir. 1994)

TORRUELLA, CIRCUIT JUDGE.

[In 1987, New England Patriots owner Billy Sullivan sought to alleviate his financial distress by putting up 49% of the team in a public stock offering. The Sullivan family's financial troubles were attributable in large part to Michael Jackson's "Victory Tour" which inflicted huge losses on Billy's son, Charles "Chuck" Sullivan, the Tour's underwriter and owner of Foxboro Stadium in which the Patriots played. The idea for a Patriots' minority-share stock offering came from the remarkable success enjoyed by the Boston Celtics when that team fashioned a similar limited partnership venture in 1986. However, allegedly because the NFL rule precluded public ownership, Sullivan decided in October 1988 to sell the Patriots (for $84 million) to a limited partnership largely owned by Victor Kiam. Then, when Kiam sold the Patriots to James Orthwein in 1992 for approximately $110 million, Sullivan sued the NFL for damages under the Sherman Act, claiming that absent the NFL's policy against public ownership he would have been able to retain the controlling interest in a rapidly-appreciating football asset, instead of having to sell it at a depressed price to private buyers. After a trial in December 1993, the jury awarded Sullivan $38 million in damages, which the trial judge remitted to $17 million, before trebling. The NFL appealed.]

III. Issues Allegedly Requiring Judgment for the NFL

A. Lack of Antitrust Injury

To establish an antitrust violation under § 1 of the Sherman Act, Sullivan must prove that the NFL's public ownership policy is "in restraint of trade." Under antitrust law's "rule of reason," the NFL's policy is in restraint of trade if the anticompetitive effects of the policy outweigh the policy's legitimate business justifications. Anticompetitive effects, more commonly referred to as "injury to competition" or "harm to the competitive process," are usually measured by a reduction in output and an increase in prices in the relevant market. Injury to competition has also been described more generally in terms of decreased efficiency in the marketplace which negatively impacts consumers. Thus, an action harms the competitive process "when it obstructs the achievement of competition's basic goals—lower prices, better products, and more efficient production methods." *Town of Concord v. Boston Edison Co.*, 915 F.2d 17, 22 (1st Cir. 1990).

The jury determined in this case, via a special verdict form, that the relevant market is the "nationwide market for the sale and purchase of ownership interests in the National Football League member clubs, in general, and in the New England Patriots, in particular." The jury went on to find that the NFL's policy had an "actual harmful effect" on competition in this market.

The NFL argues on appeal that Sullivan has not established the existence of any injury to competition, and thus has not established a restraint of trade that can be attributed to the NFL's ownership policy. The league's attack is two-fold, asserting (1) that NFL clubs do not compete with each other for the sale of ownership interests in their teams so there exists no competition to be injured in the first place; and (2) Sullivan did not present sufficient evidence of injury to competition from which a reasonable jury could conclude that the NFL's policy restrains trade.

Although we agree with the NFL that conceptualizing the harm to competition in this case is rather difficult, precedent and deference to the jury verdict ultimately require us to reject the NFL's challenge to the finding of injury to competition.

Critically, the NFL does not challenge on appeal the jury's initial finding of the relevant market and no corresponding challenge was raised at trial. . . . The NFL nevertheless maintains that NFL teams do not compete against each other for the sale of their ownership interests, even if we accept that a market exists for such ownership interests.

1.   No Competition Subject to Injury as Matter of Law

The NFL correctly points out that member clubs must cooperate in a variety of ways, and may do so lawfully, in order to make the football league a success. On the other hand, it is well established that NFL clubs also compete with each other, both on and off the field, for things like fan support, players, coaches, ticket sales, local broadcast revenues, and the sale of team paraphernalia. The question of whether competition exists between NFL teams for sale of their ownership interests, such that the NFL's ownership policy injures this competition, is ultimately a question of fact. The NFL would have us find, however, that, as a matter of law, NFL teams do not compete against each other for the sale of their ownership interests. We decline to make such a finding.

The NFL relies on a series of cases which allegedly stand for the "well established" rule that a professional sports league's restrictions on who may join the league or acquire an interest in a member club do not give rise to a claim under the antitrust laws. *Seattle Totems Hockey Club, Inc. v. National Hockey League,* 783 F.2d 1347 (9th Cir. 1986); *Fishman v. Estate of Wirtz,* 807 F.2d 520 (7th Cir. 1986); *Mid-South Grizzlies v. National Football League,* 720 F.2d 772, at 772 (3d Cir. 1983); *Levin v. National Basketball Ass'n,* 385 F. Supp. 149 (S.D.N.Y. 1974). These cases, all involving a professional sport's league's refusal to approve individual transfers of team ownership or the creation of new teams, do not stand for the broad proposition that no NFL ownership policy can injure competition. *See, e.g., North American Soccer League v. National Football League,* 670 F.2d 1249, 1259–61 (2d Cir. 1982) (finding that the NFL's policy against cross-ownership of NFL teams and franchises in competing sports leagues, which also effectively barred certain owners who owned other sports franchises from purchasing NFL teams, injured competition between the NFL and competing sports leagues and thus violated § 1 of the Sherman Act).

None of the cases cited by the NFL considered the particular relevant market that was found by the jury in this case or a league policy against public ownership. *Seattle Totems* and *Mid-South Grizzlies* considered potential inter-league competition when a sports league rejected plaintiffs' applications for new league franchises. Those decisions found no injury to competition because the plaintiffs were not competing with the defendant sports leagues, but rather were seeking to join those leagues. *Mid-South Grizzlies* left open the possibility that potential intra-league competition between NFL football clubs could be harmed by the NFL's action, but found that the plaintiff in that case had not presented sufficient evidence of harm to such competition.

The *Fishman* and *Levin* cases concerned the National Basketball Association's ("NBA") rejection of plaintiffs' attempts to buy an existing team. Those cases also based their finding that there was no injury to competition on the fact that the plaintiffs were seeking to join with, rather than compete against, the NBA. Neither case considered whether competition between teams for investment capital was injured.

The important distinction to make between the cases cited by the NFL and the present case is that here Sullivan alleges that the NFL's policy against public ownership generally restricts competition between clubs for the sale of their ownership interests, whereas in the aforementioned cases, a league's refusal to approve a given sale transaction or a new team merely prevented particular outsiders from joining the league, but did not limit competition between the teams themselves. To put it another way, the NFL's public ownership policy allegedly does not merely prevent the replacement of one club owner with another—an action having little evident effect on competition—it compromises the entire process by which competition for club ownership occurs.

* * *

2. *Insufficient Evidence of Harm to Competition*

The NFL contends that Sullivan did not present sufficient evidence concerning: (1) the existence of competition between NFL clubs for the sale of ownership interests, or (2) a decrease in output, an increase in prices, a detrimental effect on efficiency or other incidents of harm to competition in the relevant market, from which a reasonable jury could conclude that the NFL's policy injured competition. Although we agree that the evidence of all these factors is rather thin, we disagree that the evidence is too thin to support a jury verdict in Sullivan's favor.

With respect to evidence of the existence of competition for the sale of ownership interests, one of Sullivan's experts, Professor Roger Noll, testified that "one of the ways in which the NFL exercises monopoly power in the market for the franchises and ownership is by excluding certain people from owning all or part—any type part of an NFL franchise." Dr. Noll explained that this "enables a group of owners, in this case, you only need eight owners, to exclude from the League and from competing with them, people who might be more effective competitors than they are." The record also contains statements from several NFL owners which could reasonably be interpreted as expressions of concern about their ability to compete with other teams in the market for investment capital in general, and for the sale of ownership interests in particular. For example, Arthur Rooney II of the Pittsburgh Steelers stated in a letter that he did not "believe that the individually or family owned teams will be able to compete with the consolidated groups." Ralph Wilson of the Buffalo Bills stated that big corporations should not own teams because it gives them an "unfair competitive advantage" over other teams since corporations will funnel money into the team and make it "more competitive" than the other franchises. Former NFL Commissioner Pete Rozelle admitted that similar sentiments had been expressed by NFL members.

Although it is not precisely clear that the "competition" about which Noll, Rooney, and Wilson were discussing is the same competition at issue here—that is competition for the sale of ownership interests—a jury could reasonably interpret these statements as expressing a belief that the competition exists between teams for the sale of ownership interests. The statements of the two NFL owners imply that greater access to capital for all teams will put increased pressure on some teams to compete with others for that capital, and all the statements reveal that the ownership rules, particularly the rule against public ownership, are the main obstacle preventing such access. The fact that ownership by "consolidated groups" is not necessarily the same as public ownership does not affect the conclusion that teams face competitive pressure in selling their ownership interests generally to whoever might buy them. We also note that evidence of actual, present competition is not necessary as long as the evidence shows that the potential for competition exists. It would be difficult indeed to provide direct evidence of competition when the NFL effectively prohibits it.

* * *

The NFL is correct that, in one sense, the overall pool of potential output is fixed because there are only 28 NFL teams and, although their value may fluctuate, the quantity of their ownership interests cannot. However, the NFL's public ownership policy completely wipes out a certain type of ownership interest—public ownership of stock. By restricting output in one form of ownership, the NFL is thereby reducing the output of ownership interests overall. In other words, the NFL is literally restricting the output of a product—a share in an NFL team.

There was considerable testimony concerning the price effects of the NFL policy. Both of Sullivan's experts testified that the policy depressed the price of ownership interests in NFL teams because NFL franchises would normally command a premium on the public market relative to their value in the private market, which is all that the league currently permits. Professor Noll testified that fan loyalty would push up the price of ownership interests if sales to the public were allowed. Even former Commissioner Pete Rozelle acknowledged that "it was pointed out, with justification, it has been over the years, that [the ownership policy] does restrict your market and, very likely, the price you could get for one of our franchises if you wanted to sell it, because you are eliminating a very broad market. . . . And they have said that there is a depression on the price they could get for their franchise."

The NFL points out that the alleged effect of its ownership policy is to reduce prices of NFL team ownership interests, rather than to raise prices which is normally the measure of an injury to competition. *E.g., Town of Concord*, 915 F.2d at 22. We acknowledge that it is not clear whether, absent some sort of dumping or predatory pricing, *see, e.g., Monahan's Marine, Inc. v. Boston Whaler, Inc.*, 866 F.2d 525, 527 (1st Cir. 1989), a decrease in prices can indicate injury to competition in a relevant market. The Supreme Court has emphasized, however, that overall consumer preferences in setting output and prices is more important than higher prices and lower output, per se, in determining whether there has been an injury to competition. *NCAA v. Board of Regents,* 468 U.S. 85, 107 (1984). In this case, regardless of the exact price effects of the NFL's policy, the overall market effects of the policy are plainly unresponsive to consumer demand for ownership interests in NFL teams. Dr. Noll testified that fans are interested in buying shares in NFL teams and that the NFL's policy deprives fans of this product. Moreover, evidence was presented concerning the public offering of the Boston Celtics professional basketball team which demonstrated, according to some of the testimony, fan interest in buying ownership of professional sports teams. Thus, a jury could conclude that the NFL's policy injured competition by making the relevant market "unresponsive to consumer preference."[3]

As for overall efficiency of production in the relevant market[4] Sullivan's experts testified that the NFL's policy hindered efficiency gains, and that allowing public ownership would make for better football teams. Professor Noll stated that the NFL's public ownership policy prevented individuals who might be "more efficient and much better at running a professional football team" from owning teams. Dr. Noll also stated that

---

[3]   The NFL maintains that price and output are not affected because its ownership policy does not limit the number of games or teams, does not raise ticket prices or the prices of game telecasts and does not affect the normal consumer of the NFL's product in any other way. Such facts might be relevant to an inquiry of whether the NFL's policy harms overall efficiency, see infra note [4], but it is not relevant to whether the policy affects output and prices in the relevant market for ownership interests. Just because consumers of "NFL football" are not affected by output controls and price increases does not mean that consumers of a product in the relevant market are not so affected. In this case, two types of consumers are denied products by the NFL policy: consumers who want to buy stock of the Patriots or other teams, and consumers like Sullivan who want to "purchase" investment capital in the market for public financing.

[4]   Although the product at issue in the relevant market is "ownership interests," efficiency in production of that product can be measured by the value of the ownership interest. That is, an improved product produced more efficiently will be reflected in the value of the output in question (regardless of the price). In this case, the value of the product depends on the success of the Patriots' football team, the overall efficiency of its operations, and the success of the NFL in general.

publicly owned NFL teams would be better managed, and produce higher quality entertainment for the fans. Noll testified that the ownership rule excluded certain types of management structures which would likely be more efficient in running the teams, resulting in higher franchise values. One NFL owner, Lamar Hunt, acknowledged that increased access to capital can improve a team's operations and performance. A memorandum prepared by an NFL staff member stated that changes to the NFL's public ownership policy could contribute to each NFL team's own financial strength and viability, which in turn would benefit the entire NFL because the league has a strong interest in having strong, viable teams.

The NFL presented a large amount of evidence to the contrary and now claims on appeal that Sullivan's position was based on nothing more than sheer speculation. We have reviewed the record, however, and we cannot say that the evidence was so overwhelming that no reasonable jury could find against the NFL and in favor of Sullivan. We therefore refuse to enter judgment in favor of the NFL as a matter of law.

B.   Ancillary Benefits

The NFL next argues that even if its public ownership policy injures competition in a relevant market, it should be upheld as ancillary to the legitimate joint activity that is "NFL football" and thus not violative of the Sherman Act. We take no issue with the proposition that certain joint ventures enable separate business entities to combine their skills and resources in pursuit of a common goal that cannot be effectively pursued by the venturers acting alone. *See, e.g., Broadcast Music, Inc. v. Columbia Broadcasting System, Inc.,* 441 U.S. 1 (1979). We also do not dispute that a "restraint" that is ancillary to the functioning of such a joint activity—*i.e.* one that is required to make the joint activity more efficient—does not necessarily violate the antitrust laws. *Broadcast Music,* 441 U.S. at 23–25; *Rothery Storage & Van Co. v. Atlas Van Lines, Inc.,* 253 U.S. App. D.C. 142, 792 F.2d 210, at 223–24 (D.C. Cir. 1986); *see also Northwest Wholesale Stationers, Inc. v. Pacific Stationery & Printing Co.,* 472 U.S. 284, 295–96 (1985). We further accept, for purposes of this appeal, that rules controlling who may join a joint venture can be ancillary to a legitimate joint activity and that the NFL's own policy against public ownership constitutes one example of such an ancillary rule. Finally, we accept the NFL's claim that its public ownership policy contributes to the ability of the NFL to function as an effective sports league, and that the NFL's functioning would be impaired if publicly owned teams were permitted, because the short-term dividend interests of a club's shareholder would often conflict with the long-term interests of the league as a whole. That is, the policy avoids a detrimental conflict of interests between team shareholders and the league.

We disagree, however, that these factors are sufficient to establish as a matter of law that the NFL's ownership policy does not unreasonably restrain trade in violation of § 1 of the Sherman Act. The holdings in *Broadcast Music, Rothery Storage*, and *Northwest Stationers*, do not throw the "rule of reason" out the window merely because one establishes that a given practice among joint venture participants is ancillary to legitimate and efficient activity—the injury to competition must still be weighed against the purported benefits under the rule of reason. . . .

One basic tenet of the rule of reason is that a given restriction is not reasonable, that is, its benefits cannot outweigh its harm to competition, if a reasonable, less restrictive alternative to the policy exists that would provide the same benefits as the current restraint. The record contains evidence of a clearly less restrictive alternative to the NFL's ownership policy that would yield the same benefits as the current policy. Sullivan points to one proposal to amend the current ownership policy by allowing for the sale of minority, nonvoting shares of team stock to the public with restrictions on the size of the holdings by any one individual. Dividend payments, if any, would be within the firm control of the NFL majority owner. Under such a policy, it would be reasonable for a jury to conclude that private control of member clubs is maintained, conflicts of interest are avoided, and all the other "benefits" of the NFL's joint venture arrangement are preserved while at the same time teams would have access to the market for public investment capital through the sale of ownership interests.

C. Causation of Injury in Fact

[The court here addressed and rejected the NFL's claim that Sullivan's case should have been dismissed because there was no evidence to support a finding that the NFL's policy against public ownership in fact had caused economic injury to Sullivan. The court noted that "[a]lthough the evidence of causation is not overwhelming, it is nevertheless sufficient to support the verdict." With regard to the NFL's argument that Sullivan never asked for a vote, and thus the League never actually voted on whether he could sell 49% of the team through a public offering, the court concluded that the jury had sufficient evidence to find that the parties believed that a formal vote would have been futile, and thus the NFL owners' prior practice had effectively denied Sullivan permission to issue public stock in the Patriots. With respect to the NFL's second argument, that its evidence showed that a public offering of minority shares would not have raised the $70 million necessary to keep Sullivan from having to sell the team, the court stated: "[a]lthough we share the NFL's skepticism that Sullivan would have succeeded in his public offering if the NFL had allowed him to try it, we cannot say that, as a matter of law, the evidence was so overwhelming that no reasonable jury could find that the NFL's policy harmed Sullivan by preventing him from doing something he would otherwise have been able to do."]

The NFL's arguments concerning the application of § 1 of the Sherman Act to the facts of this case raise a substantial challenge to the jury verdict and are certainly weighty enough to give us pause. Upon careful consideration of the issues, however, we find Sullivan's theory of the case to be a plausible one and ultimately find the evidence sufficient to support it. For the foregoing reasons, therefore, we see no justification, as a matter of law, for ringing the death knell on this litigation.

IV. Trial Errors

Having reviewed those issues which would have warranted a judgment in favor of the NFL, had we decided any of those issues in the NFL's favor, we now turn to the NFL's claim that it is entitled to a new trial because of allegedly erroneous jury instructions and other trial errors.

* * *

D. Balancing Procompetitive and Anticompetitive Effects in the Relevant Market

As we noted above, the rule of reason analysis requires a weighing of the injury and the benefits to competition attributable to a practice that allegedly violates the antitrust laws. The district court instructed the jury on its verdict form to balance the injury to competition in the relevant market with the benefits to competition in that same relevant market. The NFL protested, claiming that all procompetitive effects of its policy, even those in a market different from that in which the alleged restraint operated, should be considered. The NFL's case was premised on the claim that its policy against public ownership was an important part of the effective functioning of the league as a joint venture. Although it was not readily apparent that this beneficial effect applied to the market for ownership interests in NFL teams, the relevant market found by the jury, the NFL argued that its justification should necessarily be weighed by the jury under the rule of reason analysis. Sullivan responded, and the district court agreed, that a jury cannot be asked to compare what are essentially apples and oranges, and that it is impossible to conduct a balancing of alleged anticompetitive and procompetitive effects of a challenged practice in every definable market.

The issue of defining the proper scope of a rule of reason analysis is a deceptive body of water, containing unforeseen currents and turbulence lying just below the surface of an otherwise calm and peaceful ocean. The waters are muddied by the Supreme Court's decision in *NCAA*—one of the more extensive examples of the Court performing a rule of reason analysis—where the Court considered the value of certain procompetitive effects that existed outside of the relevant market in which the restraint operated. NCAA, 468 U.S. at 115–20 (considering the NCAA's interest in protecting live attendance at untelevised games and the NCAA's "legitimate and important" interest in maintaining competitive balance between amateur athletic teams as a justification for a restraint that operated in a completely different market, the market for the telecasting of collegiate football games). Other courts have demonstrated similar confusion. *See, e.g., L.A. Coliseum*, 726 F.2d at 1381, 1392, 1397, 1399 (stating that the "relevant market provides the basis on which to balance competitive harms and benefits of the restraint at issue" but then considering a wide variety of alleged benefits, and then directing the finder of fact to "balance the gain to interbrand competition against the loss of intrabrand competition", where the two types of competition operated in different markets).

To our knowledge, no authority has squarely addressed this issue. On the one hand, several courts have expressed concern over the use of wide ranging interests to justify an otherwise anticompetitive practice, and others have found particular justifications to be incomparable and not in correlation with the alleged restraint of trade. *Smith v. Pro Football, Inc.*, 593 F.2d 1173, 1186 (D.C. Cir. 1978); *Brown v. Pro Football, Inc.*, 812 F. Supp. 237, 238 (D.D.C. 1992); *Chicago Pro. Sports Ltd. Partnership v. National Basketball Ass'n*, 754 F. Supp. 1336, 1358 (N.D. Ill. 1991). We agree that the ultimate question under the rule of reason is whether a challenged practice promotes or suppresses competition. Thus, it seems improper to validate a practice that is decidedly in restraint of trade simply because the practice produces some unrelated benefits to competition in another market.

On the other hand, several courts, including this Circuit, have found it appropriate in some cases to balance the anticompetitive effects on competition in one market with certain procompetitive benefits in other markets. *See, e.g., NCAA*, 468 U.S. at 115–20; *Grappone, Inc. v. Subaru of New England, Inc.*, 858 F.2d 792, 799 (1st Cir. 1988); *M & H Tire Co. v. Hoosier Racing Tire Corp.*, 733 F.2d 973, 986 (1st Cir. 1984); *L.A. Coliseum*, 726 F.2d at 1381, 1392, 1397, 1399. Moreover, the district court's argument that it would be impossible to compare the procompetitive effects of the NFL's policy in the interbrand market of competition between the NFL and other forms of entertainment, with the anticompetitive effects of the intrabrand market of competition between NFL teams for the sale of their ownership interests, is arguably refuted by the Supreme Court's holding in *Continental T.V., Inc. v. GTE Sylvania Inc.*, 433 U.S. 36 (1977). *Continental T.V.* explicitly recognized that positive effects on interbrand competition can justify anticompetitive effects on intrabrand competition. Although *Continental T.V.* can reasonably be interpreted as referring only to interbrand and intrabrand components of the same relevant market, there is also some indication that interbrand and intrabrand competition necessarily refer to distinct, yet related, markets. *Continental T.V.*, 433 U.S. at 52 n.19 ("The degree of intrabrand competition is wholly independent of the level of interbrand competition."). Arguably, the market put forward by the NFL—that is the market for NFL football in competition with other forms of entertainment—is closely related to the relevant market found by the jury such that the procompetitive benefits in one can be compared to the anticompetitive harms in the other. Clearly this question can only be answered upon a much more in-depth inquiry that we need not, nor find it appropriate to, embark upon at this time.

Finally, we note that although balancing harms and benefits in different markets may be unwieldy and confusing, such is the case with a number of balancing tests that a court or jury is expected to apply all the time.

* * *

Although the issue of the proper scope of the rule of reason analysis is more appropriately resolved in a case where it is dispositive and more fully briefed, we can draw at least one general conclusion from the case law at this point: courts should generally give a measure of latitude to antitrust defendants in their efforts to explain the procompetitive justifications for their policies and practices; however, courts should also maintain some vigilance by excluding justifications that are so unrelated to the challenged practice that they amount to a collateral attempt to salvage a practice that is decidedly in restraint of trade.

In any event, we need not enter these dangerous waters to resolve the instant dispute. The NFL wanted the jury to consider its proffered justifications for the public ownership policy—namely that the policy enhanced the NFL's ability to effectively produce and present a popular entertainment product unimpaired by the conflicting interests that public ownership would cause. These procompetitive justifications should have been considered by the jury, even under Sullivan's theory of the proper scope of the rule of reason analysis. [However], to the extent the NFL's policy strengthens and improves the league, resulting in increased competition in the market for ownership interests in NFL clubs through, for example, more valuable teams, the jury may consider the NFL's justifications as relevant factors in its rule of reason analysis. The danger of the proffered instructions on the verdict form is that they may have mislead the jury into thinking that it was precluded from considering the NFL's justifications for its ownership policy. Therefore, the relevant market language on the verdict form should be removed, or else the jury should be informed that evidence of benefits to competition in the relevant market can include evidence of benefits flowing indirectly from the public ownership policy that ultimately have a beneficial impact on competition in the relevant market itself.

[The court also found several other trial court errors that required reversal of the jury verdict; for example, the fact that the trial judge had erroneously refused to give the jury an instruction about the NFL's "equal involvement" defense, by which the league claimed that Sullivan was barred from challenging its public ownership ban because of his "complete, voluntary, and substantially equal participation" in the formulation and enforcement of the ban over his years as an NFL owner. For all of these reasons, the decision below was reversed and remanded.]

The second trial on Sullivan's claim was held during the fall of 1995 and ended in a hung jury. Before a third trial could begin, the parties settled with the help of court-ordered mediation: the NFL paid Sullivan $11 million to drop his suit. The league's ban on public ownership remains unchanged. Courts rejected follow-on litigation by other parties without reaching the merits. *See, e.g., Sullivan v. Tagliabue,* 25 F.3d 43 (1st Cir. 1994) (Sullivan's son Chuck did not suffer antitrust injury from the rule based on lack of funds for other family business ventures).

NOTES AND QUESTIONS

1. *In Which Market Was There an Anticompetitive Effect?* The only market in which the court found evidence of an anticompetitive effect was the "nationwide market for the sale and purchase of ownership interests in NFL member clubs." By restricting the number of potential buyers for interests in franchises, the court acknowledged that the effect of the ban was to lower the price NFL owners could get for their teams. Is there an antitrust concern (*i.e.,* an injury to consumer welfare) if joint venture partners impose a limitation on who can be partners, when the impact of the rule may be to *depress* the value of their own franchise interest? Do you agree with the court that a jury could reasonably find that NFL team owners compete against each other for the sale of their franchises? Why would owners agree to a scheme to lower the value of their franchises? Suppose Warren Buffet invested in the NFL, with a special stock that entitled him to 5% of all NFL revenues; would he think the cross-ownership or anti-corporate rules were good or bad for his investment?

2. *Consumers' Interest in Stock Purchases and the Antitrust Laws.* The court indicated that the anticompetitive effect of the ban was that it deprived consumers of the ability to buy shares of NFL teams, and that the rule caused the league to be "unresponsive to consumer demand for ownership interests in NFL teams." Are equity interests in a business a consumer good for which antitrust law requires the business to maintain a competitive market? How would restrictions on the sale of equity interests in any partnership, joint venture, close corporation, or limited liability company (which are pervasive in our economy) fare under the Rule of Reason inquiry recognized in *Sullivan*? Is there something distinctive about the Patriots as compared to other business ventures in Boston?

3. *Market Definition.* Is there anything distinctive about the market for NFL franchises, or is this simply a subset of the larger capital market in which investors buy and sell ownership rights in sports franchises generally—indeed,

in any part of the business world (*e.g.*, the sale of McDonald's franchises)? Is that question relevant to a court's judgment about the competitive impact of the NFL's policy against public ownership?

4. *Disconnect Between Plaintiff's Theory and Plaintiff's Expert.* Sullivan's expert witness, noted sports economist Roger Noll, opined that the ban on public ownership harmed football fans by depriving them of competition between clubs that might be more efficient or aggressively competitive. Sullivan, however, seemed to want to sell stock to the public so that he could continue personally to own and control the Patriots notwithstanding financial losses caused by family mismanagement. Is this disconnect something that should affect the court's judgment in an antitrust case?

5. *The Real Motivation Behind the NFL Policy.* Do you think that the reason for the NFL's ban on public ownership was, as Professor Noll testified, to prevent more efficient competitors from owning rival teams? Would a limit on minority investors serve legitimate interests, such as a desire for each club to have a single accountable public "face?" Or avoiding the nuisance of compliance with financial, disclosure and other regulations imposed on public traded companies or the often cumbersome process by which corporate entities make decisions? Do you agree with the testimony in *Sullivan* that corporate entities would be unduly focused on short-term, immediate shareholder-profit-maximizing thinking of corporate entities?

6. *Ongoing Impact of Ancillary Restraints Doctrine.* The relationship between the ancillary restraints doctrine and the Rule of Reason reflects a continuing imprecision in antitrust doctrine, dating back to *United States v. Addyson Pipe & Steel Co.*, 85 F. 271 (6th Cir. 1898), *aff'd*, 175 U.S. 211 (1899). Both *NASL* and *Sullivan* court's view a restraint ancillary to a legitimate underlying agreement as unlawful if there are less restrictive alternatives. For a contrary view as to the consistency of these holdings with *Addyston Pipe, see* Gabriel A. Feldman, *The Misuse of the Less Restrictive Alternative Inquiry in Rule of Reason Analysis*, 58 AM. U. L. REV. 561 (2009).

It is not clear, however, that an agreement that was both ancillary to the NFL's legitimate purpose and reasonably necessary to achieve that purpose would still be struck down because of some general balancing: there are no sports cases where we know this has occurred. With respect to its substantive reasonability, the court agreed that the league's policy against public ownership "contributes to the ability of the NFL to function as an effective sports league," and that "the policy avoids a detrimental conflict of interest between team shareholders and the league." What precisely is the positive contribution of this rule? Consider the experience in other leagues which all have publicly-owned teams—*e.g.*, baseball's Chicago Cubs, basketball's New York Knicks, hockey's Boston Bruins, indeed, even football's (not-for-profit corporation) Green Bay Packers. Are the league's fans, players, or other owners better or worse off because such public ownership has been permitted?

7. *Balancing Procompetitive Effects in One Market Against Harm in Another.* Another crucial issue in *Sullivan* was whether defendants can rely on

procompetitive effects felt in a different market to offset anticompetitive harms in the relevant market. Does this seem like a difficult question? (Remember the same issue arose in the *Yazoo Smith* case in Chapter 7.) If the only procompetitive effects a jury could consider are those in the same market as the anticompetitive effects, how would that affect the Rule of Reason analysis in the player restraint cases we considered in Chapter 7? In the *NASL* case we looked at earlier in this chapter? Keep in mind the question of what procompetitive effects a jury is allowed to consider as you assess the Rule of Reason issues in franchise relocation and television restriction cases later in this chapter, and the cases involving NCAA rules in Chapter 12.

B. ADMISSION AND RELOCATION OF SPORTS FRANCHISES

Before a competitive sports league can commence operations, someone must decide five critical questions:

(1)   how many clubs will participate;

(2)   which clubs will participate;

(3)   how many games will be played;

(4)   when will the games be played; and

(5)   where will the games be played (*i.e.*, where will each clubs' home field be located).

In North America, existing club owners make each of these determinations. These decisions are subject to limited external oversight, primarily in the form of the precedent established in the *Raiders* case excerpted below.

Not surprisingly, North American sports league clubs have adopted a policy that guarantees each club a permanent spot in the league (subject to extraordinary termination provisions). Because leagues tend to expand more slowly than the economy grows, civic leaders and local businesses in locations without franchises induce existing clubs to relocate. This surge in actual or potential franchise relocation forces cities and states seeking to obtain or retain major league franchises to spend huge amounts of money on sports facilities.

"Franchise free agency" (the idea that an owner can sell the location of his team's home games to the highest bidder) has proven to be very lucrative not just for the wealthy owners of the teams, but also for the players who can utilize their own free agency rights to extract more sizeable salary contracts from the teams that now can afford to pay even more to try to win a championship. It has not been so beneficial to the taxpayers who must foot the bill for the new stadium deals—and almost always through some version of a sales tax or a tax on visitors renting hotel rooms or cars, rather than from higher income or capital gains taxes collected from the well-to-do who watch the games from the most luxurious seats.

Teams controlled by owners who have made a sizable financial investment to acquire their club are not likely to relocate unless the move is in the team's financial interest, but the effect of relocation on the league as a whole can be less clear. In the NHL, Commissioner Gary Bettman and a majority of owners have pursued a long-term strategy of securing broader exposure in southern and western markets that were without teams, including franchise expansions as well as relocations of franchises from Winnipeg and Quebec City to Phoenix and Denver (although the Atlanta Flames returned to Manitoba as the Winnipeg Jets). Similar relocations in baseball are largely seen as enhancing the game's growth and popularity, for example, when the Giants and Dodgers moved from New York to California, and when the second team in Boston, Philadelphia, and St. Louis relocated to cities without MLB clubs. The major exception to that rule was football, where Commissioner Rozelle and the owners in the 1970s and 80s judged that few, if any, of these individual owner relocation decisions were in the best interests of the league as a whole (which found itself with no team from 1995–2017 in Los Angeles, the second largest market in the country). At the same time, even NFL leaders have been clear since the *Raiders* case in the early 1980s about their willingness to support relocations when, in their judgment, local taxpayers were being insufficiently supportive of stadium subsidies.

The internal rules and practices of each league require consent of a super-majority of club owners to create a new franchise. Once part of the league, the franchise enjoys an exclusive right (a shared-right in the largest markets) to operate a team in that geographic area. However, any attempt by an owner to move the club to a new location (whether or not occupied by another team) is also supposed to gain league-wide consent. There are a host of social, economic, and legal factors that have contributed to franchise free agency and taxpayer subsidies. The principal legal constraint on league policies is the antitrust doctrine discussed below.

1. LEAGUE REFUSALS TO PERMIT A CLUB'S RELOCATION

An early legal challenge to traditional league prerogatives came in *San Francisco Seals v. NHL*, 379 F. Supp. 966 (C.D. Cal. 1974). One of the six NHL expansion franchises created in 1967, the Seals enjoyed little success in the San Francisco Bay area. In 1969, the team sought to move to what then was still-vacant territory in Vancouver, British Columbia. The League's Board of Governors (comprised of one representative from each team) refused to approve the move, and the Seals sued under § 1 of the Sherman Act. The trial court summarily rejected this claim in a brief decision with the following key passage:

What then is the relevant market? I find that the relevant product market with which we are here concerned is the production of professional hockey games before live audiences, and that the relevant geographical market is the United States and Canada.

Now let us examine plaintiff's relationship with the defendants within the relevant market. Plaintiff, of course, wishes to participate in this market, but not in competition with the defendants. It expects to maintain its league membership and to accept and enjoy all of the exclusive territorial benefits which the National Hockey League affords. As a member team, it will continue cooperating with the defendants in pursuit of its main purpose, *i.e.*, producing sporting events of uniformly high quality appropriately scheduled as to both time and location so as to assure all members of the league the best financial return. In this respect, the plaintiff and defendants are acting together as one single business enterprise, competing against other similarly organized professional leagues.

Id. at 969–70.

Los Angeles Memorial Coliseum Comm'n v. NFL (Raiders I)
726 F.2d 1381 (9th Cir. 1984)

ANDERSON, CIRCUIT JUDGE.

[This case was precipitated by the 1978 decision of Carroll Rosenbloom, owner of the Los Angeles Rams, to move his team's home games from the Los Angeles Coliseum to Anaheim, attracted by a lucrative lease arrangement offered by that city. At the same time, Al Davis had reached a stalemate in efforts to negotiate the terms for renewal of the Raiders' lease with the Oakland Coliseum. Conversations thus began between Davis and L.A. Coliseum officials about a possible Raiders' move to the Coliseum. At the time, NFL Rule 4.1 had defined "home territory" as extending for a 75-mile radius from the boundaries of the team's home city as designated in the NFL Constitution. Thus, Los Angeles was still the home city of the Rams playing in Anaheim. Rule 4.3 then provided that any team proposing to move into another's home territory needed unanimous approval from all other teams. Other relocations required only a three-quarters vote. Concerned about the vulnerability of these rules to legal challenge, the NFL owners amended the rules in late 1978: amended Rule 4.3 applied the three-quarters formula to all relocations regardless of the new site, thus removing the possibility of a veto by an incumbent club. On March 1, 1980, Davis signed a "memorandum of agreement" to move the Raiders to the L.A. Coliseum. On March 10, 1980, the NFL took a vote on the proposed move (over Davis' objections). The result was 22–0 against, with five teams (including the Rams) abstaining and the Raiders not participating.

Shortly thereafter, the Raiders joined an amended suit filed in 1978 by the Coliseum against the NFL initially claiming that the League violated section 1 by not putting an expansion team in the Coliseum when the Rams left. Over the objections of the NFL (and the Oakland Coliseum, which intervened as a party), Los Angeles was retained as the venue for the jury trial. After a three-month jury trial in 1981 on liability alone, a trial that focused largely on the single entity defense, Judge Harry Pregerson, who had just become a Ninth Circuit judge but had retained this one case as the trial judge, granted a directed verdict for plaintiffs on this issue and thus removed it from jury consideration. Nonetheless, the jury could not reach a rule of reason verdict and a mistrial was declared. A lengthy liability retrial in 1982 resulted in a verdict that found that the NFL's action was an unreasonable restraint of trade. An injunction was entered barring the league from blocking the Raiders' relocation, and the NFL immediately appealed. The excerpt below provides the appellate court's application of the rule of reason to the NFL's refusal to approve the relocation.]

In a quite general sense, the case presents the competing considerations of whether a group of businessmen can enforce an agreement with one of their co-contractors to the detriment of that co-contractor's right to do business where he pleases. More specifically, this lawsuit requires us to engage in the difficult task of analyzing the negative and positive effects of a business practice in an industry which does not readily fit into the antitrust context. Section 1 of the Sherman Act was designed to prevent agreements among competitors which eliminate or reduce competition and thereby harm consumers. Yet, as we discussed in the context of the single entity issue, the NFL teams are not true competitors, nor can they be.

The NFL's structure has both horizontal and vertical attributes. On the one hand, it can be viewed simply as an organization of 28 competitors, an example of a simple horizontal arrangement. On the other, and to the extent the NFL can be considered an entity separate from the team owners, a vertical relationship is disclosed. In this sense the owners are distributors of the NFL product, each with its own territorial division. In this context it is clear that the owners have a legitimate interest in protecting the integrity of the League itself. Collective action in areas such as League divisions, scheduling and rules must be allowed, as should other activity that aids in producing the most marketable product attainable. Nevertheless, legitimate collective action should not be construed to allow the owners to extract excess profits. In such a situation the owners would be acting as a classic cartel. Agreements among competitors, *i.e.*, cartels, to fix prices or divide market territories are presumed illegal under § 1 because they give competitors the ability to charge unreasonable and arbitrary prices instead of setting prices by virtue of free market forces.

On its face, Rule 4.3 divides markets among the 28 teams, a practice presumed illegal, but, as we have noted, the unique structure of the NFL precludes application of the per se rule. Instead, we must examine Rule 4.3 to determine whether it reasonably serves the legitimate collective concerns of the owners or instead permits them to reap excess profits at the expense of the consuming public.

1.   Relevant Market

[The court then turned to the NFL's argument that the trial judgment should be reversed on the grounds that there had been no adverse impact on the relevant market, defined in both "product" and "geographic" terms. In the court's view, the scope of the market turned on what range of products had the ability to take significant amounts of business away from the others. This required judgments about the "reasonable interchangeability" of the products for similar uses and the "cross-elasticity of demand" for one product based on price changes in the other, which in turn depended on the "economically significant" geographic area of effective competition in which these products were traded. For their case, the Raiders claimed that the relevant market consisted just of NFL football (the product) in greater Los Angeles (the geographic area). The L.A. Coliseum claimed that its market consisted of stadiums offering facilities to NFL teams across the United States. The NFL's position was that the relevant product markets consisted of all entertainment and stadium uses across the entire country.]

* * *

That NFL football has limited substitutes from a consumer standpoint is seen from evidence that the Oakland Coliseum sold out for 10 consecutive years despite having some of the highest ticket prices in the League. A similar conclusion can be drawn from the extraordinary number of television viewers—over 100 million people—that watched the 1982 Super Bowl, the ultimate NFL product. NFL football's importance to the television networks is evidenced by the approximately $2 billion they agreed to pay the League for the right to televise the games from 1982–1986. This contract reflects the networks' anticipation that the high number of television viewers who had watched NFL football in the past would continue to do so in the future.

To some extent, the NFL itself narrowly defined the relevant market by emphasizing that NFL football is a unique product which can be produced only through the joint efforts of the 28 teams. Don Shula, coach of the Miami Dolphins, underscored this point when he stated that NFL football has a different set of fans than college football.

The evidence from which the jury could have found a narrow pro football product market was balanced, however, with other evidence which tended to show the NFL competes in the first instance with other professional sports, especially those with seasons that overlap with the NFL's. On a broader level, witnesses such as Pete Rozelle and Georgia Frontierre (owner of the L.A. Rams) testified that NFL football competes with other television offerings for network business, as well as other local entertainment for attendance at the games.

In terms of the relevant geographic market, witnesses testified, in particular Al Davis, that NFL teams compete with one another off the field for fan support in those areas where teams operate in close proximity such as New York City-New Jersey, Washington, D.C.-Baltimore, and formerly San Francisco-Oakland. Davis, of course, had firsthand knowledge of this when his team was located in Oakland. Also, the San Francisco Forty-Niners and the New York Giants were paid $18 million because of the potential for harm from competing with the Oakland Raiders and the New York Jets, respectively, once those teams joined the NFL as a result of the merger with the American Football League. Al Davis also testified at length regarding the potential for competition for fan support between the Raiders and the Los Angeles Rams once his team relocated in Los Angeles.

Testimony also adequately described the parameters of the stadia market. On one level, stadia do compete with one another for the tenancy of NFL teams. Such competition is shown by the Rams' move to Anaheim. Carroll Rosenbloom was offered what he considered to be a more lucrative situation at the Big A Stadium, so he left the L.A. Coliseum. In turn, the L.A. Coliseum sought to lure existing NFL teams to Los Angeles. Competition between the L.A. Coliseum and the Oakland Coliseum for the tenancy of the Raiders resulted.

* * *

The NFL claims that it is places, not particular stadia, that compete for NFL teams. This is true to a point because the NFL grants franchises to locales (generally a city and a 75 mile radius extending from its boundary). It is the individual stadia, however, which are most directly impacted by the restrictions on team movement. A stadium is a distinct economic entity and a territory is not.

It is also undoubtedly true, as the NFL contends, that stadia attempt to contract with a variety of forms of entertainment for exhibition in their facilities. In the case of the L.A. Coliseum, this includes college football, concerts, motorcycle races and the like. An NFL football team, however, is an especially desirable tenant. The L.A. Coliseum, for example, had received the highest rent from the Rams when they played there. We find that this evidence taken as whole provided the jury with an adequate basis on which to judge the reasonableness of Rule 4.3 both as it affected competition among NFL teams and among stadia.

We conclude with one additional observation. In the context of this case in particular, we believe that market evidence, while important, should not become an end in itself. Here the exceptional nature of the industry makes precise market definition especially difficult. To a large extent the market is determined by how one defines the entity: Is the NFL a single entity or partnership which creates a product that competes with other entertainment products for the consumer (*e.g.*, television and fans) dollar? Or is it 28 individual entities which compete with one another both on and off the field for the support of the consumers of the more narrow football product? Of course, the NFL has attributes of both examples and a variety of evidence was presented on both views. In fact, because of the exceptional structure of the League, it was not necessary for the jury to accept absolutely either the NFL's or the plaintiff's market definitions. Instead, the critical question is whether the jury could have determined that Rule 4.3 reasonably served the NFL's interest in producing and promoting its product, *i.e.*, competing in the entertainment market, or whether Rule 4.3 harmed competition among the 28 teams to such an extent that any benefits to the League as a whole were outweighed. As we find below, there was ample evidence for the jury to reach the latter conclusion.

2.   The History and Purpose of Rule 4.3

The NFL has awarded franchises exclusive territories since the 1930s. In the early days of professional football, numerous franchises failed and many changed location in the hope of achieving economic success. League members saw exclusive territories as a means to aid stability, ensuring the owner who was attempting to establish an NFL team in a particular city that another would not move into the same area, potentially ruining them both.

Rule 4.3 is the result of that concern. Prior to its amendment in 1978, it required unanimous League approval for a move into another team's home territory. That, of course, gave each owner an exclusive territory and he could vote against a move into his territory solely because he was afraid the competition might reduce his revenue. Notably, however, the League constitution required only three-quarters approval for all other moves. The 1978 amendment removed the double-standard, and currently three-quarters approval is required for all moves.

That the purpose of Rule 4.3 was to restrain competition among the 28 teams may seem obvious and it is not surprising the NFL admitted as much at trial. It instead argues that Rule 4.3 serves a variety of legitimate League needs, including ensuring franchise stability. We must keep in mind, however, that the Supreme Court has long rejected the notion that "ruinous competition" can be a defense to a restraint of trade. Conversely, anticompetitive purpose alone is not enough to condemn Rule 4.3. The rule must actually harm competition, and that harm must be evaluated in light of the procompetitive benefits the rule might foster.

3. Ancillary Restraints and the Reasonableness of Rule 4.3

The NFL's primary argument is that it is entitled to judgment notwithstanding the verdict because under the facts and the law, Rule 4.3 is reasonable under the doctrine of ancillary restraints. The NFL's argument is inventive and perhaps it will breathe new life into this little used area of antitrust law, but we reject it for the following reasons.

The common-law ancillary restraint doctrine was, in effect, incorporated into Sherman Act § 1 analysis by Justice Taft in *United States v. Addyston Pipe & Steel Co.,* 85 F. 271 (6th Cir. 1898), aff'd as modified, 175 U.S. 211 (1899). Most often discussed in the area of covenants not to compete, the doctrine teaches that some agreements which restrain competition may be valid if they are "subordinate and collateral to another legitimate transaction and necessary to make that transaction effective."

Generally, the effect of a finding of ancillary is to "remove the per se label from restraints otherwise falling within that category." R. Bork, *Ancillary Restraints and the Sherman Act,* 15 Antitrust L.J. 211, 212 (1959). We assume, with no reason to doubt, that the agreement creating the NFL is valid and the territorial divisions therein are ancillary to its main purpose of producing NFL football. The ancillary restraint must then be tested under the rule of reason, the relevance of ancillary being it "increases the probability that the restraint will be found reasonable." As we have already noted, the rule of reason inquiry requires us to consider the harms and benefits to competition caused by the restraint and whether the putative benefits can be achieved by less restrictive means.

The competitive harms of Rule 4.3 are plain. Exclusive territories insulate each team from competition within the NFL market, in essence allowing them to set monopoly prices to the detriment of the consuming public. The rule also effectively foreclosed free competition among stadia such as the Los Angeles Coliseum that wish to secure NFL tenants. The harm from Rule 4.3 is especially acute in this case because it prevents a move by a team into another existing team's market. If the transfer is upheld, direct competition between the Rams and Raiders would presumably ensue to the benefit of all who consume the NFL product in the Los Angeles area.

The NFL argues, however, that territorial allocations are inherent in an agreement among joint venturers to produce a product. This inherent nature, the NFL asserts, flows from the need to protect each joint venturer in the "legitimate fruits of the contract, or to protect him from the dangers of an unjust use of those fruits by the other party." We agree that the nature of NFL football requires some territorial restrictions in order both to encourage participation in the venture and to secure each venturer the legitimate fruits of that participation.

Rule 4.3 aids the League, the NFL claims, in determining its overall geographical scope, regional balance and coverage of major and minor markets. Exclusive territories aid new franchises in achieving financial stability, which protects the large initial investment an owner must make to start up a football team. Stability arguably helps ensure no one team has an undue advantage on the field. Territories foster fan loyalty which in turn promotes traditional rivalries between teams, each contributing to attendance at games and television viewing.

Joint marketing decisions are surely legitimate because of the importance of television. Title 15, U.S.C. § 1291 grants the NFL an exemption from antitrust liability, if any, that might arise out of its collective negotiation of television rights with the networks. To effectuate this right, the League must be allowed to have some control over the placement of teams to ensure NFL football is popular in a diverse group of markets.

Last, there is some legitimacy to the NFL's argument that it has an interest in preventing transfers from areas before local governments, which have made a substantial investment in stadia and other facilities, can recover their expenditures. In such a situation, local confidence in the NFL is eroded, possibly resulting in a decline in interest. All these factors considered, we nevertheless are not persuaded the jury should have concluded that Rule 4.3 is a reasonable restraint of trade. The same goals can be achieved in a variety of ways which are less harmful to competition.

As noted by Justice Rehnquist, a factor in determining the reasonableness of an ancillary restraint is the "possibility of less restrictive alternatives" which could serve the same purpose. *See* Justice Rehnquist's dissent from the denial of certiorari in *North American Soccer League*, 459 U.S. 1074 (1982). This is a pertinent factor in all rule of reason cases. Here, the district court correctly instructed the jury to take into account the existence of less restrictive alternatives when determining the reasonableness of Rule 4.3's territorial restraint. Because there was substantial evidence going to the existence of such alternatives, we find that the jury could have reasonably concluded that the NFL should have designed its "ancillary restraint" in a manner that served its needs but did not so foreclose competition.

The NFL argues that the requirement of Rule 4.3 that three-quarters of the owners approve a franchise move is reasonable because it deters unwise team transfers. While the rule does indeed protect an owner's investment in a football franchise, no standards or durational limits are incorporated into the voting requirement to make sure that concern is satisfied. Nor are factors such as fan loyalty and team rivalries necessarily considered.

The NFL claims that its marketing and other objectives are indirectly accounted for in the voting process because the team owners vote to maximize their profits. Since the owners are guided by the desire to increase profits, they will necessarily make reasonable decisions, the NFL asserts, on such issues of whether the new location can support two teams, whether marketing needs will be adversely affected, etc. Under the present Rule 4.3, however, an owner need muster only seven friendly votes to prevent three-quarters approval for the sole reason of preventing another team from entering its market, regardless of whether the market could sustain two franchises. A basic premise of the Sherman Act is that regulation of private profit is best left to the marketplace rather than private agreement. The present case is in fact a good example of how the market itself will deter unwise moves, since a team will not lightly give up an established base of support to confront another team in its home market.

The NFL's professed interest in ensuring that cities and other local governments secure a return on their investment in stadia is undercut in two ways. First, the local governments ought to be able to protect their investment through the leases they negotiate with the teams for the use of their stadia. Second, the NFL's interest on this point may not be as important as it would have us believe because the League has in the past allowed teams to threaten a transfer to another location in order to give the team leverage in lease negotiations.

Finally, the NFL made no showing that the transfer of the Raiders to Los Angeles would have any harmful effect on the League. Los Angeles is a market large enough for the successful operation of two teams, there would be no scheduling difficulties, facilities at the L.A. Coliseum are more than adequate, and no loss of future television revenue was foreseen. Also, the NFL offered no evidence that its interest in maintaining regional balance would be adversely affected by a move of a northern California team to southern California.

It is true, as the NFL claims, that the antitrust laws are primarily concerned with the promotion of interbrand competition. To the extent the NFL is a product which competes with other forms of entertainment, including other sports, its rules governing territorial division can be said to promote interbrand competition. Under this analysis, the territorial allocations most directly suppress intrabrand, that is, NFL team versus NFL team, competition. A more direct impact on intrabrand competition does not mean, however, the restraint is reasonable. The finder of fact must still balance the gain to interbrand competition against the loss of intrabrand competition. Here, the jury could have found that the rules restricting team movement do not sufficiently promote interbrand competition to justify the negative impact on intrabrand competition.

To withstand antitrust scrutiny, restrictions on team movement should be more closely tailored to serve the needs inherent in producing the NFL "product" and competing with other forms of entertainment. An express recognition and consideration of those objective factors espoused by the NFL as important, such as population, economic projections, facilities, regional balance, etc., would be well advised. Fan loyalty and location continuity could also be considered. Al Davis in fact testified that in 1978 he proposed that the League adopt a set of objective guidelines to govern team relocation rather than continuing to utilize a subjective voting procedure.

Some sort of procedural mechanism to ensure consideration of all the above factors may also be necessary, including an opportunity for the team proposing the move to present its case. *See Silver v. New York Stock Exchange,* 373 U.S. 341 (1963) (without procedural safeguards, the collective act of the Exchange in disconnecting the wire service to a broker constituted a boycott, per se illegal under § 1); *cf. Deesen v. Professional Golfers' Ass'n,* 358 F.2d 165 (9th Cir. 1966) (where PGA had reasonable rules governing eligibility of players for tournaments, there was not a § 1 violation). In the present case, for example, testimony indicated that some owners, as well as Commissioner Rozelle, dislike Al Davis and consider him a maverick. Their vote against the Raiders' move could have been motivated by animosity rather than business judgment.

Substantial evidence existed for the jury to find the restraint imposed by Rule 4.3 was not reasonably necessary to the production and sale of the NFL product. Therefore, the NFL is not entitled to judgment notwithstanding the verdict.

Affirmed.

[The appeals court majority concluded that the jury's verdict about the unreasonableness of this restraint—the opinion labeled this a "paradigm fact question"—was based on adequate evidence in the record.]

––––––––

The *Raiders I* decision concerned only the NFL's antitrust liability for rejecting the Raiders' proposed move to Los Angeles. Following a second trial on the damages question, the jury awarded the Raiders $11.55 million for profits lost due to the two-year delay in their move south. The NFL appealed this sizable damage award (trebled under the Sherman Act to over $34 million) on various grounds, including that the benefits the Raiders realized by taking from the NFL the opportunity to create an expansion franchise in Los Angeles should be deducted from the team's lost profits. This produced the *Raiders II* decision, *Los Angeles Memorial Coliseum Comm'n v. NFL,* 791 F.2d 1356 (9th Cir. 1986). The court of appeals there endorsed the basic premise of the NFL's argument that the NFL as a whole owned the right to expand into the Los Angeles area, a valuable right foreclosed by the Raiders' relocation. Considering the difference between the value of this right and the value to the NFL of expanding into Oakland (as the NFL has expanded to Houston, Baltimore, and Cleveland after teams in those cities relocated), the uncontradicted testimony at trial showed the Los Angeles market to be a significantly more lucrative franchise opportunity. Indeed, the Raiders' managing general partner, Al Davis, testified that the Raiders increased their value by some $25 million by moving to Los Angeles. Thus, this "windfall benefit" had to be offset against the damages awarded to the Raiders for the two-year delay in their move to Los Angeles. The court continued:

> Application of this offset rule is consistent with, and indeed, virtually compelled by, this court's *Raiders I* opinion. In analyzing the "unique" nature of professional athletic leagues vis-a-vis the antitrust laws, this panel expressly acknowledged that "the nature of NFL football requires some territorial restrictions in order both to encourage participation in the venture *and to secure each venturer the legitimate fruits of that participation.*" Here, the league owners collectively possessed the value that had accumulated in the Los Angeles expansion opportunity. This value, as indicated above, was created at least in part through the NFL's development, over the years, of a popular spectator sport with a national following. Although this panel upheld the liability jury's conclusion that Rule 4.3 as it was applied to the Raiders' move was an unreasonable restraint of trade, the opinion noted several less onerous forms of territorial restrictions that could pass muster under the rule of reason. Among these were standards restricting team movement that expressly recognized certain objective factors such as population, economic projections and the like, that the league could legitimately consider in deciding whether to permit a team to move. If such restrictions, applied in a non-arbitrary manner, would be reasonable under the Sherman Act, then *a fortiori*, a rule requiring merely an objectively-determined payment to league members as compensation for the right to take a valuable, jointly-owned franchise opportunity out of the league's hands, would also be a reasonable restriction.

791 F.2d at 1373.

————

A wave of relocations and inter-city bidding for NFL teams in the mid-1990s generated several § 1 lawsuits against the league's revised Rule 4.3, which had been amended after *Raiders I* to include several "objective" factors the owners must consider when voting on a proposed relocation. Al Davis and his Raiders continued to use the precedent to challenge a variety of league rules with which they disagreed, although none of the lawsuits yielded important sports law precedents. Another challenge was dismissed on the ground that the owner had signed a valid waiver of right to sue when he obtained the league's approval to sell the club. *VKK Corp. v. NFL*, 55 F. Supp. 2d 196 & 229 (S.D.N.Y. 1999), *aff'd*, 244 F.3d 114 (2d Cir. 2001).*

St. Louis also sued the NFL in the aftermath of the Rams move to their city, alleging that the league violated § 1 and tortiously interfered with the city's contract with the Rams by charging the Rams a $30 million relocation fee, which the team required St. Louis to subsidize. The league, which had not charged the Raiders such a fee, based it in part on anticipated reduced TV ratings and correspondingly lower broadcast rights fees. In 1997, after a lengthy trial, the trial judge granted a directed verdict for the NFL based on a lack of evidence of any conspiracy to keep other clubs from competing with the Rams for a potential St. Louis relocation opportunity. The Eighth Circuit affirmed the judgment. *St. Louis Convention & Visitors Comm'n v. NFL*, 154 F.3d 851 (8th Cir. 1998). (*See* Section B.3(b) below for subsequent litigation on non-antitrust issues.)

———

Raiders II was significant not just in sharply reducing the size of the NFL's damage liability to the Raiders, but also in offering somewhat greater support for league restraints on unilateral team movements. The latter effect became apparent soon afterwards in litigation involving the National Basketball Association and the San Diego Clippers. The Clippers decided to move their operations from San Diego to the Los Angeles Sports Arena (which was also owned by the Los Angeles Memorial Coliseum Commission), where the Clippers would compete for fans with the Los Angeles Lakers who were playing across town. After *Raiders I*, but before *Raiders II*, the NBA decided not to risk trebled damages by refusing to schedule Clippers' games in Los Angeles. Instead, the league sued the Clippers in San Diego, seeking a judicial declaration that the league could lawfully prohibit this relocation. After the district court had summarily dismissed the league's suit, the Ninth Circuit provided yet another interpretation of its holdings in *Raiders I* and *Raiders II*.

---

*   These two cases are discussed because of their significance for antitrust doctrine related to the relocation of sports league franchises. They are the tip of the iceberg, however, regarding lawsuits between the litigious Raiders owner and the NFL. Additional litigation included: *Oakland Raiders v. NFL*, 93 Cal. App. 4th 572 (2001) (affirming dismissal of a host of state law claims challenging NFL's decision to require clubs to participate in a league-owned European league); *Oakland Raiders v. NFL*, 41 Cal. 4th 624 (2007) (affirming trial verdict and judgment in favor of NFL against claims that the NFL was liable to the Raiders for the expansion opportunity given back to the league when the Raiders relocated back to Oakland from Los Angeles, and that the NFL failed to provide sufficient support for a new stadium in Los Angeles); *NFL Properties v. Superior Court*, 65 Cal. App. 4th 100 (Cal. Ct. App. 1998) (reversing discovery order in litigation challenging operation of venture controlling intellectual property rights of NFL clubs, noting that Raiders were shareholders in NFL Properties); *Oakland-Alameda County Coliseum v. Oakland Raiders,*197 Cal. App. 3d 1049 (1988) (affirming summary judgment for unpaid rent).

NBA v. SAN DIEGO CLIPPERS BASKETBALL CLUB
815 F.2d 562 (9th Cir. 1987)

FERGUSON, CIRCUIT JUDGE.

* * *

The antitrust issues are directly controlled by the two *Raiders* opinions, although the district judge had the benefit only of *Raiders I* when he rendered judgment. Collectively, the *Raiders* opinions held that rule of reason analysis governed a professional sports league's efforts to restrict franchise movement. More narrowly, however, *Raiders I* merely held that a reasonable jury could have found that the NFL's application of its franchise movement rule was an unreasonable restraint of trade. *Raiders II* confirmed that the jury's liability verdict affirmed in *Raiders I* "held Rule 4.3 [the franchise movement rule] invalid only as it was applied to the Raiders' proposed move to Los Angeles." The Clippers' and the Coliseum's efforts to characterize *Raiders I* as presenting guidelines for franchise movement rules are thus unavailing. Neither the jury's verdict in *Raiders*, nor the court's affirmance of that verdict, held that a franchise movement rule, in and of itself, was invalid under the antitrust laws . . . [T]he panel set down no absolute rule for sports leagues. Instead, it examined the facts before it and concluded that the jury's conclusion that the NFL violated the antitrust laws was supported by the record.

Yet the Clippers argue, as they must to support summary judgment, that the "NBA three-quarters rule . . . is illegal under *Raiders I*'—*i.e.*, either that the NBA rule is void as a matter of law under *Raiders I*, or that the NBA has not adduced genuine issues of fact to allow the rule to stand. The Clippers assert that the rule "is illegal as applied . . . [but that under *Raiders I*], a professional sports league's club relocation rule must at least be 'closely tailored' and incorporate objective standards and criteria such as population, economic projections, playing facilities, regional balance, and television revenues." . . . The Clippers' confusion, and that of a number of commentators, may derive from the *Raiders I* panel's painstaking efforts to guide sports leagues toward procedures that might, in all cases, withstand antitrust analysis. The objective factors and procedures recounted by the Clippers are "well advised," and might be sufficient to demonstrate procompetitive purposes that would save the restriction from the rule of reason. They are not, however, necessary conditions to the legality of franchise relocation rules.

. . . As we have demonstrated, antitrust analysis under *Raiders I* indicates that the question of what restraints are reasonable is one of fact. We believe that numerous issues of fact remain.

The NBA asserts a number of genuine issues of fact: (1) the purpose of the restraint as demonstrated by the NBA's use of a variety of criteria in evaluating franchise movement, (2) the market created by professional basketball, which the NBA alleges is substantially different from that of professional football, and (3) the actual effect the NBA's limitations on movements might have on trade. The NBA's assertions, if further documented at trial, create an entirely different factual setting than that of the Raiders and the NFL. Further, as the NBA correctly notes, the antitrust issue here is vastly different than that in the *Raiders* cases: the issue here is "whether the mere requirement that a team seek [NBA] Board of Governor approval before it seizes a new franchise location violates the Sherman Act." The NBA here did not attempt to forbid the move. It scheduled the Clippers in the Sports Arena, and when faced with continued assertions of potential antitrust liability, brought this suit for declaratory relief. Given the *Raiders I* rejection of per se analysis for franchise movement rules of sports leagues, and the existence of genuine issues of fact regarding the reasonableness of the restraint, the judgment against the NBA must be reversed.

Summary judgment reversed.

––––––––––

After this decision, the NBA and the Clippers settled their litigation, with the Clippers agreeing to make a substantial payment to the league for the right to remain in Los Angeles.

––––––––––

NOTES AND QUESTIONS

1.   *Balancing Competitive Effects.* How was the jury in the *Raiders* case supposed to balance effects on both interbrand and intrabrand competition? As for intrabrand competition, would the Raiders' presence in Los Angeles affect the competitive behavior of either the Rams or the Raiders? If so, would the Raiders absence from the San Francisco area affect the 49ers' competitive behavior in the opposite manner? What does interbrand competition mean in this context? In the *Raiders* case, how would you have balanced the intrabrand competitive effects in Los Angeles and San Francisco and the interbrand effects in the larger entertainment market? Can *Raiders* be read narrowly as an extraordinary case where the jury rejected *all* of the NFL's asserted procompetitive arguments for enhanced interbrand competition?

How would you balance the intrabrand and interbrand competitive effects in the Rams' move to St. Louis, where there was no other NFL team? Does it matter that the Patriots would have moved there from a Greater Boston market with no other NFL team, but the Rams moved there from a Los Angeles market that at the time had a second team (the Raiders) playing there? In making these determinations, should juries undertake *de novo* evaluation of the competitive effects, or should they give some deference to the judgment of the league owners?

2. *Less Restrictive Alternatives and "Due Process."* The *Raiders I* majority noted that one factor in determining reasonableness was whether less restrictive alternatives existed that could serve the same purpose. This analysis follows from the ancillary restraints doctrine of the *Addyston Pipe* case cited by the majority, limiting competitor agreements to those reasonably necessary to protect each party's "legitimate" interests. As applied to franchise relocation in sports, what does this mean? How would a jury use such an instruction in its deliberations? After the case was concluded, the NFL adopted policies that included a list of "objective factors" that club owners should consider in deciding whether to approve a franchise relocation—for example, market size, stadium adequacy, and attendance. Had this language been in the rule prior to the teams' 22–0 vote against the Raiders move, would the rule or its application in the *Raiders* case have been less restrictive? Given that the court majority perceived that the jury's conclusion was that NFL owners voted against the Raiders' relocation despite no objective harm to the league, in order to protect the Rams from competition, would this realistically have changed any votes in the *Raiders* case?

Subsequently, the Supreme Court ruled in a non-sports case that (contrary to suggestions in the *Silver* case cited in *Raiders I*) fair procedures would not shield anticompetitive agreements from antitrust liability, while unfair procedures would not condemn collective decisions that had no anticompetitive effect. *Northwest Wholesale Stationers, Inc. v. Pacific Stationery & Printing Co.*, 472 U.S. 284 (1985). However, adherence to established procedures may be relevant to protect a league from accusations that its adverse decisions were arbitrary, capricious, or malicious, under the law governing private associations considered in Chapter 1.

3. *Relocation Fees and Jury Deference to League Judgments. Raiders II* indicated that it would have been reasonable and thus legal if, instead of blocking the Raiders' move to Los Angeles, the league had merely levied a charge against the Raiders for the difference in the value of the Los Angeles and Oakland markets. How would such values be calculated? Could the Raiders refuse to pay the amount determined by the league, and then sue for treble damages under § 1, claiming that the amount charged was in fact greater than it should have been? If so, would a jury reviewing the amount of the charge substitute its own judgment of the correct amount, or should it be instructed to give some deference to the league's determination?

4. *Relocation of Bankrupt Clubs.* How should the validity of league refusals to permit relocation be affected when the franchise at issue has declared bankruptcy? When the owner of the NHL Phoenix Coyotes filed for bankruptcy in 2009, he attempted to compensate his creditors by selling the club to a Canadian businessman who would pay $212.5 million contingent on relocating the franchise from Arizona to Hamilton, Ontario. The remaining NHL owners counterbid $140 million for the purpose of keeping the Coyotes in Arizona, and argued for rejection of the Canadian bid because the NHL's Constitution reserves to the owners the right to approve any change in franchise ownership. The Canadian bidder argued that the NHL's rejection of

him as an appropriate owner was pretextual, and that the owners were really restraining trade by refusing the relocation in order to protect the nearby Toronto Maple Leafs and Buffalo Sabres from competition.

The judge sided with the NHL and refused to invoke a bankruptcy provision that would have allowed him to override NHL rules regarding transfers of ownership and franchise relocation. The judge further found that the offer of a relocation fee, per *Raiders II,* was not sufficient to adequately protect the NHL's interests. He held that the "very nature of professional sports requires some territorial restrictions in order both to encourage participation in the venture and to secure to each venturer the legitimate fruits of that participation." *In re Dewey Ranch Hockey, LLC,* 414 B.R. 577, 591 (Bankr. D. Ariz. 2009) (*Coyotes II*).

In ruling for the NHL, the bankruptcy judge declined to address the Sherman Act's limits on league relocation decisions. If, following the rejection of his bid, the Canadian bidder had filed a Sherman Act suit against the NHL, would he likely have been able to prove to a jury that the refusal was an unreasonable restraint of trade? Would it matter under U.S. antitrust law that the market that was arguably restrained was located in Canada while the city losing the team would have been in the U.S.?

5.   *Counseling Leagues After* Raiders/Clippers. What are the broader guidelines that emerge from *Raiders* and from *Clippers* for the benefit of leagues and teams that naturally want to know *before* antitrust litigation whether a team's proposed move from one city to another can either be made or be blocked? What kind of legal liability does the league—or the club—face if it guesses incorrectly about the state and application of the law?

6.   *Comparing Relocation Dynamics in NFL and MLB.* A number of owners have moved from larger to smaller markets because of more favorable stadium deals. Why is this more prevalent in the NFL, featuring 8 home games and centralized and shared television revenues, than in MLB, featuring 81 home games and largely local broadcast rights sales? Should the NFL's history be a concern of antitrust law, which is supposed to ensure that price (including tax subsidies to owners as the "price" of relocation) and output are responsive to consumer preference?

7.   *Antitrust Limits Where Fellow Owners Support Relocation.* In contrast to the owners' rejection of Al Davis' desired relocation from Oakland to Los Angeles, his son Mark Davis received league approval for a relation from Oakland to Las Vegas in conjunction with a $750 million public subsidy for stadium construction. In *City of Oakland v. Oakland Raiders,* 20 F.4th 441 (9th Cir. 2021), the court dismissed an antitrust claim challenging the move. The city attempted to claim that the other NFL owners were engaged in a group boycott, but provided no evidence that anyone other than the Raiders were "boycotting". Oakland also claimed that the NFL owners artificially limited the number of franchises in the league, but the court found the claim that the Raiders would not have relocated had there been more franchises to be unduly speculative.

2. LEAGUE CONTROLS OVER ENTRY/CONTRACTION

Three owners from the defunct World Football League took the best players from their former WFL teams and sought to persuade a federal appellate court that they were entitled to admission to the National Football League—not as purchasers of an existing team, but as creators of a new team. These owners brought with their application not just a city, a stadium, and a fan base, but also a team of players looking for a league in which to play.

MID-SOUTH GRIZZLIES V. NFL
720 F.2d 772 (3d Cir. 1983)

GIBBONS, CIRCUIT JUDGE.

[The Memphis Southmen were one of the few successful franchises in the World Football League, which opened in 1974 and closed midway through the 1975 season. The team then reorganized with players from two other WFL teams (the Philadelphia Bell and the Southern California Sun), named itself the Grizzlies, and applied for a franchise in the National Football League. The Grizzlies claimed that they were an established football enterprise operating in a city, Memphis, which had demonstrated strong popular demand for professional football, and was not included in the 75-mile "home territory" of any existing NFL franchise. The NFL rejected the Grizzlies' application; the reasons given were recent expansion to Seattle and Tampa, the scheduling need for an even number of teams, and an uncertain labor relationship with the NFLPA (the *Mackey* suit was still being litigated). The Grizzlies then filed an antitrust suit in Philadelphia. The suit relied not only on the Sherman Act, but also upon 15 U.S.C.A. § 1291 (Public Law 87–331), which gave professional sports leagues a limited antitrust exemption to pool and sell their television rights, and upon Public Law 89–800, which in 1966 amended § 1291 to permit the merger of the National and American Football Leagues "if such agreement increases rather than decreases the number of professional football clubs." The trial judge granted the NFL's motion for summary dismissal, and the Grizzlies appealed. The circuit court rejected the Grizzlies' claim that the additional monopoly power conferred on an expanded NFL by that special legislation imposed on the league an affirmative obligation, in effect, to share that power with franchise-seekers such as the Grizzlies. The court then turned to the question whether the NFL's rejection of the Grizzlies' application constituted a violation of the basic Sherman Act.]

* * *

As to the acquisition of dominant position and monopoly power, the facts are undisputed. Long before the Grizzlies and the World Football League came into existence, Congress authorized the merger of the two major football leagues extant in 1966, and granted to the merged league the power to pool television revenues. That congressional decision conferred on the NFL the market power which it holds in the market for professional football. Congress could not have been unaware that necessary effect of the television revenue sharing scheme which it approved for the NFL would be that all members of that league would be strengthened in their ability to bid for the best available playing and coaching personnel, to the potential disadvantage of new entrants.

* * *

As to competition with NFL members in the professional football market, including the market for sale of television rights, the exclusion was patently pro-competitive, since it left the Memphis area, with a large stadium and a significant metropolitan area population, available as a site for another league's franchise, and it left the Grizzlies' organization as a potential competitor in such a league. If there was any injury to competition, actual or potential, therefore, it must have been to intra-league competition.

The NFL defendants' position is that the summary judgment record establishes conclusively the absence of competition, actual or potential, among league members. Rather, they urge, the league is a single entity, a joint venture in the presentation of the professional football spectacle.

For the most part the congressionally authorized arrangements under which the NFL functions eliminate competition among the league members. Indeed it is undisputed that on average more than 70% of each member club's revenue is shared revenue derived from sources other than operations at its home location. The Grizzlies do not challenge the legality of the NFL's revenue sharing arrangements, and seek to participate in them. The Grizzlies emphasize that there nevertheless remains a not insignificant amount of intra-league non-athletic competition. We need not, in order to affirm the summary judgment, accept entirely the NFL's position that there is no intra-league competition. Conceivably within certain geographic submarkets two league members compete with one another for ticket buyers, for local broadcast revenue, and for sale of the concession items like food and beverages and team paraphernalia. Thus rejection of a franchise application in the New York metropolitan area, for example, might require a different antitrust analysis than is suggested by this record. But the Grizzlies were obliged, when faced with the NFL denial of the existence of competition among NFL members and a potential franchisee at Memphis, to show some more than minimal level of potential competition, in the product markets in which league members might compete. They made no such showing. The record establishes that the NFL franchise nearest to Memphis is at St. Louis, Mo., over 280 miles away. There is no record evidence that professional football teams located in Memphis and in St. Louis would compete for the same ticket purchasers, for the same local broadcast outlets, in the sale of team paraphernalia, or in any other manner.

The Grizzlies contend on appeal, although they did not so contend in the trial court, that league members compete in what they call the "raw material market" for players and coaching personnel. Entirely apart from the propriety of considering a legal theory not presented in the trial court, there are major defects in this Grizzlies' argument. First, the Grizzlies exclusion from the league in no way restrained them from competing for players by forming a competitive league. Second, they fail to explain how, if their exclusion from the league reduced competition for team personnel, that reduction caused an injury to the Grizzlies' business or property.

One final Grizzlies' argument in support of their § 1 Sherman Act claim bears mentioning. Relying on the essential facilities doctrine developed in cases such as *Silver v. New York Stock Exchange*, 373 U.S. 341 (1963) and *Associated Press v. United States*, 326 U.S. 1 (1945), they urge that because the NFL is a practical monopoly it had an obligation to admit members on fair, reasonable, and equal terms, absent some procompetitive justification for their exclusion. This Grizzlies argument suffers from the same defect as the others. The essential facilities doctrine is predicated on the assumption that admission of the excluded applicant would result in additional competition, in an economic rather than athletic sense. The Grizzlies have simply failed to show how competition in any arguably relevant market would be improved if they were given a share of the NFL's monopoly power.

Since on the record before us the Grizzlies have shown no actual or potential injury to competition resulting from the rejection of their application for an NFL franchise, they cannot succeed on their § 1 Sherman Act claim.

Affirmed.

————

A similar antitrust suit to force expansion in hockey was summarily dismissed in *Seattle Totems v. National Hockey League*, 783 F.2d 1347 (9th Cir. 1986).

————

The Australian Rugby League had embarked by 1995 on an ambitious expansion program that included 20 teams. When media magnates Kerry Packer and Rupert Murdoch battled over television rights, Murdoch set up his own rival Superleague. In addition to battling the ARL for the services of top players, Murdoch secured agreements with 8 of the ARL clubs to switch leagues. After a financially destructive 2-year "war," the parties entered into an agreement merging the ARL and Superleague into a new competition, the National Rugby League. Murdoch insisted, despite strong resistance from the ARL, on shrinking the NRL to 14 teams over three years. Through insolvency and mergers between traditional rivals, the NRL shrunk to 15 teams in 2000. At that time, the league's board, comprised of three officials designated by Murdoch and three designated by the old ARL, kicked the South Sydney Rabbitohs out of the competition. Souths sued under Australian competition (*i.e.*, antitrust) law, lost in the trial court, and prevailed in the appellate tribunal. At this point, the NRL gave in and agreed to re-admit South Sydney to the competition, but continued to pursue the litigation appeal.

Although the actual litigation turned on a technical point of Australian competition law not present in Sherman Act jurisprudence, Australian courts used an important concept regarding the relevant markets where competition was allegedly being restrained that has relevance for American antitrust doctrine. As the Court described the issue, sports leagues provide "competition organizing services" for clubs: "the supply of the services of organising and running top level rugby league competitions to . . . [a] rugby league club willing and able to provide a team to participate competitively in a top-level rugby league competition." In turn, clubs provide "team services" to leagues: clubs provide the actual teams to participate in competitions to be organized by those providing "competition organizing services." *South Sydney Rugby League Football Club Ltd v. News Ltd* (2003) 200 ALR 157.

We tend not to appreciate this distinction in North America, because in team sports the commercial entity that provides competition organizing services is a joint venture of the clubs providing the team services (except in auto racing, where NASCAR and the IndyCar League provide the organizing service and the individual racing teams provide the racers). In economic terms, there is a "vertical integration" between the providers of what are, analytically, two distinct services.

––––––––––

NOTES AND QUESTIONS

1.   *Admission to Monopoly Leagues.* As long as there is only one major league in each sport, should a league be required to admit any qualified applicant? How would a judgment be made as to whether an applicant was "qualified" and under what criteria?

2.   *Impact of* Grizzlies *on Other Relocations.* The court concluded in *Grizzlies* that the NFL's refusal to add this new team to the league did not affect market competition because no other NFL teams were located near Memphis, a situation that differed in this respect from the league's earlier effort to block the Raiders relocation to Los Angeles where a second NFL team was proximately located. What does the reasoning of *Raiders* and *Grizzlies* imply about the legal right of the Baltimore Colts to move (in the mid-1980s)

to Indianapolis? What about the Los Angeles Rams to St. Louis (in the mid-1990s) at a time when the Raiders were still based in Los Angeles, and the St. Louis Rams' decision to move back to Los Angeles in 2017, when the Raiders had returned to Oakland?

3. Grizzlies' *Rejection of Inter-Club Competition.* In any event, the Grizzlies also argued that NFL teams competed economically with one another in broader national markets—*e.g.*, for players, coaches, and other personnel. How did the court deal with this argument? Is the court's response persuasive?

4. *Antitrust Claims from Contraction.* The flip side of expansion is contraction, a concept largely unimagined in the major professional sports leagues in modern times—until 2001 when Commissioner Bud Selig announced MLB's decision to dissolve two of the 30 teams before the 2002 season began. Could those aggrieved by a team's elimination bring a plausible antitrust claim? Based on the *Raiders, Clippers,* and *Grizzlies* cases, what competition might arguably be restrained? Would your answer be different if the team being eliminated were playing in a one or two-team market? Or in a market in which it was the only major league sports team in any sport?

5. *How to Evaluate Antitrust Claims for Rejected Entry.* As a practical matter, the way new golfers and tennis players gain access to their respective tours differs from the manner team sports leagues add new expansion franchises. Generally, new golfers and tennis players are accepted for tournaments when they prove more competitive at the game than the people they replace. In contrast, new league franchises are added when owners of the existing teams agree that expansion to a particular area is in the league's best economic or political interests, and then only upon payment of huge expansion fees. How would the judge decide that a particular area was the best place for NFL expansion, and how would the judge calculate the appropriate franchise fee? Could the court be guided by how clubs now decide these issues?

6. *Promotion and Relegation in the Rest of the World.* For most professional sports in the rest of the western world, admission into the "major league" is determined in an entirely different way, known as "promotion and relegation." Unlike North American leagues, the major leagues sit on top of a hierarchy of lower-tier leagues, with the best teams in lower leagues being promoted to the next higher tier league at the end of each season, and the worst teams in higher leagues being relegated. These lower-tier leagues are not farm teams, although often individual players are "loaned" to lower-tier leagues for training and play much as minor leagues exist in North America. To minimize economic dislocation, most leagues arrange for "parachute payments," often 50% of television rights, if a team falls to a lower division. Rarely do top teams get relegated, but when they do, it doesn't last long as they easily dominate the lower league and get promoted within a season.

Is promotion and relegation a better way to determine entry into the major leagues? For an economic analysis of this proposal, *see* Stephen F. Ross and Stefan Szymanski, FANS OF THE WORLD, UNITE! A (CAPITALIST) MANIFESTO FOR SPORTS CONSUMERS (Stanford Univ. Press 2008). These authors sketch a legal argument on why the existing "closed league" model in the United States could be considered a violation of the Sherman Act in *Open Competition in League Sports*, 2002 WIS. L. REV. 625.

3. THE LIMITS OF ANTITRUST: ALTERNATIVE NON-ANTITRUST APPROACHES TO STAKEHOLDER INTERESTS IN FRANCHISE MOVEMENT

Reconsider the lessons learned to this point regarding the number and location of major league sports franchises. Under governance principles discussed in Chapter 1, these decisions are made collectively by the other franchise owners collectively. Under the discussion of monopoly power in Chapter 6, for a variety of reasons the usual antitrust policy of competition—in the form of rival leagues within each sport—is not available to ensure that communities that could economically support viable businesses can patronize them. Under the doctrines established in *Raiders* and *Grizzlies*, the antitrust laws only intervene to protect stakeholder interests when the league has prevented a relocation to protect existing club owners from local competition.

The result is predictable: more communities would like to support a major league franchise than there are such franchises, and as a result there is fierce financial bidding for a scarce number of sports franchises. The result of these bidding wars is that many teams, whether or not they move, are regularly favored with large public subsidies. This leverage by clubs over communities anxious to keep or acquire a professional franchise is a textbook example of exercising enormous market power, perhaps even monopoly power (lawfully acquired or not), to drive the "price" of franchises up by artificially restricting supply in the face of growing demand. With little support for a National Sports Commission to regulate this exploitation, stakeholders turn to a number of other strategies to achieve a goal that would be easily achieved in other industries where consumers and taxpayers have competitive alternatives.

These strategies are summarized in this section, for two reasons. First, they are relevant areas of law about which sports lawyers should be familiar. Second, they shape a normative evaluation about the efficacy of antitrust to protect consumers and taxpayers from monopoly power.

(a) Blocking an Undesired Relocation Based on State and Local Government Law or Federal, State, or Local Environmental Laws

Often, citizens who oppose efforts to relocate a franchise to their community resort to a variety of legal challenges based on statutes governing the operation of state or local government or judicial review of local government decisions, or based on federal, state, or local environmental laws. The former vary by state, and the latter are worthy of the entire course of Environmental Law. None have unique sports law content, and so are not discussed further in this casebook.

(b) Protective Lease Terms

Communities can try to protect themselves against departures of their "home" teams by favorable terms in leases between municipally-owned stadiums and major league clubs. Some courts have found that the city-lessor's damages from a team's breach of contract are not irreparable, and that monetary damages are sufficient. Others have granted equitable relief based on the unique and irreplaceable value of the franchise. *Compare City of New York v. New York Jets*, 394 N.Y.S.2d 799 (1977), with *HMC Management v. New Orleans Basketball Club*, 375 So.2d 700 (La. App. 1979).

After the 2001 season, MLB threatened to contract the Minnesota Twins, offering a generous buyout to the Twins' owner. However, after a Minnesota state court judge enjoined contraction based on his interpretation of the Twins' lease, the MLBPA also objected, and in the 2002 collective bargaining agreement the owners agreed to postpone contraction indefinitely. The injunction was not based on antitrust but rather on state contract and tort law. The trial judge had found that sports leases are unique, because the "welfare, recreation, prestige, prosperity, trade, and commerce of the people of the community are at stake." This argument was similar to the one that that Twins' owner Carl Pohlad had made to try to persuade the community to build a new stadium for his Twins. In *Metropolitan Sports Facilities Commission v. Minnesota Twins Partnership*, 638 N.W.2d 214 (2002), the court of appeals affirmed. Chief Judge Toussaint first synopsized the trial judge's reasons for finding irreparable harm to not only the stadium authority, but also the state and its citizens—particularly, the fans—if the Twins were to play no 2002 home games at the Metrodome. The trial judge:

> (1) cited the role of baseball as a tradition and as a national pastime, the history of the Twins in Minnesota for some 40 years, including two World Series championships, the role of Twins legends who have bettered the community by their volunteer work with children, and the availability of Twins games as affordable family entertainment; (2) noted that private buildings had been condemned to build the Metrodome; (3) found that the welfare, recreation, prestige, prosperity, trade, and commerce of the people of the community are at stake; and (4) ruled that the vital public trust outweighs any private interest.

638 N.W.2d at 221.

After then citing the legal and economic reasons why specific performance could occasionally be available as a form of equitable relief in certain exceptional commercial-lease cases, Judge Toussaint noted the state Supreme Court's decision in *Lifteau v. Metropolitan Sports Facilities Comm'n,* 270 N.W.2d 749 (Minn. 1978), which had accepted Baseball's position that "the use of public funds for construction of the Metrodome . . . constituted a public purpose for which public expenditures may legally be undertaken."

The public interest in Major League Baseball franchises in general has been recognized by others. In discussing possible effects of the potential loss of baseball's antitrust exemption, Chairman Selig stated that it could irreparably injure [fans] by leading to the removal of live professional baseball from communities that have hosted major league and minor league teams for decades. Similarly, based on his own unsuccessful efforts to stop the relocation of the Milwaukee Braves, Selig told Congress that he believed that the professional sports league and Major League Baseball should vigilantly enforce strong policies prohibiting clubs from abandoning local communities which have supported them. [Citation to Hearings omitted] He further stated that franchise relocation should be prohibited except in the most dire circumstances where the local community has, over a sustained period, demonstrated that it cannot or will not support the franchise.

638 N.W.2d of 224–25.

The Twins lease may not be typical of lease arrangements. Team owners typically possess strong leverage in lease negotiations due to the league's monopoly over the sport and the undersupply of major league franchises. The threat of relocation leads to a strong effort on the part of the city to cede favorable terms at the expense of taxpayers. Matthew J. Mitten & Bruce W. Burton, *Professional Sports Franchise Relocations From Private Law Public Law Perspectives: Balancing Marketplace Competition, League Autonomy, and the Need for Level Playing Field,* 56 MD. L. REV. 57, 70–71 (1997). For example, the City of Cleveland ultimately failed in its efforts to hold the Browns to the three years remaining on its lease of Municipal Stadium, in part because the Browns' lease was not with the City, but rather with a management corporation owned by Browns' owner Art Modell, which two decades earlier had entered into its own deal with the City to operate the stadium.

An innovative theory around an inability to secure favorable language in the stadium lease was upheld in *St. Louis Reg'l Convention & Sports Complex Auth. v. NFL,* No. ED106282, 2018 Mo. App. LEXIS 929 (Mo. App.). The stadium authority who channeled taxpayer subsidies to lure the Rams *from* Los Angeles sued when the Rams were lured *back to* Southern California in 2016. The plaintiffs did not claim a breach of their contractual relationship with the Rams, but rather that they were third-party beneficiaries of the NFL's own regulations relating to franchise relocations, which the Rams allegedly breached. The terms of the NFL regulations would have precluded the Rams from repeating the Raiders antitrust litigation strategy, requiring all parties to arbitrate disputes. But the Missouri court found that the stadium authority, albeit a beneficiary of the contract, was not bound by the arbitration clause. Faced with a trial, the league and the Rams' owner agreed to settle the case with a payment of $790 million. As this text goes to press, the owners continue to debate the validity and applicability of an agreement whereby the Rams would indemnify the rest of the league.

(c) Eminent Domain

After the Ninth Circuit upheld the antitrust challenge against the NFL's refusal to permit the Raiders from relocating to Los Angeles, the City of Oakland tried to use its power of eminent domain to purchase the club forcibly for fair market value, and then resell the club to a suitable buyer who promised to keep the club in its current location. Initially, the California Supreme Court ruled in favor of the City: it reversed the lower court's dismissal of proceedings and held that the property to be taken— the bundle of contract rights to operate a club in the NFL—were legitimate targets for the eminent domain power, and that preserving a major league football team in a city was a "public use." *City of Oakland v. Oakland Raiders*, 646 P.2d 835 (Cal. 1982), *citing with approval City of Los Angeles v. Superior Court*, 333 P.2d 745 (Cal. 1959) (upholding the use of eminent domain for the eventual use by the Los Angeles Dodgers). However, further merits proceedings resulted in defeat for the city: the court of appeals subsequently held that the use of eminent domain power to prevent a relocation within a nationwide sports league constituted an unconstitutional interference with interstate commerce. *City of Oakland II*, 220 Cal. Rptr. 153 (Ct. App. 1st Dist. 1985).

The actual use of the strategy, even if legal, is logistically problematic. In *Mayor & City Council of Baltimore v. Baltimore (Colts) Football Club*, 624 F. Supp. 278 (D. Md. 1985), the court ruled that the ordinance did not apply when, prior to the enactment of the local ordinance to acquire the Colts forcibly, owner Robert Irsay hastily arranged for all personal property of the club to be placed in moving vans and shipped to their new home in Indianapolis. Furthermore, it is conceptually problematic to think about a government "seizing" an intangible asset like the right to play games in a sports league. Even had Baltimore taken physical possession of the Colts' uniforms, blocking sleds and office equipment, the team's greatest asset is its franchise in the NFL. While the California courts have indicated that this is a legitimate target for eminent domain, how would a city "seize" that if the league scheduled the team's games in the new location?

(d) Direct State Legislation

Following the move of the Cleveland Browns to Baltimore in 1996, the Ohio state legislature enacted Ohio Revised Code § 9.67, titled "Restrictions on owner of professional sports team." Colloquially named the "Art Modell Law" after the Browns' owner who relocated the original franchise to Baltimore as the Ravens, it prohibits owners who use tax-supported facilities and accept financial assistance from the state from moving to another city without six months' notice and an opportunity being given to individuals who live in the area to purchase the team. Such law, like the use of eminent domain, raises serious questions regarding its potential interference with interstate commerce. Litigation by the MLS Columbus Crew challenging the statute was settled without a decision on constitutionality, with government support for the Crew's new stadium.

(e) Federal Legislative Reform

In order to strengthen leagues' ability to keep teams in place, politicians introduced numerous versions of antitrust reform in Congress in the mid-1990s. The prospects for actual enactment were never very promising: for every community (and politician) that loses a team, another gains one. Legislation removing antitrust scrutiny from league decisions to block a proposed regulation is only effective in preventing "bad" relocations that would actually be blocked by the league. However, as the post-*Raiders* experience has made clear, many actual or threatened moves that result in huge public subsidies are done with the full support of commissioners and fellow owners.

These and other substantive legal proposals raise an underlying institutional question. Who should make the judgment about where particular sports teams should be located? The individual owner who is most involved in and affected by the fate of his team? The league's owners, collectively deciding how the move affects the interests of all teams and owners? Or some combination of courts and lawmakers seeking to protect the interests of the affected communities? One point of view is that the people in Brooklyn, for example, should have had a "moral" right to keep their Dodgers, and the people in Cleveland their Browns. Alternatively, if the objective is to protect the broader public welfare, the ideal free-market test asks which city's fans are willing to pay the most either to gain or to keep the free-agent franchise.

Ironically, the NFL's internal revenue sharing system, one that was supposedly designed to protect smaller market teams from the competitive pressures of the bigger market teams in the players market, has actually generated movement from larger to smaller communities in the franchise market.

Although Congress considered legislation to reform the franchise relocation process, in part motivated by concerns about taxpayer subsidies, it did not exercise its authority to regulate interstate Congress to employ an extremely important tool used by the European Union to regulate trade among its member states. Article 107(1) of the EU Treaty provides:

> Save as otherwise provided in the Treaties, any aid granted by a Member State or through State resources in any form whatsoever which distorts or threatens to distort competition by favouring certain undertakings or the production of certain goods shall, in so far as it affects trade between Member States, be incompatible with the internal market.

Thus, in Europe, stadium subsidies are only permitted under limited conditions. Some general principles were laid down in a letter from the European Commission's Directorate-General for Competition to Germany regarding State funding for the Hanover football stadium. Aid for the construction of stadiums or other sports infrastructure could be argued not to constitute aid, provided it fulfills the following criteria: (1) the type of infrastructure involved is generally unlikely to be provided by the market because it is not economically viable; (2) it is not apt to selectively favour a specific undertaking: in other words, the site provides facilities for different types of activities and users and is rented out to undertakings at adequate market based compensation; (3) it is a facility needed to provide a service that is considered as being part of the typical responsibility of the public authority to the general public.

As a European White Paper explained:

> Since professional sport clubs are engaged in economic activities, there is no compelling argument why they should be exempted from the State aid rules.

> The need to ensure competitive equality between players, clubs and competitions as well as the necessity to ensure uncertainty of results can in fact be guaranteed most effectively by the application of State aid rules, which are meant to establish a level playing field and ensure that States or municipalities that are most willing or able to grant subsidies to their clubs will not disrupt fair competition.

EU Commission staff working document, The EU and Sport: Background and Context, available at http://eur-lex.europa.eu/legal-content/EN/TXT/HTML/?uri=CELEX:52007SC0935&from=EN.

———

NOTES AND QUESTIONS

1. *Are Stadium Leases Different than Other Commercial Leases?* Is it persuasive that a stadium lease with a major league sports team is substantively different from other types of commercial leases because the

consideration provided by the team is not rent to the landlord but rather entertainment for the public? If so, is the only reasonable remedy for a breach an injunction for specific performance? Would the result be different if the team is required to pay rent under the lease or any other financial terms? Would the result be different if the stadium is privately owned but was constructed with significant public subsidies?

2. *Intra-Metropolitan Relocations.* Would the rationale used by the Minnesota court in the *Twins* lease litigation apply equally in cases where a team was not attempting to go out of business, but simply to relocate to another community? If so, does this case (and the likelihood of local judges in other states threatened with the loss of their team adopting the same view) provide a vehicle for making relocations almost impossible if the stadium lease has not expired? How does this ruling affect the ability of teams to use the threat of leaving to extract huge public subsidies?

3. *State Aids.* Should Congress follow the European approach and simply ban tax subsidies? Would such a bar on state and local governments be constitutional? Would applying or enforcing it be feasible?

C. TELEVISION CONTRACTS

The primary source of soaring sports revenues has been an increasing fan appetite for watching games at home on television or on their computers and hand-held devices. A crucial condition has been the legality of teams joining together to sell a single package of broadcasting and marketing rights to the highest bidder. Consider whether such legal arrangements are in the best interests of fans of the sport and consumers of products advertised during game broadcasts. League-wide controls upon the sale of television rights has been the principal setting for this legal debate about the compatibility of league licensing packages and rules with antitrust law's commitment to a competitive consumer market.

The new television medium posed a special threat to the fundamental principle of territorial exclusivity embodied in league constitutions, a principle that insulated franchise owners from intrusion by other clubs into their home markets. Broadcasts of games involving the more successful teams (such as the New York Yankees in baseball and the Cleveland Browns in football) could be beamed into any part of the country. Thus, the earliest league television policy sought to limit the breadth of broadcasts of games played by any one team. This policy generated the first antitrust challenge encountered by leagues in their internal dealings—in fact, the one and only antitrust suit filed by the Justice Department against professional sports.

UNITED STATES V. NFL

116 F. Supp. 319 (E.D. Pa. 1953)

GRIM, DISTRICT JUDGE.

[The NFL's initial stance was to permit each individual team to contract for the telecasting (and radio broadcasting) of games in which that team was participating. However, the League's by-laws contained a blanket prohibition against teams broadcasting their games into the home territories of other teams. The Justice Department charged that this league policy constituted an agreement in restraint of trade in violation of § 1 of the Sherman Antitrust Act.]

I.

Is the provision which prevents the telecasting of outside games into the home territories of other teams on days when the other teams are playing at home illegal?

There can be little doubt that this provision constitutes a contract in restraint of trade. The market for the public exhibition of football no longer is limited to the spectators who attend the games. Since the advent of television and radio, the visual and aural projections of football games can be marketed anywhere in the world where there are television or radio facilities to transmit and receive them. When a football team agrees to restrict the projection of its games in the home areas of other teams, it thereby cuts itself off from this part of its potential market. Since the clubs of the National Football League have agreed at certain times not to project their games into the home territories of other clubs, they have given that part of their market at those certain times exclusively to other teams. In return, each of them has been given the right to market its own games without competition in its own home area under the same circumstances. The purpose and effect of this is to restrict outside competition on the part of other teams in the home area of each club. This, therefore, is a clear case of allocating marketing territories among competitors, which is a practice generally held illegal under the anti-trust laws.

An allocation of marketing territories for the purpose of restricting competition, however, is not always illegal. . . . The principal question in the present case is whether the particular restraints imposed by Article X are reasonable or unreasonable.

Professional football is a unique type of business. Like other professional sports which are organized on a league basis, it has problems which no other business has. The ordinary business makes every effort to sell as much of its product or services as it can. In the course of doing this it may and often does put many of its competitors out of business. The ordinary businessman is not troubled by the knowledge that he is doing so well that his competitors are being driven out of business.

Professional teams in a league, however, must not compete too well with each other, in a business way. On the playing field, of course, they must compete as hard as they can all the time. But it is not necessary and indeed it is unwise for all the teams to compete as hard as they can against each other in a business way. If all the teams should compete as hard as they can in a business way, the stronger teams would be likely to drive the weaker ones into financial failure. If this should happen not only would the weaker teams fail, but eventually the whole league, both the weaker and the stronger teams, would fail, because without a league no team can operate profitably.

It is particularly true in the National Football League that the teams should not compete too strongly with each other in a business way. The evidence shows that in the National Football League less than half the clubs over a period of years are likely to be financially successful. There are always teams in the League which are close to financial failure. Under these circumstances it is both wise and essential that rules be passed to help the weaker clubs in their competition with the stronger ones and to keep the League in fairly even balance.

The winning teams usually are the wealthier ones and unless restricted by artificial rules the rich get richer and the poor get poorer (as Commissioner Bell put it). Winning teams draw larger numbers of spectators to their games than do losing teams and from the larger gate receipts they make greater profits than do losing teams. With this greater wealth they can spend more money to obtain new players, they can pay higher salaries, and they can have better spirit among their players than can the weaker teams. With these better and happier players they will continue to win most of their games while the weaker teams will continue to lose most of their games. The weaker teams share in the prosperity of the stronger teams to a certain extent, since as visiting teams they share in the gate receipts of the stronger teams. But in time even the most enthusiastic fans of strong home teams will cease to be attracted to home games with increasingly weaker visiting teams. Thus, the net effects of allowing unrestricted business competition among the clubs are likely to be, first, the creation of greater and greater inequalities in the strength of the teams; second, the weaker teams being driven out of business; and, third, the destruction of the entire League.

In order to try to keep its teams at approximately equal strength and to protect weaker teams from stronger teams, a league theoretically might use a number of devices. It might (1) limit the bonus price which could be paid to new players, (2) give the weaker teams a prior right over stronger teams to draft new players, (3) prohibit the sale of players after a certain day in the playing season, (4) limit the number of players on each team, (5) limit the total amount of salaries which a team can pay, (6) give the lowest team in the league the right to draft a player from the highest team, when and if the highest team has won a certain number (three for instance) of consecutive championships, and (7) reasonably restrict the projection of games by radio or television into the home territories of other teams.

It is easy to see that the first six devices would make it easier for weaker teams to compete with stronger ones. The usefulness of the seventh device, however, in the protection of the weaker teams may not be so obvious, particularly since it prevents the weaker teams from televising into the home territories of the stronger teams as much as it prevents the stronger teams from telecasting into the home territories of the weaker ones. The evidence indicates that television audiences and sponsors have so little interest in games between weak teams that it is very difficult to obtain sponsors for outside telecasts of such games. Consequently, the weaker teams lose practically nothing by this television restriction. But they benefit greatly from it in that the restriction adds to their home game attendance by preventing potential spectators from staying at home to watch on television exciting outside head-on games between strong teams. The competitive position of the weaker teams is improved by this increase in home attendance, while the competitive position of the stronger teams is weakened somewhat by their inability to sell to sponsors the right to televise their desirable head-on games into the home territories of the weaker teams when the weaker teams are playing at home.

A large part of defendants' evidence was directed to the question of whether the televising of a team's own home games in that team's home territory has an adverse effect on attendance at these home games. The evidence on this point, particularly the evidence relating to the great decrease in home attendance of the Los Angeles Rams during the 1950 season when all its home games were televised at home, shows quite clearly that the telecasting of a home game into a home territory while the home game is being played has an adverse effect on the attendance at the game. This clearly indicates by implication that the telecast of an outside game, particularly a head-on game, also adversely affects attendance at a home game.

* * *

The greatest part of the defendant clubs' income is derived from the sale of tickets to games. Reasonable protection of home game attendance is essential to the very existence of the individual clubs, without which there can be no League and no professional football as we know it today.

This is not a case of one industry fighting the competition of another, as for instance coal fighting the competition of oil, or railroads fighting the competition of trucks, or moving pictures fighting the competition of television. Football provides a magnificent spectacle for television programs and television provides an excellent outlet and market for football. They both can use and indeed need each other. By working together intelligently each will be an important adjunct to the other. The objective of the clubs in agreeing to a television blackout of the home territory (except for the remote possibility of a home game telecast) during the day a home game is played is not to restrain competition among the individual clubs in the sale of television rights or competition among television stations and networks and advertisers and advertising agencies in the purchase of such rights. This particular restriction promotes competition more than it restrains it in that its immediate effect is to protect the weak teams and its ultimate effect is to preserve the League itself. By thus preserving professional football this restriction makes possible competition in the sale and purchase of television rights in situations in which the restriction does not apply.

The purposes of the Sherman Act certainly will not be served by prohibiting the defendant clubs, particularly the weaker clubs, from protecting their home gate receipts from the disastrous financial effects of invading telecasts of outside games. The member clubs of the National Football League, like those of any professional athletic league, can exist only as long as the league exists. The League is truly a unique business enterprise, which is entitled to protect its very existence by agreeing to reasonable restrictions on its member clubs. The first type of restriction imposed by Article X is a reasonable one and a legal restraint of trade.

II.

Is the restriction on telecasting outside games in home territories when the home teams are playing away games and telecasting them in their home territories illegal?

The reasonableness of this particular restriction must also be tested by its effect on the attendance and gate receipts of a team's home games. It is obvious that on a day when the home team is playing an away game there is no gate attendance to be harmed back in its home area and the prohibition of outside telecasts within its home area cannot serve to protect gate attendance at the away game, which is played in the opponent's home territory.

Several of defendants' witnesses attempted to justify the restriction with the opinion that it is necessary in this situation to protect the home team's "good will" by which they meant that the restriction is necessary to protect the home team from loss in gate receipts at subsequent home games. However, there is not one shred of evidence, not one specific example based on actual experience, to support this opinion which, more accurately stated, is nothing more than conjecture.

It is probably true, though not proved by the evidence, that the simultaneous telecasting of an outside game and an away game in the home area of the team playing away would result in a division of the television audience between the two games. Obviously the existence or the prospect of such competition would make the television rights to the home club's away games less attractive to sponsors and consequently less profitable to the club. But this does not concern attendance at football games. Indeed, the testimony of defendants' witnesses consistently indicates that the primary reason for the restrictions in this situation actually is to enable the clubs in the home territories to sell monopoly rights to purchasers of television rights to away games.

The record in this case contains no factual justification for Article X's suppression of competing telecasts of League games when, for example, the Philadelphia Eagles' away game is being televised in its home territory. Defendants' speculation or conjecture that without such restriction gate attendance would decline a week or two later at the Eagles' home game has little probative value. Article X's restriction on this type of competition is an unreasonable and illegal restraint of trade.

Charge upheld in part.

―――――

NOTES AND QUESTIONS

1. *Gate Protection Versus Radio Rights Protection.* In effect, Judge Grim ruled that it was lawful for the NFL to eliminate competition between member clubs when one was selling tickets to its live home games and another was selling a competing NFL game via television, but it was unlawful for the league to eliminate competition between two teams both of which were selling competing NFL games via television (or radio). What was the basis for this distinction? From an antitrust policy or Rule of Reason standpoint, does this distinction make sense?

2. *Presaging the Modern Rule of Reason.* Note that Judge Grim's decision presages the more nuanced and sophisticated Rule of Reason analysis courts would develop two decades later. In his discussion, Judge Grim reasons that the blackout to protect live gate was necessary to improve the weaker teams at the expense of the stronger teams. Is that an essential element in a competitive balance defense?

3. *Harm to Live Gate.* Do you agree that telecasting games of rival teams in the same league harms live gate in today's entertainment world?

1. COLLECTIVE SELLING OF POOLED RIGHTS AND THE SPORTS BROADCASTING ACT OF 1961

As is clear from *United States v. NFL*, the principal concern of the league as well as the district court was the perceived impact of television on the home team's game attendance, rather than on the financial value of potential television viewership and contracts. As a result, the precise decree entered in the case prohibited the National Football League and its clubs from adopting any rules or entering into any television contracts that restricted the area in which any team's games would be broadcast, *except* into a team's home territory on the day it was playing a home game.

In 1960, the American Football League (AFL) started up operations and immediately negotiated a league-wide television contract with ABC. At this time, each NFL club was still selling its television rights separately. The new NFL Commissioner, Pete Rozelle, believed that if the AFL was going to operate with the advantage of a league-wide television package, the NFL had to do the same. Such a contract, under which all clubs would share revenues equally, was becoming more important to the NFL because teams in the large markets were starting to obtain much greater revenues for their television rights than were teams in smaller cities. The resulting disparity in income, coupled with competition for players from the AFL, threatened the ability of small-market clubs to field good teams. Thus, Rozelle promptly negotiated a league-wide television contract with CBS. The NFL then petitioned Judge Grim to approve the new CBS contract.

Naturally, a provision of the NFL-CBS contract barred individual teams from selling television rights for their games to competing broadcasters. Judge Grim therefore held that the contract violated the terms of his 1953 antitrust decree. 196 F. Supp. 445 (E.D. Pa. 1961). The NFL went to the Congress and persuaded it to pass the Sports Broadcasting Act (SBA). Section 1 of the SBA, 15 U.S.C. § 1291, states that:

> The antitrust laws . . . shall not apply to any joint agreement by or among persons engaging in or conducting the organized professional team sports of football, baseball, basketball, or hockey, by which any league of clubs . . . sells or otherwise transfers all or any part of the rights of such league's member clubs in the sponsored telecasting of the games of football, baseball, basketball, or hockey as the case may be, engaged in or conducted by such clubs. . . .

Section 1292 made it clear, though, that the antitrust immunity conferred by § 1291 was only available to league-wide television contracts that limited "black-outs" of NFL games to those "home territories" in which a member club was playing a home game on the day of the blackout. At the time, the motivation of blackout rules was to protect home gate receipts and enhance the financial stability of the leagues by assuring equal distribution of broadcast revenues. *See* H. Rep. No. 87–1178, at 2–3.

These statutory prohibitions were supplemented by regulations issued by the FCC from 1971–2014. Initially designed to protect local free-to-air stations from out-of-market cable competition, the rules required a blackout if a team failed to sell a certain percentage of its tickets. *Amendment of Part 76 of the Commission's Rules and Regulations Relative to Cable Television Systems and the Carriage of Sports Programs on Cable Television Systems*, Report and Order, 54 FCC 2d 265, 285, ¶ 62. *See also* 47 C.F.R. § 76.111(a). In an order dated September 30, 2014, the FCC eliminated the sports blackout rules, finding they were no longer needed since television revenues had replaced ticket sales as the NFL's primary source of revenue. *In the Matter of Sports Blackout Rules*, FCC 14–141 at 10, ¶ 14 (2014).

———

Technological advances have generated a judicial exploration of the nature and limits of the Sports Broadcasting Act (SBA). They have also raised issues as to the application of § 1 to league contracts when the SBA does not protect them from rule of reason scrutiny. Evolving from a league playing only on Sunday afternoons, the NFL now features nationally-televised games on Thursday, Sunday, and Monday nights, and even late season Saturday games after college football's season ends. The long-time tradition remains that on Sunday afternoons, fans may watch one or two games targeted at their particular region by a national advertiser-supported television network.

Historically, fans would not be able to watch a Sunday afternoon game if it was not televised in their local market. Beginning in the mid-1990s, the NFL entered into an agreement with a satellite broadcast distributor, DirecTV, to offer fans a "NFL Sunday Ticket" package that lets them bring in through their satellite TV dish all of the games from around the country at a single subscription fee (now around $300). This would permit, for example, fans of the New England Patriots who had moved to New Orleans, or of the New Orleans Saints who had moved to Boston, to watch their favored team play every week whether or not the game was televised on a local cable or over-the-air channel.

NFL SUNDAY TICKET ANTITRUST LITIG. V. DIRECTV, LLC
933 F.3d 1136 (9th Cir. 2019)

IKUTA, CIRCUIT JUDGE:

Every Sunday during football season, millions of National Football League (NFL) fans tune in to watch their team play. If they live in the same area as their favorite team—such as Los Angeles Rams fans who live in Los Angeles—they can tune into their local Fox or CBS station to enjoy their team's game on free, over-the-air television. But if NFL fans happen to live far away from their favorite team—such as Seattle Seahawks fans residing in Los Angeles—they can watch every Seahawks game only if they purchase DirecTV's NFL Sunday Ticket, a bundled package of all NFL games available exclusively to subscribers of DirecTV's satellite television service.

The plaintiffs, a putative class of Sunday Ticket subscribers, claim that this arrangement harms NFL fans because it eliminates competition in the market for live telecasts of NFL games. Without this arrangement restricting the televising of NFL games, plaintiffs argue, the individual teams would create multiple telecasts of `each game and would compete against one another by distributing telecasts of their games through various cable, satellite, and internet channels. We conclude that at this preliminary stage, plaintiffs have stated a cause of action for a violation of Sections 1 and 2 of the Sherman Act that survives a motion to dismiss. We therefore reverse the district court's decision to the contrary.

I

To analyze the challenged arrangement between the NFL teams, the NFL, and DirecTV, it is necessary to understand the history of television broadcasting of NFL games. [The court reviewed *American Needle's* holding that the NFL is an association of "separately owned professional football teams," the initial independent licensing of telecasts by individual teams, the 1951 regulations subject to litigation in *US v. NFL*, rivalry from the AFL and the passage of the Sports Broadcasting Act, and the subsequent 25 years where the NFL teams pooled their telecasting rights to their games and sold them as a single package through free, over-the-air television. The court also reviewed the history of antitrust application to college football, not subject to the SBA.]

After *NCAA*, commentators documented the changes caused by the increased competition in college football telecasts. "With conferences and teams now free to sign their own deals, the number of televised college football games grew exponentially." Nathaniel Grow, *Regulating Professional Sports Leagues*, 72 Wash. & Lee L. Rev. 573, 617 (2015). Moreover, because college football teams could compete "against one another in the marketplace, broadcasters collectively pa[y] half as much for the rights to televise a larger number of games than the NCAA had previously received for its collective package." *Id.* By contrast, under the SBA, the NFL's control over the pooled broadcasting rights increased revenues from telecasting, *see* Michael A. McCann, American Needle v. NFL: *An Opportunity to Reshape Sports Law*, 119 Yale L.J. 726, 732 (2010), while decreasing the number of telecasts available to consumers, *see* Ariel Y. Bublick, Note, *Are You Ready for Some Football?*, 64 Fed. Comm. L.J. 223, 231, 234–36 (2011).

* * *

Courts considering challenges to the telecasting arrangements between sports leagues and satellite television services have concluded that " 'sponsored telecasting' refers to broadcasts which are financed by business enterprises (the 'sponsors') in return for advertising time and are therefore provided free to the general public." *Shaw v. Dallas Cowboys Football Club, Ltd.*, 172 F.3d 299, 301 (3d Cir. 1999).[1] Therefore, the SBA

---

[1]   **[Ed. note]:** The Third Circuit explained (172 F.3d at 301–02):

    [T]he NFL obtained in the 1961 Act an expressly limited exception to "the normal prohibition on monopolistic behavior;" one which permitted it to sell pooled rights to does not exempt league contracts with cable or satellite television services, for which subscribers are charged a fee, from antitrust liability. *Id.* at 303; *see also Chicago Prof'l Sports Ltd. P'ship v. Nat'l Basketball Ass'n*, 961 F.2d 667, 671 (7th Cir. 1992) (*Bulls I*); *Chicago Professional Sports Ltd. Pshp. v. NBA*, 95 F.3d 593, 595 (7th Cir. 1996) (*Bulls II*); *Kingray, Inc. v. NBA, Inc.*, 188 F. Supp. 2d 1177, 1183 (S.D. Cal. 2002).

[The court explained the current arrangements, whereby the 32 teams "entered into an agreement with the NFL ("Teams-NFL Agreement") to pool their telecasting rights and give the NFL the authority to exercise those rights, rather than exercising those rights individually." Then,] the NFL entered into two additional agreements licensing the teams' telecast rights: (1) "the NFL-Network Agreement," which governs "local games," and (2) "the NFL-DirecTV Agreement," which governs "out-of-market games."

Under the NFL-Network Agreement, CBS and Fox coordinate to create a single telecast for every Sunday-afternoon NFL game. Pursuant to that agreement, NFL owns the copyright in the telecasts. *See, e.g.*, U.S. Copyright Office, *NFL 2016 Season: Cowboys @ Packers, Week #6*, Reg. No. PA0002069024 (Jan. 4, 2017) (noting that copyright was held by the NFL pursuant to transfer "[b]y contract"). The NFL, in turn, permits CBS and Fox to broadcast a limited number of games through free, over-the-air television. These are the so-called local games.

Under the NFL-DirecTV Agreement, the NFL allows DirecTV to obtain all of the live telecasts produced by CBS and Fox, package those telecasts, and deliver the bundled feeds to NFL Sunday Ticket subscribers. Thus, Sunday Ticket subscribers have access to both local and out-of-market games.

As a result of these agreements, fans who do not subscribe to Sunday Ticket have access to, at most, two to three local games each Sunday afternoon, in any given geographic area. This means, for example, that Los Angeles fans would be able to use over-the-air cable to watch the Rams play the Chargers at 1:00PM E.T. on Fox, the Vikings play the Patriots at 1:00PM E.T. on CBS, and the Dolphins play the Cowboys at 4:00PM E.T. on CBS. But there is no option for NFL fans to watch any of the other 7 to 10 games played each Sunday afternoon which are not available on free, over-the-air television.

Fans who want to watch other out-of-market games cannot purchase games individually or by team, but are required to buy the entire package of NFL games. Additionally, in order to subscribe to the Sunday Ticket, consumers must also purchase a basic television package from DirecTV. In

---

sponsored telecasters and which expressly did not apply to subscription television. The NFL got what it lobbied for: it cannot now expect the federal courts to transform "narrow, discrete, special-interest" legislation [quoting the district judge] into a far broader exemption.

2015, the cost of a basic Sunday Ticket package was $251.94 annually for residential subscribers [in addition to the basic DirecTV package]. For commercial subscribers, the price varied depending on the capacity of the establishment, ranging from $2,314 to $120,000 per year.

II

* * *

The plaintiffs' consolidated complaint alleges that the defendants' interlocking agreements work together to suppress competition for the sale of professional football game telecasts in violation of Section 1 and Section 2 of the Sherman Antitrust Act. Specifically, the complaint alleges that absent the anti-competitive Teams-NFL and NFL-DirecTV Agreements, the telecasts broadcast solely on Sunday Ticket would be available through other distributors. Additionally, each NFL team could make its own arrangements for telecasts of its games, and could contract with competing distribution channels or media, including other cable, satellite or internet carriers or competing networks. As a result of competition, the complaint alleges, a greater number of telecasts of NFL games would be created, and those telecasts would be more accessible to more viewers at lower prices.

The district court dismissed the consolidated complaint for failure to state a claim under either Section 1 or Section 2 of the Sherman Act....

It is significant here that the defendants do not argue on appeal that the SBA applies to the Teams-NFL or NFL-DirecTV Agreements [and plaintiffs do not challenge the SBA's application to the NFL's agreements with Fox and CBS.]....Accordingly, our analysis of the complaint's allegations regarding those agreements is largely governed by the Supreme Court's decision in *NCAA*, 468 U.S. 85, which analyzed a similar league sport broadcasting arrangement under the Sherman Act, without any applicable statutory exemption.

III

[The court restated the basic elements of a section 1 claim outlined in Chapter 6. Recall that the court must accept all well-pleaded factual allegations as true to sustain the dismissal of the complaint under FRCP Rule 12(b)(6).]

A

[The court focused on the claim that the restraint injured competition.] An agreement between competitors (a horizontal agreement) satisfies the requirement of showing injury to competition if it reduces competitors' independent decisions about "whether and how often to offer to provide services," *F.T.C. v. Superior Court Trial Lawyers Ass'n*, 493 U.S. 411, 422 (1990), or fixes prices, *United States v. Socony-Vacuum Oil Co.*, 310 U.S. 150, 223 (1940), or otherwise limits competitors' "freedom to compete," *NCAA*, 468 U.S. at 106. In order to show that an agreement injures competition, a plaintiff must generally show that the defendants have market power within a relevant market, meaning that the defendants have "the ability to raise prices above those that would be charged in a competitive market," *NCAA*, 468 U.S. at 109 n.38. Alternatively, plaintiffs can show that a restraint injures competition if they plausibly allege "a naked restriction on price or output," such as "an agreement not to compete in terms of price or output." *Id.* at 109. An agreement between companies at different levels of a supply chain (a vertical agreement) may injure competition if it facilitates "horizontal collusion." *Brantley*, 675 F.3d at 1198.

B

In this case, the plaintiffs' allegations on their face adequately allege an injury to competition. The interlocking agreements at issue are similar to those that have historically required an exemption from antitrust liability by the SBA: they are "joint agreement[s]" whereby a "league of clubs participating in professional football . . . sells or otherwise transfers all or any part of the rights of such league's member clubs" in the telecasting of such games. 15 U.S.C. § 1291. This is the exact type of arrangement that Judge Grim concluded violated the Sherman Act—and, more importantly, that the Supreme Court held caused an injury to competition in the context of college football. *See NCAA*, 468 U.S. at 104.

Because we assume that the NFL's interlocking agreements are not protected by the SBA, the Supreme Court's decision in *NCAA* controls our analysis. . . . First, . . . the interlocking agreements in this case impose analogous limitations: plaintiffs assert that the Teams-NFL and NFL-DirecTV Agreements limit the "amount of televised [professional] football" that one team may televise because they restrict the number of telecasts made to a single telecast for each game.

Second, the Supreme Court noted that the agreements in *NCAA* provided that "[n]o member [college] is permitted to make any sale of television rights except in accordance with the basic plan." *Id.* . . . Just as the University of Oklahoma was forbidden from increasing the number of telecasts made of its games, so too are the Seattle Seahawks forbidden from selling their telecast rights independently from the NFL.

Third, . . . the NFL members vote to approve the contract between DirecTV and the NFL. Therefore, the complaint adequately alleges that the Teams-NFL Agreement is a "horizontal restraint—an agreement among competitors" that "places an artificial limit on the quantity of televised football that is available [for sale] to broadcasters and consumers." *Id.*

Finally, . . .the interlocking agreements restrain the production and sale of telecasts in a manner that constitutes "a naked restriction" on the number of telecasts available for broadcasters and consumers.

* * *

The defendants make a number of arguments against this conclusion. We consider each in turn.

1

First, the defendants argue that under *In re Musical Instruments & Equipment Antitrust Litigation*, 798 F.3d 1186 (9th Cir. 2015), it is necessary to analyze the horizontal NFL Teams agreement separately from the vertical NFL-DirecTV agreement, and when viewed in that light, the NFL-DirecTV agreement does not injure competition because it is an exclusive distribution agreement of the type that is presumptively legal. We disagree. . . .

Contrary to the defendants' argument, we are required to take a holistic look at how the interlocking agreements actually impact competition. [W]e conclude that the complaint adequately pleads that the vertical NFL-DirecTV Agreement works in tandem with the Teams-NFL agreement to restrain competition. The Supreme Court has held that a horizontal agreement among competitors to pool separate property rights and enter into an agreement to license their rights vertically can constitute a Section 1 violation. *See Am. Needle*, 560 U.S. at 201 (holding that an agreement among the NFL and its member teams to create an entity that jointly licensed their separately owned intellectual property constituted concerted action in violation of the Sherman Act). Accordingly, we reject the defendants' argument that we cannot view the effects of both the horizontal and vertical agreements working together.

2

Defendants further argue that plaintiffs have failed to allege an injury to competition because the production of the telecasts necessarily requires joint action, and therefore the restrictions are pro-competitive. According to defendants, each NFL game broadcast is a copyrighted work jointly authored by the NFL, the two competing teams, and the broadcast network, and the agreement of all participants is necessary in order to create the telecasts at all. Thus, defendants argue, the Supreme Court's decision in *American Needle* is inapposite because that decision concerned separately owned intellectual property, *id.* at 187, whereas here, the telecasts could only be created through cooperation between competitors.

We disagree. Defendants have failed to identify, and we are unaware of, any binding precedent requiring the teams and the NFL to cooperate in order to produce the telecasts.

[Here, the court reviewed the law discussed in Chapter 9 holding that "the underlying NFL game is not copyrightable subject matter" but that "the telecasts of sporting events are plainly copyrightable 'motion pictures' under the Copyright Act of 1976. 17 U.S.C. § 102(a)(6). Applying general copyright law, the court reasoned that "the team or network that creates the telecasts would be the sole owner of the copyright in the telecasts, absent some agreement to the contrary."]

In the absence of a legal requirement that the NFL teams, NFL, and broadcasters coordinate in filming and broadcasting live games, the Los Angeles Rams (for instance) could contract for their own telecast of Rams games and then register the telecasts for those games with the Rams (and perhaps the team against whom they are playing). Only the agreements that are the subject of plaintiffs' antitrust action prevent such independent actions. Thus, we reject the defendants' argument that *American Needle*, 560 U.S. at 190, is inapposite; here, like in *American Needle*, the agreements not to compete concern separately owned intellectual property, and impose an unlawful restraint on independent competition.

Indeed, the history of the NFL, as well as the practice in other professional sports leagues, supports our conclusion. As discussed above, prior to the passage of the SBA, the telecast rights in NFL games "were controlled by individual teams" and NFL teams routinely licensed telecasts of their games to television networks. *U.S. Football League*, 842 F.2d at 1346. Indeed, by the late 1950s, thirteen individual teams had signed contracts with either CBS or NBC and one team "had organized its own network." Additionally, in comparable sports leagues, namely the National Hockey League and Major League Baseball, "each team owns the initial right to control telecasts of its home games." *Laumann v. NHL*, 907 F. Supp. 2d 465, 473, 485 (S.D.N.Y. 2012); see also *New Boston Television, Inc. v. ESPN*, No. 81-1010-Z, 1981 U.S. Dist. LEXIS 15032, 1981 WL 1374, at *1 (D. Mass. Aug. 3, 1981) ("The copyright of the teleplays of all Red Sox games is owned by the Red Sox."). And in another form of media, radio broadcasting, plaintiffs allege that the NFL Teams already negotiate individual radio broadcasting contracts.

Therefore, we reject defendants' argument that the complaint fails to allege a Section 1 violation because the telecasts can be created only through cooperation among competitors.

3

Defendants next assert that plaintiffs' complaint failed to allege injury to competition because the NFL-DirecTV agreement did not reduce the output of NFL game broadcasts. From the supply side, defendants argue, every regular season NFL game is broadcast over free television in some geographic area, and therefore, the entire potential supply of NFL game broadcasts is produced and distributed to the public. From the demand side, defendants argue, NFL broadcasts receive the most views of any sports league; 202.3 million unique viewers watched an NFL football game in 2014.

* * *

The complaint alleges that defendants have limited output by restricting the quantity of telecasts available for sale, and that the NFL has set a uniform quantity of telecasts of football games—one per game—with no regard to the actual consumer demand for the telecasts. The plaintiffs plausibly allege that "if member institutions were free to sell television rights, many more games would be shown," 468 U.S. at 105, because an individual NFL team would "be free to sell the right to televise its games for whatever price it could get." *Id.* at 106 n.30 (quoting the district court's findings, 546 F. Supp. at 1318). "The prices would vary for the games, with games between prominent [NFL teams] drawing a larger price than games between less prominent [NFL teams]." *Id.* (quoting the district court's findings, 546 F. Supp. at 1318). We conclude that for purposes of determining whether plaintiffs have stated an injury to competition, the plaintiffs have plausibly alleged that the output in this case is the number of telecasts of games, and that the defendants' interlocking agreements reduce that output.

4

Finally, defendants claim that the complaint fails to allege injury to competition because it has not alleged a properly defined market in which defendants have market power. Defendants argue that the complaint failed to plausibly allege that they have market power in either the market for live video presentations of regular season NFL games or the submarket for out-of-market game broadcasts. We reject these arguments. Given that professional football games have no substitutes (as fans do not consider NFL games to be comparable to other sports or forms of entertainment), *see L.A. Mem'l Coliseum Comm'n v. Nat'l Football League*, 726 F.2d 1381, 1393 (9th Cir. 1984), the defendants in this case have effective control over the entire market for telecasts of professional football games. The complaint therefore plausibly alleges a naked restraint on output: that the defendants' interlocking agreements have the effect of limiting output to one telecast of each game, which is then broadcast in a limited manner, solely according to the NFL's agreements with CBS, Fox, and DirecTV.

We conclude that the complaint adequately alleges the element of injury to competition by alleging that the interlocking Teams-NFL and NFL-DirecTV Agreements injure competition.

C

[Discussion of "antitrust standing" omitted and monopolization claim omitted. Judge Smith's dissent on standing issues omitted.]

NOTES AND QUESTIONS

1.   *Cable Networks and the Sports Broadcasting Act.* Are league contracts with cable networks, satellite providers like DirecTV, or web-based streaming programmers covered by the SBA? By its terms, § 1291 extends antitrust immunity to a league's sale of pooled rights for "sponsored telecasting of games." The major sports cable networks such as ESPN, TNT, and Fox Sports are funded partially by subscriber's fees and partially by advertising revenues. In addition, the transmission by cable from event to television screen fits within the term "telecasting." The legislative history of the SBA, however, casts doubt on whether Congress intended to grant antitrust immunity to any league contracts other than those with the "free" over-the-air television networks. When the SBA was enacted in 1961, its chief proponent, NFL Commissioner Pete Rozelle, told Congress that "[T]his bill covers only the free telecasting of professional sports contests, and does not cover pay TV." *Telecasting of Professional Sports Contests: Hearings on H.R. 8757 Before the Subcomm. on Antitrust (Subcomm. No. 5) of the House Comm. on the Judiciary,* 87th Cong., 1st Sess. 36 (1961). In 1982, then-NFL counsel (and later Commissioner) Paul Tagliabue reiterated to a Senate Committee that "the words 'sponsored telecasting' were intended to exclude pay and cable. This is clear from the legislative history and from the committee reports. So, that statute does not authorize us to pool and sell to pay and cable." *Professional Sports Antitrust Immunity: Hearings on S. 2784 and S. 2821 Before the Senate Comm. on the Judiciary,* 97th Cong., 2d Sess. 41 (1982).

In light of these comments before and after enactment of the SBA, how should a court interpret the Act with respect to NFL television contracts with ESPN? With reference to the NHL's 1988–92 contract with SportsChannel America? With respect to any attempts to put the Super Bowl, or the NBA playoffs, or regular season games, on pay-per-view television?

2.   *Cable Contracts and the Rule of Reason.* If the SBA does not provide antitrust immunity for league broadcast contracts outside of free-to-air networks, under what conditions would these contracts, under a rule of reason analysis, violate § 1 of the Sherman Act? What is your judgment about the procompetitive and anticompetitive effects of the NFL Sunday Ticket package? How would you balance them?

3.   *Playoff Games.* Does an NFL restriction on the telecasting of a playoff game or the Super Bowl violate § 1 under the reasoning of *United States v. NFL*? If such restrictions are a violation, does the SBA exempt them? *See Blaich v. National Football League,* 212 F. Supp. 319 (S.D.N.Y. 1962) (No, and no).

4.   *Does the SBA Have Any Implications for League Revenue Sharing?* Article 10.3 of the NFL Constitution provides that all member clubs share equally in the league's television revenues. It was a major political accomplishment of new Commissioner Pete Rozelle in 1961 to persuade the Mara family (owner of the New York Giants), George Halas (Chicago Bears), and Dan Reeves (Los Angeles Rams) to agree to this policy, which transferred

significant dollar revenues from their clubs to those in smaller media markets. Similar suggestions over the years for this level of revenue sharing in other major sports leagues have been quickly killed by large market owners. Even though the legislative history makes it clear that one important rationale for the SBA was to allow NFL teams to share television revenues, does the SBA's language exempt the sharing of network television revenues? If not exempt, would such network revenue sharing, or the sharing of any other type of revenue (such as local radio and television revenues, gate receipts, luxury box rental fees, parking and concessions revenues, and trademark licensing fees), violate § 1?

5. *The SBA and Other Sports.* Section 1291 protects league pooled-rights contracts only in the "team sports of football, baseball, basketball, or hockey." If other leagues were to negotiate a league-wide contract with CBS similar to the NFL's original contract in 1961, would the SBA protect it? Is there any reason why any of these leagues should not have the same protection for their TV contracts as the NFL or NBA?

2. LEAGUE RESTRICTIONS ON THE SALE OF TELEVISION RIGHTS BY INDIVIDUAL CLUBS

In most professional sports leagues (other than the NFL), individual member clubs negotiate broadcast contracts for the majority of their games, with a minority of games televised pursuant to nationwide pooled-rights contracts. Local television rights sales account for a significant portion of each club's revenue and constitute the principal source of wide disparity in income among MLB, NBA, and NHL clubs. By way of illustration, the 2014 rights deals ranged from a $3.6 billion 20-year deal between the Lakers and Time Warner Cable to a $109 million 10-year deal between the Charlotte Bobcats and Fox Sports Carolinas.

In the 1980s, emerging satellite technology created local "superstations" whose programs could be shown nationwide, exacerbating revenue disparities among teams. A club whose local games are broadcast nationwide via a superstation is better off: it will share the higher broadcast revenues gleaned from advertising fees and cable subscription payments from viewers outside of the local market. However, the games are joint products of two clubs, and the broadcasts have the potential to affect adversely the overall value of rights to national contracts, as well as the value of each club's local broadcast rights. MLB clubs agreed to a scheme for sharing local revenues and requiring member clubs to contribute 42% of superstation revenue to that pot.

The NBA took another approach, beginning in 1991 when the NBA voted to reduce from 25 to 20 the number of games that it would allow individual teams to sell to "superstations"—local over-the-air stations whose signals are transmitted and shown on cable outlets throughout the country. The team most directly affected was the Chicago Bulls, which for the 1991–92 season had already sold to WGN the broadcast rights in 25 games. WGN and the Bulls brought launched a six-year litigation battle against the NBA's enforcement of the new rule, alleging that it was a horizontal agreement among the teams to limit competition among themselves in a way that restricted output in violation of § 1 of the Sherman Act.

The NBA sought to limit or bar superstation broadcasts of games sold by individual teams for two reasons. First, superstation telecasts allegedly cause weaker teams in smaller markets to suffer revenue losses (fewer tickets sold as fans stayed home to watch other games, and lower rights fees because of lower ratings for their own games). This competitive impact of superstation telecasts was particularly acute during the early and mid-1990s because of the tremendous popularity of then perennial NBA champion Bulls, led by Michael Jordan and Scottie Pippen. In fact, because WGN was available to about 30% of American homes, Bulls' games were viewed in an average of 650,000 homes. This was almost double the Chicago-only audience for the non-superstation Bulls' broadcasts on Chicago SportsChannel, and only slightly less than TNT's usual national cable audience of 750,000 homes under its league contract, although far less than NBC's 4.7 million viewers on regular-season Sunday afternoons.

Second, the NBA feared the impact of superstation broadcasts on the NBA's league-wide network contracts with NBC and TNT, again particularly against the popular games of the Bulls shown on WGN. The revenues generated by the league's television contracts, which all NBA teams share equally, were a crucial component (as much as 50%) of the lower-revenue teams' income.

CHICAGO PROFESSIONAL SPORTS LTD. & WGN v. NBA (BULLS I)
961 F.2d 667 (7th Cir. 1992)

EASTERBROOK, CIRCUIT JUDGE.

* * *

[T]he Sports Broadcasting Act applies only when the league has "transferred" a right to "sponsored telecasting." Neither the NBA's contract with NBC nor its contract with Turner Network Television transfers to the network a right to limit the broadcasting of other contests. Both contracts and, so far as we can tell, the league's articles and bylaws, reserve to the individual clubs the full copyright interest in all games that the league has not sold to the networks. As the "league of clubs" has not transferred to the networks either the right to show, or the right to black out, any additional games, the Sports Broadcasting Act does not protect its 20-game rule.

The NBA protests that such an approach is arbitrary. What if the league had assumed control of all broadcast rights and licensed only 20 of the Bulls' games to WGN? That would have been a "transfer" by a "league of clubs." What could be the point of forbidding a different mechanism (the rule limiting to 20 the number of games teams may sell to superstations) that leads to the same result? Other mechanisms to achieve similar outcomes abound. The league might have put a cap of 20 superstation games in its contracts with NBC and Turner, or it might have followed the path of professional baseball and allowed unlimited broadcasting over superstations while claiming a portion of the revenues for distribution among the clubs. (Sharing of revenues occurs in all team sports, although less so in the NBA than other leagues.)

Whether there are ways to achieve the NBA's objective is not the question. Laws often treat similar things differently. One has only to think of tax law, where small differences in the form of a business reorganization have large consequences for taxation. Substance then follows form. Antitrust law is no exception: agreements among business rivals to fix prices are unlawful per se, although a merger of the same firms, even more effective in eliminating competition among them, might be approved with little ado. Such distinctions are not invariably formal. The combined business entity might achieve efficiencies unavailable to the cartelists. But then the line in the Sports Broadcasting Act is not entirely formal either. Perhaps the reason the NBA has not commandeered all of the telecasting rights and sold limited numbers of games to superstations is that it cannot obtain the approval of the clubs to do this—for a change in the allocation of rights is apt to affect the allocation of revenues, making the bargaining problem difficult with 27 clubs. A league's difficulty in rearranging its affairs to obtain the protection of the Sports Broadcasting Act is one source of protection for competition.

What the NBA might have done, it did not do. The Sports Broadcasting Act is special interest legislation, a single-industry exception to a law designed for the protection of the public. When special interests claim that they have obtained favors from Congress, a court should ask to see the bill of sale. Special interest laws do not have "spirits," and it is inappropriate to extend them to achieve more of the objective the lobbyists wanted. What the industry obtained, the courts enforce; what it did not obtain from the legislature—even if similar to something within the exception—a court should not bestow . . .

III

[The appellate panel, assuming for the sake of this case that the NBA was a joint venture governed by the rule of reason, next assessed the league's market power.]

As the NBA points out, sports is a small fraction of all entertainment on TV, and basketball a small fraction of sports televising. Viewers of basketball games do not have qualities uniquely attractive to advertisers— and if they do, the advertisers can reach them via other sports programs and many other programs too. NBC advertises basketball games during sitcoms and other programs, implying that the market in viewers extends well beyond weekend sports programming. Higher prices, the hallmark of a reduction in output, are missing: advertisers pay no more per thousand viewers of NBA basketball than they do for other sports audiences, and substantially less than they pay per thousand viewers of other entertainment. During 1990 the cost per thousand viewers (CPM) of a regular-season NBA network game was $8.17. NCAA football fetched $11.50, and viewers of prime-time programs were substantially more expensive. The CPM for "L.A. Law" was $19.34, the CPM for "Coach" $13.40. The NBA hardly has cornered the market on the viewers advertisers want to reach.

According to the NBA, this means that its rules do not injure viewers or advertisers, and it makes more sense to understand them as ways to compete against other suppliers of entertainment programming, all of which—right down to the smallest producers of syndicated programs—find it in their interest to sell exclusive rights to a small number of episodes. The NBA contends that until it tried to adopt a rational structure for television it had a much smaller audience than it does now. During 1980 and 1981 CBS carried the final game of the championship series by delayed broadcast! In 1982 only five NBA games appeared on network TV. A "restraint" that in the end expands output, serves the interests of consumers and should be applauded rather than condemned. Rules keeping some popular games off superstations may help weaker teams attract the support of their local audiences, something that (like the sharing of revenues) in the longer run promotes exciting, competitive games. Teams in smaller markets depend more on live gate to finance operations that will compete with the Bulls, Lakers, and Knicks on the court. Rivalry makes for a more attractive product, which then attracts a larger audience—the very expansion of output that the antitrust laws foster.

A market defined by TV viewers is not the only way to look at things. The district court in *NCAA* defined a market of games shown. If "basketball games" are the product, then the NBA's plan cuts output by definition even if more persons watch the fewer (and more attractive) games shown on TV. The NCAA tried to persuade the Supreme Court that the plaintiffs should be required to establish power in a viewership market. The Court replied:

> We must reject this argument for two reasons, one legal, one factual. As a matter of law, the absence of proof of market power does not justify a naked restriction on price or output. . . . This naked restraint on price and output requires some competitive justification even in the absence of a detailed market analysis.

468 U.S. at 109–10. Although this passage is not entirely clear, we understand it as holding that any agreement to reduce output measured by the number of televised games requires some justification—some

explanation connecting the practice to consumers' benefits—before the court attempts an analysis of market power. Unless there are sound justifications, the court condemns the practice without ado, using the "quick look" version of the Rule of Reason advocated by Professor Areeda and by the Solicitor General's brief in *NCAA*.

The district court proceeded in this fashion, examining the league's justifications; finding each wanting, the judge enjoined the 20-game rule without defining a market. In this court, the league's lead-off justification is that the telecasting rule prevents the clubs from "misappropriating" a "property" right that belongs to the NBA: the right to exploit its symbols and success. The district court properly rejected this argument on two grounds. First, it mischaracterizes the NBA's articles and bylaws, which leave with the teams the intellectual property in their games. The NBA could acquire a property interest in all broadcasting rights but has not done so. The 20-game rule does not transfer any broadcasting rights to the league; instead it shortens the list of stations to which clubs may sell rights the teams concededly possess. Second, it has nothing to do with antitrust law. We want to know the effects of the TV policy on consumers' welfare, not whether the league possesses sufficient contractual rights that it has become the "owner" of the copyright. *See Continental T.V., Inc. v. GTE Sylvania Inc.*, 433 U.S. 36, 52–53 & n.21 (1977) (rejecting an argument that legality of restraints under the antitrust laws depends on the characterization of a transaction in the law of property). A cartel could not insulate its agreement from the Sherman Act by giving certain producers contractual rights to sell to specified customers. Agreements limiting to whom, and how much, a firm may sell are the defining characteristics of cartels and may not be invoked as justifications of a cutback in output. That the NBA's cutback is only five games per year is irrelevant; long ago the Court rejected the invitation to inquire into the "reasonableness" of price and output decisions. Competition in markets, not judges, sets price and output. A court applying the Rule of Reason asks whether a practice produces net benefits for consumers; it is no answer to say that a loss is "reasonably small." (What is more, if five superstation games is tiny in relation to the volume of telecasting, the benefits from the limitation are correspondingly small.)

[The court then addressed the NBA's argument that the reduction to 20 games that might be broadcast on superstations was justified as a restraint on "free riders."]

It costs money to make a product attractive against other contenders for consumers' favor. Firms that take advantage of costly efforts without paying for them, that reap where they have not sown, reduce the payoff that the firms making the investment receive. This makes investments in design and distribution of products less attractive, to the ultimate detriment of consumers. Control of free-riding is accordingly an accepted justification for cooperation.

Three forms of free-riding characterize the Bulls' telecasting, according to the NBA. First, the contracts with NBC and TNT require these networks to advertise NBA basketball on other shows; the Bulls and WGN receive the benefit of this promotion without paying the cost. Second, the NBA has revenue-sharing devices and a draft to prop up the weaker teams. The Bulls took advantage of these while they were weak (and through the draft obtained their current stars) but, according to the league, are siphoning viewers (and thus revenues) to their own telecasts, thus diminishing the pot available for distribution to today's weaker teams. Third, the Bulls and WGN are taking a free ride on the benefits of the cooperative efforts during the 1980s to build up professional basketball as a rival to baseball and football—efforts that bore fruit just as the Bulls produced a championship team, and which the Bulls would undermine.

Free-riding is the diversion of value from a business rival's efforts without payment. [For example, suppose there are two retailers of the same brand of electronic equipment who sell in the same neighborhood. If one provides an attractive showroom and hires salespeople to explain and demonstrate the equipment, the price of the product must build in these ancillary costs. If the other retailer simply sells the equipment off the shelf, without any ancillary services, it can sell at a lower price because it avoids these costs. Consumers can thus obtain all of the ancillary services for free from the first retailer, and then buy the product from the second at the lower price; this means that the second retailer has had a "free ride" on the services of the first. However, this will either force the first retailer to stop providing the services, which is detrimental to consumer welfare, or require the manufacturer of the brand to restrict the second retailer in some fashion, to prevent its free riding.] (brackets in original).

What gives this the name free-riding is the lack of charge. . . . Put the retailers in a contractual relation, however, and they could adjust their accounts so that the person providing a valuable service gets paid. When payment is possible, free-riding is not a problem because the "ride" is not free. Here lies the flaw in the NBA's story. It may (and does) charge members for value delivered. As the NBA itself emphasizes, there are substantial revenue transfers, propping up the weaker clubs in order to promote vigorous competition on the court. Without skipping a beat the NBA may change these payments to charge for the Bulls' ride. If the $40 million of advertising time that NBC will provide during the four years of its current contract also promotes WGN's games, then the league may levy a charge for each game shown on a superstation, or require the club to surrender a portion of its revenues. Major league baseball does exactly this and otherwise allows its teams access to superstations. Avoidance of free-riding therefore does not justify the NBA's 20-game limit.

* * *

Because of the way in which issues have become separated in this litigation, we do not decide whether revenue-sharing from superstation broadcasts is consistent with the antitrust laws. Needless to say, we also do not decide whether any of the cooperative arrangements by which the league hires the services of the players comports with the Sherman Act. (The National Basketball Players Association, concerned that we might do some such thing by accident, has filed a brief urging us to guard our tongues.) It is enough to say that if the league may levy a tax on superstation broadcasts, then there is no free-riding. And if the league may not levy a tax, then a direct limit with the same effect as a tax is unjustifiable. Either way the NBA comes up short, and under *NCAA* the failure of its justifications eliminates the need for the district judge to define a market.

The NCAA argued that restrictions on the number of games telecast spread revenues and exposure among universities, helping to produce balanced competition on the field and hence making the games actually telecast more exciting, to the benefit of fans. Distributing telecasts among schools served, in the NCAA's view, as a substitute for the draft and other controls professional leagues deployed to the same end. The Supreme Court found the argument unpersuasive. It is hard to see how similar balance arguments by professional leagues, which make the most of drafts, trades, and revenue-pooling to foster exciting games, could be more compelling. Unless the Supreme Court is prepared to modify *NCAA*, the district court did not commit clear error in applying the "quick look" version of the Rule of Reason and rejecting the NBA's arguments.

Affirmed.

The NBA's lawyers then tried a creative alternative to achieve the league's strategic objective of eliminating superstation output. They added a provision to the league's network contract with Turner Network Television (TNT) that prohibited all NBA teams from having their games televised on a superstation on the same night that another NBA game was being televised on TNT. The Bulls and WGN returned to Judge Will's courtroom to challenge this "superstation same night rule."

First, Judge Will rejected the NBA's effort to fit their revised scheme into the SBA exemption. He noted that neither the Bulls nor WGN had transferred game rights to the league or the league to any other party. As the Seventh Circuit affirmed, "the [SBA] applies only when the league has 'transferred' a right to 'sponsored telecasting.'" Moreover, because each team retains the right to televise on its particular over-the-air or cable outlet the *same games* that are televised by TNT, the league's transfer of rights to TNT cannot be characterized as exclusive." 808 F. Supp. 646, 648–49 (N.D. Ill. 1992).

As to the second issue, Judge Will ruled that the SBA would not apply, because TNT did not appear to be "sponsored telecasting."

> In its status as a cable television programming service, however, it is not clear that TNT constitutes "sponsored telecasting" as that term is used in the SBA. Although it is indeed a hybrid programming service, TNT is perhaps better characterized as subscription television for the following reasons. First, . . . a viewer must pay to receive TNT through the costs of hook-up fees, monthly cable fees and even additional monthly "premium cable" fees charged by some local cable operators for TNT. . . . Second, TNT derives its revenues predominantly from "subscriptions" [$232 million in 1991] as opposed to advertising revenues from paying "sponsors" [$138 million in 1991]. Third, prior and subsequent legislative history demonstrates that "sponsored telecasting" as used in the SBA is limited to free commercial television as opposed to cable. . . .

> . . . "Sponsored telecasting" is not expressly defined by either the SBA or by any subsequent case law. In its report on the proposed legislation, the House Judiciary Committee noted only that "[t]he bill does not apply to closed circuit or subscription television." While the plain meaning of the term "subscription television" in 1961 might arguably have referred only to a pay-per-view service, it seems equally likely that the term "sponsored telecasting" would not have included such hybrid services as TNT and ESPN. "Sponsored telecasting" in 1961 referred to "free" television—the national network and local over-the-air broadcasting provided at no direct cost to viewers. The NBA's attempt to construe TNT as such "sponsored telecasting" simply because it contains commercial advertisements and is not offered on a pay-per-view basis is unconvincing. . . .

Id. at 649–50. Because its contracts with TNT and NBC were about to expire after the 1992–93 season, the NBA did not appeal Judge Will's second ruling.

Rather, it tried a third time to legally insulate its arrangements to achieve its economic goals, by (1) amending the NBA by-laws (with the Bulls and Nets dissenting) to require teams to confer copyright in all game telecasts on the league; (2) assigning to NBC in its new television contract the exclusive right to televise all 1,100 regular season games, subject to NBC's agreement that, after selecting its 25 or so favored games, it would authorize the NBA to license Turner Broadcasting to telecast up to 85 games on its TNT cable and WTBS superstation channels; (3) permitting the NBA to authorize individual teams to telecast the remaining games on local channels—but never on superstations.

Once again, Judge Will found that this series of arrangements resulted in a superstation ban and remained unlawful. 874 F. Supp. 844 (N.D. Ill.1995). On the SBA issue, although the contract with NBC involved "sponsored telecasting," it ran afoul of § 1292's exception to the exemption by prohibiting the telecasting of games in certain areas, by limiting NBC to 25 games, and by prohibiting the games eventually reassigned to the teams from being broadcast on superstations outside the teams' local areas.

Judge Will then found the superstation ban to be illegal under antitrust law, using a "quick-look" Rule of Reason analysis. He reasoned that the league's arrangement obviously restricted broadcast output, while the league had not proven any significant procompetitive benefit. The judge did endorse the NBA position that charging some fee to the Bulls for superstation telecasts was appropriate in order to offset the free-rider effect. However, the fee could not be set at an unreasonably high level so as effectively to restrict output. *Id.* at 868–69. Judge Will ordered the NBA not to limit the Bulls to fewer than 30 superstation telecasts. He left it for the parties to try to negotiate the appropriate fee for those telecasts. Failing that, future litigation would be needed to determine if any fee the NBA in fact imposed was too high because it cut back on broadcast output; if so, the NBA would still be, *de facto*, in violation of § 1. The NBA appealed.

CHICAGO PROFESSIONAL SPORTS LTD. PARTNERSHIP & WGN v. NBA (BULLS II)
95 F.3d 593 (7th Cir. 1996)

EASTERBROOK, CIRCUIT JUDGE.

In the six years since they filed this antitrust suit, the Chicago Bulls have won four National Basketball Association titles and an equal number of legal victories. Suit and titles are connected. The Bulls want to broadcast more of their games over WGN television, a "superstation" carried on cable systems nationwide. The Bulls' popularity makes WGN attractive to these cable systems; the large audience makes WGN attractive to the Bulls. Since 1991 the Bulls and WGN have been authorized by injunction to broadcast 25 or 30 games per year. 754 F. Supp. 1336 (1991). We affirmed that injunction in 1992, *see* 961 F.2d 667, and the district court proceeded to determine whether WGN could carry even more games—and whether the NBA could impose a "tax" on the games broadcast to a national audience, for which other superstations have paid a pretty penny to the league. After holding a nine-week trial and receiving 512 stipulations of fact, the district court made a 30-game allowance permanent, 874 F. Supp. 844 (1995), and held the NBA's fee excessive, 1995–2 Trade Cas. ¶ 71,253. Both sides appeal. The Bulls want to broadcast 41 games per year over WGN; the NBA contends that the antitrust laws allow it to fix a lower number (15 or 20) and to collect the tax it proposed. With apologies to both sides, we conclude that they must suffer through still more litigation.

[The court first rejected the NBA's effort to fit its league rules within the Sports Broadcasting Act (SBA), through the new technique of transferring all broadcast rights to NBC and TBS/TNT, and having the latter return the vast majority of unused games to the individual teams, subject now to restrictions against selling those games to superstations like WGN. Echoing its earlier observation that the SBA must receive "beady-eyed reading" as a special interest exception to the antitrust laws, Judge Easterbrook asserted that "a league has to jump through every [SBA] hoop: partial compliance doesn't do the trick." The only way that the NBA could avail itself of the SBA was by itself taking over and selling broadcast rights in the games of the Bulls (and other) teams. However,] by signing a contract with NBC that left the Bulls, rather than the league, with the authority to select the TV station that would broadcast the games, the NBA made its position under the SBA untenable. For as soon as the Bulls picked WGN, any effort to control cable system retransmission of the WGN signal tripped over § 2 [of the SBA] which barred such restraints except within the home territory of clubs when they are playing.

[Judge Easterbrook next addressed Judge Will's ruling that, while the NBA did have the right to charge the Bulls a fee for sending its games out on a superstation, it should use as its calculation base the "outer market advertising revenues" that WGN generated from cable, and then split this in half with the Bulls. The upshot was that Judge Will cut the fee imposed by the league on the Bulls from roughly $138,000 to $35,000 a game.]

The district court's opinion concerning the fee reads like the ruling of an agency exercising a power to regulate rates. Yet the antitrust laws do not deputize district judges as one-man regulatory agencies. The core question in antitrust is output. Unless a contract reduces output in some market, to the detriment of consumers, there is no antitrust problem. A high price is not itself a violation of the Sherman Act. *See Broadcast Music, Inc. v. CBS, Inc.*, 441 U.S. 1, 9–10, 19–20, 22 n.40 (1979); *Buffalo Broadcasting Co. v. ASCAP*, 744 F.2d 917 (2d Cir. 1984). WGN and the Bulls argue that the league's fee is excessive, unfair, and the like. But they do not say that it will reduce output. They plan to go on broadcasting 30 games, more if the court will let them, even if they must pay $138,000 per telecast. Although the fee exceeds WGN's outer-market revenues, the station evidently obtains other benefits—for example, (i) the presence of Bulls games may increase the number of cable systems that carry the station, augmenting its revenues 'round the clock;' (ii) WGN slots into Bulls games ads for its other programming; and (iii) many viewers will keep WGN on after the game and watch whatever comes next. Lack of an effect on output means that the fee does not have antitrust significance. Once antitrust issues are put aside, how much the NBA charges for national telecasts is for the league to resolve under its internal governance procedures. It is no different in principle from the question how much (if any) of the live gate goes to the visiting team, who profits from the sale of cotton candy at the stadium, and how the clubs divide revenues from merchandise bearing their logos and trademarks. Courts must respect a league's disposition of these issues, just as they respect contracts and decisions by a corporation's board of directors. *Charles O. Finley & Co. v. Kuhn*, 569 F.2d 527 (7th Cir. 1978); cf. *Baltimore Orioles, Inc. v. Major League Baseball Players Association*, 805 F.2d 663 (7th Cir. 1986).

[The court's discussion of the single entity issue, and Judge Cudahy's concurrence on that issue, was excerpted above in Chapter 6, Section D. The conclusion was that, at a minimum, the district court judgment required reversal for consideration under a full rule of reason analysis. Thus, rather than proving anticompetitive effect simply by demonstrating that the number of NBA games on television was reduced, the plaintiffs would have to prove that the NBA had significant power in an economically relevant market.]

Substantial market power is an indispensable ingredient of every claim under the full Rule of Reason. . . . During the lengthy trial of this case, the NBA argued that it lacks market power, whether the buyers are understood as the viewers of games (the way the district court characterized things in NCAA) or as advertisers, who use games to attract viewers (the way the Supreme Court characterized a related market in *Times-Picayune Publishing Co. v. United States*, 345 U.S. 594 (1953)). College football may predominate on Saturday afternoons in the fall, but there is no time slot when NBA basketball predominates. The NBA's season lasts from November through June; games are played seven days a week. This season overlaps all of the other professional and college sports, so even sports fanatics have many other options. From advertisers' perspective—likely the right one, because advertisers are the ones who actually pay for telecasts—the market is even more competitive. Advertisers seek viewers of certain demographic characteristics, and homogeneity is highly valued. A homogeneous audience facilitates targeted ads: breakfast cereals and toys for cartoon shows, household appliances and detergents for daytime soap operas, automobiles and beer for sports. If the NBA assembled for advertisers an audience that was uniquely homogeneous, or had especially high willingness-to-buy, then it might have market power even if it represented a small portion of airtime. The parties directed considerable attention to this question at trial, but the district judge declined to make any findings of fact on the subject, deeming market power irrelevant. As we see things, market power is irrelevant only if the NBA is treated as a single firm under *Copperweld*; and given the difficulty of that issue, it may be superior to approach this as a straight Rule of Reason case, which means starting with an inquiry into market power and, if there is power, proceeding to an evaluation of competitive effects.

* * *

Vacated and remanded.

———

In December 1996, after six years of litigation on this subject, the NBA, the Bulls, and the Chicago Tribune (WGN) finally decided to compromise and settle their dispute, rather than expend even more legal resources in a full-scale rule of reason trial. The reported terms of the settlement permitted the Bulls to broadcast 35 of their games in the Chicago area over WGN, of which only 15 would go out over national cable as a superstation telecast. The league would share revenues from these national broadcasts through controlling some of the advertising spots, in return for dropping its proposed superstation tax. What do these terms indicate were the two sides' assessment of their relative prospects and benefits in settling rather than continuing to litigate this dispute? What we know for sure is that in the post-*WGN* era, the NBA was able to secure new contracts from NBC and TNT that raised the total of $275 million paid by the two networks in 1997–98 to $660 million for 1998–99 and for each of the following three seasons.

———

NOTES AND QUESTIONS

1.   *Doctrine After* Bulls. With the *Bulls* litigation finally at an end, what is the status of the various issues raised along the way concerning the interpretation of the SBA:

a.   What constitutes "sponsored telecasting?" Does the NFL's contract with ESPN qualify for the SBA? What about a league contract with a superstation like WTBS? With a premium channel like HBO?

b.   Does a league qualify for SBA protection if it incorporates a restriction on an individual team's sale of telecasting rights into a league contract with a network that is SBA-protected?

c.   Can a league avoid the limitations of the SBA by assigning exclusive rights in all games to the network, and then requiring the network to license back rights to games it does not televise to the individual clubs, but with restraints on when and how the clubs can allow their games to be telecast?

d.   What about NFL Network? Is it sponsored telecasting protected by the SBA? Is an SBA immunity required for a transfer of rights from the NFL to a wholly-owned entity?

2.   *Re-Evaluating the Sports Broadcasting Act*. Almost four decades after its enactment, is the SBA good public policy toward sports broadcasting? What

are the benefits secured by affording sports leagues this prerogative in the sale of their television rights? What has been the SBA's effect on franchise values? What are the costs of this policy? What effects has the SBA had on the number and price of games that fans can watch (in the NFL and in the NBA)? Are there other ways to secure the legitimate interests of the clubs while reducing any harmful impact on the fans? Consider the Sherman Act jurisprudence as set forth in the *NCAA* case discussed in Chapter 6.

3.   *Fees Versus Output Restraints.* After *Bulls II,* can a league charge a fee to an individual team for utilizing any source of revenue (*e.g.*, selling television rights or various stadium revenues) that arguably exploits the reputation and product of the league, without thereby violating antitrust law? Recall the "relocation fee" charged by the NFL to the Rams when it moved from Los Angeles to St. Louis. Does the same justification apply to such relocation fees? By what standard should a court judge whether a fee is legal or illegal? What does your answer imply for the concept of a league requiring any source of revenue to be shared (outside the express authorization by the SBA)?

4.   *More on Market Power Under the Rule of Reason.* Judge Easterbrook's opinions in the *Bulls* litigation illustrate the trend toward antitrust analysis founded on classical microeconomic theory. In his second *Bulls* opinion, Easterbrook held that market power was an essential element for a plaintiff to prove anticompetitive effects in a full-blown Rule of Reason case. Does the NBA have market power when selling the rights to telecast its games? What does market power mean in this context? How would a plaintiff go about proving it? Also consider the observation of Judge Richard Posner, who wrote in *Valley Liquors, Inc. v. Renfield Importers., Ltd.,* 678 F.2d 742, 745 (7th Cir. 1982), that firms without market power are unlikely to disserve consumers, and when they do, "market retribution will be swift." If the NBA were to disserve consumers, would market retribution be swift?

5.   *Sports League Decision-Making and Information Asymmetry.* Judge Will indicated on several occasions that there was no evidence that superstation telecasts actually injure other NBA teams by siphoning fans away from buying their tickets or watching them on TV. Indeed, he found that superstation telecasts have actually increased general interest in the NBA nationwide and thus enhanced the popularity of all NBA teams. If that judgment is correct, why is the NBA so adamant about abolishing superstation telecasts not controlled by the league? Are the other owners simply not as smart or perceptive as Judge Will, or do they have some ulterior unstated motive, or are they simply risk-adverse about policies that might harm their interests? Is that factual finding relevant to the case? Is a general insight from behavioral economics that people often over-estimate adverse effects of changes relevant to the analysis? If the NBA was correct that superstation telecasts were cutting into the television prices charged and revenues earned by many other teams, would that suffice to legalize its limits on those telecasts under the Sherman Act? If the benefits to the Bulls were greater than the harms to other teams, would the ban be lawful where the clubs could not agree on appropriate terms for compensation? If owners were acting from risk

aversion based on uncertain information, did the litigation serve an informative purpose?

6. *Broadcast Limits and Partnership Concepts.* The essence of the NBA's position was that efforts to limit or abolish superstation telecasts are legal because it is not unlawful for partners in a joint venture to adopt rules that limit the ways in which they are allowed to compete against one another in selling the very product that they jointly produce. Indeed, in general partnership/joint venture law there is a fiduciary duty on the partners not to compete against the venture or its other partners in the venture's line of business or to expropriate an asset belonging to the venture for the partner's own benefit without the permission of the venture. Is this a persuasive antitrust position?

Not surprisingly, Bulls (and Chicago White Sox) owner Jerry Reinsdorf did not challenge the underlying agreement among club owners to limit their "local" broadcasts to assigned geographic territories. Absent this agreement, of course, the Bulls would have been free to license their broadcasts anywhere. That agreement was later challenged in private class action litigation on behalf of sports fans, in the following case. Although this litigation also was settled, on the eve of trial, key antitrust issues were discussed by the trial judge in denying the defendants' motion to dismiss.

LAUMANN V. NHL
56 F. Supp. 3d 280 (S.D.N.Y. 2014)

SHIRA A. SCHEINDLIN, U.S.D.J.:

I. INTRODUCTION

Plaintiffs bring these putative class actions against the National Hockey League ("NHL") and various individual clubs in the league (the "NHL Defendants"); Major League Baseball ("MLB") and various individual clubs in the league (the "MLB Defendants") (together the "League Defendants"); multiple regional sports networks ("RSNs") that produce and distribute professional baseball and hockey programming;[1] two multichannel video programming distributors ("MVPDs" or "distributors"), Comcast and DIRECTV (together with the RSNs, the "Television Defendants" or "broadcasters"); Madison Square Garden Company and the New York Rangers Hockey Club (the "MSG Defendants"); and New York Yankees Partnership and Yankees Entertainment & Sports Network, LLC ("YES") (together the "Yankee

---

[1]   Several defendant RSNs are owned and controlled by defendant Comcast, several are owned and controlled by defendant DIRECTV, and two are independent of the MVPDs but share ownership with an individual club.

Defendants"). Plaintiffs allege violations under Sections 1 and 2 of the Sherman Antitrust Act (the "Sherman Act").

* * *

The Comcast Defendants, the DIRECTV Defendants, the NHL Defendants, and the MLB Defendants now move for summary judgment on the remaining claims. For the reasons that follow, all four motions are DENIED in full.

II. BACKGROUND

. . . The clubs within each League are competitors—both on the field and in the contest to broaden their fan bases. However, the clubs must also coordinate in various ways in order to produce live sporting events, including agreeing upon the game rules and setting a schedule of games for the season. Both leagues divide their member teams into geographic territories and assign each team a home television territory ("HTT") for broadcasting purposes. Neither the Comcast Defendants nor the DIRECTV Defendants played a role in the initial creation of the Leagues' HTTs.

The structure of the territorial broadcasting system is largely uncontested. By League agreement, each club agrees to license its games for telecast only within its designated HTT. The clubs then contract with RSNs through Rights Agreements. The Rights Agreements generally provide each RSN the exclusive right to produce a club's games and telecast them in the HTT.[13] The Agreements do not permit the RSNs to license telecasts for broadcast outside the HTTs. The Rights Agreements also require the RSNs to provide their telecasts to the Leagues without charge for use in the out-of-market packages ("OOM packages"). The clubs keep the revenue from their respective Rights Agreements. There are significant differences in the economic value of the various HTTs.

In order to produce the telecasts of live games, the RSNs invest in equipment, production facilities, and a large staff. They also produce "shoulder" programming such as pre-game and post-game shows. The RSNs then sell their programming to MVPDs like Comcast and DIRECTV through Affiliation Agreements, and the MVPDs televise the programming through standard packages sold to consumers within the HTT. Even when an MVPD agrees to carry a RSN, it does not always distribute that RSN throughout its entire territory. The MVPDs acquire the rights to broadcast the games subject to the territorial restrictions in the RSNs' agreements with the Leagues. The MVPDs black out games in unauthorized territories in accordance with those restrictions.

---

[13]   MLB 56.1 ¶ 93; Comcast 56.1 ¶¶ 6, 14; DIRECTV 56.1 ¶ 6; NHL Mem. at 5. Plaintiffs do not challenge the clubs' right to grant production and distribution rights for their own games to only one RSN (hereinafter "content exclusivity"). Such exclusivity is to be distinguished from the exclusivity established by the territorial rules, which prevent each RSN from televising its programming outside the HTT and protect it from competing with the programming of other teams' games within the HTT (hereinafter "territorial exclusivity").

Fans can watch out-of-market games in one of two ways. *First*, some games are televised nationally through contracts between the Leagues and national broadcasters like ESPN and Fox. The clubs have agreed to allow the Leagues to negotiate national contracts on their behalf. The Leagues' agreements with national broadcasters contain provisions requiring the Leagues to preserve the HTTs. The revenues from national broadcasts are shared equally among the clubs.

Second, the Leagues produce OOM packages in both television and Internet format. The television packages—NHL Center Ice and MLB Extra Innings—are available for purchase through MVPDs, including Comcast and DIRECTV. The Internet packages—NHL GameCenter Live and MLB.tv—are available for purchase directly from the Leagues. The OOM packages are comprised of local RSN programming from each of the clubs. As with the national broadcasts, revenues from the OOM packages are shared equally among the clubs.

Each of the OOM packages requires the purchase of the full slate of out-of-market games, even if a consumer is only interested in viewing the games of one team. The OOMs exclude in-market games to "avoid diverting viewers from local RSNs that produce the live game feeds that form the OOM packages." [Quote is from league pleadings.]

In sum, each RSN is the sole producer of its club's games[30] and the sole distributor of those games within the HTT aside from limited nationally broadcasted games. The OOM packages do not show in-market games to avoid competition with the local RSN. Additionally, the territorial broadcast restrictions allow each RSN to largely avoid competing with out-of-market games produced by other RSNs.

Internet streaming rights are owned by the Leagues and/or the clubs. The RSNs have no right to license their programming for Internet streaming directly. The Internet OOM packages are the primary way for fans to view games on the Internet. Additionally, some MVPDs have negotiated with the Leagues to provide Internet streaming of out-of-market games to subscribers of the OOM television packages. Internet streaming of in-market games remains largely unavailable to consumers.

* * *

V. DISCUSSION

* * *

B. The League Defendants Are Not Entitled to Summary Judgment

While territorial divisions of a market are normally per se violations, the Supreme Court has held that a per se approach is inappropriate in the

---

[30]   One exception is that the teams in each League have agreed to permit the visiting team to produce a separate telecast of away games.

context of sports broadcasting restrictions due to the necessary interdependence of the teams within a League. On the other hand, the procompetitive benefit of the challenged scheme here is not so obvious that the case can be resolved in favor of defendants in the " 'twinkling of an eye.' " Therefore the rule of reason is the appropriate standard in this case.

Plaintiffs have carried their initial burden of showing an actual impact on competition. The clubs in each League have entered an express agreement to limit competition between the clubs—and their broadcaster affiliates—based on geographic territories. There is also evidence of a negative impact on the output, price, and perhaps even quality of sports programming. Plaintiffs' expert, Dr. Roger G. Noll, attests that consumers pay higher prices for live game telecasts, and have less choice among the telecasts available to them, than they would in the absence of the territorial restrictions. Similarly, Dr. Noll estimates that the price of OOM packages would decrease by about fifty percent in a world without the restrictions. Finally, defendants have not argued in these motions that the Leagues lack market power.[112]

Defendants respond by identifying various procompetitive effects of the territorial broadcast restrictions. They claim that the rules: 1) prevent free riding, 2) preclude competition with joint venture products, 3) incentivize investment in higher quality telecasts, 4) maintain competitive balance, 5) preserve a balance between local loyalty and interest in the sport as a whole, and 6) increase the overall number of games that are telecast. Plaintiffs deny that the territorial rules serve the above interests and also challenge the validity of the interests in light of the territorial rules' overall economic impact on competition.

First, defendants argue that the territorial rules prevent free riding. Although avoiding free riding can be a legitimate procompetitive goal in certain contexts, it is not clear how free riding would pose a threat in this case. Defendants argue that the clubs would "free ride" on the popularity and publicity of the Leagues if they were permitted to license their games nationally. However, the same argument could be made for any revenue-producing activity that an individual team undertakes, including local ticket sales. Defendants also claim that the clubs would "free ride" off the OOM packages by nationally licensing individual club broadcasts, but it is the clubs and RSNs who create the programming in the first place. If anything, the OOM packages benefit from the labor and investment of the clubs and RSNs, not the other way around. Defendants' theory of free riding is unclear and unpersuasive.

---

[112]   *See* MLB Mem. at 12 n.22 (preserving the MLB Defendants' right to challenge plaintiffs' definition of relevant market and market power although "not addressed in this motion"); NHL Mem. at 3 n.3 ("While the NHL Defendants vigorously contest Plaintiffs' proposed market definition and the assertion that NHL Defendants possess market power in any cognizable market, they are not moving for summary judgment on these issues in this motion.").

Second, defendants argue that the Leagues have an unassailable right to prevent the clubs from competing with the "joint venture." However, no case cited by defendants stands for the proposition that a joint venture may always prevent its members from competing with the venture product regardless of anticompetitive consequences. Rather, in each case, the court concluded based on the facts presented that the restraint in question caused no actual harm to competition. "If the fact that potential competitors shared in profits or losses from a venture meant that the venture was immune from § 1, then any cartel could evade the antitrust law simply by creating a joint venture to serve as the exclusive seller of their competing products."

Third, defendants argue that territorial exclusivity encourages the RSNs to invest in higher-quality telecasts, including high-definition cameras, announcers, audio-visual effects, and related pre-game and post-game programming. However, the incentive for added investment is inflated profit stemming from limited competition. "[T]he Rule of Reason does not support a defense based on the assumption that competition itself is unreasonable." To the extent that the Leagues defend *content* exclusivity rather than territorial exclusivity, Dr. Noll predicts that increased competition would overall improve output and consumer satisfaction, an argument that applies with equal force to the quality of telecasts.

Fourth, defendants argue that the territorial restrictions foster competitive balance between the teams and prevent excessive disparities in team quality. Maintaining competitive balance is a legitimate and important goal for professional sports leagues. However, it is unclear whether the territorial restrictions at issue here really serve that purpose. On the one hand, the restrictions protect less popular clubs from competition with more popular teams in their own HTTs. On the other hand, the system requires small market teams to refrain from broadcasting in larger, more populous markets, while big market teams forego only smaller, less populous markets. It is not immediately clear whether the restrictions help or harm competitive balance overall.[120]

Defendants also claim that the revenue sharing aspects of the OOM packages and national broadcasts foster competitive balance. However, there is support in the economic community for the theory that revenue sharing in fact exacerbates competitive imbalance. Even accepting the premise that revenue sharing is beneficial, defendants have not explained why broadcasting contracts are a better mechanism than more direct, limited forms of revenue sharing.

---

[120]   *See* [Economist Roger Noll's declaration, at 117] ("Economic research provides no reason to believe that restrictions in competition for television rights contribute to competitive balance, no matter how balance is defined, and some reason to believe that these restrictions actually make balance worse.").

Fifth, defendants claim that they have a legitimate pro-competitive interest in maintaining "a balance between the promotion of [hockey and baseball] as [ ] national game[s] and the need to incentivize Clubs to build their local fan bases." Aside from the fact that these two goals appear to conflict, defendants have not explained what the ideal balance would be, or how they might quantify it. There is no objective measure the Leagues could aspire to attain. Therefore defendants cannot establish that this particular balance between local and national interests is better for consumers, or for demand, than the balance that would prevail in a free market. Moreover, the Leagues purport to bolster regional interest and team loyalty by consciously depriving consumers of out-of-market games they would prefer, which is generally not a permissible aim under the antitrust laws.

Finally, defendants argue that the number of telecasts created and broadcast is greater under the territorial restrictions than it would be in the plaintiffs' "but-for" world. According to defendants, while almost every game is currently available to consumers in one format or another (national broadcast, local RSN, or OOM package), a system dependent on consumer demand could not guarantee that every game would be available everywhere because less popular teams would struggle to get their games produced or televised on their own. Destroying the HTTs would also destroy content exclusivity because OOMs and both competing teams would be able to sell the same game in the same areas. As a result, RSNs would be loathe to give their telecasts to the Leagues to create OOM packages, depriving consumers of the ability to access any and all out-of-market games as they do now. Similarly, national broadcasters would refuse to enter into national contracts without the assurance of exclusivity. Because plaintiffs do not challenge the legality of the OOM packages or national broadcasts, defendants argue, the territorial system is also immune from challenge as a matter of law.

These arguments are far from compelling. Just because plaintiffs do not directly challenge the legality of the OOM packages and national broadcasts does not mean that preserving them is sufficient justification for the territorial rules. Even the complete disappearance of OOM packages would not necessarily cause consumer harm if the same content could be distributed in another form (such as by RSNs nationwide). The OOMs are simply one form of delivering the content to consumers—a form made necessary by the territorial rules themselves. Moreover, it is certainly conceivable that the OOMs would continue to exist absent the territorial restrictions, given the low added cost of creating the packages and the convenience of bundling to many consumers.

Defendants' assumption that market demand would be insufficient to ensure access to the same number of games is questionable. Indeed, the Television Defendants insist that the sports rights are so valuable that they would compete for those rights vigorously even in the absence of the territorial rules. Moreover, "[a] restraint that has the effect of reducing the importance of consumer preference in setting price and output is not consistent with th[e] fundamental goal of antitrust law." . . .

Defendants cite *Virgin Atlantic Airways Ltd. v. British Airways PLC,* [257 F.3d 256, 264 (2d Cir. 2001)] for the proposition that plaintiffs must identify a less restrictive alternative for any procompetitive effect defendants can identify, even if the overall effect on the economy is overwhelmingly anticompetitive. Such an interpretation, however, is inconsistent with the Supreme Court's mandate that "the essential inquiry [under the rule of reason] . . . [is] whether or not the challenged restraint enhances competition." Indeed, in *United States v. Visa U.S.A., Inc.,* [344 F.3d 229, 243 (2d Cir. 2003)], the Second Circuit balanced the alleged procompetitive and anticompetitive effects of the exclusivity rules before requiring the Government to propose any less restrictive alternatives.

* * *

C. The Television Defendants Are Not Entitled to Summary Judgment

1. Liability for the Vertical Agreements

The Television Defendants argue that downstream distributors who simply implement the restrictions of an upstream conspiracy through vertical agreements, without further involvement, cannot be deemed participants in the conspiracy as a matter of law. . . .

* * *

None of the decisions relied on by the Television Defendants held that a downstream entity must request or enforce a restraint in order to be liable for adopting it through agreement. Nor did they indicate that each party to an allegedly unlawful agreement must have equal or even substantial negotiating power in adopting the agreement's terms. Moreover, a downstream entity need not participate in the initial creation of the restraints in order to be liable for adopting them later. "It is elementary that an unlawful conspiracy may be and often is formed without simultaneous action or agreement on the part of the conspirators."

Indeed, it would defy common sense to require proof that the Television Defendants enforced the territorial restrictions when they knew that the structure would be secured through a series of parallel contracts effectively policed by the Leagues. . . . In 2008, MLB attempted to adjust the territorial lines to serve customers who could not watch local games, which would have required clubs and RSNs to cede some territory to the OOM packages. The Comcast RSNs vehemently opposed the proposal and sent the following letter to MLB:

If MLB were to adopt any new MLB rule permitting MLB Extra Innings and/or MLB.TV to be distributed in unserved or underserved portions of a club's exclusive home television territory, the scope of the exclusivity purchased by the RSN would be unilaterally changed and the financial impact on the prospects and performance of the Comcast RSNs (and, by implication, on the clubs whose rights they hold) would likely be immediate and significant. Accordingly, the Comcast RSNs are unlikely to consider favorably the release of any portion of a home television territory as to which an RSN currently has exclusive rights. In providing distribution information herewith, the Comcast RSNs specifically reserve all of their respective rights and remedies with respect to any change in MLB's current rules and practices that negatively impacts the clubs' respective home television territories and the breadth of the exclusive rights heretofore granted to their corresponding Comcast RSNs.

* * *

On the eve of trial, Judge Scheindlin approved a settlement of the class action, providing substantial fees to plaintiffs' attorneys and terms that could result in an estimated $200 million savings to consumers: a reduced price for the out-of-market package, a new option to subscribe at a $25 savings for out-of-market games of a single team, and an option to stream in-market games for those who already pay for a MVPD subscription.

A NOTE ON REVENUE SHARING

The continued use of exclusive broadcast territories after the *Laumann* settlement means that leagues (other than the NFL, where all television contracts are sold by the league) continue to struggle with the significant inequality in distribution of local broadcasting revenue. This constitutes a major source of inequality in club earnings. The problem is especially acute in MLB, where the disparity in local broadcast revenues has risen even faster than their absolute amounts, and the luxury tax is a limited restraint on the ability of broadcast-rich clubs to outspend rivals in smaller media markets. Because the clubs could no longer rely on the old reserve system to insulate equality of team playing talent from inequality in team earnings, the felt need for greater revenue sharing in Major League Baseball had become acute among small market teams. Understandably, the large market teams continued to resist the idea. Peter Bavasi, former president of the Toronto Blue Jays and the Cleveland Indians, recalled that when the subject of revenue sharing was brought up in league meetings, one of the owners of a large-market team would stand up, begin his comments with "Comrades!," and after embarrassed laughter the topic would quickly be dropped.

As detailed in John Helyar, LORDS OF THE REALM: THE REAL HISTORY OF BASEBALL (Villard, 1994), by the mid-1990s there was finally general acceptance among the owners of the value of significantly expanding the degree of revenue sharing. The small market teams secured the acquiescence of large market owners by threatening no longer to allow broadcasts from their home stadiums of games played by visiting teams like the Yankees and Dodgers. The larger market owners agreed to a new revenue-sharing formula in the spring of 1994, but only on condition that the players would accept the hard salary cap that the owners would insist upon in collective bargaining that summer, before and after the strike that eliminated that year's World Series. The players were not only strongly opposed to a hard salary cap (or tax), but were also concerned about the potential salary-constraining impact of a progressive revenue-sharing system. Finally, in December 1996, the owners ratified an agreement with the players for a luxury tax on high payroll teams and a somewhat less ambitious increase in the revenue-sharing system among the owners.

Ongoing revisions reflected in successive baseball collective agreements extended the principle of revenue sharing even further with an even more complicated set of arrangements. The complex scheme contains three main elements: (1) significant contributions from all net (deducting ballpark expenses) local revenues to a fund divided equally among all 30 teams, (2) additional payments required by high revenue teams to low revenue teams, and (3) new luxury payroll taxes on payrolls over fixed amounts. The most recent collective bargaining agreement creates a "progressive" luxury tax for teams exceeding designated payroll thresholds, up to 80% at the highest level ($290 million in 2022). MLB clubs continue to share local revenue under a complex formula designed to share money with smaller-market clubs.

3. VERTICAL INTEGRATION OF MEDIA COMPANIES AND ACCESS TO SPORTS BROADCASTING

When *United States v. NFL* was decided, clubs were licensing television rights to over-the-air networks or individual local over-the-air stations. For most of the past few decades, the dominant method of sports rights distribution was from rights holders (clubs or leagues) to programmers (including over-the-air networks like Fox, cable networks like ESPN, and internet programmers like MLB.com) to distributors (DirecTV, cable companies, internet companies). The ubiquity and improvements in internet-based streaming portends a further change, but as this book goes to print that change has yet to be fully manifested.

Antitrust economists have coined the term "serial monopoly" to describe the problems caused when consumers face limited competition at retail to buy products for which there are few close substitutes. Although economists usually focus on a nice geometric explanation of how prices are even higher than if a single monopolist is in charge of making and retailing the good, consumers often suffer even more serious harm from the bargaining costs that occur when the "upstream" and "downstream" monopolists can't agree on how to share the spoils. In the sports world, this has become unfortunately too well known to fans, when valuable sports rights are unavailable because their local cable or satellite dish provider (known as an MVPD or multichannel video programming distributor) is in a dispute with a rights seller.

For example, many of the Washington Nationals new fans were unable to view their favorite team for a significant period when the Montreal Expos relocated. To obtain the consent (based on claims of territorial exclusivity, and baseball's antitrust exemption) of Baltimore Orioles' owner Peter Angelos, MLB agreed to create a new entity, the Mid-Atlantic Sports Networks (MASN), to broadcast Nationals' games, with the Orioles initially owning 90 percent and paying the Nationals $20 million a year, and the Nationals' share eventually increasing to 33 percent. However, Comcast, the dominant local cable provider, refused to carry MASN games on its cable system because of the proposed price.

FCC regulations, 47 C.F.R. § 76.1301, prohibit MVPDs like Comcast from engaging "in conduct the effect of which is to unreasonably restrain the ability of an unaffiliated video programming vendor to compete fairly." MASN alleged that Comcast's refusal to carry Nationals and Orioles games constituted discrimination by Comcast against MASN, and in favor of other sports programming owned by Comcast. Under FCC regulations, an administrative law judge would have determined the issue; once the case was assigned, however, the parties reached an agreement for Comcast to carry these games at a price 5% lower than that demanded by MASN.

Several important issues arise from this problem. This regulation only applies to alleged discrimination by an MVPD like Comcast (owned by NBC Universal) that also owns sports programming. Is there a sufficient public interest in uninterrupted sports programming to warrant expansion of the FCC's mandatory commercial arbitration proceedings to cover all sports cases? For a number of years, over 70% of Los Angeles households lacked access to Sportsnet LA, a regional sports network with rights to carry Dodgers games. A similar legal issue concerns contractual obligations to consumers when MVPDs like Comcast or DirecTV lose retransmission rights. *See, e.g., In re Cablevision Consumer Litig.,* 864 F. Supp. 2d 258 (S.D.N.Y. 2012) (class action demanding partial refund where Comcast lost rights to NFL football for two-week period).

These issues are complicated by the MVPDs' traditional practice of requiring their customers who wish to purchase any programming other than basic free-to-air networks to acquire a package of 40–100 other programs for a single monthly fee. In turn, programmers then seek to bundle their highly popular and niche channels to compel MVPDs to carry as many as possible on their "basic premium" package. *See, e.g., Cablevision Sys. Corp. v. Viacom Int'l Inc.*, 2014-2 Trade Cas. (CCH) ¶ 78,836 (S.D.N.Y.) (denying Viacom's motion to dismiss claims for illegal bundling of various channels).

Just as contract negotiation problems between battling monopolists directly affect consumers, harm to consumers can ensue when a firm that operates in two different markets is able to use its power in one market to advantage its own products in a second market. This antitrust concern has been incorporated into communication regulation. The Cable Television Consumer Protection and Competition Act of 1992 includes various provisions to curb abuses of cable operator's "bottleneck monopoly power." Pub. L. No. 102–385, 106 Stat. 1460.

The FCC implemented this Act by issuing regulations barring MVPD discrimination against unaffiliated programming networks. Per these regulations, the Commission found that Comcast had improperly refused to broadcast the Tennis Channel as widely as its own Golf Channel and other sports programming. *See Tennis Channel, Inc. v. Comcast Cable Commc'ns, LLC*, 27 FCC Rcd. 8508 (July 24, 2012). In *Comcast Cable Comm., LLC v. FCC*, 717 F.3d 982 (D.C. Cir. 2013), the court reversed the FCC regulations. The majority, in an opinion by Judge Stephen Williams (a former antitrust professor), held that Comcast's decision was not "discriminatory" under the statute because passing on the cost to consumers of adding the Tennis Channel to its basic package would cost it money. Concurring, then-Judge Brett Kavanagh interpreted the statute more narrowly, requiring a determination that Comcast had market power "in the national video programming distribution market." Kavanagh observed:

> Not surprisingly given its procompetitive characteristics, vertical integration and vertical contracts are common and accepted practices in the American economy: Apple's iPhones contain integrated hardware and software, Dunkin' Donuts sells Dunkin' Donuts coffee, Ford produces radiators for its cars, McDonalds sells Big Macs, Nike stores are stocked with Nike shoes, Netflix owns "House of Cards," and so on. As Professors Areeda and Hovenkamp have explained, vertical integration "is ubiquitous in our economy and virtually never poses a threat to competition when undertaken unilaterally and in competitive markets." 3B Areeda & Hovenkamp, *Antitrust Law* ¶ 755c, at 6.

NOTES AND QUESTIONS

1. *FCC's Different Interpretation of § 616.* The FCC's interpretation of § 616 was significantly different than Judge Kavanagh's, a point of dispute not resolved by the panel majority. The FCC concluded:

> 41. Section 616 would serve no function if it existed simply as a redundant analogue to antitrust law. Nothing in the text of Section 616 indicates an intent to mimic existing antitrust law or the "essential facilities" doctrine. The legislative history, moreover, expressly repudiates such a design. . . .

> 42. Contrary to Comcast's arguments, our reading of the history of Section 616 reveals that it was designed to address specific concerns about vertical integration in the video distribution market. Congress was concerned that "vertical integration gives cable operators the incentive and ability to favor their affiliated programming services," thereby leading to reduced competition and diversity of programming. Congress considered prohibiting vertical integration altogether, noting that such an approach "has appeal," but ultimately decided that "[t]o ensure that cable operators do not favor their affiliated programmers over others," it was appropriate to "bar[ ] cable operators from discriminating against unaffiliated programmers." With this goal of protecting competition at its core, Section 616 is structured to prohibit discrimination on the basis of affiliation when such discrimination has the effect of "unreasonably restrain[ing] the ability of an unaffiliated . . . programming vendor to compete fairly."

2. *Is Comcast More Like Dunkin' Donuts or Sears?* Unlike Dunkin' Donuts, McDonalds, and Nike retail outlets, Comcast distributes a lot of programming produced by others and licensed by Comcast. Perhaps the better analogy would be to Sears, which offers its own blue jeans in addition to those made by Levi's or Lee. If Sears were the only retailer in town, however, and they only carried their house brand, consumers would be harmed. Likewise, if Sears contracted to sell only Lee jeans, excluding Levi's, and there were no other local retail outlets, there would likely be an antitrust violation. *Standard Fashion Co. v. Magrane-Houston Co.,* 258 U.S. 346 (1922). However, in reality, Sears could legally exclude Levi's, because consumers who wished to purchase Levi's could easily find them at other retail outlets.

In your view, is Comcast more like the only retailer in town, or like a retailer selling its own goods in competition with those of other retailers?

3. *Basic Premium or Sports Tier?* Most cable access disputes in the sports industry concern stalled negotiations over the cost per subscriber to placing a sports channel on the basic premium network. There are few issues concerning placing a sports channel on a special sports tier, where the MVPD is basically acting as a conduit for a specific monthly fee paid only by those channel's viewers. Why should *any* consumer have to pay for programming— be it Fox Sports 1 or the Disney Channel—that they don't wish to pay for? *See*

Warren S. Grimes, *The Distribution of Pay Television in the United States: Let an* Unshackled Marketplace Decide, 5 J. INT'L MEDIA & ENT. L. 1 (2013).

D. GROUP LICENSING OF MERCHANDISE AND RELATED INTELLECTUAL PROPERTY RIGHTS

While league sale of television rights is the most visible and financially significant illustration of the issues relating to a league's legal authority to pool and/or restrict its member clubs' intellectual property rights, essentially the same questions are raised by the sale of sports merchandising rights. All the North American leagues have largely centralized trademark licensing for merchandising purposes in a single league office to which every club assigns an exclusive right to market its team names and logos. (This is in marked and interesting contrast to the English Premier League, which maintains virtually no centralized marketing other than a league website that refers customers to each club's local site.) By 2016, the total consumer sales of merchandise bearing these league and team identities surged, with MLB revenue totaling $3.4 billion, with a 12% royalty for clubs.

The background source for this significant revenue is a legal system that gives clubs an exclusive property right to a variety of trademarks and copyrights associated with their teams; this system is the topic of Chapter 9, *infra*. This section focuses on the legal and policy issues concerning the ability of teams to come together to sell a single package of marketing rights to the highest bidder. In addition, because players retain some intellectual property—image rights and publicity rights, also discussed in Chapter 9—antitrust and policy considerations also apply to the collective sales of these rights by players associations.

An illustrative dispute relating to the degree of league control of intellectual property rights involves the NFL's marketing arm, NFL Properties, and the owner of the Dallas Cowboys, Jerry Jones. Among other complaints, Jones has objected to the NFL's system of dividing licensing fee revenues equally among all teams, while the Cowboys successful efforts to portray themselves as "America's Team" often leads their merchandise to account for more than 25% of total NFL sales. Jones argued that if he had the right to market the Cowboys' name and logo, he would be able to expand total Cowboys' sales and keep a lot more of the financial returns for himself. Jones was unlikely, however, to persuade three-fourths of his fellow owners to change the NFL rules as he wanted. Such intra-league competition would exacerbate revenue disparities between more popular and less popular teams, and would require other clubs to focus more time and attention on aggressively competing for merchandise as well as on-field success. In addition, league officials and other owners believe that overall revenue and economies of scale would likely diminish if the league replaced its centralized operation and marketing expertise with marketing efforts of club officials who may be more locally oriented.

In the summer of 1995, the Cowboys' owner sold to Pepsi, Nike, and American Express the right to use the name of the Cowboys' home, Texas Stadium, even though Coca Cola, Reebok, and Visa had paid NFL Properties large amounts for what was supposed to be the exclusive right to exploit the identity of all NFL teams, including the Cowboys. The league filed a $300 million lawsuit against Jones for allegedly having violated the Cowboys' contractual commitment to assign to NFL Properties the sole right to market the team's name and identity. Besides defending the contract claim on the ground that the identity of Texas Stadium was materially different from that of the Cowboys, Jones countered with a $750 million antitrust suit against his fellow owners, asserting that the agreement of the owners to give that exclusive merchandising authority to NFL Properties constituted an illegal "combination . . . in restraint of trade" under Sherman Act § 1. The matter was settled, allowing these particular deals to continue. Under revised rules, the teams and NFL Properties now can non-exclusively license marks and logos in several product categories, while in others the league retains the right to grant exclusive licenses to league sponsors.

A similar controversy arose in baseball in early 1997 when George Steinbrenner and his Yankees signed a $95 million sponsorship contract with Adidas. This deal promised the Yankees a far larger amount than its 1/30th equal share of a $325 million proposal that Nike and Reebok had together offered Major League Baseball Enterprises for sponsorship of the entire League. The Yankees and Adidas carefully worded their contract so as not to appear to infringe upon the league's exclusive authority over national and international merchandising and promotion deals. However, the MLB Executive Council judged that the sale inside Yankee Stadium of T-shirts bearing both the Yankees and Adidas logos did not come within the Yankees autonomy in its "Home Licensing Territory." In addition, the Council insisted that the Yankees-Adidas contract must include a "subservience clause" that would subject it to any future changes in the owners Agency Agreement regarding MLB Enterprise's or Properties' authority, which a three-quarters ownership vote could impose and bind the Yankees. For these and a number of other reasons, the Yankees and Adidas partnership filed a preemptive lawsuit, claiming that the entire MLB central merchandising system violated both federal and Florida antitrust law. MLB responded by suspending Steinbrenner from its Executive Council and the team from membership on any league committees. After significant pre-trial wrangling, the lawsuit was settled with MLB's exclusive licensees outfitting all on-field Yankee personnel, but Adidas becoming an MLB "marketing partner" for various other commercial opportunities.

The NFL and MLB owners were concerned that individual team exploitation of the merchandising market would increase revenue disparities in favor of the successful and popular teams, and would likely reduce the overall league revenues generated despite a broader use of team names on merchandise. Of course, the latter concern is precisely the goal that an antitrust-preserved competitive market is supposed to deliver to consumers—greater output at lower prices. There is no Sports Marketing Act that gives special antitrust immunity to leagues whose owners pool their team names and logos in a central league office that then licenses the right to outsiders.

———

In addition to collective marketing by clubs, many of the reported antitrust decisions in this area have involved players associations, all of which have persuaded almost all their player-members to assign to the union the exclusive right to grant licenses to use multiple players' names and images as a group ("group licensing" rights). Thus, any licensee that wants to use a designated number of players (it varies from three to six) from any major sports league for commercial purposes must acquire the players' publicity rights from the union, whereas merchandisers who want an endorsement from fewer players must still deal directly with the individual player(s). The revenues from these group licenses have become an important if not predominant source of revenues for the unions, and thus they vigorously defend these rights. *See, e.g., Gridiron.com, Inc. v. NFLPA*, 106 F. Supp. 2d 1309 (S.D. Fla. 2000) (individual licenses from over 150 players for separate webpages linked to Gridiron.com's home page fell within the group license agreement the players had signed with the NFLPA).

For decades, Topps Chewing Gum had dominated the market for the use of a player's likeness on a baseball trading card. For five dollars apiece, it signed up young players as they entered the minor leagues to a contract that gave Topps the exclusive right to use the player's name and likeness on cards that were sold alone or in combination with chewing gum or candy. This right was triggered when the player reached the major leagues and lasted for five years, at $125 a year. Topps then renewed the contracts for another small payment as they neared their expiration. When the increased popularity and sales of trading cards combined with the commencement of Marvin Miller's services as a professional union executive for MLBPA, Topps' plan was no longer sustainable. It agreed to a significant increase in royalty payments in return for exclusive rights to license cards. That license was upheld against antitrust attacks by Topps' competitors: *see Fleer Corp. v. Topps Chewing Gum*, 658 F.2d 139 (3d Cir. 1981).

To bolster its position in negotiations, the MLBPA subsequently obtained its members' agreement to authorize only the MLBPA to market their publicity rights on a group basis and not to renew any individual licenses inconsistent with this scheme. Topps responded with an antitrust suit, claiming violations of both §§ 1 and 2 of the Sherman Act. Following are the judge's reactions to both sides' motions for summary judgment.

TOPPS CHEWING GUM V. MAJOR LEAGUE BASEBALL PLAYERS ASS'N
641 F. Supp. 1179 (S.D.N.Y. 1986)

CONNER, DISTRICT JUDGE.

[The court initially reviewed the precedents studied in Chapter 6 where courts rejected claims that collective decisions in the sports industry were "group boycotts" that were *per se* illegal under § 1.]

The instant case differs from these classic cases in a number of important respects. First, in most of these cases the parties to the agreement were competitors of each other. This is a critical element. The per se rule is not applicable to boycotts that do not involve agreements among competitors. In this case, Topps does not and could not contend that the parties to the alleged boycott, the MLBPA and the major league baseball players, are in any sense competitors with each other.

Second, as noted above, in a classic group boycott, a group of businesses combine to exclude other competitors or potential competitors from their level of the market. Topps certainly does not compete with major league baseball players for the players' publicity rights. Topps merely purchases the rights from the players.

Topps contends, however, that it competes with the MLBPA for the players' publicity rights, and that the MLBPA has instigated the boycott in order to exclude Topps from the market except on those terms the MLBPA dictates. In light of facts set forth above, there can be little doubt that Topps and MLBPA are indeed engaged in a struggle for control of the players' rights. However, it is far from clear that Topps and the MLBPA compete economically at the same level of the market. Topps purchases the rights from the players and uses them in producing and marketing its products. Thus, it is a consumer of the rights. The MLBPA, on the other hand, does not purchase the rights from the players, and does not manufacture or market any products itself. It acts as an agent for the players in licensing manufacturers or distributors of products to use the rights. Thus, the MLBPA is more analogous to a wholesale distributor of the rights. Accordingly, it does not appear to function at the same level in the market as Topps.

Finally, a classic group boycott involves a type of arrangement that is so clearly and consistently anticompetitive that it is inherently illegal. As the Supreme Court stated recently, "[t]he decision to apply the per se rule turns on 'whether the practice facially appears to be one that would always

or almost always tend to restrict competition and decrease output.'"
Northwest Wholesale Stationers, 472 U.S. at 295 (quoting *Broadcast Music, Inc. v. Columbia Broadcasting Sys.*, 441 U.S. 1, 19–20 (1979)). I am not persuaded that the arrangement between the MLBPA and the players is one that clearly restricts competition. In fact, the MLBPA has made a strong argument that the arrangement will enhance competition for players' publicity rights for use on a group basis.

Because Topps has for many years managed to secure exclusive long-term licenses from nearly all minor and major league baseball players to use their photographs on trading cards sold alone or in combination with gum or candy, other companies have not been able to acquire similar licenses. Topps has by all appearances acquired its licenses by hard work and perseverance, and should not now be punished for having been successful in its competitive efforts. *See, e.g., United States v. Aluminum Co. of Am.*, 148 F.2d 416, 430 (2d Cir. 1945). Nonetheless, Topps' competitors are desirous of an opportunity to acquire the rights Topps holds. Topps contends that its competitors can acquire the rights in the same way Topps does—by soliciting ballplayers when they enter the minor leagues. But Topps' competitors have indicated that they are unwilling to do so since that course "would be too expensive, would take too long, and would have too little chance of success." Thus, there is currently little competition for the rights Topps acquires through its player contracts.

However, under the arrangement created by the players and the MLBPA, the tremendous expense, inefficiency, and risk in acquiring the full bundle of rights necessary to market a complete set of baseball trading cards is eliminated. A company interested in acquiring players' publicity rights would not have to solicit a contract from every individual who becomes a professional baseball player. Instead, Topps and its competitors could purchase the necessary grants from a single agent for all of the major league players. Topps' competitors apparently find this an appealing prospect, and would bid against Topps and each other for the rights Topps now acquires with little serious competition. Topps complains that this may drive up the price of the rights. But that is the natural consequence of increased competition for a limited supply of goods, and is not a ground for concluding that the arrangement between the players and the Players Association is necessarily illegal per se.

In view of the important differences between classic group boycotts and the arrangement at issue here, I conclude that *per se* treatment is inappropriate.

* * *

The first issue in any rule of reason analysis is to define the relevant market in which the competitive impact of the defendant's actions are to be examined. The parties here have devoted little attention to this question, and to the extent they have addressed it, they disagree. The

MLBPA appears to claim that the relevant market is that of publicity rights for all athletes and performers, whereas Topps contends that it is the market for the publicity rights of major league baseball players for use on a group basis. Thus, there is a disputed issue of material fact that precludes summary judgment.

Another issue in the rule of reason calculus is the intent underlying the defendant's acts. Here the MLBPA claims that its intent is to increase competition in the bidding for players' publicity rights, whereas Topps contends that the Players Association intends to obtain monopoly power over those rights. Again, this is a disputed issue of fact. Finally, rule of reason analysis looks to the effects of the defendant's acts on the relevant market. The MLBPA claims that its acts are procompetitive, while Topps asserts that it is being improperly foreclosed from competing for players' publicity rights. This is yet another question of fact. Summary judgment is obviously unavailable in these circumstances.

[For essentially the same reasons the judge dismissed the motions for summary judgment on the § 2 "monopolization" charge, and directed trials on both issues.]

Summary judgment denied.

————

The parties settled the litigation before trial, thus leaving unresolved the key legal issues posed by the case. The settlement produced a major change in the Topps-MLBPA-players relationship. Topps continued to sign individual baseball players to card licensing agreements, but these licenses were non-exclusive and paid the MLBPA directly as its members' agent for collecting and distributing their licensing fees.

————

NOTES AND QUESTIONS

1. *Applying the Rule of Reason.* Suppose the *Topps* case had gone to trial: how would you have ruled on the antitrust rule of reason issues? Should the MLB Players Association have enjoyed antitrust immunity under either the *Flood* baseball exemption or the statutory labor exemption considered in Chapters 5 and 7 respectively?

2. *Exclusive Contracts and the Rule of Reason.* Change the fact situation so that the MLBPA had made itself the sole agent for all its player-members' licensing rights (which is in fact the case today in all of the major sports for group licensing rights, except for a few star holdouts), as recognized in *Gridiron.com v. NFLPA,* 106 F. Supp. 2d 1309 (S.D. Fla. 2000), and that the Association had refused to renew the contract with Topps because another card manufacturer (*e.g.,* Fleers) was offering a large premium for an exclusive baseball cards contract. Would these hypothetical variations on the actual

scenario have exposed the Association to a much stronger Rule of Reason challenge?

———————

Another licensing-rights dispute involved NHL owners' efforts to require all clubs to migrate their websites to the league's centralized server. For years, NHL owners agreed to give the exclusive right to control the individual clubs' marks and licensing opportunities to the league for virtually all commercial purposes. Madison Square Garden, L.P., which owns the New York Rangers, objected to this arrangement, seeking to preserve its ability to sell merchandise with Rangers' logos and players' names outside the home arena and on the internet other than via NHL.com. MSG claimed that the scheme precluded the Rangers and other entrepreneurial teams from licensing arrangements with lower-cost or higher-quality licensees and from enhancing consumer options compared to those offered via NHL marketing arrangements. In *Madison Square Garden, L.P. v. NHL,* 270 F. App'x 56; 2008–1 Trade Cas. (CCH) ¶ 76,079 (2d. Cir.), the Rangers sought a preliminary injunction against the NHL's implementation of its new media strategy. The district court denied relief, and the court of appeals affirmed.

> The district court did not abuse its discretion in denying injunctive relief. First, it correctly determined that MSG failed to establish a likelihood of success or sufficiently serious questions under "quick look" analysis. "Quick look" is essentially an abbreviated form of rule of reason analysis, to be used in cases in which the likelihood of anticompetitive effects is so obvious that "an observer with even a rudimentary understanding of economics could conclude that the arrangements in question would have an anticompetitive effect on customers and markets." *Cal. Dental Ass'n v. FTC,* 526 U.S. 756 (1999). A court must abandon "quick look" and proceed to a full-blown rule of reasons analysis, however, "once the defendant has shown a procompetitive justification for the conduct." *Bogan v. Hodgkins,* 166 F.3d 509, 514 n.6 (2d Cir. 1999).

> We agree with the district court that "[i]t is far from obvious that [the NHL's ban on independent websites] has no redeeming value." Rather, the district court correctly cited "several procompetitive effects of the New Media Strategy." These procompetitive benefits preclude application of "quick look" analysis. *See Bogan,* 166 F.3d at 514 n.6 (briefly applying "quick look" but returning to Rule of Reason analysis, because the defendant offered "sound allegations of procompetitive benefit").

> The district court also did not abuse its discretion in finding that MSG did not establish a likelihood of success or sufficiently

serious questions under rule of reason analysis. Under rule of reason, a court must "determine whether restraints ... are reasonable in light of their actual effect on the market and their pro-competitive justifications." First, a plaintiff "bears the initial burden of showing that the challenged action has had an actual adverse effect on competition as a whole in the relevant market." "If the plaintiff succeeds, the burden shifts to the defendant to establish the pro-competitive redeeming virtues of the action. Should the defendant carry this burden, the plaintiff must then show that the same pro-competitive effect could be achieved through an alternative means that is less restrictive of competition."

MSG did not show that the NHL's website ban has had an actual adverse effect on competition in the relevant market. Nor did MSG demonstrate that the many procompetitive benefits of the NHL's restriction could be achieved through an alternative means that is less restrictive of competition. While there will certainly be substantive issues for the district court to address on the merits— for example, how the antitrust laws apply to the NHL as a sports league, and what the relevant market is in this case—the district court's conclusion that preliminary injunctive relief was unwarranted falls well within the range of permissible decisions, and did not constitute an abuse of discretion.

On remand, the district court granted in part the NHL's motion for summary judgment and dismissed all claims other than those relating to centralized assignment of rights to new media. The court found that MSG had waived its claims in various documents releasing the NHL and fellow owners from liability for NHL operations and activities, and that the waiver was not contrary to public policy.

With regard to new media concerns, the court denied summary judgment in a decision that was not particularly encouraging to the Rangers:

> At this early stage of litigation, there is no evidence in the record on the crucial question of market definition, let alone the inquiry into how the NHL actually operates as an economic actor in that market. . . . Therefore the NHL's arguments in favor of dismissal cannot be resolved at the pleading stage, and the motion is denied.

To be sure, MSG faces a tall order in making its case. This Court has already observed that agreements among parents of a joint venture not to compete in the market in which a joint venture operates have generally been upheld. *MSG I,* 2007 WL 3254421 at *6 n.7; *see also United States v. Addyston Pipe & Steel Co.,* 85 F. 271, 280–81 (6th Cir. 1898) (Taft, J.) (restrictions by parents were "of course, only ancillary to the main end of the union, and were to be encouraged"), *aff'd in part, modified in part on other grounds,* 175 U.S. 211 (1899). The reasonableness of the restraint, however, is evaluated under the rule of reason. *See MSG I,* 2007 WL 3254421 at *6 (observing that such agreements have typically been viewed as reasonable ancillary restraints); *Business Elecs. Corp. v. Sharp Elecs. Corp.,* 485 U.S. 717, 729 n. 3 (1988) (also observing that agreements not to compete are "classic" ancillary restraints).

2008–2 Trade Cas. (CCH) ¶ 76,346 (S.D.N.Y.).

MAJOR LEAGUE BASEBALL PROPERTIES, INC.
V. SALVINO, INC.
542 F.3d 290 (2d Cir. 2008)

KEARSE, CIRCUIT JUDGE:

Defendant Salvino, Inc. ("Salvino"), appeals from so much of a final judgment of the United States District Court for the Southern District of New York, Richard Conway Casey, Judge, as dismissed its counterclaims alleging that the organization and activities of plaintiff Major League Baseball Properties, Inc. ("MLBP"), as the exclusive licensing agent for Major League Baseball (or "MLB") clubs' intellectual property, violate § 1 of the Sherman Act, 15 U.S.C. § 1, . . . For the reasons that follow, we reject Salvino's contentions and affirm the dismissal of its antitrust claim.

I.   BACKGROUND

Viewed in the light most favorable to Salvino, as the party against which summary judgment was granted on the claim at issue on this appeal, the following facts are not in dispute.

[Salvino developed a plush, bean-filled toy bear representing various well-known sports personalities. It obtained licenses to use baseball player names and numbers from the MLB Players Association, but included some club logos without a license from MLBP. The latter, an entity in which each of the 30 current MLB clubs (the "Clubs") owns an equal interest, is, with limited exceptions, the exclusive worldwide agent for licensing the use of all names, logos, trademarks, service marks, trade dress, and other intellectual property owned or controlled by the MLB Clubs, MLB's Office of the Commissioner ("BOC"), and MLBP (collectively "MLB Intellectual Property"), on retail products. MLBP also acts as agent for the Clubs with respect to, inter alia, trademark protection, quality control, design services, royalty accounting, and auditing.

In October 1999, MLBP learned that Salvino had sold Bammers to the Arizona Diamondbacks baseball club with the Diamondbacks logo on them; Salvino had not obtained an MLBP license to use that logo. MLBP sent Salvino a cease-and-desist letter; Salvino responded by filing an antitrust claim in California. MLBP commenced the present federal trademark action (with attendant state law claims); the California lawsuit was consolidated with the New York litigation. Eventually, all of the parties' respective claims, except Salvino's counterclaims against MLBP, were either abandoned or settled. In the meantime, to the extent pertinent to this appeal from the district court's dismissal of Salvino's § 1 counterclaim, MLBP moved, following some three years of discovery, for summary judgment dismissing that claim.]

1. Major League Baseball

The Major League Baseball teams together produce an entertainment product—the "MLB Entertainment Product"—that consists of approximately 2,400 interrelated, professional baseball games per year played by the 30 MLB Clubs, leading to separate playoff games for the American and National Leagues and culminating each season with the World Series between the champion Clubs from the two Leagues. This entertainment product can be produced only by the Clubs operating together in the form of a league; it cannot be produced by any one individual Club, or even a few Clubs. While squads of players from a single Club could play each other, the organization of the Clubs into a nationwide league with geographic diversity and a common championship goal, pursued in a structured manner employing uniform rules of play, has created a vastly different and more marketable product than is created by scrimmages between squads of players from a single Club or even by ad hoc "barnstorming" games between Clubs outside of a large league structure.

The MLB Entertainment Product, for which cooperation among the Clubs is essential, affects the value of MLB Intellectual Property. For example, during the baseball players' strike in 1994 and 1995, revenues generated by sales of MLBP-licensed products decreased; after the strike ended and MLB games resumed, those revenues increased.

2. MLBP's Licensing and Policing Activities

MLBP was incorporated in 1966 by the then-existing MLB Clubs (under the name Major League Baseball Promotion Corporation) as a wholly-owned subsidiary of MLBE. Each of the current MLB Clubs owns an equal interest in MLBE and shares equally in its profits. Prior to the formation of MLBP in 1966, there had been no centralized source for the licensing of MLB Intellectual Property . . . [Some evidence suggested that the lack of centralization harmed MLB clubs' ability to participate in certain corporate promotional activities.]

When created in 1966, MLBP was given (a) the exclusive right to market and promote the official name and logo of Major League Baseball, (b) a non-exclusive right to license the names and logos of the National and American Leagues, and (c) the right to submit licensing proposals for Club marks to the Clubs for their approval. . . . In 1984, the Agency Agreement increased MLBP's authority by giving it the exclusive right—subject to limited exceptions—to license Club names and logos for use on retail products for national and international (*i.e.*, not merely local) distribution. In 1987, the Agency Agreement further expanded MLBP's authority, granting it the exclusive right (again with limited exceptions) to license Club names and logos for use on products to be sold at retail within the Clubs' respective local markets. Thus, since 1987, the retail sale of any products bearing an MLB Club's name or logos must be licensed by MLBP, even if the products are sold at a concession stand inside the Club's stadium.

[The court discussed the limited exceptions to MLBP exclusivity for a Club to grant licenses with respect to their own intellectual property: products that it gives away at a home game; intellectual property of the visiting Club in such a game may also be used on the "giveaway" product with the approval of the visiting Club and MLBP, use of its own marks to create home video products about the individual Club, to be sold or given away within the Club's home broadcasting territory (as defined for each Club in the Operating Guidelines), the use of its marks on hot dogs and similar items distributed or sold within its home broadcasting territory, and the right, within its home broadcasting territory, to use and license others to use its marks to advertise and promote the Club's cruises and fantasy, educational, or summer camps.]

3.   The Market in Which MLBP Licenses Compete

MLBP asserted the view, which Salvino criticized as "a self-serving view," that other sports leagues such as the NBA, the NFL, the NHL, and the Women's National Basketball Association, as well as non-sports entertainment purveyors such as Nickelodeon and Disney, are among MLBP's competitors in the licensing of intellectual property for use on retail products. For example, Team Beans, a competitor of Salvino that obtained licenses for MLB Intellectual Property from MLBP for use on plush toys, also held licenses to use trademarks from a variety of other licensors, including the Olympics, the NFL, the NHL, the MLB Players' Association, and NASCAR.

A market research study conducted for MLBP, whose goals included increasing game attendance, media audiences, and sales of MLB Intellectual Property, found that baseball does not compete with just one sport, or even only with sports. It found that the competitive arena for baseball is " 'a wide range of leisure and entertainment options that vary with target group and lifestyle.' " Thus, the MLBP 1996 Business Plans' list of MLBP's major competitors for intellectual property licensing included the following: branded apparel manufacturers such as Nike, Reebok, Russell, Champion, Big Dog, and No Fear; other sports entities such as the NBA, the NFL, the NHL, NASCAR, collegiate groups, and the 1996 Summer Olympics; and entities, such as Warner Brothers and

Disney, that offered licenses to use intellectual property relating to, *e.g.*, Looney Tunes, Power Rangers, Peanuts, Nickelodeon, Batman, SpaceJam, and Goosebumps.

[The court summarized evidence from plaintiff's witnesses that Salvino competed in a broad market against other producers of plush items as well as other sports collectibles. Wayne Salvino testified at his deposition that one advantage to Salvino of the NFL's centralized licensing structure was that NFL Properties offered a package of certain players and all team logos, allowing that entity to serve as a " 'one-stop shop.' "]

4. The Views of the Parties' Respective Economists

Toward the end of the discovery period, MLBP had taken the deposition of Salvino's expert economist, Louis A. Guth, who had prepared a report in which he opined that MLBP functions as an "economic cartel." The Guth Report stated that "MLBP quite likely exercises sufficient control over pricing licenses for use of club marks for plush toys and similar products so that these constitute a relevant market." In his deposition testimony . . . Guth stated that MLBP limits output and sets prices, and he opined that efficient licensing of MLB Intellectual Property could be accomplished through the use of less restrictive alternatives. He testified that the relevant market could be determined by conducting a "discrete choice survey" of consumers to determine whether changes in the prices of various products would affect the consumers' product preferences; however, Guth had conducted no empirical studies of any kind.

MLBP, in support of its motion for summary judgment, presented the April 11, 2003 report of its expert economist, Professor Franklin M. Fisher ("Fisher Report"), analyzing MLBP's functions and the product market within which MLBP operates, and disputing the views of Guth. Fisher opined, inter alia, that MLBP is not a cartel and should instead be viewed as a joint venture; that the relevant product market consists at the very least of licenses for all sports and entertainment intellectual property, rather than just for MLB Intellectual Property; and that the centralization of MLB Intellectual Property licensing and other functions in MLBP produces procompetitive efficiencies.

Fisher pointed out that "[t]he customers [for] MLB Intellectual Property are prospective licensees that use MLB Intellectual Property to sell products." Although Guth had suggested that the relevant market could be determined by conducting a survey to ascertain whether the product preferences of consumers were responsive to retail price variations, Fisher stated that "it is important to be clear that the relevant customers for MLB Intellectual Property are the prospective licensees of intellectual property and it is their demand and the alternatives that they face that determine the boundaries of the relevant market" "The demand of ultimate consumers for goods such as plush toys . . . that use intellectual property

. . . is relevant only because such demand influences the derived demand of direct customers, the licensees."

[Fisher also explained his conclusion that MLBP was a joint venture, and not a cartel, by noting that the value of MLB intellectual property is derived largely from the popularity of MLB, which is jointly created by the clubs. As an example, "no matter how successful the Yankees have been, the Yankees marks would have little value over time if the Yankees no longer competed with other Clubs in Major League Baseball. Indeed, the drop in popularity of former Club names, such as the Washington Senators, the Houston Colt 45s, and the St. Louis Browns, demonstrates this fact."

Fischer further observed that if clubs were acting solely as a cartel, they would set separate royalty rates for each club's license, to maximize overall profits. He concluded that "the very fact that MLBP does not do this indicates that it faces competition from other entertainment products and is not a cartel." At the same time, he opined that the Clubs' use of MLBP "achieve[s] numerous efficiencies and procompetitive benefits that would not exist if each Club managed and licensed its intellectual property independently." His testimony focused on "one-stop shopping" that saves transaction costs, on quality control and enforcement, and on how joint selling promoted competitive balance.

Finally, Fisher also opined that because the value of MLB Intellectual Property is dependent on the popularity of the MLB Entertainment Product, and the popularity of the MLB Entertainment Product depends in turn on the integrated efforts of the Clubs, the absence of centralized licensing could lead to various occurrences of what economists refer to as the "free-rider" problem, *i.e.*, one entity's cashing in on the efforts of another. For example, if the Clubs granted licenses directly, a Club that was popular because of its on-field success could cash in on its popularity even though its victories obviously could not have been achieved without the participation of other Clubs. . . .

* * *

Salvino presented no factual evidence to refute the evidence cited in MLBP's summary judgment motion. . . .

* * *

II. DISCUSSION

* * *

[The court rejected Salvino's claim that the MLB licensing agreement was a "naked" output restriction.] Salvino has pointed to no evidence to support its characterizations. It has not cited to any term of the Agency Agreement or to any other agreement. Nor is a reduction in output implicit in the Agency Agreement. The Clubs' agreement to make MLBP their exclusive licensor does not by its express terms restrict or necessarily reduce the number of licenses to be issued; it merely alters the identity of the licenses' issuer.

[Salvino sought to distinguish *Broadcast Music,* discussed in Chapter 5, on the basis that the challenged blanket license in that case was non-exclusive. The majority found that this distinction "loses significance in the context of the differences between the music and sports industries." In the majority's view, the "interdependent interests" of members of sports league distinguish MLBP from an association of individual music composers. This interdependence forecloses "the imposition of per se or quick-look liability." The majority also distinguished the *NCAA v. Board of Regents* case, discussed in Chapter 6.]

Whereas the Supreme Court noted that the NCAA did not act as a selling agent for those whose product was being sold, precisely the opposite is true of MLBP. A college that wished to have more than six of its games televised within a two-year period was forbidden, rather than helped, to do so by the NCAA. MLBP, in contrast, is the licensing agent for the MLB Clubs; it assists the Clubs in the licensing of their intellectual property.

Further, whereas the NCAA plan "create[d] a limitation on output" by limiting the total number of televised games and the number of times any one college's games could be televised, *NCAA,* 468 U.S. at 99, Salvino has not adduced any evidence of a limitation on the number of Club intellectual property licenses available here. . . .

* * *

Second, Salvino has presented no evidence to suggest that the licensing of MLB Intellectual Property is not entirely responsive to demand. MLBP does not issue licenses that are not requested; there is no evidence that an entity that wishes to obtain a license for particular intellectual property is required to accept or pay for a license that encompasses other intellectual property as well.

* * *

[Third, unlike *NCAA v. Board of Regents,* where the Court rejected the contention that the NCAA's restrictive television plan produced procompetitive efficiencies, here] the record shows that, similarly to the blanket licensing at issue in *Broadcast Music,* centralization of the licensing and protection of MLB Intellectual Property has produced many cost-savings and efficiencies. And, in contrast to the effect of the NCAA plan, . . . since the Clubs made MLBP their exclusive licensing agent for all retail products bearing MLB Intellectual Property, the number of licenses and licensees has multiplied.

Moreover, unlike the record in *NCAA,* the present record contains no facts to support Salvino's hypothesis that if MLBP were not the Clubs' exclusive licensor with respect to retail products, even more licenses would be granted. . . .

. . . unlike the NCAA restrictions on televising games, which were "not even arguably tailored to serve" an interest in competitive balance, 468 U.S. at 119, the Clubs' agreement that MLBP's profits from licensing MLB Intellectual Property will be distributed equally among the 30 Clubs is a precisely tailored attempt to achieve, or at least increase, competitive balance.

* * *

. . . Direct licensing by the Clubs, as recommended by Salvino and Guth, would result in the more popular Clubs granting more licenses and receiving more income for their intellectual property than the less popular Clubs would grant and receive. . . . (*See, e.g.*, Salvino brief on appeal at 30 ("If an organization is successful in . . . competition, then it should be entitled to reap the fruits of its acumen.") . . . [MLB expert Fisher replied that this] inequality in licensing income, however, would "over-compensat[e] the popular team for the joint efforts of all Clubs."

Further, the disproportionate distribution of licensing income would foster a competitive imbalance among the Clubs. The concept of "competitive balance" "reflects the expected equality of opportunity to compete and prevail on the field. Competitive balance also relates to the fans' expectations that each team is a potential champion—*i.e.* that each Club has a reasonable opportunity to win each game and also to compete for a championship."

[Because Salvino proffered no evidence that the centralization of licensing in MLBP caused any actual injury to competition or any evidence that MLBP possessed power in the relevant market, the claim fails under the Rule of Reason.]

SOTOMAYOR, CIRCUIT JUDGE, concurring in the judgment:

I concur fully in the judgment. I write separately because I believe the majority endorses an overly formalistic view of price fixing and in so doing avoids addressing directly the central contention of appellant Salvino, Inc. ("Salvino") that the exclusive arrangement between the Major League Baseball clubs (the "Clubs") and Major League Baseball Properties, Inc. ("MLBP") removes all price competition between the Clubs on the licensing of intellectual property in violation of the Sherman Act, *15 U.S.C. § 1*. Further, while I agree with the ultimate outcome of this appeal, I reach my conclusion using a different framework than the majority, applying the doctrine of ancillary restraints, which I believe more efficiently addresses the issues presented here.

* * *

Furthermore, the majority incorrectly believes that the licensing fees are "entirely responsive" to demand. A simple example displays the majority's fallacy. Take Club C, a Club that has two fans A and B. A is willing to pay $15 for a Club C hat while B is willing to pay $12 for the same hat. Assume that Producer P will sell Club C hats at its marginal cost to produce them of $10 and assume that MLBP charges a 20% license fee. Under this scenario, the price for a licensed hat would be $12.50 (price = $10/(1 − 0.20)), and only A would be willing to buy a Club C hat. However, if Club C was pricing its own licenses, it could drop the license fee to 15%, in which case both A and B would be willing to buy Club C hats for $11.76, and licensing revenue for Club C would increase from $2.50 to $3.52. As this example shows, the licensing fees here are not totally responsive to consumer demand. Basic principles of economics teach us that as royalty rates increase, the price for licensed goods will increase, and output will decline as fewer consumers are willing to purchase licensed goods at higher prices. This is Salvino's central contention—that if the Clubs were forced to compete with each other for licensing fees, they would offer licenses at lower rates, thereby resulting in lower prices (and increased output) for licensed goods.

* * *

The present dispute is significantly more complex than two competitors creating a "joint venture" for the sole purpose of fixing prices. Here, the MLBP joint venture offers substantial efficiency-enhancing benefits that the individual Clubs could not offer on their own, including decreased transaction costs on the sale of licenses, lower enforcement and monitoring costs, and the ability to one-stop shop (i.e., to purchases licenses from more than one Club in a central location). These procompetitive benefits, MLBP maintains, could not exist without the exclusivity and profit-sharing agreements, the two provisions challenged by Salvino as price fixing. In other words, MLBP argues that even if the effect of the exclusivity and profit-sharing agreements is to eliminate price competition between the Clubs, the purpose of these agreements is to achieve other significant procompetitive benefits, which outweigh any harm from the price restraint. We must decide then whether the Clubs' agreement not to compete with each other on price, which is price fixing in a literal sense, should nevertheless be reviewed under a rule of reason in light of MLBP's other efficiency-enhancing benefits. . . .

* * *

Joint ventures are typically evaluated as a whole under the rule of reason because the competitive effects of an individual restraint are intertwined with the effects of the remainder of the venture. However, under the doctrine of ancillary restraints, when a challenged restraint is not reasonably necessary to achieve any of the efficiency-enhancing purposes of a joint venture, it will be evaluated apart from the rest of the venture. [citations omitted]. This doctrine seeks to distinguish between those restraints that are intended to promote the efficiencies of a joint venture and those that are simply unrelated. . . The doctrine recognizes that a restraint that is unnecessary to achieve a joint venture's efficiency-enhancing benefits may not be justified based on those benefits. Accordingly, a challenged restraint must have a reasonable procompetitive justification, related to the efficiency-enhancing purposes of the joint venture, before that restraint will be analyzed as part of the venture. If none exists, the challenged restraint must be evaluated on its own and may be *per se* illegal even if the remainder of the joint venture is entirely lawful. . . .

In this case, the exclusivity and profit-sharing provisions of the MLBP agreement are reasonably necessary to achieve MLBP's efficiency-enhancing purposes because they eliminate several potential externalities that may otherwise distort the incentives of individual Clubs and limit the potential efficiency gains of MLBP. Most notable of these externalities is the so-called free-rider problem. Because of the interdependence of the Clubs within the setting of a sports league, free riding would occur if one of the Clubs is able to benefit disproportionately from the actions of Major League Baseball or other Clubs in the licensing of products. This may lead to inefficiencies because the Clubs' incentive to invest in the promotion and development of their intellectual property and other licensed products may be distorted. Both MLBP and Salvino recognize that without the exclusivity and profit-sharing provisions, these externalities could diminish MLBP's efficiency gains.[9] Indeed, Salvino's own expert, Louis Guth, admitted in his deposition, when asked whether there would be more or less licenses without the centralized control of MLBP, that he could not give a straight yes or no answer without empirical analysis because of these potential externalities. In other words, Guth conceded that the challenged provisions could have a procompetitive impact related to the efficiency-enhancing purposes of MLBP. Under such circumstances, the challenged restraints must be viewed as ancillary to the joint venture and reviewed under the rule of reason in the context of the joint venture as a whole. *See Rothery Storage,* 792 F.2d at 228 ("[E]limination of the free ride is an efficiency justification available to horizontal restraints that are ancillary to a contract integration.").

[Sotomayor, J., explained why she believes] the ancillary restraints framework is a superior method for analyzing the challenged restraints here because it effectively isolates when an exclusive arrangement should be reviewed under the rule of reason, as a reasonably necessary part of a

---

[9]   Salvino argues that "there are better ways to address" the externalities than these two challenged provisions. Whether the externalities could be eliminated in a substantially less restrictive manner is an inquiry that should generally be part of a rule-of-reason analysis rather than part of a per se or quick-look approach. *See, e.g., Care Heating & Cooling, Inc. v. Am. Standard, Inc.,* 427 F.2d 1008, 1012 (6th Cir. 2005).

joint venture, and when it should be reviewed as a naked restraint. Neither *Broadcast Music* nor *NCAA* offer much direct insight into the treatment of exclusivity agreements, except to emphasize the anticompetitive dangers of exclusive arrangements. . . .

Having concluded that the rule of reason is appropriate in this case, I concur fully with the majority's rule-of-reason analysis and agree that summary judgment was properly awarded to MLBP. . . .

———

Chapter 6 featured the landmark Supreme Court discussion in *American Needle,* which resolved for doctrinal purposes the question whether sports league rules should be characterized as a policy from a "single entity"—the league—or as an agreement among otherwise competing clubs. The merits of the lawsuit, which was an attack on the NFL's rule that gave an exclusive trademark license to a single clothing manufacturer, were remanded for further proceedings. The district court rejected motions for summary judgment and directed that the case proceed to trial. *American Needle, Inc. v. New Orleans La. Saints,* 2014–1 Trade Cas. (CCH) ¶ 78,729 (N.D. Ill.). First, the court conducted a "quick look" analysis that declined to condemn the exclusive licensing arrangement as obviously anticompetitive:

> defendants contend that the exclusive license arrangement encouraged additional licensee commitment and had numerous procompetitive effects, including improvements in product design, quality, distribution, and coordination of styles with other apparel items. These contentions are sufficiently supported by evidence and expert opinion to be facially plausible. The plausibility of the claims of procompetitive effect precludes abbreviated review of American Needle's claim. *California Dental Association [v. F.T.C.,* 526 U.S. 756, 778 (1999)].

Next, the court turned to the defendants' motion for summary judgment, first based on the plaintiff's alleged failure to establish an actual anticompetitive effect in a relevant market, as required under the Rule of Reason.

> Defendants assert that they are entitled to summary judgment because American Needle has failed to provide evidence of a proper product market that is sufficient to allow its claim to reach a jury. The court is not persuaded that such evidence is required here.

> "Since the purpose of the inquiry into market definition and market power is to determine whether an arrangement has the potential for genuine adverse effects on competition, proof of actual detrimental effects, such as a reduction of output, can

obviate the need for an inquiry into market power, which is but a surrogate for detrimental effects." *FTC v. Indiana Federation of Dentists*, 476 U.S. 447, 460–61 (1986) [internal citation and quotation marks omitted]. In the present case, American Needle has presented evidence that shortly following the execution of the exclusive arrangement between Reebok and NFL Properties, wholesale prices of licensed hats rose by a significant degree while output of those items dropped, and that the higher prices and lower output continued for years, never returning to their pre-exclusivity levels. These results are the direct anticompetitive effects that the Sherman Act seeks to prevent. *Law v. National Collegiate Athletic Association*, 134 F.3d 1010, 1019 (10th Cir. 1998), *Valley Liquors, Inc. v. Renfield Importers, Ltd.*, 678 F.2d 742, 745 (7th Cir. 1982).

Defendants contend that direct proof of detrimental effects obviates the need for market definition only in horizontal action cases, and that this is a vertical action case. This contention ignores the Supreme Court's holding that despite the teams' use of NFL Properties as the single agent to implement their marketing decisions, and despite the longevity of the arrangement, the decision of each of the NFL teams to grant exclusive licenses to Reebok was horizontal action. "[D]ecisons by the NFLP regarding the teams separately owned intellectual property constitute concerted action." *American Needle, Inc. v. National Football League*, 560 U.S. 183, 201 (2010). The presence of a vertical element of restraint in the form of the NFL Properties transaction with Reebok does not negate the horizontal element recognized by the Court.

Defendants also argue that American Needle's price increase analysis failed to properly assess various factors such as the quality mix of the products sold, but these arguments can be resolved only by determining which of the parties' competing inferences and experts is more credible. Such determinations are properly made by the trier of fact. The court finds that the evidence presented by American Needle would be sufficient to support a jury finding of a less competitive market following the exclusive licensing arrangement. As a result, the court also finds that American Needle need not make a specific showing of the relevant product market to survive summary judgment.

In addition, to the extent that a relevant product market definition could be considered a necessary element of American Needle's Sherman Act claim, the court is unpersuaded by defendants' contention that the market advocated by plaintiff is improper. . . .

. . .

To distinguish the market for NFL team hats from hats bearing logos of teams from other sports, American Needle has presented sales data showing that NFL hat sales are seasonal, rising with the start of the league's season and with the peak of its playoff season. It has also provided analysis purporting to show a lack of correlation between price increases for NFL hats and sales increases for other leagues' hats. Defendants argue with the validity of the analysis of American Needle's expert, but as indicated earlier, the court views this argument as raising issues not properly resolved on summary judgment.

The court noted that the Supreme Court had found college football games a distinctive market, and distinguished *Salvino,* excerpted above, because the entire case was prosecuted on a "quick look" theory rather than a rule of reason and the plaintiff "agreed with MLB's expansive market definition. 542 F.3d at 299–300."

On the eve of trial, the parties settled on terms they did not disclose. However, the NFL recently signed a new exclusive license with New Era for caps with team logos.

———

Throughout the twentieth century sports fans regularly experienced the value of new technology to enjoy the games they couldn't attend: from radio, to television, to cable, to VCR's. The computer and the internet have emerged as the predominant technology (so far) in this century. For example, in fall 2000 North American fans regularly used cyberspace to get the results of Olympic events taking place in Sydney, Australia, when it was the middle of the night on this continent. Thus, the International Olympic Committee (IOC) authorities enforced a rule that prohibited athletes from keeping a diary on their computers and releasing it over the Internet.

In 1997, the NBA, which had just settled the *WGN* lawsuit, established a much broader rule. The rule prohibited each team from operating its own website, and required the teams to assign all such functions and rights to the central league office to market and then share resulting revenues among all the teams. In early 2000, MLB and the NFL (though still not the NHL) adopted a similar policy for a single league website. The successful creation of Major League Baseball Advanced Media (MLBAM) is detailed in Andrew Zimbalist, IN THE BEST INTERESTS OF BASEBALL? THE REVOLUTIONARY REIGN OF BUD SELIG (Wiley & Co. 2006). Like the marketing arms of the other leagues, MLBAM is a distinct business entity owned by the major league clubs. However, in a significant departure from the typical governance structure, MLBAM is governed not by the entire ownership but by a Board of Directors selected by the owners (a committee of owners and an appointee of the Commissioner), who have a fiduciary duty to all shareholders to maximize the value of the company. Internet revenues have exploded during the last decade, making these entities even more significant in the future.

Owners of such small market baseball teams as the Kansas City Royals are hoping to experience the same kind of benefit from this new media as the Green Bay Packers, for example, secured in football from television four decades earlier. Indeed, MLB ex-Commissioner Selig even suggested that he might use his new powers (described in Chapter 1) to divide these revenues unequally among all teams, with larger shares for smaller-market teams. This means, though, that we may see essentially the same sports internet litigation that we did over the different league approaches to "pooling" the teams' television rights under general antitrust law. One key difference will be that there is no special Sports Broadcasting Act exemption for any type of collective selling of internet rights. Also, baseball will likely again face the question of whether its *Federal Baseball* antitrust immunity can and should cover this crucial new technology. In short, the entire range of issues noted above in the context of merchandising rights is equally presented in the context of internet rights.

———

NOTES AND QUESTIONS

1.   *Trans-Atlantic Marketing Differences?* Are North American hockey fans so very different than English soccer fans that a virtually complete centralization of licensing is most efficient on one side of the Atlantic Ocean, but a virtually complete decentralization is most efficient on the other? Why might club-run leagues select these options even if some mixed approach might be optimal?

2.   *Why Is Sports Marketing Bimodal?* Most business that operate with "franchises" have a mixed marketing scheme that attempts to optimally balance incentives for team marketing efforts without cannibalizing the national deals. Is antitrust scrutiny of this balancing effort appropriate? Are there any reasons that league owners would restrict each other's ability to market their club, other than legitimate interests in maximizing overall revenue for their league product?

3.   *Club Marketing Versus League Marketing.* Suppose that league owners in baseball or football were to adopt and enforce rules that blocked any loopholes in their merchandising programs that would permit "cherry-picking" of a few big-market and/or big-name teams. These loopholes might sharply reduce the ability of NFL or MLB Properties to negotiate valuable league-wide packages with sports footwear or other product companies that value a sports connection. Should Jerry Jones have been able to win his suit against his fellow NFL owners under antitrust law? Should George Steinbrenner have been able to sue MLB in the face of the special *Flood* baseball exemption from antitrust?

Should the Little Leagues (or their uniform manufacturers) be able to sue MLB for insisting on their purchase of a trademark license to use team names?

4. *Agreements Not to File Antitrust Suits.* In rejecting some of the New York Rangers' claims in their marketing dispute with the NHL, the district court applied a very complex body of caselaw that seeks to reconcile a policy in favor of permitting private parties to waive litigation rights and a policy that precludes members of a cartel from shielding their activities from challenge. She observed:

> Whether the enforcement of the release would violate public policy is a more difficult question. On the one hand, because "[a] no suit agreement may be one of the devices for shoring up a cartel," *see Sanjuan v. Am. Bd. of Psychiatry & Neurology, Inc.,* 40 F.3d 247, 250 (7th Cir. 1994), the Supreme Court has indicated that it would condemn as against public policy an agreement that "operated . . . as a prospective waiver of a party's right to pursue statutory remedies for antitrust violations," *Mitsubishi Motors Corp. v. Soler Chrysler-Plymouth, Inc.,* 473 U.S. 614, 637 n.19, 105 S. Ct. 3346, 87 L. Ed. 2d 444 (1985). On the other hand, despite a strong public interest in private antitrust enforcement, "this interest does not prevent the injured party from releasing his claim and foregoing the burden of litigation." *Richard's Lumber & Supply Co. v. U.S. Gypsum Co.,* 545 F.2d 18, 20 (7th Cir. 1976) ("A general release . . . is not ordinarily contrary to public policy simply because it involves antitrust claims.").
>
> Applying these well-settled principles to this case is complicated by the fact that MSG's challenge is to NHL policies, *i.e.,* restraints that form part of the structure of the joint venture and, indeed, in some cases, are built into the NHL Constitution. The Release is neither purely prospective (for this reason, the Release does not bar MSG's challenge to the New Media policy); nor is it purely retrospective in the sense that the League policies would continue to have effect after the Release's execution.

Madison Square Garden v. NHL, 2008 WL 4547518, at *7 (S.D.N.Y. Oct. 10, 2008); 2008–2 Trade Cas. (CCH) ¶ 76,346 (S.D.N.Y.).

5. *The Economics of Collective Licensing.* Do you agree with Professor Fisher's conclusion in *Salvino* that the fact that MLBP licenses all teams at the same rate, instead of charging more for a Yankees license than an Astros license, demonstrates that MLBP faces competition from non-baseball licensors? Given the strong political/business desires of club owners to split profits equally, can you think of any other reasons why MLBP might not choose to price different logos at different rates?

6. *The Merits of the NFL's Exclusive Licensing.* Consider now the merits of the challenge to the NFL's marketing policies in *American Needle.* A critical question is to identify the relevant market for licensing of intellectual property for merchandising purposes. Do you agree with the NFL's claim that it

vigorously competes in a highly competitive marketplace with all other clothing, or all other trademarked clothing? If so, restraining the ability of the Packers and Vikings to compete with each other in the sale of licensed merchandise is unlikely to affect competition. Do you agree with the plaintiff's claim that there is a market for "NFL merchandise," so that fans will switch patronage from one club's logos to another if the price is right? If the number of price-sensitive fans is too small to affect competition, and each club effectively has a monopoly for its own logo for its own avid fans, does this mean that there is no meaningful competition between the Packers and Vikings anyway, so that an agreement between the two of them has no anticompetitive effect?

7. *Antitrust Issues with Distribution of Licensed Merchandise.* Antitrust law's principal concern with exclusive distribution agreements focuses on whether the arrangements have the effect of foreclosing sources of supply to other retailers, or foreclosing sources of sale to other sellers. *See, e.g., Standard Oil Co. of California v. United States,* 337 U.S. 293, 314 (1949). Is sports merchandise so specialized that sales through Amazon and other third-party online markets have this effect on merchandise retailers? *See Casey's Distributing Inc. v. The Officer of the Commissioner, doing business as Major League Baseball et al.,* 1:22-cv-04832 (S.D.N.Y. June 9, 2022); *Santos et al. v. National Football League Inc. et al.,* 3:22-cv-00855 (N.D. Cal. Feb. 9, 2022).

E. BARGAINING DYNAMICS IN SPORTS LEAGUE DECISION-MAKING ABOUT COMMERCIAL PRACTICES

The formal topic of this chapter is antitrust scrutiny of sports league commercial rules, relating to ownership, the number and location of franchises, broadcasting, and licensing of intellectual property for sports-related merchandise. As with labor markets, studied in Chapter 7, Section D, these materials also provide rich insights into how the rules challenged in the cases studied in this chapter were enacted by the sports club owners who control the major decisions in North American sports leagues.

Two important insights by Ronald Coase are highly relevant to the bargaining dynamics of sports league governance. In "The Nature of the Firm," ECONOMICA 4 (16): 386–405 (1937), Coase wrote that the goal of reducing bargaining costs led businesses to operate within a single firm. Thus, it is less costly for General Motors Corporation to make and assemble most of the parts to an automobile, rather than have the General Auto Assembly Corporation contract with the General Auto Motors Corporation, the General Auto Chassis Corporation, the General Auto Axle Corporation, etc., for parts. This insight suggests that, if cost saving were the only concern, all sports leagues assets would be owned by a single company. For a variety of reasons (consider what they might be), the premier baseball competition is not organized by "MLB, Inc." but rather by a joint venture of independently owned clubs. Thus, rules concerning ownership, the number and location of franchises, broadcasting, and licensing of intellectual property for sports-related merchandise must be made by agreement among the owners. Moreover, many of these agreements require predictions of how business decisions will play out in the marketplace, now and in the future. As a result, league decisions involve *imperfect information* and *significant bargaining costs*. In *The Problem of Social Cost*, 3 J. L. & ECON. 1 (1960), Coase wrote that where information is imperfect and bargaining costs are significant, efficient practices may not result from the rules that govern behavior.

Sports leagues can minimize the problems caused by imperfect information and bargaining costs in a number of ways. As Coase demonstrated, when the net welfare of affected parties would be better off by a change in practices, those who are made worse off by the change can be compensated by payments from those who are made better off. If sports were run by a single corporation, the company's CEO could arrange payments in a manner designed to optimize efficient business practices of all economic actors within the firm. *See, e.g.*, Armen A. Alchian and Harold Demsetz, *Production, Information Costs, and Economic Organization*, 62 AM. ECON. REV. 777 (1972). The challenge for sports leagues controlled by club owners is to secure an agreement on these "side payments." The principal way in which today's leagues accomplish this goal is through revenue sharing.

We end this chapter with some exercises in bargaining dynamics. Re-read the introductory material on bargaining dynamics in Chapter 7, Section D, to consider how law, strategy, and dynamics would lead you to represent a stakeholder in these disputes more effectively.

First Exercise: Revenue Sharing

1. Is adoption of a rule providing for extensive revenue sharing "fair" to owners of teams in larger markets who purchased those teams before the rule was adopted? Is there a way of dealing with reliance on a property right to local revenues? *See* Louis Kaplow, *An Economic Analysis of Legal Transitions*, 99 HARVARD L. REV. 509 (1986), for a valuable analysis of this general type of problem.

2. Will extensive revenue sharing enlarge the total pie available to a league? Will this depend on which revenues are shared and the extent to which teams need to be given incentives to develop local markets? How could a revenue-sharing scheme be designed to maximize its contribution to revenue expansion?

3. Why would revenue sharing among owners have created concerns among players not only on the large market, but also on the small market teams? How could revenue sharing be designed to minimize any constraining effect on salaries from that source, particularly if the players have agreed to a direct salary cap or tax?

4. Suppose that after considerable thought and effort a new revenue-sharing scheme is devised, it proves attractive to a majority of owners, but it cannot get a necessary three-quarters approval because of opposition from the large-market clubs. Is it likely that a commissioner would step in under authority like the "best interests of baseball" authority studied in Chapter 1 to impose his revenue-sharing views?

Second Exercise: Ownership Policies

The infamous racist recordings of Los Angeles Clippers' owner Donald Sterling's opinions about his mistress' choice of escorts to basketball games led to his exclusion from the game under the broad powers conferred upon NBA Commissioner Adam Silver, discussed in Chapter 1. But consider Sterling's business practices wholly separate from racist behavior. Back in 2000, Sports Illustrated ran a story concluding that the franchise's "helplessness, so practiced and so dependable, is clearly the work of just one man—we're thinking of Donald Sterling here." Richard Hoffer, "The Loss Generation," *Sports Illustrated*, Apr. 17, 2000 at 58. SI investigative reporter George Dohrmann subsequently reviewed Sterling's record when the team was in San Diego, before the NBA settled litigation agreeing to allow Sterling to operate in Los Angeles. Incidents included policies to discourage live attendance (to hold down on security and stadium personnel), relying solely on television revenue; directing employees to disregard league rules; hiring as a de facto chief financial officer a woman he had met at the Playboy Club; failing to contribute to league pension funds; failing to pay players; making numerous player personnel decisions to save money rather than field a competitive team; and slicing scouting expenditures. "Recently banned Donald Sterling has long history of clashing with NBA," *available at* http://www.si.com/nba/2014/05/30/donald-sterling-history (updated June 23, 2014).

1. In *NASL v. NFL*, discussed in Section A, the Second Circuit recognized that new owners must be approved by a majority of other owners because "of the economic interdependence of major league team owners" and the "importance of obtaining the loyalty of partners in promoting a common business venture." Why did Sterling's fellow owners tolerate his mismanagement? If you owned an NBA franchise, would you rather have the Clippers managed by Donald Sterling or Microsoft executive Steve Ballmer?

2. In addition to fans, are there others who would benefit if the Clippers were well run?

3. Prior to the scandal, how might you advise a wealthy Angeleno who wanted to buy the Clippers on ways to persuade the league to force Sterling to sell?

Third Exercise: Franchise Relocation

Recall that when the Phoenix Coyotes were insolvent, there were two offers rejected by the bankruptcy judge: a $212.5 million offer from a Canadian bidder, conditioned on his relocating the team to Hamilton, Ontario, and a $140 million from the NHL to keep the team in Phoenix. The club was later sold to IceArizona for $170 million. Consider the following alternative explanations for this outcome, and develop ideas for how those seeking another result (hockey fans in Hamilton, creditors seeking the highest bid, broadcasters seeking the highest ratings, or others) might have changed the result.

1. Higher locally-generated revenues in Hamilton (live gate, local television and radio, and profits on retail sales operations) are estimated to be worth the extra $42.5 million, but the other NHL owners had personal disdain for the Canadian bidder.

2. Relocation to Hamilton would result in lower locally-generated revenues in Toronto and Buffalo, which were greater than $42.5 million.

3. Relocation to Hamilton would result in lower locally-generated revenues in Toronto and Buffalo, which were less than $42.5 million, but the parties could not agree on the amount to make the Maple Leafs and Sabres whole.

4. NHL Commissioner Gary Bettman believed that the addition of another Canadian team would add little to the league's contracts with the national Canadian broadcasters, but the loss of an American Sunbelt team would harm the NHL's contract with NBC.

Fourth Exercise: New Entry

The actual history of baseball in Milwaukee featured the relocation of the Boston Braves to the Midwest in 1953 and their relocation again to Atlanta in 1966, followed by the acquisition by automobile dealer Bud Selig of the bankrupt Seattle Pilots in 1970 and their relocation to Milwaukee as the Brewers. Suppose, however, that Seattle remained a viable MLB city (as it became later when the American League added a second Seattle expansion team, the Mariners, in 1977). If you were Selig's counsel in 1971, how would you advise him to pursue his dream of bringing baseball back to Milwaukee?

1. Owners and fans in Milwaukee would obviously gain from another expansion. Who would be less well off if the American League expanded? Could they be compensated?

2. Are there others who would be better off with an expansion? How might they influence the owners to add another team?

Fifth Exercise: Internet Baseball

As discussed in the *Laumann* case *supra,* in years past the only way to watch local baseball games was through a full digital subscription to your local cable retailer or DirecTV. In some cases, these games are not available when the regional sports network that owns the rights does not have a retransmission agreement. The only way to watch most out-of-market baseball games was through a package of almost all games, either on television through ExtraInnings or via the internet at mlb.com. MLB now sells games available throughout the country via Peacock (NBC streaming) and Prime Video, as well as national broadcasts on Fox, TBS, and out-of-market games on MLB network.

1. What strategies did the MLB Executive Vice President, Business, need to pursue to secure owner approval of the recent expansion in delivery?

2. Would MLB make more money offering every game on pay-per-view to anyone?

3. If a new scheme would indeed generate higher total broadcast revenues, would the owners necessarily vote to adopt the scheme? How would you advise the VP on how to create a scheme that minimized owner opposition?

4. Who else would benefit? Can their benefits be monetized and added to the pot?

Sixth Exercise: Innovative Club Marketing

The Brooklyn Nets were previously owned by Mikhail Prokhorov, who mastered the post-Soviet transition in Russia to become a multi-billionaire. Suppose that Prokhorov (a graduate of the Moscow Finance Institute), observing the huge marketing successes enjoyed by English Premier League clubs in emerging markets like China, wanted to emulate their efforts by pushing to make the Nets the "Team of Russia." Like the EPL, all NBA international television rights are sold by the league, but, unlike the EPL, merchandise rights are likewise centralized. Prokhorov believed he can significantly improve on the efforts of NBA International in sales to Russia. Although the NBA never accepted Prokhorov's proposal, the NFL has now initiated a similar idea: various countries around the world have been allocated to each NFL club for purposes of promoting their club and the NFL.

1. Assuming Prokhorov was correct, why would his fellow owners object to an exception in the NBA's scheme of centralized marketing for the Nets in Russia? Who would be worse off by granting him permission for the sale? Who else would be better off were Prokhorov permitted to market the Nets in Russia? Can their interests be monetized?

2. The NFL, like the NBA, have highly talented marketing executives in their New York offices to develop strategies for global growth. Why would the NFL owners instead adopt an initiative to delegate international growth to individual clubs?

A Final Note: Overall Restructuring of the League

The three antitrust chapters have focused to a significant degree on the challenges involved when league rules are adopted by club owners who run the league. Consider that a system where an independent commercial entity (MLB, Inc., or NHL, LLC) organizes the competition and licenses separate clubs to participate may yield several efficiency benefits:

•   The ability to draw up rules and regulations that meet the best interests of the league as a whole (consumers, owners, and players) rather than the interests of any particular group or faction.

•   The ability to market products of the league that are truly joint, such as broadcast rights, in such a way as to maximize the return to the league as a whole.

•   The ability to facilitate [welfare]-improving entry into the league through the adoption of systems such as promotion and relegation.

Suppose Warren Buffett were to agree with this analysis, and were to seek to acquire the controlling interest in the centralized organizing operation of a sports league.

1. If this analysis were correct, then the value of "MLB, Inc." plus the combined value of the 30 MLB clubs, shed of their power to run the league and split all league revenues between them, would be higher than the current combined value of all MLB clubs. If so, would owners agree to this scheme?

2. What problems would Buffett encounter in getting owners to agree to his proposal?

3. This sort of proposal would likely require a change in the MLB Constitution requiring support from three-fourths of the owners. How might Buffett secure the minimum number of yes votes?

4. What stakeholders might be worse off if MLB were restructured in this manner?

5. Who else might be better off? Can their interests be monetized and used by Buffett to provide further financial incentives?

CHAPTER 9

INTELLECTUAL PROPERTY
LAW AND SPORTS

■ ■ ■

The core business of the sports industry is to sell an intangible product—access to observe an athletic contest that can generate thrill, pride, emotional attachment, and community (as well as their antipodes). In this way the sports industry resembles other branches of the broader entertainment industry, including live theater and music concerts. Through the nineteenth century, these entertainment products were accessible only to fans who purchased tickets for live attendance, limiting the potential audience and revenue. With the invention of film, recording, radio, and television, twentieth century sports and entertainment audiences exploded, transforming the organization and economics of the industry. Sports revenue streams proliferated, including the sale of broadcasting rights, licensing of trademarks and team logos, corporate sponsorship deals, and athlete endorsement contracts. Each of these sources of revenue, and others that continue to evolve in the twenty-first century—e.g., internet-driven digital media, sports gambling, and fantasy games—depend on the definition and enforceability of intellectual property rights, primarily copyright, trademark, and rights of publicity.

To further explain, unlike a manufacturer of a tangible product such as an automobile or a pair of shoes, the sports team owner's principal product—the live athletic competition—takes no permanent material form and is highly perishable. This quality of unscripted, short-lived suspense is also a large part of sports' appeal. Of course, sports team ownership often comes with significant assets, such as player contracts; a venue lease; the right to share in league revenues and vote on league operations; equipment and uniforms; team names, marks, logos, and historical records; and a fan base. Fans attending the game might also spend money on food, beverages, and merchandise in addition to the ticket price. But the ongoing prosperity of professional and many collegiate and amateur sports enterprises depends primarily on reaching the largest possible audience for the live contest through distribution of game audio, video, and digital content, locally, nationally, and globally.

This verity is substantiated by the history of television contracts in football, baseball, basketball, and hockey. In 1962, the NFL's first league-wide television contract (with CBS) paid $4.65 million, or $320,000 for each of the 14 clubs. Major League Baseball's national contract paid $3 million to its 20 teams. For the 2022–2032 period, the NFL will earn over $110 billion in television and digital broadcast rights fees, amounting to $321 million per team each year and representing the bulk of football's total revenues. Although the other three major leagues earn significantly less from national television, that revenue combined with their local and regional television deals contributes the majority of baseball's and basketball's revenues, and a substantial percentage of hockey's. Investing in sports programming has paid off for network rights-holders, who can count on it generating the highest television ratings and corresponding advertising rates. Sports programming has also driven the development of subscription distribution channels, at first cable systems and superstations, and later satellite television providers and internet streaming services.

Public interest in sports contests, and in the leagues, teams, and athletes that produce them, has translated into other commercial opportunities. Licensing the use of sports names and logos on merchandise now generates over $25 billion annually in global retail revenue. Sports sponsorship spending in North America is expected to exceed $20 billion by 2024, after dipping during the COVID-19 pandemic when games were suspended or played without fans in the seats. Professional athletes have been among the chief beneficiaries of this marketing phenomenon, in terms of both rising salaries and the earning potential of their celebrity. All players associations now market group licenses to use union member names and likenesses on everything from trading cards to apparel to non-fungible tokens. These initiatives not so incidentally have served as a union war chest for the fierce labor struggles over player mobility and compensation, discussed in Chapters 3, 4, and 5. Since mid-2021, college athletes may also monetize their name, image and likeness, a byproduct of the incursions on the National Collegiate Athletic Association's (NCAA) amateurism principle examined in Chapter 12.

Entrepreneurs and businesses unaffiliated with sports organizations, teams, or competitions similarly seek to capitalize on sport's popularity by offering products and services that depend on and incorporate information about the games and players. These include betting operators, fantasy game providers, data aggregators and vendors, journalists and bloggers, social media influencers, and fan websites. Their activities test the boundaries of sports intellectual property rights and invite exploration of protections for fair use and freedom of expression.

Intellectual property law defines the respective rights of all those inside and outside the game who aim to profit from these intangible assets. Without intellectual property protection, these assets would reside in the public domain, available for all to exploit. Thus, to the extent this body of law grants an *exclusive* property right—in a game broadcast, a team logo, or a player's celebrity—it provides insulation from claims of monopolization that might otherwise be challenged under the antitrust laws studied in earlier chapters. Where rights holders possess exclusive control over products or services that have no reasonable substitutes, the resulting market power can disserve consumers. Meanwhile, technological advances have enlarged the popular conception of the public domain, pushing back against expansive intellectual property protection in sports.

This chapter addresses the contours of these property rights, beginning with the right to game accounts and the scope of copyright protection for game broadcasts. Next considered are the rights of individual participants, including athletes and coaches, to control and capitalize on their names, images, and identities. Finally, the chapter turns to how the law of trademark and unfair competition is applied to sports-related trademarks, logos, and other identifying symbols.

A. REAL-TIME GAME ACCOUNTS AND THE RIGHT TO BROADCAST GAMES

The first significant source of sports revenue from off-site audiences was licensed radio broadcasts, particularly of baseball games. Teams overcame initial concerns that radio broadcasts would cannibalize ticket sales when they realized that easy and regular access to games over-the-air enhanced their appeal in the local community. Radio also made it possible for fans across the country to enjoy postseason playoff and championship games. Teams gladly sold radio stations the right to install announcers with microphones inside the ballpark to describe the events of the game to the audience at home.

Keep in mind, however, that unlike seats, which only one person can occupy at the same time, a host of broadcasters can simultaneously transmit game information without physically interfering with each other. A game broadcast is thus a quasi "public good" in the sense that (a) consumption of the good—listening to or viewing the game—does not reduce its availability to others, and (b) providers of the good find it difficult to exclude from consumption those who do not pay for it. But a radio or television station is typically prepared to pay the team a substantial sum for the broadcast rights only if they are *exclusive*. Exclusivity enables the broadcaster to charge higher fees to advertisers to associate their products with the broadcast.

Furthermore, at the advent of sports broadcasting, federal copyright laws did not protect simultaneously recorded broadcasts such as sporting events. Of course, the club could limit access to the ballpark to those stations that had licensed broadcast rights. Even so, in the 1920s and 1930s, unlicensed radio stations broadcast baseball "re-creations" by announcers who lifted game descriptions from telegraph transmissions, and instantaneously relayed their own pitch-by-pitch embellishments. Indeed, in his early career as a radio announcer, former President Ronald

Reagan used to re-create Chicago Cubs and White Sox games from Des Moines, Iowa. The telegraph receiving agent would hand him a piece of paper stating "#12, out, 43," and young Reagan would tell his listeners about the hard-hit ground ball that the second baseman had fielded and then thrown to first base for the narrow out.

PROBLEM 9.1

FAN-TASTIC is a sports-specific social media platform available on a mobile application and a website. Fans create an account and then post to it by uploading written commentary and video highlights of a maximum 10-second duration. Fans create these "micro-highlights" mostly by using their smartphones to record from game telecasts or, if attending the event, to record the live action. In this way, fans can generate a personalized sports news report feed, and can follow others (just like Twitter and Instagram). The platform offers a search function so that users can find video highlights of specific sports, teams, events, or players. All uploaded micro-highlights are viewable only for 24 hours. In addition, FAN-TASTIC provides real-time scores and statistics compiled by its own employees who attend the games in person or watch them on television.

FAN-TASTIC offers an advertising supported version of its service, or an ad-free version that charges a subscription fee. Paying subscribers gain access to two special features. First, they can view a "gamecast" that displays real-time game action using graphics and digitally-generated generic avatars. Second, they can participate in a "group chat" that enables fans following an ongoing event to join a group chat and share messages and live-stream any event video to which they have access. Theoretically, and depending on what group chat members decide to live-stream, someone participating in a particular event's group chat can effectively watch the event live from the platform. Group chat messages and video are not viewable or recoverable once the event concludes.

The NFL is suing FAN-TASTIC, alleging that its platform constitutes copyright infringement and misappropriation of NFL property. How should the court rule? What additional facts would you need to know? Consider the following materials.

---

1. COMMON LAW PROPERTY RIGHTS IN LIVE GAME ACCOUNTS

During the early days of sports broadcasting, if teams were going to block free use of game information and assert a property right in the games themselves, this right was going to have to come from general common law doctrine, such as state misappropriation, unfair competition, and contract law. In what might have been a path-breaking decision, *National Exhibition v. Teleflash*, 24 F. Supp. 488 (S.D.N.Y. 1936), a federal district judge refused to enjoin a station from broadcasting a game via telephone from inside a ballpark. The judge noted that the club had failed to include a restriction on such activity on the face of the ticket the announcer had purchased to gain access to the park. The *Teleflash* contract-based analysis was overtaken by other doctrinal approaches in the next crucial ruling.

PITTSBURGH ATHLETIC CO. V. KQV BROADCASTING CO.
24 F. Supp. 490 (W.D. Pa. 1938)

SCHOONMAKER, DISTRICT JUDGE.

[For several decades prior to the construction of Three Rivers Stadium, the Pittsburgh Pirates baseball team played their home games at Forbes Field. Forbes Field was unlike its more modern counterparts in that it was simply enclosed by fences that precluded unauthorized entry, but still permitted the game to be seen from outside vantage points. By the 1930s, though, fans were admitted to the ballpark only on condition that they not give out any news of the game while it was in progress.

The Pittsburgh Athletic Company, which owned the Pirates, licensed to General Mills the exclusive right to broadcast play-by-play descriptions or accounts of Pirates games. General Mills in turn contracted with the National Broadcast Company (NBC) to broadcast the games over two Pittsburgh radio stations, KDKA & WWSW. At the same time, however, a rival radio station, KQV, was also broadcasting Pirates games. By stationing observers at leased vantage points outside Forbes Field, KQV received information about the progress of the games and provided simultaneous broadcasts.

The Pirates' owners sought an injunction to stop these "pirated" descriptions of their games, in which they asserted an underlying property right.]

* * *

It is perfectly clear that the exclusive right to broadcast play-by-play descriptions of the games played by the "Pirates" at their home field rests in the plaintiffs, General Mills, and the Socony-Vacuum Oil Company under the contract with the Pittsburgh Athletic Company. That is a property right of the plaintiffs with which defendant is interfering when it broadcasts the play-by-play description of the ball games obtained by the observers on the outside of the enclosure.

The plaintiffs and the defendant are using baseball news as material for profit. The Athletic Company has, at great expense, acquired and maintains a baseball park, pays the players who participate in the game, and has, as we view it, a legitimate right to capitalize on the news value of their games by selling exclusive broadcasting rights to companies which value them as affording advertising mediums for their merchandise. This right the defendant interferes with when it uses its broadcasting facilities for giving out the identical news obtained by its paid observers stationed at points outside Forbes Field for the purpose of securing information which it cannot otherwise acquire. This, in our judgment, amounts to unfair competition, and is a violation of the property rights of the plaintiffs. For it is our opinion that the Pittsburgh Athletic Company, by reason of its creation of the game, its control of the park, and its restriction of the dissemination of news therefrom, has a property right in such news, and the right to control the use thereof for a reasonable time following the games.

* * *

On the unfair competition feature of the case, we rest our opinion on the case of *International News Service v. Associated Press*, 248 U.S. 215 [1918]. In that case the court enjoined the International News Service from copying news from bulletin boards and early editions of Associated Press newspapers, and selling such news so long as it had commercial value to the Associated Press. The Supreme Court said:

> Regarding the news, therefore, as but the material out of which both parties are seeking to make profits at the same time and in the same field, we hardly can fail to recognize that for this purpose, and as between them, it must be regarded as quasi property, irrespective of the rights of either as against the public. . . .

248 U.S. at 236. And again:

> The right of the purchaser of a single newspaper to spread knowledge of its contents gratuitously, for any legitimate purpose not unreasonably interfering with the complainant's right to make merchandise of it, may be admitted; but to transmit that news for commercial use, in competition with complainant—which is what defendant has done and seeks to justify—is a very different matter. . . .

248 U.S. at 239–40.

* * *

Defendant contends it is not unfairly competing with any of the plaintiffs because it obtains no compensation from a sponsor or otherwise from its baseball broadcasts. It concedes, however, that KQV seeks by its broadcast of news of baseball games to cultivate the good will of the public for its radio station. The fact that no revenue is obtained directly from the broadcast is not controlling, as these broadcasts are undoubtedly designed to aid in obtaining advertising business.

Defendant seeks to justify its action on the ground that the information it receives from its observers stationed on its own property without trespassing on plaintiffs' property, may be lawfully broadcast by it. We cannot follow defendant's counsel in this contention for the reasons above stated.

* * *

Injunction granted.

———

NOTES AND QUESTIONS

1.   *Common Law Property Right in Game Broadcasts.* What rationale(s) did the *Pittsburgh Athletic* court provide for establishing a common law property right in game broadcasts? Which one do you find most persuasive? Is there something about the venue that justifies creating this property right? That is, does the right depend on the team playing in a privately owned or operated facility? If so, when the City of Hartford leased the public Civic Center to the World Figure Skating Championships, could the event organizer prohibit local telecasts in favor of ABC, the exclusive television rights-holder? *See Post Newsweek v. Travelers*, 510 F. Supp. 81 (D. Conn. 1981). Or is the right dependent on the fact that the event would not exist at all but for the organizer's efforts at staging it? If so, could the Boston Athletic Association sell exclusive rights to one local station to telecast the Boston Marathon that is being run on public streets? *See WCVB-TV v. Boston Athletic Association*, 926 F.2d 42 (1st Cir. 1991).

2.   *"Hot News" Doctrine.* The key precedent cited in *Pittsburgh Athletic* was the Supreme Court decision in *International News Service v. Associated Press*, 248 U.S. 215 (1918). The *INS* case originated the "hot news" misappropriation doctrine when it held INS liable for unfair competition for using early East Coast editions of the AP wire to rewrite World War I news stories and distribute that news the same day to its own subscribers in the western United States. The Court was concerned that allowing INS to take and sell the benefit of AP's investigations and reporting would eventually eliminate AP's incentive to invest in that effort and generate that product. Was *Pittsburgh Athletic* justified in applying *INS* to sports events and establishing a similar property right in game information?

3.   *First Amendment.* In *Zacchini v. Scripps-Howard Broadcasting Co.*, 433 U.S. 562 (1977), a decision explored further in Section C of this chapter, a narrow Supreme Court majority cited *Pittsburgh Athletic* approvingly in rejecting a First Amendment defense to liability for violating publicity rights in an athletic performance. The Court held that a television station had no free speech right to telecast the celebrated "Flying" Zacchini's entire 15-second "human cannonball" act on the local news because it would undermine his economic incentives for investing in the act. In rejecting free speech immunity for the newscast, the *Zacchini* Court emphasized that the station had broadcast the performer's entire act, not merely information about or

descriptions of the act. In delineating the property right in game broadcasts, what should the relevance be of the amount or type of information conveyed?

4.   *Off-Site Viewability of Game.* In an interesting unreported 2002 case, the Chicago Cubs sued several bars that were located on rooftops overlooking Wrigley Field and charged a premium for patrons to enter during Cubs games. The bars were not broadcasting the images or information about the games, only allowing their patrons to watch without having to pay the Cubs for a ticket. What, if any, legal theories could the Cubs assert to try to enjoin this practice? Is this case factually similar to *Pittsburgh Athletic*? Should the result be the same? What would an injunction look like—forbid the bars to be open during Cubs games? Forbid the bars to impose a cover charge? Require all patrons in the bar during games to buy a ticket from the Cubs? Would your answers be any different if the bars allowed a local TV station to set up a camera on their premises and telecast a view of the games from there?

After settlement discussions between the Cubs and the rooftop bar owners failed, the club sought and received City of Chicago approval to build more seating and erect seven new outfield signs and two Jumbotrons that would largely block the field view from the rooftop bars. The rooftop owners filed a lawsuit against the City and the Cubs claiming that the new construction would violate a 20-year revenue-sharing contract between the bars and team. Ultimately the Seventh Circuit Court of Appeals interpreted the contract to reject that claim, and also refused to subject the Cubs' alleged monopolistic behavior to antitrust scrutiny because it was part of the immunized "business of baseball." (See Chapter 5, Section D). Nonetheless, what are your views about whether it is appropriate public policy to allow businesses (or even residents) that fortuitously have a view of the playing field to enjoy and even profit from allowing people to watch the games without compensating the Cubs?

2.   CONTRACTUAL SOLUTIONS TO GAME BROADCAST OWNERSHIP

From the 1950s to the 1990s, an increasing reliance on contract sidelined the *Pittsburgh Athletic* approach to ownership of game broadcasts. Language inserted in admission tickets and media credentials restricted commercial use or distribution of live game information and depictions without the team's consent. Enforcement of these provisions was simplified by the location and design of new stadiums and arenas, which made it essentially impossible to produce a game broadcast without access to the facility.

Consider this ticket disclaimer language used by a major league sports team:

> Photographs, videos or other accounts or descriptions (whether data, textual or visual) of all or any part of the football game or of any game-related activities created by the ticket holder may be used only for personal, non-commercial uses. Any transmission or

other distribution to any commercial enterprise, and any public performance or display, are strictly prohibited.

As a practical matter in the smartphone era, how can a team and its venue enforce this provision, in particular the prohibition of "any public performance or display" of game descriptions? What legal remedies are available? Does this mean a spectator can't post a photograph or video of the game on social media? Does that depend on the spectator's privacy settings on his Instagram, Twitter, or TikTok account? Ticket disclaimers are contracts of adhesion, non-negotiable by the purchaser. Should this affect their enforceability?

Leagues and teams also resorted to contract to resolve any lingering ambiguity after *Pittsburgh Athletic* as to whether a visiting team, or the league itself, shared with the home team any ownership in the game broadcast. Each league eventually established by rule or joint venture agreement the members' respective rights in this regard. (For an early case in which the NFL had not anticipated this problem, see *Johnson-Kennedy Radio Corp. v. Chicago Bears Football Club*, 97 F.2d 223 (7th Cir. 1938), where the then-Chicago Cardinals sought to block its opponent, the Chicago Bears, from broadcasting a Cardinals home game on the Bears' licensed radio station.) As discussed in Chapter 8, when leagues periodically revisit contractual restraints on member clubs' broadcast property rights, they often must contend with intervening market developments and tensions between large and small markets, and between successful and struggling teams.

3. ADVANCING TECHNOLOGY AND APPROPRIATION OF REAL-TIME GAME ACCOUNTS

With the advance of modern communications tools, the ability to discover and disseminate game facts in new and commercially viable ways has frustrated the ownership claims of sports event producers. Case in point is the NBA's lawsuit against Motorola, Inc., and its partner, Sports Team Analysis and Tracking System, Inc. (STATS). In 1994, these two partners were licensed by Major League Baseball to provide real-time baseball game information on a portable electronic pager device—SportsTrax—that they sold to subscribers. The success of that venture led the partners to approach the NBA to expand their service into basketball. The NBA demurred, hoping to develop its own pager service. Motorola and SportsTrax nonetheless decided to generate and transmit NBA game information by themselves, without a license from the league.

In 1996, SportsTrax began offering subscribers real-time information about NBA game action, updated every two to three minutes. To obtain game information, STATS hired reporters to watch or listen to broadcasts of NBA games and continuously key into their computers the score, ball possession, shots taken and made, fouls, clock updates, and the like. A fan could use a SportsTrax pager to keep track of key elements of every NBA game being played around the country. Additional real-time game information was available on STATS's AOL website, but in the early days of the internet this was a less user-friendly option.

The NBA responded with a lawsuit alleging federal copyright and trademark infringement, and New York state common law claims of commercial misappropriation of the NBA's property rights in its games. The federal infringement claims failed because neither the underlying NBA games nor the information about those games were copyrightable "original works of authorship" under the Copyright Act. As explained in the decision below, the misappropriation claim failed because of a complex doctrine known as copyright preemption, which foils attempts to seek state law protection for uncopyrightable elements of a work.

NBA v. MOTOROLA
105 F.3d 841 (2d Cir. 1997)

WINTER, CIRCUIT JUDGE.

A.   Summary of Ruling

The issues before us are ones that have arisen in various forms over the course of this century as technology has steadily increased the speed and quantity of information transmission. . . .

With the advance of technology, radio stations began "live" broadcasts of events such as baseball games and operas, and various entrepreneurs began to use the transmissions of others in one way or another for their own profit. In response, New York courts created a body of misappropriation law, loosely based on *INS*, that sought to apply ethical standards to the use by one party of another's transmissions of events. . . . In 1976, however, Congress passed legislation expressly affording copyright protection to simultaneously-recorded broadcasts of live performances such as sports events. Such protection was not extended to the underlying events.

The 1976 amendments also contained provisions preempting state law claims that enforced rights "equivalent" to exclusive copyright protections when the work to which the state claim was being applied fell within the area of copyright protection. [Although] a "hot-news" *INS*-like claim survives preemption, . . . much of New York misappropriation law after INS goes well beyond "hot-news" claims and is preempted.

B.   Copyrights in Events or Broadcasts of Events

In our view, the underlying basketball games do not fall within the subject matter of federal copyright protection because they do not constitute "original works of authorship." . . . Unlike movies, plays, television programs, or operas, athletic events are competitive and have no underlying script. . . . For many of these reasons, Nimmer on Copyright concludes that the "[f]ar more reasonable" position is that athletic events are not copyrightable.

As noted, recorded broadcasts of NBA games—as opposed to the games themselves—are now entitled to copyright protection. . . . Although the broadcasts are protected under copyright law, the district court correctly held that Motorola and STATS did not infringe NBA's copyright because they reproduced only facts from the broadcasts, not the expression or description of the game that constitutes the broadcast.

C.   The State-Law Misappropriation Claim

1.   Preemption Under the Copyright Act

When Congress amended the Copyright Act in 1976, it provided for the preemption of state law claims that are interrelated with copyright claims in certain ways. Under 17 U.S.C. § 301, a state law claim is preempted when: (i) the state law claim seeks to vindicate "legal or equitable rights that are equivalent" to one of the bundle of exclusive rights already protected by copyright law under 17 U.S.C. § 106—styled the "general scope requirement"; and (ii) the particular work to which the state law claim is being applied falls within the type of works protected by the Copyright Act under Sections 102 and 103—styled the "subject matter requirement."

* * *

[The court first concluded that the "subject matter requirement" for preemption had been established.] Although game broadcasts are copyrightable while the underlying games are not, the Copyright Act should not be read to distinguish between the two when analyzing the preemption of a misappropriation claim based on copying or taking from the copyrightable work. We believe that:

> Once a performance is reduced to tangible form, there is no distinction between the performance and the recording of the performance for the purposes of preemption under § 301(a). Thus, if a baseball game were not broadcast or were telecast without being recorded, the Players' performances similarly would not be fixed in tangible form and their rights of publicity would not be subject to preemption. By virtue of being videotaped, however, the Players' performances are fixed in tangible form, and any rights of publicity in their performances that are equivalent to the rights contained in the copyright of the telecast are preempted.

Baltimore Orioles [*v. Major League Baseball Players Ass'n*, 805 F.2d 663, 675 (7th Cir. 1986)](citation omitted).

Copyrightable material often contains uncopyrightable elements within it, but Section 301 preemption bars state law misappropriation claims with respect to uncopyrightable as well as copyrightable elements.

* * *

Under the general scope requirement. Section 301 "preempts only those state law rights that 'may be abridged by an act which, in and of itself, would infringe one of the exclusive rights' provided by federal copyright law." [Citation omitted.] However, certain forms of commercial misappropriation otherwise within the general scope requirement will survive preemption if an "extra-element" test is met. As stated in *Altai*:

> But if an "extra element" is "required instead of or in addition to the acts of reproduction, performance, distribution or display, in order to constitute a state-created cause of action, then the right does not lie 'within the general scope of copyright,' and there is no preemption."

We turn, therefore, to the question of the extent to which a "hot-news" misappropriation claim based on *INS* involves extra elements and is not the equivalent of exclusive rights under a copyright. Courts are generally agreed that some form of such a claim survives preemption.

[The court rejected the district court's reliance on pre-1976 New York misappropriation cases that were based on "amorphous concepts" of "commercial immorality" or society's "ethics."] Such concepts are virtually synonymous for wrongful copying and are in no meaningful fashion distinguishable from infringement of a copyright. The broad misappropriation doctrine relied upon by the district court is, therefore, the equivalent of exclusive rights in copyright law.

* * *

Our conclusion, therefore, is that only a narrow "hot-news" misappropriation claim survives preemption for actions concerning material within the realm of copyright. In our view, the elements central to an *INS* claim are: (i) the plaintiff generates or collects information at some cost or expense; (ii) the value of the information is highly time-sensitive; (iii) the defendant's use of the information constitutes free-riding on the plaintiff's costly efforts to generate or collect it; (iv) the defendant's use of the information is in direct competition with a product or service offered by the plaintiff; (v) the ability of other parties to free-ride on the efforts of the plaintiff would so reduce the incentive to produce the product or service that its existence or quality would be substantially threatened.

INS is not about ethics; it is about the protection of property rights in time-sensitive information so that the information will be made available to the public by profit-seeking entrepreneurs. If services like AP were not assured of property rights in the news they pay to collect, they would cease to collect it. The ability of their competitors to appropriate their product at only nominal cost and thereby to disseminate a competing product at a lower price would destroy the incentive to collect news in the first place. The newspaper-reading public would suffer because no one would have an incentive to collect "hot news."

We therefore find the extra elements—those in addition to the elements of copyright infringement—that allow a "hot news" claim to survive preemption are: (i) the time-sensitive value of factual information, (ii) the free-riding by a defendant, and (iii) the threat to the very existence of the product or service provided by the plaintiff.

2.   *The Legality of SportsTrax*

We conclude that Motorola and STATS have not engaged in unlawful misappropriation under the "hot-news" test set out above. To be sure, some of the elements of a "hot-news" *INS*-claim are met . . .

However, there are critical elements missing in the NBA's attempt to assert a "hot-news" *INS*-type claim. As framed by the NBA, their claim compresses and confuses three different informational products. The first product is generating the information by playing the games; the second product is transmitting live, full descriptions of those games; and the third product is collecting and retransmitting strictly factual information about the games. The first and second products are the NBA's primary business: producing basketball games for live attendance and licensing copyrighted broadcasts of those games. The collection and retransmission of strictly factual material about the games is a different product: *e.g.*, box-scores in newspapers, summaries of statistics on television sports news, and real-time facts to be transmitted to pagers. In our view, the NBA has failed to show any competitive effect whatsoever from SportsTrax on the first and second products and a lack of any free-riding by SportsTrax on the third.

With regard to the NBA's primary products—producing basketball games with live attendance and licensing copyrighted broadcasts of those games—there is no evidence that anyone regards SportsTrax or the AOL site as a substitute for attending NBA games or watching them on television. In fact, Motorola markets SportsTrax as being designed "for those times when you cannot be at the arena, watch the game on TV, or listen to the radio. . . ."

The NBA argues that the pager market is also relevant to a "hot-news" *INS*-type claim and that SportsTrax's future competition with Gamestats satisfies any missing element. We agree that there is a separate market for the real-time transmission of factual information to pagers or similar devices, such as STATS's AOL site. However, we disagree that SportsTrax is in any sense free-riding off Gamestats.

An indispensable element of an INS "hot-news" claim is free-riding by a defendant on a plaintiff's product, enabling the defendant to produce a directly competitive product for less money because it has lower costs. SportsTrax is not such a product. The use of pagers to transmit real-time information about NBA games requires: (i) the collecting of facts about the games; (ii) the transmission of these facts on a network; (iii) the assembling of them by the particular service; and (iv) the transmission of them to pagers or an on-line computer site. Appellants are in no way free-riding on Gamestats. Motorola and STATS expend their own resources to collect purely factual information generated in NBA games to transmit to SportsTrax pagers. They have their own network and assemble and transmit data themselves.

To be sure, if appellants in the future were to collect facts from an enhanced Gamestats pager to retransmit them to SportsTrax pagers, that would constitute free-riding and might well cause Gamestats to be unprofitable because it had to bear costs to collect facts that SportsTrax did not. If the appropriation of facts from one pager to another pager service were allowed, transmission of current information on NBA games to pagers or similar devices would be substantially deterred because any potential transmitter would know that the first entrant would quickly encounter a lower cost competitor free-riding on the originator's transmissions.[9]

However, that is not the case in the instant matter. SportsTrax and Gamestats are each bearing their own costs of collecting factual information on NBA games, and, if one produces a product that is cheaper or otherwise superior to the other, that producer will prevail in the marketplace. This is obviously not the situation against which INS was intended to prevent: the potential lack of any such product or service because of the anticipation of free-riding.

For the foregoing reasons, the NBA has not shown any damage to any of its products based on free-riding by Motorola and STATS, and the NBA's misappropriation claim based on New York law is preempted.

Reversed.

_____

NOTES AND QUESTIONS

1. *Scope of Copyright Preemption.* Was the Second Circuit right in holding that federal copyright law preempts the NBA's state law misappropriation claim? If the NBA cannot use state law to protect uncopyrightable elements of its games, should federal law step in to give the NBA exclusive control over live descriptions and sale of game events? Does

---

[9]   It may well be that the NBA's product, when enhanced, will actually have a competitive edge because its Gamestats system will apparently be used for a number of in-stadium services as well as the pager market, resulting in a certain amount of cost-sharing. Gamestats might also have a temporal advantage in collecting and transmitting official statistics. Whether this is so does not affect our disposition of this matter, although it does demonstrate the gulf between this case and *INS*, where the free-riding created the danger of no wire service being viable.

your answer depend on whether that control is exerted before or after the information is put into the public domain by television or radio broadcasts? Would any such intellectual property conferred on the league improperly intrude upon the First Amendment rights of Motorola and STATS (an issue the Second Circuit did not have to address in this case)?

2. *Preemption Subject Matter Requirement.* The Second Circuit held that the subject matter requirement for preemption was met because the real-time data about NBA games, though not copyrightable, were contained in a copyrighted broadcast. Would the answer be different if the defendants obtained the information they put on their pager system from some means other than watching and/or listening to copyrighted broadcasts (*e.g.*, by stationing someone in the arena with a computer like in the old *Teleflash* case, or by positioning someone at a vantage point outside the facility like in the *Pittsburgh Athletic* case)? What if a game was not broadcast at all?

3. *Future of* Pittsburgh Athletic. Does *Motorola* implicitly overturn *Pittsburgh Athletic* as applied to the latter's facts? Under what circumstances can someone with access to facts about a sports event repurpose them for commercial benefit? How would this logic apply to major boxing matches, which now primarily air on pay-for-view? Consider *Twentieth Century Sporting Club v. Transradio Press Service, Inc.*, 165 Misc. 71, 300 N.Y.S. 159 (1937), which enjoined local television stations from using facts obtained from a Joe Louis fight broadcast to provide "up to the minute descriptions" in competition with NBC, the promoter's exclusive broadcast rights-holder. After *Motorola*, could a digital news service permissibly arrange for a reporter to watch a fight on pay-for-view television and simultaneously describe to the internet audience the key developments in the fight as they are taking place? Is your answer different if the reporter shared smartphone video of the television screen?

4. *Future of the Hot News Doctrine.* Has the internet made the hot news doctrine obsolete? Information, images, and video are now transmitted via satellite or the internet instantaneously at nominal cost. How does this development affect the calculus of time sensitivity in applying the hot news doctrine? Does a competitor's misappropriation of bare news facts underlying another organization's work continue to pose a significant threat to economic incentives to produce that work?

4. PROPERTY RIGHTS IN SPORTS DATA IN THE DIGITAL AGE

As internet coverage of sports events proliferated, courts confronted the "novel and compelling question of who has the 'right' to report the news, produced and gathered by others, in an age of near-instantaneous information." *Morris Commc'ns Corp. v. PGA Tour, Inc.*, 235 F. Supp. 2d 1269, 1272 (M.D. Fla. 2002), *aff'd*, 364 F.3d 1288 (11th Cir. 2004). In *Morris*, the PGA Tour successfully defended an antitrust challenge to tournament media regulations it enforced to maintain a commercial advantage for its Real-Time Scoring System (RTSS). The RTSS enabled the PGA Tour to publish "real-time" golf scores on the pgatour.com website and on the website of *USA Today*, which had paid for the privilege.

To support the RTSS, the PGA Tour had invested significant resources to monitor each golf hole during its tournaments, and collect and relay scoring information to electronic "leaderboards" throughout the golf course and to the PGA Tour's media center and website. In this way, the PGA Tour could provide up-to-date scores to both on-site spectators and television viewers for as many as 200 players on all 18 holes of its 100+ acre golf courses. The PGA Tour prohibited the use of mobile devices by the press or public during tournaments, making the RTSS the sole source of compiled golf scores for the full list of competing golfers. Beginning in 1999, the PGA Tour also conditioned media access to tournaments on agreeing to its On-Line Service Regulations (OLSR). To give pgatour.com and *USA Today* priority, the OLSR prohibited credentialed media from publishing or selling scoring information until either (1) thirty minutes after a player's shot or (2) pgatour.com published that information. In 2000, the PGA Tour amended the OLSR to allow credentialed media to instantly transmit scores on their own websites, but prohibited them from selling or syndicating scores to third parties without first purchasing a special license from the PGA Tour, as *USA Today* had.

Morris Communications was a media firm that published traditional print and web-based newspapers, and regularly covered golf events. Morris's golf reporters relied on the PGA Tour's on-site media center to obtain real-time scores, which Morris then transmitted to its own news outlets and sold to third-party subscribers. When the PGA Tour refused to allow Morris to transmit tournament scores to third parties such as the *Denver Post* and *Dallas Morning News* without first paying for a license, Morris sued under federal and state antitrust laws, claiming that the PGA Tour was leveraging its exclusive power over the gathering of the scores to suppress competition in the market for the distribution of real-time golf scores over the internet.

MORRIS COMMUNICATIONS CORPORATION V. PGA TOUR
235 F. Supp. 2d 1269 (M.D. Fla. 2002)

SCHLESINGER, DISTRICT JUDGE.

* * *

[T]he PGA Tour itself has acknowledged that the OLSR were implemented in order to maintain a commercial advantage. . . .

Thus, the record seems to clearly indicate that the OLSR have the purpose and effect of giving the PGA Tour a commercial advantage in the syndication market and disadvantaging potential competitors, including

Morris. As discussed below, this does not necessarily mean that the PGA Tour has violated any antitrust laws. . . .

* * *

III. Analysis

A. *Antitrust claims*

Morris asserts four antitrust claims: 1) monopolization of the Internet markets, 2) unlawful refusal to deal, 3) monopoly leveraging, and 4) attempted monopolization of the Internet markets. . . . [T]he Court will first address the PGA Tour's assertions that valid business reasons justify the exclusionary practice found in the OLSR, because valid business reasons are a defense to the antitrust claims. . . .

Free-riding

Morris asks the Court to force the PGA Tour to provide Morris with the compilation of scores, for which the PGA Tour spends considerable money and time creating, at no cost to Morris. While Morris does invest its own cost in re-keying the scores for syndication, Morris free-rides on the PGA Tour's efforts in compiling the scores. As Morris admits in its Memorandum of Law, "Morris cannot duplicate the functions of RTSS, which depends on the efforts of hundreds of volunteers each week." Even if it is the efforts of "volunteers", the PGA Tour has still invested time and money in the organization and technology to make RTSS possible.

[The court distinguishes *Motorola*.] [T]he information that Motorola used to create its product was in the public domain, having been broadcast on television or radio. Specifically, Motorola-paid reporters, who had heard the radio or television broadcast scores, reported the information to a central location and merely relayed what had been known to the world. Golf, unlike basketball, precludes a single person gathering all the information occurring on all 18 holes. So when television and radio cover a basketball game, the score is presented to the public through those media outlets, allowing Motorola to obtain the information and republish it. If Morris were able to gather scores from all 18 holes through a television or radio broadcast, Morris could then republish that information, absent a hot-news exception. However, golf's atypical format prevents any single television or radio broadcast from providing results from all 18 holes live. The PGA Tour does publish the scores in the media center, but the media cannot disseminate that information except as the PGA Tour's press credentials allow them to do. As a result, the scores which, are not protected by copyright, remain outside the public domain and within the PGA Tour's control, because the PGA Tour provides access with certain restrictions.

* * *

Morris additionally argues that even if there is free-riding, it must reach the level that would justify a "hot news" property right. However, the Court finds that to be a business justification free-riding does not have to reach the level that the *Motorola* court held necessary for a hot news exception. The *Motorola* court required the free-riding to be so pervasive that all incentives to undertake an activity would be lost. *See Motorola,* 105 F.3d at 853. However, to be a valid business reason, a much lower level of free riding will justify excluding competitors. *See Areeda,* Antitrust Law, Vol. III, ¶ 658(f) ("once a proffered business purpose has been accepted as asserted in good faith and not as pretense, the defense does not require 'balancing' of social gains against competitive harms . . .").

Property Right in the Scores

. . . For the following reasons, the Court finds that the PGA Tour does have a property right in the scores compiled by the use of RTSS, but that property right vanishes when the scores are in the public domain.

The PGA Tour's property right does not come from copyright law, as copyright law does not protect factual information, like golf scores. However, the PGA Tour controls the right of access to that information and can place restrictions on those attending the private event, giving the PGA Tour a property right that the Court will protect.

* * *

[T]he instant case deals with facts that are not subject to copyright protection. The compiler of the information . . . collects information, which it created, at a cost. Also the events occur on private property to which the general public does not have unfettered access, and the creator of the event can place restrictions upon those who enter the private property. The vastly increased speed that the Internet makes available does not change the calculus or the underlying property right. Accordingly, the PGA Tour, like the exchanges in the ticker cases, has a property right in the compilation of scores, but that property right disappears when the underlying information is in the public domain.

Broadcast Rights on the Internet

Whether the PGA Tour has a separate right to license or sell broadcast rights on the Internet, like sports and entertainment producers currently enjoy in dealing with television and radio, is a novel question. . . .

. . . Both parties would certainly agree that the Internet provides an opportunity to profit from a product by selling advertisement. Television, radio, and print media operate on a similar, if not identical, principle: the selling of advertisement to viewers, listeners, or readers of entertainment, be it sports, entertainment, or news. Therefore, the Court finds that the PGA Tour has a right to sell or license its product, championship golf, and its derivative product, golf scores, on the Internet in the same way the PGA Tour currently sells its rights to television broadcasting stations.[24]

Accordingly, the Court finds that the PGA Tour is justified in its restrictions because (1) Morris free-rides on the PGA Tour's efforts, (2) the PGA Tour has a property right in the scores before they are in the public domain, and (3) the PGA Tour has the right to license or sell broadcasting rights of its products over the Internet.

* * *

Unlawful Refusal to Deal

[I]n this case, Morris is seeking access to the media center and the scoring system at no cost, putting it at a competitive advantage to the PGA Tour. The PGA Tour offers access to the scores through a license as evidenced by its contract with USA Today, and Morris is free to negotiate for the purchase of a license which would put it on a competitive plane with the PGA Tour.

[The court dismisses all of Morris' antitrust claims.]

NOTES AND QUESTIONS

1. *Nature of the Property Right.* Is it significant that the PGA Tour asserted the property right as a defense to an antitrust claim? Would the *Morris Communications* court have recognized the property right if the PGA Tour had sued because Morris used camera drones above the golf course to obtain access to real-time scores without the need for a PGA Tour press credential? Could the PGA Tour in that case prohibit Morris from publishing the scores on the internet? Does the answer depend on whether state law has articulated the misappropriation tort to require the "extra elements" of a "hot news" situation?

2. *Theorizing the Property Right.* What is the basis for articulating a property right that the PGA Tour might affirmatively assert? Public policy? The moral right that the creator of a sports event has in the information about the event? The extent to which the creator has physical power to control and thus condition the right of access to that information? How does that theory operate in the digital age of instantaneous access to information and casual unauthorized retransmission of that information?

3. *Copyright Preemption.* Under what circumstances would the PGA Tour's state law misappropriation claim be preempted by the Copyright Act?

---

[24] With the emergence of "web-casting" and "streaming" video and other rapid advancements in technology, a negative answer to the question of whether the PGA Tour has broadcast rights on the Internet would stymie advancement and reduce incentive to create entertainment and sports programming by foreclosing a lucrative market. To hold otherwise would be similar to a court finding that Major League Baseball could not sell broadcasting rights to television stations in the 1940s with the advent of television.

Would this depend on whether the tournament was on television or radio in a copyrighted broadcast? If yes, would that depend on whether the real-time scores were discernible from the broadcast? Does the preemption analysis depend on the nature of the sport and how it is covered on television?

4. *Reconcilable Law?* Are the *Motorola* and *Morris Communications* decisions reconcilable? If so, what are the key distinguishing facts?

5. *Sports Data Commercial Opportunities.* Sports data present many commercial opportunities, including for third-party developers and operators of (a) sports-related applications focused on health and nutrition, performance and training regimens, scouting reports, player-trading decisions, and predictive modeling, and (b) ancillary entertainment products such as fantasy sports, video games and e-sports, augmented and virtual reality fan engagement tools, and sports betting. Should those third-parties be required to compensate the creators of the athletic contests where the data originated?

6. *Sports Gambling Data Sourcing.* With the advent of legalized sports gambling in over two-third of the United States, leagues and teams have sought to obtain—through litigation, legislation, or private ordering—intellectual property protection for the game-related statistics and information essential to setting odds and determining wager outcomes. As discussed in Chapter 1, the professional leagues intensely lobbied statehouses to require sportsbooks to use and pay for official league data. Although that effort largely failed in all but a handful of states, sports leagues and governing bodies tout the superiority, speed, and accuracy of official real-time sports data, leading many sportsbooks to voluntarily subscribe to that option. Nevada, on the other hand, notably has operated its regulated sports betting market for decades without official league data. All the major U.S. leagues have deals with data collection/analytics companies, who pay a premium to the leagues for exclusive rights to distribute official data to media outlets, gaming operators, and other data-dependent ventures. Under the decisions explored so far in this chapter, how successful would leagues be in barring sportsbooks from using unofficial game accounts and data?

B. COPYRIGHT IN THE GAME BROADCASTS

Copyright law finds its roots in the Constitution itself, which authorizes Congress "To promote the Progress of Science and useful Arts, by securing for limited Times to Authors and Inventors the exclusive Right to their respective Writings and Discoveries." Article I, § 8, cl. 8. The operating premise then and now is that granting creators exclusive right to control and license use of their works provides the incentive to invest the time, effort, and resources in production of those works for the benefit of society at large. Congress enacted the first copyright statute in 1789, and has periodically amended the law since to keep pace with technological developments.

The Copyright Act of 1976 was the first iteration to extend federal copyright protection to live sports broadcasts once they are "fixed in any tangible medium of expression," *i.e.*, recorded simultaneously with transmission. 17 U.S.C. § 102(a). As with any creative work, the owner of the copyright in telecasts of live sports events is the entity that produces the game for recording. Accordingly, and absent agreement to the contrary, the copyright in a game telecast ordinarily resides collectively in the two competing teams and the league that provides the framework and personnel to stage the contest. *See National Ass'n of Broadcasters v. Copyright Royalty Tribunal*, 675 F.2d 367 (D.C. Cir. 1982) (rejecting broadcasters' claims to copyright in game telecasts because their contributions are "de minimis"). In the modern sports industry, layers of agreements address this crucial revenue driver, primarily: (a) among the teams and the league to allocate responsibilities for staging the contest, arranging it to be fixed in a tangible medium of expression, and then exploiting the copyright; and (b) with the broadcaster or streaming service that will enter the premises to record the game and telecast it as a work for hire.

Copyright owners currently enjoy six statutorily defined exclusive rights: (1) to reproduce the copyrighted work; (2) to prepare derivative works; (3) to distribute copies; (4) to publicly perform the copyrighted work; (5) to publicly display the copyrighted work; and (6) to digitally transmit the work. 17 U.S.C. § 106. Copyright duration now lasts for the author's life plus 70 years. For a work made for hire, that is, owned by a business, the copyright endures for 95 years.

1. NO COPYRIGHT PROTECTION FOR IDEAS OR FACTS

Two key limitations on a sports event producer's "ownership" of its games nonetheless survive the 1976 Copyright Act. First, copyright protection extends only to "original works of authorship" and not "to any idea, procedure, process, system, method of operation, concept, principle, or discovery. . . ." 17 U.S.C. § 102. As explained in *Motorola*, a live sports performance cannot amount to a "work of authorship":

> Sports events are not "authored" in any common sense of the word. There is, of course, at least at the professional level, considerable preparation for a game. However, the preparation is as much an expression of hope or faith as a determination of what will actually happen. Unlike movies, plays, television programs, or operas, athletic events are competitive and have no underlying script. Preparation may even cause mistakes to succeed, like the broken play in football that gains yardage because the opposition could not expect it. Athletic events may also result in wholly unanticipated occurrences, the most notable recent event being in a championship baseball game in which interference with a fly ball caused an umpire to signal erroneously a home run.

What "authorship" there is in a sports event, moreover, must be open to copying by competitors if fans are to be attracted. If the inventor of the T-formation in football had been able to copyright it, the sport might have to come to an end instead of prospering. Even where athletic preparation most resembles authorship— figure skating, gymnastics, and, some would uncharitably say, professional wrestling—a performer who conceives and executes a particularly graceful and difficult—or, in the case of wrestling, seemingly painful—acrobatic feat cannot copyright it without impairing the underlying competition in the future. A claim of being the only athlete to perform a feat doesn't mean much if no one else is allowed to try.

105 F.3d at 846. Thus, an upstart basketball league is free to stage a basketball game for profit, employing all the same rules, mechanics, and plays as the NBA, without that league's consent. *See Hoopla Sports and Entertainment, Inc. v. Nike, Inc.*, 947 F. Supp. 347 (N.D. Ill. 1996).

Second, even after the broadcast "expression" of a game is "fixed," copyright does not protect facts or create exclusive property rights in the bare events of the game—no more than it does for the events of a war, a crime, or a political convention. *See Feist Publications v. Rural Telephone Service*, 499 U.S. 340 (1991) (telephone directory's compilation of facts— names, addresses, phone numbers—not entitled to copyright); *Miller v. Universal City Studios*, 650 F.2d 1365 (5th Cir. 1981) (docudrama may use facts it learned from book about actual kidnapping). Thus, as long as Ronald Reagan's radio recreations of baseball games comprised his own expression of what was happening, he was not violating the copyrighted expression of another announcer's broadcast a half inning or so earlier. Likewise, today's digital sports journalists do not infringe copyright when they offer real-time unique commentary on sports events, and doing so is itself a copyrightable expression.

2. FAIR USE OF COPYRIGHTED TELECASTS

Another important doctrine, now embodied in § 107 of the Copyright Act, gives everyone the right to make "fair use" of a copyrighted work. The following case provides an intriguing example of an effort to appeal to fair use in the sports broadcasting context.

NEW BOSTON TELEVISION V. ENTERTAINMENT SPORTS PROGRAMMING NETWORK (ESPN)
215 U.S.P.Q. 755, 1981 WL 1374 (D. Mass. Aug. 3, 1981)

ZOBEL, DISTRICT JUDGE:

[New Boston Television owns and operates WSBK-TV, which licensed the exclusive rights to broadcast Red Sox baseball and Bruins hockey games. The Red Sox retained the copyright in the baseball telecasts, and paid WSBK one-half of all copyright royalties. The Bruins and WSBK jointly owned the copyright in the hockey telecasts.

The recently created ESPN cable channel negotiated with WSBK to rebroadcast excerpts of the Bruins and Red Sox telecasts on its SportsCenter program, but they could not agree on terms. ESPN proceeded to use the WSBK broadcasts, which then filed suit for copyright infringement. ESPN asserted several defenses, principally fair use.]

* * *

The fair use defense is a judicially developed doctrine which is now codified in the Copyright Revision Act of 1976, 17 U.S.C. § 107. It has been defined as "a privilege in others than the owner of the copyright to use the copyrighted material in a reasonable manner without his consent; notwithstanding the monopoly granted to the owner." *Rosemont Enterprises, Inc. v. Random House, Inc.*, 366 F.2d 303, 306 (2d Cir. 1966). The doctrine "offers a means of balancing the exclusive rights of the copyright holder with the public's interest in the dissemination of information affecting areas of universal concern, such as art, science, and industry." *Wainwright Securities, Inc. v. Wall Street Transcript Corp.*, 558 F.2d 91, 94 (2d Cir. 1977).

Fair use is a question which depends on the facts of each particular case, evaluated in light of certain criteria: 1) the purpose and character of the use, including whether such use is of a commercial nature or is for nonprofit educational purposes; 2) the nature of the copyrighted work; 3) the amount and substantiality of the portion used in relation to the copyrighted work as a whole; and 4) the effect of the use upon the potential market for or value of the copyrighted work.

Defendants assert that as to the first of these factors, their use is primarily for "news" purposes and hence should be protected by the fair use doctrine in order to assure the public's right of access to newsworthy information. While protection of the public right of access to such information is a primary justification for the fair use defense, this right is sufficiently protected merely by enabling defendants to report the underlying facts which the plaintiff's videotapes record. It does not however permit defendants to appropriate the plaintiff's expression of that information by copying the plaintiff's films themselves. "The fair use doctrine is not a license for corporate theft, empowering a court to ignore a copyright whenever it determines the underlying work contains material of possible public importance." *Iowa State University v. American Broadcasting Cos.*, 621 F.2d 57, 61 (2d Cir. 1980).

Defendants rely on *Time Incorporated v. Bernard Geis Assoc.*, 293 F. Supp. 130 (S.D.N.Y. 1968), in which the Court determined that the reproduction of frames of the Zapruder film in a book inquiring into the assassination of President Kennedy was fair use. However, the unique and extraordinary nature of that historical event renders that case distinguishable from the case at bar. In addition, while the defendants in *Geis* had no opportunity to record the event themselves, defendants here are under no such impediment. Moreover, defendants are engaged in copying for commercial exploitation. That fact is not dispositive and would not preclude a finding of fair use, but it is a factor which adds to the plaintiffs' case in evaluating likelihood of their success on the merits.

Defendants assert that their use is *de minimis* because it amounts to no more than two minutes out of each videotape owned by plaintiffs. However, it is the quality of the use rather than its quantity which is determinative. The excerpts used by defendants in this case, although of relatively short duration, are the "highlights" of each broadcast and as such their use may be considered substantial.

Defendants contend that plaintiffs have failed to demonstrate that their transmission has had any effect on the present or potential market for plaintiffs' copyright in that plaintiffs have made no attempt to sell excerpts from their programming to any cable networks in the past, and have experienced no diminution in the substantial revenue that they receive from the three major television networks who do pay plaintiffs for the right to broadcast highlights on their respective news shows. Assuming it to be true that plaintiffs have made no attempt to market their broadcasts within the cable field, a fact which has not been established, this does not permit defendants to appropriate plaintiffs' copyrighted material and effectively preclude such efforts in the future. It is for plaintiffs, not defendants, to determine when and in what manner they choose to exploit their copyright. Evidence of plaintiffs' revenues from the three major networks lends further credence to their claim that defendant's use deprives them of substantial additional revenue to which they are entitled as the owners of the copyright to these materials.

* * *

Injunction granted.

———

Consider how the fair use doctrine should apply to social media sharing of sports clips. Fans now routinely share sports highlights via social media platforms such as YouTube, Twitter, Instagram, and TikTok, which the leagues tolerate as a way to drive interest and excitement in the game. It is by no means clear, however, that the highly fact-intensive fair-use inquiry protects this activity. This troubling uncertainty and its potential impact on internet service providers led to passage of the 1998 Digital Millennium Copyright Act. The DMCA provides a safe harbor from copyright liability to entities that host content if they (i) expeditiously take down potentially infringing content upon receiving notice, (ii) had no actual or constructive knowledge of the infringing behavior, and (iii) derived no financial benefit directly attributable to the infringement. While service providers are not required to self-police for infringing content, immunity is not available to websites that maintain editorial control over the posted content or actively solicit the content. *See Viacom Int'l, Inc. v. YouTube, Inc.*, 676 F.3d 19, 29 (2d Cir. 2012).

In this spirit, in 2016, an English court applying that country's fair use doctrine upheld an infringement claim against Fanatix, a social media app that invited fans to upload eight-second clips of sports broadcasts, which could then be viewed for 24 hours. Users could search for their favorite sport or team and view clips on the app or visit the Fanatix website which separately aggregated and published clips. The court found the clips were sufficiently substantial, despite their short duration, because most contained key moments of contests. Although the court acknowledged that "citizen journalism" can merit fair use protection as a form of protected news reporting, it found that the app's primary purpose was sharing clips with other users rather than reporting on them. See *England and Wales Cricket Board Ltd v Fanatix*, 2016 EWHC 575 (Ch) (March 18, 2016). What standards should U.S. courts use to assess the information sharing rights of citizen journalists?

NOTES AND QUESTIONS

1.   *Nature of Copyrighted Work.* Do you agree with the *New Boston Television* application of fair use to sports event highlights? As a matter of public policy, wouldn't consumers be better served if television newscasts could use short game clips rather than just the bare scores and statistics? How does that use compare to one television newscast reporting on current events by using clips from another station's newscasts? If intellectual property rights accommodated ESPN's use, what harm, if any, would be inflicted on WSBK, or the Red Sox and Bruins?

2.   *Game Highlights Market.* What do you think was the impact of *New Boston Television* on the marketplace? Would your views on fair use change if the marketplace no longer seemed to function and fans interested in watching highlights were required to switch multiple channels to watch highlights only on those networks that were licensees of the original broadcast? Today the major sports leagues and other sports event producers routinely grant free use of video and audio excerpts from copyrighted broadcasts subject to restrictions that, for example, limit the total number of minutes a program can use and set the usage period to expire within a few days of the game. Is this an implicit acknowledgement that sharing game highlights does not erode the market for the copyrighted broadcast, and thus such use is fair?

3.   *Amount and Substantiality of Portion Used.* Shortly after *New Boston Television*, a closely divided Supreme Court ruled that recording television

shows for later in-home, personal viewing is non-infringing fair use of a copyrighted broadcast. *See Sony Corp. of America v. Universal City Studios*, 464 U.S. 417 (1984). Significantly, the Supreme Court held the reproduction of an entire broadcast is permissible in this context. Does that logic equally apply to home taping of sports broadcasts? Consider a sports bar that did not want to pay the $1,000 business "pay-per-view" fee for a championship boxing match, and so had a patron pay the $35 residential fee, tape the fight at home, and then relay videotapes to the sports bar every few rounds. *See Cablevision of Michigan v. Sports Palace*, 27 F.3d 566 (6th Cir. 1994). Should these actions be deemed fair or unfair uses under copyright doctrine, whether by the sports bar or by the patron?

3. PUBLIC PERFORMANCE OF COPYRIGHTED TELECASTS

Public Performance. Copyright law has steadily expanded to give authors exclusive control over who can transform their work into derivative versions (via various forms of new technology), and who can publicly perform the work. Sports broadcasting in particular poses the question whether a business that simply turns on the television for its customers or retransmits game feeds has publicly performed a game telecast and thereby infringed a copyright. The Copyright Act of 1976 says yes, broadly defining "public performance" to include performance or transmission of the work to "a place open to the public or at any place where a substantial number of persons outside of a normal circle of a family and its social acquaintances is gathered." 17 U.S.C. § 101. However, the Act also granted exemptions from liability for publicly performing a copyrighted work.

Home Use Exemption. At the same time, though, Congress exempted from liability "communication of a transmission embodying a performance . . . of a work by the public reception of the transmission on a single receiving apparatus of a kind commonly used in private homes." 17 U.S.C. § 110(5). This "home use" exemption covers the local candy store whose workers listen to live game audio using a smartphone and speaker, but not a sports bar that displays NFL games on eight screens on a Sunday afternoon.

The scope and limits of the "home use" exemption have complicated efforts of leagues and teams to enforce "blackout" rules designed to control which games are going into which markets. In *NFL v. McBee & Bruno's, Inc.*, 792 F.2d 726 (8th Cir. 1986), the National Football League sought to enforce blackout rules prohibiting telecasts of home games within the team's "home territory" (*i.e.*, a 75-mile radius) unless the game is sold out 72 hours in advance. St. Louis sports bars were using satellite dish antennae to intercept the raw signal of the local NFL team's game before it reached the broadcast network, and then displayed the blacked-out home game on television screens for customers. The Eighth Circuit held that the raw game feed was sufficiently "fixed" to merit copyright protection, and that displaying it was a public performance. The court rejected the bars' argument that their actions constituted a "home use," ruling that the type of apparatus used to receive the transmission was not "commonly found in private homes" at the time. Consider whether the decision would come out the same way today when residential satellite reception is widespread.

Passive Carrier Exemption. The advent of cable television in the 1960s and 1970s raised issues under copyright law, sharpened by the retransmission of sports broadcasts. To explain, cable systems pay fees, usually per subscriber, to the television stations and networks they carry. Copyright owners of retransmitted shows demanded that cable systems also compensate them for publicly performing works that had been licensed only to the television station or network. When the Supreme Court rejected this claim, *see Fortnightly Corp. v. United Artists Television*, 392 U.S. 390 (1968), Congress stepped in with the 1976 revisions of the Copyright Act to strike a compromise.

First, Congress created a special "passive carrier exemption" for retransmission of broadcast signals by

> any carrier who has no direct or indirect control over the content or selection of the primary transmission or over the particular recipients of the secondary transmission, and whose activities with respect to the secondary transmission consist solely of providing wires, cable, or other communications channels for the use of others.

17 U.S.C. § 111(a)(3). This provision protected cable television systems that do nothing but receive and deliver an unaltered signal to the ultimate viewer, and exercise no control over the programming transmitted. *See NFL v. Insight Telecommunications Corp.*, 158 F. Supp. 2d 124 (D. Mass. 2001) (middleman that merely relayed unaltered signal from Boston television stations to Bell Canada not liable for subsequent transmission over border to Canadian cable subscribers). In effect, the passive carrier exemption amounts to a compulsory license from the owners of copyrighted television programming to the cable systems.

Second, Congress required cable systems to pay statutorily prescribed royalties into a Copyright Royalty Board, which annually distributes them to the copyright owners of sports broadcasts and other television shows. The statutory royalty scheme avoided cable systems needing to enter "unworkable separate negotiations with numerous copyright holders," and advanced the "public interest . . . in a continuing supply of varied programming to viewers." *Eastern Microwave, Inc. v. Doubleday Sports, Inc.*, 691 F.2d 125, 132 (2d Cir. 1982). While the statutory formula for royalty payments generated a total of $12 million in 1978, it produces about $300 million a year today.

Although the statutory royalty scheme simplified business for cable systems, it set copyright holders against each other as they annually petition the Board as to how this money should be divided up among the numerous copyright owners across multiple categories of programming. Sports leagues and teams are adamant that their programming has driven the growth of cable retransmission and subscriber fees, and that royalty payments should correspond to comparative market value and not sheer volume of programming. They have argued for weighing more heavily program ratings and the demographic makeup of the respective audiences, as measured by commercial advertiser preferences. Other categories of program suppliers, including movies and syndicated programs such as soap operas and game shows, prefer allocating funds based on the amount of airtime. Which approach to distributing the statutory royalties makes sense to you?

Sports Programming and Cable Superstations. The sports leagues' argument that their programming spurred cable's growth is corroborated by the "superstation" phenomenon, which arose in the early days of cable and disrupted relationships among sports rights owners and their television partners. Among the first independent local stations retransmitted widely on cable or satellite were those that carried sports broadcasts, especially baseball, basketball, and hockey, where most games aired only locally. These local stations earned the sobriquet "superstation," and in the pre-internet era, they were a game-changer, allowing fans to follow their favorite team on television from anywhere in the country. For teams whose local station became a superstation, broadcast contracts began to generate exponentially greater revenue, creating league-wide imbalances (other than in the NFL which operates primarily through national network contracts). Leagues attempted through rule-setting and other forms of private ordering to limit superstation game telecasts, but this exposed them to antitrust challenge, as with the NBA-Chicago Bulls litigation we read about in Chapter 8. The superstation issue resolved over time through contract and the emergence of other distribution channels, including regional sports networks and internet streaming services.

Internet Retransmission. Technological advances have muddied application of the "public performance" doctrine in other ways, especially as the internet has facilitated unauthorized retransmission of game feeds worldwide, including to jurisdictions with weak copyright protection. In *NFL v. PrimeTime 24 Joint Venture*, 211 F.3d 10 (2d Cir. 2000), the Second Circuit upheld an injunction against a satellite carrier that was picking up television signals of NFL games in the U.S. and then transmitting the games to cable companies and subscribers in Canada. The satellite carrier argued that its unlicensed Canadian "public performance" of the NFL's copyrighted material "does not occur until the signal is actually received by the viewing public" in their homes, and was therefore subject to more permissive Canadian rather than American copyright law. The Second

Circuit rejected this argument and ruled instead that "each step in the process by which a protected work wends its way to the audience," is part of the public performance, and that the key early "predicate act" of receiving and transmitting the signals took place south of the U.S.-Canadian border. Would the outcome be the same if a foreign carrier situated a large antenna just over the border in Canada, Mexico, or Cuba to pick up from American stations free over-the-air signals of U.S. games, and then transmitted these game signals to subscribers all over the world?

The NFL and NBA filed a similar copyright infringement claim against a Canadian company that was also picking up over-the-air U.S. game signals, but webcast them across the border to Canadian fans. *NFL v. TVRadionow Corp.*, 53 U.S.P.Q.2d 1831 (W.D. Pa. 2000). The Canadian webcaster argued that Canadian law authorized the webcasts in Canada, and that it took adequate measures to avoid infringing U.S. copyrights by requiring users to enter a Canadian area code to verify their location. That, however, did not stop a significant number of American-based football fans from entering Canadian area codes. The court held that an extra-territorial actor can be held liable for an infringing public performance that occurs within the United States, and enjoined webcasting the signal, effectively barring the webcaster's activities worldwide. With the internet enabling global webcasts, how should a court reconcile U.S. law with conflicting intellectual property protections abroad?

***Aereo* Decision.** Equipment manufacturers and service providers continue their attempts to avoid the public performance doctrine, and corresponding liability for copyright infringement, through technological work-arounds. Aereo, Inc. was one such company, which sold a service that allowed its subscribers to view live and time-shifted streams of over-the-air television on internet-connected devices. It did so by leasing to each user an individual antenna and digital video recorder (DVR) situated in a remote warehouse that they could access over the internet. The existence of an individual antenna for each user distinguished Aereo from other services that retransmit or stream video content, including sports events, because it required subscriber intervention to select and play a program. The Supreme Court sharply divided over whether this distinction made a difference in an infringement lawsuit brought by a consortium of major broadcasters, including those that broadcast all the major U.S. sports. *American Broadcasting Companies, Inc. v. Aereo, Inc.*, 573 U.S. 431 (2014).

The *Aereo* majority held that, considered in light of the 1976 Copyright Act amendments, Aereo's business model sufficiently resembled cable companies that its service must be deemed a "public performance" that infringed the copyrights of the programming it transmitted:

> In terms of the Act's purposes, these differences do not distinguish Aereo's system from cable systems, which do perform "publicly." Viewed in terms of Congress' regulatory objectives,

602 INTELLECTUAL PROPERTY LAW AND SPORTS CH. 9

why should any of these technological differences matter? They concern the behind-the-scenes way in which Aereo delivers television programming to its viewers' screens. They do not render Aereo's commercial objective any different from that of cable companies. Nor do they significantly alter the viewing experience of Aereo's subscribers. . . .And why, if Aereo is right, could not modern CATV systems simply continue the same commercial and consumer-oriented activities, free of copyright restrictions, provided they substitute such new technologies for old? Congress would as much have intended to protect a copyright holder from the unlicensed activities of Aereo as from those of cable companies. . . .

Moreover, the subscribers to whom Aereo transmits television programs constitute "the public." Aereo communicates the same contemporaneously perceptible images and sounds to a large number of people who are unrelated and unknown to each other. This matters because, although the Act does not define "the public," it specifies that an entity performs publicly when it performs at "any place where a substantial number of persons outside of a normal circle of a family and its social acquaintances is gathered." The Act thereby suggests that "the public" consists of a large group of people outside of a family and friends.

Id. at 446–48.

In a scathing dissent, Justice Scalia, joined by Justices Thomas and Alito, criticized the majority for imposing "guilt by resemblance" in order to close up a "loophole" in the Copyright Act:

I share the Court's evident feeling that what Aereo is doing (or enabling to be done) to the Networks' copyrighted programming ought not to be allowed. . . . [W]hat we have before us must be considered a "loophole" in the law. It is not the role of this Court to identify and plug loopholes. It is the role of good lawyers to identify and exploit them, and the role of Congress to eliminate them if it wishes. Congress can do that, I may add, in a much more targeted, better informed, and less disruptive fashion than the crude "looks-like-cable-TV" solution the Court invents today.

Id. at 462 (Scalia, dissenting). Many observers at the time offered dire predictions that the *Aereo* decision would stifle technological innovation and imperil the future of cloud storage services.

———

NOTES AND QUESTIONS

1. *Copyright Legislation and Technological Change.* As technology has advanced, courts have struggled to apply the Copyright Act, which has been criticized as too fact-specific and lacking provisions that articulate more general principles. For example, as cable retransmission recedes in the face of internet streaming, the compulsory cable copyright license may become a dead letter. Congress has attempted to keep pace with technology, enacting two amendments to the Copyright Act in 2020:

- Protecting Lawful Streaming Act introduced serious criminal penalties for offering or delivering unauthorized commercial streaming of sporting events and other televised entertainments.

- Copyright Alternative in Small-Claims Enforcement Act established a simpler and less expensive administrative forum to resolve smaller infringement claims.

Both 2020 enactments lowered the barriers for bringing and pursuing infringement claims, which also raises the risk of claims against legitimate users. Should we be concerned about the impact overenforcement may have on fair use and free expression? How should future amendments resolve the tension between the Copyright Act's twin goals of stimulating artistic creativity and making such works available to the public?

2. *Market Solutions.* Given the pace of technology, should we prefer the free market to generate solutions for compensating creators, rather than rely on periodic legislative updates of copyright laws? Are there any practical obstacles in the way of sports teams (or copyright owners of other programs) negotiating agreements for the showing of their events on cable or the internet? Any differences from the *New Boston Television* case we saw earlier about game highlights on the news? Precisely what kinds of economic losses does a team or league suffer by not being able to withhold its consent to internet streaming of its games? Are these the kinds of losses that the law should compensate?

3. Aereo's *Cable System Analogy.* On remand to the district court, Aereo argued that it was entitled to continue its services as long as it paid the compulsory statutory royalty required of cable systems. The district court rejected this argument as "suffer[ing] from the fallacy that simply because an entity performs copyrighted works in a way similar to cable systems it must then be deemed a cable system for all other purposes of the Copyright Act." *Am. Broad. Companies, Inc. v. Aereo, Inc.*, No. 12-CV-1540, 2014 WL 5393867, at *3 (S.D.N.Y. Oct. 23, 2014). Following this ruling, Aereo ceased operations. Given that the Supreme Court elevated function over form in applying the public performance doctrine to Aereo, should the district court have treated Aereo as a cable system for all purposes of the Copyright Act? *See Fox Television Stations, Inc v. Aereokiller, LLC*, 851 F.3d 1002 (9th Cir. 2017) (declining to treat online television streaming service as a cable company eligible for compulsory copyright licenses).

4. *Future Technological Innovation.* Has the *Aereo* ruling affected the future of cloud computing and other new technologies? Or is the holding sufficiently limited so that it is unlikely to have wider impact beyond Aereo's specific methods? How can we tell? How much longer will *Aereo* be relevant considering the "cord-cutting" phenomenon in which sports television viewers are forgoing cable television subscriptions in favor of an alternative internet-based or wireless service?

5. *Internet Streaming and Piracy.* The European Court of Justice broadly interpreted the "communication to the public" element of EU copyright infringement claims (analogous to the U.S. "public performance" requirement) to rule that it is illegal to sell streaming boxes pre-configured for piracy. *Stichting Breain v. Wullems*, C-527/15, 2017 E.C.R. I-938. Based on this ruling, the English High Court (pre-Brexit) awarded the Premier League a blocking order that requires all U.K. internet service providers (ISPs) to prevent illegal streaming of its soccer matches. Other countries have followed suit, resulting in blocking internet access to thousands of server internet protocol (IP) addresses. Unlike in the U.S., the European Union is thus forcing non-liable ISPs to assist rightsholders and target infringers. Should the U.S. weaken its longstanding restriction on injunctions against non-liable third parties to harness this copyright enforcement mechanism?

6. *Internet Streaming Services and Sports Content.* Television streaming services originally defined themselves in opposition to live viewing, with consumers subscribing to the services that offer their preferred content and watching it on their own schedule. Traditional broadcast services retained their audiences largely because of sports, which consumers have insisted on watching live. That model is changing as more sports properties are making some content exclusively available on streaming services such as Amazon Prime Video (MLB), ESPN+ (NHL), and Peacock (English Premier League).

Although it is still an open question how many sports television rights will migrate to paid subscription services, the history of television services in America is that any new service with ambitions to grow or retain audience looks to sports. As sports television increasingly fractures and spreads across broadcast, cable, and internet television, fans will face difficult technological and financial choices in order to continue to view all their favorite sports. From a fan's perspective, should the U.S. consider adopting "right-to-view" legislation, like the U.K.'s Broadcasting Act, which gives a government ministry the power to draw up a list of sporting events of national interest, for which broadcast rights must be offered to the main free-to-air terrestrial broadcasters on "fair and reasonable terms"?

C. ATHLETE PUBLICITY RIGHTS

Public interest in sports has translated into celebrity for athletes, and even coaches and other sports personalities. Companies have turned to elite athletes like LeBron James, Serena Williams, Cristiano Ronaldo, and Tiger Woods, to promote all categories of consumer products and services, from athletic equipment and apparel to car insurance. Celebrity has enabled elite athletes to match or exceed their playing salaries with revenue from endorsement contracts. Athletes who are most successful in selling their name, image, and identity are those who carefully cultivate a public persona and strategically develop multiple brand relationships. Although the vast majority of professional athletes cannot earn substantial sums from licensing publicity rights individually, players associations have proven adept at facilitating collective licensing of publicity rights that permit ordinary players to earn supplementary income in this way.

To protect the commercial value of their image and fame, athletes rely on state law rights of publicity, including the right to: (a) protect their reputation from association with uncongenial goods and services, and (b) exclusively authorize the use of their name and likeness for commercial purposes. Although the nature and scope of publicity rights vary considerably from state to state, they all are limited by First Amendment freedoms of speech and expression. This section will explore the origins and scope of the right of publicity, and the most common defenses to a publicity-right infringement claim.

PROBLEM 9.2

Giannis Alleyoopolis is a Greek professional basketball player for the NBA Milwaukee Bucks. His nationality, in addition to size, speed, strength, and ball-handling skills, have earned him the nickname "Greek Freak." On court, his signature move is the "Eurostep Dunk" in which he disorients defenders with a side-to-side stepping action. Off court, Giannis's charming personality has found an outlet in telling "dad jokes" at post-game press conferences.

Giannis has parlayed his success and fame into multiple endorsement opportunities, including with a mobile phone service provider, a television streaming service, and a gyro food company. His most lucrative deal is with Nike, which developed a line of apparel branded with the "Greek Freak" nickname, and which pays Giannis 10 percent of gross sales of those products, adding about $5 million per year to his earnings.

Public fascination with Giannis has led fans to create social media feeds dedicated to Giannis, featuring commentary, photos, and videos, some of which generate considerable advertising revenue for the operators. Online vendors have started selling shirts and mugs using phrases such as "Milwaukee Eurostep," "Greek Freak Reigns," and "I Laugh at Greek Dad Jokes." A mail-order spice company now offers a spice blend branded "Greek Freak." When Giannis caught and saved a fan's phone as he was heading to the locker room after a game, the video went viral and a phone accessory seller linked to it with the message:

"Buy our shock-absorbing protective phone cases for when Greek superheroes are not around."

Based on the following materials, how would you advise Giannis on what he can do to stop these unauthorized uses of his name, image, and likeness. What legal claims might he have, and what defenses would be available to the users?

1. ORIGINS OF THE RIGHT OF PUBLICITY

State right-of-publicity laws have their origins in the tort of defamation and in the common law right to privacy. Defamation law has long created liability for statements about anyone that are false and injurious. But defamation suits are difficult to win, especially for athletes who as public figures face a heavier burden of proof. *See New York Times v. Sullivan*, 376 U.S. 254 (1964). In addition, most commentary on athletic performance comprises opinion, which is not legally actionable even if it harms an athlete's reputation. *See Time, Inc. v. Johnston*, 448 F.2d 378, 380 (4th Cir. 1971) (derogatory description of former professional basketball player's on-court performance not actionable, even though published nine years after he retired, because he remained a public figure who assumed the risk of good or bad publicity about his public performance); *Turner v. Wells*, 879 F.3d 1254, 1271 (11th Cir. 2018) (law firm investigatory report describing conduct of professional football coach is nonactionable opinion because statements are a "subjective assessment of [the coach's] conduct . . . not readily capable of being proven true or false"). Another limitation of defamation law is that it does not cover situations where an athlete's name or likeness is merely being associated with a product, without a false statement of endorsement or quantifiable harm.

Accordingly, athletes and other celebrities initially sought to control use of their name, image, and likeness (NIL) through privacy torts, which fall into one of four categories: (1) intrusion upon seclusion or solitude; (2) public disclosure of embarrassing private facts; (3) publicity which places a person in a false light in the public eye; and (4) appropriation of name or likeness. *See* William Prosser, *Privacy*, 48 CAL. L. REV. 383, 389 (1960). The first three categories address intrusions into one's private life and affairs, and courts generally recognize that even a celebrity is entitled to some degree of personal privacy. Thus, in *Jason Pierre-Paul v. ESPN*, 2016 WL 4530884 (S.D. Fla. Aug. 29, 2016), the court allowed a professional football player to pursue invasion of privacy claims against a media company and its reporter who disclosed medical information about the player's hand injury from a fireworks mishap. The *Pierre-Paul* court held that even legitimate public interest in a celebrity athlete's medical condition must yield to limits on publication of private facts imposed by "common decency" and "regard to the feelings of the individual." *See also Bollea v. Gawker*

Media LLC, 2016 WL 4073660 (Fla. Cir. Ct. June 8, 2016) (online media company required to pay $140 million in damages to former professional wrestler Hulk Hogan for publishing unauthorized sextape); *Erin Andrews v. Marriott International Inc.*, No. 11C-4831 (Tenn. Cir. Ct. Mar. 7, 2016) (jury awarded sports reporter $55 million in damages when hotel peeping Tom posted nude videos of her on the internet); *Spahn v. Julian Messner, Inc.*, 21 N.Y.2d 124, 233 N.E.2d 840 (1967) (unauthorized falsified biography of baseball player violated statutory right to privacy).

As for the fourth privacy tort—misappropriation of name or likeness—early on celebrities who advanced such claims encountered resistance from the courts, which doubted whether protection should extend to athletes who had actively sought fame. Thus, David O'Brien, a legendary college and professional football player who had moral objections to drinking or endorsing beer was unable to stop a brewery from using his photo in its annual football calendar containing game schedules. See *O'Brien v. Pabst Sales*, 124 F.2d 167 (5th Cir. 1941). The court ruled that because O'Brien had freely permitted past publicity uses of his picture, he had no right of privacy to stop Pabst's use which, in the absence of a statement that he endorsed the beer, "could not possibly disgrace or reflect upon or cause him damage." Id. at 170–71. Do you agree that Pabst's use of O'Brien's picture could not possibly injure him? What if, as was alleged, O'Brien was a member of a temperance group and the calendar caused him great embarrassment and humiliation?

A decade later, a U.S. court dramatically altered the legal playing field in another sports-related case. In *Haelan Laboratories v. Topps Chewing Gum*, 202 F.2d 866 (2d Cir. 1953), two firms had signed agreements with baseball players authorizing use of their names and pictures on bubblegum trading cards. Haelan, the firm with the first and supposedly "exclusive" license to that effect, sued Topps for inducing breach of its contract. Topps' defense was that both sets of contracts amounted to no more than the players' release from liability for invasion of privacy, and no separate "name and likeness" property right existed. The Second Circuit disagreed, identifying an independent and assignable common law right to the publicity value of one's name and picture:

> [I]t is common knowledge that many prominent persons (especially actors and ball-players), far from having their feelings bruised through public exposure of their likenesses, would feel sorely deprived if they no longer received money for authorizing advertisements, popularizing their countenances, displayed in newspapers, magazines, busses, trains and subways. This right of publicity would usually yield them no money unless it could be made the subject of an exclusive grant which barred any other advertiser from using their pictures.

202 F.2d at 868.

This new brand of intellectual property heralded the transformation of the Major League Baseball Players Association into a real union. After *Haelan*, the Players Association took over the sale of baseball card licenses and other group marketing efforts by the players, funding a war chest that enabled tough stances at the collective bargaining table, as we saw in the chapters on labor law. Annual group licensing revenue for the major league players associations has swelled, by 2022 reaching over $60 million for the MLBPA, and over $200 million for the NFL Players Association. Indeed, a by-product of this combination of law and economics is that the Internal Revenue Service maintains that the descendible publicity right is a taxable asset in a dead celebrity's estate. *See Estate of Andrews v. United States*, 850 F. Supp. 1279 (E.D. Va.1994). Settling divisions among courts, many states now recognize that the right of publicity is descendible. *See, e.g.*, New York Civil Rights Law § 50–f (2020) (establishing post-mortem rights of publicity).

In the 65 years since *Haelan*, over 40 states have established—either through judicial pronouncement or legislative enactment—at least a narrow right to recover for misappropriation of celebrity. The Restatement (Third) of Unfair Competition § 46 defines an infringer of the right of publicity as "[o]ne who appropriates the commercial value of a person's identity by using without consent the person's name, likeness, or other indicia of identity for purposes of trade." However, states vary widely in their articulation of publicity rights and the elements of an infringement claim.

The diversity of state policy choices regarding NIL rights is manifest in over 25 state laws that, beginning in 2021, nullified the NCAA's amateurism principle to the extent it banned college athletes from profiting from their NIL. As discussed in more detail in Chapter 12, the NCAA responded to this development by withdrawing from regulating NIL and reinstating college athletes' publicity rights, subject to state law. Each such statute is unique, varying in how the state chose to address, for example, who may represent college athletes, disclosure requirements, how to resolve conflicts of interest with university values or its existing branding contracts, use of institutional intellectual property, regulation of booster involvement in NIL activities, and restrictions on activities involving "vice" products such as alcohol, tobacco, and gambling. Vindication of any athlete's publicity rights will thus necessarily depend on the applicable state law.

2. SCOPE OF THE RIGHT OF PUBLICITY

To recover on a right of publicity claim, the plaintiff typically must show that the defendant's commercial appropriation of plaintiff's identity somehow resulted in injury to plaintiff. Early cases focused on the unauthorized use of a celebrity's image for the purpose of false endorsement of or association with a good or service. The right has expanded over time, however, to protect celebrity status itself. Thus, LeBron James sought to stop a brewery from "benefitting" from his image when it retweeted a viral photo of the great basketball player taken when he jokingly swiped a "Dortmunder Gold" beer bottle from a surprised courtside server during a playoff game. Despite the photo remaining ubiquitous on social media, the brewery agreed to delete its tweet, which had added the caption "G.O.A.T. with G.O.L.D." (The first set of initials stands for "greatest of all time.") Should the law recognize and compensate this type of "injury"? Does it make a difference that the brewery's retweet added a caption? It has been argued that a celebrity's image is a public good that is infinitely consumable without being depleted, and thus James suffered no harm here. Conversely, it has been argued that a celebrity is harmed by over-exposure or low-quality exposure of his identity. Does that argument carry weight in the internet age?

One justification for the right of publicity is that every person is entitled to the fruit of her labors. *See* Melville B. Nimmer, *The Right of Publicity*, 19 Law & Contemp. Probs. 215–16 (1954). Accordingly, a celebrity is entitled to the value of her persona because she has expended considerable time, effort, skill, and resources to develop it. This theory underpins the ruling in *Uhlaender v. Henricksen*, 316 F. Supp. 1277 (D. Minn. 1970). The *Uhlaender* court upheld the MLB Players Association's publicity rights claim against the "Negamco's Major League Baseball" board game, which used the names and statistics of over 500 professional ballplayers, identified by team, uniform number, and playing positions. In a forerunner of today's fantasy sports contests, the game used playing statistics to provide computations of the relative value of players and to determine board game outcomes. In finding that a celebrity has a "legitimate proprietary interest in his public personality," the court noted:

> A celebrity must be considered to have invested his years of practice and competition in a public personality which eventually may reach marketable status. That identity, embodied in his name, likeness, statistics and other personal characteristics, is the fruit of his labors and is a type of property.

Id. at 1282. The court further held that this property interest required enjoining the unauthorized use of players' names and statistics. Must one be a celebrity to be entitled to this property right?

Other articulations of the right of publicity have emphasized the prevention of unjust enrichment. *See Midler v. Ford Motor Co.*, 849 F.2d 460, 462 (9th Cir. 1988) (comparing defendant car company's conduct in imitating singer's voice to that "of the average thief"). How can you tell when an unauthorized user of celebrity identity has been enriched in a way that is unjust? Alternatively, courts have enforced publicity rights as necessary to create economic incentives to acquire the skills and talents that generate fame, as in the *Zacchini* case discussed below. But, as one commentator suggests:

> Practically any creation of a private property right will increase the incentive of the holder to develop the underlying resource. Nevertheless, in many situations in which development incentives would be strengthened, the courts nonetheless refuse to create a private right. For instance, there might be more new football plays if courts enforced rights over them. Nevertheless, these rights do not exist.

Mark F. Grady, *A Positive Economic Theory of the Right of Publicity*, 1 UCLA ENT. L. REV. 97, 111 (1994).

Critics of the right of publicity argue that "allowing celebrities to control the meanings of their constructed personas deprives us all of the ability to 'recode' or reinterpret these texts for our own personal expression." Roberta Rosenthal Kwall, *Fame*, 73 IND. L.J. 1, 3 (1997). Professor Kwall further notes that intellectual property regimes are particularly fertile ground for exploration of a "fundamental issue pertinent to all forms of property ownership[:] what should be the appropriate degree of public access to private property." Some state publicity-rights enactments have addressed this issue by carving out the public's countervailing right to use a celebrity's NIL in a wide variety of newsworthy, public affairs, entertainment, and artistic endeavors, including broadcasting or reporting on a sports event. Publicity rights claims presenting conflicts with the First Amendment also provide some answers, as discussed later in this chapter.

3. IDENTIFIABILITY OF THE PUBLICITY-RIGHT OWNER

To vindicate a publicity right, the celebrity must show, at a minimum, that she is identifiable in the commercial promotion of a product or service. The question of "identifiability" has been answered broadly to include situations where the public would identify the celebrity even if a name or picture is not used. Consider the *Sports Illustrated* 1994 swimsuit edition, which ran an advertisement for Killian's Red Beer using a drawing of an old-time baseball game with a pitcher in an unusual windup position. Long-retired pitcher Don Newcombe was well known to fans of his era as the only player to use that peculiar style of windup. The Ninth Circuit ruled under California statutory and common law that Newcombe, who was a recovering alcoholic and upset that his identity was used to promote beer, had a triable claim for publicity right infringement. *See Newcombe v. Adolf Coors Co.*, 157 F.3d 686 (9th Cir. 1998). Is this the right result considering that the ad ran 34 years after Newcombe retired from baseball, did not show his jersey number or face, and did not depict any particular team's uniform or stadium?

Other cases address the identifiability issue in connection with:

(i) *Nicknames and Catchphrases.* Playgirl Magazine published a stylized drawing of a nude black male seated with his gloved hands on the ropes in the corner of a boxing ring, accompanied with lascivious verse that referred to the figure as "the Greatest." The court found sufficient facial resemblance to Mohammed Ali, when coupled with use of Ali's well-known appellation, to violate the fighter's publicity rights. *See Ali v. Playgirl*, 447 F. Supp. 723 (S.D.N.Y. 1978). The court also emphasized that the illustration contained no "informational or newsworthy dimension." Should such content change the analysis? *See also Johnny Carson v. Here's Johnny Portable Toilets*, 698 F.2d 831 (6th Cir. 1983) (talk show host Johnny Carson prevailed on claim against portable toilet manufacturer's use of phrases "Here's Johnny" and "The World's Foremost Commodian"); *Hirsch v. S.C. Johnson & Son, Inc.*, 90 Wis. 2d 379, 280 N.W.2d 129 (1979) (football great Elroy "Crazylegs" Hirsch prevailed on claim against "Crazylegs" women's shaving gel).

(ii) *Abandoned Name.* Basketball great Kareem Abdul-Jabbar sued for a violation of his publicity rights when General Motors used his former name, Lew Alcindor, in a car commercial. The court held that Abdul-Jabbar did not abandon the name and that the California statute's reference to "name or likeness" is a "flexible proposition" that includes indicia of identity beyond one's current use. *Abdul-Jabbar v. General Motors Corp.*, 75 F.3d 1391, 1399–1400 (9th Cir. 1996). Should it matter that the car commercial used the name Lew Alcindor in the context of an informational trivia quiz about his legendary college basketball achievements?

(iii) *Distinctive Attributes.* A cigarette commercial showed several racing cars at the track, including one that resembled the car of famed driver Lothar Motschenbacher, with its solid red color and narrow white pinstripe. Although the commercial altered Motschenbacher's car number, the court found a publicity right violation because the "distinctive decorations appearing on the car" were sufficient to cause "persons to think the car in question was plaintiff's and to infer that the person driving the car was the plaintiff." *Motschenbacher v. R.J. Reynolds Tobacco*, 498 F.2d 821, 826–27 (9th Cir. 1974); *see also Midler v. Ford Motor Co.*, 849 F.2d 460, 461 (9th Cir. 1988) (Bette Midler stated viable publicity rights claim against car company's use of "sound-alike" singer in television commercial). Would the court have reached this result if the product were not as controversial as cigarettes? *See White v. Samsung Elec. Am., Inc.*, 971 F.2d 1395 (9th Cir. 1992) (robot dressed and posed like Vanna White next to "Wheel of Fortune" set sufficiently identified her to state publicity rights claim).

4. FIRST AMENDMENT AND THE RIGHT OF PUBLICITY: INTRODUCTION

While the right of publicity has proven a financial bonanza for elite athletes, it raises public policy questions when enforcement of one person's publicity right restrains another's freedom of speech. Copyright law justifies that restraint as necessary to create incentives for more speech. But publicity rights provide no such incentive. To the contrary, restricting the use of celebrity identities impedes the communication of ideas.

The Supreme Court addressed this tension in *Zacchini v. Scripps-Howard Broadcasting*, 433 U.S. 562 (1977). As noted earlier, Hugo "the Flying" Zacchini performed a "human cannonball" act in which he was shot from a cannon in a fenced-in area of the county fair. A local television station sent a reporter to the fair to videotape Zacchini's fifteen-second act, and then showed the entire performance on its newscast. By a narrow 5–4 majority, the Supreme Court held that enforcement of Zacchini's publicity rights under Ohio state law did not abridge the television station's First Amendment rights:

> The broadcast of a film of petitioner's entire act poses a substantial threat to the economic value of that performance. . . . [T]his act is the product of [Zacchini's] own talents and energy, the end result of much time, effort, and expense. Much of its economic value lies in the "right of exclusive control over the publicity given to his performance": if the public can see the act free on television, it will be less willing to pay to see it at the fair. . . . [T]he broadcast of petitioner's entire performance, unlike the unauthorized use of another's name for purposes of trade . . . goes to the heart of petitioner's ability to earn a living as an entertainer.

433 U.S. at 575–76.

The *Zacchini* case differs in two key respects from *Haelan* and its successors. First, as the dissent emphasized, this case involved a newscast, worthy of far greater constitutional protection than commercial marketing. Second, as the majority accentuated, this broadcast was not simply an "appropriation of an entertainer's reputation to enhance the attractiveness of a commercial product, but the appropriation of the very activity by which the entertainer acquired his reputation in the first place." Like the judge in *Pittsburgh Athletic*, the Court was concerned that the latter form of appropriation would dilute the performer's economic incentives to make the necessary investment in developing the skills and appeal required for an entertainment performance that the public would watch and enjoy. Does *Zacchini* suggest that publicity rights require a balancing of the athlete's economic interests against the public's right to newsworthy information?

Consider these sports cases that explore the First Amendment limits on celebrity publicity rights:

(i) *Parody and the First Amendment.* "Cardtoons" were self-described "parody" trading cards featuring caricatures of major league baseball players who were readily identifiable despite pseudonyms that lampooned their public persona and teams (*e.g.,* Treasury Bonds for Barry Bonds, and Los Angeles Codgers for Dodgers). Language on the cards expressly disclaimed any official endorsement. Relying on the First Amendment, the Tenth Circuit dismissed the MLBPA's publicity right claim, distinguishing this branch of intellectual property as less deserving of protection, especially in the case of celebrity parodies that offer important social commentary. The court rejected the athletes' economic justifications for enforcing their publicity rights because "the commercial value of their identities are merely a by-product of their performance values," and the cards would not displace athletes' commercial opportunities given how unlikely it was that MLBPA would license self-parody. *Cardtoons L.C. v. MLB Players Association,* 95 F.3d 959, 972–75 (10th Cir. 1996). Why was Cardtoons allowed to continue operating when, as we read earlier, player publicity-right claims forced the Negamco MLB board game out of business?

(ii) *Commercial Versus Noncommercial Speech.* When is the use of a celebrity athlete's name or identity protected by the First Amendment as sufficiently informational or newsworthy, as opposed to primarily for purposes of advertising or trade? *See Titan Sports v. Comics World,* 870 F.2d 85 (2d Cir. 1989) (whether First Amendment protects a magazine's insertion of glossy, oversized posters of professional wrestlers depends on whether magazine used photos for "purposes of trade"). In *Montana v. San Jose Mercury News,* 34 Cal. App. 4th 790, 40 Cal. Rptr. 2d 639 (1995), the *San Jose Mercury News* published a special Souvenir Section of the newspaper to celebrate the San Francisco 49ers' fourth Super Bowl victory. An artistic rendition of quarterback Joe Montana appeared with reportage on the section's front page, which the Mercury later reprinted in poster form and sold for $5. Montana then sued the Mercury, not challenging the original newspaper picture and story, but just the poster reprint featuring his likeness. His claim failed on two grounds: (1) the posters reported newsworthy items of public interest and (2) a newspaper has a constitutional right to promote itself by reproducing its news stories. *See also* Complaint in *Muhammad Ali Enterprises v. Fox Broadcasting Co.,* 2017 WL 4516708 (N.D. Ill. Oct. 10, 2017) (alleging Super Bowl broadcaster's video tribute to legendary boxer Muhammad Ali was commercial speech because it was incorporated into pregame promotion).

Compare *Jordan v. Jewel Food Stores, Inc.,* 743 F.3d 509 (7th Cir. 2014), in which Michael Jordan sued Jewel Food, a Chicago grocery store, over an ad in *Sports Illustrated*'s commemorative issue, congratulating the athlete on his induction into the pro basketball hall of fame. The ad displayed basketball shoes bearing Jordan's number 23, and saluted "a fellow Chicagoan who was just around the corner for so many years," echoing the store's slogan, "good things are just around the corner." In rejecting the First Amendment defense and remanding the claim for trial, the Seventh Circuit ruled the ad "is no less 'commercial' because it promotes brand awareness or loyalty," rather than specifically proposing a commercial transaction. *Id.* at 518. Jewel Food settled with Jordan rather than go to trial, but a similar case against another Chicago grocery chain that had advertised in the commemorative issue resulted in an $8.9 million verdict for Jordan, an amount based in part on his standard endorsement contract value. *See Jordan v. Dominick's Finer Foods*, 2015 WL 5086730 (N.D. Ill. Aug. 25, 2015). Does this amount fairly reflect the injury to Jordan? What factors should determine whether a communication about an athlete's achievements has a sufficient economic motivation to defeat the speaker's First Amendment rights? *See Abdul-Jabbar v. General Motors Corp.*, 75 F.3d 1391, 1399–1400 (9th Cir. 1996) (publicity rights claim can go forward against car advertisement that incorporated trivia quiz about former basketball player's award-winning play).

(iii) *Artistic Expression.* NHL player Tony Twist earned notoriety as a brutal enforcer, inspiring the violent, Mafia-themed comic book *Spawn* to introduce a new character named "Anthony 'Tony Twist' Twistelli" who committed the most heinous crimes. While the only evident resemblance between the comic book character and the real Tony Twist was their name, the creator repeatedly told the media that he borrowed the name from the hockey player. When the real Twist learned of this, he sued claiming violation of his publicity rights through a defamatory misappropriation of his name. In *Doe, a/k/a Tony Twist v. TCI Cablevision*, 110 S.W.3d 363 (Mo. 2003), the Missouri Supreme Court ruled that the First Amendment did not immunize *Spawn*, because it used Twist's identity primarily for commercial benefit, not as a vehicle for artistic expression. The court observed:

> Twist made a submissible case that respondents' use of his name and identity was for a commercial advantage. Nonetheless, there is still an expressive component in the use of his name and identity as a metaphorical reference to tough-guy "enforcers." And yet, respondents agree (perhaps to avoid a defamation claim) that the use was not a parody or other expressive comment or a fictionalized account of the real Twist. As such, the metaphorical reference to Twist, though a literary device, has very little literary value compared to its commercial value. On the record here, the use and identity of Twist's name has become predominantly a ploy to sell comic books and related products rather than an artistic or literary expression, and under these circumstances, free speech must give way to the right of publicity.

Id. at 374.

On remand, the jury awarded $15 million in damages to Twist. An appellate court upheld the verdict based on evidence that the "predominant purpose" for using the "Tony Twist" name was "commercial gain," not "artistic expression," including evidence that *Spawn* specifically marketed its products to hockey fans. 207 S.W.3d 52, 59 (Mo. Ct. App. 2006). What are your views about the right of an author to use any celebrity names for his evil or heroic characters? Do you agree with the court that the proper measures of damages in this right of publicity case should include both emotional as well as financial harm *Spawn* inflicted on Twist?

The Masters golf tournament was the occasion for another court to balance the First Amendment right of free expression against a celebrity's right not to have his or her name or identity exploited for commercial purposes. "Sports artist" Rick Rush created a painting entitled *The Masters of Augusta* that depicted Tiger Woods mid-swing, with six other golf greats, including Jack Nicklaus and Arnold Palmer, looking down on him. Jireh Publishing Company then sold 700 serigraph prints for $700 each, and many more small lithographs for $15 apiece. Woods, who for several years had earned over $70 million from endorsements annually, sued claiming violation of both his trademark and publicity rights in his work and image.

ETW CORP. V. JIREH PUBLISHING, INC.
332 F.3d 915 (6th Cir. 2003)

GRAHAM, DISTRICT JUDGE.

* * *

II. *Trademark Claims Based on the Unauthorized Use of the Registered Trademark "Tiger Woods"*

* * *

ETW claims that Jireh infringed the registered mark "Tiger Woods" by including these words in marketing materials which accompanied the prints of Rush's painting. The words "Tiger Woods" do not appear on the face of the prints, nor are they included in the title of the painting. The words "Tiger Woods" do appear under the flap of the envelopes which contain the prints, and Woods is mentioned twice in the narrative which accompanies the prints.

The Lanham Act provides a defense to an infringement claim where the use of the mark "is a use, otherwise than as a mark, . . . which is descriptive of and used fairly and in good faith only to describe the goods . . . of such party [.]" 15 U.S.C. § 1115(b)(4). In evaluating a defendant's fair use defense, a court must consider whether defendant has used the mark: (1) in its descriptive sense; and (2) in good faith.

A celebrity's name may be used in the title of an artistic work so long as there is some artistic relevance. The use of Woods's name on the back of the envelope containing the print and in the narrative description of the print are purely descriptive and there is nothing to indicate that they were used other than in good faith. The prints, the envelopes which contain them, and the narrative materials which accompany them clearly identify Rush as the source of the print. Woods is mentioned only to describe the content of the print.

The district court properly granted summary judgment on ETW's claim for violation of its registered mark, "Tiger Woods," on the grounds that the claim was barred by the fair use defense as a matter of law.

III. *Trademark Claims Under 15 U.S.C. § 1125(a) Based on the Unauthorized Use of the Likeness of Tiger Woods*

* * *

Here, ETW claims protection under the Lanham Act for any and all images of Tiger Woods. This is an untenable claim. ETW asks us, in effect, to constitute Woods himself as a walking, talking trademark. Images and likenesses of Woods are not protectable as a trademark because they do not perform the trademark function of designation. They do not distinguish and identify the source of goods. They cannot function as a trademark because there are undoubtedly thousands of images and likenesses of Woods taken by countless photographers, and drawn, sketched, or painted by numerous artists, which have been published in many forms of media, and sold and distributed throughout the world. No reasonable person could believe that merely because these photographs or paintings contain Woods's likeness or image, they all originated with Woods.

We hold that, as a general rule, a person's image or likeness cannot function as a trademark. . . .

Here, ETW does not claim that a particular photograph of Woods has been consistently used on specific goods. Instead, ETW's claim is . . . a sweeping claim to trademark rights in every photograph and image of Woods. Woods, like [Babe] Ruth, is one of the most photographed sports figures of his generation, but this alone does not suffice to create a trademark claim.

The district court properly granted summary judgment on ETW's claim of trademark rights in all images and likenesses of Tiger Woods.

IV. *Ohio Right to Privacy Claims, and the First Amendment Defense*

* * *

B.   *First Amendment Defense*

The protection of the First Amendment is not limited to written or spoken words, but includes other mediums of expression, including music, pictures, films, photographs, paintings, drawings, engravings, prints, and sculptures. Speech is protected even though it is carried in a form that is sold for profit. The fact that expressive materials are sold does not diminish the degree of protection to which they are entitled under the First Amendment. Publishers disseminating the work of others who create expressive materials also come wholly within the protective shield of the First Amendment. Even pure commercial speech is entitled to significant First Amendment protection.

Rush's prints are not commercial speech. They do not propose a commercial transaction. Accordingly, they are entitled to the full protection of the First Amendment. Thus, we are called upon to decide whether Woods's intellectual property rights must yield to Rush's First Amendment rights.

* * *

E.   *Application of the Law to the Evidence in this Case*

The evidence in the record reveals that Rush's work consists of much more than a mere literal likeness of Woods. It is a panorama of Woods's victory at the 1997 Masters Tournament, with all of the trappings of that tournament in full view, including the Augusta clubhouse, the leader board, images of Woods's caddy, and his final round partner's caddy. These elements in themselves are sufficient to bring Rush's work within the protection of the First Amendment. The Masters Tournament is probably the world's most famous golf tournament and Woods's victory in the 1997 tournament was a historic event in the world of sports. A piece of art that portrays a historic sporting event communicates and celebrates the value our culture attaches to such events. It would be ironic indeed if the presence of the image of the victorious athlete would deny the work First Amendment protection. Furthermore, Rush's work includes not only images of Woods and the two caddies, but also carefully crafted likenesses of six past winners of the Masters Tournament: Arnold Palmer, Sam Snead, Ben Hogan, Walter Hagen, Bobby Jones, and Jack Nicklaus, a veritable pantheon of golf's greats. Rush's work conveys the message that Woods himself will someday join that revered group.

* * *

In regard to the Ohio law right of publicity claim, we conclude that Ohio would construe its right of publicity as suggested in the Restatement (Third) of Unfair Competition, Chapter 4, Section 47, Comment d., which articulates a rule analogous to the rule of fair use in copyright law. Under this rule, the substantiality and market effect of the use of the celebrity's image is analyzed in light of the informational and creative content of the defendant's use. Applying this rule, we conclude that Rush's work has substantial informational and creative content which outweighs any adverse effect on ETW's market and that Rush's work does not violate Woods's right of publicity.

We further find that Rush's work is expression which is entitled to the full protection of the First Amendment and not the more limited protection afforded to commercial speech. When we balance the magnitude of the speech restriction against the interest in protecting Woods's intellectual property right, we encounter precisely the same considerations weighed by the Tenth Circuit in *Cardtoons* [*L.C. v. Major League Baseball Players Ass'n*, 95 F.3d 959 (10th Cir. 1996)]. These include consideration of the fact that through their pervasive presence in the media, sports and entertainment celebrities have come to symbolize certain ideas and values in our society and have become a valuable means of expression in our culture. As the Tenth Circuit observed "[c]elebrities . . . are an important element of the shared communicative resources of our cultural domain." *Cardtoons*, 95 F.3d at 972.

In balancing these interests against Woods's right of publicity, we note that Woods, like most sports and entertainment celebrities with commercially valuable identities, engages in an activity, professional golf, that in itself generates a significant amount of income which is unrelated to his right of publicity. Even in the absence of his right of publicity, he would still be able to reap substantial financial rewards from authorized appearances and endorsements. It is not at all clear that the appearance of Woods's likeness in artwork prints which display one of his major achievements will reduce the commercial value of his likeness.

While the right of publicity allows celebrities like Woods to enjoy the fruits of their labors, here Rush has added a significant creative component of his own to Woods's identity. Permitting Woods's right of publicity to trump Rush's right of freedom of expression would extinguish Rush's right to profit from his creative enterprise.

After balancing the societal and personal interests embodied in the First Amendment against Woods's property rights, we conclude that the effect of limiting Woods's right of publicity in this case is negligible and significantly outweighed by society's interest in freedom of artistic expression.

Finally, applying the transformative effects test adopted by the Supreme Court of California in *Comedy III* [*Productions, Inc. v. Gary Saderup, Inc.*, 25 Cal.4th 387, 21 P.3d 797 (2001)], we find that Rush's work does contain significant transformative elements which make it especially worthy of First Amendment protection and also less likely to interfere with the economic interest protected by Woods' right of publicity. Unlike the unadorned, nearly photographic reproduction of the faces of The Three Stooges in *Comedy III,* Rush's work does not capitalize solely on a literal depiction of Woods. Rather, Rush's work consists of a collage of images in addition to Woods's image which are combined to describe, in artistic form, a historic event in sports history and to convey a message about the significance of Woods's achievement in that event. Because Rush's work has substantial transformative elements, it is entitled to the full protection of the First Amendment. In this case, we find that Woods's right of publicity must yield to the First Amendment.

* * *

Dismissal Affirmed.

NOTES AND QUESTIONS

1. *Judicial Balancing.* The Missouri Supreme Court in the Tony Twist case and the Sixth Circuit in the Tiger Woods case reached exactly opposite conclusions. The first determined that *Spawn's* use of Tony Twist's name was primarily commercial and thus not entitled to First Amendment protection, while the second concluded that Rick Rush's use of Tiger Woods' image in the painting was expressive, non-commercial, and thus protected. Is there something about the use of Woods' image that made it more worthy of constitutional immunity than the use of Twist's name in a comic book, or do the opinions simply reflect different judicial views about the balance between the right of publicity and the First Amendment?

2. *Economic Justification for Publicity Rights.* As in *Cardtoons,* the court in the Tiger Woods case discounts the economic value of publicity rights for an athlete who "engages in an activity, professional golf, that in itself generates a significant amount of income which is unrelated to his right of publicity." Why is the rights owner's wealth or alternative sources of income relevant to the balance between the First Amendment and the right of publicity? Is a wealthy rights owner less entitled to exploit his copyrights, trademarks, or publicity rights than a needier rights owner, or is this factor only relevant in cases involving celebrity rights of publicity?

3. *Consumer Welfare Concerns.* The redistribution of wealth inherent in recognition of the athlete's publicity right has made it correspondingly more expensive for fans to enjoy collecting baseball cards, wearing basketball sneakers, and swinging golf clubs. In this light, what justifies awarding athletes exclusive control over their image in cases like that of Tiger Woods where there is no association of the athlete with another product other than his own persona? Is that control necessary to provide adequate incentives for the development of the players' talents and performance? Should we want to provide additional incentives for the especially talented few to achieve celebrity status? Or does a broad right of publicity suitably recognize athletes'

"moral" right to control and exploit their own identities, rather than to enrich others?

4. *Mass-Produced Goods.* Based on the Sixth Circuit's analysis, could a self-proclaimed artist put Tiger Woods' picture on a T-shirt or coffee mug with an inspirational phrase, sell it without Woods' consent, and claim First Amendment protection because the item expresses some piety about achieving greatness? Does attaching a "message" to a mass-produced, profit-generating item immunize the inclusion of a celebrity likeness? Or must the producer be recognized in some formal way as an "artist"? How should a court or jury decide where to draw the line between art and commercial products? Is the distinction a question of fact or law?

What if the mass-produced good is a book on the history of baseball using names and pictures of former ballplayers? In *Gionfriddo v. MLB*, 94 Cal. App. 4th 400, 114 Cal. Rptr. 2d 307 (1st Dist. 2001), the court held that MLB's use of retired players' images and identifying information in its websites, documentaries, and game day programs enjoyed full First Amendment protection accorded to noncommercial speech and were "public affairs" uses exempt from consent under the California right of publicity statute. That statutory exemption is premised on the public's "right to know"—should that right extend to information about topics that concededly do not rise to the level of news? Do you agree with the court that MLB's uses did not harm the players' economic interests, and may have even enhanced their marketability?

5. *Consent to Publicity Use.* The PGA Tour membership contract with players, including Tiger Woods, authorizes the PGA to license member images for use by tournament sponsors. Despite this consent to publicity use, Woods forced the PGA to remove his image and identifying information from the advertisements of tournament sponsor Mercedes Benz. Contrast this outcome with a class action brought by PGA Tour caddies, seeking publicity rights compensation for wearing the required caddie bib that displays sponsor logos. The Ninth Circuit dismissed those claims with prejudice, holding the caddies were bound by their consent in the standard PGA Tour caddie contract to wear the uniforms prescribed by the tournament. *See Hicks v. PGA Tour, Inc.*, 897 F.3d 1109 (9th Cir. 2018). Although the caddies lost on the issue of contract construction, the court granted leave to replead antitrust and unfair competition claims. What do you make of the constraints on less-wealthy caddies in exploiting their publicity rights?

5. FIRST-SALE DOCTRINE

The "first sale" doctrine provides that those who purchase a product that contains copyrighted or trademarked material are free to resell or dispose of the particular material good as they see fit. Otherwise, every time people traded or sold a used book or a team-logo jacket, they would have to obtain a license from the author or team. Courts have extended this doctrine to the right of publicity. In *Allison v. Vintage Sports Plaques*, 136 F.3d 1443 (11th Cir. 1998), a company purchased a large group of trading cards, elaborately framed them (sometimes including a small clock), and then resold them as "Limited Edition of Authentic Collectibles" at a much higher price. The Eleventh Circuit dismissed the state-law publicity-right claims brought by the athletes depicted in the trading cards, under the "first sale" doctrine:

> Appellants argue that the right of publicity differs from other forms of intellectual property because the former protects "identity," whereas the latter protect "a particular photograph or product." The first-sale doctrine should not apply, they reason, because a celebrity's identity continues to travel with the tangible property in which it is embodied after the first sale. We find two significant problems with appellants' argument. First, the distinction that appellants draw between what is protected by the right of publicity and what is protected by other forms of intellectual property rights, such as copyright, is not sound. Copyright law, for example, does not exist merely to protect the tangible items, such as books and paintings, in which the underlying expressive material is embodied; rather, it protects as well the author's or artist's particular expression that is included in the tangible item. . . .

> Second, and more important in our view, accepting appellants' argument would have profoundly negative effects on numerous industries and would grant a monopoly to celebrities over their identities that would upset the delicate balance between the interests of the celebrity and those of the public. . . . Indeed, a decision by this court not to apply the first-sale doctrine to right of publicity actions would render tortious the resale of sports trading cards and memorabilia and thus would have a profound effect on the market for trading cards, which now supports a multi-billion dollar industry. . . . Such a holding presumably also would prevent, for example, framing a magazine advertisement that bears the image of a celebrity and reselling it as a collector's item, reselling an empty cereal box that bears a celebrity's endorsement, or even reselling a used poster promoting a professional sports team. Refusing to apply the first-sale doctrine to the right of publicity also presumably would prevent a child from selling to his friend a baseball card that he had purchased, a consequence that undoubtedly would be contrary to the policies supporting that right.

> A holding that the first-sale doctrine does limit the right of publicity, on the other hand, would not eliminate completely a celebrity's control over the use of her name or image; the right of publicity protects against unauthorized use of an image, and a celebrity would continue to enjoy the right to license the use of her

image in the first instance—and thus enjoy the power to determine when, or if, her image will be distributed. Appellants in this case, for example, have received sizable royalties from the use of their images on the trading cards at issue, images that could not have been used in the first place without permission.

* * *

The issue before us, then, is whether the district court properly resolved as a matter of law that Vintage's plaques merely are the cards themselves repackaged, rather than products separate and distinct from the trading cards they incorporate. . . .

We conclude that the district court properly determined that, as a matter of law, Vintage merely resells cards that it lawfully obtains. We think it unlikely that anyone would purchase one of Vintage's plaques for any reason other than to obtain a display of the mounted cards themselves. Although we recognize that the plaques that include a clock pose a closer case, we conclude that it is unlikely that anyone would purchase one of the clock plaques simply to obtain a means of telling time, believing the clock to be, for example, a "Hershisher Clock" or an "Allison Clock." Because reselling a product that was lawfully obtained does not give rise to a cause of action for violation of the right of publicity, we hold that the district court correctly entered summary judgment in favor of Vintage on the right of publicity claim.

136 F.3d. at 1448–51.

NOTES AND QUESTIONS

1.   *Publicity Rights Versus Copyright.* What do you make of the athletes' argument that publicity rights are entitled to greater protection than copyrights under the circumstances of *Allison*? Does the court strike the right balance here between the public interest in freely disposing of personal property and the athletes' interest in capturing the appreciation in the value of their image? How relevant is it that the athletes had already been paid a royalty for use of the image?

2.   *Same Versus New-and-Different Product.* The *Allison* court affirmed "as a matter of law" that the resold product, albeit modified, was functionally the same as the original. Was this a question of law or fact? That is, could no reasonable jury have found otherwise, or could a reasonable jury conclude that some people might buy a plaque embedded with a clock primarily to tell time? If someone took a 3" x 4" trading card and blew it up into identical 3' x 4' posters for sale, would the posters have the same function as the original trading card or a different function as a wall decoration? Other than the functionality test,

how else might you determine if the resold product is the same as the original and protected by the first-sale doctrine?

3. *Group Licensing.* The major professional league player unions administer exclusive group licensing schemes whereby a licensee pays for the right to use a certain minimum number of players' NIL in conjunction with retail or promotional products. For example, the NFLPA requires its group licensees to use at least six NFL players. NFL players retain the right to engage in individual deals, and to opt out of group license deals that conflict with those individual deals. *See generally Gridiron.com v. NFLPA*, 106 F. Supp. 2d 1309 (S.D. Fla. 2000) (unlicensed website linking to six or more separate player web pages violated NFLPA's group licensing rights). If Vintage were to take the trading cards of six or more NFL players and put them on the same plaque, would the NFLPA have a valid claim that it had the exclusive group licensing rights of the players?

6. GAME BROADCASTS AND THE RIGHT OF PUBLICITY

Whatever the intrinsic merits of publicity rights for athlete and other celebrities, these rights require accommodation of other branches of property law. Most crucial is the question whether broadcasting a game or sports events violates athlete publicity rights. That is, just as stations and networks need a license from the club to broadcast the game, do the clubs also need a license from their player-employees to display the players' likeness and performance on the screen?

Like so many other owner-player disputes in sports, this issue simmered in baseball for years before finally surfacing in *Baltimore Orioles v. Major League Baseball Players Ass'n*, 805 F.2d 663 (7th Cir. 1986). In 1982, the MLBPA announced to both clubs and broadcasters that telecasts without the players' consent constituted misappropriation of the players' property right in their performance on the field. In ensuing litigation, the Seventh Circuit disagreed, first holding that the players are employees who play ballgames within the scope of their employment as a "work for hire." Accordingly, the clubs own the game broadcast copyright under the statutory presumption, unrebutted by anything in baseball's labor agreements, that the employer owns the copyright in a work made for hire.

Second, the court agreed that the broadcasts infringed players' rights of publicity, but held that the clubs' federal copyright preempted those state law publicity claims. Addressing many of the same issues encountered in *Motorola*, the court rejected the players' reliance on *Zacchini* to assert a publicity right to control telecasts of their performances:

> Because the exercise of the Clubs' right to broadcast telecasts of the games infringes the Players' rights of publicity in their performances, the Players' rights of publicity are equivalent to at

least one of the rights encompassed by copyright, *viz.*, the right to perform an audiovisual work. Since the works in which the Players claim rights are fixed in tangible form and come within the subject matter of copyright, the Players' rights of publicity in their performances are preempted.

The Players argue that their rights of publicity in their performances are not equivalent to the rights contained in a copyright because rights of publicity and copyrights serve different interests. In their view, the purpose of federal copyright law is to secure a benefit to the public, but the purpose of state statutory or common law concerning rights of publicity is to protect individual pecuniary interests. We disagree.

The purpose of federal copyright protection is to benefit the public by encouraging works in which it is interested. To induce individuals to undertake the personal sacrifices necessary to create such works, federal copyright law extends to the authors of such works a limited monopoly to reap the rewards of their endeavors. Contrary to the Players' contention, the interest underlying the recognition of the right of publicity also is the promotion of performances that appeal to the public. The reason that state law protects individual pecuniary interests is to provide an incentive to performers to invest the time and resources required to develop such performances. In *Zacchini v. Scripps-Howard Broadcasting Co.*, 433 U.S. 562 (1977), the principal case on which the Players rely for their assertion that different interests underlie copyright and the right to publicity, the Supreme Court recognized that the interest behind federal copyright protection is the advancement of the public welfare through the encouragement of individual effort by personal gain, action for violation of the right to publicity "is closely analogous to the goals of patent and copyright law." *Id.* at 573. Because the right of publicity does not differ in kind from copyright, the Players' rights of publicity in their performances cannot escape preemption.

In this litigation, the Players have attempted to obtain *ex post* what they did not negotiate *ex ante*. That is to say, they seek a judicial declaration that they possess a right—the right to control the telecasts of major league baseball games—that they could not procure in bargaining with the Clubs. The Players' aim is to share in the increasingly lucrative revenues derived from the sale of television rights for over-the-air broadcasts by local stations and national networks and for distribution by subscription and pay cable services. Contrary to the Players' contention, the effect of this decision is not to grant the Clubs perpetual rights to the

Players' performances. The Players remain free to attain their objective by bargaining with the Clubs for a contractual declaration that the Players own a joint or an exclusive interest in the copyright of the telecasts.

———

NOTES AND QUESTIONS

1. *Implicit Contract?* An alternative theory to reject the baseball players' publicity rights claims is that they implicitly contracted those rights away when they agreed to perform in a game that they knew would be televised, in programming that they knew would exploit their names, images, and likenesses, all pursuant to broadcast contracts that largely pay their salaries. Where professional athletes are unionized and their employment is governed by an explicit contract—the collective agreement with the league, how likely is it that a court would imply such a grant of publicity rights?

2. *Derivative Works and Compilations.* Although *Baltimore Orioles* resolved team ownership of the copyright in the initial game broadcast, what about subsequent derivative uses of that footage? May the teams (or leagues) license excerpts from the telecast to filmmakers wanting to produce a docudrama about the exploits of the Manning family of NFL quarterbacks? To an athletic shoe manufacturer wanting to show Stephen Curry in a commercial advertisement? How would you distinguish these uses from what took place in *Baltimore Orioles? See Ventura v. Titan Sport, Inc.*, 65 F.3d 725 (8th Cir. 1995) (professional wrestling color commentator had publicity right to control collateral use of his videotaped performances).

This issue surfaced in *Dryer v. National Football League*, 814 F.3d 938 (8th Cir. 2016), in which a class of retired NFL players claimed that NFL Films violated their publicity rights by including game footage and player interviews in film compilations. The players sought to avoid copyright preemption by arguing that the films represent commercial speech subject to state regulation, and not artistic or informational expression. The court disagreed, finding that although the films promoted the NFL brand, they did not propose a commercial transaction or appear on other media as paid advertisements. Rather the films "tell stories," "exist as products in their own right," and "represent speech of independent value and public interest." *Id.* at 943–44 (also ruling that the players' appearance in the films did not convey a false endorsement of the NFL). Note that NFL collective bargaining agreements post-dating the retirees' playing careers expressly convey to the league non-exclusive player publicity rights for purposes such as historical films. Why do you think the league thought this was necessary given the *Dryer* analysis, as well as the *Baltimore Orioles* case? Why would the players be willing to grant those rights?

3. *Reproduction and Distribution of Copyrighted Works.* Copyright affords rights owners the exclusive right to reproduce or distribute copies of their work. Accordingly, photographers have the right to sell reprints of their photos or authorize others to do so. In *Maloney v. T3Media, Inc.*, 853 F.3d 1004

(9th Cir. 2017), the NCAA did precisely that, licensing its photo library to a website, which then sold digital copies of the photos to the public. The Ninth Circuit ruled that copyright preempted the publicity rights claims of former members of a college basketball team whose images appeared in the photos. The *Maloney* decision distinguished images used in unrelated advertising, or in "merchandise" like a coffee mug, from those incorporated into a copyrighted artistic visual work distributed for "personal use." Because the digital reprints fell in the latter category, the publicity rights claim was preempted. Do you agree with this distinction? If so, what counts as merchandise? What if the website mailed the buyer a poster of the image, rather than transmitted a digital copy? Why should a digital copy of an image be treated differently from a physical copy? Is the website's use of the images to drive sales of reprints a separate act of advertising that violates the athletes' publicity rights?

The *Maloney* decision also has uncertain implications for license negotiations involving athletes. It suggests that, absent a contractual provision to the contrary, when athletes agree to be photographed, they are giving implied consent to the holder of the copyright to use the photograph for related purposes, including distributing the photo as a product and without having to obtain publicity rights. While a professional athlete will be able to negotiate usage rights and compensation at the outset, how does this ruling impact college athletes? Even now that college athletes may monetize their NIL, the current version of NCAA amateurism, discussed in Chapter 12, still precludes the athletes from demanding payment during college from the NCAA, universities, or those institutions' photographers. How does this affect your thinking about the result in *Maloney*?

4. *Copyright Preemption.* Compare the Supreme Court's *Zacchini* decision, which addressed conduct that predated the 1976 Copyright Act's preemption provision. Does *Baltimore Orioles* imply that if a television station asserts a copyright preemption defense rather than a First Amendment right, it could now defeat Zacchini's state publicity law claim? Or is *Baltimore Orioles* distinguishable from *Zacchini* on the grounds of "authorship" of the copyrighted work? Should we treat athletes differently depending on whether they are employees of a team like a professional baseball player, independent contractors like a golfer on the PGA Tour, or ostensibly amateur athletes like a college basketball player in the Final Four?

5. *Amateur Athletes.* What if the athletes asserting a right of publicity in a game broadcast are unpaid college students? Are such claims more viable when the athletic performances are not "works for hire"? In *Marshall v. ESPN Inc.*, 111 F. Supp. 3d 815 (M.D. Tenn. 2015), *aff'd*, 668 F. App'x 155 (6th Cir. 2016), college athletes sued the conferences, networks, and licensors who profit from broadcasting college football and basketball games. With respect to their claims brought under the Tennessee right-of-publicity statute, the court held that inclusion of athlete images in a sports broadcast is a "fair use" and not an unauthorized endorsement, despite the inclusion of advertisements in the broadcast. The court noted the Tennessee statute's "legitimate goal of avoiding unreasonable impediments to the broadcasting of important matters of public

interest, including sporting events." Consider whether this public interest is as vital when athletes' performances are featured in ancillary entertainment products, as discussed below.

7. ANCILLARY ENTERTAINMENT PRODUCTS AND THE RIGHT OF PUBLICITY

In the case of professional sports game broadcasts and derivative uses of that footage that contain the likeness of the athlete-employee performing the services for which he was paid, the right of publicity yields to the contractual employment relationship. In the case of works that convey newsworthy information, artistic expression, or social commentary, such as a reprinted news article, a transformative portrait, or parody trading cards, the right of publicity defers to the First Amendment. What about ancillary entertainment products such as sports video games and fantasy sports contests, which make commercial use of player names, performance statistics, and in some cases pictures and digital representations? A series of publicity rights challenges sought to clarify under what circumstances the producer needs to obtain licenses from players or their unions for these uses, or is entitled to First Amendment immunity. As we read here, context matters, and courts to date have reached opposite conclusions in fantasy sports versus video games.

C.B.C. DISTRIBUTION AND MARKETING, INC. V. MAJOR LEAGUE BASEBALL ADVANCED MEDIA, L.P.
505 F.3d 818 (8th Cir. 2007)

ARNOLD, CIRCUIT JUDGE.

C.B.C. Distribution and Marketing, Inc., brought this action for a declaratory judgment against Major League Baseball Advanced Media, L.P., to establish its right to use, without license, the names of and information about major league baseball players in connection with its fantasy baseball products. Advanced Media counter-claimed, maintaining that CBC's fantasy baseball products violated rights of publicity belonging to major league baseball players and that the players, through their association, had licensed those rights to Advanced Media, the interactive media and Internet company of major league baseball. The Major League Baseball Players Association [PA] intervened in the suit, joining in Advanced Media's claims and further asserting a breach of contract claim against CBC. The district court granted summary judgment to CBC, *see C.B.C. Distrib. and Mktg., Inc. v. Major League Baseball Advanced Media, L.P.,* 443 F. Supp. 2d 1077 (E.D. Mo. 2006), and Advanced Media and the Players Association appealed. We affirm.

I.

CBC sells fantasy sports products via its Internet website, e-mail, mail, and the telephone. Its fantasy baseball products incorporate the names along with performance and biographical data of actual major league baseball players. Before the commencement of the major league baseball season each spring, participants form their fantasy baseball teams by "drafting" players from various major league baseball teams. Participants compete against other fantasy baseball "owners" who have also drafted their own teams. A participant's success, and his or her team's success, depends on the actual performance of the fantasy team's players on their respective actual teams during the course of the major league baseball season. Participants in CBC's fantasy baseball games pay fees to play and additional fees to trade players during the course of the season.

[From 1995–2004, the MLBPA granted CBC a license for "the names, nicknames, likenesses, signatures, pictures, playing records, and/or biographical data of each player" (the "Rights") to be used in association with CBC's fantasy baseball products.]

In 2005, after the 2002 agreement expired, the Players Association licensed to Advanced Media, with some exceptions, the exclusive right to use baseball players' names and performance information "for exploitation via all interactive media." Advanced Media began providing fantasy baseball games on its website, MLB.com, the official website of major league baseball. It offered CBC, in exchange for a commission, a license to promote the MLB.com fantasy baseball games on CBC's website but did not offer CBC a license to continue to offer its own fantasy baseball products. This conduct by Advanced Media prompted CBC to file the present suit, alleging that it had "a reasonable apprehension that it will be sued by Advanced Media if it continues to operate its fantasy baseball games."

* * *

[On appeal from the district court's grant of summary judgment to CBC, the court noted that it applies traditional *de novo* review and must predict how the Missouri Supreme Court would resolve the issue of Missouri state law.]

II.

A.

An action based on the right of publicity is a state-law claim. *See Zacchini v. Scripps-Howard Broad. Co.*, 433 U.S. 562, 566 (1977). In Missouri, "the elements of a right of publicity action include: (1) That defendant used plaintiff's name as a symbol of his identity (2) without consent (3) and with the intent to obtain a commercial advantage." *Doe v. TCI Cablevision*, 110 S.W.3d 363, 369 (Mo. 2003), *cert. denied*, 540 U.S.

1106 (2004). The parties all agree that CBC's continued use of the players' names and playing information after the expiration of the 2002 agreement was without consent. The district court concluded, however, that the evidence was insufficient to make out the other two elements of the claim, and we address each of these in turn.

With respect to the symbol-of-identity element, the Missouri Supreme Court has observed that " 'the name used by the defendant must be understood by the audience as referring to the plaintiff.' " The state court had further held that "[i]n resolving this issue, the fact-finder may consider evidence including 'the nature and extent of the identifying characteristics used by the defendant, the defendant's intent, the fame of the plaintiff, evidence of actual identification made by third persons, and surveys or other evidence indicating the perceptions of the audience.' " *Doe*, 110 S.W.3d at 370 (quoting *Restatement (Third) of Unfair Competition* § 46 cmt. d).

Here, we entertain no doubt that the players' names that CBC used are understood by it and its fantasy baseball subscribers as referring to actual major league baseball players. CBC itself admits that: In responding to the appellants' argument that "this element is met by the mere confirmation that the name used, in fact, refers to the famous person asserting the violation," CBC stated in its brief that "if this is all the element requires, CBC agrees that it is met." We think that by reasoning that "identity," rather than "mere use of a name," "is a critical element of the right of publicity," the district court did not understand that when a name alone is sufficient to establish identity, the defendant's use of that name satisfies the plaintiff's burden to show that a name was used as a symbol of identity.

It is true that with respect to the "commercial advantage" element of a cause of action for violating publicity rights, CBC's use does not fit neatly into the more traditional categories of commercial advantage, namely, using individuals' names for advertising and merchandising purposes in a way that states or intimates that the individuals are endorsing a product. *Cf. Restatement (Third) of Unfair Competition* § 47 cmt. a, b. But the Restatement, which the Missouri Supreme Court has recognized as authority in this kind of case, also says that a name is used for commercial advantage when it is used "in connection with services rendered by the user" and that the plaintiff need not show that "prospective purchasers are likely to believe" that he endorsed the product or service. *Restatement (Third) of Unfair Competition* § 47 & cmt. a. We note, moreover, that in Missouri, "the commercial advantage element of the right of publicity focuses on the defendant's intent or purpose to obtain a commercial benefit from use of the plaintiff's identity." *Doe*, 110 S.W.3d at 370–71. Because we think that it is clear that CBC uses baseball players' identities in its fantasy baseball products for purposes of profit, we believe that their identities are being used for commercial advantage and that the players therefore offered sufficient evidence to make out a cause of action for violation of their rights of publicity under Missouri law.

B.

CBC argues that the First Amendment nonetheless trumps the right-of-publicity action that Missouri law provides. . . .

The Supreme Court has directed that state law rights of publicity must be balanced against First Amendment considerations, *see Zacchini v. Scripps-Howard Broad.*, 433 U.S. 562 (1977), and here we conclude that the former must give way to the latter. First, the information used in CBC's fantasy baseball games is all readily available in the public domain, and it would be strange law that a person would not have a First Amendment right to use information that is available to everyone. It is true that CBC's use of the information is meant to provide entertainment, but "[s]peech that entertains, like speech that informs, is protected by the First Amendment because '[t]he line between the informing and the entertaining is too elusive for the protection of that basic right.'" *Cardtoons, L.C. v. Major League Baseball Players Ass'n*, 95 F.3d 959, 969 (10th Cir. 1996) [citation omitted]; *see also Zacchini*, 433 U.S. at 578. We also find no merit in the argument that CBC's use of players' names and information in its fantasy baseball games is not speech at all. We have held that "the pictures, graphic design, concept art, sounds, music, stories, and narrative present in video games" is speech entitled to First Amendment protection. Similarly, here CBC uses the "names, nicknames, likenesses, signatures, pictures, playing records, and/or biographical data of each player" in an interactive form in connection with its fantasy baseball products.

Courts have also recognized the public value of information about the game of baseball and its players, referring to baseball as "the national pastime." *Cardtoons*, 95 F.3d at 972. A California court, in a case where Major League Baseball was itself defending its use of players' names, likenesses, and information against the players' asserted rights of publicity, observed, "Major league baseball is followed by millions of people across this country on a daily basis. . . . The public has an enduring fascination in the records set by former players and in memorable moments from previous games. . . . The records and statistics remain of interest to the public because they provide context that allows fans to better appreciate (or deprecate) today's performances." *Gionfriddo v. Major League Baseball*, 94 Cal. App. 4th 400, 411, 114 Cal. Rptr. 2d 307 (2001). The Court in *Gionfriddo* concluded that the "recitation and discussion of factual data concerning the athletic performance of [players on Major League Baseball's website] command a substantial public interest, and, therefore, is a form of expression due substantial constitutional protection." *Id.* We find these views persuasive.

In addition, the facts in this case barely, if at all, implicate the interests that states typically intend to vindicate by providing rights of publicity to individuals. Economic interests that states seek to promote include the right of an individual to reap the rewards of his or her endeavors and an individual's right to earn a living. Other motives for creating a publicity right are the desire to provide incentives to encourage a person's productive activities and to protect consumers from misleading advertising. *See Zacchini,* 433 U.S. at 573, 576; *Cardtoons,* 95 F.3d at 973. But major league baseball players are rewarded, and handsomely, too, for their participation in games and can earn additional large sums from endorsements and sponsorship arrangements. Nor is there any danger here that consumers will be misled, because the fantasy baseball games depend on the inclusion of all players and thus cannot create a false impression that some particular player with "star power" is endorsing CBC's products.

Then there are so-called non-monetary interests that publicity rights are sometimes thought to advance. These include protecting natural rights, rewarding celebrity labors, and avoiding emotional harm. *See Cardtoons,* 95 F.3d at 973. We do not see that any of these interests are especially relevant here, where baseball players are rewarded separately for their labors, and where any emotional harm would most likely be caused by a player's actual performance, in which case media coverage would cause the same harm. We also note that some courts have indicated that the right of publicity is intended to promote only economic interests and that non-economic interests are more directly served by so-called rights of privacy. *See, e.g., id.* at 967; *Gionfriddo,* 94 Cal. App. 4th at 409 (2001; *see also Haelan Laboratories v. Topps Chewing Gum,* 202 F.2d 866, 868 (2d Cir. 1953). For instance, although the court in *Cardtoons,* 95 F.3d at 975–76, conducted a separate discussion of non-economic interests when weighing the countervailing rights, it ultimately concluded that the non-economic justifications for the right of publicity were unpersuasive as compared with the interest in freedom of expression. "Publicity rights . . . are meant to protect against the loss of financial gain, not mental anguish." Id. at 976. We see merit in this approach.

Because we hold that CBC's First Amendment rights in offering its fantasy baseball products supersede the players' rights of publicity, we need not reach CBC's alternative argument that federal copyright law preempts the players' state law rights of publicity.

* * *

[Affirmed.]

Mirroring the professional baseball players' claims in *C.B.C. Distribution,* former college football players sued under Indiana's publicity-rights statute to block the use of their names, pictures, and on-field statistics by fantasy sports providers FanDuel and DraftKings. *Daniels v. FanDuel, Inc.*, 2017 WL 4340329 (S.D. Ind. Sept. 29, 2017), *aff'd*, 909 F.3d 876 (7th Cir. 2018). Unlike *C.B.C. Distribution*, however, this case avoided the constitutional question because the Indiana statute contained exemptions that permit use of an individual's NIL "in material that has political or newsworthy value" or "in connection with the broadcast or reporting of an event or a topic of general or public interest." These exemptions had been interpreted to cover use by online fantasy sports operators, even though they are commercial enterprises that charge entry fees, as long as the use does not suggest unauthorized endorsement. *Daniels v. FanDuel, Inc.*, 109 N.E.3d 390 (Ind. 2018). Dispositive to the outcome here was that the fantasy sports operators relied on information in the public domain about real-world players and games, providing a resource to those interested in the athletes' sports performances and statistics. Are such statutory exemptions adequate to protect First Amendment interests?

Former college football players also asserted publicity rights claims against the NCAA and a video game developer for the game's use of avatars that closely resembled the athletes. This lawsuit, initially captioned *Keller v. Electronic Arts*, was among the many challenges to the NCAA's amateurism principle explained further in Chapter 12. Defendants moved to strike the *Keller* complaint as a strategic lawsuit against public participation (SLAPP) under California's anti-SLAPP statute, asserting First Amendment rights to their creative expression as embodied in the video game. In a landmark decision for college sports, and in stark contrast to the fantasy sports setting, the court sustained the athletes' publicity rights claims.

IN RE NCAA STUDENT-ATHLETE NAME & LIKENESS LICENSING LITIGATION
724 F.3d 1268 (9th Cir. 2013)

BYBEE, CIRCUIT JUDGE:

Video games are entitled to the full protections of the First Amendment, because "[l]ike the protected books, plays, and movies that preceded them, video games communicate ideas—and even social messages—through many familiar literary devices (such as characters, dialogue, plot, and music) and through features distinctive to the medium (such as the player's interaction with the virtual world)." *Brown v. Entm't Merchs. Ass'n*, 131 S. Ct. 2729, 2733 (2011). Such rights are not absolute, and states may recognize the right of publicity to a degree consistent with the First Amendment. *Zacchini v. Scripps-Howard Broad. Co.*, 433 U.S. 562, 574–75 (1977). In this case, we must balance the right of publicity of a former college football player against the asserted First Amendment right of a video game developer to use his likeness in its expressive works.

The district court concluded that the game developer, Electronic Arts ("EA"), had no First Amendment defense against the right-of-publicity claims of the football player, Samuel Keller. We affirm. Under the "transformative use" test developed by the California Supreme Court, EA's use does not qualify for First Amendment protection as a matter of law because it literally recreates Keller in the very setting in which he has achieved renown. The other First Amendment defenses asserted by EA do not defeat Keller's claims either.

I

[Keller played quarterback for Arizona State University and then the University of Nebraska.] EA is the producer of the *NCAA Football* series of video games, which allow users to control avatars representing college football players as those avatars participate in simulated games. In *NCAA Football,* EA seeks to replicate each school's entire team as accurately as possible. Every real football player on each team included in the game has a corresponding avatar in the game with the player's actual jersey number and virtually identical height, weight, build, skin tone, hair color, and home state. EA attempts to match any unique, highly identifiable playing behaviors by sending detailed questionnaires to team equipment managers. Additionally, EA creates realistic virtual versions of actual stadiums; populates them with the virtual athletes, coaches, cheerleaders, and fans realistically rendered by EA's graphic artists; and incorporates realistic sounds such as the crunch of the players' pads and the roar of the crowd.

EA's game differs from reality in that EA omits the players' names on their jerseys and assigns each player a home town that is different from the actual player's home town. However, users of the video game may upload rosters of names obtained from third parties so that the names do appear on the jerseys. In such cases, EA allows images from the game containing athletes' real names to be posted on its website by users. . . .

In the 2005 edition of the game, the virtual starting quarterback for Arizona State wears number 9, as did Keller, and has the same height, weight, skin tone, hair color, hair style, handedness, home state, play style (pocket passer), visor preference, facial features, and school year as Keller. In the 2008 edition, the virtual quarterback for Nebraska has these same characteristics, though the jersey number does not match, presumably because Keller changed his number right before the season started.

Objecting to this use of his likeness, Keller filed a putative class-action complaint in the Northern District of California asserting, as relevant on appeal, that EA violated his right of publicity under California Civil Code § 3344 and California common law. . .

A

The California Supreme Court formulated the transformative use defense in *Comedy III Productions, Inc. v. Gary Saderup, Inc.,* 25 Cal. 4th 387 (2001). The defense is "a balancing test between the First Amendment and the right of publicity based on whether the work in question adds significant creative elements so as to be transformed into something more than a mere celebrity likeness or imitation." The California Supreme Court explained that "when a work contains significant transformative elements, it is not only especially worthy of First Amendment protection, but it is also less likely to interfere with the economic interest protected by the right of publicity." The court rejected the wholesale importation of the copyright "fair use" defense into right-of-publicity claims, but recognized that some aspects of that defense are "particularly pertinent."

Comedy III gives us at least five factors to consider in determining whether a work is sufficiently transformative to obtain First Amendment protection. First, if "the celebrity likeness is one of the 'raw materials' from which an original work is synthesized," it is more likely to be transformative than if "the depiction or imitation of the celebrity is the very sum and substance of the work in question." Second, the work is protected if it is "primarily the defendant's own expression"—as long as that expression is "something other than the likeness of the celebrity." This factor requires an examination of whether a likely purchaser's primary motivation is to buy a reproduction of the celebrity, or to buy the expressive work of that artist. Third, to avoid making judgments concerning "the quality of the artistic contribution," a court should conduct an inquiry "more quantitative than qualitative" and ask "whether the literal and imitative or the creative elements predominate in the work." Fourth, the California Supreme Court indicated that "a subsidiary inquiry" would be useful in close cases: whether "the marketability and economic value of the challenged work derive primarily from the fame of the celebrity depicted." Lastly, the court indicated that "when an artist's skill and talent is manifestly subordinated to the overall goal of creating a conventional portrait of a celebrity so as to commercially exploit his or her fame," the work is not transformative.

[The court described four cases where California courts have applied the transformative use test to: (1) disallow T-shirts and lithographs with "literal, conventional depictions of The Three Stooges so as to exploit their fame"; (2) permit comic books that based grotesque and villainous characters on famous rock musicians because the characters "are not just conventional depictions of plaintiffs but contain significant expressive content" and distort the likeness "for purposes of lampoon, parody, or caricature" as part of "a larger story, which is itself quite expressive"; (3) permit a video game character based on a famous singer because it was a "fanciful, creative character" that was "unlike any public depiction" of the singer; (4) disallow the *Band Hero* video game's use of avatars of the rock band No Doubt that were "literal recreations of the band members," doing "the same activity by which the band achieved and maintains its fame."]

* * *

With these cases in mind as guidance, we conclude that EA's use of Keller's likeness does not contain significant transformative elements such that EA is entitled to the defense as a matter of law. The facts of *No Doubt* [*v. Activism Publishing Inc.*, 192 Cal. App. 4th 1018, 122 Cal. Rptr. 3d 397 (2011),] are very similar to those here. EA is alleged to have replicated Keller's physical characteristics in *NCAA Football,* just as the members of No Doubt are realistically portrayed in *Band Hero.* Here, as in *Band Hero,* users manipulate the characters in the performance of the same activity for which they are known in real life—playing football in this case, and performing in a rock band in *Band Hero.* The context in which the activity occurs is also similarly realistic—real venues in *Band Hero* and realistic depictions of actual football stadiums in *NCAA Football.* As the district court found, Keller is represented as "what he was: the starting quarterback for Arizona State" and Nebraska, and "the game's setting is identical to where the public found [Keller] during his collegiate career: on the football field."

* * *

The Third Circuit came to the same conclusion in *Hart v. Electronic Arts, Inc.,* 717 F.3d 141 (3d Cir. 2013). In *Hart,* EA faced a materially identical challenge under New Jersey right-of-publicity law, brought by former Rutgers quarterback Ryan Hart. *See id.* at 163 n. 28 ("*Keller* is simply [*Hart*] incarnated in California."). Though the Third Circuit was tasked with interpreting New Jersey law, the court looked to the transformative use test developed in California. *See id.* at 158 n. 23 (noting that the right-of-publicity laws are "strikingly similar . . . and protect similar interests" in New Jersey and California, and that "consequently [there is] no issue in applying balancing tests developed in California to New Jersey"); *see also id.* at 165 (holding that "the Transformative Use Test is the proper analytical framework to apply to cases such as the one at bar"). Applying the test, the court held that "the *NCAA Football* . . . games at issue . . . do not sufficiently transform [Hart]'s identity to escape the right of publicity claim," reversing the district court's grant of summary judgment to EA. *Id.* at 170.

As we have, the Third Circuit considered the potentially transformative nature of the game as a whole, *id.* at 166, 169, and the user's ability to alter avatar characteristics, *id.* at 166–68. Asserting that "the lack of transformative context is even more pronounced here than in *No Doubt,*" *id.* at 166, and that "the ability to modify the avatar counts for little where the appeal of the game lies in users' ability to play as, or alongside [,] their preferred players or team," *id.* at 168 (internal quotation marks omitted), the Third Circuit agreed with us that these changes do not render the *NCAA Football* games sufficiently transformative to defeat a right-of-publicity claim.

Given that *NCAA Football* realistically portrays college football players in the context of college football games, the district court was correct in concluding that EA cannot prevail as a matter of law based on the transformative use defense at the anti-SLAPP stage.

B

[The court considered EA's argument, predicated on *Rogers v. Grimaldi*, 875 F.2d 994 (2d Cir. 1989), that the First Amendment permits use of a celebrity's name in a creative work when doing so is artistically relevant and not misleading as to whether the celebrity endorses the work.]

The right of publicity protects the *celebrity*, not the *consumer*. Keller's publicity claim is not founded on an allegation that consumers are being illegally misled into believing that he is endorsing EA or its products. Indeed, he would be hard-pressed to support such an allegation absent evidence that EA explicitly misled consumers into holding such a belief. . . . Instead, Keller's claim is that EA has appropriated, without permission and without providing compensation, his talent and years of hard work on the football field. The reasoning of the *Rogers* and *Mattel* courts—that artistic and literary works should be protected unless they explicitly mislead consumers—is simply not responsive to Keller's asserted interests here.

* * *

C

[The court weighed EA's defenses asserted under: (a) the California common law principle that the right of publicity does not lie for the "publication of matters in the public interest," *Montana v. San Jose Mercury News, Inc.*, 34 Cal. App. 4th 790 (1995); and (b) the California statute that permits the "use of a name, voice, signature, photograph, or likeness in connection with any news, public affairs, or sports broadcast or account, or any political campaign." Cal. Civ. Code § 3344(d).]

California courts have generally analyzed the common law defense and the statutory defense separately, but it is clear that both defenses protect only the act of publishing or reporting. By its terms, § 3344(d) is limited to a "broadcast or account," and we have confirmed that the common law defense is about a publication or reporting of newsworthy items. However, most of the discussion by California courts pertains to whether the subject matter of the communication is of "public interest" or related to "news" or "public affairs," leaving little guidance as to when the communication constitutes a publication or reporting.

[I]n *Gionfriddo v. Major League Baseball*, retired professional baseball players alleged that Major League Baseball violated their right of publicity by displaying "factual data concerning the players, their performance statistics, and verbal descriptions and video depictions of their play" in game programs and on its website. The court reasoned that "[t]he recitation and discussion of factual data concerning the athletic performance of these plaintiffs command a substantial public interest, and, therefore, is a form of expression due substantial constitutional protection." And in *Montana*, former NFL quarterback Joe Montana brought a right-of-publicity action against a newspaper for selling posters containing previously published pages from the newspaper depicting the many Super Bowl victories by Montana and the San Francisco 49ers. The court found that "[p]osters portraying the 49'ers' [sic] victories are . . . a form of public interest presentation to which protection must be extended." . . .

EA is not publishing or reporting factual data. EA's video game is a means by which users can play their own virtual football games, not a means for obtaining information about real-world football games. Although EA has incorporated certain actual player information into the game (height, weight, etc.), its case is considerably weakened by its decision not to include the athletes' names along with their likenesses and statistical data. EA can hardly be considered to be "reporting" on Keller's career at Arizona State and Nebraska when it is not even using Keller's name in connection with his avatar in the game. Put simply, EA's interactive game is not a publication of facts about college football; it is a game, not a reference source. These state law defenses, therefore, do not apply.

Affirmed.

NOTES AND QUESTIONS

1. *First Amendment Balancing.* What factors did the Eighth Circuit in *C.B.C. Distribution* find determinative in ruling that the First Amendment rights of the fantasy sports provider outweigh the players' image rights? State-law protection of image rights often seeks to create incentives for individuals to make investments in their own success so that their image rights have commercial value. How would the Eighth Circuit's factors apply to the use of New York Yankee Aaron Judge's name and statistics? Does your answer depend on whether the question came up today or when he was an unknown minor leaguer investing time and effort in his baseball future?

2. *False Endorsement.* After *C.B.C. Distribution*, a football fantasy sports website relied on the decision to refuse to continue paying license fees to the NFL Players Association, and then sued for a declaration that the First Amendment superseded the football players' publicity rights. *See CBS Interactive Inc. v. Nat'l Football League Players Ass'n, Inc.*, 259 F.R.D. 398 (D. Minn. 2009). The court rejected the NFLPA's attempts to distinguish football

from baseball, including its assertion that the football fantasy site packaged player information in a way that conveyed a false endorsement. Rather, the court concluded the site was "akin to newspapers and magazines" where no one believes the subjects of news reports are endorsing either the publisher or the third-party advertisers in that publication. *Id.* at 419. Does this analogy persuade you?

3. *Transformative Use Test.* Circuit Judge Thomas dissented in *NCAA Student-Athlete*, concluding that "the creative and transformative elements of the games predominate over the commercial use of the likenesses of the athletes within the games." The dissent principally relied on the video game's omission of athlete names and provision of gamer autonomy to change athletes' abilities and appearances and to create entirely new virtual players. These and similar features convinced the dissenter that the "marketability and economic value of the game comes from the creative elements within, not from the pure commercial exploitation of a celebrity image." Did the majority or the dissent correctly apply the transformative use test? After the *NCAA Student-Athlete* ruling, EA stopped producing college athlete video games for 10 years, resuming only after the NCAA withdrew its prohibition on compensating college athletes for their NIL. Does this 10-year market void affect your view of the proper balance between athlete image rights and public access to informative and creative works?

4. *Incidental Use.* In *Davis v. Elec. Arts Inc.*, 775 F.3d 1172 (9th Cir. 2015), the Ninth Circuit replayed its *NCAA Student-Athlete* analysis to reject EA's First Amendment defenses to similar right-of-publicity claims brought by former professional football players who were depicted in a version of a video game that included "historic teams." In *Davis*, EA offered the additional defense that its use of former player likenesses was protected as "incidental" under a California doctrine that immunizes fleeting or trivial use of celebrity. EA asserted that because its game depicted several thousand players, any individual player's likeness has only a de minimis commercial value. The court rejected this argument, observing that the video games went to great lengths to achieve realism in depicting the former players, and prominently featured them as icons of the game. Recall what *Uhlaender v. Henricksen*, 316 F. Supp. 1277 (D. Minn. 1970), said about how celebrity value derives from investing "years of practice and competition in a public personality which eventually may reach marketable status." Does the *Davis* case suggest that EA's incidental use theory would prevail if the athletes were lesser known?

5. *Information in the Public Domain.* The majority in *NCAA Student-Athlete* distinguished EA's video games from the fantasy baseball products at issue in *C.B.C. Distribution* because the latter merely uses publicly available data, but the video games also use the athlete likenesses. The Ninth Circuit majority was not swayed by the argument that EA generated the likenesses from publicly available data. 724 F.3d at 1283 n.12. Does the majority's distinction make sense to you? If so, how are fantasy sports providers able to use player photographs without obtaining group licenses from the players' unions?

6. *Athlete Tattoos.* Video game developers now generally enter into license agreements with the league, players association, or individual athletes to use player NIL in games such as NBA2K. Do those licenses include portraying athletes' tattoos on the avatar bodies, or is additional permission needed from the tattoo artist? Tattoo artists have brought copyright infringement claims to establish their right to compensation in this setting. What are your views on the two principal arguments the game developers have offered in response? (1) A tattoo artist necessarily grants an implied license to famous athletes to reproduce the design, knowing that their images would appear in commercial settings like game broadcasts and video games. (2) The games' tattoo depiction is de minimis or transformative "fair use." *See Alexander v. Take-Two Interactive Software, Inc.*, 489 F. Supp. 3d 812 (S.D. Ill. 2020) (allowing discovery to proceed on claim that game portrayal of professional wrestler Randy Orton's six tattoos infringed copyright); *Solid Oak Sketches, LLC v. 2K Games, Inc.*, 449 F. Supp. 3d 333 (S.D.N.Y. 2020) (granting summary judgment in favor of game developer that reproduced tattoos on avatars of LeBron James and other NBA players). Should an individual's publicity right (or simply one's bodily autonomy) necessarily defeat copyright in this situation? What advice would you give athletes in dealing with tattoo artists?

7. *Wearable Technology and the Right to Privacy/Publicity.* Player performance information and statistics increasingly include biometric data generated by wearable (and ingestible and implantable) technology. Leagues and players unions need to negotiate exactly what information may be collected, who owns it, and how it may be shared and used. To the extent such data reveal personal health information, athletes may possess federal privacy rights against disclosure, in addition to state law privacy protections. When the data identify particular athletes, the question will inevitably arise whether players retain a publicity right in the data that requires their consent for use. Will the answer depend on whether the data are already in the public domain, for example, because somehow incorporated in game broadcasts? Or whether the data concern a topic of public interest?

8. *Sports Gambling.* As previously noted in discussion of league and team rights to game accounts and information, legalized sports gambling will further complicate the debate over the appropriate contours of sports industry intellectual property rights. (See Chapter 1, Section C.3). Have the fantasy sports disputes described here resolved all questions as to sportsbooks' use of athletes' names, pictures, and playing statistics? Is this issue more amenable to a legislative solution than to a judicial reckoning?

D. TRADEMARK RIGHTS

A trademark or service mark is a word, symbol, or logo, used to identify a particular product or service, and to distinguish that good from the products or services of another. For example, the trademark "Nike" and the Nike "swoosh" identify the shoes made by Nike and distinguish them from shoes made by other companies (*e.g.*, Puma or Reebok). Similarly, "ESPN" distinguishes the sports programming of one media company from that of another (*e.g.*, Sky Sports). In contrast, Golden State Warriors fans buy merchandise with their team's logo primarily because they want to show their affinity to the Warriors, not because they care whether the Warriors are the source or authorizing agent for the good. Accordingly, for sports franchise owners, trademark rights also offer a means of realizing the celebrity value of their team's (not their players') name and identity. Significant sports industry revenue now comes from merchandising team trademarks, logos, and other identifying insignia. The New York Yankees name and insignia is considered the single most popular sports team brand in the world, and that asset alone (apart from the team itself) has been valued at over one billion dollars.

Unlike copyright or rights of publicity which protect authorship or identity, the property right of trademark is a function of *use* of a name, logo, or design. Trademark law's primary purpose is to protect consumers from confusion in their choice or use of goods, not to protect the mark owner's business interest. Thus, mark owners do not have an absolute right to stop someone else from using their names and symbols. Rather, they can block that action only if it is likely to cause confusion or deception of consumers in the sale of competing goods. Trademarks thereby make it easier for consumers to quickly identify the source of a given good and create incentives for producers to preserve and enhance the attractive qualities of those goods.

Brand-name recognition also attracts infringers who attempt to trade on the good will and reputation of the mark owner's product, and can undermine that good will with an inferior version of the product. As long as the mark owner continues to use the mark as a source identifier, it can pursue legal remedies to stop subsequent use by a competing product. *See Nat'l Collegiate Athletic Ass'n v. Kizzang LLC*, 304 F. Supp. 3d 800 (S.D. Ind. 2018) (NCAA entitled to block sports website's use of "Final 3" and "April Madness"). As you read the cases that follow, question to what extent consumers care about the source of team logo apparel, and whether trademark protection in that setting disserves the consumer by raising prices for those goods.

Trademark protections are found in both state and federal law. The main federal statute is the Lanham Act, enacted in 1946 and periodically amended since then. 15 U.S.C. §§ 1051, *et seq.* Although the Lanham Act protects a mark regardless of whether it is federally registered, registration of a mark confers significant benefits, including presumptive nationwide ownership of the mark and exclusive rights to use the mark for the subject goods or services. Registration also enables the mark owner to bring an infringement suit in federal court and potentially recover treble damages, attorneys' fees, and other remedies.

PROBLEM 9.3

The National Women's Soccer League's Utah team, founded in 2018, has adopted the name "Royals" and uses a logo that features a crown perched on a stylized lion in royal blue, white, and gold. Like any professional sports team, the Utah Royals sell tickets to sports events and also market apparel and merchandise that feature the team name and logo. As you read the materials on trademark law, consider the following questions.

a. The Major League Baseball Kansas City Royals, founded in 1969, has a logo that features a crown on a shield in navy blue, red, and yellow. Does the baseball Royals have a right to prevent the NWSL Royals from using the team name, or any aspect of its logo?

b. Would your answer to the previous question change upon learning that the soccer Royals are affiliated with a Major League Soccer (men's) team—Real Salt Lake—which has been using a crowned lion as its logo since 2005, without complaint from MLB or the KC Royals? (NB: "real" is Spanish for royal.)

c. In 2020, Southern State College changed the name of its athletic teams from the Rebels to the Royals to discontinue using a potentially offensive name because of its associations with the Confederacy. Does SSC have the right to ban an online throwback jersey vender from selling gear labeled Rebels and using the school's red and blue color scheme? Can MLB and the KC Royals assert TM rights against SSC's use of the name?

d. Quest is a Utah-based company that sells protein bars and energy products. Since the founding of the NWSL Utah Royals soccer team, Quest has adopted the slogan, "Fill your quest for a ROYALLY energizing protein bar," and its ad campaigns, including billboards around the stadium, use colors similar to the Royals logo. Does the team have any recourse here?

e. Jane Bigelow is a film director who is making a movie about a women's soccer league. It is not authorized by the NWSL or any of its teams, who have declined to cooperate with the film or license any game footage or other intellectual property. Does Bigelow's use of store-bought official team apparel to costume her actors infringe any trademark rights?

1. SPORTS TEAM NAMES

To serve as a trademark, a name must be distinctive, that is, it must be capable of identifying the source of a particular good. The more distinctive a mark, the greater the legal protection, determined by the relationship between the mark and the underlying product. Courts group marks into four categories, from most to least distinctive: (1) arbitrary or fanciful, (2) suggestive, (3) descriptive, or (4) generic. Sports team names generally fall into one of the two most distinctive categories, earning a high degree of protection. For example, the NHL's Anaheim "Ducks" is an arbitrary name as it bears no logical relationship to the underlying product. The Nashville "Predators" and the Philadelphia "Flyers" are suggestive names, connoting desirable qualities in a hockey team. All those marks therefore receive strong legal protection. *See In Re WNBA Enterprises, LLC*, 70 U.S.P.Q.2d 1153 (T.T.A.B. June 11, 2003) (WNBA team name Orlando "Miracle" is a suggestive, not descriptive, mark). Descriptive marks, such as "National Hockey League" and the city designations in each of the above NHL team names, convey something about the product and merit protection only if they have acquired "secondary meaning" through the user's efforts to associate the mark with a particular business. *See Maryland Stadium Auth. v. Becker*, 806 F. Supp. 1236, 1241 (D. Md. 1992), *aff'd*, 36 F.3d 1093 (4th Cir. 1994) ("promotional efforts and the media coverage given to the new baseball park had conferred a secondary meaning upon the name Camden Yards").

All major U.S. sports leagues strive, though advertising and media coverage, to associate team names with member clubs and thereby acquire secondary meaning for their marks. But unrelated business decisions, such as to relocate a franchise, expand or contract the league, or build a stadium across a state line, can expose vulnerabilities in trademark ownership. For example, when the NFL's Oakland team announced its move to Las Vegas, the league had to contend with multiple earlier-filed opportunistic trademark applications for the name Las Vegas Raiders. *See also Nat'l Football League Properties, Inc. v. New Jersey Giants, Inc.*, 637 F. Supp. 507 (D.N.J. 1986) (enjoining "New Jersey Giants" mark similar to NFL New York Giants, created to take advantage of team's new home stadium location); *Johnny Blastoff, Inc. v. Los Angeles Rams Football Co.*, 188 F.3d 427 (7th Cir. 1999) (holding that someone filing a state registration for "St. Louis Rams" the day after the team announced it was moving from Los Angeles to St. Louis did not have a valid right in the mark). The following sports trademark dispute provides an apt introduction to this branch of the law, as well as a flashback to an NFL franchise move encountered in Chapter 8.

INDIANAPOLIS COLTS V. METROPOLITAN BALTIMORE FOOTBALL CLUB

34 F.3d 410 (7th Cir. 1994)

POSNER, CHIEF JUDGE.

[The Baltimore Colts had played in that city for 32 years when, in 1984, the owner, Robert Irsay, moved the team to Indianapolis, literally under cover of darkness. The NFL, worried about the prospects of an antitrust lawsuit, decided not to block the relocation of the team and allowed the team to keep its nickname as the Indianapolis Colts. The sudden and secretive move outraged Baltimore fans, who tried to get the team back through various means. They were somewhat appeased when, in 1993, the Canadian Football League (CFL) granted Baltimore a franchise, which the new owner (and the fans) wanted to name the Colts. When the NFL threatened legal action, the team adopted the name Baltimore CFL Colts. Not satisfied with that variation on the old name, the Indianapolis Colts and the NFL sued to block any use of the word "Colts" in the CFL team name. After the district judge granted a preliminary injunction, the Baltimore team appealed.]

* * *

The Baltimore team wanted to call itself the "Baltimore Colts." To improve its litigating posture (we assume), it has consented to insert "CFL" between "Baltimore" and "Colts." A glance at the merchandise in the record explains why this concession to an outraged NFL has been made so readily. On several of the items "CFL" appears in small or blurred letters. And since the Canadian Football League is not well known in the United States—and "CFL" has none of the instant recognition value of "NFL"—the inclusion of the acronym in the team's name might have little impact on potential buyers even if prominently displayed. Those who know football well know that the new "Baltimore Colts" are a new CFL team wholly unrelated to the old Baltimore Colts; know also that the rules of Canadian football are different from those of American football and that teams don't move from the NFL to the CFL as they might from one conference within the NFL to the other. But those who do not know these things—and we shall come shortly to the question whether there are many of these football illiterate— will not be warned off by the letters "CFL." The acronym is a red herring, and the real issue is whether the new Baltimore team can appropriate the name "Baltimore Colts." The entire thrust of the defendants' argument is that it can.

They make a tremendous to-do over the fact that the district judge found that the Indianapolis Colts abandoned the trademark "Baltimore Colts" when they moved to Indianapolis. Well, of course; they were no longer playing football under the name "Baltimore Colts," so could not have used the name as the team's trademark; they could have used it on merchandise but chose not to, until 1991 (another story—and not one we need tell). When a mark is abandoned, it returns to the public domain, and is appropriable anew—in principle. In practice, because "subsequent use of [an] abandoned mark may well evoke a continuing association with the prior use, those who make subsequent use may be required to take reasonable precautions to prevent confusion." J. Thomas McCarthy, *McCarthy on Trademarks and Intellectual Property* § 17.01 [2] (3d ed. 1994) at p. 17–3. This precept is especially important where, as in this case, the former owner of the abandoned mark continues to market the same product or service under a similar name, though we cannot find any previous cases of this kind. No one questions the validity of "Indianapolis Colts" as the trademark of the NFL team that plays out of Indianapolis and was formerly known as the Baltimore Colts. If "Baltimore CFL Colts" is confusingly similar to "Indianapolis Colts" by virtue of the history of the Indianapolis team and the overlapping product and geographical markets served by it and by the new Baltimore team, the latter's use of the abandoned mark would infringe the Indianapolis Colts' new mark. The Colts' abandonment of a mark confusingly similar to their new mark neither broke the continuity of the team in its different locations—it was the same team, merely having a different home base and therefore a different geographical component in its name—nor entitled a third party to pick it up and use it to confuse Colts fans, and other actual or potential consumers of products and services marketed by the Colts or by other National Football League teams, with regard to the identity, sponsorship, or league affiliation of the third party, that is, the new Baltimore team. . . .

Against this the defendants cite to us with great insistence *Major League Baseball Properties, Inc. v. Sed Non Olet Denarius, Ltd.*, 817 F. Supp. 1103, 1128 (S.D.N.Y. 1993), which, over the objection of the Los Angeles Dodgers, allowed a restaurant in Brooklyn to use the name "Brooklyn Dodger" on the ground that "the 'Brooklyn Dodgers' was a non-transportable cultural institution separate from the 'Los Angeles Dodgers.'" The defendants in our case argue that the sudden and greatly resented departure of the Baltimore Colts for Indianapolis made the name "Baltimore Colts" available to anyone who would continue the "nontransportable cultural institution" constituted by a football team located in the City of Baltimore. We think this argument very weak, and need not even try to distinguish *Sed Non Olet Denarius* since district court decisions are not authoritative in this or any court of appeals. If it were a Supreme Court decision it still would not help the defendants. The "Brooklyn Dodger" was not a baseball team, and there was no risk of confusion. . . . The only claim in our court is that a significant number of consumers will think the new Baltimore team the successor to, or alter ego of, or even the same team as the Baltimore Colts and therefore the Indianapolis Colts, which is the real successor. No one would think the Brooklyn Dodgers baseball team reincarnated in a restaurant.

A professional sports team is like Heraclitus's river: always changing, yet always the same. When Mr. Irsay transported his team, the Baltimore Colts, from Baltimore to Indianapolis in one night in 1984, the team remained, for a time anyway, completely intact: same players, same coaches, same front-office personnel. With the passage of time, of course, the team changed. Players retired or were traded, and were replaced. Coaches and other nonplaying personnel came and went. But as far as the record discloses there is as much institutional continuity between the Baltimore Colts of 1984 and the Indianapolis Colts of 1994 as there was between the Baltimore Colts of 1974 and the Baltimore Colts of 1984. . . . The Colts were Irsay's team, it was moved intact, there is no evidence it has changed more since the move than it had in the years before. There is, in contrast, no continuity, no links contractual or otherwise, nothing but a geographical site in common, between the Baltimore Colts and the Canadian Football League team that would like to use its name. Any suggestion that there is such continuity is false and potentially misleading.

Potentially; for if everyone knows there is no contractual or institutional continuity, no pedigree or line of descent, linking the Baltimore-Indianapolis Colts and the new CFL team that wants to call itself the "Baltimore Colts" (or, grudgingly, the "Baltimore CFL Colts"), then there is no harm, at least no harm for which the Lanham Act provides a remedy, in the new Baltimore team's appropriating the name "Baltimore Colts" to play under and sell merchandise under. If not everyone knows, there is harm. Some people who might otherwise watch the Indianapolis Colts (or some other NFL team, for remember that the NFL, representing all the teams, is a co-plaintiff) on television may watch the Baltimore CFL Colts instead, thinking they are the "real" Baltimore Colts, and the NFL will lose revenue. A few (doubtless very few) people who might otherwise buy tickets to an NFL game may buy tickets to a Baltimore CFL Colts game instead. Some people who might otherwise buy merchandise stamped with the name "Indianapolis Colts" or the name of some other NFL team may buy merchandise stamped "Baltimore CFL Colts," thinking it a kin of the NFL's Baltimore Colts in the glory days of Johnny Unitas rather than a newly formed team that plays Canadian football in a Canadian football league. It would be naive to suppose that no consideration of such possibilities occurred to the owners of the new Baltimore team when they were choosing a name, though there is no evidence that it was the dominant or even a major consideration.

Confusion thus is possible, and may even have been desired; but is it likely? There is great variance in consumer competence, and it would be undesirable to impoverish the lexicon of trade names merely to protect the most gullible fringe of the consuming public. The Lanham Act does not cast the net of protection so wide. The legal standard under the Act has been formulated variously, but the various formulations come down to whether it is likely that the challenged mark if permitted to be used by the defendant would cause the plaintiff to lose a substantial number of consumers. Pertinent to this determination is the similarity of the marks and of the parties' products, the knowledge of the average consumer of the product, the overlap in the parties' geographical markets, and the other factors that the cases consider. The aim is to strike a balance between, on the one hand, the interest of the seller of the new product, and of the consuming public, in an arresting, attractive, and informative name that will enable the new product to compete effectively against existing ones, and, on the other hand, the interest of existing sellers, and again of the consuming public, in consumers' being able to know exactly what they are buying without having to incur substantial costs of investigation or inquiry.

* * *

[The court then compared the market research surveys conducted by the two sides. After criticizing the methodology used by the defendant's expert, Michael Rappeport, the court analyzed the study conducted by the plaintiff's expert.]

* * *

The plaintiffs' study, conducted by Jacob Jacoby, was far more substantial and the district judge found it on the whole credible. The 28-page report with its numerous appendices has all the trappings of social scientific rigor. Interviewers showed several hundred consumers in 24 malls scattered around the country shirts and hats licensed by the defendants for sale to consumers. The shirts and hats have "Baltimore CFL Colts" stamped on them. The consumers were asked whether they were football fans, whether they watched football games on television, and whether they ever bought merchandise with a team name on it. Then they were asked, with reference to the "Baltimore CFL Colts" merchandise that they were shown, such questions as whether they knew what sport the team played, what teams it played against, what league the team was in, and whether the team or league needed someone's permission to use this name, and if so whose. . . . There were other questions, none however obviously loaded, and a whole other survey, the purpose of which was to control for "noise," in which another group of mallgoers was asked the identical questions about a hypothetical team unappetizingly named the "Baltimore Horses." The idea was by comparing the answers of the two groups to see whether the source of confusion was the name "Baltimore Colts" or just the name "Baltimore," in which event the injunction would do no good since no one suggests that the new Baltimore team should be forbidden to use "Baltimore" in its name, provided the name does not also include "Colts."

* * *

Jacoby's survey of consumers reactions to the "Baltimore CFL Colts" merchandise found rather astonishing levels of confusion not plausibly attributable to the presence of the name "Baltimore" alone, since "Baltimore Horses" engendered much less. . . . Among self-identified football fans, 64% thought that the "Baltimore CFL Colts" was either the old (NFL) Baltimore Colts or the Indianapolis Colts. But perhaps this result is not so astonishing. Although most American football fans have heard of Canadian football, many probably are unfamiliar with the acronym "CFL," and as we remarked earlier it is not a very conspicuous part of the team logo stamped on the merchandise. Among fans who watch football on television, 59% displayed the same confusion; and even among those who watch football on cable television, which attracts a more educated audience on average and actually carries CFL games, 58% were confused when shown the merchandise. Among the minority not confused about who the "Baltimore CFL Colts" are, a substantial minority, ranging from 21 to 34% depending on the precise sub-sample, thought the team somehow sponsored or authorized by the Indianapolis Colts or the National Football League. . . .

[W]e cannot say that the district judge committed a clear error in crediting the major findings of the Jacoby study and inferring from it and the other evidence in the record that the defendants' use of the name "Baltimore CFL Colts" whether for the team or on merchandise was likely to confuse a substantial number of consumers. . . .

Affirmed.

———

Coda: Baltimore fans finally saw the return of NFL football in 1996 when the historic Cleveland Browns franchise relocated there. The NFL conditioned the move on renaming the team in order to leave the name "Browns" for Cleveland to use should it ever acquire another NFL franchise (which it did in 1999 with a new expansion franchise). Baltimore's NFL football team is now called the Ravens.

The *Indianapolis Colts* decision refers to an earlier district court decision in *Major League Baseball Properties v. Sed Non Olet Denarius*, 817 F. Supp. 1103 (S.D.N.Y.1993). That case was the by-product of an even more controversial sports franchise move—the Dodgers' flight from Brooklyn to Los Angeles in 1958. The relocated baseball club had registered the word "Dodgers," and had licensed merchandisers to use both "Los Angeles Dodgers" and "Brooklyn Dodgers." On this basis, the club warned off a 1966 effort to name a Continental Football League team the Brooklyn Dodgers. However, it never challenged a Brooklyn restaurant named Dodgers Cafe during its operation from 1942 to 1968.

In 1991, though, the Dodgers filed a trademark infringement action against a new Brooklyn restaurant opened by some Dodgers fans—the

Brooklyn Dodgers Sports Bar and Restaurant. Though the original team nickname commemorated "dodging" Brooklyn streetcars, the restaurant logo included a depiction of the Artful Dodger, a character from Charles Dickens' *Oliver Twist*. The restaurant did, however, draw heavily upon the illustrious history of the city's baseball team—naming dishes after famous Dodgers players, decorating the restaurant with Dodgers memorabilia, and selling licensed Brooklyn Dodgers merchandise.

The federal judge dismissed the claim after applying the standard trademark litigation factors:

a)   Strength of the plaintiff's trademark

b)   Similarity between the parties' marks

c)   Proximity of their products

d)   Likelihood that the plaintiff will "bridge the gap" between the two markets

e)   Evidence of actual confusion

f)   Presence or absence of good faith on the part of the defendant

g)   Quality of defendant's services

———

NOTES AND QUESTIONS

1.   *Same Name, Different City or Sport.* What was the precise source of the trademark claim in the *Colts* case? Could an NFL team in a different city, *e.g.*, Green Bay, have objected to the name Baltimore CFL Packers? Or was the real issue that the two Colts teams were playing the same sport? For example, does the St. Louis baseball Cardinals have a basis for blocking use of the name by the later-established football Cardinals (or does the viability of that claim depend on whether the football team was still located in St. Louis, as opposed to its prior city of Chicago or its later location in Arizona)? Note that in 1997, a federal district judge refused to grant an injunction to the barnstorming Harlem Wizards basketball team to block the NBA's Washington franchise from changing its name from Bullets to Wizards, observing that the types of basketball entertainment offered were sufficiently dissimilar to avoid consumer confusion. *See Harlem Wizards Entertainment Basketball, Inc. v. NBA Properties*, 952 F. Supp. 1084 (D. N.J. 1997).

2.   *Historical Team Naming Customs.* Until the *Indianapolis Colts* case, trademark law long permitted legitimate applicants to register common team names in different sports and/or markets. Professional teams routinely share names, for example, MLB Texas Rangers and NHL New York Rangers, NBA Sacramento Kings and NHL Los Angeles Kings, and MLB San Francisco Giants and NFL New York Giants. Significant duplication and overlap exist among college, high school, and recreational athletics programs, who also routinely share the same names as professional teams. This practice has

slowed in the face of aggressive trademark enforcement, which has imposed costs across sport. MLB's Cleveland Guardians baseball team, formerly the Indians, had to pay off the same-named local roller derby club when it rebranded. The NHL expansion Las Vegas Golden Knights obtained only limited registration of its name in the face of opposition from the U.S. Army parachute team and a small upstate New York college with the same name. A private Florida elementary school was forced to change its 50-year-old team name from "Gators" in response to University of Florida threats of litigation. Does the *Colts* case suggest what accounts for this trademark vigilance (some might say "bullying")? Should we be concerned about trademark depletion and that the scarcity of available team names will complicate market entry and branding of new sports enterprises?

3. *Team Logos, Insignia, and Colors.* Would the Baltimore CFL team have avoided liability if it used a different nickname (*e.g.*, the "Ponies"), with a logo that incorporated a blue and white horseshoe similar to the NFL Colts logo? Courts have recognized that distinctive helmet and uniform designs and colors, and team mascots such as the chicken of the San Diego Padres and Bucky Badger of the University of Wisconsin, also serve to identify particular teams and can function as trademarks. *See Bd. of Supervisors for Louisiana State Univ. Agric. & Mech. Coll. v. Smack Apparel Co.*, 550 F.3d 465 (5th Cir. 2008) (university color schemes have acquired secondary meaning and are protected marks); *Univ. Book Store v. Board of Regents of the Univ. of Wisconsin*, 33 U.S.P.Q.2d 1385 (T.T.A.B. June 22, 1994) (although some consumers buy Bucky Badger apparel only because it's "cute," the symbol is not "merely ornamental" and signifies university sponsorship). What if a color scheme has a functional purpose, as team uniform colors do in helping team members, spectators, and officials differentiate among players on the field? Should the first team to use a particular color scheme be able to prohibit any subsequent uniform use?

4. *Disclaimers.* The Lanham Act considers a trademark abandoned when "its use has been discontinued with intent not to resume such use." Abandonment may be inferred from the surrounding circumstances, but proof of nonuse for three consecutive years is prima facie evidence of abandonment. Yet, as we saw with the Baltimore CFL Colts, a finding of abandonment does not insulate a subsequent user from infringement liability if it fails to take precautions to avoid consumer confusion. Should use of team names, logos and other insignia be permitted if the user makes clear through disclaimers that the sports entity is *not* authorizing their venture? What more should the CFL have done to communicate such a disclaimer?

5. *Trademark Abandonment and Re-establishment.* Compare the defunct 1980s United States Football League, which challenged resurrection of that name by a 2022 professional football venture. The old league claimed that even if it had abandoned the USFL name, it re-established ownership 20 years after the league's demise (and ahead of the new league) by using the name for throwback attire and reunion activities. A court found these pursuits insufficient to justify enjoining the new league's use of the name. But it also

found that the new league's reliance on nostalgia for the old USFL created a likelihood of confusion that justified monetary damages. *The Real USFL, LLC v. Fox Sports, Inc.*, 2022 WL 1134487 (C.D. Cal. Apr. 14, 2022). What precautions should the subsequent user of the USFL name have taken to avoid misleading associations with the defunct league? Given that the old league had no plans to relaunch, what should be the measure of damages?

6. *Likelihood of Confusion.* What is the relevant population for determining "likelihood of confusion" for trademark purposes? Should it be people who identify themselves as football fans? People in Indianapolis and/or in Baltimore? People who might actually buy NFL and/or CFL merchandise?

2. OTHER SPORTS PHRASES AND DESIGNATIONS

As noted, trademark in sports extends far beyond team names. Texas A&M University claims ownership of the mark "12th Man"—a phrase that recognizes fan spirit and support of the university's football team. Its vigilance in protecting that mark led to lawsuits against the NFL's Seattle Seahawks and Indianapolis Colts, both of which ultimately settled by licensing use of the phrase. *See also New York Yankees P'ship v. Evil Enterprises, Inc.*, 2013 WL 1305332 (T.T.A.B. Feb. 8, 2013) (sustaining New York Yankees' opposition to third party's registration of "Baseball's Evil Empire").

Similarly, the NFL's defense of the phrase "Super Bowl" is legendary. It has filed dozens of suits to stop unauthorized use of the phrase, including seeking to block a restaurant from trademarking its registration of "Souper Bowls." When the Philadelphia Eagles last played in the Super Bowl, a hometown sports bar resorted to identifying the annual event as the "Birds Big Game" to avoid NFL censure. In 2003, the NFL filed a trademark infringement suit against the fledgling National Women's Football League (NWFL), not for its use of that name or letters, but for using other marks, like "SupHer Bowl," and team logos that the NFL claimed were confusingly similar to its teams' marks. Although the case settled without a judicial ruling, what is your view about the legal merits of an infringement action against a new women's league that is largely unknown to the public and unlikely to survive (as the NWFL did not)? Why would the NFL bother to bring such a suit? It could not have been worried that consumers might mistakenly purchase NWFL tickets or merchandise when they meant to buy the NFL equivalents. An answer to this question is suggested in a suit involving the name of one of the sports world's most prestigious events— the men's Masters Golf Tournament at the National course in Augusta, Georgia.

Northwestern Mutual Life (NML) sponsored a Ladies Professional Golf Association Tournament, held one week after the Augusta Masters. NML named the tournament the "Ladies Masters at Moss Creek Plantation," in part to promote its new real estate development at that location. Augusta National immediately secured an injunction blocking any use of the word "Masters." *See Augusta National v. Northwestern Mutual Life Insurance*, 193 U.S.P.Q. 210 (S.D. Ga. 1976). As the judge put it:

> [T]he use of the term "Masters" by NML in the name of its planned annual tournament, "Ladies Masters at Moss Creek Plantation," is likely to confuse the public into believing that Augusta National also sponsors the women's tournament. From this factual premise, logic compels the conclusion that if Augusta National's reputation is high, defendant will be "trading" on that reputation and "reaping where it has not sown." If Augusta National's good will is of great value, defendant will be sharing in it without having contributed to its growth. Logic compels, too, the conclusion that if NML "sins," they will be "visited upon" Augusta National. If NML mismanages the tournament, Augusta National will suffer the consequences in loss of good will and reputation; and this without having a hand in it. In sum, there would be a confusion of businesses in which plaintiff would no longer be master of its own destiny.

> The case presents a classic example of the reasons for the creation of equity jurisprudence calling for the exercise of the conscience of a long-footed chancellor.

193 U.S.P.Q. at 220.

Athletes have also sought to trademark personal catchphrases, logos, and mannerisms. NBA superstar Giannis Antetokounmpo has trademarked his nickname "Greek Freak" and litigates to block any unauthorized use, including by a mail-order meal-delivery company that used that name for a spice blend. *Antetokounmpo v. Paleo Prods. LLC*, 2021 WL 4864537 (S.D.N.Y. Oct. 18, 2021). While athletes cannot trademark an actual physical pose, they can trademark symbols, words, phrases, and designs that attempt to capture that pose. For example, Olympic sprinter Usain Bolt has trademarked an icon of his signature "lightning bolt" stance. Former New England Patriots tight end Rob Gronkowski has trademarked his silhouette spiking a football. Two cautions about such personal marks: First, the U.S. Patent and Trademark Office refuses to register sports-related slogans and taglines that consist entirely of "merely informational" matter. Thus, they rejected the trademark applications of NFLer Marshawn Lynch for "I'm just here so I won't get fined" and tennis great John McEnroe for "You cannot be serious." *See* USPTO Trademark Manual of Examining Procedure 1202.04 (July 2021). Second, unlike publicity rights, to maintain control over a trademark, the athlete must use it on commercial goods or risk forfeiting the mark.

NOTES AND QUESTIONS

1. *Secondary Meaning.* In light of the *Augusta National* decision, how would you decide a case brought by the promoters of the National Invitation Tournament in New York for men's college basketball teams, against the Women's National Invitation Tournament, which held its event for several years in the 1990s in Amarillo, Texas, and invited eight women's college basketball teams that did not qualify for the NCAA tournament? What distinctions, if any, do you see between the two cases? Consider the *Augusta National* finding that "in the public's mind, the word "Masters" in the context of golf and golf tournaments, has come to mean 'a single thing coming from a single source,' that is to say, a golf tournament sponsored by Augusta National."

2. *Reverse Confusion.* "Reverse confusion" occurs when a junior (second) user of a mark is much more famous than the senior (or first) user. The problem is not that consumers will mistakenly believe that the infringer's product is affiliated with or endorsed by the trademark owner, but rather that they will mistakenly believe that the trademark owner's product originates with or is endorsed by the infringer. In *Illinois High Sch. Ass'n v. GTE Vantage, Inc.*, 99 F.3d 244 (7th Cir. 1996), the court found that even though the Illinois high school basketball tournament had used the term "March Madness" long before its association with the NCAA men's basketball tournament, the NCAA only began using the term after the media's frequent use had firmly linked it with the NCAA tournament in the minds of most consumers. That is, the broadcaster CBS, not the NCAA, caused the confusion. Thus, the court concluded that the IHSA and the NCAA had become joint owners of "March Madness," which led them to form a joint venture, the March Madness Athletic Association, to monitor and license the use of the term. *See March Madness Athletic Ass'n v. Netfire, Inc.*, 162 F. Supp. 2d 560 (N.D. Tex. 2001); *see also Dream Team Collectibles, Inc. v. NBA Properties, Inc.*, 958 F. Supp. 1401 (E.D. Mo. 1997) (factual issue whether NBA or media responsible for public association of "Dream Team" mark with NBA players).

3. MERCHANDISING OF SPORTS TRADEMARKS

The major economic value of a sports name or logo is not to adorn player uniforms in games and thereby identify teams, but rather to market sports-related merchandise valued at tens of billions of dollars annually. Thus, in the *Colts* case, the NFL's principal motivation for suing was not the likelihood that football fans would be confused about whether they were buying tickets to watch the NFL Colts or the CFL Colts on the field. Rather, NFL Properties wanted to make sure that fans would not buy T-shirts and other paraphernalia licensed by the Baltimore CFL Colts, rather than by the Indianapolis Colts. Sports entities expend large sums of money to invest their symbols and colors with a strong secondary meaning of identification with a team, and argue that because such symbols create and perpetuate the good will of the member clubs, they perform the function of valid service marks. *See Nat'l Football League Properties, Inc. v. Consumer Enterprises, Inc.*, 26 Ill. App. 3d 814 (1975) (observing that trademarks "indicate sponsorship or origin in addition to their ornamental value").

Use of trademark law to secure such protection poses an analytical problem. Recall that the nature and objective of trademark law is to encourage producers like Nike and Augusta National to develop distinctive names and symbols to identify their products, by barring other producers from attaching the same names and symbols to other products and thence misleading consumers looking to enjoy (and pay for) their favorite running shoes or golf tournament. Producers do not, however, receive a copyright-like monopoly in their name and symbol that blocks others from using it for non-confusing purposes. Pepsi, for example, can use the words "Coca Cola" in an advertisement that tries to draw an unfavorable comparison with its own product. So also could the CFL refer to the NFL's Super Bowl in advertising how closely-contested are CFL championship Grey Cup games.

In the case of sports merchandising, though, leagues and teams are selling names and symbols in and of themselves, thus allowing fans wearing a T-shirt to identify with their favorite teams and sports. If the T-shirt carried the name and likeness of a celebrated athlete, the publicity right we encountered earlier gives the individual the exclusive legal authority to license or bar use of his name and likeness for that purpose. Teams or leagues, by contrast, are business organizations, and thus cannot use this legal outgrowth of the right of personal privacy. Some other justification had to be found for granting the "right" to control merchandise that includes a team or university name. It was offered in a 1975 judicial ruling that greatly expanded trademark doctrine to protect sports merchandise and promotional goods.

BOSTON PROFESSIONAL HOCKEY ASSOCIATION V. DALLAS CAP AND EMBLEM MFG., INC.

510 F.2d 1004 (5th Cir. 1975)

RONEY, CIRCUIT JUDGE.

[Prior to this case, NHL hockey teams had organized National Hockey League Services (NHLS) to serve as their exclusive licensing agent. NHLS licensed numerous manufacturers to use the team names and symbols in various merchandise, including an exclusive license with Lion Brothers Company to manufacture embroidered emblems depicting the team logos. Between 1968 and 1971, Dallas Cap & Emblem sought to obtain a similar license. Unable to do so, the company then proceeded to manufacture the emblems for sale to sporting goods stores in various states.

When the NHL teams ultimately sued for trademark infringement, their complaint alleged that Dallas Cap's manufacture and sale of the team symbols constituted (1) an infringement of the plaintiffs' registered marks in violation of 15 U.S.C.A. § 1114; (2) false designation of origin in violation of 15 U.S.C.A. § 1125; and (3) common law unfair competition. The district court held that a disclaimer informing consumers that the products were not officially authorized by the NHL was a sufficient remedy. The NHL teams appealed.]

* * *

Nearly everyone is familiar with the artistic symbols which designate the individual teams in various professional sports. The question in this case of first impression is whether the unauthorized, intentional duplication of a professional hockey team's symbol on an embroidered emblem, to be sold to the public as a patch for attachment to clothing, violates any legal right of the team to the exclusive use of that symbol. Contrary to the decision of the district court, we hold that the team has an interest in its own individualized symbol entitled to legal protection against such unauthorized duplication.

* * *

The Case

The difficulty with this case stems from the fact that a reproduction of the trademark itself is being sold, unattached to any other goods or services. The statutory and case law of trademarks is oriented toward the use of such marks to sell something other than the mark itself. The district court thought that to give plaintiffs protection in this case would be tantamount to the creation of a copyright monopoly for designs that were not copyrighted. The copyright laws are based on an entirely different concept than the trademark laws, and contemplate that the copyrighted material, like patented ideas, will eventually pass into the public domain. The trademark laws are based on the needed protection of the public and business interests and there is no reason why trademarks should ever pass into the public domain by the mere passage of time.

Although our decision here may slightly tilt the trademark laws from the purpose of protecting the public to the protection of the business interests of plaintiffs, we think that the two become so intermeshed when viewed against the backdrop of the common law of unfair competition that both the public and plaintiffs are better served by granting the relief sought by plaintiffs.

Underlying our decision are three persuasive points. First, the major commercial value of the emblems is derived from the efforts of plaintiffs. Second, defendant sought and ostensibly would have asserted, if obtained, an exclusive right to make and sell the emblems. Third, the sale of a reproduction of the trademark itself on an emblem is an accepted use of such team symbols in connection with the type of activity in which the business of professional sports is engaged. We need not deal here with the concept of whether every artistic reproduction of the symbol would infringe upon plaintiffs' rights. We restrict ourselves to the emblems sold principally through sporting goods stores for informal use by the public in connection with sports activities and to show public allegiance to or identification with the teams themselves.

* * *

[The court turned directly to the question whether the plaintiffs had proven elements (4) and (5) of a § 1114 violation, *i.e.*, whether the symbols were used in connection with the sale of goods and whether such use was likely to cause confusion, mistake, or deception.]

* * *

The fourth requisite of a § 1114 cause of action is that the infringing use of the registered mark must be in connection with the sale, offering for sale, distribution or advertising of any goods. Although the district court did not expressly find that plaintiffs had failed to establish element four, such a finding was implicit in the court's statement that "in the instant case, the registered trade mark is, in effect, the product itself."

Defendant is in the business of manufacturing and marketing emblems for wearing apparel. These emblems are the products, or goods, which defendant sells. When defendant causes plaintiffs' marks to be embroidered upon emblems which it later markets, defendant uses those marks in connection with the sale of goods as surely as if defendant had embroidered the marks upon knit caps. *See Boston Professional Hockey Association, Inc. v. Reliable Knitting Works*, 178 U.S.P.Q. (BNA) 274 (E.D. Wis. 1973). The fact that the symbol covers the entire face of defendant's product does not alter the fact that the trademark symbol is used in connection with the sale of the product. The sports fan in his local sporting goods store purchases defendant's fabric and thread emblems because they are embroidered with the symbols of ice hockey teams. Were defendant to embroider the same fabric with the same thread in other designs, the resulting products would still be emblems for wearing apparel but they would not give trademark identification to the customer. The conclusion is inescapable that, without plaintiffs' marks, defendant would not have a market for his particular product among ice hockey fans desiring to purchase emblems embroidered with the symbols of their favorite teams. It becomes clear that defendant's use of plaintiffs' marks is in connection with the sale, offering for sale, distribution, or advertising of goods and that plaintiffs have established the fourth element of a § 1114 cause of action.

The fifth element of a cause of action for mark infringement under 15 U.S.C.A. § 1114 is that the infringing use is likely to cause confusion, or to cause mistake or to deceive. The district court decided that there was no likelihood of confusion because the usual purchaser, a sports fan in his local sporting goods store, would not be likely to think that defendant's emblems were manufactured by or had some connection with plaintiffs. . . . In this case, however, the district court overlooked the fact that the Act was amended to eliminate the source of origin as being the only focal point of confusion. The confusion question here is conceptually difficult. It can be said that the public buyer knew that the emblems portrayed the teams' symbols. Thus, it can be argued, the buyer is not confused or deceived. This argument misplaces the purpose of the confusion requirement. The confusion or deceit requirement is met by the fact that the defendant duplicated the protected trademarks and sold them to the public knowing that the public would identify them as being the teams' trademarks. The certain knowledge of the buyer that the source and origin of the trademark symbols were in plaintiffs satisfies the requirement of the Act. The argument that confusion must be as to the source of the manufacture of the emblem itself is unpersuasive, where the trademark, originated by the team, is the triggering mechanism for the sale of the emblem.

* * *

Additional Defenses to Relief

Defendant makes two arguments against an extension of Lanham Act protection to plaintiffs which need consideration. Adopting the district court's rationale, defendant asserts first, that plaintiffs' marks when embroidered on emblems for wearing apparel are functional and thus serve no trademark purpose and, second, that there is some overriding concept of free competition which, under the instant facts, would remove plaintiffs from the protective ambits of the Lanham Act.

The short answer to defendant's arguments is that the emblems sold because they bore the identifiable trademarks of plaintiffs. This fact clearly distinguishes the case from *Pagliero v. Wallace China Co.*, 198 F.2d 339 (9th Cir. 1952), relied upon by the district court. *Pagliero* involved designs on chinaware which were neither trademarked, patented nor copyrighted. The court found no unfair competition on the ground that the designs were functional, that is, they connoted other than a trademark purpose. "The attractiveness and eye-appeal of the design sells the china," 198 F.2d at 343–344, not the trademark character of the designs. In the case at bar, the embroidered symbols are sold not because of any such aesthetic characteristic but because they are the trademarks of the hockey teams. Those cases which involved utilitarian articles such as pole lamps, *Sears, Roebuck & Co. v. Stiffel Co.*, 376 U.S. 225 (1964), fluorescent lighting fixtures, *Compco Corp. v. Day-Brite Lighting, Inc.*, 376 U.S. 234 (1964), and toggle clamps, *West Point Mfg. Co. v. Detroit Stamping Co.*, 222 F.2d 581, 105 U.S.P.Q. (BNA) 200 (6th Cir. 1955), all involved products which had a consumer demand regardless of their source or origin. The principles involved in those cases are not applicable to a trademark symbol case where the design or symbol has no demonstrated value other than its significance as the trademark of a hockey team.

The argument that the symbols could be protected only if copyrighted likewise misses the thrust of trademark protection. A trademark is a property right which is acquired by use. *Trade-Mark Cases*, 100 U.S. 82 (1879). It differs substantially from a copyright, in both its legal genesis and its scope of federal protection. The legal cornerstone for the protection of copyrights is Article I, section 8, clause 8 of the Constitution. In the case of a copyright, an individual creates a unique design and, because the Constitutional fathers saw fit to encourage creativity, he can secure a copyright for his.... After the expiration of the copyright, his creation becomes part of the public domain. In the case of a trademark, however, the process is reversed. An individual selects a word or design that might otherwise be in the public domain to represent his business or product. If that word or design comes to symbolize his product or business in the public mind, the individual acquires a property right in the mark. The acquisition of such a right through use represents the passage of a word or design out of the public domain into the protective ambits of trademark law. Under the provisions of the Lanham Act, the owner of a mark acquires a protectable property interest in his mark through registration and use.

The time limit on copyright protection not being sufficient for plaintiffs' purposes, they acquainted the public with their marks and thereby created a demand for those marks. Through extensive use, plaintiffs have acquired a property right in their marks which extends to the reproduction and sale of those marks as embroidered patches for wearing apparel. What plaintiffs have acquired by use, the substantive law of trademarks as it is embodied in the Lanham Act will protect against infringement. There is no overriding policy of free competition which would remove plaintiffs, under the facts of this case, from the protective ambits of the Lanham Act.

* * *

Reversed and remanded.

———

After *Boston Hockey*, the merchandising right became entrenched in trademark practice, although the issue has never reached the Supreme Court and other circuit courts have declined to follow. *See, e.g., United States v. Giles*, 213 F.3d 1247, 1250 (10th Cir. 2000) (criticizing *Boston Hockey*'s "novel and overly broad conception of the rights that a trademark entails"); *Int'l Ord. of Job's Daughters v. Lindeburg & Co.*, 633 F.2d 912, 919–20 (9th Cir. 1980 (describing *Boston Hockey* as "an extraordinary extension of the protection heretofore afforded trademark owners"). In 1988, Congress amended the Lanham Act to expressly protect sponsorship confusion, as opposed to source confusion. The new language defined infringement to include deception as to "association . . . or as to the origin, sponsorship, or approval" of goods, services, or commercial activities. 15

U.S.C. § 1124(a). While this amendment was not necessarily intended to codify *Boston Hockey* (consumers there were not confused that the NHL team sponsored the emblem manufacturer), it did expand recognition of merchandising rights.

At least one court has expressed willingness to revisit the question: "should trademark holders... have an exclusive right to control merchandise bearing their marks when consumers are purchasing the products not for their guaranteed quality, but to signal their support for or affiliation with the trademark holder?" *Pennsylvania State Univ. v. Vintage Brand, LLC*, 2022 WL 2760233, at *3 (M.D. Pa. July 14, 2022). Penn State had sued an online retailer for selling goods with the university's marks, and moved to dismiss a counterclaim that the university's use of certain logos on merchandise is ornamental and fails to function as a trademark. The court denied that motion, and remanded for factual investigation as to whether consumers are actually confused about the source or sponsorship of the online retailer's products. The court further questioned the entire underpinning of the merchandising right, suggesting it may be "built on sand":

> As a matter of first principle, [trademark] scholars contend that a merchandising right, with its propertizing focus, is unmoored from trademark law's "twin goals of encouraging investment in product quality and preventing consumer deception." And they further assert that such a right is downright irreconcilable with these goals when consumers' confusion comes not from their belief about the source, but from their belief "that the defendant might have needed a license to use the mark." As these scholars emphasize, trademarks are not protected to dole out economic awards to the party in the case caption that is most deserving; nor are they protected to encourage entities to seek more of them. They are instead protected "to enable the public to identify easily a particular product from a particular source." This rationale separates them from patents and copyrights, which offer limited "exclusive economic rights to cure the presumed market failure that would result if copiers could replicate expressive works and inventions without the cost of their development."

> This is not a bad thing. It may disincentivize investment in the school's merchandising; but it does not discourage investment in the underlying product—the school's academic and athletic programs. And while it likewise will not encourage entities to seek out more trademarks, more trademarks have never been the goal of the law. In fact, more (particularly when they identify just one entity) may be worse. Additionally, as these scholars highlight, absent this market-correcting justification, awarding a right works an economic harm. If through trademark-created

exclusivity an entity is free from competition, consumers suffer—on price and on preference. Indeed, T-shirts are more expensive (that licensing royalty has to come out of someone's pocketbook). And as is perhaps shown by this case, which involves a company that gained a toehold by offering gear with vintage graphics, the entity may be less incentivized to come up with creative products that meet consumer demand.

... At the very least, these scholars conclude, if there is confusion about the source, but the alleged infringer is making no claim of official sponsorship, recent Supreme Court cases suggest the remedy should be a disclaimer. . . .

But the case for a disclaimer rather than an injunction lies at the base, not the margin. Consumer survey data [from earlier cases] showed widespread belief among consumers that "[n]o product can bear the name of an entertainer, cartoon character, or some other famous person unless permission is given for its use"—a belief that appears to have come from what they thought the law required. The circularity is apparent: the law only offers protection if there's belief, yet the belief comes from consumers' (mis)conception about the law. It would seem perverse to award market exclusivity based on a fake-it-until-you-make-it approach. If consumers' confusion stems from their incorrect belief that goods bearing Penn State's emblem must be licensed, shouldn't that belief be corrected, not perpetuated?

Id. at *8–9.

NOTES AND QUESTIONS

1. *Expansion of Trademark. Boston Hockey* produced a major and controversial expansion in the scope of trademark law still being debated today. Trademark law scholars have contested the misappropriation and "free-riding" theories underlying that decision, asserting the result has been to reduce market competition, chill free expression, and transfer revenue from fans to teams and their licensees. *See* Mark A. Lemley & Mark P. McKenna, *Owning Mark(et)s*, 109 MICH. L. REV. 137, 168 (2010). Nonetheless, decisions in the sports context since *Boston Hockey* routinely short-circuit the factual inquiry into consumer confusion, finding it sufficient that the sports entity's efforts generated the commercial value of the merchandise.

For example, in *Univ. of Georgia Athletic Ass'n v. Laite*, 756 F.2d 1535, 1546 (11th Cir. 1985), a brewery sold "Battlin' Bulldog Beer" with a logo that portrayed an English bulldog like the University of Georgia mascot. The court found "irrelevant" that no one believed the university had gone into the brewing business: " '[C]onfusion' need not relate to the origin of the challenged product. Rather, 'confusion' may relate to the public's knowledge that the trademark, which is 'the triggering mechanism' for the sale of the product, originates with the plaintiff." *Id.* at 1547. Do you agree that it is irrelevant whether anyone believed the university brewed the beer? If a mark owner can preclude uses even in markets it does not now and never intends to serve, what is the cost/benefit to the consumer?

2. *Lanham Act Amendment.* The 1988 Lanham Act amendment prohibits as infringing a third party's unauthorized use of a trademark as long as consumers would likely, and erroneously, mentally associate the mark's owner with that use. Consider whether this prohibition facilitates commerce or creates scarcity of critical commercial resources, *i.e.*, aesthetically functional product features such as colors and designs, as well as the language to describe one's products. Why do you think Congress believed this amendment to be necessary?

3. *Consumer Welfare Effects.* As the *Penn State* court observes, the expansion of trademark has reinforced the presumption that merchandised products are sponsored by trademark owners, thus in a circular fashion increasing the likelihood of consumer confusion. But how to correct consumers' faulty presumption? Should we allow unauthorized users to avoid liability through disclaimers of any affiliation with mark owners? The court further observed that the merchandising right harms consumers by raising prices and failing to meet demand for innovative products. Note that these are precisely the "anticompetitive effects" that the antitrust laws, discussed in Chapter 6–8, were designed to avert. What explains how far the law has traveled from trademark's consumer protection origins? Consider that consumers don't have standing to intervene in trademark disputes, and protecting their interests depends on an infringement defendant's willingness to litigate. *See* Jodi S. Balsam, *Timeout for Sports Trademark Overprotection: Comparing the United States, European Union, and United Kingdom*, 52 CAL. W. INT'L L.J. 349, 377–78 (2022).

4. *Copyright Versus Trademark.* The *Boston Hockey* court observed that copyright would not provide adequate protections for mark owners because of its finite duration, as opposed to trademark rights, which last indefinitely while the owner continues to use the mark. In addition, copyright damages in this case would likely be far less than trademark damages because copyright entitles the holder to recoup profits only to the extent attributable to the item's design. But no one was buying the emblems because of their appearance; they were buying them because of their association with a team. Thus, in *Bouchat v. Baltimore Ravens Football Club, Inc.*, 346 F.3d 514, 520 (4th Cir. 2003), a court affirmed the award of zero copyright damages to the creator of the "Flying B" logo that the NFL Ravens had copied without consent, based on the finding that the team's profits from the logo were not attributable to the copyright infringement but to its own value-creating activities. How would you go about demonstrating that fan interest in a team logo derived from associational value, and not an aesthetically appealing design? Is this always the case?

Consider also the Supreme Court's decision in *Star Athletica, LLC v. Varsity Brands, Inc.*, 137 S. Ct. 1002 (2017), which upheld a copyright in cheerleader uniforms that gave exclusive rights to one company to use the chevrons, zigzags, and stripes that characterize those uniforms. The Court held that because copyright protection extends to "pictorial, graphic, or sculptural" works, it must also cover "industrial" designs that incorporate these features. The decision prompted a highly critical reaction, pointing out that when such features have a functional purpose, the copyright monopoly is inappropriate. That said, what is your advice to sports trademark owners regarding uniform colors, designs, and other insignia? Would it be now wise to double-down and register a copyright as well?

4. FAIR USE OF A TRADEMARK

A pair of infringement suits involving the Boston Marathon invite examination of when an unauthorized user may assert a fair use defense to trademark infringement. Since 1897, the Boston Marathon has been run annually on Patriots Day, under the auspices of the non-profit Boston Athletic Association (BAA). But it was only since the 1980s that the BAA sought to assert intellectual property rights in the event. In the first case, *BAA v. Sullivan*, 867 F.2d 22 (1st Cir. 1989), the BAA sued a clothing manufacturer that sold T-shirts depicting the event, including its name and pictures of runners. Although the First Circuit acknowledged "that a trademark, unlike a copyright or patent, is not a 'right in gross' that enables a holder to enjoin all reproduction," the court concluded that "when a manufacturer intentionally uses another's mark as a means of establishing a link in consumers' minds with the other's enterprise, and directly profits from that link, there is an unmistakable aura of deception." It further observed:

> [g]iven the undisputed facts that (1) defendants intentionally referred to the Boston Marathon on its shirts, and (2) purchasers were likely to buy the shirts precisely because of that reference, we think it fair to presume that purchasers are likely to be confused about the shirt's source or sponsorship. We presume that, at the least, a sufficient number of purchasers would be likely to assume—mistakenly—that defendant's shirts had some connection with the official sponsors of the Boston Marathon. In the absence of any evidence that effectively rebuts this presumption of a "likelihood of confusion," we hold that plaintiffs are entitled to enjoin the manufacture and sale of defendant's shirts.

867 F.2d at 34.

That decision laid the groundwork for the second case, arising out of the BAA's grant of an exclusive license to WBZ-TV, the local Channel 4 station, to telecast the race. Nevertheless, WCVB-TV, Channel 5 in Boston, continued to televise the race with cameras in helicopters and along the marathon route, and regularly used the phrase Boston Marathon before, during, and after its unaffiliated telecast. The BAA went back to court, relying not on the *Pittsburgh Athletic* case, but on trademark law as interpreted in *Sullivan*. The unlicensed station, WCVB-TV argued that it was entitled to make fair use of the name Boston Marathon in reporting on the event, and the First Circuit agreed.

WCVB-TV v. BOSTON ATHLETIC ASS'N
926 F.2d 42 (1st Cir. 1991)

BREYER, CHIEF JUDGE.

* * *

[The Court initially noted the "likelihood of confusion" standard for trademark infringement cases.]

* * *

Obviously, we do not have before us the common, garden variety type of "confusion" that might arise with typical trademark infringement. This is not a heartland trademark case, where, for example, plaintiff uses the words "Big Tom" to mark his apple juice, defendant (perhaps a big man called Tom) uses the same words (or perhaps similar words, *e.g.*, "Large Tommy") on his own apple juice label, and plaintiff says customers will confuse defendant's apple juice with his own. *See, e.g., Beer Nuts, Inc. v. Clover Club Foods Co.*, 805 F.2d 920 (10th Cir. 1986) ("Beer Nuts" and "Brew Nuts" confusingly similar); 2 J. McCarthy § 23.3 at 56 ("Cases where a defendant uses an identical mark on competitive goods hardly ever find their way into the appellate reports . . . [and] are 'open and shut'. . . ."). No one here says that Channel 5 is running its own marathon on Patriot's Day, which a viewer might confuse with the BAA's famous Boston Marathon.

Rather, BAA argues that the confusion here involved is somewhat special. It points to cases where a defendant uses a plaintiff's trademark in connection with a different type of good or service and a plaintiff claims that the public will wrongly, and confusedly, think that the defendant's product somehow has the plaintiff's official "O.K." or imprimatur. The Eleventh Circuit, for example, found trademark law violated when the defendant, <u>without</u> authorization, used the plaintiff's football team mark, a bulldog, not in connection with a different football team, but, rather, on his beer mugs. *See University of Georgia Athletic Ass'n v. Laite*, 756 F.2d 1535 (11th Cir. 1985). This circuit has found trademark law violated, when the defendant, without authorization, used this very appellant's foot race mark, "Boston Marathon," on his t-shirts, sold during the event, permitting the customer to wrongly or confusedly think that his t-shirts were somehow "official." *See Boston Athletic Ass'n v. Sullivan*, 867 F.2d 22 (1st Cir. 1989). BAA goes on to say that Channel 5's use of those words will lead viewers, wrongly, and confusedly, to believe that Channel 5 (like the t-shirt seller) has a BAA license or permission or authorization to use the words, *i.e.*, that it broadcasts with the BAA's official imprimatur. It also notes that this court, in *Sullivan*, listed circumstances that create a "rebuttable presumption" of confusion. And, it quotes language from *Sullivan*, in which this court, citing *International News Service v. Associated Press*, 248 U.S. 215 (1918), said that the defendant's t-shirts were "clearly designed to take advantage of the Boston Marathon and to benefit from the good will associated with its promotion by plaintiffs," and that defendants obtained a "free ride" at the plaintiffs' expense; they "reap where [they have] not sown." *Sullivan*, 867 F.2d at 33. Appellants say that Channel 5 is doing the same here.

In our view, the cases BAA cites, and *Sullivan* in particular, do not govern the outcome of this case. Nor can we find a likelihood of any relevant confusion here. First, the *Sullivan* opinion, taken as a whole, makes clear that the court, in using the language appellants cite, referring to a "free ride," and taking "advantage" of another's good will, did not intend to depart from ordinary principles of federal trademark law that make a finding of a "likelihood of confusion" essential to a conclusion of "violation." As a general matter, the law sometimes protects investors from the "free riding" of others; and sometimes it does not. The law, for example, gives inventors a "property right" in certain inventions for a limited period of time; *see* 35 U.S.C. 101 *et seq.*; it provides copyright protection for authors; *see* 17 U.S.C. 101 *et seq.*; it offers certain protections to trade secrets. *See generally* 2 J. McCarthy § 29.16. But, the man who clears a swamp, the developer of a neighborhood, the academic scientist, the school teacher, and millions of others, each day create "value" (over and above what they are paid) that the law permits others to receive without charge. Just how, when and where the law should protect investments in "intangible" benefits or goods is a matter that legislators typically debate, embodying the results in specific statutes, or that common law courts, carefully weighing relevant competing interests, gradually work out over time. The trademark statute does not give the appellants any "property right" in their mark except "the right to prevent confusion." And, nothing in *Sullivan* suggests the contrary.

Second, the "rebuttable presumption" of confusion that this court set forth in *Sullivan* does not apply here. We concede that the *Sullivan* court said that "there is a rebuttable presumption" of confusion "about the shirts' source or sponsorship" arising from the fact that the defendants used the words "Boston Marathon" on the shirts, which use made customers more likely to buy the shirts. The court wrote that when a manufacturer intentionally uses another's mark as a means of establishing a link in consumers' minds with the other's enterprise, and directly profits from that link, there is an unmistakable aura of deception. *Sullivan*, 867 F.2d at 35. As we read these words, they mean that the *Sullivan* record indicated that the defendant wanted to give the impression that his t-shirt was an "official" t-shirt, a fact that, in the sports world, might give a shirt, in the eyes of sports fans, a special "cachet." It makes sense to presume confusion about a relevant matter (namely, official sponsorship) from such an intent, at least in the absence of contrary evidence.

Here, however, there is no persuasive evidence of any intent to use the words "Boston Marathon" to suggest official sponsorship of Channel 5's broadcasts. To the contrary, Channel 5 offered to "broadcast whatever disclaimers" the BAA might want—"every thirty seconds, every two minutes, every ten minutes"—to make certain no one thought the channel had any special broadcasting status. Nor is there any evidence that Channel 5 might somehow profit from viewers' wrongly thinking that the BAA had authorized its broadcasts. Indeed, one would ordinarily believe that television viewers (unlike sports fans who might want to buy an official t-shirt with the name of a favorite event, team or player) wish to see the event and do not particularly care about the relation of station to event-promoter.

Third, and perhaps most importantly, the record provides us with an excellent reason for thinking that Channel 5's use of the words "Boston Marathon" would not confuse the typical Channel 5 viewer. That reason consists of the fact that those words do more than call attention to Channel 5's program; they also describe the event that Channel 5 will broadcast. Common sense suggests (consistent with the record here) that a viewer who sees those words flash upon the screen will believe simply that Channel 5 will show, or is showing, or has shown, the marathon, not that Channel 5 has some special approval from the BAA to do so. In technical trademark jargon, the use of words for descriptive purposes is called a "fair use," and the law usually permits it even if the words themselves also constitute a trademark. If, for example, a t-shirt maker placed the words "Pure Cotton" (instead of the words "Boston Marathon") on his t-shirts merely to describe the material from which the shirts were made, not even a shirt maker who had a registered trademark called "Pure Cotton" could likely enjoin their sale. As Justice Holmes pointed out many years ago, "when the mark is used in a way that does not deceive the public we see no such sanctity in the word as to prevent its being used to tell the truth." *Prestonettes Inc. v. Coty*, 264 U.S. 359, 368.

This is not a case where it is difficult to decide whether a defendant is using particular words primarily as a mark, i.e., as an "attention getting symbol," or primarily as a description. Here there is little in the record before us to suggest the former (only the large size of the words on the screen); while there is much to show the latter (timing, meaning, context, intent, and surrounding circumstances). Consequently, the appellants have shown no real likelihood of relevant confusion.

We also note that the only federal court which has decided a case nearly identical to the one before us, a case in which a station planning to televise a public parade was sued by the parade's promoter who had granted "exclusive" rights to another station, reached a conclusion similar to the one we draw here. *See Production Contractors, Inc. v. WGN Continental Broadcasting Co.*, 622 F. Supp. 1500, 1504 (N.D. Ill.1985). Reviewing the promoter's Lanham Act claim that the "unauthorized" broadcast would create a "false impression" of sponsorship, the court concluded that it fell "far short of establishing likelihood of confusion" among viewers that the defendant station was the "official" or "authorized" broadcaster of the parade. Similarly, we do not see how Channel 5's broadcast could likely confuse viewers that it bore the imprimatur of the BAA.

* * *

Affirmed.

———

Fair use was interposed by the NFL Players Association in defense of an NFL lawsuit challenging a $1.6 million sponsorship agreement between the union's licensing subsidiary Players Inc. and Coors to designate it the "Official Beer of the NFL Players." *NFL v. Coors Brewing Co.*, 205 F.3d 1324 (2d Cir. 1999). In this case, however, the NFL secured a preliminary injunction barring the use. While the NFL owners said their primary concern was reputational harm from their players endorsing alcoholic beverages, they were also worried that this use of the "NFL" trademark would devalue their own deals worth millions of dollars with Miller Brewing and Anheuser-Busch. The court rejected Players Inc.'s argument that its use of "NFL" was merely descriptive, because "the record is transparent that Coors wanted to capitalize on the good will inherent in the NFL trademark." *Id.* At 1324. Was this the right decision? Would the union's licensing Coors as the "Official Beer of the NFLPA" produce the same result? What about the "Official Beer of Professional Football Players"? Would the Players Association be able to reap essentially the same return by using these alternative endorsements?

The question of whether a team name is merely descriptive has come up in other contexts. When celebrity players (or their unions) license their publicity rights to merchandisers, can those merchandisers identify the players as being "an NFL player" or a "Yankee," or must the merchandiser also obtain a trademark license from the league and/or team? In *NBA Properties and NFL Properties v. Dahlonega,* 41 F. Supp. 2d 1341 (N.D. Ga. 1998), the court granted summary judgment to the plaintiff sports leagues on the claim that trading card companies violated their trademark rights by selling cards in which players wore the full team uniform. The trading card companies had licensed player image rights, but not team trademarks. The court, however, referred to a jury whether removal of team names and logos, leaving just the uniform color and design, caused the necessary consumer "confusion" about the role of the team in this card product.

Contrast *Major League Baseball Properties v. Pacific Trading Cards*, 48 U.S.P.Q.2d 1944 (S.D.N.Y. 1998), where the court refused to restrain baseball cards displaying players in their uniforms, cards that had been licensed by the Players Association but not by MLB or its teams. As the judge explained:

> ... the reason a child may have to trade two cards of a player of lesser quality for one Cal Ripken Jr. card is found in the differences in the players' records and has nothing to do with differences in the quality of the teams' uniforms or the distinctiveness of their logos.

Id. at *2. Which of these results seems correct? More reasonable? As a practical matter, most merchandisers today now obtain both publicity rights licenses from the players and trademark licenses from the league or team before employing these marketing approaches.

Fair use of geographic names has also led to inconsistent rulings. Contrast *Resorts of Pinehurst v. Pinehurst National Corporation*, 148 F.3d 417 (4th Cir. 1998) (barring golf course's use of town's name in its title because famed neighboring course name had acquired secondary meaning), *with Pebble Beach v. Tour 18 I Ltd.*, 155 F.3d 526 (5th Cir. 1998) (permitting defendant to market—with a disclaimer—golf course built to resemble and using the names of famous holes from Pinehurst, Pebble Beach, Sea Pines, and others).

———

NOTES AND QUESTIONS

1. *Effectiveness of Disclaimers.* Are there differences in the doctrinal approaches used by the First Circuit panels in the two *Boston Marathon* cases? Between the First Circuit and the Fifth Circuit's decision in *Boston Hockey*? As a tangible test, what would have been the First Circuit's response if Sullivan had followed the suggestion of the district court in *Boston Hockey* and added to its T-shirt label the notation "*Not* sponsored or authorized by the BAA?"

2. *Descriptive Fair Use.* A junior user, even a direct competitor, may fairly use another party's descriptive trademark to describe its product. Thus, in *SportFuel, Inc. v. Pepsico, Inc. & The Gatorade Co.*, 2018 WL 2984830 (N.D. Ill. June 14, 2018), a court upheld Gatorade's fair use of the phrase "sport fuel," despite it serving as the trademark of a competing sports drink, because it is descriptive of Gatorade's products and services, and the company used the phrase in good faith. Similarly, in *Oaklawn Jockey Club, Inc. v. Kentucky Downs, LLC*, 184 F. Supp. 3d 572, 577 (W.D. Ky. 2016), *aff'd*, 687 F. App'x 429 (6th Cir. 2017), the court upheld as fair use a gambling service's display of names such as Churchill Downs in identifying the geographic origin of the

racetracks where races were held. What do these decisions tell you about the importance of adopting distinctive, rather than merely descriptive, trademarks as source identifiers?

3. *Nominative Fair Use/Parody.* Use of another's trademark for the purpose of comparative advertising, social commentary, or parody can also be a non-infringing fair use. Recall the *Cardtoons* case in which the court rejected athlete publicity-right claims against parody trading cards. The court similarly rejected trademark claims because the cards did not create consumer confusion regarding their source. The court observed that "as with all successful parodies, the effect of the cards is to amuse, rather than confuse." *Cardtoons, L.C. v. Major League Baseball Players Ass'n*, 95 F.3d 959, 967 (10th Cir. 1996).

How should courts draw the line between amusement and confusion in future cases, especially given the rapid speed of internet memes that parody sports? Does it depend on the purported social value of the commentary being offered? The golf equipment company Titleist sued a parody company I Made Bogey over gear that uses Titleist's distinct font, but swaps in the word "Titties." Does the offensiveness of the parody bolster an infringement claim? *See also Corp. of Gonzaga Univ. v. Pendleton Enterprises, LLC*, 55 F. Supp. 3d 1319 (E.D. Wash. 2014) (court blocked a radio station and bar from using university symbols where concerned fans were outraged at supposed university affiliation with scatological and sexist humor); *Dallas Cowboys Cheerleaders, Inc. v. Pussycat Cinema, Ltd.*, 604 F.2d 200 (2d Cir. 1979) (enjoining "sexually depraved film" *Debbie Does Dallas*, whose star wore uniform similar to Dallas Cowboy cheerleader).

4. *Non-Fungible Tokens.* Non-fungible tokens (NFTs) are unique digital assets that use blockchain technology to record ownership. In the sports ecosystem, they have been created for the ownership of video clips, highlights, images of iconic moments, player trading cards, and virtual real estate (e.g., stadium seat). They necessarily implicate all the intellectual property rights discussed in this chapter. Minters and sellers of NFTs must hold the requisite copyrights, publicity rights, and trademarks to create and sell the files. Buyers should understand whether the purchase permits them to display the NFT or use it for commercial purposes.

The NBA's NFT business Top Shot was an early entrant that quickly saw over $750 million in trading volume. Fans buy and sell the NFTs, and sales and transfers are recorded on a blockchain ledger for verification. Other leagues and governing bodies are planning similar NFT marketplaces. This brand extension raises a host of questions, especially for trademark owners: (a) How to best police unauthorized use of trademarks in NFTs? (b) Do existing licenses grant rights to use the marks in NFTs? (c) Does the first sale doctrine allow a sports e-commerce site to create NFTs that incorporate images of products they legally sell, just as they use images of those products on their websites? *See* Complaint in *Nike Inc. v. StockX LLC*, 1:22-cv-00983 (S.D.N.Y. Feb. 3, 2022) (alleging online sneaker reseller is selling NFTs that display Nike's sneaker designs without permission).

5.   TRADEMARK DILUTION

The Federal Trademark Dilution Act of 1995 amended the existing Lanham Act and further expanded trademark by granting the "owner of a *famous mark*" injunctive relief and potentially damages if others used its mark in ways that "cause *dilution* of the distinctive quality of the mark." Notably, the new cause of action does not require proof that an unauthorized use creates a likelihood of confusion or actual economic harm. As revised in 2006, the Act raised the bar for establishing "fame," leaving dilution claims open only to marks that are "widely recognized by the general consuming public of the United States as a designation of source of the goods or services of the mark's owner." However, the revision made it easier to establish liability by eliminating the requirements of proving actual dilution, as long as there is a "likelihood of dilution," or that the mark is inherently distinctive, as long as it has "acquired distinctiveness." 15 U.S.C. § 1125(c).

Famous sports trademarks include those of all major professional leagues and teams, national sports governing bodies such as the NCAA or the United States Olympic Committee, Division I university football and basketball teams, and signature sporting events such as the Masters golf tournament, the Kentucky Derby, major sports all-star games, and the NCAA's March Madness basketball tournament.

Dilution of a famous mark can occur either by "blurring" that "impairs the distinctiveness of the famous mark" or by "tarnishment" that "harms the reputation of the famous mark." To determine whether dilution has occurred, courts will consider the following factors:

1.   the degree of similarity between the subject mark and the famous mark;

2.   the degree of inherent or acquired distinctiveness of the famous mark;

3.   the extent to which the owner of the famous mark is exclusively using the mark;

4.   the degree of the mark's recognition;

5.   whether the use of the mark was intended to create an association with the famous mark; and

6.   any actual association between the mark and the famous mark.

In sports world cases decided under the revised Dilution Act, courts have emphasized the harm to the mark owner arising from association with the unauthorized user's inferior goods and services. *See Dallas Cowboys Football Club, Ltd. v. America's Team Properties*, 616 F. Supp. 2d 622 (N.D. Tex. 2009) (tarnishing of "America's Team" mark demonstrated by defendant's distribution of shoddy wristbands that misspelled the word "basketball"); *New York City Triathlon LLC v. NYC Triathlon Club Inc.*, 95 U.S.P.Q.2d 1451 (S.D.N.Y. 2010) (athletic club's name diluted by defendant's "pattern of sub-par business practices and poor customer support").

Consider also whether "fair use" can serve as a defense to a trademark dilution claim. In *New York Yankees Partnership v. IET Products and Services, Inc.*, No. 91189692 (T.T.A.B. May 8, 2015), the Yankees successfully opposed trademark registration for marks including "House That Juice Built" because they diluted its famous mark "House That Ruth Built." The Trademark Trial and Appeal Board firmly stated that the fair use defense in trademark dilution cases cannot succeed at the registration phase if the defendant's use is commercial. Recall that registration is not required to use and claim ownership of a trademark. So, the parody business can proceed to operate and assert the defense in court if necessary. Should a business have to take this risk? Should we be concerned that this approach to trademark registration risks chilling free expression?

Another piece of federal legislation further extended trademark protection to the internet. The Anticybersquatting Consumer Protection Act of 1999 established a cause of action for registering, trafficking in, or using a domain name confusingly similar to, or dilutive of, a trademark or personal name. 15 U.S.C. § 1125(d). In the sports industry, teams and athletes have availed themselves of the Act's protections to combat opportunists who use a domain name with the bad faith intent to profit from the goodwill of their trademarks and celebrity. Cybersquatters typically offer to sell a domain to a person or company who owns a trademark contained within the name at an inflated price, a tactic the Act can be used to defeat. But difficulties can arise when the domain owner can show it legitimately uses its domain name, as the Brooklyn Nets learned when they attempted to retrieve Nets.com from a first-user telecommunications and internet company. With the proliferation of top-level domains (*e.g.*, .com, .biz, .net), owners of famous marks will need to be ever more vigilant to protect them on the internet.

NOTES AND QUESTIONS

1. *Dilution and* Boston Hockey. The trademark dilution amendment does not necessarily endorse the broad protection of logos granted by *Boston Hockey*, because not all unauthorized uses of a mark tarnish or blur. Thus, it has been argued that the dilution provision should not provide relief in merchandising cases. Yet, in *Texas Tech Univ. v. Spiegelberg*, 461 F. Supp. 2d 510, 524 (N.D. Tex. 2006), a court held that defendant's unauthorized use of Texas Tech's famous "Double T" and "Raider Red" logos diluted those marks, even though used on precisely the same type of merchandise sold by official

licensees. The court nonetheless found that defendant's products "will likely blur the uniqueness [and] result in diminished individuality of the officially licensed products." Why did Texas Tech lodge dilution claims in addition to its fairly open-and-shut case for trademark infringement? Were the Texas Tech marks sufficiently famous to merit protection under the dilution provision? How will this interpretation of the dilution provision affect the risk tolerance of third parties who might have a legitimate fair use defense in trademark?

2. *Reputational Harm.* For many years, the NFL and other sports leagues expressed displeasure about gambling on their games, given the potential for point-shaving and game-throwing. In 1976, when the Delaware State Lottery hosted a sports lottery based on weekly results of NFL games, the League filed suit, deploring this "forced association with gambling." The League argued that Delaware's use of its game scores, listed solely by team city, misappropriated its reputation and popularity and violated its trademarks, despite the absence of any NFL team names or insignia in lottery materials. In a decision that may inform current debate over league property rights in connection with legalized sports gambling, the court permitted Delaware's usage subject to a disclaimer that the lottery had no affiliation with the NFL. *See NFL v. Governor of the State of Delaware*, 435 F. Supp. 1372 (D. Del. 1977).

How does this result square with *Pittsburgh Athletic*? The lottery case predates the Trademark Dilution Act—would the NFL have a stronger case today under that statute? Which branch of intellectual property provides the leagues with the strongest basis to assert control over use of their assets (game information, trademarks, identifying insignia) in the context of sports betting?

3. *Interests of Businesses Versus Individuals.* In appraising the desirability for sports of the expansion of trademark to protect against dilution, consider first the situation of teams and leagues. Should they be entitled to the same exclusive property rights in their names and symbols as are now given to athletes by the law of publicity rights? Even a disclaimer of endorsement will not immunize unauthorized use of an athlete's name and likeness. Are there tangible distinctions between the interests of athletes as persons and teams as business entities that warrant any difference in legal treatment?

4. *Interests of Sports Fans.* Consider now the interests of sports fans. Suppose that there are a large number of consumers in the sports market who would like to wear a shirt or cap with their favorite team's logo on it, but do not much care whether this is an "official" product—at least do not care enough to want to add the team's five to ten percent licensing fee to the purchase price of the merchandise. Should the law deny fans this informed choice in a competitive marketplace in order to ensure that hundreds of millions of dollars a year in licensing fees continue to be channeled to sports leagues? What affirmative social values are served by such a legal regime?

6. AMBUSH MARKETING

Ambush marketing is a strategy to obtain commercial benefit by creating an association with a sports event that the marketer does not officially sponsor. An ambush advertisement "may only remind customers of the event, or it may go further to create the misleading impression that the company is an official sponsor regarding these goods or services or is affiliated with the event." Ambush Advertising, 5 *McCarthy on Trademarks and Unfair Competition* § 27:66 (5th ed.). If an ambush marketing campaign creates a misleading impression, it potentially triggers a dilution claim under Lanham Act § 43(a). However, if the business does not engage in counterfeiting or illegal use of trademarks, but simply develops a creative advertising campaign around the event, it can free ride on the event's popularity and minimize legal consequences. How does it serve consumers to prohibit such creative advertising?

Famous examples of successful ambush marketing tactics include at the 2009 Wimbledon tennis tournament, when Pringles potato chips distributed to fans waiting outside specially marked tubes of its product that mirrored the packaging of tennis ball cans, with the words, "These are not tennis balls." At the 2010 South Africa World Cup, Dutch brewer Bavaria hired three dozen women to attend a soccer game clad in its signature orange color, to the dismay of the official beer sponsor Budweiser. Although FIFA, the World Cup's organizer, won civil remedies against Bavaria under the South African Merchandise Marks Act, Bavaria's website was one of the most visited worldwide in the days after the stunt. Event organizers, especially those that need sponsorship money to fund production costs, have grown increasingly wary of ambush and its potential to erode the value of official sponsorships.

A prime target of ambush marketing has been the Olympic Games, which in Winter 1992 were the setting for one of the earliest known examples. Visa, the official credit card sponsor launched an ad campaign boasting how the "Olympics don't take American Express," technically true because spectators could purchase tickets to the games only with Visa credit cards. American Express shot back during the Summer 1992 Olympics in Barcelona with a series of television spots featuring the slogan, "When you go to Spain, you'll need a passport—but you don't need a Visa." As recently as the 2018 PyeongChang Winter Olympics, Budweiser—not a sponsor—achieved ambush marketing notoriety with a television commercial featuring ice hockey legends cheering at a hockey game designed to evoke powerful memories of the legendary Olympic victory of the 1980 U.S. hockey team. Perpetually at risk of ambush, the International Olympic Committee (IOC) now insists that any nation seeking to host an Olympic Games must enact anti-ambush marketing legislation, and it regulates athlete social media use and product endorsements leading up to and during the games, at risk of expulsion from competition.

Consistent with this approach, Congress in the Amateur Sports Act of 1978 (as amended by the Ted Stevens Olympic & Amateur Sports Act of 1998), 36 U.S.C. § 371 *et seq.*, gave the U.S. Olympic & Paralympic Committee an explicit statutory right to prohibit commercial and promotional uses of the USOPC's name and emblem, the five interlocking rings symbolic of the Olympic Games, and the words Olympic or Olympiad, as well as the names and symbols of the Paralympics and Pan American Games. This right prevails irrespective of consumer confusion about use of the marks. *See San Francisco Arts & Athletics v. USOC*, 483 U.S. 522 (1987) (upholding constitutionality of Act as applied to block use of "Gay Olympic Games"). The Amateur Sports Act is addressed in greater detail in Chapter 15, Section B.

The Amateur Sports Act has also provided occasion for addressing what constitutes ambush marketing. In *United States Olympic Comm. v. American Media, Inc.*, 156 F. Supp. 2d 1200 (D. Colo. 2001), the USOPC contended that the defendant violated the Act when it published a magazine that used the Olympic name and symbol in describing Olympic events and schedules. Offering a succinct recital of the harms from ambush marketing, the USOPC claimed that this unauthorized use will "likely impair the USOPC's relationships with its existing and prospective sponsors, suppliers, and other licensees and undermine their willingness to pay . . . royalties" for their association with the Olympics. *Id.* at 1204 (citation omitted). The court, however, strictly construed the Act's special trademark rights to bar only uses for the purposes of trade or to induce a sale of some good or service, and permitted the magazine unless the USOPC could prove likelihood of confusion under the regular provisions of the Lanham Act.

Likelihood of confusion as to sponsorship remains the standard for adjudicating most ambush marketing claims. In *Fed'n Internationale De Football Ass'n v. Nike, Inc.*, 285 F. Supp. 2d 64, 66 (D.D.C. 2003), Nike was permitted to continue using "USA 03" in connection with its sponsorship of the U.S. Women's National Soccer Team, over the objections of FIFA, which sought to use a similar mark—"USA 2003"—for the 2003 Women's World Cup soccer tournament taking place across the U.S. FIFA was unable to prove the requisite consumer confusion because its mark was not inherently distinctive and FIFA had not invested much in associating those words specifically with that year's World Cup. On the issue of Nike's good faith, the court acknowledged that Nike had opportunistically established precedence in the "USA 03" mark:

> Nike's careful use of a mark that might be affiliated with both [the U.S. team and the World Cup event] is not necessarily an indication of bad faith, but instead of savvy marketing. Whenever

that team plays in this country, it is to be expected that the sponsors of both the team and the event would want to use trademarks that reflect the United States and that emphasize this year's date. Nike's doing so here thus may not indicate a deliberate attempt to deceive the buying public.

Id. at 74. *See National Hockey League v. Pepsi-Cola Canada Ltd.*, 1992 WL 1326159, 92 D.L.R. 4th 349 (Brit. Columbia Sp. Ct. 1992), *aff'd*, 1995 WL 1728674, 59 C.P.R. (3d) 216 (1995) (dismissing NHL's suit in Canada against Pepsi for running a "home team" contest promotion during the Stanley Cup playoffs because Pepsi's advertising campaign, which included a disclaimer, did not give a false impression of official sponsorship); *Mastercard Intern. Inc. v. Sprint Communications Co. L.P.*, 30 U.S.P.Q.2d 1963, 1994 WL 97097 (S.D.N.Y. 1994), *aff'd*, 23 F.3d 397 (2d Cir. 1994) (enjoining as deceptive Sprint's use of World Cup marks to convey official sanctioning of its telephone calling cards, which rights belonged to Mastercard).

NOTES AND QUESTIONS

1. *Good Faith and Savvy Marketing.* In the FIFA case discussed above, do you agree that Nike was merely "savvy" in this situation, and did not act in bad faith? What would constitute "bad faith" in this context—intent to undermine an official sponsorship? Why should we consider "bad" the competitive undermining of the monopoly conferred by an official sponsorship? On the other hand, how would you advise FIFA going forward to protect event sponsorship rights and revenues?

2. *Free Speech Concerns.* Given that sporting event producers have limited legal recourse in the case of ambush marketing, many have resorted to counter-tactics such as negotiating with broadcasters and venues to decline advertising from competitors of official sponsors. The NFL for the Super Bowl and the USOPC for the Olympic Games both demand that local governments enact ordinances that establish "clean zones" around stadia where unauthorized advertising is prohibited. Consider whether these curbs on non-sponsor activity conflict with U.S. constitutional values. Although courts have historically offered less protection to commercial speech than to noncommercial speech, such restrictions still must serve legitimate governmental interests. What interest does the government have in prohibiting non-misleading, non-safety-threatening commercial advertisements? Indeed, is the right to grant "official sponsorships" a property interest worth protecting at all from competitive advertising?

3. *Social Media and Ambush Marketing.* The rise in social media has blurred the distinction between marketing and informational content. As technology has removed economic and practical barriers to communicating with the public, brands now develop their own content that walks the line

between entertaining the consumer and soliciting a commercial relationship. Brands regularly behave like media companies in taking stands on current issues and events, including sports events, through their social media. In the information age, what social values are served by preferring the commercial interests of sports mega-events over those of unaffiliated brands?

7. FIRST AMENDMENT CONSIDERATIONS IN TRADEMARK

The discussion above leads to the question: to what extent does the First Amendment's free speech protections supersede the Lanham Act's trademark rights and restrictions? This chapter earlier discussed how the First Amendment protected artist Rick Rush from publicity-rights liability to Tiger Woods when he created and sold prints of his *Masters of Augusta* painting of Woods along with other golfing greats after the 1997 Masters Tournament. A similar case arose with respect to a series of paintings produced by artist and long-time University of Alabama football fan Daniel Moore, which he collectively called *"Great Moments in Crimson Tide Football History."* These artworks depicted scenes from Alabama football games that in various places displayed Crimson Tide logos or other trademarks on the players' uniforms, as well as the colors and design of the Crimson Tide uniforms, without a license from the University. When the University demanded Moore pay royalties, he refused, believing he did not need the University's permission to paint historical events as long as he did not use the University's marks outside the "image area" of the paintings. Furthermore, Moore gave a copyright license to a company that used reproductions of his Crimson Tide paintings on merchandise such as coffee mugs and calendars.

The University sued Moore for trademark infringement. In a split decision, the district court upheld Moore's right to use the University's marks in his paintings or prints because they were legitimate works of art entitled to First Amendment protection (as well as a fair use under the Lanham Act), but banned the use of Moore's artwork on functional merchandise. On appeal, the Eleventh Circuit affirmed the finding that the First Amendment protected Moore's paintings and prints, as well as calendars containing prints of the artwork. *University of Alabama Bd. of Trustees v. New Life Art, Inc.*, 683 F.3d 1266 (11th Cir. 2012). It adopted the Second Circuit's test for balancing the interests, articulated in *Rogers v. Grimaldi*, 875 F.2d 994 (2d Cir. 1989):

> We believe that in general the Act should be construed to apply to artistic works only where the public interest in avoiding consumer confusion outweighs the public interest in free expression. In the context of allegedly misleading titles using a celebrity's name, that balance will normally not support application of the Act unless the title has no artistic relevance to the underlying work

whatsoever, or if it has some artistic relevance, unless the title explicitly misleads as to the source of the work.

* * *

In this case, we readily conclude that Moore's paintings, prints, and calendars are protected under the *Rogers* test. The depiction of the University's uniforms in the content of these items is artistically relevant to the expressive underlying works because the uniforms' colors and designs are needed for a realistic portrayal of famous scenes from Alabama football history. Also there is no evidence that Moore ever marketed an unlicensed item as "endorsed" or "sponsored" by the University, or otherwise explicitly stated that such items were affiliated with the University. Moore's paintings, prints, and calendars very clearly are embodiments of artistic expression, and are entitled to full First Amendment protection. The extent of his use of the University's trademarks is their mere inclusion (their necessary inclusion) in the body of the image which Moore creates to memorialize and enhance a particular play or event in the University's football history. Even if "some members of the public would draw the incorrect inference that [the University] had some involvement with [Moore's paintings, prints, and calendars,] . . . that risk of misunderstanding, not engendered by any overt [or in this case even implicit] claim, . . . is so outweighed by the interest in artistic expression as to preclude" any violation of the Lanham Act.

683 F.3d at 1278–79. The Eleventh Circuit reversed the district court's judgment for the University on the placement of Moore's artwork on coffee mugs and other merchandise, but only because Moore had previously obtained a license from the University. On remand, the district court found that Moore had not violated the terms of the licensing agreement. But the issue of whether the First Amendment or fair use doctrine would protect such use in the absence of a licensing agreement was not addressed.

NOTES AND QUESTIONS

1. *Balancing First Amendment Interests.* Should the test for balancing the plaintiff's interests against the First Amendment interests be the same in trademark cases where the plaintiff's right is established by federal statute as it is in cases where the plaintiff has a right of publicity under state law? The Eleventh Circuit in *University of Alabama* avoided this question by noting that the publicity rights cases it cited as precedent, like *Rogers*, also involved claims of false endorsement under the Lanham Act, but the implication was that the

analysis of when First Amendment rights apply would be the same in all cases. Do you agree?

2. *Types of Artwork.* Should the Eleventh Circuit holding apply to all forms of artwork? This case involved a painting of scenes of Alabama football players playing in a game, which was then made into prints and sold. Would the result be different if the painting were simply a posed portrait of the star quarterback wearing his Alabama uniform? Would your answer as to whether the University's trademarks were infringed depend on whether the player had consented to the portrait (i.e., licensed his publicity rights)? What if the artworks being sold were reprints of photographs taken of famous scenes in Alabama football history rather than paintings? Are photographs any less valued works of art for purposes of the balancing test?

3. *Functional Merchandise.* How would you come out in applying the balancing test to the use of otherwise protected artwork on coffee mugs or other functional merchandise like T-shirts? If the First Amendment protects an artist's use of a celebrity's image or a team's trademark in a painting or print that can be hung on a wall, should it also protect the use of that art image when placed and then sold on a coffee mug, T-shirt, place mat, or any other type of product? If no, what would the difference in the balancing analysis be in a case involving artwork placed on a canvas whose function is to decorate a wall and a case involving artwork placed on a coffee mug whose function is to hold a beverage?

————

The First Amendment again intersects with the Lanham Act in challenges to sports teams that use racially stereotyped mascots, including the NFL team formerly known as the Washington Redskins. *See Pro-Football, Inc. v. Blackhorse,* 112 F. Supp. 3d 439 (E.D. Va. 2015), *vacated,* 709 F. App'x 182 (4th Cir. 2018). The *Blackhorse* litigation arose out of Lanham Act § 2(a), known as the "disparagement" clause. This provision authorized the federal Trademark Trial and Appeal Board (TTAB) to refuse to register a trademark, or to cancel an existing registration, if the mark:

> Consists of or comprises immoral, deceptive, or scandalous matter; or matter which may disparage or falsely suggest a connection with persons, living or dead, institutions, beliefs, or national symbols, or bring them into contempt, or disrepute. . . .

15 U.S.C. § 1152(a). On this basis, over the course of 25 years, Native Americans petitioned to cancel six trademark registrations held by Pro-Football, Inc., the owner of the Washington team. In 2014, the Board deregistered the Redskins mark as disparaging to Native Americans. That ruling was affirmed in a district court decision that rejected the team's arguments that the trademarks were intended as a tribute and that cancellation of the registrations violated the team's free speech rights.

While the *Blackhorse* case was on appeal, a separate case involving the music industry made its way to the Supreme Court, raising an identical issue. *Matal v. Tam*, 137 S. Ct. 1744 (2017), concerned a rock band named The Slants, comprised of Asian-American musicians who adopted that name as a commentary on cultural and political discussions about race and society. The TTAB denied the band's trademark registration under § 2(a), finding the name to be disparaging of Asians. In a landmark 8–0 decision, the Supreme Court invalidated the Lanham Act's disparagement clause, a decision which led to the eventual reinstatement of the Redskins trademarks as well, although the team ultimately rebranded as the Washington Commanders.

MATAL V. TAM
137 S. Ct. 1744 (2017)

JUSTICE ALITO delivered the opinion of the Court.

This case concerns a dance-rock band's application for federal trademark registration of the band's name, "The Slants." "Slants" is a derogatory term for persons of Asian descent, and members of the band are Asian-Americans. But the band members believe that by taking that slur as the name of their group, they will help to "reclaim" the term and drain its denigrating force.

The Patent and Trademark Office (PTO) denied the application based on a provision of federal law prohibiting the registration of trademarks that may "disparage . . . or bring . . . into contemp[t] or disrepute" any "persons, living or dead." 15 U.S.C. § 1052(a). We now hold that this provision violates the Free Speech Clause of the First Amendment. It offends a bedrock First Amendment principle: Speech may not be banned on the ground that it expresses ideas that offend.

I

A

"The principle underlying trademark protection is that distinctive marks—words, names, symbols, and the like—can help distinguish a particular artisan's goods from those of others." . . . A trademark "designate[s] the goods as the product of a particular trader" and "protect[s] his good will against the sale of another's product as his." . . . It helps consumers identify goods and services that they wish to purchase, as well as those they want to avoid.

"[F]ederal law does not create trademarks." . . . Trademarks and their precursors have ancient origins, and trademarks were protected at common law and in equity at the time of the founding of our country. . . . The foundation of current federal trademark law is the Lanham Act, enacted in 1946. . . .

Under the Lanham Act, trademarks that are "used in commerce" may be placed on the "principal register," that is, they may be federally registered. . . . There are now more than two million marks that have active federal certificates of registration. . . . This system of federal registration helps to ensure that trademarks are fully protected and supports the free flow of commerce.

* * *

B

Without federal registration, a valid trademark may still be used in commerce. . . . And an unregistered trademark can be enforced against would-be infringers in several ways. Most important, even if a trademark is not federally registered, it may still be enforceable under § 43(a) of the Lanham Act, which creates a federal cause of action for trademark infringement. . . . Unregistered trademarks may also be entitled to protection under other federal statutes, such as the Anticybersquatting Consumer Protection Act. . . . Federal registration, however, "confers important legal rights and benefits on trademark owners who register their marks." . . .

C

The Lanham Act contains provisions that bar certain trademarks from the principal register. . . . At issue in this case is one such provision, which we will call "the disparagement clause." This provision prohibits the registration of a trademark "which may disparage . . . persons, living or dead, institutions, beliefs, or national symbols, or bring them into contempt, or disrepute." § 1052(a). This clause appeared in the original Lanham Act and has remained the same to this day. . . .

When deciding whether a trademark is disparaging, an examiner at the PTO generally applies a "two-part test." The examiner first considers "the likely meaning of the matter in question, taking into account not only dictionary definitions, but also the relationship of the matter to the other elements in the mark, the nature of the goods or services, and the manner in which the mark is used in the marketplace in connection with the goods or services." . . . "If that meaning is found to refer to identifiable persons, institutions, beliefs or national symbols," the examiner moves to the second step, asking "whether that meaning may be disparaging to a substantial composite of the referenced group." If the examiner finds that a "substantial composite, although not necessarily a majority, of the referenced group would find the proposed mark . . . to be disparaging in the context of contemporary attitudes," a prima facie case of disparagement is made out, and the burden shifts to the applicant to prove that the trademark is not disparaging. What is more, the PTO has specified that "[t]he fact that an applicant may be a member of that group or has good intentions underlying its use of a term does not obviate the fact that a substantial composite of the referenced group would find the term objectionable."

D

Simon Tam is the lead singer of "The Slants." He chose this moniker in order to "reclaim" and "take ownership" of stereotypes about people of Asian ethnicity.... The group "draws inspiration for its lyrics from childhood slurs and mocking nursery rhymes" and has given its albums names such as "The Yellow Album" and "Slanted Eyes, Slanted Hearts."

Tam sought federal registration of "THE SLANTS," on the principal register, but an examining attorney at the PTO rejected the request, applying the PTO's two-part framework and finding that "there is ... a substantial composite of persons who find the term in the applied-for mark offensive." The examining attorney relied in part on the fact that "numerous dictionaries define 'slants' or 'slant-eyes' as a derogatory or offensive term." The examining attorney also relied on a finding that "the band's name has been found offensive numerous times"—citing a performance that was canceled because of the band's moniker and the fact that "several bloggers and commenters to articles on the band have indicated that they find the term and the applied-for mark offensive."

Tam contested the denial of registration ... to no avail. [The court describes the proceedings in the TTAB and lower federal courts.] The Government filed a petition for certiorari, which we granted in order to decide whether the disparagement clause "is facially invalid under the Free Speech Clause of the First Amendment."

* * *

III

Because the disparagement clause applies to marks that disparage the members of a racial or ethnic group, we must decide whether the clause violates the Free Speech Clause of the First Amendment. And at the outset, we must consider three arguments that would either eliminate any First Amendment protection or result in highly permissive rational-basis review. Specifically, the Government contends ... that trademarks are government speech, not private speech....

A

The First Amendment prohibits Congress and other government entities and actors from "abridging the freedom of speech"; the First Amendment does not say that Congress and other government entities must abridge their own ability to speak freely. And our cases recognize that "[t]he Free Speech Clause ... does not regulate government speech."...

As we have said, "it is not easy to imagine how government could function" if it were subject to the restrictions that the First Amendment imposes on private speech. " '[T]he First Amendment forbids the government to regulate speech in ways that favor some viewpoints or ideas at the expense of others,' " but imposing a requirement of viewpoint-neutrality on government speech would be paralyzing. When a government entity embarks on a course of action, it necessarily takes a particular viewpoint and rejects others. The Free Speech Clause does not require government to maintain viewpoint neutrality when its officers and employees speak about that venture.

Here is a simple example. During the Second World War, the Federal Government produced and distributed millions of posters to promote the war effort. There were posters urging enlistment, the purchase of war bonds, and the conservation of scarce resources. These posters expressed a viewpoint, but the First Amendment did not demand that the Government balance the message of these posters by producing and distributing posters encouraging Americans to refrain from engaging in these activities.

But while the government-speech doctrine is important—indeed, essential—it is a doctrine that is susceptible to dangerous misuse. If private speech could be passed off as government speech by simply affixing a government seal of approval, government could silence or muffle the expression of disfavored viewpoints. For this reason, we must exercise great caution before extending our government-speech precedents.

At issue here is the content of trademarks that are registered by the PTO, an arm of the Federal Government. The Federal Government does not dream up these marks, and it does not edit marks submitted for registration. Except as required by the statute involved here, an examiner may not reject a mark based on the viewpoint that it appears to express. Thus, unless that section is thought to apply, an examiner does not inquire whether any viewpoint conveyed by a mark is consistent with Government policy or whether any such viewpoint is consistent with that expressed by other marks already on the principal register. Instead, if the mark meets the Lanham Act's viewpoint-neutral requirements, registration is mandatory. . . .

In light of all this, it is far-fetched to suggest that the content of a registered mark is government speech. If the federal registration of a trademark makes the mark government speech, the Federal Government is babbling prodigiously and incoherently. It is saying many unseemly things. It is unashamedly endorsing a vast array of commercial products and services. And it is providing Delphic advice to the consuming public. . . .

* * *

Holding that the registration of a trademark converts the mark into government speech would constitute a huge and dangerous extension of the government-speech doctrine. For if the registration of trademarks constituted government speech, other systems of government registration could easily be characterized in the same way.

Perhaps the most worrisome implication of the Government's argument concerns the system of copyright registration. If federal registration makes a trademark government speech and thus eliminates all First Amendment protection, would the registration of the copyright for a book produce a similar transformation?

The Government attempts to distinguish copyright on the ground that it is " 'the engine of free expression,' " but as this case illustrates, trademarks often have an expressive content. Companies spend huge amounts to create and publicize trademarks that convey a message. It is true that the necessary brevity of trademarks limits what they can say. But powerful messages can sometimes be conveyed in just a few words.

Trademarks are private, not government, speech.

* * *

IV

Having concluded that the disparagement clause cannot be sustained under our government-speech or subsidy cases or under the Government's proposed "government-program" doctrine, we must confront a dispute between the parties on the question whether trademarks are commercial speech and are thus subject to the relaxed scrutiny outlined in *Central Hudson Gas & Elec. Corp. v. Public Serv. Comm'n of N. Y.*, 447 U.S. 557 (1980). . . . We need not resolve this debate between the parties because the disparagement clause cannot withstand even *Central Hudson* review. Under *Central Hudson*, a restriction of speech must serve "a substantial interest," and it must be "narrowly drawn." . . .

It is claimed that the disparagement clause serves two interests. First, the Government asserts an interest in preventing " 'underrepresented groups' " from being " 'bombarded with demeaning messages in commercial advertising.' " . . . But no matter how the point is phrased, its unmistakable thrust is this: The Government has an interest in preventing speech expressing ideas that offend. And, as we have explained, that idea strikes at the heart of the First Amendment. Speech that demeans on the basis of race, ethnicity, gender, religion, age, disability, or any other similar ground is hateful; but the proudest boast of our free speech jurisprudence is that we protect the freedom to express "the thought that we hate."

The second interest asserted is protecting the orderly flow of commerce. Commerce, we are told, is disrupted by trademarks that "involv[e] disparagement of race, gender, ethnicity, national origin, religion, sexual orientation, and similar demographic classification." Such trademarks are analogized to discriminatory conduct, which has been recognized to have an adverse effect on commerce.

A simple answer to this argument is that the disparagement clause is not "narrowly drawn" to drive out trademarks that support invidious discrimination. The clause reaches any trademark that disparages *any person, group, or institution*. It applies to trademarks like the following: "Down with racists," "Down with sexists," "Down with homophobes." It is not an anti-discrimination clause; it is a happy-talk clause. In this way, it goes much further than is necessary to serve the interest asserted.

The clause is far too broad in other ways as well. The clause protects every person living or dead as well as every institution. Is it conceivable that commerce would be disrupted by a trademark saying: "James Buchanan was a disastrous president" or "Slavery is an evil institution"?

There is also a deeper problem with the argument that commercial speech may be cleansed of any expression likely to cause offense. The commercial market is well stocked with merchandise that disparages prominent figures and groups, and the line between commercial and non-commercial speech is not always clear, as this case illustrates. If affixing the commercial label permits the suppression of any speech that may lead to political or social "volatility," free speech would be endangered.

For these reasons, we hold that the disparagement clause violates the Free Speech Clause of the First Amendment. The judgment of the Federal Circuit is affirmed.

JUSTICE KENNEDY, with whom JUSTICE GINSBURG, JUSTICE SOTOMAYOR, and JUSTICE KAGAN join, concurring in part and concurring in the judgment. (omitted)

JUSTICE THOMAS, concurring in part and concurring in the judgment. (omitted)

NOTES AND QUESTIONS

1. *Constitutional Challenges to Trademark Law.* In a sequel to *Matal*, the Supreme Court also struck down Lanham Act § 2(a)'s bar on registering "immoral and scandalous" marks as an unconstitutional form of discrimination against viewpoint. *Iancu v. Brunetti*, 139 S. Ct. 2294 (2019). This ruling opened the door for brands to seek federal registration of trademarks that, in the past, would have been refused as too vulgar, profane, or offensive (such as "Fuct," the mark at issue in *Brunetti*). As in *Matal*, the *Brunetti* Court avoided the question of whether trademarks are commercial speech accorded only relaxed scrutiny as free expression, an ambiguity that may invite further constitutional challenges to the Lanham Act. It's been suggested that dilution laws may provide the next battleground, given that they regulate expression based on the content of a junior use and whether it deviates from a famous mark's preferred branding message. *See* Jodi S. Balsam, *Timeout for Sports*

Trademark Overprotection: Comparing the United States, European Union, and United Kingdom, 52 CAL. W. INT'L L.J. 349 (2022).

2.   *Justice Kennedy's Concurrence.* In his concurrence, Justice Kennedy offered a different take on the issues in *Matal*, focusing on the government's argument that the law is viewpoint neutral. He rejected this assertion because "[t]o prohibit all sides from criticizing their opponents makes a law more viewpoint based, not less so," and noted that "[t]he Government may not insulate a law from charges of viewpoint discrimination by tying censorship to the reaction of the speaker's audience." 137 S. Ct. at 1766. Does this approach mean that any trademark, no matter how outrageous or offensive, should be entitled to registration? Does limiting a particular viewpoint on the basis it offends or leads to political or social "volatility" endanger all free speech? Should we be concerned about such outcomes, or can we rely on the marketplace and consumer reaction to ameliorate the risk?

3.   *Native American Mascots in Sports.* The original petition to cancel the Redskins' trademark registration was filed in 1992. In the years since then, hundreds of colleges and high schools have discontinued the use of Native American mascots. By 2005, the NCAA had adopted a policy that prohibits NCAA institutions from displaying "hostile and abusive" Native American names, mascots, or images. Some institutions were able to satisfy the NCAA that their references to Native Americans were inoffensive, but not the University of North Dakota Fighting Sioux, despite a lawsuit by members of the Sioux tribe seeking to *retain* the nickname. *See Spirit Lake Tribe of Indians ex rel. Comm. of Understanding & Respect v. Nat'l Collegiate Athletic Ass'n*, 715 F.3d 1089 (8th Cir. 2013) (dismissing claim that NCAA unlawfully discriminated against the tribe in banning UND's use of the name). Ultimately, a statewide referendum led North Dakota to retire the name.

Despite litigation success, the Redskins eventually yielded to changing social mores and voluntarily renamed the team, first as The Washington Football Team and ultimately in 2022 as the Commanders. Likewise, the MLB Cleveland Indians dropped the Chief Wahoo mascot and ultimately the team name. The team rebranded in 2021 as the Guardians, a name many derided as anodyne, but one that pays homage to statues located on the bridge leading to the team's stadium. How can trademark owners mitigate the risk that their naming choices will be overtaken by new and different perspectives on our history and culture? Consider the approach of the NBA Washington Wizards, formerly the Bullets, which in 1997 changed the club's nickname to avoid association with gun violence, and did so through a marketing campaign that included a naming contest for fans and a corporate social responsibility component.

CHAPTER 10

AGENT REPRESENTATION
OF THE ATHLETE

■ ■ ■

For most of the history of professional team sports, from the founding of the first professional baseball league in 1876 through the 1960s, the vast majority of athletes represented themselves in negotiating their player contracts. This was largely the byproduct of the industry norm that a club "owned" any player it had introduced to the major leagues and then controlled his career from that point forward. Because using a negotiating agent would not have improved the player's lot in any meaningful way, there was little incentive to retain and pay such an agent. Indeed, many teams refused to deal directly with sports agents in salary negotiations.

By the 1970s, four dramatic developments in professional sports gave agents a foothold. First, free agency allowed veteran players to sell their services on the open market. Second, upstart leagues in football, hockey, and basketball created competition for player services, driving up salaries. Both of these first two developments led players to seek assistance in navigating among competing offers for their services. Third, player unions came into their own, extracting significant concessions from ownership, while formally delegating the role of salary negotiator to individual players and their certified agents. Fourth, television revenues and endorsement deals were booming, placing even more money on the table for players.

Professional athletes came to value negotiating and money management expertise to exploit opportunity and maximize wealth creation during their usually short and always unpredictable careers. An agent with talent and experience is better equipped to deal with the seasoned general managers who bargain on behalf of the team owners. Added to this financial value is the agent's role as an emotional buffer— insulating the player's ego and relationship with the team from frank discussion about his abilities, performance, and where he fits within the club's salary scale. While negotiating the player contract remains an agent's core service, many agents now also handle endorsement deals and offer a menu of management services relating to tax and estate planning, investing and financial management, budgeting and bill paying, intellectual property protection, athletic training and health, real estate, charitable giving, and domestic arrangements. In non-team sports such as golf and tennis, where athletes' earnings from their sport depend on how they fare in tournaments and not on a negotiated employment contract, the agent's role increasingly focuses on generating revenue opportunities for their clients outside of playing the sport.

Meanwhile, rising player salaries and the commissions to be earned from negotiating those salaries and other revenue deals made the career of sports agent more appealing. By the early 2000s, the aggregate number of sports agents registered in the four major sports leagues—MLB, NBA, NFL, and NHL—amounted to almost one agent for every two players on their combined rosters. Recruiting practices became increasingly cutthroat as agencies needed to sign prominent clients to attract others. To offer the full range of now-expected services, those firms also required a deep bench of agents with knowledge of the sport, its collective bargaining agreement and player policies, applicable agent and financial advisor regulations, negotiation skills, industry norms, and revenue streams. These demands led to consolidation and corporatization of the business as smaller firms and independent agents lacked the resources to lure and keep clients. That same consolidation now means that it is more likely than ever that a sports agency represents multiple athletes in the same sport, even playing the same position or on the same team. With other participants in the industry attaining celebrity status—including coaches, managers, and owners—a sports agency also might find itself representing both athletes and management.

As the sports agent business has become more competitive and multiplex, it has also been associated with dubious competence and ethics. Among the ills that have plagued the business are conflicts of interest, fraud, self-dealing, negligence, ineptitude, client poaching, and illegal recruiting tactics that sabotage college athlete eligibility and prospects. Despite the agent's purported role as protector of athletes' interests in relation to team owners, the need arose to protect athletes' interests in relation to agents, resulting in extensive regulation of agents, first by players associations, and later by Congress and state legislatures. This chapter first sets forth basic agency law principles that underlie the athlete-agent relationship and the distinct vulnerabilities of that relationship. It next explores the role of agents in a unionized workplace, and the corresponding players association regulation of sports agents. Government regulation of sports agents is examined, as well as the additional ethical constraints on agents who are also attorneys.

A. LEGAL RELATIONSHIP BETWEEN SPORTS AGENTS AND ATHLETE-CLIENTS

1. AGENCY LAW BASICS

The sports agent-athlete relationship is subject to common law agency principles, modified in part by some of the unique structures of the sports industry. In broad terms, sports agency is a consensual, usually contractual relationship where the athlete as principal grants authority to the agent to act on behalf of and under the control of the athlete in dealing with third parties and pursuing the athlete's interests. In the case of the major professional sports leagues, the express contract creates and governs the relationship, because the players associations mandate the use of standard representation agreements and/or compliance with agent regulations. Consistent with agency law, all the players unions expressly impose on the agent the fiduciary duties of loyalty, honesty, and competence towards the athlete.

The Restatement of Agency apportions an agent's fiduciary duties into two distinct buckets. The "duty of loyalty" primarily requires an agent to avoid conflicts of interest and self-dealing, to preserve confidentiality, and to follow the principal's instructions. RESTATEMENT (THIRD) OF AGENCY §§ 8.02–8.06 (2006) (RESTATEMENT). The agent's "duty of performance" requires care, competence, and diligence, as well as acting only within the scope of actual authority granted by the principal, complying with the law, accounting for all of the principal's funds, and keeping the principal apprised of all matters that may affect the principal's interests. RESTATEMENT §§ 8.07–8.12.

Two aspects of the duty of loyalty merit closer examination in view of the economic model for today's sports agencies. First, most sports agents are paid through commissions on the athlete's earnings. This practice can risk running afoul of the agent's duty not to engage in self-dealing or acquire material benefit from a third party in connection with business conducted on behalf of the principal. RESTATEMENT § 8.02. Second, many sports agencies represent multiple clients whose interests may conflict. In such situations, the agent is duty-bound to fully disclose and obtain the athlete's informed consent to the conflict, and thereafter to deal in good faith with each principal. RESTATEMENT § 8.06.

In *Burleson v. Earnest*, 153 S.W.2d 869 (Tex. Civ. App. 1941), the court in a real estate dispute alleging agent self-dealing and conflict of interest summarized the relevant common law rules that apply equally to sports agents:

> The law is well established in this state, as well as every other jurisdiction in this country, that in all cases where the relationship of principal and agent is shown, the principal is entitled to the best efforts and unbiased judgment of his agent. For reasons founded in public policy the law denies the right of an agent to assume any relationship that is antagonistic to his duty to his principal, and it has many times been held that the agent cannot be both buyer and seller at the same time nor connect his own interests with property involved in his dealings as an agent for another.

The rule is founded on the danger of imposition and the presumption of the existence of fraud, inaccessible to the eye of the Court. The policy of the rule is to shut the door against temptation, and which, in the cases in which such a relationship exists, is deemed to be, of itself, sufficient to create the disqualification. This principle, like most others, may be subject to some qualification in its application to particular cases, but, as a general rule, it appears to be well settled in the English and in our American Jurisprudence.

The courts have, throughout the entire history of our jurisprudence, shown a jealous attitude toward an agent who becomes involved in the property of his principal and have held him to strict account for his dealings . . . . Even where the parties bargain for themselves, once the agency is established, the principal is entitled to the skill, knowledge and advice of his agent and to communicate with him without the slightest fear of betrayal. . . . The question, therefore, does not relate to the mala fides of the agent nor to whether or not a greater sum might have been procured for the property, nor even to whether or not the vendor received full value therefor. The self-interest of the agent is considered a vice which renders the transaction voidable at the election of the principal without looking into the matter further than to ascertain that the interest of the agent exists.

Id. at 874. While it may seem that in sports agency, an agent's interest is naturally aligned with the principal because they both benefit from maximizing the athlete's earnings, can you anticipate when this might not be the case?

PROBLEM 10.1

Sue Hawk, a professional basketball player with the WNBA Seattle Storm, hired Jackie Chase as her sports agent. Chase is an attorney, certified as a contract advisor with the WNBPA. Hawk and Chase entered into the WNBPA's standard representation agreement between a player and a contract advisor.

Chase negotiated Hawk's most recent contract with the Storm, a three-year deal with a base salary of $250,000/year, and workout bonuses of $100,000/year earned only if Hawk participates in at least 75 percent of the voluntary off-season workouts. Last year Hawk failed to earn the bonus because she didn't realize the contract required her to participate in those workouts at the Storm's facility in Seattle, and instead she worked out at her home in Connecticut.

In addition, Hawk instructed Chase to try to negotiate a deal for her to play in one of the European leagues during the off-season, where they pay upwards $1,000,000 per year to players coming from the WNBA. The

WNBA's new CBA permits off-season play but docks players one percent of their base salary for each day they are late to training camp, and bans for the season any player who does not arrive before the season opener. WNBA training camp typically starts in April and opening day is around May 1, while the European leagues play well into May. Chase had preliminary conversations with a team in the Latvian league, but didn't follow up when it appeared that regional political unrest might interrupt its basketball season, and most Latvian teams were demanding that WNBA players commit to play through the post-season. It turned out that the Latvian league's season was played to its conclusion, and other WNBA players were able to negotiate early departures from teams in that league in order to make it to WNBA training camp on time.

Did Chase's efforts on behalf of Hawk meet the standards for agent performance discussed below? As you read the following section, consider what claims might Hawk bring against Chase for the conduct described above, and what is the likelihood she would prevail.

2. STANDARDS FOR AGENT PERFORMANCE

Although the duty of loyalty is most often implicated in sports agent-athlete disputes, we turn briefly first to the agent's duty of performance. Consider what standard the law should establish for the level of agent competence and quality of representation owed by agents to their athlete-clients. The one appellate case that has explored this issue involved an agent for professional football players.

ZINN V. PARRISH
644 F.2d 360 (7th Cir. 1981)

BARTELS, SENIOR DISTRICT JUDGE.

This is an appeal in a diversity action by Leo Zinn from a judgment of the District Court for the Northern District of Illinois, Eastern Division, wherein he sought to recover agent fees due him under a personal management contract between him and the defendant Lemar Parrish. . . .

[The court recounted the facts of the dispute. Zinn had been managing professional athletes for two decades when he agreed to serve as agent for Parrish, who was selected by the Cincinnati Bengals in the 1970 NFL draft. Under their Professional Management Contract, Zinn received a 10% commission in return for agreeing to use his "reasonable efforts" on Parrish's behalf in "negotiating job contracts, furnishing advice on business investments, securing professional tax advice at no additional costs, and obtaining endorsement contracts." Zinn was also supposed to try to secure "gainful off-season employment" for Parrish if he so requested, from which Zinn would receive a commission only if the work was "in the line of endorsements, marketing, and the like." The agency contract automatically renewed every year, unless one side gave 30 days written notice of termination.

For Parrish's first four years with the Bengals, Zinn negotiated base salaries for his client of $16,500, $18,500, $27,000, and $35,000. By the end of the 1973 season, Parrish had become a Pro Bowl cornerback and the rival World Football League (WFL) had appeared on the scene. In the spring of 1974, Zinn had some preliminary conversations with the WFL's Jacksonville Sharks, but decided not to pursue this option, a sound decision because the WFL folded midway through the 1975 season. Instead, Zinn negotiated four new one-year contracts with the Bengals that paid $250,000 over 1974–1977, plus a $30,000 signing bonus. After signing the Bengals contracts, Parrish told Zinn by phone and letter that he "no longer needed his services." Parrish refused to pay Zinn any commission on those new contracts, and Zinn sued.

Other services Zinn performed for Parrish included arranging for tax return preparation, screening and forwarding stock market recommendations, assisting in the purchase and management of a four-unit apartment building, and procuring one endorsement contract. However, Zinn had not been able to obtain any off-season work for Parrish. Instead, he had advised his client to return to college in the off-season to secure a degree to prepare himself for life when his NFL career had ended.]

In summing up Zinn's performance under the contract, Parrish testified as follows:

Q: Did you ever ask Zinn to do anything for you, to your knowledge, that he didn't try to do?

A: I shall say not, no.

Discussion

[The court first held that the contract between Zinn and Parish was not void under federal securities law that prohibits Zinn from giving investment advice without being a registered adviser. The court said that isolated transactions with a client incident to the main purpose of a management contract to negotiate football contracts did not constitute engaging in the business of advising others on investment securities.]

We consider next the district court's judgment that Zinn failed to perform the terms and conditions of his contract. . . .

Employment Procurement

Zinn's obligation under the 1971 Management Contract to procure employment for Parrish as a pro football player was limited to the use of "reasonable efforts." At the time the contract was signed, Parrish was already under contract with the Cincinnati Bengals for the 1970–1971 season, with a one-year option clause for the 1971–1972 season exercisable by the Bengals. Parrish could not, without being in breach of his Bengals contract, enter into negotiations with other teams for the 1971–72 season. The NFL's own rules prevented one team from negotiating with another team's player who had not yet attained the status of a "free agent." At no time relevant to this litigation did Parrish become a free agent. Thus, unless he decided to contract for future services for the year following the term of the option clause with the Canadian or World Football League, Parrish's only sensible course of action throughout the time Zinn managed him was to negotiate with the Bengals.

Parrish had no objection to Zinn's performance under the professional management contract for the first three years up to 1973, during which time Zinn negotiated football contracts for Parrish. A drastic change, however, took place in 1974 when a four-season contract was negotiated with the Bengals for a total of $250,000 plus a substantial signing bonus. At that time, the new World Football League came into existence and its teams, as well as the teams of the Canadian Football League, were offering good terms to professional football players as an inducement to jump over to their leagues from the NFL. In order to persuade Parrish to remain with the team, the Bengals club itself first initiated the renegotiation of Parrish's contract with an offer of substantially increased compensation. This was not surprising.

Parrish claims, however, that Zinn should have obtained offers from the World Football League that would have placed him in a stronger negotiating position with the Bengals. This is a rather late claim. It was not mentioned in Parrish's letter of termination, and is entirely speculative. Given what Zinn accurately perceived as the unreliability of any offers he might have obtained from the WFL, his representation of Parrish during this period was more than reasonable.

* * *

Other Obligations

We focus next on the other obligations, all incidental to the main purpose of the contract. The first of these refers to "[n]egotiating employment contracts with professional athletic organizations and others." . . . [T]he evidence clearly shows that Zinn performed substantial services in negotiating with the Bengals by letter, telephone, and in person when he and Parrish were flown at the Bengals' expense to Cincinnati for the final stage of negotiations on the 1974–1977 series of contracts.

Zinn was further obligated to act in Parrish's professional interest by providing advice on tax and business matters, by "seek[ing] . . . endorsement contracts," and by making "efforts" to obtain for Parrish gainful off-season employment. Each of these obligations was subject to an implied promise to make "good faith" efforts to obtain what he sought. Under Illinois law, such efforts constitute full performance of the obligations. Until Parrish terminated the contract, the evidence was clear that Zinn made consistent, good faith efforts to obtain off-season employment and endorsement contracts. Indeed the district court found that Zinn at all times acted in good faith, with a willingness "to provide assistance within his ability." The district court confused success with good faith efforts in concluding that Zinn's failure to obtain in many cases jobs or contracts for Parrish was a failure to perform. Moreover, Zinn did give business advice to Parrish on his real estate purchases, and he did secure tax advice for him.

Parrish fully accepted Zinn's performance for the years 1970, 1971, 1972, and 1973 by remitting the 10% due Zinn under the contract. Parrish was at all times free to discharge Zinn as his agent before a new season began. Instead, he waited until Zinn had negotiated a series of contracts worth a quarter of a million dollars for him before letting Zinn know over the phone that his services were no longer required. That call, coupled with Parrish's failure to make the 10% commission payments as they came due, was a breach of the 1971 contract. . . . Therefore Zinn has a right to recover a 10% commission on all amounts earned by Parrish under the 1974, 1975, 1976, and 1977 Bengals contracts.

We must disagree with the district court's interpretation of the terms of the contract, and Zinn's obligations thereunder, and also with its findings and conclusions concerning Zinn's performance. Insofar as the district court made any findings of fact which are inconsistent with the foregoing, we find them to be clearly erroneous. [Appeal granted.]

NOTES AND QUESTIONS

1. *Standard of Performance.* How does the court formulate the standard of performance expected of a sports agent? How does this standard compare with the "duty of fair representation" imposed by labor law on the players association (see Chapter 3, Section H)? With the standard of care required of a lawyer who represents a player in any transaction? Is the standard used in *Zinn* appropriate for the sports agent business? Would it make a difference if the management contract had described the standard of performance as "best efforts"? *See Franklin v. Haak*, 499 F. Supp. 3d 379 (E.D. Mich. 2020) (equating "best efforts" language in boxer-management contract with "reasonable efforts" in finding that manager met that standard in securing remunerative bouts).

2. *Principal's Duty to the Agent.* A principal also owes a duty to the agent to deal with the agent fairly and in good faith. *See* RESTATEMENT (THIRD) OF AGENCY § 8.15 (2006). This duty requires the athlete to provide the sports agent with information about risks of physical harm or pecuniary loss that the athlete knows or should know are present in the agent's work but are unknown to the agent. *See* Chris Deubert, *What's A "Clean" Agent to Do? The Case for A Cause of Action Against A Player's Association*, 18 VILL. SPORTS & ENT. L.J. 1, 34 (2011).

How would such a duty have applied in *Bias v. Advantage International, Inc.*, 905 F.2d 1558 (D.C. Cir. 1990), where the estate of college basketball star Len Bias sued his agent, Lee Fentress, for negligent performance of agent duties? Bias died from cocaine use only two days after the Boston Celtics selected him second in the 1986 NBA draft. His survivors faulted Fentress for failing to finalize a million-dollar insurance policy and an endorsement contract with Reebok prior to Bias's death. The suit was summarily dismissed on the grounds that (a) no life insurer would have issued the policy to a drug user, and (b) the agent could not reasonably have been expected to finalize an endorsement contract in only two days. Assuming Fentress was unaware of Bias's drug use, what would Bias's duty have been to deal fairly with his agent? To what degree should an agent's duty be dependent on the principal's cooperation?

3. *Agent Malpractice in Negotiating the Playing Contract.* How can an athlete identify and protect against agent malpractice in the routine aspects of the role—*e.g.*, negligently negotiating a below-market salary, failing to seek various contract guarantees or injury protection, or giving bad advice about what salary to "hold out" for? Consider the case of NFL linebacker LaVar Arrington, who signed a Washington Redskins (now Commanders) playing contract negotiated by his agent Carl Poston, without either of them realizing that the team had failed to include a $6.5 million bonus the parties had allegedly agreed upon. Arrington ultimately settled with the Redskins to receive half the bonus amount, but he did not pursue any recourse against his agent. To the contrary, he testified on Poston's behalf in disciplinary proceedings brought against the agent by the NFLPA, which ultimately suspended the agent for two years. What explains player loyalty to the agent in this setting?

4. *Agent Obligations After Execution of the Playing Contract.* Once the playing contract is signed, what is the agent's role in explaining contract details to the athlete-client and ensuring compliance with contract obligations? Take the case of NFL cornerback Tarell Brown, who in 2013 forfeited a $2 million roster bonus because he was unaware of a contract clause that required him to participate in voluntary team workouts to earn the bonus. Brown fired his agent Brian Overstreet for not alerting him to this contract obligation, but did not bring a lawsuit. In 2004, wide receiver Dennis Northcutt lost out on potentially millions of dollars when his agent Jerome Stanley missed a deadline to void the last three years of his contract and make him a free agent eligible to renegotiate his contract. The NFLPA took disciplinary measures against Stanley, but the player brought a grievance against the team, not his agent. Consider also that most players unions, including the NFLPA, now require agents to maintain professional liability insurance, whether or not an agent is an attorney. Yet neither NFL player pursued that remedy. Why do you think players don't bring agent malpractice claims, although suits for medical and legal malpractice have become quite common?

B. BREAKDOWNS IN THE AGENT-ATHLETE RELATIONSHIP

Stories are legion of sports agent misconduct and ethical compromises. In one of the most egregious cases, William "Tank" Black, a leading football agent of the late 1990s, was sentenced to five years in prison after a federal jury convicted him of defrauding over two dozen athlete-clients of $12 million through multiple investment schemes. This sentence was imposed on top of a prior sentence of nearly seven years for Black's role in laundering over $1 million for a drug ring in Detroit. In addition, his shady practices in recruiting student athletes led to investigations by the state of Florida and the NFLPA, both of which eventually decertified him. *See generally Hilliard v. Black*, 125 F. Supp. 2d 1071 (N.D. Fla. 2000) (agent liable to athletes for investment scam). This section examines breakdowns in the relationship between an agent and the athlete-client, providing a glimpse of the working life of an agent and the degree to which many elite athletes have ceded financial autonomy to advisors.

PROBLEM 10.2

As a top-rated MLB rookie, Riley Brown hired Tripper Jackson to serve as his agent and financial advisor, and delegated all money management matters to him. Jackson received all of Brown's compensation, gave him an allowance, and invested the rest. Brown paid little attention as he never seemed to run out of money.

In his sixth year as an MLB player approaching free agency, Brown became curious that Jackson seemed to be steering him only to teams who would frontload most of his salary, meaning Jackson would receive his agent's commission earlier. After doing a little digging, Brown learned that Jackson had made risky investments on Brown's behalf, including a real estate venture in which Brown was made to be the sole guarantor on a mortgage, resulting in him losing $1,000,000 when the project defaulted. In addition, Jackson had invested in a restaurant chain that was using Brown's name, image, and likeness without any compensation to him. Jackson also procured life insurance for Brown as instructed, but it turns out Jackson signed the policy on Brown's behalf without giving him a chance to read it, by which he might have learned that the policy charged exorbitant premiums and was purchased through a brokerage run by Jackson's wife.

What is problematic about each of Jackson's actions? As you read the following material, consider the legal claims that Brown might bring against Jackson.

---

1. AGENT BREACH OF FIDUCIARY DUTIES TO ATHLETE-CLIENT

Sports agent dereliction of fiduciary duties to athlete-clients has arisen in diverse contexts. Particularly susceptible are athletes making the transition from high school or collegiate sports to the professional level, when their youth and naiveté lead them to rely heavily on the agent's care and skill in performing on their behalf. *See Jones v. Childers*, 18 F.3d 899 (11th Cir. 1994) (football player's "lack of sophistication in investment matters" cited in holding agent liable for fraud and racketeering).

To hold sports agents accountable for misconduct, athletes traditionally have relied on civil lawsuits for breach of contract, breach of fiduciary duty, and fraudulent misrepresentation. *See Terrell v. Childers*, 920 F. Supp. 854 (N.D. Ill. 1996) (professional basketball player sued agent for fraud and mismanagement of his finances and investments). Another avenue for policing agents is through reporting misdeeds to players unions and professional associations, discussed in more detail in subsequent sections of this chapter. In addition, criminal and administrative law enforcement agencies are empowered to pursue sports agents who offend laws of general applicability or specialized agent regulations. *See United States v. Dawkins*, 986 F.3d 104 (2d Cir. 2021) (affirming sports agent's conviction for bribing high school basketball players to attend specific universities and then retain agent's services); *People v. Sorkin*, 64 A.D.2d 680, 407 N.Y.S.2d 772 (1978) (upholding substantial jail term for agent who misappropriated over $1 million of client hockey players' funds).

Most player agents, however, do not rob, cheat, or steal from their clients. They are not destructive, devious, or inept. Although the practice of sports agency is not always polite and well-mannered, it is not generally sullied by criminal misconduct. The more important question posed by cases of agent misconduct is whether they manifest merely the occasional abuse that occurs in any type of commercial undertaking, or instead are symptomatic of a deeper imbalance in the player-agent relationship. Can we trust the marketplace to drive out most of the bad agents in favor of the good, relying on general criminal or civil law to deal with the few "bad apples" that remain? Or should we devise a systematic regulatory program targeted at sports agents? If the latter, who should devise and enforce the program, and with what objectives? A case of outright fraud against a young professional basketball player provoked a federal judge who had formerly served as general counsel to the Securities and Exchange Commission to recommend (in a footnote) an interesting solution to the problem.

WILLIAMS V. CWI, INC.
777 F. Supp. 1006 (D.D.C. 1991)

SPORKIN, DISTRICT JUDGE.

This claim was brought by a young professional basketball player and his wife—Reginald and Kathy Williams—against a financial advisor and his associated companies to recover $50,000 that the Williams had entrusted to the defendant, Waymon Hunt through one of his affiliated companies. Plaintiffs also seek to recover certain costs and expenses that they incurred as a result of Mr. Hunt's actions. Plaintiffs have also prayed for punitive damages.

* * *

I.   Findings of Fact

The facts clearly show that Reginald Williams, a gifted young professional basketball player, and his wife, Kathy, were unsophisticated in matters of finance and business. In the late 1980's, upon his graduation from Georgetown University where he had a distinguished career as a star basketball player, Mr. Williams signed a million-dollar-a-year contract with the Los Angeles Clippers, a National Basketball Association team. As a result of this lucrative contract, Mr. Williams and his wife were looking for opportunities to invest part of Mr. Williams substantial earnings.[1] He was directed to Waymon Hunt, a financial planner, and his company, CWI, Inc., by his wife's parents. . . .

The Williams first met Mr. Hunt in June of 1988. At that time, they agreed that Mr. Hunt would provide the Williams with financial and tax advice, including preparation of the Williams' tax returns. At approximately that time, Mr. Hunt brought to the Williams' attention an opportunity for investment involving the purchase of a product styled atmospheric reverse refrigeration heating units (hereinafter referred to as "units"). Because of how these units were supposed to perform, they were represented as being capable of producing an investment return and tax benefits.

---

[1]   Like many young professional athletes, Mr. Williams was earning a considerable salary but had no experience in making investments or managing his money. He needed reliable expert advice and did not find any readily available. Because Mr. Williams' predicament appears to be a recurring problem for basketball players and other athletes who suddenly receive large disposable incomes, it seems that it would be appropriate for either the NBA, or the player's team, or the players' organization to develop a three-pronged program to assist these young people. First, they could offer at least some rudimentary education in business and finance. Second, they could assemble a package of low risk blue-chip investments for young players that will provide for their futures as well as a system for referring them to wise and ethical professionals who can advise them on managing money. Third, they might offer a financial incentive for players to place a portion of their funds in a deferred investment program. Perhaps the League and the players' association could even establish their own high-grade, low-risk investment fund. In this way, young athletes would be protected from highly speculative ventures like the one involved in this case.

The Williams agreed to buy $1 million worth of these units through a Hunt affiliated company, Success Through Association ("STA"). [The court described how Hunt failed to disclose that he operated and controlled STA and that, as of September 1988, that company had only $301.50 in its bank account. Hunt convinced the Williams to buy $1 million worth of STA units in a deal that would be financed by the Williams paying a $50,000 deposit and borrowing $950,000 through an STA-arranged loan. The deal further stipulated that if the purchase could not be made, STA would return the Williams' deposit in full by December 16, 1988.]

Waymon Hunt agreed to arrange for the $950,000 in financing. The Williams signed a purchase agreement and forwarded $50,000 to STA, but no money was ever remitted to the purported manufacturer and seller of the units. Immediately upon STA's receipt of the $50,000, Hunt appropriated the money for his own use. Hunt did not obtain the $950,000 of financing.

Around the time of this transaction, there was an internal battle among the owners of the company that manufactured and sold the units, and the company was placed in receivership. While it later turned out that Mr. Hunt was able to contact a second seller and manufacturer, no purchase of the units ever came to pass. The parties have stipulated that the $50,000 sent to Mr. Hunt's company, STA, was never used to purchase reverse refrigeration units from any entity.

Mr. Hunt has attempted to deviate from the agreement he provided to the Williams, an agreement he drafted, by stating that he was entitled to the $50,000 as a finder's fee for locating financing for the project. He has produced two cashier's checks to show that he spent $68,000 on a fee he paid to a Georgia company, Aslanien Ltd., to obtain financing. He claims he did this on the Williams' behalf, but his testimony is not credible. While this Court cannot deny that Mr. Hunt may have discussed some financing for the purchase of the so-called reverse refrigeration units, it was clear he did not have the Williams in mind when he sent the first check for $34,000 to Aslanien, Ltd. Since he wrote that check before the Williams ever signed a contract or purchase order for the units. It is not even clear that they knew about the investment opportunity before Hunt sent the check to Aslanien. Hunt admitted that the second check for $34,000 sent in November of 1988 was sent on behalf of other clients and not the Williams. It is clear that the $50,000 sent to STA by the Williams was to be a down payment on the units. It was not a finder's fee or any other kind of advance fee. Indeed Mr. Hunt conceded in his testimony before the Court that he owes the Williams the $50,000 they sent to him. Although he testified that he does not have the funds to pay the Williams now, he clearly acknowledges that under his agreement with them, he owes them the money.

The Williams are entitled to a judgment against Mr. Hunt on both contract and fraud theories. The contract provided that the money be repaid "if for any reason [STA] cannot fulfill [the Williams] request. . . ." It is also clear that Mr. Hunt's actions with respect to the Williams prove that Mr. Hunt defrauded the Williams. Hunt flat out misappropriated the money given to him. He dissembled when the Williams periodically asked about their investment and its status. He said "things were going fine" when they were not. He never told them that the $50,000 had not been sent to the manufacturer, nor did he inform them that he had not obtained financing. Hunt misrepresented the status of the arrangement when he prepared the Williams' tax returns on which Hunt took certain deductions and credits that could only be taken if a transaction had in fact been consummated. The Williams incurred significant expenses because of Mr. Hunt's violation of the contract and fraudulent conduct.

[The court awarded $87,500 to the Williams in recovery of their $50,000 down payment, attorneys fees and litigation costs, and amounts related to rectifying their unwitting misrepresentations on their tax returns, including tax preparer fees and penalties and interest owed to the IRS and California state tax authorities.] The Williams may not collect tax savings they claim they might have enjoyed had they received legitimate financial advice. It would be too speculative to assume post hoc what investments they might have chosen and what savings they might have received.

* * *

Finally, plaintiffs seek punitive damages. The Court finds that they are warranted in this case. Mr. Hunt's egregious behavior was utterly unworthy of someone who calls himself a professional. His fraudulent conduct put the plaintiffs at risk of committing tax fraud. In recognition of these facts, the Court will award $50,000 in punitive damages, an amount that reflects the $50,000 down payment that was misappropriated and that was the basis for the grievous errors made on the Williams tax returns and caused them to incur substantial costs and expenses. . . .

NOTES AND QUESTIONS

1. *Athlete Vulnerability.* A recurring theme in civil cases involving young athletes is their relative unsophistication, as demonstrated in the *Williams* case above and the *Shaw* case discussed in Chapter 5, Section A. Do you agree that these clients more than others are vulnerable to corrupt agents and advisors, and merit additional protection from the courts?

2. *Private Efforts to Protect Athletes.* In the footnote to the *Williams* decision, the court exhorted the NBA to develop assistance programs that offer players business and finance education, low-risk investment advice, advisor

referrals, and proprietary investment opportunities. The major sports leagues all now offer their players some wealth management education, life skills training, and career transition services. The players associations have also stepped up to varying degrees. In 2002, the NFLPA specifically responded to the problem of professional athletes falling victim to poor financial advice and even outright fraud by offering its members a service to vet financial advisers. As part of that service, the NFLPA performs "[b]ackground checks and due diligence . . . to ensure that financial advisors meet our eligibility standards." NFLPA Regulations and Code of Conduct Governing Registered Player Financial Advisors 2 (2017). Financial advisors have the incentive to participate in this voluntary program because once screened, their names are included on a non-public list provided to players.

In 2006, some current and former NFL players who relied on the NFLPA's registered financial advisor list sued the NFLPA claiming it negligently performed background checks on a financial advisor who perpetrated an investment scam in which the players collectively lost over $20 million. The suit also named the NFL, alleging that its background check on the financial advisor was also inadequate. The players pursued these claims despite liability disclaimers in both the financial advisor regulations and the collective bargaining agreement that players are solely responsible for their personal finances. Ultimately, the Eleventh Circuit dismissed the players' claims because they were preempted under § 301 of the National Labor Relations Act (see Chapter 4, Section D), and must be brought under the CBA's private dispute resolution procedures. *See Atwater v. Nat'l Football League Players Ass'n*, 626 F.3d 1170 (11th Cir. 2010). Although victorious in court, the NFLPA briefly suspended its financial advisor program and strengthen its requirements. Later iterations of both the NFLPA financial advisor regulations and the labor agreement toughened the disclaimer language to further block potential liability to players for the acts of dishonest financial advisors. What role do you think the leagues and players unions should play in protecting athletes from financial harms?

3.   *Public Efforts to Protect Athletes.* Aside from agent-specific federal legislation, federal law has played an important, albeit sporadic, role in regulating athletes. Tank Black, mentioned above, was prosecuted under federal wire act and money laundering statutes. Sports agents including Fairron Newton, Myron Piggie, and Vincent Porter have been prosecuted variously under federal mail fraud, money laundering, and tax statutes. *See, e.g., United States v. Piggie*, 303 F.3d 923, 924 (8th Cir. 2002) (agent compensated elite high school basketball players in violation of NCAA rules); *Gatto* case discussed in notes at end of Section D.2 below and in Chapter 13.

The Securities and Exchange Commission has vigorously enforced its regulations in filing civil and criminal actions against agents, including accusing Donald Lukens of defrauding his numerous athlete-clients out of millions of dollars during the 1990s. Other SEC actions in the sports industry include fraud and theft charges against financial advisor Howard Golub, who was sentenced to 10 to 12 years in prison and ordered to pay restitution to athlete-clients. A 2018 report calculated that from 2004 to 2016, professional athletes suffered almost $600 million in fraud-related loss. *See* Spiegelhalter and Silvertown, *Athletes Targeted by Fraud* 2 (2018 Ernst & Young). The report identified risk factors for athletes such as shortage of time to manage their own finances, reliance on nonqualified or inexperienced people, misplaced trust, under-supervised advisors, and exploitation by family and friends. Is it possible to develop private industry standards or legislative solutions to address these risks? What would those look like?

2. DUTY TO ACT LOYALLY FOR PRINCIPAL'S BENEFIT: FEE DISPUTES

The fiduciary standard prohibits the sports agent from pursuing self-interest as a motivating force in actions taken on the athlete's behalf. One of the first major sports agents, Bob Woolf, was the target of the first major lawsuit claiming that an agent breached that duty by maximizing his own compensation at the expense of his client. Woolf represented Andrew Brown of the NHL Pittsburgh Penguins, and in that capacity fielded competing offers for the player from the Penguins and from the Indianapolis Racers of the upstart World Hockey Association. Woolf convinced Brown to accept the Racers much richer offer, perhaps because it would generate a larger agent commission. When the Racers soon after encountered financial problems, and ultimately filed for bankruptcy, Brown lost much of his promised salary, while Woolf was paid his commission in full, a disparity that led to this lawsuit.

BROWN V. WOOLF
554 F. Supp. 1206 (S.D. Ind. 1983)

STECKLER, DISTRICT JUDGE.

[Andrew Brown played hockey for the Pittsburgh Penguins during the 1973–74 season under a contract negotiated by his agent Bob Woolf. In July 1974, the Penguins offered Brown a non-guaranteed two-year contract at $80,000 a year. Woolf advised Brown to reject that offer and to sign instead with the Indianapolis Racers of the World Hockey Association, a new team in a new league. The Racers deal was a five-year guaranteed contract, at $160,000 per season.]

On July 31, 1974, plaintiff signed a five-year contract with the Racers. Thereafter, it is alleged the Racers began having financial difficulties. Plaintiff avers that Woolf continued to represent plaintiff and negotiated two reductions in plaintiff's compensation including the loss of a retirement fund at the same time defendant was attempting to get his own fee payment from the Racers. Ultimately the Racers' assets were seized and the organizers defaulted on their obligations to plaintiff. He avers that he received only $185,000.00 of the total $800,000.00 compensation under the

Racer contract but that defendant received his full $40,000.00 fee (5% of the contract) from the Racers.

Plaintiff alleges that defendant made numerous material misrepresentations upon which he relied both during the negotiation of the Racer contract and at the time of the subsequent modifications. Plaintiff further avers that defendant breached his fiduciary duty to plaintiff by failing to conduct any investigation into the financial stability of the Racers, failing to investigate possible consequences of the deferred compensation package in the Racers' contract, failing to obtain guarantees or collateral, and by negotiating reductions in plaintiff's compensation from the Racers while insisting on receiving all of his own. Plaintiff theorizes that such conduct amounts to a prima facie case of constructive fraud for which he should receive compensatory and punitive damages and have a trust impressed on the $40,000.00 fee defendant received from the Racers.

* * *

Indiana cases contain several formulizations of the tort of constructive fraud. Generally it is characterized as acts or a course of conduct from which an unconscionable advantage is or may be derived, or a breach of confidence coupled with an unjust enrichment which shocks the conscience, or a breach of duty, including mistake, duress or undue influence, which the law declares fraudulent because of a tendency to deceive, injure the public interest or violate the public or private confidence. Another formulization found in the cases involves the making of a false statement, by the dominant party in a confidential or fiduciary relationship or by one who holds himself out as an expert, upon which the plaintiff reasonably relies to his detriment. The defendant need not know the statement is false nor make the false statement with fraudulent intent.

The Court believes that both formulizations are rife with questions of fact, inter alia, the existence or nonexistence of a confidential or fiduciary relationship, and the question of reliance on false representations, as well as questions of credibility.

Defendant argues that despite the customary existence of such fact questions in a constructive fraud case, judgment is appropriate in this instance because plaintiff has produced nothing to demonstrate the existence of fact questions. He makes a similar argument in the motion for partial summary judgment on the punitive damages issue.

In this case, defendant has offered affidavits, excerpts of depositions, and photocopies of various documents to support his motions. He contends that such materials demonstrate that reasonable minds could not conclude that defendant did the acts with which the complaint charges him. In response, plaintiff rather belatedly offered portions of plaintiff's depositions as well as arguing that issues such as those raised by a complaint based on constructive fraud are inherently unsuited to resolution on a motion for summary judgment.

Having carefully considered the motions and briefs and having examined the evidentiary materials submitted, the Court concludes that summary judgment would not be appropriate in this action. The Court is not persuaded that there are no fact questions remaining unresolved in this controversy such that defendant is entitled to judgment as a matter of law.

Summary dismissal refused.

———

NOTES AND QUESTIONS

1.   *Incentives and Conflicts in Fee Structures.* What was the true source of Brown's dispute with Woolf—the agent's fee or that the agent's self-interest sabotaged the player's career? To the extent the fee is at issue, what caused the problem—the amount of the fee, how it was calculated, or when it was paid? Does a straight-commission compensation system inevitably create a conflict of interest between the agent's and the athlete's self-interests? How would you structure an agent fee system to provide the best incentives for agents to act loyally for the principal's benefit?

2.   *Constructive Fraud Theory.* The *Brown* court endorsed a theory of constructive fraud, which posits that even if the agent did not intend to deceive, the law should impose liability where the agent's actions gave him an unfair advantage over the athlete. The theory is premised on the idea that the fiduciary relationship induced the athlete to place his trust and confidence in the agent and relax the care and vigilance he would ordinarily exercise in the circumstances. Should application of this theory depend on the athlete's individual circumstances, for example his level of education and experience?

3.   *Players Union Fee Regulation.* The problem of excessive agent fees has been ameliorated by union regulation of agents. For example, the NFLPA caps the agent fee for negotiating a playing contract at three percent, with a default fee of 1.5 percent unless the agent convinces the player he's worth more. The NBPA caps such fees at four percent. These unions further lower the fee cap when the player's salary is predetermined by collective bargaining agreement pay scales or established market values, such as rookies, players earning the league minimum, and players tagged as franchise or transition players. Presumably, the idea here is that the agent's fee should be tied to the time, difficulty, and skill of the work involved. Contrast the players associations in the NHL and MLB, which set no fee caps and allow the market to dictate the fees charged by agents, typically between four and ten percent. Which of these approaches make the most sense to you? Are there differences among these sports that justify different approaches to regulating agent fees?

4.   *Demographics of Agents in Team Sports.* The demographics of agents differ noticeably between the NBA and NFL on the one hand, and the NHL

and MLB on the other. In the latter leagues, the vast majority of players are represented either by agents with many clients or by attorneys with whom they or their families had pre-existing relationships. By contrast, many more NBA and NFL players retain agents who represent a few clients and who solicited them. This difference is likely because NBA/NFL players typically come directly from college programs and choose agents under the NCAA's regulation of amateur status, while MLB/NHL players make those decisions during their multi-year minor league professional careers. Consider whether this disparity explains the different approach to agent fee regulation described in the previous note, and why.

5.   *State Regulation of Boxer Agreements.* State regulations governing boxing require promoters to file a boxer's contract with the appropriate state commission. When boxing promoter Don King failed to do so for certain one-sided and exploitative agreements with heavyweight champion Mike Tyson, a court invalidated those agreements to comply with state regulations that protect boxers from "improvident arrangements." *Tyson v. King*, 2000 WL 35572295 (S.D.N.Y. Feb. 14, 2000). The *Tyson* court observed that the agreements, which gave King more money from Tyson's fights than the boxer received, violated the "strong public policy" that prohibits a promoter from having a pecuniary interest in a boxer. Why do you think team sports are not subject to a similar public policy and regulatory regime?

6.   *Arbitration of Fee Disputes.* Arbitrators often resolve agent fee disputes pursuant to dispute resolution clauses in the union-mandated standard representation agreements. The NFLPA's arbitration clause is typical:

> Any and all disputes between Player and Contract Advisor involving the meaning, interpretation, application, or enforcement of this Agreement or the obligations of the parties under this Agreement shall be resolved exclusively through the arbitration procedures set forth in Section 5 of the NFLPA Regulations Governing Contract Advisors.

See Wichard v. Suggs, 95 F. Supp. 3d 935 (E.D. Va. 2015) (confirming arbitration award to football player's agent as consistent with "the essence" of the standard representation agreement). As stressed in Chapter 4, courts afford great deference to arbitration awards. *See Wasserman Media Grp., LLC v. Bender*, 2011 WL 1886460 (S.D.N.Y. May 16, 2011) (confirming award to basketball player's agent under Federal Arbitration Act); *Octagon, Inc. v. Richards*, 2010 WL 3932272 (E.D. Va. Oct. 5, 2010) (upholding fee award to track athlete's agent, despite evidence that agent violated state law regarding student athletes).

PROBLEM 10.3

After reading the next section, determine whether a conflict of interest exists in the following scenarios and, if so, what mechanisms might be instituted to avoid or remedy the conflict.

1.   Agent represents two football players on different NFL teams. After a trade, the two players end up on the same team. They play different positions—one on defense and one on offense—but the offensive player is far more valuable. The league has a salary cap on the total amount of monies that an individual team can allocate to player salaries. Both players are now negotiating for new contracts. The team tells Agent that they have to keep the combined salaries of the two players for the following year under $50 million to avoid cap consequences, and that they will trade the defensive player if they are unable to do so. The defensive player's value upon being traded is extremely uncertain since he is a role player on his current team.

2.   Agent represents a Division I college basketball coach who advises her stars to use Agent as their representative when they leave college for the professional ranks. After a winning season in which the team reached the NCAA Final Four, the coach is being recruited for a WNBA job at a team that is also interested in drafting one of the college players she coached.

3.   A sports management firm is purchased by a large media conglomerate which also owns: (a) an NHL franchise, and (b) a handful of regional sports networks that broadcast NHL games. Agents in the sports management firm represented hockey players before the acquisition, and continue to do so. The NHL and its players union are negotiating a new collective bargaining agreement and little progress has been made. The union is rallying its members to strike, and has provided all player agents with talking points and arguments to convince their clients to vote in favor of a strike. Note also that most game broadcast agreements require the broadcaster to continue to pay rights fees even for games canceled by a strike or lockout.

4.   A large sports management firm represents a superstar MLB player while he is a successful pitcher for a World Series winning team. After the player retires and becomes co-owner of a team in that league, the sports management firm continues to represent him, as well as many other MLB players. A national advertiser comes to the firm looking for an athlete spokesperson and the retired player/owner is angling for the opportunity, suggesting that if he serves as spokesperson he potentially could also arrange for his team to enter into an official sponsorship, a deal worth exponentially more and generating greater commissions for the sports management firm.

3. AGENT CONFLICTS OF INTEREST

A more fundamental ethical, as well as legal, issue arising in the comparatively closed sports world is agent representation of actual and potential conflicting interests. Consolidation and diversification in the industry has exacerbated this issue, with mega-agencies like Creative Artists Agency, Excel Sports Management, and Wasserman dominating the business. CAA represents almost 1,000 athletes in baseball, football, hockey, basketball, soccer, tennis, golf, and Olympic sports, in addition to coaches, broadcasters, and other sports personalities.

Consider the story of SFX Sports Group, which in the late 1990s acquired 21 smaller sports agencies. As a result, SFX Sports for a time represented approximately 16 percent of all MLB players, and significant numbers of basketball and football players. SFX Sports' parent company was then acquired by Clear Channel Entertainment (now iHeartMedia), raising the further complication that two of Clear Channel's major shareholders were owners of major league teams. In other words, the same company—Clear Channel—could be sitting on both sides of a player-team transaction. Thus, the players unions at the time insisted that Clear Channel create a separate and autonomous corporate wing to negotiate player contracts with any teams. Should the clients be satisfied that this structure adequately ameliorates any conflicts? The legal (as opposed to the ethical) reason why Clear Channel had to take that special action in sports is displayed vividly by the following case.

DETROIT LIONS AND BILLY SIMS V. JERRY ARGOVITZ
580 F. Supp. 542 (E.D. Mich. 1984)

DEMASCIO, DISTRICT JUDGE.

The plot for this Saturday afternoon serial began when Billy Sims, having signed a contract with the Houston Gamblers on July 1, 1983, signed a second contract with the Detroit Lions on December 16, 1983. On December 18, 1983, the Detroit Lions, Inc. (Lions) and Billy R. Sims filed a complaint in the Oakland County Circuit Court seeking a judicial determination that the July 1, 1983, contract between Sims and the Houston Gamblers, Inc. (Gamblers) is invalid because the defendant Jerry Argovitz (Argovitz) breached his fiduciary duty when negotiating the Gamblers' contract and because the contract was otherwise tainted by fraud and misrepresentation. Defendants promptly removed the action to this court based on our diversity of citizenship jurisdiction.

For the reasons that follow, we have concluded that Argovitz's breach of his fiduciary duty during negotiations for the Gamblers' contract was so pronounced, so egregious, that to deny rescission would be unconscionable.

Sometime in February or March 1983, Argovitz told Sims that he had applied for a Houston franchise in the newly formed United States Football

League (USFL). In May 1983, Sims attended a press conference in Houston at which Argovitz announced that his application for a franchise had been approved. The evidence persuades us that Sims did not know the extent of Argovitz's interest in the Gamblers. He did not know the amount of Argovitz's original investment, or that Argovitz was obligated for 29 percent of a $1.5 million letter of credit, or that Argovitz was the president of the Gamblers' Corporation at an annual salary of $275,000 and 5 percent the yearly cash flow. The defendants could not justifiably expect Sims to comprehend the ramifications of Argovitz's interest in the Gamblers or the manner in which that interest would create an untenable conflict of interest, a conflict that would inevitably breach Argovitz's fiduciary duty to Sims. Argovitz knew, or should have known, that he could not act as Sims' agent under any circumstances when dealing with the Gamblers. Even the USFL Constitution itself prohibits a holder of any interest in a member club from acting "as the contracting agent or representative for any player."

Pending the approval of his application for a USFL franchise in Houston, Argovitz continued his negotiations with the Lions on behalf of Sims. [The court described the offers and counter-offers that began on April 5, 1983: Argovitz (and his associate Burrough) initially asked the Lions for $6 million over four years, and the Lions responded with $1.5 million over five years. As the court remarked, "[t]he negotiating process was working. The Lions were trying to determine what Argovitz really believed the market value for Sims really was." But after confirmation of his Gamblers franchise, Argovitz reduced his demands on behalf of Sims to half of what he originally asked. The court found that, on June 1, "Argovitz and the Lions were only $500,000 apart," and on June 22, "the Lions and Argovitz were very close to reaching an agreement on the value of Sims' services."]

Apparently, in the midst of his negotiations with the Lions and with his Gamblers franchise in hand, Argovitz decided that he would seek an offer from the Gamblers. Mr. Bernard Lerner, one of Argovitz's partners in the Gamblers, agreed to negotiate a contract with Sims. Since Lerner admitted that he had no knowledge whatsoever about football, we must infer that Argovitz at the very least told Lerner the amount of money required to sign Sims and further pressed upon Lerner the Gamblers' absolute need to obtain Sims' services. In the Gamblers' organization, only Argovitz knew the value of Sims' services and how critical it was for the Gamblers to obtain Sims. In Argovitz's words, Sims would make the Gamblers' franchise.

On June 29, 1983, at Lerner's behest, Sims and his wife went to Houston to negotiate with a team that was partially owned by his own agent. When Sims arrived in Houston, he believed that the Lions organization was not negotiating in good faith; that it was not really interested in his services. His ego was bruised and his emotional outlook toward the Lions was visible to Burrough and Argovitz. Clearly, virtually all the information that Sims had up to that date came from Argovitz. Sims and the Gamblers did not discuss a future contract on the night of June 29th. The negotiations began on the morning of June 30, 1983, and ended that afternoon. At the morning meeting, Lerner offered Sims a $3.5 million five-year contract, which included three years of skill and injury guarantees. The offer included a $500,000 loan at an interest rate of one percent over prime. It was from this loan that Argovitz planned to receive the $100,000 balance of his fee for acting as an agent in negotiating a contract with his own team. Burrough testified that Sims would have accepted that offer on the spot because he was finally receiving the guarantee that he had been requesting from the Lions, guarantees that Argovitz dropped without too much quarrel. Argovitz and Burrough took Sims and his wife into another room to discuss the offer. Argovitz did tell Sims that he thought the Lions would match the Gamblers financial package and asked Sims whether he (Argovitz) should telephone the Lions. But, it is clear from the evidence that neither Sims nor Burrough believed that the Lions would match the offer. We find that Sims told Argovitz not to call the Lions for purely emotional reasons. As we have noted, Sims believed that the Lions' organization was not that interested in him and his pride was wounded. Burrough clearly admitted that he was aware of the emotional basis for Sims' decision not to have Argovitz phone the Lions, and we must conclude from the extremely close relationship between Argovitz and Sims that Argovitz knew it as well. When Sims went back to Lerner's office, he agreed to become a Gambler on the terms offered. At that moment, Argovitz irreparably breached his fiduciary duty. As agent for Sims he had the duty to telephone the Lions, receive its final offer, and present the terms of both offers to Sims. Then and only then could it be said that Sims made an intelligent and knowing decision to accept the Gamblers' offer.

During these negotiations at the Gamblers' office, Mr. Nash of the Lions telephoned Argovitz, but even though Argovitz was at his office, he declined to accept the telephone call. Argovitz tried to return Nash's call after Sims had accepted the Gamblers' offer, but it was after 5 p.m. and Nash had left for the July 4th weekend. When he declined to accept Mr. Nash's call, Argovitz's breach of his fiduciary duty became even more pronounced. Following Nash's example, Argovitz left for his weekend trip, leaving his principal to sign the contracts with the Gamblers the next day, July 1, 1983. The defendants, in their supplemental trial brief, assert that neither Argovitz nor Burrough can be held responsible for following Sims' instruction not to contact the Lions on June 30, 1983. Although it is generally true that an agent is not liable for losses occurring as a result of following his principal's instructions, this rule of law is not applicable when the agent has placed himself in a position adverse to that of his principal.

During the evening of June 30, 1983, Burrough struggled with the fact that they had not presented the Gamblers' offer to the Lions. He knew, as does the court, that Argovitz now had the wedge that he needed to bring finality to the Lions' negotiations. [The court "view[ed] with disdain" how during the crucial 24 hours in which Sims made the decision to sign with the Gamblers, Argovitz was absent and did not use the wedge of the Gamblers' offer to further negotiate with the Lions.] . . . The evidence here convinces us that Argovitz's negotiations with the Lions were ongoing and it had not made its final offer. Argovitz did not follow the common practice described by both expert witnesses. He did not do this because he knew that the Lions would not leave Sims without a contract and he further knew that if he made that type of call Sims would be lost to the Gamblers, a team he owned.

On November 12, 1983, when Sims was in Houston for the Lions game with the Houston Oilers, Argovitz asked Sims to come to his home and sign certain papers. He represented to Sims that certain papers of his contract had been mistakenly overlooked and now needed to be signed. Included among those papers he asked Sims to sign was a waiver of any claim that Sims might have against Argovitz for his blatant breach of his fiduciary duty brought on by his glaring conflict of interest. Sims did not receive independent advice with regard to the wisdom of signing such a waiver. Despite having sold his agency business in September, Argovitz did not even tell Sims' new agent of his intention to have Sims sign a waiver. Nevertheless, Sims, an unsophisticated young man, signed the waiver. This is another example of the questionable conduct on the part of Argovitz who still had business management obligations to Sims. In spite of his fiduciary relationship he had Sims sign a waiver without advising him to obtain independent counseling.

Argovitz's negotiations with Lustig, Jim Kelly's agent, illustrates the difficulties that develop when an agent negotiates a contract where his personal interests conflict with those of his principal. Lustig, an independent agent, ignored Argovitz's admonishment not to "shop" the Gamblers' offer to Kelly. Lustig called the NFL team that he had been negotiating with because it was the "prudent" thing to do. The Gamblers agreed to pay Kelly, an untested rookie quarterback, $3.2 million for five years. His compensation was $60,000 less than Sims', a former Heisman Trophy winner and a proven star in the NFL. Lustig also obtained a number of favorable clauses from Argovitz; the most impressive one being that Kelly was assured of being one of the three top paid quarterbacks in the USFL if he performed as well as expected. If Argovitz had been free from conflicting interests he would have demanded similar benefits for Sims. Argovitz claimed that the nondisclosure clause in Kelly's contract prevented him from mentioning the Kelly contract to Sims. We view this contention as frivolous. Requesting these benefits for Sims did not require disclosure of Kelly's contract. Moreover, Argovitz's failure to obtain personal guarantees for Sims without adequately warning Sims about the risks and uncertainties of a new league constituted a clear breach of his fiduciary duty.

* * *

We are mindful that Sims was less than forthright when testifying before the court. However, we agree with plaintiff's counsel that the facts as presented through the testimony of other witnesses are so unappealing that we can disregard Sims' testimony entirely. We remain persuaded that on balance, Argovitz's breach of his fiduciary duty was so egregious that a court of equity cannot permit him to benefit by his own wrongful breach. We conclude that Argovitz's conduct in negotiating Sims' contract with the Gamblers rendered it invalid.

* * *

Rescission granted.

NOTES AND QUESTIONS

1.   *Duty of Loyalty.* Identify each act (or omission) by Argovitz that breached his duty of loyalty to Sims. Would you consider any such act standing alone to be de minimis, or should any one of them justify voiding Sims's contract with the Gamblers?

2.   *Informed Consent to Conflicts of Interest.* Upon full disclosure by the agent, an athlete can consent to a conflict of interest and continue the representation, or refuse to do so and seek new representation. This assumes that athlete-clients have the sophistication and business acumen to comprehend the circumstances and nature of the conflict presented. See *Hernandez v. Childers*, 806 F. Supp. 1368 (N.D.Ill.1992) (agent's detailed disclosures regarding personal involvement in investment not sufficient to defeat baseball player's conflict of interest claim). Do you believe Sims could have made such an informed determination? Why wasn't disclosure to Sims of Argovitz's ownership of the Gamblers franchise sufficient to waive the conflict? If a player upon full disclosure effectively consents to a conflict, should that immunize the agent from the player's claims that the agent negligently performed due to the conflict? How should a court weigh the equities when the player intentionally selects a conflicted agent in the belief that the conflict helps the player, i.e., that the agent is likely to exploit the conflict for the player's benefit?

3.   *Conflict Situations.* Contrast Argovitz with the following situations:

a.   Jerry Kapstein, one of the most prominent baseball agents for two decades, married the daughter of Joan Kroc, then owner of the San Diego Padres, and regularly advised his mother-in-law about her ownership interests. Should that relationship have barred

Kapstein from representing players on the Padres? On the Dodgers? On the NFL Los Angeles Rams?

b.   Larry Fleisher and Alan Eagleson were the founders and long-time leaders of the NBA and NHL Players Associations, respectively. They were also sports agents who had full rosters of individual clients among their association members. Was this appropriate? *See Major Indoor Soccer League & Professional Soccer Players Ass'n (PROSPA)*, NLRB Ruling, Nov. 15, 1983.

c.   Tom Condon, a prominent NFL agent, represented Peyton Manning and Alex Smith when both quarterbacks were free agents looking for their next berth in 2012. Condon even arranged for Manning to work out with Smith's then team, the San Francisco Forty-Niners, although Manning ultimately took the Denver Broncos job and Alex Smith landed at the Kansas City Chiefs. Because successful agents represent a number of players, conflicts are almost inevitable and, as in the Manning/Smith situation, are compounded by the impact of a salary cap. How should Condon have negotiated with the Forty-Niners when the team was considering both quarterbacks? How should agent Drew Rosenhaus have handled his representation of DeSean Jackson and LeSean McCoy in 2012, both star players on the Philadelphia Eagles renegotiating their contracts under a tight cap?

d.   Multifaceted firms, such as International Management Group (IMG), not only represent many tennis players but they also promote, manage, and even sponsor tournaments on the tennis tour. Is this dual representation legitimate? Should the body responsible for the tour be able to impose limitations on such inter-relationships? *See Volvo North America Corp. v. Men's International Professional Tennis Council (MIPTC)*, 857 F.2d 55 (2d Cir. 1988).

4.   *Athlete Self-Management.* Some premier athletes have succeeded in avoiding the risk of conflicts of interest by founding their own management agencies to negotiate contracts and make endorsement deals for themselves. NBA great LeBron James's marketing company offers an example of this new financial model, handling all aspects of his business ventures. Similarly, golfer Rory McIlroy and tennis players Roger Federer, Andy Murray, and Rafael Nadal each left high profile companies and, taking their previous agents with them, set up their own agencies. Does this approach work only for superstar players with tremendous marketing capabilities? Or is there a version of self-management that would be equally effective for the average player? *See* Jodi S. Balsam, *"Free My Agent": Legal Implications of Professional Athletes' Self-Representation*, 16 WAKE FOREST J. BUS. & INTELL. PROP. L. 510 (2016).

5.   *Player Association Contract Assistance to Its Members.* Players associations collect and archive information about every player contract, most of which follow the standard form contract. The associations have the capability to make these data available and reasonably comprehensible to

players in the sport, ideally on a comparative basis. The NFLPA, for example, makes available to its players free advice, contract review, and statistical comparisons of contracts to ensure the player is getting fair market value. NFLPA agent regulations require agents to consult with the union before finalizing certain veteran contracts, apparently out of concern that agents were agreeing to language that placed players' guaranteed money at risk. Coincidentally, such assistance can reduce the risk that agent conflicts will shortchange some players. Given the availability of this information, what remains of an agent's value-proposition in the context of negotiating the player contract? What risks are associated with the union having access to ongoing confidential contract negotiations among multiple players and teams?

6. *Agent Representation of Coaches.* The agent business has expanded to representing coaches at both the professional and college levels. Concerns arise that those agents will try to use the coaches they represent to gain access to the players in their sport. Or conversely, that a Division I college basketball coach might pressure his stars to use his agent as their representative when they leave college for the professional ranks. And when an agent represents both coach and player, obvious conflicts arise. The players unions have tried to regulate such conflicts. The NBPA bans agents from representing both athletes and coaches, and the NFLPA requires an agent to disclose to players representation of coaches and other management personnel.

4. DISPUTES BETWEEN SPORTS AGENTS

As a result of the intense competition for clients, athletes regularly move from one agency to another, enabled by standard representation agreements that permit either party to terminate by providing short written notice (*e.g.*, five days for NFL player agents). Agents also regularly switch agencies, especially during the recent era of conglomeration of the agency business. These moves can trigger litigation about contract terms and agent fees owed, and courts have considered when aggressive business tactics cross ethical and legal boundaries.

SPEAKERS OF SPORT, INC. V. PROSERV, INC.
178 F.3d 862 (7th Cir. 1999)

POSNER, CHIEF JUDGE.

The plaintiff, Speakers of Sport, appeals from the grant of summary judgment to the defendant, ProServ, in a diversity suit in which one sports agency has charged another with tortious interference with a business relationship and related violations of Illinois law. The essential facts, construed as favorably to the plaintiff as the record will permit, are as follows. Ivan Rodriguez, a highly successful catcher with the Texas Rangers baseball team, in 1991 signed the first of several one-year contracts making Speakers his agent. ProServ wanted to expand its representation of baseball players and to this end invited Rodriguez to its office in Washington and there promised that it would get him between $2 and $4 million in endorsements if he signed with ProServ—which he did, terminating his contract (which was terminable at will) with Speakers. This was in 1995. ProServ failed to obtain significant endorsement for Rodriguez and after just one year he switched to another agent who the following year landed him a five-year $42 million contract with the Rangers. Speakers brought this suit a few months later, charging that the promise of endorsements that ProServ had made to Rodriguez was fraudulent and had induced him to terminate his contract with Speakers.

The parties agree that the substantive issues in this diversity suit are governed by Illinois law, and we do not look behind such agreements so long as they are reasonable, as this one is. . . .

Speakers could not sue Rodriguez for breach of contract, because he had not broken their contract, which was, as we said, terminable at will. Nor, therefore, could it accuse ProServ of inducing a breach of contract. . . . But Speakers did have a contract with Rodriguez, and inducing the termination of a contract, even when the termination is not a breach because the contract is terminable at will, can still be actionable under the tort law of Illinois, either as an interference with prospective economic advantage or as an interference with the contract at will itself. Nothing turns on the difference in characterization.

There is in general nothing wrong with one sports agent trying to take a client from another if this can be done without precipitating a breach of contract. That is the process known as competition, which though painful, fierce, frequently ruthless, sometimes Darwinian in its pitilessness, is the cornerstone of our highly successful economic system. Competition is not a tort, but on the contrary provides a defense (the "competitor's privilege") to the tort of improper interference. It does not privilege inducing a breach of contract—conduct usefully regarded as a separate tort from interfering with a business relationship without precipitating an actual breach of contract—but it does privilege inducing the lawful termination of a contract that is terminable at will. Sellers (including agents, who are sellers of services) do not "own" their customers, at least not without a contract with them that is not terminable at will.

There would be few more effective inhibitors of the competitive process than making it a tort for an agent to promise the client of another agent to do better by him—which is pretty much what this case comes down to. It is true that Speakers argues only that the competitor may not make a promise that he knows he cannot fulfill, may not, that is, compete by fraud. Because the competitor's privilege does not include a right to get business from a competitor by means of fraud, it is hard to quarrel with this position in the abstract, but the practicalities are different. If the argument were accepted and the new agent made a promise that was not fulfilled, the old agent would have a shot at convincing a jury that the new agent had known from the start that he couldn't deliver on the promise. Once a case gets to the jury, all bets are off. The practical consequence of Speakers' approach, therefore, would be that a sports agent who lured away the client of another agent with a promise to do better by him would be running a grave legal risk.

This threat to the competitive process is blocked by the principle of Illinois law that promissory fraud is not actionable unless it is part of a scheme to defraud, that is, unless it is one element of a pattern of fraudulent acts. By requiring that the plaintiff show a pattern, by thus not letting him rest on proving a single promise, the law reduces the likelihood of a spurious suit; for a series of unfulfilled promises is better (though of course not conclusive) evidence of fraud than a single unfulfilled promise.

Criticized for vagueness, and rejected in most states, the Illinois rule yet makes sense in a case like this, if only as a filter against efforts to use the legal process to stifle competition. Consider in this connection the characterization by Speakers' own chairman of ProServ's promise to Rodriguez as "pure fantasy and gross exaggeration"—in other words, as puffing. Puffing in the usual sense signifies meaningless superlatives that no reasonable person would take seriously, and so it is not actionable as fraud. Rodriguez thus could not have sued ProServ (and has not attempted to) in respect of the promise of $2–$4 million in endorsements. If Rodriguez thus was not wronged, we do not understand on what theory Speakers can complain that ProServ competed with it unfairly.

The promise of endorsements was puffing not in the most common sense of a cascade of extravagant adjectives but in the equally valid sense of a sales pitch that is intended, and that a reasonable person in the position of the "promisee" would understand, to be aspirational rather than enforceable—an expression of hope rather than a commitment. It is not as if ProServ proposed to employ Rodriguez and pay him $2 million a year. That would be the kind of promise that could found an enforceable obligation. ProServ proposed merely to get him endorsements of at least that amount. They would of course be paid by the companies whose products Rodriguez endorsed, rather than by ProServ. ProServ could not force them to pay Rodriguez, and it is not contended that he understood ProServ to be warranting a minimum level of endorsements in the sense that if they were not forthcoming ProServ would be legally obligated to make up the difference to him.

It is possible to make a binding promise of something over which one has no control; such a promise is called a warranty. But it is not plausible that this is what ProServ was doing—that it was guaranteeing Rodriguez a minimum of $2 million a year in outside earnings if he signed with it. The only reasonable meaning to attach to ProServ's so-called promise is that ProServ would try to get as many endorsements as possible for Rodriguez and that it was optimistic that it could get him at least $2 million worth of them. So understood, the "promise" was not a promise at all. But even if it was a promise (or a warranty), it cannot be the basis for a finding of fraud because it was not part of a scheme to defraud evidenced by more than the allegedly fraudulent promise itself.

It can be argued, however, that competition can be tortious even if it does not involve an actionable fraud (which in Illinois would not include a fraudulent promise) or other independently tortious act, such as defamation, or trademark or patent infringement, or a theft of a trade secret; that competitors should not be allowed to use "unfair" tactics; and that a promise known by the promisor when made to be unfulfillable is such a tactic, especially when used on a relatively unsophisticated, albeit very well to do, baseball player. . . . The doctrine's conception of wrongful competition is vague—"wrongful by reason of . . . an established standard of a trade or profession," or "a violation of recognized ethical rules or established customs or practices in the business community," or "improper because they [the challenged competitive tactics] violate an established standard of a trade or profession, or involve unethical conduct, . . . sharp dealing[, or] overreaching." [citations omitted] Worse, the established standards of a trade or profession in regard to competition, and its ideas of unethical competitive conduct, are likely to reflect a desire to limit competition for reasons related to the self-interest of the trade or profession rather than to the welfare of its customers or clients. [T]he tort of interference with business relationships should be confined to cases in which the defendant employed unlawful means to stiff a competitor, and . . . the case law is generally consistent with this position as a matter of outcomes as distinct from articulation.

Invoking the concept of "wrongful by reason of . . . an established standard of a trade or profession," Speakers points to a rule of major league baseball forbidding players' agents to compete by means of misrepresentations. The rule is designed to protect the players, rather than their agents, so that even if it established a norm enforceable by law Speakers would not be entitled to invoke it; it is not a rule designed for Speakers' protection. In any event its violation would not be the kind of "wrongful" conduct that should trigger the tort of intentional interference; it would not be a violation of law.

[The court evaluated Speakers' claim that ProServ violated the Illinois Consumer Fraud and Deceptive Business Practices Act, rejecting it largely because Speakers is not a consumer.]

* * *

We add that even if Speakers could establish liability under either the common law of torts or the deceptive practices act, its suit would fail because it cannot possibly establish, as it seeks to do, a damages entitlement (the only relief it seeks) to the agent's fee on Rodriguez's $42 million contract. That contract was negotiated years after he left Speakers, and by another agent. Since Rodriguez had only a year-to-year contract with Speakers—terminable at will, moreover—and since obviously he was dissatisfied with Speakers at least to the extent of switching to ProServ and then when he became disillusioned with ProServ of not returning to Speakers' fold, the likelihood that Speakers would have retained him had ProServ not lured him away is too slight to ground an award of such damages. Such an award would be the best example yet of puffing in the pie-in-the-sky sense.

Affirmed.

––––––––

NOTES AND QUESTIONS

1. *The Competitor's Privilege.* The *Speakers* court considers fierce competition to be the cornerstone of our economic system, and refuses to condemn shady conduct by sports agents in poaching clients. What limits does the court impose, if any, on the "competitor's privilege"? How do those limits circumscribe the conduct of an agent towards a prospective client? Towards a competing agent? *See Lee v. Brothers*, 2021 WL 4652336 (S.D.N.Y. Oct. 6, 2021) (dismissing claims that defendants tortiously induced top NBA draft pick to switch agents by buying the player a pick-up truck); *Bauer v. The Interpublic Group of Companies, Inc.*, 255 F. Supp. 2d 1086 (N.D. Cal. 2003) (agent unable to establish that competitor who lured away his client was responsible for anonymous letters disparaging the agent); *Wright v. Bonds*, 117 F.3d 1427 (9th Cir. 1997) (agent did not wrongfully interfere with contract by contacting baseball player represented by another agent, and then lying about it).

2. *Players Association Regulation of Sports Agents.* At least one court has held that the existence of players association regulation of sports agents is reason not to hold an agent liable under state statutory prohibitions of deceptive business practices. In *Champion Pro Consulting Grp., Inc. v. Impact Sports Football, LLC*, 845 F.3d 104 (4th Cir. 2016), a sports agency alleged that a competitor recruited college football players by using "runners," cash inducements, and other practices reviled under NFLPA regulation of agents. In view of the "well-established internal systems of governance already in place," the court declined to intervene to avoid creating overlapping and possibly conflicting mechanisms for supervision of agents. *Id.* at 110. Do you agree that courts in these situations should defer to private regulation of sports agents? The *Champion* court further observed that the allegations of agent misconduct were "indicative of the industry in which these parties operate and [therefore] outside the scope of business activities" the state statute is designed to address. *Id.* Should the standard for deceptive business practices vary with the cutthroat nature of the industry?

3. *Non-Compete Clauses.* With sports agents frequently switching agencies, non-compete clauses have become standard practice to prevent them from stealing away their old firm's clients when they move to a new firm. State

law governs non-compete clauses, and most states require them to be reasonable and to permit the departing employee to earn a living. *See Steinberg Moorad & Dunn Inc. v. Dunn*, 136 F. App'x 6 (9th Cir. 2005) (vacating $44 million judgment in favor of agent's former firm because non-competition clause was invalid to extent it prevented agent from "pursuing his trade"). Furthermore, when a non-compete clause restricts a sports agent's ability to ply his trade, it affects both athletes' rights to select the agent of their choice and players unions' federal authority to regulate agents' conduct. How would you weigh these interests against protecting an agency's investment in training an agent and supporting the agent in recruiting clients?

4.   *Athlete's Best Interests.* What are the risks to the athlete who bounces from agent to agent with little regard to loyalty or scruples? Are athletes always motivated purely by economic interests, or are there competing, highly personal considerations that can motivate their contractual decision-making? *See* Michael A. McCann, *It's Not About the Money: The Role of Preferences, Cognitive Biases, and Heuristics Among Professional Athletes*, 71 BROOK. L. REV. 1459, 1482 (2006). Consider whether there is value to professional athletes in developing long-term relationships with their advisors.

C. AGENT REPRESENTATION OF UNIONIZED ATHLETES

As explained in Chapter 3, once a workforce unionizes, the certified union has the exclusive authority to negotiate all terms and conditions of employment for all members in the bargaining unit. Like their counterparts in the entertainment industry, though, players associations have traditionally exercised this statutory authority only to the extent of negotiating minimum salaries, benefits, and job protections—a level of basic rights that is guaranteed to every player, whether a rookie or superstar. The collective bargaining agreement in each team sport allows every player to try to negotiate more advantageous terms—in particular, high guaranteed salaries. This approach is premised on the variability of player-employee talent and market value in sports, as opposed to the ordinary employment setting.

In addition, players associations delegate to player representatives—sports agents—a portion of the exclusive bargaining authority they have been granted under the Labor Act to represent all the players in their respective leagues. These representatives, however, must submit to a union certification process that can include meeting minimal education requirements, attending seminars, and passing a written examination. The first union to regulate sports agents was the NFLPA in 1983, followed by the NBPA (1985), the MLBPA (1987), and the NHLPA (1995). All four associations have adopted comprehensive regulatory schemes that address agent competence, ethics, and fair competition for athletes-clients.

Consensus has emerged over time that players associations are best equipped to regulate agents, and possess the incentives and the resources to develop the regulatory competence needed to improve the quality of agent representation. Further, once an agent has learned and complied with a union's requirements, he or she can represent any player and deal with any team in that sport.

PROBLEM 10.4

James Rickey was certified as a "contract advisor" by the NFLPA. His certification automatically expired under NFLPA rules when he was unable to negotiate an individual playing contract on behalf of a football player within three years. Rickey successfully applied for recertification, but it again lapsed when he failed to represent an NFL player in contract negotiations within another three years.

Rickey objects to the "three-year rule" as not a legitimate exercise of the union's regulatory authority. He further believes that the NFLPA, in collusion with the NFL, selectively enforces the "three-year rule" to the benefit of more established agents, who are permitted to violate the rules with impunity. He claims that the NFLPA and NFL have allowed several agents to "act as one" by signing off on the same individual player's contract to an active roster, thereby allowing some agents to avoid decertification despite minimal involvement in negotiating contracts. When reading the following material, consider how Rickey would fare if he challenged the NFLPA rule and its surrounding conduct under antitrust law, the union duty of fair representation, or state contract and tort law.

---

1.   UNION AUTHORITY TO REGULATE AGENTS

Labor law, specifically the union's exclusive bargaining authority, provides the source of an association's authority to impose binding regulations on agents. But while unions can, and do, delegate their exclusive authority to the individual athletes and their agents, a union may delegate its statutory prerogatives conditionally, and only in favor of agents of whom the union approves. When players associations adopt the latter posture, both the collective bargaining agreement and the labor laws preclude a club from negotiating individual contracts with agents who are not certified for that purpose by the association. In effect, the clubs become the enforcers of the association's regulatory program, because they must refuse to deal with any agent who has not secured and retained the association's stamp of approval.

While its bargaining relationship with the league may give the players association the leverage to impose its certification program on agents, this power secured under labor law does not necessarily insulate the regime from challenge under other laws—in particular, antitrust law. In effect, the players are agreeing to a standard set of terms upon which they will purchase the services of player agents—one term being the maximum agency fee—and the players collectively require agents to subscribe to these terms as a condition of doing business in this sport. Should such restraints on the agent market be considered an illegal restraint of trade under the Sherman Act? As one might suspect, players associations answer this question in the negative—asserting the same labor exemption from antitrust that leagues have relied on to protect their limitations on player mobility and salary based on the terms of the collective bargaining agreements negotiated with the unions.

In the following case, the NBPA attempted to ward off the first legal challenge to association regulation of agents. It arose out of accusations by basketball great Kareem Abdul-Jabbar that his agent Thomas Collins engaged in a variety of breaches of fiduciary duty and financial improprieties that cost the player close to $1 million. Although Abdul-Jabbar and Collins eventually settled these claims, Collins during the dispute had allowed his NBPA certification to lapse. When he sought recertification, the NBPA investigated the Abdul-Jabbar allegations and decided not to recertify Collins. Collins was entitled to appeal the denial to a union arbitrator, but instead brought this suit.

COLLINS V. NBPA & GRANTHAM

850 F. Supp. 1468 (D. Col. 1991), *affirmed per curiam*, 976 F.2d 740 (10th Cir. 1992)

MATSCH, DISTRICT JUDGE.

[Collins brought an antitrust challenge against the NBPA-NBA collective bargaining agreement which forbids NBA teams from negotiating with agents who are not certified by the NBPA.]

* * *

Like other sports and entertainment unions, the NBPA believes that the collective good of the entire represented group is maximized when individualized salary negotiations occur within a framework that permits players to exert leverage based on their unique skills and personal contributions. The NBPA therefore has authorized the players or their individually selected agents to negotiate individual compensation packages. This delegation of representational authority to individual players and their agents has always been limited solely to the authority to negotiate individual compensation packages, and to enforce them through the grievance-arbitration procedure established by the NBPA-NBA Agreement.

Player agents were unregulated by the NBPA before 1986. By the mid-1980s, a substantial number of players had complained to the officers of the NBPA about agent abuses. Specifically, players complained that the agents imposed high and non-uniform fees for negotiation services, insisted on the execution of open-ended powers of attorney giving the agents broad powers over players' professional and financial decisions, failed to keep players apprised of the status of negotiations with NBA teams, failed to submit itemized bills for fees and services, and, in some cases, had conflicts of interest arising out of representing coaches and/or general managers of NBA teams as well as players. Many players believed they were bound by contract not to dismiss their agents regardless of dissatisfaction with their services and fees, because the agents had insisted on the execution of long-term agreements. Some agents offered money and other inducements to players, their families and coaches to obtain player clients.

In response to these abuses, the NBPA established the Regulations, a comprehensive system of agent certification and regulation, to insure that players would receive agent services that meet minimum standards of quality at uniform rates. First, the Regulations provide that a player agent may not conduct individual contract negotiations unless he signs the "Standard Player Agent Contract" promulgated by the Committee. The "Standard Player Agent Contract" limits player agent fees by prohibiting any fee or commission on any contract which entitles the player to the minimum salary and by limiting agent fees on all contracts. Second, the Regulations contain a "code of conduct" which specifically prohibits an agent from providing or offering money or anything of value to a player, a member of a player's family or a player's high school or college coach for the purpose of inducing the player to use that agent's services. The code also prohibits agents from engaging in conduct that constitutes an actual or apparent conflict of interest (such as serving as an agent for a player while also representing an NBA team, general manager or head coach), engaging in any unlawful conduct involving dishonesty, fraud, deceit, misrepresentation, or engaging in any other conduct that reflects adversely on his fitness to serve in a fiduciary capacity as a player agent or jeopardizes the effective representation of NBA players.

Third, the Regulations restrict the representation of players to individuals who are certified player agents, and set up a program for the certification of agents who are then bound by the Regulations' fee restrictions and code of conduct. [The court listed the grounds for denying certification, including making false or misleading statements in the application for certification, misappropriated funds, engaged in fraud or other conduct that "significantly impacts adversely on his credibility, integrity or competence to serve in a fiduciary capacity on behalf of players," or is unwilling to swear to comply with agent regulations. Agents denied certification may demand final and binding arbitration.]

After unilaterally promulgating the Regulations, the NBPA obtained, in arms length collective bargaining, the NBA's agreement to prohibit all member teams from negotiating individual player salary contracts with any agent who was not certified by the NBPA.

[The court described Collins' misconduct with respect to Abdul-Jabbar as determined by an NBPA investigation, and the resulting decision to deny recertification. Collins responded with an antitrust complaint that characterized the NBPA's actions as a "group boycott" and per se violation of the Sherman Act in restraining him from representing individual basketball players in salary negotiations with their teams. The court concluded that the NBPA's actions were immune from antitrust scrutiny under the statutory and non-statutory labor exemptions.]

* * *

Both the Regulations and Article XXXI [of the CBA] are within the statutory exemption from antitrust regulation. When promulgating the Regulations and when negotiating Article XXXI, the NBPA acted in its own interest, independently of any employers and without denying access to rival employers. The number and identity of the employers remains unchanged regardless of the Regulations or Article XXXI. A union's actions are in its "self-interest" if they bear a reasonable relationship to a legitimate union interest. The NBPA regulatory program fulfills legitimate union purposes and was the result of legitimate concerns: it protects the player wage scale by eliminating percentage fees where the agent does not achieve a result better than the collectively bargained minimum; it keeps agent fees generally to a reasonable and uniform level, prevents unlawful kickbacks, bribes, and fiduciary violations and protects the NBPA's interest in assuring that its role in representing professional basketball players is properly carried out. Although Collins claims any benefit is in the *player's* self-interest, not the union's, it is impossible to separate the two—the union is composed of its members and exists solely to serve the players. When the players benefit, the union benefits as well.

The second prong of the [labor exemption] test is also met. . . . The NBPA did not combine with a non-labor group or a non-party to a labor dispute when promulgating the Regulations or negotiating Article XXXI. The NBPA unilaterally developed its Regulations in response to agent abuses and to benefit its members. It did not develop them in collusion with the employer group or to assist the employer group effort to restrain competition or control the employer group's product market.

* * *

Even if Article XXXI of the Agreement were not entitled to the statutory exemption, it would be immune from antitrust review under the nonstatutory exemption to the antitrust laws. The Supreme Court has determined that when a union-employer agreement falls within the protection of the national labor policy, a proper accommodation between the policy favoring collective bargaining under the NLRA and the congressional policy favoring free competition in business markets requires that some agreements be accorded a limited nonstatutory labor exemption from antitrust sanctions. Unlike the statutory exemption which immunizes activities that are expressly described in the Clayton and Norris LaGuardia Acts, the nonstatutory exemption immunizes labor arrangements that are the ordinary implication of activities contemplated by the federal labor laws. When the agreement is reached through bona fide, arms-length bargaining between the union and the employers, and the terms of the agreement are not the product of an initiative by the employer group but were sought by the union in an effort to serve the legitimate interests of its members, it is free from antitrust scrutiny.

* * *

The nonstatutory exemption similarly immunizes the Regulations from Sherman Act scrutiny. The Regulations were unilaterally developed in response to player complaints and to further NBPA labor policies. The NBPA-NBA Agreement, including Article XXXI, was agreed to in arms-length collective bargaining. The provision was not sought "at the behest of or in combination with" any employer or other non-labor group as forbidden by *Jewel Tea*. There is no economic benefit to the NBPA or the NBA member teams as a result of this provision and there is no effect on the employer's product or service market as a result of the provision.

Summary dismissal granted.

———

Collins appealed this ruling to the Tenth Circuit Court of Appeals, which in a non-precedential decision affirmed the district court's conclusion that "the statutory labor exemption from the Sherman Act permits the NBPA to establish a certification procedure for player agents." *Collins v. Nat'l Basketball Players Ass'n*, 976 F.2d 740 (10th Cir. 1992). That principle has been repeatedly affirmed, shielding both unions and leagues from antitrust challenge to agent regulations that interfered with an agent's livelihood. See *Dickey v. Nat'l Football League*, 2020 WL 6819135 (1st Cir. Feb. 13, 2020) (agent certification expired because unable to negotiate a contract within three-years); *Hurley v. Nat'l Basketball Players Ass'n*, 2021 WL 6065783 (N.D. Ohio Dec. 22, 2021) (agent denied certification because his law license had been suspended).

The Tenth Circuit also addressed Collins' claim that the NBPA did not have authority to discipline him for conduct unrelated to negotiating player contracts with his clients' professional teams:

> On appeal, Collins now acknowledges that the NBPA has the statutory authority to establish player agent regulations. But he maintains his attack on the Committee's decision to deny his certification because it was based in part on its finding that he had breached his fiduciary duty as an investment agent and money manager. He argues that his conduct outside of negotiations between players and their teams is not a legitimate

interest of the union because it has no bearing on the union's interest in the wage scale and working conditions of its members.

> The district court properly rejected this argument. The NBPA established the Regulations to deal with agent abuses, including agents' violations of their fiduciary duties as labor negotiators. It was entirely fair for the Committee to conclude that a man who had neglected his fiduciary duties as an investment agent and money manager could not be trusted to fulfill his fiduciary duties as a negotiator. The integrity of a prospective negotiating agent is well within the NBPA's legitimate interest in maintaining the wage scale and working conditions of its members.

Id. at 740.

NOTES AND QUESTIONS

1. *Tenth Circuit on the Scope of Union Regulatory Authority.* Should unions be allowed to regulate agents for misconduct or incompetence other than as a contract negotiator? What if union members wanted Collins to represent them in that capacity, despite his improprieties in other settings? Should certification be denied to an agent because, for example, he is convicted of drug use? Because he publicly disagrees with the union's bargaining strategy? On the other hand, what is an appropriate standard of incompetence in contract negotiations? Could certification be denied because an agent negotiated a contract the union believed was far below market value?

2. *Agents Bound by Collective Bargaining Agreement.* In *White v. Nat'l Football League,* 92 F. Supp. 2d 918 (D. Minn. 2000), the court held that NFL player agents are bound by the league's collective bargaining agreement even though they are not signatories. The court cited to Collins in finding implied consent based on agents' awareness that they are permitted to negotiate player contracts only because the players association has delegated a portion of its exclusive representational authority to them. The *White* court also relied on the fact that player agents reap significant economic benefits from their relationship with the NFLPA, and expressly agree to be bound by NFLPA agent regulations.

3. *Labor Preemption of Agents' State Law Claims Against Unions.* The labor agreement's dominion over agents was explained in *Porter v. Nat'l Football League Players Ass'n,* 2022 WL 2666060 (6th Cir. July 11, 2022). Vincent Porter sued the NFLPA when it continued to investigate him after criminal charges had been dismissed and an arbitrator had reinstated his agent certification. When the NFLPA sought to dismiss the suit as preempted under § 301 of the federal Labor Management Relations Act, the Sixth Circuit agreed, but only as to Porter's state law claims that directly challenged the NFLPA's right of exclusive representation, that is, claims of tortious interference with a business expectancy and relationship. The court allowed

Porter to proceed on his claims of negligence, breach of duty, and breach of contract. Similarly, in *Black v. NFLPA*, 87 F. Supp. 2d 1 (D.D.C. 2000), the court held that § 301 preempted Tank Black's suit against the NFLPA, in which he alleged that a three-year suspension for paying college athletes to become his clients interfered with his contractual relationships with current clients. The court ruled that any such tort claim was "inextricably intertwined with consideration of the terms of the labor contract," and the agent's only recourse was through the dispute resolution process authorized under the CBA. *See generally* Chapter 4, Section D; *cf. Indep. Sports & Entm't, LLC v. Fegan*, 2017 WL 2598550 (C.D. Cal. May 30, 2017) (in dispute between sports agency and agent who allegedly violated non-compete clause, § 301 does not preempt state contract action where no issue as to union's authority to regulate or discipline agents).

A 1993 case involving baseball agent Barry Rona produced even more challenges for association regulation and arbitral scrutiny of agent behavior. Before becoming an agent, Rona worked for the league's Player Relations Committee (PRC), the counterpart to the Players Association in collective bargaining. He was the PRC's general counsel from 1974 to 1986, and its Executive Director from 1986 to 1990. During that period, Rona had gained an enormous amount of experience and understanding of player relations in baseball, but also was present for the baseball owners' mid-1980s conspiracy to eliminate bidding for free agents and to hold down player salaries. After leaving MLB, he began to represent football and basketball players, and then filed an application for certification as a baseball player agent with the MLBPA. The MLBPA refused to certify him, based on § 2(C) of its Regulations, which barred certification of anyone whose conduct "may adversely affect his credibility [or] integrity . . . to serve in a representative and/or fiduciary capacity on behalf of players." In its rejection letter to Rona, the Players Association stated:

> In the Association's judgment, your conduct during the conspiracy cannot be explained away or excused as simply a matter of typical adversarial behavior. For the fact is that you were, if not the architect, then at least a master builder of a devastating, profound, and prolonged violation of Players' rights, the extent of which cannot be overestimated. Over an extended period of time, the Clubs undertook a scheme intended to deprive all declared free agents of the market for their services, a market that was established through the Association's good faith, arm's length negotiations with the Clubs—and you. . . .

> In sum, it is the Association's conclusion that because you engaged in the above-described conduct and, indeed, had principal responsibility for it, you are unfit to be certified to represent players. Indeed, in the circumstances, we think it is extreme ill

grace that, for your own economic interests, you now seek to align yourself with the interests of the very players you helped victimize.

Rona challenged the decision in the following arbitration.

BARRY RONA AND MAJOR LEAGUE BASEBALL PLAYERS ASSOCIATION
(Arbitration, 1993)

COLLINS, ARBITRATOR.

[The sole question for the arbitrator was whether the Association's factual findings were supported by "substantial evidence on the record as a whole," and whether its legal conclusions were "arbitrary and capricious." In his analysis, the arbitrator quoted extensively from the New York Code of Professional Responsibility which spelled out both the client's right to "zealous legal representation" and the lawyer's obligation "not to assist clients to engage in wrongful acts."]

* * *

It is clear to this Arbitrator that any institutional policy which by its terms or application would penalize a lawyer for providing, or would create a disincentive for a lawyer not to provide, zealous representation within the limits of the code, would transgress the public policy on which the Code rests. A corollary to this is that lawyers acting as such can only be judged, in terms of the ethics of their behavior, by the standards set forth in the Code. In addition there would seem to be serious questions whether determinations as to whether or not a lawyer has acted ethically can be made by other than the courts and whether or not such determinations can be based on anything less than a preponderance of the evidence.

The evidence in this proceeding establishes that the PRC [Major League Baseball Player Relations Committee] is a New York corporation domiciled in New York, that from 1974 or 1975 until late 1985, sometime before January 1, 1986, Rona served the PRC only in a legal capacity, first as Counsel and later General Counsel, and that from late 1985 until his termination in December 1989 he also was the PRC's Executive Director, a post to which he was formally named in August 1986. Thus the collusion that . . . existed in the 1985 free agent market must have been devised and implemented when Rona was acting solely in a legal capacity for the PRC. While he thereafter assumed an additional leading role in the PRC, the evidence establishes only that his subsequent relationship to the collusion in the 1985 and 1986 free agent markets was only in his capacity as a lawyer—evaluating his clients' cases, advising them, questioning them, speaking publicly on their behalf, and serving on the [arbitration panels that resolved the collusion disputes]. In fact neither [panel] mentioned Rona in their opinions dealing respectively with the 1985 and 1986 free agent markets. As to 1987, there is evidence that Rona was a knowing participant in activities that related directly to the collusion that the [panel] found existed in that year's free agent market. However, all such activities by Rona, whatever their propriety, were conducted by Rona in his capacity as the principal inside lawyer for the PRC, working in conjunction with PRC outside counsel. . . . While the Players Association asserts that Rona bore some other responsibility for the collusion because of his role as PRC Executive Director, that is purely speculative. Since Rona's relationship to the collusion was only that of lawyer representing clients, the significance of Rona's actions for his credibility and integrity, in this Arbitrator's opinion, had to be judged solely in terms of the applicable New York law—the New York Code of Professional Responsibility.

It is mystifying why the Players Association failed to measure Rona's actions against the standards in the Code or even to acknowledge that such standards existed. . . . The Arbitrator is strongly inclined to view the Players Association's evaluation of Rona's credibility and integrity without any reference to the applicable official standards as itself constituting arbitrary and capricious action within the meaning of the Regulations. In any event, even when the evidence is measured by the Code's standards, the Arbitrator finds that the Players Association acted arbitrarily and capriciously in rejecting Rona's application.

The Players Association's conclusion that Rona was part of the collusion in the 1985 and 1986 free agent markets because he was a leading figure in the PRC is fundamentally at odds with the Code's very clear position that lawyers do not act unethically merely because they represent individuals or institutions that are found to have engaged in wrongful activities. And there is no evidence, nor any finding . . . that it was or should have been obvious to Rona that his clients were acting "merely for the purpose of harassing or maliciously injuring any person" within the meaning of DR2–110 or DR7–102. On the contrary, he expressed his "concerns" to his clients, asked them directly whether they were involved in collusion to destroy the free agent markets in 1985 and 1986 and, when they replied negatively, allowed them to so testify under oath. . . . Rona acted entirely properly within the meaning of EC7–5—his allowing his clients to have their day in court to attempt under oath to refute the circumstantial evidence that they were engaged in collusion can hardly be termed taking a "frivolous legal position" in contravention of EC7–5. This Arbitrator believes that these are not even close questions. For the foregoing reasons the Arbitrator concludes that the Players Association's rejection of Rona's application because of his alleged involvement in the 1985 and 1986 collusion was arbitrary and capricious.

* * *

Under the Regulations the Arbitrator has no jurisdiction to judge the merits of Rona's argument; he only has jurisdiction to review, on a substantial evidence, arbitrary-capricious basis the Association's response to Rona's argument. However, Rona's argument is not [in] the Arbitrator's opinion frivolous—he was entitled to have the Association consider the merits of his argument. That the Association never considered the argument, and could not have considered it, is clear to the Arbitrator. The Association's denial letter makes no effort to treat Rona's activities in 1987 separate and apart from his alleged participation in the 1985 and 1986 collusion. On the contrary, it refers to 1987 as a "graphic illustration of [his] central role . . . in the conspiracy." And, even more importantly, the Association never considered the possibility that Rona could be viewed as not bearing any responsibility for the 1985 and 1986 collusion. On the contrary, in its rejection letter, in its statements to this Arbitrator, and in the testimony in this proceeding of its representatives, it has heaped extraordinary opprobrium on Rona, much of which . . . is referable only to the events in 1985 and 1986, and not 1987, or is explainable only in terms of Rona's alleged involvement in the collusion in all three years. Having failed to consider, in fact having been incapable of fairly considering the arguments Rona advanced in support of his application, the Association acted, in this Arbitrator's opinion, arbitrarily and capriciously.

Agent certification ordered.

NOTES AND QUESTIONS

1. *Analysis of Rona.* The MLBPA objected to the arbitrator's ruling in Rona on the ground that he had exceeded his arbitral authority by focusing on external law, rather than on the standards the union established in the Player Agent Regulations. Do you agree with that objection? What are the odds that the union would win a challenge in court, given the standards for judicial review of arbitration awards?

2. *Players as Agents.* During his playing career, Jose Canseco, then with the Boston Red Sox (and before he admitted steroid use), tried to create a new sports management firm targeted especially at Latin American players. Canseco proposed to hire a certified agent to represent players in their direct negotiations with clubs. The plan foundered, though, when the MLBPA deemed it to be an unacceptable conflict of interest for one player's firm to be representing other players. Do you agree with that judgment, at least from the point of view of the Players Association (as distinct from the league)?

3. *Agents and Player Work Stoppages.* During the 1994 season-ending player strike, the owners briefly considered staging baseball replacement games. In response, the MLBPA reportedly considered a ban against any of its certified agents representing replacement players. Would such a ban have violated the union's duty of fair representation, as explained in Chapter 3, Section H? Or would it have invited antitrust scrutiny, given that it foreclosed access by the replacement players to the most experienced and skilled

representation? Would the labor exemption, explained in Chapter 7, Section D, insulate the players association rule from antitrust challenge?

4.   *Agent Loyalty to the Union.* A lengthy 1998–99 labor battle between NBA owners and NBPA player-members generated another union-agent conflict and arbitration ruling, *In re NBPA Committee on Agent Regulation and Stephen M. Woods* (1999). Agent Woods had been a fervent and publicly outspoken dissenter from the negotiating strategy of NBPA President Patrick Ewing and Executive Director Billy Hunter. Indeed, on behalf of his basketball clients, he even filed some unfair labor practice charges with the NLRB alleging unfair NBPA representation of its members, although these charges were all eventually withdrawn. An NBPA arbitrator upheld the NBPA's decision to decertify Woods as an agent, on the premise that a certified player agent owed a fiduciary duty of loyalty to the players union as well as to his player clients. Woods had apparently violated this duty not just by filing the unfair labor practice charges, but also by making public statements that attacked the union's bargaining positions, were derogatory of the union leaders, and often contained false as well as confidential information. How does the decertification in the *Woods* case compare with the *Rona* ruling we have just read? Does Woods have a viable antitrust claim that this union action is an unreasonable restraint of player agent free trade?

2.   EXAMPLES AND IMPACT OF PLAYER ASSOCIATION AGENT REGULATION

Despite the agent litigation described above, players association regulation has evoked remarkably little complaint from established practitioners in this field, many of whom have served as advisers to the unions in the development and administration of these programs. Most of the regulatory schemes comprise four essential elements:

(i)   Application form and approval process;

(ii)   Standards of conduct including duty of loyalty and fiduciary duties;

(iii)   Continuing duty to disclose information to the union; and

(iv)   Dispute resolution process.

In designing these elements of agent regulation, the unions must grapple with the tension between the goal of "consumer protection" of their athlete members and the desire to allow each member to select an agent of his choosing.

The NFLPA offers a model of agent regulation, periodically reexamining and amending its regulations as needed to address persistent and emerging problems with agent competence and ethics. Over the years these amendments have included, for example, requiring agents to have negotiated at least one contract during a three-year period in order to retain certification; imposing heightened educational requirements including a postgraduate degree or demonstrated negotiation experience; prohibiting recruitment of clients while an agent is suspended; requiring written disclosure to clients of representation of any college or professional coaches; imposing a continuing duty to inform the union of criminal offenses and civil complaints; and passing a re-certification test of CBA knowledge every two years. As you review the regulation excerpts below, consider the design choices made by the NFLPA and what motivated them.

NFLPA REGULATIONS GOVERNING CONTRACT ADVISORS
(as amended through August 2016)

Section 1: Scope of Regulations

A.   Persons Subject to Regulations

No person (other than a player representing himself) shall be permitted to conduct individual contract negotiations on behalf of a player* and/or assist in or advise with respect to such negotiations with NFL Clubs after the effective date of these Regulations unless he/she is (1) currently certified as a Contract Advisor pursuant to these Regulations; (2) signs a Standard Representation Agreement with the player (See Section 4; Appendix D); and (3) files a fully executed copy of the Standard Representation Agreement with the NFLPA, along with any contract(s) between the player and the Contract Advisor for other services to be provided.

B.   Activities Covered

The activities of Contract Advisors which are governed by these Regulations include: the providing of advice, counsel, information or assistance to players with respect to negotiating their individual contracts with Clubs and/or thereafter in enforcing those contracts; the conduct of individual compensation negotiations with the Clubs on behalf of players; and any other activity or conduct which directly bears upon the Contract Advisor's integrity, competence or ability to properly represent individual NFL players and the NFLPA in individual contract negotiations, including the handling of player funds, providing tax counseling and preparation services, and providing financial advice and investment services to individual players.

. . .

Section 2: Certification

After the effective date of these Regulations, any person who wishes to perform the functions of a Contract Advisor as described in Section 1 above must be certified by the NFLPA. . . .

C. Grounds for Denial of Certification

Grounds for denial of Certification shall include, but not be limited to, the following:

- The applicant has made false or misleading statements of a material nature in his/her application;

- The applicant has misappropriated funds, or engaged in other specific acts such as embezzlement, theft or fraud, which would render him/her unfit to serve in a fiduciary capacity on behalf of players;

- The applicant has engaged in any other conduct that significantly impacts adversely on his/her credibility, integrity or competence to serve in a fiduciary capacity on behalf of players;

- The applicant is unwilling to swear or affirm that he/she will comply with these Regulations and any amendments hereto and/or that he/she will abide by the fee structure contained in the Standard Representation Agreement incorporated into these Regulations;

- The applicant has been denied certification by another professional sports players association;

- The applicant directly or indirectly solicited a player for representation as a Contract Advisor during the period of time between the filing of his/her Application for Certification and Certification by the NFLPA;

- The applicant has not received a degree from an accredited four-year college/university and a post-graduate degree from an accredited college/university. . . .

Section 3: Standard of Conduct for Contract Advisors

A. General Requirements

A Contract Advisor shall be required to:

(1) Disclose on his/her Application, and thereafter upon request of the NFLPA, all information relevant to his/her qualifications to serve as a Contract Advisor, including, but not limited to, background, special training, experience in negotiations, past representation of professional athletes, and relevant business associations or memberships in professional organizations;

(2) Pay an application fee pursuant to Section 2 above unless waived;

(3) Pay the annual fee and provide proof of any required insurance documents in a timely manner;

(4) Attend an NFLPA seminar on individual contract negotiations each year;

(5) Comply with the maximum fee schedule and all other provisions of these Regulations and any amendments thereto;

(6) Execute and abide by the printed Standard Representation Agreement with all players represented, and file with the NFLPA a copy of that fully executed agreement along with any other agreement(s) for additional services that the Contract Advisor has executed with the player. . .

(9) Provide on or before May 1 each year, to every player who he/she represents, with a copy to the NFLPA, an itemized statement covering the period beginning March 1 of the prior year through February 28 or 29 of that year, which separately sets forth both the fee charged to the player for, and any expenses incurred in connection with, the performance of the following services:

    (a) individual player salary negotiations,

    (b) management of the player's assets,

    (c) financial, investment, legal, tax and/or other advice to the player, and

    (d) any other miscellaneous services;

(10) Permit a person or firm authorized by a former or current player-client to conduct an audit of all relevant books and records pertaining to any services provided to that player;

(11) Complete a notarized updated Application for Certification on or before an annual date to be determined by the NFLPA. Such annual update shall include, without limitation, disclosure of the names of any financial advisors the Contract Advisor is recommending or has recommended to players within the past year. A failure to comply with this Section 3(A)(11) shall result in immediate suspension of the Contract Advisor's Certification.

(13) Provide the NFLPA with all materials that the NFLPA deems relevant with respect to any investigation conducted pursuant to these Regulations and in all other respects cooperate fully with the NFLPA;

(14) Fully comply with applicable state and federal laws;

(15) Become and remain sufficiently educated with regard to NFL structure and economics, applicable Collective Bargaining Agreements and other governing documents, basic negotiating techniques, and developments in sports law and related subjects. To ascertain whether the Contract Advisor is sufficiently educated with regard to the above-related subjects, the NFLPA may require a Contract Advisor to pass a Contract Advisor examination. A failure to pass an examination administered pursuant to this Section 3(A)(15) shall result in immediate suspension of the Contract Advisor's Certification. . . .

(16) Disclose . . . the names and current positions of any NFL management personnel, NFL Coaches, other professional league coaches or college coaches whom Contract Advisor represents or has represented in matters pertaining to their employment by or association with any NFL club, other professional league club or college;

(17) Act at all times in a fiduciary capacity on behalf of players;

(18) Comply with and abide by all of the stated policies of the NFLPA;

(19) In connection with payments for assistance in recruiting any player: [prepare disclosure forms identifying other contract advisors who helped recruit the player, and provide the form to the player and have him sign it].

B. Prohibited Conduct

Contract Advisors are prohibited from:

(1) Representing any player in individual contract negotiations with any Club unless he/she (i) is an NFLPA Certified Contract Advisor; (ii) has signed the Standard Representation Agreement with such player; and (iii) has filed a copy of the Standard Representation Agreement with the NFLPA along with any other contract(s) or agreement(s) between the player and the Contract Advisor;

(2) Providing or offering money or any other thing of value to any player or prospective player to induce or encourage that player to utilize his/her services;

(3) Providing or offering money or any other thing of value to a member of the player's or prospective player's family or any other person for the purpose of inducing or encouraging that person to recommend the services of the Contract Advisor;

(4) Providing materially false or misleading information to any player or prospective player in the context of recruiting the

player as a client or in the course of representing that player as his Contract Advisor;

(5) Representing or suggesting to any player or prospective player that his/her NFLPA Certification is an endorsement or recommendation by the NFLPA of the Contract Advisor or the Contract Advisor's qualifications or services;

(6) Directly or indirectly borrowing money from any player (whether or not the player is a client), either by receiving the funds directly from the player or by the player providing collateral for or agreeing to guarantee a loan to the Contract Advisor by another party;

(7) Holding or seeking to hold, either directly or indirectly, a financial interest in any professional football club or in any other business entity when such investment could create an actual conflict of interest or the appearance of a conflict of interest in the representation of NFL players;

(8) Engaging in any other activity which creates an actual or potential conflict of interest with the effective representation of NFL players;

(9) Soliciting or accepting money or anything of value from any NFL Club in a way that would create an actual or apparent conflict with the interests of any player that the Contract Advisor represents;

(10) Negotiating and/or agreeing to any provision in a player contract which deprives or purports to deprive that player of any benefit contained in any collectively bargained agreement between the NFL and the NFLPA or any other provision of any applicable documents which protect the working conditions of NFL players;

(11) Negotiating and/or agreeing to any provision in any agreement involving a player which directly or indirectly violates any stated policies or rules established by the NFLPA;

(12) Concealing material facts from any player whom the Contract Advisor is representing which relate to the subject of the player's individual contract negotiation;

(13) Failing to advise the player and to report to the NFLPA any known violations by an NFL Club of a player's individual contract;

(14) Engaging in unlawful conduct and/or conduct involving dishonesty, fraud, deceit, misrepresentation, or other activity which reflects adversely on his/her fitness as a Contract

Advisor or jeopardizes his/her effective representation of NFL players;

(15) Failure to comply with the maximum fee provisions contained in Section 4 of these Regulations;

(16) Circumventing the maximum fee provisions contained in Section 4 of these Regulations by knowingly and intentionally increasing the fees that Contract Advisor charges or otherwise would have charged the player for other services including, but not limited to, financial consultation, money management, and/or negotiating player endorsement agreements; . . .

(18) Filing any lawsuit or other proceeding against a player for any matter which is subject to the exclusive arbitration provisions contained in Section 5 of these Regulations; . . .

(21) (a) Initiating any communication, directly or indirectly, with a player who has entered into a Standard Representation Agreement with another Contract Advisor and such Standard Representation Agreement is on file with the NFLPA if the communication concerns a matter relating to [that player's current contract advisor, SRA, status with an NFL club, or services to be provided under an SRA or otherwise. However, the ban doesn't apply when: the player initiates such communications, the player has less than 60 days remaining on his current NFL Player Contract and has not yet signed a new SRA, and when the agent is sending general advertising directed at players in general.] . . .

(26) Directly or indirectly soliciting a prospective rookie player for representation as a Contract Advisor (a "rookie" shall be defined as a person who has never signed an NFL Player Contract) if that player has signed a Standard Representation Agreement prior to a date which is thirty (30) days before the NFL Draft and if thirty (30 days have not elapsed since the Agreement was signed and filed with the NFLPA.

A Contract Advisor who engages in any prohibited conduct as defined above shall be subject to discipline [including fines, suspension of certification, and decertification].

———

As the NFLPA excerpt illustrates, in designing an agent regulatory program, key issues include:

a. *Coverage.* Who is an "agent" for purposes of such regulation? Union authority to regulate extends only to people who represent players in connection with their employment contracts with teams. Who serves as such a representative? What about the "runners" who assist in recruiting clients? How should such regulation resolve conflicts with state bar codes governing agents who are also lawyers licensed to practice in the relevant jurisdiction? Should unions defer to state regulations that govern dealings between agents and college players or graduates who are not yet on a professional roster?

b.   *Eligibility.* What qualifications should be demanded of someone seeking certification as an approved agent? A law degree? Participation in a training program? A passing score on a test of knowledge of the relevant material in this area of practice? (Should such a test be a one-time entrance exam or one that has to be taken and passed periodically?) A probationary term until successful negotiation of a certain number of player contracts?

c.   *Financial Responsibility.* Should the agent have to demonstrate financial responsibility to practice in this field? Through posting a surety bond? For how large an amount? Just for money managers or also for contract negotiators?

d.   *Solicitation of Business.* Should any active solicitation of players by agents be permitted? Should the agent be permitted to provide something of value to a player as an inducement to sign the agency contract? Should the agent be able to pay third parties for referrals of players? Most important of all, should agents be restricted from even contacting college players whose eligibility has not yet expired?

e.   *Fees.* Within the players associations, the driving force behind regulatory efforts tends to be player concerns about the size of agent fees. An important issue is whether any ceiling at all should be imposed on agent fees, especially a ceiling devised by the players association. If there is to be such a fee scale, should it be based on an hourly rate or a percentage figure? If a percentage, should it be a single rate or one that rises and falls depending on the size of the underlying contract? What is the appropriate percentage figure? Should the base exclude the minimum salary amounts mandated by the collective agreement or amounts paid as incentive bonuses? What about non-guaranteed contract amounts, especially those contained in long-term deals?

Is the same fee percentage appropriate for the negotiation of a player's contract with the team as for the negotiation of an endorsement contract with a product manufacturer or a promotional contract with an outside business? (Players associations do not have authority to regulate these fees, and they generally run in the 10–20% range.) How will the association's answer to these issues likely influence the agent's incentives in negotiations (*e.g.*, to pursue incentive bonuses and long-term deals)?

———————

NOTES AND QUESTIONS

1. *NFLPA Discipline of Agents.* Among the disciplinary measures the NFLPA can impose under its agent regulations are suspension and decertification, during which time the agent may not represent an NFL player or engage in "recruiting activities." At the prospect of losing one's livelihood, most agents appeal such discipline, but rarely gain relief. See *Kivisto v. Nat'l Football League Players Assoc.*, 435 F. App'x 811 (11th Cir. 2011) (dismissing agent's complaint seeking to avoid arbitration of his decertification). Since 2010, the NFLPA has cracked down on agents who violate its rules, including suspending agents who misappropriated or comingled client funds, failed to submit required paperwork for playing contracts, failed to pay fees owed to another agent, failed to disclose interests in a company that separately provided services to athletes, violated NCAA recruiting rules, and were under indictment for fraud and tax evasion. What do you think is driving this crackdown—the union, the players, the honest agents? How do you think the NFLPA's tough regulatory stance has affected its relationship with the agency industry?

2. *Discipline by Other Player Unions.* The NBPA has also toughened its agent regulation, most recently in 2016 when it reinforced its ban on an agent representing both an NBA player and a coach or general manager. The 2016 amendments to NBPA agent regulations also require: decertifying agents who haven't represented a player in a five-year period, disclosure of the use of paid recruiters, and disclosure when an agent refers players to financial advisers. In addition, new agents will now need to pass a written examination to become certified, as in the NFL. Whether these revisions will bring greater vigor to NBPA disciplinary activity has yet to be seen. The NBPA has rarely suspended an agent, a recent notable exception being its 2008 year-long suspension of Calvin Andrews for illegal recruiting tactics and payments involving the University of Southern California basketball star O.J. Mayo.

The MLBPA has also periodically updated its agent regulations, with 2010 additions that primarily address fair competition for clients, a 2013 prohibition against agents lending money to players without the union's approval, and the introduction in 2015 of a written exam and background check for agent applications. In a bizarre 2018 case, the MLBPA suspended agent Jason Wood for allegedly filming his clients with a hidden camera.

3. *Agent Pushback.* As agent regulation has tightened, agents have protested that the rank and file are not making enough money to stay in business, ultimately to the detriment of players who will have fewer agents to choose among. Some NFLPA-certified agents proposed establishing an agent association to advocate for relaxing certification rules and permitting higher commissions. To the extent that such an association works to countermand the union's efforts to protect players from agent incompetence and overreaching, how would it square with the agents' fiduciary duties to their principals?

4. *Which Regulations Matter Most?* Note that players association activity in enforcing agent regulations seems to tilt towards disciplining agent

misconduct in representing a player in contract negotiations or managing a client's finances. When it comes to consumer protection in the recruiting of athletes, unions seem more reluctant to suspend an agent. What explains or justifies this imbalance?

5.   *Agents Representing Athletes in International Sport.* The Fédération Internationale de Football Association (FIFA) withdrew from licensing and overseeing football (soccer) agents in 2015, deputizing its 211 affiliated national football associations to regulate in this area. Five years later it conceded that the move was a mistake, as the resulting system exposed FIFA players and clubs to grossly permissive standards and wildly inconsistent enforcement approaches, and decreased the quality, transparency, and ethics of the services provided. Reregulation is forthcoming as of this casebook edition, with proposals that would cap commissions at three percent of a player's salary, ban clubs from owning a stake in player agencies, and prohibit agents from representing all three parties in a player transfer. What other NFLPA regulations would you advise FIFA to emulate? As FIFA is not a union, and is subject to international competition law, how can it justify regulations that on their face fix prices and exclude participation of some would-be agents?

D. AGENT RECRUITING OF COLLEGE ATHLETES

One feature of the sports agent business that contributes to its characterization as sleazy is the way some agents recruit clients from college. Rather than the athlete paying the agent above the table for his services, the agent pays the athlete below the table to induce the athlete to sign a representation agreement, a practice that violates NCAA regulations requiring students to compete as amateurs. This is a particular problem in football and basketball, where these regulations require rule-abiding athletes to select an agent in a very narrow time frame following completion of intercollegiate eligibility and prior to pursuing their professional career; abuses are less likely in baseball and hockey where players have more time during minor league careers to make a prudent selection.

The NCAA's regulations have been evolving to permit college athletes to hire sports agents to represent them in connection with name, image, and likeness (NIL) deals and, in limited circumstances, to advise regarding turning pro. Chapter 12 examines in more detail the evolution of the NCAA amateurism principle, along with the legal and policy issues it provokes, especially in commercialized college sports like football and basketball. College athletes nonetheless continue to risk their eligibility if they sign with an agent or accept benefits from an agent other than for the stated limited purposes.

To establish prohibited relationships with college athletes, agents will often rely on an intermediary (their "runner"), who is typically around the same age as the athletes. The runner befriends an athlete, picks up the bills for his entertainment, and then delivers the athlete as a client to the agent when the athlete is about to relinquish his college eligibility and turn professional. If these payments are ever disclosed (even after the fact), negative consequences ensue for the agent, the player, and the school, which can incur significant penalties for having played in NCAA-regulated events using athletes who were no longer amateurs. Questions of agent integrity thus frequently arise in the context of college athletics.

PROBLEM 10.5

Ginger Dodge and her sports marketing agency have been representing Zayne Winters, an Ohio State football player, in connection with exploiting his NIL. In the middle of his final season, anticipating selection in the first round of the NFL draft, Winters orally promised to use Dodge as his agent for navigating the draft and negotiating his first playing contract. In exchange, Dodge bought Zayne a pick-up truck and agreed to cover all expenses relating to draft preparation. The agreement was not reduced to writing, and Dodge did not register as an athlete-agent in Ohio.

Just before the draft, Winters switched to another agent for all purposes, including playing contracts and marketing deals. Considering the following public and private law regulation of agent relationships with college athletes, how would you answer these questions:

- Did Dodge violate any rules, regulations, or laws? If so, what are the consequences of any such violations?

- Is Dodge entitled to any remedy here or to compensation based on the contracts negotiated by Winters' new agent?

---

1. AGENT RECRUITING TACTICS AND ENFORCEABILITY OF REPRESENTATION AGREEMENTS

Predating enactment of government regulation of agents discussed later in this chapter, a 1980s case of agent corruption of college athletes produced notoriety and multiple lawsuits. Norby Walters was a successful representative of musicians and entertainers. With Lloyd Bloom, a young acquaintance, Walters expanded into representing athletes, especially football players. Acting as Walters' "runner," Bloom approached college players and offered a cash sum and subsequent monthly payments, in return for the player signing an agency contract post-dated to January 2nd of the player's senior year (after the player's final football season). All agreed to keep the whole arrangement confidential so that the player would not lose his collegiate eligibility, something that would diminish his professional marketability.

Walters and Bloom quickly enjoyed remarkable success. In 1985, they signed ten college players, two of whom were 1986 first-round NFL draft picks. In 1986, they signed 35 players, eight of whom were 1987 first round draft picks. All in all, Walters and Bloom invested roughly $800,000 in recruiting some 60 college players, most in football and a handful of basketball players. However, this economic venture unraveled and spawned numerous legal proceedings for reasons explained in the next case.

NORBY WALTERS AND LLOYD BLOOM V. BRENT FULLWOOD
675 F. Supp. 155 (S.D.N.Y. 1987)

BRIEANT, CHIEF JUDGE.

[In the summer of 1986, Norby Walters and Lloyd Bloom induced Brent Fullwood, star running back for Auburn University, to sign a post-dated representation agreement in return for an immediate payment of $4,000 (secured by a promissory note) and another $4,000 during the fall football season. That spring, the Green Bay Packers selected Fullwood as the fourth pick in the 1987 NFL draft. By that time, however, Fullwood had defected to another agent and repudiated his deal with Walters and Bloom. Thus, Walters and Bloom sued Fullwood, seeking not only to recover the $8,000 they had already paid him, but also to collect the promised 5% commission on Fullwood's multi-million-dollar contract. The key issue posed to the federal judge was whether the secret arrangement between the agents and Fullwood, which had put the player in violation of NCAA regulations, was an enforceable contract under New York law.]

* * *

"We are living in a time when college athletics are honeycombed with falsehood, and when the professions of amateurism are usually hypocrisy. No college team ever meets another today with actual faith in the other's eligibility."

—President William Faunce of Brown University, in a speech before the National Education Association, 1904.

The N.C.A.A. was organized in 1906 largely to combat such evils. Its constitution provides in relevant part that:

Any individual who contracts or who has ever contracted orally or in writing to be represented by an agent in the marketing of the individual's athletic ability or reputation in a sport no longer shall be eligible for intercollegiate athletics in that sport.

N.C.A.A. Constitution, sec. 3–1–(c). Section 3–1–(a) prohibits any player from accepting pay in any form for participation in his college sport, with an exception for a player seeking, directly without the assistance of a third party, a loan from an accredited commercial lending institution against future earnings potential solely in order to purchase insurance against disabling injury.

This Court concludes that the August 1986 loan security agreement and the W.S. & E. agency agreement between Fullwood and the plaintiffs violated Secs. 3–1–(a) and 3–1–(c) of the N.C.A.A. Constitution, the observance of which is in the public interest of the citizens of New York State, and that the parties to those agreements knowingly betrayed an important, if perhaps naive, public trust. Viewing the parties as *in pari delicto*, we decline to serve as "paymaster of the wages of crime, or referee between thieves." We consider both defendant Fullwood's arbitration rights under the N.F.L.P.A. Agents' Regulations, and plaintiffs' rights on their contract and promissory note with Fullwood, unenforceable as contrary to the public policy of New York. "The law 'will not extend its aid to either of the parties' or 'listen to their complaints against each other, but will leave them where their own acts have placed them.' "

Absent these overriding policy concerns, the parties would be subject to the arbitration provisions set forth in section seven of the N.F.L.P.A. Agents' Regulations, and plaintiffs' rights under the contract and promissory note with Fullwood also would be arbitrable. However, under the "public policy" exception to the duty to enforce otherwise-valid agreements, we should and do leave the parties where we find them.

It is well settled that a court should not enforce rights that arise under an illegal contract.

* * *

An agreement may be unenforceable in New York as contrary to public policy even in the absence of a direct violation of a criminal statute, if the sovereign has expressed a concern for the values underlying the policy implicated. In *In re Estate of Walker*, 476 N.E.2d 298, 301 (1985), the Court of Appeals refused to enforce a bequest of adoption decrees to the testator's adopted daughters, concluding that such a bequest, though not criminal, was contrary to public policy. The court concluded, " '[W]hen we speak of the public policy of the state, we mean the law of the state, whether found in the Constitution, the statutes or judicial records.' Those sources express the public will and give definition to the term. A legacy is contrary to public policy, not only if it directly violates a statutory prohibition . . . but also if it is contrary to the social judgment on the subject implemented by the statute."

* * *

The New York State legislature has spoken on the public policies involved in this case, by expressing a concern for the integrity of sporting events in general, and a particular concern for the status of amateur athletics. *See, e.g.*, New York Tax Law sec. 1116(a)(4) (McKinney's supp. 1987) (granting tax exemption to any organization "organized and operating exclusively . . . to foster national or international amateur sports competition"); New York Penal Law Secs. 180.35, 180.40 (McKinney's supp. 1987) (establishing criminal sanctions for sports bribery).

Even were we not convinced of the legislative concern for the values underlying sec. 3–1–(c) of the N.C.A.A. Constitution, New York case law prevents judicial enforcement of contracts the performance of which would provoke conduct established as wrongful by independent commitments undertaken by either party. Not all contracts inducing breaches of other agreements fall within this rule, but those requiring fraudulent conduct are unenforceable as contrary to the public policy of New York.

* * *

In the case before us, no party retains enforceable rights. To the extent plaintiffs seek to recover on the contract or promissory note signed by Fullwood, their wrongful conduct prevents recovery; to the extent Fullwood seeks to compel arbitration, as provided for in the N.F.L.P.A. Agents' Regulations, his own wrongs preclude resort to this Court.

All parties to this action should recognize that they are the beneficiaries of a system built on the trust of millions of people who, with stubborn innocence, adhere to the Olympic ideal, viewing amateur sports as a commitment to competition for its own sake. Historically, amateur athletes have been perceived as pursuing excellence and perfection of their sport as a form of self-realization, indeed, originally, as a form of religious worship, with the ancient games presented as offerings to the gods. By demanding the most from themselves, athletes were believed to approach the divine essence. Through athletic success, the Greeks believed man could experience a kind of immortality.

There also is a modern, secular purpose served by Secs. 3–1–(a) and 3–1–(c) of the N.C.A.A. Constitution. Since the advent of intercollegiate sports in the late 19th century, American colleges have struggled, with varying degrees of vigor, to protect the integrity of higher education from sports-related evils such as gambling, recruitment violations, and the employment of mercenaries whose presence in college athletic programs will tend to preclude the participation of legitimate scholar-athletes.

Sections 3–1–(a) and 3–1–(c) of the N.C.A.A. Constitution were instituted to prevent college athletes from signing professional contracts while they are still playing for their schools. The provisions are rationally related to the commendable objective of protecting the academic integrity of N.C.A.A. member institutions. A college student already receiving payments from his agent, or with a large professional contract signed and ready to take effect upon his graduation, might well be less inclined to observe his academic obligations than a student, athlete or not, with uncertainties about his future career. Indeed, he might not play at his college sport with the same vigor and devotion.

The agreement reached by the parties here, whether or not unusual, represented not only a betrayal of the high ideals that sustain amateur athletic competition as a part of our national educational commitment; it also constituted a calculated fraud on the entire spectator public. Every honest amateur player who took the field with or against Fullwood during the 1986 college football season was cheated by being thrown in with a player who had lost his amateur standing.

In August 1986, Brent Fullwood was one of that select group of college athletes virtually assured of a lucrative professional sports contract immediately upon graduation, absent serious injury during his senior year. The fruits of the system by which amateur players become highly paid professionals, whatever its flaws, were soon to be his. That is precisely why plaintiffs sought him out. Both sides of the transaction knew exactly what they were doing, and they knew it was fraudulent and wrong. This Court and the public need not suffer such willful conduct to taint a college amateur sports program.

[Suit dismissed.]

NOTES AND QUESTIONS

1. *Public Policy Analysis.* The Fullwood decision rests heavily on a perceived New York public policy to protect the integrity of amateur athletics. Do you agree that such a state policy existed at the time? Does one exist today, and if so, where is it manifested? Why is violation of this policy so abhorrent that it justifies nullification of a contract? Would your answer be different for an agent representation agreement entered in a state that has enacted legislation that permits college athletes to monetize their NIL?

2. *Arbitration Requirement.* As an NFLPA-certified agent, Walters was subject to agent regulations that require arbitration of disputes with a player. Accordingly, Fullwood sought to defend Walters' suit in arbitration, a request the federal court denied, holding "[t]he principles requiring non-enforcement of contracts on public policy grounds apply equally to arbitration agreements." Was this a decision the court was entitled to make? How should we reconcile the court's approach with the favoring of arbitration required by federal labor law, as highlighted in Chapter 4?

A state court judge disagreed with the *Fullwood* decision on the arbitration issue, sending to an NLFPA arbitrator claims involving yet another player recruited by Walters through illicit payments and a post-dated representation contract. *See Walters v. Harmon,* 135 Misc.2d 905, 416 N.Y.S.2d 874 (1987). The arbitrator voided the representation agreement between Walters and Ron Harmon, but on totally different grounds. Although the arbitrator acknowledged that the contract violated NCAA rules, he did not take those rules into consideration. Nor did he regard Harmon as an innocent victim of fraud or unequal bargaining power. Instead, he held that the agency agreement was null and void under NFLPA regulations, which if not enforced could lead to "unfettered bribery" and "bidding wars between contract advisors for the rights to represent athletes." The arbitrator did find that Walters had provided valuable services to Harmon, who was required to pay for them in *quantum meruit*, along with reimbursement of Walters's out-of-pocket representation expenses.

3. *Agent Redress in Case of Unenforceable Representation Agreement.* As in *Harmon*, the court in *Total Economic Athletic Management of America v. Pickens*, 898 S.W.2d 98 (Mo. 1995), agreed that an agent is owed something, even if the representation agreement is not enforceable. There, agent Howard Misle sued college football star Bruce Pickens for repudiating an agency contract that Misle had induced with gifts of cash and a luxury car, in violation of both NCAA and NFLPA regulations. Misle sought contract damages of the specified agent fee of four percent of the value of the multi-million-dollar contract Pickens ultimately signed with the Atlanta Falcons. A jury declined to enforce the contract as written, but awarded $20,000 in damages. Affirming the award on appeal, the court held:

> In the context of. professional sports, the player's breach of an agency agreement does not necessarily entitle the agent to commission. Technically, the agent is only entitled to damages for breach of contract, i.e., the value of the promised performance reduced by any expenses saved. In addition, the agent is entitled to his commission only if he can show that, had he been permitted to continue performance, he would have been able to consummate the contracts upon which he claims commission.

Id. at 108.

These and similar cases involving soured relationships between college players and agents pose the question whether rogue agents should be awarded any compensation or reimbursement for their efforts? Or should they receive no redress as a punitive deterrent against such behavior? To what extent should your answer depend on the degree of "innocence" of the college player involved? What about similar advance payments to athletes who never had or have now exhausted college eligibility (*e.g.*, minor league baseball players)? Current union regulations of agents typically bar such payments as well. Why do you suppose they do so?

4. *Ethics of Illicit Payments to College-Athletes.* Walters and Bloom were not unique in paying college players money to sign post-dated agency contracts. Even aside from its deceptive nature, this practice raises significant ethical and legal questions. Why would Walters and Bloom believe it was financially worthwhile to pay clients to sign with them? If a player takes a "signing bonus" from an agent, shouldn't that obligate the player to honor the contract later on? How does that situation differ from a player contract with a team that pays a signing bonus? Even when the agent offers no money, is it ever proper for an agent to pursue college athletes as potential clients? Should it matter whether the athlete's college eligibility has expired?

2. ENFORCING NCAA AMATEURISM RULES AGAINST AGENT MISCONDUCT

Rulings in both the *Fullwood* and *Harmon* cases demonstrate that an agent who pays off student-athletes risks only losing that money and being unable to enforce the agency contract. This risk has proven to have little deterrent value against such agent misconduct. Furthermore, while judge-made contract law and player association regulations attempt to protect the interests of the athlete in this situation, they do not address the interests of the college, which is not a party to the agency relationship.

Because agent payments to athletes (other than for legitimate NIL deals) constitute violations of the NCAA amateurism principles, they also subject the college to a considerable risk of tangible loss. For example, Walters and Bloom secretly signed Alabama's star basketball forward, Derrick McKey, to an agency contract, after which the unknowing school used McKey in the next NCAA tournament. When the NCAA discovered this fact, it required Alabama to forfeit two games it had won and repay the $250,000 the university had received from the tournament. Even if the university learns of an agency contract in time to declare the player ineligible, the university loses one of its best players and thus the chance for a successful season, both athletically and financially. Of course, the risk of loss of eligibility will deter some student-athletes from violating NCAA agent rules, and university compliance efforts often include educating students to these risks.

Yet, the question arises how to put legal teeth behind the surviving NCAA eligibility rules that ban receiving benefits from agents. As a private association, the NCAA lacks the authority to directly regulate the agent industry or sanction agents who impair a college athlete's eligibility, and its eligibility rules are not directly enforceable in court. Many agents candidly treat the NCAA rules as optional. Norby Walters stated that he believed that ignoring the NCAA code was "no different than bending the Knights of Columbus rules." However, federal law enforcement authorities took interest in Walters's sports practice when they learned that members of a New York organized crime family were his partners and investors, and they helped enforce player contracts with physical threats and violence. This connection came to light in March 1987, when a masked man beat the wife of a former Notre Dame quarterback because she was an associate of a Chicago-based sports agent that had attracted a client away from Walters and Bloom. The Chicago U.S. Attorney's office and FBI opened an investigation and ultimately brought criminal charges against Walters.

To establish its jurisdiction in the *Walters* case, the government developed the theory that it was criminal fraud for the player and his agent to hide their relationship in order to maintain the player's scholarship and his NCAA eligibility. This constituted federal mail fraud by virtue of the school mailing the player's annual signed eligibility form to the NCAA head office. Repeated use of this practice further constituted a violation of the Racketeer Influenced and Corrupt Organizations Act (RICO). Under that theory, any time an agent signed a contract with a player who continued to play college ball, both the player and the agent were committing a federal crime, irrespective of whether any money was changing hands. After a long and complex journey through the criminal justice system, the Seventh Circuit was finally required to appraise the legal validity of that theory.

UNITED STATES V. NORBY WALTERS
997 F.2d 1219 (7th Cir. 1993)

EASTERBROOK, CIRCUIT JUDGE.

* * *

"Whoever, having devised . . . any scheme or artifice to defraud, or for obtaining money or property by means of false or fraudulent pretenses, representations, or promises . . . places in any post office or authorized depository for mail matter, any matter or thing whatever to be sent or delivered by the Postal Service . . . or knowingly causes [such matter or thing] to be delivered by mail" commits the crime of mail fraud. Norby Walters did not mail anything or cause anyone else to do so (the universities were going to collect and mail the forms no matter what Walters did), but the Supreme Court has expanded the statute beyond its literal terms, holding that a mailing by a third party suffices if it is "incident to an essential part of the scheme," *Pereira v. United States*, 347 U.S. 1, 8 (1954). While stating that such mailings can turn ordinary fraud into mail fraud, the Court has cautioned that the statute "does not purport to reach all frauds, but only those limited instances in which the use of the mails is a part of the execution of the fraud." *Kann v. United States*, 323 U.S. 88, 95 (1944). Everything thus turns on matters of degree. Did the schemers foresee that the mails would be used? Did the mailing advance the success of the scheme? Which parts of a scheme are "essential?" Such questions lack obviously right answers, so it is no surprise that each side to this case can cite several of our decisions in support. . . .

"The relevant question . . . is whether the mailing is part of the execution of the scheme as conceived by the perpetrator at the time." *Schmuck v. United States*, 489 U.S. 705, 715 (1989). Did the evidence establish that Walters conceived a scheme in which mailings played a role? We think not—indeed, that no reasonable juror could give an affirmative answer to this question. Walters hatched a scheme to make money by taking a percentage of athletes' pro contracts. To get clients he signed students while college eligibility remained, thus avoiding competition from ethical agents. To obtain big pro contracts for these clients he needed to keep the deals secret so the athletes could finish their collegiate careers. Thus deceit was an ingredient of the plan. We may assume that Walters knew that the universities would ask athletes to verify that they were eligible to compete as amateurs. But what role do the mails play? The plan succeeds so long as the athletes conceal their contracts from their schools (and remain loyal to Walters). Forms verifying eligibility do not help the plan succeed; instead they create a risk that it will be discovered if a student should tell the truth. And it is the forms, not their mailing to the Big Ten, that pose the risk. For all Walters cared, the forms could sit forever in cartons. Movement to someplace else was irrelevant. In *Schmuck*, where the fraud was selling cars with rolled-back odometers, the mailing was essential to obtain a new and apparently "clean" certificate of title; no certificates of title, no marketable cars, no hope for success. Even so, the Court divided five to four on the question whether the mailing was sufficiently integral to the scheme. A college's mailing to its conference has less to do with the plot's success than the mailings that transferred title in *Schmuck*.

* * *

No evidence demonstrates that Walters actually knew that the colleges would mail the athletes' forms. The record is barely sufficient to establish that Walters knew of the forms' existence; it is silent about Walters' knowledge of the forms' disposition. The only evidence implying that Walters knew that the colleges had students fill out forms is an ambiguous reference to "these forms" in the testimony of [one of the student-athletes]. . . . Recall that Walters was trying to break into the sports business. Counsel specializing in sports law told him that his plan would not violate any statute. These lawyers were unaware of the forms (or, if they knew about the forms, were unaware that they would be mailed). The prosecutor contends that Walters neglected to tell his lawyers about the eligibility forms, spoiling their opinion; yet why would Walters have to brief an expert in sports law if mailings were foreseeable even to a novice?

* * *

There is a deeper problem with the theory of this prosecution. The United States tells us that the universities lost their scholarship money. Money is property; this aspect of the prosecution does not encounter a problem under *McNally v. United States*, 483 U.S. 350 (1987). Walters emphasizes that the universities put his 58 athletes on scholarship long before he met them and did not pay a penny more than they planned to do. But a jury could conclude that had Walters' clients told the truth, the colleges would have stopped their scholarships, thus saving money. So we must assume that the universities lost property by reason of Walters' deeds. Still, they were not out of pocket to Walters; he planned to profit by taking a percentage of the players' professional incomes, not of their scholarships. Section 1341 condemns "any scheme or artifice to defraud, or for obtaining money or property" (emphasis added). If the universities were the victims, how did he "obtain" their property? Walters asks.

* * *

In this case the mail fraud statute has been invoked to shore up the rules of an influential private association [the NCAA]. [The court compares the NCAA to a cartel whose rules are designed to deter "cheaters" who undermine the profitability of participating universities.] . . . Fanciful? Not at all. Many scholars understand the NCAA as a cartel, having power in the market for athletes. The NCAA depresses athletes' income—restricting payments to the value of tuition, room, and board, while receiving services of substantially greater worth. The NCAA treats this as desirable preservation of amateur sports; a more jaundiced eye would see it as the use of monopsony power to obtain athletes' services for less than the competitive market price. Walters then is cast in the role of a cheater, increasing the payments to the student athletes. Like other cheaters, Walters found it convenient to hide his activities. If, as the prosecutor believes, his repertory included extortion, he has used methods that the law denies to persons fighting cartels, but for the moment we are concerned only with the deceit that caused the universities to pay stipends to "professional" athletes. For current purposes it matters not whether the NCAA actually monopsonizes the market for players; the point of this discussion is that the prosecutor's theory makes criminals of those who consciously cheat on the rules of a private organization, even if that organization is a cartel. We pursue this point because any theory that makes criminals of cheaters raises a red flag.

Cheaters are not self-conscious champions of the public weal. They are in it for profit, as rapacious and mendacious as those who hope to collect monopoly rents. Maybe more; often members of cartels believe that monopoly serves the public interest, and they take their stand on the platform of business ethics, while cheaters' glasses have been washed with cynical acid. Only Adam Smith's invisible hand turns their self-seeking activities to public benefit. It is cause for regret if prosecutors, assuming that persons with low regard for honesty must be villains, use the criminal laws to suppress the competitive process that undermines cartels. Of course federal laws have been used to enforce cartels before. . . . But what is it about [the mail fraud statue] that labels as a crime all deceit that inflicts any loss on anyone? Firms often try to fool their competitors, surprising them with new products that enrich their treasuries at their rivals' expense. Is this mail fraud because large organizations inevitably use the mail? "Any scheme or artifice to defraud, or for obtaining money or property by means of false or fraudulent pretenses, representations, or promises" reads like a description of schemes to get money or property by fraud rather than methods of doing business that incidentally cause losses.

* * *

Reversed.

NOTES AND QUESTIONS

1. *Future of Criminal Prosecution for NCAA Violations.* The *Walters* decision suggests that federal prosecution of agent misbehavior under federal law is not a viable option. *See also Abernathy v. State*, 545 So.2d 185 (Ala. Crim. App. 1988) (unsuccessful prosecution of agent for "tampering with a sporting contest" by paying Auburn football star). Yet, in 2017 the Manhattan U.S. Attorney's office revived the theory underlying the *Walters* prosecution, criminalizing NCAA amateurism violations and indicting college basketball coaches, shoe company marketing executives, and sports agents for bribery, honest services wire fraud, and travel act conspiracy. In one alleged scheme, the coaches took cash bribes from financial advisers, business managers and others, and facilitated bribes directly to student-athletes in exchange for pressuring those athletes to retain the services of these advisers once they entered the NBA. In a second alleged scheme, a top Adidas executive worked in connection with the advisers to funnel bribes to high-school players and their families to induce them to attend universities sponsored by Adidas, and to choose Adidas as their sponsor when they turned pro. A third alleged scheme involved bribes to assistant coaches and youth basketball coaches to steer athletes to particular schools. *See United States v. Gatto*, 295 F. Supp. 3d 336 (S.D.N.Y. 2018) (sustaining indictment). Convictions were obtained in all the prosecutions, and affirmed on appeal. *See United States v. Gatto,* 986 F.3d 104 (2d Cir. 2021). Is it appropriate to use criminal law in this sphere? How should we view these prosecutions now that the NCAA's amateurism principle has been significantly diluted by college athlete NIL exploitation?

2. *Honest Services Fraud Theory.* In *Skilling v. United States,* 561 U.S. 358 (2010), the Supreme Court scaled back the prosecution theory that the mail fraud statute covers schemes to defraud a private-sector employer where the "loss" sustained is not monetary, but rather an intangible right to "honest services." The Court allowed honest service fraud prosecutions of offenders who, in violation of a fiduciary duty, participated in bribery or kickback schemes, but excluded more "amorphous" cases involving conflicts of interest and undisclosed self-dealing. In which category would you place the schemes alleged in the NCAA basketball indictment described in the previous note?

3. *Student-Athlete Antitrust Challenges to NCAA Regulation.* The *Walters* decision observes that "a more jaundiced eye would see [the NCAA rules] as the use of monopsony power to obtain athletes' services for less than the competitive market price." This statement anticipates by almost 30 years the Supreme Court's decision in *Nat'l Collegiate Athletic Ass'n v. Alston,* 141 S. Ct. 2141 (2021), which struck down under the antitrust laws NCAA limits on education-related benefits that schools can offer to recruit and retain student-athletes. (See Chapter 12, Section D). Although the NCAA has relaxed aspects of the "no-agent" rule since *Walters,* it continues to attempt to control when and which agents can provide advisory services to student-athletes. If elite college basketball players want to test the draft, they can hire only agents

who obtain NCAA certification by paying a fee and passing a test. By what authority, if any, does the NCAA purport to certify sports agents? What does this additional layer of agent regulation add to that already imposed by professional sports players unions and state and federal statutory schemes? As a private association that does not enjoy a union's labor law immunity from antitrust, do the NCAA's agent rules risk challenge as a group boycott of uncertified agents?

E. GOVERNMENT REGULATION OF AGENTS

The substantive issues and cases presented in the prior sections raise a broader systemic question: what role should government play—at both the federal and state levels—in directly regulating agents to secure high quality and ethical representation of athletes? As it turns out, that role has been largely confined to protecting universities from the single problem exemplified by the *Walters* case—agent recruiting of college athletes whose eligibility has not yet expired. The states entered the field first.

1. STATE LEGISLATION

The representation of athletes is an occupation subject to the kinds of legal controls that now govern activities ranging from medicine to hairdressing. While some agents have argued that such regulatory and licensing schemes violate the federal Constitution's "dormant" commerce clause by imposing an unreasonable burden on interstate commerce, this argument seems unlikely to prevail under current constitutional standards. *See South Dakota v. Wayfair, Inc.*, 138 S. Ct. 2080 (2018) (internet seller's physical presence in taxing state is not necessary for state to require seller to collect and remit its sales tax). Labor law preemption, however, poses a higher barrier to state regulation of agents' representation of *unionized* athletes. Because NLRB-certified unions are the exclusive bargaining representatives of employees, and they delegate some of this authority to their certified agents, state regulation of any of these agents' representation of union members would interfere with the exercise of protected concerted activity.

The pioneer in regulating sports agents was the California legislature, which in 1982 enacted the Athlete Agents Act that required agents engaging in activities in the state to register with the Secretary of State and to follow the rules set forth in the statute. Numerous states adopted similar laws, resulting in a patchwork of agent regulation with varying definitions of covered student-athletes, registration procedures and renewals, disclosure requirements, educational prerequisites, exemptions (*e.g.*, for attorneys), procedures for notifying educational institutions of agency contracts with college-athletes, and enforcement methods. By the 1990s, 28 states were in the business of regulating sports agents, most of which were home to one or more colleges that are traditional powers in

either football or basketball. However, this regulation was largely
ineffective, with few agents bothering to register and few states dedicating
resources to law enforcement.

The Uniform Athlete Agent Act

In 2000, a commission on uniform state laws promulgated the Uniform
Athlete Agent Act (UAAA), a version of which has been adopted in 42
jurisdictions as of 2022. The UAAA is periodically revised, most recently in
2019, and has been restyled the Revised Uniform Athlete Agent Act
(RUAAA). The prefatory note to the RUAAA reads:

> With the immense amount of money at stake for a wide
> variety of professional athletes and those who represent them, the
> commercial marketplace in which athlete agents operate is
> extremely competitive. While seeking to best position one's clients
> and to maximize their potential income is both legal and good
> business practice, the recruitment of a student athlete while he or
> she is still enrolled in an educational institution can and will
> cause substantial eligibility problems for both the student and the
> institution, which can in turn lead to severe economic sanctions
> and loss of scholarships. The problem is more acute where an
> unscrupulous agent misleads a student, especially where the
> athlete is not aware of the implications of signing the agency
> agreement or where an agency contract is entered without notice
> to the institution. In response to these issues, the Uniform Athlete
> Agents Act (UAAA) was promulgated by the Uniform Law
> Commission (ULC) in 2000. . . .

> [S]everal states have amended the act to, among other things,
> deal with a perceived lack of enforcement, broaden the coverage
> of the act to individuals who do not necessarily recruit or solicit a
> student athlete to enter into an agency contract, and require
> notice to educational institutions prior to contact. It became
> evident that the variations from state to state put uniformity at
> risk and may have discouraged reputable agents from complying
> with the act. To deal with these issues, the Uniform Law
> Commission adopted the Revised Uniform Athlete Agents Act
> (RUAAA) in July of 2015.

The RUAAA, like its predecessors and like agent regulation in non-
adopter states, focuses on the harm done to amateur athletes and their
universities when athletes sign with agents before their eligibility has
expired. To protect against this harm, the RUAAA regulates agent
interactions with amateur athletes in several ways, including:

1.   Agents must register with the state and disclose training,
experience, education, criminal convictions, civil determinations of false or

deceptive representations, and any disciplinary action against the agent. Agents may not contact a student-athlete without first being registered. To encourage compliance with the Act, registration in one state entitles the agent to reciprocity in other RUAAA states.

2.   All representation agreements must be in writing, signed by both parties, with clear provisions specifying agent compensation and a statement as to the athlete agent's registration status.

3.   All representation agreements must contain an explicit bold warning, signed by the student-athlete, that by entering into the agreement, the athlete may be forfeiting any further NCAA eligibility. The athlete is then given a 14-day "cooling off" period within which to change his mind and cancel the agreement.

4.   Agents are prohibited from offering "anything of value to any person to induce a student athlete" to enter into a representation agreement.

5.   The agent and/or the athlete must notify the educational institution within 72 hours that a representation agreement has been signed.

The RUAAA's restrictions on agent dealings with college athletes are enforced by a variety of sanctions, including criminal prosecution with the possibility of imprisonment or fines, and a right conferred on the institution and the student-athlete to sue the agent for damages suffered as the result of the agent's conduct. A university's damages can include financial losses associated with NCAA discipline. Finally, there is an administrative penalty of up to $50,000 for violation of the statute.

At least three states, including California, continue to regulate agents under non-UAAA laws. California has periodically reformed its agent legislation, now known as the Miller-Ayala Act, to enlarge substantive requirements and impose stiffer penalties for violations than does the UAAA. The Miller-Ayala Act includes a cause of action against agents; it empowers not just institutions and athletes, but any "adversely affected" party to file a state court suit for actual and punitive damages arising out of an agent's violation, specifying a minimum award of $50,000. In addition, if a court finds that an agent violated the Miller-Ayala Act, it *must* revoke that agent's privileges to do business in the state for at least one year and order the agent to disgorge fees. The University of Southern California availed itself of these remedies in the 1990s, suing sports agent Robert Caron after learning that he had given three USC football players benefits that rendered them ineligible to play. USC settled out of court, receiving $50,000 in damages from the agent.

Enforcement of State Agent Regulations

The appropriate scope and practical effects of such state regulation raise serious questions. For example, given the national cast to professional sports, should the reach of the state regulation turn on the agent's home base, or the player's home base, or the location of the college from which the player is coming, or the location of the team to which he is going, or all of the above? With nearly every state insisting on agent registration, each requiring its own registration fees, surety bonds, and administrative paperwork, the cumulative cost of such regulation inevitably reduces either the number of agents who are competing to work on behalf of athletes or the number of active agents who are complying with the licensing requirements.

Further, despite legislative consensus on the need for agent regulation, it has neither served as a significant deterrent to agent misconduct nor resulted in significant enforcement. On the criminal side, only a handful of UAAA prosecutions have been brought, including:

- 2017 North Carolina prosecution of Terry Watson for providing thousands of dollars in improper benefits to three former UNC players to induce them to sign with him.

- 2008 Alabama prosecution of Raymond Savage, a Virginia-based agent, and his runner Jason Goggins, for failing to register under Alabama's UAAA and initiating contact with a student athlete.

- 2006 Louisiana prosecution of Charles Taplin for violating the Act's registration and notification provisions by texting to Louisiana State University football players on behalf of an agent, and of former LSU strength coach Travelle Gaines for inviting players to his home to meet an agent.

A 2010 Associated Press study found that more than half of the states that had enacted a version of the UAAA had yet to revoke or suspend any agent registrations, or impose any sort of penalty on agent misconduct. According to the AP study, Texas was a lone outlier, with 31 agents receiving civil discipline and paying fines totaling $17,500. Why aren't states doing more to enforce the UAAA? How should state-level investigators and prosecutors prioritize these cases against high-level felonies and violent crime?

A form of private civil enforcement of the UAAA has emerged in lawsuits contesting the enforceability of representation agreements signed while the athlete was still a college student. In UAAA states, agents have learned the hard way the importance of meticulous compliance with those regulations. An Ohio court threw out the CSE Talent agency's lawsuit seeking to enforce its oral agreement with high school baseball standout Nick Northcut because the agency failed to register with the state under its "athlete-agent" statute, and to reduce the representation agreement to writing using statutorily-required language. *CSE Talent, LLC v. Northcut*, No. 20-CV93505 (Ohio Ct. Comm. Pl. Oct. 12, 2020). CSE had provided services to Northcut to prepare for MLB's amateur draft, in exchange for a 10 percent commission on his first contract. When Northcut was drafted by the Boston Red Sox, he switched agents to negotiate his contract and declined to repay CSE the $55,000 it had invested in him. Because the Ohio statute rendered the contract void ab initio, the court declined to award any compensation even under an unjust enrichment theory. Notably, the Ohio statute contemplates prosecution of agent noncompliance as misdemeanors subject to a 180-day jail term, which might explain why CSE cut its losses and did not appeal the ruling.

Likewise, Duke basketball star Zion Williamson obtained a declaratory judgment voiding a written marketing agreement with agent Gina Ford, signed just before he entered the NBA draft. The court found that Ford had violated the North Carolina Uniform Athlete-Agent Act by failing to register as an agent in the state or to include required warnings in the agreement. *Williamson v. Prime Sports Mktg., LLC*, 2021 WL 201255 (M.D.N.C. Jan. 20, 2021). Grasping to uphold the contract, Ford argued that Williamson had forfeited his status as an "eligible student-athlete" protected under the North Carolina Act because Duke allegedly paid family members to recruit him in violation of NCAA rules. The court rejected this argument:

> Defendants have not alleged or provided any facts to plausibly support their conclusory claims that Plaintiff [Williamson] was permanently ineligible to compete in intercollegiate athletics at the time the parties entered into the Agreement. Defendants' listing of purported offenses are insufficient to raise a genuine issue of material fact as to whether Plaintiff had been deemed permanently ineligible during the time period in question and thus no longer a student-athlete under the UAAA. Defendants have provided no authority, caselaw or otherwise, that suggests that it is for a court to adjudicate the details of a student-athlete's eligibility under NCAA rules. Rather, in applying the statute, it would appear that the Court's role is to determine whether the student-athlete has been either determined to be or declared "permanently ineligible" by the governing body authorized to do so. Defendants have not alleged that this has occurred.

Should the court have deferred to the NCAA's disinclination to pursue allegations of recruiting violations that would have forfeited Williamson's eligibility? Having determined the underlying contract was void, the court ruled that North Carolina law required dismissal of Ford's counterclaims for unjust enrichment. *See Williamson v. Prime Sports Mktg., LLC*, 2022

WL 2802611 (M.D.N.C. July 18, 2022) (granting summary judgment dismissing Ford's counterclaims).

2. FEDERAL LEGISLATION

In 2004, Congress entered the agent regulation field by enacting the Sports Agent and Responsibility Trust Act (SPARTA). 15 U.S.C. §§ 7801 *et seq*. This Act brought sports agent activity under the regulatory jurisdiction of the Federal Trade Commission and imposed disclosure and conduct duties on agents that can be enforced by state attorneys general or the FTC. As a federal enactment, SPARTA is not vulnerable to the possible constitutional and labor law impediments facing state regulation.

SPARTA emulates much of the original UAAA and forbids sports agents from: (1) giving false or misleading information to a student-athlete; (2) making false or misleading promises or misrepresentations to a student-athlete; (3) providing anything of value to the student or any individual associated with the student, including friends and family; (4) failing to disclose in writing that the student may lose eligibility to compete as a student-athlete if he or she signs an agency contract; and (5) predating or postdating contracts. The act also requires the agent and athlete to notify the athletic director at the student's school within 72 hours of signing a contract. Violations can be enforced under the Federal Trade Commission Act as unfair or deceptive acts or practices punishable by fines of up to $11,000 per incident, to be paid by the sports agent. The Act expressly supplements current state agent regulation laws; it does not replace or preempt these laws since nothing in it is inconsistent with any state requirements.

Although SPARTA appears to provide a national, uniform standard and framework for deterring unethical agent conduct, the FTC to date has not taken any action against an agent under SPARTA. Does this suggest to you important differences in the competence and concern of the respective government sources of regulation? What explains the federal government's total lack of enforcement of SPARTA?

3. ETHICS RULES GOVERNING ATTORNEY-AGENTS

Many sports agents are also attorneys who must also comply with rules of professional conduct. These ethical obligations are potentially a competitive disadvantage insofar as non-attorney agents are not equally bound. While some attorney-agents have argued that they should not be subject to professional codes with respect to non-legal work for athletes, that theory largely has been rejected. *See, e.g., Matter of Frederick J. Henley*, 478 S.E.2d 134 (Ga. 1996); *Cuyahoga County Bar Assoc. v. Glenn*, 649 N.E.2d 1213 (Ohio 1995); Illinois State Bar Assoc., Op. No. 700 (Nov. 4, 1980) (attorneys who act as sports agents are subject to bar rules). In any event, it is incumbent on attorney-agents to make clear that athletes who hire them gain an advantage by retaining an agent who is held to a higher standard in terms of both ethics and competence. Consider some of the attorney rules most relevant in this context, from the American Bar Association's Model Rules of Professional Conduct (2020):

Rule 1.1 Competence

A lawyer shall provide competent representation to a client. Competent representation requires the legal knowledge, skill, thoroughness and preparation reasonably necessary for the representation.

Rule 1.5 Fees

(a) A lawyer shall not make an agreement for, charge, or collect an unreasonable fee or an unreasonable amount for expenses. The factors to be considered in determining the reasonableness of a fee include the following:

(1) the time and labor required, the novelty and difficulty of the questions involved, and the skill requisite to perform the legal service properly; . . .

(3) the fee customarily charged in the locality for similar legal services; . . .

(6) the nature and length of the professional relationship with the client;

(7) the experience, reputation, and ability of the lawyer or lawyers performing the services; . . . .

Rule 1.7 Conflict of Interest: Current Clients

(a) Except as provided in paragraph (b), a lawyer shall not represent a client if the representation involves a concurrent conflict of interest. A concurrent conflict of interest exists if:

(1) the representation of one client will be directly adverse to another client; or

(2) there is a significant risk that the representation of one or more clients will be materially limited by the lawyer's responsibilities to another client, a former client or a third person or by a personal interest of the lawyer.

(b) Notwithstanding the existence of a concurrent conflict of interest under paragraph (a), a lawyer may represent a client if:

(1) the lawyer reasonably believes that the lawyer will be able to provide competent and diligent representation to each affected client;

(2) the representation is not prohibited by law;

(3) the representation does not involve the assertion of a claim by one client against another client represented by the lawyer in the same litigation or other proceeding before a tribunal; and

(4) each affected client gives informed consent, confirmed in writing.

Rule 1.8 Conflict Of Interest: Current Clients: Specific Rules

(a) A lawyer shall not enter into a business transaction with a client or knowingly acquire an ownership, possessory, security or other pecuniary interest adverse to a client unless:

(1) the transaction and terms on which the lawyer acquires the interest are fair and reasonable to the client and are fully disclosed and transmitted in writing in a manner that can be reasonably understood by the client;

(2) the client is advised in writing of the desirability of seeking and is given a reasonable opportunity to seek the advice of independent legal counsel on the transaction; and

(3) the client gives informed consent, in a writing signed by the client, to the essential terms of the transaction and the lawyer's role in the transaction, including whether the lawyer is representing the client in the transaction.

(b) A lawyer shall not use information relating to representation of a client to the disadvantage of the client unless the client gives informed consent, except as permitted or required by these Rules.

(c) A lawyer shall not solicit any substantial gift from a client, including a testamentary gift, or prepare on behalf of a client an instrument giving the lawyer or a person related to the lawyer any substantial gift unless the lawyer or other recipient of the gift is related to the client. . . .

Rule 5.5 Unauthorized Practice Of Law; Multijurisdictional Practice Of Law

(a) A lawyer shall not practice law in a jurisdiction in violation of the regulation of the legal profession in that jurisdiction, or assist another in doing so.

(b) A lawyer who is not admitted to practice in this jurisdiction shall not:

(1) except as authorized by these Rules or other law, establish an office or other systematic and continuous presence in this jurisdiction for the practice of law; or

(2) hold out to the public or otherwise represent that the lawyer is admitted to practice law in this jurisdiction.

Rule 7.3 Solicitation of Clients

. . .

(b) A lawyer shall not by in-person, live telephone or real-time electronic contact solicit professional employment from a prospective client when a significant motive for the lawyer's doing so is the lawyer's pecuniary gain, unless the person contacted is with a:

> (1) lawyer;

> (2) a person who has a family, close personal, or prior professional relationship with the lawyer or law firm; or

> (3) person who routinely uses for business purposes the type of legal services offered by the lawyer.

(c) A lawyer shall not solicit professional employment even when not otherwise prohibited by paragraph (b), if:

> (1) the target of the solicitation has made known to the lawyer a desire not to be solicited by the lawyer; or

> (2) the solicitation involves coercion, duress or harassment. . . .

NOTES AND QUESTIONS

1.   *Competence.* A non-lawyer has no formal competency requirement such as those contained in the Model Rules. However, under common law, an agent is under the legal duty to represent an athlete with competence on par with that displayed by others who represent athletes. As discussed above, athletes can bring malpractice claims against negligent non-attorney agents. Why might this remedy be less effective than a similar claim against an attorney-agent? What other ways can athletes hold accountable attorneys who have not adequately served their interests?

2.   *Fees.* Although some leagues fix agent fees for player contract negotiation services, other leagues leave that up to the player and agent to negotiate. And fees for management services and negotiating other revenue deals are similarly unregulated for non-attorney agents. An attorney, however, may charge only a "reasonable" fee. How do you think that affects, in practice, the way attorneys structure revenue deals for their athlete-clients?

3.   *Conflicts of Interest.* An attorney-agent is ostensibly more sensitive to the potential for conflicts of interest in representing different athletes and other sports industry participants. Thus, an attorney-agent arguably will not give one athlete-client precedence over another in negotiating a deal based on their relative star quality. In negotiating an endorsement deal, an attorney-agent will avoid recommending a deal in order to collect a fee, and must consider the athlete's long-term interests. In obtaining informed consent from an athlete-client to a potential or actual conflict of interest, an attorney-agent

is more likely to provide the necessary disclosures and ensure the client's consent is fully knowledgeable. Do you agree that attorney-agents will in reality conduct themselves and their athlete-clients' business more ethically and loyally?

4. *Unenforceable Representation Agreement.* Agents who are also attorneys run the risk that they will not be able to enforce representation agreements that do not strictly comply with professional conduct codes. That fate befell the attorney-agent at the helm of Sports Management Network, which represented stock car racer Kurt Busch in negotiating with racing teams without disclosing that it also represented many of those teams. After learning of the conflicts, Busch refused to pay commissions and fees owed to SMN, and obtained a court ruling that Michigan attorney conduct rules negated the representation agreement and his obligation to pay. *Sports Mgmt. Network v. Busch*, 2019 WL 1057314 (E.D. Mich. Mar. 6, 2019). Consider whether Busch's victory would have been as complete if the agent were not an attorney and Busch could only rely on agency and fiduciary duty law.

5. *Solicitation.* Identify the ways that the Model Rules ban on attorney solicitation is more restrictive and less restrictive than UAAA and SPARTA regulation of recruitment of college athletes. In what ways do you think the professional rules compel attorney-agents to vary their recruitment practices from non-attorneys? While there is no guarantee that attorney-agents will avoid aggressive recruitment practices, consider how much more the lawyer has to lose if caught.

6. *Unauthorized Practice of Law.* Attorney-agents with active sports practices will unavoidably serve athlete-clients in multiple jurisdictions as players move from college to the pros and from team to team. How can an attorney in this situation comply with the requirement to be licensed as a lawyer everywhere she actually practices? Implicit in the competitive tension between non-attorney agents and attorney agents is that non-attorney agents themselves are engaging in unauthorized practice of law. However, few jurisdictions actively enforce their UPL restrictions, and have little incentive to do so against sports agents increasingly subject to parallel—if similarly rarely enforced—ethical regulations. To what extent has this regulatory failure allowed non-attorney agents to exploit their "operational" freedom vis-à-vis attorney agents to dominate the business and possibly its reputation?

CHAPTER 11

INTERCOLLEGIATE SPORTS: THE STUDENT-ATHLETE

■ ■ ■

A. THE NCAA

The National Collegiate Athletic Association ("NCAA") is an organization comprised of around 1,200 member institutions—colleges and universities—in roughly 100 athletics conferences allocated over three Divisions. While the employees of the NCAA interpret and support member legislation, run championships, and manage programs that benefit student-athletes, the college and university presidents work through a committee structure to create the rules and regulations that govern athletic competition and eligibility requirements.

This large operation annually involves almost 500,000 athletes on 19,500 teams, with 90 championships in 24 sports. Division I includes 37% of NCAA athletes, with 57% receiving athletics aid, usually in the form of multiyear, cost-of-attendance athletics scholarships. Division II includes 25% of NCAA athletes, with 60% of athletes receiving athletics aid, usually in the form of partial athletics scholarships. Finally, Division III includes 39% of NCAA athletes, of whom 80% receive non-athletics financial aid. The funding for the NCAA comes almost entirely from the NCAA Division I basketball tournament, March Madness, which generates over $1 billion annually, mostly through television contracts.

Critics of the NCAA treat it as a monolithic institution with top-down, staff-directed directed decision-making, but in reality, its governance structure is a complicated one, involving a number of different entities. The Board of Governors oversees the organization as a whole and help set Association-wide policy. To aid in this process, there are a number of Association-wide committees to address specific issues. To enact legislation, however, the Board of Governors sends proposals to the legislative branches of each of the three divisions. In addition, the Division I Board of Directors, the Division II Presidents Council, and the Division III Presidents Council set policies for their respective divisions.

The NCAA's membership has attempted to balance tensions between variant and often conflicting interests, particularly as college sports has become more commercialized. Members, not surprisingly, aim to shape policy in their own institutional interests, which sometimes conflict with the best interests of intercollegiate sports and typically conflict with the institutional interests of other members. Part of this tension lies in the less commercially successful schools seeking to place competitive balance limitations on the more commercially successful schools.

In 2014, the NCAA passed a new model giving the Power 5 conferences—the Southeastern Conference (SEC), the Big Ten, the Pac-12, the Atlantic Coast Conference (ACC), and the Big Twelve—autonomy to create their own legislation and voting rights with respect to particular governance issues, including offering students the full cost of attendance, allowing students to borrow against future earnings when obtaining insurance, and monitoring time athletes spend on their sports.

In 2022, the NCAA adopted a new constitution, streamlining some of its processes, providing for increased athlete participation in governance, and accounting for state laws that empower college athletes to monetize their name, image, and likeness. Significantly, Article II of the new constitution decentralizes the NCAA's authority, delegating to each division the task of setting its own rules and shifting power to schools and conferences. This delegation includes the ability of the divisions to establish and enforce eligibility and academic standards.

For instance, Division I convened a "Transformation Committee" still at work at the time of this edition's publication, but the committee's name foretells the significance of the changes to expect. This new NCAA is likely to look very different, even in the near future, as it is moving from a one-size-fits-all approach to one that creates different sets of rules for different subgroups of institutions. As discussed in Chapter 13, the major moves in conference realignment certainly threaten the status quo at the more commercial end of the spectrum.

Generally, NCAA members still embrace the policy that college athletes should not receive compensation from their institution beyond the cost of their education. The actual rationales of individual university presidents and athletic directors vary. Many remain philosophically committed to the concept of the amateur "student-athlete" who participates in intercollegiate sports for the intrinsic benefits the student receives. Many are philosophically committed to a broad program allowing hundreds of athletes to compete with high levels of training, traveling, and financial support, and fear that this would not be possible if they paid athletes in commercially-successful sports. In a similar vein, many believe that the budgetary pressures of paying athletes will lead universities to abandon academic and social service programs that support those very athletes. Many live in fear that their university's program is barely able to compete at its current level, and paying athletes will give currently dominant programs an additional advantage. Some fear that paying athletes will lead to unionization of players, adding costs and ceding power. As a result, the NCAA as an institution continues to articulate a policy that their players are "student-athletes" who participate in sports as part of their education.

Historically, the NCAA model has endeavored to "protect" student-athletes from exploitation by professional and commercial enterprises. Thus, it banned from competition any individuals who receive significant financial benefits outside of tuition, room, board, books, and cost of attendance. Because the approved financial benefits all relate to education, they did not, from the NCAA's perspective, compromise the amateur status of the athletes.

Since the 1990s, this model has faced external pressure because of the significant amount of money that the revenue sports—college football and college basketball—generate, with both being multi-billion dollar industries. These soaring financial figures have caused many to claim that commercialization jeopardizes the principles that supposedly make intercollegiate sports unique, including amateurism. Serious questions arise as to whether the mass public appeal and commercial opportunities in big-time college sports, particularly in Division I-A football and Division I men's basketball, are in fundamental tension with the NCAA's stated purpose of conducting intercollegiate sports in a manner designed to protect and enhance the physical and educational welfare of student-athletes.

Advocates of pay for play find the NCAA's rhetoric dubious. They characterize college athletics as a big business with the luxury of largely free labor, or at the very least, labor with a restricted salary cap of tuition, room, board, books, and cost of attendance. They stress that many athletes come to the university to enhance their ability to become a professional athlete, despite the slim odds of realizing that dream. These critics claim that the NCAA and its member institutions exploit the revenue sport athletes by denying them a share in the profits they generate. For some the solution is paying the athletes; for others it is reducing the commercial pressure on the current model to develop a better version of the status quo.

Others question the educational opportunities offered to revenue sport athletes, who often spend sixty or more hours per week on athletics during the season. Even with tutors, the time demands of sports participation—particularly the revenue sports—can make academic performance very challenging, especially where the student involved struggled to qualify academically in the first place. Certainly, universities have incentive to compromise academic integrity, especially where an athlete's eligibility is at stake.

There are, however, success stories that occur at the intersection of academics and athletics. The NCAA and its member institutions point out that athletes graduate at a higher rate than non-athletes, though in many cases, it is the success of the non-revenue sport athletes that makes the difference. In addition, it is clear that the overall academic profile of many institutions has risen because athletics attracts strong non-athlete students to attend, as the proverbial "front porch" of the university.

Nonetheless, athletics can sometimes pose a problem for the academic pursuits of strong students, where the demands of the athletic team make taking certain classes or enrolling in certain majors virtually impossible. The recent phenomenon of clustering, where many members of one athletic team all major in the same discipline and/or take the same series of pre-approved classes, bears this out. Even where academic advisors, students, tutors, and faculty are all working together to ensure athletes have a legitimate and robust academic experience, the pressure generated by intercollegiate athletics raises serious questions about the NCAA's narrative with respect to certain institutions.

The NCAA, to its credit, is considering reforms related to limiting the amount of time athletes can spend on their sports. While there are limits on formal practice time, informal participation can result in athletes spending in excess of fifty hours per week on their sport during the season. Under the new constitution, the results may differ among the different divisions, but new legislation on this issue is likely in 2023.

Finally, it is no secret that some athletes attend universities as a required stepping stone to a professional career given that they are not draft eligible until they have been out of high school for at least one year for the NBA and three years for the NFL. Elite athletes in football and basketball thus choose NCAA athletics largely because there is no other established route to become a high draft pick, although that is changing in the NBA with the growth of its development league and international playing opportunities. Not surprisingly, the use of college athletics as a professional stepping stone creates tension with the education and amateurism ideals advanced by the NCAA.

The summer of 2021 marked a major transformation in college athletics away from amateurism. The Supreme Court in *NCAA v. Alston*, 141 S. Ct. 2141 (2021), ruled that the Sherman Act barred NCAA limits on universities providing college athletes with benefits "related to education." That means universities can now provide college athletes with a wide range of additional inducements such as musical instruments, computers, expenses related to study abroad, paid internships, and tuition for post-graduate programs and vocational schools.

Perhaps more importantly, many states adopted name, image, and likeness (NIL) laws that went into effect on July 1, 2021. These NIL laws reinstated college athletes' right to exploit their celebrity and receive third-party compensation for doing so, and barred the NCAA from punishing athletes or their institutions for such activities. The NCAA subsequently changed its rules to allow for all college athletes to receive third-party NIL compensation, even in states that did not pass NIL laws. Even so, college athletes are still amateurs in that NCAA rules continue to prohibit universities from compensating their athletes for playing their sport, or providing benefits unrelated to education.

The future of college sports remains unknown. What is clear is that the NCAA's amateurism model is facing the possibility of significant change in the near future.

B. ADMISSIONS AND ELIGIBILITY

NCAA rules specify the academic credentials required of athletes who graduate from high school and want to play in intercollegiate athletics. In order to facilitate this process, the NCAA runs a clearinghouse of information to help high school students through the process of obtaining eligibility. As explored below, the NCAA has adopted a sliding scale through which a student must receive a minimum combination of high school grades and test scores. In addition, the students must achieve a minimum grade point average in a number of required high school courses.

For years, university admissions departments have struggled with the weight and value ascribed to standardized admissions tests. With athletes, these conflicts can become more pronounced as some athletes in revenue sports have test scores that fall below some institutions' requirements. Much of the controversy in placing too much weight on standardized tests stems from empirical data showing that test outcomes are disparate based on race, and have built-in biases.

With the COVID-19 pandemic, the NCAA suspended the standardized test requirement for athletes beginning with the 2020–21 academic year. The NCAA has continued this no test requirement policy through the 2023–24 academic year, and some are advocating for a permanent abolition of this requirement. As you read the following materials, consider whether the NCAA should abandon its testing requirement.

The future of this legislation may be more diffuse in light of the new 2022 constitution which reallocates this legislation to the three different divisions. The divisions will now have their own ability to set admissions and eligibility standards, which could create significant variation.

In its early days, the NCAA followed a policy of college "home rule" in allowing schools to make the judgment about whether or not to admit athletes into their classes. At its 1964 Convention, though, the membership adopted a "1.6 Predictor Rule" that conditioned eligibility for participating in intercollegiate sports upon the student-athlete's academic prospects for meeting a minimum 1.6 predicted grade point average (GPA) in college. This prediction was based on the student's high school GPA and class ranking, combined with their Scholastic Aptitude Test (SAT) or American College Test (ACT) scores, as assessed through expectancy tables that incorporated statistics for over 40,000 students at more than 80 colleges.

The debate about the impact of this rule surfaced in the federal courts in a case involving Centenary College's effort to play a center who had not met this 1.6 Predictor standard—future NBA Hall of Famer Robert Parish, who would later help lead the Boston Celtics to three NBA championships in the 1980s.

PARISH V. NCAA
361 F. Supp. 1220 (W.D. La. 1973)

DAWKINS, CHIEF JUDGE.

* * *

Parish, 7′ 1″ in height, denominated a "super-athlete," was recognized during his last high school year by national magazines, newspapers, and sports columnists as probably the number one or number two leading basketball prospect in the United States, in the manner of Wilt Chamberlain and Lew Alcindor. He was named to several All-American high school teams and chosen by the Basketball News as the number one high school graduate basketball player in the country. Of course, he was recruited, even courted, by almost every major college in the nation.

In order to fulfill the requirements of NCAA's 1.600 Rule, Parish took the ACT twice, his score being an 8. Regrettably, before achieving such prominence, he had been somewhat deprived, both educationally and economically; and probably began to aspire ambitiously toward a full higher education only after "the baskets began to swish." With this score, most colleges "backed off" because they felt Parish could not meet the 1.600 requirement.

* * *

[Centenary, however, did sign Parish up to the then-standard four-year athletic scholarship after converting his ACT test scores to SAT scores (which he still did not meet). Though he did have significantly higher college grades than the NCAA minimum, the Association suspended him and several of his teammates from playing basketball, and so they went off to court. As the judge put it, he was facing] a "Hobson's choice," which we do not relish at all, considering the empathy we hold for all of these competing interests: 1) the careers of these young athletes; 2) their present and future prospects; 3) the outstanding degree of culture contributed by the institution known as Centenary College, locally, regionally, and nationally, since well before the War Between the States; and finally, 4) the nationwide elevation of scholastic and athletic standards developed by NCAA for so many years.

* * *

Addressing the merits, even if [education] is a right or privilege protected by the Constitution, we hold that the 1.600 Rule withstands the denial of equal protection attack because it has a rational relationship to legitimate State (or national) purposes. Obviously, the challenged action by NCAA is not subject to strict judicial scrutiny. Therefore, we turn to the traditional standard of review which requires only that the NCAA's system be shown to bear some rational relationship to legitimate purposes. NCAA adopted the 1.600 Rule as a means of insuring that the athlete be an integral part of the student body and to maintain intercollegiate athletics as an integral part of the education program. Mr. Byers, of NCAA, summarized the need for these rules, as establishing a minimum standard which would prevent exploitation of athletes by the college or university, that is, setting up and agreeing to the prediction process by NCAA's members in order to prevent recruitment for athletic purposes alone of young men who had relatively poor chances of obtaining academic degrees; to encourage institutions with lower standards to elevate those standards to be more compatible with other institutions; and to discourage the unsound academic and economic practices of the past which had allowed indiscriminate granting of scholarships, resulting in too many athletes dropping out after their freshman or sophomore years. This rule was adopted to prevent abuses and at the time it was thought that this rule would solve the problem.

Notwithstanding, NCAA now has determined (since its action involving Centenary, Parish, and his teammates) that the rule was inadequate. This is based upon the fact that the 1.600 Rule was repealed and the 2.00 Rule was enacted in its stead. In *Associated Students v. NCAA* (May 25, 1973, Civil No. S-2754, E.D. Cal.), Judge McBride stated:

> Without deciding the question, it appears that this classification is reasonably related to the purposes of the 1.600 Rule.

However, he concluded that the 1.600 Rule, as interpreted by Official Interpretation 418 (O.I. 418) did not meet muster as to equal protection constitutional requirements. We agree that the 1.600 Rule's classification is reasonable, not arbitrary, and rests upon a ground having a fair and substantial relation to NCAA's object in enacting the legislation, so that all persons similarly circumstanced shall be treated alike, *i.e.*, the Rule bears a rational relationship to the legitimate purposes for which it was enacted. Although application of the Rule may produce seemingly unreasonable results in certain situations, this is not unusual, for use of generalized rules frequently produces irrational results in isolated circumstances. Such results do not condemn those rules under traditional equal protection scrutiny. Here, NCAA has advanced one step at a time, addressing itself to the phase of the problem which then seems most acute to it.

Plaintiffs also presented evidence to show that the SAT and ACT tests discriminated against all of them in some form. One (Parish) came from a minority group, one from a rural school, etc. This type of evidence was rejected as having no weight in [controlling precedent].

We take judicial notice of the fact that, at the time in question, the particular tests involved here under NCAA's Rule 1.600 were administered throughout the nation; almost every college in the United States required a score from one test or the other for admission purposes. We, therefore, must reject plaintiffs' claim as to this issue. We also note that members of the black race have been perhaps the greatest beneficiaries of numerically disproportionate participation in intercollegiate athletics; and they have done so under the aegis of the 1.600 Rule.

In *Associated Students*, supra, the Court stated:

* * *

Bearing in mind that the central purpose of the 1.600 Rule is to ensure that the individual who participates in intercollegiate athletics is capable of succeeding academically at the college level, this new classification is over-inclusive and not rationally related to the objective of the rule insofar as it declares ineligible not only those student athletes who fail to predict a minimum 1.600 grade point average and who have not yet completed their first year in college, and not only those student athletes who fail to achieve a minimum 1.600 grade point average for the first year in college, but additionally those student athletes who demonstrated by the conclusion of the first year that they have the ability to achieve academic success by actually earning at least a 1.600 grade point average. Once a student has an earned grade point average achieved over a reasonable period of time, then it is unreasonable, in light of the purposes of the rule, to impose sanctions against the student based on the fact that he failed to predict a certain grade point average. Instead, any sanctions imposed should be predicated on the actual grade point average attained by the student.

* * *

With this conclusion, we respectfully but regretfully disagree. It is our considered view that the Court in the just quoted decision overlooked the fact that one of the purposes of the official interpretation of the 1.600 Rule is to prevent schools from granting scholarships to those students who, after taking part in testing procedures, do not show a possibility of attaining a degree before entering college.

Under that decision, all member schools could recruit all those athletes whose entrance examinations did not predict successful graduation and then, if they did obtain a higher grade-point average than 1.600 after the first year in school, they would be entitled to participate in NCAA sponsored athletic events thenceforth. The Court's decision there effectively would prevent enforcement of the 1.600 Rule, which the Court already had determined to be rational in order to achieve NCAA's stated objective.

We cannot fathom how the official interpretation creates a classification which is in nonconformance with equal protection standards. In order to meet that objective, determination of eligibility must be made at the time of application and certification; to make it at a later date simply destroys the classification which the Court already had conceded to be reasonable. This decision in effect would allow colleges to recruit ineligible athletes and hope they will meet graduation prediction standards after their first year grades are in, thus becoming eligible for their entire collegiate athletic life. As stated, it is our considered opinion that NCAA's official interpretation of its 1.600 Rule does not create a classification which violates the equal protection requirements of the Constitution.

Case dismissed.

NOTES AND QUESTIONS

1. *Aftermath.* Although the Fifth Circuit upheld the lower court's decision in favor of the NCAA on appeal, *see Parish v. NCAA*, 506 F.2d 1028 (5th Cir. 1975), the NCAA repealed the 1.600 Rule in the early 1970s. Instead, the NCAA required scholarship athletes to have only a minimum 2.0 GPA from high school. Why do you think the NCAA changed its rules after *Parish*? Is "home rule" a good approach or is it problematic?

2. *Development of the Rule.* In 1983, the NCAA adopted Proposition 48, which required that the mandatory 2.00 high school GPA had to come from core academic courses in English, mathematics, science, history, and other subjects reviewed and approved by the NCAA. Most significantly, student-athletes also had to score a minimum of 700 on the SAT or 15 on the ACT. Unlike the 1.6 Predictor Rule in the *Parish* case, the original version of Proposition 48 did not make the standardized test (or GPA) minimum an absolute barrier to college sports. A student-athlete who met either of, though not both, the standardized test and GPA criteria received "partial qualifier" status and could still enroll in college on an athletic scholarship. Partial qualifiers, though, were not eligible to play (though they could practice) in their freshman year, during which they had to demonstrate satisfactory progress in the college's academic program.

In 1992, the NCAA further tightened athlete eligibility standards by adopting Proposition 16. For Division I colleges, the minimum high school GPA standard was raised from 2.00 to 2.50 in 13, not just 11, core academic courses. Athletes who had higher than minimum test scores could have a somewhat lower GPA (and vice versa): *e.g.*, the minimum GPA was 2.00 for an athlete who scored 900 on the SAT. In 1995, the NCAA adopted a sliding scale requiring minima in both areas. Although used until recently, this approach may not survive a decision by the different divisions of the NCAA to abandon standardized testing requirements.

———

As explored in Chapter 12, the Supreme Court held in *NCAA v. Tarkanian*, 488 U.S. 179 (1988), that the NCAA was not a state actor, foreclosing the kind of constitutional challenge Parish brought to the NCAA's eligibility requirements. Title VI of the Civil Rights Act of 1964, in theory, provided another avenue to challenge eligibility rules believed to be discriminatory.

The limits of a Title VI challenge, though, were demonstrated in *Cureton v. NCAA*, 37 F. Supp. 2d 687 (E.D. Pa., 1999), *rev'd on other grounds*, 198 F.3d 107 (3d Cir. 1999). The question in *Cureton* was whether Title VI prohibited the NCAA from requiring students to achieve a minimum score on either of two standardized tests as a condition of eligibility to participate in intercollegiate athletics and/or receive athletically related financial aid during their freshman year.

The two named plaintiffs, Leatrice Shaw and Tai Kwan Cureton, had graduated with honors from their Philadelphia high school in June 1996, ranking 5th and 27th respectively in their senior year class of 305 students. Both Shaw and Cureton were also topflight track and field runners who had been actively recruited by Division I colleges around the country. They failed, however, to achieve the minimum SAT or ACT required to qualify for participation in NCAA athletics. Shaw still secured an athletic scholarship as a "partial qualifier" with Miami University's Division I track and field team, although she was not able to compete in her 1996–97 freshman year. Cureton's athletic ineligibility as a freshman rendered him unattractive to Division I schools, and he ended up at Division III Wheaton College, which does not offer any athletic scholarships.

Their Title VI challenge relied on a disparate impact theory of discrimination, meaning that the NCAA policy was not discriminatory on its face, but had the effect of discriminating based on race. The disparate impact theory is premised upon the notion that some employment practices, adopted without a deliberately discriminatory motive, may in operation be functionally equivalent to intentional discrimination.

The court took note of 1994 and 1998 NCAA memoranda and a U.S. Department of Education report that found Proposition 16 standards disproportionately impact African-American and low-income student-athletes. With clear prima facie evidence of a discriminatory effect, the question became whether the NCAA could prove that Proposition 16 was an "educational necessity."

The NCAA argued that the standardized test requirements accomplished the goals of (1) raising student-athlete graduation rates, and

(2) closing the gap between black and white student-athlete graduation rates. The Court accepted the first justification and rejected the second one. But it found that there was not a manifest relationship between test scores and graduation rates that justified the use of Proposition 16 in light of its discriminatory effect. Further, the plaintiffs demonstrated a number of alternatives for determining eligibility that could achieve the goal of improving graduation rates without relying on test scores.

The plaintiff's victory was short-lived. On appeal, the Third Circuit held that Title VI did not apply to the NCAA. Another decision of the Supreme Court, *Alexander v. Sandoval*, 532 U.S. 275 (2001), similarly barred student-athletes from suing specific Division I schools under a Title VI disparate impact theory. In *Sandoval*, a narrowly divided Court held that Title VI, unlike Title VII, does not afford a private right of action based on disparate impact. After *Sandoval*, student-athletes bringing Title VI actions against universities have to prove intentional discrimination.

For purposes of initial freshman eligibility, the NCAA made some important revisions to Propositions 48 and 16 after the *Cureton* decision. First, the core curriculum requirement in high school has been raised again to sixteen academic courses (four years of English, three years of Math, two years of Science, one additional course in either English, Math, or Science, two years of social science, and four years of "additional academic coursework"). Second, in these core courses, students must secure at least a 2.00 cumulative grade point average to be eligible. The NCAA has a pure sliding scale on the SAT or ACT side, one that requires a student who receives no more than a 400 SAT for just signing his name to have at least a 3.55 GPA in his sixteen core high school courses.

In January 2005, the NCAA adopted another landmark reform with regard to academic progress. Each university team must satisfy an official Academic Progress Rate (APR) or have its permitted scholarships reduced. This APR consists roughly of a fifty percent graduation rate over a five-year period and involves complex calculations and penalty determinations. If a school's average falls below a minimum APR, and a player becomes academically ineligible and then leaves the school, the school cannot replace him for at least one year. There is a ten percent ceiling on the total number of team scholarships that can be lost; *i.e.*, nine of football's eighty-five scholarship ceiling and two of basketball's twelve.

In addition, if the deficiency continues, there are further penalties that can come into play, including a reduction in the amount of time a team can practice each week (with the time spent instead on academic activities), a reduction in number of competitions in which the team can participate, and a variety of other penalties, including coaching suspensions and restricted NCAA membership privileges.

And starting with the 2008–09 season, the additional penalty of a ban on postseason play was added for a team that did not achieve a 900 APR four-year average or above a 930 APR average in the previous two years. This penalty has been assessed most notably against the men's team at the University of Connecticut in 2012–13, two years after it won the NCAA Division I men's championship and the year before it won that title again. Finally, the ultimate possible penalty is a one-year suspension for a school's entire athletic program from NCAA membership.

As noted above, the recently adopted NCAA constitution opens the door to significant changes in the admissions, eligibility, and APR rules. This is because all of the membership will no longer necessarily operate under the same set of rules. In addition, the recent decision to make standardized tests optional during the Covid pandemic may accelerate changes in this area.

NOTES AND QUESTIONS

1. *Purpose of Regulation.* What are the purposes of the NCAA's eligibility regulations for both the admission and academic progress of college athletes? Could they be better served by some type of federal government legislation and regulation?

2. *Sliding Scale.* If the NCAA does need to regulate the admission of college athletes, must it consider standardized tests as well as high school grades and courses? Does the NCAA's sliding scale striking an appropriate balance by allowing sufficiently high grades in core courses to compensate for any standardized test score? Or should standardized tests be eliminated from eligibility requirements?

3. *Eligibility Versus Academic Progress.* Should the NCAA be concerned only with the academic progress of the athletes its member schools choose to admit rather than with the pre-college academic records and potential of these athletes? Why does it need to regulate the latter as well as the former? Is regulation of the former more difficult and demanding of more administrative resources? Are the NCAA's current academic progress standards and incentives adequate and appropriate?

The other long-time key feature of Proposition 48–16 is its insistence upon a minimum GPA in a host of "core courses" in high school to permit a student to compete in college sports in his or her freshman year. This initially much less controversial provision has already generated extensive litigation under a different branch of antidiscrimination law, the one designed to protect the disabled.

As mentioned above, the NCAA requires students to have passed 16 core courses. Excluded from this *academic* standard are not only courses that are for vocational or personal service purposes, but also those that are "remedial, special education, or compensatory courses" designed for high school students with special learning problems. But the federal Rehabilitation Act of 1973 has long applied to all institutions that receive financial assistance from the government (*de facto*, encompassing all private as well as public colleges with students, not just professors, who receive any federal funding). The Americans with Disabilities Act of 1990 (ADA) expanded this federal antidiscrimination policy to cover a large array of purely private institutions that operate a place of "public accommodation" (including perhaps the NCAA). These laws protect not just those with physical disability, but also those with certain forms of learning disability (*e.g.*, dyslexia or attention deficit disorder). Chapter 14 explores further some applications of the ADA and Rehabilitation Act.

It took some time for the NCAA to focus its attention on the implications of Proposition 48–16 for the disabled. By the mid-1990s, though, the Association had not only recognized that those student-athletes would often have to take the SAT or ACT in a non-standard format, but they also might need a specially designed high school curriculum. The NCAA established a Special Subcommittee on Initial-Eligibility Waivers to conduct case-by-case reviews of the administrative exclusion of certain high school courses that did not seem to meet the academic core course standard. The Subcommittee decided that in order to accommodate the learning disabled, a "remedial" course could be treated as "core" if the course was designed to help the student proceed in a different format at a slower pace, but was aimed at the same intellectual content as the basic course at that school. The following judicial opinion addressed the question of whether this somewhat more flexible NCAA regime had sufficiently accommodated the needs of this legally protected minority group.

GANDEN V. NCAA

1996 WL 680000 (N.D. Ill. 1996)

MANNING, DISTRICT JUDGE.

[Chad Ganden graduated at the age of 18 from Naperville North High School in June 1996, and was recruited by Michigan State as one of the fastest young swimmers in the United States. Even so, Ganden's learning disability—a "decoding" problem that primarily affects reading and writing skills—had seriously impeded Ganden's success in his suburban Chicago classroom. From his freshman through junior years, Ganden's cumulative GPA was just 2.09. That learning condition was diagnosed at the end of his junior year, and the high school devised an Individualized Education Plan (IEP) for Ganden. With the help of additional resources, Ganden's GPA reached 3.0 in his senior year. Ganden took the ACT three times under special testing standards for his disability, and achieved a "compiled" score of 76. Under the NCAA bylaws, this ACT score required a GPA of 2.275 in

13 core courses. Unfortunately, only 11 of Ganden's high school courses met the general NCAA standard, and his cumulative GPA in these was just 2.136. Ganden could neither receive an athletic scholarship nor compete in intercollegiate sports.

Michigan State, supported by the U.S. Department of Justice applied to the NCAA Subcommittee on Initial-Eligibility Waivers for a waiver for Ganden as a disabled student-athlete. The Subcommittee agreed to count additional courses as "core courses," raising Ganden's GPA to 2.153, still below the 2.275 required for someone with his 76 ACT. That meant that Ganden was a "partial qualifier" who was able to receive a Michigan State scholarship and practice with its swimming team, but was not permitted to compete during his freshman year.

The Subcommittee then granted Ganden's request to include LRC Typing and Computing courses in his core academic component, further raising his cumulative GPA to 2.21. But the Subcommittee would not let him replace other courses as part of the top 13 academic courses, which would have move Ganden's cumulative GPA to above the 2.275 minimum required of someone at his ACT score level. Ganden thus filed suit under the ADA, seeking an injunction that would permit him to compete in his freshman year as a full qualifier under NCAA rules that were made compatible with his learning disability, his improved academic record after this disability had been diagnosed, and other external factors indicating he would succeed in college.

The district judge concluded that if Ganden were likely to succeed on the merits, he should be entitled to interim injunctive relief, because "an elite level swimmer only has a competitive life span of a few years, peaking between the ages of nineteen and twenty-one." If Ganden had to wait for trial, he would "lose an entire year of competitive competition . . . that was likely to inhibit his development as a swimmer during a critical point in his career." The judge also concluded that the NCAA was governed by the ADA, as a private body that "*operates* . . . a place of public accommodation." The NCAA's certification rules function as a "ticket" for effective student-athlete use of Michigan State's physical facilities, because the rules determine whether the university can give them financial support, coaching, practice time, and competitive performance in athletic events taking place in those facilities.

The judge then turned to the crucial substantive issue whether the NCAA bylaws and procedures had the effect of "screening" Ganden out of college sports because of his learning disability, and if so, whether the NCAA had refused to take reasonable steps to accommodate its standards to Ganden's disability.]

1. Discrimination on the Basis of Disability.

The court rejects the NCAA's contention that Ganden cannot establish a causal link between its denial of Ganden's waiver application and his learning disability. The NCAA asserts that it denied Ganden's waiver application because he failed to meet the minimum eligibility requirements through his combined GPA and ACT scores. In support, the NCAA cites to *Sandison v. Michigan High School Athletic Ass'n*, 64 F.3d 1026 (6th Cir. 1995), in which two learning disabled students argued that a high school athletic association's age limitation excluded them from competition on the basis of their disabilities. Dismissing their claims under the ADA and the Rehabilitation Act of 1973, *Sandison* explained that "the plaintiffs' respective learning disability does not prevent the two students from meeting the age requirements, the passage of time does . . ." *Id.* at 1033 & 1036; *Johannesen v. NCAA*, No. 96 C 197 PHX ROS, p. 7 (D.C.Ariz.1996).

The court respectfully disagrees with this analysis. In implementing civil rights legislation for the disabled, Congress recognized that discrimination on the basis of a disability is "most often the product, not of invidious animus, but rather of thoughtlessness and indifference—of benign neglect." *Alexander v. Choate*, 469 U.S. 287, 297 & n. 12 (1985). Accordingly, the ADA and Rehabilitation Act focus on whether the defendant has provided a reasonable accommodation to an individual on the basis of a known disability. In the instant case, the evidence strongly suggests that Ganden failed to take the requisite "core courses" or satisfy the remaining eligibility criteria because of his disability. When they reviewed his waiver application, the NCAA Subcommittee was aware of this condition and how it affected his ability to meet their eligibility requirements. Consequently, Ganden has presented a strong prima facie case that there is a causal link between the NCAA refusal to certify Ganden a "qualifier" and his learning disability.

2. Reasonable Modifications.

The court next addresses whether Ganden's requested modifications are reasonable or would "fundamentally alter" the nature of the privilege or accommodation to which he has been denied access. . . .

This analysis requires that the court examine the particular eligibility criteria and the nature of the privilege that it monitors. The criteria at issue are the minimum GPA requirements and the "core course" definition that is instrumental in computing a student's GPA. The privilege at issue is the NCAA's intercollegiate athletic program. Ganden narrowly characterizes this privilege as swimming competitions. However, this cramped view ignores the broader nature and role of NCAA intercollegiate athletics. The NCAA is not merely a swimming group, but an integral part of the college community. The NCAA was created to promote the concept of the student-athlete through both athletic excellence and academic development. It offers its competitors more than an opportunity to swim, but also to represent the NCAA's member institutions. Towards this general purpose of the privilege, the eligibility requirements (1) ensure that student-athletes are representative of the college community and not recruited solely for athletics; (2) ensure that a student-athlete is academically prepared to succeed at college; and (3) preserve amateurism in intercollegiate sports.

As an initial matter, the court does not believe that any alteration to the NCAA's eligibility requirements would "fundamentally alter" the nature of the privilege offered. In support of this position, the NCAA cites to two recent decisions holding that any waiver to an age cap for high school sports leagues would "fundamentally alter" the high school programs. *See Sandison*, 64 F.3d 1026 (Title II); *Pottgen*, 40 F.3d 926 (Title II). First, those cases found that requiring an individual assessment of each overage student would constitute an undue burden for the defendant. *Sandison*, 64 F.3d at 1034; *see also Pottgen*, 40 F.3d at 931 (refusing to assess eligibility criteria in light of plaintiffs' circumstances because it would [require] exhaustive evidentiary investigation by defendant for each disabled student). In contrast, the NCAA already has instituted an individual assessment process particularly intended to review student-athletes academic records and abilities. More importantly, the court believes that these decisions failed to adequately analyze the purposes of the act in light of the specific claims for modifications; *i.e.*, the circumstances of the plaintiff and learning disabled students. *Johnson*, 899 F. Supp. at 584. Rather, these courts simply asked whether the eligibility requirement served any important interests of the program. Like most rationally created procedural requirements, the court found that the age requirement did, and concluded that any alteration to those rules would fundamentally alter the program. *Pottgen*, 40 F.3d at 930 ("Waiving an essential eligibility standard would constitute a fundamental alteration in the nature of the [athletic] program."); *see Sandison*, 64 F.3d at 1035.

This analysis ignores the central issue under the ADA: Are reasonable accommodations possible in light of the disability. . . .

Although the court does not believe that any modification to the NCAA's eligibility requirements would "fundamentally alter" the nature of its accommodation, the court finds that Ganden does not have a reasonable likelihood of demonstrating that his requested modification would not "fundamentally alter" that accommodation. There is little doubt that the GPA and "core course" requirements generally serve important interests of the NCAA athletics. Because of its dual mission, the NCAA has an important interest in insuring that its student-athletes are prepared to succeed at college. Whatever criticism one may level at GPA and the national standardized tests, these provide significant objective predictors of a student's ability to succeed at college. The "core course" criteria further serves the dual interest of insuring the integrity of that GPA and independently insuring that the student has covered the minimum subject matter required for college.

However, in the case of learning disabled students, the NCAA may be able to serve these purposes and ensure that a student has the necessary academic capabilities through consideration of additional factors. In fact, through its waiver application process, the NCAA provides such individualized consideration. In the case of learning disabled students, a generally improving academic record may indicate that prior remedial courses adequately substituted for earlier "core courses," even if not qualitatively and quantitatively identical to other "core courses." In such circumstances, some remedial courses may have served the same role as approved "core courses" to other students. Therefore, the record indicates that Title III requires the NCAA to consider a students' progress in his or her IEP courses and overall high school career.

Ganden could only satisfy the required GPA if the Subcommittee actually counted his two LRC courses as "core:" if the Subcommittee replaced other "core course" grades with the grades from the LRC courses. However, in contrast to Ganden's other remedial courses, neither of the LRC courses appear remotely similar to the subject areas of "core courses." While Title III may require the NCAA to count courses as "core" even if they are not substantively identical to approved "core courses," it does not require the NCAA to count courses with little substantive similarity. Whatever skills such a course may provide to the student, they cannot be said to substitute for earlier "core courses." Similarly, the grades from such courses do not provide valid indications of the student's academic potential. Based upon the current record, the court finds that this modification would "fundamentally alter" the privilege of participation in intercollegiate swimming.

The court also finds that lowering the minimum GPA for Ganden would "fundamentally alter" the nature of the privilege. Unlike a modification to the "core course" definition, lowering the GPA minimum directly removes the NCAA's primary objective tool to determine a student's academic capabilities. While circumstances may exist where such a modification are necessary, the court finds that it is generally unreasonable to require the NCAA to lower this basic standard. Instead, Title III would focus on less drastic modifications affecting the computation of the GPA, such as modifications to the "core course" requirement.

As Ganden argues, Title III requires the NCAA to individually assess his request for modifications. However, the NCAA provided such an assessment. The Subcommittee reviewed Ganden's case for over one hour. It received an application prepared by a member institution with a strong interest in procuring a waiver on his behalf. This package included his academic record, a psychological report focusing on his disability as well as his efforts and successes in overcoming it, and arguments on his behalf from MSU. In addition, the record indicates that the Subcommittee was aware of the Department of Justice's efforts and arguments on his behalf. After this review, the Subcommittee accommodated Ganden through granting him "partial qualifier" status.

While there is some doubt whether the NCAA actually counted Ganden's three "Basic" courses as "core" in consideration of his disability or MSU's reliance argument, the record reveals that the Subcommittee did consider Ganden's disability, his efforts to overcome it, and his impressive academic gains during his final two years of high school. Even though he did not meet the minimum GPA, it still granted Ganden "partial qualifier" status. Title III does not require the NCAA to simply abandon its eligibility requirements, but only to make reasonable modifications to them. The record reveals that the NCAA did precisely that.

* * *

4.   Conclusion.

Although Ganden has demonstrated some likelihood of success on the merits with respect to questions of subject matter jurisdiction, the court finds that he has not shown a reasonable likelihood of success on the critical allegation that the NCAA's denial of his waiver application constituted "discrimination" under § 12182(b)(2) of Title III . . .

Injunction denied.

NOTES AND QUESTIONS

1.   *Aftermath.* In the fall of 1997, just before Ganden was to begin varsity swimming for Michigan State in his sophomore year, the Department of Justice announced that its Civil Rights Division had concluded that the NCAA's eligibility rules and procedures did not adequately accommodate the situation and needs of Ganden and other learning-disabled athletes. The remedies proposed by the Department for this alleged ADA violation were to restore a fourth year of eligibility for Ganden and 33 other learning-disabled athletes who had lost their freshman athletic year, plus financial compensation for Ganden and four others who had filed complaints under this federal law. When the NCAA did not immediately accept this proposal, the Clinton Justice Department filed its own lawsuit under the ADA, forcing the NCAA to agree to settle all these cases in May 1998. While not admitting that it was a "place of public accommodation" subject to the ADA, the NCAA not only paid some money to each of these disabled plaintiffs, but it also altered its rules to accommodate their successors.

2.   *A Different View of the NCAA and the ADA.* In *Butler v. NCAA*, 1996 WL 1058233 (W.D.Wash.1996), a federal district judge reached a contrary conclusion to that of *Ganden*. This unpublished opinion granted the plaintiff's

motion for a preliminary injunction, finding that the NCAA was subject to the ADA because it "operated" a facility of "public accommodation."

3.   *Current Approach.* Since *Ganden,* the NCAA deems certain special education high school courses to be core academic classes, but only for documented learning-disabled student-athletes. And even if the latter cannot become eligible as college freshmen, they are given a fourth year of athletic eligibility if they have completed a substantial part of their college degree by the time that they have reached their fifth year. Under the current practice, the NCAA typically grants most waiver requests from learning disabled students for an initial eligibility waiver.

4.   *Impact on Disabled.* Assuming the NCAA is governed by Title III of the Americans with Disabilities Act as an operator of a "place of public accommodation," what responsibilities does it have toward students with learning disabilities to provide reasonable accommodation to their disabilities when applying its regulations on admission standards, including those defining requisite "core" high school courses? Must it give individualized consideration to each applicant with learning disabilities rather than apply strictly its standards? If so, should the critical question be whether the learning disabled student's record is as predictive of academic success in college as the minimum required of the non-disabled? Or does the reasonable accommodation requirement demand taking greater risk with the disabled? Does the NCAA now provide adequate accommodation to the learning disabled?

C. THE NATIONAL LETTER OF INTENT

Assuming the athlete meets the eligibility requirements, the athlete can enter into an agreement with the University that operates much like a unilateral contract. This agreement has three separate parts: the national letter of intent, the financial aid agreement, and the university's rules and regulations. Major universities participate in the Collegiate Commissioners Association (CCA) and all agree to use the same contractual language in the letter of intent.

Generally speaking, the university agrees to provide the athlete with tuition, room, board, books, and in some cases, cost of attendance. In exchange, the athlete agrees to attend the university, meet the university's academic requirements, and participate in intercollegiate athletics. Historically, these agreements had a one-year term, renewable annually for up to four years of eligibility. Now, universities can provide a legally-enforceable guarantee that athletes abiding by university rules will receive promised financial aid for four years.

The National Letter of Intent (NLI) is the initial agreement that the athlete enters into during high school. The primary functions of the letter are to bar other schools from recruiting the athlete and secure a scholarship for the athlete. If the athlete decides not to honor the letter of intent, the athlete must sit out a year unless the athletic director releases him or her from that agreement. A number of rules govern the execution of the national letter of intent. First and foremost, each sport has one or two "signing periods" when athletes can sign the letter. If the athlete is a minor, the parent must also sign the letter. Also, coaches cannot be present at the signing of the letter.

The NCAA has made it clear that the athlete remains bound to the letter even if the coach decides to leave the university, though schools presumably could release an athlete in such a case. From the perspective of the NCAA, the NLI is an agreement between the athlete and the university, even though the coach may be the central reason the athlete signs the NLI. Beyond the NLI, the athlete-university relationship is an agreement that governs the interaction between the athlete and the institution during his or her time as a student. The next case explores the scope of this relationship.

TAYLOR V. WAKE FOREST
191 S.E.2d 379 (N.C. Ct. App. 1972)

CAMPBELL, JUDGE.

[Gregg Taylor was recruited by and signed a letter of intent to play football for Wake Forest University. The grant—in—aid, or athletic scholarship, provided as follows:

> This Grant, if awarded, will be for 4 years provided I conduct myself in accordance with the rules of the Conference, the NCAA, and the Institution. I agree to maintain eligibility for intercollegiate athletics under both Conference and Institutional rules. Training rules for intercollegiate athletics are considered rules of the Institution, and I agree to abide by them. If injured while participating in athletics supervised by a member of the coaching staff, the Grant or Scholarship will be honored; and the medical expenses will be paid by the Athletic Department. This grant, when approved, is awarded for academic and athletic achievement and is not to be interpreted as employment in any manner whatsoever.

Taylor played for Wake Forest's football team in his freshman year. During the fall semester he compiled a grade point average of 1.0 (out of 4.0), far below the 1.35 the school required all students to have at the end of the freshman year. Taylor did not attend the spring football practices, and his GPA for the spring semester rose to 1.9. He then decided not to play football in the fall of his sophomore year; his GPA rose again, to 2.4.

Because of his refusal to play football, Wake Forest's Scholarship Committee, on the recommendation of the Faculty Athletic Committee, revoked his scholarship as of the end of his sophomore year. Taylor nevertheless remained at Wake Forest and graduated on time. He sued to recover $5,500 in expenses incurred during his last two years because he had lost his scholarship. Faced with Wake Forest's motion for summary dismissal, Taylor contended that under the relevant contract doctrines there was a genuine issue for a jury to determine—whether or not he had "acted reasonably and in good faith in refusing to participate in the football program at Wake Forest when such participation interfered with reasonable academic progress."]

* * *

The plaintiffs' position depends upon a construction of the contractual agreement between plaintiffs and Wake Forest. As stated in the affidavit of George J. Taylor, the position of the plaintiffs is that it was orally agreed between plaintiffs and the representative of Wake Forest that:

> [I]n the event of any conflict between educational achievement and athletic involvement, participation in athletic activities could be limited or eliminated to the extent necessary to assure reasonable academic progress.

And plaintiffs were to be the judge as to what "reasonable academic progress" constituted.

We do not agree with the position taken by plaintiffs. The scholarship application filed by Gregg Taylor provided:

> I agree to maintain eligibility for intercollegiate athletics under both Conference and Institutional rules. Training rules for intercollegiate athletics are considered rules of the Institution, and I agree to abide by them.

Both Gregg Taylor and his father knew that the application was for "Football Grant-In-Aid Or A Scholarship," and that the scholarship was "awarded for academic and athletic achievement." It would be a strained construction of the contract that would enable the plaintiffs to determine the "reasonable academic progress" of Gregg Taylor. Gregg Taylor, in consideration of the scholarship award, agreed to maintain his athletic eligibility and this meant both physically and scholastically. As long as his grade average equaled or exceeded the requirements of Wake Forest, he was maintaining his scholastic eligibility for athletics. Participation in and attendance at practice were required to maintain his physical eligibility. When he refused to do so in the absence of any injury or excuse other than to devote more time to studies, he was not complying with his contractual obligations.

Summary judgment granted.

———

NOTES AND QUESTIONS

1. *The Move to Multi-Year Scholarships.* Sometime after *Taylor* (and after a similar verdict in *Begley v. Mercer University*, 367 F. Supp. 908 (E.D. Tenn.1973)), the NCAA amended its Division I rules to provide that "where a student's athletic ability is taken into consideration in any degree in awarding financial aid, such aid shall not be awarded in excess of one academic year." Article 15.3.3.1. While high school athletes could learn that the practice of the athletic department is to recommend renewal of financial aid, this rule explicitly forbade any assurance that renewal is automatic (even for an athlete who suffers a career-ending injury). Why would the NCAA impose these constraints on its own members' freedom of action? Could the NCAA justify these constraints if challenged in an antitrust suit?

In 2012, the NCAA amended its rule to allow (but not require) member institutions in Division I to give multi-year scholarships not to exceed five years and to provide continued financial aid to student-athletes who had exhausted their playing eligibility but needed more time to graduate. By 2015, all of the Power 5 conference schools (as well as Notre Dame) had agreed to offer multi-year athletic scholarships.

2. *Grounds for Alleging Breach of Promise and Tortious Conduct by Universities.* A similar case, *Jackson v. Drake University*, 778 F. Supp. 1490 (S.D. Iowa 1991), involved contract and tort claims by Terrell Jackson in a dispute with Drake University. Jackson claimed that when Drake recruited him, basketball coach Tom Abatemarco promised him both the right to play basketball and an environment conducive to high academic achievement. When Jackson got to Drake, the coaches allegedly pressured him to take easy courses and submit plagiarized papers, and denied him adequate study time. When Jackson complained about the situation, Abatemarco was said to have harassed him at practice, called him foul names, and made him run extra drills and do extra exercises. In the middle of his sophomore year, Jackson quit the team. He filed suit against the school alleging breach of contract, educational malpractice, negligent misrepresentation in recruiting, and fraud. The court dismissed the contract claim because the entitlements upon which it was based, especially the right to play basketball, were not expressly contained in Jackson's scholarship documents. Citing Ross, *see infra* Section B.2., the court dismissed the educational malpractice claim, finding it was not a viable tort in Iowa. The court did, however, order a trial of the negligent misrepresentation and fraud claims, according to the following legal specifications:

> To properly state a claim of negligent misrepresentation, Jackson must allege that the defendant, in the course of its business or profession or employment, supplied false information for the guidance of others in their business transactions, that the information was justifiably relied on by the plaintiff, and the defendant failed to exercise reasonable care or competence in communicating the information. To state a claim for fraud, Jackson must allege a material misrepresentation, made knowingly, with the

intent to induce Jackson to act, upon which he justifiably relied, with damages.

Id. at 1494.

D. ACADEMIC OPPORTUNITY

As part of the contractual relationship with the university, the student-athlete has a claim to a legitimate opportunity to an education. The university, as an institution of higher learning, bears significant responsibility in affording such opportunities to intercollegiate athletes, while also ensuring that athletes do not engage in academic fraud. Some fear that the university's real interest may lie in athletic performance, not academic competence, despite the rhetoric of the NCAA and its member institutions. The next case explores a challenge to a university's failure to provide academic opportunity followed by an example of widespread academic fraud.

ROSS v. CREIGHTON UNIV.

740 F. Supp. 1319 (N.D. Ill. 1990)

NORDBERG, DISTRICT JUDGE.

One day in July 1987, Kevin Ross, a former college basketball player, barricaded himself in a high-rise hotel room in downtown Chicago and threw assorted pieces of furniture out the window. As Ross currently recalls it, the defenestrated furniture "symbolized" the employees of Creighton University, whose alleged misdeeds he blames for the onset of this "major depressive episode." Ross now sues the university in contract and tort. The gist of Ross's Amended Complaint is that Creighton caused this episode and otherwise injured him by recruiting him to attend the school on a basketball scholarship while knowing that Ross, who scored nine points out of a possible 36 on the American College Test, was pitifully unprepared to attend Creighton, which is a private school whose average student in the year Ross matriculated, 1978, scored 23.2 points on the ACT.

COMPLAINT

Ross, who is six feet and nine inches tall, was a high school basketball star in Kansas City, Kansas, when Creighton recruited him. Creighton knew that Ross could not handle college-level studies, but kept him eligible for the basketball team by recommending that he enroll in "bonehead" (Ross's description) courses, such as ceramics, marksmanship, and the respective theories of basketball, track and field, and football. Under its rules, the university would not have accepted the pursuit of this esoteric curriculum by a non-athlete. After four years, when his basketball eligibility expired, Ross had earned only 96 of the 128 credits required to graduate, maintaining a "D" average. His reading skills were those of a seventh-grader; his overall language skills, those of a fourth-grader.

In order to get Ross remedial education, representatives of Creighton made arrangements for Ross to attend Chicago's Westside Preparatory School, an elementary and high school whose founder, Marva Collins, has drawn national attention for her abilities as an educator. As its name suggests, Westside Prep is a school for children, not for adults. Ross says that Creighton representatives made four trips to Chicago to discuss Ross's enrollment. The agreement to enroll Ross is spelled out in a letter dated July 29, 1982, from Collins to Creighton's athletic director. The letter, countersigned by a Creighton official and returned to Collins, obligated Creighton to pay for Ross's tuition, special tutoring, books and living expenses. Ross attended Westside in 1982 and 1983. He later attended Roosevelt University, also located in Chicago, but dropped out after 1985 for want of money. Ross's furniture-throwing outburst took place on July 23, 1987. He was arrested and ordered to make restitution in the amount of $7,500.

* * *

ROSS'S TORT CLAIM

... Ross says [his tort] claim is a hybrid of "negligent infliction of emotional distress" and "educational malpractice." These strands of tort law "intertwine" to form the novel tort of "negligence in recruiting and repeatedly re-enrolling an athlete utterly incapable—without substantial tutoring and other support—of performing the academic work required to make educational progress," exacerbated by the enrollment of plaintiff in a school with children half his age and size. Before considering the merits of this tort, the Court must unravel its separate threads.

Educational malpractice is a tort theory beloved of commentators, but not of courts. While often proposed as a remedy for those who think themselves wronged by educators (see, e.g., J. Elson, *A Common Law Remedy for the Educational Harms Caused by Incompetent or Careless Teaching,* 73 Nw. U. L. Rev. 641 (1978)), educational malpractice has been repeatedly rejected by the American courts.

* * *

Whether to create a cause of action for educational malpractice is, of course, a question for the Court, which determines as a matter of law whether a duty runs from defendant to plaintiff. It is a matter of considering sound social policy, guided by looking to " '[t]he likelihood of injury, the magnitude of the burden of guarding against it and the consequences of placing that burden upon defendant.' "

* * *

This Court believes the same general concerns would lead the Illinois courts to reject the tort of educational malpractice. Admittedly, the term "educational malpractice" has a seductive ring to it; after all, if doctors, lawyers, accountants and other professionals can be held liable for failing to exercise due care, why can't teachers? The answer is that the nature of education radically differs from other professions. Education is an intensely collaborative process, requiring the interaction of student with teacher. A good student can learn from a poor teacher; a poor student can close his mind to a good teacher. Without effort by a student, he cannot be educated. Good teaching methods may vary with the needs of the individual student. In other professions, by contrast, client cooperation is far less important; given a modicum of cooperation, a competent professional in other fields can control the results obtained. But in education, the ultimate responsibility for success remains always with the student. Both the process and the result are subjective, and proof or disproof extremely difficult.

* * *

It also must be remembered that education is a service rendered on an immensely greater scale than other professional services. If every failed student could seek tort damages against any teacher, administrator and school he feels may have shortchanged him at some point in his education, the courts could be deluged and schools shut down. The Court believes that Illinois courts would avert the flood and the educational loss. This is not to say that the mere worry that litigation will increase justifies a court's refusal to remedy a wrong; it is to say that the real danger of an unrestrained multiplication of lawsuits shows the disutility of the proposed remedy. If poor education (or student laziness) is to be corrected, a common law action for negligence is not a practical means of going about it.

* * *

[Having rejected both the general tort of educational malpractice and Ross's claim for negligent infliction of emotional distress, the court then asked whether Ross nonetheless has a cause] of action that is *sui generis*? Ross argues that he does, contending that "the present case is so unique and egregious that, despite the lack of precedent, a cause of action should be found to exist." Ross basically argues that a special tort be created for the benefit of student athletes, or more precisely, for the benefit of student athletes whose academic performance would not have qualified them to be students had they not been athletes. In Ross's view, "The present case does not question classroom methodology or the competence of instruction. Rather the issue is whether Plaintiff should ever have been admitted to Creighton and whether, once admitted, Creighton had a duty to truly educate Plaintiff and not simply to maintain his eligibility for basketball. . . ."

Ross's inability to plead a cause of action under existing law strongly counsels against creating a new cause of action in his favor. Rules serve little purpose if they are not reasonably predictable and if they do not apply across the board, for one cannot conform behavior to the unknowable. *See*

A. Scalia, *The Rule of Law as a Law of Rules*, 56 U. CHICAGO L. REV. 1175, 1178–79 (1989). Even a new rule declared through the evolutionary process of the common law ought fairly be deduced from existing doctrine— something that cannot be said for Ross's claim. The policy reasons considered by the Illinois courts further counsel against recognition of this new duty. Schools would be forced to undertake the delphic science of diagnosing the mental condition of potential recruits. And why should the cause of action be limited to student athletes? Shouldn't all students who actually pay tuition also have an equal right to recover if they are negligently admitted, and once negligently admitted, have a right to recover if the school negligently counsels and educates them? To allow Ross to recover might redress a wrong (assuming, for sake of argument, that he was in fact exploited), but it would also endanger the admissions prospects of thousands of marginal students, as schools scrambled to factor into their admissions calculations whether a potentially "negligent admission" now could cost unforeseeable tort damages later. The Court should not and will not craft a new tort for Ross.

———

On appeal, the Seventh Circuit Court of Appeals upheld the summary dismissal of Ross' tort theory of educational malpractice, but took a somewhat different view of Ross' contract claim.

ROSS V. CREIGHTON UNIV.
957 F.2d 410 (7th Cir. 1992)

RIPPLE, CIRCUIT JUDGE.

* * *

It is held generally in the United States that the "basic legal relation between a student and a private university or college is contractual in nature. The catalogues, bulletins, circulars, and regulations of the institution made available to the matriculant become a part of the contract." Indeed, there seems to be "no dissent" from this proposition. As the district court correctly noted, Illinois recognizes that the relationship between a student and an educational institution is, in some of its aspects, contractual. It is quite clear, however, that Illinois would not recognize all aspects of a university-student relationship as subject to remedy through a contract action. "A contract between a private institution and a student confers duties upon both parties which cannot be arbitrarily disregarded and may be judicially enforced." However, "a decision of the school authorities relating to the academic qualification of the students will not be reviewed. . . . Courts are not qualified to pass an opinion as to the attainments of a student . . . and . . . courts will not review a decision of the school authorities relating to academic qualifications of the students."

There is no question, we believe, that Illinois would adhere to the great weight of authority and bar any attempt to repackage an educational malpractice claim as a contract claim. As several courts have noted, the policy concerns that preclude a cause of action for educational malpractice apply with equal force to bar a breach of contract claim attacking the general quality of an education. "Where the essence of the complaint is that the school breached its agreement by failing to provide an effective education, the court is again asked to evaluate the course of instruction . . . [and] is similarly called upon to review the soundness of the method of teaching that has been adopted by an educational institution."

To state a claim for breach of contract, the plaintiff must do more than simply allege that the education was not good enough. Instead, he must point to an identifiable contractual promise that the defendant failed to honor. Thus, . . . if the defendant took tuition money and then provided no education, or alternately, promised a set number of hours of instruction and then failed to deliver, a breach of contract action may be available. *See Zumbrun v. University of Southern California*, 101 Cal. Rptr. 499 (1972) (breach of contract action allowed against university when professor declined to give lectures and final exam, and all students received a grade of "B"). Similarly, a breach of contract action might exist if a student enrolled in a course explicitly promising instruction that would qualify him as a journeyman, but in which the fundamentals necessary to attain that skill were not even presented. In these cases, the essence of the plaintiff's complaint would not be that the institution failed to perform adequately a promised educational service, but rather that it failed to perform that service at all. Ruling on this issue would not require an inquiry into the nuances of educational processes and theories, but rather an objective assessment of whether the institution made a good faith effort to perform on its promise.

We read Mr. Ross' complaint to allege more than a failure of the University to provide him with an education of a certain quality. Rather, he alleges that the University knew that he was not qualified academically to participate in its curriculum. Nevertheless, it made a specific promise that he would be able to participate in a meaningful way in that program because it would provide certain specific services to him. Finally, he alleges that the University breached its promise by reneging on its commitment to provide those services and, consequently, effectively cutting him off from any participation in and benefit from the University's academic program. To adjudicate such a claim, the court would not be required to determine whether Creighton had breached its contract with Mr. Ross by providing deficient academic services. Rather, its inquiry would be limited to whether the University had provided any real access to its academic curriculum at all.

Accordingly, we must disagree respectfully with our colleague in the district court as to whether the contract counts of the complaint can be dismissed at the pleadings stage. In our view, the allegations of the complaint are sufficient to warrant further proceedings. We emphasize, however, the narrow ground of our disagreement. We agree—indeed we emphasize—that courts should not "take on the job of supervising the relationship between colleges and student-athletes or creating in effect a new relationship between them." We also recognize a formal university-student contract is rarely employed and, consequently, "the general nature and terms of the agreement are usually implied, with specific terms to be found in the university bulletin and other publications; custom and usages can also become specific terms by implication." Nevertheless, we believe that the district court can adjudicate Mr. Ross' specific and narrow claim that he was barred from any participation in and benefit from the University's academic program without second-guessing the professional judgment of the University faculty on academic matters.

Affirmed in part, remanded in part.

NOTES AND QUESTIONS

1. *Aftermath.* Despite Creighton's failure to educate him, Mr. Ross returned to grade school and after learning to read, received his college degree. His case also created change within the NCAA, which responded by establishing the Eligibility Center to ensure that college-bound student-athletes understand the requirements to participate in NCAA athletics.

2. *Pressure to Win.* To what extent does the pressure to win undermine the athlete's pursuit of an education? When athletes spend 60 hours a week on athletics, is education possible? Do you think the increased commercialism of college sports adds to such pressure?

3. *Tutoring.* Most Power 5 universities have extensive academic tutoring programs to help student-athletes. To what extent does this approach create a great educational value for student-athletes and help make their educational experience robust? Alternatively, does such an approach encourage institutions to cut corners academically? The next case is an example of an institution cutting corners, or at the very least, allowing corners to be cut.

A case that reveals the NCAA's approach to academic support for student-athletes and its particular emphasis on preventing what members believe to be unfair competitive advantage arose from an academic scandal at the University of North Carolina. A number of so-called "paper courses" were offered by the Department of African and Afro-American Studies. The courses involved no class attendance; limited, if any, faculty oversight; and liberal grading. The paper courses included both independent studies and courses listed as standard lectures but taught as independent studies. Although the exact number of paper courses is unknown, a report following an independent investigation by a national law firm (the "Cadwalader Report") conservatively estimated 3,100 students, including athletes, took a paper course involving irregular instruction. These so-called classes never met and rarely involved a faculty member. They typically required the submission of a paper, or two shorter papers. The papers were often graded by the secretary, who admitted she did not read every word and occasionally did not read every page. The papers consistently received high grades.

UNIVERSITY OF NORTH CAROLINA AT CHAPEL HILL PUBLIC INFRACTIONS DECISION

NCAA Committee on Infractions, 2017

* * *

III. FINDINGS OF FACT

* * *

At the hearing, UNC stood by its paper courses. UNC indicated that the work was assigned, completed, turned in and graded under the professor's guidelines. UNC also asserted that the grades are recorded on the students' transcripts and continue to count.

* * *

While independent studies and lecture courses are regular experiences for students on college campuses, the paper courses were, as UNC defined them, "irregular." UNC's chancellor elaborated on that characterization at the infractions hearing, succinctly describing them as having "inconsistent professorial involvement in teaching and grading." She and others further explained that the courses failed to meet UNC's high standards and expectations. Although the courses failed to meet UNC's own expectations, UNC repeatedly stressed at the infractions hearing that nothing about the courses themselves, the way they were administered or the way they were graded, violated then-existing policies. UNC admitted the courses would violate its current policies.

Enrollment in the courses literally began, continued and ended with the secretary. Generally, she controlled the administration of department offerings, administration of courses and, eventually, grading of many of the submitted papers. In both her written response and at the infractions hearing, she identified that the courses were meant to assist all UNC students who had difficult circumstances. If any student had extenuating circumstances, the secretary would accommodate them with a paper course. For students, those circumstances included schedule and work conflicts, campus obligations and, on occasion, difficult personal circumstances. For student athletes, those circumstances included athletic obligations (*i.e.*, practice, meetings, games and other athletically related activity). These arrangements started with a case-by-case approach, but as word spread and popularity soared, the secretary had to adjust her approach to handle the demand. To facilitate that demand, the secretary relied on academic counselors (both academic counselors for students and [special Academic Support Services for Student-Athletes (ASPSA)] counselors) to identify extenuating circumstances. . . .

Once enrolled in the courses, student-athletes or ASPSA staff usually received the assigned topic from the secretary. During her interview, she acknowledged that she would provide paper topics but indicated that all paper topics were faculty approved. ASPSA records indicate that while student-athletes may not have met with faculty members, they did work with ASPSA staff on writing and structuring research papers. Further, sometimes ASPSA staff turned in student athletes' completed papers. As it relates to the quality of the work, at least some interviewees suggested that the courses required little academic work and substance.

Most ASPSA counselors knew that papers would likely receive an A or a B. Others knew, or had suspicions, that the secretary actually graded the papers.

* * *

As far as her grading method, the secretary admitted that she did not read every word of every paper submitted. But in following the department chair's instructions, if the paper met his stated requirements, she gave it an A or a B.

ASPSA personnel recognized the positive impact the paper courses had on student-athletes' grade-point averages (GPAs). Around the time of the secretary's retirement, a former ASPSA associate director met with the football staff regarding promoting academic responsibility among its student-athletes. In that presentation, she included a slide that indicated the paper courses were part of the "solution in the past" but no longer existed. The slide specifically indicated four characteristics of the courses where student-athletes were not required to: (1) go to class; (2) take notes or stay awake; (3) meet with professors; and (4) pay attention or necessarily engage with the material. The presentation also included comparisons of student-athletes' GPAs with and without paper courses. Of the eight examples, all had AFAM GPAs of 3.2 or higher and other GPAs lower than 2.036, with six of the eight student-athletes' other GPAs falling below 2.0.

* * *

[The report discussed the violations by the University officials that failed to report the academic fraud. The panel then considered the other allegations.]

The case involved three other allegations: (1) unethical conduct and extra benefits related to student-athletes' access to and assistance in the paper courses; (2) unethical conduct by the instructor/counselor for providing impermissible academic assistance to student-athletes; and (3) a failure to monitor and lack of institutional control.

* * *

The enforcement staff identified six actions that taken alone or in combination purportedly constituted active management of the courses and extra benefit violations. In part, UNC claimed that there were no extra benefit violations because its actions were required and/or permitted under Bylaw 16.3.1.1. [This Bylaw mandates "academic counseling and tutoring services" and permits "other academic and support services that the institution, at its discretion, determines to be appropriate and necessary for the academic success of its student-athletes."] UNC mischaracterized the bylaw and its obligations. Bylaw 16.3.1.1 is not without limits. And it is not intended to be used as a shield for an academic program gone awry. It is intended to support, not replace, student-athletes' academic efforts. Supplanting student-athletes' academic efforts, responsibilities and educational experiences can violate NCAA legislation. Regardless, the panel cannot conclude that ASPSA's or athletics personnel's actions taken alone, in combination or in totality resulted in extra benefits. The record covers nearly two decades of information. It touches broad concepts but fails to establish specific or systemic activities limited to student-athletes. While student-athletes certainly benefited from the courses and ASPSA assistance, the record indicates that similar assistance was generally available to all students. Therefore, the panel cannot conclude that violations occurred.

* * *

[The Cadwalader report concluded that systematic academic fraud had occurred at UNC. The University initially affirmed these findings, but later attempted to recharacterize what happened on its campus as academically honest. Even so, the panel concluded] that it is more likely than not that student-athletes received fraudulent credit by the common understanding of what that term means. It is also more likely than not that UNC personnel used the courses to purposely obtain and maintain student-athletes' eligibility. These strong possibilities, however, are not the operative or controlling starting points to the membership's academic fraud analysis. What ultimately matters is what UNC says about the courses. In addition to rejecting its early admissions and distancing itself from the Cadwalader report in the infractions process, UNC took the firm position that the courses were permissible and UNC will continue to honor the grades. Despite the fact that the courses failed to meet, involved little, if any, faculty engagement, and were often graded by the secretary, UNC argued the courses violated no UNC policy. UNC further claimed that work was assigned, completed and graded, and the grades counted towards a UNC degree.

* * *

The [Committee on Infractions (COI)], however, has not confirmed allegations on such a broad and convoluted set of facts or on academic allegations where the institution repeatedly affirms during the infractions process that the conduct did not violate its policies in place at the relevant time.

UNC has offered two diametrically opposed characterizations of the courses, seemingly dependent on the venue. Even if the panel were to assign more credibility to UNC's initial admissions to SACS [the Southern Association of Colleges and Schools which accredits the University of North Carolina], the case record does not support overriding UNC's recent positions. The record was voluminous. It also included information spanning nearly two decades and interviews where subjects had difficulty recalling circumstances and events. This lack of specificity inhibited the panel's ability to test and probe certain theories. Therefore, the panel cannot confirm the allegations and conclude that academic fraud occurred. Further, the record's limitations did not establish a firm basis for the panel issuing new allegations.

* * *

As the panel previously noted, the NCAA's role in academic violations is limited. While the NCAA defers academic fraud determinations to member institutions, there is no such deference requirement for impermissible academic assistance. But there are circumstances where the question whether impermissible academic assistance occurred itself requires academic judgments. In those circumstances, the COI must tread carefully. A violation must be clear on its face. Here, there are gaps in the record. . . .

Considering the record and the instructor/counselor's credible statements at the hearing, the panel cannot conclude that she committed unethical conduct. Similarly, because she thoroughly explained her approach to all students and student-athletes she encountered, which is not refuted by the record material, the panel cannot conclude that she provided women's basketball student-athletes with extra benefits. It is not clear on the face of the record that the conduct supported impermissible academic assistance. The dual role as instructor and academic counselor is a significant issue, one that member institutions must approach with caution. Proper policies and procedures regarding appropriate behaviors are essential to ensure individuals have a clear understanding of what is appropriate and what is not.

* * *

The record, however, does not establish specific, intentional or systemic efforts tied to athletics motives. The record was full of email chains, missing academic work and interviews conducted, in some circumstances, more than five years after the classes ceased. Those materials required the panel to, at best, infer motives based on the large number of student-athletes who took the courses and received high marks. While student-athletes and athletics programs likely benefitted from utilizing the courses for eligibility purposes, regular students likely benefitted from them as well. Without the proper athletics touchpoints, however, the COI cannot conclude free-standing failure to monitor or lack of institutional control violations occurred based solely on deficient administrative structures. Here, absent the attenuated fact that potentially around two thousand student-athletes took these courses, the record does not demonstrate that those failures had an athletics motive. Based on the posture of the record and in light of the secretary's statements at the hearing related to the nature of the courses, the conduct did not involve those athletics touchpoints. . . .

Although the panel could not conclude academic, failure to monitor or lack of institutional control violations occurred, UNC originally adopted SACS' characterization of the conduct as academic fraud. UNC also admitted that the courses did not meet its standards and it let its students down. Bylaw 19.9.10 permits panels to recommend that the NCAA president forward a copy of the public infractions decision to accrediting bodies when the panel determines academic violations or questionable academic conduct occurred. Those circumstances are present here. Therefore, the panel will recommend that the NCAA president forward a copy of the public infractions decision to SACS.

NOTES AND QUESTIONS

1. *Lack of Consequences?* Which university's academic malfeasance was worse—Creighton's or UNC's? To what extent do such attempts to cut corners undermine the NCAA's narrative of education and student-athlete? In order to protect that narrative, do they require the imposition of stiff penalties? Is it troubling that neither Creighton nor North Carolina suffered any major athletic consequences for their academic fraud?

2. *Adequacy of Self-Policing?* Should the NCAA's role be to hold universities accountable? Or is the better model to defer to the university's policing of itself? Universities have strong motivations to conduct their academic programs with honesty. On the other hand, the pressure to win is

non-ceasing. Did North Carolina adequately self-police before being prodded by the NCAA?

3.   *Pressure of Athletics on Academics*. As discussed in the next chapter, athletes at Northwestern seeking union representation questioned the balance between academics and athletics, particularly in big-time revenue sports. Do the demands of college athletics make academic fraud likely or even inevitable? Could the NCAA create rules that might reduce the pressure on athletes in this context? How would you frame such rules?

4.   *Role of the NCAA*. Do you agree with the COI's characterization of its role in the North Carolina case? Or should it take a more active role in regulating academic fraud? Also, do you buy the COI's reasoning that making an opportunity available to non-athletes somehow removes it from NCAA scrutiny because it is not a "benefit" given just to athletes?

5.   *Athlete Versus Non-Athlete Benefits*. Part of the COI's reasoning related to the neutrality of the benefit offered, *i.e.*, it was provided to athletes and non-athletes alike. Why should it matter that non-athletes enjoyed the same benefits? Could a booster avoid scrutiny under recruiting rules by buying a car for a recruit and another car for the recruit's non-athlete friend?

E. COMPENSATION AND BENEFITS

For much of its history, the NCAA limited the compensation and benefits a university could provide its athletes to tuition, room, board, and books ("grant-in-aid"). Any other benefit provided by the university or a third-party, even if de minimis, constituted an illegal benefit that threatened the eligibility of the athlete. For decades, NCAA rules were exceedingly specific and sought to preserve its conception of amateurism at all costs. The rules have broadened considerably, as a result of judicial decisions and legislation explored in Chapter 12.

A question examined in the next two cases is whether receiving compensation related to prior athletic participation bars an athlete from intercollegiate competition.

NCAA v. LASEGE

53 S.W.3d 77 (Ky. 2001)

I.   INTRODUCTION

The National Collegiate Athletic Association ("NCAA") moves this Court for interlocutory relief under [Court Rule] 65.09 and asks us to vacate the Jefferson Circuit Court's temporary injunction which (1) declares Respondent Lasege eligible to participate in NCAA intercollegiate basketball and (2) prohibits the NCAA from imposing future sanctions against Lasege or Respondent University of Louisville ("U of L") pursuant to its NCAA Bylaw 19.8 restitutionary powers. We find that the NCAA has demonstrated "extraordinary cause" justifying CR 65.09 relief and we vacate the temporary injunction in its entirety.

* * *

[Lasege, a citizen of Nigeria, a country in West Africa, enrolled at the University of Louisville during the 1999–2000 academic year with the intention of playing for its intercollegiate men's basketball team. In March 2000, U of L declared Lasege ineligible to play intercollegiate basketball because he had previously entered into professional basketball contracts and had received preferential benefits that compromised his amateur status. The NCAA declined to reinstate Lasege].

The NCAA described the factual basis for its findings as follows:

Prior to enrollment, SA [Student Athlete] asserts he left his home in Nigeria to go to Russia in order to obtain a visa to come to the U.S. so that SA could go to school. SA was provided with an airline ticket ($800) to Russia from Nigeria by the Russian Sports Agency, New Sport. While in Russia, SA signed a contract with New Sport in Russia to represent SA regarding playing basketball for the professional club system in Moscow. As a result of the New Sport three-year contract, SA was to receive a salary of $9,000 a year with additional monetary incentives based on athletic performance. SA asserts he did not receive a salary but did receive living accommodations and meals for approximately 18 months valued at $1,170. SA was provided a driver, a cook, a visa to Russia ($70), clothing ($75) and a round-trip ticket from Moscow to Nigeria ($798). SA signed a second contract with a professional basketball team, which was to provide SA with a salary, furnished apartment, utilities but no telephone, two round-trip airline tickets to return to Nigeria and a car for personal needs if SA should obtain a Russian driver's license. SA asserts he did not receive a salary from the second contract. SA competed with two junior teams in 13 contests. One of the teams was a junior team of the professional team SA signed the second contract with, and both junior teams were financially supported by professional teams. SA practiced with two professional teams but did not compete. SA was provided an airline ticket ($750) and visa ($50) to Canada from Moscow by an individual in Canada who knew of SA due to his athletics ability, which constituted a violation of 12.1.1.6. This individual provided SA with lodging and meals ($2,000) for approximately eight months. Individual also provided SA with automobile transportation to and lodging while at institution for an unofficial visit ($342.50), airline tickets, meals and lodging at another collegiate institution for an unofficial visit ($538) and a one-way airline ticket to institution for initial college enrollment ($101.50) for the 1999–00 academic year.

* * *

On November 27, 2000, Lasege filed a Motion and Complaint in Jefferson Circuit Court seeking a temporary injunction requiring the NCAA to reverse its decision as to U of L's request and to immediately reinstate his eligibility to play basketball at U of L. After conducting an evidentiary hearing, the trial court found that the complaint presented a substantial question as to whether the NCAA's ruling was arbitrary and capricious. Specifically, the trial court: (1) suggested that the NCAA had ignored what it described as "overwhelming and mitigating circumstances," including economic and cultural disadvantages, a complete ignorance of NCAA regulations, and elements of coercion associated with execution of the contracts; (2) believed the NCAA's determination to conflict with the NCAA's own amateurism guidelines and past eligibility determinations regarding athletes who had engaged in similar violations; (3) expressed its doubts about whether the first contract signed by Lasege was legally enforceable as an agency contract both because of Lasege's minority at the time he executed it and because the trial court disputed that the contract created an agency relationship; and (4) opined that a clear weight of evidence suggested Lasege committed these violations not in order to become a professional athlete, but only to obtain a visa which would allow him to become a student-athlete in the United States.

The trial court found that Lasege would suffer substantial collateral consequences from an erroneous and adverse eligibility determination, balanced the equities in favor of Lasege, and ordered "the NCAA and its members ... to immediately restore the intercollegiate eligibility of Muhammed Lasege so as to allow him to participate in all NCAA basketball contests." The trial court also addressed U of L's concern that the NCAA could impose sanctions under NCAA Bylaw 19.8 if the injunction was subsequently vacated. NCAA Bylaw 19.8 allows the NCAA to seek restitution from member institutions who permit student-athletes found ineligible by the NCAA to compete for their athletic teams pursuant to court orders which are later vacated. The trial court therefore "declare[d] that NCAA Bylaw 19.8 is invalid because it prevents parties from availing themselves of the protections of the courts" and ordered:

> ... that the University of Louisville shall abide by this injunction and shall not prohibit Muhammed Lasege from engaging in intercollegiate basketball;
>
> IT IS FURTHER ORDERED AND ADJUDGED that the NCAA and its members are hereby ordered to take no action to prevent or interfere with the University of Louisville's ability to abide by this Order by attempting to enforce NCAA Bylaw 19.8.

After the trial court entered the temporary injunction, Lasege played basketball for U of L during the 2000–2001 season.

While Lasege played, the NCAA sought interlocutory relief under CR 65.07, but the Court of Appeals found the trial court's findings supported by substantial evidence and denied the NCAA's motion. . . .

The NCAA thus seeks interlocutory relief from this Court.

III. DISCUSSION

III(A)—STANDARD OF REVIEW

Cases involving challenges to eligibility decisions made by voluntary athletic associations such as the Kentucky High School Athletic Association ("KHSAA") or, as in this case, the NCAA, pose special difficulties for our circuit courts. Such cases are invariably time-sensitive as they are typically filed in the midst of an athletic season, often on the cusp of postseason competition. Because athletic seasons are usually completed before either a final decision on the merits by the trial court or appellate review, a circuit court's ruling granting or denying a temporary injunction will typically, as a practical matter, decide the issue of whether a student-athlete competes. In *KHSAA v. Hopkins County Board of Education*, [552 S.W.2d 685, 690 (Ky. App. 1977)], the Court of Appeals recognized the inherent limitations courts face in such determinations:

> This case demonstrates that courts are a very poor place in which to conduct interscholastic athletic events, especially since this type of litigation is most likely to arise at playoff or tournament time. If an injunction or restraining order is granted erroneously, it will be practically impossible to unscramble the tournament results to reflect the ultimate outcome of the case.

Since, by definition, temporary injunctions attempt to place the parties in a position most likely to minimize harm before the court can finally decide the issues raised in a complaint, trial courts are asked to make significant decisions with less-than-complete information. As such, these determinations differ from most decisions reached by trial courts. There are no "drive-through windows" on courthouses for a good reason—judicial decision making demands thought and deliberation of all relevant evidence. The problem is further magnified by the fact that challenges to a voluntary athletic association's eligibility decision typically present issues which require considerable reflection. In general, the members of such associations should be allowed to "paddle their own canoe" without unwarranted interference from the courts. Nonetheless, relief from our judicial system should be available if voluntary athletic associations act arbitrarily and capriciously toward student-athletes. Thus, cases involving challenges to a voluntary athletic association's eligibility decisions involve difficult assessments of a plaintiff's probability of succeeding on his or her claim and complex balancing of competing interests. Because the values a trial court assigns to these competing interests will depend, in part, upon the trial court's assessment of the probability that the athletic association's determination was correct, a circuit court's ruling as to temporary injunctive relief largely hinges upon its preliminary determination of the merits of the plaintiff's claim. Claimants will generally demonstrate potential injuries which justify injunctive relief only when they can show a substantial probability that the athletic association's ruling was arbitrary and capricious. "Longshot" claims which have little hope of prevailing when the buzzer sounds will not justify injunctive relief.

* * *

In this case, we find that the trial court abused its discretion by: (1) substituting its judgment for that of the NCAA on the question of Lasege's intent to professionalize; (2) finding that the NCAA has no interest in this case which weighs against injunctive relief; and (3) declaring NCAA Bylaw 19.8 invalid. This combination of clearly erroneous conclusions constitutes extraordinary cause warranting CR 65.09 [interlocutory] relief.

III(B)—REINSTATEMENT OF LASEGE'S ELIGIBILITY

. . . The trial court made a preliminary determination/n that "the arbitrary nature of the enforcement of its by-laws by the members of the NCAA and its committees raises a substantial issue concerning the merits of their rules." The trial court further found that "Mr. Lasege faces irreparable harm because without reinstatement, he will not be able to continue in classes, and may be deported back to Nigeria." Although we agree with the trial court's assessment of the magnitude of the harm from an erroneous NCAA eligibility decision, we find that Lasege's chances of prevailing on the merits of his claim are too remote to justify injunctive relief. We believe the trial court clearly erred when assessing the merits of Lasege's claim.

In our opinion, the trial court wrongfully substituted its judgment for that of the NCAA after it analyzed the evidence and reached a different conclusion as to Lasege's intent to professionalize. The mere fact that a trial court considering mitigating evidence might disagree with the NCAA's factual conclusions does not render the NCAA's decision arbitrary or capricious. We have held that a ruling is arbitrary and capricious only where it is "clearly erroneous, and by 'clearly erroneous' we mean unsupported by substantial evidence." Here, the NCAA's ruling has strong evidentiary support—Lasege unquestionably signed contracts to play professional basketball and unquestionably accepted benefits. Contrary to the trial court's allegations of disparate treatment, the NCAA submits that no individual has ever had his or her eligibility reinstated after committing a combination of rules violations akin to those compiled by Lasege. The NCAA's eligibility determinations are entitled to a presumption of correctness—particularly when they stem from conceded violations of NCAA regulations. Although we recognize that Lasege's mitigation evidence is relevant to a review of the NCAA's determination, we believe the trial court simply disagreed with the NCAA as to the weight which should be assigned to this evidence. Accordingly, we believe the trial court abused its discretion when it found that Lasege had a high probability of success on the merits of his claim.

We also find "extraordinary cause" warranting CR 65.09 relief in the trial court's balancing of the equities. The trial court's order contrasts Lasege's risk of irreparable injury with the NCAA's interest and states that "the NCAA, on the other hand, will not suffer any potential harm by this court's order." We find this conclusion clearly erroneous, and accordingly believe the trial court's subsequent balancing of the equities suffers from an inherent computational error.

The NCAA unquestionably has an interest in enforcing its regulations and preserving the amateur nature of intercollegiate athletics. As the trial court entered a *temporary* injunction on the basis of its *preliminary* findings, the trial court could eventually determine that the NCAA properly denied the reinstatement request. If that is the case, the trial court's order would have erroneously allowed an ineligible player to participate in intercollegiate athletics. While the NCAA has no identifiable interest in the arbitrary application of its regulations to the detriment of a student-athlete, it certainly has an interest in the proper application of those regulations to ensure competitive equity.

* * *

III(C)—PROHIBITION OF NCAA BYLAW 19.8 RESTITUTION

[T]he trial court's order "that the NCAA and its members are hereby ordered to take no action to prevent or interfere with the University of Louisville's ability to abide by this Order by attempting to enforce NCAA Bylaw 19.8" declares an NCAA Bylaw invalid within the Commonwealth of Kentucky and insulates U of L from restitutionary sanctions for allowing Lasege to participate as a member of its intercollegiate men's basketball team.

At the outset, we observe that the trial court's order gives no indication that it engaged in a CR 65.04 analysis before enjoining the NCAA in this regard, and that reason standing alone would require us to vacate this portion of the injunction. It appears that the trial court included this prophylactic measure, at U of L's urging, simply to facilitate its other order by permitting U of L the "risk-free" right to allow Lasege to play basketball. In any event, we can find no interest which would justify such injunctive relief. Accordingly, we find that the trial court abused its discretion when it prohibited the NCAA from seeking NCAA Bylaw 19.8 restitution.

By becoming a member of the NCAA, a voluntary athletic association, U of L agreed to abide by its rules and regulations. NCAA Bylaw 19.8 is one of those regulations, and it specifically provides that the NCAA can attempt to restore competitive equity by redistributing wins and losses and imposing sanctions upon a member institution which allows an ineligible player to participate under a subsequently-vacated court order, even if that order requires the institution to allow the player to participate. [The court quoted from an Indiana Supreme Court decision that deferred to a high school athletic association's contractual risk allocation in its Restitution Rule:]

> While schools will contend that is unfair when they have to forfeit victories earned with an ineligible player on the field because they complied with a court order, competing schools will reply that it is unfair when they have to compete against a team with an ineligible student athlete because a local trial judge prohibited the school or the [Association] from following the eligibility rules. The Restitution Rule represents the agreement of [Association] members on how to balance those two competing interests. The Restitution Rule may not be the best method to deal with such situations. However, it is the method which the member schools have adopted. And in any event, its enforcement by the [Association] does not impinge upon the judiciary's function.[18]

In fact, contrary to the belief of the trial court the concept of "risk-free" injunctive relief is unheard of—CR 65.05 requires the party in whose favor the injunction is granted to post a bond and wrongfully enjoined parties may recover compensatory damages. Here, U of L and the other NCAA members reached an agreement as to how competitive equity should be restored in the event of an erroneous court determination regarding a player's eligibility, and the trial court simply released U of L from that obligation.

The trial court's belief that the NCAA's Restitution Rule "thwarts the judicial power" is simply without foundation. NCAA Bylaw 19.8, like the Restitution Rules enforced by many state high school athletic associations "does not purport to authorize interference with any court order during the time it remains in effect, but only authorizes restitutive penalties when a temporary restraining order is ultimately dissolved and the challenged eligibility rule remains undisturbed in force." The authority of the courts is thus in no way compromised, and NCAA Bylaw 19.8 merely allows for post-hoc equalization when a trial court's erroneously granted temporary injunction upsets competitive balance. If the trial court's preliminary conclusions carry the day, and a student-athlete's eligibility is confirmed by final determination, no restitutionary remedy is warranted or appropriate, and NCAA Bylaw 19.8 provides for none.

* * *

[Dissenting opinion by JOHNSTONE, J., omitted].

---

18   *IHSAA v. Reyes*, 694 N.E.2d 249, 257–8 (Ind. 1997). See also *Cardinal Mooney High School v. Michigan High School*, 437 Mich. 75, 467 N.W.2d 21 (Mich. 1991). * * *

NOTES AND QUESTIONS

1. *Aftermath.* The decision of the Kentucky Supreme Court effectively ended Lasege's college basketball career. He did not make it to the NBA. An excellent student, Lasege later received an MBA from the Wharton school.

2. *Pre-NCAA Remuneration.* Should receiving money for athletics prior to coming to college disqualify an athlete from NCAA participation? Do you agree with the NCAA that Lasege's prior experiences should remove his amateur status? Or should past experience be irrelevant to the amateurism determination?

3. *Benefit?* Did the benefit received by Lasege somehow create an unfair playing field with respect to other amateur athletes? Was the pre-Louisville benefit to Lasege really just the experience itself or the actual compensation?

4. *An Alternative Solution?* NCAA By-law 19.08 responds to concerns that a "home court" local judge would distort intercollegiate competition by injunctive relief that permitted ineligible players to participate, but does so at the expense of any meaningful review of NCAA eligibility decisions. Would a preferable alternative be an NCAA rule that both required all prospective athletes and schools to agree to arbitrate any legal claims regarding eligibility, and also created an impartial tribunal that could render a quick and final judgment?

BLOOM V. NCAA

93 P.3d 621 (Colo. Ct. App. 2004)

Opinion by JUDGE DAILEY.

In this dispute concerning eligibility to play college football, plaintiff, Jeremy Bloom, appeals the trial court's order denying his request for a preliminary injunction against defendants, the National Collegiate Athletic Association (NCAA) and the University of Colorado (CU). We affirm.

[Bloom, a world-class skier and a very gifted football player, had failed in his attempt to comply with NCAA rules that permit student-athletes to maintain their amateur eligibility in one sport while turning professional in another sport. Although Stanford Quarterback John Elway was permitted to receive a huge bonus check to play minor league baseball for a New York Yankees farm team, and Bloom was allowed to receive prize money for skiing, NCAA rules barred him from earning endorsement income from ski-related products, which is a principal source of income for professional skiers.]

* * *

IV. Standing

We reject the NCAA's assertion that Bloom lacked standing to pursue claims for breach of contract or arbitrary and capricious action on the part of the NCAA [because] . . . the NCAA's constitution, bylaws, and regulations evidence a clear intent to benefit student-athletes. And because each student-athlete's eligibility to compete is determined by the NCAA, we conclude that Bloom had standing in a preliminary injunction hearing to contest the meaning or applicability of NCAA eligibility restrictions.

* * *

V. Probability of Success

Bloom contends that the trial court erred in assessing the probability of success on his contract claims. We disagree. . . .

A. Interpretation of NCAA Bylaws

* * *

Bloom relies on NCAA Bylaw 12.1.2, which states that "[a] professional athlete in one sport may represent a member institution in a different sport." He asserts that, because a professional is one who "gets paid" for a sport, a student-athlete is entitled to earn whatever income is customary for his or her professional sport, which, in the case of professional skiers, primarily comes from endorsements and paid media opportunities.

We recognize that, like many others involved in individual professional sports such as golf, tennis, and boxing, professional skiers obtain much of their income from sponsors. We note, however, that none of the NCAA's bylaws mentions, much less explicitly establishes, a right to receive "customary income" for a sport.

To the contrary, the NCAA bylaws prohibit every student-athlete from receiving money for advertisements and endorsements. . . . Additionally, while NCAA Bylaw 12.5.1.3 permits a student-athlete to continue to receive remuneration for activity initiated prior to enrollment in which his or her name or picture is used, this remuneration is only allowed, if, as pertinent here, "the individual became involved in such activities for reasons independent of athletics ability; . . . no reference is made in these activities to the individual's name or involvement in intercollegiate athletics; [and] . . . the individual does not endorse the commercial product."

* * *

In our view, when read together, the NCAA bylaws express a clear and unambiguous intent to prohibit student-athletes from engaging in endorsements and paid media appearances, without regard to: (1) when the opportunity for such activities originated; (2) whether the opportunity arose or exists for reasons unrelated to participation in an amateur sport; and (3) whether income derived from the opportunity is customary for any particular professional sport.

The clear import of the bylaws is that, although student-athletes have the right to be professional athletes, they do not have the right to simultaneously engage in endorsement or paid media activity and maintain their eligibility to participate in amateur competition. And we may not disregard the clear meaning of the bylaws simply because they may disproportionately affect those who participate in individual professional sports.

Further, the record contains ample evidence supporting the trial court's conclusion that this interpretation is consistent with both the NCAA's and its member institutions' construction of the bylaws. . . . Thus, even if the bylaws were viewed as ambiguous, the record supports the trial court's conclusion that the bylaws would ultimately be interpreted in accordance with the NCAA's and its member institutions' construction of those bylaws.

B.   Application of Bylaws to Bloom

The United States Supreme Court has recognized the NCAA as "the guardian of an important American tradition," namely, amateurism in intercollegiate athletics. *See NCAA v. Bd. of Regents,* 468 U.S. 85, 101 (1984).

[The court found that the NCAA seeks to keep student participation in intercollegiate athletics as an "avocation" and pursued the "legitimate purpose of retaining the 'clear line of demarcation between intercollegiate athletics and professional sports.' "]

The trial court noted that salaries and bonuses are an acceptable means for attaining income from professional sports, but endorsement income is not acceptable if a student-athlete wishes to preserve amateur eligibility. According to NCAA officials: (1) endorsements invoke concerns about "the commercial exploitation of student-athletes and the promotion of commercial products"; and (2) it is not possible to distinguish the precise capacity in which endorsements are made. A CU official related that generally, the endorsement rule prevents students from becoming billboards for commercialism, and in Bloom's case, there would "be no way to tell whether he is receiving pay commensurate with his . . . football ability or skiing ability."

* * *

In this case, Bloom presented evidence that some of his acting opportunities arose not as a result of his athletic ability but because of his good looks and on-camera presence. However, the record contains evidence that Bloom's agent and the Tommy Hilfiger company marketed Bloom as a talented multi-sport athlete, and a representative from a talent agency intimated that Bloom's reputation as an athlete would be advantageous in obtaining auditions for various entertainment opportunities. Further, the NCAA indicated, when asked to interpret its rules, that it was unable, due to insufficient information, to determine which of Bloom's requested media activities were, in fact, unrelated to his athletic ability or prestige.

Under these circumstances, we perceive no abuse of the trial court's discretion in failing to fault the NCAA for refusing to waive its rules, as requested by CU, to permit Bloom "to pursue any television and film opportunities while he is a student-athlete at CU." *See Cole v. NCAA,* 120 F. Supp. 2d 1060, 1071–72 (N.D.Ga.2000) (NCAA decisions regarding "challenges of student-athletes are entitled to considerable deference," and courts are reluctant to replace the NCAA as the "decision-maker on private waiver applications"); *see also NCAA v. Lasege, supra,* 53 S.W.3d at 83 (voluntary athletic associations "should be allowed to 'paddle their own canoe' without unwarranted interference from the courts").

Bloom also asserts that the NCAA is arbitrary in its application of the endorsement and media bylaws. He notes that, while the NCAA would bar him from accepting commercial endorsements, it will allow colleges to commercially endorse athletic equipment by having students wear the equipment, with identifying logos and insignias, while engaged in intercollegiate competition. But the trial court determined, and we agree, that this application of the bylaws has a rational basis in economic necessity: financial benefits inure not to any single student-athlete but to member schools and thus to all student-athletes, including those who participate in programs that generate no revenue.

* * *

The record thus supports the trial court's findings that the NCAA's administrative review process is reasonable in general and that it was reasonably applied in this case. As such, these findings, as well as those with respect to the NCAA's application of its bylaws, are not manifestly arbitrary, unreasonable, or unfair. *See Bd. of County Comm'rs v. Fixed Base Operators, Inc., supra,* 939 P.2d at 467.

For these reasons, we agree with the trial court that Bloom failed to demonstrate a reasonable probability of success on the merits.

———

NOTES AND QUESTIONS

1.   *Aftermath.* Following this decision, Bloom decided not to appeal any further. He had success playing football, but was unable to sustain a pro career, and also failed in his later attempt at Olympic skiing. Should the NCAA have previously granted the University of Colorado's petition for a waiver of its rule, given Bloom's unique situation? On what basis could the NCAA grant

the petition without creating a precedent that would effectively undermine the rule? Is the NCAA rule sensible?

2.   *State NIL Laws.* With the adoption of state laws prohibiting the NCAA from interfering with state NIL compensation, the NCAA would no longer be able to restrict Bloom from receiving endorsements. Do you think this is a positive development?

3.   *Amateurism and Use of Name, Image, Likeness.* Do you agree that Bloom receiving endorsements would compromise his amateur status in such a way that the NCAA is right to prohibit it under the old rule? What about compensation for modeling? Is it a fair characterization of the situation that the NCAA rule served to protect Bloom from exploitation by third parties? Do you find the old rule justifiable or paternalistically unreasonable?

F.   RECRUITING AND TRANSFERRING

The NCAA's new constitution and bylaws still contain regulations concerning the recruiting of student-athletes and limits on benefits available to recruits. The NCAA continues to prohibit pay for play:

> Student-athletes may not be compensated by a member institution for participating in a sport but may receive educational and other benefits in accordance with guidelines established by their NCAA division.

NCAA Constitution, Article § 1.B (2022).

It also requires universities to continue to exercise institutional control over their athletic programs:

> It is the responsibility of each member institution to monitor and control its athletics program and to provide education and training to ensure compliance with the rules established by the Association, its division and conference. It is the responsibility of each member institution to report all rules violations to its NCAA division and conference in a timely manner and to cooperate fully with enforcement efforts. Responsibility for maintaining institutional control ultimately rests with the institution's campus president or chancellor.

NCAA Constitution, Article § 1.E (2022).

And it makes clear that recruiting standards still exist, albeit in a more decentralized manner:

> Divisional bylaws shall be designed to promote informed decisions and balance the interests of prospective and current (or transfer) student-athletes, their educational institutions and intercollegiate athletics as a whole.

NCAA Constitution, Article § 1.H (2022).

These rules have long existed both to preserve the ideal of the student-athlete and to promote competitive equity among schools. One university should not be able, under the NCAA's amateurism approach, to buy all of the best high school players.

The adoption of NIL laws has created challenges for distinguishing between acceptable recruiting practices and NCAA violations. Universities cannot compensate athletes beyond benefits related to education, but third parties can as long as that remuneration is compensation for NIL use. Further, universities and third parties cannot use NIL contracts or compensation as an inducement for an athlete to choose a particular school but by all appearances it is difficult to separate the decision to attend a school from the perceived endorsement opportunities that athletes can receive by attending that school.

In an NIL world, though, athletes can receive outside income for their name, image, and likeness, which would have previously violated NCAA rules. Thus, endorsement deals from third parties no longer cross this line, as a result of state laws and the NCAA policy which incorporates them.

Nonetheless, student athletes still bear a significant degree of responsibility for preserving their amateur status. The general bylaw principle explains:

> The recruitment of a student-athlete by a member institution or any representative of its athletics interests in violation of the Association's legislation, as acknowledged by the institution or established through the Association's infractions process, shall result in the student athlete becoming ineligible to represent that institution in intercollegiate athletics. . . A student is responsible for his or her involvement in a violation of NCAA regulations during the student's recruitment, and involvement in a Level I or Level II violation may cause the student to become permanently ineligible for intercollegiate athletics competition at that institution.

NCAA Article 13.01.1 (2022). Athletes accepting improper benefits thus might not only lose the ability to play for a particular school, but also can lose the ability to compete altogether. Under NCAA rules, once an athlete accepts improper benefits, his or her amateur status can be lost forever. The likelihood of a university paying such benefits after the adoption of NIL is negligible, particularly since third-party boosters are not only available but also likely to have more resources.

It is important to note that improper benefits restrictions do not mean that the universities cannot benefit athletes in other ways. Over the past decade or more, universities have been in an "arms-race" of sorts to provide better and better facilities for athletes with an increased range of amenities. In addition to spending millions on facilities, universities also provide athletes with tutoring services and other forms of academic support.

———

Historically, the NCAA required transfers in certain sports—baseball, basketball, men's ice hockey, and bowl subdivision football—to spend an academic year in residence before being eligible to play for the new university. Over time, the NCAA began granting waivers to particular students, and ultimately became overwhelmed by the waiver process.

Effective beginning with the 2021–22 academic year, the NCAA adopted a one-time transfer rule, and instituted a transfer portal. Under the one-time transfer rule, athletes are eligible to play immediately at their new schools.

To qualify for the one-time transfer, an athlete must:

- Transfer from a four-year collegiate institution to an NCAA Division I school;

- Leave their current four-year school academically eligible;

- Have not transferred previously from another four-year institution; and

- Certify in writing, along with their new head coach, they did not have direct or indirect communication with the new school's athletics staff prior to entering the NCAA Transfer Portal.

The deadline to enter the transfer portal is May 1 for fall or winter sports, and July 1 for spring sports. Further, the one-time transfer rule also applies to post-graduate transfers. Finally, athletes who have exercised the one-time transfer rule would have to spend a year in academic residence prior to eligibility on subsequent transfers. The NCAA may waive this requirement on a case-by-case basis.

The effect of this rule change has been to introduce greater freedom of player movement into intercollegiate athletics, particularly college football and college basketball. Coaches have opted to recruit less than a full class of high school athletes to reserve scholarship spaces for transfers. And teams have an instant way to become competitive again, through the acquisition of stars from other universities.

G. GOING PRO

From the perspective of labor or employment law, college athletes become professional when they sign contracts of employment with a professional club. NCAA regulations, however, continue to maintain three key thresholds that relate to athletes' continued eligibility for intercollegiate athletics—becoming eligible for the draft, entering the draft, and retaining an agent. College football players cannot enter the National Football League draft until three years after they have graduated high school. If the athlete has not used up their college eligibility, the league must approve the request to enter the draft early. (For a failed challenge to this rule, see the *Clarett* case in chapter 7.) College basketball players cannot enter the draft until the calendar year that they turn 19 years old and one season has passed since graduation from high school. Baseball players can enter the Major League Baseball draft after high school, and again after their third year of college.

Alternative professional sports leagues have begun to provide options for athletes that want to spend less time in college or avoid college altogether. The NBA's well-established Gatorade League (G-League) allows athletes to play basketball in their league once they turn 18. In 2022, the XFL and the USFL started new iterations, with the XFL having no age requirement and the USFL requiring two years out of high school instead of the three required by the NFL. Athletes in baseball, basketball, hockey, and soccer can also play professionally outside the United States.

In the past, NCAA regulations terminated amateur status once the athlete declared for the draft. Over time, the NCAA relaxed the rule to allow athletes to declare for the draft and enjoy an exploratory period in which pro scouts could evaluate them and provide feedback before then deciding to enter the draft or withdraw their declaration. Recent college basketball reforms allow college basketball players to enter the draft and then return to college without losing their eligibility. The athletes have 10 days after the conclusion of the NBA draft to withdraw from the draft process and return to their college team. These reforms, however, have not yet reached college football players. Once the cutoff for withdrawing from the draft passes (which occurs prior to the draft), college football players lose their amateur football status and become ineligible to play college football.

Perhaps even more confusing are the NCAA's rules about agents. Historically, the NCAA rules provided that retaining an agent would cost an athlete their eligibility. State NIL laws have complicated this picture. Athletes are allowed to use agents to negotiate their NIL deals. In addition, as with the draft, the NCAA has recently changed its rules to allow basketball players to hire agents. They have not, to date, changed these rules with respect to college football players. With the widespread use of agents for NIL, it seems like it is only a matter of time before the NCAA will abandon all restrictions on agents, particularly because the NFLPA has authorized NFL agents to represent college athletes in NIL deals.

The two cases below explore the potential limits on the NCAA regulation of agents.

SHELTON V. NCAA
539 F.2d 1197 (9th Cir. 1976)

WRIGHT, CIRCUIT JUDGE.

The principal issue in this appeal is whether the NCAA rule declaring ineligible for intercollegiate athletics in a particular sport any student who has ever signed a contract to play that professional sport violates the Equal Protection Clause of the constitution.

* * *

Appellee Shelton does not deny that he signed a professional contract with an American Basketball Association team which resulted in his being declared ineligible by Oregon State University. Indeed, he contends that the contract is unenforceable because he was induced to sign it by fraud and undue influence. The legal enforceability of the contract is the subject of a separate action brought by Shelton against the professional team which is now pending before the district court. Shelton urges that the NCAA rule making him ineligible despite the alleged defects in the contract creates an impermissible classification in violation of the Equal Protection Clause. He wants the rule suspended while his litigation and the college basketball season continue.

Our review on such questions is limited. None of the parties contends that the NCAA rule infringes upon a fundamental right which would necessitate strict judicial scrutiny. Instead, we must examine the rule to determine whether it rationally furthers some legitimate purpose. If it does, then our review is complete.

The rule purports to promote and protect amateurism in intercollegiate athletics. None of the parties seriously contends that this goal is illegitimate. Instead they dispute the means chosen by the NCAA to achieve it.

Shelton believes that it is unreasonable to treat as a professional one who alleges that the contract which he signed is unenforceable. In effect, he contends that the NCAA rule is overinclusive because if he is successful in his other action and the contract is declared unenforceable he is not nor would he ever have been a professional.

In a similar case two years ago, *Associated Students, Inc. v. NCAA*, 493 F.2d 1251 (9th Cir. 1974), this court reviewed another NCAA eligibility rule which was challenged on equal protection grounds. We recognized that the application of such rules may produce unreasonable results in certain situations. Nonetheless, we found that the rule did not violate the equal protection clause. Moreover, we did so although we recognized that the rule and its enforcement provisions might not be the best means for achieving the desired goal. It is not judicial business to tell a voluntary athletic association how best to formulate or enforce its rules.

We believe that the present appeal is controlled by *Associated Students*. The general rule under which Shelton was declared ineligible may from time to time produce unfortunate results. If an individual were subsequently successful in gaining a legal declaration that a professional contract was in fact void from its inception, a ruling that he was ineligible in the interim between his signing and the court's judgment might cause hardship. But the potential hardship does not make the rule irrational or unrelated to its goal. Moreover, hardship could be avoided by not signing a pro-contract. Reliance on a signed contract as an indication that a student's amateur status has been compromised is rationally related to the goal of preserving amateurism in intercollegiate athletics.

While our function is to determine only if the NCAA has selected a method of protecting amateurism which is reasonably related to that goal, an examination of the alternatives suggested by Shelton supports the conclusion that the rule in question withstands an equal protection challenge. Shelton argues that the rule should allow for cases such as his own where alleged defects in formation of the contract render it a nullity. The NCAA and its member institutions cannot simply take an athlete's word that his signed contract is void. An eligibility rule limited to contracts that would withstand a court test would be no rule at all. One could sign a contract, then allege that it was unenforceable and participate at will in college athletics while maintaining an option to enter the professional ranks at any time. Clearly, this would obliterate any remaining distinctions between amateur and professional athletes.

The alternative would be extremely burdensome. In the context of this appeal, for instance, the NCAA and its member institutions would be placed in the position of having to predict the outcome of Shelton's action against the professional basketball team. In order to do so they would likely have to undertake extensive investigations of the facts and time consuming hearings involving the parties. Even then, they would have no assurance that their decision would be compatible with the ultimate determination of the courts.

We hold that an effort to avoid this tangled set of affairs through the use of an easily applied and generally reliable criterion is rationally related to a legitimate purpose and does not, therefore, violate the equal protection clause.

Case dismissed.

NOTES AND QUESTIONS

1. *Aftermath.* After *Shelton*, the NCAA amended the rule to make clear that merely *signing* a professional contract will cost the student-athlete his

amateur status, "regardless of [the contract's] legal enforceability or any consideration received." Article 12.1.3.

2. *The Scope of Amateurism.* The NCAA rules concerning signing a professional contract seemed justified in an era when college sports was not a multi-billion dollar industry. As explored in Chapter 12, to what extent has the increase in commercialism in college sports made such rules less justifiable?

OLIVER V. NCAA
920 N.E.2d 203 (2009)

TONE, JUDGE.

* * *

FACTS

The plaintiff, Andrew Oliver, is a resident of Vermilion, Erie County, Ohio. In 2006, the plaintiff graduated from Vermilion High School, where he was the primary pitcher for its baseball team. The plaintiff is currently in his junior year of college at Oklahoma State University ("OSU"). Since August 2006, the plaintiff has pitched for the baseball team at OSU.

The defendant, the National Collegiate Athletic Association ("NCAA"), is an unincorporated business association having its principal place of business in Marion County, Indiana; it has member institutions not only in Oklahoma but also in Ohio. . . .

The plaintiff, in February 2006, retained the services of Robert M. Baratta, Tim Baratta, and Icon Sports Group, d.b.a. Icon Law Group, as his sports advisors and attorneys. In June of the same year, the Minnesota Twins of Major League Baseball drafted the plaintiff in the 17th round of the draft. At the end of the summer, the Minnesota Twins met with the plaintiff and his father at the Oliver family home in Vermilion before the plaintiff left for his freshman year of college. Tim Baratta also attended the meeting, at his own request, at the Oliver home. During the meeting the Minnesota Twins offered the plaintiff $390,000 to join their organization. After heeding the advice of his father, the plaintiff rejected the offer and chose to attend OSU in the fall on a full scholarship for which he had already signed a letter of intent in the fall of 2005.

As a result of deciding to go to OSU and accepting amateur status, the plaintiff would not be eligible for the draft again until his junior year of college in June 2009. The plaintiff played his freshman and sophomore years for OSU, and during that period he never received any invoices requesting payment for any services rendered by his advisors. In fact, the plaintiff avers that the advisors provided nothing of value to him.

In March 2008, plaintiff decided to terminate the Barattas and Icon Sports and retain the Boras Corporation. The plaintiff communicated his intentions of termination to Robert Baratta. At that time, Robert Baratta attempted to reconnect with the plaintiff and his father, but to no avail. In April 2008, the plaintiff received a letter and an invoice from the Barattas for $113,750 for legal services. . . . The plaintiff has argued that the contract is fictitious and the assistance stated in it was in fact never performed.

On May 19, 2008, the previous attorneys mailed, faxed, and e-mailed a letter to the defendant complaining about the plaintiff and reporting alleged violations by the plaintiff, *i.e.* the meeting at the Olivers' home that Tim Baratta had attended. As a result of the allegations, OSU and the defendant investigated the alleged violations in relationship to the plaintiff's amateur status. In May 2008, the plaintiff was indefinitely suspended from playing baseball and was informed by OSU staff that he had violated NCAA Bylaw 12.3.1 by (1) allowing his previous attorneys to contact the Minnesota Twins by telephone and (2) by allowing Tim Baratta to be present in his home when a representative from the Minnesota Twins tendered an offer to him.

On August 18, 2008, the plaintiff was reinstated as a result of a temporary restraining order issued by this court. However, in October 2008, OSU filed for reinstatement of the plaintiff with the NCAA even though the temporary restraining order had reinstated the plaintiff. Subsequently, in December 2008, the plaintiff was suspended for one year and charged a year of eligibility by the defendant. The penalty was subsequently reduced to 70 percent of the original suspension and no loss of eligibility for the plaintiff.

* * *

To the extent that the plaintiff's claim of arbitrary and capricious action asserts a violation of the duty of good faith and fair dealing that is implied in the contractual relationship between the NCAA and its members, his position as a third-party beneficiary of that contractual relationship affords him standing to pursue his claims.

* * *

III. GOOD FAITH AND FAIR DEALING

Even though the obligation of good faith exists in a contractual relationship, this is not an invitation for this court to rewrite the benefit bestowed on the parties. The court agrees with the defendant that this is not a case about whether the court agrees or disagrees with the bylaws in question. * * * Therefore, the defendant, and for that matter OSU, was required to deal honestly and reasonably with the plaintiff as a third-party beneficiary regarding their contractual relationship. Surely each party is entitled to the benefit of its bargain. With that stated, if this court determines that Bylaw 12.3.2.1 is void because it is against the public policy of Ohio or because it is arbitrary and capricious, and Bylaw 19.7 interferes with the delegation of judicial power to the courts of this state, then the defendant has not dealt with the plaintiff honestly or reasonably and the defendant has breached the contract.

The court continues this analysis by examining the plaintiff's argument that he retained lawyers to represent him and that those lawyers are subject to the exclusive regulation of the Ohio Supreme Court. Thus the defendant, according to the plaintiff, had no authority to promulgate Bylaw 12.3.2.1. The plaintiff asserts that the bylaw promulgated by the defendant prevented his lawyers from competently representing him. Therefore the plaintiff argues, the bylaw is void because it is against public policy. Bylaw 12.3.2.1 states:

> A lawyer may not be present during discussions of a contract offer with a professional organization or have any direct contact (in person, by telephone or by mail) with a professional sports organization on behalf of the individual. A lawyer's presence during such discussions is considered representation by an agent.

In contrast, the defendant argues that Bylaw 12.3.2.1 helps to retain a clear line of demarcation between collegiate and professional sports that is a fundamental goal of the member institutions. Furthermore, according to the defendant, it preserves an amateur model of collegiate athletics, and the defendant contends that this court should not intervene since the bylaw is the will of the NCAA membership.

It is important to fully understand the fact pattern of what transpired and what caused the plaintiff to be pronounced ineligible. At the end of the summer of 2006, representatives from the Minnesota Twins met with the plaintiff and his father at the Oliver home. According to the plaintiff's testimony, the plaintiff's father contacted the Barattas to inform them of the meeting. Tim Baratta told the plaintiff's father that he thought he should be there. While all the parties were at the Oliver home, the Twins offered the plaintiff a $390,000 contract, which he rejected after seeking the advice of his father. However, Tim Baratta's presence at the Oliver home, even though no testimony ever portrayed that Mr. Baratta was involved in any of the conversations between the plaintiff and the Twin's representative, just Baratta's presence (the presence of an attorney/advisor who advised the plaintiff that he would keep his amateurism status safe) in that room, violated Bylaw 12.3.2.1 and stripped the plaintiff of his eligibility to play baseball through the entire season.

Let us also remember that the rules and testimony are clear that amateurism is the bedrock and founding principle of the NCAA. And so, the court has listened to and read much about Bylaw Article 12, set forth in the NCAA division manual, which is entitled "Amateurism" and sets forth the rules governing the protection of a student-athlete's amateur status that must be maintained in order for an athlete to participate in an intercollegiate sports program.

* * *

[T]he crux of this case falls under Bylaw 12.3.2, which carves out an exception to the no agent rule by allowing a student-athlete to retain a lawyer (not even the defendant can circumvent an individual's right to counsel). Yet, the exception to the rule, *i.e.*, NCAA Bylaw 12.3.2 which allows legal counsel for student-athletes attempts to limit an attorney's role as to that representation and, in effect, such as in the case here, puts the onus on the student-athlete.

The status of the no-agent rule, as firmly pointed out in the direct testimony of Kevin Hennon, vice president of membership services, is a prohibition against agents, not lawyers. Therein lies the problem.

It is impossible to allow student-athletes to hire lawyers and attempt to control what that lawyer does for his client by Bylaws 12.3.2 or 12.3.2.1. These rules attempt to say to the student-athlete that he or she can consult with an attorney but that the attorney cannot negotiate a contract with a professional sport's team. This surely does not retain a clear line of demarcation between amateurism and professionalism. The student-athlete will never know what his attorney is doing for him or her, and quite frankly neither will the defendant. The evidence is very clear that this rule is impossible to enforce and as a result is being enforced selectively. Further, as in this case, it allows for exploitation of the student-athlete "by professional and commercial enterprises," in contravention of the positive intentions of the defendant.

Was Baratta's presence in that room a clear indication that the plaintiff, a teenager who had admitted at trial that he was in no position to negotiate a professional contract and whose father testified to the same, was a professional? According to Bylaw 12.3.2.1, the no-agent rule, he was. As such the following issues must be resolved: Is the no-agent rule against the public policy of Ohio? Is it arbitrary? Is it capricious?

The plaintiff testified that he hired the Barattas in part because they were attorneys and they promised that they would protect his amateur status. From the testimony given at trial, the court is aware that the defendant permits student-athletes and their parents to negotiate contracts while in the presence of a sports representative but to have an attorney present in the room would in some way smear the line of demarcation between what is amateurism and what is professionalism. An attorney's duty, in Ohio, in Oklahoma, in all 50 states, is to represent his client competently. . . .

For a student-athlete to be permitted to have an attorney and then to tell that student-athlete that his attorney cannot be present during the discussion of an offer from a professional organization is akin to a patient hiring a doctor, but the doctor is told by the hospital board and the insurance company that he cannot be present when the patient meets with a surgeon because the conference may improve his patient's decision-making power. Bylaw 12.3.2.1 is unreliable (capricious) and illogical (arbitrary) and indeed stifles what attorneys are trained and retained to do.

The process advanced by the NCAA hinders representation by legal counsel, creating an atmosphere fraught with ethical dilemmas and pitfalls that an attorney consulting a student-athlete must encounter. Will the attorney be able to advance what is best for the client or will a neutral party, the NCAA, tie his hands? What harm could possibly befall the student-athlete if such a rule were not found? What occurs if the parents of a student are attorneys or for that matter sport agents? What would have happened if Tim Baratta had been in the kitchen or outside or on the patio instead of in the same room as His client when the offer from the Minnesota Twins was made to the plaintiff?

This court appreciates that a fundamental goal of the member institutions and the defendant is to preserve the clear line of demarcation between amateurism and professionalism. However, to suggest that Bylaw 12.3.2.1 accomplishes that purpose by instructing a student-athlete that his attorney cannot do what he or she was hired to do is simply illogical. . . . [N]o entity, other than that one designated by the state, can dictate to an attorney where, what, how, or when he should represent his client. With all due respect, surely that decision should not be determined by the NCAA and its member institutions, no matter what the defendant claims is the purpose of the rule. If the defendant intends to deal with this athlete or any athlete in good faith, the student-athlete should have the opportunity to have the tools present (in this case an attorney) that would allow him to make a wise decision without automatically being deemed a professional, especially when such contractual negotiations can be overwhelming even to those who are skilled in their implementation.

* * *

After this court has engaged in a balancing process that was designed to weigh the equities between the parties, the court determines by clear and convincing evidence that the plaintiff would suffer immediate and irreparable injury, loss, or damage if injunctive relief is not granted. If an injunction is not granted, the plaintiff would suffer loss of his college baseball experience, impairment or loss of his future baseball professional career, loss in being available for the upcoming draft because he is less likely to be seen, and ongoing damage to the plaintiff's reputation and baseball career.

In comparison, the defendant's witnesses stated that if relief were granted, it would be confusing as to which institutions would have to follow this court's ruling. Would it be Ohio members, Oklahoma members, all institutions? However, since this court has personam jurisdiction, this argument is not as persuasive as the plaintiff's and the scales of justice have tilted in the plaintiff's favor.

Judgment accordingly.

NOTES AND QUESTIONS

1. *Loss of Amateur Status.* Should hiring an agent make an athlete lose amateur status? What is the justification for this rule? Do you find it persuasive?

2. *The Line Between Amateur and Professional.* The NCAA's strict definition of "amateur" status has historically sought to maintain a clear line of demarcation between college athletics and professional sports. In that regard, is there a defensible reason for the very different treatment afforded to baseball players who are drafted without their permission by a MLB team after three years in college (which by itself does not cost them their college eligibility), basketball players who elect into the NBA draft (who can now retrieve their eligibility if no team picks them), and football players (who give up any college football future when they participate in the NFL draft)?

3. *The Need for an Agent.* With respect to any or all of the leagues, should a player be free to hire a real "agent" to determine his true market value in professional sports before deciding whether to enter or return to college sports? Indeed, suppose a player is picked low in the draft, is offered and signs a contract to play with that team eventually (but with no money paid now), and wants to return to college to finish both his athletic and academic careers there. Is it vital for the NCAA to bar any such contract for *future* professional services in order to maintain its "clear line of demarcation" from professional leagues? Certainly, there is a great deal of movement of highly-paid coaches (such as Rick Pitino and Nick Saban) between these two settings, with the college programs often outbidding the professional teams for highly-valued coaches' services. The broader issue that runs through all of these questions and cases in the intercollegiate sports chapters is whether, given the financial stakes now riding on big-time college sports, courts should defer to NCAA efforts to maintain the *amateur* status of its players (as opposed to the *academic* status discussed above).

CHAPTER 12

INTERCOLLEGIATE SPORTS: THE EVOLUTION OF AMATEURISM

■ ■ ■

A. NCAA AMATEURISM

The concept of amateurism derives from England, where the wealthy would engage in sport "for the love of the game" without compensation. The modern NCAA has historically defined amateurism to allow universities to cover the cost of education, but otherwise proscribe other benefits.

The new NCAA constitution both clearly bars pay for play as well as emphasizes the importance of the academic experience. It provides:

> Intercollegiate student-athletes are matriculated, degree-seeking students in good standing with their institutions who choose voluntarily to participate in NCAA sports. It is the responsibility of each member institution to establish and maintain an environment in which a student-athlete's activities are conducted with the appropriate primary emphasis on the student-athlete's academic experience. Intercollegiate athletics programs shall be maintained as a vital component of each institution's broader educational program. The admission, academic standing and academic progress of student-athletes shall be consistent with the policies and standards adopted by the institution.

NCAA Constitution, Article § 1.A (2022).

The NCAA's amateurism principle has long emphasized education—amateur athletes come to the university campus to receive an education, with athletics merely being part of that education.

Over the past two decades, however, the commercialization of college sports has led to repeated calls for college athletes to receive payment for participating in sports outside of the educational compensation that universities provide. Lawyers and athletes have challenged the NCAA's amateurism rules through a number of methods, including legislation. The current iteration of college sports amateurism, which allows for third-party compensation for uses of athlete name, image, and likeness and bars any restriction of benefits "related to" education, represents a meaningful departure from the NCAA's historical approach. This chapter tells the story of those changes and the current legal landscape.

B. LIMITS ON NCAA POWER

Before examining the specific challenges to the NCAA's amateurism model, it is instructive to study two Supreme Court cases that frame its power under federal law—*NCAA v. Tarkanian* and *Board of Regents v. NCAA*.

The NCAA's oversight of college athletics has been the subject of a number of legal challenges. One of the most important came in the late 1970s when Jerry Tarkanian, the basketball coach of the University of Nevada at Las Vegas (UNLV), challenged a suspension resulting from alleged rules violations. The two main charges against Tarkanian were that he had arranged for payment of a flight home for one of his players, and that he had arranged for an instructor to give another player a passing grade in a course the player did not attend. The NCAA's Committee on Infractions put UNLV's basketball program on probation for two years and required the university to suspend Tarkanian as coach for those two years or face further penalties. Both federal constitutional and state statutory law required UNLV, a state university, to give Tarkanian, its tenured coach, a due process hearing before suspending him. Although the hearing officer did not believe that any violations had occurred, he concluded that UNLV had no choice but to suspend Tarkanian if the school wanted to remain part of the NCAA.

In response, Tarkanian sued both UNLV and the NCAA. The Nevada courts found that the NCAA proceedings had denied Tarkanian procedural "due process" guaranteed by the Fourteenth Amendment. Operating on the assumption that the NCAA was a "state actor" governed by the federal constitution, the trial court issued injunctions barring UNLV's suspension of Tarkanian and NCAA retaliation against UNLV. The Nevada Supreme Court affirmed. The case finally reached the United States Supreme Court in 1988; by then Tarkanian had amassed one of the highest winning percentages of all active coaches in college basketball.

NCAA v. TARKANIAN
488 U.S. 179 (1988)

JUSTICE STEVENS for the Court.

* * *

II

Embedded in our Fourteenth Amendment jurisprudence is a dichotomy between state action, which is subject to scrutiny under the Amendment's Due Process Clause, and private conduct, against which the Amendment affords no shield, no matter how unfair that conduct may be. As a general matter the protections of the Fourteenth Amendment do not extend to "private conduct abridging individual rights." *Burton v. Wilmington Parking Authority*, 365 U.S. 715, 722 (1961).

"Careful adherence to the 'state action' requirement preserves an area of individual freedom by limiting the reach of federal law" and avoids the imposition of responsibility on a State for conduct it could not control. When Congress enacted § 1983 as the statutory remedy for violations of the Constitution, it specified that the conduct at issue must have occurred "under color of" state law; thus, liability attaches only to those wrongdoers "who carry a badge of authority of a State and represent it in some capacity, whether they act in accordance with their authority or misuse it." *Monroe v. Pape*, 365 U.S. 167, 172 (1961). As we stated in *United States v. Classic*, 313 U.S. 299, 326 (1941):

> Misuse of power, possessed by virtue of state law and made possible only because the wrongdoer is clothed with the authority of state law, is action taken "under color of" state law.

In this case Tarkanian argues that the NCAA was a state actor because it misused power that it possessed by virtue of state law. He claims specifically that UNLV delegated its own functions to the NCAA, clothing the Association with authority both to adopt rules governing UNLV's athletic programs and to enforce those rules on behalf of UNLV. Similarly, the Nevada Supreme Court held that UNLV had delegated its authority over personnel decisions to the NCAA. Therefore, the court reasoned, the two entities acted jointly to deprive Tarkanian of liberty and property interests, making the NCAA as well as UNLV a state actor.

These contentions fundamentally misconstrue the facts of this case. In the typical case raising a state action issue, a private party has taken the decisive step that caused the harm to the plaintiff, and the question is whether the State was sufficiently involved to treat that decisive conduct as state action. This may occur if the State creates the legal framework governing the conduct; if it delegates its authority to the private actor; or sometimes if it knowingly accepts the benefits derived from unconstitutional behavior. Thus, in the usual case we ask whether the State provided a mantle of authority that enhanced the power of the harm-causing individual actor.

This case uniquely mirrors the traditional state action case. Here the final act challenged by Tarkanian—his suspension—was committed by UNLV. A state university without question is a state actor. When it decides to impose a serious disciplinary sanction upon one of its tenured employees, it must comply with the terms of the Due Process Clause of the Fourteenth Amendment to the Federal Constitution. Thus when UNLV notified Tarkanian that he was being separated from all relations with the University's basketball program, it acted under color of state law within the meaning of 42 U.S.C. § 1983.

The mirror image presented in this case requires us to step through an analytical looking glass to resolve it. Clearly UNLV's conduct was influenced by the rules and recommendations of the NCAA, the private party. But it was UNLV, the state entity, that actually suspended Tarkanian. Thus the question is not whether UNLV participated to a critical extent in the NCAA's activities, but whether UNLV's actions in compliance with the NCAA rules and recommendations turned the NCAA's conduct into state action.

We examine first the relationship between UNLV and the NCAA regarding the NCAA's rulemaking. UNLV is among the NCAA's members and participated in promulgating the Association's rules; it must be assumed, therefore, that Nevada had some impact on the NCAA's policy determinations. Yet the NCAA's several hundred other public and private member institutions each similarly affected those policies. Those institutions, the vast majority of which were located in States other than Nevada, did not act under color of Nevada law. It necessarily follows that the source of the legislation adopted by the NCAA is not Nevada but the collective membership, speaking through an organization that is independent of any particular State.

State action nonetheless might lie if UNLV, by embracing the NCAA's rules, transformed them into state rules and the NCAA into a state actor. UNLV engaged in state action when it adopted the NCAA's rules to govern its own behavior, but that would be true even if UNLV had taken no part in the promulgation of those rules. In *Bates v. State Bar of Arizona*, 433 U.S. 350 (1977), we established that the State Supreme Court's enforcement of disciplinary rules transgressed by members of its own bar was state action. Those rules had been adopted in toto from the American Bar Association Code of Professional Responsibility. It does not follow, however, that the ABA's formulation of those disciplinary rules was state action. The State Supreme Court retained plenary power to reexamine those standards and, if necessary, to reject them and promulgate its own. So here, UNLV retained the authority to withdraw from the NCAA and establish its own standards. The University alternatively could have stayed in the Association and worked through the Association's legislative process to amend rules or standards it deemed harsh, unfair, or unwieldy. Neither UNLV's decision to adopt the NCAA's standards nor its minor role in their formulation is a sufficient reason for concluding that the NCAA was acting under color of Nevada law when it promulgated standards governing athlete recruitment, eligibility, and academic performance.

Tarkanian further asserts that the NCAA's investigation, enforcement proceedings, and consequent recommendations constituted state action because they resulted from a delegation of power by UNLV. UNLV, as an NCAA member, subscribed to the statement in the Association's bylaws that NCAA "enforcement procedures are an essential part of the intercollegiate athletic program of each member institution." It is, of course, true that a state may delegate authority to a private party and thereby make that party a state actor. Thus, we recently held that a private physician who had contracted with a state prison to attend to the inmates' medical needs was a state actor. But UNLV delegated no power to the NCAA to take specific action against any University employee. The commitment by UNLV to adhere to NCAA enforcement procedures was enforceable only by sanctions that the NCAA might impose on UNLV itself.

Indeed, the notion that UNLV's promise to cooperate in the NCAA enforcement proceedings was tantamount to a partnership agreement or the transfer of certain University powers to the NCAA is belied by the history of this case. It is quite obvious that UNLV used its best efforts to retain its winning coach—a goal diametrically opposed to the NCAA's interest in ascertaining the truth of its investigators' reports. During the several years that the NCAA investigated the alleged violations, the NCAA and UNLV acted much more like adversaries than like partners engaged in a dispassionate search for the truth. The NCAA cannot be regarded as an agent of UNLV for purposes of that proceeding. It is more correctly characterized as an agent of its remaining members which, as competitors of UNLV, had an interest in the effective and evenhanded enforcement of NCAA's recruitment standards. Just as a state-compensated public defender acts in a private capacity when she represents a private client in a conflict against the State, the NCAA is properly viewed as a private actor at odds with the State when it represents the interests of its entire membership in an investigation of one public university.

The NCAA enjoyed no governmental powers to facilitate its investigation. It had no power to subpoena witnesses, to impose contempt sanctions, or to assert sovereign authority over any individual. Its greatest authority was to threaten sanctions against UNLV, with the ultimate sanction being expulsion of the University from membership. Contrary to the premise of the Nevada Supreme Court's opinion, the NCAA did not—indeed, could not—directly discipline Tarkanian or any other state university employee.[18] The express terms of the Confidential Report did

---

[18]   Tarkanian urges us to hold, as did the Nevada Supreme Court, that the NCAA by its rules and enforcement procedures has usurped a traditional, essential state function. Quite properly, he does not point to the NCAA's overriding function of fostering amateur athletics at the college level. For while we have described that function as "critical," *NCAA v. Board of Regents of the University of Oklahoma*, 468 U.S. 85, 120 (1984), by no means is it a traditional, let alone an exclusive, state function. Cf. *San Francisco Arts & Athletics, Inc. v. United States Olympic Committee*, 483 U.S. 522, 545 (1987) ("Neither the conduct nor the coordination of amateur sports has been a traditional government function."). Tarkanian argues instead that the NCAA has assumed the state's traditional and exclusive power to discipline its employees. "[A]s to state employees connected with intercollegiate athletics, the NCAA requires that its standards, procedures and determinations become the State's standards, procedures and determinations for disciplining state employees," he contends. "The State is obligated to impose NCAA standards, procedures and determinations making the NCAA a joint participant in the State's suspension of Tarkanian." This argument overlooks the fact that the NCAA's own legislation prohibits it from taking any direct action against Tarkanian. Moreover, suspension of Tarkanian is one of many recommendations in the Confidential Report. Those recommendations as a whole were intended

not demand the suspension unconditionally; rather, it requested "the University . . . to show cause" why the NCAA should not impose additional penalties if UNLV declines to suspend Tarkanian. Even the University's vice president acknowledged that the Report gave the University options other than suspension: UNLV could have retained Tarkanian and risked additional sanctions, perhaps even expulsion from the NCAA, or it could have withdrawn voluntarily from the Association.

Finally, Tarkanian argues that the power of the NCAA is so great that the UNLV had no practical alternative to compliance with its demands. We are not at all sure this is true,[19] but even if we assume that a private monopolist can impose its will on a state agency by a threatened refusal to deal with it, it does not follow that such a private party is therefore acting under color of state law.

In final analysis the question is whether "the conduct allegedly causing the deprivation of a federal right [can] be fairly attributable to the State." It would be ironic indeed to conclude that the NCAA's imposition of sanctions against UNLV—sanctions that UNLV and its counsel, including the Attorney General of Nevada, steadfastly opposed during protracted adversary proceedings—is fairly attributable to the State of Nevada. It would be more appropriate to conclude that UNLV has conducted its athletic program under color of the policies adopted by the NCAA, rather than that those policies were developed and enforced under color of Nevada law.

Reversed.

JUSTICE WHITE dissented and filed an opinion in which JUSTICES BRENNAN, MARSHALL and O'CONNOR joined.

All agree that UNLV, a public university, is a state actor, and that the suspension of Jerry Tarkanian, a public employee, was state action. The question here is whether the NCAA acted jointly with UNLV in suspending Tarkanian and thereby also became a state actor. I would hold that it did.

I agree with the majority that this case is different on its facts from many of our prior state action cases. As the majority notes, in our "typical case raising a state action issue, a private party has taken the decisive step that caused the harm to the plaintiff." In this case, however, which in the majority's view "uniquely mirrors the traditional state action case," the final act that caused the harm to Tarkanian was committed, not by a private party, but by a party conceded to be a state actor. Because of this

---

to bring UNLV's basketball program into compliance with NCAA rules. Suspension of Tarkanian was but one means toward achieving that goal.

[19]   The University's desire to remain a powerhouse among the nation's college basketball teams is understandable, and nonmembership in the NCAA obviously would thwart that goal. But that UNLV's options were unpalatable does not mean that they were nonexistent.

difference, the majority finds it necessary to "step through an analytical looking glass" to evaluate whether the NCAA was a state actor.

* * *

On the facts of the present case, the NCAA acted jointly with UNLV in suspending Tarkanian. First, Tarkanian was suspended for violations of NCAA rules, which UNLV embraced in its agreement with the NCAA. As the Nevada Supreme Court found in its first opinion in this case, "[a]s a member of the NCAA, UNLV contractually agrees to administer its athletic program in accordance with NCAA legislation." Indeed, NCAA rules provide that NCAA "enforcement procedures are an essential part of the intercollegiate athletic program of each member institution."

Second, the NCAA and UNLV also agreed that the NCAA would conduct the hearings concerning violations of its rules. Although UNLV conducted its own investigation into the recruiting violations alleged by the NCAA, the NCAA procedures provide that it is the NCAA Committee on Infractions that "determine[s] facts related to alleged violations," subject to an appeal to the NCAA Council. As a result of this agreement, the NCAA conducted the very hearings the Nevada Supreme Court held to have violated Tarkanian's right to procedural due process.

Third, the NCAA and UNLV agreed that the findings of fact made by the NCAA at the hearings it conducted would be binding on UNLV. By becoming a member of the NCAA, UNLV did more than merely "promise to cooperate in the NCAA enforcement proceedings." It agreed, as the University Hearing Officer appointed to rule on Tarkanian's suspension expressly found, to accept the NCAA's "findings of fact as in some way superior to [its] own." By the terms of UNLV's membership in the NCAA, the NCAA's findings were final and not subject to further review by any other body, and it was for that reason that UNLV suspended Tarkanian, despite concluding that many of those findings were wrong.

In short, it was the NCAA's findings that Tarkanian had violated NCAA rules, made at NCAA-conducted hearings, all of which were agreed to by UNLV in its membership agreement with the NCAA, that resulted in Tarkanian's suspension by UNLV. On these facts, the NCAA was "jointly engaged with [UNLV] officials in the challenged action," and therefore was a state actor.

* * *

The majority states in conclusion that "[i]t would be ironic indeed to conclude that the NCAA's imposition of sanctions against UNLV— sanctions that UNLV and its counsel, including the Attorney General of Nevada, steadfastly opposed during protracted adversary proceedings—Is fairly attributable to the State of Nevada." I agree. Had UNLV refused to suspend Tarkanian, and the NCAA responded by imposing sanctions against UNLV, it would be hard indeed to find any state action that harmed Tarkanian. But that is not this case. Here, UNLV did suspend Tarkanian, and it did so because it embraced the NCAA rules governing conduct of its athletic program and adopted the results of the hearings conducted by the NCAA concerning Tarkanian, as it had agreed that it would. Under these facts, I would find that the NCAA acted jointly with UNLV and therefore is a state actor.

NOTES AND QUESTIONS

1. *Aftermath.* While the NCAA won this major legal victory over Tarkanian, it was not able to remove him immediately from the college basketball court. Further litigation in the lower courts kept Tarkanian in place through the 1989–90 season, which UNLV capped with its first national championship.

2. *On the Merits.* In appraising the merits of the *Tarkanian* ruling, consider the following issues:

    a. What claims could be made by Jerry Tarkanian, had the NCAA been found to be a state actor, that cannot be made by him with the NCAA found to be a private association? (The latter treatment is considered below.)

    b. Should NCAA action toward a student-athlete at a private school such as Duke or Notre Dame constitute state action, or is it indistinguishable from a baseball commissioner's action toward a Pete Rose or an Alex Cora? In other words, is there anything special about the function of regulating sports in educational institutions? Are there any material legal differences in the structures of the NCAA and of a professional sports league and in the manner in which the respective members conduct their athletic businesses?

    c. When the NCAA takes action against a state university such as UNLV or UCLA, is there a stronger case for judicial scrutiny than when the NCAA imposes sanctions on its private members? How much choice did UNLV have to defy the NCAA and respect Tarkanian's due process rights? On the other hand, could the NCAA afford to have different procedural rules for disciplining state and private schools and their personnel? Are there legal instruments more appropriate than the Constitution for challenging NCAA restraints on institutional or personal choices?

3. *When Do State Actors Bind Themselves to Private Decision-Making?* The constitutional doctrine concerning when state involvement with private parties constitutes "state action" is a difficult one, more fully explored in courses in constitutional law. *Tarkanian* holds that state actors are free to bind themselves to decisions of a private actor, the NCAA. Suppose the NCAA adopted a rule requiring racial discrimination in athletics? Of course, member schools couldn't adhere to such a rule under numerous civil rights and

education statutes, but if these statutes did not exist, do you think the Supreme Court would follow *Tarkanian* and hold that public universities were free to impose such a rule at the behest of a private party?

4. *Revisiting the Law of Private Associations*. Recall the discussion from Chapter 2 about private associations. Should courts always defer to such associations? In *Gulf South Conference v. Boyd*, 369 So.2d 553 (Ala. 1979), the Alabama Supreme Court declined to defer to the rules of the Gulf South Conference (GSC) in reinstating the eligibility of Boyd.

Boyd had played football one season at a Livingston University, a GSC member, spent a year at junior college, and then transferred to Troy State University, also a GSC member. Boyd's Livingston University scholarship had been a one year renewable scholarship, but Boyd declined Livingston's offer to renew his scholarship after his freshman season. The GSC rules provided that transfers from one GSC school to another would be ineligible to play at the second school unless the first school did not renew their grant-in-aid. Because Boyd's grant-in-aid had been renewed, the GSC declared Boyd ineligible to play football at Troy State.

The court decided that it had jurisdiction to interfere with the GSC's decision and reversed it, declaring Boyd eligible to play at Troy State. The court explained:

> The contention by the GSC that the lower court did not have jurisdiction basically stems from a body of common law involving private associations. The general rule is that courts should not interfere with the internal management of such associations. Even though we recognize the existence of this non-interference principle, nevertheless this Court has sanctioned judicial review when the actions of an association are the result of fraud, lack of jurisdiction, collusion, arbitrariness, or are in violation of or contravene any principle of public policy.

> We hold that the general non-interference doctrine concerning voluntary associations does not apply to cases involving disputes between college athletes themselves and college athletic associations. There is a cogent reason for this position. In such cases the athlete himself is not even a member of the athletic association; therefore, the basic "freedom of association" principle behind the non-interference rule is not present. The athlete himself has no voice or bargaining power concerning the rules and regulations adopted by the athletic associations because he is not a member, yet he stands to be substantially affected, and even damaged, by an association ruling declaring him to be ineligible to participate in intercollegiate athletics. Thus he may be deprived of the property right eligibility to participate in intercollegiate athletics.

* * *

It should be noted that the relationship between a college athlete who accepts an athletic scholarship and the college which awards such an athletic scholarship is contractual in nature. The college athlete agrees to participate in a sport at the college, and the college in return agrees to give assistance to the athlete. The athlete also agrees to be bound by the rules and regulations adopted by the college concerning the financial assistance. Most of these rules and regulations are promulgated by athletic associations whose membership is composed of the individual colleges. The individual athlete has no voice or participation in the formulation or interpretation of these rules and regulations governing his scholarship, even though these materially control his conduct on and off the field. Thus in some circumstances the college athlete may be placed in an unequal bargaining position. The GSC's interpretation of the bylaws in question was that a student football athlete who transfers from one GSC school to another will not be eligible to participate in football at the second school unless the first school drops football or unless the first school *does not* (merely) *offer to renew* the grant-in-aid scholarship of the student-athlete.

Should courts follow the approach of the Alabama Supreme Court and make an exception to the law of private association in disputes between athletes and athletic associations? What would the consequences of such an approach be?

————

The Supreme Court in *Brentwood Academy v. Tennessee Secondary Schools Athletic Ass'n*, 531 U.S. 288 (2001), added another layer to the law of whether the Constitution (and 42 U.S.C. § 1983) applies to sports governing organizations as "state actors," this time involving an association that governs high school sports. At the time, the Tennessee Secondary Schools Athletic Association ("TSSAA") consisted of about 350 public and private high schools in the state of Tennessee, with 84 percent of its members being public and the other 16 percent being private schools. One of the latter, Brentwood Academy, is an affluent Christian school just outside Nashville, and a long-time football powerhouse in the state.

The TSSAA charged the Brentwood football coach, Carlton Flatt, with violating several rules in 1996. One alleged violation involved an invitation sent to 13 notable eighth-grade student players to come to a spring training practice. Another involved giving some students free tickets to the Brentwood games. After it found Brentwood guilty of these violations, the TSSAA stripped the school of its 1996 state football championship, fined it $3,000, and placed it on probation for four years. Brentwood then went to federal court to challenge the legality of the TSSAA action on several grounds, including under the federal Constitution's due process and free speech protections.

The district court, at 13 F. Supp. 2d 670 (M.D. Tenn. 1998), found the TSSAA to be a "state actor," and that a ban on recruiting potential high school students on the basis of athletics (rather than academics and the like) violated the school's First Amendment right to free speech. The Sixth Circuit, at 180 F.3d 758 (6th Cir. 1999), reversed on the ground that the TSSAA was just as much a private actor as the NCAA (whose member colleges are also largely public, although by a much smaller majority) and thus not subject to any constitutional restraints. The Supreme Court took the case for review of that issue.

In February 2001, the Court issued a 5–4 decision, this time holding that the TSSAA was indeed a state actor. Justice Stevens was the only justice that switched his vote from the *Tarkanian* case, amidst several court retirements and appointments. Justice Souter explained the Court's decision as follows:

> To be sure, it is not the strict holding in *Tarkanian* that points to our view of this case, for we found no state action on the part of the NCAA. We could see, on the one hand, that the university had some part in setting the NCAA's rules, and the Supreme Court of Nevada had gone so far as to hold that the NCAA had been delegated the university's traditionally exclusive public authority over personnel. But on the other side, the NCAA's policies were shaped not by the University of Nevada alone, but by several hundred member institutions, most of them having no connection with Nevada, and exhibiting no color of Nevada law. Since it was difficult to see the NCAA, not as a collective membership, but as surrogate for the one State, we held the organization's connection with Nevada too insubstantial to ground a state action claim.

> But dictum in *Tarkanian* pointed to a contrary result on facts like ours, with an organization whose member public schools are all within a single State. "The situation would, of course, be different if the [Association's] membership consisted entirely of institutions located within the same State, many of them public institutions created by the same sovereign." . . .

> B

> Just as we foresaw in *Tarkanian,* the "necessarily fact-bound inquiry," leads to the conclusion of state action here. The nominally private character of the Association is overborne by the pervasive entwinement of public institutions and public officials in its composition and workings, and there is no substantial reason to claim unfairness in applying constitutional standards to it.

> The Association is not an organization of natural persons acting on their own, but of schools, and of public schools to the extent of 84% of the total. Under the Association's bylaws, each member school is represented by its principal or a faculty member,

who has a vote in selecting members of the governing legislative council and board of control from eligible principals, assistant principals and superintendents.

Although the findings and prior opinions in this case include no express conclusion of law that public school officials act within the scope of their duties when they represent their institutions, no other view would be rational, the official nature of their involvement being shown in any number of ways. Interscholastic athletics obviously play an integral part in the public education of Tennessee, where nearly every public high school spends money on competitions among schools. Since a pickup system of interscholastic games would not do, these public teams need some mechanism to produce rules and regulate competition. The mechanism is an organization overwhelmingly composed of public school officials who select representatives (all of them public officials at the time in question here), who in turn adopt and enforce the rules that make the system work. Thus, by giving these jobs to the Association, the 290 public schools of Tennessee belonging to it can sensibly be seen as exercising their own authority to meet their own responsibilities. Unsurprisingly, then, the record indicates that half the council or board meetings documented here were held during official school hours, and that public schools have largely provided for the Association's financial support. . . .

In sum, to the extent of 84% of its membership, the Association is an organization of public schools represented by their officials acting in their official capacity to provide an integral element of secondary public schooling. There would be no recognizable Association, legal or tangible, without the public school officials, who do not merely control but overwhelmingly perform all but the purely ministerial acts by which the Association exists and functions in practical terms. Only the 16% minority of private school memberships prevents this entwinement of the Association and the public school system from being total and their identities totally indistinguishable.

To complement the entwinement of public school officials with the Association from the bottom up, the State of Tennessee has provided for entwinement from top down. State Board members are assigned ex officio to serve as members of the board of control and legislative council, and the Association's ministerial employees are treated as state employees to the extent of being eligible for membership in the state retirement system.

* * *

The entwinement down from the State Board is therefore unmistakable, just as the entwinement up from the member public schools is overwhelming. Entwinement will support a conclusion that an ostensibly private organization ought to be charged with a public character and judged by constitutional standards; entwinement to the degree shown here requires it.

531 U.S. at 297–302 (2001). Justice Thomas, writing for Justices Rehnquist, Scalia, and Kennedy, dissented, arguing that

[w]e have never found state action based upon mere "entwinement." Until today, we have found a private organization's acts to constitute state action only when the organization performed a public function; was created, coerced, or encouraged by the government; or acted in a symbiotic relationship with the government. [This decision] not only extends state-action doctrine beyond its permissible limits but also encroaches upon the realm of individual freedom that the doctrine was meant to protect.

Id. at 305.

NOTES AND QUESTIONS

1. *Comparing the NCAA and the TSSAA.* What are the distinctions between the TSSAA and the NCAA that led the Court to different results? Are those distinctions persuasive? Is there any merit to Justice Thomas' warning, 531 U.S. at 314 n.7, that "it is not difficult to imagine that application of the majority's entwinement test could change the result reached in [*Tarkanian*], so that the National Collegiate Athletic Association's actions could be found to be state action given its large number of public institution members that virtually control the organization"? For a further limitation, see the not-for-citation "unpublished" opinion in *Cohane v. NCAA*, 215 F. App'x 13 (2d Cir. 2007), allowing a complaint to proceed based on allegations that, unlike UNLV, Cohane's employer (Buffalo, a New York public university) did not contest charges adversely to the NCAA, but rather colluded with the NCAA and fired Cohane in an attempt to placate the Infractions Committee, in addition to compelling witnesses to testify and suborning perjury. The Second Circuit concluded, "at this point in the litigation, it was error for the District Court to interpret Tarkanian as holding categorically that the NCAA can never be a state actor when it conducts an investigation of a state school."

2. *Scope of Brentwood Academy.* How broadly does *Brentwood Academy* sweep? Does it now render all state high school athletic governing associations state actors subject to the Constitution, or is it narrowly limited to its specific facts? Again, Justice Thomas' dissent offers a view: "Because the majority never defines 'entwinement,' the scope of its holding is unclear. If we are fortunate, the majority's fact-specific analysis will have little bearing beyond

this case." 513 U.S. at 314. How might a state association structure itself and operate in such a way to avoid the conclusion reached in *Brentwood Academy*?

3.   *Aftermath.* The Supreme Court revisited this controversy six years later. *Tennessee Secondary Sch. Ath. Ass'n v. Brentwood Academy,* 551 U.S. 291 (2007). The Court held that the TSSAA's procedures were consistent with constitutional requirements of due process and that the substance of the anti-recruiting rule did not violate the First Amendment.

While the Constitution does not restrict the actions of the NCAA (assuming *Tarkanian* was correct in holding it is not a state actor), antitrust law does place limits on its power and authority. Antitrust law can restrict the manner in which the NCAA governs its member institutions.

NCAA v. BOARD OF REGENTS OF THE UNIV. OF OKLAHOMA & UNIV. OF GEORGIA ATHLETIC ASS'N
468 U.S. 85 (1984)

[*See supra* Chapter 6, Section C for text of case.]

NOTES AND QUESTIONS

1.   *Effect of Television on Attendance.* Part of the NCAA's antitrust defense rested on its claim that televising the games would decrease attendance at football games. This defense has two elements, a factual and a legal one. Factually, over forty years later, do you agree that widespread television coverage of almost all NCAA football games in Power 5 conference schools has harmed attendance at those games? Or was the NCAA argument clearly wrong? As to the legal question, if the evidence showed that widespread television coverage increased the total number of consumers watching college football, but reduced the number attending games, particularly at schools below the top 40, would that be a valid defense?

2.   *Economic Competition, Academic Competition, or Athletic Competition?* If an NCAA rule fixing the level of output of the NCAA members' athletic programs is anticompetitive on its face, as Justice Stevens opines, and thus can be declared in violation of section 1 under a "quick look" rule of reason, how would the NCAA rules that fix the maximum number of contests every school's teams in each sport can play survive a challenge by a member school that wanted its football team to play 20 games every year, or its baseball team to play 80 games every year? What procompetitive arguments could the NCAA make in defense of these output limiting rules? Would such arguments be any more persuasive than those rejected by the Court in *Board of Regents*? How do rules about athletic competition or academic competition differ from rules about economic competition under antitrust law?

3. *Defining the NCAA "Product."* The Court in *Board of Regents* refers to the "revered tradition of amateurism in college sports" and observes, "In order to preserve the character and quality of the 'product,' athletes must not be paid." The NCAA relied on that language for years in defending against litigation challenges to its amateurism principle. Consider how the Court's view of the NCAA's product has changed as you read the *Alston* decision excerpted in Section D of this chapter.

4. *The NCAA After* Board of Regents. The practical effect of *Board of Regents* is that the NCAA lost the opportunity to receive revenue from college football, which currently is an industry worth billions annually. It learned from its mistakes quickly, though, and has been able to leverage the NCAA March Madness basketball tournament into a corporate blockbuster, alone worth over $1 billion annually. Ironically, in light of *Board of Regents*, it is the television ratings that drive this economic windfall. Most of the money is sent to the member institutions, but the NCAA retains enough to cover its entire annual operating budget.

C. ATHLETES AS EMPLOYEES?

In light of the growing commercialism of college sports, athletes have challenged and continue to challenge the student-athlete model on both labor and antitrust grounds. As we will see, antitrust has to date provided a more promising path to upend the current model.

Employment law challenges to NCAA rules have centered on the argument that athletes should be treated as university employees, not mere student-athletes. In *Waldrep v. Texas Employers Insurance Ass'n*, 21 S.W.3d 692 (2000), for instance, an athlete attempted to claim employee status in order to receive workers compensation benefits for a football injury. The Texas Court of Appeals rejected the claim, finding the athlete to be only a student. *See also Rensing v. Indiana State Univ.*, 444 N.E.2d 1170 (Ind. 1983) (holding that an injured college football player was not entitled to workers compensation because he was not an employee of the university).

More recently, athletes at Northwestern University had greater initial success making a similar claim that they were university employees. In March 2014, the NLRB's regional director in Chicago ruled that the scholarship recipient members of the Northwestern football team were employees of the university and thus were eligible to hold a representation election to determine if a majority of the employees wanted to be represented for purposes of collective bargaining by a union (CAPA) that would serve as their exclusive bargaining representative. Although the full Board ultimately overturned this decision, the opinion matters for its rhetoric, which informs the antitrust question explored in *O'Bannon*, *supra*. The regional director's rhetoric suggested that the ideal of the student-athlete does not exist for Northwestern football players. He opined that they attend Northwestern primarily for athletics, not for education.

The essence of the decision was that the scholarship football players met the criteria for being classified as employees in light of the following: (1) they provide a valuable service to the university (as demonstrated by the substantial revenue and public relations benefits the university receives), (2) they are compensated (with scholarships that include tuition, fees, books, room and board), (3) they are required to perform services for the university as a condition of receiving that compensation, and (4) their "work" is controlled by supervisors employed by the university (their coaches).

The regional director also stressed: (a) the players spend huge amounts of time on their football duties, sometimes as much as 40 to 50 hours a week, which is far more than they spend on their studies; (b) the work for which the players are compensated, playing football, has no relationship to their degree-seeking academic work and they receive no academic credit for it; (c) the university employees who supervise the players are not faculty, but rather non-academic coaches; and (d) the compensation the players receive is not financial aid for academic purposes.

One month after the regional director's decision was announced, a representation election was held by secret ballot. During that month, Northwestern football coach Pat Fitzgerald and other university officials tried to persuade the players to vote against recognizing the union by telling them that a union would not be able to obtain anything more for them than they already received and that unionization of college athletes would destroy college athletics. Similarly, football coaches, athletics directors, and university presidents, as well as several politicians, publicly derided the decision, some going so far as to suggest that their schools might shut down their scholarship athletic programs rather than face collective bargaining with a players union. The NLRB then announced the day before the election that the ballots would be impounded and no results announced pending the decision by the full Board on appeal.

Two years later, the NLRB vacated the regional director's decision and the election, deciding that whether or not the athletes were university employees, a bargaining unit including only them and not players for the other universities in the Big Ten would not be appropriate. The Board noted these other universities are all public institutions over which the Board has no jurisdiction. The Board offered no opinion on whether athletes were employees for purposes of the NLRA.

In 2021, however, the NLRB General Counsel, Jennifer Abruzzo, opined that college athletes are employees for purposes of the NLRA. She further indicated a willingness to bring actions against institutions classifying college athletes as "student-athletes" to the extent that such classifications chill athletes' section 7-protected activity under the NLRA or otherwise violate athletes' right to organize pursuant to section 8(a)(1).

A determination that college athletes are university employees would have significant and far-reaching consequences. Athletes would have to pay taxes on their remuneration, and their university employers would have to accord all of the human resource benefits it accords other employees. This would likely include health insurance. In addition, a series of federal and state employment laws, not just the NLRA, would apply to athletes. These include workers' compensation, unemployment compensation, anti-discrimination, health and safety, and disability laws. Finally, as explored in several cases below, the Fair Labor Standards Act (FLSA) and parallel state laws would apply, requiring colleges and universities to pay athletes minimum wages that would vary with the jurisdiction.

NOTES AND QUESTIONS

1. *A Northwestern Bargaining Unit?* If the NLRB had ruled that the Northwestern football players were employees for purposes of the NLRA, and the union had won the certification election, what would the practical effect have been on the Northwestern football program? About what could the players have bargained with the university? Presumably they could not bargain effectively about being compensated beyond NCAA rules. Could they have bargained to lighten practice schedules without putting their team at a competitive disadvantage against their Big Ten rivals? Would any ruling in favor of the union also have meant that other Northwestern teams could organize unions? That teams at other private universities could do so?

2. *Limited to Private Institutions.* Because the NLRA governs only private employers, the legal impact of the decision could have potentially applied only to private colleges and universities. The athletes at the public universities that make up a majority of all NCAA divisions would be governed by the public sector labor laws of their various states. How likely do you think it is that the agencies and courts in the various states would apply their public employee labor laws consistently in the same way as the NLRB applied the federal law? If some or all states took a different view and found student-athletes not to be employees of their universities, what would the system look like, and with what consequences, with athletes at private schools eligible to unionize under federal law but those in many state universities barred from doing so?

3. *Non-Revenue Sport Employees?* To what degree should the reasoning that led the Regional Director NLRB to find the Northwestern football players to be employees apply equally to athletes on the other Northwestern athletic teams who receive scholarships? Should student-athletes on the men's and women's basketball teams, which are so-called "head count" sports where every

scholarship recipient receives a full grant-in-aid like football players, also be eligible to organize a union? What about the student-athletes on the so-called "equivalency" sport teams like tennis and golf that receive only partial, often very small, tuition waivers? What about the players on any of these teams who are "walk-ons" and receive no athletic scholarships but do receive some other types of benefits like special academic tutoring and individualized weight training, or who receive academic scholarships not tied directly to their athletic performance? Might your answer to all of these questions turn on whether the athletes on any particular team are providing a valuable service for the university, one of the criteria relied on by the NLRB regional director?

4.   *Title IX Implications.* If some or all of the student-athletes at a particular university are deemed to be employees, how does that impact the application of Title IX requirements to that school? Title IX prohibits gender discrimination in "educational programs." Are athletes deemed to be employees then not considered to be in educational programs so that they would not be counted in any Title IX analyses? Would your answer depend on whether the "employee" athletes elected to form a union?

5.   *Effect on Antitrust.* Perhaps most significantly, how would the NLRB's classification of student-athletes as employees for labor law purposes affect whether NCAA rules that limit how and how much student-athletes can be compensated are found to violate § 1 of the Sherman Act? For a proposal concerning how the NCAA could use labor law as a shield against antitrust claims, *see* William W. Berry III, *How Labor Law Could Save the NCAA*, Slate.com, March 31, 2014.

6.   *Loss of Eligibility Concerns.* Finally, if the student-athletes at some private universities elect to be represented by a union, would any NCAA or conference restraints on how much they can be compensated or when they forfeit their eligibility be immune from antitrust challenge because of the labor exemption that applies to unionized professional athletes, as explained in Chapter 7? If any such restraints were otherwise found to be antitrust violations, how would any remedy be structured if the violation applied to student-athletes at public universities who were not recognized as employees but not to employee student-athletes at private universities where the labor exemption protected the rule?

7.   *Unfair Labor Practice?* In February 2022, the College Football Players Association filed an unfair labor practice charge with the NLRB against USC and UCLA, also naming the Pac-12 and the NCAA. The allegation claims that the schools have misclassified the athletes as "student-athletes." Encouraged by the NLRB General Counsel's statement, the advocacy group seeks to have the NLRB revisit the question from *Northwestern* of whether college athletes are employees.

BERGER V. NCAA

843 F.3d 285 (7th Cir. 2016)

KANNE, CIRCUIT JUDGE.

Former student athletes at the University of Pennsylvania ("Penn") sued Penn, the National Collegiate Athletic Association ("NCAA"), and more than 120 other NCAA Division I universities and colleges alleging that student athletes are employees who are entitled to a minimum wage under the Fair Labor Standards Act ("FLSA"). The district court disagreed. We agree with the district court and hold that student athletes are not employees and are not covered by the FLSA.

1.   Background

Gillian Berger and Taylor Hennig ("Appellants") are former students at Penn who participated on Penn's women's track and field team. Like many collegiate athletic teams across the country, Penn's women's track and field team is regulated by the NCAA. The NCAA is a member-driven, unincorporated association of 1121 colleges and universities. It is divided into three divisions—Divisions I, II, and III—based roughly on the size of the schools and their athletic programs. Penn's women's track and field team competes in Division I, which includes the largest colleges and universities in the country.

Appellants sued Penn, the NCAA, and more than 120 other NCAA Division I member schools ("Appellees"), alleging that student athletes are "employees" within the meaning of the FLSA, 29 U.S.C. § 201. Accordingly, Appellants contend that the NCAA and its member schools violated the FLSA by not paying their athletes a minimum wage. Appellees moved to dismiss under Federal Rules of Civil Procedure 12(b)(1) and 12(b)(6).

The district court granted Appellees' motions, holding that (1) Appellants lacked standing to sue any of the Appellees other than Penn, and (2) Appellants failed to state a claim against Penn because student athletes are not employees under the FLSA. This appeal followed.

II.   Analysis

[The court affirmed the district court's dismissal of claims against parties other than Penn for lack of standing.]

* * *

We now turn to the merits with regard to Penn, over which no one disputes that we have jurisdiction. The district court dismissed Appellants' suit against Penn for failure to state a claim. [The court summarized judicial interpetations of this standard, construing the complaint in the light most favorable to the non-moving party and accepting well-pleaded facts as true.]

* * *

The FLSA requires "[e]very employer" to pay "his employees" a minimum wage of $7.25 per hour. 29 U.S.C. § 206(a)(1)(c). Section 203(e)(1) defines "employee" in an unhelpful and circular fashion as "any individual employed by an employer." 29 U.S.C. § 203(e)(1). Section 203(g) broadly defines "employ" as "to suffer or permit to work." 29 U.S.C. § 203(g). Thus, to qualify as an employee for purposes of the FLSA, one must perform "work" for an "employer." "Work" is not defined by the Act.

Under the FLSA, the plaintiff bears the burden of establishing that he or she performed work for an employer and is therefore entitled to compensation. *Melton v. Tippecanoe Cty.*, 838 F.3d 814, 818 (7th Cir. 2016). Here, to survive the motions to dismiss, Appellants had to allege facts, which taken as true, establish that they were employees and performed work for Penn.

Although "[t]he Supreme Court has instructed the courts to construe the terms 'employee' and 'employer' expansively under the FLSA," *Vanskike v. Peters*, 974 F.2d 806, 807 (7th Cir. 1992) (citing *Nationwide Mut. Ins. Co. v. Darden*, 503 U.S. 318, 326 (1992)), the Court has also held that the definition of "employee" "does have it" limits." *Tony & Susan Alamo Found. v. Sec'y of Labor*, 471 U.S. 290, 295 (1985). "Because status as an 'employee' for purposes of the FLSA depends on the totality of circumstances rather than on any technical label, courts must examine the 'economic reality' of the working relationship" between the alleged employee and the alleged employer to decide whether Congress intended the FLSA to apply to that particular relationship. *Vanskike*, 974 F.2d at 808.

To guide this inquiry, courts have developed a variety of multifactor tests. For example, we have applied a seven-factor test to determine whether migrant laborers are employees for purposes of the FLSA. *Sec'y of Labor v. Lauritzen*, 835 F.2d 1529, 1535–1538 (7th Cir. 1987). Similarly, the Second Circuit created a "non-exhaustive set of [seven] considerations" to help determine when an intern is an employee under the FLSA. *Glatt v. Fox Searchlight Pictures, Inc.*, 811 F.3d 528, 536–37 (2d Cir. 2015). Appellants liken student athletes to interns and contend that we should use the Second Circuit's test set forth in *Glatt* to determine whether student athletes are employees under the FLSA. We disagree.

It is true, as Appellants note, that the district court cited the Second Circuit's test favorably. But the district court also declined to follow that test here. Instead, the court concluded correctly that our approach "to determining who is an employee under the FLSA is . . . a flexible one." (R. 238 at 15.) The court then discussed our decision in *Vanskike*, in which we rejected the strict application of a similar multifactor test in favor of a more flexible standard. 974 F.2d at 809.

We have declined to apply multifactor tests in the employment setting when they "fail to capture the true nature of the relationship" between the alleged employee and the alleged employer. *Id.* In *Vanskike*, we considered whether an inmate at a state prison was an employee under the FLSA. *Id.* at 806. Like Appellants here, the inmate in *Vanskike* urged us to apply a multifactor test to determine whether an employment relationship existed. We rejected the application of that test because it was "not the most helpful guide in the situation presented." *Id.* at 809. Rather than follow a specific test, we examined the economic reality of the alleged employment relationship and concluded that the prisoner was not an employee. *Id.* at 809–10.

The district court followed the reasoning of *Vanskike* and held that the "factors used in the trainee and private-sector intern context fail to capture the nature of the relationship between the Plaintiffs, as student athletes, and Penn." (R. 238 at 15). We agree with the district court and decline to apply the test set forth in *Glatt* here.

As the Supreme Court has noted, there exists "a revered tradition of amateurism in college sports." *Nat'l Collegiate Athletic Ass'n v. Bd. of Regents of Univ. of Okla.*, 468 U.S. 85, 120 (1984). That long-standing tradition defines the economic reality of the relationship between student athletes and their schools. To maintain this tradition of amateurism, the NCAA and its member universities and colleges have created an elaborate system of eligibility rules. *See O'Bannon v. Nat'l Collegiate Athletic Ass'n*, 802 F.3d 1049, 1054–55 (9th Cir. 2015) (outlining the development of these rules). We have held that these rules "define what it means to be an amateur or a student-athlete, and are therefore essential to the very existence of" collegiate athletics. *Agnew v. Nat'l Collegiate Athletic Ass'n*, 683 F.3d 328, 343 (7th Cir. 2012). The multifactor test proposed by Appellants here simply does not take into account this tradition of amateurism or the reality of the student-athlete experience. In short, it "fail[s] to capture the true nature of the relationship" between student athletes and their schools and is not a "helpful guide." *Vanskike*, 974 F.2d at 809.

* * *

[The court reviewed prior decisional law interpreting workers' compensation statutes, and concluded that student athletes are not employees in that context.]

The Department of Labor, through its Field Operations Handbook ("FOH"), has also indicated that student athletes are not employees under the FLSA. The FOH "is an operations manual that provides Wage and Hour Division . . . investigators and staff with interpretations of statutory provisions, procedures for conducting investigations, and general administrative guidance." . . . We agree with Appellants that the provisions in this handbook are not dispositive, but they certainly are persuasive. . . .

Chapter ten of the FOH "contains interpretations regarding the employment relationship required for the [FLSA] to apply." *Field Operations Handbook (FOH)*, § 10a00. Section 10b24 specifically addresses the employment status of university or college students. This section is broken into two subsections—subsection (a) and subsection (b).

Subsection (a) discusses situations when university or college students are not treated as employees under the FLSA. Under this subsection, "University or college students who participate in activities generally recognized as *extracurricular* are generally not considered to be employees within the meaning of the [FLSA]." § 10b24(a) (emphasis added). This subsection then cross-references another section, § 10b03(e), which states the following:

> As part of their overall educational program, public or private schools . . . may permit or require students to engage in activities in connection with dramatics, student publications, glee clubs, bands, choirs, debating teams, radio stations, intramural and *interscholastic athletics* and other similar endeavors. Activities of students in such programs, conducted primarily for the benefit of the participants as a part of the educational opportunities provided to the students by the school or institution, are not work of the kind contemplated by [the FLSA] and do not result in an employer-employee relationship between the student and the school. . . ." (emphasis added).

Subsection (b), "[o]n the other hand" discusses situations in which "an employment relationship will generally exist with regard to students. . . ." § 10b24(b). Under this subsection, students who participate in a work-study program and, for example, "work at food service counters or sell programs or usher at athletic events, or who wait on tables or wash dishes in dormitories in anticipation of some compensation" are "generally considered employees under the [FLSA]." *Id.*

Appellants compare NCAA-regulated athletes to the work-study participants of § 10b24(b) and argue that these athletes should be deemed employees under the FLSA. In so doing, Appellants contend that § 10b24(a)'s reference to "extracurricular" activities and § 10b03(e)'s reference to "interscholastic athletics" refer only to "student-run, interscholastic club sports," and not to NCAA-regulated sports. (Appellants' Br. at 18).

To support this argument, Appellants point to the many differences between club sports and NCAA-regulated sports—the most obvious of which being that club sports are largely student-run, whereas NCAA-regulated sports are heavily supervised by university-employed staff. We agree that NCAA-regulated sports are very different from club sports, but we disagree that this warrants different treatment under the clear language of the FOH.

Section 10b24(a) categorically states that students who participate in "extracurricular" activities are generally not considered employees. Section 10b03(e) includes "interscholastic athletics" in a list of activities that do not constitute "work." These references are not limited to activities that are entirely student run. In fact, most of the activities included in § 10b03(e)'s list are not student run. Appellants have not presented any persuasive argument to suggest that the Department of Labor intended to limit this language to student-run activities. We therefore reject Appellants' linguistic limitation.

Because NCAA-regulated sports are "extracurricular," "interscholastic athletic" activities, we do not believe that the Department of Labor intended the FLSA to apply to student athletes. We find the FOH's interpretation of the student-athlete experience to be persuasive.

Appellants in this case have not, and quite frankly cannot, allege that the activities they pursued as student athletes qualify as "work" sufficient to trigger the minimum wage requirements of the FLSA. Student participation in collegiate athletics is entirely voluntary. Moreover, the long tradition of amateurism in college sports, by definition, shows that student athletes—like all amateur athletes—participate in their sports for reasons wholly unrelated to immediate compensation. Although we do not doubt that student athletes spend a tremendous amount of time playing for their respective schools, they do so—and have done so for over a hundred years under the NCAA—without any real expectation of earning an income. Simply put, student-athletic "play" is not "work," at least as the term is used in the FLSA. We therefore hold, as a matter of law, that student athletes are not employees and are not entitled to a minimum wage under the FLSA. . . .

III. Conclusion

For the foregoing reasons, we AFFIRM the district court's grant of Appellees' motions to dismiss.

HAMILTON, CIRCUIT JUDGE, concurring.

I join Judge Kanne's opinion for the court but wish to add a note of caution. The plaintiffs in this case were students who participated in track and field at the University of Pennsylvania. Like other Ivy League schools, Penn does not offer athletic scholarships. Also, as far as I know, track and field is not a "revenue" sport at Penn or any other school. In this case, therefore, the economic reality and the sometimes frayed tradition of amateurism both point toward dismissal of these plaintiffs' claims. *See generally, e.g., O'Bannon v. National Collegiate Athletic Ass'n*, 802 F.3d 1049, 1054–55 (9th Cir. 2015) (holding that NCAA compensation rules for Division I men's basketball players and Football Bowl Subdivision football players violated federal antitrust laws).

Because the plaintiffs in this case did not receive athletic scholarships and participated in a non-revenue sport, they pursued a broad theory. The logic of their claim would have included not only any college athlete in any sport and any NCAA division, but also college musicians, actors, journalists, and debaters. That broad theory is mistaken, as Judge Kanne's opinion explains. I am less confident, however, that our reasoning should extend to students who receive athletic scholarships to participate in so-called revenue sports like Division I men's basketball and FBS football. In those sports, economic reality and the tradition of amateurism may not point in the same direction. Those sports involve billions of dollars of revenue for colleges and universities. Athletic scholarships are limited to the cost of attending school. With economic reality as our guide, as I believe it should be, there may be room for further debate, perhaps with a developed factual record rather than bare pleadings, for cases addressing employment status for a variety of purposes.

DAWSON V. NCAA
932 F.3d 905 (9th Cir. 2019)

THOMAS, CHIEF JUDGE:

We consider whether Lamar Dawson and Division I Football Bowl Subdivision ("FBS") Football Players are employees of the National Collegiate Athletic Association ("NCAA") and PAC-12 Conference ("PAC-12") within the meaning of the Fair Labor Standards Act ("FLSA"), 29 U.S.C. §§ 201–219, and California labor law. We have jurisdiction pursuant to 28 U.S.C. § 1291. Because the claims fail as a matter of law, we affirm the judgment of the district court.

I

Dawson played football for the University of Southern California ("USC"), a Division I FBS member of the NCAA's PAC-12 Conference. In this putative class action case, Dawson does not allege that he was an employee of USC, so the pure question of employment is not before us, and we need not consider whether he had employment status as a football player, nor whether USC was an employer. That question is left, if at all, for another day. Rather, the only issue before us is whether the NCAA and PAC-12 were his employers under federal and state law.

The NCAA is an "unincorporated not-for-profit educational organization" comprised of more than 1,100 colleges and universities throughout the United States. NCAA member schools are organized into three Divisions based on the number and quality of opportunities that the schools provide to participate in intercollegiate athletics. Division I consists of approximately 351 schools. Approximately 253 Division I schools have Division I football programs, of which approximately 128 fall within the FBS. The PAC-12 is an unincorporated association which operates a multi-sport collegiate athletic conference, and is a formal conference member of the NCAA Division I FBS.

NCAA member schools "agree to administer their athletics programs in accordance with the constitution, bylaws, and other legislation of the [NCAA]." The NCAA's constitution and bylaws establish academic eligibility requirements, provide guidelines and restrictions for recruitment, impose limits on the number and size of athletic scholarships, and regulate the scheduling and conditions of practice and games. [The court recited NCAA bylaws that govern financial aid and prohibit compensation for student-athletes, and the complaint's allegation that such regulation establishes the NCAA and PAC-12 as joint employers whose failure to pay wages to student athletes violates federal and state labor laws.]

II

The district court properly concluded that Division I FBS Football Players are not employees of the NCAA or PAC-12 as a matter of federal law.

A

The FLSA provides that "employers" must pay their "employees" a minimum wage and overtime pay for hours worked in excess of the statutory workweek. 29 U.S.C. §§ 206(a), 207(a)(1). The statute defines an "employee" as "any individual employed by an employer." 29 U.S.C. § 203(e)(1). To "employ" means "to suffer or permit to work." 29 U.S.C. § 203(g) . . .

Ultimately, "[t]he test of employment under the [FLSA] is one of 'economic reality.'" *Id.* at 301 (quoting *Goldberg v. Whitaker House Cooperative, Inc.*, 366 U.S. 28, 33 (1961)). Economic reality accounts for "the circumstances of the whole activity" rather than considering "isolated factors" determinative. *Rutherford Food Corp. v. McComb*, 331 U.S. 722, 730 (1947).

The Supreme Court has found a number of circumstances relevant in evaluating economic reality, including: (1) expectation of compensation, *Portland Terminal*, 330 U.S. at 152; (2) the power to hire and fire, *Goldberg*, 366 U.S. at 33; (3) and evidence that an arrangement was "conceived or carried out" to evade the law, *Portland Terminal*, 330 U.S. at 153. We apply these guiding principles in our analysis, and conclude that the economic reality of the relationship between the NCAA/PAC-12 and student-athletes does not reflect an employment relationship.

1

We need not address whether Dawson's scholarship engendered an "expectation of compensation" or whether his scholarship amounted to compensation because he did not receive the scholarship from the NCAA or the PAC-12. The NCAA Bylaws reveal that member schools themselves award and distribute the financial aid Dawson alleges constitutes expected compensation. *See* 2015–16 NCAA Division I Manual, NCAA Bylaw 15.01.6 (prohibiting "institutions" from awarding aid to a student-athlete in excess of cost of attendance).

Dawson's theory is that NCAA regulations prohibit NCAA student-athletes from accepting compensation beyond scholarships limited to cost of attendance. He does not claim that the defendants provide scholarships; whether "compensation" or not, scholarship funding comes from his school. The limitation on scholarships does not, as a matter of law, create any expectation of compensation from the NCAA/PAC-12.

Thus, on the undisputed facts, neither the NCAA nor PAC-12 provided Dawson with a scholarship or any expectation of a scholarship.

2

Similarly, on this record, Dawson cannot demonstrate that the NCAA or the PAC-12 had the power to fire or hire him. Dawson alleges that the NCAA/PAC-12 assert complete control over the lives of student-athletes, on and off campus, including a student-athlete's: "(a) living arrangements; (b) athletic eligibility; (c) permissible compensation; (d) allowable behavior; (e) academic performance; (f) use of alcohol and drugs; and (g) gambling." Dawson alleges that the penalties for violating these rules include "loss of financial aid and eligibility for sports." Dawson also alleges that the NCAA/PAC-12 control and regulate student-athletes' "training and game schedules, academic schedules, and other collegiate activities."

The NCAA Bylaws pervasively regulate college athletics. The complaint, however, does not allege that the NCAA/PAC-12 "hire and fire," or exercise any other analogous control, over student-athletes. The complaint does not allege, and moreover, the record does not demonstrate, that the NCAA and PAC-12 choose the players on any Division I football team, nor that they engage in the actual supervision of the players' performance. Rather, the allegations of the complaint, taken as true, demonstrate that the NCAA functions as a regulator, and that the NCAA member schools, for whom the student-athletes allegedly render services, enforce regulations.

In sum, on this record, Dawson cannot demonstrate that the NCAA or the PAC-12 had the power to fire or hire him.

3

Finally, there is no evidence tendered by Dawson that the NCAA rules were "conceived or carried out" to evade the law. The relevant rules were first promulgated in the early 1920's, and some version of them has "existed for a long time." *Hale v. State of Ariz.*, 993 F.2d 1387, 1398 (9th Cir. 1993). In contrast, Congress enacted the FLSA in 1938. *Rutherford*, 331 U.S. at

723. Even though "economic reality" in college sports is much different today, there is no evidence on this record that the NCAA rules were "conceived or carried out" to evade the law.

4

The Supreme Court has also considered more specific factors when helpful to probe the economic reality of a particular situation. *See, e.g., Rutherford,* 331 U.S. at 730 (considering whether an employment relationship existed versus independent contractor status); *Goldberg,* 366 U.S. at 32–33 (evaluating whether members of a cooperative may also be employees of the same). In this context, Dawson argues that the labor of student-athletes generates substantial revenue for the NCAA and PAC-12, and that this "economic reality" alters the analysis.

However, precedent demonstrates that revenue does not automatically engender or foreclose the existence of an employment relationship under the FLSA. The Supreme Court has held self-proclaimed volunteers to be employees of a nonprofit religious organization. *Alamo,* 471 U.S. at 296–97. Conversely, we recently held that cosmetology students were not employees entitled to minimum wage despite the fact that they performed services for paying customers at salons run by their schools. *Benjamin v. B&H Education, Inc.,* 877 F.3d 1139, 1148 (9th Cir. 2017). Therefore, in the context of our preceding analysis, the revenue generated by college sports does not unilaterally convert the relationship between student-athletes and the NCAA into an employment relationship.

B

Bonnette v. California Health and Welfare Agency, 704 F.2d 1465, 1470 (9th Cir. 1983), *abrogated on other grounds by Garcia v. San Antonio Metro. Transit Auth.,* 469 U.S. 528 (1985), does not compel a contrary conclusion, as Dawson contends. In *Bonnette,* we applied a four-factor test to probe the economic reality of the relationship between state agencies and chore workers hired to perform in-home care for disabled public service recipients. *Id.* at 1470.

The *Bonnette* factors ask "whether the alleged employer (1) had the power to hire and fire the employees, (2) supervised and controlled employee work schedules or conditions of employment, (3) determined the rate and method of payment, and (4) maintained employment records." *Id.* at 1470. These factors prove "particularly appropriate where (as in *Bonnette* itself) it is clear that some entity is an 'employer' and the question is which one." *Hale,* 993 F.2d at 1394 (quoting *Vanskike v. Peters,* 974 F.2d 806, 809 (7th Cir. 1992)). Under the *Bonnette* test, however, the NCAA and PAC-12 are clearly not Dawson's employers. They do not admit him to the school or pick him for the team; they cannot remove him from the team; they do not supervise his schedules or activities in practices or games; they do not maintain his scholastic records; and, although they put caps on what he may receive as a scholarship, they do not determine whether he gets a scholarship or in what amount.

Similarly, *Benjamin* does not alter our conclusion. In *Benjamin*, we applied a seven-factor "primary beneficiary test" to evaluate economic reality in the vocational student-employee context. 877 F.3d at 1147. The primary beneficiary test looks to "seven non-exhaustive factors for courts to weigh and balance[.]" *Id.* at 1146 (discussing *Glatt v. Fox Searchlight Pictures, Inc.*, 791 F.3d 376 (2d Cir. 2015), *amended and superseded by* 811 F.3d 528 (2d Cir. 2016)).

Benjamin is not useful in determining whether an employment relationship exists between Dawson and the defendants. *Benjamin* involved vocational students earning academic credit necessary to take a state licensing exam. *Id.* at 1142. In contrast, student-athletes are participating in highly regulated extra-curricular activities. Thus, *Benjamin's* "primary beneficiary test" fails to "capture the true nature" of the relationship at issue here. *Hale*, 993 F.2d at 1394.

III

The district court also correctly dismissed Dawson's California law claims for failure to state a claim, relying on the California Legislature's decision to except student-athletes from workers compensation benefits and decisions of the California Courts of Appeal that interpret the student-athlete exception. Dawson argues that the district court erred in dismissing his state law claims because the exception does not apply to the wage and hour provisions at issue here.

The status of student-athletes under California labor law has a storied history. In 1963, the California Court of Appeal determined that the estate of a state college football player, killed with his team in a plane crash while returning from a football game, was entitled to death benefits from his college under the state's Workmen's Compensation Act. *Van Horn v. Indus. Acc. Comm'n*, 219 Cal. App. 2d 457, 465 (1963). The California Legislature responded in 1965 by amending the Workmen's Compensation Act to exclude explicitly " '[a]ny person, other than a regular employee, participating in sports or athletics who receives no compensation for such participation other than the use of athletic equipment, uniforms, transportation, travel, meals, lodgings, or other expenses incidental thereto.' " *Graczyk v. Workers' Comp. Appeals Bd.*, 184 Cal. App. 3d 997, 1005 (1986). The amendment intended to "clarify the position" of athletic sponsors, and noted the "absence of the usual elements of the employment relationship." *Id.* (citation omitted). The Legislature again amended the Act in 1981 to "more specifically clarify the exclusion of athletic participants." *Id.*

To be sure, the exclusion of student-athletes from the Workmen's Compensation Act at Section 3352(k) of the Labor Code is informed by

Section 3350, which provides that "[u]nless context otherwise requires, the definitions set forth in this article shall govern the construction and meaning of the terms and phrases used in this division." Cal. Labor Code § 3350. Dawson emphasizes the Legislature's use of the phrase "this division," and argues that *expressio unius est exclusio alterius*—the expression of one thing excludes the expression of another—"confirms that Section 3352(k) is confined" to the Worker's Compensation section of the Labor Code. However, California's appellate courts have interpreted the Legislature's actions differently.

[The court summarizes California case law broadly interpreting Labor Code § 3350 "to prevent the student-athlete from being considered an employee of an educational institution for any purpose which could result in financial liability on the part of the university." The court also described California's subsequent enactment of a Student Athlete Bill of Rights that compensates injured student-athletes through scholarship funds and payment of insurance deductibles and medical expenses, rather than extending employment-related protections.] Thus, ... [t]here is no authority that supports an inference that, even though the student-athletes are not considered to be employees of their schools under California law, the NCAA and the PAC-12 can nevertheless be held to be "joint employers" with the students' schools. Consequently, we must hold that student-athletes are not employees of the NCAA/PAC-12 under the California Labor Code.

IV

For the foregoing reasons, we affirm the district court's dismissal of Dawson's FLSA and California state law claims against the NCAA and PAC-12. We need not, and do not, reach any other issue urged by the parties, nor do we express an opinion about student-athletes' employment status in any other context.

AFFIRMED.

————

NOTES AND QUESTIONS

1. *Employee-Athletes?* Do you agree with the Seventh Circuit and the Ninth Circuit's conclusions that college athletes are not employees? Does the NLRB regional director's analysis of the Northwestern football program provide a more persuasive counter view?

2. *Revenue Versus Non-Revenue.* To what extent is the employee-athlete argument limited to revenue sport athletes? The concurrence in *Berger* suggests that the outcome might be different in the case of revenue sport athletes. Do you agree? How could revenue-producing athletes be distinguished for purposes of the FLSA, which does not contain any applicable exemption?

3. *Effect of Applying the FLSA to College Athletes?* What would be the likely effect on college athletic programs if they were forced to compensate all participants? Would it be likely that teams would be eliminated by many universities and colleges, most of which must subsidize their athletic department?

_____

While courts have generally rejected the idea that college athletes are university employees, a recent district court case found otherwise. Pending on a rare interlocutory appeal to the Third Circuit at the time of publication, *Johnson v. NCAA*, 556 F. Supp. 3d 491 (E.D. Pa. 2021), considered whether college athletes were employees for purposes of claims made under the Fair Labor Standards Act (FLSA). The plaintiffs' class action complaint involved the NCAA and all Division I universities, and sought damages for violations of the FLSA, as well as for unjust enrichment. The defendants moved to dismiss under Rule 12(b)(6) on the grounds that the plaintiffs were not employees, but the court denied their motion.

The district court first rejected the defendants' argument that the plaintiff athletes were not employees because they are amateurs. Citing *Alston*, the district court found this argument "circular and unpersuasive." It found that the "long-standing tradition of amateurism in NCAA interscholastic athletics that defines the economic reality of the relationship" between athletes and universities did not foreclose a determination that they were employees for purposes of the FLSA.

The district court next rejected the defendants' claim that the language of the Field Operations Handbook (FOH) of the Department of Labor foreclosed the plaintiffs claim that they were university employees. The relevant section of the FOH, § 10b03(e), provides:

> As part of their overall educational program, public or private schools and institutions of higher learning may permit or require students to engage in activities in connection with dramatics, student publications, glee clubs, bands, choirs, debating teams, radio stations, intramural and interscholastic athletics and other similar endeavors. Activities of students in such programs, conducted primarily for the benefit of the participants as a part of the educational opportunities provided to the students by the school or institution, are not work of the kind contemplated by . . . the Act and do not result in an employer-employee relationship between the student and the school or institution.

But court found that the athletes were engaged in athletics primarily for the benefit of the *university*, not the athlete. It explained:

> [W]e find that the Complaint plausibly alleges that NCAA D1 interscholastic athletics are not conducted primarily for the

benefit of the student athletes who participate in them, but for the monetary benefit of the NCAA and the colleges and universities that those student athletes attend. We further find that the Complaint plausibly alleges that the NCAA D1 interscholastic athletics are not part of the educational opportunities provided to the student athletes by the colleges and universities that they attend but, rather, interfere with the student athletes' abilities to participate in and get the maximum benefit from the academic opportunities offered by their colleges and universities. Accordingly, we conclude that the Complaint plausibly alleges that NCAA D1 interscholastic athletics are not the types of activities listed in FOH § 10b03(e) that "do not result in an employer-employee relationship between the student and the school or institution." FOH § 10b03(e). We further conclude, accordingly, that FOH § 10b03(e) does not require us to find, as a matter of law, that Plaintiffs cannot be employees of the ASD.

Id. at 506.

Finally, the district court found that under the multifactor test used by the Second Circuit (*Glatt v. Fox Searchlight Pictures*, 811 F.3d 528 (2d Cir. 2015)) to determine whether an individual is an employee that plaintiffs had provided enough evidence to survive a motion to dismiss.

NOTES AND QUESTIONS

1. *Same Question, Different Outcome?* What convinced the district court to allow the plaintiffs' claim to proceed? How does the court's view of the FLSA differ from those of the Seventh and Ninth Circuits?

2. *Settling Versus Litigating.* Should the NCAA settle in *Johnson* given the good precedents it has in *Berger* and *Dawson*? The Third Circuit's upholding of a trial victory in *Johnson* would create a circuit split. After you read *Alston* in the next section, consider whether the NCAA would be eager to litigate the FLSA employee question before the Supreme Court.

D. ANTITRUST LIMITS ON NCAA AMATEURISM REGULATIONS

The traditional approach of courts to applying antitrust law to the NCAA's amateurism regulations has been one of judicial deference. Specifically, courts found that amateurism provided a sufficient pro-competitive justification for the NCAA's rules. A Seventh Circuit case, *Banks v. NCAA*, 977 F.2d 1081 (7th Cir. 1992), is instructive on this point.

Braxston Banks was an oft-injured running back at Notre Dame who decided to forego his final year of eligibility to enter the NFL draft. After going undrafted, Banks tried to return to the university to play one more season, but NCAA rules barred him from returning. By hiring an agent and entering the draft, Banks lost his amateur status under NCAA rules.

Banks subsequently filed an antitrust suit, challenging the NCAA's rules, but the court dismissed his case for failure to state a claim under Rule 12(b)(6). The Court found that Banks had failed to allege an anti-competitive effect on a relevant market. In explaining that athletes would have to be employees to have a valid antitrust claim, the court stated:

> Because the no-draft rule represents a desirable and legitimate attempt "to keep university athletics from becoming professionalized to the extent that profit making objectives would overshadow educational objectives," the no-draft rule and other like NCAA regulations preserve the bright line of demarcation between college and "play for pay" football. We consider college football players as student-athletes simultaneously pursuing academic degrees that will prepare them to enter the employment market in non-athletic occupations, and hold that the regulations of the NCAA are designed to preserve the honesty and integrity of intercollegiate athletics and foster fair competition among the participating amateur college students.

Id. at 1090.

The dissent found that the NCAA's no-draft rule did have an anti-competitive effect in the market for college football players. Its view, which the majority chastised as "surprisingly cynical," focused more on the economic aspects of college sports and found that Banks had alleged a plausible claim. The dissent explained:

> The NCAA continues to purvey, even in this case, an outmoded image of intercollegiate sports that no longer jibes with reality. The times have changed. College football is a terrific American institution that generates abundant nonpecuniary benefits for players and fans, but it is also a vast commercial venture that yields substantial profits for colleges. The games provide fans with entertaining contests to watch, and athletes with an opportunity to display and develop their strength, skills and character, but they are saleable products nonetheless. An athlete's participation offers all of the rewards that attend vigorous competition in organized sport, but it is also labor, labor for which the athlete is recompensed. The no-draft and no-agent rules may, ultimately, pass muster under the rule of reason. But, putting the adequacy of Banks' complaint to the side, contending that they have no commercial effect on competition in the college football labor market, or that there is no market of that type at all, is chimerical:

The true stake Is this decades-long gentleman's agreement between the NFL and the college powers-that-be that has kept all but a handful of football playing collegians from turning pro before their four-year use to their schools is exhausted. The pros get a free farm system that supplies them with well-trained, much publicized employees. The colleges get to keep their players the equivalent of barefoot and pregnant.

Klein, *College Football: Keeping 'em Barefoot*, Wall St. J., Sept. 4, 1987, at 15.

Id. at 1099–1100.

A more recent case that involved a challenge to the NCAA's transfer rules met a similar outcome.

DEPPE V. NCAA

893 F.3d 498 (7th Cir. 2018)

SYKES, CIRCUIT JUDGE.

This case raises an antitrust challenge to the NCAA's "year in residence" rule, which requires student-athletes who transfer to a Division I college to wait one full academic year before they can play for their new school. A Division I football player filed a class-action lawsuit alleging that the rule is an unlawful restraint of trade in violation of § 1 of the Sherman Act. The district court dismissed the suit on the pleadings.

We affirm. The year-in-residence requirement is an eligibility rule clearly meant to preserve the amateur character of college athletics and is therefore presumptively procompetitive under *NCAA v. Board of Regents of University of Oklahoma*, 468 U.S. 85 (1984), and *Agnew v. NCAA*, 683 F.3d 328 (7th Cir. 2012).

1.   Background

The case comes to us from a dismissal on the pleadings, *see* FED. R. CIV. P. 12(b)(6), so we take the following factual account from the complaint, accepting the allegations as true. Peter Deppe was a star punter in high school, and several schools recruited him to play college football. He chose Northern Illinois University ("NIU"), a Division I school, and enrolled in June 2014 as a preferred walk-on. In other words, NIU invited him to join the football team but did not offer him an athletic scholarship. Deppe decided to "red shirt" his first year; this meant that he practiced with the team during the 2014 season but did not compete, and the clock did not run on his four years of NCAA athletic eligibility.

Shortly after Deppe enrolled, an NIU football coach told him that he would start receiving an athletic scholarship in January 2015. That coach soon left NIU, however, and the head football coach later informed Deppe that he would not receive the scholarship after all. Sometime in 2015 NIU signed another punter, reducing Deppe's chances of getting playing time or receiving an athletic scholarship, so in the fall of 2015 he started shopping around for a new football program.

The University of Iowa, another Division I school, was interested. Coaches at Iowa told Deppe they wanted him to join the team if he would be eligible to compete during the 2016–2017 season. Deppe's parents asked the NCAA about their son's eligibility to play. The NCAA responded that under its year-in-residence rule, Deppe would be ineligible to compete for one year following his transfer.

The year-in-residence bylaw appears in the eligibility section of the *NCAA Division I Manual*. It provides:

> 14.5.5.1 General Rule. A transfer student from a four-year institution shall not be eligible for intercollegiate competition at a member institution until the student has fulfilled a residence requirement of one full academic year (two full semesters or three full quarters) at the certifying institution.

... The NCAA permits a one-time transfer with immediate athletic eligibility in certain limited circumstances. The so-called one-time transfer exception is available to a Division I football player only if he transfers from a school in the Football Bowl Subdivision to a school in the Football Championship Subdivision with two or more seasons of athletic eligibility remaining, or if he transfers from a Football Championship school that offers athletic scholarships to a Football Championship school that does not. *Id.*, 184–85, § 14.5.5.2.10. The exception was unavailable to Deppe because he intended to transfer from one Football Bowl school to another.

In addition, a player who transfers due to difficult personal or family circumstances or other extenuating circumstances may apply for a waiver of the NCAA's requirement that a student-athlete's four years of playing time be completed in five calendar years. *Id.*, 79, § 12.8.1; *Id.*, 81, § 12.8.1.7; *Id.*, 88–89, § 12.8.6. The NCAA informed Deppe that if he wanted to try to obtain a waiver, the school to which he planned to transfer would have to initiate the process on his behalf. In November 2015 the University of Iowa granted Deppe academic admission. But a few days later, Iowa football staff notified him that the team had decided to pursue another punter who had immediate eligibility and the school would not initiate the waiver process for him.

Deppe sued the NCAA on behalf of himself and a proposed class alleging that two of the Association's bylaws violate § 1 of the Sherman Act: the year-in-residence requirement, and a rule capping the number of athletic scholarships a school can grant each year. He dropped his challenge to the scholarship cap; only the year-in-residence rule remains at issue. Deppe argued that the bylaw is an unlawful restraint of trade and that student-athletes would receive more generous athletic scholarships if they could transfer more freely.

The NCAA moved to dismiss the complaint under Rule 12(b)(6), arguing that the year-in-residence bylaw is an eligibility rule and thus is presumptively procompetitive under *Board of Regents* and *Agnew* and need not be tested for anticompetitive effect under a full rule-of-reason analysis. The district judge agreed and dismissed the case.

II. Discussion

* * *

The Supreme Court considered the antitrust implications of NCAA regulations in [NCAA v.] *Board of Regents*. The case raised a Sherman Act challenge to the Association's restrictions on televising college football games. 468 U.S. at 91–92. The details are not important here; for our purposes, it's enough to note that the Court found the restrictions unlawful under § 1 of the Act. *Id.* at 120. Along the way to that holding, the Court had this to say about antitrust challenges to the NCAA's bylaws more generally:

> It is reasonable to assume that most of the regulatory controls of the NCAA are justifiable means of fostering competition among amateur athletic teams and therefore procompetitive because they enhance public interest in intercollegiate athletics. The specific restraints on football telecasts that are challenged in this case do not, however, fit into the same mold as do rules defining the conditions of the contest, the eligibility of participants, or the manner in which members of a joint enterprise shall share the responsibilities and the benefits of the total venture.

Id. at 117. The Court closed its decision by observing that "[t]he NCAA plays a crucial role in the maintenance of a revered tradition of amateurism in college sports" and "needs ample latitude" to play that role, and that "the preservation of the student-athlete in higher education adds richness and diversity to intercollegiate athletics and is entirely consistent with the goals of the Sherman Act." *Id.* at 120.

In *Agnew* we read this language from *Board of Regents* to mean that although the Sherman Act applies to the NCAA, "most [of the Association's] regulations will be a 'justifiable means of fostering competition among amateur athletic teams[ ]' and are therefore procompetitive." 683 F.3d at 341 (quoting *Bd. Of Regents*, 468 U.S. at 117). We also understood these passages as "a license to find certain NCAA bylaws that 'fit into the same mold' as those discussed in *Board of Regents* to be procompetitive . . . at the motion-to-dismiss stage" without the need for analysis under the rule-of-reason framework. *Id.* (internal citation omitted) (quoting *Bd. Of Regents*, 468 U.S. at 117, 110 n.39). Accordingly, we held that "the first—and possibly only—question to be answered when NCAA bylaws are challenged is whether the NCAA regulations at issue are of the type that have been blessed by the Supreme Court, making them presumptively procompetitive." *Id.*

Agnew involved a challenge to the NCAA's scholarship cap and its prohibition of multiyear scholarships. *Id.* at 332. Extrapolating from *Board of Regents*, we distilled the following legal standard for determining whether a § 1 challenge in this context may go forward or should be dismissed on the pleadings: an NCAA bylaw is presumptively procompetitive when it is "clearly meant to help maintain the 'revered tradition of amateurism in college sports' or the 'preservation of the student-athlete in higher education.'" *Id.* at 342–43 (quoting *Bd. Of Regents*, 468 U.S. at 120). On the other hand, "if a regulation is not, on its face, helping to 'preserve a tradition that might otherwise die,'" no such presumption is warranted. *Id.* at 343 (quoting *Bd. Of Regents*, 468 U.S. at 120).

Importantly here, we also explained that "[m]ost—if not all—eligibility rules . . . fall within the presumption of procompetitiveness" established in *Board of Regents. Id.* After all, "the Supreme Court explicitly mentioned eligibility rules as a type that 'fit[s] into the same mold' as other procompetitive rules." *Id.* (alteration in original). And because eligibility rules "define what it means to be an amateur or a student-athlete," they are "essential to the very existence of the product of college football." *Id.*

The rules challenged in *Agnew* did not govern athletic eligibility or otherwise "fit into the same mold" of the presumptively procompetitive regulations mentioned in *Board of Regents. Id.* at 344–45. But the absence of a procompetitive presumption did "not equal a finding that [the rules] are anticompetitive;" rather, it simply meant that they could not be presumed procompetitive at the pleadings stage. *Id.* at 345. So we moved to the next step in the § 1 analysis and determined that the complaint failed to identify a relevant cognizable market and affirmed the dismissal of the suit on that basis. *Id.* at 345–47.

Unlike the bylaws at issue in *Agnew*, the year-in-residence requirement is plainly an eligibility rule. It appears in the eligibility section of the NCAA Division I Manual. On its face, it governs a transfer student's eligibility for intercollegiate athletic competition. In particular, the bylaw suspends a transfer student's athletic eligibility until the student has spent one full academic year at his new college.

Deppe insists that the year-in-residence rule does not "fit within the contours of a traditional eligibility bylaw." On the contrary, the rule falls neatly in line with other rules courts have characterized as eligibility rules. In *Agnew* we gave the example of a class-attendance requirement to explain why eligibility rules are entitled to a procompetitive presumption. We said: "There may not be such a thing as a student athlete, for instance, if it was not for the NCAA rules requiring class attendance, and thus no detailed analysis would be necessary to deem such rules procompetitive." *Id.* at 343 (internal quotation marks and citation omitted). Bylaws that have been classified as eligibility rules include: a bylaw revoking a student-athlete's eligibility to compete if he enters the professional draft or hires a professional agent, *Banks v. NCAA*, 977 F.2d 1081, 1082–83 (7th Cir. 1992); a rule allowing the suspension of a college football program for illicitly compensating players beyond scholarships, *McCormack v. NCAA*, 845 F.2d 1338, 1343 (5th Cir. 1988); and a bylaw making student-athletes ineligible to compete at a graduate school different from their undergraduate institution, *Smith v. NCAA*, 139 F.3d 180, 186 (3d Cir. 1998), *vacated on other grounds by NCAA v. Smith*, 525 U.S. 459 (1999). We have no difficulty concluding that the year-in-residence bylaw is an eligibility rule.

As we've noted, most NCAA eligibility rules are entitled to the procompetitive presumption announced in *Board of Regents* because they define what it means to be a student-athlete and thus preserve the tradition and amateur character of college athletics. *Agnew*, 683 F.3d at 343. Deppe has not persuaded us that the year-in-residence requirement is the rare exception to this general principle. Indeed, the complaint alleges that Division I football student-athletes would transfer more often if not for the year-in-residence rule. Without it student-athletes could be "traded" from year to year like professional athletes. A college player could begin the season playing for one school and end the season playing for its rival. Uninhibited transfers with immediate eligibility to play would risk severing the athletic and academic aspects of college sports, threatening the character of intercollegiate athletics. The year-in-residence rule guards against that risk and thus is "clearly meant to help maintain the 'revered tradition of amateurism in college sports.'" *Id.* at 342 (quoting *Bd. Of Regents*, 468 U.S. at 120).

Deppe points to the exceptions and the possibility of a waiver of the Association's five-year rule, arguing that if these forms of relief are available, then the year-in-residence requirement is actually unnecessary to the survival of college football. This argument is a nonstarter. To begin, the test under Agnew is not whether college athletics could survive without this bylaw, but rather whether the rule is clearly meant to help preserve the amateurism of college sports. And scrutinizing the NCAA's bylaws as Deppe suggests conflicts with the Supreme Court's admonition in *Board of Regents* that the NCAA needs "ample latitude" to preserve the product of college sports. 468 U.S. at 120. That the NCAA allows some avenues for relief does not suggest that the year-in-residence requirement is aimed at an objective other than the maintenance of the amateur character of the college game. Instead it suggests that the NCAA is willing to allow players certain flexibility where doing so will not damage the product of college football.

Next, Deppe argues that the NCAA enforces the year-in-residence requirement for economic reasons and not to preserve the product of college football. He asks us to infer an economic motive from the fact that the one-time transfer exception is unavailable to most Division I football, basketball, and ice-hockey players—the highest-revenue sports programs in the NCAA. This argument ignores the innocent explanation that these are precisely the athletes who are most vulnerable to poaching. Without transfer restrictions, the players in these high-revenue sports could be traded like professional athletes.

Deppe also argues that because the year-in-residence requirement impedes transfers, it lowers the administrative costs associated with player movement, including recruiting and retention expenditures. That is, schools are saving money they would otherwise need to spend on more generous scholarships to tempt their student-athletes to stay, as well as money necessary to recruit and train new players to replace those who leave. But the fact that colleges may save money as a consequence of the year-in-residence requirement does not mean that the bylaw is fundamentally aimed at containing costs rather than preserving the amateur character of college football.

Last, Deppe argues that at bottom, the year-in-residence rule serves economic interests because it "preserves the hegemony of the top 'Power 5' conferences"—the most powerful group of schools in the NCAA. He asserts that these schools recruit the most talented high-school athletes and that the year-in-residence rule prevents those student athletes from transferring to less powerful schools. But the rule impedes transfers in both directions. Without it, the "Power 5" schools could poach rising stars from smaller schools, which would risk eroding the amateur character of the college game.

In sum, the year-in-residence rule is, on its face, a presumptively procompetitive eligibility rule under *Agnew* and *Board of Regents*. Accordingly, a full rule-of-reason analysis is unnecessary. Deppe's Sherman Act challenge to the NCAA's year-in-residence bylaw fails on the pleadings. AFFIRMED.

NOTES AND QUESTIONS

1. *Eligibility Rules (Athletic Competition) Versus Economic Rules (Economic Competition)*. The court in *Deppe* held that eligibility rules do not even require analysis under the Sherman Act because they are procompetitive in nature. By contrast, economic rules face more intense antitrust scrutiny. Why?

2. *Extending Prior Precedent*. The court in *Deppe* also distinguished its 2012 decision in *Agnew v. NCAA*, 683 F.3d 328 (7th Cir. 2012), where it reached

the same result but not at the 12(b)(6) stage of the pleadings. In *Agnew*, athletes challenged the then-prohibition against multiyear scholarships and the cap on the number of scholarships as antitrust violations under the Sherman Act. The court found that these were not eligibility rules, like in *Deppe*, but still upheld the rules as procompetitive. The *Agnew* court relied on language from *Board of Regents*, explaining that NCAA rules have a procompetitive purpose when they manifest the " 'revered tradition of amateurism in college sports' or the 'preservation of the student-athlete in higher education.' " *Agnew*, 683 F.3d at 342–43.

O'BANNON V. NCAA
802 F.3d 1049 (9th Cir. 2015)

BYBEE, CIRCUIT JUDGE.

[In 2008, Ed O'Bannon saw his likeness in an EA Sports video game, with the avatar mimicking his basketball moves and mannerisms. O'Bannon sued EA Sports and the NCAA, who had sold his likeness to EA Sports. The suit grew, with the case becoming a class action. EA Sports settled, leaving the case as an antitrust challenge against the NCAA and its amateurism rules. The district court held that the NCAA's amateurism rule violated antitrust law, but concluded that $5,000 per year, held until students finished school, would remedy the antitrust issue. The Ninth Circuit affirmed the determination that NCAA rules violated the Sherman Act, but reversed the remedy, finding that athletes were entitled to cost of attendance but not $5,000 payments.]

[The NCAA argued that *Board of Regents* precluded the court from reaching the merits of the antitrust claim.]

* * *

Applying the Rule of Reason, the Court struck down the television rules on the ground that they did not serve any legitimate procompetitive purpose. *Id.* at 113–20. It then concluded its opinion by stating:

> The NCAA plays a critical role in the maintenance of a revered tradition of amateurism in college sports. There can be no question but that it needs ample latitude to play that role, *or that the preservation of the student-athlete in higher education adds richness and diversity to intercollegiate athletics and is entirely consistent with the goals of the Sherman Act.* But consistent with the Sherman Act, the role of the NCAA must be to preserve a tradition that might otherwise die; rules that restrict output are hardly consistent with this role. Today we hold only that the record supports the District Court's conclusion that by curtailing output and blunting the ability of member institutions to respond to consumer preference, the NCAA has restricted rather than enhanced the place of intercollegiate athletics in the Nation's life.

Id. at 120 (emphasis added).

Quoting heavily from the language in *Board of Regents* that we have emphasized, the NCAA contends that any Section 1 challenge to its amateurism rules must fail as a matter of law because the *Board of Regents* Court held that those rules are presumptively valid. We disagree.

The *Board of Regents* Court certainly discussed the NCAA's amateurism rules at great length, but it did not do so in order to pass upon the rules' merits, given that they were not before the Court. Rather, the Court discussed the amateurism rules for a different and particular purpose: to explain why NCAA rules should be analyzed under the Rule of Reason, rather than held to be illegal per se.

* * *

Board of Regents, in other words, did not approve the NCAA's amateurism rules as categorically consistent with the Sherman Act. Rather, it held that, because many NCAA rules (among them, the amateurism rules) are part of the "character and quality of the [NCAA's] 'product,'" *Id.* at 102, no NCAA rule should be invalidated without a Rule of Reason analysis. The Court's long encomium to amateurism, though impressive-sounding, was therefore dicta.

* * *

[The court next rejected the NCAA's claim that its rules do not regulate "commercial activity"—its eligibility rules *are* compensation rules, before reaching the merits of the antitrust claim.]

Like the district court, we follow the three-step framework of the Rule of Reason: "[1] The plaintiff bears the initial burden of showing that the restraint produces significant anticompetitive effects within a relevant market. [2] If the plaintiff meets this burden, the defendant must come forward with evidence of the restraint's procompetitive effects. [3] The plaintiff must then show that any legitimate objectives can be achieved in a substantially less restrictive manner." *Tanaka v. Univ. of S. Cal.*, 252 F.3d 1059, 1063 (9th Cir. 2001) (citations and internal quotation marks omitted).

A.   *Significant Anticompetitive Effects Within a Relevant Market*

As we have recounted, the district court made the following factual findings: (1) that a cognizable "college education market" exists, wherein colleges compete for the services of athletic recruits by offering them scholarships and various amenities, such as coaching and facilities; (2) that if the NCAA's compensation rules did not exist, member schools would compete to offer recruits compensation for their NILs; and (3) that the compensation rules therefore have a significant anticompetitive effect with respect on the college education market, in that they fix an aspect of the "price" that recruits pay to attend college (or, alternatively, an aspect of the price that schools pay to secure recruits' services). These findings have substantial support in the record.

* * *

Because we agree with the district court that the compensation rules have a significant anticompetitive effect on the college education market, we proceed to consider the procompetitive justifications the NCAA proffers for those rules.

B.   *Procompetitive Effects*

. . . the NCAA focuses its arguments to this court entirely on the first proffered justification—the promotion of amateurism. . . .

The NCAA is correct that a restraint that broadens choices can be procompetitive. The Court in *Board of Regents* observed that the difference between college and professional sports "widen[s]" the choices "available to athletes." *Bd. Of Regents,* 468 U.S. at 102. But we fail to see how the restraint at issue in this particular case—*i.e.,* the NCAA's limits on student-athlete compensation—makes college sports more attractive to recruits, or widens recruits' spectrum of choices in the sense that *Board of Regents* suggested.

* * *

We thus turn to the final inquiry—whether there are reasonable alternatives to the NCAA's current compensation restrictions.

C.   *Substantially Less Restrictive Alternatives*

The third step in the Rule of Reason analysis is whether there are substantially less restrictive alternatives to the NCAA's current rules. We bear in mind that—to be viable under the Rule of Reason—an alternative must be "virtually as effective" in serving the procompetitive purposes of the NCAA's current rules, and "without significantly increased cost." *Cnty. Of Tuolumne v. Sonora Cmty. Hosp.,* 236 F.3d 1148, 1159 (9th Cir. 2001) (internal quotation marks omitted). We think that plaintiffs must make a strong evidentiary showing that its alternatives are viable here. Not only do plaintiffs bear the burden at this step, but the Supreme Court has admonished that we must generally afford the NCAA "ample latitude" to superintend college athletics. . . .

The district court identified two substantially less restrictive alternatives: (1) allowing NCAA member schools to give student-athletes grants-in-aid that cover the full cost of attendance; and (2) allowing member schools to pay student-athletes small amounts of deferred cash compensation for use of their NILs. *O'Bannon,* 7 F. Supp. 3d at 1005–07. We hold that the district court did not clearly err in finding that raising the grant-in-aid cap would be a substantially less restrictive alternative, but that it clearly erred when it found that allowing students to be paid compensation for their NILs is virtually as effective as the NCAA's current amateur-status rule.

1. Capping the permissible amount of scholarships at the cost of attendance

. . . All of the evidence before the district court indicated that raising the grant-in-aid cap to the cost of attendance would have virtually no impact on amateurism: Dr. Mark Emmert, the president of the NCAA, testified at trial that giving student-athletes scholarships up to their full costs of attendance would not violate the NCAA's principles of amateurism because all the money given to students would be going to cover their "legitimate costs" to attend school. Other NCAA witnesses agreed with that assessment. *Id.* at 983. Nothing in the record, moreover, suggested that consumers of college sports would become less interested in those sports if athletes' scholarships covered their full cost of attendance, or that an increase in the grant-in-aid cap would impede the integration of student-athletes into their academic communities. *Id.*

. . . We agree with the NCAA and the *amici* that, as a general matter, courts should not use antitrust law to make marginal adjustments to broadly reasonable market restraints. . . .The particular restraint at issue here, however—the grant-in-aid cap that the NCAA set below the cost of attendance—is not such a restraint. To the contrary, the evidence at trial showed that the grant-in-aid cap has no relation whatsoever to the procompetitive purposes of the NCAA: by the NCAA's own standards, student-athletes remain amateurs as long as any money paid to them goes to cover legitimate educational expenses.

2. Allowing students to receive cash compensation for their NILs

In our judgment, however, the district court clearly erred in finding it a viable alternative to allow students to receive NIL cash payments untethered to their education expenses. Again, the district court identified two procompetitive purposes served by the NCAA's current rules: "preserving the popularity of the NCAA's product by promoting its current understanding of amateurism" and "integrating academics and athletics." *O'Bannon,* 7 F. Supp. 3d at 1005; *see also Board of Regents,* 468 U.S. at 117 ("It is reasonable to assume that most of the regulatory controls of the NCAA are justifiable means of fostering competition among amateur athletic teams and therefore procompetitive because they enhance public interest in intercollegiate athletics."). The question is whether the alternative of allowing students to be paid NIL compensation unrelated to their education expenses, is "virtually as effective" in preserving amateurism as *not* allowing compensation. *Cnty. Of Tuolumne,* 236 F.3d at 1159 (internal quotation marks omitted).

We cannot agree that a rule permitting schools to pay students pure cash compensation and a rule forbidding them from paying NIL compensation are both *equally* effective in promoting amateurism and preserving consumer demand. Both we and the district court agree that the NCAA's amateurism rule has procompetitive benefits. But in finding that paying students cash compensation would promote amateurism as effectively as not paying them, the district court ignored that not paying student-athletes is *precisely what makes them amateurs.*

Having found that amateurism is integral to the NCAA's market, the district court cannot plausibly conclude that being a poorly-paid professional collegiate athlete is "virtually as effective" for that market as being as amateur. Or, to borrow the Supreme Court's analogy, the market for college football is distinct from other sports markets and must be "differentiate[d]" from professional sports lest it become "minor league [football]." *Bd. Of Regents,* 468 U.S. at 102.

Aside from the self-evident fact that paying students for their NIL rights will vitiate their amateur status as collegiate athletes, the court relied on threadbare evidence in finding that small payments of cash compensation will preserve amateurism as well the NCAA's rule forbidding such payments. Most of the evidence elicited merely indicates that paying students large compensation payments would harm consumer demand more than smaller payments would—not that small cash payments will preserve amateurism. . . . But there is a stark difference between finding that small payments are less harmful to the market than large payments— and finding that paying students small sums is virtually as effective in promoting amateurism as not paying them.

Finally, the district court, and the dissent, place particular weight on a brief interchange during plaintiffs' cross-examination of one of the NCAA's witnesses, Neal Pilson, a television sports consultant formerly employed at CBS. Pilson testified that "if you're paid for your performance, you're not an amateur," and explained at length why paying students would harm the student-athlete market. Plaintiffs then asked Pilson whether his opinions about amateurism "depend on the level of the money" paid to players, and he acknowledged that his opinion was "impacted by the level." When asked whether there was a line that "should not be crossed" in paying players, Pilson responded "that's a difficult question. I haven't thought about the line. And I haven't been asked to render an opinion on that." When pressed to come up with a figure, Pilson repeated that he was "not sure." He eventually commented that "I tell you that a million dollars would trouble me and $5,000 wouldn't, but that's a pretty good range." When asked whether deferred compensation to students would concern him, Pilson said that while he would not be as concerned by deferred payments, he would still be "troubled by it."

So far as we can determine, Pilson's offhand comment under cross-examination is the sole support for the district court's $5,000 figure. But even taking Pilson's comments at face value, as the dissent urges, his testimony cannot support the finding that paying student-athletes small sums will be virtually as effective in preserving amateurism as not paying them. Pilson made clear that he was not prepared to opine on whether pure cash compensation, of any amount, would affect amateurism. Indeed, he was never asked about the impact of giving student-athletes small cash payments; instead, like other witnesses, he was asked only whether big payments would be worse than small payments. Pilson's casual comment— "[I] haven't been asked to render an opinion on that. It's not in my report"— that he would not be troubled by $5,000 payments is simply not enough to support the district court's far-reaching conclusion that paying students $5,000 per year will be as effective in preserving amateurism as the NCAA's current policy.

The difference between offering student-athletes education-related compensation and offering them cash sums untethered to educational expenses is not minor; it is a quantum leap. Once that line is crossed, we see no basis for returning to a rule of amateurism and no defined stopping point; we have little doubt that plaintiffs will continue to challenge the arbitrary limit imposed by the district court until they have captured the full value of their NIL. At that point the NCAA will have surrendered its amateurism principles entirely and transitioned from its "particular brand of football" to minor league status. *Bd. Of Regents,* 468 U.S. at 101–02. In light of that, the meager evidence in the record, and the Supreme Court's admonition that we must afford the NCAA "ample latitude" to superintend college athletics, *Bd. Of Regents,* 468 U.S. at 120, we think it is clear the district court erred in concluding that small payments in deferred compensation are a substantially less restrictive alternative restraint. We thus vacate that portion of the district court's decision and the portion of its injunction requiring the NCAA to allow its member schools to pay this deferred compensation.

THOMAS, CHIEF JUDGE, concurring in part and dissenting in part:

. . . I respectfully disagree with the majority's conclusion that the district court clearly erred in ordering the NCAA to permit up to $5,000 in deferred compensation above student-athletes' full cost of attendance.

* * *

The disagreement between my view and the majority view largely boils down to a difference in opinion as to the procompetitive interests at stake. The majority characterizes our task at step three of the Rule of Reason as determining "whether the alternative of allowing students to be paid NIL compensation unrelated to their education expenses is 'virtually as effective' in preserving *amateurism* as not allowing compensation." Op. at 1076 (emphasis added). This conclusion misstates our inquiry. Rather, we must determine whether allowing student-athletes to be compensated for their NILs is 'virtually as effective' in preserving *popular demand for college sports* as not allowing compensation. In terms of antitrust analysis, the concept of amateurism is relevant only insofar as it relates to consumer interest.

* * *

The NCAA insists that consumers will flee if student-athletes are paid even a small sum of money for colleges' use of their NILs. This assertion is contradicted by the district court record and by the NCAA's own rules regarding amateurism. . . .

____

NOTES AND QUESTIONS

1. *Aftermath.* The practical effect of *O'Bannon* was that institutions could provide the cost of attendance to student-athletes, an amount between $1,500 and $6,000 per year, depending on locale. In 2017, the NCAA settled part of another class action lawsuit, *NCAA v. Alston* (including the *White v. NCAA* plaintiffs) for $208 million, but the residual part of the case continued to the Supreme Court. This compensation provided for cost of attendance (in the amount of $5,000 to $7,500) for all men's and women's basketball players, and FBS football players from the 2008–09 season until the 2016–17 season.

2. *Effect of* O'Bannon. The *O'Bannon* case is particularly significant because it holds that the NCAA's amateurism rules violated antitrust law. Nonetheless, based on the way the case was litigated by plaintiffs' counsel, the district court held that providing cost of attendance to athletes is sufficient to remedy that violation. It is clear that the NCAA rules are anti-competitive, but the case turns on the extent of the pro-competitive justification. Do you agree with the court's conclusion that paying athletes could affect the product of intercollegiate athletics? Do you think many people would stop attending or watching games if universities paid athletes? Could payment lead to many universities not being able to compete financially? Might this all depend on how much the athletes were paid and under what system?

3. *District Court Opinion.* The Ninth Circuit opinion did not address a couple of important holdings of the district court. First, the district court held that the NCAA restrictions on athletes' ability to obtain group licenses using their name, image, and likeness do not violate the Sherman Act. This was irrespective of whether the use was live telecasts, videogames, or archival footage. Second, the district court rejected NIL as a legitimate alternative remedy. This holding gave rise to the state statutes that allow for NIL discussed below.

Finally, the district court opinion makes clear that it is not a valid antitrust defense to restrain trade in order to reallocate revenue from one sport in order to pay for another. This point echoes a long tradition in antitrust law finding that the reallocation of revenue to more socially worthy cause did not provide an adequate justification for an anti-competitive market restraint. While most cartels restrain trade to increase profits, in the case of the NCAA, the NCAA members restrain trade to reallocate profits, including paying for scholarships in non-revenue sports.

4.   *Slippery Slope.* Judge Bybee's opinion characterizes the district court's decision to allow a direct $5,000 per year payment as opening a Pandora's box and sliding down a slippery slope to professionalism in college sports. Do you agree with Bybee's characterization?

NCAA V. ALSTON
141 S.Ct. 2141 (2021)

JUSTICE GORSUCH for the Court.

[The Court summarized the history leading to the NCAA's restrictions on athlete compensation. It described the evolution of student-athlete compensation from tuition, room, board, and fees to the increase to full cost of attendance, followed by the Student Assistance Fund, and other forms of remuneration. It then described the size of the NCAA's business, with $1.1 billion annually received from the March Madness basketball tournament, and the millions of dollars made by conferences, athletic conference commissioners, athletic directors, and college coaches.

The Court next summarized the district court decision, which held that the NCAA's amateurism rules violated the Sherman Act's Rule of Reason to the extent that they placed limits on the ability of student-athletes to receive education-related benefits, such as scholarships for graduate or vocational school, payments for academic tutoring, or paid post-eligibility internships. As a result, the district court enjoined the NCAA from limiting education-related compensation or benefits that conferences and schools may provide to student-athletes playing Division I football and basketball. The court's injunction further specified that the NCAA could continue to limit cash awards for academic achievement—but only so long as those limits are no lower than the cash awards allowed for athletic achievement (currently $5,980 annually). The Ninth Circuit affirmed this injunction.

The Court then highlighted what the parties agreed to with respect to the application of antitrust law: the relevant market, that the NCAA enjoys monopoly control in the labor market, that schools compete for athletes but are subject to NCAA caps on compensation (horizontal price fixing), and that the NCAA can justify these restraints by showing pro-competitive effects in another market.]

* * *

[W]e focus only on the objections the NCAA *does* raise. Principally, it suggests that the lower courts erred by subjecting its compensation restrictions to a rule of reason analysis. In the NCAA's view, the courts should have given its restrictions at most an "abbreviated deferential review," or a " 'quick look,' " before approving them.

The NCAA offers a few reasons why. Perhaps dominantly, it argues that it is a joint venture and that collaboration among its members is necessary if they are to offer consumers the benefit of intercollegiate athletic competition. We doubt little of this. There's no question, for example, that many "joint ventures are calculated to enable firms to do something more cheaply or better than they did it before." 13 Areeda & Hovenkamp ¶ 2100c, at 7. And the fact that joint ventures can have such procompetitive benefits surely stands as a caution against condemning their arrangements too reflexively. See *Dagher*, 547 U.S. at 7; *Broadcast Music, Inc. v. Columbia Broadcasting System, Inc.*, 441 U.S. 1, 22–23 (1979).

But even assuming (without deciding) that the NCAA is a joint venture, that does not guarantee the foreshortened review it seeks. Most restraints challenged under the Sherman Act—including most joint venture restrictions—are subject to the rule of reason. . .

[The Court noted that the application of the rule of reason can vary in scrutiny.]

None of this helps the NCAA. The NCAA *accepts* that its members collectively enjoy monopsony power in the market for student-athlete services, such that its restraints can (and in fact do) harm competition. Unlike customers who would look elsewhere when a small van company raises its prices above market levels, the district court found (and the NCAA does not here contest) that student-athletes have nowhere else to sell their labor. Even if the NCAA is a joint venture, then, it is hardly of the sort that would warrant quick-look approval for all its myriad rules and restrictions.

Nor does the NCAA's status as a particular type of venture categorically exempt its restraints from ordinary rule of reason review. We do not doubt that some degree of coordination between competitors within sports leagues can be procompetitive. Without some agreement among rivals—on things like how many players may be on the field or the time allotted for play—the very competitions that consumers value would not be possible. See *Board of Regents*, 468 U.S. at 101 (quoting R. Bork, The Antitrust Paradox 278 (1978)). Accordingly, even a sports league with market power might see some agreements among its members win antitrust approval in the " 'twinkling of an eye.' " *American Needle*, 560 U.S. at 203.

But this insight does not always apply. That *some* restraints are necessary to create or maintain a league sport does not mean *all* "aspects of elaborate interleague cooperation are." While a quick look will often be enough to approve the restraints "necessary to produce a game," a fuller review may be appropriate for others . . .

The NCAA's rules fixing wages for student-athletes fall on the far side of this line. Nobody questions that Division I basketball and FBS football can proceed (and have proceeded) without the education-related compensation restrictions the district court enjoined; the games go on. Instead, the parties dispute whether and to what extent those restrictions in the NCAA's labor market yield benefits in its consumer market that can be attained using substantially less restrictive means. That dispute presents complex questions requiring more than a blink to answer.

B

Even if background antitrust principles counsel in favor of the rule of reason, the NCAA replies that a particular precedent ties our hands. The NCAA directs our attention to *Board of Regents*, where this Court considered the league's rules restricting the ability of its member schools to televise football games. 468 U.S. at 94. On the NCAA's reading, that decision expressly approved its limits on student-athlete compensation—and this approval forecloses any meaningful review of those limits today.

We see things differently. *Board of Regents* explained that the league's television rules amounted to "[h]orizontal price fixing and output limitation[s]" of the sort that are "ordinarily condemned" as " 'illegal *per se.*' " The Court declined to declare the NCAA's restraints *per se* unlawful only because they arose in "an industry" in which some "horizontal restraints on competition are essential if the product is to be available at all." Our analysis today is fully consistent with all of this. Indeed, if any daylight exists it is only in the NCAA's favor. While *Board of Regents* did not condemn the NCAA's broadcasting restraints as *per se* unlawful, it invoked abbreviated antitrust review as a path to condemnation, not salvation. If a quick look was thought sufficient before rejecting the NCAA's procompetitive rationales in that case, it is hard to see how the NCAA might object to a court providing a more cautious form of review before reaching a similar judgment here.

To be sure, the NCAA isn't without a reply. It notes that, in the course of reaching its judgment about television marketing restrictions, the *Board of Regents* Court commented on student-athlete compensation restrictions. Most particularly, the NCAA highlights this passage:

> "The NCAA plays a critical role in the maintenance of a revered tradition of amateurism in college sports. There can be no question but that it needs ample latitude to play that role, or that the preservation of the student-athlete in higher education adds richness and diversity to intercollegiate athletics and is entirely consistent with the goals of the Sherman Act."

See also *id.*, at 101, 102, (the NCAA "seeks to market a particular brand of football" in which "athletes must not be paid, must be required to attend class, and the like"). On the NCAA's telling, these observations foreclose any rule of reason review in this suit.

Once more, we cannot agree. *Board of Regents* may suggest that courts should take care when assessing the NCAA's restraints on student-athlete compensation, sensitive to their procompetitive possibilities. But these remarks do not suggest that courts must reflexively reject *all* challenges to the NCAA's compensation restrictions. Student-athlete compensation rules were not even at issue in *Board of Regents*. And the Court made clear it was only assuming the reasonableness of the NCAA's restrictions: "It is reasonable to *assume* that most of the regulatory controls of the NCAA are justifiable means of fostering competition among amateur athletic teams and are therefore procompetitive . . . ." Accordingly, the Court simply did not have occasion to declare—nor did it declare—the NCAA's compensation restrictions procompetitive both in 1984 and forevermore.

[The Court also emphasized that market realities are very different than in 1984].

. . . The NCAA submits that a rule of reason analysis is inappropriate for still another reason—because the NCAA and its member schools are not "commercial enterprises" and instead oversee intercollegiate athletics "as an integral part of the undergraduate experience." The NCAA represents that it seeks to "maintain amateurism in college sports as part of serving [the] societally important non-commercial objective" of "higher education."

> . . . it is unclear exactly what the NCAA seeks. To the extent it means to propose a sort of judicially ordained immunity from the terms of the Sherman Act for its restraints of trade—that we should overlook its restrictions because they happen to fall at the intersection of higher education, sports, and money—we cannot agree. This Court has regularly refused materially identical requests from litigants seeking special dispensation from the Sherman Act on the ground that their restraints of trade serve uniquely important social objectives beyond enhancing competition . . .

To be sure, this Court once dallied with something that looks a bit like an antitrust exemption for professional baseball. In *Federal Baseball Club of Baltimore, Inc. v. National League of Professional Baseball Clubs*, 259 U.S. 200 (1922), the Court reasoned that "exhibitions" of "baseball" did not implicate the Sherman Act because they did not involve interstate trade or commerce—even though teams regularly crossed state lines (as they do today) to make money and enhance their commercial success. But this Court has refused to extend *Federal Baseball's* reasoning to other sports leagues—and has even acknowledged criticisms of the decision as "'unrealistic'" and "'inconsistent'" and "aberration[al]." *Flood v. Kuhn*, 407 U.S. 258, 282 (1972) (quoting *Radovich v. National Football League*, 352 U.S. 445, 452 (1957)); see also Brief for Advocates for Minor Leaguers as *Amicus Curiae* 5, n. 3 (gathering criticisms). Indeed, as we have seen, this Court has already recognized that the NCAA itself *is* subject to the Sherman Act.

The "orderly way" to temper that Act's policy of competition is "by legislation and not by court decision." *Flood*, 407 U.S. at 279. The NCAA is free to argue that, "because of the special characteristics of [its] particular industry," it should be exempt from the usual operation of the antitrust laws—but that appeal is "properly addressed to Congress." *National Soc. Of Professional Engineers*, 435 U.S. at 689. . . .

III

A

While the NCAA devotes most of its energy to resisting the rule of reason in its usual form, the league lodges some objections to the district court's application of it as well.

When describing the rule of reason, this Court has sometimes spoken of "a three-step, burden-shifting framework" as a means for " 'distinguish[ing] between restraints with anticompetitive effect that are harmful to the consumer and restraints stimulating competition that are in the consumer's best interest.' " *American Express Co.*, 138 S.Ct., at 2284. As we have described it, "the plaintiff has the initial burden to prove that the challenged restraint has a substantial anticompetitive effect." Should the plaintiff carry that burden, the burden then "shifts to the defendant to show a procompetitive rationale for the restraint." If the defendant can make that showing, "the burden shifts back to the plaintiff to demonstrate that the procompetitive efficiencies could be reasonably achieved through less anticompetitive means."

These three steps do not represent a rote checklist, nor may they be employed as an inflexible substitute for careful analysis. As we have seen, what is required to assess whether a challenged restraint harms competition can vary depending on the circumstances. The whole point of the rule of reason is to furnish "an enquiry meet for the case, looking to the circumstances, details, and logic of a restraint" to ensure that it unduly harms competition before a court declares it unlawful. *California Dental*, 526 U.S. at 781

. . . In the proceedings below, the district court followed circuit precedent to apply a multistep framework closely akin to *American Express*'s. As its first step, the district court required the student-athletes to show that "the challenged restraints produce significant anticompetitive effects in the relevant market." . . . As we have seen, based on a voluminous record, the district court held that the student-athletes had shown the NCAA enjoys the power to set wages in the market for student-athletes' labor—and that the NCAA has exercised that power in ways that have produced significant anticompetitive effects. Perhaps even more notably, the NCAA "did not meaningfully dispute" this conclusion.

Unlike so many cases, then, the district court proceeded to the second step, asking whether the NCAA could muster a procompetitive rationale for its restraints. This is where the NCAA claims error first crept in. On its account, the district court examined the challenged rules at different levels of generality. At the first step of its inquiry, the court asked whether the NCAA's entire package of compensation restrictions has substantial anticompetitive effects *collectively*. Yet, at the second step, the NCAA says the district court required it to show that each of its distinct rules limiting student-athlete compensation has procompetitive benefits *individually*. The NCAA says this mismatch had the result of effectively—and erroneously—requiring it to prove that each rule is the least restrictive means of achieving the procompetitive purpose of differentiating college sports and preserving demand for them.

We agree with the NCAA's premise that antitrust law does not require businesses to use anything like the least restrictive means of achieving legitimate business purposes. To the contrary, courts should not second-guess "degrees of reasonable necessity" so that "the lawfulness of conduct turn[s] upon judgments of degrees of efficiency." *Rothery Storage*, 792 F.2d at 227; *Continental T. V., Inc. v. GTE Sylvania Inc.*, 433 U.S. 36, 58, n. 29 (1977).

. . . While we agree with the NCAA's legal premise, we cannot say the same for its factual one. Yes, at the first step of its inquiry, the district court held that the student-athletes had met their burden of showing the NCAA's restraints collectively bear an anticompetitive effect. And, given that, yes, at step two the NCAA had to show only that those same rules collectively yield a procompetitive benefit. The trouble for the NCAA, though, is not the level of generality. It is the fact that the district court found unpersuasive much of its proffered evidence. Recall that the court found the NCAA failed "to establish that the challenged compensation rules . . . have any direct connection to consumer demand."

To be sure, there is a wrinkle here. While finding the NCAA had failed to establish that its rules collectively sustain consumer demand, the court did find that "some" of those rules "may" have procompetitive effects "to the extent" they prohibit compensation "unrelated to education, akin to salaries seen in professional sports leagues." The court then proceeded to what corresponds to the third step of the *American Express* framework, where it required the student-athletes "to show that there are substantially less restrictive alternative rules that would achieve the same procompetitive effect as the challenged set of rules." And there, of course, the district court held that the student-athletes partially succeeded—they were able to show that the NCAA could achieve the procompetitive benefits it had established with substantially less restrictive restraints on education-related benefits.

Even acknowledging this wrinkle, we see nothing about the district court's analysis that offends the legal principles the NCAA invokes. The court's judgment ultimately turned on the key question at the third step: whether the student-athletes could prove that "substantially less restrictive alternative rules" existed to achieve the same procompetitive benefits the NCAA had proven at the second step. Of course, deficiencies in the NCAA's proof of procompetitive benefits at the second step influenced the analysis at the third. But that is only because, however framed and at whichever step, anticompetitive restraints of trade may wind up flunking the rule of reason to the extent the evidence shows that substantially less restrictive means exist to achieve any proven procompetitive benefits. See, *e.g.*, 7 Areeda & Hovenkamp ¶ 1505, p. 428 ("To be sure, these two questions can be collapsed into one," since a "legitimate objective that is not promoted by the challenged restraint can be equally served by simply abandoning the restraint, which is surely a less restrictive alternative").

Simply put, the district court nowhere—expressly or effectively—required the NCAA to show that its rules constituted the *least* restrictive means of preserving consumer demand. Rather, it was only after finding the NCAA's restraints "'patently and inexplicably stricter than is necessary'" to achieve the procompetitive benefits the league had demonstrated that the district court proceeded to declare a violation of the Sherman Act. That demanding standard hardly presages a future filled with judicial micromanagement of legitimate business decisions.

B

In a related critique, the NCAA contends the district court "impermissibly redefined" its "product" by rejecting its views about what amateurism requires and replacing them with its preferred conception.

This argument, however, misapprehends the way a defendant's procompetitive business justification relates to the antitrust laws. Firms deserve substantial latitude to fashion agreements that serve legitimate business interests—agreements that may include efforts aimed at introducing a new product into the marketplace. But none of that means a party can relabel a restraint as a product feature and declare it "immune from § 1 scrutiny." *American Needle*, 560 U.S. at 199, n. 7. In this suit, as in any, the district court had to determine whether the defendants' agreements harmed competition and whether any procompetitive benefits associated with their restraints could be achieved by "substantially less restrictive alternative" means.

The NCAA's argument not only misapprehends the inquiry, it would require us to overturn the district court's factual findings. While the NCAA asks us to defer to its conception of amateurism, the district court found that the NCAA had not adopted any consistent definition. Instead, the court found, the NCAA's rules and restrictions on compensation have shifted markedly over time. The court found, too, that the NCAA adopted these restrictions without any reference to "considerations of consumer demand," and that some were "not necessary to preserve consumer demand." None of this is product redesign; it is a straightforward application of the rule of reason.

C

Finally, the NCAA attacks as "indefensible" the lower courts' holding that substantially less restrictive alternatives exist capable of delivering the same procompetitive benefits as its current rules. The NCAA claims, too, that the district court's injunction threatens to "micromanage" its business.

Once more, we broadly agree with the legal principles the NCAA invokes. As we have discussed, antitrust courts must give wide berth to business judgments before finding liability. Similar considerations apply when it comes to the remedy. Judges must be sensitive to the possibility that the "continuing supervision of a highly detailed decree" could wind up impairing rather than enhancing competition. *Trinko*, 540 U.S. at 415. . . . And throughout courts must have a healthy respect for the practical limits of judicial administration: "An antitrust court is unlikely to be an effective day-to-day enforcer" of a detailed decree, able to keep pace with changing market dynamics alongside a busy docket. *Trinko*, 540 U.S. at 415. Nor should any court " 'impose a duty . . . that it cannot explain or adequately and reasonably supervise.' " In short, judges make for poor "central planners" and should never aspire to the role.

Once again, though, we think the district court honored these principles. The court enjoined only restraints on education-related benefits—such as those limiting scholarships for graduate school, payments for tutoring, and the like. The court did so, moreover, only after finding that relaxing these restrictions would not blur the distinction between college and professional sports and thus impair demand—and only after finding that this course represented a significantly (not marginally) less restrictive means of achieving the same procompetitive benefits as the NCAA's current rules.

Even with respect to education-related benefits, the district court extended the NCAA considerable leeway. As we have seen, the court provided that the NCAA could develop its own definition of benefits that relate to education and seek modification of the court's injunction to reflect that definition. The court explained that the NCAA and its members could agree on rules regulating how conferences and schools go about providing these education-related benefits. The court said that the NCAA and its members could continue fixing education-related cash awards, too—so long as those "limits are never lower than the limit" on awards for athletic performance. And the court emphasized that its injunction applies only to the NCAA and multiconference agreements; individual conferences remain free to reimpose every single enjoined restraint tomorrow—or more restrictive ones still.

In the end, it turns out that the NCAA's complaints really boil down to three principal objections.

First, the NCAA worries about the district court's inclusion of paid post-eligibility internships among the education-related benefits it approved. The NCAA fears that schools will use internships as a way of circumventing limits on payments that student-athletes may receive for athletic performance. The NCAA even imagines that boosters might promise post-eligibility internships "at a sneaker company or auto dealership" with extravagant salaries as a "thinly disguised vehicle" for paying professional-level salaries.

This argument rests on an overly broad reading of the injunction. The district court enjoined only restrictions on education-related compensation or benefits "that may be made available *from conferences or schools*." Accordingly, as the student-athletes concede, the injunction "does not stop the NCAA from continuing to prohibit compensation from" sneaker companies, auto dealerships, boosters, "or anyone else." The NCAA itself seems to understand this much. Following the district court's injunction, the organization adopted new regulations specifying that only "a conference or institution" may fund post-eligibility internships. See Decl. of M. Boyer in No. 4:14-md-02541, ECF Doc. 1302-2, p. 6 (ND Cal., Sept. 22, 2020) (NCAA Bylaw 16.3.4(d)).

Even when it comes to internships offered by conferences and schools, the district court left the NCAA considerable flexibility. The court refused to enjoin NCAA rules prohibiting its members from providing compensation or benefits unrelated to legitimate educational activities— thus leaving the league room to police phony internships. As we've observed, the district court also allowed the NCAA to propose (and enforce) rules defining what benefits do and do not relate to education. Accordingly, the NCAA may seek whatever limits on paid internships it thinks appropriate. And, again, the court stressed that individual conferences may restrict internships however they wish. All these features underscore the modesty of the current decree.

Second, the NCAA attacks the district court's ruling that it may fix the aggregate limit on awards schools may give for "academic or graduation" achievement no lower than its aggregate limit on parallel athletic awards (currently $5,980 per year). This, the NCAA asserts, "is the very definition of a professional salary." The NCAA also represents that "[m]ost" of its currently permissible athletic awards are "for genuine individual or team *achievement*" and that "[m]ost . . . are received by only a few student-athletes each year." Meanwhile, the NCAA says, the district court's decree would allow a school to pay players thousands of dollars each year for minimal achievements like maintaining a passing GPA.

The basis for this critique is unclear. The NCAA does not believe that the athletic awards it presently allows are tantamount to a professional salary. And this portion of the injunction sprang directly from the district court's finding that the cap on athletic participation awards "is an amount that has been shown not to decrease consumer demand." Indeed, there was no evidence before the district court suggesting that corresponding academic awards would impair consumer interest in any way. Again, too, the district court's injunction affords the NCAA leeway. It leaves the NCAA free to reduce its athletic awards. And it does not ordain what criteria schools must use for their academic and graduation awards. So, once more, if the NCAA believes certain criteria are needed to ensure that academic awards are legitimately related to education, it is presently free to propose such rules—and individual conferences may adopt even stricter ones.

Third, the NCAA contends that allowing schools to provide in-kind educational benefits will pose a problem. This relief focuses on allowing schools to offer scholarships for "graduate degrees" or "vocational school" and to pay for things like "computers" and "tutoring." But the NCAA fears schools might exploit this authority to give student-athletes "'luxury cars'" "to get to class" and "other unnecessary or inordinately valuable items" only "nominally" related to education.

Again, however, this over-reads the injunction in ways we have seen and need not belabor. Under the current decree, the NCAA is free to forbid in-kind benefits unrelated to a student's actual education; nothing stops it from enforcing a "no Lamborghini" rule. . .

When it comes to fashioning an antitrust remedy, we acknowledge that caution is key. Judges must resist the temptation to require that enterprises employ the least restrictive means of achieving their legitimate business objectives. Judges must be mindful, too, of their limitations—as generalists, as lawyers, and as outsiders trying to understand intricate business relationships. Judges must remain aware that markets are often more effective than the heavy hand of judicial power when it comes to enhancing consumer welfare. And judges must be open to clarifying and reconsidering their decrees in light of changing market realities. Courts reviewing complex business arrangements should, in other words, be wary about invitations to "set sail on a sea of doubt." *United States v. Addyston Pipe & Steel Co.*, 85 F. 271, 284 (CA6 1898) (Taft, J.). But we do not believe the district court fell prey to that temptation. Its judgment does not float on a sea of doubt but stands on firm ground—an exhaustive factual record, a thoughtful legal analysis consistent with established antitrust principles, and a healthy dose of judicial humility.

Some will think the district court did not go far enough. By permitting colleges and universities to offer enhanced education-related benefits, its decision may encourage scholastic achievement and allow student-athletes a measure of compensation more consistent with the value they bring to their schools. Still, some will see this as a poor substitute for fuller relief. At the same time, others will think the district court went too far by undervaluing the social benefits associated with amateur athletics. For our part, though, we can only agree with the Ninth Circuit: " 'The national debate about amateurism in college sports is important. But our task as appellate judges is not to resolve it. Nor could we. Our task is simply to review the district court judgment through the appropriate lens of antitrust law.' " 958 F.3d at 1265. That review persuades us the district court acted within the law's bounds.

The judgment is *Affirmed.*

JUSTICE KAVANAUGH, concurring.

The NCAA has long restricted the compensation and benefits that student athletes may receive. And with surprising success, the NCAA has long shielded its compensation rules from ordinary antitrust scrutiny. Today, however, the Court holds that the NCAA has violated the antitrust laws. The Court's decision marks an important and overdue course correction, and I join the Court's excellent opinion in full.

But this case involves only a narrow subset of the NCAA's compensation rules—namely, the rules restricting the *education-related* benefits that student athletes may receive, such as post-eligibility scholarships at graduate or vocational schools. The rest of the NCAA's compensation rules are not at issue here and therefore remain on the books. Those remaining compensation rules generally restrict student athletes from receiving compensation or benefits from their colleges for playing sports. And those rules have also historically restricted student athletes from receiving money from endorsement deals and the like.

I add this concurring opinion to underscore that the NCAA's remaining compensation rules also raise serious questions under the antitrust laws. Three points warrant emphasis.

First, the Court does not address the legality of the NCAA's remaining compensation rules. As the Court says, "the student-athletes do not renew their across-the-board challenge to the NCAA's compensation restrictions. Accordingly, we do not pass on the rules that remain in place or the district court's judgment upholding them. Our review is confined to those restrictions now enjoined."

Second, although the Court does not weigh in on the ultimate legality of the NCAA's remaining compensation rules, the Court's decision establishes how any such rules should be analyzed going forward. After today's decision, the NCAA's remaining compensation rules should receive ordinary "rule of reason" scrutiny under the antitrust laws. The Court makes clear that the decades-old "stray comments" about college sports and amateurism made in *National Collegiate Athletic Assn. v. Board of Regents of Univ. of Okla.*, 468 U.S. 85 (1984), were dicta and have no bearing on whether the NCAA's current compensation rules are lawful. And the Court stresses that the NCAA is not otherwise entitled to an exemption from the antitrust laws. See also *Radovich v. National Football League*, 352 U.S. 445, 449–452 (1957). As a result, absent legislation or a negotiated agreement between the NCAA and the student athletes, the NCAA's remaining compensation rules should be subject to ordinary rule of reason scrutiny.

Third, there are serious questions whether the NCAA's remaining compensation rules can pass muster under ordinary rule of reason scrutiny. Under the rule of reason, the NCAA must supply a legally valid procompetitive justification for its remaining compensation rules. As I see it, however, the NCAA may lack such a justification.

The NCAA acknowledges that it controls the market for college athletes. The NCAA concedes that its compensation rules set the price of student athlete labor at a below-market rate. And the NCAA recognizes that student athletes currently have no meaningful ability to negotiate with the NCAA over the compensation rules.

The NCAA nonetheless asserts that its compensation rules are procompetitive because those rules help define the product of college sports. Specifically, the NCAA says that colleges may decline to pay student athletes because the defining feature of college sports, according to the NCAA, is that the student athletes are not paid.

In my view, that argument is circular and unpersuasive. The NCAA couches its arguments for not paying student athletes in innocuous labels. But the labels cannot disguise the reality: The NCAA's business model would be flatly illegal in almost any other industry in America. All of the restaurants in a region cannot come together to cut cooks' wages on the theory that "customers prefer" to eat food from low-paid cooks. Law firms cannot conspire to cabin lawyers' salaries in the name of providing legal services out of a "love of the law." Hospitals cannot agree to cap nurses' income in order to create a "purer" form of helping the sick. News organizations cannot join forces to curtail pay to reporters to preserve a "tradition" of public-minded journalism. Movie studios cannot collude to slash benefits to camera crews to kindle a "spirit of amateurism" in Hollywood.

Price-fixing labor is price-fixing labor. And price-fixing labor is ordinarily a textbook antitrust problem because it extinguishes the free market in which individuals can otherwise obtain fair compensation for their work. See, *e.g.*, *Texaco Inc. v. Dagher*, 547 U.S. 1, 5 (2006). Businesses like the NCAA cannot avoid the consequences of price-fixing labor by incorporating price-fixed labor into the definition of the product. Or to put it in more doctrinal terms, a monopsony cannot launder its price-fixing of labor by calling it product definition.

The bottom line is that the NCAA and its member colleges are suppressing the pay of student athletes who collectively generate *billions* of dollars in revenues for colleges every year. Those enormous sums of money flow to seemingly everyone except the student athletes. College presidents, athletic directors, coaches, conference commissioners, and NCAA executives take in six- and seven-figure salaries. Colleges build lavish new facilities. But the student athletes who generate the revenues, many of whom are African American and from lower-income backgrounds, end up with little or nothing. See Brief for African American Antitrust Lawyers as *Amici Curiae* 13–17.

Everyone agrees that the NCAA can require student athletes to be enrolled students in good standing. But the NCAA's business model of using unpaid student athletes to generate billions of dollars in revenue for the colleges raises serious questions under the antitrust laws. In particular, it is highly questionable whether the NCAA and its member colleges can justify not paying student athletes a fair share of the revenues on the circular theory that the defining characteristic of college sports is that the colleges do not pay student athletes. And if that asserted justification is unavailing, it is not clear how the NCAA can legally defend its remaining compensation rules.

If it turns out that some or all of the NCAA's remaining compensation rules violate the antitrust laws, some difficult policy and practical questions would undoubtedly ensue. Among them: How would paying greater compensation to student athletes affect non-revenue-raising sports? Could student athletes in some sports but not others receive compensation? How would any compensation regime comply with Title IX? If paying student athletes requires something like a salary cap in some sports in order to preserve competitive balance, how would that cap be administered? And given that there are now about 180,000 Division I student athletes, what is a financially sustainable way of fairly compensating some or all of those student athletes?

Of course, those difficult questions could be resolved in ways other than litigation. Legislation would be one option. Or colleges and student athletes could potentially engage in collective bargaining (or seek some other negotiated agreement) to provide student athletes a fairer share of the revenues that they generate for their colleges, akin to how professional football and basketball players have negotiated for a share of league revenues. Cf. *Brown v. Pro Football, Inc.*, 518 U.S. 231, 235–237 (1996); *Wood v. National Basketball Assn.*, 809 F.2d 954, 958–963 (CA2 1987) (R. Winter, J.). Regardless of how those issues ultimately would be resolved, however, the NCAA's current compensation regime raises serious questions under the antitrust laws.

To be sure, the NCAA and its member colleges maintain important traditions that have become part of the fabric of America—game days in Tuscaloosa and South Bend; the packed gyms in Storrs and Durham; the women's and men's lacrosse championships on Memorial Day weekend; track and field meets in Eugene; the spring softball and baseball World Series in Oklahoma City and Omaha; the list goes on. But those traditions alone cannot justify the NCAA's decision to build a massive money-raising enterprise on the backs of student athletes who are not fairly compensated. Nowhere else in America can businesses get away with agreeing not to pay their workers a fair market rate on the theory that their product is defined by not paying their workers a fair market rate. And under ordinary principles of antitrust law, it is not evident why college sports should be any different. The NCAA is not above the law.

———

NOTES AND QUESTIONS

1. *Aftermath.* The practical effect of *Alston* is that institutions now may provide student-athletes with all costs "related to education." These include computers, summer abroad programs, and graduate school tuition.

2. *Effect of Amateurism on Attendance.* In *O'Bannon v. NCAA*, 802 F.3d 1049 (9th Cir. 2015) and *NCAA v. Alston*, 141 S. Ct. 2141 (2021), discussed in Part D, the NCAA relied heavily on the following language from *Board of Regents* in arguing that compensating intercollegiate athletics would destroy the product of college football:

> Moreover, the NCAA seeks to market a particular brand of football—college football. The identification of this "product" with an academic tradition differentiates college football from and makes it more popular than professional sports to which it might otherwise be comparable, such as, for example, minor league baseball. In order to preserve the character and quality of the "product," athletes must not be paid, must be required to attend class, and the like. And the integrity of the "product" cannot be preserved except by mutual agreement; if an institution adopted such restrictions unilaterally, its effectiveness as a competitor on the playing field might soon be destroyed. Thus, the NCAA plays a vital role in enabling college football to preserve its character, and as a result enables a product to be marketed which might otherwise be unavailable. In performing this role, its actions widen consumer choice—not only the choices available to sports fans but also those available to athletes—and hence can be viewed as procompetitive.

NCAA v. Bd. of Regents, 468 U.S. at 101–02. Do you think the amateur character of intercollegiate athletics (at least as the NCAA defines it) is quintessential to the product on the field? If universities started paying their athletes, would that affect attendance? Is this argument any different than the one with respect to television that the Court rejected in *Board of Regents*? Why or why not?

3. *Kavanaugh's Concurrence.* Justice Kavanaugh's concurrence proclaimed that the "NCAA is not above the law." It will be interesting to see whether this language will encourage additional antitrust challenges to the NCAA's bar on universities paying players unrelated to education. Do you find the majority opinion or his concurrence more persuasive?

––––––––

In 2020, before the *Alston* Supreme Court decision and the rise of name, image, and likeness commercialization discussed in Section E, *infra*, student-athletes filed putative class actions alleging that NCAA prohibitions on receiving compensation for their NIL violated Sherman Act § 1. The NCAA moved to dismiss the complaints and found themselves again in front of Judge Wilken.

HOUSE V. NCAA
545 F.Supp.3d 804 (N.D. Cal. 2021)

WILKEN, JUDGE.

[Plaintiff athletes challenged the NCAA rules that "prohibit student-athletes from receiving anything of value in exchange for the commercial use" of their names, images, and likenesses (NIL).]

. . . According to Plaintiffs, the rules they challenge cannot be justified on the basis that they are necessary to preserve consumer demand for college sports as a distinct product because any such procompetitive effect, to the extent that it exists, would fall outside of the scope of the relevant market and is therefore irrelevant to the Rule of Reason analysis.

Alternatively, Plaintiffs allege that, to the extent that the preservation of consumer demand for college sports as a distinct product is deemed to be a procompetitive effect within the relevant market, the challenged rules are not necessary to achieve that effect because . . . [the NCAA has granted waivers to some athletes and allowing NIL would not affect consumer demand.]

Plaintiffs allege that the challenged rules violate federal antitrust laws and the common law because they (1) fix at zero the amount that student-athletes may be paid for the licensing, use, and sale of their NIL; and (2) foreclose student-athletes from the market for licensing, use, and sale of their NIL. Plaintiffs assert claims for (1) conspiracy to fix prices in violation of Section 1 of the Sherman Act, 15 U.S.C. § 1; (2) group boycott or refusal to deal in violation of Section 1 of the Sherman Act; and (3) unjust enrichment. Plaintiffs assert these claims on their own behalf and on behalf of the following proposed class and sub-classes.

The "Declaratory and Injunctive Relief Class" is comprised of:

All current and former student-athletes who compete on, or competed on, an NCAA Division I athletic team at any time between four (4) years prior to the filing of this Complaint and the date of judgment in this matter.

Plaintiffs request an injunction permanently restraining Defendants from enforcing their alleged agreements to restrict the amount of NIL compensation that members of this proposed class can receive.

The "Social Media Damages Sub-Class" is comprised of:

All current and former student-athletes who compete on, or competed on, an NCAA Division I athletic team at a college or university that is a member of one of the Power Five Conferences, at any time between four (4) years prior to filing of this Complaint and the date of judgment in this matter.

On behalf of this sub-class, Plaintiffs seek the social media earnings that members of this sub-class would have received absent Defendants' unlawful conduct.

The "Group Licensing Damages Sub-Class" is comprised of:

All current and former student-athletes who compete on, or competed on, an NCAA Division I men's or women's basketball team or an FBS football team, at a college or university that is a member of one of the Power Five Conferences, at any time between four (4) years prior to the filing of this Complaint and the date of judgment in this matter.

On behalf of this sub-class, Plaintiffs seek the share of game telecast group licensing revenue that members of this sub-class would have received absent Defendants' unlawful conduct.

* * *

III. DISCUSSION

Defendants argue that the complaints in *House* ... are subject to dismissal with prejudice because (1) the complaints are barred under the doctrine of stare decisis ... [in light of *O'Bannon* and *Alston*]; (2) the claims of the "Group-Licensing Damages Sub-Class" fail as a matter of law because the members of that sub-class have no publicity rights in game broadcasts, and even if they did, Plaintiffs have not alleged injury to competition in the "Group Licensing Market" that was adjudicated in O'Bannon ...

As an initial matter, the Court is not persuaded by Defendants' contention ... The Ninth Circuit made clear in both *O'Bannon II* and *Alston II* that any holdings in those cases with respect to whether certain NCAA limits on student-athlete compensation could be enjoined as anticompetitive were based on, and limited to, the record presented in those cases. The Ninth Circuit thus left open the possibility for reaching a different conclusion in future litigation to the extent that the parties present a different record. Indeed, the court of appeals recognized in both *O'Bannon II* and *Alston II* that, because the analysis demanded by the Rule of Reason requires the evaluation of "dynamic market conditions and consumer preferences" and is "inherently fact-dependent," "courts must continue to subject NCAA rules, including those governing compensation, to antitrust scrutiny." *Id.* at 1254 (citing *O'Bannon II*, 802 F.3d at 1064 ("The amateurism rules' validity must be proved, not presumed.")).

Here, Plaintiffs' allegations, which the Court must construe in their favor at this juncture, raise the reasonable inference that material differences exist between *House*, on the one hand, and *O'Bannon* and *Alston*, on the other hand, that distinguish the former from the latter on a principled basis. [The court identifies four material differences between *House* and the latter cases to reject the stare decisis defense. The first three are that *House*: (1) challenges different rules, (2) relies on facts that post-date the earlier cases, (3) and advances a different legal theory, namely, that any procompetitive effects of the NIL ban in preserving consumer demand for college sports are immaterial because they fall outside the alleged relevant market for the labor of DI college athletes. The court acknowledges that plaintiffs' legal theory is based on Judge Milan Smith's concurrence in *Alston II*, which disagreed with the majority's consideration of procompetitive effects in collateral markets:]

> ... Our Rule of Reason framework has shifted toward this cross-market analysis without direct consideration or a robust justification. ... Lacking a robust justification, I fear that our cross-market Rule of Reason analysis frustrates the very purpose of the antitrust laws, in this case to the great detriment of Student-Athletes. I hope our court will reconsider this issue in a case that squarely raises it.

.... because of the distinct factual and legal differences that exist between *House* and *O'Bannon* and *Alston*, Plaintiffs here have proposed less restrictive alternatives that were not considered in the prior cases. One proposed less restrictive alternative here is to require the NCAA to permit its members to allow student-athletes to receive compensation from third parties for the use of their NIL. ...

B.   Group-Licensing Damages Sub-Class

Defendants argue that the claims of the "Group Licensing Damages Sub-Class" are subject to dismissal for two reasons. First, Defendants argue that the proposed members of the sub-class have no publicity rights in broadcasts of football or basketball games, which precludes them from alleging the requisite injury to their "business or property" under the Clayton Act, 15 U.S.C. § 15(a). Second, Defendants contend that, even if the sub-class members had such rights, Plaintiffs cannot establish injury to competition because they have not alleged the same "Group Licensing Market" that was adjudicated in *O'Bannon*. Defendants argue that, because Plaintiffs' request for a share of broadcasting revenue here is "in all material respects identical" to the request for a share of broadcasting revenue in *O'Bannon*, Plaintiffs must allege injury to competition "in the relevant market for that claim," which Defendants contend is, and can only be, the "Group Licensing Market" defined and adjudicated in *O'Bannon*. . . .

Here, Plaintiffs allege that, absent the challenged rules, "Division I conferences and schools would compete amongst each other by allowing their athletes to . . . share in the conferences' and schools' commercial benefits received from exploiting student-athletes names, images, and likenesses," which include broadcasting revenue. These allegations are sufficient to raise the reasonable inference that competition among schools and conferences would increase in the absence of the challenged rules, and that this increased competition would incentivize schools and conferences to share their broadcasting and other commercial revenue with student-athletes even if the student-athletes lacked publicity rights in broadcasts. These allegations are sufficient to claim injury in fact at this juncture.

* * *

Defendants also argue that the claims of the sub-class at issue are subject to dismissal because Plaintiffs have not alleged facts showing that the challenged rules harm competition in the "Group Licensing Market" that was adjudicated in *O'Bannon*. This argument is premised on the theory that, because Plaintiffs here seek a share of broadcasting revenue just like the plaintiffs in *O'Bannon* sought a share of broadcasting revenue, then Plaintiffs are required to allege and rely on the same relevant market for group licenses adjudicated in *O'Bannon*, as the request for a share of broadcasting revenue in both actions is essentially "identical."

Here, Plaintiffs have adequately pleaded a relevant market, as well as injury to competition in that market. Plaintiffs allege that the relevant market is the nationwide market for the labor of Division I college athletes, wherein Division I members compete with each other to purchase through bundles of goods and services student-athletes' labor and the right to use their NIL. Plaintiffs further allege that, because Division I members have overwhelming market power as a result of the absence of reasonable substitutes for the opportunities offered by Division I members, the challenged rules allow Division I members to suppress competition that would otherwise exist among them by artificially fixing the price of the bundle of goods and services offered to student-athletes. In the absence of the challenged rules, Plaintiffs allege, competition among Division I members would increase, resulting in an increase in the price of the bundle of goods and services that Division I members would offer to student-athletes. Plaintiffs allege that one of the ways in which Division I members could increase the price of the bundle of goods and services in the absence of the challenged rules would be to offer student-athletes a share of the revenue that Division I members derive from the licensing or commercializing of student-athletes' NIL.

The injury to competition that Plaintiffs allege here is the artificial suppression of the price of the bundle of goods and services that student-athletes can receive in exchange for their labor and the right to use their NIL within the nationwide labor market just described. This alleged injury is cognizable and sufficient to survive the present motion to dismiss.

. . .Defendants . . . have cited no authority to support the proposition that Plaintiffs in *House* are required to adopt the same market definition that another set of plaintiffs relied upon in a different case. To avoid dismissal at the pleading stage, Plaintiffs are required to "identify a relevant market" and plead injury to competition within that market. *Tanaka*, 252 F.3d at 1063. For the reasons discussed above, they have done so here. Plaintiffs are not required to do more.

This conclusion is not altered by the fact that the Court ruled after a bench trial in *O'Bannon* that the plaintiffs in that case had failed to show that the rules challenged there had harmed competition in a sub-market for group licenses. Defendants have not shown that the Court's post-trial analysis of the evidence presented in another case with respect to a market different from the one that Plaintiffs allege here is relevant to its determination of the present motions.

Accordingly, the Court denies Defendants' motion to dismiss the claims of the "Group Licensing Damages Sub-Class."

———

NOTES AND QUESTIONS

1. *Relevant Market.* How does the relevant market identified by the plaintiffs shape their antitrust claim? How is it different than the market in *O'Bannon*?

2. House *as the next* Alston? What are the consequences if the plaintiffs prevail at trial? Which of their claims is the most significant threat to the future of the NCAA?

E. THE RISE OF NAME, IMAGE, AND LIKENESS

After the Ninth Circuit's decision in *O'Bannon*, the California legislature passed a bill in 2019 that gave California athletes the right to monetize their name, image, and likeness (NIL) without penalty from the NCAA or their colleges and universities. Set to go into effect in 2023, the California law spurred activity across the United States. Florida adopted a similar law, but set the effective date on July 1, 2021. Most other states adopted similar laws and amended their effective dates.

In response, the NCAA adopted the following interim NIL rules:

1.   NCAA Bylaws, including prohibitions on pay-for-play and improper recruiting inducements, remain in effect, subject to the following:

- For institutions in states without NIL laws or executive actions or with NIL laws or executive actions that have not yet taken effect, if an individual elects to engage in an NIL activity, the individual's eligibility for intercollegiate athletics will not be impacted by application of Bylaw 12 (Amateurism and Athletics Eligibility).

- For institutions in states with NIL laws or executive actions with the force of law in effect, if an individual or member institution elects to engage in an NIL activity that is protected by law or executive order, the individual's eligibility for and/or the membership institution's full participation in NCAA athletics will not be impacted by application of NCAA Bylaws unless the state law is invalidated or rendered unenforceable by operation of law.

- Use of a professional services provider is also permissible for NIL activities, except as otherwise provided by a state law or executive action with the force of law that has not been invalidated or rendered unenforceable by operation of law.

2.   The NCAA will continue its normal regulatory operations but will not monitor for compliance with state law.

3.   Individuals should report NIL activities consistent with state law and/or institutional requirements.

These rules provided all college athletes with the right to monetize their NIL, even if their state did not have a law. The NCAA otherwise left the oversight of NIL to conferences, individual institutions, and state law. Under the interim NIL rules, the NCAA continues to prohibit:

1. NIL compensation contingent on enrollment at a particular institution.

2. NIL compensation for athletic participation or achievement.

3. NIL compensation for work not performed.

State laws add other requirements including reporting contracts to the university, prohibiting NIL deals with certain kinds of companies—alcohol, tobacco, and gambling, and avoiding contracts in conflict with university contracts. States have modified their laws to keep a competitive advantage, including giving college coaches and university officials a more active role in NIL deals. Other states, like Alabama, have repealed their NIL laws in light of the NCAA's permissive approach to NIL. The NCAA and conference leaders have advocated for a federal NIL law, but to date there has been no consensus on such a law.

A number of open legal questions remain with the passage of NIL laws and the NCAA's interim NIL guidelines. They include:

1. Will there be any limitation on the use of NIL deals to recruit college athletes and transfers? With the creation of the transfer portal, athlete free agency and movement from one institution to another is pervasive, and the availability of NIL deals is clearly driving some of this activity. And yet, how does one prove that the motivation was financial and that a particular NIL deal induced an athlete to attend a particular university? As explored in the Chapter 13, this question has implications not only for NCAA compliance, but also for federal criminal law.

2. How much of a role can universities play in establishing NIL opportunities? Universities have set up co-operatives or other arrangements with third parties to endorse their athletes. Coaches increasingly are helping to connect boosters with their athletes to help generate endorsements. To the extent that universities do participate, does such participation violate NCAA compliance rules? What if boosters pay for individual or group NIL rights at above a fair market value? Or is the calculation of such value not practical in any event? At what point do the university's efforts in procuring NIL deals trigger Title IX's gender equity requirements?

3. To what extent does allowing NIL deals weaken the NCAA's policy against pay-for-play? Does NIL make it more likely that the NCAA will lose an antitrust challenge to its amateurism rules?

4. To what extent does university participation in NIL deals weaken the argument that athletes are not university employees? Will courts move away from *Berger* and towards *Johnson*?

5. Given the discussion of labor unions in the context of professional sports in earlier chapters, do you think collective bargaining agreements will become a part of intercollegiate athletics?

In October 2022, the NCAA announced plans to enforce its amateurism rules with respect to NIL. Specifically, this is likely to mean that evidence of using NIL deals to recruit athletes will violate NCAA rules. As the book goes to press, it is uncertain where and how the NCAA will draw that line in practice, and what limits universities must place on NIL deals for prospective athletes.

CHAPTER 13

INTERCOLLEGIATE SPORTS: COACHES, CONFERENCES, AND COMPLIANCE

■ ■ ■

Having explored the legal issues related to college athletes in Chapters 11 and 12, this chapter concludes the discussion of intercollegiate athletics by examining three other categories of cases—those involving college coaches, athletic conferences, and NCAA compliance—the last of which is its own body of law.

A. COACHES

College coaches, particularly in the revenue sports, have benefitted significantly from the economic model that limits the compensation received by college athletes. The result has been a robust free market in which college coaches have seen significant salary increases. To be sure, some of this increase has also resulted from the public roles coaches take in their universities and communities, as well as the connection between athletic success and enrollment at some universities.

Reformers have called for the NCAA to place caps on coach compensation. The next case illustrates the legal roadblock to such limits.

LAW v. NCAA
134 F.3d 1010 (10th Cir. 1998)

EBEL, CIRCUIT JUDGE.

[In late 1989, the NCAA created a Cost Reduction Committee to address what many of its members felt was a "catastrophic cost spiral" affecting their athletic programs. In 1992, the NCAA adopted the Committee' "Restricted Earnings Coach Rule," (REC rule) which required that institutions designate one of the coaches in each sport as a "restricted earnings coach." The NCAA set a salary limit of $12,000 during the academic year and $4,000 during the summer months. NCAA basketball coaches brought an antitrust class action, challenging the REC rule under the Sherman Act.]

[The first issue was whether plaintiffs had to prove that this NCAA rule made a tangible difference in the market for their services, given that this particular category of coach made up just 8% of the overall number of basketball coaching positions after adding in Division II and III, high schools, and professional teams.]

The NCAA misapprehends the purpose in antitrust law of market definition, which is not an end unto itself but rather exists to illuminate a practice's effect on competition. In *Board of Regents*, the Court rejected an early identical argument from the NCAA that a plan to sell television rights could not be condemned under the antitrust laws absent proof that the NCAA had power in the market for television programming. "As a matter of law, the absence of proof of market power does not justify a naked restriction on price or output. To the contrary, when there is an agreement not to compete in terms of price or output, 'no elaborate industry analysis is required to demonstrate the anticompetitive character of such an agreement.'" No "proof of market power" is required where the very purpose and effect of a horizontal agreement is to fix prices so as to make them unresponsive to a competitive marketplace. Thus, where a practice has obvious anticompetitive effects—as does price-fixing—there is no need to prove that the defendant possesses market power. Rather, the court is justified in proceeding directly to the question of whether the procompetitive justifications advanced for the restraint outweigh the anticompetitive effects under a "quick look" rule of reason.

We find it appropriate to adopt such a quick look rule of reason in this case. Under a quick look rule of reason analysis, anticompetitive effect is established, even without a determination of the relevant market, where the plaintiff shows that a horizontal agreement to fix prices exists, that the agreement is effective, and that the price set by such an agreement is more favorable to the defendant than otherwise would have resulted from the operation of market forces. *See* Gary R. Roberts, *The NCAA, Antitrust, and Consumer Welfare*, 70 TUL. L. REV. 2631, 2636–39 (1996) (citing *Board of Regents*, 468 U.S. at 109–10). Under this standard, the undisputed evidence supports a finding of anticompetitive effect. The NCAA adopted the REC Rule to reduce the high cost of part-time coaches' salaries, over $60,000 annually in some cases, by limiting compensation to entry-level coaches to $16,000 per year. The NCAA does not dispute that the cost-reduction has effectively reduced restricted-earnings coaches' salaries. Because the REC Rule was successful in artificially lowering the price of coaching services, no further evidence or analysis is required to find market power to set prices. Thus, in the case at bar, the district court did not need to resolve issues of fact pertaining to the definition of the relevant market in order to support its decision on summary judgment that the REC Rule is a naked price restraint.

The NCAA contends that the district court misapplied *Board of Regents*, a case in which the Court had before it detailed factual findings that resulted from a trial. The NCAA is right about the procedural posture of *Board of Regents*, but wrong about its significance. In *Board of Regents* the Supreme Court relied on the district court's findings that the television plan in fact resulted in horizontal price restraints. Because the REC Rule is a horizontal price restraint on its face, similar factual findings are not required in this case. Further, although in *Board of Regents* the Court found that the parties had proven factually that the NCAA had market power in the defined market of college football, the Court said that as a matter of law it did not need to analyze market power because horizontal price restraints are so obviously anticompetitive.

Finally, the NCAA cites *Hennessey v. NCAA*, 564 F.2d 1136 (5th Cir. 1977) (per curiam). In Hennessey, assistant football and basketball coaches challenged a NCAA bylaw limiting the number of assistant coaches member institutions could employ at any one time. The Fifth Circuit upheld the rule, concluding that the plaintiff failed to show that the rule was an unreasonable restraint of trade after weighing the anticompetitive effects with the procompetitive benefits of the restriction.

Hennessey is not controlling for a variety of reasons. First, the REC Rule is distinguishable from the agreement at issue in *Hennessey*. *Hennessey* addresses a restriction on the number of assistant coaches that a Division I school could employ whereas the REC Rule limits salary of a certain category of coaches. Therefore, the analysis of the reasonableness of the restraint in *Hennessey*, which did not involve a naked restriction on price, will not control the analysis of the reasonableness of the REC Rule.

Second, the *Hennessey* court placed the burden of showing the unreasonableness of the coaching restriction in that case on the plaintiff and then found that the plaintiff could not make such a showing because the rule had only recently been implemented. In our analysis, the plaintiff only has the burden of establishing the anticompetitive effect of the restraint at issue. Once the plaintiff meets that burden, which the coaches have done in this case by showing the naked and effective price-fixing character of the agreement, the burden shifts to the defendant to justify the restraint as a "reasonable" one. It is on this step that the defendant NCAA stumbles. Thus, we disagree with the Fifth Circuit's allocation of the burden of proof in *Hennessey*, and we note that this shift in the burden of proof could explain the difference in outcome between our case and *Hennessey*.

B.   Procompetitive Rationales

Under a rule of reason analysis, an agreement to restrain trade may still survive scrutiny under Section 1 if the procompetitive benefits of the restraint justify the anticompetitive effects. Justifications offered under the rule of reason may be considered only to the extent that they tend to show that, on balance, "the challenged restraint enhances competition." *Board of Regents*, 468 U.S. at 104.

In *Board of Regents* the Supreme Court recognized that certain horizontal restraints, such as the conditions of the contest and the eligibility of participants, are justifiable under the antitrust laws because they are necessary to create the product of competitive college sports. Thus, the only legitimate rationales that we will recognize in support of the REC Rule are those necessary to produce competitive intercollegiate sports. The NCAA advanced three justifications for the salary limits: retaining entry-level coaching positions; reducing costs; and maintaining competitive equity. We address each of them in turn.

1. Retention of Entry-Level Positions

The NCAA argues that the plan serves the procompetitive goal of retaining an entry-level coaching position. The NCAA asserts that the plan will allow younger, less experienced coaches entry into Division I coaching positions. While opening up coaching positions for younger people may have social value apart from its effect on competition, we may not consider such values unless they impact upon competition . . . .

The NCAA also contends that limiting one of the four available coaching positions on a Division I basketball team to an entry level position will create more balanced competition by barring some teams from hiring four experienced coaches instead of three. However, the REC Rule contained no restrictions other than salary designed to insure that the position would be filled by entry-level applicants; it could be filled with experienced applicants. In addition, under the REC Rule, schools can still pay restricted-earnings coaches more than $16,000 per year by hiring them for physical education or other teaching positions. In fact, the evidence in the record tends to demonstrate that at least some schools designated persons with many years of experience as the restricted-earnings coach. The NCAA did not present any evidence showing that restricted-earnings positions have been filled by entry-level applicants or that the rules will be effective over time in accomplishing this goal. Nothing in the record suggests that the salary limits for restricted-earnings coaches will be effective at creating entry-level positions. Thus, the NCAA failed to present a triable issue of fact as to whether preserving entry-level positions served a legitimate procompetitive end of balancing competition.

2. Cost Reduction

The NCAA next advances the justification that the plan will cut costs. However, cost-cutting by itself is not a valid procompetitive justification. If it were, any group of competing buyers could agree on maximum prices. Lower prices cannot justify a cartel's control of prices charged by suppliers, because the cartel ultimately robs the suppliers of the normal fruits of their enterprises. Further, setting maximum prices reduces the incentive among suppliers to improve their products. Likewise, in our case, coaches have less incentive to improve their performance if their salaries are capped. As the Supreme Court reiterated in *Superior Court Trial Lawyers*, 493 U.S. at

423, "the Sherman Act reflects a legislative judgment that ultimately competition will produce not only lower prices, but also better goods and services ... This judgment recognizes that all elements of a bargain—quality, service, safety, and durability—and not just the immediate cost, are favorably affected by the free opportunity to select among alternative offers."

The NCAA adopted the REC Rule because without it competition would lead to higher prices. The REC Rule was proposed as a way to prevent Division I schools from engaging in behavior the association termed "keeping up with the Joneses," *i.e.*, competing. However, the NCAA cannot argue that competition for coaches is an evil because the Sherman Act "precludes inquiry into the question whether competition is good or bad." *National Soc'y of Prof'l Engineers*, 435 U.S. at 695.

While increasing output, creating operating efficiencies, making a new product available, enhancing product or service quality, and widening consumer choice have been accepted by courts as justifications for otherwise anticompetitive agreements, mere profitability or cost savings have not qualified as a defense under the antitrust laws. The NCAA's cost containment justification is illegitimate because the NCAA

> ... improperly assumes that antitrust law should not apply to condemn the creation of market power in an input market. The exercise of market power by a group of buyers virtually always results in lower costs to the buyers—a consequence which arguably is beneficial to the members of the industry and ultimately their consumers. If holding down costs by the exercise of market power over suppliers, rather than just by increased efficiency, is a procompetitive effect justifying joint conduct, then section 1 can never apply to input markets or buyer cartels. That is not and cannot be the law.

Roberts, 70 TUL. L. REV. at 2643. Reducing costs for member institutions, without more, does not justify the anticompetitive effects of the REC Rule.

The NCAA argues that reducing costs can be considered a procompetitive justification because doing so is necessary to maintain the existence of competitive intercollegiate sports. Emphasizing the deficits many college sports programs faced prior to the adoption of the REC Rule, the NCAA quotes with approval language from the opinion in *Hennessey* to support its claim that reducing costs serves as a procompetitive benefit:

> Colleges with more successful programs, both competitively and economically, were seen as taking advantage of their success by expanding their programs, to the ultimate detriment of the whole system of intercollegiate athletics. Financial pressures upon many members, not merely to "catch up", but to "keep up," were beginning to threaten both the competitive, and the

amateur, nature of the programs, leading quite possibly to abandonment by many. "Minor" and "minority" sports were viewed as imperiled by concentration upon the "money makers," such as varsity football and basketball.

Bylaw 12–1 [the rule at issue in *Hennessey*] was, with other rules adopted at the same time, intended to be an "economy measure". In this sense it was both in design and effect one having commercial impact. But the fundamental objective in mind was to preserve and foster competition in intercollegiate athletics-by curtailing, as it were, potentially monopolistic practices by the more powerful, and to reorient the programs into their traditional role as amateur sports operating as part of the educational process.

564 F.2d at 1153.

We are dubious that the goal of cost reductions can serve as a legally sufficient justification for a buyers' agreement to fix prices even if such cost reductions are necessary to save inefficient or unsuccessful competitors from failure. Nevertheless, we need not consider whether cost reductions may have been required to "save" intercollegiate athletics and whether such an objective served as a legitimate procompetitive end because the NCAA presents no evidence that limits on restricted-earning coaches' salaries would be successful in reducing deficits, let alone that such reductions were necessary to save college basketball. Moreover, the REC Rule does not equalize the overall amount of money Division I schools are permitted to spend on their basketball programs. There is no reason to think that the money saved by a school on the salary of a restricted-earnings coach will not be put into another aspect of the school's basketball program, such as equipment or even another coach's salary, thereby increasing inequity in that area.

3. Maintaining Competitiveness

We note that the NCAA must be able to ensure some competitive equity between member institutions in order to produce a marketable product: a "team must try to establish itself as a winner, but it must not win so often and so convincingly that the outcome will never be in doubt, or else there will be no marketable 'competition.'" Michael Jay Kaplan, *Annotation, Application of Federal Antitrust Laws to Professional Sports*, 18 A.L.R. Fed. 489 § 2(a) (1974). The NCAA asserts that the REC Rule will help to maintain competitive equity by preventing wealthier schools from placing a more experienced, higher-priced coach in the position of restricted-earnings coach. The NCAA again cites *Hennessey* to support its position, and again we find *Hennessey* to be unpersuasive for the reasons previously articulated.

While the REC Rule will equalize the salaries paid to entry-level coaches in Division I schools, it is not clear that the REC Rule will equalize the experience level of such coaches.[15] Nowhere does the NCAA prove that the salary restrictions enhance competition, level an uneven playing field, or reduce coaching inequities. Rather, the NCAA only presented evidence that the cost reductions would be achieved in such a way so as to maintain without "significantly altering," "adversely affecting," or "disturbing" the existing competitive balance. The undisputed record reveals that the REC Rule is nothing more than a cost-cutting measure and shows that the only consideration the NCAA gave to competitive balance was simply to structure the rule so as not to exacerbate competitive imbalance. Thus, on its face, the REC Rule is not directed towards competitive balance nor is the nexus between the rule and a compelling need to maintain competitive balance sufficiently clear on this record to withstand a motion for summary judgment.

Affirmed.

NOTES AND QUESTIONS

1. *Aftermath.* After the Tenth Circuit rejected the NCAA's appeal of the liability verdict in this case, the district court held a trial on damages. This 1996 jury verdict awarded $22.3 million in actual damages, which was automatically trebled to $66.9 million by the Clayton Antitrust Act, with legal fees also added. The NCAA then filed an appeal of the damage calculation, but the parties settled the case in the spring of 1999 with the NCAA agreeing to pay a total of $54.5 million to the plaintiffs and their lawyers. It took another year for the groups on both sides (both the coaches and the schools) to decide how to divide up this settlement and its costs.

2. *What's Really Going on Here?* The Cost Reduction Commission found that many schools were spending money on coaches' salaries that were not being recouped by revenues from big-time sports. Why do universities spend more on money-losing programs?

3. *Why Limit College Coaches' Salaries?* Advocates of a fully free market in college sports do not support limiting coaches' salaries, preferring instead to permit a competition for players' services that should result in some reduction of salaries paid to coaches. Today, consider the following arguments for legislation that would permit the NCAA to restrict competition for coaches in

---

[15] For example, some more-experienced coaches may take restricted-earnings coach positions with programs such as those at Duke or North Carolina, despite the lower salary, because of the national prominence of those programs. In fact, absent the REC Rule, the market might produce greater equity in coaching talent, because a school with a less-prominent basketball program might be able to entice a more-experienced coach away from a prominent program by offering a higher salary.

order to limit the salaries they are paid; how many of them are persuasive as a matter of policy? How many are valid antitrust defenses?

(a) It is outrageous that college coaches are paid so much more than distinguished university professors, often even the university president, and that the highest paid public employee in most states is a college football or basketball coach.

(b) University athletics programs cannot afford high salaries for football and basketball coaches and still provide full scholarships and expenses for national travel for golf, tennis, lacrosse, and most women's teams.

(c) University presidents and trustees (like baseball owners who appointed a commissioner as described in Chapter 1) need a law to save them from themselves and inhibit unsound investments in big-time sports that divert monies from educational programs.

With the removal of any restrictions on coach salaries, the free agent market for coaches has exploded in recent years. The top college football coaches now make over $10 million per year, and the growth in salaries has also extended to assistant football coaches, many of whom make over $1 million per year. The highest paid public employee in most states is a college football or basketball coach. Critics have decried this increase in pay, but after *Law v. NCAA*, antitrust law prohibits any sort of salary cap or agreed-upon limit on coach pay. Thus, contract law has become increasingly important. Unfortunately for universities, the bargaining power lies with the coaches in large part because of external pressure on university presidents to have competitive athletic programs, particularly in football and/or basketball.

Besides salary and duration, another important provision of coaching contracts addresses termination. When institutions terminate coaches, they often must pay out the remainder of the salary due under the contract, unless the coach has behaved in a way that results in him being fired for cause. Having an unsuccessful team on the field typically does not constitute "cause" for termination under most contracts, which limit for cause termination to unethical behavior or moral turpitude of some sort. The institution, though, has the second worry of the coach leaving to coach a higher paying or more athletically prominent institution. The next case examines one university's attempt to address that issue.

VANDERBILT UNIVERSITY V. DiNardo
174 F.3d 751 (6th Cir. 1999)

GIBSON, CIRCUIT JUDGE.

Gerry DiNardo resigned as Vanderbilt's head football coach to become the head football coach for Louisiana State University. As a result,

Vanderbilt University brought this breach of contract action. The district court entered summary judgment for Vanderbilt, awarding $281,886.43 pursuant to a damage provision in DiNardo's employment contract with Vanderbilt. DiNardo appeals, arguing that the district court erred in concluding: (1) that the contract provision was an enforceable liquidated damage provision and not an unlawful penalty under Tennessee law; (2) that Vanderbilt did not waive its right to liquidated damages; (3) that the Addendum to the contract was enforceable; and (4) that the Addendum applied to the damage provision of the original contract. DiNardo also argues that there are disputed issues of material fact precluding summary judgment. We affirm the district court's ruling that the employment contract contained an enforceable liquidated damage provision and the award of liquidated damages under the original contract. We conclude, however, that there are genuine issues of material fact as to whether the Addendum was enforceable. We therefore reverse the judgment awarding liquidated damages under the Addendum and remand the case to the district court.

On December 3, 1990, Vanderbilt and DiNardo executed an employment contract hiring DiNardo to be Vanderbilt's head football coach. Section one of the contract provided:

> The University hereby agrees to hire Mr. DiNardo for a period of five (5) years from the date hereof with Mr. DiNardo's assurance that he will serve the entire term of this Contract, a long-term commitment by Mr. DiNardo being important to the University's desire for a stable intercollegiate football program. . . .

The contract also contained reciprocal liquidated damage provisions.

Vanderbilt agreed to pay DiNardo his remaining salary should Vanderbilt replace him as football coach, and DiNardo agreed to reimburse Vanderbilt should he leave before his contract expired. Section eight of the contract stated:

> Mr. DiNardo recognizes that his promise to work for the University for the entire term of this 5-year Contract is of the essence of this Contract to the University. Mr. DiNardo also recognizes that the University is making a highly valuable investment in his continued employment by entering into this Contract and its investment would be lost were he to resign or otherwise terminate his employment as Head Football Coach with the University prior to the expiration of this Contract. Accordingly, Mr. DiNardo agrees that in the event he resigns or otherwise terminates his employment as Head Football Coach (as opposed to his resignation or termination from another position at the University to which he may have been reassigned), prior to the expiration of this Contract, and is employed or performing services for a person or institution other than the University, he

will pay to the University as liquidated damages an amount equal to his Base Salary, less amounts that would otherwise be deducted or withheld from his Base Salary for income and social security tax purposes, multiplied by the number of years (or portion(s) thereof) remaining on the Contract.

During contract negotiations, section eight was modified at DiNardo's request so that damages would be calculated based on net, rather than gross, salary. Vanderbilt initially set DiNardo's salary at $100,000 per year. DiNardo received salary increases in 1992, 1993, and 1994.

[In August, 1994, DiNardo signed a two year contract extension with Vanderbilt. In November 1994, Louisiana State University contacted Vanderbilt in hopes of speaking with DiNardo about becoming the head football coach for L.S.U. On December 12, 1994, DiNardo announced that he was accepting the L.S.U. position.]

Vanderbilt sent a demand letter to DiNardo seeking payment of liquidated damages under section eight of the contract. Vanderbilt believed that DiNardo was liable for three years of his net salary: one year under the original contract and two years under the Addendum. DiNardo did not respond to Vanderbilt's demand for payment.

Vanderbilt brought this action against DiNardo for breach of contract. DiNardo removed the action to federal court, and both parties filed motions for summary judgment. The district court held that section eight was an enforceable liquidated damages provision, not an unlawful penalty, and that the damages provided under section eight were reasonable. *Vanderbilt University v. DiNardo,* 974 F. Supp. 638, 643 (M.D. Tenn. 1997). The court held that Vanderbilt did not waive its contractual rights under section eight when it granted DiNardo permission to talk to L.S.U. and that the Addendum was enforceable and extended the contract for two years. *Id.* at 643–45. The court entered judgment against DiNardo for $281,886.43. *Id.* at 645. DiNardo appeals.

I.

DiNardo first claims that section eight of the contract is an unenforceable penalty under Tennessee law. DiNardo argues that the provision is not a liquidated damage provision but a "thinly disguised, overly broad non-compete provision," unenforceable under Tennessee law.

* * *

Contracting parties may agree to the payment of liquidated damages in the event of a breach. *See Beasley v. Horrell,* 864 S.W.2d 45, 48 (Tenn.Ct.App.1993). The term "liquidated damages" refers to an amount determined by the parties to be just compensation for damages should a breach occur. *See id.* Courts will not enforce such a provision, however, if the stipulated amount constitutes a penalty. *See id.* A penalty is designed to coerce performance by punishing default. *See id.* In Tennessee, a provision will be considered one for liquidated damages, rather than a penalty, if it is reasonable in relation to the anticipated damages for breach, measured prospectively at the time the contract was entered into, and not grossly disproportionate to the actual damages. *See Beasley,* 864 S.W.2d at 48; *Kimbrough & Co. v. Schmitt,* 939 S.W.2d 105, 108 (Tenn.Ct.App.1996). When these conditions are met, particularly the first, the parties probably intended the provision to be for liquidated damages. However, any doubt as to the character of the contract provision will be resolved in favor of finding it a penalty. *See Beasley,* 864 S.W.2d at 48.

The district court held that the use of a formula based on DiNardo's salary to calculate liquidated damages was reasonable "given the nature of the unquantifiable damages in the case." 974 F. Supp. At 642. The court held that parties to a contract may include consequential damages and even damages not usually awarded by law in a liquidated damage provision provided that they were contemplated by the parties. *Id.* at 643. The court explained:

> The potential damage to [Vanderbilt] extends far beyond the cost of merely hiring a new head football coach. It is this uncertain potentiality that the parties sought to address by providing for a sum certain to apply towards anticipated expenses and losses. It is impossible to estimate how the loss of a head football coach will affect alumni relations, public support, football ticket sales, contributions, etc. . . . As such, to require a precise formula for calculating damages resulting from the breach of contract by a college head football coach would be tantamount to barring the parties from stipulating to liquidated damages evidence in advance.

Id. at 642.

DiNardo contends that there is no evidence that the parties contemplated that the potential damage from DiNardo's resignation would go beyond the cost of hiring a replacement coach. He argues that his salary has no relationship to Vanderbilt's damages and that the liquidated damage amount is unreasonable and shows that the parties did not intend the provision to be for liquidated damages.

DiNardo's theory of the parties' intent, however, does not square with the record. The contract language establishes that Vanderbilt wanted the five-year contract because "a long-term commitment" by DiNardo was "important to the University's desire for a stable intercollegiate football program," and that this commitment was of "essence" to the contract. Vanderbilt offered the two-year contract extension to DiNardo well over a year before his original contract expired. Both parties understood that the extension was to provide stability to the program, which helped in recruiting players and retaining assistant coaches. Thus, undisputed evidence, and reasonable inferences therefrom, establish that both parties understood and agreed that DiNardo's resignation would result in Vanderbilt suffering damage beyond the cost of hiring a replacement coach.

This evidence also refutes DiNardo's argument that the district court erred in presuming that DiNardo's resignation would necessarily cause damage to the University. That the University may actually benefit from a coaching change (as DiNardo suggests) matters little, as we measure the reasonableness of the liquidated damage provision at the time the parties entered the contract, not when the breach occurred, *Kimbrough & Co.*, 939 S.W.2d at 108, and we hardly think the parties entered the contract anticipating that DiNardo's resignation would benefit Vanderbilt.

The stipulated damage amount is reasonable in relation to the amount of damages that could be expected to result from the breach. As we stated, the parties understood that Vanderbilt would suffer damage should DiNardo prematurely terminate his contract, and that these actual damages would be difficult to measure. *See Kimbrough & Co.*, 939 S.W.2d at 108.

Our conclusion is consistent with a decision by the Tennessee Court of Appeals in *Smith v. American General Corporation,* No 87-79-II, 1987 WL 15144 (Tenn. Ct. App. Aug.5, 1987). In that case, an individual sued his former employer for breach of an employment contract. *Id.* at *1. The employee had a three-year contract, and the contract provided for a single lump sum payment of all remaining compensation in the event of a breach by the employer. *Id.* at *1–2. When the employer reduced the employee's duties, he quit, and sued seeking to enforce the liquidated damage provision. The employer argued the provision was a penalty, and that the employee should only be able to recover his total salary under the contract reduced by the employee's earnings in his new job. The Tennessee court rejected these arguments, concluding that even though the usual measure of damage is the difference between an employee's old and new salaries, here, the parties reasonably contemplated "special damage," including the intangible damage to the employee's prestige and career. *Id.* at *6. The court found that the parties expressly recognized the importance to the employee of the continuation of his employment, and it was "clearly within the contemplation of the parties that, if [the employee] should not be retained in his position ... he would suffer unliquidated damages which would be difficult of proof." *Id.* at *7.

Our reasoning follows that of *Smith*. Vanderbilt hired DiNardo for a unique and specialized position, and the parties understood that the amount of damages could not be easily ascertained should a breach occur. Contrary to DiNardo's suggestion, Vanderbilt did not need to undertake an analysis to determine actual damages, and using the number of years left on the contract multiplied by the salary per year was a reasonable way to calculate damages considering the difficulty of ascertaining damages with certainty. *See Kimbrough & Co.*, 939 S.W.2d at 108. The fact that liquidated damages declined each year DiNardo remained under contract, is directly tied to the parties' express understanding of the importance of a long-term commitment from DiNardo. Furthermore, the liquidated damages provision was reciprocal and the result of negotiations between two parties, each of whom was represented by counsel.

We also reject DiNardo's argument that a question of fact remains as to whether the parties intended section eight to be a "reasonable estimate" of damages. The liquidated damages are in line with Vanderbilt's estimate of its actual damages. *See Kimbrough & Co.*, 939 S.W.2d at 108–09. Vanderbilt presented evidence that it incurred expenses associated with recruiting a new head coach of $27,000.00; moving expenses for the new coaching staff of $86,840; and a compensation difference between the coaching staffs of $184,311. The stipulated damages clause is reasonable under the circumstances, and we affirm the district court's conclusion that the liquidated damages clause is enforceable under Tennessee law.

* * *

[The Court rejected DiNardo's argument that Vanderbilt waived its right to liquidated damages when it granted DiNardo permission to discuss the coaching position with L.S.U. The Court, by contrast accepted DiNardo's argument that there was a factual dispute with respect to the enforceability of an addendum to the contract, and remanded that part of the case to the district court for trial. The parties settled subsequent to the Sixth Circuit's decision.]

* * *

We affirm in part, reverse in part, and remand the case to the district court for further proceedings consistent with this opinion.

DAVID A. NELSON, CIRCUIT JUDGE, concurring in part and dissenting in part.

If section eight of the contract was designed primarily to quantify, in an objectively reasonable way, damages that the university could be expected to suffer in the event of a breach, such damages being difficult to measure in the absence of an agreed formula, the provision is enforceable as a legitimate liquidated damages clause. If section eight was designed primarily to punish Coach DiNardo for taking a job elsewhere, however, the provision is a penalty unenforceable under Tennessee law. My colleagues on the panel and I are in agreement, I believe, on both of these propositions. We disagree, however, as to section eight's primary function.

It seems to me that the provision was designed to function as a penalty, not as a liquidation of the university's damages. Insofar as the court holds otherwise, I am constrained to dissent. In all other respects, I concur in Judge Gibson's opinion and in the judgment entered pursuant to it.

My principal reasons for viewing section eight as a penalty are these: (1) although the damages flowing from a premature resignation would normally be the same whether or not Coach DiNardo took a job elsewhere, section eight does not purport to impose liability for liquidated damages unless the coach accepts another job; (2) the section eight formula incorporates other variables that bear little or no relation to any reasonable approximation of anticipated damages; and (3) there is no evidence that the parties were attempting, in section eight, to come up with a reasonable estimate of the university's probable loss if the coach left. I shall offer a few words of explanation on each of these points.

Section eight does not make Coach DiNardo liable for any liquidated damages at all, interestingly enough, unless, during the unexpired term of his contract, he "is employed or performing services for a person or institution other than the University. . . ." But how the coach spends his post-resignation time could not reasonably be expected to affect the university's damages; should the coach choose to quit in order to lie on a beach somewhere, the university would presumably suffer the same damages that it would suffer if he quit to coach for another school. The logical inference, therefore, would seem to be that section eight was intended to penalize the coach for taking another job, and was not intended to make the university whole by liquidating any damages suffered as a result of being left in the lurch.

This inference is strengthened, as I see it, by a couple of other anomalies in the stipulated damages formula. First, I am aware of no reason to believe that damages arising from the need to replace a prematurely departing coach could reasonably be expected to vary in direct proportion to the number of years left on the coach's contract. Section eight, however, provides that for every additional year remaining on the contract, the stipulated damages will go up by the full amount of the annual take-home pay contemplated under the contract. Like the "other employment" proviso, this makes the formula look more like a penalty than anything else.

Second, the use of a "take-home pay" measuring stick suggests that the function of the stick was to rap the coach's knuckles and not to measure the university's loss. Such factors as the number of tax exemptions claimed by the coach, or the percentage of his pay that he might elect to shelter in a 401(k) plan, would obviously bear no relation at all to the university's anticipated damages.

Finally, the record before us contains no evidence that the contracting parties gave any serious thought to attempting to measure the actual effect that a premature departure could be expected to have on the university's bottom line. On the contrary, the record affirmatively shows that the university did not attempt to determine whether the section eight formula would yield a result reasonably approximating anticipated damages. The record shows that the university could not explain how its anticipated damages might be affected by the coach's obtaining employment elsewhere, this being a subject that the draftsman of the contract testified he had never thought about. And the record shows that the question of why the number of years remaining on the contract would have any bearing on the amount of the university's damages was never analyzed either.

In truth and in fact, in my opinion, any correspondence between the result produced by the section eight formula and a reasonable approximation of anticipated damages would be purely coincidental. What section eight prescribes is a penalty, pure and simple, and a penalty may not be enforced under Tennessee law. On remand, therefore, in addition to instructing the district court to try the factual questions identified in Judge Gibson's opinion, I would instruct the court to determine the extent of any actual damages suffered by the university as a result of Coach DiNardo's breach of his contract. Whether more than the section eight figure or less, I believe, the university's actual damages should be the measure of its recovery.

NOTES AND QUESTIONS

1. *Aftermath.* DiNardo's tenure at LSU was mixed. He had a promising start, reversing six straight LSU losing seasons with two Independence Bowl wins and a Peach Bowl win. This was enough to convince LSU boosters to pay Vanderbilt his damages after he lost the lawsuit. After two consecutive losing seasons, though, LSU fired DiNardo and replaced him with Nick Saban, who won a national championship at LSU.

2. *Enforceable Liquidated Damages?* The court held that the contractual provision was an enforceable liquidated damages provision because the damages that DiNardo owed were in reasonable relation to the damages actually suffered. Do you agree with the court's reading of the facts? On the field, one can make a case that DiNardo's performance (19 wins in 4 years) was significantly better than the coaches immediately before (10 wins in 5 years) or after (9 wins in 4 years), but as the court indicated, the damages issue goes beyond wins and losses. Nonetheless, Vanderbilt did not have a winning season or go to a bowl game until 2008, almost 15 years after DiNardo left. In light of *DiNardo*, how should universities draft contract provisions covering coaches leaving? Is the model Vanderbilt used one you would follow?

3. *Effect of Athletics on Contract Interpretation.* To what degree did the nature of DiNardo's job as a football coach shape the outcome of this case? Does the speculative nature of the true cost of replacing a football coach inform the liquidated damages determination? If a university put a similar provision in an academic dean's contract, would a court view it the same way?

4. *Property Interests.* Do coaches have constitutional property interests in their positions arising out of their contracts? It depends upon the language

used by the parties in drafting the contract. If a university cannot fire a coach without cause, then the coach retains a property interest in the salary due to him under the contract. On the other hand, if the coach has a contract that is "not continuing in nature" or "may be terminated at the pleasure of the board," then no property interest exists. *See Kish v. Iowa Central Community College*, 142 F. Supp. 2d 1084, 1097 (N.D. Iowa 2001) (citing *Board of Regents v. Roth*, 408 U.S. 564 (1972) ("To succeed on a procedural due process claim, [a public employee] must establish that he had a constitutionally protected property interest, that is, a 'legitimate claim of entitlement' to continued employment by the [public entity].")).

5. *Contract Perquisites.* In addition to salary, college football and basketball coaches often receive a package of benefits, some through the university, some through third parties. These can include radio and television shows, automobiles, and country club memberships. The contractual language that delineates these benefits is important, particularly when the university terminates the coach. Georgia Tech fired its head football coach, Franklin "Pepper" Rodgers in 1979. Rodgers' contract, however, continued through 1981, and his contract was with the athletic association.

Rodgers sued to retain the perquisites listed in his contract until its end date, even though he was no longer the head football coach. In *Rodgers v. Georgia Tech Athletic Association*, 303 S.E.2d 467 (1983), the Georgia Court of Appeals held that Rodgers was not entitled to any perquisites related to the performance of the job as head coach, such as a secretary and funds to attend football conferences, but reversed summary judgment with respect to items that did not relate directly to the job of coaching the team, such as tickets to professional sporting events and use of an automobile.

6. *Sovereign Immunity.* Mike Leach was the successful coach of the Texas Tech football team from 2000–09. In 2009, however, Texas Tech fired Leach for cause following an incident involving one of his players, Adam James. James accused Leach of forcing him to stand in an equipment room for the duration of practice when James refused to practice while suffering from a concussion. Texas Tech subsequently fired Leach, calling his refusal to apologize to James "an act of insubordination."

Leach sued Texas Tech for wrongful termination, alleging that his firing related to acrimonious contract negotiations, not the James incident. Unfortunately for Leach, the Texas Court of Appeals held that the common law doctrine of sovereign immunity, based on language in the Texas Constitution, barred Leach's suit against Texas Tech. *See Leach v. Texas Tech University*, 335 S.W.3d 386 (2011). Specifically, the court held that the university did not waive its sovereign immunity with respect to breach of contract claims. If certain state universities are immune from breach of contract suits, how does the negotiation of a contract between a coach and a university change?

Even though constitutional claims against the NCAA are foreclosed by *Tarkanian*, discussed in Chapter 12, coaches still have other tools to challenge the NCAA's actions, including tort law. Todd McNair, a former assistant football coach at the University of Southern California (USC), for instance, filed a defamation case against the NCAA that lasted almost a decade. The lawsuit arose from the NCAA's finding that McNair violated ethical conduct regulations during the NCAA's investigation into whether team member and Heisman Trophy winner Reggie Bush received improper benefits while he was a student-athlete at USC.

The NCAA Committee on Infractions (COI) issued a report imposing significant sanctions against USC's football program. As a result of the COI's findings and after a "Show-Cause" hearing, the NCAA prohibited McNair from engaging in recruiting activities or contacting prospective student athletes for one recruiting season, from April 29, 2011 to April 28, 2012. While the NCAA did not prohibit McNair from coaching, USC did not renew McNair's contract. McNair had difficulty finding another college or professional coaching job and was initially reduced to coaching at a local high school, before ultimately becoming an NFL assistant coach.

According to the COI, Lloyd Lake (Lake), a convicted felon, and his associate Michael Michaels (Michaels) formed a sports agency and marketing company and began giving Bush and his parents cash and other benefits such as merchandise, housing, lodging, and transportation in exchange for Bush's promise to sign with Lake's agency when he began playing professional football. Although this arrangement rendered Bush ineligible to participate in college football, he continued to play for USC. The NCAA's evidence against McNair consisted of a late-night call that demonstrated McNair knew of the benefits Lake's agency gave Bush and lied about his knowledge to USC and the NCAA. The COI report stated:

> At least by January 8, 2006, the assistant football coach [McNair] had knowledge that [Bush] and [Lake and Michaels] likely were engaged in NCAA violations. At 1:34 a.m. he had a telephone conversation for two minutes and 23 seconds with [Lake] during which [Lake] attempted to get [McNair] to convince [Bush] either to adhere to the agency agreement or reimburse [Lake and Michaels] for money provided to [Bush] and his family. Further, during his September 19, 2006, and February 15, 2008, interviews with the enforcement staff, [McNair] violated NCAA ethical conduct legislation by providing false and misleading information regarding his knowledge of this telephone call and the NCAA violations associated with it. [McNair] failed to alert the institution's compliance staff of this information and later attested falsely, through his signature on a certifying statement, that he had no knowledge of NCAA violations.

* * *

The [COI] nonetheless remains particularly troubled by the two minute and 32 second telephone call from [Lake] to [McNair] that took place at 1:34 a.m. on January 8, 2006. [McNair] claimed that he did not remember the phone call and denied [Lake's] description of what was said. The committee finds [Lake] credible in his report of the call. [Lake] said that he phoned [McNair] to ask him to intercede with [Bush] and get him to adhere to the agency agreement that he made with [Lake and Michaels]. [Lake] said he also told [McNair] that he did not intend to lose the money he had given [Bush] and his parents and preferred not to go public with the matter and implicate [USC].

The COI report listed facts to justify the COI's doubt about McNair's credibility. Those facts were: (1) that McNair and Lake were both friends with Faizon Love, a comedian and actor, who grew up with Lake; (2) a photograph of McNair, Love, Lake, and Michaels (the photograph), which was taken on Michaels' telephone and which the NCAA did not believe McNair would have agreed to without having at least been introduced to Lake; (3) three one-minute telephone calls McNair made to Lake on March 29, 2005, despite denying he ever knew or spoke to Lake, and (4) the late-night call that served as the exclusive basis for the finding against McNair. The COI found it implausible that McNair would have stayed on the late-night call for two minutes and 34 seconds with someone he claimed not to know.

McNair disputed the findings of the COI and sued the NCAA. The complaint alleged that the NCAA's false and malicious statements that McNair was unethical and had committed unethical acts damaged his reputation and ruined his career as a college football coach by making him toxic to USC and to any potential future college employers.

After a tortured procedural history, the case finally went to trial on the defamation claim in 2018, with the jury deciding in favor of the NCAA. The trial court, however, reversed the jury verdict. The trial court also granted McNair declaratory relief based on its finding that the NCAA's "Show-Cause" order violated section 16600 of the California Business and Professions Code, because such restraints "constitute an unlawful restraint on engaging in a lawful profession."

On appeal, the California Court of Appeal upheld McNair's motion for a new trial, finding that the evidence at trial was insufficient to justify the verdict. The Court explained:

The NCAA acknowledges that the late-night call was the "linchpin" on which it sanctioned McNair, and the only evidence of the *content* of the late-night call was the Lake interview. Comparing the [COI's] operative statement to the transcript of Lake's interview, the court found that the operative statement's summary of the late-night call was "false in at least the following ways:" (1) it falsely stated who initiated the call; (2) it falsely related the purpose Lake ascribed to the call; and (3) it falsely stated that McNair and Lake discussed the agency agreement and improper benefits during the late-night call. Therefore, the court found the operative statement did not "paraphrase" the Lake interview, but was "a fictional account of the Lake version" of the late-night call that was the impetus for the sanctions imposed on McNair.

Having granted a new trial, the appellate court vacated the declaratory judgment. McNair and the NCAA subsequently settled the lawsuit in the summer of 2021.

————

NOTES AND QUESTIONS

1. *The Cost of Litigation.* As in *Tarkanian* and *Brentwood Academy*, discussed in Chapter 12, the litigation in *McNair* lasted over a decade. As compared to labor arbitration as the tool for resolving disputes in professional sports, litigation is both more costly and time-consuming. Would a collective bargaining approach be better for college sports?

2. *The Limits of COI Fact-Finding.* As explored later in this chapter and in Chapter 12, the NCAA's Committee on Infractions does not have subpoena power. It took 18 months for the NCAA enforcement staff to convince Lake, who was in prison, to provide them just one opportunity to talk. How might this explain the confusion surrounding the Lake interview?

3. *Ollie Arbitration.* University of Connecticut men's basketball coach Kevin Ollie challenged his firing from the university based on alleged NCAA violations during his time as a head coach. The arbitrator found that UConn had violated Ollie's procedural due process rights and awarded the coach $11 million. In particular, the arbitrator cited the failure of the university to wait until it had made a determination concerning whether Ollie had violated NCAA rules (he had not). In light of the *McNair* and *Ollie* cases, what approach should universities take with respect to coaches accused of violating NCAA rules?

B. CONFERENCES

In addition to coach contracts, conferences have, in recent years, engaged in more robust contractual arrangements with their member institutions. The first wave of conference realignment occurred in 1991, with Arkansas and South Carolina moving to the Southeastern Conference (SEC), expanding it to 12 teams and allowing for a lucrative conference championship game in football. Soon after, Florida State joined the Atlantic Coast Conference (ACC) and Penn State joined the Big Ten. In

1996, the Big 8 Conference and the Southwest Conference joined to form the Big 12.

In 2003–04, Boston College, Miami, and Virginia Tech all left the Big East to join the ACC. The ACC paid $5 million to settle a lawsuit filed by the Big East over the defections. Conferences began to restructure their contracts with member institutions, imposing economic penalties for leaving and instituting waiting periods.

As television money increased, however, further shifts became inevitable. The rise of the Big Ten Network, and the University of Texas's own network opened the door to more lucrative arrangements that depended on having access to major media markets. The SEC, ACC, and Pac-12 have all followed suit, establishing their own television networks.

The next major shift of schools came during this growth, beginning in 2011, with the SEC expanding to add Missouri and Texas A&M; the Big Ten expanding to include Rutgers, Nebraska, and Maryland; the ACC again raiding the Big East in welcoming Louisville, Pittsburgh, Syracuse, and Notre Dame (in basketball only).

Most recently, the SEC expanded again to add Texas and Oklahoma, arguably the two strongest football programs in the Big 12, in the fall of 2021, with the membership scheduled to commence in 2025. This addition makes the SEC a superconference of 16 teams. This move threatened the landscape of major college football so significantly that three of the other four power conferences—the Big Ten, the ACC, and the Pac-12 subsequently announced an "alliance," presumably to defend against the SEC in the market.

This alliance was short-lived, however, as the USC and UCLA announced in the summer of 2022 that they were leaving the Pac-12 to join the Big Ten in 2024. The current map remains uncertain, other than that the SEC and the Big Ten will thrive with long-term lucrative television deals. The SEC reported revenue of $777.8 million for the 2020–21 fiscal year; the Big Ten signed a $1.2 billion annual television deal in 2022 (for 2023 through 2030). The expansion of the college football playoff seems like a distinct possibility as well.

The Pac-12 and the Big-12 have, to date, opted not to merge, and have also not successfully recruited schools from each other. The ACC likewise has not made a significant move.

What is clear is that football television revenue is driving the conference realignment and threatens the status quo of college sports. For this reason, the Knight Commission has called for separating out college football from the NCAA and the rest of intercollegiate athletics. The CFP, which oversees the college football playoff, discussed this option of college football leaving the NCAA in August 2022. It subsequently voted to expand the college football playoff from four to twelve teams.

One wonders whether many institutions will be cut out of the big paydays likely to come. The lack of diversity of teams participating in the college football playoff underscores this point, with the move toward a super-league or two super-leagues seeming imminent. It is also not clear that schools currently in the Big Ten or SEC are safe. One could imagine a new league that takes the most marketable programs and leaves out other, less successful programs.

Notre Dame, which as of the summer of 2022 remained independent, remains the university arguably with the most power to affect the landscape in the near future in the way that Oklahoma, Texas, UCLA, and USC have. If Notre Dame joins the Big Ten, it will help consolidate a two-power conference model. If Notre Dame joins the ACC, with whom it played during the pandemic year and participates in other sports with, then the ACC would be resuscitated.

The ACC has two major issues, though. First, its current television deal runs through 2036, which means that it is likely to continue to fall behind the SEC and the Big Ten in terms of annual revenue. Second, it has a restrictive contract that makes it very difficult for institutions to leave without incurring punitive financial costs. The next case illustrates this issue.

ACC v. UNIVERSITY OF MARYLAND
751 S.E.2d 612 (2013)

HUNTER, J.

[In 2012, the University of Maryland decided to end their long-standing affiliation with the Atlantic Coast Conference to join the Big Ten Conference. The ACC filed a lawsuit in North Carolina state court seeking a declaration that the substantial financial penalties for withdrawing from the conference provided for in Conference policies were legally valid. Maryland contested the court's jurisdiction, and this appeal followed.]

* * *

The ACC is a North Carolina unincorporated nonprofit association with its principal place of business in Greensboro, North Carolina. When the complaint in this action was filed, the ACC's membership consisted of twelve colleges and universities located along the eastern seaboard. In addition to the University of Maryland, the ACC's membership included Boston College, Clemson University, Duke University, Florida State University, the Georgia Institute of Technology, the University of Miami, the University of North Carolina, North Carolina State University, the University of Virginia, Virginia Polytechnic Institute and State University, and Wake Forest University.

On 13 September 2011, in response to a growing concern that a member institution's withdrawal from the ACC could cause financial damage to the conference, the Council unanimously voted to amend the ACC Constitution to establish a mandatory withdrawal payment at one and one-quarter times the total operating budget of the ACC. Defendants' representative on the Council proposed the factor used in the calculation and voted for the amendment.

The ACC alleges that after the September 2011 vote, the potential financial damage that would result from a member institution's withdrawal substantially increased. In response, the Council voted in September 2012 to change the formula used to calculate the withdrawal payment from one and one-quarter to three times the total operating budget of the ACC. Defendants' representative on the Council voted against this measure.

Not long after the Council voted to increase the withdrawal payment, Defendants informed the ACC on 19 November 2012 of their decision to withdraw from the ACC. On the same day, Defendants held a press conference publicly announcing their decision to withdraw from the ACC and to join the Big Ten Conference.

The ACC alleges that the University of Maryland's withdrawal from the ACC subjects them to a mandatory withdrawal payment in the amount of $52,266,342. [Maryland objected on grounds of lack of personal jurisdiction and "based upon the sovereign immunity of the State of Maryland."]

* * *

[The Court found that it had jurisdiction to hear the interlocutory appeal, and should review the question of law de novo.]

IV. Analysis

Having determined that this Court has jurisdiction to hear Defendants' appeal and the appropriate standard of review, we now address whether the trial court erred in denying Defendants' motion to dismiss on the grounds of sovereign immunity. Defendants contend that the extension of comity in this case would not violate public policy and that they are entitled to sovereign immunity under the laws of Maryland. We disagree and affirm the trial court's order.

As previously stated, under the rule of comity in North Carolina, rights acquired under the laws or judgments of a sister state will be given force and effect in North Carolina if not against public policy. *See, e.g., Cox v. Roach*, 723 S.E.2d 340, 346 (N.C. App. 2012). Moreover,

> [t]o render foreign law unenforceable as contrary to public policy, it must violate some prevalent conception of good morals or fundamental principle of natural justice or involve injustice to

the people of the forum state. This public policy exception has generally been applied in cases such as those involving prohibited marriages, wagers, lotteries, racing, gaming, and the sale of liquor.

Id. (quoting *Boudreau v. Baughman*, 368 S.E.2d 849, 857–58 (N.C. 1988)) (quotation marks omitted).

In the context of the sovereign immunity doctrine, our Supreme Court has used public policy to effectively waive the State's sovereign immunity in causes of action grounded in contract. *Smith v. State*, 222 S.E.2d 412, 423–24 (1976). In making this decision, the *Smith* Court was moved by the following public policy considerations:

(1) To deny the party who has performed his obligation under a contract the right to sue the state when it defaults is to take his property without compensation and thus to deny him due process; (2) To hold that the state may arbitrarily avoid its obligation under a contract after having induced the other party to change his position or to expend time and money in the performance of his obligations, or in preparing to perform them, would be judicial sanction of the highest type of governmental tyranny; (3) To attribute to the General Assembly the intent to retain to the state the right, should expedience seem to make it desirable, to breach its obligation at the expense of its citizens imputes to that body "bad faith and shoddiness" foreign to a democratic government; (4) A citizen's petition to the legislature for relief from the state's breach of contract is an unsatisfactory and frequently a totally inadequate remedy for an injured party; and (5) The courts are a proper forum in which claims against the state may be presented and decided upon known principles.

Id. at 423–24. Accordingly, public policy is violated in North Carolina when the State is allowed to assert sovereign immunity as a defense to causes of action based on contract. It would seem plain, then, that because the ACC is seeking a declaration as to the parties' rights and obligations under the terms of the ACC Constitution, it would violate public policy to extend comity to Defendants' claim of sovereign immunity. To this line of reasoning, Defendants raise three objections that we address in turn.

First, Defendants contend that *Boudreau* limits the public policy exception to matters of marriages, family, and morals. *See Boudreau*, 322 N.C. at 342, 368 S.E.2d at 858 ("This public policy exception has generally been applied in cases such as those involving prohibited marriages, wagers, lotteries, racing, gaming, and the sale of liquor."). However, as the language of *Boudreau* makes clear, the examples provided therein are nonexclusive and merely represent what has qualified under the exception as a general matter. Moreover, other language in *Boudreau* is consistent with the policy considerations at issue in *Smith*. Compare *id.* at 342, 368

S.E.2d 849, 368 S.E.2d at 857–58 ("To render foreign law unenforceable as contrary to public policy, it must violate some prevalent conception of good morals or fundamental principle of natural justice or involve injustice to the people of the forum state." (emphasis added)), with *Smith*, 289 N.C. at 320, 222 S.E.2d at 423 ("To hold that the state may arbitrarily avoid its obligation under a contract . . . would be judicial sanction of the highest type of governmental tyranny."). Thus, the language of *Boudreau* explicitly provides that any injustice to the people of the forum state implicates the public policy exception, not merely matters of marriages, family, and morals. Here, Defendants' are attempting to immunize themselves from a determination of their responsibilities under an alleged contract with the ACC—a North Carolina entity. Under the rationale of *Smith*, such an action violates public policy.

Second, Defendants contend that Cox stands for the proposition that "North Carolina courts extend sovereign immunity to and are to dismiss an action brought by North Carolina residents in North Carolina Courts against the educational institutions of sister states which enjoy sovereign immunity in the courts of those states." In Cox, this Court extended comity to the University of Virginia's claim of sovereign immunity and affirmed the trial court's decision to grant the University's motion to dismiss. *Cox*, 723 S.E.2d at 346–47.

However, it does not follow that because we decided to extend comity to the University of Virginia in *Cox* we must, ipso facto, extend sovereign immunity to all the educational institutions of our sister states irrespective of the attendant circumstances. *Cox* is distinguishable from the present case because it dealt with tort claims being asserted against the University of Virginia, not a cause of action on a contract. *See id.* at 342; *see also Kawai*, 567 S.E.2d at 217 (" 'Suits against the State, its agencies and its officers for alleged tortious acts can be maintained only to the extent authorized by the Tort Claims Act, and that Act authorizes recovery only for negligent torts. Intentional torts committed by agents and officers of the State are not compensable under the Tort Claims Act.' " (quoting *Wojsko v. State*, 47 N.C. App. 605, 610, 267 S.E.2d 708, 711 (1980)). Thus, at least with respect to torts not covered by the Torts Claims Act, the state is entitled to defend tort suits by claiming sovereign immunity. Such a defense does not contravene public policy in North Carolina. Thus, this Court properly extended comity to the University of Virginia in *Cox*. Here, however, extending comity to Defendants in a cause of action based on an alleged contract would violate the clear public policy articulated in *Smith*. For these reasons, the same principles that we applied in *Cox* lead us to the opposite conclusion here—comity will not be extended to allow Defendants to escape a determination as to their rights and obligations under an alleged contract.

Third, Defendants contend that the holding in *Smith*—that the State has no sovereign immunity defense in causes of action based on contract—is limited to actions claiming a breach of contract. Accordingly, Defendants contend that because the ACC seeks declaratory relief, the waiver found in *Smith* does not apply and Defendants are entitled to sovereign immunity.

As an initial matter, we note that even though the underlying claim in Smith was for breach of contract, our Supreme Court did not limit its holding to such actions:

> We hold, therefore, that whenever the State of North Carolina, through its authorized officers and agencies, enters into a valid contract, the State implicitly consents to be sued for damages on the contract in the event it breaches the contract. Thus, in this case and in causes of action on contract arising after the filing date of this opinion, ... the doctrine of sovereign immunity will not be a defense to the State. The State will occupy the same position as any other litigant.

* * *

Furthermore, even though the underlying claim in *Smith* was for breach of contract, the public policy considerations underlying the Court's rationale are equally persuasive here. Specifically, we are moved by the consideration in *Smith* that

> [t]o hold that the state may arbitrarily avoid its obligation under a contract after having induced the other party to change his position or to expend time and money in the performance of his obligations, or in preparing to perform them, would be judicial sanction of the highest type of governmental tyranny.

Smith, 289 N.C. at 320, 222 S.E.2d at 423. The Court's holding in *Smith* explicitly waived the State's sovereign immunity in "causes of action on contract" and we can discern no sound reason to limit that language to breach of contract claims when the Court's stated rationale is equally persuasive with respect to declaratory relief actions seeking to ascertain the rights and obligations owed under an alleged contract. *See Ferrell v. Dep't of Transp.*, 334 N.C. 650, 654–55, 435 S.E.2d 309, 312–13 (1993) (relying on the public policy considerations articulated in *Smith* to find a waiver of the State's sovereign immunity in a declaratory judgment action). Such declaratory relief actions are a "cause of action on contract" sufficient to waive the State's sovereign immunity.

Accordingly, because the public policy of this state does not allow the State of North Carolina to avoid its obligations in contract, we cannot extend comity to Defendants' claim of sovereign immunity. Furthermore, because we find that the extension of comity in this case would violate public policy, we decline to consider—as would be required if we had reached the opposite conclusion—whether Defendants would be entitled to sovereign immunity as a matter of Maryland law.

V. Conclusion

For the foregoing reasons, we affirm the order of the trial court denying Defendants' motion to dismiss and terminate the stay entered by this Court on 18 April 2013.

Affirmed.

———

NOTES AND QUESTIONS

1. *Aftermath.* Soon after the court's decision, Maryland and the ACC settled their case, with Maryland paying a $31.3 million exit fee to the ACC.

2. *Sovereign Immunity in Interstate Contracts.* Here, the Court denied Maryland's claim for sovereign immunity. Unlike Texas (*see Leach* case in notes above), North Carolina does not allow the state to claim immunity in breach of contract cases. Might a difference here be the interstate (instead of intrastate) nature of the contract? If a school was leaving the Big 12 instead of the ACC, and the case was brought in Texas, same result? What if the ACC was headquartered in Maryland instead of North Carolina? Same result?

3. *Changed Circumstances as Non-Performance?* The Maryland-ACC case was not the only litigation that emerged from conference realignment. In 2011, West Virginia left the Big East for the Big 12. When the Big East attempted to enforce its contractual relationship with West Virginia to delay its move and force it to pay an exit fee, West Virginia filed suit challenging the contract itself. Arguing that the Big East was "no longer a viable and competitive football conference," West Virginia argued that the court should set aside its agreement because the Big East's implosion amounted to a breach of contract. West Virginia also argued that the contract violated antitrust law as an unreasonable restraint of trade, even though it had willingly agreed to the bylaws. The case, however, soon settled, with the Big 12 schools contributing $20 million of the $31 million exit fee paid by West Virginia in exchange for immediate release from its contract with the Big East.

4. *Past Conduct as Estoppel?* Not long after West Virginia left the Big East, Rutgers left as well, joining the Big Ten. Recognizing the bylaw requirements of a $10 million exit fee and a 27-month waiting period. Rutgers immediately filed suit against the Big East, seeking release from the contract. Part of their complaint argued that the Big East was estopped from enforcing the contract based on the prior exits of Pittsburgh, Syracuse, and West Virginia, none of which waited the full 27 months before leaving. Rutgers also argued that the Big East failed to collect the full amount of exit fees from other institutions, such that its exit bylaws were "void and of no effect as between the parties."

The parties eventually settled the lawsuit, with Rutgers paying an $11.5 million exit fee, and being able to participate the next season in the Big Ten. Rutgers officials estimated that the move to the Big Ten would result in it making an additional $200 million over the next 12 years. The Big East subsequently reorganized, dropping football completely and moving forward as a basketball league largely made up of Catholic institutions.

C. COMPLIANCE

Historically, one of the NCAA's primary roles has been to monitor rules infractions and punish institutions that transgress its rules. The radical changes to the college sports environment in the 2020s led to the adoption of a new NCAA constitution in January 2022, and the delegation of rulemaking and enforcement proceedings to the three divisions. Division I convened a Transformation Committee whose work is ongoing at the time of this edition's publication and whose remit includes modernizing the rulebook and restructuring the infractions process. While compliance in the future NCAA may look different than it does today, this section looks at the range of available sanctions, and the scope of the enforcement power.

The worst penalty that the NCAA has given is the "death penalty"—a requirement that an institution cease playing a particular sport for a year or more. The "death penalty" rule (in NCAA By-law Art. 19.6.2.3.2(a)) allowed the NCAA to terminate for up to two years a school's program in a sport in which a major rules violation is committed within five years of another major rules violation in any sport. In the cases below, pay attention to whether the NCAA chose to impose the death penalty, and assess whether its decision was proper.

Second, this section examines situations where the conduct of the university falls outside the typical provision of economic benefits to students and instead involves some other shortcoming. In these cases, which involve the intersection of athletics with criminal conduct, the core questions are whether the NCAA ought to police such behavior, and if so, what kind of standard or approach it should use.

SOUTHERN METHODIST UNIVERSITY INFRACTIONS REPORT
NCAA Committee on Infractions, February 25, 1987

I. Origin of the Case.

On October 21, 1986, an NCAA enforcement representative interviewed a former football team member from the university (and the young man's mother) who reported possible major violations of NCAA legislation. On October 27, a television sportscaster and film crew interviewed the university's former director of athletics, former head football coach and the former administrative assistant to the director of athletics concerning possible payments of cash to the young man.

* * *

II. Findings of Violations as Stipulated by Southern Methodist University and the NCAA Enforcement Staff.

Violations of the principles governing amateurism and extra benefits to student-athletes [NCAA Constitution 3–1–(a)–(1), 3–1–(a)–(3) and 3–1–(g)–(5)]—During the period September 1985 through December 1986, monthly payments ranging from $50 to $725 were made to numerous student-athletes in the sport of football from funds provided by an outside representative of the university's athletics interests.

Specifically, subsequent to the conclusion of an NCAA infractions case in August 1985, certain key athletics department staff members agreed that promises made to student-athletes prior to the 1984–85 academic year during the young men's recruitment should continue to be fulfilled. Previous cash payments to the student-athletes had gone undetected by the NCAA, and the involved staff members agreed to continue the payments and to distribute them to the young men. It was understood that such payments would not be made to new student-athletes. An outside athletics representative who had been disassociated from the university's athletics program for involvement in the NCAA infractions case provided the funds for these payments.

As a result of these arrangements, 13 football team members received payments during the 1985–86 academic year that totaled approximately $47,000, and eight student-athletes continued to receive payments from September through December 1986 that totaled approximately $14,000. Payments were not continued subsequent to December 1, 1986, and reportedly, all but three of the student-athletes have exhausted their eligibility.

III. Factors Considered in Judgment of Case.

A. At the June 1985 NCAA special Convention, the NCAA membership enacted a series of mandatory penalties applicable to member institutions found guilty of repeat major violations. A "repeat major violation" is a second major violation found at an institution within a five-year period following the starting date of a major penalty.

At the February 13, 1987, hearing before the Committee on Infractions, the university agreed that repeat major violations had been committed by key members of both the football coaching staff and the athletics administrative staff, and another person for whose actions Southern Methodist University is responsible. A statement of the violations that the university agrees took place is set forth in Part II of this Infractions Report.

The issue, therefore, that the Committee on Infractions has confronted is whether to impose the mandatory penalties, the so-called "death penalty," or to exercise its discretion to impose less serious penalties because of unique circumstances in the case.

B. The present infractions case does present some unique circumstances that arguably call for the committee to exercise its discretion to impose less than the mandatory penalties. The efforts of the university in this investigation are commendable, and the dedicated work of the university's faculty athletics representative, Lonnie Kliever, went far beyond what could fairly be expected of a single faculty athletics representative. So impressed was the NCAA enforcement staff with the efforts of Mr. Kliever that the staff joined in the university's request that the committee impose penalties that were substantially less severe than those prescribed by the membership for a repeat major violation. Specifically, the staff joined with the university in urging that no football season be canceled. The university recommended a cancellation of two nonconference games for two seasons, while the enforcement staff recommended that all nonconference games be canceled for two years. Otherwise, the university and enforcement staff were in agreement with regard to coaching staff, grant-in-aid and recruiting reductions. The penalties recommended by the university are attached as Appendix A.

C. The committee gave serious and prolonged consideration to the recommendations of both the university and the enforcement staff, but declined to accept either recommendation. Factors that the committee believes call for more substantial penalties than those recommended include the following:

1. As a committee of the Association, the Committee on Infractions is bound by the judgment of the membership. That judgment was made absolutely clear in the recently adopted legislation and provides that serious repeat violators are to receive heavy penalties. That legislation was passed by an overwhelming majority of the membership.

2. Not only is Southern Methodist University a repeat major violator, but its past record of violations is nothing short of abysmal. Both the current infractions case and the university's 1985 infractions case involved major violations that occurred at times when the university was on NCAA probation for previous serious violations. These violations and additional past infractions cases demonstrate that numerous individuals associated with the university's athletics program, including key staff members and outside representatives, have been committed to achieving athletics success through deliberate and flagrant violations of fundamental NCAA rules that were designed to maintain equal and fair competition.

3. Past efforts at the university to design a program to gain a competitive advantage over the university's competitors by cheating did achieve its apparent goal—a winning record and national prominence for its football program.

4. As recently as September 1986, the university requested the committee to grant relief from an earlier penalty. This request was made at a time when some key athletics department staff members knew full well the cheating that caused the penalty to be imposed was continuing, and those individuals deliberately failed to disclose this fact.

5. Three unidentified enrolled student-athletes with eligibility remaining who have received improper payments refuse to identify themselves despite efforts by the university to persuade them to do so and despite the fact that they were offered limited immunity by the Committee on Infractions.

6. Although institutional personnel who were responsible for the football program have been separated from the university, the terms of their separation are unknown, and there has been no acknowledgment of the identity of those staff members who are most responsible for the flagrant, continuing violations found in this case.

7. There was no explanation in this case from the former director of athletics or the former head football coach regarding the reasons violations continued to occur after the appearance of the university's representatives before the committee in April 1985. During that appearance, assurances were given to the committee that all known violations had been disclosed and that every effort would be made to avoid violations in the future. Both assurances turned out to be false.

8. The continuing source of the funds for the violations found in this case was a university booster who the institution assured the committee in 1985 had been disassociated from the athletics program. The fact of this disassociation was stressed by the university as evidence of institutional remedial action at the time of its April 1985 hearing. Yet, when it subsequently became apparent in August 1985 that payments to football team members had not stopped, this booster was requested by key athletics department staff members to continue to fund the payments that were distributed through the athletics department. This arrangement was concealed by certain institutional staff members.

D. The penalties that the committee determined to be appropriate in this case are severe, but they differ in some respects from the prescribed repeat major violator penalties set forth in Section 7–(d) of the NCAA enforcement procedures. The committee accepted the view that there are uniquenesses in this case, but concluded that the university should be permitted to rebuild a football program only under carefully controlled conditions. The committee is satisfied that the university went to extraordinary efforts to uncover wrongdoing in its program in this case, and the committee is encouraged that there is evidence of actions by the university to obtain full compliance with NCAA regulations. Therefore, although the committee's penalties are intended to eliminate a program that was built on a legacy of wrongdoing, deceit and rule violations, the penalties also are intended to permit a new beginning for football at the university under a timetable that provides some relief from the recovery period required by the prescribed penalty structure. In addition, it should be noted that one of the prescribed penalties would have prohibited the university's membership on NCAA committees and denied institutional voting privileges for four years. These penalties were not imposed, in part because the institution's actions in this case demonstrate that it should be permitted to participate in the consideration of significant issues facing NCAA athletics programs.

IV. Committee on Infractions Penalties.

A. <u>Probation</u>. The university shall be placed on probation until September 1, 1990, it being understood that should any of the penalties in this case be set aside for any reason other than by appropriate action of the Association, the penalties shall be reconsidered by the Committee on Infractions; further, the university shall conduct annual audits of the expenses and income of its football team members during the probationary period (*i.e.*, by September 1, 1988, 1989 and 1990) to ensure that these student-athletes can meet their financial obligations without improper financial assistance, and the university shall report the results of these audits in writing to the NCAA enforcement staff, and finally, the NCAA shall conduct a review of the university's athletics policies and procedures prior to the expiration of this probationary period, which shall include an in-person visit to the university.

B. <u>Football Games</u>. The university shall be prohibited from participating in any football game or scrimmage with outside competition in 1987. During the 1988 football season, the university shall be limited to no more than seven games or scrimmages against outside competition, none of which shall be a "home" game; further, the university shall not be permitted to participate in "live" television appearances in the 1988 season or in postseason competition following that season.

C. <u>Practice</u>. During the 1987 calendar year, practice in the sport of football at the university shall be limited to conditioning programs only, and no football equipment may be used other than helmets and shoes. Teaching of football fundamentals or techniques shall be prohibited; no instruction, including walking through plays or watching films, shall be permitted. The university shall be permitted to resume normal practice activities in the spring of 1988.

D. <u>Coaches</u>. The university shall be limited to the use of no more than one head football coach and five full-time assistant football coaches until August 1, 1989.

E. <u>Grants-in-Aid</u>. No student-athlete in the sport of football shall receive initial, athletically related financial aid (as set forth in O.I. 600) that would be countable in the 1987–88 academic year at the university;

further, no more than 15 student-athletes shall be recipients of initial, athletically related financial aid that would be countable in the 1988–89 academic year, and finally, no student-athlete who receives countable financial aid for the 1988–89 academic year shall be permitted to receive such aid until at least the beginning of that academic year at the university.

F.   Recruiting. No member of the university's football coaching staff shall be permitted to participate in any off-campus recruiting activities (except the evaluation of prospects during football evaluation periods only) until August 1, 1988. Further, no prospective student-athlete in the sport of football shall be provided an expense-paid recruiting visit to the university until the beginning of the 1988–89 academic year, and no more than 45 such visits shall be permitted during that academic year.

G.   Disassociation. The university shall show cause within 15 days of receipt of this report why additional institutional penalties should not be imposed upon the university if it fails to take further corrective action in regard to the nine outside representatives who were disassociated for varying periods of time in the university's 1985 infractions case. In the committee's view, such action should permanently prohibit these individuals from providing the university's athletics program with any financial contributions or other support services for any purpose. These individuals should not be permitted to retain membership in the university's booster organizations and should not be permitted to receive any special athletics benefits from the university other than those available to the general public. . . .

The committee's penalties in this case are severe, and they are designed to compensate for the great competitive advantage that Southern Methodist University has gained through long-term abuses and a pattern of purposeful violations of NCAA regulations. The penalties also have deterrent value for others who might be tempted to follow the example set by Southern Methodist University; however, the penalties also are intended to achieve a long-term rehabilitative objective. The present administration of the university has expressed its hope for a new beginning in athletics, and canceling the football season in 1987 will afford an opportunity for the university to start a new football program based on integrity and fair play rather than on wrongdoing and deception.

———

NOTES AND QUESTIONS

1.   *Aftermath.* The SMU case was unprecedented at the time, and has never been replicated. The decision destroyed the SMU football program for a generation, with its next bowl game coming in 2009.

2. *The Death Penalty*. Given the crippling effect of the death penalty, should the NCAA ever impose it? If so, did SMU deserve it? Why or why not?

3. *NCAA Appellate Model*. The NCAA's current process has 2 levels: the Committee on Infractions (COI) and the NCAA Infractions Appeals Committee (IAC). As is typical with lower courts, the COI performs all of the fact finding in the case, while the IAC reviews the sanctions to determine if they are appropriate. After a COI decision, the institution and any penalized individuals have the ability to appeal to the IAC. The IAC reviews the COI decision using a clear error deferential standard as to the findings of the COI.

The NCAA created the IAC in 1992 in the aftermath of the Tarkanian litigation. SMU thus could not have appealed the COI decision above. If it could have appealed, do you think the outcome would have been the same?

UNIVERSITY OF ALABAMA, TUSCALOOSA PUBLIC INFRACTIONS APPEALS COMMITTEE REPORT
NCAA Infractions Appeals Committee, September 17, 2002

[The COI accused Alabama of violating NCAA bylaws on recruiting, honesty standards, salary control, and extra benefits. Specifically, three athletics department representatives paid a football recruit $20,000 as well as additional benefits. There were numerous other examples of benefits being provided to football recruits.

Further, an athletics department representative paid a high school football coach a significant amount of money to induce a star lineman to attend Alabama. Finally, strippers entertained recruits in university housing during their official visit.

Prior to the case, the university took a number of corrective actions, including self-imposing penalties. These included a reduction in scholarships and recruiting limitations.

The COI imposed a 2-year post-season ban and a 5-year probation term.]

* * *

We have addressed violations by athletics representatives in a number of prior cases. The issue in the University of Nevada, Las Vegas, case was whether it was appropriate to impose a ban on postseason competition against an institution whose athletics representatives had made cash payments to a prospective student-athlete and an enrolled student-athlete. We held that such a penalty was appropriate as a deterrent to future violations by bringing the "violations to the attention of the institution's boosters as well as the institution." (UNLV Public Infractions Appeals Committee Report, page 11, February 16, 2001) In that case, we discussed the application of Bylaw 19.6.2.1–(f). We found it unnecessary to decide there whether one of the three conditions of the bylaw must be satisfied as a condition to imposing a postseason ban because the case was subject to the repeat violator Bylaw 19.6.2.3.

In this case, we have a similar situation because the institution is subject to the repeat violator bylaw. The Committee on Infractions has discretion to ban postseason competition under this bylaw if such a penalty is not excessive or inappropriate. We have already concluded that such a ban is not inappropriate in a case involving violations by athletics representatives.

A ban on postseason competition is one of the most serious penalties that can be imposed on an institution. It deprives the institution and its student-athletes of the opportunity to achieve the highest level of success in their sport. It also prevents the fans and other supporters of the program from enjoying the full success of a season of competition. Because the violations in this case were numerous and particularly egregious, we conclude that the imposition of such a penalty is appropriate under the facts of the case.

The institution contended that, although it is responsible for the conduct of its athletics representatives, it was not, and was not found to be, at fault with respect to their actions. Without institutional fault, the institution argued that it is inappropriate to impose penalties on it for violations committed by its athletics representatives. This argument is based on the fact that the Committee on Infractions did not make a finding of lack of institutional control. As discussed above, we upheld the institutional sanction of a postseason ban in the UNLV case based on athletics representative violations for a repeat violator where there were no findings of lack of institutional control. Moreover, the Committee on Infractions noted in this case that the athletics representatives were "not the typical representatives" due to their "favored access and 'insider status'." (Committee on Infractions report page 3) The Committee found this status:

> "... not only gives credence to their claims of authority within a program but also, and however unintended, serves to reward them for the illicit activities in which they engage. Moreover, special access and insider status likely ease the way for illicit conduct by rogue representatives both by identifying prospects for them and by fostering (or contributing to) the belief of prospects and their parents that the representative's conduct is sanctioned by the university and in its best interest as well as that of the prospect." (Committee on Infractions report page 3).

The Committee concluded that this favored access and insider status created "greater university responsibility for any misconduct in which they engage." (Committee on Infractions report page 3) We agree.

The remaining question is whether the penalty is excessive. The two-year postseason ban imposed here is one of the longest imposed by the Committee on Infractions. However, in its report, the Committee on Infractions indicated that it seriously considered imposing the repeat violator penalty set forth in Bylaw 19.6.2.3.2–(a) and prohibiting outside competition in football (the "death penalty"). Its articulated bases for considering this penalty were the institution's status as a "two-time repeat violator" (1995 and 1999), the very serious nature of the recruiting violations and its view that the institution "bears some responsibility for the special status ... within the athletics department" enjoyed by two of the athletics representatives. (Committee on Infractions report page 29)

Although finding this a "very close question," the Committee on Infractions declined to impose the death penalty due to "the particular circumstances of this case and of the university's infractions history." (Committee on Infractions report page 29) Although the Committee did not elaborate in the report on what it meant by the "particular circumstances" of the institution's infractions history, it appears that the Committee considered cooperation of the institution in reporting the 1999 violation as a mitigating factor. This is consistent with the view the Committee took in its 1999 report on this matter. In that report, the Committee recognized that the institution had made great strides after the 1995 violation by creating "an environment of compliance" and stated: "Rather than impose institutional penalties, the Committee commends the university for its effective institutional control and proactive compliance ...." (Public Infractions Report for the University of Alabama, Tuscaloosa, page 3, February 9, 1999). The Infractions Appeals Committee agrees with this assessment of the 1999 report. However, even if the nature of the 1999 case mitigates the institution's status as a two-time repeat violator, the institution remains a repeat violator as a result of the 1995 report.

In further explaining why it did not impose the death penalty, the Committee on Infractions contrasted this case with the prior case (Southern Methodist University, February 25, 1987) in which this penalty was imposed. In that case, the Committee noted that there was "a demonstrated blatant disregard for NCAA rules that permeated throughout the entire university and its governance structure." (Committee on Infractions report page 29) The Committee found the circumstances of this case in sharp contrast. Here "university officials cooperated fully with the enforcement staff, often at great personal criticism, in a diligent effort to develop complete information regarding the violations." (Committee on Infractions report page 29) The Committee concluded "[h]ad this candor and cooperation been lacking, the death penalty (as well as substantial penalties in addition to those imposed in this case) would have been imposed." (Committee on Infractions report pages 29–30)

In the recent Howard University case, we encouraged the Committee on Infractions "to include in its report in future cases a fuller explanation of the basis of the penalties imposed and the extent of the consideration given to any degree of institutional cooperation sufficient to be a mitigating factor." (Howard Public Infractions Appeals committee Report, page 31, July 16, 2002). The Infractions Appeals Committee commends the Committee on Infractions for its explanation of the rationale for the penalties it imposed and the extent to which the institution's cooperation operated to mitigate those penalties. It is clear from the Committee's report that it did properly consider institutional cooperation as a "significant factor" and accorded it "substantial weight in determining and imposing" penalties here. (Mississippi page 19)

Finally, the institution argued that the two-year postseason ban and five-year probation are excessive compared to the penalties imposed in other cases involving repeat violators. Consistency in penalties so that comparable cases receive comparable penalties is a factor to consider in determining whether a penalty is excessive or inappropriate. We recognize that it is difficult to meaningfully compare cases because there are so many disparate variables in the cases. We also recognize that the Committee on Infractions must have latitude in tailoring remedies to the particular circumstances involved in each case and that the universe of relevant cases is not static, but evolving. In this case, the Committee on Infractions carefully considered the nature, number and seriousness of the violations, the conduct and motives of those involved in the violations, the corrective actions taken by the institution, the institution's exemplary cooperation and its repeat violator status.

The Committee on Infractions compared this case with the only case in which the death penalty was imposed and appropriately distinguished this case from that one. In the hearing on appeal, it adequately demonstrated the consistency of the result in this case with other recent cases.

* * *

For all of the foregoing reasons, we conclude that the two-year postseason ban and five-year period of probation imposed in this case are not excessive or inappropriate, and affirm Penalties III-B-3 and III-B-2.

NOTES AND QUESTIONS

1. *Aftermath.* Unlike SMU's program, Alabama's football program recovered quickly. After missing two years of bowls, it returned to a bowl game in 2004. It hired Nick Saban in 2007, and won six national championships in the next thirteen years.

2.   *When to Impose the Death Penalty.* Do you think the COI and IAC were correct here in choosing not to impose the death penalty? Note the factual similarities between the SMU and the Alabama cases: repeat offenders, paying recruits, multiple new violations. What in the NCAA COI's eyes was different here? Do you find that distinction persuasive?

3.   *Cooperation as Mitigation.* One of the distinctions that the COI found between SMU and Alabama (and the IAC found persuasive) was the full cooperation by University of Alabama officials who provided complete information to the NCAA enforcement staff. Indeed, the COI intimated that absent this cooperation, Alabama might have received the death penalty. The NCAA COI often rewards university compliance departments for self-reporting violations, and imposes more serious punishments (as with SMU) where universities do not disclose violations. Should the degree to which a university is forthcoming about violations and/or cooperates with NCAA enforcement staff factor into the sanction for violations? Why or why not?

4.   *Due Process and Subpoena Power.* One reason that the NCAA COI rewards self-reporting is its lack of subpoena power. The COI cannot force anyone not associated with a university to testify, provide information, or otherwise cooperate with investigators. As a result, obtaining evidence is often a problem in compliance cases, particularly when the athlete that received improper benefits has completed his or her eligibility and is no longer a student.

Further, the NCAA procedures do not provide many of the evidentiary protections that civil or criminal lawsuits do, including the ability to cross-examine all witnesses interviewed by the enforcement staff. As we have learned, though, the NCAA is not a state actor, and its procedures thus do not have to meet constitutional due process requirements. On the other hand, the NCAA does not have the subpoena power of a public authority. In your view, are such limitations significant enough to undermine the legitimacy of the process? Why or why not?

5.   *Lack of Institutional Control.* A second core principle, the requirement of institutional control, has emerged in part from the lack of subpoena power and the resulting dependence of the NCAA on institutional self-reporting of violations. Thus, where a university does not put in place adequate safeguards to monitor possible violations, it is guilty of exercising a lack of institutional control. In such cases, universities face additional sanctions, beyond the sanctions for the violations themselves.

The idea is that an institution's carelessness or failure to monitor adequately fosters an environment where violations are more likely to occur and more likely to go undetected. As you read the excerpt from the Miami case below, pay attention to the discussion concerning the lack of institutional control. Should institutions face a second punishment for failing to prevent and/or monitor violations? Keep in mind such violations can be as simple as improper phone calls, text messages, or de minimis benefits provided to recruits and/or student-athletes.

This is also true for head coaches. Head coaches are responsible for controlling their programs and face vicarious liability for infractions that occur on their watch. Knowledge of such violations is presumed because of the head coach's role in supervising the program.

UNIVERSITY OF MIAMI PUBLIC INFRACTIONS REPORT
NCAA Committee on Infractions, October 22, 2013

[The COI accused Miami of 18 allegations that primarily involved widespread and significant recruiting inducements and extra benefits. Many of the allegations centered around a known representative of the institution's athletics interests ("the booster") freely entertaining numerous prospects and student-athletes at his home, on his yacht and in various public settings. The booster paid for entertainment, food and various gifts. This booster also was a significant donor of the football and men's basketball programs and had a visible presence around the programs.]

* * *

The committee concludes that former assistant football coaches B and C were involved in unethical conduct by providing impermissible benefits or inducements and providing false or misleading information to the enforcement staff and the institution. The former head men's basketball coach's violations were the result of his failure to promote an atmosphere for compliance. The committee also concludes that former assistant men's basketball coaches A and B were involved in recruiting violations by providing impermissible benefits or inducements and in some instances using the booster to facilitate the provision of those benefits or inducements. Former assistant men's basketball coach B committed unethical conduct in connection with those recruiting violations. The institution demonstrated a failure to monitor its programs and the booster's activities. The institution also failed to have the proper policies and procedures in place during the relevant time period, which led to the committee concluding that there was a lack of institutional control.

The committee acknowledges and accepts the extensive and significant self-imposed penalties by the institution, and prescribes the following principal penalties: three years of probation, a reduction in the maximum number of athletics awards in football and men's basketball, restrictions on unofficial visits, a five-game suspension for the former head men's basketball coach, and two-year show-cause orders for former assistant football coaches B and C and former assistant men's basketball coach B.

III. FINDINGS OF FACT

The committee divides the institution's major infractions case into four distinct areas. The first and second areas involve major infractions in connection with two of the institution's highly visible sports programs, football (Part A) and men's basketball (Part B). Many of the violations in the football and men's basketball program are separate and distinct violations with one common link. That common link is the booster who, over a series of interviews, reported nearly a decade's worth of violations. The violations came to light primarily as a result of the reporting provided by the booster.

A third area involves major infractions investigated and initially submitted to the NCAA by way of the summary disposition process. These violations are largely the result of telephone and text-messaging violations in nearly all sport programs and included an admission on the part of the institution that it failed to monitor its programs. The violations were contained within the unprocessed June 2011 Summary Disposition Report and later incorporated in the enforcement staff's notice of allegations as allegations 15, 16 and 17. *See* Section C.

The fourth area concerns the institution's administration and overall control of its intercollegiate athletics program and commitment to rules education, monitoring and compliance.

* * *

IV. ANALYSIS

The violations in this case fall largely into the following areas: recruiting violations and the provision of impermissible benefits to student-athletes and prospects by representatives of the institution's athletics interests and prospective sports agents; the provision of impermissible supplemental income to assistant coaches; recruiting violations and the provision of impermissible benefits by assistant coaches; unethical conduct by former assistant football coaches and an assistant men's basketball coach; the former head men's basketball coach's failure to promote an atmosphere for compliance; telephone and text-messaging violation; and a lack of institutional control.

* * *

L. LACK OF INSTITUTIONAL CONTROL. [NCAA Constitution 2.8.1, 6.01.1.]

From 2002 through 2010, the institution failed to exercise institutional control and failed to monitor the administration of football and the men's basketball programs. The institution also failed to exercise control and failed to monitor the conduct of the highly recruited prospects, enrolled student-athletes, and coaching staffs in those high-profile programs. The institution did very little to control or to monitor the conduct of the booster. In fact, it was the institution that encouraged the booster to become connected to those sport programs, but provided no oversight to identify any potential concerns or violations. Additionally, the institution failed to monitor football and all of its other sports programs to ensure compliance with telephone and text-messaging legislation. None of the eight coaches or the approximately 30 student-athletes involved in the numerous major violations in this case took any meaningful steps to report the events. The failures of the coaches and student-athletes were either the result of a lack of understanding of the rules, or an attitude of indifference towards compliance. The failings of the institution enabled a culture of noncompliance to exist within the institution. The committee concludes that the facts found and the violations set forth in the Analysis sections above constitute a lack of institutional control.

* * *

The NCAA Constitution requires that each member institution comply with all applicable rules and regulations of the NCAA. It also requires that each institution monitor its programs to ensure compliance and to identify and report to the NCAA any instances where compliance has not been achieved. *See* NCAA Constitution 2.8.1. Further, the Constitution mandates that the institution's administration or faculty "or a combination of the two," exercise control and responsibility for the conduct of intercollegiate athletics. NCAA Constitution 6.01.1

The committee, however, does not base its conclusion that the institution failed to exercise institutional control solely on the booster's status or failing to monitor him. In assessing whether a member lacks institutional control, the committee considers whether adequate compliance measures exist; whether those compliance measures were appropriately conveyed to those who need to be aware of them; whether the compliance measures are monitored to ensure they are followed; and whether upon learning that a violation may have occurred, the institution takes timely and appropriate action.

The committee is concerned that former assistant football coach C reported being told to discuss violations or potential violations with the recruiting coordinator, a colleague on the coaching staff, and not a compliance officer. An institution should have policies and procedures for staff members to seek guidance on compliance related issues and report potential violations confidentially. As demonstrated by the majority of the widespread unreported violations identified in this case, the institution did not have adequate policies and procedures in place for staff members to report potential violations without fear of consequence.

The failure to implement proper policies, procedures and an internal monitoring system is one measure the committee has identified as an indicator that an institution lacks control over its intercollegiate athletics program. In this case, policies that the institution did have in place were disregarded or unevenly applied.

Policies and procedures that effectively deter and detect violations are essential to an internal monitoring system. As provided in allegations 15,

16 and 17, the institution also lacked the personnel, policies, and monitoring systems to ever detect text messages or to regularly detect improper or ill-timed recruiting telephone calls.

Further, the former associate director of athletics / compliance took the position that the compliance staff monitored sidelines, stands, suite areas, and bus-loading zones at home and away football games. However, these efforts failed to detect and deter a number of violations that occurred during football contests, including but not limited to prospects access to suite areas, interactions between the booster and prospects and the receipt of extra benefits and inducements.

The institution did not routinely compare telephone logs and telephone bills to ensure that the coaching staff was properly recording or logging telephone contacts and also that those contacts were consistent with NCAA legislative requirements. The committee has consistently concluded that rules education alone is not enough. The institution did not fully meet its responsibility to monitor its programs to ensure compliance and to identify and report those instances where "compliance has not been achieved." *See* NCAA Constitution 2.8.1. Because the institution lacked an adequate monitoring system and had policies that were disregarded or not communicated, it failed to establish a proper internal monitoring system.

Aside from the texting and telephone violations, the reports of secondary violations during the relevant time period, the institution did not identify a single instance of the booster's impermissible benefits or recruiting activity, separate from the enforcement staff's investigation and as identified in this report. According to the institution, the booster's access through the student-athlete scholarship program did not contribute to the violations. The committee concludes to the contrary because for years, the booster was able to meet and develop relationships with student-athletes. Some of these relationships enabled the booster to provide impermissible benefits to numerous student-athletes resulting in violations of NCAA bylaws.

Without monitoring systems or other internal controls, the chain of introductions that began between the booster and the student-athlete scholarship program were permitted to grow over time. While the institution contends that the booster operated "in the shadows" in places "that institutional eyes don't often frequent," the committee concludes otherwise. The booster visibly entertained small and large groups of student-athletes and operated in the public view of the institution and the nearby city of Miami. . . .

The institution's documentation program did not adequately monitor the athletics department's activities. As a result, numerous violations went undetected. . . .

For nearly a decade, the booster provided, and student-athletes received a range of impermissible benefits. For nearly a decade, those benefits were completely undetected. It does not appear that the institution conducted an assessment of the effectiveness of its compliance program, particularly in its high-profile sports to determine whether there was any concern for potential violations. Had the institution routinely examined its sports programs, it may have been alerted to the potential for NCAA violations and amended its policies and procedures to combat those identified risks.

Either way, the institution is responsible for the conduct of its intercollegiate athletics program. The scope of that responsibility covers the actions of staff and individuals representing the institution's athletics interests.

In this case it is apparent that individuals within and outside of the program were involved with, and aware of numerous violations. It is also apparent that the former head men's basketball coach failed to promote an atmosphere of compliance. There is nothing to suggest, however, that the institution failed to take timely and appropriate action when it became clear that these violations had occurred. Notwithstanding that, however, an institution is required to put adequate systems in place to prevent and detect violations, as well as take action when they occur.

The committee finds that the institution is responsible for the conduct of individuals in their sports programs, if adequate compliance measures are not in place; they are not effectively communicated to the individuals, or, they are not monitored to ensure that such measures are being followed. The committee concludes that adequate compliance measures did not exist to prevent or effectively deter the violations from occurring in this case.

Institutional Control and Representatives of an Institution's Athletics Interests

As the committee has stated in previous infractions cases, institutions have a greater responsibility to monitor athletics representatives with "insider" or favored status. *See University of Alabama,* Case No. M173 (February 1, 2002), *University of Arkansas,* Case No. M183 (April 17, 2003), *University of Michigan,* Case No. M191 (May 8, 2003), *University of Central Florida,* Case No. M361 (July 31, 2012). In some of those cases, the committee specified that a failure to monitor and control these athletics representatives is demonstrative of either an institutional failure to monitor (*Arkansas*) or a lack of institutional control (*Central Florida*). . . .

The booster at the center of this case was extremely "visible," as reflected in the above activities. By granting him special access and celebrating him with the naming of a student lounge, it is clear that the institution embraced him. He certainly did not "fly under the radar," as the institution asserts but rather was a major supporter of their athletics programs, which creates a greater responsibility to monitor.

Moreover, the record establishes that a former associate director of athletics / compliance had general concerns about donors being provided "way too much access" to the student-athletes, and he voiced those concerns to the athletics administration in place at the time. In November 2007, the former associate director of athletics/compliance actually had an altercation with the booster and again raised those concerns with senior athletics administrators. There is nothing in the record that suggests institutional steps were taken to address the concerns raised by the former associate director of athletics.

The institution failed to exercise control over its football and men's basketball programs. The institution lacked sufficient institutional policies and procedures, as well as lacked adequate monitoring efforts, both of which contributed to their lack of control. The facts as found demonstrate that a number of the indicia of institutional control were absent at the institution. Finally, the committee looked to past cases to analyze the booster's activities. Considering the facts as found and past cases as guidance, the committee concludes that the institution lacked institutional control. The committee concludes that the facts as found constitute violations of NCAA Constitution 2.8.1 and Bylaw 6.01.1.

* * *

V. PENALTIES.

The committee considered the institution's cooperation in the processing of all parts of this case. Cooperation during the infractions process is addressed in NCAA Bylaw 19.01.3—Responsibility to Cooperate and NCAA Bylaw 32.1.4—Cooperative Principle (2011–12 Division I NCAA Manual). The committee finds that the cooperation exhibited by the institution was consistent with its obligation under Bylaws 19.01.3.3 and 32.1.4.

In addition to its cooperation, the committee notes that the institution understood the nature and the scope of the allegations that were pending. It is clear that the institution substantially agreed with a majority of the violations. It is also clear that the institution, even before the committee conducted the June 2013 hearing, took responsibility for violations, particularly in the football program. For two seasons, the institution limited its football program to regular season competition only, eliminating any postseason competition opportunities, including the 2012 Atlantic Coast Conference Championship game.

Finally, in full consideration of the institution's presentation at the hearing, submissions into the record and conduct to date, the committee prescribes the following sanctions.

Those self-imposed by the institution are so noted:

1. Public reprimand and censure.

2. Three years of probation from October 22, 2013, through October 21, 2016.

Football Program

3. Reduction in Athletics Awards. The total number of athletically related financial aid awards in football shall be reduced by a combined total of nine during the 2014–15, 2015–16 and 2016–17 academic years. The institution shall reduce the total number of athletics awards during each academic year. The institution has the option of assigning the reductions during those years.

4. During the 2014–15 and 2015–16 academic years, the institution shall be limited when providing complimentary admissions to prospects on unofficial visits. The institution may provide a prospect with complimentary admissions for a maximum of one home athletics event. All other restrictions for unofficial visits, not addressed in the committee's decision, may be found in the applicable bylaws, including NCAA Bylaw 13.7.

5. The institution imposed bans on the football team's participation in postseason bowl games following both the 2011 and 2012 seasons, and withheld the football team from participating in the 2012 ACC Championship game.

6. The institution reduced official paid visits for 2012–13 by 20 percent. The reduction resulted in a total of 36 visits. The institution shall certify that this penalty has been fulfilled in its first annual compliance report.

7. The institution reduced fall evaluations in 2012–13. The institution therefore used 36 of the permissible 42. The institution shall certify that this penalty has been fulfilled in its first annual compliance report.

8. The institution limited coaches during the 2012–13 contact period. The institution reduced available contact days by 20 percent. The institution shall certify that this penalty has been fulfilled in its first annual compliance report.

* * *

[Miami self-imposed a series of penalties and show cause bans on its former assistant football coaches involved in the violations]

Men's Basketball Program

12. Reduction in Athletics Awards. The total number of athletically related financial aid awards in men's basketball shall be reduced by a

combined total of three during the 2014–15, 2015–16 and 2016–17 academic years. The institution shall reduce the total number of athletics awards by one during each academic year.

* * *

[Miami self-imposed a series of penalties and show cause bans on its former head men's basketball coach and the assistant basketball coach involved in the violations. In addition, the Report provided a long list of minor penalties related to the sports listed above as well as a series of institutional penalties.]

———

NOTES AND QUESTIONS

1. *Aftermath.* Miami's athletic programs did not suffer as much as SMU's football team did, but they were not able to bounce back as quickly as Alabama's football team did. In 2017–18, however, its football team returned to national prominence, and its basketball team made the NCAA tournament for the third year in a row.

2. *When to Impose the Death Penalty, Part II.* How do you compare the violations at Miami with the violations at SMU and Alabama? The extensive and flagrant nature of Miami's violations would seem to make the death penalty at least a possibility, but the NCAA did not think so. How did they distinguish this case? Are these cases all similar? Or are there important differences?

3. *Subpoena Power, Part II.* The difficulties imposed by the NCAA's lack of subpoena power surfaced again in the Miami case, where the COI investigators went too far and broke the NCAA's own rules in investigating the case. The NCAA admitted that its investigators "improperly" obtained information by working too closely with a criminal defense attorney for Nevin Shapiro. In addition, the NCAA paid Miami attorney Maria Elena Perez for taking two depositions in a bankruptcy case involving one of Shapiro's companies and sharing information from that case. Do you think that the NCAA's malfeasance affected the outcome in the Miami case?

4. *Lack of Institutional Control.* The lack of institutional control found here had as much to do with the lack of safeguards within the athletic department, as with the rampant disregard for the rules displayed by the booster in question and other members of the athletic department and coaching staffs. Should the focus here be more on the quantity and frequency of the benefits? Or on the lack of a system to monitor phone calls? To what extent do the proof problems present in compliance cases make the presence or absence of monitoring systems an easy target by which to assess compliance?

———

Around the time of the Miami case, an unprecedented number of major infractions cases occurred at high profile programs, including Ohio State, Tennessee, Auburn, Southern California, Georgia Tech, West Virginia, and Syracuse. In response, the NCAA implemented a new punishment structure in 2013.

The new structure separated infractions into four tiers: (1) Level I: Severe Breach of Conduct; (2) Level II: Significant Breach of Conduct; (3) Level III: Breach of Conduct; and (4) Level IV: Incidental Issues, with Level I being the most serious.

Level I violations (Severe Breach of Conduct) are those that:

". . . seriously undermine or threaten the integrity of the NCAA collegiate model as set forth in the Constitution and bylaws, including any violation that provides or is intended to provide a substantial or extensive recruiting, competitive or other advantage, or a substantial or extensive impermissible benefit."

Examples of Level I violations include: lack of institutional control, academic fraud, failure to cooperate in an enforcement investigation, unethical or dishonest conduct, and head coach responsibility for a Level I violation by a member of his staff.

Level II violations (Significant Breach of Conduct) are those that:

"Violations that provide or are intended to provide more than a minimal but less than a substantial or extensive recruiting, competitive or other advantage; includes more than a minimal but less than a substantial or extensive impermissible benefit; or involves conduct that may compromise the integrity of the NCAA collegiate model as set forth in the Constitution and bylaws."

Examples of Level II violations include: failure to monitor, systemic violations not rising to the level of lack of institutional control, multiple recruiting violations, and collective Level III violations. Level III violations (Breach of Conduct) are those that:

"are isolated or limited in nature; provide no more than a minimal recruiting, competitive or other advantage; and do not include more than a minimal impermissible benefit. Multiple Level IV violations may collectively be considered a breach of conduct."

Finally, Level IV violations (Breach of Conduct) are those that:

"are inadvertent and isolated, technical in nature and result in a negligible, if any, competitive advantage. Level IV infractions generally will not affect eligibility for intercollegiate athletics."

The goal of this structure is to add legitimacy to the infractions system by creating a more uniform way of categorizing behavior and promoting consistency in sanctioning. In the words of the NCAA, the COI is seeking to provide "credible accountability." In addition, this revised system has placed more responsibility on head coaches for infractions that occur in their programs. New penalties have included suspension of coaches for multiple games during the season, as in the case of basketball coaches Jim Boeheim of Syracuse and Rick Pitino of Louisville (before he was fired). The core sanctions remain—postseason bans, scholarship reductions, and financial sanctions—with the stated goal of deterring misconduct and preventing advantages stemming from providing improper benefits to athletes.

In 2019, the NCAA subsequently adopted another layer to its compliance system to counter two major criticisms—the relative lack of speed of the process and the lack of independence of the members of the COI. This new unit was the Independent Accountability Review Process (IARP), reserved for particularly complicated cases to be decided by the Independent Resolution Panel (IRP). The standard for referral to the IRP included "when a case involves unique policy issues or factors that when weighed in totality could impede accurate and effective resolution of the case under the current internal infractions resolution structure." Six cases from major programs were referred to the IRP in 2020–21: LSU, North Carolina State, Kansas, Louisville, Arizona, and Memphis, many of which resulted from the federal investigation in the *Gatto* case discussed below. After the 2022 adoption of the new NCAA constitution, Division I suspended referrals to the IARP, and the IRP was later disbanded other than to conclude its work on previously referred cases.

Historically, recruiting rules violations have made up a significant portion of the COI caseload. Even after the NIL changes discussed in Chapter 12, the NCAA still places significant limits on recruiting. The next case is an example of a serious recruiting violation that would still violate the rules after the NIL changes.

UNIVERSITY OF LOUISVILLE PUBLIC INFRACTIONS APPEALS COMMITTEE REPORT

NCAA Infractions Appeals Committee, February 20, 2018

* * *

VI. PENALTIES IMPOSED BY THE COMMITTEE ON INFRACTIONS. * * *

Financial penalties (VI-3): The institution shall pay a financial penalty of $5,000 (institution imposed). The former operations director knew that his actions violated NCAA legislation. The student-athletes who participated in the striptease dances, prostitution and "tipping" of the strippers became ineligible for competition. They knew or should have known that their actions were contrary to NCAA legislation. Therefore, consistent with former Bylaw 19.5.2–(i) and Bylaw 31.2.2.4, the IAC's [Infractions Appeals Committee] report in *Purdue University* (2000), IAC Report No. 306 in *University of Memphis* (2010) and IAC Report No. 414 in *Syracuse University* (2015), the institution shall return to the NCAA all of the monies it has received to date through conference revenue sharing for its appearances in the 2012, 2013, 2014 and 2015 NCAA Men's Basketball Tournaments. Future revenue distributions that are scheduled to be provided to the institution from those tournaments shall be withheld by the conference and forfeited to the NCAA. A complete accounting of this financial penalty shall be included in the institution's annual compliance reports and, after the conclusion of the probationary period, in correspondence from the conference to the Office of the Committees on Infractions.

Vacation of records (VI-12): The COI has not previously dealt with a case like this. A team staff member arranged striptease dances and acts of prostitution for enrolled student-athletes and prospects who eventually enrolled at the institution. Some of the prospects were minors. By his actions, the former operations director rendered those student-athletes and prospects ineligible for competition. The violations were serious, intentional, numerous and occurred over multiple years. Therefore, pursuant to former Bylaw 19.5.2–(h) and Bylaw 31.2.2.3, and consistent with IAC Report No. 306 in *University of Memphis* (2010) and IAC Report 414 in *Syracuse University* (2015), the institution shall vacate all regular season and conference tournament wins in which ineligible student-athletes competed from the time they became ineligible through the time they were reinstated as eligible for competition through either the student-athlete reinstatement process or through a grant of limited immunity. Further, if any of the student-athletes competed in the NCAA Division I Men's Basketball Championships at any time they were ineligible, the institution's participation in the championships shall be vacated. The individual records of the ineligible student-athletes shall also be vacated. Further, the institution's records regarding men's basketball, as well as the record of the head coach, will reflect the vacated records and will be recorded in all publications in which men's basketball records are reported, including, but not limited to, institutional media guides, recruiting material, electronic and digital media plus institutional, conference and NCAA archives. * * * Any public reference to these vacated contests shall be removed from athletics department stationery, banners displayed in public areas and any other forum in which they may appear. Any trophies or other team awards attributable to the vacated contests shall be returned to the Association. * * *

VII. ISSUES RAISED ON APPEAL. In its written appeal, Louisville asserted that the Committee on Infractions abused its discretion when prescribing penalties VI-3 and VI-12.

* * *

IX. INFRACTIONS APPEALS COMMITTEE'S RESOLUTION OF THE ISSUES RAISED ON APPEAL. In reviewing this case, a penalty prescribed by the hearing panel, including determinations regarding the existence and weighing of any aggravating or mitigating factors, shall not be set aside on appeal except on a showing by the appealing party that the hearing panel abused its discretion. The hearing panel determines the credibility of the evidence. [The standard on review is abuse of discretion].

As we stated in the *Alabama State University* case:

". . .we conclude that an abuse of discretion in the imposition of a penalty occurs if the penalty: (1) was not based on a correct legal standard or was based on a misapprehension of the underlying substantive legal principles; (2) was based on a clearly erroneous factual finding; (3) failed to consider and weigh material factors; (4) was based on a clear error of judgment, such that the imposition was arbitrary, capricious, or irrational; or (5) was based in significant part on one or more irrelevant or improper factors." [*Alabama State University, Infractions Appeals Committee Public Report*, June 30, 2009, Page No. 23].

Louisville challenged the vacation of records from the 2011–12, 2012–13, 2013–14 and 2014–15 academic years, as well as having to return the revenue earned from its appearances in the 2012, 2013, 2014 and 2015 NCAA Men's Basketball Tournaments.

* * *

In its review of the case, the committee agreed with the Committee on Infractions that the involved student-athletes knew or should have known they were receiving improper benefits in violation of NCAA legislation. In fact, the institution conceded the student-athletes received improper benefits during the oral argument. [Infractions Appeals Committee Oral Argument Transcript, Page Nos. 8, 19–23]. Because the student-athletes received improper benefits, it follows they competed while ineligible, which in turn supports the vacation of records and financial penalties imposed by the Committee on Infractions. In response to the institution's argument that one of the involved student-athletes who competed while ineligible would have been reinstated, it is the committee's position there is no guarantee regarding the reinstatement process. [*Georgia Institute of Technology Infractions Appeals Committee Public Report* March 9, 2012, Page No. 14]. The institution is not free from punishment now based on an assumption regarding the reinstatement process with respect to other student-athletes at different institutions.

Pursuant to Bylaw 19.9.7–(g), a vacation of records penalty is appropriate when there are ineligible student-athletes involved in competition. The Committee on Infractions has significant discretion to fashion appropriate penalties for the overall infractions at issue in a case. [*St. Mary's College of California Infractions Appeals Committee Public Report* October 14, 2013, Page No. 6]. While the Committee on Infractions retains discretion to apply (or not apply) the vacation penalty under any circumstances it believes appropriate, this committee has indicated the likelihood of such a penalty is significantly increased when any of the following aggravating factors are present:

1.   Academic fraud;

2.   Serious intentional violations;

3.   Direct involvement of a coach or high-ranking school administrator;

4.   A large number of violations;

5.   Competition while academically ineligible;

6.   Ineligible competition in a case that includes a finding of failure to monitor or a lack of institutional control; or

7.   When vacation of a similar penalty would be imposed if the underlying violations were secondary.

[*Georgia Tech Infractions Appeals Committee Public Report* Page No. 14].

This committee recognizes the factors involved in vacation of records cases continue to evolve and expand. Because this case involved serious and intentional violations, which Louisville agreed were reprehensible and inexcusable [Infractions Appeals Committee Oral Argument Transcript, Page No. 9], direct involvement of an institutional staff member, and a large number of violations, the Committee on Infractions was within its legislated authority to impose the vacation of records penalty. Given the reprehensible nature of the violations, which resulted in ineligible student-athletes competing over a four-year time period, the Committee on Infractions was also within its authority to impose the financial penalties assessed in this case. For this reason, the committee did not find an abuse of discretion in the imposition of the penalties in this case.

* * *

X.   CONCLUSION. The penalties are affirmed.

_____

NOTES AND QUESTIONS

1.   *Aftermath*. Louisville fired its head basketball coach, Rick Pitino, soon after the decision came down. The reason for his termination, though, was

the discovery of a new set of violations related to the recruitment of an athlete allegedly compensated with $100,000. These allegations emerged as part of a federal probe that so far has involved the arrest of 10 individuals for corruption and bribery. The case of one of these individuals, Joe Gatto, is explored below.

2. *Louisville Recruiting Violations.* While the presence of violations is clear here (and in most cases), the real question is whether the sanction is appropriate. Do you agree with the decision of the IAC? Why or why not?

3. *Bag Man? University of Mississippi Infractions Case.* Also in 2018, the NCAA COI held that recruiting violations by the University of Mississippi warranted a two-year post-season ban in football, a decision largely upheld by the IAC. At the heart of the case was the allegation that an assistant coach had helped arrange for a booster to pay a recruit $10,000. The recruit, who incidentally enrolled at archrival Mississippi State, was granted immunity for his testimony. The case raised the issue of "bag men," wealthy donors who provide money to recruits and their families as an inducement to attend their university. Many believe that this practice is widespread, particularly in the SEC, and that Ole Miss was the unfortunate institution to be caught. An incident from months earlier made an investigation more likely. Laremy Tunsil was interviewed on the night of the NFL draft. He had dropped multiple spots in the draft after an anonymous hacker released a photo on social media of him smoking marijuana. He admitted during the ensuing press conference that he had received money from Ole Miss assistant coaches, but the NCAA was unable to prove that to be true, even with text messages that hinted as much.

4. *Recruiting Barbeques?* The University of Tennessee basketball infractions case from 2011 sheds additional insight into the restrictions of the NCAA recruiting rules. Coach Bruce Pearl hosted a barbeque at his house for prospective players and their families in violation of NCAA rules. Pearl lied about the party to investigators, who ultimately found pictures on social media of the party on social media. Pearl received a show cause order and was unable to coach for several years.

5. *Fair Play or Paternalism?* The NCAA recruiting rules discussed above exist to promote fair play in recruiting in light of the amateurism rules. Are such rules appropriate or paternalistic? Are the rules too restrictive, applying so broadly as to limit basic human contact? Should athletes be prevented from receiving any valuable benefits during recruitment in light of the millions of dollars that coaches earn annually? Or does the amount of money on the line for coaches require the NCAA's regulation?

6. *Can Lines Be Drawn Between Recruitment Benefits?* If the NCAA allowed barbecues at coaches' houses, could they effectively distinguish dinners at fancy restaurants or parties with prostitutes? How would you draw lines in recruitment rules?

Beyond serious infractions cases and the challenge of finding appropriate sanctions, the NCAA has faced a different kind of issue in recent years where criminal conduct has been connected to athletic programs. The Penn State scandal in particular provided a very serious challenge to the NCAA. In 2011, the NCAA (and the general public) learned that a former Penn State assistant football coach, Jerry Sandusky, had sexually molested young boys in various locations, including locker rooms in Penn State athletic facilities. These incidents spanned a decade, and some Penn State employees at least had reason to suspect that these criminal acts were occurring.

Sandusky was eventually convicted of multiple counts of unlawful contact with minors, corruption of minors, and endangering the welfare of children, and sentenced to 30 to 60 years in prison. In addition, Penn State Athletic Director Tim Curley and Vice President Gary Schultz pled guilty to child endangerment, and President Graham Spanier was convicted on that charge (after an acquittal on more serious conspiracy allegations). All three began serving prison sentences of between 4 months and 2 years in 2018.

Any scrutiny of the involvement of Penn State's legendary football coach, Joe Paterno, ended with his death in January 2012, three months after the scandal broke. Shortly after the scandal erupted, the Penn State Board of Trustees commissioned an investigation of the entire episode by former FBI director Richard Freeh, who issued a lengthy report. It concluded that the Penn State officials noted above had failed to disclose information they knew concerning Sandusky's sexual abuse.

Relying primarily on the Freeh Report, President Mark Emmert announced on July 23, 2012 that the NCAA's Executive Committee was levying several sanctions against Penn State for fostering an unhealthy culture that allowed the Sandusky crimes to happen and go unreported. The sanctions included: (a) a fine of $60 million; (b) banning the football team from post-season play for five seasons (through the 2016 season); (c) reducing the number of football scholarships Penn State could give from 2012 through 2015 to 15 a year and a total of no more than 65 (the normal maximum for a Division I-A school is 85); and (d) requiring Penn State retroactively to forfeit 112 wins earned from 1998 through 2011 (the years that Sandusky was committing his crimes), which caused Coach Paterno to lose his status as the winningest Division I-A football coach of all time. Emmert stated at the same time as he announced the sanctions that the Penn State Board of Trustees had agreed to sign a consent form accepting the penalties and agreeing not to contest them.

Later, the media reported that new Penn State President Rodney Erickson's decision to accept the sanction was significantly affected by NCAA leaders' threats to impose the "death penalty" (shutting the football program down entirely), although Penn State's defenders questioned whether such a sanction would have been consistent with NCAA rules or sustainable through internal NCAA appeals. In 2014, the NCAA began restoring some of the football scholarships so that Penn State was able to give 20 in 2014 (for a total of 75), and 25 (a full complement) thereafter so it would have a full allotment of 85 by the 2016 season. The stated reason for reducing this penalty was that the University had made strong good-faith efforts to change its culture by adopting many of the 119 recommendations the Freeh Report had made. In September 2014, the NCAA lifted the ban on post-season play two years earlier than originally imposed, allowing the Penn State football team to play and defeat Boston College by one point in overtime in the New Era Pinstripe Bowl in Yankee Stadium two days after Christmas in 2014.

The legal fallout from all these events was extensive. Many victims of Sandusky's crimes filed lawsuits against Penn State, with the university settling those claims for damages in over 30 cases. Pennsylvania Governor Tom Corbett filed an antitrust suit against the NCAA in January 2013 claiming that its sanctions against Penn State constituted an illegal restraint of trade. The district court granted the NCAA's motion to dismiss on the ground that none of the sanctions had any plausible anticompetitive effect in any relevant market. *Pennsylvania v. NCAA*, 948 F. Supp. 2d 416 (M.D. Pa. 2013).

In February 2013, a report commissioned by Joe Paterno's family found that the Freeh Report was in many respects factually wrong, speculative, and fundamentally flawed. Based on this Report, Coach Paterno's wife and children, his estate, and five members of the Penn State Board filed a lawsuit in Pennsylvania state court claiming that by rushing to judgment and falsely publicly accusing Joe Paterno of covering up Sandusky's criminal behavior, the NCAA and President Emmert had committed various torts and interfered with the NCAA's contract with the University. The plaintiffs in that case sought an injunction setting aside the consent agreement between the NCAA and the Penn State trustees (that it claimed was coerced) and several of the sanctions, including the one that vacated 112 of Coach Paterno's victories.

That same month, the Pennsylvania legislature passed Senate Bill 187, called the Endowment Act, requiring that any fines assessed against Penn State by the NCAA be put into a special trust fund and distributed to the Pennsylvania Commission on Crime and Delinquency to be thereafter paid out to Pennsylvania organizations that fight or treat child abuse.

State Senator Jake Corman and Treasurer Rob McCord then filed suit against the NCAA in state court in Harrisburg seeking to require the NCAA to spend the $60 million in fines collected from Penn State exclusively in Pennsylvania, not only because of the Endowment Act, but also because the monies are state funds legally under the oversight of the Senate Appropriations Committee that Corman chairs. The NCAA then filed a separate suit in federal district court in Harrisburg claiming that the Endowment Act violates the U.S. Constitution because it interferes with a private contract.

In January 2015, the NCAA settled these lawsuits by agreeing to restore the 112 wins it had previously struck from the records (thereby once again making Joe Paterno the winningest Division I-A football coach in history) and to spend the $60 million fine on child abuse prevention and treatment programs in Pennsylvania. Thus, by 2015, the NCAA had either lifted, substantially reduced, or modified all the sanctions imposed against Penn State. Most of the reforms Penn State introduced to persuade the NCAA to lift sanctions remain in place.

In 2018, another sex abuse scandal followed this sordid saga; it involved Larry Nassar, a Michigan State physician. Nassar, a team doctor for USA Gymnastics, molested hundreds of mostly female young athletes, as part of his "medical care." Nassar pleaded guilty to seven counts of criminal sexual conduct, admitting to sexually assaulting and abusing young girls under the guise of providing medical treatment. As part of his plea deal, 144 victims gave victim impact statements. In all, Nassar will be serving three prison sentences, two of 40–125 years for molestation and abuse, and another 60-year sentence for child pornography.

Nassar had been an associate professor at Michigan State since 1997. Questions immediately arose, as with the Penn State scandal, concerning whether the university knew about Nassar's criminal behavior. In the wake of the revelations about Nassar, both the Michigan State president and athletic director resigned. The NCAA sent a letter in January 2018 asking for more information concerning the scandal. Unlike Penn State, it did not commission a law firm to prepare an outside report. In May 2018, Michigan State reported that it did not find any NCAA rules violations in relation to the Larry Nassar case, and in August 2018, the NCAA's enforcement unit confirmed that conclusion. Michigan State agreed in 2018 to pay $500 million to settle claims with more than 300 women and girls who said they were assaulted by Nassar.

The University of Michigan had a similar issue with one of its doctors. Dr. Robert Anderson, a sports doctor, abused over 1,000 people, mostly men during routine medical examinations over a four-decade career. Anderson died in 2003 before the allegations became public, but the University of Michigan agreed to pay victims $490 million in 2022. Many former Michigan football players were among Anderson's victims.

NOTES AND QUESTIONS

1. *Role of the NCAA.* Should the NCAA regulate and punish universities for the criminal activity that occurs in their athletic departments or with their

athletes? Or should the punishments merely be what the criminal justice system elects to impose? In the Penn State case, for instance, the criminal law was able to reach the alleged malfeasance of the administrators, not just Sandusky. Does this make the NCAA's punitive actions not only inappropriate, but also unnecessary? Or should the NCAA intervene as the governing body for intercollegiate sports?

2. *Appropriate Sanctions*. If the NCAA should regulate the criminal conduct of members of university athletic departments, how should it punish any malfeasance? There is a strong case that current athletes should not suffer for the sins of others in the athletic department, but perhaps there should be some sanction, particularly where university officials engage in wrongful or criminal behavior. Do you agree with the NCAA's actions in punishing Penn State? Do you agree with the NCAA's ultimate decision to mitigate Penn State's punishment?

3. *Penn State Versus Michigan State*. What facts might differentiate these cases? What facts might make them similar? Do the NCAA's actions in the *Penn State* case constitute a binding precedent requiring some response?

4. *Role of Infractions*. One of the criticisms of the Penn State decision was that it was made outside of the NCAA's normal infractions process. Was this a wise approach? Why do you think the NCAA did not follow a similar approach with Michigan State?

5. *Oversight*. While the NCAA has clearly distinguished criminal cases from recruiting violation cases, both types of cases assume university responsibility for oversight of third-party behavior. Nevin Shapiro, for instance, was engaged in rules violations for which the university was responsible, because he paid athletes in violation of the amateurism rules.

With respect to Sandusky, and perhaps with respect to Nassar, the basis for NCAA sanctions would be the failure of the university to intervene and stop the behavior at issue. Is holding the university liable for the criminal acts of its employees under NCAA rules the same as holding the university liable for amateurism violations by boosters? What if the acts of the boosters (as in Shapiro's case) involve some kind of criminal activity?

———

Can violating NCAA rules be criminal? In 2017, the U.S. Attorney's for the Southern District of New York filed a number of indictments against basketball coaches, runners, and shoe company executives alleging mass corruption, bribery, and wire fraud. The criminal law theory was that by paying athletes to choose a particular university, these actors deprived the university of an amateur athlete, thereby defrauding the institution.

UNITED STATES V. GATTO

986 F.3d 104 (2nd Cir. 2021)

CHIN, CIRCUIT JUDGE:

In this case, defendants-appellants James Gatto, Merl Code, and Christian Dawkins ("Defendants") were convicted of engaging in a scheme to defraud three universities by paying tens of thousands of dollars to the families of high school basketball players to induce them to attend the universities, which were sponsored by Adidas, the sports apparel company, and covering up the payments so that the recruits could certify to the universities that they had complied with rules of the National Collegiate Athletic Association (the "NCAA") barring student-athletes and recruits from being paid.

At trial, Defendants admitted that they engaged in the scheme and broke NCAA rules, but argued that what they did was not criminal. On appeal, they contend that the government failed to prove that they intended to defraud the universities—North Carolina State University ("N.C. State"), the University of Kansas ("Kansas"), and the University of Louisville ("Louisville") (collectively, the "Universities")—and that their intent instead was to help the Universities by bringing them top recruits to ensure winning basketball programs. They contend that, "in the real world, . . . universities engage in an all-out arms race to recruit the best talent, motivated by the tens of millions of dollars that can be earned each year by a successful men's basketball program," and that they "broke NCAA rules out of a genuine desire to see the Universities' basketball teams succeed." They argue that under-the-table payments to student-athletes are widespread in college sports, and that, indeed, many college coaches are aware of and endorse the practice. And they argue, as they did in their opening statements at trial, that "[t]he kids on the court, . . . the ones whose blood, sweat and tears is making this game a billion dollar industry, they are not allowed to earn a dime."

We have no doubt that a successful men's basketball program is a major source of revenue at certain major universities, but we need not be drawn into the debate over the extent to which college sports is a business. Instead, our task is to determine whether the government proved beyond a reasonable doubt that Defendants knowingly and intentionally engaged in a scheme, through the use of wires, to defraud the Universities of property, *i.e.*, financial aid that they could have given to other students.

* * *

The NCAA . . . promulgates rules that its member universities must follow, among which is the requirement that all student-athletes must remain amateurs to be eligible to compete for their schools. This means that the student-athletes—and their families—may not accept payments of any form for the student-athletes' playing or agreeing to play their sport.

This rule extends from the time when the student-athletes are still in high school and are being recruited to play at the collegiate level.

There are, however, exceptions. Colleges are permitted, for example, to offer athletic-based aid to a certain number of student-athletes, to cover tuition, room, and board. And the schools themselves are permitted to enter into sponsorship agreements with sports apparel brands, which allow them to provide their student-athletes with clothing and footwear that they receive from their corporate sponsors. Essentially, these sponsorship agreements are marketing deals. Major sports apparel brands, including Adidas, Nike, and Under Armour, enter into such contracts to promote their brands. Under these agreements, student-athletes must wear the brand of the company their school has partnered with when they compete for their school—that is, at practice and during games.

II. *The Scheme*

Gatto was Adidas's director of global sports marketing for basketball. He managed the sports marketing budget, and part of his job entailed overseeing the relationship that Adidas had with various schools, including N.C. State, Kansas, and Louisville. This included helping to ensure the success of the sponsorship agreements Adidas signed with the Universities pursuant to which Adidas paid the Universities for the right to provide their NCAA sports teams with Adidas apparel.

Gatto worked with Code and Thomas Joseph Gassnola, both Adidas consultants. He also worked informally with Dawkins, an aspiring sports agent, and Munish Sood, a financial advisor. Together, these men paid the families of top-tier high school basketball recruits—including Dennis Smith Jr., Billy Preston, and Brian Bowen Jr. (collectively, the "Recruits")—to entice those players to enroll at one of the Universities. This activity violated NCAA rules, and if the NCAA were to discover the payments, the players would not be permitted to play in games and the Universities would be subject to penalties. As a result, Defendants and those who assisted them concealed these payments by falsifying Adidas invoices to make it seem as though the payments were going to youth basketball teams affiliated with the Amateur Athletic Union ("AAU"), a non-profit, multi-sport organization that, among other things, facilitates youth basketball tournaments. In reality, the money was being funneled through AAU teams with which some Defendants were affiliated to the families of top basketball prospects. In addition to creating fake expense reports to mask these payments, Defendants used phones that were not registered in their names while communicating with the Recruits' families.

Per the NCAA bylaws, every member institution must certify that its prospective student-athletes are amateurs and thus eligible to compete. Consequently, the Universities required all their recruits to sign paperwork attesting that they were aware of and in compliance with the NCAA bylaws. By signing the certifications, the recruits affirmed, among other things, that they had not used their "athletics skill (directly or indirectly) for pay in any form in that sport." A recruit's athletic-based aid was contingent upon his certifying his eligibility. Those in charge of compliance at the Universities explained that they would have never awarded athletic-based aid to the Recruits had they known they were ineligible to compete, and the head coaches' contracts required the coaches to be stewards of the NCAA rules and report any suspected violations.

A. N.C. State

Smith verbally committed to play basketball for N.C. State in September 2015. At the time, he was one of the top recruits in North Carolina, but, according to Gassnola, there were rumors that he was going to change his mind about which college he would attend. To ensure that Smith enrolled at N.C. State, Gassnola gave the Smith family $40,000 in the Fall 2015. He was reimbursed by Adidas via Gatto, who filed false invoices to facilitate the repayment. Shortly after the Smith family received the $40,000 payment, Smith signed forms enrolling at N.C. State indicating that he was compliant with the NCAA eligibility rules. He played one season at N.C. State before being selected as the ninth overall pick in the 2017 NBA Draft.

B. Kansas

Preston verbally committed to play for Kansas in Fall 2016. After Preston committed, however, Gassnola heard that the Preston family was accepting money from sports agents and financial advisors, thereby putting Preston's eligibility in jeopardy. Because, according to Gassnola, he thought that he was better-equipped to prevent illicit payments from being discovered, Gassnola arranged to pay the Preston family to stop them from taking money from others and preserve Preston's NCAA eligibility. With Gatto's permission, Gassnola paid the Preston family around $50,000. Gassnola paid the money and then, with the help of Gatto, submitted false AAU expense reports to Adidas for reimbursement. In November 2016, Preston signed forms indicating that he was compliant with the NCAA eligibility rules. His ineligibility, however, was discovered, and he never played for Kansas.

C. Louisville

Bowen committed to play for Louisville in May 2017. Around the same time, Bowen's family agreed to accept $100,000 from Adidas, to be paid in four installments. These payments were to be funneled through an AAU program with which Code was affiliated. On June 1, 2017 and June 9, 2017, Bowen signed forms accepting athletic-based aid and indicating that he was compliant with the NCAA eligibility rules. Around a month later, on July 13, 2017, Bowen's father was paid the first installment of $25,000. Defendants were arrested before any other payments were made, and

Bowen, whom Louisville decided to withhold from competition, withdrew from Louisville after one semester to play professional basketball.

* * *

On October 24, 2018, the jury found Defendants guilty of wire fraud and conspiracy to commit wire fraud. . . . Defendants were sentenced in March 2019—Gatto principally to nine months' imprisonment and Code and Dawkins principally to six months' imprisonment each.

* * *

On appeal, Defendants raise three principal arguments: (1) there was insufficient evidence to sustain their wire fraud and conspiracy to commit wire fraud convictions; (2) the district court abused its discretion in excluding evidence; and (3) the district court erroneously instructed the jury. . . .

* * *

To convict a defendant of wire fraud, the government must prove beyond a reasonable doubt: "(1) a scheme to defraud, (2) money or property as the object of the scheme, and (3) use of the . . . wires to further the scheme." . . .

As to the "scheme to defraud" element, there must be "proof that defendants possessed a fraudulent intent." *United States v. Starr*, 816 F.2d 94, 98 (2d Cir. 1987). Accordingly, defendants must either intend to harm their victim or contemplate that their victim may be harmed. ("Although the government is not required to prove actual injury, it must, at a minimum, prove that defendants *contemplated* some actual harm or injury to their victims. . . .") . . .

As to the "object of the scheme" element, a defendant need not literally obtain money or property—in the sense of putting money into his own pocket—to violate the wire fraud statute. . . . And because individuals have the right to control their property, depriving the victim of "economic information it would consider valuable in deciding how to use its assets" satisfies the object-of-the-scheme element. *United States v. Finazzo*, 850 F.3d 94, 111 (2d Cir. 2017). Still, as the Supreme Court recently noted, "a property fraud conviction cannot stand when the loss to the victim is only an incidental byproduct of the scheme." *Kelly v. United States*, ___ U.S. ___, 140 S. Ct. 1565, 1573 (2020). Loss to the victim "must play more than some bit part in a scheme: It must be an object of the fraud."

. . . Defendants argue that they "were convicted of a fraud they did not know about." In other words, they contend that there was no scheme to defraud because Defendants did not know that false representations would be made to the Universities. Defendants also argue that even if there were such a scheme, the government failed to prove that the Universities' athletic-based aid was an object of that scheme. We disagree in both respects.

1. *Scheme to Defraud*

Defendants have not shown that the government failed to present enough evidence for "*any* rational trier of fact," *Jackson*, 443 U.S. at 319, to find, beyond a reasonable doubt, that there was a scheme to defraud . . .

First, Defendants were sophisticated actors who were involved in all aspects of top-tier basketball in America, including the amateur grassroots leagues, college basketball programs, and the NBA. Gatto was the head of global sports marketing for Adidas, one of the top sports apparel companies in the world, and he was in charge of Adidas's entire basketball marketing budget. Code worked for Nike, another top apparel company, for fourteen years where he cultivated relationships with grassroots, high school, and college basketball programs before he began consulting for Adidas. And Dawkins spent time working for a sports agency recruiting NBA prospects. The jury was therefore presented with evidence of Defendants' proximity to—and involvement in—all things basketball.

Second, Defendants went to great lengths to prevent both Adidas and the Universities from discovering that they were paying the Recruits' families. Defendants worked together to disguise their funneling of tens of thousands of dollars to the Recruits' families to induce the Recruits to enroll at Adidas-sponsored schools. Indeed, Defendants had to lie to Adidas to get reimbursed for these secretive payments, as those in charge of the budget at Adidas knew the payments violated both "NCAA regulation and Adidas policy" and would not have signed off on them had they known the truth. Their furtive behavior indicates that they knew their actions were wrong. When coupled with their sophistication, it was reasonable for the jury to infer they knew the Recruits had to deceive the Universities about their eligibility.

Third, Defendants' co-conspirators admitted on wiretaps that their conduct violated NCAA rules. Gassnola, who worked directly under Gatto, explained to the jury that had the Universities learned that Smith's family had been paid, he "would have been deemed ineligible" and "would never have played [at N.C. State]." Sood, another co-conspirator, stated that he knew that giving money to NCAA athletes was not permitted under NCAA rules and could have led to those players losing their scholarships. . . .

Fourth, Code and Dawkins acknowledged that Bowen had to sign an NCAA form for his commitment to Louisville to be complete. And Dawkins was recorded on a wiretap discussing the need to avoid a paper trail "because some of it is whatever you want to call it, illegal, against NCAA rules, or whatever." Accordingly, these statements, together with Defendants' sophistication, steps taken to conceal their actions, and co-conspirators' statements, surely show that Defendants knew that the

Recruits had to sign eligibility forms to compete in the NCAA, and constituted sufficient evidence for the jury to find that Defendants knew a materially false representation had to be made for the scheme to succeed. *See United States v. Reifler*, 446 F.3d 65, 96 (2d Cir. 2006).

2. *Object of Scheme*

Similarly, the jury was also presented with enough evidence for a rational trier of fact to find that the Universities' athletic-based aid was "an object" of their scheme. *See Kelly*, 140 S. Ct. at 1573; *see also* 18 U.S.C. § 1343. In *Kelly*, better known as the "Bridgegate" case, state officials devised a scheme to punish the mayor of Fort Lee, New Jersey, for declining to endorse the incumbent New Jersey governor in his reelection bid. To do so, politically appointed Port Authority officials closed traffic lanes that led from Fort Lee to the George Washington Bridge for four days under the guise that they were conducting a traffic study. The study, however, was a sham; no official was interested in the data it produced. The government charged the officials with property fraud, arguing that they commandeered the traffic lanes and deprived the state of property by paying extra wages to perpetuate the scheme. The officials who did not plead guilty went to trial and were convicted, but the Supreme Court overturned their convictions.

The unanimous *Kelly* Court found that property was not an object of the scheme. It explained that the traffic study was a "sham," intended only to cover up the defendants' misconduct and the additional wages were "implementation costs" that only became necessary because an additional toll booth operator was needed after the original plan was altered to avoid traffic accidents. Because the officials' only goal was political retaliation—to create a headache for the Fort Lee mayor—and the officials were indifferent about the unintended additional costs of carrying out the plan, they were not guilty of property fraud. The *Kelly* Court held that "a property fraud conviction cannot stand when the loss to the victim is only an incidental byproduct of the scheme."

This case is different from *Kelly*. Here, the loss of property—the Universities' funds set aside for financial aid—was at the heart of Defendants' scheme. Their original plan included inducing the Universities to give the Recruits financial aid by concealing from the Universities the payments made to the Recruits' families in fear that if they were discovered the Recruits would not be permitted to compete. Importantly, the scheme depended on the Universities awarding ineligible student-athletes athletic-based aid; without the aid, the recruits would have gone elsewhere. And if the Recruits' ineligibility had been discovered by the schools, the scheme would have failed. After all, the Recruits would have never been permitted to play in the NCAA for Adidas-sponsored schools, defeating the purpose of the payments and potentially derailing the Recruits' professional careers.

Defendants have asserted that they intended to "assist the Universities' recruiting efforts" by luring the best basketball players to Adidas-sponsored schools to better market their brand. Defendants may have had multiple objectives, but property need only be "*an* object" of their scheme, not the sole or primary goal. Unlike in *Kelly*, where there was a sham study and additional wages were paid only after the original plan was scaled back due to safety concerns, here, depriving Universities of athletic-based aid was at the *center* of the plan.

Finally, the evidence, construed in the government's favor, showed that Defendants deprived the Universities of information that would have helped them decide whether to award the Recruits athletic-based aid. This deprivation was enough to support a wire fraud conviction. *See Finazzo*, 850 F.3d at 111. As discussed above, hiding the Recruits' ineligibility was essential to Defendants' scheme—had the Universities known the Recruits were ineligible, they would not have offered them athletic-based aid or roster spots on their basketball teams. Similarly, it was reasonable for the jury to find that Defendants knew the Recruits had to misrepresent their eligibility to deceive the Universities into giving them athletic-based aid. Thus, it is evident that Defendants' scheme facilitated the withholding of valuable information that would have caused the Universities not to dispense with their property. *See United States v. Lebedev*, 932 F.3d 40, 48–49 (2d Cir. 2019). Accordingly, we conclude that the jury rationally found that Defendants committed wire fraud.

[The Court rejected the Defendants' argument that it erroneously excluded expert testimony about the benefits of a basketball program to a university. The Court also upheld the district court's decision to bar evidence of phone calls to recruits not at issue in the case and evidence of other recruiting violations. The Court also concluded that there were no errors in the jury instructions.]

* * *

1. *Phone Calls*

... Defendants also take issue with the district court's exclusion of other phone calls in which various NCAA coaches purportedly encouraged Defendants to violate the amateurism rules. Defendants contend that this evidence proved they were doing "what the Universities wanted and expected their corporate apparel sponsors to do." Appellants' Br. at 114. They also argue that the calls would have contradicted the testimony of Gassnola, one of the government's cooperating witnesses. The district court, however, found the prejudicial effect of these calls to substantially outweigh their probative value, and it did not admit them. This was not an abuse of discretion.

First, at least one coach on these calls worked at a school not involved in this case, and therefore his discussion of practices elsewhere had little relevance here. Second, to the extent the calls were relevant, allowing such testimony could have confused the jury, as it would have required the jury to learn about individuals not involved in the case. Third, even if we accept that coaches encouraged NCAA recruiting violations—there was testimony, for example, that Pitino, Louisville's coach, needed "[p]lausible deniability,"—that the coaches asked Defendants to pay the Recruits' families was *not* a defense unless, as we discuss further below, the coaches were unconflicted and acting in good faith on behalf of their Universities, *see D'Amato*, 39 F.3d at 1257–58. In addition, a closer examination of the calls Defendants sought to admit further refutes this argument. When the topic of compensating recruits came up, for example, one coach said: "I have got to shut my door." That this coach did not want to have a conversation about violating NCAA rules with his door open indicates that his school did not condone such behavior. Another coach said he kept his relationship with Dawkins "off the book," which the jury reasonably could have understood to mean off the record. Thus, this evidence is of limited utility to the extent it supposedly proves that Defendants believed they were doing what the Universities here wanted, as it cuts against any argument that the coaches were unconflicted and acting in good faith. *See D'Amato*, 39 F.3d at 1257–58. Accordingly, the district court did not abuse its discretion in excluding the evidence.

* * *

B. *"Obtain"*

A defendant is guilty of wire fraud if he "devises or intends to devise any scheme or artifice to defraud, or for *obtaining* money or property by means of false or fraudulent pretenses, representations, or promises" and uses wires to further that scheme. 18 U.S.C. § 1343. Defendants argue that a plain reading of the statute makes it clear that the law requires that property or money be obtained *by* the defendant *from* the victim, and the district court erred by not making this clear to the jury. We are not persuaded.

* * *

Nor are we bound or persuaded by the out-of-circuit precedent that Defendants cite.... In *United States v. Walters*, the Seventh Circuit explained that "[l]osses that occur as byproducts of a deceitful scheme do not satisfy the statutory requirement" for property fraud. 997 F.2d 1219, 1227 (7th Cir. 1993). We do not quarrel with this rule, which was recently reaffirmed by the Supreme Court. *See Kelly*, 140 S. Ct. at 1573. The facts of *Walters*, however, are distinguishable.

Norby Walters was an aspiring sports agent who gave NCAA student-athletes cars and money with the hope that they would retain him as their agent when they turned professional. *Walters*, 997 F.2d at 1221. This, of course, violated the NCAA's amateurism rules. The Seventh Circuit noted that because "[t]he athletes' pro prospects depended on successful completion of their collegiate careers," it could "assume that Walters knew that the universities would ask [the] athletes to verify that they were eligible to compete as amateurs," and Walters "promised to lie to the universities" about the payments if asked.

The *Walters* Court acknowledged that the case was close: "Everything . . . turns on matters of degree. Did the schemers foresee that the mails would be used? Did the mailing advance the success of the scheme? Which parts of a scheme are 'essential'? Such questions lack obviously right answers." Ultimately, the Court found that Walters did not "conceive a scheme in which mailings played a role." In other words, Walters did not satisfy a critical element of the mail fraud statute: he did not intend to mail anything. ("For all Walters cared, the [eligibility] forms could sit forever in cartons. Movement to someplace else was irrelevant."). Here, the equivalent element in the wire fraud statute is the use of wires, which Defendants do not—and cannot—dispute. Accordingly, Defendants' reliance on *Walters* is misplaced, and, for the reasons noted above, the district court did not err in its instructions on the meaning of "obtain."

* * *

At trial, Defendants argued that their intent was not to harm but to help the Universities, and they also sought to offer evidence that they were not the only individuals who have paid high school basketball recruits to attend certain universities. The ends, however, do not justify the means, and that others are engaging in improper behavior does not make it lawful. . . .

Defendants concede that they broke the NCAA rules, but contend that they did not act criminally. But "the essence of fraud is misrepresentation, made with the intent to induce another person to take action without the relevant facts necessary to make an informed . . . decision." *United States v. Rutigliano*, 887 F.3d 98, 109 (2d Cir. 2018). Fraud involves "a departure from fundamental honesty, moral uprightness, or fair play," *United States v. Ragosta*, 970 F.2d 1085, 1090 (2d Cir. 1992), and depriving one of property through "dishonest methods or schemes" or "trick, deceit, chicane or overreaching." Here, as the jury could have reasonably found, Defendants deprived the Universities of property—athletic-based aid that they could have awarded to students who were eligible to play—by breaking NCAA rules and depriving the Universities of relevant information through fundamentally dishonest means.

For the foregoing reasons, the judgments of the district court are **AFFIRMED**.

* * *

GERARD E. LYNCH, CIRCUIT JUDGE, concurring in part and dissenting in part:

* * *

B. *Calls Between Defendants and Coaches*

The district court also excluded certain calls between a defendant and a representative of a school. The defendants argue that these calls corroborated their claim "that the basketball coaches at the Universities specifically asked them to break NCAA rules" and helped refute testimony from a witness who testified that Kansas basketball coaches "wouldn't have liked it very much" if they had been told of the payments to the recruits' families. The district court excluded the calls as irrelevant and prejudicial, and the majority lumps them together and upholds the district court's decision. . . .

But two of the excluded calls involved coaches from the universities in this case, and the majority glosses over the probative value of those calls. In one, Dawkins and a Louisville assistant coach discussed a recent business dinner the coach had attended where one of his associates "was trying to pick [his] brain on [Dawkins]." The coach told the associate that he "[doesn't] really talk about" his and Dawkins's relationship; he keeps that connection "off the book[s]." In another call, a Kansas assistant coach called Code to discuss a different recruit who is not implicated in the conduct charged in this case. In that call, the coach described the recruit's family "ask[ing] about some stuff." The coach told the family "we'll talk about that if you decide [to come to Kansas]." The coach then told Code "I've got to just try to work and figure out a way. Because if that's what it takes to get him[,] . . . we're going to have to do it some way." The coach stated that he would "talk with Jimmy [Gatto]" about funneling money to the family through an amateur team. Code says he will "talk to Jim today too." The coach then described how he might also ask Gatto to help pay for the recruit's brother to visit Kansas despite acknowledging "not [being] allowed to pay for it."

. . . The evidence from which the majority infers that these coaches were *not* unconflicted and were acting in bad faith should have been left to the jury. The majority cites a conversation between Code and Dawkins in which they reference their understanding that Head Coach Rick Pitino of Louisville wanted "plausible deniability" about recruiting infractions. But that Pitino wanted plausible deniability does not necessarily mean that he knew Louisville would not tolerate cheating. It could equally well mean that he was speaking for the university itself, which (the defendants' theory held) wanted to get winning players but also wanted precisely such deniability.

The majority also cites the coaches' conduct on two of the excluded calls as indicative of conflict. In one call, the coach closed his door while talking on the phone. In another, the coach made statements about keeping his relationship with Dawkins off the books. But while these actions could be construed, as the majority interprets them, as "cut[ting] against any argument that the coaches were unconflicted and acting in good faith," they could also have indicated that the universities wanted deniability as to impropriety that they condoned. It all depends on from whom the coaches wanted to keep things secret. A reasonable jury could infer that the coaches were afraid not that the universities would disapprove of their condoning the defendants' conduct, but that the coaches knew—as defendants argued—that the universities could not tolerate *having it known* that they were condoning it. This is a subtle but important distinction. A coach would not be conflicted if he was doing exactly what the university wanted: winking at the defendants' off-the-books payments to players' families, but preserving the façade that he was not involved and did not know what was going on. . . .

But was the probative value of these two calls high enough to make the district court's decision under Rule 403 arbitrary and irrational? In the first call, the coach implied that his relationship with Dawkins was something that he needed to hide by keeping it "off the book[s]." On the call, the coach referred to Louisville's success in recruiting "five-stars" that year and opined that this was the "[b]est class in Coach Pitino's history." Dawkins then replies "[o]n the heels of a . . . whore scandal," referencing the misconduct reported in the COI findings. The call did not directly implicate the assistant coach (or Louisville) in Dawkins's rule-breaking. The coach did not say, for example, that he kept his relationship with Dawkins off the books because Dawkins was assisting his team to recruit players in ways that broke NCAA rules—though of course the jury could have certainly inferred as much from the call. The call's probative value is also reduced by the fact that the coach in question was only a young assistant, far removed from the policy-making apparatus of the university.

Still, the conversation cannot be considered mere evidence of generalized corruption in college athletics. It involves statements made to one of the defendants by a basketball coach who was a key point of contact for that defendant with Louisville. If the government is going to prosecute people at Dawkins's level, who are not likely to have direct contact with university presidents, athletic directors, or even head coaches, excluding evidence of what such defendants were told by university officials at their own level cannot be justified.

In the second call, an assistant coach from Kansas directly discussed rule-breaking with Code, though the recruit at issue was not implicated in the conduct charged in this case. The coach said that he needed "to figure out a way" to get money and housing for a recruit's family, and admitted that he would have to route the money through a third party to avoid detection by the NCAA. The coach then mentioned that he would talk with

Jimmy Gatto—another defendant in this case—about how to get the money to the family. Surely a conversation in which a coach from a victim university discusses with one defendant soliciting help from another defendant to break the NCAA rules would be extremely relevant to whether those defendants believe that the university the coach represents condones such rule-breaking.

On the one hand, the defendants' case hinged on showing that they believed they were not deceiving the universities, but they had few opportunities to make their case to the jury. On the other hand, the government was able to prove intent from "the scheme itself" if "the necessary result of the . . . scheme [was] to injure others." *D'Amato*, 39 F.3d at 1257. Thus, the probative value of these calls, when considering that the central defense was to challenge scienter, was high. Though these are close and difficult judgments to make, I respectfully conclude that the district court's evidentiary rulings failed to appreciate the substantial probative value of these calls.

* * *

I cannot find, with high probability, that the district court's exclusion of the call between Code and the assistant coach from Kansas did not affect Gatto's conviction for wire fraud as to Kansas. . . .

The district court's exclusion of the call between Dawkins and the assistant coach from Louisville was not harmless as to Dawkins's convictions . . .

In excluding the call, the district court may have substantially affected the jury's decision to find Dawkins guilty of wire fraud as to Louisville, and the error also necessarily affected Dawkins's conviction on the conspiracy count. . . . By excluding the calls, the district court erroneously deprived Gatto and Dawkins of a fair opportunity to convince the jury that they did not intend to deceive the victim universities. Thus, I would overturn Gatto's conviction on count three and Dawkins's convictions on counts one and two.

* * *

Here, the defendants' argument was that the things the government said they stole from the universities—the scholarship money provided to the athletes and the university's ability to comply with NCAA rules and avoid penalties—were things that they reasonably believed the universities were in fact happy enough to give up in the pursuit of greater financial benefit. The defendants claimed to believe that by not openly acknowledging the rules violations they committed, they were deceiving no one, because the universities in fact knew that such violations happened regularly. The universities did not know of the specific payments made by these particular defendants not because the defendants pulled the wool over the victims' eyes, but because the alleged victims desired not to know too much, in order to preserve a hypocritical pretense of compliance while pursuing the financial and reputational benefits of maintaining successful athletic programs without paying the athletes whose skills and hard work generate the profits that go to the adult coaches and schools.

Such a cynical theory may be a caricature of how college sports are in fact conducted. No doubt many university officials and athletic coaches genuinely attempt to comply with rules derived from a model of amateurism that some others desecrate, and that is difficult to maintain in a world where winning games and making money can come to be seen as the highest goals. To whatever extent the defendants' professed beliefs correspond to reality, evidence to that effect would be difficult to come by; the essence of the defense is that the universities *pretended* to want to run clean programs, and that this pretense required those who funneled payments to hard-pressed families of student athletes to operate in secret, *as if* they were deceiving universities that themselves were trying to hide what makes their programs successful. And in the absence of evidence directly supporting their claims, defendants fell back on evidence that provides only limited, indirect support for their specific theory, and that does so by painting a grim picture of widespread corruption and hypocrisy without quite engaging the government's evidence suggesting that at least these particular victims were genuinely defrauded.

The district court was ultimately right to try to prevent the defendants from putting the entire NCAA system on trial for its exploitation of athletes under circumstances that make violations of the sort in which these defendants engaged all but inevitable, or even to appear morally justified in providing some recompense to those whose labor generates the money that enriches others. . . .

By the same token, a venture into the underside of college athletic recruiting opens up significant questions about the motivations and beliefs of the participants. We should be particularly careful not to sweep too broadly in declaring out of bounds evidence that does indeed support the defendants' claims about what they believed. The cynicism of their claimed beliefs does not do them much credit, but on this record one is left with a queasy feeling that the deeper cynicism may be in the system within which they operate.

People like the defendants operate at the seamiest margin of amateur sports. They (and the athletes and their families who succumb to their offers) are violating the rules by which the universities, cynically or sincerely, have agreed to be bound—rules of which the athletes are well aware, and with which they are required to represent that they have complied. And such violations are not victimless. Only a few athletes have the talent to skip the college game and succeed at the highest professional level. A few more are realistic candidates for such success, if they are properly trained and groomed by the opportunity to compete in college programs. Most who compete in college have an opportunity to earn a degree that will stand them in good stead even if they do not play professional sports—but only if they can pay for their education with their labor on behalf of the school's teams. But all are vulnerable to losing those scholarships, and having their vocational training disrupted, if they are publicly known to have violated the rules. Whether or not those who bribe aspiring athletes to sign onto a particular college's basketball program have defrauded the universities, they expose the youthful athletes to a high degree of risk.

It is not for judges to decide whether it makes sense to use federal law enforcement revenues to pursue the relatively low-level agents of corruption in this system. Our only responsibility is to decide whether the defendants have been tried and convicted on the charges brought against them in accordance with the law, including the applicable rules of evidence. . . .

NOTES AND QUESTIONS

1.   *Aftermath.* The NCAA responded swiftly to the announcement of the investigation, as it was clearly keen on protecting March Madness, its entire source of revenue. It created the Independent Commission on College Basketball led by Condoleezza Rice. The Commission proposed a number of reforms subsequently adopted by the NCAA, including the creation of the IARP discussed in Section C, *supra*, and allowing basketball players to hire agents and enter the NBA draft without losing their eligibility.

2.   *After NIL.* After the passage of state NIL laws (discussed in Chapter 12), boosters providing payments to prospective college athletes does not violate NCAA rules and would not presumably be criminal as long as the remuneration was for use of the athlete's NIL. NCAA rules, though, bar using these deals as an inducement to sign with a particular school or transfer to a particular school. As with *Gatto*, this behavior could, in theory, be criminal. Is there a clear way to distinguish between what conduct follows NCAA rules as opposed to what violates them with these NIL deals? Is there a similarly thin line separating what NIL conduct is legal and what is felonious?

3.   *The Peculiar Dynamics of the Shoe Industry's Involvement in Youth Basketball.* Under the NBA collective bargaining agreement, players are free to select their own shoes and are free to endorse shoe and apparel companies independently of club or league sponsorships. For the overwhelming majority of NBA players, their professionally chosen shoe of choice is from the shoe company that sponsored their youth sports team or that is the official sponsor of the university where they played college basketball.

CHAPTER 14

EQUITY IN SPORTS

■ ■ ■

A. RACE

1. DESEGREGATION AND AMERICAN ATHLETICS

Athletic competitions provided some of the most important cultural events of the twentieth century for Black Americans as they struggled to emerge from the injustices of Jim Crow segregation and subordination. Three events stand out. Two of them were in the 1930s and involved individual sports: Jesse Owens capturing four gold medals in the 1936 Olympics held in Berlin in front of one of the century's most vicious racists, Adolf Hitler, and Joe Louis's first round knockout of the German Max Schmeling in1938 to retain the heavy weight-boxing crown. The latter may have been even more meaningful for most Black Americans, as boxing was second only to baseball in popularity as a professional American sport at the time and Louis was a hero throughout many Black communities. His enlistment in the World War II armed forces extended his popularity.

The third event involved the team sport of baseball, what was then called the National Pastime. In April 1947, Branch Rickey, the General Manager of the Brooklyn Dodgers, took the first step in desegregating major league baseball by adding Jackie Robinson to the Dodgers roster. It should and could have happened sooner, as there were many great ball players in the Negro Leagues, whose earlier excellence has now been recognized by the Baseball Hall of Fame. That competitive clubs did not desegregate sooner shows that competition is not always sufficient to eliminate injustices caused by cultural norms and the tacit agreements they support. That the desegregation of baseball happened when it did proves that cultural change can precede and even spur legal change. Joe Louis and many other Black athletes had fought in World War II, a war against a particularly horrible, racist regime. When they came home, their claim for change was stronger than ever. With Robinson making an impact at the plate and on the bases for the Dodgers, competition spurred desegregation in both leagues. The Cleveland Indians and St. Louis Browns followed in the American League later in 1947. The New York Giants, the Dodgers cross-town rival, added a Black player in 1949 and several more, including Willie Mays, in 1951. When the Boston Red Sox finally enlisted utility infielder Pumpsie Green in 1959, every major league franchise had at least one Black player.

954   EQUITY IN SPORTS   CH. 14

In the three decades from 1968 to 1998, Black baseball players comprised between 14.5% and 19% of MLB rosters. That percentage has declined over the past quarter century. Black players in 2022 constituted only 7.2% of major league rosters. Latino players, many of whom have some African heritage, now constitute over 25% of such rosters, however, and no one claims that MLB teams are still discriminating in their selection of players.[1]

The two North American professional sports leagues in which Black athletes now play a dominant role were not yet as popular as baseball in the post-war years, but their post-war story of integration spurred by competition for the sports dollar is similar. The NBA was formed in 1949 by a merger of two smaller predecessor leagues that did not employ Black basketball players. By the following year, three Black athletes were under contract with three different teams. By the end of the decade, several Black stars had emerged, including Maurice Stokes (whose career lasted only three years because of a tragic on-court brain injury), Bill Russell, Elgin Baylor, and Wilt Chamberlin, with Oscar Robertson waiting to join in 1960. In 1964, Celtic coach Red Auerbach substituted recently acquired veteran Willie Naulls for an injured Tommy Heinsohn to form the NBA's first all-Black starting five (Naulls, Russell, Sam and K.C. Jones, and Satch Sanders), apparently breaking a "gentleman's agreement" between the clubs to have one white player on the court at all times. Two years later Russell became the Celtic's coach, the first Black coach of a major American sports franchise's team.

Although the NFL had some Black players in the early years of the twentieth century, by the 1930s the league had fully succumbed to Jim Crow rules as it attempted to grow. This also changed in the aftermath of the War, however. In 1946, the Los Angeles Rams, under pressure from the publicly owned L.A. Coliseum where they played, brought two Black ex-UCLA stars, Kenny Washington and (future Hollywood actor) Woody Strode on to their squad. (This was a few months before the Dodgers played Jackie Robinson, Washington's and Strode's 1939 UCLA "Gold Dust Trio" backfield-mate, as their 1947 opening day first baseman.) The Cleveland Browns of the competing professional All-American Football Conference (AAFC) also brought two black players on to their team in 1946, Marion Motley and Bill Willis. With Willis blocking in front of him, Motley became the most productive running back in professional football as the Browns

---

[1]   There have been many reasons offered for the decline in the percentages of Black North Americans in baseball, including competition from youth basketball and football, and the urbanization of African American culture. MLB has made greater recent efforts to appeal to inner city youth. One of the authors of this casebook proposes providing teams with the same incentives to recruit and develop American Blacks that the teams have had to recruit international players not subject to the MLB draft. See Stephen F. Ross and Michael James, Jr., *A Strategic Legal Challenge to the Unforeseen Anticompetitive and Racially Discriminatory Effects of Baseball's North American Draft*, 115 COL. L. REV. sidebar 129 (2015). The institution over the next few years of an international draft, however, is probable, while the elimination of the domestic draft is hard to imagine.

won four consecutive AAFC championships and then an NFL crown in 1950 after the AAFC folded and the Browns were absorbed by the NFL. In 1952, other NFL teams started signing more and more successful Black players, except for the Washington Redskins, whose overtly segregationist owner only relented in 1962 under pressure from the federal government, the lessor of the stadium used by the Redskins. The integration of NFL teams was a gradual process, more rapid in the AFL before the 1970 merger. Some positions seemed resistant to change, however. This was particularly true for quarterbacks, at least until a gradual change after the success of Warren Moon and Randall Cunningham in the 80s and 90s, and the success of Doug Williams in Super Bowl XXII in 1987, appropriately enough for the Redskins, under new ownership.

The post-war story in college sports is similar. Competition and the lure of enhanced revenue, not law, spurred change. Prior to World War II, prominent Black athletes competed in football, basketball, baseball, and track at many non-Southern schools. Yet, most of these athletes were isolated players on their teams and campuses. After the war opportunities started to gradually expand with the appeal of college sports and their potential as revenue generators.

It was not until the 1960s, however, as the post-war Civil Rights movement reached its zenith that Southern schools eased their rigid application of Jim Crow to college sports. The color line was broken in 1963 in the Atlantic Coast Conference and two years later in the then primarily Texan Southwest Conference. The University of Kentucky signed the Southeastern Conference's first two black football recruits for the 1966 season, but it was the loss of the all-White Kentucky basketball team in the finals of the NCAA tournament that same year that is remembered as the final turning point. Kentucky's loss was to Texas Western, whose coach Don Haskins started five Black basketball players for the first time in NCAA tournament history. Adolph Rupp, Kentucky's coach, then started to recruit Black players to remain competitive. And so did Alabama's famed Bear Bryant after Sam Cunningham, an All-American running back at the University of Southern California, helped embarrass Bryant's all-White defensive unit in a lopsided 1970 football game. By 1971, all SEC schools had integrated their football squads.

2. TITLE VII OF THE 1964 CIVIL RIGHTS ACT

The Civil Rights movement and cultural change that yielded this desegregation of professional and college sports was not dependent upon any new laws or judicial rulings. The same movement and change, however, did lead to important legal changes that are important for racial equity in sports. Most important was Title VII of the 1964 Civil Rights Act, which prohibits race-based (as well as color, national origin, religion and sex-based) discrimination in employment. Title VII, beyond the cultural and political change that helped generate it, may be more important to the control of race discrimination in the employment of coaches and other managerial personnel than for athletes in competition. The costs of discrimination in the selection of those not in direct competition on the playing field or court are less obvious.

Proving a violation of Title VII and other anti-discrimination laws predictably is difficult to the extent it depends on the proof of internal motivation that is not always made manifest by speech or external actions. In its first interpretations of Title VII, however, the Supreme Court provided two alternative routes to proving discrimination that have assisted many plaintiffs. Those alternative routes are both described in the following unsuccessful case involving a claim of race discrimination by a Black applicant for a coaching position.

JACKSON V. UNIVERSITY OF NEW HAVEN

228 F.Supp.2d 156 (D. Conn. 2002)

DRONEY, DISTRICT JUDGE.

I. *Introduction*

James C. Jackson ("Jackson") brought this action against the University of New Haven ("UNH") and Deborah Chin, the Athletic Director of UNH, alleging racial discrimination in hiring in violation of 42 U.S.C. § 1981, 42 U.S.C. § 2000d (Title VI) [prohibiting discrimination by entities receiving federal financial assistance], and 42 U.S.C. § 2000e–5 (Title VII). Jackson seeks damages as well as equitable relief, costs, and attorney's fees. Pending before the Court is Defendants' Motion for Summary Judgment. For the following reasons, the motion is GRANTED.

II. *Facts*

In February 1999 the head football coach at the University of New Haven ("UNH") left to take a position with the Cleveland Browns of the National Football League. This dispute arises out of the ensuing search for a new head coach at UNH.

Beginning in early February of 1999, UNH posted the head coach position both internally and with the "NCAA market," an online professional publication for university and college athletics. The postings for the head coaching position listed the following requirements:

> A bachelors degree is required, master's degree preferred. *Successful collegiate coaching experience required.* Experience in recruiting, game coaching and knowledge of NCAA rules and regulations is essential.

Further, the duties were listed as follows:

Implement and manage all aspects of a national caliber Division II football program in accordance with NCAA and university regulations. Areas of responsibility include, but are not limited to coaching, recruiting qualified student athletes, budget management, scheduling, hiring and supervising coaching staff, academically monitoring student-athletes, and promotions and fund-raising.

After receiving 36 applications, UNH's Search Committee, which had been established to select a new head coach, decided to interview six applicants-all of whom had college coaching experience and are Caucasian. Jackson, an African-American, was not among the six applicants interviewed. Jackson had no college experience, but had been a professional minor league football coach, earned several "coach of the year" honors as such a coach, and was inducted into the minor league football hall of fame. The defendants assert that they decided not to interview Jackson because he lacked the requisite collegiate coaching experience. From the six applicants interviewed, the Search Committee ultimately selected Darren Rizzi, who had been an assistant coach at UNH for four years, to fill the position of head coach.

At the heart of this dispute lies the "collegiate coaching experience" requirement. The parties are in agreement that the posted job qualifications included that requirement and that all of the applicants selected for interviews possessed such experience. However, the parties differ markedly in their characterizations of that prior experience requirement. The defendants maintain that prior NCAA coaching experience was essential to ensure the selection of a candidate sufficiently well-versed in NCAA rules and regulations to both pass the NCAA's annual tests on such regulations and manage the UNH football team successfully. Jackson, however, asserts that the requirement of previous collegiate coaching experience was not necessary to ensure familiarity with NCAA rules and regulations and that it served to exclude otherwise qualified minority applicants, such as himself.

Jackson asserts that the requirement that applicants have prior college coaching experience amounts to discrimination in violation of 42 U.S.C. § 1981, 42 U.S.C. § 2000d (Title VI), and 42 U.S.C. § 2000e–5 (Title VII).[3] Jackson asserts all three of these statutory causes of action against

---

[3]   Title 42 U.S.C. § 1981 provides that "[a]ll persons within the jurisdiction of the United States shall have the same right in every State and Territory . . . to the full and equal benefit of all laws." Title 42 U.S.C. § 2000d (Title VI) provides that "No person in the United States shall, on the ground of race . . . be excluded from participation in, be denied any benefits of, or be subject to discrimination under any program or activity receiving Federal financial assistance." Here, the parties do not dispute that defendant UNH is an entity receiving federal funds that is subject to the provisions of Title VI. . . .

defendant UNH. However, only the § 1981 claim is asserted against defendant Chin.[4]

Jackson appears to base his complaint on both the "disparate treatment" and "disparate impact" theories of recovery in that he alleges both that the challenged qualification had a discriminatory effect upon African Americans (disparate impact) and that the defendants intentionally discriminated against him based on his race (disparate treatment).

III. *Summary Judgment Standard* [The court explains the general summary judgment standard used in the federal court system].

IV. *Analysis*

A. *Disparate Treatment Claim*

As mentioned, Jackson alleges that he has been discriminated against in violation of 42 U.S.C. §§ 1981, 2000d (Title VI), and 2000e–5 (Title VII). To the extent that he claims that he has been discriminated against intentionally, the U.S. Supreme Court has developed a "burden shifting framework" for claims brought under Title VII alleging "disparate treatment." *McDonnell Douglas Corp. v. Green*, 411 U.S. 792, 802 (1973). Courts have subsequently applied the same burden-shifting framework articulated in *McDonnell Douglas* to disparate treatment claims arising under 42 U.S.C. §§ 1981 and 2000d (Title VI). . . . .Thus, because the test is the same under each of the three statutes, this Court will apply the same *McDonnell Douglas* burden-shifting framework to the plaintiff's disparate treatment claim.

Under the burden-shifting framework of *McDonnell Douglas*, a plaintiff alleging disparate treatment based on race and national origin must first establish a prima facie case of discrimination. 411 U.S. at 802.[5] The burden then shifts to the defendant to offer a legitimate, nondiscriminatory rationale for its actions. *See James v. New York Racing Ass'n*, 233 F.3d 149, 154 (2d Cir.2000). Finally, if the defendant does offer a non-discriminatory reason for its decision, the burden again shifts to the plaintiff to show that the defendant's stated reason is a mere pretext for discrimination. *See Id.* (citing *St. Mary's Honor Ctr. v. Hicks*, 509 U.S. 502, 506–10 (1993)). In some circumstances, under *Reeves v. Sanderson Plumbing Products, Inc.*, 530 U.S. 133 (2000), after the plaintiff offers evidence to show that the defendant's asserted non-discriminatory reason for the hiring is pretextual, the evidence that established the prima facie case will be sufficient to survive a summary judgment motion. 530 U.S. at

---

[4] Even if the plaintiff had asserted his Title VI and VII claims against defendant Chin, she would not have been a proper defendant under either title of the Civil Rights Act.

[5] The McDonnell Douglas burden-shifting framework is only necessary when the plaintiff has failed to offer direct evidence of discriminatory intent. See Johnson v. New York, 49 F.3d 75, 78 (2d Cir.1995) . . . Here, the plaintiff has not offered any evidence of discriminatory intent; thus, the McDonnell Douglas inquiry is appropriate.

148 ("a plaintiff's prima facie case, combined with sufficient evidence to find that the employer's asserted justification is false, may permit the trier of fact to conclude that the employer unlawfully discriminated."). Here, the burden-shifting framework does not reach this stage because Jackson has failed to establish a prima facie case.

To establish a prima facie case of discrimination, a plaintiff must show (1) membership in a protected class, (2) qualification for the employment, (3) an adverse employment decision, and (4) circumstances that give rise to an inference of discrimination. *McDonnell Douglas*, 411 U.S. at 802. *See also Weinstock v. Columbia Univ.*, 224 F.3d 33, 42 (2d Cir. 2000). . . .

The parties do not dispute that Jackson is a member of a protected class. Nor do they dispute that the defendants' decision to hire Rizzi instead of Jackson was adverse to him. However, the parties disagree as to whether Jackson meets the second prong of *McDonnell Douglas:* qualification for the position. In their Motion for Summary Judgment, the defendants assert that Jackson was not qualified because he failed to meet an express condition of the employment, that he did not have prior NCAA coaching experience. Although he maintains that he is qualified, Jackson does not dispute that prior collegiate coaching was an expressly listed qualification for the UNH head coach position, nor does he contend that he had any prior experience coaching in college. However, Jackson's subjective determination that he is qualified for the position is not enough to carry his burden of making out a prima facie case. The Second Circuit, in the context of an age discrimination suit, elaborated on the definition of the "qualification" requirement of the *McDonnell Douglas* prima facie case in *Thornley v. Penton Publ'g*, 104 F.3d 26 (2d Cir.1997): "As we understand this element, being 'qualified' refers to the criteria the employer has specified for the position." 104 F.3d at 29. The Court further explained that broad deference should be afforded to employers in selecting hiring criteria: "Absent a showing by the plaintiff that the employer's demands were made in bad faith . . . an employer . . . is not compelled to submit the reasonableness of its employment criteria to the assessment of either judge or jury." *Id.* (citations omitted). *See also Gonzalez v. Connecticut*, 151 F.Supp.2d 174, 180–81 (D.Conn.2001) (applying *Thornley* to a Title VII racial discrimination case).

. . . [Thus], deference must be given the defendants in selecting college coaching experience as a qualification for the position of head coach. Nor is it appropriate for this Court to mandate that the defendants equate Jackson's experience in coaching minor league football with college coaching experience. *See also Bennett v. Roberts*, 295 F.3d 687, 695–96 (7th Cir.2002)(holding that the plaintiff, who was seeking a teaching position, had not met the "qualification" prong of the prima facie case under Title VII despite holding a teaching certificate and a master's degree, when she had not alleged that she met the specific criteria in the job postings). . . .

There are, however, limits to an employer's latitude in selecting hiring criteria. For example, in *Howley v. Town of Stratford*, 217 F.3d 141 (2d Cir. 2000) the Second Circuit rejected the defendant's argument that the plaintiff, a female firefighter, was "ineligible" for a promotion to assistant-chief because she did not have the required four years of line-officer experience. 217 F.3d at 151. The Court acknowledged that the town was "entitled to set its own criteria" for the position, but held that because the Town had "relaxed" that standard for two male firefighters, the plaintiff's lack of experience should not have resulted in summary judgment for the defendant. *Id.* at 151–52.

Here there is no claim, and Jackson has put forth no evidence, that the defendants failed to apply the prior college coaching experience requirement uniformly to African-Americans and others. Absent any such showing, the defendants are entitled to the deference in selecting hiring criteria recognized in *Thornley*. Moreover, the prior college coaching experience requirement at issue here appears reasonable on its face. There is an obvious and significant nexus between the defendants' need to select a head coach well-versed in NCAA regulations and the requirement that candidates have actual experience in college coaching. Thus, Jackson has failed to make out a prima facie case of disparate treatment in that he has failed to demonstrate that he was qualified for the position of head coach. As Jackson has failed to meet his burden, this Court grants summary judgment as to his disparate treatment claim brought pursuant to 42 U.S.C. §§ 1981, 2000d (Title VI), and 2000e–5 (Title VII).

B. *Disparate Impact*

Unlike disparate treatment, in asserting a claim of disparate impact under Title VII a plaintiff need not allege that the discrimination was intentional. *Griggs v. Duke Power Co.*, 401 U.S. 424, 430–32 (1971) ("[G]ood intent or absence of discriminatory intent does not redeem employment procedures or testing mechanisms that operate as 'built in head winds' "). It is enough that a facially-neutral policy, such as the prior college coaching experience requirement at issue here, be shown to have an adverse impact on a protected group. *Id.* at 431 (noting that Title VII "proscribes not only overt discrimination but also practices that are fair in form, but discriminatory in operation").

However, unlike disparate treatment, the disparate impact theory of recovery is available only for claims brought pursuant to Title VII, and not for claims under 42 U.S.C. § 1981 or § 2000(d) (Title VI). The U.S. Supreme Court has held that these latter provisions can only be violated by intentional discrimination and that they therefore cannot support a "disparate impact" claim. *See Alexander v. Sandoval*, 532 U.S. 275, 280–85 (2001)(holding that § 2000d (Title VI) proscribes only intentional discrimination and therefore does not support a disparate impact theory of recovery)(citing *Regents of Univ. of Cal. v. Bakke,* 438 U.S. 265 (1978));

General Bldg. Contractors Ass'n v. Pennsylvania, 458 U.S. 375, 391 (1982)(holding that § 1981 is only violated by a showing of intentional discrimination). Thus, to the extent that Jackson alleges a disparate impact theory of recovery, his claim is cognizable only under Title VII.

Disparate impact cases, like disparate treatment cases, are governed by a "burden-shifting" framework. The Second Circuit reviewed the disparate impact burden-shifting framework in *NAACP, Inc. v. Town of East Haven,* 70 F.3d 219, 225 (2d Cir.1995): "[A] plaintiff may establish a prima facie case of disparate impact by showing that use of the test causes the selection of applicants . . . in a racial pattern that significantly differs from that of the pool of applicants." *Bridgeport Guardians, Inc. v. City of Bridgeport,* 933 F.2d 1140, 1146 (2d Cir.1991), *cert. denied,* 502 U.S. 924 (1991). Such a showing can be established through the use of statistical evidence which discloses a disparity so great that it cannot reasonably be attributed to chance. *See Hazelwood Sch. Dist. v. United States,* 433 U.S. 299, 307–08 (1977). To establish a prima facie case, the statistical disparity must be sufficiently substantial to raise an inference of causation. *Watson v. Fort Worth Bank and Trust,* 487 U.S. 977, 994–95 (1988). After a prima facie case is established, the employer has the burden of coming forward with evidence to show that the test has " 'a manifest relationship to the employment in question.' " *Albemarle Paper Co. v. Moody,* 422 U.S. 405, 425 (1975) (quoting *Griggs v. Duke Power Co.,* 401 U.S. 424, 432 (1971)). If the employer can make such a showing, the plaintiff may nonetheless prevail if he can suggest alternative tests or selection methods that would meet the employer's legitimate needs while reducing the racially disparate impact of the employer's practices. *Bridgeport Guardians, Inc.,* 933 F.2d at 1147. *Id.* at 225. *See also Robinson v. Metro-North Commuter R.R. Co.,* 267 F.3d 147, 160–61 (2d Cir.2001). As the Court noted in *East Haven,* this framework was statutorily enacted by the Civil Rights Act of 1991. *Id.* at 225 fn. 6. *See also* 42 U.S.C. § 2000e–2(k).

Here, as in the disparate treatment context, Jackson has failed to meet his burden of setting forth a prima facie case of disparate treatment. In making out a prima facie case for disparate impact under Title VII, the plaintiff bears the burden of demonstrating that a specific policy or practice of the defendant has had a disproportionately negative impact on the plaintiff's protected class. 42 U.S.C. Section 2000e–2(k)(1)(A); *Albemarle Paper Co. v. Moody,* 422 U.S. 405, 425 (1975) (superseded by statute on other grounds); *Griggs,* 401 U.S. at 432. "To make this showing, a plaintiff must (1) identify a policy or practice, (2) demonstrate that a disparity exists, and (3) establish a causal relationship between the two." *Robinson,* 267 F.3d at 160 (citing 42 U.S.C. § 2000e–2(k)(1)(A)(I)). *See also Brown v. Coach Stores, Inc.,* 163 F.3d 706, 712 (2d Cir.1998) ("plaintiff must show that a facially neutral employment policy or practice has a significant disparate impact"). Here, Jackson alleges that the defendants' facially neutral hiring criteria (requiring prior college coaching experience), had a discriminatory impact on African-Americans. Specifically, Jackson asserts that because African-Americans have historically been under-represented in the ranks of NCAA coaches this requirement disproportionately excludes African-Americans from consideration.

Statistics are often an important component of a disparate impact claim. . . . The defendants here attack the sufficiency of the plaintiff's statistics. They argue that the plaintiff has not offered any statistical evidence to indicate a causal link between UNH's prior college coaching experience requirement and its negative impact on African-Americans. However, in its memorandum in opposition to the defendants' motion for summary judgment, Jackson does offer statistics suggesting a causal link between the prior experience requirement and its impact on African-Americans, by comparing the pool of applicants to those who were ultimately selected for interviews. Jackson notes that, of the 14 applicants whose race was identified, only 10% of the Caucasians (1 out of 10) did not have college coaching experience, but 50% of the African-American candidates (2 out of 4) did not have college coaching experience. Further, Jackson noted that all six of the applicants selected for interviews were Caucasian. However, this statistical evidence fails to establish a sufficient causal link between the defendants' employment criterion and its impact on African-Americans. The Second Circuit has recognized that exceedingly small sample sizes often result in statistically unreliable evidence. *Lowe v. Commack Union Free Sch. Dist.*, 886 F.2d 1364, 1371–72 (2d Cir.1989) (holding that the fact that two out of three candidates under age 40 received favorable ratings while only 16 out of 34 candidates over age 40 received such ratings did not support a disparate impact claim in part because of "the unreliability of such a small statistical sample") (superseded by statute on other grounds). The Second Circuit has also indicated that a plaintiff's statistics must meet a certain threshold level of substantiality. *See Smith*, 196 F.3d at 365 ("Statistical data may be admitted to show a disparity in outcome between groups, but to make out a prima facie case the statistical disparity must be sufficiently substantial to raise an inference of causation."); *E.E.O.C. v. Joint Apprenticeship Comm. of the Joint Indus. Bd. of the Elec. Indus.*, 164 F.3d 89, 95 (2d Cir.1998) ("[A] plaintiff's statistical evidence must reflect a disparity so great it cannot be explained by chance.") Here, the relevant sample size is only 14 (of the 36 applicants, the race of only 14 has been identified), which is too small to yield a statistically significant result.

In *Smith*, the Second Circuit cautioned that in assessing whether a statistical disparity is "sufficiently substantial to establish a prima facie case of disparate impact, there is no one test that always answers that question." *Smith*, 196 F.3d at 366. "Instead," the Court reasoned, "the substantiality of a disparity is judged on a case-by-case basis." *Id.* (citing *Watson v. Fort Worth Bank & Trust*, 487 U.S. 977, 996 n. 3 (1988)). In this case, the plaintiff has failed to provide a sufficiently substantial disparity to survive summary judgment, because the sample is too small.

In addition to the statistics discussed above, the plaintiff has presented an article from the *Sports Business Journal,* which purportedly demonstrates the disparity of college football coaches that are African-American. However, this article-without more-does not present the type of substantial statistical evidence contemplated by the Second Circuit in *Smith.* It is only two pages long, and most of it is an opinion piece rather than a scientific statistical analysis. Even when the author does cite statistics, he does not disclose the basis for them or reveal their methodology. Also, the article fails to set forth the type of statistics that are appropriate in a disparate impact analysis. The only statistics in the article concern the percentages of coaches in the various NCAA divisions that are African-American. However, the essence of a disparate impact analysis is a *comparison.* In *Carter v. Ball,* 33 F.3d 450 (4th Cir.1994) the plaintiff brought a Title VII discrimination suit against the Secretary of the Navy. The plaintiff in that case attempted to offer statistical evidence "which purportedly demonstrate[d] a statistical imbalance in the Navy's promotional practices." 33 F.3d at 456. The Fourth Circuit upheld the district court's exclusion of the statistical evidence. In so holding, the Court emphasized that "[i]n a case of discrimination in hiring or promoting, the relevant comparison is between the percentage of minority employees and the percentage of potential minority applicants in the qualified labor pool. . . . The mere absence of minority employees in upper-level positions does not suffice to prove a *prima facie* case of discrimination without a comparison to the relevant labor pool." *Id.; see also Wards Cove Packing Co. v. Atonio,* 490 U.S. 642 (1989) ("the proper basis for the initial inquiry in a disparate-impact case" is "between the racial composition of the qualified persons in the labor market and the persons holding at issue jobs"). 490 U.S. at 650.[9] Here, the article offered by Jackson makes no such comparison. It simply recites the percentages of college coaches that are African-American. It does not offer statistics on the percentage of African-Americans that would be otherwise qualified for head coaching positions, but were not hired.

Finally, also in support of his disparate impact claim, the plaintiff asserts that the use of the prior college coaching experience requirement has yielded discriminatory results when applied to other athletic programs at UNH. The plaintiff contends that only one out of 23 coaches hired since 1993, when the plaintiff asserts the prior college coaching experience requirement was adopted for most head coaching positions at UNH, has been African-American. However, even if true, the Supreme Court held in

---

[9] The Court did observe that in some cases such statistics on the labor market would be "difficult if not impossible to ascertain" and that in those instances, other statistical comparisons might be appropriate. Wards Cove, 490 U.S. at 651. Here, the plaintiff has not made any showing that statistics on the relevant labor market would be difficult to produce.

Wards Cove that "[t]he percentage of nonwhite workers found in other positions in the employer's labor force is irrelevant to the question of a prima facie statistical case of disparate impact." 490 U.S. at 653. Thus, the plaintiff has failed to meet his burden of establishing a prima facie case of disparate impact, and this Court also grants summary judgment as to that claim.

For the foregoing reasons, the defendant's Motion for Summary Judgment is GRANTED and the case is DISMISSED.

NOTES AND QUESTIONS

1. McDonnell Douglas *Indirect Proof Option.* The burden-shifting method of proof described and applied in the *Jackson* decision affords plaintiffs the option of making a demonstration of discriminatory intent without any direct proof of a prohibited discriminatory motive. A plaintiff can do so by proving the likelihood of such a discriminatory motive through proof of the absence of a non-discriminatory motive. The plaintiff can do this in a hiring case like *Jackson* first by proving that he adequately applied and had the basic qualifications for a job he did not get and then by proving that any alternative good motive offered by the defendant employer, such as the superior qualifications of another applicant, was pretextual. In other words, the *McDonnell Douglas* methodology offers the plaintiff an option of proving bad motivation by disproof of good motivation. Jackson could not do so because he could not prove the absence of the good motive of his failure to have the basic qualification of past college coaching experience. He might have proven this motive was pretextual by demonstrating that UNH had hired other coaches without such experience, but such comparators probably were not available to him so he could not do so.

As the *Jackson* court stated in its footnote 5, *McDonnell Douglas* pretext proof is not the only kind of proof that is relevant to demonstrating discriminatory motive. Plaintiffs also may prove a bad discriminatory motive directly, for instance, by evidence of a decision-maker's racist comments or by some overtly racist formal policy. The Supreme Court has held that a complaint need not allege a *McDonnell Douglas* prima facie case even in order to survive a motion to dismiss on the pleadings. *Swierkiewicz v. Sorema*, 534 U.S. 506 (2002). Jackson, however, in addition to offering no proof that the college experience qualification was pretextual, also offered no direct proof of a discriminatory motive.

2. *Proving Pretext in Hiring for High Status Positions.* Jackson likely would not have had an easier time proving discrimination if he had been rejected for a higher paying coaching job, such as a head coach of a leading Division I football program or an NFL coaching position. When hiring for premium positions in any profession, employers are likely to use some

subjective criteria on which courts understandably are more hesitant to substitute their comparative judgments. Proving pretext is thus more difficult.

3. *Disparate Impact Proof.* Title VII also offers the plaintiffs another proof option not dependent upon proof of discriminatory motivation. As the *Jackson* decision notes, this alternative disparate proof option was first formulated by the Supreme Court in *Griggs v. Duke Power,* 401 U.S. 424 (1971), and then codified by the Civil Rights Act of 1991's amendments to Title VII. See 42 U.S.C. § 2000e–2(k). The latter clarified that the purpose of disparate impact proof is not only to uncover discriminatory intent, but also to eliminate unnecessary barriers to the employment of protected groups. The 1991 amendments, however, also limited the availability of legal damages to disparate treatment cases that demonstrate discriminatory intent. Successful disparate impact plaintiffs can only obtain equitable relief, including instatement and back pay. See 42 U.S.C. § 1981A(a).

As the *Jackson* court stresses, to advance a disparate impact case a plaintiff must demonstrate that a particular employment practice of a defendant disproportionately disadvantages members of the plaintiff's protected class, not just the plaintiff individually. Thus, Jackson had to demonstrate the general impact of UNH's college coaching experience requirement on Blacks, not just the impact of the requirement on him. The *Jackson* court says that he did not do so by demonstrating the disproportionate impact on the fourteen-person applicant pool whose race could be identified. Why not? Was it simply because this pool was too small to be statistically significant? What larger relevant pool could Jackson have used? The pool of all football coaches, including on the high school and professional level, who met UNH qualifications other than prior college experience? Is it obvious that use of such a pool would demonstrate that the college experience requirement disparately excluded Black coaches?

If Jackson had adequately demonstrated that the college experience requirement disparately excluded Black coaches, UNH would have had the opportunity to defend the requirement as "job related" and "consistent with business necessity." If UNH had done so, Jackson still could have prevailed by demonstrating that an "alternative employment practice" could have served the same business purposes without the same disparate impact. Do you think Jackson might have convinced this court that such an alternative existed?

4. *Proving a "Pattern or Practice" of Discrimination.* Title VII also authorizes government actions against employers who engage in a "pattern or practice" of discrimination, and the Supreme Court has approved private class actions to establish systemic disparate treatment in such cases. See *Franks v. Bowman,* 424 U.S. 747 (1976). To do so, the government or private plaintiff must use a somewhat different statistical proof than that used in disparate impact cases. Statistical proof of pattern or practice discrimination compares the percentage of the plaintiff's protected class in the jobs for which discrimination is alleged with the percentage of the plaintiff's class in the relevant qualified labor market from which employees are selected for those jobs. The comparison uses a statistical method called binomial distribution

analysis to determine the likelihood that random distribution would produce such a disparity. If the likelihood is small, generally less than two standard deviations or five per cent, the defendant will have to provide some other explanation for the disparity other than randomness to dispel the inference of a general practice of discrimination. At least absent egregious statistical disparities, plaintiffs have needed further evidence of discrimination, including examples of individual cases, to prove systemic disparate treatment. Furthermore, even when a general practice is proven, a defendant has the opportunity to prove that the practice did not cause an adverse action against particular members of plaintiff's protected class.

Jackson probably could not have successfully advanced a systemic disparate treatment case in a class action. He would have had to develop statistics comparing the proportion of Black coaches at UNH with the proportion of Black coaches in the national college and professional football coach workforce. He probably would have had to demonstrate particular examples of intentional discrimination. In the actual case, he was not even successful proving his own disparate treatment.

5. *Section 1981 and Title VI.* Note that Jackson brought claims under two other anti-discrimination provisions in addition to Title VII. Section 1981, 42 U.S.C. § 1981, quoted by the *Jackson* court in its footnote 3, was originally part of the Civil Rights Act of 1866. It now prohibits racial and ethnic discrimination in all contracting by private and public employers. Unlike Title VII, it allows direct private rights of action without any exhaustion of administrative remedies. It also affords the remedy of unlimited compensatory damages, while Title VII compensatory damages are capped based on the size of the employer. Disparate impact actions, however, cannot be based on § 1981. The provision proscribing discrimination by federal fund recipients in Title VI of the 1964 Civil Rights Act is also quoted in the *Jackson* court's footnote 3. Title VI also has been interpreted by the Supreme Court to allow a direct private right of action for compensatory damages in disparate treatment claims of intentional discrimination. *See Alexander v. Sandoval*, 532 U.S. 275 (2001).

Apart from any impetus from Title VII or other anti-discrimination laws, cultural developments and practical considerations, such as the growing pool of experienced retired Black athletes, should result in at least a gradual increase in the number of minority coaches and athletic administrators. That has been true, for instance, in the NBA. Almost every franchise has had a Black coach; indeed, during the 2021–2022 season, half of the teams were led by a Black head coach.

The NFL's coaching ranks have not been filled with as high a proportion of Black coaches. Though Black coaches now constitute about 70% of NFL players, the thirty-two NFL teams had only three Black head coaches in 2021 and 2022. There were six Black general managers, four

Black offensive coordinators, and eleven Black defensive coordinators. Black coaches were selected to fill fewer than one in six open head coaching positions in the previous two decades. Twelve of the 32 NFL teams have never hired a Black head coach.

These figures suggest the limited effectiveness of the league's "Rooney Rule." After the 2002 firing of two successful Black coaches, Tony Dungy and Dennis Green, resulted in criticism from civil rights advocates and some players, the NFL adopted a policy, suggested by Pittsburgh Steelers' owner Dan Rooney, requiring teams to interview at least one minority applicant for any open head coach position. The League fined the Detroit Lions $200,000 for violating the Rooney Rule in 2003. It also expanded the Rule in 2020 to require the interviewing of two external minority candidates for head coach openings and a minority interview for all senior coaching and football operations positions. The League in 2020 also adopted a resolution to award third round draft picks to teams whose employee is hired by another team to fill a head coaching or general manager position. The Rooney Rule's interviewing obligation, however, only is part of an agreement between the owners and can only be enforced by the League; it is not an external law, like Title VII, or even a contractual commitment against discrimination, that can be enforced by any applicant for a coaching job.

Nonetheless, in February of 2022, Brian Flores, a Black head coach who had coached the Miami Dolphins for three years before being dismissed, alleged that the New York Giants in 2022 and the Denver Broncos in 2019 interviewed him only for facial compliance with the Rooney Rule after the teams had already selected a nonminority head coach. The allegations were made in a federal complaint against the NFL and its thirty-two franchises, seeking certification of a class action claiming race discrimination on behalf of all Black NFL head coaches, coordinators, and general managers, and applicants for those positions. Flores's class action cannot be certified under governing Supreme Court decisions such as *Wal-Mart Stores, Inc. v. Duke*, 564 U.S. 338 (2011), but the suit garnered substantial publicity and perhaps again focused the League's attention on the Rooney Rule. In March 2022 the League announced that each team must have at least one minority, or woman, on their offensive coaching staff, where a majority of recently hired NFL head coaches have had some experience. (Though this minimal quota requirement might not be able to withstand judicial scrutiny, any challenge seems doubtful.)

———

Another lawsuit brought against the NFL in November 2020 better indicates the continued legal relevance of statutory anti-discrimination commands, even against sophisticated sports entities like the NFL. See *Henry v. NFL*, 2020 WL 5076071 (E.D. Pa.). As explained more fully in Chapter 16, in 2015 the NFL settled consolidated multidistrict litigation

(MDL) cases brought by retired players who claimed the NFL breached duties to protect them from various brain injuries caused by playing-related concussions. The settlement provided for the administration of claims based on various types of injuries, including levels of cognitive decline. The settlement provided that cognitive declines would be based on and "in accordance with the standardized neuropsychological testing protocol." Under this protocol eligibility for cognitive decline benefits would be determined by the standard deviation of an applicant's test scores from the mean of scores of the relevant population for that applicant. In litigation of claims under the agreement, race-based definitions of the relevant population were used. Because the general Black population has lower mean scores on cognitive tests than has the White population, this meant that a retired Black player had to have a lower score to recover for cognitive decline than did a retired White player.

The November 2020 lawsuit challenging this "race-norming" was brought by two Black claimants of cognitive decline seeking class certification for a claim of race discrimination in violation of § 1981. (Title VII was not invoked, presumably to avoid that statute's requirement of exhaustion of administrative remedies.) The lawsuit was filed with the court with jurisdiction over the MDL and settlement, and was dismissed in March 2021 by that court with an order that the claim be settled through mediation between the NFL and the lead counsel for the plaintiffs in the MDL. On June 2, 2021, the NFL announced that it would no longer request race-norming in future cases and would evaluate the treatment of past cognitive decline cases for any racial bias.

The NFL's agreement to cease using race norming may have settled a meritorious case. To be sure, the NFL's prior insistence on race-norming was supported by accepted medical practice designed to avoid the over diagnosis of dementia in Black patients. Moreover, assuming the questionable premise that Black NFL players, most of whom are college-educated, are as different in cognitive levels from White NFL players, as is the relatively poorly educated general Black population from the better educated general White population, race-norming would help ensure that the same proportion of Black and White retired players would be able to establish cognitive decline. In other words, there would be the same proportion of Black and White player false positives and false negatives because of outliers from the cognitive mean before NFL concussions. Nonetheless, the Supreme Court has made clear that race or sex-based employment practices constitute illegal discrimination, regardless of the absence of malice and the presence of benign motive. Moreover, the Court in *Arizona Governing Committee v. Norris*, 463 U.S. 1073 (1983), held (unanimously on this point) that an employer's sex-based pension annuities were illegal even though using sex-based tables resulted in the same proportion of female and male annuity beneficiaries and an equal aggregate payout to women and men. Such "statistical discrimination" is illegal because of its impact on protected individuals, even if the discrimination is not malign and even if it has an equal impact in the aggregate on classifications protected from discrimination. Is there any way that the NFL could have distinguished the *Norris* decision?

B. SEX

The historic segregation of and discrimination against Blacks have not been the only aspects of American society presenting barriers to equitable opportunities in sports. Females of all ages have suffered historically from limited opportunities to gain the benefits of athletic competition. For instance, in 1972, fifty years before the preparation of this Seventh Edition, there were only around 300,000 females, compared to almost four million males, participating in interscholastic athletic competitions in high school and college. Universities allotted college women only 2% of college athletic budgets. Women's sports in college did not even come within the purview of the NCAA. Instead, there was a separate and severely under-funded Association of Intercollegiate Athletic Women (AIAW). Most high school girls and college women interested in sports were relegated to the subordinate supportive role of cheering for males.

1.   TITLE IX—APPLICATION TO ATHLETICS

The relegation of females to subordinate supportive roles in athletics was not addressed by the 1964 Civil Rights Act. That Act included a Title VI that prohibited discrimination by "any program or activity receiving federal financial assistance," but unlike Title VII's prohibition of employment discrimination, Title VI did not include sex as a protected category. It was not until eight years later, in Title IX of the Education Amendments Act of 1972, that Congress passed legislation that has led to a fifty-year surge in athletic opportunities and resources for female interscholastic athletes, now numbering over three and half million.

Title IX prohibits discrimination in federally funded educational programs based on sex:

> No person ... shall, on the basis of sex, be excluded from participation in, be denied the benefit of, or be subjected to discrimination under any education program or activity receiving federal financial assistance.

The relevance of this statute to athletics was not immediately recognized, but when the Senate reconsidered the statute in 1974, Sen John Tower (R-Texas) offered an amendment (supported by NCAA leadership) that would have excluded revenue-generating college sports from the purview of Title IX's coverage of "education program or activity." Title IX's original sponsor, Sen. Birch Bayh (D-Indiana), strongly opposed the amendment, arguing that Title IX should be comprehensive in scope and not exclude sports. 118 Cong. Rec. 5804 (1972). The Senate rejected the Tower Amendment. Instead, it adopted an amendment introduced by Sen. Jacob Javits (R-NY) that required the Department of Health, Education and Welfare (HEW) to issue regulations to include "reasonable provisions considering the nature of particular sports." P.L. 93–380, Title VIII, Part D, § 844, 88 Stat. 612 (1974). Before such regulations could be effectuated, the Supreme Court seemed to secure for sports essentially the same result that Senator Tower sought. In *Grove City College v. Bell*, 465 U.S. 555 (1984), the Court read Title IX as governing only the specific college programs that received federal financial assistance, which did not include athletic departments. The Civil Rights Restoration Act of 1987, 20 U.S.C.A. § 1681, et seq. (1988)), in response extended Title IX's coverage to *all* the operations of an educational institution that receive *any* federal aid (including grants or loans to its students), bringing Title IX fully into play for college sports.

What that entailed depended greatly on the content of the Regulation promulgated by HEW pursuant to the Javits amendment in 1975, as further elaborated by a Policy Interpretation from the HEW's Office of Civil Rights (OCR) in 1979 in response to hundreds of complaints. As quoted above, Title IX states only a very general statutory prohibition of sex-based exclusion from participation, denial of benefits, or discrimination under educational programs. There was very little congressional material (*e.g.*, no Committee Report) about what was envisaged for the bill as a whole, and only two mentions of college sports in the entire congressional deliberations. The Act did state that Title IX was not to

> . . . be interpreted to require any educational institution to grant preferential or disparate treatment to the members of one sex on account of an imbalance which may exist with respect to the total number or percentage of persons of that sex participating in or receiving the benefits of any federally supported program or activity, in comparison with the total number or percentage of persons of that sex in any community, state, section, or other area: Provided, that this subsection shall not be construed to prevent the consideration in any hearing or proceeding under this chapter of statistical evidence tending to show that such an imbalance exists with respect to the participation in, or receipt of the benefits of, any such program or activity by the members of one sex.

Even the latter provision, however, did no more than reject pure statistical disparities as themselves a violation of the statute; such statistical material can be and is regularly used (along with other factors) to find "discrimination."

The OCR's 1979 Policy Interpretation elaborates in much greater detail the meaning of equal educational opportunity in college and high school sports programs. Quoting from the 1975 Regulation, the interpretation states that the statutory requirement of "equality" is not necessarily violated by "unequal aggregate expenditures for members of each sex or unequal expenditures for male and female teams." 34 C.F.R. § 106.41(c). Instead, the test for compliance is a comparison of the

> ... availability, quality and kinds of benefits, opportunities and treatment afforded members of both sexes. Institutions will be in compliance if the compared program components are equivalent, that is, equal or equal in effect. Under this standard, identical benefits, opportunities or treatment are not required, provided the overall effect of any differences is negligible.

44 Fed. Reg. 71,415 (1979). Quoting again from the Regulation, 34 C.F.R. § 106.41(c), the Policy Interpretation states that for purposes of judging whether there actually is "equal athletic opportunity," the following program factors must be taken into account:

1. Whether the selection of sports and levels of competition effectively accommodate the interests and abilities of members of both sexes;

2. Provision of equipment and supplies;

3. Scheduling of games and practice time;

4. Travel and per diem allowance;

5. Opportunity to receive coaching and academic tutoring;

6. Assignment and compensation of coaches and tutors;

7. Provision of locker rooms, practice and competitive facilities;

8. Provision of medical training services;

9. Provision of housing and dining facilities and services;

10. Publicity.

44 Fed. Reg. 71,414 (1979). The Policy Interpretation further directs that the amounts spent on athletic scholarships be on a "substantially proportional basis to the number of male and female participants in the institution's athletic programs." Id.

Most significantly, the Policy Interpretation also set out a three-prong test to determine whether an institution is equalizing participation opportunities for women and men. The test is that a school complies with Title IX with respect to participation opportunities if any of the following questions can be answered affirmatively:

> (1) Whether intercollegiate level participation opportunities for male and female students are provided in numbers substantially proportionate to their respective enrollments; or

(2) Where the members of one sex have been and are underrepresented among intercollegiate athletes, whether the institution can show a history and continuing practice of program expansion which is demonstrably responsive to the developing interest and abilities of the members of that sex; or

(3) Where the members of one sex are underrepresented among intercollegiate athletes, and the institution cannot show a continuing practice of program expansion such as that cited above, whether it can be demonstrated that the interests and abilities of the members of that sex have been fully and effectively accommodated by the present program.

44 Fed. Reg. 71,414, 71,423 (1979).

This test reflected a recognition that in order to provide women significantly more equitable opportunities and resources for interscholastic sports, Title IX had to be interpreted to do more than simply apply Title VII's race and sex-blind anti-discrimination principle to the competition for participation on men's interscholastic teams. Because of the different development of men's and women's bodies during and after puberty, few women can hope to compete on most teams open to men. The post-puberty athletic differences become more obvious the higher the level of competition. Women's world record times in most pure athletic competitions, such as track and swimming, are about 10% slower than men's record times. In 2018, 275 high school boys had a better time in a 400-meter race than the personal best of the great female sprinter Allyson Felix, who has earned the most medals in world competition in history. Requiring schools to provide equal educational opportunities to women in sports had to entail requiring them to provide an equal number of spots on teams open only to women.

Not surprisingly, the bulk of the cases and controversies generated by Title IX's regulation of college sports have involved the implementation of, or challenges to, the equalization of opportunities for women to play on women's-only teams through the OCR's three prong test. Most of the legal cases have been private rights of action brought after the Supreme Court in 1992 authorized private suits for damages and attorney fees by anyone asserting that they had been personally harmed by the school's violation of Title IX. *See Franklin v. Gwinnett County Public Schools*, 503 U.S. 60 (1992) (involving a high school student's claim of sexual harassment by a teacher).

That same year, Congress split HEW into a Department of Health and Human Services (HHS) and a Department of Education (DOE). The latter department, through its OCR, is responsible for the continued monitoring of universities' compliance with Title IX. The OCR requires reports and responds to specific complaints of possible violations. The OCR has authority to demand reforms as a condition of continuing eligibility for receiving federal funds. Also, the NCAA requires every Division I school to go through a certification process once every ten years that essentially requires compliance with the same standards as those set by Title IX.

Although critics point to the inadequacy and under funding of these enforcement systems and to continuing violations at many universities, athletic departments have come much closer to achieving gender equity in the half century since Title IX's enactment. In 2020–21, 44% of college athletes were women, receiving around a third of overall athletic expenditures. At schools without football, spending is now virtually equal between the genders. (Football schools spend an average of 60% of their budget on that one sport.) The impact of Title IX also is manifest in high schools where few girls competed in 1972, while over 300,000 do now. The changes in female athletics wrought in large part by Title IX have also been significant for Olympic competitions. In 1972, the U.S. team had 339 males and 90 females; fifty years later at the 2021 Tokyo Olympics the U.S. team carried 284 males and 329 females.

2.   EQUALITY OF OPPORTUNITY THROUGH TITLE IX

The first prominent use of the OCR Policy Interpretation in Title IX litigation was in an action to prevent Brown University from eliminating two women's teams. Brown is a member of the Ivy League, where college sports first began in the 1850s, and where American-style football evolved in the 1870s. Not until the late 1960s and early 1970s did all Ivy League universities finally integrate their undergraduate colleges by accepting women into their academic as well as athletic programs. By that time, the Ivy League was no longer part of the NCAA's highly commercialized Division I-A, and it did not provide athletic scholarships as such to its students.

In 1971, Brown University merged with Pembroke College, a women's-only school. One of the early steps in that joint venture was to increase substantially the athletic opportunities for its new female students; by 1977, Brown had created 14 women's varsity teams. Over the next decade, however, just a single women's team was added, such that by 1991–92 Brown had 15 women's teams and 16 men's teams. Even so, Brown did not have equity, as the total number of participants on all teams was 328 women (37%) and 566 men (63%).

At the time, though, the NCAA and most of its members were engaged in a cost reduction program. Like a number of schools, the Brown administration announced that it was going to reduce its athletic budget by cutting four varsity sports—two women's teams in volleyball and gymnastics (which would generate savings of approximately $37,000 and $24,000) and two men's teams in water polo and golf (which would save $9,000 and $7,000 respectively). While significantly more dollars were cut from the women's than the men's programs, the relative number of team positions remained essentially the same, at 37%–63%; however, women made up approximately 48% of Brown's student body. The university told the team members that they could continue playing in those sports as "intercollegiate clubs," but without financial assistance or support services from the school, and likely with sharply reduced opportunities to compete against varsity teams at other schools. The members of the women's teams (led by gymnast Amy Cohen) chose, instead, to file suit under Title IX, and they won a preliminary injunction against Brown's elimination of the women's varsity teams. Brown appealed that decision, and received the first circuit court opinion about how Title IX applied to intercollegiate athletics.

COHEN V. BROWN UNIVERSITY
991 F.2d 888 (1st Cir. 1993)

SELYA, CIRCUIT JUDGE.

* * *

III. Title IX and Collegiate Athletics

* * *

A. Scope of Title IX.

At its inception, the broad proscriptive language of Title IX caused considerable consternation in the academic world. The academy's anxiety chiefly centered around identifying which individual programs, particularly in terms of athletics, might come within the scope of the discrimination provision, and, relatedly, how the government would determine compliance. The gridiron fueled these concerns: for many schools, the men's football budget far exceeded that of any other sport, and men's athletics as a whole received the lion's share of dedicated resources—a share that, typically, was vastly disproportionate to the percentage of men in the student body.

[The judge then described the evolution of the Title IX legislation and its administrative interpretation. After quoting the key passage from the OCR Policy Interpretation set out above, the court continued.]

. . . The first benchmark furnishes a safe harbor for those institutions that have distributed athletic opportunities in numbers "substantially proportionate" to the gender composition of their student bodies. Thus, a university which does not wish to engage in extensive compliance analysis may stay on the sunny side of Title IX simply by maintaining gender parity between its student body and its athletic lineup.

The second and third parts of the accommodation test recognize that there are circumstances under which, as a practical matter, something short of this proportionality is a satisfactory proxy for gender balance. For example, so long as a university is continually expanding athletic opportunities in an ongoing effort to meet the needs of the underrepresented gender, and persists in this approach as interest and ability levels in its student body and secondary feeder schools rise, benchmark two is satisfied and Title IX does not require that the university leap to complete gender parity in a single bound. Or, if a school has a student body in which one sex is demonstrably less interested in athletics, Title IX does not require that the school create teams for, or rain money upon, otherwise disinterested students; rather, the third benchmark is satisfied if the underrepresented sex's discernible interests are fully and effectively accommodated.[13]

It seems unlikely, even in this day and age, that the athletic establishments of many coeducational universities reflect the gender balance of their student bodies. Similarly, the recent boom in Title IX suits suggests that, in an era of fiscal austerity, few universities are prone to expand athletic opportunities. It is not surprising, then, that schools more often than not attempt to manage the rigors of Title IX by satisfying the interests and abilities of the underrepresented gender, that is, by meeting the third benchmark of the accommodation test. Yet, this benchmark sets a high standard: it demands not merely some accommodation, but full and effective accommodation. If there is sufficient interest and ability among members of the statistically underrepresented gender, not slaked by existing programs, an institution necessarily fails this prong of the test.

Although the full-and-effective-accommodation standard is high, it is not absolute. Even when male athletic opportunities outnumber female athletic opportunities, and the university has not met the first benchmark (substantial statistical proportionality) or the second benchmark (continuing program expansion) of the accommodation test, the mere fact that there are some female students interested in a sport does not ipso facto require the school to provide a varsity team in order to comply with the third benchmark. Rather, the institution can satisfy the third benchmark by ensuring participatory opportunities at the intercollegiate level when, and to the extent that, there is "sufficient interest and ability among the members of the excluded sex to sustain a viable team and a reasonable expectation of intercollegiate competition for that team. . . ." Staying on top of the problem is not sport for the short-winded: the institution must remain vigilant, "upgrading the competitive opportunities available to the historically disadvantaged sex as warranted by developing abilities among

---

[13] OCR also lists a series of illustrative justifications for the disparate treatment of men's and women's athletic teams, including (1) sports that require more resources because of the nature of the game (e.g., contact sports generally require more equipment), (2) special circumstances, such as an influx of first-year players, that may require an extraordinary infusion of resources, (3) special operational expenses (e.g., crowd control at a basketball tournament), as long as special operational expense needs are met for both genders and (4) affirmative measures to remedy past limitations on athletic opportunities for one gender.

the athletes of that sex," until the opportunities for, and levels of, competition are equivalent by gender.[15]

Brown argues that DED's Policy Interpretation, construed as we have just outlined, goes so far afield that it countervails the enabling legislation. Brown suggests that, to the extent students' interests in athletics are disproportionate by gender, colleges should be allowed to meet those interests incompletely as long as the school's response is in direct proportion to the comparative levels of interest. Put bluntly, Brown reads the "full" out of the duty to accommodate "fully and effectively." It argues instead that an institution satisfactorily accommodates female athletes if it allocates athletic opportunities to women in accordance with the ratio of interested and able women to interested and able men, regardless of the number of unserved women or the percentage of the student body that they comprise.

Because this is mountainous terrain, an example may serve to clarify the distinction between Brown's proposal and our understanding of the law. Suppose a university (Oooh U.) has a student body consisting of 1,000 men and 1,000 women, a one to one ratio. If 500 men and 250 women are able and interested athletes, the ratio of interested men to interested women is two to one. Brown takes the position that both the actual gender composition of the student body and whether there is unmet interest among the underrepresented gender are irrelevant; in order to satisfy the third benchmark, Oooh U. must only provide athletic opportunities in line with the two to one interested athlete ratio, say, 100 slots for men and 50 slots for women. Under this view, the interest of 200 women would be unmet—but there would be no Title IX violation.

We think that Brown's perception of the Title IX universe is myopic. The fact that the overrepresented gender is less than fully accommodated will not, in and of itself, excuse a shortfall in the provision of opportunities for the underrepresented gender. Rather, the law requires that, in the absence of continuing program expansion (benchmark two), schools either meet benchmark one by providing athletic opportunities in proportion to the gender composition of the student body (in Oooh U.'s case, a roughly equal number of slots for men and women, as the student body is equally divided), or meet benchmark three by fully accommodating interested athletes among the underrepresented sex (providing, at Oooh U., 250 slots for women).

---

[15] If in the course of adding and upgrading teams, a university attains gender parity between its athletic program and its student body, it meets the first benchmark of the accommodation test. But, Title IX does not require that a school pour ever-increasing sums into its athletic establishment. If a university prefers to take another route, it can also bring itself into compliance with the first benchmark of the accommodation test by subtraction and downgrading, that is, by reducing opportunities for the overrepresented gender while keeping opportunities stable for the underrepresented gender (or reducing them to a much lesser extent).

In the final analysis, Brown's view is wrong . . . as a matter of law, for DED's Policy Interpretation, which requires full accommodation of the underrepresented gender, draws its essence from the statute. Whether Brown's concept might be thought more attractive, or whether we, if writing on a pristine page, would craft the regulation in a manner different than the agency, are not very important considerations. Because the agency's rendition stands upon a plausible, if not inevitable, reading of Title IX, we are obligated to enforce the regulation according to its tenor.

* * *

The record reveals that the court below . . . properly recognized that even balanced use of the budget-paring knife runs afoul of Title IX where, as here, the fruits of a university's athletic program remain ill-distributed after the trimming takes place. Because the district court understood this principle, and because its findings of fact as to the case's probable outcome are based on substantial evidence, the court's determination that plaintiffs are likely to succeed on the merits is inexpugnable.

Injunction affirmed.

Brown University's athletic program was also the subject of the first full-scale trial of a Title IX case. By this time, Amy Cohen and her gymnastic and volleyball classmates had long since graduated from Brown. Instead, the lawsuit had become a class action on behalf of all present and future Brown women students who might want to participate in intercollegiate sports. While the percentage of women among Brown's varsity athletes had increased slightly from 37% in 1990–91 to 38% in 1993–94, the percentage of women in Brown's classes had increased from 48% to 51% in that same period. Thus, while Brown had 16 varsity *teams* both for men and for women students-athletes, there was a 13-point gap between the percentage of women team *members* and students.

Brown now pressed an argument that had been alluded to in the earlier case—that the latter gap actually reflected a disparity in male and female student *interests* in varsity sports, and that Brown's programs provided more than "equal accommodation" to the female interests. The trial judge rejected this argument: in his view, not only was measurement of such true student interests inherently difficult, but it was legally irrelevant under the OCR standard. Since Brown had stopped expanding women's sports, while still leaving this statistical disparity between its female athlete and student ratios, the university had to meet *all* existing women student interests and abilities in any particular varsity sport (which clearly existed at Brown in volleyball and gymnastics).

The reaction of Brown President Vartan Gregorian to the trial verdict was that this reading of Title IX was "tantamount to quotas." In filing its appeal, Brown's counsel also placed some hope in two major Equal Protection decisions rendered by the Supreme Court since the First Circuit's initial *Cohen* decision. In *Adarand Constructors, Inc. v. Pena*, 515 U.S. 200 (1995), the Court had overruled *Metro Broadcasting v. FCC*, 497 U.S. 547 (1990) (a case that had been relied on by the First Circuit in *Cohen*); the Court there required that even benign federal affirmative action programs in favor of previously discriminated-against groups— there a racial group—have to pass the same "strict scrutiny" standard that is applied to negative state discrimination. A year later came *United States v. Virginia*, 518 U.S. 515 (1996), which dealt with the state of Virginia's effort to preserve its all-male Virginia Military Institute (VMI), and to offer women with military aspirations a female-only program instead. In this case, the Supreme Court did not utilize the traditional "intermediate scrutiny" to judge whether gender-based classifications were "substantially related to an important government objective." Instead, the Court majority subjected Virginia's actions to "skeptical scrutiny of official action denying rights or opportunities based on sex" (518 U.S. at 531), and eventually concluded that the state did not provide the "exceedingly persuasive justification" needed for its exclusion of female applicants from VMI. Brown University asserted that *Virginia* and *Adarand* required the First Circuit to take a second look at the application of Title IX to its case. The following opinion (by a new circuit panel) produced the first Title IX division within an appeals court.

COHEN V. BROWN UNIVERSITY
101 F.3d 155 (1st Cir. 1996)

BOWNES, CIRCUIT JUDGE.

* * *

IV.

* * *

A.

Title IX is not an affirmative action statute; it is an anti-discrimination statute, modeled explicitly after another anti-discrimination statute, Title VI. No aspect of the Title IX regime at issue in this case—inclusive of the statute, the relevant regulation, and the pertinent agency documents— mandates gender-based preferences or quotas, or specific timetables for implementing numerical goals.

Like other anti-discrimination statutory schemes, the Title IX regime permits affirmative action. In addition, Title IX, like other anti-discrimination schemes, permits an inference that a significant gender-based statistical disparity may indicate the existence of discrimination. Consistent with the school desegregation cases, the question of substantial proportionality under the Policy Interpretation's three-part test is merely the starting point for analysis, rather than the conclusion; a rebuttable presumption, rather than an inflexible requirement. *See, e.g., Swann v. Charlotte-Mecklenburg Bd. of Educ.*, 402 U.S. 1, 25 (1971). In short, the substantial proportionality test is but one aspect of the inquiry into whether an institution's athletics program complies with Title IX.

* * *

[The court then retraced and reaffirmed the earlier *Cohen* panel's treatment of the Title IX regulatory issues. In particular, the majority here specifically rejected Brown's principal argument—that the existing demands of its women students for varsity athletic opportunities were being accommodated as much if not more than were the demands of its male students. This position, the Court said, did not satisfy the third prong of the Policy Interpretation that required "full and effective" accommodation of all the athletic demands of the currently under-represented female student. The court dismissed Brown's effort to use the Title VII equal employment opportunity analogy to try to paint the Policy Interpretation as creating an illegitimate quota system in the athletic sphere.]

* * *

E.

* * *

It is imperative to recognize that athletics presents a distinctly different situation from admissions and employment and requires a different analysis in order to determine the existence vel non of discrimination. While the Title IX regime permits institutions to maintain gender-segregated teams, the law does not require that student-athletes attending institutions receiving federal funds must compete on gender-segregated teams; nor does the law require that institutions provide completely gender-integrated athletics programs. To the extent that Title IX allows institutions to maintain single-sex teams and gender-segregated athletics programs, men and women do not compete against each other for places on team rosters. Accordingly, and notwithstanding Brown's protestations to the contrary, the Title VII concept of the "qualified pool" has no place in a Title IX analysis of equal athletics opportunities for male and female athletes because women are not "qualified" to compete for positions on men's teams, and vice-versa. In addition, the concept of "preference" does not have the same meaning, or raise the same equality concerns, as it does in the employment and admissions contexts.

Brown's approach fails to recognize that, because gender-segregated teams are the norm in intercollegiate athletics programs, athletics differs from admissions and employment in analytically material ways. In providing for gender-segregated teams, intercollegiate athletics programs necessarily allocate opportunities separately for male and female students, and, thus, any inquiry into a claim of gender discrimination must compare the athletics participation opportunities provided for men with those provided for women. For this reason, and because recruitment of interested athletes is at the discretion of the institution, there is a risk that the institution will recruit only enough women to fill positions in a program that already underrepresents women, and that the smaller size of the women's program will have the effect of discouraging women's participation.

In this unique context, Title IX operates to ensure that the gender-segregated allocation of athletics opportunities does not disadvantage either gender. Rather than create a quota or preference, this unavoidably gender-conscious comparison merely provides for the allocation of athletics resources and participation opportunities between the sexes in a non-discriminatory manner. . . .

* * *

F.

Brown has contended throughout this litigation that the significant disparity in athletics opportunities for men and women at Brown is the result of a gender-based differential in the level of interest in sports and that the district court's application of the three-part test requires universities to provide athletics opportunities for women to an extent that exceeds their relative interests and abilities in sports. Thus, at the heart of this litigation is the question whether Title IX permits Brown to deny its female students equal opportunity to participate in sports, based upon its unproven assertion that the district court's finding of a significant disparity in athletics opportunities for male and female students reflects, not discrimination in Brown's intercollegiate athletics program, but a lack of interest on the part of its female students that is unrelated to a lack of opportunities.

We view Brown's argument that women are less interested than men in participating in intercollegiate athletics, as well as its conclusion that institutions should be required to accommodate the interests and abilities of its female students only to the extent that it accommodates the interests and abilities of its male students, with great suspicion. To assert that Title IX permits institutions to provide fewer athletics participation opportunities for women than for men, based upon the premise that women are less interested in sports than are men, is (among other things) to ignore the fact that Title IX was enacted in order to remedy discrimination that results from stereotyped notions of women's interests and abilities.

Interest and ability rarely develop in a vacuum; they evolve as a function of opportunity and experience. The Policy Interpretation recognizes that women's lower rate of participation in athletics reflects women's historical lack of opportunities to participate in sports. *See* 44 Fed. Reg. at 71,419 ("Participation in intercollegiate sports has historically been emphasized for men but not women. Partially as a consequence of this, participation rates of women are far below those of men"). . . .

Thus, there exists the danger that, rather than providing a true measure of women's interest in sports, statistical evidence purporting to reflect women's interest instead provides only a measure of the very discrimination that is and has been the basis for women's lack of opportunity to participate in sports. Prong three requires some kind of evidence of interest in athletics, and the Title IX framework permits the use of statistical evidence in assessing the level of interest in sports.[15] Nevertheless, to allow a numbers-based lack-of-interest defense to become the instrument of further discrimination against the underrepresented gender would pervert the remedial purpose of Title IX. We conclude that, even if it can be empirically demonstrated that, at a particular time, women have less interest in sports than do men, such evidence, standing alone, cannot justify providing fewer athletics opportunities for women than for men. Furthermore, such evidence is completely irrelevant where, as here, viable and successful women's varsity teams have been demoted or eliminated. We emphasize that, on the facts of this case, Brown's lack-of-interest arguments are of no consequence. As the prior panel recognized, while the question of full and effective accommodation of athletics interests and abilities is potentially a complicated issue where plaintiffs seek to create a new team or to elevate to varsity status a team that has never competed in varsity competition, no such difficulty is presented here, where

---

[15] Under the Policy Interpretation, institutions may determine the athletic interests and abilities of students by nondiscriminatory methods of their choosing provided:

  a. The processes take into account the nationally increasing levels of women's interests and abilities;

  b. The methods of determining interest and ability do not disadvantage the members of an underrepresented sex;

  c. The methods of determining ability take into account team performance records; and

  d. The methods are responsive to the expressed interests of students capable of intercollegiate competition who are members of an underrepresented sex.

44 Fed. Reg. at 71,417.

The 1990 version of the Title IX Athletics Investigator's Manual, an internal agency document, instructs investigating officials to consider, inter alia, the following: (i) any institutional surveys or assessments of students' athletics interests and abilities, see Valerie M. Bonnette & Lamar Daniel, *Department of Education, Title IX Athletics Investigator's Manual* at 22 (1990); (ii) the "expressed interests" of the underrepresented gender, *id.* at 25; (iii) other programs indicative of interests and abilities, such as club and intramural sports, sports programs at "feeder" schools, community and regional sports programs, and physical education classes, *id.*

As the district court noted, however, the agency characterizes surveys as a "simple way to identify which additional sports might appropriately be created to achieve compliance. . . . Thus, a survey of interests would follow a determination that an institution does not satisfy prong three; it would not be utilized to make that determination in the first instance." *Cohen III*, 897 F. Supp. at 210 n.51; see 1990 *Investigator's Manual* at 27 (explaining that a survey or assessment of interests and abilities is not required by the Title IX regulation or the Policy Interpretation but may be required as part of a remedy when OCR has concluded that an institution's current program does not equally effectively accommodate the interests and abilities of students).

plaintiffs seek to reinstate what were successful university-funded teams right up until the moment the teams were demoted. . . .[16]

On these facts, Brown's failure to accommodate fully and effectively the interests and abilities of the underrepresented gender is clearly established. . . . Under these circumstances, the district court's finding that there are interested women able to compete at the university-funded varsity level is clearly correct. Finally, the tremendous growth in women's participation in sports since Title IX was enacted disproves Brown's argument that women are less interested in sports for reasons unrelated to lack of opportunity. *See, e.g.,* Mike Tharp et al., *Sports crazy! Ready, set, go. Why we love our games,* U.S. News & World Report, July 15, 1996, at 33–34 (attributing to Title IX the explosive growth of women's participation in sports and the debunking of "the traditional myth that women aren't interested in sports"). [Note that in a portion of *Brown I* not included in the prior excerpt, the First Circuit had observed, in this regard, that Brown University had introduced no "evidence in the record that men are any more likely to engage in athletics than women, absent socialization and disparate opportunities." 991 F.2d at 900.]

Brown's relative interests approach is not a reasonable interpretation of the three-part test. This approach contravenes the purpose of the statute and the regulation because it does not permit an institution or a district court to remedy a gender-based disparity in athletics participation opportunities. Instead, this approach freezes that disparity by law, thereby disadvantaging further the underrepresented gender. Had Congress intended to entrench, rather than change, the status quo—with its historical emphasis on men's participation opportunities to the detriment of women's opportunities—it need not have gone to all the trouble of enacting Title IX.

* * *

Of course, a remedy that requires an institution to cut, add, or elevate the status of athletes or entire teams may impact the genders differently, but this will be so only if there is a gender-based disparity with respect to athletics opportunities to begin with, which is the only circumstance in which prong three comes into play. Here, however, it has not been shown that Brown's men students will be disadvantaged by the full and effective accommodation of the athletics interests and abilities of its women students.

---

[16] The district court found that the women's gymnastics team had won the Ivy League championship in 1989–90 and was a "thriving university-funded varsity team prior to the 1991 demotion;" that the donor-funded women's fencing team had been successful for many years and that its request to be upgraded to varsity status had been supported by the athletics director at the time; that the donor-funded women's ski team had been consistently competitive despite a meager budget; and that the club-status women's water polo team had demonstrated the interest and ability to compete at full varsity status. *Cohen III,* 879 F. Supp. at 190.

VII.

[While the circuit court majority upheld the district court's ruling that Brown's athletic program was in violation of Title IX, the panel refused to endorse the remedial order that required Brown to upgrade its existing women's gymnastics, fencing, skiing, and water polo teams to university-funded varsity status. The Court said that Brown should have the option to cut back, instead, on its men's varsity slots in order to put itself in compliance with the law.]

* * *

There can be no doubt that Title IX has changed the face of women's sports as well as our society's interest in and attitude toward women athletes and women's sports. In addition, there is ample evidence that increased athletics participation opportunities for women and young girls, available as a result of Title IX enforcement, have had salutary effects in other areas of societal concern.

One need look no further than the impressive performances of our country's women athletes in the 1996 Olympic Summer Games to see that Title IX has had a dramatic and positive impact on the capabilities of our women athletes, particularly in team sports. These Olympians represent the first full generation of women to grow up under the aegis of Title IX. The unprecedented success of these athletes is due, in no small measure, to Title IX's beneficent effects on women's sports, as the athletes themselves have acknowledged time and again. What stimulated this remarkable change in the quality of women's athletic competition was not a sudden, anomalous upsurge in women's interest in sports, but the enforcement of Title IX's mandate of gender equity in sports.

Affirmed in part, reversed in part, and remanded for further proceedings. No costs on appeal to either party.

TORRUELLA, CHIEF JUDGE (Dissenting).

Because I am not persuaded that the majority's view represents the state of the law today, I respectfully dissent.

* * *

II. Brown's Equal Protection Challenge

* * *

A. The District Court's Construction of the Three-Prong Test

1. Prong One

A central issue in this case is the manner in which athletic "participation opportunities" are counted. During the 1990–91 academic year, Brown fielded 16 men's and 15 women's varsity teams on which 566 men and 328 women participated. By the 1993–94 year, there were 12 university-funded men's teams and 13 university funded women's teams. These teams included 479 men and 312 women. Based on an analysis of membership in varsity teams, the district court concluded that there existed a disparity between female participation in intercollegiate athletics and female student enrollment.

Even assuming that membership numbers in varsity sports is a reasonable proxy for participation opportunities—a view with which I do not concur—contact sports should be eliminated from the calculus. The regulation at 34 C.F.R. § 106.41 (1995)(b) provides that an academic institution may operate separate teams for members of each sex "where selection of such teams is based upon competitive skill or the activity involved is a contact sport." 34 C.F.R. § 106.41(b). . . . The regulation, therefore, allows schools to operate single-sex teams in contact sports. In counting participation opportunities, therefore, it does not make sense to include in the calculus athletes participating in contact sports that include only men's teams. For example, if a university chooses to sponsor a football team, it is permitted to sponsor only a men's team. Not all sports are the same and the university should be given the flexibility to determine which activities are most beneficial to its student body. By including in its accounting a contact sport that requires very large numbers of participants, e.g., football, the district court skews the number of athletic participants—making it impossible for the university to provide both men's and women's teams in other sports.

If the athletes competing in sports for which the university is permitted to field single-sex teams are excluded from the calculation of participation rates, the proportion of women participants would increase dramatically and prong one might be satisfied. If so, the inquiry ends and Brown should be judged to be in compliance.

2. Prong Two

The district court concluded, and the majority appears to agree, that Brown failed to satisfy prong two because "merely reducing program offerings to the overrepresented gender does not constitute program expansion for the underrepresented gender." This is a curious result because the entire three-prong test is based on relative participation rates. Prong one, for example, requires that participation opportunities be provided proportionately to enrollment, but does not mandate any absolute number of such opportunities. The district court's conclusion with respect to prong two, however, implies that a school must not only demonstrate that the proportion of women in their program is growing over time, it must also show that the absolute number of women participating is increasing.[26]

---

[26] This requirement presents a dilemma for a school in which women are less interested in athletics, as Brown contends is the case. Under such conditions, a school may be unable to succeed under the second prong because there may not be enough interested female students to achieve a continuing increase in the number of female participants.

Under the district court's interpretation, a school facing budgetary constraints must, in order to comply with prong two, increase the opportunities available to the underrepresented gender, even if it cannot afford to do so. . . . I see no possible justification for this interpretation—the regulation is intended to protect against discrimination, not to promote athletics on college campuses. A school is not required to sponsor an athletic program of any particular size. It is not for the courts, or the legislature, for that matter, to mandate programs of a given size. The most that can be demanded is that athletics be provided in a non-discriminatory manner.

* * *

3. Prong Three

Prong three of the three-prong test states that, where an institution does not comply with prongs one or two, compliance will be assessed on the basis of

> whether it can be demonstrated that the interests and abilities of the members of the [proportionately underrepresented] sex have been fully and effectively accommodated by the present program.

44 Fed. Reg. 71,413, 71,418 (December 11, 1979).

* * *

. . . Brown argues that prong three is in fact ambiguous with respect to whether "fully" means (1) an institution must meet 100% of the underrepresented gender's unmet reasonable interest and ability, or (2) an institution must meet the underrepresented gender's unmet reasonable interest and ability as fully as it meets those of the overrepresented gender. I agree with Brown that, in the context of OCR's Policy Interpretation, prong three is susceptible to at least these two plausible interpretations.

Additionally, § 1681(a), a provision enacted by Congress as part of Title IX itself, casts doubt on the district court's reading of prong three. 20 U.S.C. § 1681(a) (1988). As Brown points out, Title IX, of which the Policy Interpretation is an administrative interpretation, contains language that prohibits the ordering of preferential treatment on the basis of gender due to a failure of a program to substantially mirror the gender ratio of an institution. Specifically, with respect to Title IX's guarantee that no person shall be excluded on the basis of sex from "participation in, denied the benefits of or subjected to discrimination under any education program or activity receiving Federal financial assistance," 20 U.S.C. § 1681(a),

> nothing contained [therein] shall be interpreted to require any educational institution to grant preferential or disparate treatment to the members of one sex on account of an imbalance which may exist with respect to the total number or percentage of persons of the sex participating in or receiving the benefits of any

federally supported program or activity, in comparison with the total number or percentage of persons of that sex in any community.

Id. § 1681(b). Section 1681(b) provides yet another reason why the district court's reading of prong three is troublesome and why Brown's reading is a reasonable alternative.

* * *

B.   *The District Court's Interpretation and the Resulting Equal Protection Problem*

* * *

1.   *The Quota*

I believe that the three prong test, as the district court interprets it, is a quota. I am in square disagreement with the majority, who believe that "no aspect of the Title IX regime at issue in this case . . . mandates gender-based preferences or quotas." Put another way, I agree that "Title IX is not an affirmative action statute," but I believe that is exactly what the district court has made of it. As interpreted by the district court, the test constitutes an affirmative action, quota-based scheme.

* * *

The majority claims that "neither the Policy Interpretation nor the district court's interpretation of it, mandates statistical balancing." The logic of this position escapes me. A school can satisfy the test in three ways. The first prong is met if the school provides participation opportunities for male and female students in numbers substantially proportionate to their enrollments. This prong surely requires statistical balancing. The second prong is satisfied if an institution that cannot meet prong one can show a "continuing practice of program expansion which is demonstrably responsive to the developing interest and abilities of the members of the underrepresented sex." 44 Fed. Reg. at 71,418. It can hardly be denied that this prong requires statistical balancing as it is essentially a test that requires the school to show that it is moving in the direction of satisfying the first prong. Establishing that a school is moving inexorably closer to satisfying a requirement that demands statistical balancing can only be done by demonstrating an improvement in the statistical balance. In other words, the second prong also requires balancing. Finally, the third prong, interpreted as the majority advocates, dispenses with statistical balancing only because it chooses to accord zero weight to one side of the balance. Even a single person with a reasonable unmet interest defeats compliance. This standard, in fact, goes farther than the straightforward quota test of prong one. According to the district court, the unmet interests of the underrepresented sex must be completely accommodated before any of the interest of the overrepresented gender can be accommodated.[28]

A pragmatic overview of the effect of the three-prong test leads me to reject the majority's claim that the three-prong test does not amount to a quota because it involves multiple prongs. In my view it is the result of the test, and not the number of steps involved, that should determine if a quota system exists. Regardless of how many steps are involved, the fact remains that the test requires proportionate participation opportunities for both sexes (prong one) unless one sex is simply not interested in participating (prong three). It seems to me that a quota with an exception for situations in which there are insufficient interested students to allow the school to meet it remains a quota. All of the negative effects of a quota remain, and the school can escape the quota under prong three only by offering preferential treatment to the group that has demonstrated less interest in athletics.

2. *"Extremely Persuasive Justification" Test*

In view of the quota scheme adopted by the district court, and Congress' specific disavowal of any intent to require quotas as part of Title IX, appellees have not met their burden of showing an "exceedingly persuasive justification" for this gender-conscious exercise of government authority. As recently set forth in *Virginia*, "parties who seek to defend gender-based government action must demonstrate an 'exceedingly persuasive justification' for that action." *Virginia*, 116 S. Ct. at 2274. . . .

* * *

III. Evidentiary Issues

* * *

The refusal to accept surveys of interest levels as evidence of interest raises the question of what indicators might be used. The majority offers no guidance to a school seeking to assess the levels of interest of its students. Although the three-prong test, even as interpreted by the district court, appears to allow the school the opportunity to show a lack of interest, the majority rejects the best—and perhaps the only—mechanism for making such a showing.

Brown claims that the district court erred in excluding evidence pertaining to the relative athletic interests of men and women at the

---

[28] The problem with the majority's argument can be illustrated with a hypothetical college admissions policy that would require proportionality between the gender ratio of the local student aged population and that of admitted students. This policy is comparable to prong one of the three prong test and is, without a doubt, a quota. It is no less a quota if an exception exists for schools whose gender ratio differs from that of the local population but which admit every applicant of the underrepresented gender. It remains a quota because the school is forced to admit every female applicant until it reaches the requisite proportion. Similarly, the district court's interpretation requires the school to accommodate the interests of every female student until proportionality is reached.

university. Brown sought to introduce the NCAA Gender Equity Study and the results of an undergraduate poll on student interest in athletics, but was not permitted to do so. The majority is unsympathetic to Brown's claim that the disparity between athletic opportunities for men and women reflect a gender-based difference in interest levels. Indeed, despite Brown's attempt to present evidence in support of its claim, the majority characterizes Brown's argument as an "unproven assertion."[30]

* * *

Accordingly, I would reverse and remand for further proceedings

———

NOTES AND QUESTIONS

1. *Meaning of the OCR Test.* What do the opinions in the two *Brown* cases explain about the meaning of the three-pronged OCR Test? Do they clarify that an institution must meet only one of the prongs? Do they clarify the meaning of any phrases in one of the prongs, such as "substantially proportionate" in the first or "program expansion which is demonstrably responsive to . . . developing interest and abilities" in the second? How about "fully and effectively accommodated" in the third?

2. *Affirmative Action Review of the OCR Test?* Does Judge Torruella correctly assess the Test by constitutional equal protection standards set by the Supreme Court in cases involving admissions to sex segregated schools, like *Virginia (VMI)*, and in cases involving race-conscious or gender-conscious school admissions, employment hiring, and government contract selections, like *Adarand*? The OCR Policy Interpretation certainly constitutes state action and it is overtly gender-conscious, but does it operate differently than previously challenged race or gender-conscious standards because it is framed to provide separate but equal opportunities?

Asked differently, does the Test have an "extremely persuasive" or even "compelling" justification—other than remedying past or avoiding future discrimination—that would not be available in prior "affirmative action" cases? Given that justification, is the question of whether the Test imposes something that could be termed a "quota" relevant? And if enrollment-based proportionality is treated as imposing a quota, why does interest-based

---

[30] Among the evidence submitted by Brown are: (i) admissions data showing greater athletic interest among male applicants than female applicants; (ii) college board data showing greater athletic interest and prior participation rates by prospective male applicants than female applicants; (iii) data from the Cooperative Institutional Research Program at UCLA indicating greater athletic interest among men than women; (iv) an independent telephone survey of 500 randomly selected Brown undergraduates that reveals that Brown offers women participation opportunities in excess of their representation in the pool of interested, qualified students; (v) intramural and club participation rates that demonstrate higher participation rates among men than women; (vi) walk-on and try-out numbers that reflect a greater interest among men than women; (vii) high school participation rates that show a much lower rate of participation among females than among males; (viii) the NCAA Gender Equity Committee data showing that women across the country participate in athletics at a lower rate than men.

proportionality not also do so? How likely do you think it is that even a conservative Supreme Court suspicious of affirmative action in educational admissions would find enforcement of the Test to be unconstitutional?

3. *Substantially Proportionate to Enrollment or to Interests?* The primary early policy debate about the Test was whether the substantially proportionate standard should relate to the gender-based *interests* of a current student body rather than to the gender balance in the student body's total enrollment. *See, e.g., Pederson v. Louisiana State University,* 912 F. Supp. 892 (M.D. La. 1996), *rev'd,* 201 F.3d 388 (5th Cir. 2000). Those who favor using current student interests rather than total enrollment cite statistics showing that a substantially higher proportion of male college students are interested in intercollegiate competition. The response of those who defend the current use of enrollment is that the level of opportunities ultimately will determine the level of interests, as the growth of female sports on the high school as well as college level since the passage of Title IX demonstrates. Can the lack of the potential for proportionate female interests in intercollegiate competition be assumed in the absence of proportionate opportunities? Should the Test be amended because of the kind of data cited in footnote 30 of Judge Tottuella's dissent? Can such data be the basis for a determination of the interests of a school's potential applicant pool? Finally, consider whether the argument for using the interests of a current student body is particularly weak for elite Division I programs whose athletes come to the school primarily because of the program.

4. *Meeting the Test Through Elimination of Men's Teams.* In order to meet the substantial proportionality requirement, schools in addition to adding women's teams have eliminated many men's teams, often provoking protests from the male athletes. There have been several unsuccessful challenges to this approach to Title IX compliance. *See, e.g., Boulahanis v. Board of Regents of Illinois State Univ.,* 198 F.3d 633 (7th Cir.1999); *Neal v. Board of Trustees of California State Universities,* 198 F.3d 763 (9th Cir.1999); *Kelley v. University of Illinois,* 35 F.3d 265 (7th Cir. 1994). The challenges have failed to convince courts that the test denies equal protection to male athletes or that Title IX cannot be used to achieve equality through the contraction rather than only the addition of programs. Is there any text in Title IX that promotes the expansion or maintenance rather than equalization of athletic programs?

5. *Reconsidering the Tower Amendment?* University compliance with Title IX and the impact on the number of men's intercollegiate sports teams would have been eased considerably if Senator Tower's amendment to exempt revenue producing sports had been adopted. Division I football rosters typically number more than 100, including 85 scholarship student-athletes permitted by NCAA regulations. Schools have had to balance these huge rosters with more and larger female teams in other sports.

Should the Tower amendment be reconsidered? Is there a case to be made that a sport that produces enough revenue to at least support itself should not be included in the calculation of whether an educational institution is providing equal opportunities to female students? Or is a position on the football team like any other opportunity for intercollegiate competition that schools should be required to compare to the other athletic opportunities that they could instead provide their male students? Why should the fact that 85 male football players help create millions of dollars in revenue ultimately determine how the university allocates this revenue to non-revenue sports?

6. *What Does the Third Prong Require?* The "fully and effectively accommodated" requirement in the third prong of the Test poses an analogous question to that posed in the debate addressed in Note 3 above: Should the "interests and abilities" that must be accommodated only be ones of current students or also ones of potential students? If a university was required to consider the latter, it would be required to consider whether the establishment of a new women's team would attract enough new students to support the team's intercollegiate competition.

But the current interpretation does not seem to require the consideration of the potential to attract new students. In 2005, a Bush Administration official in the Department of Education's Office of Civil Rights issued a clarification to the three-prong approach providing:

> Under the third compliance option, an educational institution is in compliance with Title IX's mandate to provide equal athletic participation opportunities if, despite the underrepresentation of one sex in the intercollegiate athletics program, the institution is fully and effectively accommodating the athletic interests and abilities of its students who are underrepresented in its current varsity athletic program offerings. An institution will be found in compliance with part three unless there exists a sport (s) for the underrepresented sex for which all three of the following conditions are met: (1) unmet interest sufficient to sustain a varsity team in the sport(s); (2) sufficient ability to sustain an intercollegiate team in the sport(s); and (3) reasonable expectation of intercollegiate competition for a team in the sport(s) within the school's normal competitive region. Thus, schools are not required to accommodate the interests and abilities of all their students or fulfill every request for the addition or elevation of particular sports, unless all three conditions are present. In this analysis, the burden of proof is on OCR (in the case of an OCR investigation or compliance review), or on students (in the case of a complaint filed with the institution under its Title IX grievance procedures), to show by a preponderance of the evidence that the institution is not in compliance with part three.

Moreover, the letter indicated that a properly devised survey can demonstrate

> insufficient interest to support an additional varsity team for the underrepresented sex will create a presumption of compliance with part three of the three-part test and the Title IX regulatory requirement to provide nondiscriminatory athletic participation opportunities. The presumption of compliance can only be overcome if OCR finds direct and very persuasive evidence of unmet interest

sufficient to sustain a varsity team, such as the recent elimination of a viable team for the underrepresented sex or a recent, broad-based petition from an existing club team for elevation to varsity status.

In 2010, the Obama Administration's Assistant Secretary of Education for Civil Rights announced that this letter had been withdrawn. The policy change reflected in the letter seems to be that email or internet surveys can no longer be the principal basis for demonstrating the absence of unmet need under Prong Three. The letter, however, reaffirmed that the OCR would find a violation only if (1) there was unmet interest in a particular sport, (2) there is sufficient ability to sustain a team in the sport, and (3) there was reasonable expectation of competition for the team.

Title IX litigation has further considered two questions posed by the first prong: (1) how strictly to define "substantially proportionate," and (2) which activities should count as "participation opportunities."

BIEDIGER V. QUINNIPIAC UNIVERSITY
691 F.3d 85 (2d Cir. 2012)

RAGGI, CIRCUIT JUDGE.

Quinnipiac University appeals pursuant to 28 U.S.C. § 1292(a)(1) from a permanent injunction ordered on July 22, 2010, by the United States District Court for the District of Connecticut (Stefan R. Underhill, *Judge*), after a bench trial at which Quinnipiac was found to have violated Title IX of the Education Amendments of 1972 ("Title IX") by failing to afford equal participation opportunities in varsity sports to female students. *See Biediger v. Quinnipiac Univ.*, 728 F. Supp. 2d 62 (D. Conn. 2010). Quinnipiac argues that the injunction, which prohibits any such future discrimination, should be vacated because it is based on a Title IX ruling infected by errors in counting the varsity athletic participation opportunities afforded Quinnipiac's female students in the 2009–10 school year.

Specifically, Quinnipiac faults the district court for excluding from its count of the total athletic participation opportunities afforded female students: (1) 11 roster positions on the women's indoor and outdoor track and field teams, held by members of Quinnipiac's women's cross-country team who were required to join the track teams even though they were unable to compete in 2009–10 because they were injured or "red-shirted"; and (2) all 30 roster positions on Quinnipiac's nascent women's competitive cheerleading team, based on a finding that the team did not afford the athletic participation opportunities of a varsity sport. Quinnipiac further contends that, even if these 41 roster positions should not count as varsity athletic participation opportunities for women, the district court erred in concluding that (3) the resulting 3.62% disparity between the percentage of all participation opportunities in varsity sports afforded female students (58.25%) and the percentage of enrolled female undergraduates (61.87%) established a Title IX violation warranting the challenged injunctive relief.

We identify no merit in these arguments, and we affirm the challenged injunction substantially for the reasons stated by the district court in its comprehensive and well reasoned opinion.

I.   *Background*

A.   *Quinnipiac's Decision To Eliminate Women's Volleyball Prompts This Title IX Action*

This lawsuit has its origins in Quinnipiac's March 2009 announcement that in the 2009–10 academic year, it would eliminate its varsity sports teams for women's volleyball, men's golf, and men's outdoor track and field, while simultaneously creating a new varsity sports team for women's competitive cheerleading. Plaintiffs, five Quinnipiac women's volleyball players and their coach, Robin Sparks, filed this action in April 2009, charging the university with violating Title IX by denying women equal varsity athletic participation opportunities, and seeking an injunction that, among other things, prevented Quinnipiac from eliminating its women's volleyball team. After a hearing, the district court preliminarily enjoined Quinnipiac from withdrawing support from its volleyball team, finding that Quinnipiac systematically and artificially increased women's teams' rosters and decreased men's teams' rosters to achieve the appearance of Title IX compliance. *See Biediger v. Quinnipiac Univ.*, 616 F. Supp. 2d 277 (D.Conn.2009). The district court subsequently certified a plaintiff class of all present and future female Quinnipiac students who had been or would be harmed by the alleged Title IX discrimination and sought injunctive relief. *See Biediger v. Quinnipiac Univ.*, No. 3:09-cv-621 (SRU), 2010 WL 2017773 (D. Conn. May 20, 2010). In June 2010, the district court conducted a bench trial on plaintiffs' claim of disproportionate allocation of athletic participation opportunities and, finding in their favor, granted permanent injunctive relief.

* * *

[The Court recounted the basic provisions of Title IX.]

In 1996, the DOE's Office of Civil Rights ("OCR"), which is responsible for enforcement of Title IX, *see* 20 U.S.C. § 3441(a)(3), clarified that the analysis for determining whether a university affords substantially proportionate participation opportunities to athletes of both sexes under the first prong of the three-part test—the prong relied on by Quinnipiac in defending against plaintiffs' Title IX effective accommodation claim— "begins with a determination of the number of participation opportunities afforded to male and female athletes in the intercollegiate athletic program." OCR, U.S. DOE, *Clarification of Intercollegiate Athletics Policy Guidance: The Three-Part Test*, at 2–3 (Jan. 15, 1996) ("1996

Clarification"). OCR explained that, "[a]s a general rule, all athletes who are listed on a team's squad or eligibility list and are on the team as of the team's first competitive event are counted as participants." *Id.* at 3. Further, "an athlete who participates in more than one sport will be counted as a participant in each sport in which he or she participates." *Id.* It is not necessary for an athlete to meet minimum criteria of playing time or athletic ability to count as a participant. As OCR explained, "athletes who practice but may not compete" nevertheless "receive numerous benefits and services, such as training and practice time, coaching, tutoring services, locker room facilities, and equipment, as well as important non-tangible benefits derived from being a member of an intercollegiate athletic team." *Id.* Thus, "it is necessary to count all athletes who receive such benefits when determining the number of athletic opportunities provided to men and women." *Id.* In a letter accompanying the 1996 Clarification, however, OCR sounded a note of caution: for an athlete to be counted, he or she must be afforded a participation opportunity that is "real, not illusory," in that it offers the same benefits as would be provided to other *bona fide* athletes. *See* Letter from Norma V. Cantú, Assistant Sec'y for Civil Rights, OCR, U.S. DOE, to Colleagues, at 4 (Jan. 16, 1996) ("1996 OCR Letter").

In a 2008 letter, OCR explained that a genuine athletic participation opportunity must take place in the context of a "sport." Letter from Stephanie Monroe, Assistant Sec'y for Civil Rights, OCR, U.S. DOE, to Colleagues, at 1–2 (Sept. 17, 2008) ("2008 OCR Letter"). If a school is a member of a recognized intercollegiate athletic organization, such as the National Collegiate Athletic Association ("NCAA"), that subjects the activity at issue to its organizational requirements, OCR will "presume" that the activity is a sport and that participation can be counted under Title IX. *Id.* at 1–2. But if that presumption does not apply or has been rebutted, OCR will determine whether the activity qualifies as a sport by reference to several factors relating to "program structure and administration" and "team preparation and competition." *Id.* at 1–4.

Eight years earlier, in 2000, OCR had issued two letters stating that cheerleading, whether of the sideline or competitive variety, was presumptively not a sport, and that team members could not be counted as athletes under Title IX. While the letters indicated OCR's willingness to review particular cheerleading programs on a case-by-case basis, the parties stipulated in the district court that, since 2000, OCR has never recognized an intercollegiate varsity cheerleading program to be a sport for Title IX purposes. *See Biediger v. Quinnipiac Univ.*, 728 F. Supp. 2d at 92. Nor has Quinnipiac ever sought OCR recognition of its competitive cheerleading program as a sports activity. *See id.* at 85.

* * *

[The court reviewed the district court opinion, which held that Quinnipiac had improperly double counted track athletes and members of the cheerleading squad. It also explained that it deferred to the OCR's interpretation of its own guidelines.]

Here, Quinnipiac elected to defend against plaintiffs' discrimination claim *only* by reference to the first safe harbor created by the three-part test, arguing that its athletics program provided "substantially proportionate" athletic participation opportunities to women. For reasons we discuss *infra* at 99–108, the district court reasonably found to the contrary, thus simultaneously rejecting Quinnipiac's defense and finding for plaintiffs on the first element of their disparate treatment claim. To the extent that plaintiffs further offered evidence that Quinnipiac's disproportionate provision of athletic participation opportunities failed fully and effectively to accommodate the athletic interests and abilities of its female undergraduates insofar as it eliminated the women's volleyball team, Quinnipiac did not dispute the point. Nor did it attempt to argue that the school has a history of expanding women's athletic participation opportunities.

In sum, as a matter of Quinnipiac's litigation strategy, resolution of this case effectively turned on whether Quinnipiac's sex based treatment of varsity athletes provided its female students with genuine athletic participation opportunities substantially proportionate to their enrollment. Because the district court found that it did not, plaintiffs carried their burden to prove unlawful disparate treatment. In these circumstances, *amicus curiae's* challenge to the judicial deference accorded the agency's 1979 Policy Interpretation generally, or its articulated three-part test specifically, is unpersuasive.

* * *

[The Court rejected Quinnipiac's method of counting track athletes.]

D. *Athletic Participation Opportunities for Women in Competitive Cheerleading: The Determination That the Activity Does Not Yet Qualify as a "Sport"*

Competitive cheerleading, which Quinnipiac decided to create as a new women's varsity sport team for 2009–10, is a late twentieth-century outgrowth of traditional sideline cheerleading. Whereas sideline cheerleaders generally strive to entertain audiences or solicit crowd reaction at sport or school functions, a competitive cheerleading team seeks to pit its skills against other teams for the purpose of winning. *See Biediger v. Quinnipiac Univ.*, 728 F. Supp. 2d at 78. Thus, to distinguish the two activities, competitive cheerleaders

> do not attempt to elicit crowd response; generally do not use pom-poms, megaphones, signs, or other props associated with [sideline] cheerleading teams; . . . wear uniforms consisting of

shorts and jerseys, much like what women's volleyball players don; and emphasize the more gymnastic elements of sideline cheerleading, such as aerial maneuvers, floor tumbling, and balancing exercises, to the exclusion of those activities intended to rally the watching audience.

Id. (observing that competitive cheerleading is an "athletic endeavor" that might be described as "group floor gymnastics" (internal quotation marks omitted)).

The district court nevertheless concluded that the 30 roster positions that Quinnipiac assigned competitive cheerleading for 2009–10 could not be counted under Title IX because the activity did not yet afford the participation opportunities of a varsity "sport." *See id.* at 101.

Preliminary to reaching this conclusion, the district court observed that competitive cheerleading is not yet recognized as a "sport," or even an "emerging sport," by the NCAA action that would have triggered a presumption in favor of counting its participants under Title IX. *See id.* at 93–94 (citing 2008 OCR Letter). Nor has DOE recognized competitive cheerleading as a sport; to the contrary, in two letters in 2000, OCR indicated competitive cheerleading is presumptively not a sport, while leaving open the possibility for a different conclusion with respect to a particular cheerleading program. *See* April 2000 OCR Letter at 3; May 2000 OCR Letter at 1. There is, however, no record evidence of any competitive cheerleading program being recognized by DOE as a sport. *See Biediger v. Quinnipiac Univ.*, 728 F. Supp. 2d at 92.

Mindful of these circumstances, the district court proceeded carefully to review the structure, administration, team preparation, and competition of Quinnipiac's competitive cheerleading program to determine whether it nevertheless qualified as a sport whose athletic participation opportunities should be counted for purposes of Title IX. *See* 2008 OCR Letter at 2–4 (listing factors relevant to identifying activity as sport). Again, we only briefly summarize the district court's detailed findings, which find ample support in the record evidence. The district court found that in terms of the team's operating budget, benefits, services, and coaching staff, competitive cheerleading was generally structured and administered by Quinnipiac's athletics department in a manner consistent with the school's other varsity teams. *See Biediger v. Quinnipiac Univ.*, 728 F. Supp. 2d at 95. The district court noted two "minor" exceptions to this conclusion: Quinnipiac did not afford its competitive cheerleading team locker space; and because the NCAA did not recognize competitive cheerleading as a sport, the team did not receive NCAA catastrophic injury insurance and had to obtain it from a separate provider. *Id.* at 99; *see id.* at 95. With respect to factors relating to the team's preparation and competition, the district court found that the competitive cheerleading team's practice time, regimen, and venue were consistent with other varsity sports. *See id.* at 96. Further, as with other varsity sports, the length of the competitive cheerleading season and the minimum number of competitions in which a team would participate were pre-determined by a governing athletic organization, the recently formed National Competitive Stunt and Tumbling Association, of which Quinnipiac was a founding member. *See id.* at 82–83, 96–97. Finally, the purpose of the team—to compete athletically at the intercollegiate varsity level—was akin to that of other varsity sports. *See id.* at 99.

At the same time, however, the district court identified a number of circumstances that sufficiently distinguished Quinnipiac's competitive cheerleading program from traditional varsity sports as to "compel[ ] the decision that, for the 2009–10 season," the program could not "be counted as a varsity sport for purposes of Title IX." *Id.* First, Quinnipiac did not—and, in 2009–10, could not—conduct any off-campus recruitment for its competitive cheerleading team, in marked contrast not only to the school's other varsity sports teams but also to a typical NCAA Division I sports program. *See id.* at 95–96, 99. The district court explained the significance of this circumstance: "Although the women on the Quinnipiac competitive cheer team were athletically able, they would have been all the more talented had [Coach] Powers been able to seek out the best competitive cheerleaders around the country, as any other varsity coach would have been able to do." *Id.* at 99.

More important, no uniform set of rules applied to competitive cheerleading competition throughout the 2009–10 season. Indeed, in the ten competitions in which the Quinnipiac team participated during the regular season, it was judged according to five different scoring systems. *See id.* at 97. Further, in these competitions, Quinnipiac did not face only varsity intercollegiate competitive cheerleading teams. Rather, it was challenged by "a motley assortment of competitors," *id.* at 98, including collegiate club opponents who did not receive varsity benefits, collegiate sideline cheerleading teams, and all-star opponents unaffiliated with a particular academic institution, some of whom may still have been high-school age, *see id.* at 97–98. As the district court observed, "application of a uniform set of rules for competition and the restriction of competition to contests against other varsity opponents" are the "touchstones" of a varsity sports program. *Id.* at 99–100. "Those features ensure that play is fair in each game, that teams' performances can be compared across a season, and that teams can be distinguished in terms of quality." *Id.* at 100.

The concerns raised by these irregularities in season competition were only aggravated by aspects of post-season play. Notably, competitive cheerleading offered no progressive playoff system leading to a championship game. *See id.* at 98. Rather, it provided an open invitational, which neither excluded any team on the basis of its regular season performance nor ranked or seeded participating teams on that basis. *See id.* Instead, all entrants competed in a single championship round in which the team with the highest score won. *See id.* That round, moreover, was subject to a new rule of competition that had not applied to Quinnipiac in any of its regular season competitions: a mandatory 45–60 second "spirit" segment in which a team was judged by the intensity of the response it elicited from the crowd and the number of the sponsoring brand's props that it employed, features that Quinnipiac's coach confirmed were more characteristic of sideline rather than competitive cheerleading. *See id.* at 98–99. Viewing the totality of these circumstances, the district court concluded that the competitive cheerleading team's post-season competition did not conform to expectations for a varsity sport.

Most other varsity sports would have used some system to separate teams and competitors in terms of quality, and would have ranked, seeded, or excluded teams on the basis of their performances during the regular season. Moreover, any other varsity sport would not have imposed new rules of competition in the post-season that teams did not follow during the regular season. *Id.* at 100.

Based on these findings, as well as those pertaining to regular season play, the district court concluded that Quinnipiac's competitive cheerleading team did not compete in circumstances indicative of varsity sports. Thus, it ruled that Quinnipiac's 30 roster positions for competitive cheerleading could not be counted for Title IX purposes because the activity did not yet afford women genuine participation opportunities in a varsity sport. *See id.* at 100–01.

In challenging this conclusion, Quinnipiac questions the weight the district court assigned the various factors it identified as supporting or undermining recognition of competitive cheerleading as a genuine varsity sport. Quinnipiac argues that this court should decide the question *de novo.* We generally accord considerable discretion to a factfinder in deciding what weight to assign competing evidence pointing toward different conclusions. *See Diesel Props. S.r.l. v. Greystone Bus. Credit II LLC,* 631 F.3d at 52 (" 'Where there are two permissible views of the evidence, the factfinder's choice between them cannot be clearly erroneous.' ") (quoting *Anderson v. Bessemer City,* 470 U.S. 564, 574 (1985)). But the point merits little discussion here because, even assuming that *de novo* review were warranted, we conclude for the same reasons stated in detail by the district court and summarized in this opinion that, although there are facts on both sides of the argument, in the end, the balance tips decidedly against finding competitive cheerleading presently to be a "sport" whose participation opportunities should be counted for purposes of Title IX. Like the district court, we acknowledge record evidence showing that competitive cheerleading can be physically challenging, requiring competitors to possess "strength, agility, and grace." *Biediger v. Quinnipiac Univ.,* 728 F. Supp. 2d at 101. Similarly, we do not foreclose the possibility that the activity, with better organization and defined rules, might some day warrant recognition as a varsity sport. But, like the district court, we conclude that the record evidence shows that "that time has not yet arrived." *Id.*

Accordingly, we conclude that the district court was correct not to count the 30 roster positions assigned to competitive cheerleading in determining the number of genuine varsity athletic participation opportunities that Quinnipiac afforded female students.

E.   *Finding a Title IX Violation Based on a 3.62% Disparity*

Having reduced Quinnipiac's claimed athletic participation opportunities for women by 41—representing 30 competitive cheerleaders and 11 cross-country runners required to join the indoor and outdoor track teams but unable to compete on those teams because of their injuries or red-shirt status—the district court correctly found that the school had a total of 400 varsity athletic participation opportunities, of which 233, or 58.25%, were assigned to women. Because enrollment data established that 61.87% of Quinnipiac's undergraduate population were women, this indicated a 3.62% disparity in the athletic opportunities that Quinnipiac afforded women. *See id.* The district court concluded that this disparity was sufficient to support a finding that Quinnipiac had failed to afford female students varsity athletic participation opportunities substantially proportionate to their enrollment. *See id. at 113.*

Quinnipiac argues that a 3.62% disparity is too small to support such a finding. In any event, it submits that the district court erred in holding Quinnipiac responsible for the disparity in light of fluctuations in enrollment and Quinnipiac's good faith reliance on the district court's statement at the time of the preliminary injunction decision that it would likely count all women members of the cross-country, indoor track, outdoor track, and competitive cheerleading teams as athletic participants for purposes of Title IX. Further, Quinnipiac contends that the district court erroneously accorded dispositive weight to the fact that the number of additional female roster spots needed to achieve exact proportionality— 38—would have been sufficient for Quinnipiac to field an additional varsity team.

Quinnipiac's arguments fail to persuade. First, its emphasis on the relatively small percentage of disparity is unwarranted. The district court itself recognized that "in strictly numerical terms," a 3.62% disparity presents "a borderline case of disproportionate athletic opportunities." But as the 1996 Clarification makes clear, substantial proportionality is not determined by any bright-line statistical test. *See* 1996 Clarification at 4; *see also Equity in Athletics, Inc. v. DOE,* 639 F.3d 91, 110 (4th Cir.2011) ("DOE has not specified a magic number at which substantial proportionality is achieved."). While a district court outside this circuit reports finding no case in which a disparity of two percentage points or less has been held to manifest a lack of substantial proportionality, *see Equity in Athletics, Inc. v. DOE,* 675 F.Supp.2d 660, 682–83 (W.D.Va.2009), *aff'd,* 639 F.3d 91 (4th Cir.2011), we do not pursue the issue because the disparity in this case is greater than 2%, and we do not, in any event, understand the 1996 Clarification to create a statistical safe harbor at this or any other percentage. Instead, the Clarification instructs that substantial proportionality is properly determined on a "case-by-case basis" after a careful assessment of the school's "specific circumstances," including the causes of the disparity and the reasonableness of requiring the school to add additional athletic opportunities to eliminate the disparity. 1996 Clarification at 4; *see also* Amicus Br. of U.S. 23–25. The district court's challenged ruling was based on precisely this analysis.

Specifically, the district court pointed to record evidence showing that the 3.62% identified disparity was almost entirely attributable to Quinnipiac's own careful control of its athletic rosters. *See Biediger v. Quinnipiac Univ.,* 728 F.Supp.2d at 111–12. Although Quinnipiac claims that, but for a 0.27% increase in female enrollment in 2009–10 beyond its control, the disparity would have been only 3.35%, the difference is not one that undermines the district court's conclusion that Quinnipiac's voluntary actions largely caused the disparity.

While Quinnipiac professes to have relied on the district court's observation at the time of the preliminary injunction ruling that it would likely count all women members of the cross-country, indoor track, outdoor track, and competitive cheerleading teams as athletic participants for purposes of Title IX, Quinnipiac—or certainly its able counsel—surely knew the risks of such reliance. . . . In any event, the 1996 Clarification indicates only that a school will not be held responsible under Title IX for disparities caused by matters outside its control. *See* 1996 Clarification at 4. Nowhere does it indicate that a school can avoid responsibility for *future* remediation of Title IX disparities caused by its own choices if it can show that those choices were made in good faith.

Finally, we do not understand the district court to have ruled, as Quinnipiac suggests, that no matter how small a disparity, if it can be closed by the creation of a new sports team, a school will be found not to have afforded substantially proportionate athletic opportunities. Rather, we understand the court to have discussed the possible creation of a new sports team only to explain why it was reasonable to expect Quinnipiac to add additional athletic opportunities for women to close the identified 3.62% disparity. In so concluding, the district court noted that, insofar as the gap reflected 38 positions, each of Quinnipiac's women's varsity teams had 30 or fewer roster spots, making it "certain that an independent sports team could be created from the shortfall of participation opportunities." *Biediger v. Quinnipiac Univ.,* 728 F.Supp.2d at 112 & n. 27. Moreover, the district court observed that little effort was required for Quinnipiac to afford the additional participation opportunities of an independent sports team: "That independent sports team would be the eliminated women's volleyball squad, a team that, based on Quinnipiac's 2010–11 roster target, requires a mere 14 players to compete." *Id.* at 112. Of course, the district court did not suggest that Quinnipiac's compliance with Title IX was dependent on it forever fielding a women's volleyball team. *See id. at 113–14.* But the ease with which Quinnipiac could afford these particular additional varsity athletic opportunities was a "specific circumstance[ ]" that, pursuant to the 1996 Clarification, supported the conclusion that a 3.62% disparity in this case demonstrated that Quinnipiac was not affording substantially proportionate varsity athletic participation opportunities to its female students. 1996 Clarification at 4.

Accordingly, we reject Quinnipiac's challenge to the district court's finding that the school engaged in sex discrimination in violation of Title IX, and we affirm the order enjoining Quinnipiac from continuing such discrimination.

III. Conclusion

To summarize, we conclude as follows:

1.   For purposes of determining the number of genuine varsity athletic participation opportunities that Quinnipiac afforded women students, the district court correctly declined to count:

a.   five roster positions on the women's indoor track team and six roster positions on the women's outdoor track team because these were held by cross-country runners who (i) were required to join the indoor and outdoor track teams even though they could not compete on those teams because they were injured or red-shirted and (ii) did not receive any additional benefits from membership on the track teams beyond those received as injured or red-shirted off-season members of the cross-country team;

b.   any of the 30 roster positions for women's competitive cheerleading because that activity was not yet sufficiently organized or its rules sufficiently defined to afford women genuine participation opportunities in a varsity sport.

2.   Where the 3.62% disparity between the percentage of women students enrolled at Quinnipiac and the percentage of women listed on varsity sports teams was largely caused by Quinnipiac's voluntary decisions with respect to its athletics programs and reasonably remedied by the addition of more athletic opportunities for women, the district court correctly concluded that the disparity demonstrated a failure to provide substantially proportionate athletic participation opportunities as required by Title IX.

Accordingly, the district court's order enjoining Quinnipiac from continuing to discriminate against female students by failing to provide them with equal athletic participation opportunities is AFFIRMED.

NOTES AND QUESTIONS

1. *How to Define Athletic Participation Opportunities?* What makes participation on intercollegiate athletic teams sufficiently special to require schools to provide equal opportunities to both genders? Why should participation in other extra-curricular activities, like intramural sports or debate or band or drama, not be part of the calculus? Some of these other activities can be as competitive and time consuming as traditional athletics. Furthermore, intramural sports may involve as much physical activity. Does the distinction turn on the involvement of coaching staffs paid to train and discipline participants to achieve competitive physical goals against opponents with similar training and discipline? Is there an assumption that this type of competition provides a uniquely valuable experience?

Consider the factors identified by the *Biediger* court as relevant to the exclusion of Quinnipiac's competitive cheerleading squad from the calculus. Why should the absence of recruitment be relevant? Why should the variant rules of competition? The "motley assortment of competitors"? The absence of a "progressive playoff system"? Note, as does the court, that these factors could cut in favor of inclusion of competitive cheerleading in the future? Can you envisage cheerleading even as an Olympic sport?

Ultimately, how would you decide whether, and under which conditions, cheerleading and dance should be included in Title IX participation calculations? Note that the inclusion could affect the number of opportunities afforded female athletes in more traditional sports. Consider also the following note.

2. *Title IX as Cultural Change?* Northwestern Professor Kimberly Yuracko, in her article *One For You and One For Me: Is Title IX's Sex-Based Proportionality Requirement for College Varsity Athletic Positions Defensible*, 97 Nw. U.L. Rev. 731 (2003), argues that

> The proportionality requirement may be best understood and explained as an attempt to promote certain widely shared values about the kinds of skills and attributes that girls and boys should be encouraged to develop. It may be, in other words, that the strongest and the most honest justification for proportionality is that it encourages girls to develop a sense of their own bodily agency and to develop a conception of themselves as agents in their social and physical world.

Id. at 791. Title IX accomplishes this, Yuracko suggests, by creating athletic role models for girls, and proportionality may be one part of a social reconstruction project aimed at changing the cultural tags associated, not only with competitive athletics, but also with physical agency more generally. Proportionality may encourage girls to think of themselves and their bodies in a different way by tagging competitive physical activity as in equal part female, rather than exclusively male. Proportionality may, therefore, be part of a larger project to change the social meaning attached to femaleness from passive beauty or sex object to strong physical agent.

Id. at 796. Do you find Yuracko's argument persuasive? How might it apply to the treatment of dance teams or cheerleading squads?

3.   *Should Non-Competing Players Be Included?* Note the *Biediger* court's conclusion that Quinnipiac could not include injured or red-shirted cross-country runners on the indoor or outdoor track teams. If they were not able to compete, why were they included as members of the cross-country team?

Should athletes who never do more than practice, who never engage in interschool competitions, be included? *See, e.g., Balow v. Michigan State University*, 24 F.4th 1051, 1056 (7th Cir. 2022) ("Title IX does not require that athletes participate in competitions to be counted").

4.   *How Much of a Disparity in Participation Negates Substantial Proportionality?* How does the court treat Quinnipiac's argument that a 3.62% disparity is too small to constitute a violation of Title IX? Does the court adopt a bright line rule or does it embrace the case-by-case approach recommended in the OCR's 1996 Clarification Letter? What is relevant to the latter approach? Does it inquire whether the school could choose to be closer to exact proportionality by not eliminating or by adding a women's team? By focusing on numbers rather than percentages, does it highlight whether a school could add a women's team whose size is not greater than a numerical disparity? For further treatment of these questions, see the majority and dissenting opinions in *Balow, supra.*

———————

As stated in the OCR Policy Interpretation quoted at the beginning of Section B.1, *supra*, Title IX requires more than the equal provision of opportunities to participate in competitive athletics. It also requires schools (1) to provide financial assistance to men's and women's athletic programs proportionate to the numbers of male and female participants in the programs and (2) to ensure that the availability and quality of the program factors listed on pages 19–19 are "equivalent." While these additional requirements have not generated the same frequent litigation as that based on the equal provision of participation opportunities, each may be enforced by the OCR through compliance reviews.

The Policy Interpretation does not require a proportionate number of scholarships for men and women or individual scholarships of equal dollar value. Rather, it requires only that the total amount of scholarship aid made available to men and women be substantially proportionate to their athletic participation numbers. This requirement nonetheless may present a challenge for many universities for several reasons. First, like the proportionate opportunities requirement considered above, it is easy to monitor through the reporting of numbers. Second, unlike the opportunities requirement as qualified by the three-prong test, there is no need to qualify the proportionate requirement by a best efforts alternative. And, most importantly, in allocating scholarship dollars, athletic departments must also contend with NCAA rules governing the number and type of scholarships that universities may provide in various sports in order to compete in NCAA contests in those sports.

The NCAA distinguishes between two different kinds of sports: one labeled "head count," which requires full scholarships for any athlete receiving one, and the other "equivalency," which permits partial scholarships that divide up the available maximum numbers among a large roster of players. Football, with its 85 permitted full scholarships, is the major "head count" sport, with basketball (at 13 scholarships) being the only other men's sport in this category. The four women's head count sports—basketball (15), volleyball (12), gymnastics (12), and tennis (8)— together comprise 47 positions. If these were the only sports involved, the award of 98 full-time scholarships (68%) to male athletes and 47 (or 32%) to female, might, it could be argued, satisfy the Title IX scholarship proportionality test since every athlete, male and female, would be receiving a full grant-in-aid. Of course, unless the university's enrollment was 68% male, providing for only these sports would instead violate the school's obligation—considered in detail above—to provide equal opportunities to participate.

In order to provide such equal opportunities, schools must offer many women's sports that the NCAA covers under "equivalency" scholarship rules. This increase in the female participation rate in equivalency sports, however, aggravates the disparity between the proportion of scholarship dollars allocated and the proportion of participation by women. The only ways to address this disparity while maintaining equal opportunities for women to participate is to reduce the amount of aid to men's equivalency sports relative to the participants in those sports compared to the aid offered to the participants in female sports. The NCAA could alleviate the problem by making more female sports head count sports or at least raising the number of equivalency scholarships for female sports, but this would impose further costs on resistant member institutions. So again, Title IX's proportionate scholarship requirement ultimately forces universities to choose between support for large football squads and support for varied athletic opportunities for its male students.

Title IX's regulations prohibit institutions "[t]hrough solicitation, listing, approval, provision of facilities or other services, assist[ing] any foundation, trust, agency, organization, or person which provides assistance to any of such recipient's students in a manner which discriminates on the basis of sex." 34 C.F.R. § 106.37(a). The 1979 Policy Interpretation on the regulations further states that "[w]hen financial assistance is offered in forms other than grants, the distribution of non-grant assistance will also be compared to determine whether equivalent benefits are proportionately available to male and female athletes. A disproportionate amount of work-related aid or loans in the assistance made available to the members of one sex, for example, could constitute a violation of Title IX." Would these interpretations of Title IX challenge a school's participation in the facilitation of greater opportunities for a football team's collective sale of name, image, and likeness than those afforded to the school's female athletes?

The Regulation's requirement that the other program factors be "equivalent" rather than strictly proportional also is subject to OCR compliance reviews. The Policy Interpretation states that "[if] comparisons of program components reveal that treatment, benefits, or opportunities are not equivalent in kind, quality or availability, a finding of compliance may still be justified if the differences are the result of nondiscriminatory factors." 44 Fed. Reg. 71,414 (1979). The Interpretation lists some of those nondiscriminatory factors. These "include rules of play, nature / replacement of equipment, rates of injury resulting from participation, nature of facilities required for competition, and the maintenance / upkeep requirements of those facilities." Id. The Interpretation acknowledges that differences in these factors will occur in football and thus will favor men. The Interpretation also states that the costs of managing athletic events that draw large crowds, such as football and basketball, may be justified.

The NCAA has been subjected to protests from female athletes and criticisms from journalists and other commentators for failing to provide facilities and benefits in national competitions of women's teams equal to those provided for men's teams competing in comparable sports. For instance, women's basketball competitors have not been treated as well as men's basketball competitors and women's softball teams have not been treated as well as men's baseball teams. The protests and criticisms may achieve greater parity from the NCAA, but Title IX does not require it; the Supreme Court, in a unanimous decision penned by Justice Ginsburg, held that the NCAA's acceptance of membership dues from regulated universities does not make it a federal fund recipient subject to Title IX. *NCAA v. Smith*, 525 U.S. 459 (1999).

3. NON-DISCRIMINATORY ACCESS

Recall that Title IX prohibits sex discrimination using the same words as Title VI does in prohibiting race discrimination. Thus, while Title IX (because of the gender-based differences in post-puberty physical development) requires the equal opportunities afforded by female-only teams, it also supports application of the same anti-discrimination model that would prevent any school from preventing athletes from competing for positions on particular teams because of their skin color.

The federal regulations adopted under Title IX in 1975 balanced this tension in the following manner:

(b) *Separate teams.* Notwithstanding the requirements of paragraph (a) of this section, a recipient may operate or sponsor separate teams for members of each sex where selection for such teams is based upon competitive skill or the activity involved is a contact sport. However, where a recipient operates or sponsors a team in a particular sport for members of one sex but operates or sponsors no such team for members of the other sex, and athletic opportunities for members of that sex have previously been limited, members of the excluded sex must be allowed to try-out for the team offered unless the sport involved is a contact sport. For the purposes of this part, contact sports include boxing, wrestling, rugby, ice hockey, football, basketball and other sports the purpose or major activity of which involves bodily contact.

34 C.F.R. § 106.41(d).

This regulation was cited in a Title IX suit against Duke University in September 1997 by a woman who claimed that she had not been given a fair opportunity to make the Duke football team. Heather Mercer had been the place-kicker for her Yorktown Heights high school team that won the New York State Class B championship in 1993, with Mercer named as the third-team All-State place-kicker. After enrolling at Duke in the fall of 1994, Mercer sought to make the Blue Devils football squad. At the end of Duke's 1995 spring training session, Mercer was the first place-kicker selected by the "rising seniors" to play in the Blue-White game, and her last-minute, 28-yard field goal won the game for the Blues. While Blue Devils coach Fred Goldsmith apparently said after that game that Mercer had made the team (for the first time in Division I college football history), she was not invited to the team's summer football camp, nor permitted that fall to wear a football uniform and sit on the sidelines even during home games (an opportunity given to all male walk-ons, including place-kickers). When that situation continued into her 1997 senior year, Mercer sued Duke under Title IX, seeking monetary damages that Mercer said she would use to create a scholarship fund for future female place-kickers.

Duke's legal defense was that football—a contact sport—was expressly excluded from the HEW regulation requiring that if a school did not offer a separate team for each sex, it must allow members of the "excluded sex" whose "athletic opportunities . . . have previously been limited" to try out for the other sex's team. In *Mercer v. Duke University*, 190 F.3d 643 (4th Cir.1999), the Fourth Circuit rejected that position even for what Duke had characterized as the "traditionally all-male bastion of college football." *Id.* at 648. The reason is that

> [o]nce an institution has allowed a member of one sex to try out for a team operated by the institution for the other sex in a contact sport, subsection (b) is no longer applicable, and the institution is subject to the general antidiscrimination provision of sub-section (a).

Id.

This still left open the question of whether Duke had actually been discriminating against Mercer because of her gender. The case went to trial in October 2000 and it took the North Carolina jury just two hours to find Duke liable. Goldsmith, dismissed in 1998 for coaching a losing team, testified to embarrassment at teasing from rival coaches for including a woman on his squad. The coach had apparently told Mercer to sit in the stands rather than be on the sidelines where she was a "distraction" to the players, and was invited to give up this "little boys' sport" in favor of girls' beauty pageants and the like. Thus, the jury rejected Duke's claim that Mercer had simply been released from the team (as were several other male place kickers) because of her lack of relative skills.

While Mercer was able to secure only $1 in compensatory damages for her actual financial losses, the jury found that Duke had engaged in intentional and malicious discrimination against Mercer and awarded her $2 million in punitive damages. After the verdict, Mercer immediately said she would donate that award to create a new college scholarship program for female high school place kickers. The University, though, appealed this damages judgment to the Fourth Circuit. In *Mercer v. Duke University*, 50 F. App'x 643 (2002), the Circuit panel rendered a brief *per curiam* opinion on the damages issue, holding that because the Supreme Court had just ruled in *Barnes v. Gorman*, 536 U.S. 181 (2002), that punitive damages are not available to private plaintiffs under Title VI of the Civil Rights Act, they cannot be awarded under Title IX either. After a brief career on Wall Street, Mercer returned to the sports field as a world-class poker player.

NOTES AND QUESTIONS

1.   *Can Equality of Access Substitute for Equality of Opportunity?* Should a college be able to meet its Title IX obligations by allowing female students to

compete for positions on enough male teams to give them potential access to a proportionate number of athletic positions?

2. *Male Access to Female Teams?* The primary reason for not allowing male access to female teams derives from concerns that such access would deprive females of competitive opportunities. Consider, however, that Department of Education's Title IX Regulations at 34 C.F.R. § 106.41 allow a school to maintain a single sport only for one sex without allowing members of the opposite sex to try out only if it is a "contact sport" and "athletic opportunities for members of [the excluded] sex have previously been limited." Does this suggest that schools that do not offer a male team in a non-contact sport, such as volleyball or crew, should allow boys to try out for spots on a female team? Even if the school offers males an equal number of other athletic opportunities?

3. *Female Access to Male Teams?* What exactly is the justification for preventing a capable female from competing against males, even in contact sports, if she wants to do so? Can it be concerns about injuries? Do not such concerns stereotype and stigmatize women, many of whom are stronger and less likely to be injured than many males who are allowed to compete? Is it based on a principle of symmetry so that there is a neutral veneer over the blocking of male access to female teams? Should it matter at what age level, or competition level, the school participates?

While issues of gender integration of sports have been rarely tested in college athletics, female high school athletes have on occasion filed suit under Title IX to require their schools to integrate the teams in certain sports. The following decision is one judicial response.

HOOVER V. MEIKLEJOHN

430 F. Supp. 164 (D. Col. 1977)

MATSCH, DISTRICT JUDGE.

[The plaintiff, a 16-year-old eleventh grade student, was barred from playing for her public high school's junior varsity soccer team. She challenged a rule adopted by the Colorado High School Activities Association that limited soccer (but not baseball or cross country running) to males. The Association had relied on advice from its medical committee that girls playing soccer on mixed-sex teams risked their health and safety.]

* * *

Primarily, the committee was concerned with risks attendant upon collisions in the course of play. While the rules of soccer prohibit body contact (except for a brush-type shoulder block when moving toward the ball), there are frequent instances when players collide in their endeavors to "head" the ball. In those instances, contact is generally in the upper body area.

There is agreement that after puberty the female body has a higher ratio of adipose tissue to lean body weight as compared with the male, and females have less bone density than males. It is also true that, when matured, the male skeletal construct provides a natural advantage over females in the mechanics of running. Accordingly, applying the formula of force equals mass times acceleration, a collision between a male and a female of equal weights, running at full speed, would tend to be to the disadvantage of the female. It is also true that while males as a class tend to have an advantage in strength and speed over females as a class, the range of differences among individuals in both sexes is greater than the average differences between the sexes. The association has not established any eligibility criteria for participation in interscholastic soccer, excepting for sex. Accordingly, any male of any size and weight has the opportunity to be on an interscholastic team and no female is allowed to play, regardless of her size, weight, condition or skill.

* * *

The defendants on the board of education and the professional educators in control of the activities association have concluded that the game of soccer is among those which serve an educational purpose and governmental funds have been provided for it. It is a matter of common knowledge that athletics are a recognized aspect of the educational program offered at American colleges and universities and that many of them offer scholarships to males and females for their agreement to participate in intercollegiate sports competition. Such offers result from organized recruiting programs directed toward those who have demonstrated their abilities on high school teams. Accordingly, the chance to play in athletic games may have an importance to the individual far greater than the obvious momentary pleasure of the game.

Accordingly, the claim of the plaintiff class in this case is properly characterized as a denial of an equal educational opportunity.

* * *

Brown v. Board of Education, 347 U.S. 483 (1954), held that blacks were denied a constitutionally protected equality when they were forced to attend schools established only for those of the same race. As suggested by Justice Brennan in *Frontiero v. Richardson*, 411 U.S. 677, 686 (1973), a classification according to sex is comparable to race in that it is "an immutable characteristic determined solely by the accident of birth."

* * *

The Supreme Court has exhibited an obvious reluctance to label sex as a "suspect" classification because the consequences of the application of the many "invidious" discrimination precedents to all separations by sex could lead to some absurd results. For example, would the Constitution preclude separate public toilets?

* * *

In a very recent Supreme Court opinion, *Craig v. Boren*, 429 U.S. 190 (1976), Mr. Justice Brennan, writing for the Court, attempted to define a new standard of review, saying:

> To withstand constitutional challenge, previous cases establish that classifications by gender must serve important governmental objectives and must be substantially related to achievement of those objectives.

That language may be considered a "middle-tier approach," requiring something between "legitimate" and "compelling," viz., "important," and something more than a "rational" relationship but less perhaps than "strict scrutiny," viz., "substantially" related.

* * *

... Because of its flexibility and sensitivity to the notion of equality itself, [the following three-pronged] method of analysis is particularly appropriate to the present case.

1. The Importance of the Opportunity Being Unequally Burdened or Denied

The opportunity not merely burdened but completely denied to the plaintiff and the class she represents is the chance to compete in soccer as a part of a high school educational experience. Whether such games should be made available at public expense is not an issue. The content of an educational program is completely within the majoritarian control through the representatives on the school board. But, whether it is algebra or athletics, that which is provided must be open to all. The Court in *Brown* expressed a constitutional concern for equality in educational opportunity and this controversy is squarely within that area of concern. Accordingly, without reference to any label that would place this opportunity on one of two or more "tiers," it must be given a great importance to Donna Hoover and every other individual within her class. Surely it is of greater significance than the buying of beer, considered in *Craig*, supra.

2. The Strength of the State Interest Served in Denying It

The defendants in this case have sought to support the exclusionary rule by asserting the state interest in the protection of females from injury in this sport. While the evidence in this case has shown that males as a class tend to have an advantage in strength and speed over females as a class and that a collision between a male and a female would tend to be to the disadvantage of the female, the evidence also shows that the range of differences among individuals in both sexes is greater than the average differences between the sexes. The failure to establish any physical criteria to protect small or weak males from the injurious effects of competition with larger or stronger males destroys the credibility of the reasoning urged in support of the sex classification. Accordingly, to the extent that governmental concern for the health and safety of anyone who knowingly and voluntarily exposes himself or herself to possible injury can ever be an acceptable area of intrusion on individual liberty, there is no rationality in limiting this patronizing protection to females who want to play soccer.

3.   The Character of the Group Whose
Opportunities Are Denied

* * *

It is an inescapable conclusion that the complete denial of any opportunity to play interscholastic soccer is a violation of the plaintiff's right to equal protection of the law under the Fourteenth Amendment. This same conclusion would be required under even the minimal "rational relationship" standard of review applied to classifications which are not suspect and do not involve fundamental rights. The governmental purpose in fielding a soccer team is to enhance the secondary school educational experience. The exclusion of girls to protect them from injury cannot be considered to be in furtherance of that educational objective. If the purpose of the exclusionary rule is the protection of health, safety and welfare of the students, it is arbitrary to consider only the general physiological differences between males and females as classes without any regard for the wide range of individual variants within each class.

While Rule XXI is invalid under either method of analysis, there is a difference between them which is revealed in considering both the remedy required here and the possible ramifications of this case for future controversies.

There is no contention in this case that the Constitution compels soccer competition with teams composed of the best players, regardless of sex. Donna Hoover sought a chance to play on the boys' team only because there is no girls' team. The parties here agree that the effective equalization of athletic opportunities for members of both sexes would be better served by comparable teams for members of each sex and that under current circumstances mixed-sex teams would probably be dominated by males. Accordingly, it is conceded that "separate but equal" teams would satisfy the equality of opportunity required by the Constitution. The "separate but equal" doctrine was articulated in *Plessy v. Ferguson*, 163 U.S. 537 (1896), approving racial separation in transportation facilities. The doctrine was rejected for education in *Brown*, supra, upon the conclusion that racial separation was inherently unequal because it involved a stigmatizing inferiority for the minority race. No such effect is conceivable for a separation of athletic teams by sex.

* * *

Given the lack of athletic opportunity for females in past years, the encouragement of female involvement in sports is a legitimate objective and separation of teams may promote that purpose. It may also justify the sanction of some sports only for females, of which volleyball may be an example.

Separate soccer teams for males and females would meet the constitutional requirement of equal opportunity if the teams were given substantially equal support and if they had substantially comparable programs. There may be differences depending upon the effects of such neutral factors as the level of student interest and geographic locations. Accordingly, the standard should be one of comparability, not absolute equality.

In arriving at the conclusion that the defendants are in violation of the Fourteenth Amendment by providing interscholastic soccer only for male high school students, I am aware that there will be many concerned about the ramifications of this ruling. Football, ice hockey and wrestling are also made available only for males in Colorado, and volleyball is provided only for females. While there is now no reason to rule beyond the specific controversy presented by the evidence, it would seem appropriate to make some general observations about constitutional concerns in athletic programs supported by public funds.

The applicability of so fundamental a constitutional principle as equal educational opportunity should not depend upon anything so mutable as customs, usages, protective equipment and rules of play. The courts do not have competence to determine what games are appropriate for the schools or which, if any, teams should be separated by sex. What the courts can and must do is to insure that those who do make those decisions act with an awareness of what the Constitution does and does not require of them. Accordingly, it must be made clear that there is no constitutional requirement for the schools to provide any athletic program, as it is clear that there is no constitutional requirement to provide any public education. What is required is that whatever opportunity is made available be open to all on equal terms. It must also be made clear that the mandate of equality of opportunity does not dictate a disregard of differences in talents and abilities among individuals. There is no right to a position on an athletic team. There is a right to compete for it on equal terms.

* * *

Order granted.

———

NOTES AND QUESTIONS

1. *Effect on Colorado High Schools?* What actions does this ruling allow Colorado high schools to take? Consider each of the following scenarios: (1) a school allows girls to try out for the school's only soccer team, but over a period of several years few girls try out and none make the team; (2) a school requires half the players on the school's only soccer team to be girls; (3) a school has both boys' and girls' soccer teams, but disbands the girls' team when only three girls come out for the team, and then refuses to let the three girls try out for the boys' team; (4) a school has a boys-only soccer team and a girls-only field hockey team (each team has the same number of players).

2. *Risk of Injury in Mixed Sports?* In the present, unlike the 1970s, few would argue that mixed soccer poses a serious risk of injury to young girls. But what about football or ice hockey? Should either of these sports be mixed-sex or just single sex? How should the court rule in a case involving a sixteen-year-old girl who wants to try out for the men's wrestling team when the school has no women's wrestling program? *See Saint v. Nebraska School Activities Ass'n*, 684 F. Supp. 626 (D. Neb.1988) (granting a temporary order requiring the state association to allow a girl to compete on the high school wrestling team because there was no showing that the ban promoted the stated goal of protecting the health and safety of girls). How about a case in which a young woman sues to be permitted to compete in the regional Golden Gloves boxing competition?

3. *Males in Female Sports?* The opposite question arises if a boy wishes to participate in a sport for which his school offers only a girls' team—for example, in field hockey or volleyball. Should courts allow high school boys to try out for spots on a "girls" team if there is no "boys" team in that sport? What would likely happen if that were the rule? Should it matter whether the sport is a "contact sport?" *Compare Kleczek v. Rhode Island Interscholastic League*, 612 A.2d 734 (R.I. 1992) (holding that boys do not have any right to play on the girls' field hockey team), *with Williams v. School District of Bethlehem*, 799 F. Supp. 513 (E.D. Pa.1992), *rev'd*, 998 F.2d 168 (3d Cir.1993) (holding that it is a factual question whether field hockey is a "contact sport" that would justify a girls-only team under Title IX or the Pennsylvania Constitution).

In *Clark v. Arizona Interscholastic Ass'n*, 695 F.2d 1126 (9th Cir.1982), a group of boys sued when they were barred by Arizona rules from playing on their school's volleyball team, which was limited to girls. In dismissing the suit, the court asserted:

> The record makes clear that due to average physiological differences, males would displace females to a substantial extent if they were allowed to compete for positions on the volleyball team. Thus, athletic opportunities for women would be diminished. As discussed above, there is no question that the Supreme Court allows for these average real differences between the sexes to be recognized or that they allow gender to be used as a proxy in this sense if it is an accurate proxy. This is not a situation where the classification rests on " 'archaic and overbroad' generalizations" or "the baggage of

sexual stereotypes." Nor is this a situation involving invidious discrimination against women, or stigmatization of women. The [Arizona Interscholastic Association] is simply recognizing the physiological fact that males would have an undue advantage competing against women for positions on the volleyball team. The situation here is one where there is clearly a substantial relationship between the exclusion of males from the team and the goal of redressing past discrimination and providing equal opportunities for women.

. . . While equality in specific sports is a worthwhile ideal, it should not be purchased at the expense of ultimate equality of opportunity to participate in sports. As common sense would advise against this, neither does the Constitution demand it.

Id. at 1131.

4.   *Horner v. KHSAA.* The Kentucky High School Athletic Association (KHSAA) serves as the agent of the Kentucky State Board for Elementary and Secondary Education, for regulation of interscholastic sports in Kentucky. The KHSAA grants official "sanction" to a sport for purposes of creating a state tournament only when the sport has secured interest in participation among at least 25% of member schools (though such sanction, once granted, is preserved as long as at least 15% of members maintain their participation). The KHSAA had sanctioned ten sports for boys, including baseball, and eight for girls, including slow-pitch softball. The latter sport was first approved in 1982, after a school survey found that 44% of Association members wanted to play it. A 1988 survey found just nine percent membership interest in girls' fast-pitch softball, which had risen to 17% (or 50 schools around the state) by 1992. Because the minimum 25% figure had not been met, the KHSAA refused to grant "sanction" to the sport. Member schools did retain the freedom to compete among themselves in such a non-sanctioned sport, and girls had the freedom to play on a boys' baseball team if their member schools did not offer girls' fast-pitch softball.

Lori Ann Horner and eleven other female student athletes in Kentucky filed suit against both the KHSAA and its parent Board, alleging that the failure to sanction girls fast-pitch softball violated both their Equal Protection and Title IX rights. The plaintiffs' concern was that in college sports, both the NCAA and the NAIA had sanctioned women's fast-pitch, but not slow-pitch, softball. This meant that Kentucky girls who were playing softball were at a disadvantage relative to their classmates in other sanctioned sports (boys or girls) in securing athletic scholarships when they went to college. Should the KHSAA's "25 percent" rule be found in violation of the constitutional right to equal protection? Or of the Title IX jurisprudence expressed in the DOE Regulations and in *Cohen* and other circuit court opinions? *See also Horner v. Kentucky High School Athletic Ass'n,* 43 F.3d 265 (6th Cir.1994); *Gordon v. Jordan,* 522 F.Supp.3d (D. Utah 2021) (high school students seeking to establish sufficient interest for competitive girls' football teams).

5. *Michigan HSAA*. The Michigan High School Athletic Association serves the same role in its state as the KHSAA does in Kansas. For years, it had scheduled the girls' season in basketball, volleyball, soccer, golf, swimming, and tennis to be played during a time of the year normally not associated with the sport, primarily to allow schools to offer girls' sports without having to duplicate facilities that the boys utilized during their more traditional seasons. The mothers of several girls filed a class action lawsuit on behalf of their daughters claiming that requiring them to play during nontraditional and less advantageous seasons disadvantaged them in a variety of ways. The district court held that such off-season scheduling of girls' sports, while boys' sports were always played during the traditional seasons, violated Title IX, the Equal Protection clause of the 14th Amendment, and the Michigan Civil Rights Act. *See Communities for Equity v. Michigan High School Athletic Ass'n*, 178 F. Supp. 2d 805 (W.D. Mich. 2001). What would the MHSAA and its member schools have to do to correct this violation? Must it schedule both boys' and girls' sports in the traditional seasons, even if many schools lack the facilities adequately to accommodate both at the same time? Would it be sufficient if some boys' sports were switched to nontraditional seasons so the girls in those sports could play during the traditional seasons? What if the boys' sports switched were golf, swimming, and tennis, while the girls still played nontraditional seasons in basketball, soccer, and volleyball?

4. TRANSGENDER AND INTERSEX ATHLETES

The tension between the goals of equal access to athletic competitions and of equal opportunity for athletic participation for women may be particularly salient when devising policy for the treatment of transgender athletes. The Court's opinion in *Bostock v. Clayton County,* 140 S. Ct. 1731 (2020), holding that Title VII's prohibition of sex discrimination encompasses the protection of transgender as well as sexual orientation status, would seem to apply to the similar anti-discrimination language in Title IX. The OCR issued a statement taking this position in June 2021, noting support in several lower federal court decisions.

This coverage, however, does not necessarily mean that schools cannot or even must not attempt to ensure that transgender athletes, though protected from discrimination, also do not use their superior muscular development to encroach upon the competitive opportunities of cisgender women. In 2010, the NCAA announced a policy to balance the two goals by requiring transgender females who wish to compete in female-only competitions to document both a year of testosterone suppression treatment and a one-time testosterone test that falls below a maximum level set for the sport for which they are competing.

Lia Thomas, a female transgender swimmer for the University of Pennsylvania, complied with this policy before winning the 100 meter, 200 meter, and 500 meter freestyle races in the female-only Ivy League competitions. Thomas also won the 500-meter freestyle ace in the NCAA national completion, before finishing fifth in the 200 and eighth in the 100-meter national freestyle female-only competitions. Thomas reported that the hormone therapy had weakened her muscles; the therapy thus raised the times she had set competing as a male, but her slower times still compared more favorably to other female times. For instance, she ranked only 554 among males in the 200-meter swim in which she finished fifth in the national female competition. Of further interest in the Ivy League competition was the first-place finisher in the 50 meter freestyle and second place finisher in the 100 meter female competition, Iszac Henig, a transgender male who also complied with NCAA policies by not having hormone therapy to enhance his musculature.

Beginning the 2023–24 year, the NCAA implemented a new policy that requires each sport to conform to the policy of the National Governing Body (NGB) for that sport, or in the absence of such a NGB, to an international federation's policy or the policy of the International Olympic Committee. Transgender athletes have to provide documentation of meeting a sport-specific testosterone level at the beginning of the sports season and again six months later. The athlete also must provide laboratory documentation within four weeks of participation in an NCAA championship.

Before the NCAA announced its new policy, the IOC had issued a new "Framework on Fairness, Inclusion, and Non-Discrimination" in November 2021 that set forth several principles to guide the treatment of transgender athletes by the various international sports federations. These principles include not assuming that any athlete has a "disproportionate competitive advantage due to their sex variations, physical appearance and/or transgender status." The principles also state that "any restrictions arising from eligibility criteria should be based on robust and peer reviewed research that ... demonstrates a consistent, unfair, disproportionate competitive advantage in performance and/or an unpreventable risk to the physical safety of other athletes."

These guidelines, however, do not dictate the use of any particular criteria for the federations that govern international sports. In June 2022, the International Swimming Federation (FINA), which governs diving, water polo and artistic swimming, as well as swimming racing, announced that transgender women could not compete in female competitions unless they transitioned before the age of 12 or an early stage of puberty. FINA also stated that it would establish a working group to explore developing an open category of events for athletes who do not meet its eligibility criteria for men's and women's competitions.

Another federation, World Athletics, formerly known as IAAF, which governs international track and field competitions announced that the IOC's new guidelines would not cause it to change its particular regulation governing female competitions in races between 400 meters and one mile. These regulations require athletes who sign a declaration that they are a transgender female to demonstrate that their testosterone level has been less than 5 nanomoles per liter for six months before a competition. (The normal female range for elite athletes is between .12 and 1.79, while the normal male range for elite athletes is between 7.7 and 29.4). This regulation has been particularly controversial because it was applied to disqualify from 800-meter races an intersex athlete who had been a dominant competitor at this distance in female races, but who had refused to suppress her hormone level to continue to compete. This woman, Caster Semenya, was classified as a DSD (Difference of Sexual Development) athlete because she has an XY chromosome and, rather than ovaries, internal testes that generated testosterone during her physical development in puberty. Semenya challenged her disqualification before the Court of Arbitration for Sport. Excerpts from its opinion follow.

SEMENYA V. INT'L ASS'N OF ATHLETICS FED'NS (IAAF)

CAS 2018/0/5794, Court of Arbitration of Sport, 2018

Panel: The Hon. Dr. Annabelle Bennett AO SC (Retired Judge, Sydney, Australia), The Hon. Hugh L. Fraser (Judge, Ottawa, Ontario, Canada), Dr. Hans Nater (Attorney-at-Law, Zurich, Switzerland)

* * *

THE DSD REGULATIONS

* * *

Regulation 1.1 of the DSD Regulations *("Introduction")* explains that: *These Regulations reflect the following imperatives:*

(a) To ensure fair and meaningful competition in the sport of athletics, competition has to be organised within categories that create a level playing field and ensure that success is determined by talent, dedication, hard work, and the other values and characteristics that the sport embodies and celebrates. In particular:

> *(i) The IAAF wants athletes to be incentivised to make the huge commitment and sacrifice required to excel in the sport, and so to inspire new generations to join the sport and aspire to the same excellence. It does not want to risk discouraging those aspirations by having unfair competition conditions that deny athletes a fair opportunity to succeed.*

> *(ii) Because of the significant advantages in size, strength and power enjoyed (on average) by men over women from puberty onwards, due in large part to men's much higher levels of circulating testosterone, and the impact that such advantages can have on sporting performance, it is generally accepted that competition between male and female athletes would not be fair and meaningful, and would risk discouraging women from*

participation in the sport. Therefore, in addition to separate competition categories based on age, the IAAF has also created separate competition categories for male and female athletes.

(b) The IAAF also recognises, however, that:

(i) Biological sex is an umbrella term that includes distinct aspects of chromosomal, gonadal, hormonal and phenotypic sex, each of which is fixed and all of which are usually aligned into the conventional male and female binary.

(ii) However, some individuals have congenital conditions that cause atypical development of their chromosomal, gonadal, and/or anatomic sex (known as differences of sex development, or DSDs, and sometimes referred to as 'intersex').

(iii) As a result, some national legal systems now recognise legal sexes other than simply male and female (for example, 'intersex', 'X', or 'other').

(c) The IAAF respects the dignity of all individuals, including individuals with DSDs. It also wishes the sport of athletics to be as inclusive as possible, and to encourage and provide a clear path to participation in the sport for all. The IAAF therefore seeks to place conditions on such participation only to the extent necessary to ensure fair and meaningful competition. As a result, the IAAF has issued these Regulations, to facilitate the participation in the sport of athletes with DSDs.

(d) There is a broad medical and scientific consensus, supported by peer-reviewed data and evidence from the field, that the high levels of endogenous testosterone circulating in athletes with certain DSDs can significantly enhance their sporting performance. These Regulations accordingly permit such athletes to compete in the female classification in the events that currently appear to be most clearly affected only if they meet the Eligibility Conditions defined below.

(e) These Regulations exist solely to ensure fair and meaningful competition within the female classification, for the benefit of the broad class of female athletes. In no way are they intended as any kind of judgement on or questioning of the sex or the gender identity of any athlete. To the contrary, the IAAF regards it as essential to respect and preserve the dignity and privacy of athletes with DSDs, and therefore all cases arising under these Regulations must be handled and resolved in a fair, consistent and confidential manner, recognising the sensitive nature of such matters. Any breach of confidentiality, improper discrimination, and/or stigmatisation on grounds of sex or gender identity will amount to a serious breach of the IAAF Integrity Code of Conduct and will result in appropriate disciplinary action against the offending party.

Regulation 1.2 provides that the DSD Regulations *"operate globally"* and therefore *"are to be interpreted and applied not by reference to national or local laws, but rather as an independent and autonomous text, and in a manner that protects and advances the imperatives identified above"*.

* * *

Regulation 2 is headed *'Special Eligibility Requirements for Restricted Events at International Competitions"*. Regulation 2.1 explains that the special rules set out in the DSD Regulations *apply only to participation by a Relevant Athlete in the female classification in a Restricted Event at an International Competition. They do not apply to any other athletes, or to any other events, or to any other competitions (although/ a Relevant Athlete does not meet the Eligibility Conditions then she will not be eligible to set a World Record in a Restricted Event at a competition that is not an International Competition).*

Regulation 2.2(a) defines a *'Relevant Athlete'* as [one who has DSD and high testosterone levels].

Regulation 2.2(b) defines *'Restricted Events'* as . . . *400m races, 400m hurdles races, 800m races, 1500m races, one mile races, and all other Track Events over distances between 400m and one mile (inclusive), whether run alone or as part of a relay event or a Combined Event.*

Regulation 2.3 specifies [that Relevant Athletes] must: *To be eligible to compete in the female classification in a Restricted Event at an International Competition, or to set a World Record in a competition that is not an International Competition, a Relevant Athlete must meet each of the following conditions (the Eligibility Conditions):*

(a)   she must be recognised at law either as female or as intersex (or equivalent);

(b)   she must reduce her blood testosterone level to below five (5) nmol/L8 for a continuous period of at least six months (e.g., by use of hormonal contraceptives); and

(c)   thereafter she must maintain her blood testosterone level below five (5) nmol/L continuously (i.e., whether she is in competition or out of competition) for so long as she wishes to maintain eligibility to compete in the female classification in Restricted Events at International Competitions (or to set a World Record in a Restricted Event at a competition that is not an International Competition).

[Regulation 2.6 emphasizes that a Relevant Athlete who does not meet eligibility conditions remains eligible to compete in female classifications in all competitions other than international competitions.]

* * *

Regulation 3.5 states that cases will be investigated/assessed as quickly as reasonably practicable and that an athlete who is under investigation/assessment must cooperate in good faith including by *"providing blood and/or urine samples upon request for analysis, and if needed, by submitting to medical physical examination"*.

* * *

Regulation 3.18 provides that an athlete who wishes to participate . . . must agree to comply fully with the DSD Regulations and to cooperate promptly and in good faith with the IAAF Medical Manager and Expert Panel including by: (i) *providing them with all of the information and evidence they request to determine whether she is a Relevant Athlete and (if so) to assess her compliance and to monitor her continuing compliance with the Eligibility Conditions, including (without limitation) submitting to testing in accordance with these Regulations; (ii) ensuring that all information and evidence provided is accurate and complete, and that nothing relevant is withheld;(iii) providing appropriate consents and waivers (in a form satisfactory to the IAAF Medical Manager) to enable her physician(s) to disclose to the IAAF Medical Examiner and the Expert Panel any information that the Expert Panel deems necessary to its assessment.*

In addition, under Regulation 3.18(d) such an athlete is also required to follow the dispute resolution procedures set out in Regulation 4 (see below) and must *'not . . .bring any proceedings in any court or other forum that are inconsistent'* with that provision.

* * *

Regulation 4 concerns confidentiality. It provides that all cases, results of investigations and assessments conducted under the DSD Regulations will be dealt with in strict confidence at all times. . .

Regulation 5 contains provisions concerning dispute resolution. Regulation 5.2 provides that any dispute in connection with the DSD Regulations arising between the IAAF and an affected athlete (and/or her member federation) shall be subject to the exclusive jurisdiction of the CAS. . . .

IX. MERITS

A. Introduction

Ms. Semenya is a woman. At birth, it was determined that she was female, so she was born a woman. She has been raised as a woman. She has lived as a woman. She has run as a woman. She is—and always has been—recognised in law as a woman and has always identified as a woman.

As an athlete, she says that she was born to run. She has undoubtedly had outstanding success in her career as an elite middle-distance runner, winning multiple Olympic, World, Commonwealth and regional championship titles. She is, today, a strong and dignified woman and one of the most famous and accomplished female athletes in the history of the sport.

The IAAF is entrusted with enacting regulations to facilitate and ensure the fair and principled administration of the sport of athletics for the benefit of all athletes. To this end, the IAAF has for some years, if not decades, struggled to deal with a problem that the IAAF believes must be solved. While children manifest similar athletic ability pre-puberty, this changes significantly post-puberty. Later in this Award, some of those changes are discussed but, at this point, suffice to say that post-puberty, generally speaking, male athletes outperform female athletes and, at elite level, this difference is insurmountable. Accordingly, in order to enable women to compete at elite level, with all of the benefits that result from such competitions and success in such competitions, it has been considered necessary to provide for what the IAAF calls *'a protected class'* of female athletes. Without the protection of restricted entry to that class, the IAAF says, women athletes would be at risk of being denied the right to compete and succeed at the highest levels. It would follow that women athletes would cease to compete in events where that protection is not available. Accordingly, the "protected class" must exist, and some workable and effective condition(s) must be established to regulate who may, and may not, participate within it.

The answer, at first, seems to be logical and straightforward: restrict entry to that "protected class" to female athletes and deny entry to male athletes, who have their own category in which to compete. In short, require like to compete against like. However, that straightforward answer assumes that sex is binary for all purposes, which it is not. It is not so simple. While elite competitive athletics has been divided into discrete binary categories of male and female, a neat and discrete boundary between male and female does not exist in nature. The male/female categorisation at the heart of competitive athletics thus does not map perfectly onto the diverse spectrum of sex characteristics that exists in natural human biology.

In recent years, a further complicating factor has begun to emerge. Laws governing the assignment of legal sex have begun to evolve in a number of jurisdictions around the world. In some jurisdictions legal sex is no longer exclusively confined to the statuses of "male" and "female". Other legal sex statuses—such as "intersex"—are now recognised in some countries. Moreover, in some jurisdictions, an individual born as one sex may change their legal sex in certain circumstances. The circumstances where this is possible vary across those jurisdictions that permit such changes to occur. The present case is not concerned with athletes who change their legal sex. Separate regulations cater specifically for such cases. The IAAF nonetheless points in this case to the growing divergence in the national rules governing legal sex as a further factor that means that the right to participate in the female class cannot simply depend on whether an athlete is recognised in national law as female.

* * *

This case therefore involves a collision of scientific, ethical and legal conundrums. It also involves incompatible, competing, rights. It is not possible to give effect to, or endorse, one set of rights without restricting the other set of rights. Put simply, on one hand is the right of every athlete to compete in sport, to have their legal sex and gender identity respected, and to be free from any form of discrimination. On the other hand, is the right of female athletes, who are relevantly biologically disadvantaged vis-a-vis male athletes, to be able to compete against other female athletes and not against male athletes and to achieve the benefits of athletic success, such as positions on the podium and consequential commercial advantages. This right of competition is often described (although not so easily defined) as the right to compete on a "level playing field".

* * *

C.   The factual and scientific issues in this case

* * *

In respect of the role of testosterone in athletic performance, the following points of agreement emerged during the relevant hot tub (in which Prof. Holt, Prof. Hackney, Prof. Handelsman, Prof. Baggish and Prof. Tucker participated):

- Differences in testosterone levels are the primary, but not the exclusive, cause of the recorded gap in performance between males and females.

- The main physical attributes that contribute to elite athletic performance include power generation, aerobic power, body composition, fuel utilisation and economy of motion. They also include neuromuscular function, tendon function and innate immunity.

- 46 XY individuals generally have greater lean body mass, larger hearts, higher cardiac output, larger haemoglobin mass and larger VO2 max than 46 XX individuals. The single biggest reason for the sex differences in these physical attributes is exposure in 46 XY individuals with functional androgen receptors to much higher levels of testosterone during growth and development (puberty) and throughout the athletic career.

The experts did not reach agreement, however, regarding:

- the magnitude of the performance advantage that is derived by having endogenous testosterone in the normal male range of 7.7 to 29 nmol/L;

- the strength of the correlation between levels of endogenous testosterone and lean body mass in adult males;

- whether the fact that 46 XY DSD athletes are overrepresented only in some track events constitutes a paradox that suggests the IAAF's hypothesis concerning the relationship between high endogenous testosterone and athletic performance is incorrect; and

- whether differences in exposure to growth hormone may account for some of the differences in athletic performance between men and women.

* * *

D. What is the role of testosterone in male/female sporting ability?

The role of testosterone in determining sporting ability was a major focus of each party's submissions and evidence. A fundamental feature of the Claimants' case is that there is no single determinant in defining sex as male or female and no single determinant for sporting ability. In respect of the latter, the Claimants contend that natural genetic variation can provide many examples of enhanced athletic ability that has led to outstanding success for particular individual athletes or groups of athletes.

It is accepted by all parties that circulating testosterone has an effect from puberty, in increasing bone and muscle size and strength and the levels of haemoglobin in the blood. . . .

Testosterone may not be the only factor that results in an increase in lean body mass, higher levels of haemoglobin and increased sporting ability, but the expert evidence explains that it is the primary factor. The IAAF cited the view, endorsed by some 42 leading international experts in sports science and sports medicine, that [the main physical attributes that contribute to elite athletic performance are power generation, aerobic power, body composition, fuel utilization, and economy of motion. These experts also conclude that] biological males and biological females are materially different with respect to these attributes . . . The primary reason for these sex differences in the physical attributes that contribute to elite (> 99th percentile) athletic performance is exposure in gonadal males with function at androgen receptors to much higher levels of testosterone during growth and development (puberty), and throughout the athletic career. No other endogenous physical or physiological factors have been identified as contributing substantially and predominantly to these differences. As a policy matter, the exogenous factors that influence elite athletic performance—nutrition, training, sports psychology, environmental manipulation, sports medicine techniques, etc.—should be equally accessible to biological male and biological female athletes. . . .

Having considered all of the scientific evidence adduced by the parties, the Panel accepts this conclusion.

E.   What is the role of DHT in male/female sporting ability?
     (omitted)

F.   What are the main characteristics of an athlete with a 46 XY DSD (in particular 5-ARD)?

. . . all 46 XY DSD such as 5-ARD are forms of genetic mutation that can affect testosterone levels. Individuals with 5-ARD have what is commonly identified as the male chromosomal sex (XY and not XX), male gonads (testes not ovaries) and levels of circulating testosterone in the male range (7.7–29.4 nmol/L), which are significantly higher than the female range (0.06–1.68 nmol/L).

In individuals with 5-ARD, the deficiency in 5-alpha reductase affects the conversion of the male foetus's testosterone into DHT, with the result that the external genital tissues do not develop normally. At birth, depending on physical examination of external genitalia and often in consultation with the parents and other experts, such a person may be assigned the female sex or the male sex. While the enzyme deficiency affects the development of male gonads in utero, following the onset of puberty circulating testosterone has the same virilising effect on the body of an individual with 5-ARD as it does on males without 5-ARD. The testes produce normal male levels of testosterone. According to the IAAF's expert evidence, a reported 58–63% of 5-ARD persons who were assigned the female sex at birth change to the male sex when these secondary sex characteristics develop at puberty.

It is not disputed that a person, whether a man or a woman, with 5-ARD is a person who is XY, with testes and not ovaries and levels of endogenous circulating testosterone in the male range. What is in dispute is whether these differences, and particularly testosterone levels, do in fact affect body composition, muscle mass and haemoglobin levels to the same or similar extent as in the male adult population and whether such differences have an impact on sports performance. The Panel addresses these disputed issues further below.

G.   Can it be said, as advanced by the IAAF, that a woman can have a "male sports sex"?

* * *

The IAAF contends that, for sporting purposes, individuals with 5-ARD are biologically indistinguishable from males without a DSD and have been shown to dominate in sport over "biological females" who, the IAAF asserts, have no chance to win when competing against such "biologically male" athletes. This is because, it says, from a biological perspective 5-ARD athletes are the same in every material respect to male athletes without DSD. They have the same biological and physiological features that confer the same ergogenic effect. The only material physical difference is the size and shape of external genitalia which, the IAAF emphasises, has no impact on sport performance.

The IAAF submits that it is a matter of unfairness to "biological females"—using that term to encompass XX women born with female gonads and low levels of circulating testosterone from puberty—to require them to compete against "biological males" with a female legal sex and gender identity. The IAAF does not deny the right of "biological males" with a female legal sex/female gender identity to compete in the female category but, it says, such an athlete must do the minimum necessary to ensure that their participation does not defeat the purpose of the category. If there is to be a female category the purpose of which is to protect "biological females" against unfair competition, then the IAAF submits that eligibility to compete in that category must be based on the relevant differences between "biological males" and "biological females".

* * *

H. Did the athletes whose data were the subject of BG17 provide informed consent for those data to be used by the IAAF for the purposes they are now relied on? (omitted)

I. Do women with a 46 XY DSD such as 5-ARD have an athletic advantage over other female athletes? If so, what is the magnitude of that advantage?

The role of evidence and scientific assessment to support regulatory decision-making is obviously of great importance. This has resulted in detailed focus on the evidence relied upon by the IAAF to support the DSD Regulations, in particular the evidence concerning the existence and extent of the alleged athletic advantage that female athletes with 46 XY DSD enjoy over other female athletes without such DSD. The evidence adduced by the IAAF in respect of this issue comes from a variety of sources. . . .

The IAAF also places substantial reliance on the Handelsman Paper, published in Endocrine Reviews, which is a peer-reviewed journal. This paper contains a review of the available literature up to 2018. The authors concluded, in effect, that the available evidence supports the link between circulating testosterone of adults and the sex differences in sports performance in most sports, that is, that testosterone was a causative factor. The main physiological factors affected were muscle size and strength, bone size and strength, and haemoglobin, each of which, alone, were said to increase athletic ability.

[The Panel discusses specific criticism of Semenya's counsel directed to these papers, and responded to some of them.]

. . . The Panel has carefully considered all of the scientific evidence adduced by the parties in these proceedings. On the basis of that analysis, the majority of the Panel accepts that the preponderance of the evidence is that female athletes with 5-ARD and other 46 XY DSD have high levels of circulating testosterone in the male range and that this does result in a significantly enhanced sports performance ability, for example, by action in the body to increase muscle mass and size and levels of circulating haemoglobin.

The majority of the Panel further concludes that that enhanced performance ability translates in practice to a significant performance advantage in certain athletics events covered by the DSD Regulations. . . .

J. The legal issues regarding the validity of the DSD Regulations

(i) **Where does the burden of proof lie?** [The parties agreed that the regulations discriminate on the basis of sex.]

(ii) Do the DSD Regulations constitute discrimination?

The conclusion that the DSD Regulations are prima facie discriminatory is merely the starting point, and not the end, of the Panel's legal analysis. In particular, it is common ground that a rule that imposes differential treatment on the basis of a particular protected characteristic is valid and lawful if it is a necessary, reasonable and proportionate means of attaining a legitimate objective. It is to these questions that the Panel must therefore now turn. . . .

(iii) Are the DSD Regulations necessary?

There is no dispute that ensuring fair competition in the female category of elite competitive athletics is a legitimate objective for the IAAF to pursue. . . . The Panel accepts that this is an important and legitimate objective. The more difficult (and disputed) question is whether the DSD Regulations are necessary for this purpose.

* * *

Once it is recognised that the reason for organising competitive athletics into separate male and female categories rests on the need to protect one group of individuals against having to compete against individuals who possess certain insuperable performance advantages derived from biology rather than legal status, it follows that it may be legitimate to regulate the right to participate in the female category by reference to those biological factors rather than legal status alone. Since those biological factors do not correspond perfectly with legal sex in every case, the Panel accepts the IAAF's submission that it is sometimes necessary to devise eligibility conditions that are not exclusively based on legal sex. . . .

Ms. Semenya argues that genetic difference and outstanding success is by no means uncommon in elite sport. Indeed, it is generally and rightly celebrated. Her evidence supports the submission that a 46 XY DSD is a form of genetic mutation that is not qualitatively different form other genetic differences that are accepted in sport and which in many instances may be determinative of athletic success. She submits that human diversity should be celebrated through inclusiveness and points to her own success in overcoming adversity through strength and perseverance. . . .

Ms. Semenya points out that her fastest time in her best event, the 800 metres, has been beaten by almost 3,000 men and that she is consistently between 9% and 14% slower than the comparable men's performances. The evidence also demonstrates that the margin by which she finishes ahead of the second place is, on average, just 1.03%—a margin that is not a statistical outlier in comparison with the history of track events analysed in the same timeframe. . . .

[T]he IAAF emphasised that, while this may be so, there is still a difference and a performance advantage between "second tier" male athletes and elite female athletes. The magnitude of that difference would not be of the order of 10–12% but would still be relevant and sufficient to deny female athletes the fair opportunities to win. That is, male athletes do not have to be elite to surpass even the very best female athletes. Dr Berman pointed out that, in a race such as the 800m, a 1.6% advantage, as calculated in BG 17, was sufficient to determine first place by in the region of nine metres.

Thus, with the benefit of further evidence and submissions, it can be accepted that the relevant male performance advantage should not be limited to one of 10–12%. Rather, a lower percentage advantage may still be sufficiently significant as to render competition meaningless. . . .

On this basis, the majority of the Panel accepts that the IAAF has discharged its burden of establishing that regulations governing the ability of female athletes with 46XY DSD to participate in certain events are necessary to maintain fair competition in female athletics by ensuring that female athletes who do not enjoy the significant performance advantage caused by exposure to levels of circulating testosterone in the adult male range do not have to compete against female athletes who do enjoy that performance advantage.

The next question, therefore, is whether the IAAF has discharged its burden of establishing that the DSD Regulations are both reasonable and proportionate.

(iv) Are the DSD Regulations reasonable and proportionate?

The majority of the Panel . . . concludes that the DSD Regulations are necessary and reasonable. The area that has given rise to the greatest difficulty is that of proportionality. . . .

* * *

a. The effect of the DSD Regulations on society generally
(omitted)

b. The effects of testosterone-suppressing medical treatment

The Claimants submit that, in order to be eligible to compete in a Restricted Event, Relevant Athletes must undergo testosterone-suppressing treatment that is both medically unnecessary and has serious and potentially dangerous side effects. The Claimants argue that this is a factor of very great significance when it comes to an assessment of the reasonableness and proportionality of the impugned Regulations.

* * *

The evidence of Ms. Semenya was, of its nature, anecdotal but real. However, it is not possible for the Panel to conclude that all of the symptoms that she encountered while attempting to reduce her levels of testosterone were due to the medication, or that they could not otherwise be controlled, or that they would continue, or that other athletes . . . would experience exactly the same side effects (different women react differently to different forms of oral contraceptive), or that another form of oral contraceptive, if prescribed, would result in the same side effects.

In any event, there is also the evidence of clinicians who say that the side effects are not different in nature to those experienced by the many thousands, if not millions, of . . . XX women, who take oral contraceptives. . . .

In the majority of the Panel's view, requiring 46 XY DSD athletes to take oral contraceptives to lower testosterone in order to compete in the female category in Restricted Events at International Competitions is not, of itself, disproportionate. In the circumstances, the majority of the Panel is of the view that, on the present evidence, the side effects that may be experienced by such athletes . . . as a result of taking an oral contraceptive do not outweigh the need to give effect to the DSD Regulations in order to attain the legitimate objective of protecting and facilitating fair competition in the female category.

c. The effect of requiring Relevant Athletes to undergo intimate medical examinations and assessments of virilisation

The Claimants submit that the requirement to undergo intimate personal examination to determine the extent of virilisation if an athlete does have high levels of testosterone is another form of sex or gender testing and is both subjective and inappropriate. It can also be highly intrusive and is an infringement of bodily integrity that can result in psychological harm. This harm would be repeated were an athlete to appeal to the CAS, where further examination may be required, and further detailed discussion of her body would take place. The Claimants also submit that psychological harm may arise from an athlete being labelled as having a DSD and from learning that they have such a condition.

* * *

Having regard to all these factors, the majority of the Panel therefore concludes that the provisions in the DSD Regulations dealing with the assessment of virilisation do not render the DSD Regulations disproportionate.

d. The risk that the confidentiality of Relevant Athletes will be compromised.

The Panel does accept that the IAAF has been successful in preserving the confidentiality of DSD athletes covered by the predecessor to the DSD Regulations. Neveliheless, the exclusion of athletes from Restricted Events in International Competitions where, for example, the athlete has qualified in National Competitions would be likely to render confidentiality meaningless in some cases. In those situations, it would not be difficult for an informed observer to infer from the absence of that athlete at subsequent International Competitions that the athlete has a relevant 46 XY DSD and has declined (or been unable) to reduce their endogenous testosterone to within the prescribed level. The Panel considers this is likely to be an inevitable detrimental effect of the DSD Regulations as they are currently framed. The Panel does not consider that this factor of itself renders the DSD Regulations disproportionate having regard to the countervailing legitimate interests pursued by the Regulations. It neveliheless has regard to the likelihood of some harm arising from the inferential disclosure of confidential medical information in reaching its overall conclusion as to the proportionality of the Regulations.

e. The application of the DSD Regulations to only the Restricted Events (omitted)

f. The rationale and effect of the 5 nmol/L threshold

A further issue of concern relates to the level of endogenous testosterone permitted under the DSD Regulations. The upper level of testosterone permitted in the Hyperandrogenism Regulations . . . was 10 nmol/L. The rationale for that former limit was that 10 nrnol/L is at the lower end of the normal male range. The upper level in the DSD Regulations has been lowered to 5 nrnol/L. The IAAF's explanation for the change is that it has determined a level by reference to XX female levels of testosterone. Thus, this lower threshold represents a level that is significantly higher than the upper limit of the normal range for the female XX population (0.06 to 1.68 nrnol/L), adjusted upwards to allow for increased levels of testosterone in female XX athletes with PCOS. The IAAF points out that individuals with levels above 5 nrnol/L will either have a testosterone-secreting tumour in the adrenal glands or ovaries, be taking exogenous testosterone, or be a male-to-female transgender athlete or a 46 XY DSD individual who is not suppressing their testosterone levels. The IAAF has not provided any further concrete explanation for why the level was lowered or why it is not, for example, 7.7 nmol/L (which is the accepted lower limit of the normal male range).

There are statements in the IAAF's evidence as to a performance advantage when the level of an individual's endogenous testosterone increases from 5 nrnol/L to 10 nrnol/L. There is some evidence that exogenous doses to increase women's circulating testosterone to 7.3 nrnol/L resulted in 4.4% increased muscle mass and 12–26% increased muscle strength and that increasing endogenous testosterone from 0.9 to 5, 7 and 10 nrnol/L increased circulating haemoglobin by 6.5%, 7.5% and 8.9% respectively. The Panel is therefore satisfied that the decision to reduce the testosterone threshold from 10 nrnol/L to 5 nrnol/L was not arbitrary.

g.   The ability of the athlete to maintain a level of testosterone below 5 nmol/L

[Semenya argued that training regimes could result in an athlete inadvertently breaching the 5 nrnol/L maximum level under the DSD Regulations even if the treatment regime of oral contraceptives designed to reduce the level of testosterone sufficiently was followed diligently.]

For the purposes of the proportionality assessment, a balance must be struck between countervailing factors. On one hand is the imposition of a new maximum threshold of 5 nmol/L which was rationally selected because it represents the highest level well above the normal female range (allowing for athletes with PCOS). On the other hand, there are the side effects of using medication to lower testosterone levels coupled with the risk of inadvertent fluctuations above the 5 nmol/L threshold and, potentially, the difficulty for an elite athlete in competition to keep their testosterone consistently below 5 nmol/L, to monitor that level adequately in real time and to pay for that monitoring.

The matters of compliance are clearly very important. If the DSD Regulations cannot be implemented fairly in practice, that could render them disproportionate at a later stage, since a regulation which is impossible or excessively difficult to apply fairly cannot be characterised as a proportionate interference with the rights of those who are subjected to it.

* * *

The Panel does not, of course, have direct evidence of compliance with the DSD Regulations, which have not yet been implemented. Nevertheless, the Panel does have concerns as to the maximum level of 5 nmol/L and the practical ability of female athletes with 46 XY DSD to ensure that their levels of testosterone do not exceed that level. These matters will necessarily require oversight by the IAAF to ensure that this requirement is workable in practice.

* * *

h.   Conclusion on reasonableness and proportionality

The majority of the Panel concludes that, on the evidence before it, the IAAF has shown that the DSD Regulations are reasonable and proportionate on their face. Nevertheless, the Panel has some grave concerns as to the future practical application of the DSD Regulations. While the evidence has not established that those concerns are justified, or that they negate the conclusion of *ex facie* proportionality, this may change in the future unless constant attention is paid to the fairness of how they are implemented. In this regard, reference is made to the matters discussed above.

———

NOTES AND QUESTIONS

1.   *A Reasonable Balance?* Does the type of testosterone testing considered in the *Semenya* decision provide a reasonable way to balance the tension between the service of non-discrimination and fair opportunity goals in elite female athletic competitions? Would your view on whether testosterone suppression provides an adequate balance be influenced by research on whether such suppression substantially eliminates the advantages, such as size and bone structure, provided by testosterone production during puberty? Consider also whether there is any reason why a sport should have different rules for transgender females like Lia Thomas than for intersex or DSD females like Semenya.

Note Semenya's argument that her natural biological advantage should not be treated differently than the natural biological advantages that enable other athletes to be elite. Given the justification for female-only competitions, is there a relevant difference between Semenya's intersex developmental advantage and the biological advantages of height or hand size or even an especially high natural male testosterone level of a male athlete?

2.   *Relevance of Semenya's Success in Female Competition?* Is the level of Caster Semenya's success in female-only competitions relevant to whether she should be allowed to continue to race in them? Or should the decision turn only on scientific calculations of the impact of testosterone? Does your answer apply also to Lia Thomas?

3.   *Treatment of Transgender Males?* Note the participation in the Ivy League female swimming competition of Iszac Henig, a transgender male. Is there any reason why such males, if they have not undergone hormone enhancement and can pass testosterone tests, should not be able to compete against females?

4.   *Application to Non-Elite Sports?* Should the same standards for transgender and intersex athletes apply regardless of the level of competition? Should the NCAA follow the leads of international sports federations for all

levels of college competitions? Should high school athletic associations? Are the costs of regulation the same for younger athletes?

5.   *Relevance of Title IX?* Do schools violate Title IX when they require transgender females to comply with testosterone standards as a condition for competing in female-only sports? What if they prohibit transgender females from competing in female-only sports regardless of their compliance with testosterone standards? Some states have enacted laws prohibiting such competition regardless of testosterone testing. Are such laws preempted by Title IX?

6.   *Should World Athletics Serve Only Elite Cisgender Athletes?* World Athletics (formerly IAAF) seems to embrace the view that, because of genetic differences, elite cisgender female athletes would not be able to compete at the highest level of athletics without a separate category of competition to protect them. Should World Athletics also provide other categories of competition for other athletes? Should it follow the lead of FINA and at least explore the possibility of developing events for athletes who do not meet eligibility criteria for men's and women's competitions? Should it even adopt the approach of paralympic sport (or wrestling and boxing) and give multiple types of athletes, such as those with shorter legs, an opportunity to compete?

5.   REGULATING SEX DISCRIMINATION IN EMPLOYMENT

In addition to Title IX, two other important federal statutes prohibiting sex discrimination in employment, and similar non-preempted state laws, are relevant to the achievement of equality in sports for women. The first of course is Title VII of the 1964 Civil Rights Act, which prohibits sex-based as well as race-based discrimination in employment. The second is the Equal Pay Act, which in effect prohibits sex discrimination in the compensation of employees. Both statutes protect only those who work as employees and thus provide no protection to college athletes, unless they achieve the status of employees through developments treated in Chapter 12. These statutes are, however, relevant to professional athletes.

Given the gender-segregated nature of most sports competitions, Title VII has greater potential relevance today for female coaches and sports administrators than for female athletes just as it has greater potential relevance for race discrimination in coaching and sports administration. The growth of athletic opportunities for girls and women, due in large part to Title IX, has not led to a proportionate growth in female coaches. Quite the contrary. In 1972, prior to Title IX, 90% of the head coaching positions for women's college teams were held by women. In 2021, women held only 41% of such positions and less than 50% of assistant coaching positions in women sports. The source of this development is easy to trace. The Title IX-enlargement of resources devoted to female sports, including in coaches' salaries, led more men to desire and obtain positions leading female teams. And most university athletic directors, who remain predominantly male themselves, seem to prefer them. Nor have women gained coaching positions in men's college teams. Only about 5% of men's teams have female head coaches.

In recent years women have done better securing head coaching positions in the limited number of female professional teams. Two-thirds of the head coaches in the WNBA were women in 2022, as were half of the head coaches in the NWSL (National Women's Soccer League). Women also have started to fill at least some assistant coaching positions in men's team sports. The NBA has had fifteen female assistant coaches, including six in the 2021–2022 season, and a record eight-year run with the San Antonio Spurs for Becky Hammon before her transition to a head coaching post in the WNBA. From having no female coaches in 2014, in 2022 MLB teams had a record number of thirty-three female coaches somewhere in their systems, including the Yankees' Rachel Balkovic, the first minor league female manager, and the Giants' Alyssa Nakken, the first female major league coach. Even the NFL, without the benefit of a pool of female college footballers, had twelve female assistants, including interns, in some coaching capacity in 2022.

Women who are not hired for a coaching position they feel they observe may advance a complaint under Title VII. They can use the same doctrinal tools available for Black athletes claiming race discrimination, as discussed previously in this chapter. National hiring statistics, such as those cited above for college coaching, would not be relevant in a law suit against a particular school, however, and even statistics about the hiring done at a particular school would not be determinative. Each hiring decision ultimately must be considered on its own merit. Thus, female coaches have the same difficult challenge as do minority coaches proving discrimination in coaching hiring, especially for the most highly salaried positions with the least objective hiring criteria. Nonetheless, female coaching applicants have had occasional success in some litigation, at least on the high school level. *See, e.g., Joll v. Valparaiso Cmty. Schs.*, 953 F.3d 923 (7th Cir. 2021) (denying defendant summary judgment against female coach's claim that defendant had used sex-based hiring criteria to deny her applications to be assistant track coach for female and male teams); *Wynn v. Columbus Municipal Separate School Dist.*, 692 F. Supp. 672 (N.D. Miss.1988) (qualified female plaintiff proved that school's reason for not hiring her for the position of athletic director was pretextual).

Because of Title VII, women cannot ask schools to provide them preference for coaching women's teams. Title VII prohibits discrimination against males as well as against females. Though it provides a narrow "bona fide occupational qualification" defense to sex discrimination in hiring, the Supreme Court has held that this defense is only available for jobs that "all or substantially" members of the excluded sex cannot perform. Thus, a male applicant to coach a female team can claim unlawful discrimination if a less qualified female is hired for the job. See, e.g., *Medcalf v. Trustees of the Univ. of Pennsylvania*, 71 F. App'x 924 (3d Cir. 2003) (affirming a jury verdict that the University of Pennsylvania violated Title VII when it discriminated against Andrew Medcalf, an assistant coach of the women's crew team, by hiring a clearly less qualified woman as the head coach without even granting him an interview.)

The Equal Pay Act (EPA), the other federal statute regulating sex discrimination in employment, was passed in 1963, the year before the Civil Rights Act. The EPA only addresses sex discrimination in compensation; it does not cover discrimination in other employment decisions, such as hiring or termination. The EPA was a one paragraph addition to the Fair Labor Standards Act, 29 U.S.C. § 206 (introduced in Congress by Rep. Charles Goodell, the father of the then future NFL Commissioner.) Thus, the EPA applies the FLSA procedural and remedial provisions, including the availability of a direct private right of action in federal court, opt-in collective actions, and the doubling of damages for violations not in good faith. The EPA imposes strict liability on employers who pay different wages to employees "of the opposite sex" in the same "establishment for equal work on jobs the performance of which requires equal skill, effort, and responsibility, and which are performed under similar working conditions." The Act, however, also offers employers the opportunity to prove one of four affirmative defenses, one of which is that the difference was "based on any other factor other than sex." In an important decision, *County of Washington v. Gunther*, 452 U.S. 161 (1981), Justice Brennan explained for the Court that the "factor other than sex" defense effectively eliminates disparate impact sex compensation discrimination actions under the EPA (or Title VII which incorporates the defense for these actions) by requiring courts to accept an employer's proven non-discriminatory reasons for a pay differential.

In sum, the EPA provides a legal remedy for female coaches who are paid less than male coaches in comparable positions by the same employer. The remedy, however, requires them to prove that their work "requires equal skill, effort, and responsibility" and is "performed under similar working conditions" as that of their male comparators. And it also allows employers to defeat such pay discrimination claims by demonstrating other reasons for any differential. Consider the example of this early case involving then prominent coaches.

STANLEY V. UNIVERSITY OF SOUTHERN CALIFORNIA
13 F.3d 1313 (9th Cir. 1994)

ALARCON, CIRCUIT JUDGE.

* * * Coach Stanley has not offered proof to contradict the evidence proffered by USC that demonstrates the differences in the responsibilities of the persons who serve as head coaches of the women's and men's

basketball teams. Coach Raveling's responsibilities as head coach of the men's basketball team require substantial public relations and promotional activities to generate revenue for USC. These efforts resulted in revenue that is 90 times greater than the revenue generated by the women's basketball team. Coach Raveling was required to conduct twelve outside speaking engagements per year, to be accessible to the media for interviews, and to participate in certain activities designed to produce donations and endorsements for the USC Athletic Department in general. Coach Stanley's position as head coach did not require her to engage in the same intense level of promotional and revenue-raising activities. This quantitative dissimilarity in responsibilities justifies a different level of pay for the head coach of the women's basketball team. See *Horner v. Mary Inst.*, 613 F.2d 706, 713–14 (8th Cir.1980) (evidence that male physical education teacher had a different job from a female physical education teacher because he was responsible for curriculum precluded finding that jobs were substantially similar; court may consider whether job requires more experience, training, and ability to determine whether jobs require substantially equal skill under EPA).

The evidence presented by USC also showed that Coach Raveling had substantially different qualifications and experience related to his public relations and revenue-generation skills than Coach Stanley. Coach Raveling received educational training in marketing, and worked in that field for nine years. Coach Raveling has been employed by USC three years longer than Coach Stanley. He has been a college basketball coach for 31 years, while Coach Stanley has had 17 years' experience as a basketball coach. Coach Raveling had served as a member of the NCAA Subcommittee on Recruiting. Coach Raveling also is the respected author of two bestselling novels. He has performed as an actor in a feature movie, and has appeared on national television to discuss recruiting of student athletes. Coach Stanley does not have the same degree of experience in these varied activities. Employers may reward professional experience and education without violating the EPA.

Coach Raveling's national television appearances and motion picture presence, as well as his reputation as an author, make him a desirable public relations representative for USC. An employer may consider the marketplace value of the skills of a particular individual when determining his or her salary. *Horner*, 613 F.2d at 714. Unequal wages that reflect market conditions of supply and demand are not prohibited by the EPA. *EEOC v. Madison Community Unit Sch. Dist. No. 12*, 818 F.2d 577, 580 (7th Cir.1987).

The record also demonstrates that the USC men's basketball team generated greater attendance, more media interest, larger donations, and

produced substantially more revenue than the women's basketball team.[1]
As a result, USC placed greater pressure on Coach Raveling to promote his
team and to win. The responsibility to produce a large amount of revenue
is evidence of a substantial difference in responsibility. *See Jacobs v.
College of William and Mary*, 517 F. Supp. 791, 797 (E.D. Va.1980) (duty
to produce revenue demonstrates that coaching jobs are not substantially
equal), aff'd without opinion, 661 F.2d 922 (4th Cir.), *cert. denied*, 454 U.S.
1033 (1981).

Coach Stanley did not offer evidence to rebut USC's justification for
paying Coach Raveling a higher salary. Instead, she alleged that the
women's team generates revenue, and that she is under a great deal of
pressure to win.[2]

We agree with the district court in *Jacobs* that revenue generation is
an important factor that may be considered in justifying greater pay. We
are also of the view that the relative amount of revenue generated should
be considered in determining whether responsibilities and working
conditions are substantially equal. The fact that the men's basketball team
at USC generates 90 times the revenue than that produced by the women's
team adequately demonstrates that Coach Raveling was under greater
pressure to win and to promote his team than Coach Stanley was subject
to as head coach of the women's team.

Coach Stanley's reliance on *Burkey v. Marshall County Board of
Education*, 513 F. Supp. 1084 (N.D. W. Va.1981), and *EEOC v. Madison
Community Unit School District No. 12*, 818 F.2d 577 (7th Cir.1987), to
support her claim of sex discrimination is misplaced. In *Burkey*, the women
coaches were "uniformly paid one-half (1/2) of the salary which male

---

[1]   The total average attendance per women's team game during Coach Stanley's tenure was
751 as compared to 4,035 for the men's team during the same period. The average sales of season
ticket passes to faculty and staff for women's games were 13, while the average sales for men's
games were 130. Alumni and other fans, on average, purchased 71 passes for women's home games
as compared to over 1,200 season passes for men's home games during the same period. A season
pass to the men's home games was more than double the price of a season pass to women's home
games.

The same disparity exists with respect to media interest in the men's and women's basketball
teams. Television and radio stations paid USC to broadcast the men's basketball games; all of the
home games and many games off campus were broadcast on network or cable stations. All of the
games were broadcast on commercial radio. Approximately three of the women's basketball games
were broadcast on cable stations as part of a contract package that also covered several other
sports.

Donations and endowments were likewise greater for the men's basketball team, totaling
$66,916 during the time period of Coach Stanley's contract, as compared to $4,288 for the women's
basketball team. The same was true for revenue production. While the women's basketball team
produced a total revenue of $50,262 during Coach Stanley's four years, the men's team generated
$4,725,784 during the same time period.

[2]   Coach Stanley also alleged that, as head coach, she had won four national women's
basketball championships, but that Coach Raveling had won none. In addition, while head coach
at USC, Coach Stanley was named PAC-10 Coach-of-the-Year in 1993 and the women's basketball
team played in the last three NCAA Tournaments and advanced to the NCAA Sweet Sixteen in
1993 and the NCAA Elite Eight in 1992. She also described numerous speaking engagements in
which she had participated.

coaches of comparable or identical boys' junior high school sports were paid." Here, however, Coach Stanley has not shown that her responsibilities were identical.

Coach Stanley argues that *Jacobs* is distinguishable because, in that matter, the head basketball coach of the women's team was not required to produce any revenue. Coach Stanley appears to suggest that a difference in the amount of revenue generated by the men's and women's teams should be ignored by the court in comparing the respective coaching positions. We disagree.

In *Madison*, the Seventh Circuit held that the plaintiff established a prima facie EPA claim because "male and female coaches alike testified that the skill, effort, and responsibility required were the same and the working conditions [were] also the same—not merely similar—which is all the Act requires." In the instant matter, the uncontradicted evidence shows that Coach Raveling's responsibilities, as head coach of the men's basketball team, differed substantially from the duties imposed upon Coach Stanley.

Coach Stanley contends that the failure to allocate funds in the promotion of women's basketball team demonstrated gender discrimination. She appears to argue that USC's failure to pay her a salary equal to that of Coach Raveling was the result of USC's "failure to market and promote the women's basketball team." The only evidence Coach Stanley presented in support of this argument is that USC failed to provide the women's team with a poster containing the schedule of games, but had done so for the men's team. This single bit of evidence does not demonstrate that Coach Stanley was denied equal pay for equal work. Instead, it demonstrates, at best, a business decision to allocate USC resources to the team that generates the most revenue.

The district court also was "unconvinced" by Coach Stanley's claim that USC's disparate promotion of men's and women's basketball teams had "caused the enormous differences in spectator interest and revenue production." The court rejected Coach Stanley's assertion that the differences were due to societal discrimination and that this was evidence of a prima facie case under the EPA. The court reasoned that societal discrimination in preferring to witness men's sports in greater numbers cannot be attributed to USC. We agree.

At this preliminary stage of these proceedings, the record does not support a finding that gender was the reason that USC paid a higher salary to Coach Raveling as head coach of the men's basketball team than it offered Coach Stanley as head coach of the women's basketball team. Garrett's affidavit supports the district court's conclusion that the head coach position of the men's team was not substantially equal to the head coach position of the women's team. The record shows that there were significant differences between Coach Stanley's and Coach Raveling's public relations skills, credentials, experience, and qualifications; there also were substantial differences between their responsibilities and working conditions. The district court's finding that the head coach positions were not substantially equal is not a "clear error of judgment."

* * *

Affirmed.

NOTES AND QUESTIONS

1.   *Aftermath.* After failing to obtain immediate injunctive relief, Stanley filled in during the 1995–96 season at Stanford, temporarily replacing its women's basketball coach who had taken a year's leave of absence to coach the women's team at the 1996 Atlanta Olympics. Stanley was then hired to coach the University of California team, beginning in the 1996–97 season. Eventually her quest for damages from USC was summarily dismissed, a judgment that was affirmed 2–1 in *Stanley v. University of Southern California*, 178 F.3d 1069 (9th Cir. 1999). There, the court explained,

> Both sides agreed that "the men's and women's coaching jobs share a common core of tasks ... recruiting athletes and administering the basketball programs. USC's basic defense, though, was that Raveling had 'greater revenue generating responsibilities, that he is under greater media and spectator pressure to produce a winning program, and that he actually generates more revenue for the University.' Relying on an October 1997 Notice issued by President Clinton's Equal Employment Opportunity Commission (EEOC) as interpretation guidelines for 'sex discrimination in the compensation of sports coaches in educational institutions,' Stanley claimed that these differences between the two jobs resulted from the University's historically disparate treatment of male and female teams; namely, its decision to invest in and promote the men's program more than the women's program." USC's response was that this disparity in coaching responsibilities and team revenues was because even now "there simply is not a sufficient spectator or media market for women's basketball games."

> Because that essentially factual issue could not be decided on a motion for summary dismissal, the majority instead based its decision on another "factor other than sex." The salary differential between the female and male coaches could instead be explained by the fact that Raveling had coached for 14 more years than Stanley, had twice been named national coach of the year, had once coached the men's Olympic team, had authored several books on basketball, and had many years more experience in marketing and promotion.

> Coaches with substantially more experience and significantly superior qualifications may of course be paid more than their less

experienced and qualified counterparts, even when it is the male coach who has the greater level of experience and qualifications.

Id. at 1079–80.

2. *Relevance of Differentiating Factors in* Stanley. Were Raveling's television, movie and publishing experiences relevant to whether his job was equal in skill, effort, and responsibility and performed under similar working conditions to that of Stanley? Was his greater experience as a coach? The fact that his team produced substantially more revenue for USC? How about USC's requirement that he spend extra time in public relations to generate revenue? In any event, were all these factors "other than sex" and thus possible nondiscriminatory explanations for the pay differential? If so, are female coaches of nonrevenue producing women's teams ever likely to be successful challenging a compensation disparity with a coach of a men's revenue producing team?

Note, however, that these factors would not necessarily be available as defenses in a typical pay discrimination suit against a high school that paid its male and female coaches differently, such as the *Marshall County Board of Education* and *Madison Community Unit School District* cases cited in the *Stanley* decision.

3. *Relevance of Prior Pay?* The highest salaries in college sports often derive from efforts by one university to attract coaches who have been successful at another school. Should prior salary thus be treated as a factor other than sex in a defense against any EPA claim? What if a school uses prior salary as a starting basis for all its coaching salaries? Should it matter if such a policy leads generally to lower pay for female coaches because of past discrimination in the external coaching market? Judge Pregerson's dissent in the panel decision in the *Stanley* case stressed not only USC's greater marketing of the men's program, but also the "formidable obstacles Stanley faced as a female coach in a male-dominated profession." Are obstacles in the external labor market relevant to an EPA claim?

4. *State Anti-Discrimination Employment Laws as an Alternative Remedy?* The Bennett Amendment, interpreted by the Court in the *Gunther* decision noted above, incorporated the EPA's affirmative defenses into Title VII for purposes of pay discrimination claims. Thus, Title VII does not offer a route around the "factor other than sex" defense. However, a few states, including California, have anti-discrimination laws that require any non-discriminatory explanation to be job-related, consistent with business necessity and not avoidable by an alternative practice

5. *Title IX as an Alternative Remedy?* Could Stanley have been successful using Title IX to attack her pay's disparity with that of Raveling? A disparity between the compensation for the coaches of the men's and women's basketball teams—regardless of the coaches' gender—might constitute evidence of a violation of the school's Title IX obligation to direct equal resources toward the support of its female and male *athletes*. Indeed, the Title IX regulations list "compensation of coaches" as a factor relevant to whether

equal athletic opportunities are being provided. But how would the plaintiff coach of the women's basketball team argue that his/her players were discriminated against or injured because he or she was paid less than the men's team's coach? Because he or she didn't work as hard as if he or she had been paid more? Because the school could have hired a better coach than him or her had the salary been higher?

Furthermore, it is doubtful that a coach would even have standing to assert a Title IX claim for a higher salary. Title IX is framed to protect from sex discrimination the student participants and beneficiaries of educational programs and activities. The employees who are responsible for those programs and activities are not within the zone of interests protected by Title IX. The Court did hold in *Jackson v. Birmingham Bd. of Educ.*, 544 U.S. 167 (2005), that a coach of a public high school girls' team was protected by Title IX from the school's retaliation for complaining that his team was not receiving equal funding and equal access to athletic equipment and facilities. The Court, by a 5–4 majority, ruled that retaliation against a person because he or she complains of sex discrimination constitutes intentional "discrimination" "on the basis of sex," in violation of Title IX. The narrow decision, however, did not address whether a coach would have standing under Title IX to bring an action complaining of unequal treatment of female athletes, and none of the Justices in the majority remain on the Court.

The EPA does not provide a useful tool for most female professional athletes. Few are employed by an entity that also employs male athletes whose work can be compared to theirs. The National Women's National Soccer Team's members, however, are employed by the same United States Soccer Federation that employs the Men's National Soccer Team. Perhaps because other, more soccer-focused nations have nothing comparable to Title IX to encourage the development of their female players, for many years the women's team has been more successful than the men's team in international competition. This success has translated into greater prominence in popular culture. In the following litigation the women attempted to leverage that success and prominence through the EPA.

MORGAN V. UNITED STATES SOCCER FEDERATION
445 F. Supp.3d 635 (C.D. Cal. 2020)

KLAUSNER, DISTRICT JUDGE.

I. INTRODUCTION

On March 8, 2019, Plaintiffs, who are female professional soccer players on the United States Senior Women's National Soccer Team ("WNT"), filed a putative collective action and class action against the United States Soccer Federation, Inc. ("Defendant" or "USSF"). Plaintiffs assert two claims against Defendant: (1) violation of the Equal Pay Act

("EPA"), 29 U.S.C. § 206; and (2) violation of Title VII of the Civil Rights Act of 1964 ("Title VII"), 42 U.S.C. § 2000e.

* * *

II. FACTUAL BACKGROUND

The following facts are undisputed unless otherwise indicated.

A. The United States Soccer Federation

USSF is the national governing body for the sport of soccer in the United States. USSF selects, funds, trains, and manages the various United States national soccer teams, including the WNT and its male counterpart, the United States Senior Men's National Soccer Team ("MNT"). The MNT and the WNT are each represented by a separate union and compensated under the terms of a separate collective bargaining agreement ("CBA").

B. The Men's National Team

The MNT competes in a variety of events throughout the world. Since 2015, the MNT has competed for USSF in (1) friendly matches ("friendlies"); (2) FIFA World Cup qualifying matches; and (3) a variety of other tournaments such as the Gold Cup, Concacaf Cup, Copa America Centenario, and the Concacaf Nations League. In addition to playing for USSF, members of the MNT also play with professional soccer clubs. Indeed, since 2013, almost all MNT players have played for a club team in a professional soccer league, such as Major League Soccer (in the United States), LigaMX (in Mexico), the Eredivisie (in the Netherlands), the Premier League (in England), and the Bundesliga (in Germany). USSF does not compensate MNT players for playing with professional soccer clubs.

USSF recognizes the United States National Soccer Team Players Association ("USNSTPA") as the exclusive representative of all MNT players for collective bargaining. The most recent CBA between the USNSTPA and USSF was executed on November 20, 2011 and remained in effect through December 31, 2018. USSF has continued to compensate the MNT according to the terms of the 2011–2018 CBA since it expired, with some exceptions.

The MNT CBA is structured as a "pay-to-play" agreement, meaning that players are not compensated unless they participate in a training camp or make a particular roster. Under the CBA, USSF has "no obligation to hold any matches, tournaments, or events or to field a team for any match, tournament, or event." MNT players also do not receive an annual salary. Instead, they receive bonuses based on the team's performance in different matches. For example, from 2011 through 2014, if a player made the roster for a friendly against a team with a FIFA ranking of 1–10 and the team won, that player would receive a $14,100 bonus. If there was a tie, the same player would receive a $6,500 bonus, and if the team lost (regardless of the opponent's FIFA ranking), the player would receive a $4,000 bonus. These bonuses increased to $17,625 for a win, $8,125 for a tie, and $5,000 for a loss during the period from 2015 through 2018.

The highest bonuses available to MNT players under their CBA are bonuses related to the FIFA World Cup, which takes place every four years. For example, under the MNT CBA, if the team qualified for the 2018 World Cup (which it did not), USSF would have paid $2.5 million to the MNT player pool. Each player on the roster for the World Cup would have received an additional bonus of $68,750. If the team advanced to the semifinals, USSF would have paid the player pool $5.625 million. If the team won first place, USSF would have paid the player pool $9.375 million.

C.   The Women's National Team

Like the MNT, the WNT participates in competitions around the world. Unlike the MNT, the WNT has achieved largely unrivaled success, winning four FIFA Women's World Cup titles and four Olympic gold medals. Since 2015, the WNT has competed for USSF in (1) friendlies; (2) the Olympics and associated qualifying matches; (3) the FIFA Women's World Cup and associated qualifying matches; and (4) a variety of other tournaments such as the She Believes Tournament, the Tournament of Nations, and the Algarve Cup. Since 2013, most WNT players have not only played for USSF, but also for a club team in a professional soccer league. Many WNT players participate in the National Women's Soccer League ("NWSL")—the top-tier professional women's soccer league in the United States.

USSF recognizes the United States Women's National Soccer Team Players Association ("WNTPA") as the exclusive representative of WNT players for purposes of collective bargaining. The first CBA between the WNTPA and USSF expired at the end of 2004. The second CBA covered the period from 2005 through 2012.

[The court next describes in detail the extensive five year collective bargaining negotiations between the USSF and the WNTPA, culminating in the 2017 CBA.]

* * *

IV.   DISCUSSION

A.   Equal Pay Act

As the Supreme Court has explained, the EPA's structure is straightforward. *See Corning Glass*, 417 U.S. [188,]195. First, the plaintiff bears the burden to establish a prima facie case of wage discrimination. *Id.* If the plaintiff establishes a prima facie case, the burden shifts to the defendant to show that the wage differential is justified by one of the EPA's four exceptions. *Id.* at 196.

Here, Plaintiffs have the initial burden to establish a prima facie case of wage discrimination under the EPA. To do this, Plaintiffs must show that (1) they performed substantially equal work as MNT players, (2) under similar working conditions, and (3) MNT players were paid more. *See* 29 U.S.C. § 206(d)(1); *Riser v. QEP Energy*, 776 F.3d 1191, 1196 (10th Cir. 2015). The Court begins with the third element—whether MNT players were paid more than WNT players.

To establish a prima facie case of wage discrimination, Plaintiffs must show that Defendant pays wages to WNT players "at a rate less than the rate at which [it] pays wages to employees of the opposite sex." 29 U.S.C. § 206(d). "The term wage 'rate,' as used in the EPA, refers to the standard or measure by which an employee's wage is determined [.]" 29 C.F.R. § 1620.12(a). Meanwhile, "the term 'wages' generally includes all payments made to [or on behalf of] an employee as remuneration for employment." 29 C.F.R. § 1620.10 (bracketing in original). Wages include "*all forms of compensation* irrespective of the time of payment, whether paid periodically or deferred until a later date, and whether called wages, salary, profit sharing, expense account, monthly minimum, bonus, uniform cleaning allowance, hotel accommodations, use of company car, gasoline allowance, or some other name." *Id.* (emphasis added). Wages also include fringe benefits, which include "medical, hospital, accident, life insurance and retirement benefits; profit sharing and bonus plans; leave; and other such concepts." *Id.*; 29 C.F.R. § 1620.11(a).

Plaintiffs contend that "the written terms of the relevant CBAs establish as a matter of undisputed fact that USSF has paid WNT players at a rate less than MNT players throughout the class period." In support, Plaintiffs make two primary arguments. First, Plaintiffs focus on the CBAs' bonus provisions, arguing that the WNT CBA provides for lower bonuses than the MNT CBA for friendlies, World Cup-related matches, and other tournaments. Second, Plaintiffs point to what WNT players *would have received* had they been compensated under the terms of the MNT CBA. Plaintiffs' expert opines that had WNT players been compensated under the MNT CBA, they would have received more money over the class period than they did under the WNT CBA, even when all fringe benefits are considered.

Defendant disputes that USSF pays WNT players at a rate less than the rate it pays MNT players. Unlike Plaintiffs, Defendant focuses on the total compensation paid to the players under the terms of the respective CBAs. Defendant contends that when total compensation is considered, it is apparent that WNT players received *more* money than MNT players on both a cumulative and an average per-game basis. Indeed, Defendant's expert opines that from 2015 to 2019, payments to the WNT totaled approximately $24 million and averaged $220,747 per game, whereas payments to the MNT totaled approximately $18 million and averaged

$212,639 per game. (Irwin Expert Report at 17, ECF No. 171-4.) Defendant's expert also opines that the average per-game compensation received by the four class representatives exceeds the average per-game compensation received by the four highest-paid MNT players. (*Id.* at 18–19 (finding that the four WNT class representatives made an average of $11,356 to $17,416 per game, while the four highest-paid MNT players made an average of $10,360 to $13,964 per game).) Defendant argues that total compensation is the appropriate method for comparison where, as here, plaintiffs receive more than one category of wages and "higher pay in one category can offset lower pay in another category for purposes of the Equal Pay Act[.]" Defendant also avers that this method of comparison is appropriate where men and women "do not have a parallel standard or measure of pay . . . that can be directly compared for the purpose of the anti-discrimination laws."

* * *

Since the Court's class certification ruling, "Plaintiffs have had ample time and opportunity to develop evidence showing that the fact that the WNT was paid more than the MNT was due solely, or in material part, to the WNT working more than the MNT." Now, at the summary judgment stage, Plaintiffs have the burden to "show what evidence" they have on this issue. Plaintiffs have not satisfied this burden. It is undisputed that, during the class period, the WNT played 111 total games and made $24.5 million overall, averaging $220,747 per game. By contrast, the MNT played 87 total games and made $18.5 million overall, averaging $212,639 per game. Based on this evidence, it appears that the WNT did not make more money than the MNT solely because they played more games. Rather, the WNT both played more games and made more money than the MNT per game. . . .

Consider, for example, Plaintiffs' reliance on the bonuses received by WNT players for friendlies, World-Cup-related games, and other tournaments. Plaintiffs ask the Court to find an EPA violation because the WNT CBA provides for lower bonuses in these categories of compensation than the MNT CBA. But this approach ignores other benefits received by WNT players, such as guaranteed annual salaries and severance pay— benefits that MNT players do not receive. To consider these bonus provisions in isolation would run afoul of the EPA, which expressly defines "wages" to include all forms of compensation, including fringe benefits. 29 C.F.R. § 1620.12(a); 29 C.F.R. § 1620.11(a); *see Diamond v. T. Rowe Price Assocs., Inc.*, 852 F. Supp. 372, 395 (D. Md. 1994) (granting summary judgment to employer on plaintiff's EPA claim where although plaintiff did not receive stock options and larger annual bonuses, plaintiff received more total compensation than her alleged comparators). The Court therefore finds that Plaintiffs cannot establish that they were paid less than MNT players solely by reference to these bonus provisions.

Plaintiffs also ask the Court to conclude that WNT players are paid less than MNT players because had they been paid under the MNT CBA, they would have made more than they did under their own CBA. But Defendant has submitted evidence showing that had MNT players been paid under the terms of the WNT's 2017 CBA, they too would have made more than they did under their own CBA. Is this sufficient to demonstrate that Defendant compensates MNT players at a rate less than the rate it pays wages to WNT players? The Court thinks not. This approach—merely comparing what each team would have made under the other team's CBA—is untenable in this case because it ignores the reality that the MNT and WNT bargained for different agreements which reflect different preferences, and that the WNT explicitly rejected the terms they now seek to retroactively impose on themselves. The first time the WNT requested bonuses equivalent to those received by the MNT was in January 2016. USSF rejected that proposal, however, because the WNT was not asking for a pay-to-play arrangement similar to the MNT CBA; instead, it was asking for all of the upsides of the MNT CBA (namely, higher bonuses) without any of the drawbacks (e.g., no base salary). In May 2016, USSF offered the WNT a pay-to-play proposal similar to the MNT CBA but the WNT rejected it, preferring an agreement that involved some element of guaranteed compensation. The parties attempted to work out such an agreement and, in February 2017, USSF made a proposal which included, (1) a commitment to have 15 contracted players, (2) annual WNT salaries ranging from $70,000 to $90,000, and (3) bonuses for friendlies of $9,000 per win and $2,000 per tie for teams ranked 1–4. In response, the WNT offered a counterproposal which included *lower* bonuses for friendlies, but a higher number of contracted players with higher base salaries. Ultimately, the parties agreed to a compromise whereby there would be 20 contracted players in 2017, each of whom would receive a base salary of $100,000, with friendly bonuses of $8,500 per win and $1,750 per tie against teams ranked 1–4.

This history of negotiations between the parties demonstrates that the WNT rejected an offer to be paid under the same pay-to-play structure as the MNT, and that the WNT was willing to forgo higher bonuses for other benefits, such as greater base compensation and the guarantee of a higher number of contracted players. Accordingly, Plaintiffs cannot now retroactively deem their CBA worse than the MNT CBA by reference to what they *would have made* had they been paid under the MNT's pay-to-play structure when they themselves rejected such a structure. This method of comparison not only fails to account for the choices made during collective bargaining, it also ignores the economic value of the "insurance" that WNT players receive under their CBA. One of the defining features of the WNT CBA is its guarantee that players will be compensated regardless of whether they play a match or not. This stands in stark contrast to the MNT CBA, under which players are only compensated if they are called into camp to play and then participate in a match. It is difficult to attach a dollar value to this "insurance" benefit, and neither party attempts to do so here. However, there is indisputably economic value to this type of "fixed pay" contract, as compared to a "performance pay" contract. Indeed, the WNT clearly attached significant economic value to this contractual arrangement because it was willing to agree to lower bonuses in exchange for higher fixed payments in its 2017 CBA. Merely comparing what WNT players received under their own CBA with what they would have received under the MNT CBA discounts the value that the team placed on the guaranteed benefits they receive under their agreement, which they opted for at the expense of higher performance-based bonuses.

In sum, Defendant has offered evidence in support of its Motion for Summary Judgment that the WNT has been paid more on both a cumulative and an average per-game basis than the MNT over the class period. In response, Plaintiffs have offered evidence that (1) WNT players are paid lower bonuses for friendlies, World Cup-related games, and other tournaments; (2) WNT players would have made more under the MNT CBA than they did under then own CBA, and; (3) USSF agents made statements to the effect that WNT players are paid less than MNT players. As set forth above, this evidence is insufficient to create a genuine issue of material fact for trial. Accordingly, the Court grants summary judgment to Defendant on Plaintiffs' EPA claim. The Court need not address the remaining elements of Plaintiffs' prima facie case.

B. Title VII

The Court next turns to Plaintiffs' remaining claim for discrimination in violation of Title VII. Plaintiffs bring their Title VII claim on two theories of disparate treatment. First, Plaintiffs allege that Defendant intentionally discriminated against them by paying them less than similarly situated MNT players. Second, Plaintiffs allege that Defendant intentionally discriminated against them by subjecting them to unequal working conditions. The Court addresses each theory in turn.

1. *Discriminatory Compensation*

Plaintiffs first contend that Defendant discriminated against them by paying them less than similarly situated players on the MNT. However, the Court has already held that Plaintiffs have not demonstrated a triable issue that WNT players are paid less than MNT players. Accordingly, the Court grants summary judgment to Defendant on this claim.

2. *Discriminatory Working Conditions*

Plaintiffs also allege that Defendant subjected WNT players to discriminatory working conditions. . . .

Upon review, the Court finds that Plaintiffs' Complaint fairly encompasses a claim for discriminatory working conditions with respect to

(1) field surfaces; (2) travel conditions (specifically, charter flights and hotels), and; (3) support services (specifically, medical and training support).

* * *

Plaintiffs contend that USSF made the WNT play on inferior surfaces such as artificial turf more frequently than the MNT. Essentially, Plaintiffs contend that USSF made two decisions about field surfaces, either one or both of which must have been plagued by discriminatory animus. First, when deciding the venue for matches, USSF chose turf venues more frequently for WNT matches than for MNT matches. Second, if either team was scheduled to play at a turf venue, USSF chose to install temporary grass over the turf more frequently for the MNT than for the WNT. According to Plaintiffs, playing on artificial turf can lead to significant injuries and can also affect fundamentals of the game, including the way the ball bounces and how the ball can be struck. . . .

Once a plaintiff has established a prima facie case of discrimination, "the burden of production shifts to the defendant, who must offer evidence that the adverse action was taken for other than impermissibly discriminatory reasons." Here, Defendant has satisfied this burden. It is undisputed that, during the relevant time period, the MNT and WNT played the vast majority of their matches on grass rather than turf. Defendant has submitted evidence that there were only two time periods when Defendant subjected the WNT to games on artificial turf more frequently than the MNT. First, after the 2015 Women's World Cup, the WNT played on artificial turf seven times during their 10-game Victory Tour. It should be noted that the MNT did not play in any corresponding Victory Tour. Second, the WNT played three friendlies on artificial turf during the period between July 27 and October 19, 2017. With respect to the Victory Tour, Defendant submits evidence that USSF's desire "to spread its Senior National Team games across various cities in various regions of the country, the relatively large number of games required to be played in a relatively short period of time during fall and winter, and the desire to prioritize venues with grass fields for 2016 in preparation for the Olympic Games all played a role in the number and concentration of games on artificial turf [during the Victory Tour]" As for why it did not install temporary grass over the turf at these venues, Defendant submits evidence that it did not anticipate generating enough revenue from those matches to make it financially prudent to install temporary grass over the turf at those venues, nor did USSF believe doing so would be necessary to attract opponents. With respect to the three friendlies between July 27 and October 19, 2017, again Defendant submits evidence that it did not anticipate generating enough revenue from these matches to justify the cost of installing temporary grass.

* * *

Even viewing the evidence cumulatively and in the light most favorable to Plaintiffs, the Court finds that Plaintiffs have failed to raise a triable issue as to pretext. . . .

Based on the evidence submitted by Plaintiffs, a reasonable trier of fact could not conclude by a preponderance of the evidence that Defendant intentionally discriminated against the WNT by subjecting them to turf surfaces more frequently than the MNT. The Court therefore grants summary judgment to Defendant on this claim.

Defendant also moves for summary judgment on Plaintiffs' charter-flights claim, which is one aspect of Plaintiffs' broader theory that Defendant discriminated against the WNT by subjecting them to inferior travel conditions relative to the MNT. Indeed, not only do Plaintiffs allege that Defendant provided the MNT with charter flights more frequently than the WNT, Plaintiffs also allege that Defendant budgeted and spent more money on airfare and hotels for the MNT than the WNT. For example, Plaintiff allege that from 2015 to 2020, USSF spent approximately $9 million on airfare for the MNT, while spending approximately $5 million on airfare for the WNT, even though the WNT played more games during this period.

* * *

Upon review, the Court finds that Plaintiffs' evidence is sufficient to raise a genuine dispute as to pretext. The most common explanation provided by Defendant for the charter-flight disparity is rooted in the MNT's "competitive need." To be sure, this is a legitimate nondiscriminatory explanation for the disparity. However, this explanation is "so weak" and "implausible" "that a reasonable fact finder could conclude that it was not an honestly held belief but rather was subterfuge for discrimination." *Young v. Dillon Companies, Inc.*, 468 F.3d 1243, 1250 (10th Cir. 2006). For one, this rationale does not fully explain the gross disparity in money spent on airfare and hotels for the teams. Additionally, it compels the implausible conclusion that the WNT never faced a similar situation during the relevant time period when it too would have benefited from the "competitive advantage" that comes from charter flights. A rational fact finder could infer that the disparity in charter flights, coupled with the disparity in funds allocated for travel more broadly and Defendant's weak explanations for these discrepancies, gives rise to an inference of discriminatory motive. . . .

The Court does not specifically address the merits of Plaintiffs' remaining claims regarding travel conditions more broadly and support services. In its Motion for Summary Judgment, Defendant asked the Court to enter summary judgment only on Plaintiffs' claims related to artificial turf and charter flights. Defendant did not address Plaintiffs' allegations about money spent on airfare and hotel accommodations or Plaintiffs' allegations about support services until its Reply. . . .

VI. CONCLUSION

For the foregoing reasons, the Court DENIES Plaintiffs' Motion and GRANTS in part Defendant's Motion. Plaintiffs' Title VII claim for discriminatory working conditions survives only insofar as it is based on (1) travel conditions (specifically, charter flights and hotel accommodations), and (2) personnel and support services (specifically, medical and training support).

———

NOTES AND QUESTIONS

1. *Aftermath.* After avoiding a trial by settling the working conditions claim with the USSF, the women appealed the EPA decision to the Ninth Circuit Court of Appeals. Before the appellate court could consider the case, however, the USSF announced new collective bargaining agreements in May 2022 with both the women's and men's teams. The agreements, which will run simultaneously through the end of 2028, provide for identical game bonuses and appearance fees and for the two teams to share equally the prize money from their respective World Cups. The women gave up their guaranteed salaries, but retained some special benefits the men do not have, including for health care, vision and dental, parental leave for up to six months, and short-term disability payments. Each agreement specifies minimum working conditions standards, including for venue and surfaces, travel, and accommodations.

2. *Determination of Pay Rate.* Do you understand how the women in their EPA action could claim that their "rate" of compensation was below that of the men if they were paid more in total than the men over the relevant period and were also paid more on average per game? The women argued that bonuses are part of the rate that the EPA requires to be equal. Should the structuring of the pay through different bonus systems make a difference if the structuring does not lead to lower pay per time of work, whether the time is calculated by hours or by games played? Should it matter that the women would have made more if they worked under the men's collective agreement? Note the court's citation of evidence that the men also would have earned more had they worked under the women's collective agreement.

3. *Relevance of Collective Bargaining?* Did the decision turn on the fact that the men's and women's different compensation structures were both the product of arms-length collective bargaining? If the women had not chosen collective bargaining and the USSF had offered the men's pay-for-play system to each woman player individually, would those who rejected it to retain a guaranteed salary be able to advance an EPA claim if they were paid less than they would have been paid had they accepted it? Or was it critical that the USSF offered the women's team the collective option of the men's pay-for-play system without guaranteed salaries?

Alternatively, should the fact of arms-length collective bargaining be treated as a factor-other-than-sex defense to any pay disparities? A collective bargaining agreement that intentionally provides women with different pay than it provides men is not a factor other than sex. But in this case, there were two collective agreements negotiated with two separate bargaining units. The women did not advance evidence of discriminatory intent in bargaining, such as proof that the USSF bargained less flexibly with the women's team. (While the two teams were appropriately in separate bargaining units, a merged unit also probably would have been appropriate. See the discussion of appropriate units in Chapter 3.)

4. *Equal Skill, Effort, and Responsibility?* At one point in the litigation the USSF's lawyers argued that the women could not demonstrate the equality required for the EPA prima facie case. This provoked vehement protests of "misogyny" from the women and led to the USSF restructuring their legal team. Even if politically unacceptable, however, did the argument have any legal merit? Presumably the women could not match the speed and strength of the men. But are attributes like speed and strength relevant to skill in athletic competition, or should skill be treated as separate from raw athleticism?

5. *Application to Other Sports.*

a. The Women's National Basketball Association (WNBA) was created by and has been subsidized by the NBA. While the NBA owners collectively retain a fifty percent ownership of the women's league, the NBA and WNBA do not have the common ownership on which an EPA case can rest. Assuming there were common ownership, however, would the EPA provide a basis for female players to claim a compensation structure that mirrors that of the male players in the NBA?

b. Professional tennis players are not employees of the tours on which they play. They are independent contractors who employ their own support staffs and decide which tournaments to play. Thus, they are not covered by either the EPA or Title VII. All four Grand Slam tournaments now pay women and men equal prize money, though the men play best-of-five set matches while the women play only best-of-three. Some American tournaments, however, still do not offer the same prize money to women that they offer to men, though both play best out of three set matches. Should the law require equal prize money? Should that depend upon whether the revenue streams can be separated? Should the EPA be amended to cover independent contractors generally?

C. DISABILITY

Athletes with disabilities are protected from discrimination under two federal statutes: the Rehabilitation Act of 1973 (Rehabilitation Act) and the Americans with Disabilities Act of 1990 (ADA). In addition, state human rights laws may provide impaired athletes with legal rights to participate in sports. The Rehabilitation Act, like Title IX for sex discrimination and Title VI for race discrimination, covers programs of entities that receive federal financial assistance, such as the sports programs of colleges and universities. The ADA includes provisions that cover discrimination by employers, state and local government services, and public accommodations such as hotels and restaurants.

The requirements for a claim under both Acts are similar—the plaintiff must show he or she: (a) is an individual with a "disability"; (b) is "otherwise qualified" to participate, with or without reasonable accommodations; and (c) was excluded from participation because of that disability. Before 2009, the statutes defined a disabled person to include (1) someone who has "a physical or mental impairment that substantially limits one or more major life activities," (2) someone who had a record of such an impairment, or (3) someone who was regarded as having such an impairment. However, in response to judicial decisions that had narrowed its coverage, Congress amended the ADA in 2008.

The 2008 amendments retained the same structure for the definition of "disability" but broadened that term's coverage in several ways. Most importantly, the amendments expanded the class of individuals protected from discrimination by modifying the definition of "regarded as" having a disability, the third prong of the definition of disability. 42 U.S.C. § 12102(3). To be protected from discrimination under the amended acts, an actual or perceived impairment does not have to "limit" or "be perceived to limit a major life activity," as long as the impairment is not both transitory (six months or less) and minor. This makes critical the definition of "impairment" included in an applicable regulation adopted soon after passage of the Rehabilitation Act and approved by the Supreme Court. That definition defines impairment to be "[a]ny physiological disorder or condition, cosmetic disfigurement, or anatomical loss affecting one or more body systems" or "[a]ny mental or psychological disorder." See 29 C.F.R. § 1630.2(H).

The amendments also enlarge the class of individuals who may claim reasonable accommodation as well as protection from discrimination because they qualify as disabled under the first or second prongs. The amendments do so first by expanding the statute's nonexclusive list of major life activities to include "caring for oneself, performing manual tasks, seeing, hearing, eating, sleeping, walking, standing, lifting, bending, speaking, breathing, learning, reading, concentrating, thinking, communicating and working," as well as "[m]ajor bodily functions." Major bodily functions include "functions of the immune system, normal cell growth, digestive, bowel, bladder, neurological, brain, respiratory, circulatory, endocrine, and reproductive functions." 42 U.S.C. § 12102(2). Second, the amendments clarify that the substantially-limits determination "shall be made without regard to the ameliorative effects of mitigating measures," such as medication, equipment, prosthetics and hearing aids, but not ordinary eyeglasses or contact lenses. 42 U.S.C.

12102(4)(E). Third, the amendments provide that an "impairment that is episodic or in remission is a disability if it would substantially limit a major life activity when active." 42 U.S.C. § 12102(4)(D). Finally, the amendments provide that the "definition of disability . . . shall be construed in favor of broad coverage." 42 U.S.C. § 12102(4)(A).

We consider how the ADA and the Rehabilitation Act apply to three issues made salient by the effort to provide equitable opportunities for the disabled in athletic competitions: (1) how to weigh any increased risk to other participants; (2) how to weigh any increased risk to an impaired athlete; and (3) how much the rules of competition should be modified to accommodate the disabled.

1. INCREASED RISK TO OTHER PARTICIPANTS

A disabled athlete may endanger other participants beyond the risks inherent in a given sport. For example, some athletes have expressed concern about perceived health risks from playing sports with an athlete diagnosed as HIV-positive, the virus that causes AIDS (acquired immunodeficiency syndrome). This became a major sports issue in 1991 when Earvin "Magic" Johnson announced that he was retiring from the L.A. Lakers because he had just been diagnosed as HIV-positive. Several months later, Johnson returned to the basketball court for the 1992 NBA All-Star game, and then to the "Dream Team" in the Summer Olympics in Barcelona. Johnson again dropped out of the game in the fall of 1993 when a number of other NBA players (most prominently the Utah Jazz's Karl Malone) raised concerns about the risks of playing against an HIV-infected opponent.

Such concerns arose again in 1995 when Greg Louganis, Olympic gold medalist in diving, announced that he had learned he was HIV-positive sometime before he competed in the 1988 Seoul Games. At the Seoul Olympics, Louganis hit his head on a diving board during a preliminary event, and he bled profusely into the pool, as well as on the hands of the team physician who was treating him. HIV anxiety surfaced again in the winter of 1996, when former WBC heavyweight champion Tommy Morrison was scheduled for a comeback fight in Las Vegas. However, the blood test required by Nevada's state boxing commission disclosed that Morrison was HIV-positive: Nevada revoked Morrison's license to fight in that state, a decision all other states honored. Commissioners in New Jersey, New York, and most other states quickly instituted the same mandatory testing and HIV-positive bans.

The following case considers the legality of excluding an athlete known to be HIV positive from participation in a contact sport.

MONTALVO V. RADCLIFFE
167 F.3d 873 (4th Cir. 1999)

NIEMEYER, CIRCUIT JUDGE.

Michael Montalvo, a 12-year old boy with AIDS, was denied admission to a traditional Japanese style martial arts school because of his HIV-positive status. In this action, brought under Title III of the Americans with Disabilities Act (prohibiting discrimination on the basis of disability by places of public accommodation), the district court denied Montalvo relief because his condition posed a significant risk to the health or safety of other students and no reasonable modification could sufficiently reduce this risk without fundamentally altering the nature of the program. We affirm.

I

Southside Virginia Police Karate Association, Inc. operates a karate school in Colonial Heights, Virginia, known as U.S.A. Bushidokan, which is owned by James P. Radcliffe, II. The school teaches exclusively traditional Japanese, combat-oriented martial arts rather than the more prevalent, family-oriented fitness programs offered by most martial arts schools. Within the first three weeks of lessons at U.S.A. Bushidokan, students learn techniques that involve substantial body contact, and within the first few months they apply these techniques to spar in actual combat situations. Radcliffe testified at trial that the sparring often results in injuries which, while minor, are bloody. . . .

He explained that to progress "through the belt," a level of achievement, a student must "engage in combat activity fighting. You have to do the self-defense. It involves contact, that's what we do." Radcliffe noted that inherent in this form of karate are "consistently scratched skin, scratches, gouges, bloody lips, bloody noses, things of that nature."

In May 1997, Luciano and Judith Montalvo applied to enter their 12-year old son, Michael, into group karate classes at U.S.A. Bushidokan because Michael wanted to learn karate with some friends who had already begun lessons there. Luciano Montalvo signed a "Membership Application and Agreement" form in which he warranted that Michael was "in good health and that [he] suffer[ed] from no illness or condition . . . which would possibly be infectious to others" and that the Montalvos understood that "no member [would] use the facilities with any open cuts, abrasions, open sores, infections, [or] maladies with the potential of harm to others." In fact, however, Michael had AIDS. The Montalvos did not disclose that fact to U.S.A. Bushidokan because they were afraid that U.S.A. Bushidokan would not enroll Michael if it knew of his HIV-positive status.

[The court explained that USA Bushidokan learned about Michael's HIV status from an "anonymous source." Radcliffe informed that

Montalvos that Michael would not be allowed to participate in group karate classes, but offered private lessons.]

* * *

II

Title III of the Americans with Disabilities Act ("ADA") was enacted to facilitate disabled individuals' access to places of public accommodation. Consistent with this goal, the Act states broadly:

> No individual shall be discriminated against on the basis of disability in the full and equal enjoyment of the goods, services, facilities, privileges, advantages, or accommodations of any place of public accommodation by any person who owns, leases (or leases to), or operates a place of public accommodation.

42 U.S.C. § 12182(a). The ADA defines "denial of participation" in a program offered by a place of public accommodation to be an act of discrimination. 42 U.S.C. § 12182(b)(1)(A)(i).

Recognizing that the need to protect public health may at times outweigh the rights of disabled individuals, Congress created a narrow exception to this broad prohibition against discrimination based on disability in places of public accommodation. Thus, a place of public accommodation is entitled to exclude a disabled individual from participating in its program "where such individual poses a direct threat to the health or safety of others." 42 U.S.C. § 12182(b)(3) (emphasis added). The Act defines "direct threat" as "a significant risk to the health or safety of others that cannot be eliminated by a modification of policies, practices, or procedures or by the provision of auxiliary aids or services." *Id.*

When determining whether an individual poses a "direct threat," a place of public accommodation must not base its calculus on stereotypes or generalizations about the effects of a disability but rather must make "an individualized assessment, based on reasonable judgment that relies on current medical knowledge or on the best available objective evidence." 28 C.F.R. § 36.208(c). The relevant factors which the place of public accommodation must weigh and balance are "the nature, duration, and severity of the risk [and] the probability that the potential injury will actually occur."

If the place of public accommodation determines that the individual would pose a significant risk to the health and safety of others, it must then ascertain "whether reasonable modifications of policies, practices, or procedures will mitigate the risk," 28 C.F.R. § 36.208(c), to the point of "eliminat[ing]" it as a "significant risk," 42 U.S.C.§ 12182(b)(3). Under the ADA, a failure to make a reasonable modification is itself an act of discrimination unless the place of public accommodation can demonstrate that implementing the modification would fundamentally alter the nature of the program. *See* 42 U.S.C. § 12182(b)(2)(A)(ii).

In this case, U.S.A. Bushidokan concedes that its karate school is a place of public accommodation subject to the requirements of Title III and that Michael Montalvo is disabled for purposes of the ADA by virtue of being HIV-positive or having AIDS. Bushidokan also concedes that it denied Michael participation in group karate classes on the basis of his HIV-positive status, the condition that concededly constitutes his disability. But U.S.A. Bushidokan contends that its exclusion of Michael was legally justified because Michael posed a "direct threat" to other members of the karate class. This contention presents two issues: (1) whether Michael's condition posed a significant risk to the health or safety of others and (2) whether reasonable modifications of policies, practices, or procedures were available to eliminate the risk as a significant one. *See* 42 U.S.C. § 12182(b)(3).

A

While the question of whether Michael's HIV-positive status posed a significant risk to the health or safety of others is a "fact intensive determination," *Rizzo v. Children's World Learning Centers, Inc.*, 84 F.3d 758, 764 (5th Cir. 1996), the evidence in the record before us is ample to support the district court's conclusion that Michael posed such a risk.

First, both the Montalvos' and U.S.A. Bushidokan's medical experts testified that blood-to-blood contact is a means of HIV transmission, and both experts agreed that AIDS is inevitably fatal. In addition, U.S.A. Bushidokan's expert testified without challenge that it was possible to become infected with the virus from blood splashing into the eyes or onto seemingly intact skin.

Second, the type of activity offered at U.S.A. Bushidokan emphasized sparring, attack drills, and continuous body interaction with the result that the participants frequently sustained bloody injuries, such as nose bleeds, cuts inside the mouth, and external abrasions. Radcliffe testified that blood from those injuries is "extremely likely" to come in contact with other students' skin. Even though U.S.A. Bushidokan had a policy of constantly monitoring for bloody injuries and removing for treatment participants with those injuries, the fast-paced, continuous combat exercises hampered U.S.A. Bushidokan's efforts to eliminate contact when such injury occurred. . . .

The nature, duration, and severity of the risk and probability of transmission—factors outlined by *Arline* and the ADA regulations—indicate that a significant risk to the health and safety of others would exist if Michael were allowed to participate in the group karate classes. The nature of the risk, which *Arline* defines as the mode of transmission of the disease, is blood-to-blood or blood-to-eye contact, according to the testimony of both sides' experts. The duration of the risk, which *Arline* defines as how long the carrier is infectious, *see id.*, is for the length of Michael's life. The severity of the risk is extreme because there is no known cure for AIDS, and, as the Montalvos concede, AIDS is inevitably fatal. And although the exact mathematical probability of transmission is unknown, the mode of transmission is one which is likely to occur in U.S.A. Bushidokan's combat-oriented group karate classes because of the frequency of bloody injuries and body contact. Thus, the nature of the risk, combined with its severity, creates a significant risk to the health and safety of hard-style karate class members.

When balancing the *Arline* factors to determine whether a risk is significant, one need not conclude that each factor is significant on its own. Rather, the gravity of one factor might well compensate for the relative slightness of another. Thus, when the disease at risk of transmission is, like AIDS, severe and inevitably fatal, even a low probability of transmission could still create a significant risk. In this case, therefore, we agree with the district court that Michael's condition posed a significant risk to the health and safety of others. . . .

* * *

The experts in this case agreed that HIV can be transmitted through blood-to-blood contact, and the evidence showed that this type of contact occurred frequently in the karate classes at U.S.A. Bushidokan. Thus, the district court's finding that Michael Montalvo posed a significant risk to the health or safety of others is amply supported by the evidence.

B

Even though Michael Montalvo's condition posed a significant risk to the health or safety of others, U.S.A. Bushidokan would still be required to admit him to group karate classes if a reasonable modification could have eliminated the risk as a significant one. The only modification which was both effective in reducing risk to an insignificant level and in maintaining the fundamental essence of U.S.A. Bushidokan's program was its offer of private karate classes to Michael.

In considering other modifications, U.S.A. Bushidokan was entitled to reject the modification that would soften the teaching style of its program. U.S.A. Bushidokan's unique niche in the martial arts market was its adherence to traditional, "hard-style" Japanese karate, and the contact between participants, which causes the bloody injuries and creates the risk of HIV transmission, was an integral aspect of such a program. To require U.S.A. Bushidokan to make its program a less combat-oriented, interactive, contact intensive version of karate would constitute a fundamental alteration of the nature of its program. The ADA does not require U.S.A. Bushidokan to abandon its essential mission and to offer a fundamentally different program of instruction. *See* 42 U.S.C. § 12182(b)(2)(A)(ii).

Similarly, U.S.A. Bushidokan was not required to implement further "universal precautions" such as using eye coverings and wearing gloves. The district court found as a fact that these modifications would not accomplish their goal of eliminating or reducing the otherwise significant risk Michael would pose to his classmates. As Radcliffe testified on behalf of U.S.A. Bushidokan, the suddenness of injuries, the tendency of some wounds to splatter blood, the continuing movement and contact, and the inability to detect injuries immediately all would undermine the effectiveness of these precautions, particularly for places not protected by eye coverings, gloves, or other similar coverings. . . .

U.S.A. Bushidokan did propose the effective modification of giving Michael private karate lessons, and the district court found this modification reasonable. But the Montalvos rejected this proposal. While an ADA plaintiff is under no obligation to accept a proffered, otherwise reasonable modification, *see* 28 C.F.R. § 36.203(c)(1) ("Nothing in this part shall be construed to require an individual with a disability to accept an accommodation . . . under this part that such individual chooses not to accept"), such rejection does not impose liability on U.S.A. Bushidokan for failure to modify its program.

Accordingly, we conclude that U.S.A. Bushidokan, in excluding Michael Montalvo from participating in its combat-oriented group karate classes, did not violate Title III of the ADA because Michael posed a significant risk to the health and safety of others that could not be eliminated by a reasonable modification.

The judgment of the district court is AFFIRMED.

NOTES AND QUESTIONS

1. *Medical Evidence of Risk.* A year before the *Montalvo* decision, the Court in *Bragdon v. Abbott*, 524 U.S. 624, 626–27 (1998), had held that the assessment of "risk to the health of others" under the ADA direct threat defense is to be "based on the medical or other objective, scientific evidence available . . . not simply on . . . good-faith belief that a significant risk existed." Was the approach of the *Montalvo* court consistent with this ruling? Was the medical evidence in *Montalvo* sufficient?

2. *What Level of Risk Is Significant?* The *Bragdon* decision does not state how much risk is "significant." The court, however, does cite a regulation that lists relevant factors to be balanced, including "the nature, duration, and severity of the risk [and] the probability that the potential injury will actually occur." Is this helpful? What probability of infection, for instance, should be deemed "significant" for a potentially fatal disease like HIV?

3. *HIV/AIDS and Major Sports Leagues.* Over time, increased consciousness of the scope and limits of the risk of transmission of HIV/AIDS, led various leagues to announce they would not mandate testing of players for HIV and, in any event, the condition would not bar their playing. There has never been a documented case of HIV transmission during a sporting event. What level of risk would require a sport governing body to ban the athlete or to alter the rules of the sport to avoid the risk? How feasible might it be for a sport to offer a "reasonable accommodation?"

2. INCREASED RISK TO THE IMPAIRED ATHLETE

Because college sports are sponsored by institutions that receive federal aid, they are governed by § 504 of the Rehabilitation Act, 29 U.S.C. § 794, which offered the legal basis for the next case.

KNAPP V. NORTHWESTERN UNIVERSITY
101 F.3d 473 (7th Cir. 1996)

EVANS, CIRCUIT JUDGE.

Nicholas Knapp wants to play NCAA basketball for Northwestern University—so badly that he is willing to face an increased risk of death to do so. Knapp is a competent, intelligent adult capable of assessing whether playing intercollegiate basketball is worth the risk to his heart and possible death, and to him the risk is acceptable. Usually, competent, intelligent adults are allowed to make such decisions. This is especially true when, as here, the individual's family approves of the decision and the individual and his parents are willing to sign liability waivers regarding the worst-case scenario should it occur.

Northwestern, however, refuses to allow Knapp to play on or even practice with its men's basketball team. Knapp, currently a sophomore at Northwestern, has the basketball skills to play at the intercollegiate level, but he has never taken the court for his team. Although Northwestern does not restrict him from playing pick-up basketball games, using recreational facilities on campus, or exerting himself physically on his own, the university disqualified Knapp from playing on its intercollegiate basketball team. The issue in this case boils down to whether the school—because of § 504 of the Rehabilitation Act of 1973, as amended, 29 U.S.C. § 794—will be forced to let Knapp don a purple uniform and take the floor as a member of Northwestern's basketball team.

Prior to his senior year of high school Knapp was rated among the best basketball players in Illinois. He was recruited by numerous universities, including Northwestern. At the end of Knapp's junior year at Peoria's Woodruff High School, Northwestern orally offered him an athletic scholarship to play basketball. Knapp orally accepted the offer.

A few weeks into his senior year, Knapp suffered sudden cardiac death—meaning his heart stopped—during a pick-up basketball game. Paramedics used cardiopulmonary resuscitation, defibrillation (*i.e.*, electric shocks), and injections of drugs to bring Knapp back to life. A few weeks later, doctors implanted an internal cardioverter-defibrillator in Knapp's abdomen. The device detects heart arrhythmia and delivers a shock to convert the abnormal heart rhythm back to normal. In other words, if Knapp's heart stops again the device is supposed to restart it.

On the day following his sudden cardiac death, Northwestern informed Knapp and his family that whatever the ultimate medical decision, Northwestern would honor its commitment for a scholarship. Seven weeks after his collapse Knapp signed a national letter of intent to attend Northwestern.

Knapp did not play basketball during his senior year in high school, but he was always a superb student, and in June 1995 he graduated as the valedictorian of his class. In September 1995 he enrolled as a Northwestern student.

On November 7, 1995, Dr. Howard Sweeney, Northwestern's head team physician, declared Knapp ineligible to participate on Northwestern's men's basketball team for the 1995–96 school year. Dr. Sweeney based his decision on Knapp's medical records in which several treating physicians recommended that Knapp not play competitive basketball, the report of team physician Dr. Mark Gardner following a physical examination of Knapp, published guidelines and recommendations following two national medical conferences known as the Bethesda Conferences regarding eligibility of athletes with cardiovascular abnormalities, and recommendations of physicians with whom Dr. Gardner and Dr. Sweeney consulted. After the basketball season ended, Northwestern and the Big Ten declared Knapp permanently medically ineligible to play basketball. Northwestern's athletic director, Rick Taylor, later confirmed that Northwestern will never voluntarily let Knapp play intercollegiate basketball as a Wildcat.

As a result, Knapp has never practiced with the Northwestern team nor played in a college game. His scholarship nevertheless continues and he attends practices (though he is not allowed to do anything but watch, apparently). He also receives other benefits afforded to athletes (such as tutoring, counseling, and training table), in addition to the full range of academic and nonacademic offerings the university provides to all students.

[On the day he was declared ineligible, Knapp filed a federal lawsuit and secured an injunction that barred Northwestern from excluding him from its basketball team for any reason related to his cardiac condition. Northwestern immediately appealed this order to the Seventh Circuit. The circuit court noted that the Rehabilitation Act was the sole basis for

Knapp's claim and required him to prove that he has a physical impairment which substantially limits one or more of his major life activities, is otherwise qualified to play basketball, and has been excluded from doing so solely because of his disability. The circuit court also noted that the Act defines "major life activities" to include basic functions "such as caring for one's self, performing manual tasks, walking, seeing, hearing, speaking, breathing, learning, and working," and that they are "those basic activities that the average person in the general population can perform with little or no difficulty."]

* * *

This case is difficult because it does not fit neatly under the Rehabilitation Act. The "disability" Knapp claims is the basis for discrimination against him is not a continuing one like blindness or deafness. At any given moment in time when Knapp's heart is functioning properly his disability does not affect him. He is truly disabled only when his heart stops, which may or may not happen to him again. The disability regarding which Northwestern allegedly discriminates, therefore, actually is the greater risk of harm for Knapp than the risk faced by other male college basketball players. In addition, other impairments usually do not have as severe a result as is possible in this case. A person who is deaf, for instance, will not suddenly die on the basketball court because of that disability. Here, Knapp's disability is all or nothing. Finally, because Knapp's disability affects one of the most central organs of the body, his disability to some extent affects all major life activities—if his heart stops, he will not breathe, see, speak, walk, learn, or work. Once again it is all or nothing—either his heart is functioning and no major life activities are limited at that moment, or it has stopped and the most major life activity of all—living—has been affected.

In any event, the parties here have framed their arguments as involving solely the major life activity of learning. Knapp contends that playing an intercollegiate sport is an integral part of his major life activity of learning and that his education will be substantially limited if he cannot play on the team. He states that he does not believe he can obtain confidence, dedication, leadership, perseverance, discipline, and teamwork in any better way. The district court agreed with him, determining that for Knapp, playing on the Northwestern basketball team was part of the major life activity of learning and that he was substantially limited from such learning by the university. . . .

We do not think that the definition of "major life activity" can be as particularized as Knapp wants it to be. Playing intercollegiate basketball obviously is not in and of itself a major life activity, as it is not a basic function of life on the same level as walking, breathing, and speaking. Not everyone gets to go to college, let alone play intercollegiate sports. We acknowledge that intercollegiate sports can be an important part of the college learning experience for both athletes and many cheering students—especially at a Big Ten school. Knapp has indicated that such is the case for him. But not every student thinks so. Numerous college students graduate each year having neither participated in nor attended an intercollegiate sporting event. Their sheepskins are no less valuable because of the lack of intercollegiate sports in their lives. Not playing intercollegiate sports does not mean they have not learned. Playing or enjoying intercollegiate sports therefore cannot be held out as a necessary part of learning for *all* students.

* * *

We decline to define the major life activity of learning in such a way that the Act applies whenever someone wants to play intercollegiate athletics. A "major life activity," as defined in the regulations, is a basic function of life "such as caring for one's self, performing manual tasks, walking, seeing, hearing, speaking, breathing, learning, and working." These are basic functions, not more specific ones such as being an astronaut, working as a firefighter, driving a race car, or learning by playing Big Ten basketball. . . .

[A]ny narrowing of what constitutes learning for a particular individual occurs within reasonable limits—coverage of the Rehabilitation Act is not open-ended or based on every dream or desire that a person may have. Not every impairment that affects an individual's major life activities is a substantially limiting impairment. The key obviously is the extent to which the impairment restricts the major life activity. . . . An impairment that interferes with an individual's ability to perform a particular function, but does not significantly decrease that individual's ability to obtain a satisfactory education otherwise, does not substantially limit the major life activity of learning.

Because learning through playing intercollegiate basketball is only one part of the education available to Knapp at Northwestern, even under a subjective standard, Knapp's ability to learn is not substantially limited. Knapp's scholarship continues, allowing him access to all academic and—except for intercollegiate basketball—all nonacademic services and activities available to other Northwestern students, in addition to all other services available to scholarship athletes. Although perhaps not as great a learning experience as actually playing, it is even possible that Knapp may "learn" through the basketball team in a role other than as a player. Knapp is an intelligent student and athlete, and the inability to play intercollegiate basketball at Northwestern forecloses only a small portion of his collegiate opportunities. . . . Knapp has not shown that his education and training limit him to do nothing but play basketball. The fact that Knapp's goal of playing intercollegiate basketball is frustrated does not substantially limit his education. The Rehabilitation Act does not guarantee an individual the exact educational experience that he may desire, just a fair one. Consequently, we hold that Knapp as a matter of law is not disabled within the meaning of the Rehabilitation Act.

Even if we were inclined to find Knapp disabled under the Rehabilitation Act, he would still come up short because we also hold as a matter of law that he is not, under the statute, "otherwise qualified" to play intercollegiate basketball at Northwestern. . . .

Section 794 does not compel educational institutions to disregard the disabilities of disabled persons. It requires only that an "otherwise qualified" disabled person not be excluded from participation in a federally funded program solely because of the disability. In other words, although a disability is not a permissible ground for assuming an inability to function in a particular context, the disability is not thrown out when considering if the person is qualified for the position sought. "An otherwise qualified person is one who is able to meet all of a program's requirements in spite of his handicap" with reasonable accommodation.

Legitimate physical qualifications may in fact be essential to participation in particular programs. . . .

A significant risk of personal physical injury can disqualify a person from a position if the risk cannot be eliminated. But more than merely an elevated risk of injury is required before disqualification is appropriate. Any physical qualification based on risk of future injury must be examined with special care if the Rehabilitation Act is not to be circumvented, since almost all disabled individuals are at a greater risk of injury. . . .

In this case, the severity of the potential injury is as high as it could be—death. [The court summarized the expert testimony that playing intercollegiate basketball would expose Knapp to a risk of death between one in 34 and one in 100.] These estimates took into account Knapp's internal defibrillator, apparently the only "accommodation" possible for Knapp's condition. Although the doctors indicated that these numbers were merely estimates, all agreed that the risk to Knapp is higher than to the average male collegiate basketball player. Knapp's experts believed it was an acceptable level of risk. Northwestern's experts agreed with the school's team doctors that Knapp's participation in competitive Big Ten basketball presented an unacceptable level of risk. . . .

The district court judge in this case believed that in the face of conflicting opinion evidence regarding risk, and the fact that no scientific data existed to quantify that risk, the decision on whether Knapp should play falls in the lap of the court. . . .

We disagree with the district court's legal determination that such decisions are to be made by the courts and believe instead that medical determinations of this sort are best left to team doctors and universities as long as they are made with reason and rationality and with full regard to possible and reasonable accommodations. In cases such as ours, where

Northwestern has examined both Knapp and his medical records, has considered his medical history and the relation between his prior sudden cardiac death and the possibility of future occurrences, has considered the severity of the potential injury, and has rationally and reasonably reviewed consensus medical opinions or recommendations in the pertinent field—regardless whether conflicting medical opinions exist—the university has the right to determine that an individual is not otherwise medically qualified to play without violating the Rehabilitation Act. The place of the court in such cases is to make sure that the decision-maker has reasonably considered and relied upon sufficient evidence specific to the individual and the potential injury, not to determine on its own which evidence it believes is more persuasive.

* * *

We do not believe that, in cases where medical experts disagree in their assessment of the extent of a real risk of serious harm or death, Congress intended that the courts—neutral arbiters but generally less skilled in medicine than the experts involved—should make the final medical decision. Instead, in the midst of conflicting expert testimony regarding the degree of serious risk of harm or death, the court's place is to ensure that the exclusion or disqualification of an individual was individualized, reasonably made, and based upon competent medical evidence. So long as these factors exist, it will be the rare case regarding participation in athletics where a court may substitute its judgment for that of the school's team physicians.

* * *

In closing, we wish to make clear that we are not saying Northwestern's decision necessarily is the right decision. We say only that it is not an illegal one under the Rehabilitation Act. On the same facts, another team physician at another university, reviewing the same medical history, physical evaluation, and medical recommendations, might reasonably decide that Knapp met the physical qualifications for playing on an intercollegiate basketball team. Simply put, all universities need not evaluate risk the same way. What we say in this case is that if substantial evidence supports the decision-maker—here Northwestern—that decision must be respected.

Section 794 prohibits authorities from deciding without significant medical support that certain activities are too risky for a disabled person. Decisions of this sort cannot rest on paternalistic concerns. Knapp, who is an adult, is not in need of paternalistic decisions regarding his health, and his parents—more entitled to be paternalistic toward him than Northwestern—approve of his decision. In regard to cases involving risk of future injury, a school's perception of the threat of such injury cannot be based on unfounded fears or stereotypes; it must be based on objective evidence. But here, where Northwestern acted rationally and reasonably rather than paternalistically, no Rehabilitation Act violation has occurred. The Rehabilitation Act "is carefully structured to replace . . . reflexive actions to actual or perceived handicaps with actions based on reasoned and medically sound judgments. . . ." *Arline*, 480 U.S. at 284–85.

Reversed.

————

NOTES AND QUESTIONS

1. *Decision Under Current Law?* The *Knapp* decision preceded the 2008 amendments to the ADA, which also apply to the Rehabilitation Act. How would the case be analyzed under these amendments as explained earlier in the chapter? Did Knapp seek an accommodation, such as special practice aids or court-side medical attention, or did he only ask to be treated without regard to his heart condition—clearly an impairment under the regulatory definition? If he sought to be treated without regard to this impairment, he sought only to be protected from discrimination and thus would not have had to demonstrate substantial limitation of a major life activity under the third prong of the definition of disability. Even if he had sought some type of special accommodation to protect him from the risk of heart failure, would the 2008 amendments, including the listing of bodily functions as major life activities, have provided him with a strong case for that accommodation?

2. *Relevance of Risk to* Knapp. Does the protection of Knapp as disabled under the 2008 amendments necessarily mean that the Rehabilitation Act would prevent Northwestern from keeping him from playing basketball because of the risk to him? Acceptance of the *Knapp* court's assertion that the risks posed by Knapp's heart condition kept him from being "otherwise qualified" would seem to allow a school or employer to discriminate by defining a qualification based on the absence of some disabilities. Would it have been better to analyze the case under the "direct threat" defense considered in the *Montalvo* case? The defense provides that a qualification standard "may include a requirement that an individual . . . not pose a direct threat to the health or safety of *other individuals*" (emphasis added). In *Chevron U.S.A. Inc. v. Echazabal*, 536 U.S. 73 (2002), however, a unanimous Court sustained an EEOC regulation stating that an employer can guard against a "direct threat" to the health or safety of the impaired individual as well as to others. 29 C.F.R. § 1630.2(r).

Application of the "direct threat" defense now would be controlled by the Court's interpretation of that defense in *Bragdon v. Abbott, supra*. That decision required courts to determine, without any deference, whether the defendant's challenged decision was reasonable based on then available objective medical or other evidence. Does this mean that Northwestern's admittedly reasonable assessment of the risk was sufficient regardless of the court's appraisal of whether it was more reasonable than that of Knapp's medical experts? If so, is this compatible with the legislative policy of providing opportunity to the disabled? Or should a disabled athlete be able to compete if a judge determines that the athlete's assessment of medical risk is reasonable?

3. *Liability Waivers.* Schools might enlarge opportunities for the disabled by requiring some more marginally impaired students to sign liability waivers. Why are schools reluctant to take that route? Are they concerned that such waivers may be deemed unenforceable in the event of a tort suit? Or are schools concerned that by agreeing to liability waivers for some athletes, they open the door for other athletes with more serious medical conditions to sign similar waivers and compete against the advice of their doctors?

4. *Reasonable Accommodation Requirement for Those with Substantially Limited Life Activities.* Both the ADA and the Rehabilitation Act require covered entities to make reasonable accommodations or modifications to participation requirements to enable disabled athletes to play sports. *Alexander v. Choate*, 469 U.S. 287, 300 (1985) ("while a [school] need not be required to make 'fundamental' or 'substantial' modifications to accommodate the handicapped, it may be required to make 'reasonable' ones"); *Grube v. Bethlehem Area Sch. Dist.*, 550 F. Supp. 418, 424 (E.D. Pa. 1982) (requiring high school to reasonably accommodate student with one kidney to play football if he wore a protective flak jacket).

3. ACCOMMODATION THROUGH RULE MODIFICATION

Sports competitions require all participants to play by the same rules and be subject to the same eligibility requirements. This can create tension with federal disability discrimination laws that mandate reasonable accommodation to enable an impaired athlete to play. The next case focuses on the extent to which a sport must adjust its playing rules to accommodate a disabled athlete.

Professional golfer Casey Martin suffers from the Klippel-Trenaunay-Weber syndrome, a congenital malformation of his veins that curtails blood circulation and that gradually atrophied the calf muscles and tibia bones in his right leg. Notwithstanding this condition and the resulting pain, Martin excelled at playing golf, a sport that typically permits the amateur golfer to ride a cart rather than require walking from shot to shot. During his college career, Martin was permitted to use a cart when he was experiencing severe pain. When he turned pro after college, he had to comply with PGA Tour rules for elite golfers that prohibited riding in carts.

Martin sought to qualify for the PGA Tour in 1997, attending "Q School" where early rounds of play permitted, and sometimes required, riding in a cart. In the final rounds of play, Tour rules required walking and barred Martin from using a cart. However, Martin's lawyer secured a preliminary injunction against enforcement of this rule. *Martin v. PGA Tour, Inc.*, 984 F. Supp. 1320 (D. Ore. 1998). Using a cart, Martin nonetheless narrowly missed making the regular Tour, but he did qualify for a lower-tier tour that allowed carts and where he had some success in 1998. Then Martin and his lawyers went back to court to try to obtain a permanent ruling on whether the ADA mandated a rules change to permit Martin to use a cart.

As explained above, Title I of the ADA requires employers to reasonably accommodate employees with disabilities. However, in professional golf, players are not employees of the PGA Tour, but rather independent contractors. Thus, Martin sued under Title III, which prohibits disability discrimination in places of "public accommodation." The PGA Tour argued that tournament golf courses are public accommodations only with respect to the space made available to spectators behind the ropes, and not to eligible players out on the course. Martin argued that he was also a "customer" of the PGA, because he paid $3,000 to compete in Q School. The district court agreed with Martin.

As Martin undeniably suffered from a severe physical disability, the next legal question was whether the ADA required the PGA Tour to allow Martin to use a cart as a "reasonable accommodation," or whether cart use would fundamentally alter the game by giving Martin an unfair competitive advantage over his fellow Tour members who had to walk rather than ride from shot to shot. A number of major golfing figures, led by Arnold Palmer, Jack Nicklaus, and Ken Venturi, testified in favor of the PGA rule as one designed to preserve golf as "a game of stamina." The district court disagreed, rejecting the PGA's argument that full adherence by everyone to its "walking rule" was necessary to fairly "inject the element of fatigue into the skill of shotmaking." Martin won a permanent order allowing him the cart accommodation on the Tour. *Martin v. PGA Tour, Inc.*, 994 F. Supp. 1242 (D. Ore. 1998).

When the Ninth Circuit affirmed the judgment, *Martin v. PGA Tour, Inc.*, 204 F.3d 994 (9th Cir. 2000), and the Seventh Circuit reached the exact opposite conclusion in a similar case, *Olinger v. United States Golf Association*, 205 F.3d 1001 (7th Cir. 2000), the Supreme Court granted certiorari.

PGA TOUR, INC. V. MARTIN

532 U.S. 661 (2001)

MR. JUSTICE STEVENS, delivered the opinion of the Court.

[After describing the Americans With Disabilities Act, the professional golf tours, and the treatment of the *Olinger* and the *Martin* cases by the lower courts, the majority opinion continued.]

* * *

It seems apparent, from both the general rule and the comprehensive definition of "public accommodation," that petitioner's golf tours and their qualifying rounds fit comfortably within the coverage of Title III, and Martin within its protection. The events occur on "golf course[s]," a type of place specifically identified by the Act as a public accommodation. § 12181(7)(L). In addition, at all relevant times, petitioner "leases" and "operates" golf courses to conduct its Q-School and tours. § 12182(a). As a lessor and operator of golf courses, then, petitioner must not discriminate against any "individual" in the "full and equal enjoyment of the goods, services, facilities, privileges, advantages, or accommodations" of those courses. Certainly, among the "privileges" offered by petitioner on the courses are those of competing in the Q-School and playing in the tours; indeed, the former is a privilege for which thousands of individuals from the general public pay, and the latter is one for which they vie. Martin, of course, is one of those individuals. It would therefore appear that Title III of the ADA, by its plain terms, prohibits petitioner from denying Martin equal access to its tours on the basis of his disability. . . .

According to petitioner, Title III is concerned with discrimination [only] against "clients and customers" seeking to obtain "goods and services" at places of public accommodation, whereas it is Title I that protects persons who work at such places. . . . Martin therefore cannot bring a claim under Title III because he is not one of the " 'clients or customers of the covered public accommodation.' " Rather, Martin's claim of discrimination is "job-related" and could only be brought under Title I— but that Title does not apply because he is an independent contractor (as the District Court found) rather than an employee.

* * *

We need not decide whether petitioner's construction of the statute is correct, because petitioner's argument falters even on its own terms. If Title III's protected class were limited to "clients or customers," it would be entirely appropriate to classify the golfers who pay petitioner $3,000 for the chance to compete in the Q-School and, if successful, in the subsequent tour events, as petitioner's clients or customers. In our view, petitioner's tournaments (whether situated at a "golf course" or at a "place of exhibition or entertainment") simultaneously offer at least two "privileges" to the public—that of watching the golf competition and that of competing in it. . . . That petitioner identifies one set of clients or customers that it serves (spectators at tournaments) does not preclude it from having another set (players in tournaments) against whom it may not discriminate.

* * *

As we have noted, 42 U.S.C. § 12182(a) sets forth Title III's general rule prohibiting public accommodations from discriminating against individuals because of their disabilities. The question whether petitioner has violated that rule depends on a proper construction of the term "discrimination," which is defined by Title III to include "a failure to make reasonable modifications in policies, practices, or procedures, when such modifications are necessary to afford such goods, services, facilities, privileges, advantages, or accommodations to individuals with disabilities, *unless the entity can demonstrate that making such modifications would fundamentally alter the nature* of such goods, services, facilities, privileges, advantages, or accommodations." § 12182(b)(2)(A)(ii) (emphasis added).

... Petitioner does not contest that a golf cart is a reasonable modification that is necessary if Martin is to play in its tournaments. ... In this case [ ] the narrow dispute is whether allowing Martin to use a golf cart, despite the walking requirement ... is a modification that would "fundamentally alter the nature" of those events.

In theory, a modification of petitioner's golf tournaments might constitute a fundamental alteration in two different ways. It might alter such an essential aspect of the game of golf that it would be unacceptable even if it affected all competitors equally; changing the diameter of the hole from three to six inches might be such a modification. Alternatively, a less significant change that has only a peripheral impact on the game itself might nevertheless give a disabled player, in addition to access to the competition as required by Title III, an advantage over others and, for that reason, fundamentally alter the character of the competition. We are not persuaded that a waiver of the walking rule for Martin would work a fundamental alteration in either sense.

As an initial matter, we observe that the use of carts is not itself inconsistent with the fundamental character of the game of golf. From early on, the essence of the game has been shot-making—using clubs to cause a ball to progress from the teeing ground to a hole some distance away with as few strokes as possible. ... Over the years, there have been many changes in the players' equipment, in golf course design, in the Rules of Golf, and in the method of transporting clubs from hole to hole. ... Golf carts started appearing with increasing regularity on American golf courses in the 1950's. Today they are everywhere. And they are encouraged. For one thing, they often speed up play, and for another, they are great revenue producers. There is nothing in the Rules of Golf that either forbids the use of carts, or penalizes a player for using a cart. That set of rules, as we have observed, is widely accepted in both the amateur and professional golf world as the rules of the game. The walking rule that is contained in petitioner's hard cards, based on an optional condition buried in an appendix to the Rules of Golf, is not an essential attribute of the game itself.

Indeed, the walking rule is not an indispensable feature of tournament golf either. As already mentioned, petitioner permits golf carts to be used in the SENIOR PGA TOUR, the open qualifying events for petitioner's tournaments, the first two stages of the Q-School, and, until 1997, the third stage of the Q-School as well. Moreover, petitioner allows the use of carts during certain tournament rounds in both the PGA TOUR and the NIKE TOUR. In addition, although the USGA enforces a walking rule in most of the tournaments that it sponsors, it permits carts in the Senior Amateur and the Senior Women's Amateur championships.

Petitioner, however, distinguishes the game of golf as it is generally played from the game that it sponsors call golf at the "highest level." According to petitioner, "[t]he goal of the highest-level competitive athletics is to assess and compare the performance of different competitors, a task that is meaningful only if the competitors are subject to identical substantive rules." The waiver of any possibly "outcome-affecting" rule for a contestant would violate this principle and therefore, in petitioner's view, fundamentally alter the nature of the highest level athletic event. The walking rule is one such rule, petitioner submits, because its purpose is "to inject the element of fatigue into the skill of shot-making," and thus its effect may be the critical loss of a stroke. As a consequence, the reasonable modification Martin seeks would fundamentally alter the nature of petitioner's highest level tournaments even if he were the only person in the world who has both the talent to compete in those elite events and a disability sufficiently serious that he cannot do so without using a cart.

The force of petitioner's argument is, first of all, mitigated by the fact that golf is a game in which it is impossible to guarantee that all competitors will play under exactly the same conditions or that an individual's ability will be the sole determinant of the outcome. For example, changes in the weather may produce harder greens and more head winds for the tournament leader than for his closest pursuers. A lucky bounce may save a shot or two. Whether such happenstance events are more or less probable than the likelihood that a golfer afflicted with Klippel-Trenaunay-Weber Syndrome would one day qualify for the NIKE TOUR and PGA TOUR, they at least demonstrate that pure chance may have a greater impact on the outcome of elite golf tournaments than the fatigue resulting from the enforcement of the walking rule.

Further, the factual basis of petitioner's argument is undermined by the District Court's finding that the fatigue from walking during one of petitioner's 4-day tournaments cannot be deemed significant. . . .

Even if we accept the factual predicate for petitioner's argument—that the walking rule is "outcome affecting" because fatigue may adversely affect performance—its legal position is fatally flawed. Petitioner's refusal to consider Martin's personal circumstances in deciding whether to accommodate his disability runs counter to the clear language and purpose of the ADA. As previously stated, the ADA was enacted to eliminate discrimination against "individuals" with disabilities, and to that end Title III of the Act requires without exception that any "policies, practices, or procedures" of a public accommodation be reasonably modified for disabled "individuals" as necessary to afford access unless doing so would fundamentally alter what is offered. To comply with this command, an individualized inquiry must be made to determine whether a specific modification for a particular person's disability would be reasonable under the circumstances as well as necessary for that person, and yet at the same time not work a fundamental alteration.

To be sure, the waiver of an essential rule of competition for anyone would fundamentally alter the nature of petitioner's tournaments. As we have demonstrated, however, the walking rule is at best peripheral to the nature of petitioner's athletic events, and thus it might be waived in individual cases without working a fundamental alteration. Therefore, petitioner's claim that all the substantive rules for its "highest-level" competitions are sacrosanct and cannot be modified under any circumstances is effectively a contention that it is exempt from Title III's reasonable modification requirement. But that provision carves out no exemption for elite athletes. . . .

Under the ADA's basic requirement that the need of a disabled person be evaluated on an individual basis, we have no doubt that allowing Martin to use a golf cart would not fundamentally alter the nature of petitioner's tournaments. As we have discussed, the purpose of the walking rule is to subject players to fatigue, which in turn may influence the outcome of tournaments. Even if the rule does serve that purpose, it is an uncontested finding of the District Court that Martin "easily endures greater fatigue even with a cart than his able-bodied competitors do by walking." The purpose of the walking rule is therefore not compromised in the slightest by allowing Martin to use a cart. A modification that provides an exception to a peripheral tournament rule without impairing its purpose cannot be said to "fundamentally alter" the tournament. What it can be said to do, on the other hand, is to allow Martin the chance to qualify for and compete in the athletic events petitioner offers to those members of the public who have the skill and desire to enter. That is exactly what the ADA requires. As a result, Martin's request for a waiver of the walking rule should have been granted.

* * *

The judgment of the Court of Appeals is affirmed.

JUSTICE SCALIA, with whom JUSTICE THOMAS joins, dissenting.

In my view today's opinion exercises a benevolent compassion that the law does not place it within our power to impose. The judgment distorts the text of Title III, the structure of the ADA, and common sense. I respectfully dissent.

I

* * *

For many reasons, Title III will not bear such an interpretation. The provision of Title III at issue here (§ 12182, its principal provision) is a public-accommodation law, and it is the traditional understanding of public-accommodation laws that they provide rights for customers. . . . Surely this has nothing to do with employees and independent contractors.

If there were any doubt left that § 12182 covers only clients and customers of places of public accommodation, it is eliminated by the fact that a contrary interpretation would make a muddle of the ADA as a whole. . . . Congress expressly excluded employers of fewer than 15 employees from Title I. The mom-and-pop grocery store or laundromat need not worry about altering the nonpublic areas of its place of business to accommodate handicapped employees—or about the litigation that failure to do so will invite. Similarly, since independent contractors are not covered by Title I, the small business (or the large one, for that matter) need not worry about making special accommodations for the painters, electricians, and other independent workers whose services are contracted for from time to time. It is an entirely unreasonable interpretation of the statute to say that these exemptions so carefully crafted in Title I are entirely eliminated by Title III (for the many businesses that are places of public accommodation) because employees and independent contractors "enjoy" the employment and contracting that such places provide. The only distinctive feature of places of public accommodation is that they accommodate the public, and Congress could have no conceivable reason for according the employees and independent contractors of such businesses protections that employees and independent contractors of other businesses do not enjoy.

* * *

[The dissent then addressed the majority's point that Martin was. . .] a "customer" of the PGA TOUR or of the golf courses on which it is played. That seems to me quite incredible. The PGA TOUR is a professional sporting event, staged for the entertainment of a live and TV audience, the receipts from whom (the TV audience's admission price is paid by advertisers) pay the expenses of the tour, including the cash prizes for the winning golfers. The professional golfers on the tour are no more "enjoying" (the statutory term) the entertainment that the tour provides, or the facilities of the golf courses on which it is held, than professional baseball players "enjoy" the baseball games in which they play or the facilities of Yankee Stadium. To be sure, professional ballplayers participate in the games, and use the ballfields, but no one in his right mind would think that they are customers of the American League or of Yankee Stadium. They are themselves the entertainment that the customers pay to watch. And professional golfers are no different. . . . Respondent did not seek to "exercise" or "recreate" at the PGA TOUR events; he sought to make money (which is why he is called a professional golfer). He was not a customer buying recreation or entertainment; he was a professional athlete selling it. . . .

II

* * *

[E]ven if respondent here is a consumer of the "privilege" of the PGA TOUR competition, I see no basis for considering whether the rules of that competition must be altered. It is as irrelevant to the PGA TOUR's compliance with the statute whether walking is essential to the game of golf as it is to the shoe store's compliance whether "pairness" is essential to the nature of shoes. If a shoe store wishes to sell shoes only in pairs it may; and if a golf tour (or a golf course) wishes to provide only walk-around golf, it may. The PGA TOUR cannot deny respondent access to that game because of his disability, but it need not provide him a game different (whether in its essentials or in its details) from that offered to everyone else. . . .

[As for the Court's conclusion that allowing Martin to use a cart would not "fundamentally alter the nature" of the PGA Tour game], it is worth pointing out that the assumption which underlies that question is false. Nowhere is it writ that PGA TOUR golf must be classic "essential" golf. Why cannot the PGA TOUR, if it wishes, promote a new game, with distinctive rules (much as the American League promotes a game of baseball in which the pitcher's turn at the plate can be taken by a "designated hitter")? If members of the public do not like the new rules—if they feel that these rules do not truly test the individual's skill at "real golf" (or the team's skill at "real baseball") they can withdraw their patronage. But the rules are the rules. They are (as in all games) entirely arbitrary, and there is no basis on which anyone—not even the Supreme Court of the United States—can pronounce one or another of them to be "nonessential" if the rulemaker (here the PGA TOUR) deems it to be essential.

If one assumes, however, that the PGA TOUR has some legal obligation to play classic, Platonic golf—and if one assumes the correctness of all the other wrong turns the Court has made to get to this point—then we Justices must confront what is indeed an awesome responsibility. It has been rendered the solemn duty of the Supreme Court of the United States . . . to decide What Is Golf. I am sure that the Framers of the Constitution, aware of the 1457 edict of King James II of Scotland prohibiting golf because it interfered with the practice of archery, fully expected that sooner or later the paths of golf and government, the law and the links, would once again cross, and that the judges of this august Court would some day have to wrestle with that age-old jurisprudential question, for which their years of study in the law have so well prepared them: Is someone riding around a golf course from shot to shot really a golfer? The answer, we learn, is yes.

The Court ultimately concludes, and it will henceforth be the Law of the Land, that walking is not a "fundamental" aspect of golf.

Either out of humility or out of self-respect (one or the other) the Court should decline to answer this incredibly difficult and incredibly silly question. To say that something is "essential" is ordinarily to say that it is necessary to the achievement of a certain object. But since it is the very nature of a game to have no object except amusement (that is what distinguishes games from productive activity), it is quite impossible to say that any of a game's arbitrary rules is "essential." Eighteen-hole golf courses, 10-foot-high basketball hoops, 90-foot baselines, 100-yard football fields—all are arbitrary and none is essential. The only support for any of them is tradition and (in more modern times) insistence by what has come to be regarded as the ruling body of the sport—both of which factors support the PGA TOUR's position in the present case. . . .

In an apparent effort to make its opinion as narrow as possible, the Court relies upon the District Court's finding that even with a cart, respondent will be at least as fatigued as everyone else. This, the Court says, *proves* that competition will not be affected. . . . In . . . determining whether waiver of the "nonessential" rule will have an impermissible "competitive effect" by measuring the athletic capacity of the requesting individual, and asking whether the special dispensation would do no more than place him on a par (so to speak) with other competitors, the Court guarantees that future cases of this sort will have to be decided on the basis of individualized factual findings. Which means that future cases of this sort will be numerous, and a rich source of lucrative litigation. One can envision the parents of a Little League player with attention deficit disorder trying to convince a judge that their son's disability makes it at least 25% more difficult to hit a pitched ball. (If they are successful, the only thing that could prevent a court order giving the kid four strikes would be a judicial determination that, in baseball, three strikes are metaphysically necessary, which is quite absurd.)

The statute, of course, provides no basis for this individualized analysis that is the Court's last step on a long and misguided journey. The statute seeks to assure that a disabled person's disability will not deny him equal access to (among other things) competitive sporting events—not that his disability will not deny him an equal chance to win competitive sporting events. The latter is quite impossible, since the very nature of competitive sport is the measurement, by uniform rules, of unevenly distributed excellence. This unequal distribution is precisely what determines the winners and losers—and artificially to "even out" that distribution, by giving one or another player exemption from a rule that emphasizes his particular weakness, is to destroy the game. . . . In the Court's world, there is one set of rules that is "fair with respect to the able-bodied" but "individualized" rules, mandated by the ADA, for "talented but disabled athletes." The ADA mandates no such ridiculous thing. Agility, strength, speed, balance, quickness of mind, steadiness of nerves, intensity of concentration—these talents are not evenly distributed. No wild-eyed dreamer has ever suggested that the managing bodies of the competitive sports that test precisely these qualities should try to take account of the uneven distribution of God-given gifts when writing and enforcing the rules of competition. And I have no doubt Congress did not authorize misty-eyed judicial supervision of such a revolution.

* * *

And it should not be assumed that today's decent, tolerant, and progressive judgment will, in the long run, accrue to the benefit of sports competitors with disabilities. Now that it is clear courts will review the rules of sports for "fundamentalness," organizations that value their autonomy have every incentive to defend vigorously the necessity of every regulation. They may still be second-guessed in the end as to the Platonic requirements of the sport, but they will assuredly lose if they have at all wavered in their enforcement. The lesson the PGA TOUR and other sports organizations should take from this case is to make sure that the same written rules are set forth for all levels of play, and never voluntarily to grant any modifications. The second lesson is to end open tryouts. I doubt that, in the long run, even disabled athletes will be well served by these incentives that the Court has created.

* * *

NOTES AND QUESTIONS

1. *Aftermath.* After his victory in the Supreme Court, Martin played in only a few tournaments on the PGA Tour, never finishing higher than 65th. He qualified for the U.S. Open in 2012 by winning a sectional tournament, but did not make the cut. In 2006 he became the head golf coach at the University of Oregon and led the team to a national championship in 2016. After breaking his impaired leg in a fall in 2019, he had the leg amputated and successfully replaced by a prosthetic in 2021.

2. *Authority Under ADA to Assess Reasonable Modifications and Fundamental Alteration.* Justice Scalia in dissent asserts that the courts do not have authority to require ADA defendants offering opportunities in competitive sports to modify the rules that define those sports in order to provide opportunities to the disabled. Is Justice Scalia correct? The statutory provision in Title III quoted in the majority opinion requires "reasonable modifications" that do not "fundamentally alter" the nature of the sport. Does not this require courts to assess what would fundamentally alter a sport? Even if the inquiry is made under Title I, which does not use the "fundamentally alter" phrase as a qualification for reasonable accommodation of the disabled

in employment, would it not be necessary for a court to assess the fundamental nature of a sport to determine what is reasonable? Justice Scalia asserts that the statute does not even require offering the disabled modification in a sport's "details." If so, what meaning is left for the "reasonable accommodation" and "fundamentally alter" language?

3.   *Defining "Fundamentally Alter."* How does the majority approach determining what would fundamentally alter the nature of the sport of golf offered for competition? Does it imagine a preexisting "Platonic" essence of the game, as Justice Scalia charges, or does it analyze what is important to competition in the game as played? Did its analysis provide adequate guidance to future courts?

4.   *Not Providing an Unfair Advantage.* Note how Justice Stevens in the majority opinion responds to the PGA Tour's argument that the fatigue from walking may be part of the challenge in competitive golf. Justice Stevens stresses that Martin gains no competitive advantage from riding because his condition creates more fatigue. Does this mean that another golfer with a different disability would not be able to ride in a cart if doing so would protect him from the threat of fatigue confronted by those who walked? Is there any reason why such an individualized inquiry is not consistent with the statute?

Must the unfair advantage standard in any case be limited? Could a golfer with a muscular impairment that weakens his strength use such a standard to justify teeing off closer to the hole? Or is the weakened golfer's case different because the accommodation, rather than making him stronger, would change what the game assesses? How would the following other hypotheticals be treated under the *Martin* decision?

a.   A professional baseball player is weakened by a disease causing muscular degeneration in his arms that has sapped him of 25% of his strength. He asks that he be allowed to use an aluminum or corked bat that generates 25% greater average exit velocity than that from the required wood bats.

b.   A professional tennis player suffers from a moderately crippling disease that limits his ability to move about on his feet quickly. He argues that he can hit the ball as effectively as anyone but has 25% less mobility than his average non-disabled competitors. He asks that the sidelines on his side of the court be moved in 25% during his matches.

c.   A professional golfer has permanent shoulder problems preventing him from swinging his arms with a full rotation. He is able to putt and chip and take half swings as well as anyone, but he cannot drive or take a full swing. He asks that for distances of over 75 yards he be allowed to use a large slingshot that he has devised that would enable him to propel the ball up to a maximum of 300 yards.

d.   A basketball player with a severe and sensitive skin condition on his arms and legs asks that he able to play with his limbs completely covered with a nonabrasive fabric, contrary to league game dress rules.

5. *Place of Public Accommodation.* The dissent also contends that the ADA's "place of public accommodation" requirement in Title III covers only businesses that offer to sell or lease goods or services to the public—*i.e.,* the obligation not to discriminate on the basis of disability extends only to a business's "clients or customers." The majority does not disagree with this, but rather argues that Casey Martin is a "client or customer" of the PGA Tour because he had to pay $3,000 in order to sign up for Qualifying School. Is this persuasive? Would the outcome then be different for a sporting tour or governing body that did not require a fee of any kind from those seeking to qualify for a spot on the tour? If the PGA Tour dropped the $3,000 Q-School registration fee, could it again apply its "no cart" policy against Casey Martin?

6. *Floodgates Argument.* Justice Scalia also expressed concern that the *Martin* ruling would lead to a flood of claims by disabled athletes asking for all sorts of modifications to rules. It has not done so. Only a handful of such claims have been litigated to a published decision. In *Kuketz v. Petronelli*, 443 Mass. 355, 821 N.E.2d 473 (2005), the court dismissed a wheelchair user's ADA claim against a private racquetball league that refused to allow him two bounces of the ball while his able-bodied opponents received one bounce, because that accommodation would fundamentally alter the nature of the game.

7. *Prosthetics as Reasonable Accommodations?* Oscar Pistorius was born with congenital absence of the fibula bone in both legs and had them both amputated before he was a year old. Using prosthetic legs, he became an elite runner, taking the gold in Paralympic competitions. He sought to compete against able-bodied athletes; and in 2008, the Court of Arbitration for Sport (CAS) ruled that he could do so, over the objections of the International Association of Athletics Federation, which considered the prosthetics to offer a competitive advantage. Pistorius qualified for the 2012 London Olympics and represented South Africa in both individual and relay races. In another case in 2021, however, CAS upheld a decision of World Athletics not to allow Blake Leeper, an American born without either leg below the knee, from competing with the aid of prosthetics as a sprinter in the 2021 Tokyo Olympics or other sanctioned international competitions. The decision was based on a determination that the length of Leeper's prosthetics gave him a competitive advantage by enabling him to run "unnaturally tall" relative to the rest of his anatomy.

How should the CAS judge whether prosthetic legs provide athletes like Pistorius and Leeper an unfair competitive advantage? Should judgments turn on whether the prosthetics provide assistance beyond that provided by average legs or by the legs of average elite athletes? Do we want success in athletic competitions to depend on the special nature or quality of external enhancements rather than on any superior ability and conditioning of the athletes?

Consider also the relevance of the *Martin* decision to the use of prosthetics. Presumably a golf event covered as a public accommodation by the ADA would be required now to allow Casey Martin to compete walking on his new prosthetic leg. Would the *Martin* decision's interpretation of the ADA also require a track event to allow at least some prosthetic legs in a track event, or might this require an alteration of the fundamental nature of the competition? How would the Court's interpretation apply to the use of prosthetics in a football or basketball game?

For cases involving wheelchair competitors, *see McFadden v. Grasmick*, 485 F. Supp. 2d 642 (D. Md. 2007) (granting elite wheelchair racer right to compete alongside footed athletes in high school track meets, but denying preliminary injunction to require state athletic association to count her points in separate wheelchair racing events in determining team track and field state champion); *Badgett v. Alabama High School Athletic Assn.*, 2007 WL 2461928 (N.D. Ala. May 3, 2007) (denying preliminary injunction to enable wheelchair athlete to compete against able-bodied runners in state tournament because doing so would raise legitimate competitive fairness and safety concerns).

CHAPTER 15

INTERNATIONAL AND OLYMPIC SPORTS

■ ■ ■

In most areas of international law, it is difficult to create a set of principles that all countries will agree to in writing, much less actually enforce. Sport is perhaps unique in this sense. For the most part, all of the countries that participate in Olympic sports agree to and abide by (at least presently) the authority of the Court of Arbitration of Sport (CAS) as a decision-making body with respect to disputes in international and Olympic sports. Created by the International Olympic Committee (IOC) and operated by the International Council of Arbitration for Sport (ICAS) in Lausanne, Switzerland, the CAS conducts arbitrations of international disputes related to sport. Countries have increasingly deferred to its arbitral decisions, as explored in *Pechstein* later in the chapter. The CAS has in many ways relieved the inherent tension between the external legal regulation and the internal governance of sport.

As we will see, having a centralized adjudicatory tribunal is essential in light of the extraordinarily complex structure that governs international and Olympic sports. At the apex of the Olympic structure is the IOC, headquartered in Lausanne, Switzerland, which owns and controls the Olympic Games. The IOC in turn entrusts the various national Olympic committees (NOCs) to oversee the process of determining which athletes will compete for their respective countries in the Olympics. In the United States, this governing body is the United States Olympic & Paralympic Committee (USOPC). Under the Amateur Sports Act of 1978 (as amended by the Ted Stevens Olympic & Amateur Sports Act of 1998), 36 U.S.C. § 371 *et seq.*, the USOPC oversees all matters relating to U.S. participation in the Olympic, Pan American, and Paralympic Games, as well as with performing several other specific functions related to the promotion of "amateur athletic activity" in the United States.

In addition to the NOCs, each sport has its own governing body, both on the international (international sports federations or ISFs) and national levels (national governing bodies or NGBs). There are almost one hundred different ISFs, running the spectrum from the most widely known in highly commercialized sports like soccer, gymnastics, track and field, and ice skating, to the most obscure like fistball, muaythai, wushu, and flying disc. The IOC recognizes 41 of these ISFs as governing Olympic sports eligible to participate in the Olympic Games, 34 in the Summer Olympics and seven in the Winter Olympics.

Each of the ISFs conducts its own world championships and sanctions other independently operated contests. The ISFs also determine and enforce eligibility standards for participation in those contests. With respect to the Olympics, the ISFs also determine eligibility for participation by individual athletes in the Olympic Games within the context of the broader rules established by the IOC. The ISFs thus play a significant role in determining who can participate in their sport in the Olympics and other international competitions.

In addition to the ISFs, most sports have national federations, often called "national governing bodies" (NGBs) that operate under the umbrella of the international federation (the ISF). The NGB exercises many of the eligibility and promotional functions of the international body. The NGB in each sport in each country holds the qualifying events that determine which athletes are to represent the country in the Olympic Games (and in many sports, the world championships sponsored by the international federation). As with the IOC, governments (at least in theory) do not control the NGBs, which are private entities. In some countries, the NGBs control power and money through their role in overseeing commercialized professional sport (as is the case with European soccer), in some cases using a portion of professional revenues to organize and support youth and recreational sport in their country (as is the case with New Zealand rugby). By contrast, American NGBs function independently of major professional sports leagues.

As explained below, the burden of regulating performance-enhancing drugs has become increasingly difficult, and so the IOC established the World Anti-Doping Agency (WADA) in 1999 to help address this issue. An independent non-profit like the CAS, WADA establishes the doping rules for international sports and the Olympics, while also participating in the policing of doping violations. As with the IOC-NOCs and the ISF-NGBs, there are national anti-doping agencies that report to WADA and help implement its rules and guidelines. In the United States, the anti-doping agency is the United States Anti-Doping Agency (USADA).

Having provided an overview of the constellation of national and international organizations involved in regulating the Olympics and many international competitions, we now take a brief look at the ways in which two of these entities work in practice before exploring some consequences of their decision-making processes later in the chapter.

A. ROLE OF INTERNATIONAL ORGANIZATIONS

The nature of international competitions necessitates a governing body that can adopt and implement eligibility rules while avoiding review by courts or administrative agencies in individual countries. As with other areas of international law, finding a way in which to establish legitimacy and authority to which others would submit was a central concern.

Specifically, there was a need for an institution to standardize the venue and the procedures used to resolved sports disputes without leaving individual disputes to the inconsistencies and biases of national courts in countries that had a vested interest in the outcome of the cases. Further, there was a need to set standardized substantive doping rules rather than leave the burden of adopting and enforcing such rules to the individual sport federations that often lacked the resources or the expertise to be effective and that occasionally even failed to recognize basic principles of fairness and due process. In light of this challenge, the IOC created the CAS is to adjudicate the disputes, and WADA to develop the doping rules.

1. THE COURT OF ARBITRATION FOR SPORT (CAS)

Established by the IOC in Delhi, India in 1984, the CAS initially consisted of around 60 selected arbitrator members, almost all of whom were European. In 1994, the IOC created the International Council of Arbitration for Sport (ICAS) to oversee the CAS. Governed by its own self-perpetuating, 20-person board of highly respected jurists, ICAS was a new, independent organization under Swiss law, and gave the CAS new legitimacy and separation from the IOC.

The success of the CAS in becoming the forum of choice for almost all sports disputes depended on the willingness of various sports federations to amend their rules to require that the CAS adjudicate the disputes within their respective sports. While few had done so under the old structure when the CAS was simply a division of the IOC, the IOC now began to pressure and influence federations to do so. One by one, the international federations amended their rules, and required national federations, event organizers, and individual athletes to sign contracts agreeing to submit any disputes they have with one another to the CAS. By the end of the 20th Century, most federations had recognized the jurisdiction of the CAS to settle disputes internal to their sports, even long-time hold outs World Athletics (track & field) and FIFA (soccer). Even if a federation does not submit to the CAS directly, the CAS may hear that federation's disputes involving doping if it is a signatory to the WADA Code.

Some of the salient procedural aspects of the CAS are as follows:

- The official languages of the CAS are English and French, and the CAS conducts its proceedings in one of these two languages.

- The Code of Sports-Related Arbitration (The CAS Code) governs the CAS's structure, operation, and procedure. As is typical for an arbitral tribunal, there are no fixed rules of evidence, with each three-arbitrator panel able to consider or exclude what it believes appropriate under the circumstances.

- The CAS Code distinguishes between an Ordinary Division and an Appeals Division. Both sets of proceedings are closed.

  o The Ordinary Division hears cases in the first instance that typically relate to a contractual relationship between the parties such as those involving television or sponsorship rights, athlete-agent contracts, or disputes between a national and international federation.

  o The Appeals Division hears appeals from the decisions of arbitral tribunals established either in a country or within a sports federation. Most typically these involve challenges brought by athletes to sanctions imposed on them by their sport's NGB or their national anti-doping authority.

- Although the CAS Code distinguishes between these two internal divisions, as a practical matter the procedures followed are nearly identical for both, and even cases heard on appeal from an earlier arbitration panel are heard by the CAS panel de novo without giving any deference to the earlier factual or legal findings.

- The CAS also has what it calls "consultation procedures" that create a method for parties to seek an advisory opinion about a sports legal issue, and more recently it has established a Mediation Division where parties can seek the assistance of CAS appointed mediators to help resolve disputes without formal litigation.

- Beginning with the Atlanta Olympics in 1996, the CAS has sent a group of CAS arbitrators to the site of the Games to be available to hear and resolve on an expedited basis (within 24 hours) any emergency disputes. The CAS Ad Hoc Division panels also have heard disputes at other international sporting events.

- Cases heard by the Ad Hoc Division generally fall into two categories—appeals by athletes who have been denied access to compete in the Games for any of a variety of reasons and appeals to the outcome of an event for such reasons as failure by judges to adhere to the rules, equipment failure, discovery corrupt judging, or cheating.

The "law" that the CAS generally interprets and enforces derives from the private rules established by the various organizations that make up the world sports movement, including the Olympic Charter, the constitutions and rules of the IOC and international federations, the World Anti-Doping Agency Code, and the rules of national sports and anti-doping agencies. In interpreting and applying the relevant rules in a given case, CAS arbitrators look to the CAS Code for procedural guidance, but employ general principles of substantive law, and if there is no generally accepted principle then the arbitrators must look to the law of the country most directly involved in the case.

Because they are arbitration awards, CAS decisions technically are not binding precedent. Even so, the CAS publishes and indexes digests of all Appeals Division and Ad Hoc Division awards, which parties often cite in subsequent CAS cases. CAS arbitrators typically attempt to make their awards consistent with previous decisions. As such, the growing body of published CAS awards has created a *lex sportiva*—a coherent body of international sports law that is "anational" in that it transcends national laws and applies uniformly throughout the world.

All CAS awards are appealable to the Swiss Federal Tribunal (SFT), and parties cannot waive that right. *See Canas v. ATP Tour* (Swiss Federal Tribunal 2007). Nonetheless, the grounds for a successful appeal are very narrow. The SFT has held that under Swiss law the only grounds upon which it may grant an appeal are: (1) the appealing party was effectively denied the right to be heard before the arbitral tribunal; (2) the arbitral panel was constituted irregularly; (3) the panel lacked impartiality; (4) the panel erred in finding that it had jurisdiction over the matter decided; (5) the panel's award exceeded its authority as submitted to it; and (6) the panel's award contravened public policy as defined under Swiss law (which the court has defined very narrowly because "it must be understood as a universal rather than a national concept, intended to penalize incompatibility with the fundamental legal or moral principles acknowledged in all civilized states"). *N.J.Y.W. v. Fédération Internationale de Natation (FINA)*, 5P.83/1999/Translation (Switz.), 31 March 1999, in DIGEST OF CAS AWARDS II: 1998–2000 at 775, 779 (Matthieu Reeb ed., 2002). The SFT's recognition of the CAS as a legitimate independent arbitral body whose decisions receive the full recognition under Swiss law has served as an international certification of the CAS's authority. *See, e.g. Lazutina* and *Danilova v. IOC* cases, [Swiss Federal Tribunal 2003], (explaining that in a case appealing an IOC decision, the CAS is a legitimate and independent arbitral body whose decisions must "be considered true awards, equivalent to the judgments of State courts.").

Litigants have appealed less than five percent of CAS determinations, with less than one percent of those appeals being successful. In short, the CAS decisions are, for all practical purposes, final decisions.

2. THE WORLD ANTI-DOPING AGENCY (WADA)

As with the CAS, countries have generally accepted the authority of WADA, albeit with the IOC's insistence. Headquartered in Montreal, Canada, WADA's importance lies in its ability to establish and develop a set of uniform and transparent rules to address the issue of doping. The mission of the WADA includes research, education, development of anti-doping capacities, and monitoring and enforcing the World Anti-Doping Code (WADA Code).

As mentioned above, most countries have a national anti-doping organization that reports to WADA. The national anti-doping organizations are often responsible for testing athletes and imposing sanctions with the NGB, as well as investigating potential WADA violations. For example, the USADA's investigation of Lance Armstrong, discussed in Chapter 1, exposed his doping that had previously avoided detection.

WADA has an extensive set of complex rules. The most basic rule is that its scheme is a strict liability one. If athletes test positive for a banned substance, they have violated the Code, irrespective of their intent. Even if one ingests a substance unknowingly or accidentally, they have violated WADA. Mitigation, to the extent any exists, comes with respect to the sanction, not the guilt determination.

The original WADA Code underwent a substantial revision that became effective as of January 1, 2015. The new document governs all aspects of the effort to combat the use of banned substances in sport throughout the world, except the professional unionized sports leagues in the United States that have collectively bargained rules dealing with drugs and drug testing. The 2015 WADA Code sets forth detailed rules that:

- list all of the substances that are banned from being artificially put into an athlete's body,

- establish the procedures for determining when and under what conditions athletes are to be tested for banned substances,

- provide for the procedures and methods by which selected laboratories will scientifically evaluate urine or blood samples for banned substances,

- establish the scientific thresholds that define a violation for each substance, and

- set forth the penalties for violations.

Some other general principles include:

- Article 2 of the WADA Code requires athletes randomly selected for testing to report their location at all times during the window between selection and testing.

- Testing can consist of urine or blood samples, or both. WADA immediately divides the sample into 2 containers, the A sample and the B sample. For a positive test, both samples must be positive.

- Article 3 of the Code establishes evidentiary burdens and the standards of proof. All burdens of proof must meet the standard of "comfortable satisfaction," which WADA officials regard as the functional equivalent of "clear and convincing evidence" in the United States—something between a preponderance of the evidence and beyond a reasonable doubt.

- To the extent that an athlete wants to mitigate his or her sanction, the athlete must likewise prove any underlying facts or evidence by "comfortable satisfaction."

- Article 4 of the Code establishes the criteria and procedures by which WADA determines which substances to include on the "prohibited list," as well as any acceptable uses of such substances.

- Article 5 of the Code covers all of the testing rules, Articles 6 and 7 address the technical aspects of testing and the handling of results, and Article 8 addresses the appellate procedure.

- Article 10 provides the sanctions for violations. The presence of a banned substance during a qualification results in immediate disqualification. A first out-of-competition violation of the Code by an athlete triggers an automatic four-year suspension from the sport. The automatic suspension may be reduced by half if the athlete can establish with comfortable satisfaction that the presence of the banned substance in the body was not intentional, and it may be eliminated entirely if the athlete can establish with comfortable satisfaction that he/she bears no fault or negligence whatsoever for the banned substance being in the body. The penalties for repeat violations increase sharply, with a third intentional violation resulting in a lifetime ban.

One final consideration is worth noting with respect to WADA and drug testing generally. It is not a black and white question of whether a substance is present; instead, it is a question of whether the amount of a substance exceeds a certain threshold. This is because many of the banned substances increase the amounts of hormones that already exist naturally in the body.

———

NOTES AND QUESTIONS

1. *Centralized Tribunal.* What are the advantages of having a centralized international tribunal in the CAS? Are there disadvantages? Would national courts be preferable?

2.   *Arbitration Versus Judicial Proceeding.* In a CAS arbitration, three arbitrators are chosen from an approved list of over 300 neutrals. The decision of the three individuals is essentially not appealable and does not require use of the rules of evidence. Is this approach preferable to a judicial proceeding? Preferable to case decided by a jury? If some kind of judicial proceeding is preferable, which court?

3.   *Double Jeopardy?* In cases where an athlete wins an appeal from a positive drug test in neutral arbitration proceedings in her home country or within her sports federation, WADA can force relitigation of that case *de novo* in an appeal to the CAS. Does this constitute double jeopardy? Or is the determination of a national arbitration proceeding different than a criminal jury finding of not guilty? This scenario played itself out in cases involving U.S. distance runner Mary Decker Slaney (for excessive testosterone levels), Scotland's 200-meter European champion Doug Walker (for nandrolone), and British 100-meter champion Linford Christie (for nandrolone). Should national courts refuse to recognize the international panel's decision as being fundamentally unfair because of its double-jeopardy nature? Or should national courts defer to the judgment of the international tribunal because national arbitrators may be biased in favor of their country's athletes and potentially inconsistent results may also result from different national standards? Does this perhaps explain why the CAS requires that appeals from national or federation arbitration decisions be heard *de novo?*

4.   *Considering WADA's List of Banned Substances.* Another set of questions arises out of WADA's now standardized list of banned substances for all sports. For one, is it appropriate to have the same substances banned in every sport, even though it is generally recognized that some substances only give a competitive advantage in some, but not all, sports? In addition, some drugs on the list, like cocaine and marijuana, may not provide a competitive advantage but WADA proscribes them nonetheless. Is this necessary? Why or why not? To what extent should WADA's list consider changing laws toward these drugs? In 2022, WADA initiated a scientific review of whether marijuana should be removed from its list.

B. A HISTORY OF INTERNATIONAL CORRUPTION AND POLITICAL INTERFERENCE

Chapter 1 explored a number of corruption issues in domestic sports. If anything, corruption on the international sports stage has, at times, been even worse. On one level this is not surprising as the countries that compete in competitions for Olympic medals or soccer trophies also have political rivalries that can make the sports more about international relations than the competitions themselves.

Indeed, it is hard to ignore the potential for politicization of the Games. Such attempts date back to the first modern Olympic Games in Athens in 1896, when the British compelled an Australian athlete to declare himself British. Other prominent examples of Olympic politicization include the

Nazi propaganda that pervaded the 1936 Berlin Games, the Soviet-Hungarian friction at the 1956 Melbourne Games following the USSR's suppression of a revolution in Hungary, the murder of Israeli athletes by terrorists at the 1972 Munich Games, the controversy between China and Taiwan leading up to the 1976 Montreal Games, the disputes resulting from South Africa's apartheid policy from 1968 to 1988, the U.S.-led boycott of the 1980 Moscow Games (explored below) in protest of the Soviet invasion of Afghanistan, and the retaliatory boycott of the 1984 Los Angeles Games by the Soviet bloc.

The most recent international conflict to similarly interfere with international sports competitions has been the Russia-Ukraine war. At the conclusion of the 2022 Winter Olympic Games in Beijing, China, Russia invaded Ukraine. Russia had stationed its armies on the Ukrainian border for weeks, but waited until the conclusion of the Olympics to invade. The world responded by banning Russian athletes from international competitions. FIFA and UEFA banned all Russian club and national teams from international competition, including the 2022–23 season. In July, 2022, the CAS rejected Russia's appeal of these soccer bans.

In addition, the ISU, figure skating's governing body, banned Russian and Belarusian athletes from competition. The IIHF, ice hockey's governing body, stripped Russia of the hosting of the 2023 world championships. The world governing body for track and field barred athletes from Russia and Belarus for the foreseeable future. Wimbledon similarly prohibited Russian athletes from participating, meaning that Daniil Medvedev, world number 1 and the prior year's finalist, could not play in the summer of 2022. And Formula One pulled out of Russia, including canceling the Russian Grand Prix.

1. IOC CORRUPTION

The IOC has a history of corruption. In December 1998, allegations surfaced that IOC members had accepted bribes from members of the Committee that had successfully advanced the bid of Salt Lake City, Utah as the host site for the 2002 Winter Olympic Games. The IOC expelled six committee members, adopted an extensive reform package, and established an independent IOC Ethics Commission.

One questions how well this IOC Ethics Commission has worked in practice. In 2021, Carlos Arthur Nuzman, the head of the Brazilian Olympic Committee for more than two decades, received a sentence of over 30 years incarceration for buying votes for Rio de Janeiro to host the 2016 Olympics. The Brazilian court found Nuzman guilty of corruption, criminal organization, money laundering, and tax evasion. Others sentenced in connection with the same payoff scheme included former Rio Gov. Sergio Cabral, businessman Arthur Soares, and Leonardo Gryner, the Rio committee director general of operations. Investigators testified that all four individuals coordinated to bribe the former IAAF president, Lamine Diack and his son, Papa Massata Diack, for votes. Rio's corrupt bid defeated the competing bids of Chicago, Tokyo, and Madrid.

A similar bribery scandal surrounded Japan's successful 2013 bid to host the 2020 Tokyo Olympics, which took place in 2021 as a result of the Covid pandemic. According to French prosecutors, Haruyuki Takahashi spent $8.2 million from the Toyko bid committee to help secure IOC votes. Others indicated that individuals acting on behalf of Tokyo's bidding team made payments of around €1.3m to a hidden account linked to Papa Massata Diack, who was banned from athletics for life in 2015. Japanese police raided the home of Takahashi in the summer of 2022 after Takahashi reportedly received $300,000 in bribe money from Olympic sponsor Aoki, despite his role as a quasi-civil servant not permitted to accept money related to his position.

2. FIFA CORRUPTION

In December 2010, FIFA awarded the hosting rights for the 2018 World Cup to Russia and the 2022 World Cup to Qatar. Around the same time, European media reported that three of the voting officials—Nicolas Leoz, Issa Hayatou, and Ricardo Teixeira—had received bribes in the 1990s in choosing host venues.

In February 2011, FIFA's ethics committee upheld bans for executive committee members Amos Adamu (three years) and Reynard Temarii (one year) for breaches of the code of ethics during the World Cup 2018 and 2022 bidding campaigns. In June 2011, the same committee banned FIFA presidential candidate Mohamed Bin Hammam for life for bribery related to his campaign as well as his role in securing the World Cup for Qatar. Vice-president Jack Warner resigned before his activities could be investigated.

In July 2012, FIFA commissioned a report by former U.S. attorney Michael Garcia into the World Cup 2018 and 2022 bidding campaigns in response to growing public criticism. The report was completed in September 2014, with FIFA issuing a summary statement in November that the breaches of ethics were "of very limited scope" and effectively confirming Russia and Qatar as hosts, despite Garcia's objections to the summary's characterization of his report. The ethics commission subsequently banned long time FIFA president Sepp Blatter in 2016.

In May 2015, seven FIFA officials were arrested in a dawn raid in Zurich. They were indicted in federal court along with seven other FIFA officials for racketeering, wire fraud, and money laundering conspiracies spanning over two decades. A superseding indictment charged another 16 FIFA officials. The criminal investigation has resulted in 27 individual FIFA defendants pleading guilty to federal crimes. Two other FIFA officials, Juan Ángel Napout and José Maria Marin, were convicted of racketeering conspiracy and related offenses in December 2017.

To date, the prosecutions have resulted in charges against more than 50 individual and corporate defendants from more than 20 countries, primarily in connection with the offer and receipt of bribes and kickbacks paid by sports marketing companies to soccer officials in exchange for the media and marketing rights to various soccer tournaments and events and the laundering of those payments. The arrests in the U.S. case triggered Australia, Columbia, Costa Rica, Germany, and Switzerland to open or expand separate criminal investigations into top FIFA officials for corruption.

FIFA, CONCACAF (North and Central America federation), and CONMEBOL (South America federation) have received over $201 million from criminal asset forfeiture to remit losses incurred as a result of this criminal activity. FIFA, CONCACAF, and CONMEBOL have committed to distributing funds received through the remission process to and through a newly created World Football Remission Fund focused on women's / girl's football (soccer), education, safeguarding, youth programs, community outreach, and humanitarian needs. The Fund has been established under the FIFA Foundation, an independent foundation that uses soccer, and sport in general, as a tool for social development.

One explanation of the widespread nature of FIFA corruption relates to its organization model. Each of the 209 member nations gets a single vote when electing a federation president and executive committee. That means that Maldives, Andorra, and Trinidad & Tobago have the same voting power as Brazil, England, and Germany. The smaller countries and their federations receive an equal share of FIFA's revenues. In theory, it is easier to bribe a number of smaller countries and be able to influence outcomes rather than to try to bribe much larger and wealthier countries.

NOTES AND QUESTIONS

1. *Is Corruption Inevitable?* The economic benefits for cities and countries in hosting Olympic games or World Cups can be significant. The long history of representatives bribing voters indicates an international view for some that this is simply how business is done. Is such corruption inevitable? Is there an effective way to police it? Will the criminal convictions, prison sentences, and asset forfeitures deter future unethical conduct?

2. *A New System?* Should the IOC or FIFA adopt a rotational system that mandates which cities get to host over time? Or is that approach unrealistic given the four year gap between the competitions?

3. *Relationship Between Politics and Corruption.* Should there be a stronger relationship between politics and corruption? In other words, should there be punitive bans on countries hosting where corruption is discovered?

4. *Punishing Political Acts.* Are the punishments different international sporting bodies have placed on Russian athletes appropriate? Or are they unfair? To what extent should individual athletes bear the cost of decisions by their political leaders?

C. THE UNITED STATES IN INTERNATIONAL SPORTS

The federal statute that governs Olympic sports in the United States is the Amateur Sports Act of 1978, 36 U.S.C. § 371, *et seq.* The legislation expanded the USOPC's power to coordinate all amateur athletic activity in the United States. It also gave the USOPC the power to recognize (or to withdraw recognition from) an amateur sports organization as the NGB in each sport. Under the statute, there exists an arbitration remedy for dispute resolution among members as well as those "relating to the opportunity of any amateur athlctc, coach, trainer, or other person to participate in certain protected competitions."

Further, the Act empowers these governing bodies to perform various functions related to their sports:

- to conduct "amateur athletic competition" in the United States; to sanction other such competitions inside and outside the United States;

- to determine eligibility standards for participation in such competitions;

- to select the athletes to represent the United States in the Olympic, Paralympic, and Pan American Games;

- to represent or to select a representative for the United States in the international federations; and

- generally to govern and promote all "amateur athletic activities" in their respective sports in the United States.

In 1998, Congress passed sweeping amendments to the Amateur Sports Act (ASA) affecting a number of significant matters. In addition to renaming it the Ted Stevens Olympic and Amateur Sports Act (ASA), the amendments:

- formalized the rights and procedures available to athletes in challenging eligibility decisions;

- expanded the list of protected trademarks that the USOPC controls (whether or not an alleged infringement creates any consumer confusion);

- brought the Paralympic Games and issues relating to disabled athletes within the scope of the Act;

- formalized the involvement of athletes and national sports governing bodies in the USOPC's governing process;

- gave federal courts exclusive jurisdiction over ASA cases, but banned the issuance of injunctions within 21 days of the start of an Olympic event;

- codified extensive prior case law that the ASA does not create a private right of action; and

- created the office of an ombudsman to provide independent advice and counsel to athletes about applicable laws and procedures.

In 2020, Congress passed the Empowering Olympic, Paralympic and Amateur Athletes Act which established new safeguards and powers to protect American amateur athletes from abuse. The law builds on the Protecting Young Victims from Sexual Abuse and Safe Sport Authorization Act of 2017 (SafeSport Act), which established the United States Center for SafeSport as an independent investigative body tasked with combatting abuse in the world of amateur sports. Both laws were part of the response to the Larry Nassar-USA Gymnastics scandal in 2017, that revealed Nassar's sexual abuse of hundreds of female athletes.

The Empowering Athletes Act signals a more active approach by Congress in that it assumes authority over amateur sports associations and federations. Specifically, the Act aims to expand the role of the Center for SafeSport by:

- imposing an annual mandate of at least $20 million in annual grants by USOPC to the Center;

- as the USOPC does not receive federal funds, the NGBs of various sports will need to contribute to the Center;

- in addition to receiving funding from the USOPC and NGBs, the Center will undertake annual SafeSport compliance audits of these organizations;

The Act provides for a broad increase in congressional oversight, in part through a new committee—"Commission on the State of the U.S. Olympics and Paralympics" which is to complete a nine-month audit of all of the activities of USOPC.

The Act also gives Congress the power to directly dissolve the board of directors of the USOPC and even terminate federal recognition of individual NGBs. If Congress were to act to dissolve the USOPC under this trigger provision, it might violate the Olympic Charter, and result in the IOC suspending the USOPC. Finally, the Act also places structural limitations on the USOPC and the NGBs, including requiring increased participation by the athletes in governance.

1. JUDICIAL REVIEW OF SPORTS GOVERNING BODIES

A crucial legal issue is when, under what legal theories, and under what standard of review, an American court should overturn a decision by one of these governing bodies. The following highly publicized case depicts some of the key legal arguments that have been made about this issue.

DEFRANTZ V. UNITED STATES OLYMPIC COMMITTEE
492 F. Supp. 1181 (D.D.C.), *aff'd*, 701 F.2d 221 (D.C. Cir. 1980)

PRATT, JUDGE.

Plaintiffs, 25 athletes and one member of the Executive Board of defendant United States Olympic Committee (USOC), have moved for an injunction barring defendant USOC from carrying out a resolution, adopted by the USOC House of Delegates on April 12, 1980, not to send an American team to participate in the Games of the XXII Olympiad to be held in Moscow in the summer of 1980. Plaintiffs allege that in preventing American athletes from competing in the Summer Olympics, defendant has exceeded its statutory powers and has abridged plaintiffs' constitutional rights.

* * *

According to its Rules and By-laws, the International Olympic Committee (IOC) governs the Olympic movement and owns the rights of the Olympic games. IOC Rules provide that National Olympic Committees (NOC) may be established "as the sole authorities responsible for the representation of the respective countries at the Olympic Games," so long as the NOC's rules and regulations are approved by the IOC. The USOC is one such National Olympic Committee.

The USOC is a corporation created and granted a federal charter by Congress in 1950. This charter was revised by the Amateur Sports Act of 1978. Under this statute, defendant USOC has "exclusive jurisdiction" and authority over participation and representation of the United States in the Olympic Games.

* * *

On December 27, 1979, the Soviet Union launched an invasion of its neighbor, Afghanistan. That country's ruler was deposed and killed and a new government was installed. . . .

President Carter termed the invasion a threat to the security of the Persian Gulf area as well as a threat to world peace and stability, and he moved to take direct sanctions against the Soviet Union. These sanctions included a curtailment of agricultural and high technology exports to the Soviet Union, and restrictions on commerce with the Soviets. The Administration also turned its attention to a boycott of the summer Olympic Games [in Moscow] as a further sanction against the Soviet Union.

* * *

[The President put great pressure on the USOC not to send a team to the 1980 Games, even to the point of threatening to withhold federal funding from the USOC, to revoke its tax exemptions, and to invoke the International Emergency Economic Powers Act to forbid any athletes from traveling to the Soviet Union during the games. In addition, the House of Representatives passed a resolution, by a vote of 386 to 12, opposing U.S. participation in the Games.]

* * *

[On April 12, 1980], [a]fter what USOC President Kane describes in his affidavit as "full, open, complete and orderly debate by advocates of each motion," the House of Delegates, on a secret ballot passed, by a vote of 1,604 to 798, a resolution [declaring that the USOC would not send a team to Moscow unless international conditions changed dramatically.]

* * *

1.   The Amateur Sports Act of 1978

Plaintiffs allege in their complaint that by its decision not to send an American team to compete in the summer Olympic Games in Moscow, defendant USOC has violated the Amateur Sports Act of 1978. . . . Reduced to their essentials, these allegations are that the Act does not give, and that Congress intended to deny, the USOC the authority to decide not to enter an American team in the Olympics, except perhaps for sports-related reasons, and that the Act guarantees to certain athletes [a right to compete in the Olympic Games.] . . .

* * *

The principal substantive powers of the USOC are found in § 375(a) of the Act.[12] In determining whether the USOC's authority under the Act encompasses the right to decide not to participate in an Olympic contest,

---

[12]   They are to: "(1) serve as the coordinating body for amateur athletic activity in the United States directly relating to international amateur athletic competition; (2) represent the United States as its national Olympic committee in relations with the International Olympic Committee . . . ; (3) organize, finance, and control the representation of the United States in the competitions and events of the Olympic Games . . . and obtain, either directly or by delegation to the appropriation national governing body, amateur representation for summer games." 36 U.S.C. § 375(a)(1), (2), (3). The "objects and purposes" section of the Act includes the provision, also found in the 1950 Act, that the USOC shall "exercise exclusive jurisdiction . . . over all matters pertaining to the participation of the United States in the Olympic Games . . . including the representation of the United States in such games." *Id.* § 374(3).

we must read these provisions in the context in which they were written. In writing this legislation, Congress did not create a new relationship between the USOC and the IOC. Rather, it recognized an already long-existing relationship between the two and statutorily legitimized that relationship with a federal charter and federal incorporation.[13] The legislative history demonstrates Congressional awareness that the USOC and its predecessors, as the National Olympic Committee for the United States, have had a continuing relationship with the IOC since 1896. Congress was necessarily aware that a National Olympic Committee is a creation and a creature of the International Olympic Committee, to whose rules and regulations it must conform. The NOC gets its power and its authority from the IOC, the sole proprietor and owner of the Olympic Games.

In view of Congress' obvious awareness of these facts, we would expect that if Congress intended to limit or deny to the USOC powers it already enjoyed as a National Olympic Committee, such limitation or denial would be clear and explicit. No such language appears in the statute. Indeed, far from precluding this authority, the language of the statute appears to embrace it. For example, the "objects and purposes" section of the Act speaks in broad terms, stating that the USOC shall exercise "exclusive jurisdiction" over ". . . all matters pertaining to the participation of the United States in the Olympic Games. . . ." We read this broadly stated purpose in conjunction with the specific power conferred on the USOC by the Act to "represent the United States as its national Olympic committee in relations with the International Olympic Committee," and in conjunction with the IOC Rules and By-laws, which provide that "representation" includes the decision to participate. In doing so, we find a compatibility and not a conflict between the Act and the IOC Rules on the issue of the authority of the USOC to decide whether or not to accept an invitation to field an American team at the Olympics. The language of the statute is broad enough to confer this authority, and we find that Congress must have intended that the USOC exercise that authority in this area, which it already enjoyed because of its long-standing relationship with the IOC. We accordingly conclude that the USOC has the authority to decide not to send an American team to the Olympics.

Plaintiffs next argue that if the USOC does have the authority to decide not to accept an invitation to send an American team to the Moscow Olympics, that decision must be based on "sports-related considerations." In support of their argument, plaintiffs point to §§ 392(a)(5) and (b) of the Act, which plaintiffs acknowledge "are not in terms applicable to the

---

[13]   To the extent the USOC was granted extended power by the 1978 Act, the legislative history makes clear, and the plaintiffs do not dispute the fact, that these powers were primarily designed to give the USOC supervisory authority over United States amateur athletic groups in order to eliminate the numerous and frequent jurisdictional squabbles among schools, athletic groups and various national sports governing bodies.

USOC," but rather concern situations in which national governing bodies of various sports, which are subordinate to the USOC, are asked to sanction the holding of international competitions below the level of the Olympic or Pan American Games in the United States or the participation of the United States athletes in such competition abroad. These sections provide that a national governing body may withhold its sanctions only upon clear and convincing evidence that holding or participating in the competition "would be detrimental to the best interests of the sport." Plaintiffs argue by analogy that a similar "sports-related" limitation must attach to any authority the USOC might have to decide not to participate in an Olympic competition. We cannot agree.

The provision on which plaintiffs place reliance by analogy is specifically concerned with eliminating the feuding between various amateur athletic organizations and national governing bodies which for so long characterized amateur athletics. As all parties recognize, this friction, such as the well-publicized power struggles between the NCAA and the AAU, was a major reason for passage of the Act, and the provisions plaintiffs cite, among others, are aimed at eliminating this senseless strife, which the Senate and House Committee reports indicate had dramatically harmed the ability of the United States to compete effectively in international competition. In order to eliminate this internecine squabbling, the Act elevated the USOC to a supervisory role over the various amateur athletic organizations, and provided that the USOC establish procedures for the swift and equitable settlement of these disputes. As indicated above, it also directed that the national governing bodies of the various sports could only withhold their approvals of international competition for sports-related reasons. Previously, many of these bodies had withheld their sanction of certain athletic competitions in order to further their own interests at the expense of other groups and to the detriment of athletes wishing to participate.

In brief, this sports-related limitation is intimately tied to the specific purpose of curbing the arbitrary and unrestrained power of various athletic organizations subordinate to the USOC not to allow athletes to compete in international competition below the level of the Olympic Games and the Pan American Games. This purpose has nothing to do with a decision by the USOC to exercise authority granted by the IOC to decide not to participate in an Olympic competition.

* * *

We therefore conclude that the USOC not only had the authority to decide not to send an American team to the summer Olympics, but also that it could do so for reasons not directly related to sports considerations.

(b) Athletes' Statutory Right to Compete in the Olympics

* * *

Plaintiffs argue that the Report of the President's Commission on Olympic Sports, which was the starting point for the legislation proposed, and the legislative history support their argument that the statute confers an enforceable right on plaintiffs to compete in Olympic competition. Again, we are compelled to disagree with plaintiffs.

The legislative history and the statute are clear that the "right to compete," which plaintiffs refer to, is in the context of the numerous jurisdictional disputes between various athletic bodies, such as the NCAA and the AAU, which we have just discussed, and which was a major impetus for the Amateur Sports Act of 1978. Plaintiffs recognize that a major purpose of the Act was to eliminate such disputes. However, they go on to argue that the Report which highlighted the need for strengthening the USOC in order to eliminate this feuding, made a finding that there is little difference between an athlete denied the right to compete because of a boycott and an athlete denied the right to compete because of jurisdictional bickering.

The short answer is that although the Congress may have borrowed heavily from the Report of the President's Commission, it did not enact the Report. Instead, it enacted a statute and that statute relates a "right to compete" to the elimination of jurisdictional disputes between amateur athletic groups, which for petty and groundless reasons have often deprived athletes of the opportunity to enter a particular competition. . . .

The Senate Report makes clear that the language relied on by plaintiffs is not designed to provide any substantive guarantees, let alone a Bill of Rights. Further, to the extent that any guarantees of a right to compete are included in the USOC Constitution as a result of this provision, they do not include a right that amateur athletes may compete in the Olympic Games despite a decision by the USOC House of Delegates not to accept an invitation to enter an American team in the competition. This provision simply was not designed to extend so far. Rather, it was designed to remedy the jurisdictional disputes among amateur athletic bodies, not disputes between athletes and the USOC itself over the exercise of the USOC's discretion not to participate in the Olympics.

* * *

Because we conclude that the rights plaintiffs seek to enforce do not exist in the Act, and because the legislative history of the Act nowhere allows the implication of a private right of action, we find that plaintiffs have no implied private right of action under the Amateur Sports Act of 1978 to maintain this suit.

2.   Constitutional Claims

Plaintiffs have alleged that the decision of the USOC not to enter an American team in the summer Olympics has violated certain rights guaranteed to plaintiffs under the First, Fifth and Ninth Amendments to the United States Constitution. . . .

(a)   State Action

Although federally chartered, defendant is a private organization. Because the Due Process Clause of the Fifth Amendment, on which plaintiffs place great reliance, applies only to actions by the federal government, plaintiffs must show that the USOC vote is a "governmental act," *i.e.*, state action. In defining state action, the courts have fashioned two guidelines. The first involves an inquiry into whether the state

> . . . has so far insinuated itself into a position of interdependence with (the private entity) that it must be recognized as a joint participant in the challenged activity.

Here, there is no such intermingling, and there is no factual justification for finding that the federal government and the USOC enjoyed the "symbiotic relationship" which courts have required to find state action. The USOC has received no federal funding[25] and it exists and operates independently of the federal government. Its chartering statute gives it "exclusive jurisdiction" over "all matters pertaining to the participation of the United States in the Olympic Games. . . ." 36 U.S.C. § 374(3). To be sure, the Act does link the USOC and the federal government to the extent it requires the USOC to submit an annual report to the President and the Congress. But this hardly converts such an independent relationship to a "joint participation."

The second guideline fashioned by the courts involves an inquiry of whether:

> . . . there is a sufficiently close nexus between the state and the challenged action of the regulated entity so that the action of the latter may be fairly treated as that of the state itself.

> . . . In the instant case, there was no requirement that any federal government body approve actions by the USOC before they become effective.

Plaintiffs argue that by the actions of certain federal officials, the federal government initiated, encouraged, and approved of the result reached (i.e., the vote of the USOC not to send an American team to the summer Olympics). Plaintiffs advance a novel theory. Essentially, their

---

[25]   Federal funds were authorized under the Amateur Sports Act of 1978 but have never been appropriated. But the mere receipt of federal funds by a private entity, without more, is not enough to convert that entity's activity into state action. *Spark v. Catholic University of America,* 510 F.2d 1277 (D.C. Cir. 1975).

argument is that the campaign of governmental persuasion, personally led by President Carter, crossed the line from "governmental recommendation," which plaintiffs find acceptable and presumably necessary to the operation of our form of government, into the area of "affirmative pressure that effectively places the government's prestige behind the challenged action," and thus, results in state action. We cannot agree.

* * *

Here there is no [requisite governmental] control. The USOC is an independent body, and nothing in its chartering statute gives the federal government the right to control that body or its officers. Furthermore, the facts here do not indicate that the federal government was able to exercise any type of "de facto" control over the USOC. The USOC decided by a secret ballot of its House of Delegates. The federal government may have had the power to prevent the athletes from participating in the Olympics even if the USOC had voted to allow them to participate, but it did not have the power to make them vote in a certain way. All it had was the power of persuasion. We cannot equate this with control. To do so in cases of this type would be to open the door and usher the courts into what we believe is a largely nonjusticiable realm, where they would find themselves in the untenable position of determining whether a certain level, intensity, or type of "Presidential" or "Administration" or "political" pressure amounts to sufficient control over a private entity so as to invoke federal jurisdiction.

We accordingly find that the decision of the USOC not to send an American team to the summer Olympics was not state action, and therefore, does not give rise to an actionable claim for the infringements of the constitutional rights alleged.

(b) Constitutionally Protected Rights

. . . Were we to find state action in this case, we would conclude that defendant USOC has violated no constitutionally protected right of plaintiffs.

We note that other courts have considered the right to compete in amateur athletics and have found no deprivation of constitutionally protected rights. As the Government has pointed out in *Parish v. National Collegiate Athletic Association*, 506 F.2d 1028 (5th Cir. 1975), basketball players sought an injunction to prevent the NCAA from enforcing its ruling declaring certain athletes ineligible to compete in tournaments and televised games. The court stated that:

> the privilege of participation in interscholastic activities must be deemed to fall . . . outside the protection of due process.

Plaintiffs have been unable to draw our attention to any court decision which finds that the rights allegedly violated here enjoy constitutional protection, and we can find none. Plaintiffs would expand the constitutionally-protected scope of liberty and self-expression to include the denial of an amateur athlete's right to compete in an Olympic contest when that denial was the result of a decision by a supervisory athletic organization acting well within the limits of its authority. Defendant has not denied plaintiffs the right to engage in every amateur athletic competition. Defendant has not denied plaintiffs the right to engage in their chosen occupation. Defendant has not even denied plaintiffs the right to travel, only the right to travel for one specific purpose. We can find no justification and no authority for the expansive reading of the Constitution which plaintiffs urge. To find as plaintiffs recommend would be to open the floodgates to a torrent of lawsuits. The courts have correctly recognized that many of life's disappointments, even major ones, do not enjoy constitutional protection. This is one such instance.

Case dismissed.

NOTES AND QUESTIONS

1.   *State Action?* Should the federal government be able to enact a law delegating what in many countries is a governmental function to a private group, then exert enormous political pressure on that group to make a certain decision, and still argue that there is insufficient government involvement to trigger constitutional protections for those adversely affected by that decision? The courts have uniformly refused to recognize as state action the decisions of any of the national or international athletic governing bodies. *See, e.g., Behagen v. Amateur Basketball Ass'n of the United States*, 884 F.2d 524 (10th Cir. 1989); *International Olympic Comm. v. San Francisco Arts & Athletics*, 781 F.2d 733 (9th Cir. 1986), *aff'd*, 483 U.S. 522 (1987). Thus, like the NCAA after the *Tarkanian* decision in Chapter 12, these organizations do not have to provide constitutional due process or equal protection to those affected by their decisions. Does this mean that these bodies can do whatever they want? Could the USOPC decide not to send a team to the Olympics in retaliation for an IOC decision not to award the 2016 Games to Chicago, or because the IOC refused to enter a licensing agreement with an American company? If constitutional arguments are unavailable, what other legal claims are available to disappointed athletes?

2.   *Constitutional Violation?* Even if the court had found that the USOC was a state actor, would the plaintiffs have prevailed on their constitutional claims? What constitutional rights, if any, did the USOC arguably violate?

3.   *Antitrust Law?* One question stemming from the Amateur Sports Act is the extent to which the USOC, a national sports governing body, or its international counterparts, are subject to American antitrust law, especially since the courts have found such bodies to be private, non-governmental actors. The American courts have not really addressed the issue, with the exception of

Cady v. TAC, No. C 89-1737 (N.D. Cal. May 25, 1989), an unpublished opinion holding that The Athletics Congress (TAC) was exempt from antitrust law because of the power Congress vested in it. Was this the proper result?

In Europe, by contrast, there is a rich jurisprudence on this topic where courts have drawn a distinction between "purely sporting" rules that are not subject to competition law and commercial rules that are subject to competition law. Should antitrust law apply here? Is the USOPC fundamentally similar to or different than the NCAA?

2. ATHLETE ELIGIBILITY STANDARDS

Some of the most controversial decisions by sports federations involve athlete eligibility—either establishing eligibility standards or applying the standards in individual cases. Prior to the widespread agreement to submit to the CAS, conflicts arose between the decisions of international governing bodies and interpretation of the same evidence by national courts.

REYNOLDS V. INTERNATIONAL AMATEUR ATHLETIC FEDERATION
841 F. Supp. 1444 (S.D. Ohio 1992)

KINNEARY, DISTRICT JUDGE.

[Harold "Butch" Reynolds was the world track and field record holder at 400 meters who had won the silver medal at the 1988 Olympic Games in Seoul, South Korea. Following the "Herculis Meet" event in Monte Carlo, Monaco, on August 12, 1990, Reynolds was randomly selected to provide a urine sample. In October 1990, Reynolds was informed that he had tested positively for the anabolic steroid nandrolone, and was suspended by the IAAF (now called World Athletics) for two years, which would have cost him a spot in the 1992 Olympic Games in Barcelona, Spain.

Reynolds brought suit in federal court in his home state of Ohio, arguing that the test results were erroneous—based in part on the fact that a urine sample from an August 19 track meet in Berlin one week after the Monte Carlo meet had tested negative. The district judge dismissed this initial suit on the ground that Reynolds first had to use the athletic system's administrative process. Reynolds thus sought an arbitration hearing pursuant to the Amateur Sports Act of 1978 and the constitution of the U.S. Olympic Committee (USOC). Following a hearing in June 1991, the arbitrator issued an opinion that exonerated Reynolds.

> The arbitrator finds that the Respondent's suspension of Mr. Reynolds was improper; that there is clear and convincing evidence that the "A" sample and the "B" sample did not emanate from the same person and the "B" sample did not confirm the "A" sample; that there is substantial evidence that neither the "A" sample or the "B" sample emanated from the Claimant; and that

Claimant should be declared eligible to compete in the qualifying rounds for the World Game Championships on June 12, 1991.

Both TAC and the IAAF refused to accept this ruling because it had not complied with the adjudicative procedures under IAAF Rule 59, which were initially administered by the domestic track and field body (in the U.S., this was TAC). Reynolds thus asked TAC to conduct a hearing, which took place that September. After 12 hours of testimony and arguments and two weeks of deliberation, the three person TAC panel also exonerated Reynolds. They wrote:

> The panel, after hearing the matters before it, the testimony of witnesses and expert witnesses from both sides, documents and exhibits, hereby finds that Mr. Harry "Butch" Reynolds has cast substantial doubt on the validity of the drug test attributed to him. The panel finds that the "B" sample positive result reported by the Lafarge Laboratory has been impeached by clear and convincing evidence.

This time, the IAAF refused to accept the TAC verdict and, under its Rule 20, ordered yet another arbitration of this dispute. In a two-day hearing in London, England, on May 11–12, 1992, counsel for TAC and the IAAF presented their respective positions; after just two hours of deliberations, the three-member panel issued a seven-page decision that found "no doubt" about Reynolds' guilt.

With the Olympic trials to select members of the U.S. track and field team for the Games in Barcelona scheduled just two weeks later, Reynolds went back to court in Ohio, suing the IAAF for breach of contract, defamation, tortious interference with a business relationship, and denial of contractual due process. The IAAF refused to participate in these proceedings, contending that an American court had no jurisdiction over its international regime. This time, the district judge found that Reynolds' claim satisfied Ohio's "long-arm" statutory jurisdiction, which covered nonresident defendants who "transact any business in the state," or who "cause tortious injury" to someone in the state even by out-of-state actions, as long as the defendant regularly engages in business in the state. This finding raised the more fundamental question of whether such a state jurisdictional rule complied with the Due Process standard in the U.S. Constitution, one that requires out-of-state defendants to have sufficient minimum contact with the state such "that the maintenance of the suit does not offend 'traditional notions of fair play and substantial justice.'" *International Shoe Co. v. Washington*, 326 U.S. 310, 316 (1945).]

* * *

I.   Personal Jurisdiction of This Court Over the IAAF

The Court believes that it may constitutionally exercise personal jurisdiction over the IAAF. Initially, the Court must sharply reject the

IAAF and TAC's position that the IAAF is not subject to the jurisdiction of *any* court *anywhere* in the world. At the hearing, TAC's counsel expressed the view that the IAAF is "infallible" and its decisions must not be reviewable by this Court—or any other. Indeed, IAAF vice president Arne Ljungqvist has been quoted as stating:

> Civil courts create a lot of problems for our anti-doping work, but we have said we don't care in the least what they say. We have our rules, and they are supreme....

... It is simply an unacceptable position that the courts of this country cannot protect the individual rights of United States citizens where those rights are threatened by an association which has significant contacts with this country, which exercises significant control over both athletes and athletic events in this country, which acts through an agent organization in this country,[6] and which gains significant revenue from its contracts with United States companies.

Regarding the inquiry which this Court must make ..., it is manifest that the IAAF has purposefully availed itself of the privilege of acting in Ohio, and has caused direct consequences to the Plaintiff in Ohio. This Court has previously listed in detail the facts supporting this conclusion and they will not be recounted here. Suffice it to say, as a general matter, Ohio athletes are subject to the Rules of the IAAF, the IAAF gains substantial revenue from the activities of these athletes, and the IAAF has recognized a track and field event to be held in Ohio. With respect to Mr. Reynolds specifically, the IAAF has contributed expense money so that Mr. Reynolds could compete in two events recognized by the IAAF, has published arguably defamatory statements which were circulated in Ohio publications, and has committed acts which may be found to have tortiously interfered with Mr. Reynolds' business relationships with both United States and Ohio companies.

Furthermore, this Court believes that as the IAAF acts through its member organizations, it is reasonable to subject the IAAF to jurisdiction anywhere its member organizations may be subject to suit. The evidence before the Court establishes that the IAAF distributes money to athletes through its member organizations, notifies athletes of positive drug test results through its member organizations, and provides adjudication of disputed drug test results in the first instance through its member organizations. Essentially, the IAAF refuses to have any contact with individual athletes, instead forcing such athletes to approach the IAAF

---

6   The Court finds untenable what is apparently the tactic of the IAAF to insulate itself from the jurisdiction of any court: despite the incredible power and influence which it directly wields over track and field athletics in the United States and throughout the world, the IAAF continually maintains that it has no direct contact with any country or athlete, and that it only acts or has any outside contact through its member organizations, such as TAC. While that may be true, it must then be conceded that TAC is an agent of the IAAF and personal jurisdiction may be found to exist through TAC's contacts with this forum.

through the national organizations. Thus, this Court holds, as the Tenth Circuit held in *Behagen v. Amateur Basketball Ass'n*, [744 F.2d 731 (10th Cir. 1984)], that an international organization which acts through its members may be subject to the jurisdiction of a particular court based upon a member's contacts with, and activity in, the forum. Where, as here, the member organization has intervened as a Defendant in the action, the exercise of personal jurisdiction is beyond question.

* * *

In accordance with all of the foregoing . . . , this Court holds that the IAAF's failure to enter a timely objection to personal jurisdiction, which failure resulted in the inability of the Plaintiff to obtain the necessary discovery to establish the facts upon which he asserts the jurisdiction of this Court rests, results in the waiver of the IAAF's right to contest the personal jurisdiction of this Court. . . .

II.   The Preliminary Injunction

* * *

The issue of greatest import to this Court, to the parties, and to *amicus*, is the threat of the IAAF to "contaminate," or in other words, suspend any athlete who competes against Mr. Reynolds knowing that he is currently deemed ineligible to participate in IAAF track and field events. The Court not only finds the threat unconvincing, it finds it to be an inappropriate consideration to weigh against the harm which will befall Mr. Reynolds if he is wrongfully prevented from participating in track and field competitions due to his IAAF Ineligibility status.

The IAAF's threat is unconvincing for several reasons. First, it is not at all clear that IAAF's contamination rule is mandatory in nature. Indeed, documents and testimony adduced at the preliminary injunction hearing cast considerable doubt upon this proposition, and lead this Court to conclude that it is not always strictly enforced. Furthermore, it is equally unclear that the IAAF would attempt to prevent United States track and field athletes uninvolved in this litigation from participating in the Olympics on the basis of Rule 53(ii) alone. The loss of some of the event's top competitors, the resulting public outcry, and the possible loss of substantial revenue to the IAAF, all lead this Court to conclude that widespread "contamination" of American athletes by the IAAF is unlikely.

Even if, however, this Court considered such contamination to be the likely result if an injunction were to issue, the Court finds such a threat *by the Defendant IAAF* to be an entirely inappropriate consideration. It is, of course, axiomatic that in considering the merits of a preliminary injunction, the Court must consider whether the injunction will harm others. However, it is the impassioned conviction of the Court that such harm to others does not, and indeed, should not, include harm to others *caused by the voluntary and intentional acts of the Defendant*. To hold otherwise would be to allow the IAAF to hold the entire American Olympic team against an unfavorable decision from this Court. . . .

This Court also believes that Reynolds has established a likelihood of success on the merits of his claims. With respect to the validity of the drug test performed at the Lafarge Laboratory on the urine sample provided by Reynolds in Monte Carlo, this Court believes—as did the American Arbitration Association arbitrator and the TAC hearing panel—that Reynolds has created a substantial doubt as to the accuracy of the reported results. Not only did Reynolds' expert testify as to numerous deficiencies in the Lafarge Laboratories' testing procedure,[9] he also testified as to several inconsistencies with the actual test results which make it highly unlikely that both samples actually originated with Mr. Reynolds.[10] Finally, and perhaps most egregious of all, Plaintiff's expert testified that nandrolone is known to remain in an individual's body for a considerable period of time, and the fact that Reynolds' urine allegedly tested positive for two metabolites of nandrolone on August 12, 1990, and tested negative for nandrolone one week later on August 19, 1990, casts considerable doubt on the validity of the August 12 test.

With respect to the claims in Reynolds Complaint, the Court finds it likely that they are meritorious. First, it appears likely that a contractual relationship exists between the Plaintiff and both the IAAF and TAC, and it further appears that the IAAF breached this contract when it departed from its own guidelines and regulations regarding appropriate drug testing procedures. Second, it appears likely that the IAAF—with disregard for its own policy of confidentiality—maliciously released to the world media information that Reynolds had tested positive for the steroid nandrolone *before* Reynolds was accorded a hearing before TAC as prescribed by IAAF rules. It is reasonable to infer that the IAAF knew that such information would cause third parties to void existing endorsement contracts and prevent others from entering into such contracts. As such, Reynolds is likely to succeed on his claim of defamation and tortious interference with a business relationship.

* * *

Injunction granted.

————

[9]   For instance, Plaintiff's expert testified that the laboratory failed to attach proper chain of custody documentation to the urine samples provided by Reynolds, failed to use an "internal standard" to assist it in interpreting the results, and failed to use a positive quality control.

[10]   Plaintiff's expert testified that the "picture" of naturally occurring steroids should be relatively the same for both samples of urine if, as alleged, they were both supplied by Reynolds. He concluded, however, that because the naturally occurring steroids in the two samples created extremely different "pictures," the two could not have originated with the same individual.

NOTES AND QUESTIONS

1. *Aftermath*. The court in *Reynolds* enjoined the IAAF and TAC "from interfering, impeding, threatening to impede or interfere in any way [with] the Plaintiff's ability to compete in all international and national amateur track and field competitions. . ." TAC allowed Reynolds to run in the 400-meter race at the Olympic trials in New Orleans, at which Reynolds qualified only as an alternate on the 4x400 meter relay team. But the USOC refused to grant Reynolds credentials to travel with the U.S. Olympic team to Barcelona, based on the IAAF's refusal to allow him to compete. After the Olympics, the IAAF announced that because of Reynolds' legal challenge, it was extending his suspension from August 1992 through the end of that year. In December 1992, Judge Kinneary, finding that the IAAF had "purposefully avoided the truth," entered a default damages award of $27.3 million (approximately $7 million in compensatory damages and $20 million in punitive damages), and made his earlier injunction permanent.

2. *Enforcement of $27 Million Judgment*. Reynolds had the practical problem of how to enforce his $27 million judgment. He began garnishment proceedings against four American corporations (including Coca-Cola) that owed the IAAF money for sponsorship deals. The IAAF argued that the Ohio federal courts lacked personal jurisdiction. In finding for the IAAF on appeal, the Sixth Circuit explained:

> In short, the IAAF is based in England, owns no property and transacts no business in Ohio, and does not supervise U.S. athletes in Ohio or elsewhere. Its contacts with Reynolds in Ohio are superficial, and are insufficient to create the requisite minimum contacts for personal jurisdiction.

Reynolds v. IAAF, 23 F.3d 1110 (6th Cir. 1994).

3. *Minimum Contacts?* The Sixth Circuit did not hold that an international governing federation would never be subject to the personal jurisdiction of any American court; it held only that, on the facts of this case, the IAAF was not subject to the jurisdiction of the Ohio courts. Under what circumstances would an international governing body be subject to a state's jurisdiction in cases like *Reynolds*? Consider the following scenarios:

    a. Reynolds sues the World Athletics in Georgia, where World Athletics (the new name for IAAF), the USOPC, and other federations were engaged in extensive preparation for the 1996 Atlanta Olympics.

    b. Reynolds sues the World Athletics in Indiana, where TAC's (now USAT&F's) headquarters and offices are located.

    c. Reynolds sues the World Athletics in New York, where several corporations that sponsor World Athletics events, and TV networks that purchase television rights to World Athletics events, are headquartered? Would it matter if the contracts with these entities were negotiated or signed in New York?

    d.   Reynolds sues the World Athletics in California, where World Athletics has sanctioned track meets and held its own World Track & Field Championships in the recent past.

    e.   Reynolds sues World Athletics in Ohio, but the meet at which he was alleged to have tested positive occurred in Texas, and the laboratory at which the sample was tested was located in Louisiana. What if the meet or the laboratory were in Ohio?

    4.   *Nationalism Versus Deference to International Institutions.* Should courts in the United States—or in any country—review and overturn the decisions of an international sports governing body? If so, under what standard of review and on what grounds? World Athletics contends that if the courts of every nation could overturn its decisions, the Federation could not govern effectively because national political interests would influence many courts to overturn any World Athletics decision contrary to the interests of their country's athletes. Therefore, World Athletics does not recognize the jurisdiction of any court, anywhere.

LINDLAND V. UNITED STATES WRESTLING ASSOCIATION
227 F.3d 1000 (7th Cir. 2000)

EASTERBROOK, CIRCUIT JUDGE.

    Readers of our prior opinions (or the sports pages) know that Keith Sieracki and Matt Lindland both believe that they are entitled to be the U.S. entrant in the 76 kilogram weight class of Greco-Roman wrestling at the 2000 Olympic Games. They have met twice in championship bouts where the Olympic spot was the victor's reward: Sieracki won the first by a score of 2–1; Lindland won the second by a score of 8–0. Each claims that his victory entitles him to the slot in Sydney. Lindland protested the result of the first match through the hierarchy of USA Wrestling, the national governing body for amateur wrestling. After USA Wrestling rejected his protests, Lindland commenced arbitration, which was his right under the Ted Stevens Olympic and Amateur Sports Act. *See* 36 U.S.C. § 220529(a). Arbitrator Burns ordered the rematch, which Lindland won. USA Wrestling was unwilling to accept this outcome; instead of sending Lindland's name to the United States Olympic Committee (USOC) as its nominee for the Games, it told the USOC to send Sieracki and listed Lindland only as a person eligible to compete in the event of injury. Lindland then sought confirmation of the Burns Award under § 9 of the Federal Arbitration Act, 9 U.S.C. § 9, and in an opinion issued on August 24 we held that Lindland is entitled to that relief-which, we pointedly added, means that he is entitled to be USA Wrestling's nominee to the USOC. *Lindland v. USA Wrestling Association, Inc.,* 230 F.3d 1036 (7th Cir. 2000).

    Later that day, USA Wrestling informed the USOC that Sieracki remained its nominee. Its explanation for this defiance was that a second arbitrator, in a proceeding initiated by Sieracki, had disagreed with Arbitrator Burns and directed USA Wrestling to make Sieracki its nominee on the basis of his victory in the first match. USA Wrestling had no excuse for following Arbitrator Campbell's unreviewed award rather than a decision of a federal court confirming Arbitrator Burns's award, and on August 25 we issued a writ of mandamus requiring the district court to ensure that USA Wrestling implemented the Burns Award "immediately and unconditionally." *Lindland v. US Wrestling Association, Inc.*, 228 F.3d 782 at 783 (7th Cir. 2000), On August 26 USA Wrestling finally complied, but the USOC then refused to accept Lindland as a member of the team, asserting that USA Wrestling's nomination of Lindland was untimely because Sieracki's name already had been sent to the International Olympic Committee (IOC) in Lausanne, Switzerland.

Lindland then returned to the district court, asking it to compel the USOC to send his name to the IOC. Sieracki fought back by asking a different district court (in Denver, Colorado) to confirm the Campbell Award. The district judge in Denver sensibly transferred that request to the Northern District of Illinois under 28 U.S.C. § 1404, consolidating all proceedings arising out of the dispute. The Northern District ordered the USOC to request the IOC to substitute Lindland for Sieracki. The USOC has done so, and the IOC has made the substitution. The Northern District also denied Sieracki's petition to confirm the Campbell Award. Two appeals ensued. We expedited the briefing and affirmed both decisions on September 1, promising that this opinion would follow with an explanation.

Although Lindland now is a member of the U.S. team, and the IOC's deadline for making changes has expired, the dispute is not moot. The Games begin at 4 A.M. on September 15 (Chicago time), and the 76 kilogram classification in Greco-Roman Wrestling does not get underway until September 24. The IOC accepted a substitution of Lindland for Sieracki after its deadline, remarking that it was willing to make the change because the USOC acted under judicial order. This implies that if we now confirmed the Campbell Award (including its provision annulling the Burns Award) and directed the USOC to substitute Sieracki for Lindland, the IOC would accept that change as well. We therefore address the merits-starting with what is logically the first issue, whether to confirm the Campbell Award.

Lindland had argued to Arbitrator Burns that USA Wrestling's grievance proceedings were flawed. Arbitrator Burns agreed and ordered the rematch as a remedy in lieu of directing USA Wrestling to reconsider Lindland's protest to the judging of his match with Sieracki. Arbitrator Campbell went over the same ground, disagreed with Arbitrator Burns about the adequacy of USA Wrestling's processes and adding that in his view the result of the first match (which everyone calls "Bout # 244") had not been affected by any errors in applying the scoring rules for Greco-

Roman Wrestling. It is not a surprising view for Arbitrator Campbell to have taken, because the proceedings began amicably. Sieracki initiated the arbitration to defend his initial victory, and USA Wrestling, the respondent, likewise defended both the scoring of the match and the conduct of its internal appeals. (Lindland intervened to defend the Burns Award, but, having already won the rematch, was more interested in preserving that victory than in litigating from scratch.) What is surprising was that Arbitrator Campbell not only approved the result of the original Bout # 244 and the adequacy of USA Wrestling's grievance procedures but also directed it to ignore the result of the rematch-that is, Arbitrator Campbell directed USA Wrestling not to implement the Burns Award.

Sieracki argues that the Campbell Award is no less confirmable under the standards of the Federal Arbitration Act than was the Burns Award, *see* 9 U.S.C. § 10, and if he is entitled to confirmation of the Campbell Award then we should set aside the confirmation of the Burns Award (because relief from the Burns Award is part of the Campbell Award). Certainly there is no evidence that the Campbell Award is the result of "corruption," "fraud," "evident partiality," or any similar bar to confirmation. The district court refused to enforce the Campbell Award because the Burns Award had been enforced already, and it read *Consolidation Coal Co. v. United Mine Workers*, 213 F.3d 404 (7th Cir. 2000), as precluding enforcement of incompatible awards. Only one of these athletes can be on the Olympic Team, and the district judge thought that federal courts should not order the USOC to send both. Sieracki replies that arbitrators need not follow judicial notions of preclusion-a good point about arbitrators, *see Brotherhood of Maintenance of Way Employees v. Burlington Northern R.R.*, 24 F.3d 937 (7th Cir. 1994), but not about judges. Once the Burns Award was confirmed, it was no longer simply the view of a fellow arbitrator with which Campbell could disagree. But this may not be a complete answer. If the Campbell Award is understood to vacate the Burns Award, then confirmation of the Campbell Award logically entails vacating the prior confirmation of the Burns Award. That step would not leave USA Wrestling under conflicting judicial instructions. (Nor is it clear that conflict is an irremediable evil. Injunctions create property rights, which may be altered by private agreements. Bargaining among Sieracki, Lindland, and USA Wrestling could lead to a settlement that would relieve USA Wrestling of any incompatible obligations. *See* Guido Calabresi & A. Douglas Melamed, *Property Rules, Liability Rules, and Inalienability: One View of the Cathedral*, 85 Harv. L. Rev. 1088 (1972).)

Definitive resolution of the right way to handle conflicting awards, after one has been confirmed, may await another day. The Campbell Award could not be confirmed even if it were the sole award. It is doubly flawed: first, the entire proceeding appears to have been ultra vires; second, the award violates the Commercial Rules of the American Arbitration

Association, under which the proceeding was conducted. 36 U.S.C. § 220529(b)(2). Because Arbitrator Campbell exceeded his powers, his award cannot be confirmed. 9 U.S.C. § 10(a)(4).

Sieracki initiated an arbitration not to contest a final decision by USA Wrestling but to protest the Burns Award. Sieracki filed his demand for arbitration on August 11, two days after the Burns Award and three days before his rematch with Lindland (and thus before any issues associated with that bout could have arisen). The Stevens Act does not authorize arbitration about the propriety of another arbitrator's decision. Section 220529(a) provides:

> A party aggrieved by a determination of the corporation under section 220527 or 220528 of this title may obtain review by any regional office of the American Arbitration Association.

What is arbitrable is "a determination of the corporation under section 220527 or 220528 of this title". Arbitrator Burns is not "the corporation" (a term defined in § 220501 as the USOC, though some of its powers have been delegated to national governing bodies such as USA Wrestling); what is more, neither he nor USA Wrestling (in implementing the Burns Award to the extent of scheduling the rematch) rendered "a determination under section 220527 or 220528 of this title". Section 220528 deals with applications to replace national governing bodies. Section 220527 specifies remedies that athletes have within national governing bodies such as USA Wrestling. Lindland exhausted his remedies within USA Wrestling and obtained "a determination of the corporation under section 220527 of this title", and thus was entitled to arbitrate his grievance. Sieracki, by contrast, did not initiate any proceedings within the scope of § 220527. Although § 220527(b)(1) allows athletes to forego exhaustion when time is too short to allow decision, it does not allow bypass of a claim under § 220527—that is, a contention that a national governing body has failed "to comply with sections 220522, 220524, and 220525 of this title". 36 U.S.C. § 220527(a). Sieracki did not have such a claim and therefore was not entitled to arbitration under the Stevens Act even if it was proper to pretermit administrative remedies. No other provision of which we are aware supports arbitration whose sole subject is the decision of a prior arbitrator. The Stevens Act would be self-destructive if it authorized such proceedings, which would lead to enduring turmoil (as happened here) and defeat the statute's function of facilitating final resolution of disputes, *see* § 220529(d).

Even if the second arbitration had been authorized, however, the outcome would have been forbidden by the rules under which it was conducted. Rule 48 of the AAA's Commercial Rules provides that an "arbitrator is not empowered to redetermine the merits of any claim already decided." Sieracki stresses, as our opinion of August 24 acknowledged, that judicial ideas about issue and claim preclusion need not apply in arbitration. But arbitrators assuredly are bound by the contracts and other rules that give them power to act. An arbitrator who throws aside those rules and implements his "own brand of industrial justice" oversteps his powers, and the resulting award must be set aside. *Steelworkers v. Enterprise Wheel & Car Corp.*, 363 U.S. 593, 597 (1960); *Paperworkers v. Misco, Inc.*, 484 U.S. 29, 36 (1987). What the Steelworkers Trilogy declared about "industrial justice" is equally true of commercial or athletic justice. Arbitrators are not ombudsmen; they are authorized to resolve disputes under contracts and rules, not to declare how the world should work in the large. Arbitrator Campbell did not misinterpret Rule 48; he decided to ignore it utterly. The whole point of the Campbell proceeding was to redecide the issues that had been before Arbitrator Burns, and the Campbell Award directs USA Wrestling to disregard the Burns Award. Campbell observed, correctly, that Sieracki was not a party to the Burns proceedings, but the other participants in the proceedings before Arbitrator Campbell were parties to the Burns proceedings. By the time Campbell acted, the Burns Award had "already decided" that the nomination to the Olympic team would depend on a rematch between Sieracki and Lindland. Whatever powers Campbell possessed via-à-vis Sieracki, he lacked the power to order USA Wrestling to nominate anyone other than the winner of the rematch. The Campbell Award therefore is not entitled to confirmation.

This conclusion makes it unnecessary to decide whether, by participating in the Campbell proceedings, Lindland waived or forfeited his entitlement to the benefits of the Burns Award. The Campbell Award is invalid, so it does not bind Lindland or anyone else. But we shall not conceal our doubt about this argument. The "waiver" to which Sieracki and USA Wrestling point is simply Lindland's assent to the terms of participation in the Olympic Games, one of which is submitting to final and binding arbitration of disputes. How such a document can surrender the final and binding effect of the Burns Award is a mystery. When Sieracki and USA Wrestling entered into their friendly arbitration in an effort to escape from the unwelcome Burns Award, Lindland was in a tough spot. It would not be sensible to say that he waived the benefits of an award already in hand by trying to persuade Arbitrator Campbell to follow his duties under AAA Rule 48 or by attempting to persuade Campbell that Burns acted wisely (and thus to avert the problems that have ensued from Campbell's contrary decision). Nor is it sensible to say, as Sieracki does, that Lindland won a race to the courthouse. The Campbell Award is invalid, so timing is immaterial. Lindland is entitled to USA Wrestling's nomination because (a) Arbitrator Burns ordered USA Wrestling to hold a rematch, and (b) Lindland won that rematch. If Sieracki had prevailed in the rematch, he would be on the Olympic Team today. Athletic disputes should be settled on the playing field-as the Burns Award provided.

* * *

Lindland and USA Wrestling were the only parties to the Burns proceedings. All the Burns Award (coupled with Lindland's victory in the rematch of Bout #244) requires is that USA Wrestling send Lindland's name to the USOC as USA Wrestling's nominee for the team. By the time USA Wrestling finally complied with the Burns Award—11 days after Lindland won the rematch, and 2 days after we enforced the Burns Award—the deadline for making nominations had passed, and the USOC declared that it would send Sieracki to Sydney. The district court's injunction, the IOC's acceptance of Lindland, and the USOC's appeal followed.

Most of the USOC's submission on appeal misunderstands the basis of the injunction. Consider, for example, the USOC's lengthy argument, based on *Michels v. United States Olympic Committee*, 741 F.2d 155 (7th Cir. 1984) (which interpreted the predecessor to § 220527), that there is no private right of action to enforce the Stevens Act. That may or may not be so under the current version of the statute; we need not decide, because Lindland did not file suit to enforce the Stevens Act. He sued to enforce the Burns Award, and the Federal Arbitration Act provides the necessary private right of action. The dispositive question is whether the order (and eventually the injunction) entered against USA Wrestling binds the USOC too. This depends on Fed.R.Civ.P. 65(d):

> Every order granting an injunction and every restraining order ... is binding only upon the parties to the action, their officers, agents, servants, employees, and attorneys, and upon those persons in active concert or participation with them who receive actual notice of the order by personal service or otherwise.

The USOC, as a party to the proceedings to enforce the Burns Award, received actual notice of our decision on August 24 requiring USA Wrestling to nominate Lindland forthwith. USA Wrestling tarried, but the USOC knew what USA Wrestling was required to do and easily could have taken our decision as equivalent to a formal nomination by USA Wrestling on August 24—when it would have been timely under the USOC's rules. The district court's injunction requires the USOC to do what it should and would have done had USA Wrestling timely complied with the decision of August 24. This order is proper if the USOC is a person "in active concert or participation with" USA Wrestling.

Briefing the "active concert or participation" issue at our instructions, the USOC contends that it is an independent organization, entitled to make the final decision. No one doubts this, but the "active concert or participation" clause supposes legal distinctiveness; if USA Wrestling and the USOC were the same party, the order would be binding directly. The "active concert or participation" clause is designed to prevent what may well have happened here: the addressee of an injunction, eager to avoid its obligations, persuades a friendly third party to take steps that frustrate the injunction's effectiveness. *See Reich v. Sea Sprite Boat Co.*, 50 F.3d 413

(7th Cir. 1995). The USOC has given every indication of willingness to lend a hand. For example, it responded to the initiation of the Campbell proceedings by promising to respect their outcome-which entails a promise to ignore the outcome of the Burns proceedings. The events of August 24 also imply that USA Wrestling and the USOC acted in concert. On the evening of August 24 USA Wrestling sent the USOC one document "notifying" it of this court's decision and a second document nominating Sieracki. The USOC decided to accept the nomination of Sieracki, knowing full well that this nomination violated a decision of this court. The inference that USA Wrestling and the USOC undertook a joint effort to defeat the Burns Award (and our decision) is very strong.

That inference could be overcome by a demonstration that the USOC had an independent ground of decision. No one doubts that the USOC may adopt its own criteria and make its own selections. 36 U.S.C. § 220505(c). Thus if, for example, Lindland failed a drug test, or if his behavior at past international competitions had brought shame on the team (as the U.S. Olympic hockey team did en masse in 1998), then the USOC could have sent Sieracki to the Games. Similarly, if the USOC regularly made its own judgments about athletic prowess, then a determination that Sieracki is the wrestler most likely to succeed in Sydney would be respected by the federal judiciary. Yet in response to a question posed by this court (and a similar one posed by the district court), the USOC failed to identify even a single instance in which it has not forwarded to the IOC the nomination of a national governing body such as USA Wrestling. Its promise to send whichever athlete Arbitrator Campbell selected abjures any independent role; indeed, that promise is the best evidence that USA Wrestling and the USOC have acted jointly to implement the Campbell Award despite judicial enforcement of the Burns Award.

When on August 15 it originally sent to the IOC the full list of USA Wrestling's nominees (a list that included Sieracki despite Lindland's victory on August 14), the USOC did not make an independent decision about their athletic skills; instead the certification says that the list (and the USOC's approval) is "based on the selection criteria devised and previously approved by the USOC" and in particular that "[t]he selection of the NGB athlete nominations were [sic] conducted in our estimation according to the policies and procedures approved by the USOC for the 2000 Olympic Summer Games." In other words, the USOC investigated only to ensure that USA Wrestling followed the rules for selecting its nominees. One of these rules (quoted in our August 24 opinion) specifies that the winner of Bout # 244 would be USA Wrestling's nominee in the 76 kilogram classification. Lindland is the winner of Bout # 244 and the recipient of USA Wrestling's (belated) nomination. Under the USOC's own rules, therefore, Lindland is entitled to the position on the Olympic Team. This makes it very hard to understand the USOC's position as anything other than a continuation of the view disparaged in our August 24 opinion:

a belief by the USOC that athletes who pursue their rights under the Stevens Act should be penalized. The district court was entitled to prevent the USOC from carrying out that view under the pretext that USA Wrestling's nomination of Lindland arrived too late.

Nonetheless, the USOC insists, it is entitled to do as it pleases-defying injunctions to its heart's content-if it manages to stall until only three weeks remain before the Games.   For this proposition it relies on another part of the Stevens Act, 36 U.S.C. § 220509(a):

> The corporation shall establish and maintain provisions in its constitution and bylaws for the swift and equitable resolution of disputes involving any of its members and relating to the opportunity of an amateur athlete, coach, trainer, manager, administrator, or official to participate in the Olympic Games, the Paralympic Games, the Pan-American Games, world championship competition, or other protected competition as defined in the constitution and bylaws of the corporation. In any lawsuit relating to the resolution of a dispute involving the opportunity of an amateur athlete to participate in the Olympic Games, the Paralympic Games, or the Pan-American Games, a court shall not grant injunctive relief against the corporation within 21 days before the beginning of such games if the corporation, after consultation with the chair of the Athletes' Advisory Council, has provided a sworn statement in writing executed by an officer of the corporation to such court that its constitution and bylaws cannot provide for the resolution of such dispute prior to the beginning of such games.

Saturday, August 26, was the 21st day before the "beginning" of the Sydney Olympics. The USOC filed in the district court an affidavit parroting the statutory terms and insists that, as a result, the district court was powerless to enforce the Burns Award.

Section 220509(a) is designed to prevent a court from usurping the USOC's powers when time is too short for its own dispute-resolution machinery to do its work. The premise of the USOC's argument is that the dispute among Lindland, Sieracki, and USA Wrestling is one to be resolved by the USOC's internal processes, which can't be done at this late date. This is just another variation of the USOC's misunderstanding about the genesis of the district court's order. Lindland has not asserted a private right of action to enforce the Stevens Act, nor has he attempted to initiate a new dispute-resolution process before the USOC. His claim depends on the Burns Award, which was issued on August 9, well outside the 21-day window, and the decision of this court, also issued before the 21st day. The only question on the table is whether USA Wrestling and the USOC will comply with obligations that had been established before that three-week period. The USOC's liability stems from its obligation as an entity "in active concert or participation with" USA Wrestling to avoid frustrating the order enforcing the Burns Award.

We do not for one second believe that Congress set out to reward intransigence, so that the USOC can protect scofflaws among the national governing bodies, or itself defy judicial orders if, on the 21st day before the Olympic torch enters the stadium, the President of the USOC is not already in prison for contempt. There is no dispute for the USOC to resolve, so its inability under its constitution and bylaws to act on short notice is not important. All the USOC had to do was implement this court's decision of August 24 (enforcing the Burns Award of August 9); all we hold is that delay in compliance with an obligation judicially articulated before the 21st day does not entitle the USOC to escape that obligation. To put this in the statutory language, the prohibition applies only if "such dispute"-that is, a dispute to be handled under the USOC's procedures-can't be resolved in the time remaining before the games. When no "such dispute" survives into the three-week period (because it had been resolved earlier), § 220509(a) does not preclude enforcement of the outstanding decision.

* * *

Affirmed.

NOTES AND QUESTIONS

1. *Aftermath.* Lindland won the silver medal at the summer 2000 Olympics in Sydney, and followed it up with a silver medal in the 2001 World Championships. Nicknamed "The Law," Lindland became the coach of the U.S. Olympic Greco-Roman Wrestling team in 2014.

2. *Which Award?* Was the court correct in adopting the Burns report and rejecting the Campbell report? Does it matter that Sieracki was not present at the Burns hearing? Why or why not?

3. *Lindland or Sieracki.* If you were choosing which wrestler should represent the U.S. team, which one would you pick? Why?

D. THE PECHSTEIN SAGA

As with other areas of international law, international sports law can create enforcement issues. The CAS provides a tribunal under which enforcement is possible. But is international enforcement preferable? Or should national courts have a say? The *Pechstein* case explores these questions.

Claudia Pechstein, a very successful German speed skater, competed in the World Championships in Hamar, Norway on February 7–8, 2009. In order to compete, Pechstein signed the form of the International Skating

Union (ISU) which required her to comply with the ISU's anti-doping regulations and included an arbitration agreement giving CAS jurisdiction over any dispute arising out the regulations.

During the World Championships in Hamar, blood samples were taken from the Plaintiff; these samples showed elevated reticulocyte counts. ISU interpreted the samples as evidence of doping and decided to ban Pechstein for two years (including the 2010 Olympics) and annul her results at the Championships. The German National Association for Skating subsequently banned Pechstein from training with the team.

Pechstein appealed to CAS, which upheld the ISU's determination, and the appealed to the Swiss federal tribunal, which also upheld the suspension.

Pechstein then challenged the CAS decision in the German courts. She argued that the German courts had jurisdiction over her case, that the arbitration agreement was invalid under German antitrust law, and that her suspension was incorrect on the merits.

The German Court of Appeal found for Pechstein, finding that the arbitration clause violated antitrust law because Pechstein was required to sign it to participate. The Court also found that the CAS did not foreclose lawsuits on the merits challenging eligibility determinations.

The German Federal Court of Justice, its highest court, reversed the decision of the Court of Appeal and reinstated the decision by the CAS. The Court found that the CAS was a "true" court of arbitration in the way that it sets up a neutral and independent arbitration system. It then explained why national courts should not intervene in CAS arbitrations:

> If this task were left to the courts in the individual states, the goal of international sporting arbitration would be jeopardised. No one has succeeded as yet in drawing up a system of rules capable of maintaining international sports arbitration, while, at the same time, completely avoiding the deficiencies in connection with the appointment of independent arbitrators and the proceedings in general that results from the significant influence exercised by the international sports federations and the Olympic Committees. . . .
> The statutes of the CAS, as they currently stand, contain procedural rules for the appointment of arbitrators which can be considered as acceptable.

Because the CAS served to adjudicate doping disputes in a fair and impartial, it did not violate German antitrust law.

Having lost in the German courts, Pechstein subsequently brought suit in the European Court of Human Rights. She alleged that her CAS arbitration violated section 6 § 1 of the European Convention on Human Rights. That section provides:

In the determination of his civil rights and obligations or of any criminal charge against him, everyone is entitled to a fair and public hearing within a reasonable time by an independent and impartial tribunal established by law. Judgment shall be pronounced publicly but the press and public may be excluded from all or part of the trial in the interests of morals, public order or national security in a democratic society, where the interests of juveniles or the protection of the private life of the parties so require, or to the extent strictly necessary in the opinion of the court in special circumstances where publicity would prejudice the interests of justice.

Specifically, Pechstein claimed that she had the right to a trial before an impartial tribunal with a public hearing, and the private CAS arbitration violated that right.

MUTU AND PECHSTEIN V. SWITZERLAND

European Court of Human Rights 2018

[The first issue on the merits was whether Pechstein could waive her right to a court under Article 6 § 1 of the Convention through an arbitration agreement and whether her decision to sign the arbitration agreement was made under duress. Pechstein's co-plaintiff Mutu made similar arguments about the arbitration clause in his Chelsea football contract.]

* * *

92. The Court reiterates that Article 6 § 1 of the Convention secures to everyone the right to have any claim relating to his civil rights and obligations brought before a court or tribunal. . . .

94. This access to a court is not necessarily to be understood as access to a court of law of the classic kind, integrated within the standard judicial machinery of the country; thus, the "tribunal" may be a body set up to determine a limited number of specific issues, provided always that it offers the appropriate guarantees. Article 6 does not therefore preclude the establishment of arbitral tribunals in order to settle certain pecuniary disputes between individuals. . . .

[The Court then distinguished voluntary and compulsory arbitration explaining that greater safeguards with respect to the impartiality of the arbitral tribunal were required in compulsory situations. It found that Pechstein's arbitration agreement was compulsory.]

* * *

150. The second applicant began by arguing that the president of the arbitral panel which decided her case had previously always refused to be appointed as an arbitrator by any athlete accused of doping and had preferred to represent the sports federations. She inferred that this

arbitrator was biased against athletes accused of doping and therefore that he lacked impartiality.

The Court notes that, before the Federal Court, the applicant had used another argument in seeking to demonstrate a lack of impartiality on the part of the president of the arbitral panel. She had argued that, in the past, he had represented the "hard line" in the fight against doping (see paragraph 23 above).

In any event, like the Federal Court, the Court does not see any factual element that could cast doubt on the independence or impartiality of the arbitrator in question. The applicant's allegations are too vague and hypothetical and must therefore be rejected.

151. As regards the financing of the CAS by sports bodies, the Court notes, like the Government, that national courts are always financed by the State budget and yet this fact does not imply that those courts lack independence and impartiality in disputes between litigants and the State. By analogy, the CAS cannot be said to lack independence and impartiality solely on account of its financing arrangements.

152. The Court further notes the applicant's position that the CAS cannot be regarded as an independent and impartial tribunal on account of a structural problem stemming from an imbalance between federations and athletes in the mechanism for appointing arbitrators.

153. The Court would point out that at the relevant time, in accordance with Article S14 of the Code of Arbitration, the list of CAS arbitrators was established by the ICAS and was to be composed as follows: three fifths of arbitrators selected from among the persons proposed by the IOC, Ifs and NOCs, chosen from within their membership or outside; one fifth of arbitrators chosen by the ICAS "after appropriate consultations, with a view to safeguarding the interests of the athletes"; and one fifth of arbitrators chosen, again by the ICAS, from among "persons independent" of the above-mentioned bodies (paragraph 33 above). The ICAS was therefore only required to choose one-fifth of the arbitrators from among persons independent of the sports bodies which could be involved in disputes with athletes before the CAS. The Court further notes that this mechanism of appointment by fifths was abolished in 2012 and replaced by a more general wording (see paragraph 38 above).

154. In addition, the Court notes that even the appointment of one-fifth of arbitrators who were independent of sports bodies was at the discretion of the ICAS. Moreover, the ICAS itself was composed entirely of figures from those bodies (see paragraph 32 above), thus revealing the existence of a certain link between the ICAS and organisations that might be involved in disputes with athletes before the CAS, especially those of a disciplinary nature.

155. Furthermore, first, the arbitrators were appointed for a renewable term of four years, without any limitation on the number of terms of office, and secondly, the ICAS had the power to remove, by a decision with "brief reasons" under Article R35 of the Code of Arbitration, any arbitrator who refused to perform or was prevented from performing his duties, or who failed to fulfil his duties pursuant to that Code.

156. In the present case, the arbitral panel which ruled on the dispute between the second applicant and the ISU was made up of three arbitrators, all chosen from the list drawn up by the ICAS, in accordance with the procedures described above, and subject to the ICAS' power of removal. Even the applicant's ability to appoint the arbitrator of her choosing was limited by the obligation to use this list (see Articles R33, R38 and R39 of the Code of Arbitration), such that the applicant did not have full freedom of choice—whereas such freedom is the rule, for example, in commercial arbitration, under Article 12 of the ICC Rules.

157. That being said, the Court notes that the list of arbitrators drawn up by the ICAS included, at the relevant time, some 300 arbitrators (see paragraph 37 above), yet the applicant did not submit any factual evidence such as to cast any general doubt on the independence and impartiality of these arbitrators. Even with regard to the arbitral panel which ruled on her case, the applicant only actually impugned one arbitrator, namely the president of the panel, without substantiating her allegations (see paragraph 150 above).

While the Court is prepared to acknowledge that the organisations which were likely to be involved in disputes with athletes before the CAS had real influence over the mechanism for appointing arbitrators, as applicable at the relevant time, it cannot conclude that, solely on account of this influence, the list of arbitrators, or even a majority thereof, was composed of arbitrators who could not be regarded as independent and impartial, on an individual basis, whether objectively or subjectively, vis-à-vis those organisations.

In the Court's view, therefore, there are insufficient grounds for it to reject the settled case-law of the Federal Court to the effect that the system of the list of arbitrators meets the constitutional requirements of independence and impartiality applicable to arbitral tribunals, and that the CAS, when operating as an appellate body external to international federations, is similar to a judicial authority independent of the parties (see paragraph 44 above).

* * *

159. Having regard to the foregoing, the Court finds that there has been no violation of Article 6 § 1 of the Convention on account of an alleged lack of independence and impartiality on the part of the CAS.

* * *

[Pechstein then argued that she was entitled to a public hearing under Article 6 § 1].

172. At the outset, the Court would draw attention to its previous finding as to the compulsory nature of the arbitration to which the second applicant was a party.

173. The second applicant submitted that in her case the CAS had held two days of hearings during which many experts had given testimony on complex scientific questions. She argued in this connection that the points made by the experts that she herself had called had been rejected in a non-objective manner and mockingly, and that this would not have been the case if the CAS had allowed the public to attend.

* * *

175. The Court reiterates that the public character of proceedings constitutes a fundamental principle enshrined in Article 6 § 1 of the Convention. It protects litigants against the administration of justice in secret with no public scrutiny and is thus one of the means whereby confidence in the courts can be maintained. By rendering the administration of justice visible, it contributes to the achievement of the aim of Article 6 § 1, namely a fair trial, the guarantee of which is one of the fundamental principles of any democratic society. . .

* * *

182. The Court is of the view that the questions arising in the impugned proceedings—as to whether it was justified for the second applicant to have been penalised for doping, and for the resolution of which the CAS heard testimony from numerous experts—rendered it necessary to hold a hearing under public scrutiny. The Court notes that the facts were disputed and the sanction imposed on the applicant carried a degree of stigma and was likely to adversely affect her professional honour and reputation (see, mutatis mutandis, Grande Stevens and Others v. Italy, nos. 18640/10, 18647/10, 18663/10, 18668/10 and 18698/10, § 122, 4 March 2014). Moreover, in spite of its somewhat formalistic conclusion, the Federal Court itself, in its judgment of 10 February 2010, expressly recognised in an obiter dictum that a public hearing before the CAS would have been desirable.

183. Having regard to the foregoing, the Court finds that there has been a violation of Article 6 § 1 of the Convention on account of the fact that the proceedings before the CAS were not held in public.

* * *

[The Court found that Article 6 § 1 did not require a decision by a Federal Court and that an arbitral panel was sufficient]

IV. APPLICATION OF ARTICLE 41 OF THE CONVENTION

192. Article 41 of the Convention provides:

"If the Court finds that there has been a violation of the Convention or the Protocols thereto, and if the internal law of the High Contracting Party concerned allows only partial reparation to be made, the Court shall, if necessary, afford just satisfaction to the injured party."

A. Damage

193. By way of just satisfaction the second applicant claimed the sum of 3,584,126.09 euros (EUR), plus interest, for pecuniary damage and EUR 400,000 for non-pecuniary damage. For the breakdown of the pecuniary damage claim she referred to her submissions in the civil proceedings against the ISU in the German courts.

* * *

194. The Court fails to see any causal link between the violation found and the pecuniary damage alleged by the second applicant (see Gajtani v. Switzerland, no. 43730/07, § 125, 9 September 2014). There is no evidence to suggest that, if the award had been made by an arbitral tribunal after a public hearing, the findings of that tribunal would have been in favour of the second applicant.

195. As to the claim for non-pecuniary damage, ruling on an equitable basis, the Court awards the second applicant EUR 8,000 for the violation found in respect of her application.

———

NOTES AND QUESTIONS

1. *Aftermath.* Even after the decision of the European Court of Human Rights, Pechstein's case is not over. She had previously challenged the 2016 decision of the Federal Court of Justice by filing a constitutional complaint in the German Federal Constitutional Court. In July 2022, the Federal Constitutional Court held that the Federal Court of Justice had not adequately considered the significance of the right to have public proceedings. The Court thus held that the prior decision of the Federal Court of Justice interfered with Pechstein's constitutional rights. The case has been submitted to the Higher Regional Court of Munich for further evaluation.

It appears that the German Constitutional Court adopted some of the reasoning of the European Court of Human Rights, at least with respect to the right to have one's trial in public. Is this an essential right in your view? Should it be grounds for retrying Pechstein's case in the German courts? Or is the European Court of Human Rights correct in finding that a failure to have a public trial can give rise to money damages but not a new trial?

2.   *Arbitration as Compulsory?* The European Court of Human Rights found the arbitration clause signed by Pechstein to be compulsory, triggering the application of Article 6 § 1. Do you agree? Are arbitrations stemming from collective bargaining agreements different? Why or why not?

3.   *The Right to a Public Hearing.* The Court found that Pechstein's human rights were violated by the private nature of the CAS hearing. Why might a public hearing be important? Could it affect the outcome? The CAS has altered its procedures in response to this decision to allow for the option of a public hearing.

4.   *The Dissent, Part I.* The Court's decision was 5–2. The two dissenting justices questioned whether the CAS is an independent and impartial tribunal. In particular, they found fault with 60% of the pool of CAS arbitrators being appointed by international governing bodies (IFs, IOCs, and NOCs). The ability of these organizations to exercise influence over the selection of arbitrators for a particular case likewise troubled the dissenters. Do you agree with the dissent?

5.   *The Dissent, Part II.* The two dissenting justices questioned whether the CAS is "established by law." In particular, the compulsory nature of the arbitration suggested to the dissent that the arbitral panel was not established by law but an instrument of private Swiss law. The dissenters wanted the majority to provide some criteria required to consider a private entity to be a public tribunal established by law. What might some applicable criteria be?

6.   *Implications of* Pechstein? In 2020, a lower German court in Frankfurt, read the European Court of Human Rights' *Pechstein* decision to mean that compulsory arbitration clauses were invalid. Two beach volleyball players won a $17,000 preliminary judgment against the German volleyball federation because their complaint was handled in arbitration instead of by a court. Do you think this judgment will survive on appeal? Why or why not?

E. THE RUSSIAN DOPING SAGA

In 2014, Russia hosted the Winter Olympics in its city of Sochi, Russia. During the Winter Games, the Russian Olympic team won 33 medals, topping all other countries. This was a surprising result, as Russia more than doubled its medal count from the 2010 Winter Games in Vancouver.

In December 2014, former Russian Anti-Doping Agency (RUSADA) official Vitaly Stepanov and his wife Yuliya, a former middle-distance runner, appeared in a German documentary, in which they alleged that Russia sponsored systematic doping for its athletes. Another Russian athlete said that "99 percent" of Russian Olympians had used performance-enhancing drugs.

In November 2015, an independent commission from WADA accused Russia of running a state-sponsored doping program. The commission's report highlighted the use of shadow laboratories, destruction of urine samples, and surveillance of lab workers by Russian intelligence agents. In the aftermath the international governing body for track and field banned Russia's team from international athletic competitions. This ban remained in effect through 2022.

In May 2016, the International Olympic Committee (IOC) began retesting old samples from Russian athletes dating back to the 2008 Beijing Summer Olympics. The *New York Times* interviewed the former director of the anti-doping lab, Grigory Rodchenkov. Rodchenkov testified to switching out dirty samples for clean ones and claimed that at least 15 medalists from the Sochi Games were part of the state-run doping program.

In August 2016, Russia competed in the Summer Olympic Games in Rio de Janeiro. While the track and field athletes were banned, the rest of the Russian team competed and won 19 medals, finishing fourth in the medal count. The IOC left the decision of whether to allow Russia to participate up to the individual sporting federations and most allowed participation.

In December 2017, the IOC banned Russia from the 2018 Winter Olympics in Pyeongchang. The severity of the ban was an historic and unprecedented. The IOC did allow 168 Russian athletes to compete as "Olympic Athletes from Russia." With the ban, the Russian flag and national anthem were absent from the Games. Also, some of the country's most accomplished winter athletes did not compete.

In September 2018, the WADA executive committee reinstated RUSADA against strong opposition from a number of athletes. This reinstatement was conditioned upon Russia giving officials access to data from the Moscow lab where the samples were doctored. Interestingly, several members of the WADA committee also served as IOC members responsible for staging the upcoming Olympics. Eight months later, WADA said the lab data that Russia provided may have been tampered with and reconsidered the RUSADA reinstatement.

In December 2019, WADA imposed a four-year ban against Russia, including the 2020 Tokyo Summer Olympics and the 2022 Beijing Winter Olympics, and major international competitions through 2023, including FIFA's World Cup, the Youth Olympic Games, and the Paralympics. In 2020, the CAS considered the Russian appeal challenging the appropriateness of the four-year ban.

WADA v. RUSADA
Court of Arbitration of Sport, 2020

[As part of its investigation into systemic Russian doping, WADA alleged non-compliance on the part of RUSADA with respect to a critical requirement of the International Standard for Code Compliance by Signatories (ISCCS). Specifically, WADA alleged that RUSADA failed to provide authentic data from its laboratory and sought to have the CAS issue an award finding non-compliance and imposing continued sanctions on RUSADA.

On the merits, RUSADA challenged the validity of the 2018 WADA code and the ISCCS and argued that neither was binding against it. The CAS rejected that argument because Russia was a signatory to the ISCCS. The panel also found that RUSADA was obligated to comply with the WADA Post-Reinstatement Data requirements after its 2018 suspension.

It found, however, that RUSADA did not comply with requirements. Russia submitted manipulated data designed to incriminate some lab employees and exonerate others. The question then became what the appropriate sanction should be.]

* * *

702. Although this case primarily concerns data manipulation and the non-compliance by RUSADA with the Post-Reinstatement Data Requirement, in accordance with the WADA submission, these must be considered in the context of an attempt to:

1.   cover up evidence of the doping and anti-detection scheme described in early reports;

2.   exculpate the Russian authorities implicated in that scheme;

3.   inculpate the whistle-blowers who exposed it; and

4.   undermine evidence that could be used to prosecute anti-doping cases covered up by the scheme.

703. The forensic and investigative reports show that the data manipulations and deletions affect thousands of athletes' samples, of which 298 cases have been specifically targeted by WADA for further investigation. As a result of the deletions of parts of the Moscow Data, it will never be possible to know the number of cheating athletes or officials who may have escaped detection. . . .

709. The data manipulation is the culmination of a fraudulent scheme that sought to undermine the fundamental tenets of anti-doping regulation and of sporting values. . . .

710. These manipulations show that the Russian authorities remain as willing as ever to interfere with, and corrupt, the anti-doping system. Having done so in the past (in a manner previously considered unthinkable), it is necessary to take robust action to attempt to deter any repetition. . . .

711. The Panel accepts that it is necessary to impose serious consequences not only in the interest of the fight against doping in general, but also specifically in the long-term interest of RUSADA, the protection of Russian athletes, and clean Russian sport. To attempt to ensure that RUSADA can fulfil its role of fighting against doping in Russia, it is

necessary to effect a fundamental change in attitude at the level of public authorities in Russia, who have demonstrated frequently that they are able and willing to interfere with the anti-doping infrastructure and processes and also in respect of those athletes who have been willing to engage in doping. It is necessary to impose meaningful consequences to attempt to ensure the confidence of clean athletes, stakeholders and the wider public in the ability of WADA to defend the integrity of sport against doping. Otherwise, the clear message will be that governments and public authorities can corrupt and manipulate anti-doping programs and that WADA is unable to do anything about it. The Panel accepts that WADA is motivated not by ill will against Russia or Russians, but rather by the desire for an effective and independent Russian anti-doping program, to protect a new generation of Russian athletes and for clean Russian sport.

* * *

719. The Panel bears firmly in mind at all times the paramount need to consider notions of proportionality in the imposition of Signatory Consequences. . . .

725. The Panel also endorses the statements made [in a previous decision regarding proportionality]:

> *The principle of proportionality implies that there must be a reasonable balance between the nature of the misconduct and the sanction. In order to be respected, the principle of proportionality requires that (i) the measure taken by the governing body is capable of achieving the envisaged goal, (ii) the measure taken by the governing body is necessary to reach the envisaged goal, and (iii) the constraints which the affected person will suffer as a consequence of the measure are justified by the overall interest to achieve the envisaged goal. In other words, to be proportionate a measure must not exceed what is reasonably required in the search of the justifiable aim. . . .*

739. WADA has sought to have the Signatory Consequences imposed for a four-year period. However, it noted that the four-year period was only ever intended to cover one edition of each of the summer and winter Olympic/Paralympic Games, which it reflected in its revised prayers for relief in its Reply. . . .

743. However, notwithstanding the Panel's view that:

a. a four-year period is permissible; and

b. having regard to the seriousness of the non-compliance, Signatory Consequences must be imposed for a significant period, the Panel is nonetheless required to consider the appropriate period for which the Signatory Consequences it imposes should have effect.

744. In doing so, the Panel has had regard to:

1.   The *prima facie* periods for noncompliance with critical requirements set out in Articles B.3.1(c) and B.3.1(d)(2) of Annex B to the ISCCS (respectively, one year and until the next edition of the Olympic Games, Paralympic Games and/or any World Championships);

2.   the fact that the imposition of the Signatory Consequences was only ever intended by WADA to cover one edition of each of the summer and winter Olympic and Paralympic Games (as WADA confirmed in its revised prayers for relief);

3.   principles of proportionality, in particular noting that proportionality must be assessed in light of the Signatory Consequences the Panel has decided to impose as a whole.

745. Accordingly, the Panel has decided that an appropriate period for imposition of Signatory Consequences in the present circumstances is two years from the date of this Award.

[The consequence for Russian signatories of the ISCCS included (1) restrictions on representatives of the Russian Federation; (2) restrictions on Russia hosting international events; (3) restrictions on the use of the Russian flag at competitions; restrictions on the Russian Olympic Committee officers and executives; (5) and (7) restrictions on participation and attendance of Russian athletes and support personnel; (6) notice of non-compliance; and (8) a fine of $100,000 per signatory.]

* * *

785. A number of Russian athletes provided statements and gave evidence at the hearing. They were all elite competitors in their chosen field, with unchallenged drug free records, and with ambitions to represent their country for the first or subsequent times at future Olympic Games, Paralympic Games and World Championship events. There was no cross examination of any of the athletes. Much of their evidence was addressed to the potential consequence of their exclusion from events. However, given that they are presumed to be unaffected by any anti-doping violations, and in light of the modified neutrality consequence to be imposed by the Panel, it is only necessary to consider those parts of their evidence which concerns the neutrality criteria. All of the athletes express an understandable desire to compete under their national flag and colours and accompanied by the national anthem at medal ceremonies. They all express, in differing terms, the disappointment that they would feel if they were not able to do so. Many of them express concerns that they may lose

sponsorship or other financial support if they are required to complete as neutral athletes. . . .

791. The Panel finds that it is appropriate to impose a modified and less restrictive version of the NPIC [Neutral Participation Implementation Criteria] to that proposed by WADA. The Panel considers that the conditions under which Russian athletes may participate should allow some limited association with the name (for example, "Neutral Athlete from Russia") and colours of their homeland where necessary, but subject to restrictions as to the use of the Russian flag, national symbols and the Russian national anthem in a sport, recognition or awards capacity. This accommodates a balance between the WADA submission that the purpose of the consequences is that the athlete will not be associated with Russia, and the opposing concern that clean athletes should not be affected by neutrality conditions for any longer than is justified. . . .

810. WADA refers to CAS precedent which establishes that the ECHR [European Convention on Human Rights] does not apply directly to CAS or WADA, but that regard should be had to the ECHR as certain fundamental tenets of it may be considered within the context of any review by the Swiss Federal Tribunal. The Panel is satisfied that the requirement to compete as neutral athletes, in the manner determined by the Panel (which permits use of national colours and the name Russia on a limited basis), does not violate the human dignity or any other right of Russian athletes. . . .

811. With respect to the question of collective punishment, this is primarily a principle of international humanitarian law or criminal law, and there is no specific prohibition on collective punishment in the ECHR. . . . The Panel does, however, accept that Article 8 of the ECHR requires measures to be proportionate. The Signatory Consequences imposed by the Panel meet have been determined having regard to the principle of proportionality.

* * *

858. The saga that has followed the exposure of systemic doping practices in Russian sport, including the matters which are the subject of this arbitration, has considerably damaged the history of Russian and international sport.

859. This Panel has found that, despite having an opportunity to come clean and draw a line under this scandal by providing access to the Moscow Data, Russian authorities engaged in an extensive manipulation of that data. This conduct is likely to thwart or at least substantially hinder the ability to identify those athletes who participated in the doping scheme.

860. Having further found that RUSADA failed to comply with the Post-Reinstatement Data Requirement, this Panel has accordingly imposed consequences to reflect the nature and seriousness of the non-

compliance and to ensure that the integrity of sport against the scourge of doping is maintained.

861. The consequences which the Panel has decided to impose are not as extensive as those sought by WADA. This should not, however, be read as any validation of the conduct of RUSADA or the Russian authorities. In making its orders, the Panel is limited by the powers granted under the applicable law, in particular the WADC and the ISCCS. It has considered matters of proportionality and, in particular, the need to effect cultural change and encourage the next generation of Russian athletes to participate in clean international sport.

862. It is the Panel's hope that this Award will mark a new path towards reconciliation and allow Russian athletes a fresh start to contribute to their otherwise proud sporting history.

_____

NOTES AND QUESTIONS

1. *Reduction of Ban from Four Years to Two Years.* Did the CAS impose a fair punishment? Or did it let the Russians off the hook? Is a two year ban appropriate or should the CAS have imposed the four years that WADA requested?

2. *Proportionality.* The panel's decision to reduce the ban from four years to two rested on its application of the principle of proportionality. How did they use this principle to reach their result? Is proportionality an effective tool to use to determine a punishment? Why or why not?

3. *Aftermath.* In July 2021, more than 300 Russian athletes competed at the Tokyo Olympics under the Russian Olympic Committee flag. The ROC athletes finished with 20 gold and 71 total medals in third place behind the United States and China.

_____

In December 2021, Kamila Valieva, a 15-year-old Russian prodigy favored to win the women's figure skating gold medal performed at the Russian national championships, where she won the national championship. RUSADA collected a sample from Valieva to be tested for illegal substances.

In February 2022, Valieva began competing in the Beijing Olympics. She became the first woman to land a quadruple jump at the Olympics, and led the ROC team to a gold medal. The IOC then delayed the medal ceremony when the test results came back positive for the hormone trimitazidine from the RUSADA-collected samples in December 2021. The CAS conducted an expedited hearing to determine whether Valieva should be provisionally suspended from the individual skating events in Beijing.

Valieva claimed that she could have been exposed to the drug through interactions with her grandfather. In assessing Valieva's case, the CAS noted that she was a "Protected Person" for purposes of WADA because she was a minor. Specifically, sanctions for protected persons are limited to a range of reprimand up to two years in cases where no fault is found. Interestingly, the CAS panel found that the RUSADA Anti-Doping Rules and the WADC are silent with respect to Provisional Suspensions imposed on Protected Persons. The panel explained:

> As a result, it appears to the Panel there is a lacuna, or a gap, in the Russian ADR, and indeed the WADC 2021. When CAS panels find a lacuna in the WADC, this has been the basis for a CAS panel to find a gap filling construct that would ameliorate an overly harsh or inconsistent outcome: "[W]hen there is a gap or lacuna in the WADC, that gap or lacuna must be filled by the Panel ... applying the overarching principle of justice and proportionality on which all systems of law, and the [WADC] itself, is based." ... Accordingly, the Panel determines that in cases involving Protected Persons, their Provisional Suspensions should be evaluated as optional Provisional Suspensions under WADC 2021 Article 7.4.2 and its progeny. The Panel determines that Ms Valieva was entitled to benefit from being subject to an optional Provisional Suspension as a Protected Person and that, under the facts and circumstances, the option not to impose a Provisional Suspension should have been exercised so that she would not be prevented to compete in the OWG 2022.

The Panel noted that the Stockholm lab had taken an extensive amount of time to review the sample so that the results were not reported until the middle of the Olympics. The CAS also weighed whether imposing a provisional suspension would create a likelihood of irreparable harm, and concluded that it would irreparably harm Valieva. Given all of these considerations and emphasizing the narrow nature of its decision, the CAS allowed Valieva to skate in the remainder of the Olympics.

———

NOTES AND QUESTIONS

1. *Aftermath.* Kamila Valieva skated in the individual competition and finished a disappointing fourth, just out of the medals. Her ROC teammates won gold and silver. The question of whether Valieva faces additional discipline is undecided at the time of publication.

2. *Protected Persons.* What do you think of the rules concerning protected persons? Does Valieva's age reduce her culpability?

3. *Statutory Interpretation.* The CAS panel had to interpret a code provision that was silent on the issue of whether provisional suspensions apply

differently to protected persons. Did the panel act correctly in reading in a rule? Or should they have read the statute's silence differently?

4. *Imminent. Harm.* Would the outcome have been different if the positive test were discovered in December instead of during the Olympics? Should it matter?

CHAPTER 16

HEALTH AND SAFETY ISSUES IN SPORTS

■ ■ ■

Participation in sports can be risky. Sports-related injuries—to athletes, spectators, and other participants—are ubiquitous. In other contexts, a person who suffers an injury might have a tort action alleging negligence or intentional harm. Conduct that amounts to battery or assault can lead to criminal charges. But in athletic competition, injuries that result from otherwise tortious physical contact are generally not actionable if they fall within the inherent risks of the sport. In other words, the duties of care owed in the context of sport accommodate the special characteristics of athletic competition and the public policy favoring it.

This chapter first examines the application of tort and criminal law principles to injury-causing conduct during athletic competition, and how courts have modified those principles in this distinctive setting. It next addresses health and safety off the field as it relates to the unique concerns of professional athletes.

A. INJURIES FROM PLAYING THE GAME

PROBLEM 16.1

Should any of the following conduct give rise to tort or criminal liability? Consider the category of tort or crime, the requisite state of mind, possible defenses, and any public policy concerns.

(i) After an MLB pitcher gives up a three-run home run, he throws a ball far inside the plate that strikes the next batter. In weighing liability, consider whether your analysis would differ if the batter was seriously injured? If the batter—uninjured but livid—turns around and swats the catcher with his bat? If it was a Little League game?

(ii) In an MLB game, a runner from first base slides, with spikes up, into the second baseman some distance away from the base, to break up a double play in a close late-inning game. The slide fractures the second baseman's femur, sidelining him for the next two seasons. Would your analysis change if the following season, MLB amends the "slide rule" to expressly ban a runner from changing his path for the purpose of initiating contact with the fielder?

> (iii) An NFL free safety forcibly hits a wide receiver with his helmet, breaking up a reception and inflicting a concussion. A game official flags the play as a violation of the rule prohibiting helmet contact against a defenseless opponent, and the NFL later fines the safety.
>
> (iv) An NHL coach tells a player to start a fight with the opposing players to disrupt their game plan. During the fight, the instigator slashes an opponent with his stick, breaking his nose. Would your analysis change if this were a college hockey game?
>
> Consider also whether any of the above actions should warrant Commissioner discipline and the extent to which that discipline should be a consideration in adjudicating tort or criminal liability.

1. INJURY TO ATHLETES—TORT LIABILITY

The special problems that sports pose to tort litigation occur most vividly in cases in which an injured athlete files suit against another athlete whose actions during the game allegedly caused the injury. The aim of a sporting event is to produce spirited athletic competition on the field, the ice, or the floor. In sports such as boxing, football, and ice hockey, a central feature of the contest is the infliction of violent contact on the opponent. This is not the anticipated outcome of ordinary interactions in society. In other sports, such as basketball and baseball, violent contact is an expected risk, if not a desired outcome, of intense competition. The question arises—when does such contact fall so far outside the rules of the game that the injury-inflicting player is liable for damages or criminal penalties for his conduct?

HACKBART v. CINCINNATI BENGALS, INC. (HACKBART I)
435 F. Supp. 352 (D. Col. 1977)

MATSCH, DISTRICT JUDGE.

This case arises as a result of an incident which occurred in the course of a professional football game played between the Denver Broncos and the Cincinnati Bengals, in Denver, Colorado, on September 16, 1973.

* * *

The incident which gave rise to this lawsuit occurred near the end of the first half of the game at a time when the Denver team was leading by a score of 21 to 3. Dale Hackbart was playing a free safety position on the Broncos' defensive team and Charles Clark was playing fullback on the Bengals' offensive team. The Cincinnati team attempted a forward pass play during which Charles Clark ran into a corner of the north end zone as a prospective receiver. That took him into an area which was the defensive responsibility of Mr. Hackbart. The thrown pass was intercepted near the goal line by a Denver linebacker who then began to run the ball upfield. The interception reversed the offensive and defensive roles of the two teams. As a result of an attempt to block Charles Clark in the end zone, Dale Hackbart fell to the ground. He then turned and, with one knee on the ground and the other leg extended, watched the play continue upfield. Acting out of anger and frustration, but without a specific intent to injure, Charles Clark stepped forward and struck a blow with his right forearm to the back of the kneeling plaintiff's head with sufficient force to cause both players to fall forward to the ground. Both players arose and, without comment, went to their respective teams along the sidelines. They both returned to play during the second half of the game.

Because no official observed it, no foul was called on the disputed play and Dale Hackbart made no report of this incident to his coaches or to anyone else during the game. Mr. Hackbart experienced pain and soreness to the extent that he was unable to play golf as he had planned on the day after the game, he did not seek any medical attention and, although he continued to feel pain, he played on specialty team assignments for [two more games]. The Denver Broncos then released Mr. Hackbart on waivers and he was not claimed by any other team. After losing his employment, Mr. Hackbart sought medical assistance, at which time it was discovered that he had a neck injury. When that information was given to the Denver Broncos Football Club, Mr. Hackbart received his full payment for the 1973 season pursuant to an injury clause in his contract.

* * *

The claim of the plaintiff in this case must be considered in the context of football as a commercial enterprise. . . . Football is a recognized game which is widely played as a sport. . . . The basic design of the game is the same at the high school, college and professional levels. The differences are largely reflective of the fact that at each level the players have increased physical abilities, improved skills and differing motivations.

Football is a contest for territory. . . . The most obvious characteristic of the game is that all of the players engage in violent physical behavior.

The rules of play which govern the method and style by which the NFL teams compete include limitations on the manner in which players may strike or otherwise physically contact opposing players. During 1973, the rules were enforced by six officials on the playing field. The primary sanction for a violation was territorial, with the amounts of yardage lost being dependent upon the particular infraction. Players were also subject to expulsion from the game and to monetary penalties imposed by the league commissioner. . . .

Many violations of the rules do occur during each game. . . . Disabling injuries are also common occurrences in each contest. Hospitalization and surgery are frequently required for repairs. Protective clothing is worn by all players, but it is often inadequate to prevent bodily damage. . . .

The violence of professional football is carefully orchestrated. Both offensive and defensive players must be extremely aggressive in their actions and they must play with a reckless abandonment of self-protective instincts. The coaches make studied and deliberate efforts to build the emotional levels of their players to what some call a "controlled rage." . . .

The large and noisy crowds in attendance at the games contribute to the emotional levels of the players. Quick changes in the fortunes of the teams, the shock of violent collisions and the intensity of the competition make behavioral control extremely difficult, and it is not uncommon for players to "flare up" and begin fighting. The record made at this trial indicates that such incidents as that which gave rise to this action are not so unusual as to be unexpected in any NFL game.

The end product of all of the organization and effort involved in the professional football industry is an exhibition of highly developed individual skills in coordinated team competition for the benefit of large numbers of paying spectators, together with radio and television audiences. It is appropriate to infer that while some of those persons are attracted by the individual skills and precision performances of the teams, the appeal to others is the spectacle of savagery.

Plaintiff's Theories of Liability

[T]he plaintiff contends that Charles Clark's foul was so far outside of the rules of play and accepted practices of professional football that it should be characterized as reckless misconduct . . . .

Alternatively, the plaintiff claims that his injury was at least the result of a negligent act by the defendant. The difference in these contentions is but a difference in degree. Both theories are dependent upon a definition of a duty to the plaintiff and an objective standard of conduct based upon the hypothetical reasonably prudent person. Thus, the question is what would a reasonably prudent professional football player be expected to do under the circumstances confronting Charles Clark in this incident?

* * *

It is wholly incongruous to talk about a professional football player's duty of care for the safety of opposing players when he has been trained and motivated to be heedless of injury to himself. The character of NFL competition negates any notion that the playing conduct can be circumscribed by any standard of reasonableness.

Both theories of liability are also subject to the recognized defenses of consent and assumption of the risk. Here the question is what would a professional football player in the plaintiff's circumstances reasonably expect to encounter in a professional contest?

All of the witnesses with playing or coaching experience in the NFL agreed that players are urged to avoid penalties. The emphasis, however, is on the unfavorable effects of the loss of yardage, not the safety of the players. It is undisputed that no game is without penalties and that players frequently lose control in surges of emotion.

The conflict in the testimony is the difference in the witnesses' opinions as to whether Mr. Clark's act of striking the plaintiff on the back of the head in reaction to anger and frustration can be considered as "a part of the game." Several former players denounced this incident and said that Mr. Clark's conduct could not be considered customary or acceptable.

It is noteworthy that while this incident was clearly shown on the Denver Broncos' defensive game films, which were routinely reviewed by the defensive players and coaching staff, none of them made it a matter of special attention or concern.

Upon all of the evidence, my finding is that the level of violence and the frequency of emotional outbursts in NFL football games are such that Dale Hackbart must have recognized and accepted the risk that he would be injured by such an act as that committed by the defendant Clark on September 16, 1973. Accordingly, the plaintiff must be held to have assumed the risk of such an occurrence. Therefore, even if the defendant breached a duty which he owed to the plaintiff, there can be no recovery because of assumption of the risk.

* * *

The Application of Tort Principles to Professional Football. A Question of Social Policy

While the foregoing findings of fact and conclusions of law are determinative of the claim made by Dale Hackbart against Charles Clark and his employer, this case raises the larger question of whether playing field action in the business of professional football should become a subject for the business of the courts. . .

To this time professional football has been a self-regulated industry. The only protection which NFL contract players have beyond self-defense and real or threatened retaliation is that which is provided by the league rules and sanctions. It may well be true that what has been provided is inadequate and that these young athletes have been exploited and subjected to risks which should be unacceptable in our social order. In this respect, it is interesting to compare football with boxing. Because of the essential brutality of the contest, prize fighting has been held to be unlawful unless conducted under the sanction and authority of a governmental commission.

Football has been presumed to be lawful and, indeed, professional football has received the implicit approval of government because these contests take place in arenas owned by local governments and the revenues are subject to taxation. Like coal mining and railroading, professional football is hazardous to the health and welfare of those who are employed as players.

What is the interest of the larger community in limiting the violence of professional football? That question concerns not only the protection of the participants, but also the effects of such violence on those who observe it. Can the courts answer this question? I think not. An ordinary citizen is entitled to protection according to the usages of the society in which he lives, and in the context of common community standards there can be no question but that Mr. Clark's blow here would generate civil liability. It would involve a criminal sanction if the requisite intent were present. The difference here is that this blow was delivered on the field of play during the course of action in a regularly scheduled professional football game. . . .

There is no discernible code of conduct for NFL players. The dictionary definition of a sportsman is one who abides by the rules of a contest and accepts victory or defeat graciously. That is not the prevalent attitude in professional football. There are no Athenian virtues in this form of athletics. The NFL has substituted the morality of the battlefield for that of the playing field, and the "restraints of civilization" have been left on the sidelines.

Mr. Justice Holmes' simple statement of the function of tort law and the evidentiary record now before me clearly reveal the density of the thicket in which the courts would become entangled if they undertook the task of allocation of fault in professional football games. The NFL rules of play are so legalistic in their statement and so difficult of application because of the speed and violence of the play that the differences between violations which could fairly be called deliberate, reckless or outrageous and those which are "fair play" would be so small and subjective as to be incapable of articulation. The question of causation would be extremely difficult in view of the frequency of forceful collisions. The volume of such litigation would be enormous and it is reasonable to expect that the court systems of the many states in which NFL games are played would develop differing and conflicting principles of law. It is highly unlikely that the NFL could continue to produce anything like the present games under such multiple systems of overview by judges and juries. If there is to be any governmental involvement in this industry, it is a matter which can be best considered by the legislative branch.

My conclusion that the civil courts cannot be expected to control the violence in professional football is limited by the facts of the case before me. I have considered only a claim for an injury resulting from a blow, without weaponry, delivered emotionally without a specific intent to injure, in the course of regular play in a league-approved game involving adult, contract players. Football as a commercial enterprise is something quite different from athletics as an extension of the academic experience and what I have said here may have no applicability in other areas of physical competition.

Judgment for defendants.

HACKBART V. CINCINNATI BENGALS, INC. (HACKBART II)
601 F.2d 516 (10th Cir. 1979)

DOYLE, CIRCUIT JUDGE.

The question in this case is whether in a regular season professional football game an injury which is inflicted by one professional football player on an opposing player can give rise to liability in tort where the injury was inflicted by the intentional striking of a blow during the game.

* * *

The evidence at the trial uniformly supported the proposition that the intentional striking of a player in the head from the rear is not an accepted part of either the playing rules or the general customs of the game of professional football. . . .

[T]he district court's assumption was that Clark had inflicted an intentional blow which would ordinarily generate civil liability and which might bring about a criminal sanction as well, but that since it had occurred in the course of a football game, it should not be subject to the restraints of the law; that if it were it would place unreasonable impediments and restraints on the activity. The judge also pointed out that courts are ill-suited to decide the different social questions and to administer conflicts on what is much like a battlefield where the restraints of civilization have been left on the sidelines. . . .

III.

WHETHER INTENTIONAL INJURY IS ALLOWED BY EITHER WRITTEN RULE OR CUSTOM

Plaintiff . . . maintains that tort law applicable to the injury in this case applies on the football field as well as in other places. On the other hand, plaintiff does not rely on the theory of negligence being applicable. This is in recognition of the fact that subjecting another to unreasonable risk of harm, the essence of negligence, is inherent in the game of football, for admittedly it is violent. . . .

Contrary to the position of the court then, there are no principles of law which allow a court to rule out certain tortious conduct by reason of general roughness of the game or difficulty of administering it.

Indeed, the evidence shows that there are rules of the game which prohibit the intentional striking of blows. Thus, Article 1, Item 1, Subsection C, provides that:

> All players are prohibited from striking on the head, face or neck with the heel, back or side of the hand, wrist, forearm, elbow or clasped hands.

Thus the very conduct which was present here is expressly prohibited by the rule which is quoted above.

The general customs of football do not approve the intentional punching or striking of others. That this is prohibited was supported by the testimony of all of the witnesses. They testified that the intentional striking of a player in the face or from the rear is prohibited by the playing rules as well as the general customs of the game. Punching or hitting with the arms is prohibited. Undoubtedly these restraints are intended to establish reasonable boundaries so that one football player cannot intentionally inflict a serious injury on another. Therefore, the notion is not correct that all reason has been abandoned, whereby the only possible remedy for the person who has been the victim of an unlawful blow is retaliation.

* * *

V.

IS THE STANDARD OF RECKLESS DISREGARD OF THE RIGHTS OF OTHERS APPLICABLE TO THE PRESENT SITUATION?

The Restatement of Torts Second, § 500, distinguishes between reckless and negligent misconduct. Reckless misconduct differs from negligence, according to the authors, in that negligence consists of mere inadvertence, lack of skillfulness or failure to take precautions; reckless misconduct, on the other hand, involves a choice or adoption of a course of action either with knowledge of the danger or with knowledge of facts which would disclose this danger to a reasonable man. Recklessness also differs in that it consists of intentionally doing an act with knowledge not only that it contains a risk of harm to others as does negligence, but that it actually involves a risk substantially greater in magnitude than is necessary in the case of negligence. The authors explain the difference, therefore, in the degree of risk by saying that the difference is so significant as to amount to a difference in kind.

Subsection (f) also distinguishes between reckless misconduct and intentional wrongdoing. To be reckless the *act* must have been intended by the actor. At the same time, the actor does not intend to cause the harm which results from it. It is enough that he realized, or from the facts should have realized, that there was a strong probability that harm would result even though he may hope or expect that this conduct will prove harmless.

Nevertheless, existence of probability is different from substantial certainty which is an ingredient of intent to cause the harm which results from the act.

Therefore, recklessness exists where a person knows that the act is harmful but fails to realize that it will produce the extreme harm which it did produce. It is in this respect that recklessness and intentional conduct differ in degree.

In the case at bar the defendant Clark admittedly acted impulsively and in the heat of anger, and even though it could be said from the admitted facts that he intended the act, it could also be said that he did not intend to inflict serious injury which resulted from the blow which he struck.

In ruling that recklessness is the appropriate standard and that assault and battery is not the exclusive one, we are saying that these two liability concepts are not necessarily opposed one to the other. Rather, recklessness under § 500 of the Restatement might be regarded, for the purpose of analysis at least, a lesser included act.

Assault and battery, having originated in a common law writ, is narrower than recklessness in its scope. In essence, two definitions enter into it. The assault is an attempt coupled with the present ability to commit a violent harm against another. Battery is the unprivileged or unlawful touching of another. Assault and battery then call for an intent, as does recklessness. But in recklessness the intent is to do the act, but without an intent to cause the particular harm. It is enough if the actor knows that there is a strong probability that harm will result. Thus, the definition fits perfectly the fact situation here. Surely, then, no reason exists to compel appellant to employ the assault and battery standard which does not comfortably apply fully in preference to the standard which meets this fact situation. . . .

* * *

The cause is reversed and remanded for a new trial. . . .

NOTES AND QUESTIONS

1. *Football as a "Commercial Enterprise."* The court in *Hackbart I* was reluctant to apply tort doctrine to professional football because it is a commercial enterprise built on abandoning the "restraints of civilization." The court also worried that judges, who may not be football fans, would not be able to determine whether a rules violation has occurred. Instead, the court deferred to the NFL's internal disciplinary mechanisms, including on-field penalties and league suspensions and fines, to "carefully orchestrate" the violence. Should a particular judge's familiarity with the game make a difference in the outcome of the litigation?

2. *League Self-Policing.* Do you agree that leagues such as the NFL are capable of self-policing for excessive violence so that participants should be excused from civil tort liability? Should tort liability turn on the quality of the league's self-policing? Does it inform your thinking that some leagues, including the NFL, review all game footage after-the-fact, in part for the purpose of identifying and penalizing foul play, whether or not it was flagged during the game?

3. *Conduct Not "Part of the Game."* An issue both *Hackbart I* and *II* confronted is how to distinguish between aggressive conduct that is "part of the game," and reckless conduct that is not. Note that in concluding that Clark was reckless, the *Hackbart II* court relied on the fact that Clark's conduct "is expressly prohibited by the rule [against striking with a forearm]." Note also that no official saw or penalized the conduct during the game. Even with instant replay review, experienced game officials struggle with applying the playing rules. Furthermore, every off-season, the NFL tweaks its playing rules for a variety of reasons, including to control the violence of the game. Given the uncertainty about rules interpretation this produces, are courts competent to assess whether a player's conduct violates a game rule?

Furthermore, is it possible to draw a line between permitted aggressiveness and prohibited recklessness in football? The *Hackbart II* court concluded that Clark's conduct fit the definition of recklessness because he intended the act and should have known "there was a strong probability that harm would result." Given the emotional content of the game—stirred up by coaches, teammates, and the crowd—is it fair to infer in the moment of contact that a player has constructive knowledge of probable harm? If not, what sort of evidence would be necessary to infer that knowledge? Consider *Green v. Pro Football, Inc.*, 31 F. Supp. 3d 714 (D. Md. 2014), where the court allowed an injured professional football player to pursue his intentional tort claim against an opposing team and its coach for instituting a bounty program wherein that team's players were given financial rewards for deliberately injuring opposing players. In that case, a by-product of the 2012 revelations of the New Orleans Saints bounty scandal discussed in Chapter 2, Section D, substantial evidence of specific intent to injure existed. What should an injured player's recourse be shy of such evidence?

4. *Compensating the Injured Athlete.* After the *Hackbart II* court remanded the case for trial, Hackbart settled his claim for $200,000. How would you allocate this payment between the joint tortfeasors, Clark and the Bengals? *See Tomjanovich v. California Sports, Inc.*, 1979 WL 210977 (S.D. Tex. Oct. 10, 1979) (Los Angeles Lakers liable to pay $3 million damage award when its player punched opposing player during on-court fight, resulting in career-ending injuries); *Averill v. Luttrell*, 44 Tenn. App. 56, 311 S.W.2d 812 (1957) (team vicariously liable for catcher's conduct when he slugged a batter who threw his bat at pitcher in response to several "brush-back" pitches); *Nathans v. Offerman*, 922 F. Supp. 2d 271 (D. Conn. 2013) (club might be held vicariously liable when its batter charges the mound, bat in hand, after being hit by a pitch). Should this type of liability be addressed and compensated

through other mechanisms, such as the league's labor agreement and medical and pension benefits, or state workers' compensation benefits? Why shouldn't a coparticipant shoulder liability for on-field conduct that would get him arrested if he did it in the parking lot?

5. *Standard of Liability for Professional Athletes.* In post-*Hackbart* cases, courts have been reluctant to impose tort liability on professional athletes for playing field injuries in the absence of intentional or reckless conduct beyond a mere rules violation. *See, e.g., McKichan v. St. Louis Hockey Club, L.P.,* 967 S.W.2d 209 (Mo. Ct. App. 1998) (hockey goaltender could not recover for injuries from severe body check after referee's whistle had blown because "rough play is commonplace in professional hockey"). The logic underpinning this standard was explained in *Turcotte v. Fell,* 68 N.Y.2d 432, 502 N.E.2d 964 (1986). There, the court absolved a professional jockey who crossed lanes during a race, in violation of the "foul riding" rules governing the sport, and severely injured another jockey. The court held that professional athletes consent to the risk of injury even from conduct that violates the rules:

> Manifestly, a professional athlete is more aware of the dangers of the activity, and presumably more willing to accept them in exchange for a salary, than is an amateur. . . . The rules of the sport, however, do not necessarily limit the scope of the professional's consent. Although the foul riding rule is a safety measure, it is not by its terms absolute for it establishes a spectrum of conduct and penalties, depending on whether the violation is careless or willful and whether the contact was the result of mutual fault. As the rule recognizes, bumping and jostling are normal incidents of the sport. . . . Plaintiff does not claim that Fell intentionally or recklessly bumped him, he claims only that as a result of carelessness, Fell failed to control his mount as the horses raced for the lead and a preferred position on the track. While a participant's "consent" to join in a sporting activity is not a waiver of all rules infractions, nonetheless a professional clearly understands the usual incidents of competition resulting from carelessness, particularly those which result from the customarily accepted method of playing the sport, and accepts them. They are within the known, apparent and foreseeable dangers of the sport and not actionable and thus plaintiffs' complaint against defendant Fell was properly dismissed.

Id. at 441. What differentiates this case from the facts in *Hackbart*?

6. *Recreational Athletes.* Recreational sports similarly raise the issue of the appropriate standard for coparticipant liability for on-field injury. In *Knight v. Jewett,* 3 Cal. 4th 296, 834 P.2d 696 (1992), the California Supreme Court denied the claim of a coparticipant who lost a finger as a result of a collision in a touch football game, holding that she assumed the risk of injury from "normal energetic conduct [that] often includes accidentally careless behavior":

[L]iability properly may be imposed on a participant only when he or she intentionally injures another player or engages in reckless conduct that is totally outside the range of the ordinary activity involved in the sport. . . . The courts have concluded that vigorous participation in such sporting events likely would be chilled if legal liability were to be imposed on a participant on the basis of his or her ordinary careless conduct. . . . [E]ven when a participant's conduct violates a rule of the game and may subject the violator to internal sanctions prescribed by the sport itself, imposition of *legal liability* for such conduct might well alter fundamentally the nature of the sport by deterring participants from vigorously engaging in activity that falls close to, but on the permissible side of, a prescribed rule.

Id. at 318; *see also Gauvin v. Clark*, 404 Mass. 450, 537 N.E.2d 94 (1989) (applying reckless disregard standard in denying recovery to hockey player against opponent who struck him in the abdomen in violation of rules).

Contrast *Nabozny v. Barnhill*, 31 Ill. App. 3d 212, 334 N.E.2d 258 (1975), in which an Illinois court allowed a claim arising out an amateur soccer match where one player, in clear violation of safety rules, kicked the other team's goaltender in the head:

This court believes that the law should not place unreasonable burdens on the free and vigorous participation in sports by our youth. However, we also believe that organized, athletic competition does not exist in a vacuum. Rather, some of the restraints of civilization must accompany every athlete onto the playing field. One of the educational benefits of organized athletic competition to our youth is the development of discipline and self-control. . . . A reckless disregard for the safety of other players cannot be excused. To engage in such conduct is to create an intolerable and unreasonable risk of serious injury to other participants. We have carefully drawn the rule announced herein in order to control a new field of personal injury litigation.

Id. at 260; *see also Bourque v. Duplechin*, 331 So. 2d 40 (La. Ct. App. 1976) (softball second baseman could recover for injuries caused by baserunner who ran out of his way to cause the collision). How would you strike the right balance between encouraging participation in sports and deterring reckless play? Which sports rules violations should trigger tort liability—only those related to player safety?

7. *Non-Contact Sports.* Courts have also examined whether the assumption of the risk doctrine absolves negligence in non-contact sports, largely concluding it does. In *Shin v. Ahn*, 42 Cal. 4th 482, 165 P.3d 581 (2007), the California Supreme Court extended the logic of the *Knight* case noted above to the sport of golf, rejecting the argument that liability should be imposed because the defendant failed to observe golf's rules of etiquette in hitting his tee shot without first ascertaining plaintiff's whereabouts. *See also Anand v. Kapoor*, 15 N.Y.3d 946, 942 N.E.2d 295 (2010) ("The manner in which Anand

was injured—being hit without warning by a 'shanked' shot while one searches for one's own ball—reflects a commonly appreciated risk of golf."); *Bowman v. McNary*, 853 N.E.2d 984 (Ind. App. 2006) (denying recovery to a member of a high school girls' golf team, blinded when her teammate unintentionally struck her in the head with a golf club during a driving-range practice).

2. INJURY TO ATHLETES—CRIMINAL LIABILITY

When an athlete sustains an injury not during the ordinary course of play but from contact that the rules directly prohibit or that occurred during stoppages from play, criminal liability might be considered. Ice hockey has attracted the most attention from law enforcement, given the accepted practice of in-game fights. When those fights involve prohibited stick slashes, criminal prosecutions have ensued.

Regina v. Green and *Regina v. Maki* were two such prosecutions that arose from a single incident during a 1969 preseason game between the Boston Bruins and the St. Louis Blues in Ottawa, Canada. A routine fight got out of hand when the Bruins' Ted Green and the Blues' Wayne Maki both slashed each other with their sticks, conduct specifically prohibited by the rules. So violent was the exchange that Green sustained a skull fracture. Canadian law enforcement filed criminal charges against both Maki and Green for conduct that exceeded the contact permitted by the rules and to which the players ostensibly consented. In separate decisions, the provincial court judges who tried the cases acquitted both players. In *Regina v. Green*, 16 D.L.R.3d 137 (Can. Ont. Prov. Ct. 1970), the judge addressed the "consent" defense as follows:

> There is no doubt that the players who enter the hockey arena consent to a great number of assaults on their person, because the game of hockey as it is played in the National Hockey League, which is the league I am dealing with, could not possibly be played at the speed at which it is played and with the force and vigour with which it is played, and with the competition that enters into it, unless there were a great number of what would in normal circumstances be called assaults, but which are not heard of. No hockey player enters onto the ice of the National Hockey League without consenting to and without knowledge of the possibility that he is going to be hit in one of many ways once he is on that ice.

> I think it is notable that Mr. Maki in his evidence, when he was questioned about the fact that he was struck in the face by Mr. Green's glove, said this had happened to him hundreds of times. I think within our experience we can come to the conclusion that this is an extremely ordinary happening in a hockey game and the players really think nothing of it. If you go in behind the net with a defenseman, particularly one who is trying to defend

his zone, and you are struck in the face by that player's glove, a penalty might be called against him, but you do not really think anything of it; it is one of the types of risk one assumes.

One now gets the most difficult problem of all, in my opinion: since it is assumed and understood that there are numerous what would normally be called assaults in the course of a hockey game, but which are really not assaults because of the consent of the players in the type of game being played, where do you draw the line? It is very difficult in my opinion for a player who is playing hockey with all the force, vigour and strength at his command, who is engaged in the rough and tumble of the game, very often in a rough situation in the corner of the rink, suddenly to stop and say, "I must not do that. I must not follow up on this because maybe it is an assault; maybe I am committing an assault." I do not think that any of the actions that would normally be considered assaults in ordinary walks of life can possibly be, within the context that I am considering, considered assaults at all.

See also *Regina v. Maloney*, 28 C.C.C.2d 323 (Can. Ont. 1976) (players are presumed to consent to conduct "inherent in and reasonably incidental to the normal laying of the game").

In *Regina v. Maki*, 14 D.L.R.3d 164 (Can. Ont. Prov. Ct. 1970), the judge expressed a different view, concluding that a hockey fight could amount to criminal assault, but acquitting Maki on the grounds of self-defense:

If the fact situation in this case had been such that no doubt was raised in my mind regarding self defense, I would not have hesitate[d] to convict the accused. The defense of consent would in my opinion have failed. Although no criminal charges have been laid in the past pertaining to athletic events in this country, I can see no reason why they could not be in the future where the circumstances warrant and the relevant authorities deem it advisable to do so. No sports league, no matter how well organized or self policed it may be, should thereby render the players in that league immune from criminal prosecution. . . .

Thus all players, when they step onto a playing field or ice surface, assume certain risks and hazards of the sport, and in most cases the defense of consent as set out in 230 of the Criminal Code would be applicable. But as stated above there is a question of degree involved, and no athlete should be presumed to accept malicious, unprovoked or overly violent attack.

But a little reflection will establish that some limit must be placed on a player's immunity from liability. Each case must be decided on its own facts so it is difficult, if not impossible, to decide how the line is to be drawn in every circumstance. But injuries inflicted in circumstances which show a definite resolve to cause serious injury to another, even when there is provocation and in the heat of the game, should not fall within the scope of the implied consent. [citation omitted]

The adoption of such principles in the future, would, I feel certain, be a benefit to the players, of course, to the general public peace and, in particular, to young aspiring athletes who look to the professionals for guidance and example.

Consider the implications of the two defenses offered in these cases: consent and self-defense. One could read the *Green* decision as implying that we are not always expected to control ourselves—so long as we are playing sports. Relying on the defense of consent in sports violence cases is in tension with societal interest in controlling violence, on and off the ice. A promoter who wants to attract "full-blooded" fans can make the sport really violent and no crimes would be committed since all the participants "consented." By this reasoning self-defense might be a better approach to avoiding criminal liability for sports violence. But then, did the acquittal of Maki on self-defense grounds mean that Green did assault Maki? Or vice versa?

Although the Ontario courts acquitted Green and Maki, a British Columbia judge took Canadian law in a different direction reviewing the actions of Boston Bruin Marty McSorley in a fight against Vancouver Canucks Donald Brashear. McSorley had lost an earlier fight against Brashear, who later taunted McSorley on the bench when his Bruins were losing the game. Just seconds before the end of the contest with the Canucks three goals ahead, the Bruins' coach sent McSorley back onto the ice to instigate another confrontation. To get Brashear's attention and provoke the fight, McSorley swung his stick and hit him on the head, giving Brashear a concussion that left him unable to play for several weeks. This time in addition to the standard five minutes penalty for fighting—which both players had received earlier in the game—the NHL Commissioner suspended McSorley for the remainder of the season. There was no right to appeal the Commissioner's discipline to an arbitrator under hockey's collective bargaining agreement.

Despite what the NHL called unusually "harsh and decisive" action against the player, the British Columbia Crown Prosecutor's office charged McSorley with "criminal assault with a weapon." At the criminal trial, the critical issue was whether McSorley had intended to hit Brashear on the shoulder or on the head (and helmet) with his stick.

REGINA V. MCSORLEY

2000 British Columbia Prov. Ct. 116 (Criminal Div. 2000)

KITCHEN, JUDGE.

This is my decision on the charge against Marty McSorley that he assaulted Donald Brashear with his hockey stick during a hockey game on February 21, 2000. . . .

Some may view the matter as a trial of the game of hockey itself. If that is the expectation, my decision will be a disappointment. My only concern is whether Marty McSorley is guilty of the specific charge alleged against him. That is not to say that the McSorley/Brashear incident should not prompt a healthy discussion of hockey and the role of violence in the sport. . . .

A related issue includes the question of whether the criminal law process should be preempted where discipline procedures have been taken by the hockey authorities. Again, I must emphasize that this is not an issue related to a determination of whether Mr. McSorley has committed a crime.

There are many groups that claim authority to discipline their members. Some are statutory, such as law societies and judicial councils, and some exist by virtue of private contractual arrangements such as in the case of the National Hockey League. . . . In my view, there should be a heavy onus on those purporting to preempt the normal criminal process, particularly where it is a private organization such as a group of hockey owners. Statutory bodies must act in the public interest; businessmen have no such obligation. . . .

[T]he object of the game of hockey is to put the puck in the net—the opposing net. Many of the written rules of the game deal with the legitimate means by which that may be done. Many other written rules deal with the consequences that will follow if the rules are not obeyed. . . . But those written rules are only part of the picture. There is also an unwritten code of conduct, agreed to by the players and officials, that is superimposed on the written rules. This code of conduct deals mainly with situations where the written rules are breached, and the code then comes into play. For example, the written rules prohibit slashing with the stick, but the unwritten code says that slashing is permissible as long as it is during play, and not to the head. Of course, when a slash is employed, and it is observed by the referee, there are consequences; a penalty is called. . . .

There is a further complication. The referees and linesmen exercise considerable discretion in assessing penalties. This exercise of discretion is seen by them as setting guidelines for the players so that the players will know what tolerance there will be for breaches of the written rules. Presumably the players are then expected to govern themselves accordingly. This requires the players to have a thorough knowledge of the written rules, a familiarity with the unwritten code, and an understanding of the guidelines the referee is signaling to the players during the game through his assessment and non-assessment of penalties. . . . It is within this somewhat indefinite framework that players must play the game.

It is the position of the Crown that this body of evidence permits only two possibilities—that McSorley deliberately struck Brashear to the head without Brashear's consent, or that he recklessly struck him to the head, not necessarily aiming for the head directly. Recklessness in this case may be likened to wilful blindness—ignoring a known risk. . . . If the blow to the head was intentional, it is common ground that it was an assault. Brashear himself said in evidence that he did not consent to being struck in that manner. The other witnesses agreed that stick blows to the head were not permitted in either the written rules, or the unwritten code. [E]vidence [established] that players in the NHL would not accept a blow such as that as part of the game

If the slash was intended for the shoulder, delivered with the intention of starting a fight, my conclusion would be that it was within the common practices and norms of the game.

I conclude that the following occurred. McSorley had fought Brashear and he had been briefly hurt. He was nevertheless prepared to fight him again, but Brashear frustrated his attempts to do so. Brashear taunted the Boston players and was seen to be responsible for taking the Boston goalie out of the game. This was all fairly routine for McSorley. He was credible when he said he was prepared to let things wind down at the end of the game.

Then [the Bruins coach] effectively directed him to get Brashear with about twenty seconds left. This was really too little time to fight but he felt himself pressured to do something. He found himself gliding in from centre ice toward Brashear, sizing him up for possible ways to confront him. Brashear crossed directly in front of him, presenting an easy target. Brashear was the focus of all of McSorley's and Boston's frustrations. McSorley had to do something; he might still be able to start a fight. . . . He had an impulse to strike him in the head. His mindset, always tuned to aggression, permitted that. He slashed for the head. A child, swinging as at a Tee ball, would not miss. A housekeeper swinging a carpetbeater would not miss. An NHL player would never, ever miss. Brashear was struck as intended.

Mr. McSorley, I must find you guilty as charged.

———

The judge in *McSorley* declined to impose a fine or jail sentence, instead agreeing to a "conditional discharge"—a probationary term that required 18 months of good behavior. The judge based this gentle penalty on his belief that McSorley's "act was unpremeditated. It was impulsive, committed when McSorley was caught in a squeeze—attempting to follow an order [from his coach] to fight with Brashear when there was too little time to do so." When is leniency in criminal sentencing justified by the convict's claim that he was "just following orders"?

———

NOTES AND QUESTIONS

1. *Application of Criminal Law to Competition Violence.* Clearly the typical punching and shoving that occurs during a hockey fight would not produce criminal liability, while a hockey player pulling out a gun and shooting a competitor to death undoubtedly would. But at what point does on ice violence cross the line to where it is appropriate to use the criminal courts to punish or deter it? Does your answer turn on the nature of the act or on the motives of the perpetrator—or both? Should the standard be different from sport to sport: *i.e.*, should violence by a hockey player against a competitor be viewed differently than violence by a basketball or baseball player? Or a golfer or tennis player?

2. *Home Versus Away Team.* It is exceedingly rare for a prosecutor to bring criminal charges against a home-team player for in-competition violence. Consider whether this is because the psychology of sport creates a disproportionate tendency to use excessive force when playing on the road or before a neutral audience. Or does this imbalance result, in the United States at least, from the fact that most local prosecutors are elected? The one case of home-team criminal prosecution occurred in Canada, where career government attorneys customarily make prosecutorial decisions. In *Regina v. Bertuzzi*, 2004 BCPC 472 (Can. B.C. Prov. Ct. 2004), British Columbia authorities charged the Vancouver Canucks' Todd Bertuzzi with criminal assault for his vicious attack on the Colorado Avalanche's Steve Moore, which ended Moore's career. Bertuzzi pled guilty and received a conditional discharge and one year's probation. In addition, the NHL suspended Bertuzzi indefinitely and fined his club $250,000 for "failure to prevent the atmosphere that may have led to" the incident.

Compare this outcome to the New Orleans Saints bounty scandal where for three seasons, Saints coaches allegedly established a bonus pool to pay team members for injuring opposing star players. (See Chapter 2, Section D). Although the NFL Commissioner imposed harsh punishments on the players and other team personnel involved, no local prosecutor—either home or away—brought any criminal charges.

3. *Tort Versus Criminal Liability.* In the Bertuzzi case described above, Moore, the injured player, also brought a civil suit seeking $38 million in pecuniary and punitive damages against Bertuzzi, the Canucks coach, and the team, which they ultimately settled confidentially. Consider the differences between the elements and burdens of proof for tort and criminal liability. As noted in *McSorley*, and in the tort cases we read, coparticipant sports violence that results in injury is not culpable if it is "within the common practices and

norms of the game." Criminal law provides for the defense of consent just as tort law provides for the defense of assumption of the risk. In a criminal prosecution, however, any reasonable doubt as to any element of the offense will result in acquittal. Does this alone explain why so few prosecutors pursue incidents of sports violence?

4. *Consent to Physical Contact Outside the Rules.* While consent is a defense in prosecutions of sports violence, courts have held that in some circumstances, coparticipants could not legally consent to overly violent contact. In an early prosecution of a professional boxer for a blow that killed his opponent, the jury was instructed that "the public has an interest in the personal safety of its citizens" and that citizens "cannot lawfully engage in" a sport so dangerous that it is likely to cause death. *People v. Fitzsimmons*, 34 N.Y.S. 1102, 1109 (1895); *see People v. Freer*, 381 N.Y.S.2d 976 (1976) ("[T]here is a limit to the magnitude and dangerousness of a blow to which another is deemed to consent."); *State v. Shelley*, 85 Wash. App. 24, 33, 929 P.2d 489 (1997) ("There is nothing in the game of basketball, or even rugby or hockey, that would permit consent as a defense to [intentionally punching an opponent].")). The difficulty is in drawing the boundaries of that consent in accordance with the "reasonably foreseeable hazards of joint participation in a lawful, athletic contest." *Id.* at 26. Given this difficulty, how should we apply criminal law's rule of lenity that requires a court to apply any unclear or ambiguous law in the manner most favorable to the defendant?

5. *Recreational Sports.* Would you expect prosecutions of sports violence to be more or less frequent in the recreational sports setting? In *People v. Schacker*, 670 N.Y.S.2d 308 (1998), the court dismissed criminal charges against a recreational hockey player who struck an opponent in a game, after the play was over and the whistle had blown, causing minor injuries. Expressing concern that the prosecution would undermine public policy "intended to facilitate free and vigorous participation in athletic activity," the court observed:

> [A]thletic competition includes intentional conduct that has the appearance of criminal acts.... Thus, in order to allege a criminal act which occurred in a hockey game, the factual portion of the information must allege acts that show that the intent was to inflict physical injury which was unrelated to the athletic competition. Although play may have terminated, the information herein does not show that the physical contact had no connection with the competition. Furthermore, the injuries must be so severe as to be unacceptable in normal competition, requiring a change in the nature of the game. That type of injury is not present in this case.

Id. at 309–10. Contrast *People v. Hall*, 999 P.2d 207 (Col. 2000), in which a court reinstated a reckless manslaughter charge against a skier who was moving so fast and out of control that he collided with and killed another skier. The court found probable cause to believe that the defendant, a former ski racer, consciously disregarded the substantial and unjustifiable risk of injury to others. What explains the different outcomes in these two cases? The degree of injury inflicted? The level of the athlete's skill? Using the language of *Schacker*, does the prosecution of the skier in *Hall* require a change in the nature of the sport?

6. *Legislative Solutions.* The policy question posed by these cases has periodically interested the U.S. Congress in legislating against sports violence. One 1980 bill, the Sports Violence Act, would have created a new federal criminal offense of "excessive violence during professional sporting events," defined as force that "has no reasonable relationship to the competitive goals of the sport; is unreasonably violent; and could not be reasonably foreseen, or was not consented to, by the injured person, as a normal hazard to such person's involvement in such sports events." All major sports league commissioners opposed the bill, which died in committee and was never revived. If the bill had passed, would it be easier to resolve the factual issues, such as consent, raised by these incidents? Would a Sports Violence Act serve as a criminal court test run, at taxpayers' expense, for potential tort claims by injured athletes? Why did the major sports commissioners oppose the Sports Violence Act? Does this imply that federal intervention to deal with sports violence is not in the best interests of the game?

3. INJURY TO SPECTATORS

Cases involving injuries to spectators at sports events also take a distinctive approach to tort law. Spectator injuries typically involve a flying object that has entered the stands. Because this happens so frequently in baseball, courts refer to the legal doctrine as the "baseball rule."

JANE COSTA V. THE BOSTON RED SOX BASEBALL CLUB
61 Mass. App. Ct. 299, 809 N.E.2d 1090 (2004)

COHEN, J.

On a September evening in 1998, the plaintiff and three companions attended a Boston Red Sox baseball game at Fenway Park. They arrived late, at the top of the fifth inning. The plaintiff took her seat in an unscreened area in the upper box section on the first base line, more or less behind the Red Sox dugout. Several players from the visiting team, the Detroit Tigers, batted before their side was retired. In the bottom of the fifth, the first batter for the Red Sox was Darren Lewis. On a count of one ball and two strikes, Lewis hit a line drive foul ball into the stands along the first base line. The ball struck the plaintiff in the face, causing severe, permanent injuries. She had been in the ballpark no more than ten minutes when she was hurt.

It is not disputed that, while passively watching the game, the plaintiff's life was forever changed by this tragic event. What is disputed is whether the defendant Boston Red Sox Baseball Club may be compelled to compensate the plaintiff for her injuries. A judge of the Superior Court granted the defendant's motion for summary judgment. We agree that, as matter of law, the plaintiff may not recover on the only theory she advances—negligent failure to warn of the danger of being hit by a foul ball—and, accordingly, we affirm.

We view the summary judgment record, as we are required to do, in the light most favorable to the plaintiff. In addition to the facts outlined above, the record reveals the following.

Foul ball injuries occur with some regularity at Fenway Park. A spreadsheet produced by the defendant, summarizing five years of data during the 1990's, showed that the annual number of injuries sustained by patrons from foul balls ranged from thirty-six to fifty-three, with a substantial number requiring medical attention. While some of these incidents were listed as involving patrons who were injured while attempting to catch the ball, many others were not. Moreover, avoiding injury from a ball hit into the stands sometimes may be close to impossible. According to a professor of engineering retained by the plaintiff, the plaintiff had virtually no time to react to the ball that came her way. He determined, with the help of a range finder, that the distance from the plaintiff's seat to home plate was forty-seven yards, or 141 feet. By analyzing a videotape of the game, he also determined that the minimum speed of the baseball at the time it struck the plaintiff was ninety miles per hour, or 132 feet per second. Thus, he concluded, the plaintiff had no more than 1.07 seconds from the time Lewis hit the ball to take evasive action.

At her deposition, the plaintiff professed marked ignorance of the sport of baseball. Except for one occasion when she sat in the bleachers with her father when she was eight years old, she had never attended a baseball game prior to the night of the accident. She had not seen baseball on television except while changing channels, and did not watch sports reports or read about sports in the newspaper. Before the evening of her injury, she understood a foul ball to be one that simply rolled off to the side after being hit. As atypical as this may seem in "Red Sox Nation," we accept for present purposes (as we must) that the plaintiff had no subjective understanding of the risks posed by an errant foul ball.

There is an area behind home plate where netting protects approximately 2,511 seats; however, the plaintiff does not contend that the netting should have extended to the area where she was seated, or otherwise question the design of the ballpark. She claims only that she was entitled to an adequate warning of the dangers of sitting in an unprotected location so that she could have made an informed choice whether to remain there. She acknowledges the existence of a disclaimer printed on her admission ticket but maintains that she did not look at the ticket and that, in any event, the disclaimer was not adequate to discharge the defendant's duty to warn, particularly since the print was extremely small. She notes that, after the date of her injury, signage was installed along the first base line reading "BE ALERT. FOUL BALLS AND BATS HURT." Such signage, according to the plaintiff, was feasible and necessary before her accident. She claims that had she been adequately informed of the danger, she would not have exposed herself to the risk of injury presented by the location of her seat.

We turn now to the relevant law. It has been more than fifty years since a case like the plaintiff's has been considered on appeal in Massachusetts. In *Shaw v. Boston Am. League Baseball Co.*, 325 Mass. 419, 90 N.E.2d 840 (1950), the Supreme Judicial Court held, as matter of law, that a baseball club was not liable to a spectator who was injured by a foul ball. Shaw rested on the doctrine of assumption of risk and therefore turned on the plaintiff's subjective knowledge and appreciation of the danger. The plaintiff in Shaw was an admitted "fan" who had attended many baseball games and who knew that fast-moving foul balls often landed in the stands. On those facts, the court had little difficulty concluding that the defendant was shielded from liability because the "plaintiff's position [was] that of a spectator familiar with the game who was injured by an ordinary risk of the game which she had voluntarily assumed."

The present case stands on a different footing from Shaw, both legally and factually. As to claims arising on or after January 1, 1974, assumption of risk was abolished as an affirmative defense, . . . and here the plaintiff must be taken as ignorant of the danger of being hit by a foul ball. In spite of these distinctions, however, we conclude that the plaintiff still cannot recover . . . "Before liability for negligence can be imposed, there must first be a legal duty owed by the defendant to the plaintiff, and a breach of that duty proximately resulting in the injury." Here, the asserted duty is the duty to warn of the dangers of foul balls. Although an owner or possessor of land owes to all persons lawfully on the premises a common law duty of reasonable care to maintain the property in a reasonably safe condition and "to warn visitors of any unreasonable dangers of which the landowner is aware or reasonably should be aware," the duty to warn does not extend to dangers that would be obvious to persons of average intelligence. "Where a danger would be obvious to a person of ordinary perception and judgment, a landowner may reasonably assume that a visitor has knowledge of it and, therefore, 'any further warning would be an empty form' that would not reduce the likelihood of resulting harm."

This principle exists independently of the doctrine of assumption of risk. . . . As the Supreme Judicial Court explained, the abolition of assumption of risk as an affirmative defense did "not alter the plaintiff's burden in a negligence action to prove that the defendant owed him a duty of care in the circumstances, and thus [left] intact the open and obvious danger rule, which operates to negate the existence of a duty of care," at least insofar as a duty to warn is concerned.

Viewing the present case through the lens of the defendant's duty, we are persuaded that the potential for a foul ball to enter the stands and injure a spectator who is seated in an unscreened area is, as matter of law, sufficiently obvious that the defendant reasonably could conclude that a person of ordinary intelligence would perceive the risk and need no additional warning. Even someone of limited personal experience with the sport of baseball reasonably may be assumed to know that a central feature of the game is that batters will forcefully hit balls that may go astray from their intended direction. We therefore hold that the defendant had no duty to warn the plaintiff of the obvious danger of a foul ball being hit into the stands.

The result we reach is consistent with the vast majority of reported decisions involving injuries to spectators at baseball games. Although cases in other jurisdictions have turned on a variety of tort doctrines, they reflect a consensus that baseball stadium owners should not be held responsible for injuries to spectators that result from balls leaving the field during play—at least if adequate safety screening has been provided to protect areas of the stadium in the vicinity of home plate, where the danger is thought to be most acute. As a consequence, injured fans like the plaintiff are left to bear the costs of their injuries, even though they played no role in causing them except by choosing to attend the game.

In its amicus brief, the office of the commissioner of baseball, paraphrasing Justice Cardozo, justifies this result with the cavalier observation that "the timorous may always choose to stay at home." Perhaps a more gracious approach would be for major league baseball to elect to internalize the costs of unavoidable injuries sustained by fans through no fault of their own. On the theory the plaintiff has asserted, however, we do not so require.

Judgment affirmed.

Although declining to impose tort liability, dicta in *Costa* urged Major League Baseball to "internalize the costs of unavoidable injuries sustained by fans through no fault of their own." MLB finally did so in 2020, after a spate of injuries to fans, requiring all ballparks to have protective netting reaching at least the far ends of both dugouts. A number of teams have extended that netting to the foul poles. This step, however, further eroded the baseball rule as at least one court has construed the MLB edict to be a concession that ballparks should do more to reduce spectator injuries.

In *Summer J. v. United States Baseball Fed'n*, 45 Cal. App. 5th 261, 258 Cal. Rptr. 3d 615 (2020), a California court held that the baseball rule did not bar claims on behalf of a 12-year-old girl attending a U.S. Baseball event at a college ballpark when a foul ball struck her in the face, damaging her optic nerve. MLB's requirement of protective netting weighed heavily in the court's reassessment of the baseball rule, along with a changing ballpark environment that has shifted how spectators understand the risks inherent in attending a baseball game:

> Installing protective netting down the first- and third-base lines at least to the dugouts would certainly increase safety and minimize risk to fans sitting in those areas. Would it alter the nature of the game? [Prior decisions] surmised . . . if foul balls hit into the stands were eliminated, "it would be impossible to play the game" [as] protective screens would interfere with the players' ability to reach into the spectator area to catch foul balls, "changing the very nature of the game itself." . . . Commissioner Rob Manfred, the 30 Major League Baseball teams and many minor league teams disagree, all of them planning to expand protective netting in their stadiums substantially beyond the end of the dugouts for the upcoming 2020 season. See generally Grow & Flagel, *The Faulty Law and Economics of the "Baseball Rule"* (discussing developments during the past 25 years that have increased the risk of being injured by foul balls at professional baseball games, including changes in stadium construction that bring spectators closer to the playing field, elevated velocity of pitched balls and increased distractions such as free Wi-Fi). Allegations incorporating the views of experienced baseball professionals that extending protective netting along the first- and third-base lines will minimize the inherent risk of being injured by a foul ball without fundamentally changing the game adequately identify an enforceable duty, at least for pleading purposes. Accordingly, Summer should be permitted to file an amended pleading alleging US Baseball had a duty to ensure there was adequate protective netting at Blair Field on August 17, 2013 and acted unreasonably, breaching that duty of care, by failing to provide netting on the field level along the first- and third-base lines at least from home plate to the dugouts.

Id. at 273–74, 625–26.

A second California court relied on the *Summer* court's reasoning in rejecting the baseball rule as a bar to a similar foul ball injury claim against a college ballpark at La Sierra University. In *Mayes v. La Sierra Univ.*, 73 Cal. App. 5th 686, 288 Cal. Rptr. 3d 693 (2022), the court held that the widespread installation of protective netting at other ballparks raised a triable issue of fact as to whether La Sierra had a duty to invest in similar improvements. The court cautioned, however, that such a duty may depend on whether the upgrade "would have been too expensive or was otherwise unwarranted for an NAIA or smaller college like La Sierra." Should a duty of care depend on the resources available to improve ballpark conditions? The *Mayes* court also deemed triable issues of fact whether La Sierra had a duty to (a) warn spectators about the lack of protective netting, (b) provide more screened seats, and (c) exercise crowd control to minimize distractions from the game. All these alternatives may be more cost-efficient than protective netting, but similarly shift safety responsibility from the fans to the ballpark, in defiance of the baseball rule.

In other industries, when a risk is characteristic of an enterprise, courts have been willing to hold the enterprise strictly liable for resulting injury. That is, nonnegligent accident costs are imposed on the activity, not on the random victim. Why not in sports? What more could baseball stadiums do to protect fans from stray balls, and would those measures appreciably detract from spectator enjoyment of the game? See *Benejam v. Detroit Tigers, Inc.*, 246 Mich. App. 645, 651, 635 N.W.2d 219 (2001) (rejecting liability for injury from flying shard of a broken bat and noting the "inherent value in having most seats unprotected by a screen because baseball patrons generally want to be involved with the game in an intimate way"); *cf. Payne v. Office of the Comm'r of Baseball*, 2016 WL 6778673 (N.D. Cal. Nov. 16, 2016), *aff'd*, 705 F. App'x 654 (9th Cir. 2017) (dismissing class action suit seeking to compel MLB to expand protective netting in its ballparks). Why do most courts continue to prefer a policy favoring spectator enjoyment over risk avoidance?

NOTES AND QUESTIONS

1.   *Open and Obvious Danger.* In declining to impose a duty to warn on the baseball club, the *Costa* court held that the risk of foul balls is open and obvious to anyone attending a baseball game. Should it matter whether a spectator is sufficiently knowledgeable about the game? Should it matter where the spectator is sitting or how early in the game the injury occurred? Should it matter that errant baseballs are not just a common, expected danger of baseball, but actually one of the reasons why fans come to games? *See Rudnick v. Golden West Broadcasters*, 156 Cal. App. 3d 793, 202 Cal. Rptr. 900 (Ct. App. 1984) ("the chance to apprehend a misdirected baseball is as much a part of the game as the seventh inning stretch or peanuts and Cracker Jack").

2.   *Ticket Disclaimer.* Costa's game ticket included a disclaimer that read in relevant part: "The holder assumes all risk and danger incidental to the game of baseball including specifically (but not exclusively) the danger of being injured by thrown bats and thrown or batted balls and agrees that the participating clubs, their agents and players are not liable for injuries resulting from such causes." What is the legal import of this language? Should courts permit a facility operator to contractually modify its duty of care?

3.   *Recreational Sports.* Should the *Costa* reasoning apply to a backyard pick-up softball game? *Judge v. Carrai*, 77 Mass. App. Ct. 803, 934 N.E.2d 276 (2010) (both organizer of the game and hosts, as owners of the softball equipment, owed guest a duty of care).

4.   *Duty of Care to Spectators and Inherent Risks.* Under the traditional baseball rule, a ballpark's duty is merely not to act in a way that increases the risk of injury beyond what is inherent in the sport. As the *Summer* court noted, recent developments have increased the risk that fans will be struck by foul balls, including: (a) new stadium construction places fans closer to the field, (b) the ever-intensifying power and velocity of pitching and hitting gives fans less reaction time, (c) foul balls have increased more than 10 percent since Costa, and (d) fans are faced with more distractions from the action on the field in the form of video scoreboards, colorful advertising, mascots and other entertainment activities, and smartphone usage encouraged by free Wi-Fi. Do these developments require a shift in the legal system's application of the baseball rule, or even argue for its abolition?

Regarding mascot antics, courts are split as to whether this type of distraction should limit the scope of the baseball rule. *Compare Lowe v. California League of Prof. Baseball*, 56 Cal. App. 4th 112, 65 Cal. Rptr. 2d 105 (1997) (fan struck by flying ball when distracted by team mascot permitted to sue because mascot's presence was not necessary to the game), *with Harting v. Dayton Dragons Prof'l Baseball Club, L.L.C.*, 171 Ohio App. 3d 319, 870 N.E.2d 766 (2007) (given prevalence of team mascots at sporting events, mascot's antics did not excuse fan from paying attention to action on the field).

5.   *Facility Amenities and Architecture.* Courts are willing to deviate from the baseball rule's quasi-immunity when facility amenities increase the dangers associated with game attendance. The Idaho Supreme Court, in a case of first impression, declined to adopt the baseball rule where a foul ball flew into a "multi-purpose" club area and hit a spectator, causing him to lose an eye. *Bud Rountree v. Boise Baseball*, 154 Idaho 167, 296 P.3d 373 (2013). The New Mexico Supreme Court similarly rejected the baseball rule in a case where a child sitting in a picnic area was struck by a baseball:

> [A]n owner/occupant of a commercial baseball stadium owes a duty that is symmetrical to the duty of the spectator. Spectators must exercise ordinary care to protect themselves from the inherent risk of being hit by a projectile that leaves the field of play and the owner/ occupant must exercise ordinary care not to increase that inherent risk.

Edward C. v. City of Albuquerque, 148 N.M. 646, 658–59, 241 P.3d 1086 (2010). *See also Maisonave v. Newark Bears Professional Baseball Club, Inc.*, 185 N.J. 70, 881 A.2d 700 (2005) (spectator did not assume the risk of being hit by a foul ball when he was at a concession stand in the concourse and not at his seat); *Jones v. Three Rivers Mgmt. Corp.*, 483 Pa. 75, 394 A.2d 546 (1978) (fan struck when standing in concourse allowed to sue because architectural features of stadium impaired sightlines to field).

Contrast *Turner v. Mandalay Sports Entertainment, LLC*, 124 Nev. 213, 180 P.3d 1172 (2008), in which the Nevada Supreme Court narrowly reaffirmed the baseball rule to immunize stadium operators for foul-ball injuries to fans struck at any location inside the stadium, not just when sitting in their seats. The court held that a fan assumed the risk of being hit by a ball even while eating at a picnic area with restricted views of the field. The dissent in *Turner* would have followed *Maisonave*, the New Jersey case cited above. Which is the best approach for determining the duty of a baseball club towards spectators?

6.   *Other Sports Projectiles.* The baseball rule has been applied to hockey pucks, even when a spectator was hit during pre-game warmups when crowds of fans obstructed her view. *See Nemarnik v. Los Angeles Kings Hockey Club, L.P.*, 103 Cal. App. 4th 631, 638, 127 Cal. Rptr. 2d 10 (2002) ("it is undisputed that ice hockey spectators face a known risk of being hit by a flying puck"). Similarly, a spectator at a football game was deemed to have assumed the risk of being hit by a football punted on the sidelines during player introductions. *See Callinan v. Nat'l Football League*, 2021 WL 6081473 (Md. Ct. Spec. App. Dec. 23, 2021). Notably, the *Callinan* court relied heavily on the spectator's acknowledged familiarity with the sport and the risk of errant footballs to fans sitting only six rows from the field. Should a novice spectator's claim have been allowed to proceed?

Contrast *Allred v. Capital Area Soccer League, Inc.*, 194 N.C. App. 280, 669 S.E.2d 777 (2008), where the court held that a spectator at a soccer game injured by a struck ball was entitled to pursue her claim based on lack of knowledge of the risk of injury. At the time of this ruling, soccer was still emerging as a spectator sport in the U.S. Do you think that was outcome determinative? *See also Coomer v. Kansas City Royals*, 437 S.W.3d 184 (Mo. 2014) (rejecting application of the baseball rule when a fan was hit by a flying hotdog thrown by team mascot).

7.   *Premises Liability in General.* Beyond a sport's known projectile hazards, facility operators are subject to standard premises liability principles in force in their jurisdiction. Generally, facility operators have a duty to maintain a reasonably safe environment for invitees. This includes using reasonable care to regulate crowd control and invitee conduct during sporting events. *See Brisbin v. Washington Sports & Entm't, Ltd.*, 422 F. Supp. 2d 9, 13 (D.D.C. 2006) (spectator injured when another spectator fell on her could pursue her negligence claim only if supported by expert testimony on "the appropriate standard of care Washington Sports should have met based on the Center's physical layout"). This principle is discussed further in Section B.4.

B.   HEALTH AND SAFETY OFF THE FIELD

Injuries and medical conditions from playing sports can be precipitated or exacerbated by the off-field decisions and practices of leagues, teams, and their personnel. Leagues closely monitor their game presentations and periodically adjust their playing rules to enhance both entertainment value and player safety. Leagues hire and train game officials to enforce those playing rules and keep the game safe. Teams hire health care professionals, including physicians, physical therapists, and athletic trainers, to provide for the physical well-being of their athletes.

Playing surfaces and equipment are inspected and upgraded to promote safety as well as to improve athletic performance. The discharge of these duties and many other functions of sports leagues and teams is subject to the standard of reasonable care to avoid foreseeable harm to the athletes.

PROBLEM 16.2

Deion Fleet is a college football cornerback anticipated to be a first-round NFL draft pick. He recently learned he has a variant of a gene associated with a predisposition to concussions. When this was disclosed, his draft stock plummeted, but one team was willing to take a chance on him as long as he followed a regimen of targeted neck muscle strengthening recommended by the athletic training staff. He was also encouraged to use a specially designed helmet among those approved by the NFL.

Fleet found that as a result of the exercises, he experienced some discomfort in rotating his neck, flexibility that is essential to defending the pass. He decreased the strengthening exercises and also obtained painkillers from the team physician to mask the discomfort during games. Midway through his first season, an on-field collision resulted in a concussion from which he never fully recovered, ending his NFL career. What claims could Fleet bring for his career-ending injury, and in what forum? What defenses might be available to the NFL and its teams?

---

1. MEDICAL MALPRACTICE

Sports teams usually employ physicians and other health care professionals to provide athletes with a range of services, including prevention, diagnosis, treatment, and rehabilitation of injuries and medical conditions. Regardless of who pays their salary, team physicians are first and foremost bound by their professional code and legal duty to prioritize the patient-athlete's health. Even so, the singular relationship among a team, its players, and the team doctor is susceptible to conflicts of interest arising out of the need for the athlete to heal quickly and help the team win. Team medical staff face undeniable pressure to subordinate the athlete's well-being to the team's and often the athlete's own strong desire that he or she return to play. Athletes may pursue malpractice claims when the team physician's judgment appears compromised by the team's need for the player's services. Recovery for malpractice against team medical professionals, however, is complicated in team sports by (1) league collective bargaining agreements and standard playing contracts, and (2) state workers' compensation rules.

First, in unionized sports, the labor agreement typically provides contractual injury protection guarantees and disability benefits to athletes for playing injuries. *See Giles v. Bert Bell/Pete Rozelle NFL Player Ret. Plan*, 2013 WL 6909200 (D. Md. Dec. 31, 2013) (interpreting NFL players' disability benefits plan). As discussed in Chapter 4, Section D, players who dispute the team's assessment of their rights under those agreements must submit their claims to binding arbitration under federal labor law that preempts tort suits. *See Smith v. Houston Oilers, Inc.*, 87 F.3d 717 (5th Cir. 1996) (requiring arbitration of claims arising out of allegedly abusive rehabilitation program); *Boogaard v. Nat'l Hockey League*, 126 F. Supp. 3d 1010 (N.D. Ill. 2015) (requiring arbitration of claims arising out of hockey players' substance abuse); *Sherwin v. Indianapolis Colts, Inc.*, 752 F. Supp. 1172 (N.D.N.Y. 1990) (requiring arbitration of claims of inadequate medical care and intentionally withholding information about player's injury). A tort claim is available only if the player's allegations do not implicate the collective bargaining agreement (CBA). *See Bentley v. Cleveland Browns Football Co.*, 194 Ohio App. 3d 826, 958 N.E.2d 585 (2011) (claims for fraud and negligent misrepresentation in treating player's staph infection do not implicate the CBA); *Brown v. Nat'l Football League*, 219 F. Supp. 2d 372 (S.D.N.Y. 2002) (allowing player's tort claim for career-ending eye injury caused when referee struck him with penalty flag because based on state law duty independent of CBA).

Second, in most states, businesses that employ workers must purchase workers' compensation insurance. Where an employer team pays for this coverage and provides the benefits to an injured player, those benefits become the player's exclusive remedy. Injured players are statutorily barred from bringing tort suits against the team and co-employees. Thus, in *Stringer v. Minnesota Vikings Football Club, LLC*, 705 N.W.2d 746 (Minn. 2005), the Minnesota Supreme Court held that when a Vikings team member died of heat stroke during training camp, his survivors could not recover in a tort action against the team medical staff who treated him. *See also DePiano v. Montreal Baseball Club, Ltd.*, 663 F. Supp. 116 (W.D. Pa. 1987), *aff'd*, 838 F.2d 1205 (3d Cir. 1988) (workers' compensation was exclusive remedy for team doctor's negligent medical treatment of minor league baseball player).

An injured athlete may be able to recover in tort against team medical personnel who are independent contractors, rather than co-employees. In *Bryant v. Fox & Chicago Bears*, 162 Ill. App. 3d 46, 515 N.E.2d 775 (1987), the court held that two Bears players were not limited to statutory remedies, and reinstated their medical malpractice claims against the team physician because the team treated the doctor as an independent contractor, paying him fees for services provided, without issuing a W-2 or making Social Security deductions. In addition, some states have been willing to carve out exceptions from workers' compensation exclusivity for claims that an employer intentionally inflicted physical injury.

KRUEGER v. SAN FRANCISCO FORTY NINERS
189 Cal. App. 3d 823, 234 Cal. Rptr. 579 (Ct. App. 1987)

NEWSOM, ASSOCIATE JUSTICE.

Appellant began playing professional football with the San Francisco 49'ers (hereafter respondent or the 49'ers) in 1958. He was a defensive lineman for the 49'ers until retiring in 1973, missing only parts of two seasons due to injuries. During his career, however, appellant played despite suffering numerous injuries. . . .

The injuries and damages to appellant's left knee are the focus of the present suit. While in college in 1955, appellant had surgery on his left knee to repair a torn meniscus. Then, in October of 1963, he ruptured the medial collateral ligament in his left knee. Dr. Lloyd Taylor, a physician who treated 49'ers' players, performed an operation on the knee which, appellant was told, effectuated a "good repair." Thereafter, appellant engaged in rehabilitative therapy with the team trainer and was given a knee brace which he later wore while playing until he removed it in 1967.

Dr. Taylor noted in his report of the operation that the anterior cruciate ligament—the function of which is to prevent the tibia from shifting forward on the femur—"appeared to be absent" from appellant's left knee. Such an injury can produce instability in the knee, particularly if combined with other injuries. According to appellant, he was not told that his left knee evidently lacked the anterior cruciate ligament.

In the spring of 1964, appellant began experiencing pain and considerable swelling in his left knee. He again received treatment from physicians retained by the 49'ers, specifically Dr. Taylor and Dr. Lloyd Milburn, which consisted of aspiration of bloody fluid from the knee by means of a syringe and contemporaneous injection of novocain and cortisone, a steroid compound. Appellant testified that he received approximately 50 such "Kepplemann" treatments during 1964, and an average of 14 to 20 per year from 1964 to 1973. Dr. Milburn could not recall administering Kepplemann treatments with such frequency, and testified that his records indicated only seven such treatments. Appellant also testified that he was never advised by the 49'ers medical staff of the dangers associated with steroid injections in the knee, such as possible rupturing of tendons, weakening of joints and cartilage, and destruction of capillaries and blood vessels. He also offered expert medical testimony that the adverse effects of steroids were known at that time. The same medical expert also testified that the number of steroid injections appellant claimed to have undergone would have been inappropriate and quite "unusual."

Appellant's left knee continued to plague him during his football career, and in 1971 he underwent another operation performed by Dr. Taylor to remove "loose bodies" in the knee resulting from chronic chondromalacia patella—thinning and loss of cartilage on the undersurface of the kneecap, a condition fully consistent with known adverse reaction to prolonged steroid use. X-rays taken between 1964 and 1971 revealed "degenerative post-traumatic changes" in appellant's left knee joint. Appellant testified—without contradiction—that he was not told of either of these afflictions by the 49'ers medical staff.

Krueger also testified that he suffered a "hit" on the outside of the knee during a game in 1970. He felt a piece of the knee break off. Notwithstanding the obvious severity of the injury, appellant was given Empirin codeine and directed to return to the game. For the remainder of the season, he could feel a "considerable piece of substance" dislodged on the outside of his left knee joint; nevertheless, he played the remaining five games of the season. At no time did the team doctors ever advise him that he risked permanent injury by continuing to play without surgery. Krueger testified unequivocally that, had he been advised not to play, he would have followed that advice. . . .

Appellant retired from football following the 1973 season. . . . Not until 1978 was appellant treated again for his injured knee. At that time, he received a Kepplemann treatment from Dr. Milburn, and x-rays were taken of both legs. According to appellant it was not until this visit to Dr. Milburn in 1978 that he was shown x-rays of his knees and advised for the first time that he suffered from chronic and permanent disability in the knee.

Defendant was referred to Dr. Taylor, who subsequently performed on him a tibial osteotomy, which is a shaving of planes from the leg bone followed by regrafting of the tendons and ligaments to the bone. The operation did nothing to alleviate appellant's severe discomfort, and in fact, he thereafter developed calcification in the knee and suffered greater pain than had been the case before the surgery. He presently suffers from traumatic arthritis and a crippling degenerative process in the left knee. He cannot stand up for prolonged periods, and cannot run. He is also unable to walk on stairs without severe pain. His condition is degenerative and irreversible.

Appellant's action was for fraud or deceit. . . . "Deceit may be negative as well as affirmative; it may consist in suppression of that which it is one's duty to disclose, as well as in the declaration of that which is false." [citation omitted] [T]he intentional concealment of a material fact is actionable fraud only if there is a fiduciary relationship giving rise to a duty to disclose it. The relationship between physician and patient is fiduciary in nature and creates a duty to disclose. . . .

As to the crucial issue of full disclosure, . . . we find the evidence uncontradicted; as will appear, the requisite disclosure was never made. That the team physicians *withheld* no material information from Krueger is not, in our view, the proper focus of inquiry. The critical question is whether full *disclosure* of his medical condition was ever made to Krueger. . . .

The physician must disclose to the patient all information necessary to make a knowledgeable decision about proposed treatment. The duty to disclose is imposed so that patients might meaningfully exercise their right to make decisions affecting their own bodies. Hence, even if the patient rejects a recommended procedure, the duty to disclose is nonetheless recognized.

* * *

In our opinion, the duty of full disclosure within the context of a doctor-patient relationship defines the test for concealment or suppression of facts under Civil Code section 1710, subdivision (3). The failure to make such disclosure constitutes not only negligence, but—where the requisite intent is shown—fraud or concealment as well. A physician cannot avoid responsibility for failure to make full disclosure by simply claiming that information was not withheld.

The testimony that, following his knee surgery in 1963, Krueger was not advised of the adverse effects of steroid injections, or of the risks associated with the continued pursuit of his profession, was uncontradicted. That is, while respondent produced testimony that the physicians treating appellant told him of the general nature of his injury, and did not conceal certain information from him, there is no evidence that appellant was ever informed of the continuing risks associated with his injuries. Hence, the requisite disclosure was never made. . . .

[W]e think the record unequivocally demonstrates that, in its desire to keep appellant on the playing field, respondent consciously failed to make full, meaningful disclosure to him respecting the magnitude of the risk he took in continuing to play a violent contact sport with a profoundly damaged left knee. . . . [I]t is in this palpable failure to disclose, viewed in the light of the 49'ers compelling obvious interest in prolonging appellant's career, that we find the intent requisite for a finding of fraudulent concealment. . . . [Krueger] was entitled . . . to rely upon respondent's physicians for medical treatment and advice without consulting outside sources or undertaking independent investigation.

Turning to the issues of proximate cause and damages, we note the trial court's finding that appellant's desire to continue playing was so intense that he would have continued even had he been informed of the magnitude of the risk involved. This finding seems to us mere conjecture. Appellant demonstrated throughout his football career a courageous—some might say foolhardy—willingness to endure pain and injuries for the sake of his team and employer, but no credible evidence suggests that he ever assessed and accepted the prospect of permanent disability. On the contrary, he testified that he would have retired had respondent's physicians recommended that course of action, and no contrary evidence was offered by respondent.

Motion for dismissal denied.

————

The 49ers paid Krueger more than $1 million to settle the litigation. Numerous other notable athletes have successfully sued their team doctors for medical malpractice in the treatment (or non-treatment) of their injuries. *See Rolle v. Brigham*, No. 11 CVS 11278 (Sup. Ct. N.C. Sept. 5, 2014) (Baltimore Ravens cornerback won $650,00 jury award against team doctor who cleared him to return to play too soon after spinal surgery); *Babych v. Comcast-Spectator*, No. ATL-L-1365-00 (Sup. Ct. N.J. Oct. 31, 2002) (Philadelphia Flyer won $1.37 million jury award against team physician for forcing him to play with a broken foot in the 1998 NHL playoffs); *Novak v. Lucie*, No. 00-04156 (Circ. Ct. Fl. July 19, 2002) (Jacksonville Jaguars offensive lineman received $2.2 million settlement from team doctor who cleared him to play pre-season game that severely aggravated an earlier leg injury and ended his career); *Hoge v. Munsell*, No. 2-01-0214 (Cty. Ct. Ill. July 21, 2000) (Chicago Bears running back won $1.55 million jury award against team doctor who failed to properly treat concussions and cleared him to play, resulting in further career-ending injury); *Barrett v. Pappas*, No. 92-CV-40076 (D. Mass. Oct. 26, 1995) (Red Sox infielder won $1.7 million jury award against team doctor who diagnosed only torn cartilage so he would return to play, when he actually tore his anterior crucial ligament).

Cases like these have led several malpractice insurers to stop covering doctors who provide medical care to professional athletes, or to require team physicians to sign explicit employment agreements with their teams. In *Daniels v. Seattle Seahawks*, 92 Wash. App. 576, 968 P.2d 883 (1998), a player who was misdiagnosed, and whose subsequent injury prematurely ended his career, sued the Seahawks' team physician for malpractice. The court found that the physician's detailed employment contract with the Seahawks controlled the physician's conduct while performing his contractual duties, and as a result, the player could bring only workers' compensation claims against the team. Even though team physicians under employment contracts retain sole responsibility for medical decisions, the courts have continued to find that the teams maintain the requisite control over the team physicians to qualify them as employees.

Collective bargaining agreements increasingly articulate and expand upon players' rights with respect to medical care. The NFL's 2020–2030 Collective Bargaining Agreement entitles players to seek second medical opinions from independent providers at the team's expense. In Article 39, Section 1(e), it further spells out the relationship between team doctor and athlete-patient:

Medical Providers and Allegiance. The cost of medical services rendered by Club physicians, Club Athletic Trainers,

Physical Therapists, and other medical providers (together, "Club medical personnel") will be the responsibility of the respective Clubs, but the Club medical personnel's primary duty in providing player medical care shall be not to the Club but instead to the player-patient regardless of the fact that he/she or his/her hospital, clinic, or medical group is retained by the Club to diagnose and treat players. The Club medical personnel shall not disclose confidential player health information except as permitted. In addition, all Club medical personnel shall comply with all federal, state, and local requirements, including all ethical rules and standards established by any applicable government and/or other authority that regulates or governs the medical profession in the Club's city. All Club physicians are required to disclose to a player any and all information about the player's physical condition that the physician may from time to time provide to a coach or other Club representative, whether or not such information affects the player's performance or health. If a Club physician advises a coach or other Club representative of a player's serious injury or career threatening physical condition which significantly affects the player's performance or health, the physician will also advise the player in writing. The player, after being advised of such serious injury or career-threatening physical condition, may request a copy of the Club physician's record from the examination in which such physical condition was diagnosed and/or a written explanation from the Club physician of the physical condition.

NOTES AND QUESTIONS

1. *Physician-Patient Relationship.* The *Krueger* court described the physician-patient relationship as a fiduciary one, imposing a duty of full disclosure and informed consent for medical treatment. Liability, however, depended on Krueger showing that the physician's breach of the duty *caused* his injury, that is, he would have made other treatment decisions or quit playing the sport if he were fully informed. Should an athlete be permitted to continue playing against medical advice, at a risk of permanent disability? What is the team's responsibility here? In competitive sports cultures, some athletes may dissemble about symptoms or pain they are experiencing to hasten return to play. And for a variety of reasons, some athletes simply fail to follow treatment instructions. Such conduct may amount to contributory negligence that bars or limits recovery.

2. *Standard of Care for Malpractice Suits.* Medical negligence is measured by the standard of care that applies in the specific treatment setting. Different states impose different tests for physician conduct, which can depend on the field of medicine and whether the doctor's skill and care is measured

against national or local standards. Sports medicine is increasingly recognized as a distinct specialization subject to national standards. *See Zimbauer v. Milwaukee Orthopaedic Grp., Ltd.*, 920 F. Supp. 959 (E.D. Wis. 1996) (requiring baseball pitcher to submit expert testimony on standard of care physician owed for sports medical treatment).

3. *Sports Medicine Malpractice Reform.* What more can sports leagues do to assure appropriate medical care beyond spelling out players' rights and team physician duties in the labor agreement? Options for sports malpractice reform include having the leagues hire doctors as part-time employees, not just independent contractors, to eliminate negligence suits while insulating physicians from team pressure to return athletes to play quickly. Alternatively, players unions could hire the physicians, eliminating the co-employee immunity under workers' compensation and giving players a chance to receive adequate compensation for the premature ending of their careers. This proposal would require some level of league or union financial support for malpractice insurance, in order to give physicians the incentives and protection necessary to continue treating professional athletes.

4. *Physically Impaired Athletes.* What if the physicians who treated Krueger correctly diagnosed his injury and declared him physically unfit to return to play, over his objection? That is, what if an athlete with a physical impairment is fully informed of the risks and nonetheless wants to participate in a sport? Is the team required to let him or her play? This issue arose in the 1990 case of Mark Seay, a wide receiver for the Long Beach State College football team, who was struck by a stray bullet meant for a street gang member. Seay lost a kidney, and the bullet remained lodged near his heart. The school refused to allow Seay to return to the football team because of the risk of aggravating his injury. Seay sued and, on the eve of trial, the school relented and allowed him to play football again—but only in return for a signed waiver of liability. What explains the school's reluctance to take this route in the first place? Concern that California courts would deem such a waiver unenforceable in the event of a tort suit? Concern that by agreeing to the liability waiver, schools open the door for other athletes with serious medical conditions to sign similar waivers and compete against the advice of their doctors?

2. LEAGUE AND TEAM POLICIES AND PRACTICES THAT AFFECT PLAYER HEALTH AND SAFETY

League and team policies and practices also have serious repercussions on player well-being. While injuries are inevitable in sports, especially those like football and hockey that mandate physical collisions, the way that leagues and teams manage player injuries and return-to-play can determine long-term health outcomes. Accusations that injury management practices prioritize team interests over player health and safety have surfaced in a range of lawsuits involving prescription drug medication and concussions.

(a) Prescription Drug Abuse Litigation

In 2014, nine former NFL players brought a putative class action against the league, and *not* the member clubs, alleging a policy and practice of encouraging abuse of painkillers to keep players on the field at all costs. The lawsuit alleged both negligent and intentional tortious conduct and violations of federal regulation of prescription drugs:

> [Plaintiffs] alleged that since 1969, the NFL has distributed controlled substances and prescription drugs to its players in violation of both state and federal laws, and that the manner in which these drugs were administered left the players with permanent injuries and chronic medical conditions. . . .

> [D]uring their years in the NFL, they received copious amounts of opioids, non-steroidal anti-inflammatory medications, and local anesthetics. The complaint claims the NFL encouraged players to take these pain-masking medications to keep players on the field and revenues high, even as the football season got longer and the time between games got shorter, increasing their chances of injury. According to the players, they "rarely, if ever, received written prescriptions . . . for the medications they were receiving." Instead, they say they were handed pills in "small manila envelopes that often had no directions or labeling" and were told to take whatever was in the envelopes. During their years of consuming these powerful medications, it is further alleged that no one from the NFL warned them about potential side effects, long-term risks, interactions with other drugs, or the likelihood of addiction. The plaintiffs claim that as a result of their use (and overuse) of these drugs, retired players suffer from permanent orthopedic injuries, drug addictions, heart problems, nerve damage, and renal failure.

Dent v. Nat'l Football League, 902 F.3d 1109, 1114–15 (9th Cir. 2018) (lawsuit not preempted under labor law to extent alleges direct participation by NFL in providing medical care and supplying drugs to players).

After multiple rounds of pleading and discovery, the lawsuit was whittled down to a single negligence claim against the NFL. That claim rested on a "voluntary undertaking" theory that the NFL had assumed a "duty to ensure the proper recordkeeping, administration and distribution" of prescription medications. These voluntary undertakings included a drug oversight program that required clubs to report to the NFL, audits of club compliance with federal drug laws, mandated registration of facilities used to store controlled substances, annual meetings between club medical personnel and NFL officials, and NFL-funded studies on prescription drug use. *Dent v. Nat'l Football League*, 968 F.3d 1126 (9th Cir. 2020). Ultimately, even this claim failed because barred by the relevant statutes of limitations. *Dent v. Nat'l Football League*, 2021 WL 5987260 (N.D. Cal. Dec. 17, 2021) (on appeal as this edition goes to press).

Former players also pursued virtually identical painkiller abuse claims against individual NFL clubs. *See Evans v. Arizona Cardinals Football Club LLC*, 2016 WL 3566945 (N.D. Cal. July 1, 2016) (holding that players' claims against teams were not preempted by § 301, and denying teams' motion to dismiss). Discovery had sufficiently advanced in that suit to permit the district court to grant summary judgment to the defendant clubs, dismissing all claims. *See* 231 F. Supp. 3d 342 (N.D. Cal. 2017), *aff'd*, 761 F. App'x 701 (9th Cir. 2019) (dismissing RICO claims); 252 F. Supp. 3d 855 (N.D. Cal. 2017) (dismissing fraudulent concealment claims); 262 F. Supp. 3d 935 (N.D. Cal. 2017) (dismissing remaining claims because no intentional misconduct sufficient to fall within exceptions to workers' compensation exclusivity).

Despite their inefficacy in obtaining compensation for the plaintiffs, the prescription drug lawsuits got the attention of the federal Drug Enforcement Agency, which conducted a few surprise inspections of NFL locker rooms to investigate the misuse of prescription drugs. In addition, the NFLPA filed a grievance alleging the overprescription of painkillers violates the CBA, including the "Medical Providers and Allegiance" provision excerpted above.

Consider what is the best forum to redress the former players' torts claims as well as systemic issues regarding player healthcare—the courts or the collectively bargained arbitral tribunal? Consider also how the NFL collective agreement might address the incentives to over-medicate players.

(b) Concussion Litigation

Systemic threats to player health and safety are also the subject of concussion litigation mounted by both professional and amateur athletes against multiple sports entities. Lawsuits were filed in the wake of scientific advances that suggest that repeated traumatic brain injuries can have latent consequences, including a host of cognitive impairments, degenerative diseases, mental illness, and a condition known as chronic traumatic encephalopathy (CTE).

Starting in 2011, retired NFL players filed lawsuits claiming that the NFL had a duty to address the risks of brain injuries to protect players. Hundreds of similar suits followed, including some styled as class actions. In June 2012, they were consolidated in the Eastern District of Pennsylvania and captioned *In re National Football League Players' Concussion Injury Litigation*, 842 F. Supp. 2d 1378 (U.S. Jud. Pan. Mult. Lit. 2012). The master complaint sought to impose liability on the NFL and its member clubs for negligence, fraud, and misrepresentation in connection with warning players about the risk of head injuries, conducting and disseminating relevant scientific research, developing playing rules and equipment designed to protect players from concussion-related health risks, and developing policies and procedures for dealing with player head injuries and return-to-play. Claims were also lodged against Riddell, the NFL's helmet manufacturer, accusing it of designing a defective product and failing to adequately warn players about its inherent deficiencies.

While motions were pending to dismiss the litigation as to the NFL parties based on § 301 labor preemption (see Chapter 4), the judge ordered mediation and a settlement resulted. *In re Nat. Football League Players' Concussion Injury Litig.*, 307 F.R.D. 351, 363 (E.D. Pa. 2015), *aff'd*, 821 F.3d 410 (3d Cir. 2016). In its final iteration, the settlement offered over 20,000 former NFL players both medical monitoring and compensation for cognitive injuries from an uncapped settlement fund. Money was also set aside for medical research. By 2022, the NFL had paid out over $1 billion to affected players, with awards ranging from $27,000 to $5.3 million depending on years in the league, age at the time of onset of symptoms, and severity of impairment. Although about 100 former players opted out of the class settlement, most of those cases also eventually settled, making it increasingly unlikely that the litigation will ever produce judicial decisions on issues such as labor preemption and causation.

The merits of the case against the NFL suggest that it had a good chance of ultimately prevailing on those issues. The NFL argued that the players knew the risks of playing the game at the highest level, and were aware of the effect of repeated impacts to their heads. As an evidentiary matter, retirees who continued to pursue litigation would have had to establish actual causation—*e.g.*, that their conditions resulted from concussions received while playing the NFL as opposed to in high school or college. And finally, labor preemption of most claims was likely, given collective bargaining agreements that specifically addressed player health and safety. Consider then the strategic value of the concussion litigation, aimed not necessarily at obtaining a court judgment but at putting the defendant in a public relations situation where it concludes it must do the "right thing" even if not legally compelled to do so.

Hence, both sides in the NFL concussion litigation were highly motivated to reach a settlement. The former players faced debilitating neurological problems that needed immediate attention. Pursuing a remedy through litigation might have taken years of discovery, a trial, and inevitable appeals, with a favorable outcome far from certain. By reaching the settlement, the NFL hoped to avoid opening its files to pre-trial discovery and continuing to experience bad public relations for the League and the sport. However, the NFL settlement did not resolve the former players' cases against helmet manufacturer Riddell. While a settlement is possible, Riddell has less incentive to resolve the claims because of its potential extensive exposure to litigation, pending as well as future, brought on behalf of high school and college athletes who use its helmets.

Meanwhile, the claims process for the NFL concussion settlement fund has been plagued with allegations of fraud perpetrated by and against players. The independently administered fund has mechanisms in place to detect fraudulent claims, and hundreds of submissions have been flagged as suspicious. In addition, unscrupulous lenders and lawyers have induced hundreds of retired players to sign dubious contracts for settlement advances and claims services that charge exorbitant fees. Given these complications and delays, consider whether the players back in 2011 would have been better served by pursuing relief in the first instance through their collectively bargained grievance procedures. Notably, beginning with the NFL 2011–2020 CBA, former players may apply for a "neuro-cognitive disability benefit," a feature designed both to compensate deserving players and firmly preempt future litigation.

With the litigation largely behind it, the NFL invested in a $60,000 initiative called "Engineering Roadmap" to advance the understanding of biomechanics in football and encourage development of new and improved protective equipment. Starting with the 2015 season, the NFL has studied video of every reported concussion, which at that time averaged about 250 per year, and categorized them by the type of play, the positions of the players involved (cornerbacks top the victim list), and the site of helmet impact. The review led to revised training methods, reduced use of high-impact practice drills, better-performing helmets, and safety-focused rules changes. Five years later, for the 2021 season, the NFL recorded 187 concussions during games and practices, a 25 percent decrease.

Concussion lawsuits were also lodged against the NHL and the NCAA. Former NHL players claimed that the league did not do enough to protect them from the dangers of head trauma, especially in sending them out to fight and expecting them to shake off resulting injuries. In contrast to the NFL, the NHL adopted an aggressive litigation strategy of fighting the claims on all fronts, generating multiple substantive rulings. Notably, the league defeated class certification on the grounds that state legal standards vary too widely to satisfy the class action requirement that common questions of law predominate. *See In re: Nat'l Hockey League Players' Concussion Injury Litig.*, 2018 WL 3421343 (D. Minn. July 13, 2018). *See also* 189 F. Supp. 3d 856 (D. Minn. 2016) (denying labor preemption motion pending additional discovery); 2015 WL 1334027 (D. Minn. Mar. 25, 2015) (denying motion to dismiss).

The NHL cases were consolidated as a multidistrict litigation for the purpose of procedural motions and discovery, and unlike the NFL litigation, the NHL parties took extensive document and deposition discovery of league executives, team owners, and players, most of which has been kept confidential. While the league settled these claims for $19 million, this modest payout bought an equally modest release from further liability as it covered only named plaintiffs, and not the entire class of potentially injured former players. Thus, new cases continue to arise, and the league continues to press its defenses, primarily based on labor preemption and statutes of limitation. At least one court has ruled that negligence claims based on voluntary undertakings, duty to disclose, failure to warn, and misrepresentation were all preempted under the NHL CBA, and players were required to resolve those claims according to mandatory grievance and arbitration procedures. *Carcillo v. Nat'l Hockey League*, 529 F. Supp. 3d 768 (N.D. Ill. 2021).

College-athletes also filed concussion suits against the NCAA, which were consolidated in 2013 into *In re Nat'l Collegiate Athletic Ass'n Student-Athlete Concussion Injury Litigation*. The athletes' claims track those of NFL and NHL players, alleging that the NCAA failed in its duty to protect them from the risks of traumatic brain injury. The parties reached a settlement agreement that received final approval in 2019. *In re Nat'l Collegiate Athletic Ass'n Student-Athlete Concussion Inj. Litig.*, 332 F.R.D. 202, 207 (N.D. Ill. 2019), *aff'd sub nom. Walker v. Nat'l Collegiate Athletic Ass'n*, No. 19-2638, 2019 WL 8058082 (7th Cir. Oct. 25, 2019). The settlement provides $75 million for medical monitoring and research and requires member schools to institute return-to-play guidelines under concussion management policies. Although the settlement did not include damages for the plaintiffs, individual athletes were free to pursue compensatory damages in separate personal injury lawsuits, and many did. *See, e.g., Rose v. Nat'l Collegiate Athletic Ass'n*, 346 F. Supp. 3d 1212 (N.D. Ill. 2018) (dismissing contract claims and allowing fraudulent concealment claim to proceed on basis of NCAA's superior knowledge of risks of repetitive head impacts in football games).

Concern about traumatic brain injury has now spread across sport, including wrestling, water polo, rugby, and cheerleading. In soccer (internationally known as football), the concern arises primarily from the risk of subconcussive trauma from repetitive heading of the ball. In the United States, youth soccer players brought a putative class action against FIFA, the sport's international governing body, and other soccer entities, alleging that they failed to adopt and enforce rules that would reduce the risk of preventable injuries resulting from concussions and heading the ball. The court declined to impute "a legal duty to reduce the risks inherent in the sport of soccer" in the absence of facts showing that any defendant took any action that increased those risks. *Mehr v. Féderation Internationale de Football Ass'n*, 115 F. Supp. 3d 1035 (N.D. Cal. 2015) (dismissing suit for lack of personal jurisdiction, lack of subject matter jurisdiction, and failure to state a claim). Nonetheless, the United States Soccer Federation responded with a series of safety initiatives that set strict limits on youth players heading balls. In 2022, England's Football Association instituted a trial program that prohibits players under the age of 12 to head the ball in training. The FA's guidelines further recommend that all players, including professionals, should be exposed to a maximum of 10 high-force headers a week in training. Heading is still permitted in competition, but a future devoid of heading is not unthinkable; consider the repercussions that would have across the sport.

———

NOTES AND QUESTIONS

1. *Existential Threat to Contact Sports.* The concussion litigation poses a fundamentally different and possibly existential challenge to contact sports. Most civil and criminal suits involving sports spring from prohibited conduct, both on and off the field. Liability can be avoided when the athlete has given informed consent to the risk. By contrast, the concussion class actions arise from injuries sustained while playing the sport according to its rules and within the participants' reasonable expectations. Avoiding those injuries requires more than simply enforcing existing rules of the game. Furthermore, it may not be possible to obtain informed consent to head injuries where the medical science is still emerging or where society is not willing to tolerate the risk. Should public policy demand radically changing the rules of the game—or even banning the sport—to avoid head injury risk? Consider that game rules inevitably affect amateur and youth participants as well as professionals.

2. *Game Rules Changes.* Since 2002, the NFL has made over 50 rules changes intended to eliminate potentially dangerous tactics and reduce the risk of injuries. These changes include prohibiting use of the helmet as a weapon against defenseless players, banning "horse-collar" tackles when a defender grabs a player's jersey from the back of the neck, and moving the touchback forward to discourage the kickoff return. Other sports have also tinkered with rules to improve player safety. Beginning with the 2014 season, Major League Baseball outlawed collisions at home plate: a baserunner may not barrel through the catcher and catchers may not block the plate without holding the ball. As of the 2016 season, MLB banned rolling block slides at second base to break up potential double plays. Both rules changes stemmed from game incidents in which players suffered serious orthopedic injuries. Were any of these revised rules fundamental to the game? As professional athletes grow bigger and stronger, with improved nutrition and training, should leagues be anticipating injury risks and proactively adjusting their rules? Should leagues face tort liability for creating rules that put athletes at an undue risk, or should juries stay out of the business of second-guessing competition rules?

3. *Game-Day and Medical Protocols.* In addition to rules changes, the NFL has instituted protocols to monitor and safeguard player health. Game-day staffing rules now mandate an unaffiliated neurotrauma consultant and athletic trainers to assist team medical staffs in identifying concussions and other potential player injuries. When traveling across state lines, every visiting team must retain a local licensed emergency physician affiliated with a nearby

trauma center. Dedicated video monitors are provided for injury review. Concussion diagnosis and return-to-participation protocols, including mandatory sit-time, are strictly enforced. What more should the NFL be doing?

Consider the analysis offered by a football players' health study: *Protecting and Promoting the Health of NFL Players* (Harvard Univ. 2016). Among its recommendations are: a ban on adversarial collective bargaining over player health issues; flexible roster caps to encourage players with concussions to sit without penalty to teams; guaranteeing more of player compensation; and fining teams and team doctors for violating rules that protect player health. In addition, every state has enacted some form of legislation requiring monitoring and protection against concussions in youth sports. *See* National Conference of State Legislatures, *Traumatic Brain Injury Legislation*, http://www.ncsl.org/research/health/traumatic-brain-injury-legis lation.aspx.

4.   *Players Association Exposure.* Some NFL ex-players also sued the NFLPA for complicity in concealing the risk of concussions. A court ruled those claims preempted by federal labor law requiring the players to pursue relief through an unfair representation charge before the NLRB. *See Ballard v. Nat'l Football League Players Ass'n*, 123 F. Supp. 3d 1161 (E.D. Mo. 2015). What more should the players associations be doing to protect player health and safety? Why do you think they have not been more aggressive in advocating for safer sport?

5.   *Medical Marijuana Use.* In response to the marijuana legalization movement, professional sports leagues have re-evaluated their approaches to drug testing and discipline, and athlete use of cannabis for pain management. In the 2020–30 NFL CBA, the league and players agreed to quadruple the threshold for positive marijuana tests and eliminate suspensions for positive tests. MLB removed marijuana from its list of banned substances. But neither league has committed to therapeutic use of cannabis products. What, then, if players self-medicate without informing team medical personnel? Who should assume the risk of adverse health outcomes in this scenario?

6.   *Sexual Abuse and Harassment of Athletes.* Another off-field health and safety risk that has mushroomed since this casebook's last edition is the vulnerability of young athletes to sexual abuse and harassment by their physicians and coaches. High-profile abuse cases have rocked the sports world and resulted in criminal charges and civil suits. *See, e.g., Michigan v. Nassar*, 17-20217-FC (Circ. Ct. Eaton Cty. Mich. 2018) (sentencing Dr. Larry Nassar to 40 to 175 years on sexual abuse charges); *Doe MC-1 v. Univ. of Michigan*, 2:20-cv-10568 (E.D. Mich. 2021) (civil action arising out Dr. Robert Anderson's abuse of student athletes, ultimately settled for $490 million); *Frederick v. USOC*, 1:18-cv-11299 (D. Mass 2018) (class action on behalf of former gymnasts against the sport's governing bodies and training facilities). These scandals have awakened private and public governing bodies to the need to develop safeguards and mechanisms to report and protect against abuse. In 2018, Congress authorized the U.S. Center for SafeSport to serve as a centralized authority with jurisdiction over reports of abuse and misconduct in

Olympic, Paralympic and amateur sports. This entity has been criticized, however, for mishandling complaints, lack of transparency, and inconsistent arbitral results. Why should criminal activity of this nature be referred to a semi-private forum rather than handled by the relevant law enforcement and prosecutorial agencies? Is there something different or special about sports participation that justifies this approach rather than, for example, state-by-state legislation to protect against abuse in youth sports, just as states have acted to protect against concussions?

3.   DEFECTIVE PRODUCTS AND HAZARDOUS FACILITIES

Another attractive third-party target for a tort suit by an injured athlete is the manufacturer of a product used in the game. Sports law was certain to gain a share of expanding product liability litigation. Prime examples are lawsuits against helmet manufacturers, which over the years have been largely unsuccessful. These claims typically rest on theories of defective design and failure to warn, as did the following lawsuit against Riddell brought by high school football players who had suffered mild traumatic brain injuries [MTBIs].

ADAMS V. BRG SPORTS, INC.
2021 WL 1517881 (N.D. Ill. Apr. 17, 2021)

KENNELLY, J.

The plaintiffs in these cases, all of whom played high school football, sued BRG Sports, Inc. and Riddell, Inc., which design, manufacture, and sell football helmets. . . .

[T]he plaintiffs allege that the defendants' negligence (design defect and failure to warn) caused them to suffer brain and neurocognitive injuries. The Court, with the assistance of the parties, then selected a number of "bellwether" cases, in which full discovery, including expert discovery, would be taken. That process has been completed through the deadline for the plaintiffs to designate experts. . . .

For the reasons set forth below, the Court grants summary judgment in favor of the defendants on the plaintiffs' design defect claims but denies the motion on the plaintiffs' failure to warn claims.

Background

. . .Each plaintiff wore a Riddell helmet during the time period relevant to these lawsuits; some as early as 1975 and others as late as 2002 or even later. The purpose of a football helmet is to mitigate the risk of head injuries and ensure safety during game play. The National Operating Committee on Standards for Athletic Equipment (NOCSAE), formed in 1969, implemented football helmet safety standards in 1973; its standards cover Riddell helmets. The plaintiffs contend that as football players, they sustained various head injuries during game play—namely from blows to the head.

A. Riddell adds warning labels

Beginning in 1983 and until the late 1990s, Riddell affixed warning labels onto the back of their football helmets. The warning stated: "Do not use this helmet to strike an opponent. Such an action is against football rules and may cause severe brain or neck injury. Playing the game of football in itself can cause injury, and no helmet can prevent all such injuries." The plaintiffs contend that Riddell's warnings were insufficient and that a better warning would have prompted them to avoid playing football altogether, choose a safer helmet, or play football differently. Riddell disputes these contentions and says that without evidence of a causal link between the plaintiffs' alleged injuries and Riddell helmets, the adequacy of warnings do not matter.

B. Riddell introduces new Revolution helmet

In 2002, Riddell introduced a new product—the "Riddell Revolution Helmet"—which it claimed to be 31% safer than other helmets on the market. The plaintiffs contend that they suffered brain injuries caused by Riddell's football helmets—older Riddell products and the Revolution line of helmets—because these helmets did not adequately protect them against injuries from concussive and sub-concussive blows to the head. The design defects alleged by the plaintiffs include (1) padding liner systems that lacked newer, safer, and better energy absorbing materials; (2) substandard foams that did not reduce force to the forehead; (3) insufficiently thick padding; and (4) the lack of safer and better energy absorbing systems, such as air-filled chamber-based systems. The plaintiffs say that Riddell marketed all of their helmets as safe equipment that would protect football players—especially from concussions. . . .

Discussion

A. Riddell's motion for summary judgment on general causation

1. Design defect claims

Under both Texas and Iowa law, which collectively govern all of the bellwether plaintiffs' claims, a plaintiff alleging design defect—based on theories of negligence and strict liability—must provide evidence of causation. In Texas, "[t]o recover for a products liability claim alleging a design defect, a plaintiff must prove that (1) the product was defectively designed so as to render it unreasonably dangerous; (2) a safer alternative design existed; and (3) the defect was a producing cause of the injury for which the plaintiff seeks recovery." *Timpte Indus., Inc. v. Gish*, 286 S.W.3d 306, 311 (Tex. 2009). Negligent design defect claims similarly require evidence that the negligent design caused the plaintiff's injuries. . . .

Iowa law likewise imposes these requirements on plaintiffs asserting such claims, although the Iowa Supreme Court has explained that it "prefer[s] to label a claim based on a defective product design as a design defect claim without reference to strict liability or negligence." *See Wright v. Brooke Group Ltd.*, 652 N.W.2d 159, 169 (Iowa 2002). . . .

In count 1 of the first amended master complaint, the plaintiffs assert a negligent design defect claim and contend that Riddell was "negligent in the design, testing, marketing, and engineering of the helmets warn [sic] by Plaintiffs.". . . In count 2, the plaintiffs assert a design defect claim sounding in strict liability; they allege that the Riddell helmets worn by the plaintiffs were "defective in design, unreasonably dangerous, unsafe for their intended purpose, and failed to perform as safely as an ordinary consumer would expect . . . because the helmets did not provide adequate protection against the foreseeable risk of concussive brain injury." They further allege that "[t]he design defects created an unavoidable and unreasonable risk of long-term health consequences arising from repeated concussive and sub-concussive blows to the head during football play and practice." "These risks," the plaintiffs allege, "could have been significantly reduced through the implementation of reasonable, relatively affordable, and technologically and scientifically feasible alternative designs.". . .The plaintiffs contend that they suffered long-term brain injuries caused by Riddell's defective helmets and that an alternative design—such as one with superior padding—could have reduced their risk of injury.

Riddell argues that the plaintiffs' design defect theory "depends on [an] . . . attenuated causal chain" encompassing "complex issues involving medicine, epidemiology, neuroscience and brain injury mechanism, and football helmet design and engineering." Riddell contends that the plaintiffs' theory of causation needs to be supported by sufficient expert testimony but that "nothing in [Dr. Benson's report] comes close to the level the plaintiffs need to set forth a triable issue on general causation.". . .

In response, the plaintiffs cite, in addition to Dr. Benson's report, a number of scientific studies in support of their claims that football participation and helmet design are causally linked to MTBIs. But none of these scientific studies concern Riddell helmets; many do not even address football helmets at all. . . .

The Court concludes that to prevail on their design defect claims, the plaintiffs need expert testimony on general causation [and] that Dr. Benson's expert report falls short of providing evidence sufficient to permit a reasonable jury to find the required connection between Riddell's helmet designs and the plaintiffs' injuries. Dr. Benson's report is sufficient to permit a reasonable finding that a person may suffer brain and/or neurocognitive injuries from playing football. But his report does nothing to connect the plaintiffs' injuries with Riddell's designs. Indeed, the most that Dr. Benson has said regarding design is, in essence, that good helmet design can mitigate the risk of head injuries. That's all well and good, but it does not advance the ball in establishing that Riddell's designs were deficient, let alone how they were deficient. Without such evidence, the plaintiffs cannot meet their evidentiary burden on general causation regarding their design defect claims. *See, e.g., Williams v. City of Baytown*, 467 S.W.3d 566, 578 (Tex. App. 2015) (noting that the plaintiffs' "expert could not connect his general causation theory . . . to any specific fact . . . in this case"). For this reason, Riddell is entitled to summary judgment on the bellwether plaintiffs' design defect claims.

———

After the *Adams* court rejected the design defect claims against Riddell, it issued a second summary judgment against the failure to warn claims, again faulting expert testimony on the adequacy of the warnings and their causal link to the injuries. *See Adams v. BRG Sports, Inc.*, 2022 WL 93497 (N.D. Ill. Jan. 10, 2022). Causation continues to be the stumbling block for product liability claims against helmet manufacturers as plaintiffs must show that defendants' conduct did more than "furnish the condition that makes plaintiff's injury possible," but was a "substantial factor" in causing the injury. *Wilbourn v. BRG Sports, Inc.*, 569 F.Supp.3d 445 (N.D. Tex. 2021) (internal quotations omitted).

———

NOTES AND QUESTIONS

1. *Football Helmet Design Standards.* A single standard governs football helmet design, established by the National Operating Committee on Standards for Athletic Equipment (NOCSAE). It applies to all helmets—for adult and youth football. Consider whether manufacturers should establish and utilize a specific youth standard for minor athletes, such as the *Adams* plaintiffs, given their different proportions and fitting needs.

2. *Adequacy of Warnings.* As the *Adams* court noted, in 2002, Riddell introduced "The Revolution," a helmet it promoted as reducing concussions by 31 percent. Each Riddell helmet contained a label warning about head, neck, and concussive brain injuries. (Schutt, a rival manufacturer, went even further with its warning: "To avoid these risks, do not engage in the sport of football.") It is often easy to find an expert engineer to criticize safety warnings and suggest alternatives; it is harder to establish proximate cause between the warnings and the injurious event. What would the proof entail? That more alarming warnings would have dissuaded the plaintiffs from playing football? That Schutt used more detailed warnings?

3. *Expert Testimony.* The *Adams* court rejected the design defect claims because expert testimony failed to establish a causal chain encompassing "complex issues involving medicine, epidemiology, neuroscience and brain injury mechanism, and football helmet design and engineering." The *Wilbourn* court (cited above) similarly derogated the expert report for failing to "address

the key question: whether [plaintiff's injury] still would have occurred without the use of Riddell's helmets." What does an expert report need to substantiate to allow such claims to advance to a jury? That reasonable alternative designs exist that could diminish risk? That there was a safer helmet available from Riddell's competitors, such as Schutt Sports?

4.   *League-Approved Helmets.* How should risk of head injury be apportioned when the league mandates that players choose among NOCSAE-approved helmets? In 2019, NFL wide receiver Antonio Brown filed a grievance based on the league's refusal to let him continue wearing a Schutt helmet model that had been discontinued because of advances in helmet technology, and no longer met NOCSAE certification standards. Brown complained that NFL-approved helmets interfered with his vision. What if the NFL backed down and permitted Brown to use the old Schutt helmet and he suffers a debilitating concussion? What if while using a new league-mandated helmet, Brown is injured when the reduced visibility contributes to a collision with another player?

Like any employee, professional athletes who perform their job at an employer-furnished workplace are entitled to protection from hazards that might foreseeably cause injury. For professional athletes, their workplaces are the facilities where they train, practice, and play in games. When those facilities are not properly designed or maintained, resulting in injury to the athlete, there is potential for tort recovery. San Francisco 49ers running back Reggie Bush brought a premises liability case in Missouri state court against the St. Louis Rams and their facility when he suffered a season-ending knee injury during a road game. After surgery, he attempted a comeback, but retired a year later.

The gravamen of Bush's complaint alleged:

36.   The Rams owed a duty to the general public and specifically those invited on the field, including, but not limited to, players, coaches, trainers, media, youth football players, cheerleaders, fans, and referees to remove or warn of dangerous conditions in the Dome and to maintain the Dome, including the playing surface and surrounding areas, in a reasonably safe condition.

37.   In violation of this duty, the Rams negligently permitted and maintained a dangerous condition to exist at the Dome, creating an unreasonable risk of injury to those invited on the field and surrounding surfaces, including Mr. Bush. Specifically, the turf playing field was surrounded by a slippery concrete surface. This abrupt change in surface was not reasonably safe.

38.   As described above, Mr. Bush slipped and fell on the slippery concrete surface, injuring his left knee.

* * *

47. The Rams breached the duty owed to Mr. Bush by one or more of the following negligent acts or omissions:

a. Designing, constructing, and/or setting up the playing field such that it was surrounded by a slippery concrete surface;

b. Failing to cover the slippery concrete surface with padding;

c. Failing to provide warnings related to the concrete surface. . . .

Bush v. St. Louis Rams, LLC., 2016 WL 11295572 (Mo. Cir. Ct. 2016). The Rams responded to the suit by removing it to federal court on the grounds that the collective bargaining agreement governs the terms and conditions of Bush's employment, and as such his state law tort claims would be preempted under § 301 of the Labor Management Relations Act. Bush moved to remand to state court.

BUSH V. ST. LOUIS RAMS

2016 WL 3125869 (E.D. Mo. June 3, 2016)

HAMILTON, JUDGE.

At all times relevant to this action, Plaintiff Reginald Bush was a professional football player employed by the San Francisco 49ers. On November 1, 2015, Plaintiff played as a running back for the 49ers in a game against the St. Louis Rams that took place at the Edward Jones Dome in St. Louis, MO. According to Plaintiff, while trying to slow down out-of-bounds after a play had concluded in the first quarter, Plaintiff slipped on a concrete surface surrounding the turf playing field at the Dome. Plaintiff maintains the resultant injury to his left knee ended his football season.

* * *

[T]he Court begins its section 301 preemption analysis with the claim itself, negligence. . . . Plaintiff's negligence claims are premised on the common law duty of care that sports teams owe to their invitees. According to Plaintiff, this duty required the Rams "to remove or warn of dangerous conditions in the Dome and to maintain the Dome, including the playing surface and surrounding areas, in a reasonably safe condition." . . . [T]he Court now must evaluate whether the CBA is the source of Plaintiff's claims, or whether the claims are substantially dependent upon an interpretation of the CBA.

[The court quoted extensively from CBA provisions on: (i) players' rights to medical care and treatment, including club payment of healthcare costs and adherence to the recommendations of the Accountability and Care Committee; (ii) workers' compensation; (iii) injury grievances; and (iv) the joint NFL-NFLPA Committee on Player Safety and Welfare.]

Upon consideration, the Court finds an interpretation of the above provisions is not essential to Plaintiff's case. For example, with respect to Article 39, Sections 1 and 3, the Court finds that neither the cost of medical services rendered by Club physicians (to be paid for by the Club, *i.e.*, the 49ers), nor the provision of preventive, medical, surgical, or rehabilitative care for players by clubs is at issue in Plaintiff's suit. In other words, Plaintiff does not claim he failed to receive contractually mandated care; instead, he claims he was not warned of a dangerous condition existing at the stadium. The same holds true for any responsibilities imposed on the Accountability and Care Committee; in other words, the Court finds the Rams' duty to warn exists independently of the Committee's responsibility to develop a standardized preseason and postseason physical examination, and to develop an educational protocol to inform players of the primary risks associated with playing professional football.

With respect to Articles 41 and 44 of the CBA, and section 9 of the NFL Player Contract, the Court finds those provisions speak to the player's ability to perform under his contract, or otherwise to recover from, his own NFL team. Plaintiff is not a player with the Rams, and so the provisions do not apply.

The strongest argument put forth by the Rams involves Article 50, Section 1. As noted above, that provision requires the establishment of a Joint Committee for the purpose of discussing, among other things, the player safety and welfare aspects of playing equipment, playing surfaces, and stadium facilities. The Joint Committee does not have the power to commit or bind any of the signatories to the CBA, however, nor does the CBA establish a contractually agreed upon standard of care applicable to Plaintiff's claims. . . .

Thus, the Court agrees with Plaintiff that the duties at issue here arise out of the common law duty of care sports teams owe to their invitees, and not out of any particular terms in the CBA. A substantial dependence upon an analysis of the CBA thus cannot serve as a basis for removal, and so Plaintiff's Motion to Remand must be granted.

Reggie Bush tried his claims in front of a St. Louis state court jury in the spring of 2018, a year after the Rams had decamped to Los Angeles. During the trial, the Rams argued that Bush failed to prove the fall caused his injury because he had a long history of knee problems. Missouri law, however, rejects the "eggshell" plaintiff theory, and dictates that a negligent defendant is responsible for all of the harm it causes even when the plaintiff is more susceptible to a worse injury than the average person. The jury found the Rams liable, awarding Bush a total of $12.5 million in compensatory and punitive damages.

NOTES AND QUESTIONS

1. *Athlete Suits Involving Hazardous Playing Surfaces.* Professional athletes who suffer serious injuries while playing games typically have limited recourse to the courts. Either they have assumed the risk or must resolve their claims through collectively bargained grievance procedures. But hazardous facilities claims offer a loophole. New York Yankee Dustin Fowler was allowed to proceed in state court with his claim against the Chicago White Sox and its facility for a season-ending injury suffered when, as he chased a foul ball, he ran into an unpadded metal electrical box protruding onto the field. *Fowler v. Illinois Sports Facilities Auth.*, 338 F. Supp. 3d 822 (N.D. Ill. 2018) (clubs retained duty for playing field safety and did not delegate it to collectively bargained joint player-league committee); *but see Houston NFL Holding L.P. v. Ryans*, 581 S.W.3d 900 (Tex. App. 2019) (compelling Philadelphia Eagles linebacker DeMeco Ryans to arbitrate claim that the Houston Texans patchy grass field caused a torn Achilles tendon). What justifies the different treatment of game injuries caused by contact with other players and those caused by contact with playing surfaces?

2. *Other Workplace Facilities.* Given the earning potential and asset value of professional athletes, you would think that their workplaces would be maintained in pristine condition. Yet, Tampa Bay Buccaneers players Lawrence Tynes and Carl Nicks each received multi-million-dollar settlements from the team after a 2013 staph infection outbreak in the team's facilities resulted in career-ending disabilities. The lawsuits claimed that the Bucs actively concealed ongoing incidents of the infection among other individuals who used and visited the team's facilities, and failed to employ necessary sterile techniques. *See Tynes v. Buccaneers Ltd. P'ship*, 134 F. Supp. 3d 1351 (M.D. Fla. 2015) (holding that player's premises liability claims did not arise from CBA).

At the 2015 United States Tennis Open, Canadian player Eugenie Bouchard slipped on a cleaning substance that had been applied to the floor of the trainer's room and sustained a concussion that stalled her career for over two years. As an independent contractor playing an individual, not team, sport, Boucher faced no statutory obstacles to her claims, and a liability-only trial was conducted in early 2018. The jury found the tournament organizer, the United States Tennis Association, 75% liable for negligence, and Bouchard 25% liable because she broke the rules when she entered the trainer's room unaccompanied. The parties reached a confidential settlement prior to the damages phase.

4. KEEPING SPORTING EVENTS SAFE FROM VIOLENCE, DISORDER, AND PUBLIC HEALTH RISKS

Sporting events organizers generally owe a duty of care to both participants and spectators to keep the facility reasonably safe. At its most basic, this duty requires taking measures to avert or mitigate predictable spectator conduct that might cause injury to others, for example when spectators scramble to claim a football that goes into the stands, causing injury to those in their way. *See Hayden v. University of Notre Dame*, 716 N.E.2d 603 (Ind. App. 1999) (university has duty to protect spectators from that foreseeable risk by attempting to recover errant balls). This duty may also include taking precautions if it is foreseeable that a third party will commit a criminal or violent act injuring a player or spectator, or that a public health risk threatens those in attendance.

(a) Fan Violence

The potential for fan violence presents a premises liability risk unique to sporting events, often arising out of excessive alcohol use, a mob mentality tied to team allegiance, and the aggression and violence inherent in sports themselves. The most extreme fan violence has regularly occurred in international soccer, where rabid fans known as "hooligans" have instigated violent altercations resulting in property damage, severe bodily injuries and even death. Most infamous is an incident at the 1985 European Cup final in Belgium, where English hooligans attacked fans from Italy, leaving 39 people dead and 470 injured. Following that tragedy, the Fédération Internationale de Football Association (FIFA) banned England from participating in the European Cup for five years. In its turn, England expedited passage of public reforms to combat the ongoing hooliganism problem at home, among them the Sporting Events Act of 1985, which banned the worst offenders from matches and limited alcohol consumption, and the Public Disorder Act of 1986, which updated penal code offenses relating to riot and unlawful assembly.

Fan violence has unfolded with disturbing regularity in the United States as well. Some professional teams have developed reputations for unruly fans, notably the NFL Philadelphia Eagles. Violence in the Eagles stands got so out of hand that in 1998, the team installed a court and jail under its stadium to arrest, detain, and try their fans on the spot. Eagles fans even took their violence on the road, assaulting Dallas Cowboys fans in the stands at the Cowboys stadium while security personnel looked on and failed to intervene. The resulting negligence lawsuit alleged that the team failed to properly monitor the premises, train its security personnel, provide adequate security equipment, and respond to the incident. *See Kennedy v. Dallas Cowboys Football Club*, 017-304020-18 (Tex. Dist. Ct. Oct. 30, 2018).

Los Angeles Dodgers Stadium has also been the site of repeated vicious attacks by hometown fans on rivals, notoriously the savage beating of San Francisco Giants fan Bryan Stow in the stadium parking lot on 2011 MLB opening day. Stow suffered severe brain damage requiring long term care. His negligence suit against the Dodgers resulted in a $13.9 million verdict for failure to provide adequate security and lighting. *Stow v. Los Angeles Dodgers*, 2014 WL 3387350 (Cal. Super. July 8, 2014). Dodgers home-team fans committed assaults that again sent victims to hospitals in 2015 (Mets fan) and 2019 (Diamondbacks fan), and resulted in more lawsuits alleging inadequate security and lighting. *See Reyna v. Los Angeles Dodgers*, 20 StCv15459 (Cal. Super. Apr. 23, 2020); *see also Bergin v. The Los Angeles Rams*, 2019 WL 13125771 (Cal. Super. Apr. 9, 2019) (alleging foreseeability of violence at highly anticipated NFL night game). Intense rivalries like that between the NFL 49ers and Raiders have spawned brutal encounters including in 2011 a shooting in Candlestick Park and brawl at Oakland Stadium.

What is the obligation of facilities, leagues, and teams in response to fan violence? The major leagues have all adopted alcohol control policies for their games, including forbidding outside alcohol, limiting each purchase to two beverages, and discontinuing service well before the end of the game. The smartphone era has enabled "tattle-text" programs, where spectators can anonymously inform stadium security of problematic fans in their section. Other measures include expanded video surveillance, greater security and police presence especially at key rivalry games, and fan ejections. The NFL has instituted a fan code of conduct that provides for ejecting unruly fans and then temporarily banning any such misbehaving fans until they attend a fan-conduct-awareness class and formally request to lift the ban.

The enforceability of league codes of conduct for fans is untested, and encountered a setback in a case involving a fan at a 2009 Kansas City Chiefs-San Diego Chargers game in San Diego. Stadium guards attempted to remove Jason Ensign after he yelled obscenities and flipped his middle finger at other fans. A fracas ensued and a stadium guard was seriously injured. A San Diego Superior Court judge threw out battery charges against Ensign, ruling that he was rightfully defending his First Amendment rights against overzealous security, and that the stadium code of conduct was unenforceable in a publicly owned facility. Ensign in turn brought false arrest and excessive force claims against the Chargers and City of San Diego, which were ultimately dismissed on the merits. *See Baker v. Ensign*, 2015 WL 5568044 (S.D. Cal. Sept. 22, 2015). Should it make a difference whether the sports facility is public or private in enforcing a fan code of conduct?

(b) Public Health Risks

When the World Health Organization declared COVID-19 a pandemic on March 11, 2020, nearly all competitive sports suspended, postponed, or cancelled play. Like every sector of society, sports had to re-evaluate business as usual and deal with unprecedented financial and legal challenges, which have outlasted the pandemic. Those challenges include mitigating risk of exposure and illness for players and spectators.

When players returned to the diamond, field, or arena, leagues and sport governing bodies took measures to avoid infection with COVID-19 through contact with other players, staff, or training equipment. Return to play in the NBA, NHL, and MLS initially occurred in "bubbles" where teams were sequestered to play in specific centralized locations and required to follow detailed health protocols. When spectators were allowed back in the stands to watch live sporting events, municipalities and teams at first imposed mask mandates, social distancing, and vaccination requirements, returning to normal operations only as the virus abated. Despite these measures, leagues were plagued with major outbreaks, game postponements and cancellations, and roster depletions. Notably, in the 2021 season, the NFL had to shift games around to Tuesday and Wednesday evenings, and the Denver Broncos had to start a non-quarterback because all the quarterbacks on their roster were disqualified from play due to the league's COVID-19 protocols.

Beyond protecting the health of game participants and fans, league protocols sought to mitigate the risk of and establish defenses to potential tort suits by anyone who might be able to trace an infection to game attendance. Leagues and teams have traditionally relied on disclaimers and waivers of liability in game tickets to manage risk to spectators (*e.g.*, foul balls at baseball games). Despite doubts as to the enforceability of such waivers, in 2021, Walt Disney World revised its theme park pass to announce that guests "voluntarily assume any and all risks in any way related to exposure to COVID-19."

Meanwhile, courts across the country have allowed lawsuits to move forward seeking to impose liability for the negligent transmission of COVID-19. *See, e.g., Kantrow v. Celebrity Cruises Inc.*, 533 F. Supp. 3d 1203 (S.D. Fla. 2021) (alleging plaintiff contracted COVID-19 on cruise ship); *Evans v. Walmart, Inc.*, 2020 WL 1697022 (Ill. Cir. Ct. Apr. 6, 2020) (alleging store's lax safety and cleanliness standards caused employee to be infected, leading to his death). Especially given the 2020–21 pandemic experience, facilities, leagues, and teams are on notice that they have a duty to fans, players, and staff to mitigate the risk of infection.

While "negligent COVID-19 transmission" lawsuits against sporting events have been rare, high school and college student-athletes brought lawsuits during the pandemic to *compel* the resumption of sports that had been shut down. Illinois high school students and their parents argued that suspension of sports violated the bylaws of the state's high school athletic association. *See Ruggles v. Ill. High Sch. Ass'n*, No. 2020CH00552 (Ill. Cir. Ct. Oct. 1, 2020) (denying students' request for temporary restraining order). Parents of another group of Illinois high school students brought equal protection claims against the governor and high school athletic association after disaster declarations shut down the 2020–21 winter sports season. The complaint alleged irrational differential treatment of high school athletes while allowing college and professional athletes to play the same sports. One parent alleged the ban caused her son's suicide. *See*

Moore v. Pritzker, 2021-MR-000295 (Ill. Cir. Ct. Dec. 12, 2020). Football players at the University of Nebraska sued the Big Ten Conference when it canceled the 2021 football season, alleging tortious interference and breach of contract. *Snodgrass v. The Big Ten Conference, Inc.*, 2020 WL 5076062 (Neb. Dist. Ct. Aug. 27, 2020) (case mooted by resumption of football season). How best should sport governing bodies navigate the oddly competing interests of athletic participation and public health?

Vaccine mandates offered another source of controversy and litigation during the COVID-19 pandemic. These mandates issued from both government authorities and private entities, requiring game participants, and in some places also fans, to be immunized against the virus. When Western Michigan University required varsity student-athletes to be vaccinated in order to play their sports, students with religious objections won an injunction against the mandate as violating their free exercise rights. *See Dahl v. Bd. of Trustees of W. Michigan Univ.*, 558 F. Supp. 3d 561 (W.D. Mich. 2021), *aff'd*, 15 F.4th 728 (6th Cir. 2021). The court held that the mandate was not narrowly tailored, as it permitted unvaccinated students to participate in intramural sports. What does a narrowly tailored vaccine mandate look like? The NBA questioned New York City's vaccine mandate for professional athletes because it applied only to home teams, resulting in Kyrie Irving, the unvaccinated Brooklyn Nets star, sitting out most of the 2021–22 season, while unvaccinated visiting team players could take the court.

NOTES AND QUESTIONS

1.   *Foreseeability of Fan Violence.* The return of fans to stadiums in 2021 after the worst of the COVID-19 pandemic brought with it even more aggressive behavior, perhaps triggered by pandemic-related stress and frustration. Incidents including a brawl at an Astros game and a fan dumping popcorn on NBA star Russell Westbrook during a playoff game led to ticket-holder ejections and bans. Given what we know about the psychology of sports fandom, what other proactive steps should facilities and teams be taking, and to what extent should spectators assume the risk of rowdy fan behavior? Why are courts willing to impose liability on facilities and teams for foreseeable fan violence when they decline to do so, under the baseball rule, for foreseeable errant balls?

2.   *Spectator Attacks on Game Participants.* Less foreseeable are spectator attacks on game participants, as when number one tennis player Monica Seles was stabbed in the neck by a Steffi Graf fan in the middle of a 1993 match in Germany. Although her physical recovery was quick, the psychological scars kept her from playing for two years. She received no satisfaction in the German courts, which imposed only a suspended sentence on her attacker and dismissed her lost income claims against the German

Tennis Federation whose inadequate security led to the attack. Was the unprecedented nature of the attack, by a mentally ill fan, a sound basis for refusing compensation?

A violent and equally unprecedented altercation occurred between players and fans at a 2004 Detroit Pistons home game against the Indiana Pacers. After two players engaged in a shoving match, a home-team fan threw a beverage at Pacers forward Ron Artest. Artest responded by entering the stands and attacking one spectator. Other players and spectators joined the fray, resulting in NBA suspensions for all the players and injuries for some of the fans. (See Chapter 4, Section B). In one of the resulting spectator tort suits, *Haddad v. O'Neal*, 2006 WL 3532686 (E.D. Mich. Oct. 19, 2006), a federal jury found the player and team were not liable for the spectator's injuries because the player was acting in defense of teammates. Should athletes be free to meet violence with violence in defending themselves from spectator assault, even when other options are available (such as walking away or deferring to security)?

3. *Infectious Disease and Sporting Events.* In March 2020, Atalanta, a soccer team from Bergamo, Italy, played in a Champions League match against Valencia. Two days earlier, as COVID-19 cases mounted, Italy had established a quarantine zone around Bergamo, yet 40,000 Bergamo fans traveled to the match in Milan. The result has been called a "biological bomb" as the virus spread rapidly among players on both teams, and devastated Bergamo, a city of 120,000, which counted 4,000 COVID-19 deaths in March 2020 alone. While this tragedy may not have been foreseeable in the early days of the pandemic, other Champions League matches had already banned spectators. With this history behind us, consider how leagues should manage public health risk going forward. What degree of risk should interrupt a season? How soon should a league restart games while a pandemic lingers? Should that depend on federal and state guidelines? How effective are league screening procedures and safety measures? What happens when players are allowed to play despite the presence of symptoms? Or when a player hides his or her symptoms to remain in the game?

INDEX

References are to Pages
